Servitude and Greatness 1832–1869

it is possible to have an unflawed human endeavour, then this is
. This may be a book that satisfies the scholar but in every sense
the word it is a special work; it is a book which will also seduce
he general reader' Nigella Lawson, Samuel Johnson Prize judge

'One of the masterpieces of modern biography . . . as broad in its
perspectives on nineteenth-century culture as it is deep in its
understanding of one of Romanticism's most dogged and lovable
individualists . . . [it has] a richness and wholeness which renders
Berlioz more vividly and intimately real than ever before'
Rupert Christiansen, *Daily Telegraph*

'David Cairns wins this year's Whitbread Biography Award for his
masterly evocation of the inner man as well as the outer world in
which he lived and worked. The judges felt that his biography is a
work of art in itself which will still be enjoyed and admired for
centuries to come' Whitbread judges on David Cairns's
Berlioz: Servitude and Greatness

'He able to . . . assess his achievements as conductor, entrepreneur,
journalist, and of course composer, with long and trenchant essays
on the great works . . . Cairns has never penetrated to the essence of
the masterpieces so deeply as he does here, in the context of a
life in which the music was an essential integrated part'
Hugh Macdonald, *The Times Literary Supplement*

immensely readable. The descriptions of time and place are
atmospheric . . . the treatment of the music is illuminating . . . the
judgements are admirably clear and admirably forthright . . . the
product of a lifetime's study, understanding and love'
Terry Barfoot, *Classical Music*

'Berlioz himself described his life as "an improbable novel". You may, as I did, break off to play a recording of the work under discussion (which is a tribute to the way it is discussed), but the sheer human interest of the tale has you plunging back in'
Francis Carlin, *Opera Now*

'Monumental . . . How fortunate Berlioz has been in his latest, perhaps definitive, biographer' George Steiner, *Observer*

'One of the most difficult, and possibly useless, activities is commenting on a perfect work of art. What words can add anything to Ravels *L'enfant et les sortilèges* or Mozart's *Le nozze di Figaro*? It is in such a spirit that I salute David Cairns's biography of Hector Berlioz' Robert Tear, *Oldie*

ABOUT THE AUTHOR

David Cairns was chief music critic of the *Sunday Times* from 1983 to 1992, having earlier been music critic and arts editor of the *Spectator* and a writer on the *Evening Standard*, the *Financial Times* and the *New Statesman*. From 1967 to 1972 he worked for the London branch of Phonogram, where he was involved in planning and carrying out large-scale recordings of Haydn, Mozart, Berlioz and Tippett. He has been Distinguished Visiting Professor at the University of California at Davis, a visiting scholar at the Getty Center in Santa Monica, and a visiting fellow of Merton College, Oxford. In 1991, in recognition of his services to French music, he was made Officier de l'Ordre des Arts et des Lettres. He has always been actively involved in music making; he was co-founder of the Chelsea Opera Group and is now conductor of the Thorington Players.

Berlioz: The Making of an Artist 1803–1832 won the Royal Philharmonic Society's Music Award, the *Yorkshire Post* Book of the Year and the British Academy's Derek Allen Prize. *Berlioz: Servitude and Greatness 1832–1869* won the Samuel Johnson Prize for Non-fiction, the Whitbread Biography of the Year and the Royal Philharmonic Society's Music Award.

DAVID CAIRNS

Berlioz

VOLUME TWO

Servitude and Greatness 1832–1869

PENGUIN BOOKS

PENGUIN BOOKS

Published by the Penguin Group
Penguin Books Ltd, 27 Wrights Lane, London W 8 5 TZ, England
Penguin Putnam Inc., 375 Hudson Street, New York, New York 10014, USA
Penguin Books Australia Ltd, Ringwood, Victoria, Australia
Penguin Books Canada Ltd, 10 Alcorn Avenue, Toronto, Ontario, Canada M 4 V 3 B 2
Penguin Books India (P) Ltd, 11, Community Centre, Panchsheel Park, New Delhi – 110 017, India
Penguin Books (NZ) Ltd, Private Bag 102902, N S M C, Auckland, New Zealand
Penguin Books (South Africa) (Pty) Ltd, 5 Watkins Street, Denver Ext 4, Johannesburg 2094, South Africa

Penguin Books Ltd, Registered Offices: Harmondsworth, Middlesex, England

First published by Allen Lane The Penguin Press 1999
Published in Penguin Books 2000
1

Copyright © David Cairns, 1999
All rights reserved

To Rosemary
and to Isaac, Joseph, Molly, Laura, Isobel,
Maisie and Oliver

Contents

CONTENTS

List of Illustrations

Thanks are due to the following for permission to reproduce the above-named illustrations: Richard Macnutt (1, 3b, 4, 5d, 6, 21a), The Bibliothèque Nationale de France, Paris (5b, 5c, 7, 9b, 13a, 16, 19, End-papers), The Association Nationale Hector Berlioz (8, 14a, 14b, 14c, 15, 21b, 22), The Leeds City Art Gallery and the Bridgeman Art Library (9a), Photo AKG London (9b), The Hulton Getty Picture Collection (11a, 11b, 17), Museum of Fine Arts, Boston (13b), François Lesure (23).

Berlioz and his orchestra, caricature by Grandville, 1846

I

Harriet

Harriet Smithson's presence in the Conservatoire Hall on the afternoon of 9 December 1832 set the seal on one of the high dates of the Romantic calendar. Few can have missed the symbolism. Berlioz had not exactly kept his infatuation with *la belle Irlandaise* to himself, and though d'Ortigue's biographical essay in the *Revue de Paris* telling the story of the symphony's genesis had not yet appeared, many in the audience would have known it or would have been apprised of it by their neighbours, as Heinrich Heine was by the man next to him. The sudden appearance of the actress herself in a prominent place just above the orchestra, with the composer no longer metaphorically but physically at her feet, had the hall buzzing. Here was the living original of the *idée fixe*, the inspirer of the symphony, come to receive back the music she had called into being. The passions she evoked were returning, if not to "plague the inventor", then to trouble and perhaps inspire her in her turn.

All over the hall people were staring at her. She could hardly mistake their glances; Paris audiences had long ceased to show her that kind of attention – not since the great days of 1827 and 1828 had she been the object of such excitement. Though her knowledge of French was as yet sketchy she knew enough to grasp the gist of the literary programme she held in her hand, even without the thinly veiled allusions of Maurice Schlesinger, and the English journalist Schutter, to the emotional origins of the work. If there was still any doubt who its heroine was, none was possible when in the sequel to the symphony she heard Bocage, the actor who took the role of the composer-hero, speak of his longing for "the Juliet, the Ophelia that my heart cries out for". From that moment "she felt the room reel about her; she heard no more, but sat in a dream, and at the end went home like a sleepwalker, hardly aware of what was happening". The words are Berlioz's, not Harriet's, but there is no reason to think them exaggerated. As Peter Raby remarks, it is not everyone who is wooed by a full orchestra.

For Berlioz it brought five years of disdain and indifference to an abrupt end. His life was revolutionized. Even the revenge against Fétis, target of Bocage's fiercest tirade, was forgotten. Within hours Miss Smithson had sent him her congratulations on his success. Next day he was granted permission to be introduced to her and they met. From now on he called every evening the English company was not performing. When he could not see her he wrote, in French, and she answered in English. Less than a week after the concert, "like Othello" he was telling her the story of his life since the day he had first set eyes on her, and she was weeping. "You can imagine with what intoxication I saw her tears flow." On 18 December, scarcely able to believe it, he heard her say, "Eh bien, Berlioz . . . Je vous aime": his feelings were answered at last. It did not matter that hers were not of the same intensity as his, but rather – he told his sister Nancy – "feelings which combine love, friendship and gratitude". The agonizing hopelessness was over and past. She loved him.

Yet it was not till nine and a half months later, after a series of delays only partly external in origin, that they were married. Looking back on it many years later, Berlioz recalled it as a time of continual, almost unbearable agitation in his life; he was alternately "elated with wild hopes and racked with fearful apprehensions". The course of true love never ran less smooth.

During those fraught, protracted months they did not become lovers, though gossip assumed they were. Whatever he may have desired, to her it would have been unthinkable. Her reserve often drove him to distraction – even his most restrained caresses alarmed her – yet at the same time he admired it and marvelled to find such innocence in a woman whose whole life had been lived in the theatre. It was bitterly ironic, he told his father, that Dr Berlioz should consent to his engagement to Camille Moke, a thoroughly promiscuous woman (as he had since discovered), but should oppose his marrying Harriet Smithson, whose behaviour had always been irreproachable.

The family's opposition was the first obstacle. Berlioz did not break the news to his father until the beginning of February, nearly eight weeks after he had begun courting Harriet; but Nancy's reply to an earlier letter in which he opened his heart to her (as in the old days) gave a taste of what the reaction would be. She dismissed it as a passing fancy, adding a warning – like Germont *père* in *La Dame aux camélias* – that such an alliance would jeopardize Adèle's chance of making a good marriage.

As actress, Protestant and penniless woman, Miss Smithson was trebly obnoxious. Félix Marmion, who was in Paris (Berlioz watched him parade down the boulevard at the head of his regiment on 23 January), characteristically fastened on this last objection. It was not even a speculation on his nephew's part, he wrote to Nancy: "the actress is ruined". Colonel Marmion pinned his hopes on certain "information" about Miss Smithson, which according to Alphonse Robert had reached Hector and was causing him to think again. (This is a recurring note in the correspondence. Berlioz's Côtois friend Edouard Rocher hints darkly to him about "fears" – presumably as to Harriet's virtue – which the inquiries of "well-informed persons" have confirmed.) In the second week of February Marmion took himself to the minor theatre in the Rue Chantereine where the English company had been playing for the past month, and sent a report to Nancy next day.

> I was very curious to analyse the potent charms which have wrought such havoc. Her features are indeed remarkable, she has an exquisite voice, and her gestures are noble. The theatre is so small that it's not at all favourable to illusion. Miss Smithson is necessarily at a disadvantage there. On that stage she doesn't even appear young. Without having my nephew's eyes or unique nature, I nevertheless understand the impression this woman must have made on his artist's soul. But has sober reflection, have the entreaties of his family no weight with him? We must see that he does not lack for either, so that we may have no reason to reproach ourselves. I confess that I do not hold out much hope.

Dr Berlioz remained studiedly calm. He accepted that their only weapon was time. "Our one resource," he wrote to Nancy on 20 February, "is to multiply the obstacles." He would not be swayed by threats. Hector talked of blowing his brains out; but Dr Berlioz declined to believe that his son would take his own life rather than lose so totally unsuitable a woman. Delay the marriage, withhold all financial support, and justice, common sense, family sentiment, might yet prevail. Meanwhile it was agreed they should keep the news from his mother as long as possible.

By refusing his consent the doctor forced Berlioz to resort to legal means, whereby a son who married against his parents' wishes was not disinherited – a process which, requiring the presenting of three separate *sommations respectueuses*, took three months. During that time the wind might change. And for a while there did seem a serious possibility that before the period of waiting expired and they could be married, Harriet would be forced by her financial losses to leave Paris and return to England.

In the end, just as it had been with the issue of music as a career eight or ten years earlier, family pressure achieved nothing; but the marriage was delayed. Berlioz was forced to go to elaborate lengths to find a justice of the peace and a notary prepared to serve the summonses; his friends Just Pion and Edouard Rocher either refused point-blank or agreed and then backed down.

During those months his natural affection for his parents and his strong sense of family loyalties were stretched to breaking-point. Saddest of all was to realize yet again how little his beloved father really knew him.

Saturday 23 February [1833]

Oh my father, my father, this is appalling! You go so far as to slander my future. Me a gambler! In God's name, how can you say that? Have I not been through every possible ordeal that might have tempted me to become one? When I had nothing, did I gamble? No – I preferred the humiliation of being a chorister in a vaudeville theatre; I lived on fifty francs a month, but I never gambled. You speak of my love for Harriet as if it dated from yesterday. But for heaven's sake, I told you about it; it began on 6 September 1827, and tortured my life for five whole years. The passionate episode which you use against me was itself occasioned by that love. It was all the talk about my obsession for Miss Smithson, my desolate constancy, that attracted the capricious attentions of Mlle Moke. She wrote to me, asked for a rendezvous, *made me a verbal declaration, came for me in my room, got me to elope with her*, etc., etc., and finally inspired me with a violent physical passion which I embraced with all the more ardour in that it seemed the only way of being cured of the other. You know the vile behaviour of that madwoman and her mother. But the horrible tempest was powerless to uproot the love that I still had in the depths of my heart for Harriet.

He thought he would never be loved by her in return. But now she loves him. His constancy has vanquished her.

I told her the whole story of Camille; I was completely frank about it. I knew who I was talking to. Harriet has a noble and lofty soul, but gentle and unassertive, for all her rich and varied genius.

Her conduct, in the world she lives in, lends her character a particular merit.

Father, you are utterly mistaken about her. It's heartbreaking; but that is how it is. As nothing will disabuse you, I have one last prayer to make to you: not to destroy the affection my heart holds for you. I love you, father, with all the love naturally inspired in me by the tender care with which you surrounded my childhood. Don't take it away from me; don't, I beg you, make me an unfeeling son.

You can be sure that, rightly or wrongly, there is nothing you can do that will separate me from Harriet. When I say I would do anything to win her, I mean exactly that; but it is utterly inhuman to drive out the natural and loving feelings from my heart, to replace them with despair and all its frightful train. If you are going to say to me again that "in marrying Miss Smithson I shall bring her misfortune" and that "I will abandon her for another", then I must tell you that in order not to lose my affection for you I shall not open any more letters from La Côte and there is no point in writing to me. I have sent Edouard a procuration, in order that, with the help of a notary, he can present you with my first summons. I have nothing to add; if you don't understand me, it would all be to no purpose. H. B.

"In the last resort," he asks his father in another letter, "what will be gained by prolonging my torment for three months?" And to Adèle, who alone of the family is not treating him like a pariah: "After everything that our parents have inflicted on me since I was twenty, one might have thought they would finally let me be." "Will they prevent my marrying Harriet?" he writes to Adèle, a few weeks later. "No, a thousand times no. Today I feel so outraged by this abuse of legal force on my account that even if I ceased to love and respect Mlle Smithson and all my feelings for her turned to *hatred* and *contempt*, I *should still marry her*. But I love her with a deep and tender love which, now that it is shared, no longer has the dreadful bitterness of the first five years; and curses without end on all obstacles which delay what I regard as the moment of my supreme happiness."

On her side Harriet was subjected by her family to direct and continuous pressure which played on her natural uncertainties. Her mother had not come to Paris with her but her sister Anne had. Though younger, and crippled, she had long assumed the dominant role in their relationship, and Harriet, preoccupied with her work and used to leaving all domestic arrangements and decisions to others, had let her. In opposing the marriage tooth and nail she spoke for their absent mother as well. Harriet was the family breadwinner and, until her recent troubles, a successful one. They depended on her. Marriage of any kind would mean upheaval to lives built around her career as an actress. Marriage to a Frenchman of doubtful prospects and erratic temperament would be a disaster and must not be allowed to happen. In addition, Anne had taken an instant dislike to Berlioz. She was often in and out of the room during their têtes-à-têtes, watching with exasperation as he knelt, tears in his eyes, gazing up into her sister's face. Once, when he had talked Harriet into letting him have a civil licence drawn up, Anne seized it from her and tore it up in front of them. When Berlioz was not there and Harriet was not at the theatre, she kept up a barrage of waspish comments, dinning into her the reasons why such a match was impossible and assuring her that Berlioz was actually mad; someone had written from London saying that it was a fact and all Paris knew it.

From the beginning of March Anne had her even more at her mercy. Returning on the afternoon of 1 March from a meeting at the Ministry of Commerce and Public Works, where she had been discussing arrangements for a benefit, Harriet caught her dress on the carriage door as she was stepping down and, twisting her right foot, fractured both bones just above the ankle. Two passers-by caught her as she fell and carried her into the house.

The accident, the climax of three and a half months of misfortune and the death blow to the English company, may or may not have been psychologically motivated; but its consequence was a long and painful convalescence, during which Harriet was confined to the house in acute discomfort, a passive listener to her sister's diatribes. The leg, broken in the worst place, healed very slowly. Three months later she could walk only with crutches. It was July before she ventured out, on Berlioz's arm, to the nearby Tuileries Gardens.

The news was reported by Félix Marmion in a letter of 6 March to his sister Joséphine Berlioz, who by now knew the worst. Marmion remained pessimistic:

Only chance can save us – for it's an illusion to believe that Hector will make the least sacrifice to the wishes and misgivings of his family. His madness is in the head, which is even worse than if his heart were caught. One can't begin to reason with him; he doesn't want to hear, gets easily irritated, and regards us as his enemies. Fearing probably that I'll raise the matter when we meet, he appears to be avoiding me. I've not seen him once chez moi since I arrived in Paris. We've written to each other, and Alphonse and I have met him a few times, to get information and to try to forestall disaster. Up till now the only hope we had was in the delay caused by his negotiations with his father and by the accident which has just befallen Miss Smithson: four days ago she broke her leg while getting out of a carriage. I was naturally anxious at the effect the news of this event would have on his volcanic temperament; but I found him, though much affected, calmer than I expected. I had written two days before to say that he and Alphonse absolutely must come and dine with me, and I gave them both a rendezvous – to which only Alphonse turned up. Hector didn't even respond to my invitation but merely sent me, by a musician we both know, two tickets for a concert at which a piece of his is being played.* It was last Sunday [3 March] that we were supposed to meet. I found Alphonse at our rendezvous; and after walking up and down for a while, with no sign of your son, we decided we would go and see him, to distract him from his gloom and force him to come and cheer up a little with us; for that was our plan of campaign: we were not going to treat the affair tragically but, on the contrary, to combat his absurd project by laughing at it. We found him in; he paced up and down the room, hardly speaking to us, visibly affected but none the less quite calm. We had agreed, Alphonse and I, to pretend not to know about Miss S.'s accident, so as to make our planned meeting more natural. I began by saying, "Well, we're going to have dinner together, you must have had my letter, why didn't you reply?" He answered, "I couldn't. So you don't know about the accident." (Then he described it.) "But," I said, "one has to have dinner, so come on." "No," he said, "I have to go and fetch a young man, we're dining together." "Can't you put him off?" "I could, but I'm not going to, because you would involve me in a conversation that I don't want to listen to." At that Alphonse and I sadly took our leave, to talk over dinner about our abortive expedition

---

* The *Francs-juges* overture, at a charity concert arranged by Liszt, 12 March 1833, at Vauxhall.

and how little hope we still had. I had been thinking of attempting a visit to Miss S., to try to break down her resolution by telling her about the family's unconquerable repugnance to the marriage, but hadn't yet fixed a day. In addition I have to find an interpreter, and the move must be made with care. The recent accident gives me time to reflect. They both live a long way from me, which is another difficulty, not to mention that my work rarely allows me to get off before five or six in the evening. I may write to her. It's vital not to make a false move, and above all not to aggravate that deranged mind any further.

With Harriet incapacitated, Berlioz assumed full responsibility for the benefit which they had both been organizing in the hope of paying off some of her debts – debts now swollen still more by her medical bills. He wrote letters in her name, which she signed, and saw to the practical details of the event. The intended gala performance of *Romeo and Juliet*, with a miniature concert in one of the entr'actes, was replaced by a miscellaneous evening involving many of the brightest stars of the theatrical and musical worlds – Mlle Mars, Mlle Duchesnois, Samson, Arnal, Rubini, Tamburini, Giulia Grisi, Liszt, Chopin, Urhan (Théâtre-Italien, 2 April) – which realized 6,500 francs.

After the accident Berlioz became if anything an even more assiduous visitor at the apartment in the Rue Castiglione, the street running north from the Rue de Rivoli, just round the corner from their old lodgings at the Hôtel du Congrès, where Harriet and her sister had moved not long before. For the time being, however, her invalid condition ruled out any decisive change. Worse, the weeks of discomfort and immobility further sapped her confidence, making her still less able to assert herself against her sister or respond to Berlioz's ardour, let alone nerve herself to the momentous step of marriage. Even when she had recovered sufficiently to walk with only a slight limp, and the legal obstacles had been surmounted, she continued to hesitate. Whereas he had satisfied himself that the rumours he kept hearing about her were false, she had to go on listening to equally damaging charges against him which, reject them as she might, were persistent and insidious enough to leave a lingering doubt. Above all, not being used as he was to a hand-to-mouth existence, the prospect of marrying on nothing terrified her.

As the weeks dragged on he was several times on the point of forcing himself to a separation. Always it was she who drew them back. In late February, just before her accident, the daily scenes with her sister of which he was the cause had become so acrimonious that he told her that rather than estrange her totally from her family he was ready to give her up ("which wasn't true – I should die") – only to abandon the idea in the face of the extreme distress and heart-warming display of affection it prompted. "The one thing that frightens me is her faintheartedness," he had written during the first weeks of their relationship; and it becomes a motif of his letters. At times he felt he would never succeed in overcoming it.

In the immediate aftermath of the accident he hesitated again. On 12 March he wrote to Edouard Rocher telling him "not to go on" with the legal submissions "for the moment; *I have no further need to get married just now*. If, later, Harriet absolutely wants it, I imagine the first submission you made will still count." The letter, shown to Dr Berlioz, was taken by the family as a sign that the immediate danger was over. Nancy regretted only that the submission had to be presented in a centre of gossip like La Côte, "where the houses are made of glass and domestic life is exposed to the four winds". Ten days later Berlioz was telling Rocher to forget what he had said and present the second submission.

In the spring a separation did take place. It did not last. Though Berlioz, in response to a desperate note from Harriet, remained "cold and impassive as a marble statue" when they met, she persuaded him to see her a second time and poured out a flood of "protestations and explanations" which at least partly reassured him. Lack of money was now their biggest stumbling-block. In July, and again in August, he attempted to raise a few thousand francs from his connections in Dauphiné, both times apparently in vain. A friend went to see Nancy's husband Camille Pal to negotiate a loan. Even Nancy was touched by her brother's plight, though such a loan was of course out of the question – the very thought of the money being used to "support Miss Smithson" was "revolting". Harriet's financial state was indeed desperate; she was still heavily in debt and talked once more of returning to England. She refused, however, to accept a penny of Berlioz's money. Instead he managed to get her a grant of 1,000 francs from the Fund for the Encouragement of the Arts, and in response to her plea for help the Duc d'Orléans sent 200. Yet by the end of July Berlioz was again near to breaking free. He understood her difficulties; but she was wearing him out. "This evening I shall see Harriet perhaps for the *last time*. She is so unhappy that my heart bleeds for her. Her timid, vacillating character makes her unable to take the least decision. But it must reach a conclusion; I cannot live like this."

Once again he stayed. The scenes with her sister grew more violent. He wished he could "exterminate that bloody little hunchback". She told him to his face that if only she were strong enough she would throw him out of the window. Each time he persuaded Harriet to the verge of marriage she shrank back.

He could bear it no longer. When she accused him of not loving her he took an overdose of opium on the spot, followed – in response to her cries and protestations of love – by an emetic. In an access of remorse she said yes, then "once more hesitated, her resolve shaken by her sister's attacks and her alarm at the wretched state of our fortunes. She has nothing, yet I love her; but she cannot bring herself to entrust her fate to me. She wants to wait a few more months. Months! Damnation take it! I cannot wait any longer." He had, after all, waited nearly six years. On Thursday 29 August he wrote telling her that he would call for her on Saturday, to take her to the *mairie*: if she refused, he would leave the following Thursday for Berlin. (By the regulations of the Prix de Rome he should have gone there in January.) "She doesn't believe in my resolution, and has sent me word that I will have her reply today. It will be the same phrases – begging me to come and see her, saying she is ill, etc. But I shall stand firm, and she will see that if I have been weak and dying at her feet all this time, I can get up again, shun her, and live for those who love and understand me. I have done all I can for her, and she dares not take a risk for me. It's too fainthearted, too *reasonable*. So I am going." But he didn't. Instead, she came.

A few days before, he had been approached by a group of friends on behalf of a young woman of eighteen, a fugitive from a brute who had been keeping her prisoner. The poor girl, terrified of falling into the man's clutches again, was set on leaving the country. Would he help her get away?

It is quite possible that the romantic circumstances were invented by Janin and the others to appeal to his chivalrous nature and thus liberate him from Miss Smithson. But the girl was real enough. Berlioz met her, found her intelligent, charming and musical, and agreed to take her with him to Berlin and, with Spontini's help, try to get her a place in one of the choruses.

This intriguing idyll would certainly have changed the story if it had happened, as it nearly did. Quite apart from the attractions of the young fugitive, he had finally made up his mind.

> My passport is ready, I have a few things left to settle, and then I'm off. It must be ended. I'm leaving poor Harriet really unhappy, her position is appalling; but I have nothing to reproach myself with and I can't do any more for her. I would still give my life for *one month* spent at her side, loved as I must be. She'll weep and she'll despair. It will be too late. She will suffer the consequences of her unfortunate character, weak and incapable of high feelings or resolute action . . . Then she'll get over it and find that I was wrong. That's how it always is. As for me, I must go forward, turning a deaf ear to the clamour of my inner voice, which tells me that I am indeed wretched and that life is an atrocity.

Harriet, however, must have realized that this time he meant it. Whether or not she found out about the travelling companion, his ultimatum brought her at last to the point. At the beginning of September she took the plunge. Their banns were published. (The fugitive was provided for by a subscription among his friends, and thereafter disappears from the scene.) A month later, on Thursday, 3 October 1833, Berlioz and Harriet Smithson were married at the British Embassy in the Rue du Faubourg St Honoré, with Liszt one of the witnesses and Hiller and Heine in attendance.

The account in the *Memoirs*, though written after the disillusionment of their broken marriage, relives the unbelievable elation of that moment so long dreamed of and fought for, so long denied:

> On our wedding day she had nothing in the world except her debts and the dread that because of her accident she would never be able to make a successful return to the stage. I on my side possessed the total sum of three hundred francs, lent me by my friend Gounet; and once again I had quarrelled with my family. But she was mine and I defied the world.

What of Harriet? What did it do for her? Because we have only his side of the story, not hers, because her career as an actress went into eclipse, and because Berlioz, though he never abandoned her, did eventually leave her "for another" as his father predicted, she has taken on the pathos and passive air of one to whom events happen; she is the irrevocably fading star, the helpless object of another's fantasies, dragooned into a marriage she did not really desire – the "unfortunate

Harriet Smithson" on whom, in Barzun's phrase, Berlioz, "so constituted that his 'tenacity' would not let him yield anything on which he had once set his heart", had fastened a love image that was the pure product of his imagination. "Berlioz," says Hippeau, "is less to be pitied than the unhappy actress at whose feet he threw himself without knowing whether, once the splendid dream had become reality, domestic life would give him the satisfaction his ardour demanded." Instead of the Juliet, the Ophelia he yearned to possess, says Tiersot, he found – "ô déception!" – that he had married "une dame anglaise".

In all this, knowledge of the tragic end colours our attitude. The evidence suggests a different picture. Certainly Harriet, during these months, vacillated and drew back several times from the brink; but her hesitancy was perfectly natural. Her life had long been centred on her family; marriage was not a state that either circumstances or personal history inclined her to. To marry an impoverished foreign artist of no assured income when you yourself are deep in debt and have no immediate financial prospects, to start a new life and a new home under those conditions, would have seemed a questionable step even without a demoralizing physical injury and even without the propaganda she was daily subjected to – "the thousand and one absurd slanders", as Berlioz wrote after their marriage, "which, she has since explained, were used to put her off me and which were the cause of her frequent indecisiveness, among them one that really frightened her: the assertion, which she was told categorically was true, that I was liable to epileptic fits". No wonder she wavered. But Berlioz's letters reveal another Harriet: a Harriet who, despite everything, could not bear to be parted from him and who, loving him, took the initiative in their reconciliations; who stuck rigorously to her principle of never accepting the smallest sum of money from him and once, discovering that he had given her sister a few hundred francs, forced him to take them back on pain of never seeing her again; who was "glad he had nothing, for at least he could not doubt that it was for himself that she loved him"; who insisted that he got to know her as she was and not as the incarnation of the Shakespearean heroines she played, and for that reason forbade him to go and see her act. This does not sound like a weak-minded woman who allows herself to be used by a man for his own egotistical fancy, nor like a woman who (as has been said) in her extremity turns to him for material support – in Berlioz's case hardly the likeliest source of it. Her imagination, like his, was enthralled by his Romantic attachment and by the sense of their converging destinies. But everything we know about her indicates a person of spirit with a mind of her own.

Except for a single performance of *Romeo and Juliet* at the Salle Chanteraine which he may have attended (Harriet appeared once each in *Romeo*, *Hamlet* and *Othello* during the month of January 1833), Berlioz, who had last seen her on stage in 1827, did not see her act again until after they were married. Had he done so he would not have found an artist past her best. It is commonly assumed that Harriet had lost her power to appeal to the French (something the English professed to find totally mysterious in any case): at thirty-two, Sainte-Beuve's "céleste Smithson" had aged and coarsened. Berlioz himself reported, just before he fell under the old spell, that she was "changed in every respect". Without doubt Harriet was a good deal stouter than she used to be (a lighter person might not have broken her leg when she stepped awkwardly on to the pavement). But her Parisian peers did not find her any less remarkable. For them she remained not just a name but a living force. And when she was in extreme need they gave their aid as to an equal.

Jules Janin, in a bravura review in the *Journal des débats*, might argue that it was too late to revive the glories of 1827 – the vogue for Shakespeare had been submerged in the torrential if melodramatic passions of modern French drama – but the great Marie Dorval knew that Smithson had as much as ever to teach her about the technique and emotional expression of tragic acting, and she watched her whenever she could. She was with Auguste Barbier and her lover Alfred de Vigny in Antoine Fontenay's box on 26 December 1832 when Smithson played the last two acts of *Romeo and Juliet* at a benefit evening at the Vaudeville. In January Dorval went to the Salle Chantereine, writing a day or two later to Vigny: "If you had come to the English theatre with me we could have visited her together in her dressing-room and then afterwards, together, at her place. [. . .] You know how keen I am to see Smithson." Five years later, by which time she is reduced to performing isolated scenes with inadequate supporting actors, her lustre in the eyes of her fellow-artists is undimmed. Adèle Hugo, conveying Victor Hugo's congratulations to Berlioz on the success of his Requiem, goes out of her way to praise, on her own and her husband's behalf, Harriet's wonderful performance in the fifth act of *Jane Shore*, which they had seen seven months earlier and wish they could see again.

The newspaper accounts of her acting in the winter of 1832-3 are of an actress still at the height of her powers. Miss Smithson, the *Débats* reported,

> has more élan and passion than most English actresses. She is a tragedienne in the genre of Mme Dorval. Pathetic, gifted with the gift of tears, real tears, she expresses grief in all its anguish and intensity with a heartfelt truthfulness. Sometimes she exaggerates the tears and the cries; as Shakespeare says, "she o'ersteps the modesty of nature". But she remains a remarkable actress, admirable above all in her mastery of shades of expression and in her extraordinary ability to pass from tender feelings to paroxysms of rage and despair. When she does, her features become contorted, transformed, with the practised skill that only the greatest actors possess.

A month later, in January 1833, another critic writes that Miss Smithson is "not only one of those tragic actresses who speak clearly and project well, but an artist. And what is rarer than an artist in the theatre? To an exact and profound observation of nature – a quality found especially among English actors – she adds something of that élan and spontaneous passion of the south which has few examples or models in England."

From such testimony we can see that Berlioz, in Raby's words, "was not simply living in the past, reviving out of pity memories, distorted by time, of a few freak performances". His faith in her genius was widely shared.

That she was a genius in adversity gave her a yet deeper appeal. Her troubles only made her more dear. They stirred his sense of chivalry: it was for him to rebuild Ophelia's shattered fortunes, to repay her debts, to provide her with a new and happier life. Through all her years of decline the image of the Ophelia and the Juliet through whom the light of Shakespeare had first shone, "illuminating the whole heaven of art", never faded.

Ophelia and Juliet – Desdemona too (a role for which, though he never saw her play it, Harriet was celebrated) – weave their way into the texture of Berlioz's letters during the year 1833. When he has seen her play Juliet (he writes to Albert Du Boys in January) – the one performance she is allowing him to attend – then, "after the tragedy, the *real Romeo*, the Romeo Shakespeare created, that is me, yes me, I shall be there at the feet of my Juliet, ready to die, ready even to live if she wishes it". Then, breaking into a rapturous montage of phrases in

English from the play, "I am mad, dearest, I am dead!! Sweetest Juliet! My life, my soul, all, all, 'tis heaven!"; and, in French, "speak then, my orchestra." When, "like Othello", he tells her of the long years of trial and adversity during which he loved her without hope, she weeps "abundant tears". Later, as he sings her the Fantastic Symphony while she leans against his shoulder, her hand on his brow, she is "Ophelia in person – not Juliet, she does not have her fire and passion: she is gentle, tender, *timid*".

Did Berlioz in these months, while they grappled with the challenge but also the stimulus of the lack of a common language – did he get to know Harriet Smithson as she was and as she wished him to? Or do such outpourings show him still so dazzled by the literary prototype that he is blind to the person herself? I think it is easy to be misled by the language of his mythopoeic imagination. If on one level Harriet is "Ophelia" (or "Oph."), "Juliet", Shakespeare's representative on earth, she is also very much a woman of flesh and blood and her own identity who, as he clearly recognizes, is no longer the slim and graceful beauty she was when he first set eyes on her five years before, yet whom he loves not less deeply but more. The protracted courtship, whatever else he had against it, gave him the opportunity to begin to find out what she was like. "Hers is a true and deep sensibility, such as I didn't suppose she had". "She is no Camille – she has a heart and a noble soul." These were first impressions, seized amid the almost incredulous delight of being loved in return. As the days went by he could observe her more closely, above all during the months of pain and convalescence, when the vision of the fair Ophelia was brought down to earth, to the realities of the sickroom. "Her character is really amazing; every day I make the most enchanting discoveries." The opinions his friends had formed of her could not be more wrong. Her life was "quite another story; and the way she sees, feels and thinks is not the least fascinating part of it". Later he realized that the indecisiveness that had tormented him had a particular cause and was not characteristic of her. But the sensitivity was. The life of the theatre had not hardened her heart any more than it had corrupted her morals. With all her generosity of spirit she was easily wounded, and not naturally assertive. Her insecurity – did he sense it already? – gave her a potentially jealous nature. "One day she saw me so moved in speaking of you," he tells Adèle, "that several times since then she has said to me, 'Oh, you don't love me as much as you love your sister, I see it clearly, I'm just second best.'"

Yet it is his destiny to marry her. She is his "star", who will "beautify the last days of my life, which I trust will not be long".

For anyone wishing to highlight the "excessive" Berlioz the texts are there. "If you do not desire my death," he writes to Harriet (when and on what occasion we do not know), "in the name of pity – I dare not say of love – let me know when I can see you. I ask your mercy, your forgiveness on bended knees, with sobs!!! Oh, wretch that I am I did not think I deserved all that I suffer, yet I bless the blows I receive from your hands." To Adèle: "I am absorbed continually by the strangeness, the romanticness of my situation." To Du Boys: "What an improbable novel my life is!" To Edouard Rocher: "The novel that is my life is drawing to its close." To Ferrand: "She reproached me with not *loving* her. At that, for the sake of peace and quiet I riposted by poisoning myself before her eyes. Frantic cries from Harriet – sublime despair – horrible laughter from me – desire to recover on seeing her impassioned protestations of love – emetic – ipecacuanha – vomiting for two hours. Two grains of opium was all that was left. I was ill for three days, but I survived."

Berlioz certainly made the most of his situation, mixing the sublime and the grotesque in the approved style, playing the role of star-crossed lover for all it was worth – sobbing in Liszt's arms, telling Hiller to "keep this letter so that, if some terminal misfortune befalls me, you can claim *all my musical manuscripts, which I bequeath and entrust to you*". If he hadn't he would not have been the person he was. But that he relished doing so, between whiles, doesn't make the issue any less real or any less crucial. It was for him literally a matter of life and death, a prize to risk everything for, a loss to break one's heart over – the "supreme drama" of his existence, as he wrote many years later. We should also remember his lifelong ability to stand back from his emotions and observe them, objectively, ironically, even as they engulfed him. The detachment coexisted with the passionate involvement. He was at once the curious reader turning the pages of the novel and the hero involuntarily living its agonies and exaltations in his own person. "Speak then, my orchestra": as he spews out a torrent of *Romeo* quotations, his mind is thinking of the symphony he will create from the play. He swallowed the opium, but had the antidote with him just in case.

Half a century later, in *Soixante ans de souvenirs*, Ernest Legouvé recalled a dramatic late-night session with Berlioz and the novelist

Eugène Sue. Legouvé is a witness to be wary of, whose memory in old age was ready to distort details if not invent them. Dr Berlioz never "said yes" to the marriage and his son never said he did. The news he was full of that day, when he rushed round to the Rue Castiglione a few short streets away to tell Harriet, must have been the presenting of the third *sommation respectueuse*, which meant that they were free to marry. Legouvé's account also conforms to the rather partial view he had of his friend, that of the "slave of his every impression", "at the mercy of his nerves". But it evokes not inaccurately, I think, the fever pitch of Berlioz's existence in those summer months when the drama was nearing its dénouement and Legouvé, finding the job of confidant too much to cope with on his own, recruited Sue to help him.

One morning I got a note from Berlioz written in an agitated scrawl: "I absolutely must speak to you. Let Sue know. Oh my friends, what anguish!"

I wrote straight off to Sue: "Gale warning! Berlioz has summoned us. Midnight tonight, supper, at my place."

At midnight Berlioz arrived, his look darkly clouded, his hair falling over his face like a weeping willow, fetching sighs that seemed to come from his boots.

"Well, what is it now?"

"Oh my friends, this is not living."

"Is your father still implacable?"

"My father," cried Berlioz in a fury, "my father says yes. He sent me word this morning."

"Well, in that case – "

"Wait! Mad with joy at getting the letter, I hurried round to see her, I arrived in a whirl, tears flowing, and called out to her, 'My father consents, he consents!' And do you know what she said? 'Not yet, Hector, not yet! My foot hurts too much.' What do you say to that?"

"We say, my friend, that the poor woman was no doubt in great pain."

"Is one in pain," he replied, "does pain exist when one is in a state of ecstasy? I, I – if someone had stabbed me in the chest at the moment she told me she loved me, I would not have felt it. But she . . . she was capable . . . she dared to . . ." Then, all at once, interrupting himself: "How could she dare? How did she not think I might strangle her?" At these words, uttered with the simplicity of total conviction, Eugène Sue and I burst out laughing. Berlioz stared at us with stupefaction. To him, what he had said was the most natural thing in the world; and we had the greatest difficulty getting him to understand that a woman complaining that her foot hurts and a woman risking being strangled are two completely different things, and that Miss Smithson would have been utterly dumbfounded if he had sprung at her throat like Othello. The poor man listened to us without comprehension, his head lowered; tears trickled down his cheeks. "All the same," he said, "she doesn't love me – she doesn't love me."

"She doesn't love you as you love her," Sue replied. "That's clear, and a good thing too – two lovers like you would make a very strange couple." He could not repress a smile. "Look here, my dear friend," I added, "your mind is full of Shakespeare's Portia, who stabs herself in the thigh to induce Brutus to trust her. But Miss Smithson doesn't play your Portias – she plays Ophelia, Desdemona, Juliet, that is to say delicate, tender, timorous creatures, essentially feminine in fact; and I am sure her character resembles her roles."

"That's true."

"And that she has a sensitive spirit like the persons she represents."

"Yes, that's right. Oh, sensitive is the word."

"And that if you had been worthy of her – or to put it better, if you had been worthy of yourself – instead of flinging this joy in her face you would have laid it gently on her pain like balm. Your divine Shakespeare, if he'd had this scene to do, wouldn't have failed to do it like that."

"You're right!" exclaimed the poor fellow. "I'm a brute, a savage! I don't deserve to be loved by such a soul. If you knew all the wealth of affection she has in her. Oh, how I shall beg her forgiveness tomorrow! But just think – what a good thing I consulted you, my friends. I arrived in despair, and now look at me, happy, laughing, full of optimism!" And suddenly, with the naivety, the changeability of a child, he was plunging into the joy of his approaching marriage.

Seeing this, I added, "Very well, let's celebrate the marriage now, without delay: let's have some music."

He assented enthusiastically. But how were we to do so? I had no piano in my bachelor quarters and even had I had one, what good would it have done? Berlioz could only play with one finger. Happily there remained one triumphant resource, the guitar. For him the guitar comprised all the instruments, and he played it very well. He took it and began to sing. What? Boleros, dance tunes, songs? Nothing like that.

The finale of the second act of *La Vestale*! The high priest, the vestal virgins, Julia – he sang it all, every character, every part. Unhappily he had no voice. No matter – he made himself one. Thanks to a method of singing with closed mouth which he practised with extraordinary skill, and thanks to the passion and the musical genius that animated him body and soul, his chest, his throat and his guitar gave forth unknown sounds, penetrating laments which – mixed here and there with exclamations of admiration, enthusiastic interruptions, even eloquent commentaries – produced a total effect so extraordinary, a whirlwind of passion and high spirits so unbelievable, that no performance of the great work even at the Conservatoire has ever moved and enchanted me as much as that voiceless singer and his guitar.

After *La Vestale* we had a movement from his Fantastic Symphony. It was his first big creation. It had only been performed once so far in public [actually three times], and I had written an article, full of excited expectation, on the work and its author. Finally, after all this music and as though inspired by it, we threw ourselves into talk of our futures. Eugène Sue told us his plans for novels, I my dramatic projects and Berlioz his dreams of opera. We cast about for subjects for him and constructed him a scenario on *The Brigands* of Schiller, a work he adored. At four in the morning we separated, intoxicated with poetry and music, trembling with the fine fever of art. Next day Miss Smithson saw this strange being arrive at her house remorseful but radiant, who the day before had parted from her in fury and desolation.

Legouvé was not alone, among the amused but fascinated circle of writers and musicians who were privy to it, in thinking the match unsuitable. Liszt, in the first days of the relationship, tried to dissuade his friend from marriage (drawing from Berlioz a moving affirmation of his love and a plea to Liszt "in the name of our friendship not to speak again *to me or to others* of what you have said to me [. . .] Suppress, I beg you, all talk on the subject with Dumas, and with Hiller when he is here; say even the opposite of what you think – you must, I ask you on bended knee"). Edouard Rocher also urged him to think again: "You were called to do honour to your career in an art which seemed bound to make great progress under the stimulus of your genius; and you are sacrificing this entire future to a fatal love affair which halts you in your tracks, causing you to lose interest and deflecting you from your true destiny, and makes you the unhappiest of men. Is there no way of escaping from this ruinous influence?" Hiller described Berlioz's marrying Harriet as "the most high-minded and at the same time the most disastrous step he ever took". At the wedding, after the bride and bridegroom had gone off to Vincennes for their honeymoon, Heine – according to Hiller – was at his "most melancholy and sarcastic". To Legouvé, Harriet, with her other disadvantages, "was already too old when she married him". The sensible arguments were all against it.

Posterity has agreed with the Jeremiahs: such a marriage was doomed from the start. How could it have worked? The causes of its failure were inherent.

In much of what has been written about the Berlioz–Smithson union there is an element of moralizing after the fact, not unmixed with satisfaction – the satisfaction of being able to prove Berlioz mistaken and demonstrate that his dream of passion could only end – how else? – in disaster. But did it have to? Marrying Harriet Smithson was certainly in bourgeois terms an act of folly. As Félix Marmion said, it wasn't even a speculation. Taking on her debts – 14,000 francs at the time of their marriage – was high-minded to the point of being quixotic. It would be five years before they were paid off – years of intermittent privation and constant anxiety. Aspiring to "reconstruct her happiness" (in Etienne Rey's phrase) was magnificent, but was too much even for Berlioz. And in "sacrificing everything" for Harriet he was, in a sense, laying an extra burden on her. Besides, if he hadn't married her, if he had remained single, he would have had only his own more manageable debts to worry about, he needn't have squandered on the hack work of journalism time and energy meant for writing music, and he would have gone to Germany nine years sooner, with who knows what consequences for his art and his life. As for Harriet, she would presumably have returned to England where, though she was not recognized as she was in France, she could have continued working.

All this is true – up to a point. But Harriet was naturally drawn to Paris, where her talents were honoured and where she had become a great tragic actress. She didn't want to return. And to do what Berlioz did, to take her troubles on himself, was so much in character with what Jonathan Keates has called his "noble, unselfish egoism" that it is idle to complain about it. It was a condition of his being, one of the things, if you like, that made him the artist he was. He would also never have been satisfied with casual affairs. A temporary liaison – which

Harriet for her part would not have countenanced – was alien to him. Love was, with music ("they are the two wings of the soul"), the purpose and meaning of life, and now at last it had come. He had never truly been loved before; the previous experience had ended in nightmare, leaving him more solitary than ever. He could only go all out for it and stake everything, his future and hers. It was his "sole and unique chance of happiness". He had no choice but to seize it, whatever the risk.

Yet reading his letters written during their first years together – say from 1834 to 1839, the year when, finally free of debt, he composed *Romeo and Juliet* and performed it three times to a full and enthusiastic hall – I do not have the impression of a marriage that was bound to fail; rather, of one that failed not because of glaring incompatibilities which any commentator could have told them would be fatal but because of pressures external and internal which in the long run they did not know how to deal with. Longer than most biographers have given it credit for, the marriage brought a degree of fulfilment to them both. It may well be that the damage inflicted on Harriet in her early childhood – left by her parents before she was two in the care of a saintly old man to whom she became devoted and who died suddenly when she was barely eight – predisposed her, unconsciously, to a victim's role in life, to expect rejection; we might even say that choosing to live in France, where there were no obvious opportunities for her as an actress, she made sure she was rejected. But that lay in the future. To begin with, in the warmth of her husband's love, her nature flowered as never before. And these years coincide – despite all the exigencies of a busy journalistic career – with Berlioz's period of greatest productivity.

The year 1833, occupied as it was with his courtship of Harriet and with complicated arrangements for concerts and benefit performances, did indeed produce little: some work on *Le dernier jour du monde*, in which Emile Deschamps and Jules de Saint-Félix replaced the dilatory Ferrand as librettists but which Véron, the director of the Opéra, turned down; discussions with Gounet about an opera on Schiller's *The Brigands*; one song, *Le jeune pâtre breton*; and a new scene for *Les francs-juges*; otherwise nothing. But he had predicted as much, writing to Nancy: "At present I am not undertaking anything; I'm leaving everything, music, theatres, etc., till the moment when I can be sure of not losing her." (It may have been this information that prompted Rocher's accusation that he was throwing away his future.) Once he was sure, however, it would be "an eagle's flight".

He was right. The accusation was answered in the most emphatic fashion. These are the years of *Harold in Italy*, of *Benvenuto Cellini*, of what became the Symphonie funèbre, of the Requiem, of *Romeo and Juliet*. Without Harriet and her debts he might have written a greater quantity of music. But it is what he wrote with Harriet that concerns us. There is an exuberance of colour, of melody and above all rhythm in the works of the first few years that cannot be entirely a coincidence. Their *joie de vivre* must be more than just his response to the poetic demands of the works in question, more than the reawakened memory of the freedom and animation of "wild Italy" that suffuses so much of them or than an artist's delight in the consciousness of mastery. Berlioz could write music that had no relation to his state of mental or physical health and that existed as though independently of its creator, in its own domain. But the *Harold* symphony, full of sonorities and rhythms new to the orchestra and with a sense of well-being not heard before in his music; *Benvenuto Cellini*, the most brilliantly inventive score he had yet produced, extending the sonic and rhythmic explorations of the symphony and its celebratory mood; *Sara la baigneuse*, with its glinting strings and piccolo and lilting gait, "lovely and lazy" as the daydreaming bather of Victor Hugo's poem, a study in almost unshadowed euphony and concord – these are the compositions of a happy man.

A few weeks before the wedding, Harriet and her sister moved to the village of Vincennes, outside the city walls to the south-east; and it was there, in a "jolie petite maison de campagne", that she and Berlioz spent their brief honeymoon. At least on the day of the wedding Anne left them alone. For their first meal as a married couple they had the main dish sent over from the local restaurant but picked their dessert themselves in the garden, in autumn weather at its most serene and lovely. That night, at long last, they became lovers. Berlioz found that his wife – as he told Ferrand, and as he had hoped and believed against all the knowing slanders – was "as pure, as virginal as it is possible to be". To Liszt, who had been among the slanderers, he wrote the same, expressing it less discreetly: "a virgin, in every meaning of the word"; he could not resist adding, "My trial has succeeded – yes, in token of which I am quite worn out with my exertions." Vincennes, by ironic coincidence, was where he and Camille had eloped three years before, in June 1830; but Camille was forgotten now. At last he had an outlet for the untapped tenderness within him, and a wealth of healing affection in return such as he had not experienced before from any woman except his sister Adèle. He wrote elatedly to his friends to tell them of his immense good fortune – among them Chopin, who wrote back on 10 October: "Your charming letter gave me great pleasure. Nothing is more precious than the happiness of one's friends. My warmest greetings to Madame Berlioz."

The honeymoon could only be brief: their joint affairs demanded urgent attention. They were less than two weeks at Vincennes, and during that time he was quite often in Paris. On days when he didn't have to go they took restorative walks in the glow of a celestial Indian summer. Years later he recalled the ancient cannon in the park at Vincennes, "sleeping harmlessly in the sun, with hens nesting in their mouths".

Berlioz threw himself into the cause of coaxing Harriet back to physical and psychological health. "When I feel I have misspent an hour that I could have devoted to her happiness I reproach myself the whole day." Before their marriage he had "followed the progress of her recovery with the anxiety of a mother who watches her child's first steps". The leg had now mended but she was in great need of emotional support and encouragement; the accident, her traumatic financial losses and the collapse of her company had between them undermined her morale. "She thinks the whole world has forgotten her," he wrote to Vigny a fortnight before the wedding; she was so lacking in confidence that he begged his friend, if possible, to receive them without other company present. "The vague hope I gave her of a play by you in which she would make a reappearance is so enticing that she dare not give way to it, and a few more words from you on this occasion, even if only to calm her a little, would be of inestimable value to me." He must neglect no chance to relaunch Harriet's career. One way was to cultivate the friendship of men of letters who could be of help to her – not only Vigny but also Victor Hugo: within a few days of the wedding he was at Hugo's house in the Place des Vosges to attend a reading of his new play *Marie Tudor*, and soon after was making himself useful by acting as go-between for Schutter, who wanted to translate the play into English. On 23 October husband and wife were again at Vigny's house, 3 Rue des Ecuries d'Artois in the Faubourg St Honoré, where they inscribed the Comtesse de Vigny's album, Berlioz with the "Chant de bonheur" from *Lélio*, words and music, together with the text of the succeeding monologue and a few bars of "The Harp's Last Sigh", Harriet with the whole of "To be or not to be".

For the moment, though, it looked as if her immediate future as an actress lay not in Paris but in Berlin. Livius, the director of an English company touring Germany, had written to ask if she would be interested in taking part in a season of twelve performances there that winter.

Her debts, however, *their* debts – though she had insisted on a clause in the marriage contract exempting him from legal responsibility, he considered them his as well now – were too pressing to wait. By the second week of October Berlioz was planning a fund-raising concert, featuring the Fantastic Symphony, with himself conducting, and solos by Liszt. A few days later the event had changed into a theatrical evening, with some music, including Weber's Concertstück played by Liszt but without the symphony. Marie Dorval, attentive to Harriet as ever, agreed to take part in one of her most famous roles, Adèle in Dumas' domestic drama *Antony*. And Harriet, encouraged by Berlioz, nerved herself to risk a reappearance in the celebrated Ophelia scenes from the fourth act of *Hamlet*.

By now they had left Vincennes and were back in Paris, at 1 Rue Neuve St Marc, Berlioz's – and Harriet's former – lodgings. (Nothing more is heard of Anne's presence in their lives; she had presumably returned to England.) The next few weeks were hectic with arrangements. Supporting actors to play in the *Hamlet* scenes had to be recruited from among the best amateurs available. (We hear of the English company still in Paris in April, when Harriet asked Mlle Mars to use her influence to prevent two of their number from being excluded from a forthcoming benefit; but by November it had long since dispersed.) Meanwhile the venue, originally the Odéon, had been altered to the Théâtre-Italien; and the Fantastic Symphony had been reinstated, making it a kind of public celebration of their marriage, husband and wife appearing at the same event. The date, too, had gone through several changes. At first planned for 12 November, then the 10th, then postponed till the 17th, the benefit finally took place on Sunday the 24th. The start was scheduled for 7 p.m.

These hesitations, in retrospect, augured ill for the success of the evening. The disaster of 24 November 1833 – the worst Berlioz ever suffered at a musical event organized by himself – was due more than anything to bad planning. He had learned from his first débâcle, the abortive rehearsal of his Mass in 1824, to have the musical material thoroughly prepared, and from the chaotic try-out of the Fantastic Symphony at the Nouveautés in May 1830 to get all the rest of the practical details of concert-giving right in advance. (As a freelance musician he had to make himself personally responsible for the arrangements which today are looked after variously by orchestral managers, librarians, publicity officers, accountants, secretaries and the like.) What was wrong this time was simply the dimensions of the evening, consequent on the decision to combine concert and theatrical entertainment. There was too much of everything. The musical items alone made a complete programme: the *Francs-juges* overture, *Sardanapale* (with Alexis Dupont), the Concertstück, a Weber hunting chorus, and the symphony. And instead of putting together an orchestra of the best players in Paris, as he usually did, Berlioz – presumably as an economy – engaged for a lump sum the orchestra and chorus of the Théâtre-Italien, adding a few key musicians of his own choice from the Opéra. This was a dangerous mixture. Whereas the Opéra musicians were being paid for their work, the local players, by the terms of their contract with the house, were not; and, unused to Berlioz's music, with only a brief time allotted for rehearsal, they made a poor showing of it.

The newspaper accounts of the evening disagree as to the exact timing of events, as newspaper accounts generally do. But it is clear that, for whatever reason, the start was delayed by as much as an hour, during which the pit became increasingly restive and (according to the *Revue musicale*) broke into raucous renderings of the *Marseillaise*, Méhul's *Chant du départ, Ça ira,* and "songs of a disreputable nature", to the consternation of the smart spectators in the boxes. How much of *Antony* was given is nowhere specified, but it was enough to have included an interval, of inordinate length, and there was another, as long, between Dumas' play and the scenes from *Hamlet*, with the result that the concert did not get under way until at least half past eleven – well over four hours after the evening was supposed to have begun. Berlioz on his own admission conducted badly – he had conducted in public only once before, when his Mass was given at St Eustache in 1827. By the time the concert began he was on edge with nerves. The Weber Concertstück – brilliantly played by Liszt (all accounts agree) and, the *Revue musicale* noted, without the "grotesque facial contortions" which had previously been such a blemish on his talent – was the one musical success of the evening and was received with enthusiasm. But *Sardanapale*, which followed, though competently sung by Dupont, was a failure. Under-rehearsed and badly played, even the famous conflagration made no effect.

Worse, during the next piece, Weber's *Chasse de Lützow* ("execrably" sung by the theatre chorus), most of the orchestra got up and filed out through the understage exit while Berlioz, conducting the singers at the front, had his back turned. They were within their rights: contractually they were not obliged to play after midnight, and by then it must have been at least half past. Any hope of an orderly departure was doomed when one of the harpists, manoeuvring his harp through the narrow passage, tripped and blocked the way. During the ensuing hubbub the pit rose and demanded the Fantastic Symphony. Berlioz could only apologize to the audience: he "could not perform it without an orchestra". "Then give us the March to the Scaffold!" "As the clamour increased," wrote d'Ortigue, "he cried out, 'Gentlemen, have pity on me!'" A supporter yelled from the gallery, "Next time, the Conservatoire!", and the audience went home. The critic of the *Revue musicale*, remarking that many of the spectators left well before the end, confessed to being "of their number. I am therefore unable to tell you how the evening finished. It is said that, some musicians of the orchestra having decided like me that it was time to go home, the symphony could not be performed." It seemed that Berlioz's music positively drove the players away. According to d'Ortigue, "certain persons unfortunately not without influence in musical affairs" openly expressed pleasure at his discomfiture.

The only consolation for the humiliated composer-conductor-promoter were the box-office takings of 5,000 francs. The cost of the theatre and of other expenses came to 2,500, but the actors and the soloists had given their services and Dumas had waived his royalties, which left 2,500 for the repayment of Harriet's most pressing debts. In addition, the Duc d'Orléans, whom Berlioz had invited but who fortunately seems not to have come, again sent an honorarium of 200 francs.

If the evening was an embarrassment for Berlioz, it was a serious setback for his wife. Whatever the weaknesses of the supporting cast, she herself had apparently lost none of her skill as a dramatic artist. D'Ortigue's review, which does not read as though he were putting the best face on things in order to soothe her feelings, claimed that she "made a profound and vivid impression, I will not say on the audience as a whole but on the élite spectators who were present at the performance".

After a long and admiring description of her acting, he concluded: "One can say of Madame Berlioz-Smithson what Laertes says of his sister: 'Thoughts and afflictions, passion, hell itself / She turns to favour and to prettiness.'" Yet – as d'Ortigue conceded – such fragmentary scenes, played cold, out of context, could only be unsuccessful, quite apart from the ill humour of this particular audience, forced to wait so long for them, and the paucity of people who understood the language: it being a Sunday, the English community had mostly stayed at home.

Dorval, in fiery form (despite her "monotonous, droning delivery", the *Revue musicale* added), was given an ovation; Harriet was not recalled once. It was to be the first of several such wounds to her pride and self-confidence – wounds which, unlike her leg, never healed. How deep it cut for both of them is shown by the way Berlioz treats it in the *Memoirs*. He calls it "her last appearance on the Paris stage" and a "heartbreaking" experience for the actress – who, though she no longer walked with a limp, had lost the ease and certainty of some of her movements. "Poor Ophelia! Your star was setting." In fact he would continue to campaign energetically for her return to the stage and she would make several more appearances in isolated scenes. But, for want of a professional English company for her to appear with or a role in a French drama, Harriet would never again act in a full-length play in Paris.

For Berlioz himself a swift riposte to the Théâtre-Italien disaster was both possible and imperative. It was a gamble – the receipts might not cover the cost of a large hand-picked orchestra adequately rehearsed, which would leave them deeper in debt – but it had to be taken. Harriet was equally insistent that he must do it, and to his delight "showed herself, as from then on she always would, the sworn enemy of all half-measures and, where the interest of art or the reputation of an artist was at stake, bold to the point of recklessness in the face of penury and privation". She told him they could "sleep on straw" if they had to.

Her boldness was vindicated. The cry of "the Conservatoire" was taken up. Schlesinger, writing to Meyerbeer on the morning of the concert (22 December), announced that there were "no more tickets to be had". And the full house gave the music a tremendous reception. "It was like being at one of those splendid concerts where the name of Beethoven arouses a magical enthusiasm," wrote d'Ortigue in the *Quotidienne*. Under Narcisse Girard, Berlioz's violinist-conductor friend (he himself had not ventured to conduct, after his recent experience), the ardent young orchestra played like men inspired. There were three premières: the *King Lear* overture, composed in Nice two and a half years before, the *Jeune pâtre*, to words by the young Breton poet Auguste Brizeux, and another song, a setting of lines from Victor Hugo's current play *Marie Tudor*. After that the violinist Théodore Hauman played his own variations on a theme from Auber's *La fiancée*, and then Liszt again carried all before him in the Weber Concertstück, making his Erard piano rival the orchestra with its power, the audience frequently breaking in with clapping and bravos ("only Listz [*sic*] is applauded in a *tutti*!"). Finally, the Fantastic Symphony, and the biggest success Berlioz had yet had, the hall resounding again and again to prolonged acclamation. "Well, was I wrong," wrote d'Ortigue, "when I recommended to those captious gentlemen who were congratulating themselves on the downfall of a young artist as if it was a victory for them, that they moderate their song of triumph and beware of a comeback?"

Harriet shared in her husband's rehabilitation. Berlioz described her to Adèle as "overjoyed, on leaving the hall, to find herself congratulated on all sides, by A. de Vigny, Hugo, E. Deschamps, Legouvé, Eugène Sue – for I must tell you that all the Paris poets were at the concert. Oh my dear Adèle, if only you had been there!"

How much the concert made we do not know. But there seems to have been a slight easing of financial pressure in the winter of 1833–4. He was still drawing his six-monthly Prix de Rome stipend of 1,500 francs, the latest instalment of which was due in January (though he felt pressed enough to write twice to the Minister of Trade and Public Works to ask for it, the second time stating that he was "on the point of leaving for Germany"). He was beginning to earn money from journalism. The previous summer he had written a couple of well-paid pieces for the new arts weekly *L'Europe littéraire*, a prestigious journal which during its short existence offered subscribers musical evenings on Thursdays in May and June 1833 at its premises in the Rue de la Chaussée d'Antin. (All four concerts were probably organized by Berlioz, two of them featuring his music and perhaps doing something to offset the failure of his *Rob Roy* overture at a Conservatoire concert in April.) In December 1833 he became music critic of the *Rénovateur*, a newspaper of the right-wing, Legitimist or pro-Bourbon opposition – "but as I couldn't care less about political opinions, you can imagine how much the colour of the paper matters to me". The pay was pretty meagre; but from the beginning of January he was writing once a week. The authority and ease of these weekly articles (signed at first "H. B.", and then "Hector Berlioz" or "H. Berlioz") quickly earned him a name and he was soon in demand as a writer. By midsummer 1834 he was contributing regularly to Schlesinger's new specialist journal, the *Gazette musicale*, which had been founded in competition with Fétis' *Revue musicale* (and would soon absorb its ailing rival). *L'Italie pittoresque*, a lavishly illustrated travel book issued in instalments, commissioned him to recount his experiences as a Prix de Rome, and he produced two long pieces, "Voyage musical" and "L'Académie de France à Rome", which when published would further enhance his reputation.

This same year, 1834, two songs, *Les champs* and *Je crois en vous*, appeared as supplements in the fashion magazines *La Romance* and *Le Protée*, making a modest addition to his income. One way and another Berlioz had more freedom than he would have later to compose new works for his coming series of concerts, due in November and December. Though the Berlin project had fallen through, the household could relax a little and face the prospect of another mouth to feed. By the end of January Harriet was expecting a baby.

Berlioz and his wife had been hoping for much from Berlin. He had written to Spontini, the Generalmusikdirektor at the opera, asking him to use his influence on her behalf. But he was probably not sorry on his own account that it came to nothing: his immediate future was in Paris. And Harriet's condition was now an additional argument against their going; at thirty-four she was old to be experiencing her first pregnancy. So they stayed and settled into a contented routine. Sometimes she accompanied him to the opera. More often she preferred to remain at home and read by the fire. But friends came to see them: Berlioz's letters mention Liszt, Chopin, Alfred de Vigny, Brizeux, Legouvé and the brothers Emile and Antoni Deschamps. From time to time they dined with Alphonse Robert and his wife. Alphonse was a special favourite with Harriet, in addition to his potential usefulness as a source of free medical advice. "Harriet, who has an incredible instinct with new faces," wrote Berlioz to Adèle, "was impressed instantly with his kindness and became fond of him from the very first conversation they had together."

Though one or two biographers have scoffed at the notion of Berlioz of all people being happy with such tranquil domestic bliss, that is exactly what the correspondence of this period conveys. He too liked sitting by the fire; it was there, one February evening, that he sketched the Pilgrims' March, the second movement of his *Harold* symphony. He was in love with his wife and she with him. She still thought of her retirement as temporary; he had the conditions he needed for his work. "Oph.'s love has multiplied my capabilities a hundred-fold": that was four years before, when he briefly imagined that the distant beloved of his dreams returned his love. But now it was true. Sometimes he wrote for twelve hours at a stretch. Most of the drafting of the symphony was done in less than two months; 1834 was the best, most fulfilling year of his married life and, until 1839, of his career. Before *Romeo and Juliet* no series of Berlioz concerts was as successful as the one he gave at the end of 1834. The prospects for an opera – still the accepted goal of a composer – seemed distinctly good; the stir caused by the recent Conservatoire concert had slightly, perhaps significantly, improved them. There was serious talk of his being commissioned to compose a *Hamlet* for the Opéra, and other projects were in the wind. Véron, the director, was being difficult, but rumour predicted that he was about to resign. And the powerful Bertin family, owners of the influential high-circulation daily newspaper the *Journal des débats*, were interested in Berlioz and were taking up his cause. One of them, Edouard Bertin, was on the committee of the Opéra.

As always, there were days when he was out of sorts with everything, including himself. A letter to Ferrand written that spring speaks of his feeling "horribly sad today, why I don't know, incapable of replying to you as I should like". Another, to Liszt, tells of "wounds to my artistic affections" – evidently someone had been dismissing Spontini as outmoded –

> which have made me wretched to the point of tears and which all my reason (for I have much more than you may think), and all my dear Harriet's reasoning, cannot make me forget or surmount. I wish I could see you. Is de Vigny coming? There is something gentle and affectionate in his character which I always find very attractive but which today I have special need of . . . Why aren't you both here? . . . Tomorrow my state of mind may have changed . . . Are we really "the playthings of the air"? Is Shakespeare right? Is Moore also right when he says, "And false the light on Glory's plumes / And Fancy's flash and Reason's ray / Seem

but to light the troubled way – / There's nothing true, there's nothing *bright* but Heaven"? But I don't believe in heaven. It's awful! My heaven is the poetic world, and there's a caterpillar on every flower. Do come and see me, bring de Vigny with you. I miss you, I miss both of you . . . Why can't I stop myself adoring with so obstinate a passion certain works which after all are frail, impermanent things – as we ourselves are, as is everything that exists? [Berlioz then quotes a favourite passage from Spontini's *La Vestale*]. Here is M. Lammenais who has again written an inspired book in support of an idea which to me is absurd. Is he being honest? Equality! Is there such a thing? Was Shakespeare born equal to M. Scribe? Or Beethoven to Rossini?

Extreme fluctuations of mood were the pattern of his life. A few days later, when Liszt and Vigny and several other friends did come, he had recovered his spirits.

The breach with his family was a cause of continued anger and sadness; but at least it brought him closer to Adèle. She, he told her, would be his family; and he arranged secretly for her to receive an engraved portrait of Harriet ("a very good likeness"). *She* had strength of character, she was "a good sister, who doesn't give in to crass prejudice; you don't play the prude, the dolt, unlike our honourable sister Nanci, who didn't deign to reply to the letter I was fool enough to send her at the time of my marriage. I'm not writing to my father, although I am quite sure that today a letter would not be badly received: my father has too lofty a mind and heart to remain susceptible for long to the ideas which estranged him from his son. But I'm afraid of his attributing my natural impulse to mercenary motives, so I shall refrain until times are less hard." Berlioz's letters to Adèle are our chief source of information about his life and Harriet's in their first year of married life. With all the problems of daily existence described in them, they breathe an atmosphere of contentment.

The year 1834 begins with Paganini. The great violinist had been in the audience at the concert of 9 December 1832 in which Berlioz reasserted his presence after two years away from the capital. It was almost certainly then and not after the "concert de revanche" a year later (where the *Memoirs* locate the encounter) that Berlioz was accosted by "a man with flowing hair, piercing eyes and a strange ravaged countenance, a creature haunted by genius, a Titan among giants", who stopped him as he was leaving the hall and "seizing my hand, uttered eulogies that set my heart and mind on fire". But Paganini was certainly at the concert of 22 December 1833 as well.

In the interim he had fallen foul of the Paris press for failing to play at the bedridden Miss Smithson's benefit of 2 April 1833 along with Liszt, Chopin and the stars of theatre and opera. *L'Europe littéraire*, with which Berlioz was closely associated in the spring and summer of 1833, waxed sarcastic at the great violinist's expense in its issue of 19 April: "*Primo mihi*, that watchword of egoism, may be justified, but not this time. It appears that Mr Paganini has made the adamantine resolution never to proceed to *cras tibi*; that would be, on his musical scale, to play out of tune, and we know how exquisite his intonation is." The attack doesn't read as if written by Berlioz, though he may have prompted it. If so, Paganini's admiration for his music was not affected. About four weeks after the December 1833 concert he called on Berlioz in the Rue Neuve St Marc and asked him to write a work for him to play on the Stradivarius viola he had recently acquired. A day or two later (21 January) the *Rénovateur*, the paper for which Berlioz was music critic, carried a news item, copied in the *Gazette musicale* and elsewhere: "Paganini, whose health is beginning to improve, has just requested from Berlioz a new composition in the genre of the Fantastic Symphony, which the celebrated virtuoso intends to perform at his next concert in England. The work will be entitled 'The Last Moments of Mary Stuart, dramatic fantasy for orchestra, chorus and solo viola'. Paganini will play the viola part at the first public performance."

How far Berlioz went with "The Last Moments of Mary Stuart" before abandoning it for the symphony with obbligato viola, *Harold in Italy,* we do not know. The form "the last day/hour of " was enjoying a vogue; so were the two sixteenth-century Marys. But we should not assume that it was a mere convenience title, thought up for reasons of publicity. The fusion of chorus, orchestra and soloist suggests at least an intention to develop the idea of the all-inclusive dramatic concert work, which will lead to *Romeo and Juliet* and then to *The Damnation of Faust* and *The Childhood of Christ*. It may have also been influenced by Beethoven's choral symphony, which Berlioz heard for the first time that month and which left its mark on the review of themes at the beginning of the finale of *Harold*. His original scheme for *Harold* – which was first planned as a work in only two movements – sounds more like a dramatic fantasy than a symphony. It is possible that the discarded *Rob Roy* overture, which he decided to scrap immediately after hearing it at the Conservatoire and from which he took material for *Harold*, was a source common to the symphony and to the fantasy. He may have intended reworking the "Scotch" motif of the overture for a movement or section evoking the remembered happiness of Mary's youth – a motif which, in his review of *Harold*, d'Ortigue regretted Berlioz had not used along with the other *Rob Roy* tunes that reappeared in the symphony, one as motto for the work, the other as second theme of the opening allegro.

In retrospect *Rob Roy* can more easily be seen as a sketch for *Harold* than for a work celebrating Mary Queen of Scots. The Scotch motif may well have been left out of the symphony just because it had so strong a local colour; but the melody which became the symphony's motto theme was too deeply impregnated with the world of Berlioz's Abruzzian wanderings to find fulfilment in any but an Italian setting. It was ideally cast for a central role in a work arising out of them – a role both as recurring melody and as generator of other melodic ideas. Unlike the Fantastic Symphony's *idée fixe*, the *Harold* theme associated with the solo viola preserves its form and character unchanged. At the same time, being the source from which much of the thematic material of the work is derived, it functions as metaphor of the poetic consciousness through which the various scenes of Italian life and landscape are presented, thus helping to link them not just on the surface, by a recurring theme, but organically. The solo viola is what Berlioz calls it, "a kind of melancholy dreamer in the style of Byron's Childe Harold". "I live not in myself, but I become / Portion of that around me", the aphorism of Byron's autobiographical hero, could be the epigraph of the symphony: the principle behind the symphony is exactly analogous, and the compositional procedures reflect it. In calling the work "Harold", Berlioz was not merely making a gesture to fashion and capitalizing on the popularity of Byron's narrative poem, nor simply paying tribute – though he does that too – to the poet who, on the passage to Leghorn, on the tragicomic escapade to Nice, in the confessional at St Peter's, in the Campagna, in the Abruzzi, was the patron saint of his Italian journey. The title is apt at every level. It describes what happens.

While he was there Berlioz could create almost nothing from his experiences of Italy. Recollected in tranquillity a few years later, they flowed freely. What he had seen and felt and heard became music: the lowering presence of mountains in cloud; the moment when the sun strikes through and parts the curtain on a shining perspective of land or sea; the delight of serene skies and wide horizons; voices from far off coming through the warm air; bells tolling at dusk; darkness gathering in the valley while, high above, a crag still glows with light; peasants dancing; the animation of "wild Italy". The symphony also drew on music he encountered there. For the third movement, "Serenade of a mountain-dweller of the Abruzzi to his mistress", he took as his starting-point the *pifferari*, the strolling wind-players he had met in Rome and in the hills, absorbing into his own style and into the melodic patterns of the work their candid open-hearted tunes and exuberant ornamentation. The Pilgrims' March, the second movement, grew out of memories of reapers chanting their litanies as they trudged home to the hilltop villages; different musically developed ideas – the regular tramp of the procession approaching, passing close by, fading from earshot, the bell-like notes punctuating the melody and bringing it back each time to the home key, the chanted prayer, the gradual onset of night, the curve of feeling in the solitary observer, from pleasure to angst and isolation – were combined into a single arch-shaped structure.

By the time Berlioz and Harriet moved to Montmartre, at the end of March, the score was more than half done.

2

Friends and Enemies

The house stood on the northward slope of the village; their furnished four-room apartment occupied two floors. From the vine-wreathed windows of the upper storey you looked far out over the plain, beyond the silver Seine to the great basilica of St Denis. The walled garden was large and leafy, with fruit trees and an ancient well. In the spring nightingales sang day and night. The streets – Rue St Denis, where they lived (at No. 10), Rue St Vincent, which crossed it just by their house – were unpaved lanes. They were practically in the country. Montmartre, like Auteuil, Neuilly, Longchamps, La Villette, was not Paris then but a separate commune, well outside the city on its high hill, with farms and windmills and goats. Life was less expensive than in town, and the amiable old proprietor, M. Thorelle, charged a rent of only 70 francs a month. It was their home for six months in 1834, and they would return to Montmartre for a longer period in 1835 and 1836.

The peace and seclusion suited Berlioz as well as Harriet. Living a good half or three quarters of an hour from the centre of Paris he was safe from the casual callers who were forever interrupting him in the Rue Neuve St Marc. Their friends on the other hand were happy to come and visit them. On one such excursion, about five weeks after they moved, Liszt, Chopin, Hiller, Vigny and Antoni Deschamps spent the day with them; they sat in the garden and "talked and argued art, poetry, ideas, music, theatre, in fact everything that constitutes life, in the presence of the beauties of nature and this Italian sunshine we've been having the last few days".

Business took Berlioz down the hill into the city quite often: to attend the operas and concerts which provided material for his weekly reviews in the *Rénovateur*; to discuss subjects for an opera with librettists and theatre directors; to see Schlesinger, his publisher and editor of the new *Gazette musicale* for which he began to write regularly that summer;

to deliver copy; to collect mail at the Rue Neuve St Marc; to dine with friends like d'Ortigue and Robert, sometimes together with Harriet, sometimes, if she felt too sick to go out, on his own. But in the spring and summer months the trip to Paris was no great hardship and the return at night to their fragrant hilltop always a pleasure.

Harriet's solitariness during his absence was lessened, soon after they went to live there, by the company of an Englishwoman, Mrs Butler, and her young children, who rented lodgings in the same house. Much of the time, though, he was working at home. He had a good deal still to do for his winter concerts. *Harold* was completed at 10 Rue St Denis – the manuscript bears the inscription "Montmartre, 22 juin 1834" – and *Sara la baigneuse* and the first orchestral versions of *La captive* and *La belle voyageuse* were written there. So, soon after *Harold*, was a scene for *Benvenuto Cellini*. And Harriet's career seemed at last on the move again. She was engaged to appear that autumn in a leading mime role at the Théâtre Nautique, a new venture about to open in the Salle Ventadour – "nautique" because aquatic entertainments, enacted on a basin of water, would form one of the main attractions, along with more conventional forms of mime, including ballet. Though a far from ideal way of returning to the stage, it was a first step. Alphonse Robert found them the nurse they would need for the baby, due in the first half of August.

For Harriet, Montmartre with the shady garden and country air was a better place to be expecting a child than Paris. We catch a glimpse of her two weeks before the birth, described by her husband as "pastorally seated in the garden" with him, "not under a *beech* [as in Virgil's *Eclogues*] but under a plum tree", where Edouard Rocher's elder brother Firmin finds them one evening when he calls unexpectedly. But it was a hard pregnancy. The correspondence is full of references not only to severe morning-sickness but, throughout, to pains of all kinds. The confinement, when it came at last, was long and difficult. At one point Berlioz thought she would not survive. In the end, at eleven on the morning of 14 August, after forty hours' labour, Harriet was safely delivered of a baby boy. Berlioz promptly wrote the long-delayed letter to his father, receiving an immediate reply which, he told Ferrand, was as "kind and good" as he had hoped. Though relations with Nancy would take another year and a half to re-establish, the breach with his parents was healed. But it was to his faithful Adèle, the baby's godmother, that he continued to send his most intimate thoughts, writing her long and loving accounts of their life.

Montmartre, 23 Sept. [1834]

Yes, my dear Adèle, I am frantically busy and for several weeks have been trying to find a moment to write to you. Today finally, not having a score to orchestrate or some work of my copyist's to check or a meeting with the director of the Opéra or a session with my poet playwrights or any proofs to correct or newspaper articles to scribble, I am using this leisure to reply to you. First, you may set your mind at rest: our boy has been baptized. He's not called Hercule, Jean-Baptiste, César, Alexandre or Magloire, but just plain Louis. He doesn't cry at all during the day but he does at night, which is a rather sore point with his mother and his nurse. I, on the other hand, don't hear him in my room, where I sleep peacefully like a savage after his wife's confinement. He is a charming boy, strong, with superb blue eyes, the suspicion of a dimple in his chin,* fair hair with a touch of red, like mine when I was a child, ears with a piece of pointed cartilage, just as I have, and a slightly short lower half of the face.** Those are all the points of resemblance to his father. Sadly, he doesn't look at all like his mother. Harriet is besotted with him. She's quite recovered. When I have been to Paris she comes with her son and the nurse to wait for me halfway down the Montmartre hill, in a shaded walk where I often used to come seven years ago and look down over Paris, dreaming of *her*. If anyone had told us that in 1834 we would come and sit here *en famille* on these rocks . . . Yesterday while she was waiting for me several English ladies went past; the nurse was a short distance away with the little one. They went close to have a look at the child, and pronounced him superb.*** All their questions, in bad French, were met by Marie with wide-eyed incomprehension. Harriet listened entranced to their exclamations and asides, but then couldn't contain herself and announced in English, half laughing, half crying, that he was only five weeks old, that he was French, born in Montmartre and *she was his mother*. She burst with pride as she told me. It's the event of the day. Harriet thanks you warmly for the interest you take in her and Louis in your last letter. If you weren't so far away she would ask you to make him a bonnet, so as to have something of yours. We didn't have a lavish baptism, as you can imagine, but we shall make up for it this winter. Yes, of course, you know his godfather: it's Gounet. There are all your questions answered! In a week we shall be in Paris, at 34 Rue de Londres. We've taken an unfurnished apartment, which is much cheaper at the end of the year; but to begin with it's hard: we have to buy furniture, wine, wood, and all the other tiresome things one doesn't have to think of in furnished accommodation.

As for you, poor sister, life's boring as ever – I understand it, La Côte must be a depressing place. My father, as you read this letter, is no doubt buried in his wine harvest, and Mama worrying that he's exhausting himself. This morning early we went for a long walk, Harriet and I, on the plain of St Denis and talked about "young Prosper, who's not afraid of the open air", while we watched the larks rising around us. Just tell him, if his snares leave him free for an instant, to do me the honour of writing and letting me know how his hunting has gone this year, I'm still very interested in it. Farewell, good Adèle, all my love.

Your affectionate brother
Hector Berlioz

*By order of his mother I add a note to say he has "a very handsome forehead" – which happens to be true.
**Second note by mother's orders: "he is well made, with sturdy limbs".
***Third note by order of Harriet: "Many French ladies too, and the women of Montmartre, have stopped to admire Louis."

The beginning of the letter gives a summary of Berlioz's work at this juncture – as at many others – of his life: completing the orchestration of newly composed scores; going through his copyist's work to see that it is correct; working with librettists on ideas for operas (including *Benvenuto Cellini*, whose inception dates from the spring of 1834) and trying to persuade theatre directors to commission one from him; checking proofs of concert handbills, posters and programmes; writing articles for the press. Much of this could be done from Montmartre. By now, however, the move back to Paris had become unavoidable. The following year, 1835, they would return to Montmartre and stay there through the winter season; but with Harriet's rehearsals for the Théatre Nautique due to start at the beginning of October a Paris domicile was for the moment essential. They chose a small apartment in a new residential quarter in the north-west part of the city, reasonably close to both the Conservatoire Hall and the Salle Ventadour, and not far from the present Gare St Lazare. (This is the district where Berlioz would live for the remainder of his life.) They could afford to buy only the bare minimum of furniture; the rest would have to wait till they had earned the necessary money: Harriet from her theatrical performances, Berlioz from his forthcoming concerts, from which he hoped to make a profit despite the heavy copyist's bill.

Berlioz's expectations were fulfilled; but once again Harriet's venture turned out badly. She was hardly to blame, except for associating herself with a doubtful enterprise and with a role that (Berlioz told his father) was "below the level of her talents". But its failure dealt a fresh blow to her hopes and her confidence. Since its opening in June, the Nautique had been giving a series of ballet-pantomimes: *Les ondines*, a short curtain-raiser extracted from E. T. A. Hoffmann's opera, which made use of the water-tank; *William Tell*, a full-length ballet with music by the German composer and impresario Jacques Strunz (one of the witnesses at Berlioz's and Harriet's wedding); a one-act ballet with more water, *Le nouveau Robinson*; and a piece of chinoiserie called *Chao-Kang*. The orchestra was in the hands of Berlioz's friend and collaborator Girard. It performed Weber's *Oberon* overture as an entr'acte, and room was found for choruses by Weber and others, sung by members of the German company then being assembled in Paris. There was just enough here for Berlioz to give discreet encouragement to in his weekly column in the *Rénovateur*, especially as Strunz and Girard had plans to put on productions of *Oberon*, *Freischütz* and *Fidelio* once the ballet season was over. Janin, in the *Débats*, enjoyed himself at the expense of *William Tell*, which despite constant occasions for water, and after Paris had been all agog at the prospect, proved to be enacted entirely non-aquatically, and he rubbished *Le nouveau Robinson*; but he liked *Chao-Kang* and was full of praise for the work of the resident choreographer Louis Henry and the energy and discipline of his troupe. Most of the reviews, however, were distinctly unenthusiastic, and audiences declined. By the time Harriet's show opened on 22 November the company was on its last legs.

La dernière heure d'un condamné, a one-act pantomime devised by Henry (who also played in it), with music by Pugni, exploited the actress's famous gift for portraying madness. The heroine was a woman who loses her reason on learning that her husband, a cavalry colonel and the father of her child, has been condemned to execution. The part called on a generous repertoire of tears, cries, maniacal laughter, hand-wringing and infant-cradling, with a final despairing shriek as the fatal discharge of musket-fire offstage announced the end – what Janin in his notice called "the two or three dozen contortions that are known as the art of mime". Harriet did her best with it. It was only the third time she had appeared in a non-speaking, pantomime role. Though deprived of her beautiful voice – "they have cut Miss Smithson's tongue out", Janin complained – she still made a vivid impression. The anonymous review in the *Gazette musicale* spoke of the "sustained pathos" of her acting; at the end, "asked for loudly and repeatedly", she reappeared on stage "to receive the bravos of the whole audience". The review, admittedly, was written by Berlioz; but *Galignani's Messenger* confirmed the undiminished powers of Harriet Smithson as well as the mediocrity of the work: "The single feature worth naming of this piece is the performance of Madame Berlioz, as the wife of the *condamné*, in which the agony and despair of such a situation is depicted with a fidelity and painful truth only within the reach of a perfect artiste." But it was not enough to save the show or the company. In December the season closed and the management declared bankruptcy. Harriet was not paid a penny. Berlioz did what he could to console his wife, as well as instituting legal proceedings to recover the money owed her. His unsigned article in the *Gazette* was, I have no doubt, designed to lay balm to her wound. More than half of it comprised a detailed account of Miss Smithson's triumph on the first night of *Hamlet* at the Odéon in 1827, her revolutionary conception of the role of Ophelia and the new style of acting it inaugurated in France, from which so many imitators had benefited. It ended with melancholy reflections on "the cruel laws that innovators in every genre are subject to: they profit little from their innovation, while others appropriate it, abuse it and turn it into gold".

It was all the more vital to make a profit on the three concerts for which he had hired the Conservatoire Hall. The household had been counting on Harriet's fees to settle long-standing bills. He had also to recoup the large outlay on the copying of orchestral parts: there were six new works in the programme. A good house was essential.

Paganini's participation as soloist in the new symphony would have guaranteed it. But at some stage he had dropped out of the reckoning, in circumstances and for reasons that remain obscure. In August Berlioz's correspondence was still mentioning him in connection with the work, if without much expectation that he would actually play it. "Paganini, I think, will find that the viola is not treated enough in concerto style; it's a symphony on a new plan and not at all a composition written with the aim of showing off a brilliantly individual talent like his." Paganini may well have looked at the score subsequently and decided that it was not for him, though d'Ortigue's review of the first performance has him lavishing "fresh eulogies and fresh encouragement" on the composer after examining the completed manuscript, the implication being that Paganini had agreed to perform the work and it had been expected he would do so. In the meantime, however, he had come once again under fire from the French press. His fame and wealth and the aura of necromancer that surrounded him in the public imagination tended to bring out the tabloid journalist even in so supposedly serious a critic as Jules Janin (who loved putting the boot in), and this time the opportunity was irresistible. In July the Boulogne press carried a report, copied by the Paris papers, that the violinist had lured an innocent English girl away from her father and abducted her to France. Paganini's reply, to the effect that the man was an unmitigated scoundrel and was maltreating and exploiting his daughter, who had fled of her own accord, made a dignified and convincing rebuttal of the charge; but the press kept up the hunt. And in September a triumphantly indignant Janin pilloried him for refusing to appear at a concert in aid of the workers of St Etienne, victims of the recent Rhône floods, when so many other famous artists were giving their services. In vain Paganini protested that he was too ill to play. He left for Italy soon afterwards, pursued by Janin's most lethal darts.

Berlioz may well have felt let down. D'Ortigue, whom he often supplied with information as well as technical advice, clearly implies that Paganini is *persona non grata* in the Berlioz camp: "Just when the symphony was ready to be performed and the double triumph of composer and performer seemed assured: where is Paganini? They search for Paganini. Paganini is nowhere to be found." Urhan, who performs in his place, "is not an egoist; amour propre, if he suffers from it at all, is something to sacrifice in the service of a friend, of a poor hard-working young artist".

Urhan, though an admired player, was no Paganini. But Chopin appeared at the third concert, playing the slow movement of his E minor piano concerto, and for the second Véron lent Berlioz Cornélie Falcon, the star of the Opéra, who sang *La captive* and *Le jeune pâtre breton* and an aria by Bellini. Friendly newspapers stirred up interest in the concerts; the infant art of public relations, of which Meyerbeer was the master but Berlioz no mean practitioner, was set to work. He also wrote to the Duc d'Orléans inviting him to attend the première of *Harold*. The year before, he had had to ask his friend Gounet, a civil servant, for advice on the correct way of addressing royalty. Now he suffers no inhibitions in its presence:

Sire, it is unlikely that my name has come to Your Highness's attention unaccompanied by the epithets of lunatic and extravagant. Though my friends and the tiny fraction of the public known as my fanatics keep assuring me that artists who stray even slightly from the beaten track have been denounced for their extravagance and lunacy from time immemorial, the fact remains that every avenue is closed to me by stubborn and vigilant opposition.

I write therefore to beg Your Royal Highness to be so good as to attend the concert I am giving at the Conservatoire, the programme of which is enclosed with this letter. Perhaps, having heard my music performed by a hundred and thirty young men who are all more or less touched by the same faults for which I am rebuked, Your Highness will conclude, like my friends, that a place in the asylum at Charenton is not what I am most urgently in need of. Resolved as I am to strive with unswerving determination till I reach my goal, even if I have to use my teeth and nails to force a way through the door that refuses to open, I firmly believe I shall get there one day. Unhappily it is quite possible that, by the time I do, I shall no longer have either teeth or nails. That is a terrible thought for an artist who is conscious that his powers are at their height yet has the fear that the only way forward is downhill.

The duke duly came, and stayed long enough at least to hear *Harold*, the first work in the programme on Sunday 23 November 1834. Afterwards he sent a cheque for 300 francs (the receipt for the cheque – which arrived at the house while Berlioz was out – was signed by Harriet). This second concert, with the new symphony and Mlle Falcon on the programme, did better business than the first a fortnight earlier, when there were the premières of *Sara* and the four-voice, orchestral version of *La belle voyageuse* but no stars.

How well attended the concerts were is, as so often, difficult to judge. Fétis' *Revue musicale* took pleasure in observing that "there was no lack of seats" at any of them. The *Revue du théâtre*, on the other hand, implied that the hall was packed even at the first; and Janin in the *Débats* reported quite a crowd at the first but said it was "even bigger at the second", when "for the first time the receipts exceeded the expenses".

Such testimonies are suspect on both sides. Berlioz told Ferrand that the receipts at the second concert – 2,400 francs – were twice those at the first (though it is not always clear whether by receipts he means gross takings or net). At any rate, when the orchestra offered to play a further time for nothing he did not hesitate to accept; and it seems likely that it was thanks to this fourth concert, on 28 December, at which Liszt performed two movements of the Fantastic Symphony in his newly published piano arrangement and *Harold* was given for the third time, that he was able to come out at the end 2,000 francs to the good. He informed d'Ortigue that he was giving the extra concert "in order to make a bit of money"; and he did (as Schlesinger wrote to Meyerbeer, "sein letztes Concert hat ihm Geld eingetragen"). The implication is that if the musicians hadn't given their services there would have been little if any profit on the whole venture. Concert promotion by an individual, even an individual of Berlioz's reputation, was a risky business. (The third concert, announced for Sunday 7 December, had to be postponed by a week when the Opéra chose that day for a crowd-pulling gala featuring its two star dancers, Fanny Ellsler and Mlle Taglioni.) But the musicians did give their services. They were on his side; they believed in him; he was one of them – literally so at the first concert, where Janin described him as just visible behind the bass drum, playing the cymbals ("since the orchestra performs at our composer's expense, one fewer cymbal player to pay is that much gain for M. Berlioz"). They evidently revelled in his difficult but rewarding music, and their skill and enthusiasm made up for some of the technical deficiencies of Girard, the conductor, as well as for Urhan's hesitant account of the viola part at the first performance of the symphony.

It is true that Girard drove Berlioz to distraction by never achieving the necessary accelerando in the coda of the first movement of *Harold*. Like other more famous conductors since then, he also had trouble with the end of the Serenade, where the tempos and metres of the two sections are superimposed. And at the première he failed to correct the harpist when the player came in wrong halfway through the encore of the Pilgrims' March. Instead, after allowing the cacophony to proceed unchecked for several bars, he called out "Last chord!" and brought the movement to an abrupt end. But the March *was* encored, and at every subsequent performance. So was the March to the Scaffold at the first concert. According to the *Revue du théâtre*, each movement of the Fantastic Symphony provoked "an avalanche of frantic applause" and the feeling in the hall was "electric". The critics as usual were divided – Fetis' son Edouard attempted to take Berlioz apart in the *Revue musicale*, and another hostile journal began its notice of the second concert "Ha! ha! ha! haro! haro! haro! Harold!" ("haro" being the shout which raises a hue and cry after a fugitive from justice) – but the mood of excitement in the hall is unmistakable in review after review.

As before it was an audience full of famous names. "All the great artists of Paris were there," wrote Janin after the second concert. Meyerbeer attended the first two, and their final rehearsals. (In *Lettres d'un voyageur*, a few years later, George Sand recalled running into him at the second concert: "They played the March to the Scaffold. I shall never forget how you grasped my hand, and the warmth of feeling with which those hands laden with honours applauded the great misunderstood artist.") Antoni Deschamps responded to the first by publishing an ode in the *Revue de Paris*, "To Hector Berlioz after hearing his *King Lear* overture".

For the audiences at Berlioz's concerts in 1834 the atmosphere, in the hot proximity of the Conservatoire Hall, had something of the shared sense of momentousness, of new and great things coming to birth, that d'Ortigue evoked when he spoke of the "magical moment" at the Société des Concerts just before a Beethoven symphony, when "the orchestra waits motionless, hardly breathing, for its conductor to give the signal; a prolonged murmur passes through the hall, to die away in a rapt silence, and I could imagine myself in the palace of the Queen of Tyre at the moment when, the banquet being over and Iopas having sung to his golden harp of great Atlas and the wandering moon and the course of the sun, all the guests lean forward to hear Aeneas tell the story of his voyage and of his sufferings".

The tide seemed to be running for him. The papers were full of rumours of an opera commission. More and more critics were of the same mind: the authorities must yield to the growing pressure of his public, the doors of the Opéra cannot be closed to him any longer. Yet until *Romeo and Juliet* – a work whose existence was due to exceptional circumstances – Berlioz never again achieved this pitch of success at his winter concerts nor gave so many. There were two each in 1835 and 1836, none in 1837, two in 1838. The reason is obvious when you look at their programmes: the sole new score that he could offer the Conservatoire public in these years was the twelve-minute cantata *Le cinq mai*. Otherwise, the same works were repeated: *Harold*, the Fantastic, and the three overtures, *Waverley*, *Francs-juges*, *King Lear*. He could not afford to compose.

To have the necessary time and freedom of mind to write his opera

Benvenuto Cellini he had to borrow money from a friend. He composed the Requiem in the spring of 1837 to a government commission and with the certainty (on paper at least) of prompt payment; and even then, to survive while he was composing it he had to borrow and get further into debt. The score was completed by June; yet for want of funds he wrote nothing in the second half of the year and, having no new works to perform, gave no Conservatoire concert that winter. No doubt he reasoned that, though he had got away with it the previous December when, encouraged by Harriet, he had risked programming the two symphonies once again, he could not do so two years running.

In 1835 the facts of life begin to close in on Berlioz. His situation is horribly simple. Journalism pays on the spot, composition is an investment — one that he can rarely afford to risk, because you wait too long for a return. The correspondence of 1835 makes it all too clear. "If I had the time I should already have begun on the work for next season; but I am forced to scribble wretched articles" (10 January). "The necessity of earning all the money I can in order to buy the innumerable things for our little household that we lack and that we will lack for a long while to come, and in order quite simply to *keep alive*, forces me to exploit my pen to the limit" (17 April). "For me time is now money, and the money I earn is the family's livelihood, so much so that for want of having enough to tide me over for a few months, it's quite impossible for me to work at a large composition which I've begun and of which I have high hopes. I have to write the whole time for my newspapers, on pain of not having a penny to my name if I don't. [. . .] I have my audience, which gets bigger all the time but which also gets more demanding. 'Are you working on something? When are we going to have a new symphony? When is the next concert?' Those are the questions I'm bombarded with when I go to Paris. But I am unable to compose" (2 August). "I'm working like a dog for the four papers which give me my daily bread: the *Rénovateur*, which pays badly, the *Monde dramatique* and the *Gazette musicale*, which pay little, the *Débats* which pays well. With all this I have to struggle against the horror of my musical position: I can't find time to compose" (August). "I can't begin working at the music [of *Benvenuto Cellini*] – like my hero I'm *short of metal*" (16 December). "The necessity of sacrificing not only my art but also a sure profit, because of the impossibility of waiting for it and not having anything to live on during the period of composition, is one of the most revolting tricks that fate can inflict on a man" (24 December).

No wonder he thought of journalism as servitude. That he was good at it didn't make it any less so: he would hardly have been in such demand if he hadn't been. But his very skill and the quality of his writing dug the trap deeper. It became for him his one reliable source of income, an occupation which he could no longer escape from, which was even considered by many his *raison d'être*. When he eventually became a member of the Institute, twenty years later, the critic Scudo objected that "They were supposed to elect a musician, they have elected a journalist" – a well-worn gibe used against Delacroix when the absence of any canvas of his at the 1846 salon was attributed to the fact that "M. Delacroix is not a painter but a journalist", and curiously paralleled by General Weygand's comment on de Gaulle's appointment in 1940 as Under-Secretary for Defence: "more a journalist than an officer".

It may be said that making a living putting on orchestral concerts of contemporary music has not been possible in any period since Mozart's brief successes in the 1780s and Haydn's in London a decade later. Berlioz, however, was not trying to do that. He wrote symphonic works because it was the modern medium par excellence and because music, as he said, had "wings too wide to be spread fully within the confines of a theatre". When he had them performed they made a modest profit and won him the support of a small but enthusiastic public. But, for him, as for everyone who aspired to be more than a composer of drawing-room ditties, the way to material prosperity lay through opera. It was on the royalties of their operatic works that Rossini lived in regal state at Passy and Auber maintained a town house and a country house and a stable of horses. Berlioz never remotely achieved that, nor the sudden affluence that could come from an isolated hit in the theatre, such as enabled Clapisson to carpet his apartment and instal a heater in the dining-room on the strength of the success of his *Gibby la cornemuse*. Berlioz's studio, as described by Léon Gastinel, who visited him in the Rue de Londres in 1840, consisted of an attic room with a table and chair for furniture.

It was not that he didn't try. The search for an opera commission, and to that end a suitable libretto, was a constant preoccupation of these years. *Benvenuto Cellini* was the one eventually accepted, but other projects were pursued, though none of them got very far. At the same time he was continually on the lookout for the security of a salaried position, and sometimes came close to getting it. Things could have worked out differently.

We tend to think of Berlioz as the predestined outcast, as he says of himself when commenting on the fact that his prizewinning cantata began with a sunset, not with the traditional dawn: "doomed to be different from everybody else, for ever at odds with life and the Academy". Such a person, surely, could only remain outside the system.

In the early 1830s he sometimes acts as if this were so. By allowing, almost encouraging, the image of a bizarre and extreme artist to take root in the popular consciousness he accustoms people to look for and find only the bizarre and the extreme in his music. Especially in the overwrought months of his courtship of Harriet Smithson, his behaviour is reckless in its Dauphinois zeal for settling old scores whatever the consequences. At the première of Cherubini's *Ali-Baba* (Opéra, 22 July 1833) he causes offence by shouting out during the first act, "Ten francs for an idea!", then raising his bid in each subsequent act and finally announcing that he can't afford to go any higher and is giving up. "Everyone has heard about my joke," he tells Ferrand, "even Véron and Cherubini, who love me as you can imagine." At the concert of 9 December 1832, which re-establishes his presence in Paris after two years' absence, he takes open revenge on Fétis for his attacks on Beethoven by having Bocage mimic him to his face during the monologue in *Lélio* which likens "improvers" of masterpieces to the birds that soil the statues of the Olympian gods in public gardens. In doing so he makes of Fétis a dangerous enemy for much of the rest of his career. His two articles on the administration of the Prix de Rome competition, written for *L'Europe littéraire* in the summer of 1833, are unabashedly provocative. In the first of them, in which Cherubini is thinly disguised as "the grand old man", the preliminary exam or *concours d'essai* is held up to ridicule.

> The other members of the music section – some of whom, still virgin and unspotted from all contact with quadruple counterpoint, have never written a fugue in their lives (which hasn't prevented them enriching the French stage with a number of fine works) – leave the task of unravelling the candidates' unholy scrawls to their grand old colleague: a task, it is only fair to say, that he discharges with loving devotion. Fugue is his joy; it is his native element. He plays with it, caresses it, hugs it, grapples

it to him, bestrides it like Quasimodo on the great bell of Notre-Dame. In due course the other musician-jurors assemble, all but one; he [Le Sueur], in some ways the most distinguished, whose fame was at its brilliant height during the Empire, has a habit of arriving when it is all over.

The session begins. The judges sit round a large table littered with the lamentable manuscripts. Only the grand old man remains standing, glaring through his lorgnette at the pile of fugues which he has already scrutinized and compared. [. . .] The jurors refer almost blindly to him for the choice of the seven or eight "best fugues" (as they still say at the Conservatoire); and, while the candidates wait pale and tense in the next room, these gentlemen calmly re-enact the consultation scene in Molière's *L'Amour médecin*.

Eventually, when the jurors have held forth to their satisfaction on M. Tomes' mule, M. Macroton's horse and the dispute between Artemius and Theophrastes, they address themselves to the business of the meeting and select four or five fugues from among the seven which the grand old man has picked out and dissected. Their choice is determined by factors such as: "No.3 is in my class; it is two years since a pupil of mine won a prize – it's my turn." Or, "No.4 has already competed six times and so far has only won second prize; he's twenty-nine; if we don't admit him he can never win – this is his last competition." Or, "No.1 is eligible for conscription this year; you know candidates are excused; we shouldn't deprive him of this chance of exemption." Or, "No.2 is a good fellow, he only wants to compete once, so as to make a bit of a name and acquire some pupils; he'll be quite satisfied with a second prize" – and other considerations of the sort. But while each one's claims are being urged in this way, the missing academician, whom everyone had forgotten about, has arrived at the Institute. The door opens. His colleagues call out to him: "I say – you've come too late, we've finished without you." And he, his hand on the door handle, absent-minded as ever, goes on with the conversation he has started outside with one of his favourite pupils: "Yes, my dear friend, the true artist must raise the public to his own level, not lower himself to theirs. Ah, if Napoleon were to come back, I should have no anxieties about your future."

The irreverent candour of this article – and, still more, of the second one, later incorporated in the *Memoirs*, about the Institute usher, Pingard, and his revelation of horse-trading among the members of the

Academy – may have amused the journal's readers and won him the reputation of a lively writer, but was hardly calculated to allay official doubts about his soundness; and, as he acknowledged, it made the "Opéra and Conservatoire crowd" more hostile than ever. It was surely because of these two articles that Habeneck, who had championed him up till then, didn't conduct the concert of December 1833, so that he was forced to turn to the less able Girard.

Berlioz gives the impression, in these years, that he is single-handedly taking on the world. He will reconstruct Harriet's career and restore her happiness. He will write the truth about the way the musical scene is run. Though for the moment he has to "continue working outside the theatre", the time is drawing near when he will overcome the opposition of those "idiot directors" and "place his foot on their necks". Like a young Balzac character from the provinces, he will conquer Paris. And like a Balzac character he is defeated.

Defeated – but not without a prolonged and heroic struggle, nor before he has won many individual victories. In retrospect his defeat may seem a foregone conclusion: in reality it was due to the interaction of many different factors, political as well as artistic. Some were connected with his personality and his art and with what he was thought to stand for – the subversion of musical values, the sins against the sacred doctrine of regular phrase structure ("la carrure"). Others were impersonal, institutional, bureaucratic.

Berlioz had many supporters, among ordinary music-lovers and musicians and among the great. The committee of the Société des Concerts was against him (and after its performance of the Rob Roy overture in 1833 did not touch his music again for sixteen years, nor after that for another fourteen); but the orchestral musicians were mostly on his side, as were many of the leading artists, his peers. Paganini believed in him; so did Meyerbeer; so did Liszt, passionately, and helped him, in public and in private, with the generosity that was characteristic of him. They and others were not only admirers, applauders of him and his music: they acted on their belief – Paganini to such effect (as we shall see) and so much against the received idea of the great violinist that many people refused to credit it. Meyerbeer used his influence at the Opéra to help get Benvenuto Cellini finally commissioned after months of managerial and ministerial shilly-shallying. Liszt shut himself away in the spring and summer of 1833, allowing no one to see him except his mother and Berlioz (everyone else was told he was in the country), so as to make his piano transcription of the Fantastic Symphony, and then published it at his own expense. For more than a decade, until Berlioz brought out the full score in 1845, this edition was the only form in which the work was available. Through Schumann's review of it, it was crucial in getting its composer known in Germany and in paving the way for the epoch-making German tours of the 1840s and 1850s. Others who, like Chopin, did not care for Berlioz's music nevertheless recognized his integrity and the force of his creative personality. (Chopin, similarly, admired Delacroix while disliking his paintings.) The writers – Hugo, Balzac, Alfred de Vigny, Dumas, Gautier, George Sand, Emile Deschamps and, later, Flaubert – treated him as an equal. George Sand gave "la fraternité d'artistes" as the reason for leaving her sickbed to attend a Berlioz concert in December 1836 when she was feeling so ill that she got dressed for it "with the alacrity of a whipped dog". They all thought of themselves as belonging to a fellowship of free spirits, united, whatever their differences, in the common fight against a philistine society which the July Revolution had left essentially untouched. Berlioz had not got as far as most of the others – he had yet to storm the composer's citadel, the Opéra – but he was one of them.

Outside the ranks of the Romantic artists too there were people, men in prominent positions, who were for him: administrators like Baron Taylor, scholars like Auguste Bottée de Toulmon, above all politicians like the Comte de Gasparin, the Minister of the Interior who commissioned the Grande messe des morts and allocated substantial sums of government money for its composition and performance. Paris officialdom did its best to frustrate the minister – some of the opposition was deliberate, some simply the organic inertia and obstructionism familiar in all ages of French bureaucracy – but the gesture was of symbolic as well as practical importance. A composer distinguished by the state in such a way was not an outsider; indeed his enemies saw it as proof of the special standing he enjoyed with the regime. The rich, well-connected Bertin family were his allies. They moved in circles of power and influence, social and ministerial, to which Berlioz did not normally have access. The salon in the Rue Louis-le-Grand presided over by Bertin de Vaux, brother of the editor of the *Journal des débats*, was a rendezvous of the great and good, where governments were made and unmade. It was through the Bertins as well as Meyerbeer that the Opéra was finally induced to put on *Benvenuto Cellini*, and very probably thanks to them that Berlioz was able to go on drawing his Prix de Rome grant in Paris when by the regulations he should have been in Germany.

The Bertins' influence, however, went only so far. In the last resort it was subject to the diurnal shifts, the superior calculations of political advantage and the innate conservatism of French artistic institutions. The deal arranged with the Minister of the Interior, Montalivet, in 1838 or 1839, whereby Berlioz was to have a professorship of composition at the Conservatoire and an annual pension, was heard of no more when the wheel of fortune removed Montalivet from office before it could be signed and sealed. An equally promising and lucrative arrangement, the directorship of the Gymnase Musical, which would have given him the freedom he needed, came to nothing because the then Minister, Adolphe Thiers, refused to allow choral music to be performed at its concerts, thereby strangling the infant enterprise. This was a crucial failure, and not the least of the crimes against France committed by the butcher of the Paris Commune in his long and distinguished career; but I doubt if it was personal. The project was unacceptable because it was thought to infringe certain sacred privileges which Thiers, as (in Edmond Goncourt's phrase) "the most complete representative of the bourgeoisie", must necessarily uphold, not because Berlioz was in charge of it. Despite his bad relations with Cherubini, it was not under Cherubini but under his successor Auber that he was excluded from using the Conservatoire Hall for his concerts. By no means everybody in high places considered him the madman, the subverter of musical law and order, the noise-maker and figure of fun pictured by the caricaturists and the more virulent critics. The Duc d'Orléans did not think him ripe for a place in the madhouse; he took a sympathetic interest in his doings and gave him his patronage throughout this period. Guizot told Legouvé that of all the famous artists he had met at his house Berlioz was the one who impressed him most: "There is a truly original being!" Legouvé goes on:

> Guizot was right. Everything in Berlioz was original. An extraordinary mixture of enthusiasm and mockery; a mind that you could never predict; conversation that had you constantly on the alert by its very changeability; long brooding silences, with lowered eyes and a glance that seemed to plumb unimaginable depths; then a sudden dazzling recovery of spirits, a stream of brilliant, amusing or touching remarks, bursts of Homeric laughter, and a delight like a child's.

What attracted some repelled others; he made enemies as easily as he made friends. Some were against him on principle, because of what he was believed to personify: for his music which, even if they hadn't heard it, they knew was cacophonous and without melody; for his crazy view that music could depict life; for his known contempt for the composers of the past. Berlioz might write the Pilgrims' March, *La captive*, *Les nuits d'été*; he might demonstrate, in a long essay, his really quite traditional ideas on tone-painting and musical "imitation"; he might write admiring articles on Dalayrac and the old French pastoral school, and d'Ortigue might tell the story of the young Berlioz moved to tears at a performance of Sacchini's *Oedipe* – it was to no avail. Prejudice that ran so deep could not be reasoned away.

Others were against him for specific and, from their point of view, well-founded reasons: political, because he was the employee and pro-tégé of the pro-government *Journal des débats*; aesthetic, because of his blasphemous attacks on the modern Italian school of opera, to them the *ne plus ultra* of musical beauty and the absolute antithesis of his music, which they could only actively dislike; personal, because his reviews damned their compositions with faint praise. Others from pure envy; others from the Parisian spirit of contradiction, in sceptical reaction to the claims of his supporters, whom they regarded as having fabricated a purely coterie reputation; others because he was there, asking to be shot at. It was an age when few holds were barred, malice was freely indulged, and the more flamboyant journalists were tiger-cats "seeking whom they might devour", as Berlioz said to Heine, only half teasingly. Heine could be extraordinarily bitchy – about Liszt, for example, or about Victor Hugo. Few critics had his style; but they tried to make up for it by their ferocity.

Of course the great innovators of the nineteenth century routinely drew the fire of reactionary or mediocre minds fearful of the new in art. Vicious attacks on composers whose greatness we take for granted – Wagner, Chopin, the Beethoven of the final period – were routine. In an era of constant and rapid artistic change, innovation, throughout Europe, was in itself anathema to many creators as well as critics. Ingres thought Courbet's *Après-dîner à Ornans*, exhibited in 1849, pernicious, a threat to the very future of art. The scribes, in their more or less scurrilous way, reflected such attitudes. Most criticism of Balzac in France in the 1830s and 1840s was cheap and nasty. Chopin was savaged by Rellstab, Verdi by Davison, Wagner by Hanslick. Berlioz as the arch innovator among French composers was automatically the object of scathing reviews – from Fétis, from Alphonse Karr, Azevedo and many lesser critics, and later from the appalling Scudo, whose jeering critiques in the otherwise rather respectable *Revue des deux mondes* were extreme even by the most scabrous standards of the age. (Berlioz himself, often thought of then and now as a very caustic critic, never wrote anything half as violent.) Quite apart from what he actually did, it was enough that he was identified with change. The article he wrote in the *Débats* in 1837 advocating a new and emancipated treatment of rhythm in musical composition was widely regarded as a scandal and a confirmation of his shocking disruptiveness.

Mixed up with their rejection of him was an element of unconscious fear: fear not just of his music and what it expressed, what it portended, but fear of the man. The unease that he inspired in many people sprang, I think, not so much from his personal manner (though he could be abrasive and also forbiddingly withdrawn, as well as captivatingly high-spirited) as from his integrity, his incorruptibility of vision and purpose, his fundamental lack of *arrière-pensée* – something that placed him apart from the values and venalities of contemporary society and in implicit criticism of them. Legouvé was not entirely exaggerating when he said that "few felt easy with him" and even "the most eminent artists" experienced "a kind of awkwardness in his presence". In his reminiscences Legouvé describes seeing Adolphe Nourrit, one morning, launch into a Schubert song with gusto, then suddenly grow nervous on noticing Berlioz enter the room, "so that having begun like a master he finished like a schoolboy". The sense of someone who did not really play the game as everyone else played it, who did not take bribes, who put his ideals higher than personal gain, gave an extra edge to his adversaries' hostility.

Such attacks, no matter how disagreeable they were for him and for his friends to read, conferred a certain topicality and distinction, as did the endless sallies of the caricaturists ("Cab, sir?" "My man, I see that you are addressing me, but I have just come from a Berlioz concert and cannot hear a word you are saying.") To be forgotten was the worst of all fates in Paris, that great Babylon, as Napoleon called it, where notoriety soon languished unless constantly replenished, and one reputation was quickly superseded by another. Berlioz, in these early years, did not have to suffer that.

By the beginning of 1835 he was notorious enough to be chosen for lampooning at the first of the Opéra's annual new-year masked balls. The actor Arnal, in flaming auburn wig, impersonated him conducting his "symphonie pittoresque et imitative", *Episode in the Life of a Gambler* (composed for the occasion by Adolphe Adam), with *Lélio*-like commentary on the new kind of music which rendered words, singers, actors, costumes and décor superfluous.

> It's all in my orchestra, gentlemen. You will see the character in action, you will hear him speak, I shall portray him from head to foot; in the second reprise of the first allegro I will show you how he ties his cravat. The marvels of instrumental music! But that is only the beginning. Wait till you hear my second symphony on . . . the Civil Code. What a contrast between this kind of music, which dispenses with all those accessories that true genius has no need of, and to be understood merely requires – er – three hundred musicians – what a contrast, I say, with the ditties of Rossini. Rossini! Don't talk to me of him: an adventurer who presumes to have his music performed in every corner of the globe so as to acquire a reputation! A man who writes things any fool can understand! The charlatan!

Berlioz went along to the Opéra and wrote about it afterwards, contriving both to laugh with a reasonably good grace and to doubt "whether the assembly quite grasped the satirical point of the monologue or the orchestra's musical jokes". He also wondered whether, with all their splendour, their tombola prizes, and their leading ballerinas dancing Musard gallops to a sumptuous orchestra, these masked balls had much to offer anyone except the *flâneur* bent on amorous adventure. For the rest, the relentless brilliance of the lighting, the deafening thumps of the bass drum, and the coating of dust which neither punch nor ices could dislodge from one's throat, ruled out any possibility of pleasure. (Janin was more censorious, demanding to know "What is this passion for sordid enjoyment, this wretched itch for joyless delights?") However, though people always went away declaring there was nothing more tedious, they came back; and he hoped to be able to write another suitable composition in time to provide material for next year's festivities.

The composition he intended to write was a seven-movement work for soloists, chorus and orchestra entitled *Fête musicale funèbre à la mèmoire des hommes illustres de la France*. Such a work had been taking shape for some time. Part of it can be traced to the Napoleonic symphony whose movement titles he jotted down in his notebook three years before, on the journey home from Italy in the spring of 1832. And out of its unfinished, fragmentary state came, almost certainly, the opening march of the Symphonie funèbre et triomphale as well as part of the idea for the Te Deum. Though never completed, it was at the time a very real project to Berlioz. The austere ceremonial work is a constant preoccupation of his career as a composer, answering a deep-seated need which his studies with Le Sueur made conscious but did not create. Throughout, the monumental and the richly coloured and passionate alternate in an almost continuous sequence: the Fantastic Symphony followed by *Le dernier jour du monde*, *Harold* by the *Fête musicale funèbre*, *Benvenuto Cellini* by the Grande messe des morts, *Roméo* by the Symphonie funèbre, itself followed by *Les nuits d'été* and *La mort d'Ophélie*, *The Damnation of Faust* by the Te Deum, until the two streams unite in *The Trojans*, whose grandeur in turn gives rise to the mercurial *Beatrice and Benedick*. That two of the ceremonial works, the Grande messe and the Symphonie funèbre, were commissioned, and two, *Le dernier jour* and the *Fête musicale funèbre*, were unrealized, does not make the pattern any less striking.

Berlioz set his heart on this "symphony on a new and large-scale plan". It was not from any lack of commitment on his part that it remained a fragment. But 1835 was the year not of the *Fête musicale funèbre* but of the *Journal des débats*.

3

The Music Critic malgré lui

Already by the spring of 1834 Berlioz had met the proprietors of the *Journal des débats*, Bertin *aîné* and his son Armand, and they were taking an active interest in his career. He had been drawn quite naturally into their orbit. Jules Janin was the paper's drama and opera critic; and his new acquaintance Léon de Wailly, novelist, playwright, translator and one of the librettists of *Benvenuto Cellini*, was an intimate of the family.

He had also attracted the Bertins' notice as a writer. They had had ample opportunity to assess his capabilities and to decide that he was the man they wanted. Since the end of 1833 he had been writing a weekly column in the *Rénovateur*; more recently he had become a contributor to the *Gazette musicale*. The retirement of Castil-Blaze from the *Débats* had left the paper too long without anyone to review concerts – much less important than opera in the great Parisian scheme of things no doubt but, since the founding of the Conservatoire series and the advent of instrumentalists like Liszt and Paganini, of concern to a growing number of people, not least among the *Débats*' twenty thousand subscribers. Janin, though he sometimes ventured into the concert hall and was never at a loss for words, was hardly the man to fill the gap. Berlioz was. In a short time he had made himself master of the field. No one else combined his knowledge of music and the musical world with his command of the French language. He wrote "as one having authority, not as the scribes". He was ideally qualified, if not to "make musical criticism intelligible to the deaf" (as Shaw would claim to be able to), then to arouse the curiosity and sustain the interest of his readers with a style which leavened the evocative with a flattering dash of the technical and which used a virtuoso mixture of irony, rhetoric, humour, enthusiasm, mockery and passionate conviction to propagate a view of music at once exalted and practical.

It was precisely this opportunity to coax and coerce his readers into thinking and feeling as he did, to treat them to a virtual course in the art of music, that appealed to him. The *Débats'* feuilletons were given prominent billing, starting towards the foot of the front page – where they occupied the last three or four inches of all five columns – and usually spreading on to page 2. They could be anything up to five thousand words long.

Berlioz's connection with the *Débats* began in October 1834. On the 10th of that month the paper reproduced as its feuilleton of the day a piece that had appeared in the *Gazette* a few days before, prefacing it with the announcement that " 'Rubini at Calais' is the title of an anecdote which we find in the latest number of the *Gazette musicale*, where it is recounted, with wit and verve, by M. Hector Berlioz." The story, written when he was "desperate for a few francs", tells of a Calais impresario providentially rescued from the tight spot he finds himself in when his plan to present the great tenor to the admiring inhabitants goes awry. It is a minor example of a genre of journalistic novella that was popular at the time and that normally was designed to include a moral of topical importance: in this case the iniquities of the poor tax, which took 9 per cent of an opera's receipts but 25 per cent of a concert's.

> Since our honoured representatives (whom God confound) passed a law on a subject as foreign to them as are so many others on which they legislate, a duty – did I say a duty? a power of plunder – is unleashed on all who put on concerts. Say a composer, with scarcely sufficient to live on, wishes to perform a work on which his future depends. He arranges a grand musical ceremony and engages a splendid orchestra. His score, executed with vigour and precision, has a great success. But the takings are only 2,000 francs, the expenses were 1,900, and lo and behold the tax-farmer claims 500 francs for the poor – the quarter of the gross receipts that the law entitles him to; with the result that the unfortunate artist, instead of making a modest hundred francs from having composed a remarkable work and succeeded in getting it worthily performed at his own peril, is robbed of his profit and becomes, by law, the loser to the tune of 400 francs. It is the due of the poor, or rather the due of the tax-farmer for the poor, who, while not himself putting on concerts, finds it all too convenient that they should be put on for him, and pockets a quarter of the takings without including in the reckoning the least part of what they cost to put on.

The day after "Rubini at Calais" was reprinted in the *Débats* Berlioz called at the office in the Rue des Prêtres St Germain l'Auxerrois, by the Louvre, to thank Armand Bertin. Armand replied by offering him the job. It was agreed he should take on the musical feuilleton. (Janin would retain his "ius primae noctis" over the Opéra, including ballets, and Etienne Delécluse would continue to cover the Théâtre-Italien.) He was to start in January at the exceptionally high rate of 100 francs an article.

The first feuilleton, more than four thousand words long, was devoted to the Société des Concerts (as were many of its successors) and appeared on Sunday 25 January 1835; the society's season, its eighth, had opened a week before. The piece is not Berlioz at his best. You can sense a constraint as he feels his way into the new context and strives to catch a tone appropriate to it and at the same time his own. Compared with his later articles, or with the ones he was doing in the *Rénovateur*, it is the work of a writer who is trying too hard. The ironies and sarcasms lack the glancing touch which would later become familiar. But central Berliozian themes are set out in it. The long introductory section on the reception of Beethoven in France and the vital role of the Société des Concerts in transforming the composer's image from incoherent barbarian to transcendent genius – a process aided by his timely demise (he had to "die in order to earn our esteem") – contains a nice vignette of Boieldieu at a Beethoven rehearsal, here used to tilt at academic orthodoxy.

> A celebrated composer, whose recent death the arts deplore, was present, in his hand the score of the symphony about to be played. Indicating a particular passage, he declared he could not conceive how it could possibly be bearable. The orchestra commenced. "But it works," he cried, "it works very well! How extraordinary – that a harmony incomprehensible to the eye should produce such an effect in performance!" This naive exclamation is a damning indictment of the restrictive systems adopted by the professors of the French school, which they impose on their pupils as sacred dogmas.

Significantly, in view of the assertion often made that Berlioz was not interested in any recent music but his own (Cherubini? Rossini? Mendelssohn? Chopin? Verdi? Wagner?), there is an enthusiastic couple of paragraphs on Schubert, whose *Young Nun* was sung at the concert by Adolphe Nourrit in an orchestral arrangement which Berlioz evidently believed was the work of Schubert himself. After giving a synopsis of the words, he goes on:

> Such is the subject of the little poem that the composer had to treat. He made a masterpiece of it. The persistent violin tremolos, the dark phrase of the bass which answers every interjection of the nun, the outbursts in the brass which seem to be attempting to overpower the singer but in vain, above all the admirable expressiveness of the voice part, all combine to make a consummate dramatic achievement. Poor Schubert! To die at twenty-five [thirty-one], with a musical future like that before one! This young composer, cut off, in Vienna, before his time, left two volumes of pieces for one or several voices – music which is to our feeble French romances as *Coriolan* is to the overture to [Lebrun's] *The Nightingale* – and several string quartets and septets [*sic*] whose loftiness of style is equalled by their formal originality. In a few years artistic Europe will come to appreciate the richness of the heritage that Schubert has bequeathed it. No doubt we too shall not restrict ourselves to the *Nun* but will go on to perform the rest and do justice to the composer, now that he is dead.*

The article attacks the practice of including trivial display pieces in programmes of serious music – Urhan had played some Mayseder variations for violin – and looks forward to the day when the Société des Concerts feels able to do without such concessions to mass taste. And it gives another outing to a favourite hobby-horse, the tyranny of the interminable anti-musical fugue on the word "Amen", this time apropos of the conclusion of the Credo of the Missa Solemnis (!). Berlioz recalls a conversation he had with a learned but enlightened professor (Reicha), compatriot and colleague of Beethoven, during which he asked him "what he thought of those fugal and vocalized Amens. He answered very frankly, 'Oh, they're barbarous.' 'Then why persist in writing them?' 'Good Lord – what do you mean? It's customary. All composers have done so.' How depressing that routine should still be so powerful that even a Beethoven will bow down, for a moment, before it!"

However sad, this at least shows him not blindly uncritical in his adoration of Beethoven. But Beethoven and the need to expound and celebrate his music and raise the public, as far as possible, to a love

---

* When Schubert's Great C major symphony was eventually performed in Paris, twenty years later, Berlioz recognized it as one of the supreme orchestral works of the century.

and understanding of it, is none the less for Berlioz the single most important *raison d'être* of his work as a critic. The analysis of the Eroica that ends this opening *Débats* salvo is the first in a long line of "critiques admiratives" in which he will seek to educate his readers in the beauties and splendours of the symphonies – the greatest of all works of their kind and the true beginning of modern music – and to dissipate the many prejudices that still obscure them. He will pursue the same campaign on behalf of high art and against vulgar commercialism in the columns of the *Gazette musicale*, the journal founded by Maurice Schlesinger to promote his own publications but also to champion symphonic music and combat the low taste of the piano music industry and the excessive influence of the Italian school on Parisian musical life.

Given Berlioz's values, the vogue for Italian music – common to this whole period but reaching its apogee in 1840 when seven Donizetti operas were staged in Paris – could only provoke his dissenting voice. His view of contemporary Italian musical culture was shared by other musicians – by Liszt, Schumann and Mendelssohn, for example. It did not prevent him admiring individual works. But the enormous extent of the vogue explains why this dissent annoyed so many people, and why critics like Scudo and Karr, devotees of Italian music, attacked his compositions so ferociously. He was their enemy before he had written a note. That what he said was quite mild by the journalistic standards of the time, in manner at least, made no difference; the fact that he said it at all was enough to make them feel their sacred cows had been violated. And the mildness was often deceptive; it was criticism which understands that laughter is a more effective weapon than heated indignation.

Here he is, in the *Rénovateur*, on a new work by the Italian composer Vincenzo Gabussi:

> The other day I went to the Théâtre-Italien – something that doesn't often happen to me; but when all is said, with a new opera, and an opera entitled *Ernani*, with the composer making his Paris début, and Rubini, Tamburini, Santini and Grisi on the bill, a visit to the Salle Favart was clearly in order.
>
> Ye gods! What gilded visions the young composer must have had before his eyes. No doubt he had heard all about the literary feud generated by Hugo's play; echoes of the tumult that engulfed the pit at

every performance, the sarcastic laughter of the hostile faction, the furious threats and passionate enthusiasm of the new school's champions, had reached him and set his heart aflame with noble emulation. "I shall make Victor Hugo's play into an opera," will have been his response. "I shall find a way of getting it put on at the Théâtre-Italien in Paris. I shall rekindle the great conflict that the French poet provoked not long ago. There will be confrontations, shouting matches, duels for and against me. And, with a company formed of the finest singers in Europe, I cannot fail to have all my intentions brought out and displayed in the best possible light."

Poor maestro! What a sad awakening. Nothing could have been cooler and more docile than the audience at the fourth performance of *Ernani*: no trace of confrontation, not a whisper of an argument, everyone on the contrary in perfect agreement. On the way out we talked of everything but the opera we had just heard. It might have been the hundredth performance of a long-established work. That is cruel for a composer. But in all honesty, what can one say of this *Ernani*, which is no more Ernani than I am the Pope? Where are the volcanic passions, the fierce vengefulness, the impetuous, consuming love, the pure and noble devotion of Doña Sol, and the other outstanding features that made Victor Hugo's play absurd to some, sublime to others, remarkable to all? The physiognomy of the Italian drama is such that it might just as well be called *Francesco* or *Pietro*. And the music shares this fault. It wants distinctive colour. The cavatinas are tailored to the pattern of every other example of the kind. The ritornellos have the form used by every other maestro of the Italian school: the same modulation appears exactly at the point where custom decrees it should appear. The tunes have sisters and cousins in every corner of the globe. And this fault, which is a very serious one to our way of thinking in any composition, becomes shocking in a subject as extreme as that of *Ernani*.

In fact, to speak our mind fully, *Ernani* cannot be treated by an Italian composer who wishes to succeed with his fellow-countrymen. The music such a drama demands would be hooted off the stage; the maestro who wrote it would be ill-advised to show himself at the keyboard on the day of the first performance: one couldn't answer for his not being assassinated. Besides, if the score of *Ernani* had been written in such a way as to produce, at the Favart, the sort of advance rumours provoked by Victor Hugo's play at the Théâtre-Français, you may be sure the Théâtre-Italien's management wouldn't have touched it. Opera directors have unerring tact. Put a commonplace piece among four works of originality, and instinct will infallibly guide them to choose the commonplace. All in all, one cannot absolutely blame M. Gabussi for not treating his subject in a fresh and poetic manner. He has made an Italian opera that is no worse than many I could mention, and that our dilettanti find very capital.

It would be interesting to know how Berlioz responded to the *Ernani* which Verdi composed ten years later, and which reached the Paris stage in 1846; but his opinion is not recorded.

His review of Donizetti's new opera at the Théâtre-Italien in March 1835, a few months after Gabussi's, though containing nothing abusive, would have certainly failed to satisfy the composer's many admirers:

Marino Faliero achieved a thorough success; several numbers were encored, and the maestro himself took two or three bows; all of which demonstrates the very real merit of the score. Before examining it, however, we should like to associate ourselves with some of our colleagues in deploring the ludicrous practice, recently introduced here by the Italians, of insisting on calling the authors and the performers on stage at the drop of a cavatina and according them ovations or even triumphs apropos of nothing – a practice which has the effect of pre-empting any genuine, well-earned display of enthusiasm.

Berlioz then digresses to his experiences of opera in Rome, and describes an occasion when, at a performance of a work of no account, everyone from the librettist to the machinist was made to take a curtain call, and only the wig-maker held back.

And this same Roman public, a few years earlier, pursued the young composer of *The Barber of Seville* with boos and catcalls. Which shows how much the approval of the crowd is worth and why Rossini (if what they say is true) despises it so profoundly.

After discussing the work in some detail, he concludes that

the new opera does credit to M. Donizetti's facility; it is clear that the composer did not have to wait for his ideas or search for them laboriously. All the same we do not think *Marino Faliero* is destined for a long life. The lack of originality evident throughout the work is treated indulgently by the regulars of the Théâtre-Italien, but in the last resort it is what a musical production has most to fear.

He also criticizes Donizetti for "not attending sufficiently to his orchestra".

> I realize that in Italy an opera is considered well instrumented when it contains elegant solos for flute and horn and cello. But in Paris, where you can hear Beethoven and Weber and Mozart every day, a lot of people know that instrumentation means something very different.

He probably did himself no good either by his review in the *Réno-vateur*, later the same year, of *La grande duchesse* by Rossini's friend the Italian-born composer Michele Enrico Carafa. But with Bossuet's funeral oration for "Madame la grande duchesse", the young Henrietta of England, ready to hand – "Madame se meurt, Madame est morte" – the opportunity was heaven-sent and not to be resisted:

> *La grande duchesse* is not making money for the Opéra-Comique. "Madame is dying. Madame is dead." Yet the score was written exactly as the director wanted, with just the degree of originality he required. The music contained nothing to shock the expectations of the dilettanti of the place. The singers should have found it absolutely to their taste, since it cost no effort to learn. Why then its lack of success? I confess to having no idea; I no longer understand what is going on in our musical world. The other day the Opéra was full for *William Tell*. Yet M. Crosnier's theatre empties when they give *La grande duchesse*. Masterpieces are doing well while platitudes flop. *Don Juan* itself draws the crowds at the Opéra. Some strange influence is at work. Can it be the comet?

The notice which caused the greatest offence of all, however, was his article in the *Débats* on Herold's *Zampa*, occasioned by a revival of the work at the Opéra-Comique in September 1835.

> Until the recent revival – which I could not discuss without poaching on the preserves of my gifted colleague M. Jules Janin – all I knew of Herold's opera were the scraps extracted from it for the vaudevilles and quadrilles and barrel-organs. At the time of its first performances I was in Italy, giving little thought to what went on at the Opéra-Comique in Paris. I frequented the theatres – not the San Carlo, the Fondo, the Valle, the Pergola or the Scala but the antique theatres of Pompeii, San Germano, Tusculum and Rome, where the evening breeze playing along the deserted tiers sings airs more expressive than Coccia, Schiafogatti, Focolo, or Vaccai himself could hope to achieve. True, the performance and the staging were

a not unimportant part of the magic of that nocturnal music. The wind changes nothing in the text which the great composer of the universe has entrusted to it; it is gay or melancholy, violent or playful, as the eternal maestro commands; it howls, weeps, sighs but never embellishes, never defaces its primordial melodies with nauseating appoggiaturas, and adds no cadenzas. As for the scenery, it beggars description: above all at the tragic theatre of Pompeii, where to your right Vesuvius towers up, roaring and brandishing its fearsome plume while a crimson necklace of lava lies majestically on its exhausted breast, and to your left, on the gleaming bay of Naples, "the moon spreads its silver fan across the sea"*; and over all that sublimity of sky and earth and fire and water a deep enchanted silence – no distracting chatter, no idiotic remarks, no irritating applause, no audience at all, at most a solitary spectator.

Oh memories! oh Italy! oh liberty! oh poetry! oh damnation! – I have to apply myself to the Opéra-Comique! But I have read and seen the piece, so the worst is over. *Zampa, or the Marble Fiancée*: I shall probably be stoned for saying what I think of this much-acclaimed work. So be it. Herold is no more, and though according to the man who reversed the proverb we owe respect to the dead, I consider I owe it to art – living, progressive art – to be truthful. The long and short of it is that I do not like *Zampa*, and here is why. There is – as doesn't often happen at the Opéra-Comique – some real music in it, there are even some fine ensembles; but as a work, as a score which by its subject, whatever anyone may say, lays a barely concealed claim to be the counterpart of Mozart's *Don Juan*, *Zampa* seems to me a poor piece. The one is as true, as dazzling and noble as the other is bogus, vulgar and commonplace.

A comparison between the words will better convey the difference between the two scores. Everyone is familiar with the originality, the pungent directness of the language of Mozart's protagonist. Here is the language of Herold's, during an orgy:

> A fig for storm and sorrow!
> For when the cup
> Such wine fills up,
> Come, let us drink!
> Who knows? To sink
> May be our fate tomorrow.

* Victor Hugo, "La captive".

Elsewhere, on the point of violating a young maiden, he says, in all seriousness: "Yield, yield to my laws!", to which his breathless victim replies:

> Dispel these my fears.
> 'Tis not thus, with tears,
> That happiness comes.
> Subscribe to my prayers.

Nowhere else in the world but the Opéra-Comique do you hear lines like that. Well: the music of *Zampa* is not generally speaking much more elevated in idea, much more truthful in expression or more distinguished in form. But whereas we may be sure the author of the words attached no importance whatever to the rhymes he threw at the composer, the composer sweated blood in a vain attempt to rise above his collaborator. The music, at any rate, has exactly the same effect on me as the lines I have quoted would have on a poet. Its style, moreover, has no distinct character. It is neither pure and austere like Méhul's, brilliant and exuberant like Rossini's, nor dreamy, passionate and brusque like Weber's. Neither Italian, French nor German, Herold takes something from each of the three schools but has no style of his own. His music is just like those industrial products manufactured in Paris on foreign models and adapted with minor modifications. It is Parisian music. That is why it goes down so well with the Opéra-Comique audience, which in our view represents the middle class of the inhabitants of the capital, and why those artists and music-lovers whose radically different nature and taste and intelligence set them apart from the multitude think so little of it.

Berlioz then analyses the score in detail, praising some numbers, including the quartet in Act 1 – "incomparably the best thing in the opera, decisive in style, genuinely dramatic, with strong momentum and striking modulations, and free of those terrible appoggiaturas which the author is so prone to" – but finding fault with many more, and concluding:

For the rest, I find only the flower of the Parisian style, tricked out with the patent embellishments of Italian orchestration and the chromatic harmonies, bristling with dissonances, which Spohr and Marschner have so abused, to the reproach of the German school. I should add that in employing these chords of wild and fantastic aspect Herold rarely hits the mark. The weapon is one that he has not learned to use. Almost always it is the handle and not the blade that strikes; and, in contrast to Mozart, Beethoven and Weber, his blows bruise but fail to draw blood.

Matters are made no better by the final paragraph:

> If anything can soften the harshness of these opinions in the eyes of Herold's admirers, let me say in conclusion that the score fulfils every condition required of an opéra-comique in Paris today, and that its authors have entirely succeeded in their intentions, having won the undisputed approval of that section of the public to which they were appealing.

If we compare Berlioz's criticism with that of most of his colleagues and rivals – Janin, Karr, Azevedo, Blaze de Bury, Louis Desnoyers, Joseph Mainzer, Charles Maurice, Scudo, to name a cross-section of the motley fraternity writing musical criticism in the burgeoning newspaper and periodical press of Paris – we can only be struck not just by the far greater knowledge of music and grasp of the entire musical scene it reveals but also by its more civilized tone. Even at his most severe, he criticizes, like Shaw, without malice or brutality. He draws blood but does not bruise; his weapon is the rapier, not the cosh. He writes like a man in thorough command of his material, and seemingly as he pleases.

Yet Berlioz himself is forever complaining about the inhibiting restraints under which he operates and which prevent him from speaking his mind. Criticism, he says, is like "walking on eggshells". Occasionally he will contrive not to write at all about the work in question. "I find Paër's opera [*Un caprice de femme*] stale and colourless," he says in a letter to Maurice Schlesinger; "in consequence, as an article *against* would not suit you, I can't take it on." Or: "Despite M. Bertin's request, I wouldn't write a notice of *I puritani* nor of that wretched *Juive*; I had too many bad things to say about them – it would have been put down to jealousy." More frequent is the avowal that "my position has not allowed me to admit that without exception all the singers [in the Opéra's 1834 revival of *Don Giovanni*], and Nourrit most of all, are a thousand miles below their roles". And again (in a letter to the poet and critic Rellstab): "There are very few living composers about whom I can say at all candidly what I think. People know this; and as a result, when I do succeed in saying what I really feel [i.e. in praise], many assume I am not being sincere."

"Don't believe what I wrote in my notice" of such and such a new opera is a refrain of his correspondence, especially where the *Journal des débats* is concerned.

Recently Jules Janin handed over to me (with a very good grace) the reviewing of opera in the *Débats* – only the Théâtre-Italien and the ballet remain outside my domain – with the result that I now hold sway over the Opéra and the Opéra-Comique; but it's a position that's very hard to maintain without all sorts of disagreeable concessions. In a few days' time I have to find a way of writing indulgent nonsense about an appalling non-work called *Stradella*, of which I saw a rehearsal yesterday evening at the Opéra. A thousand reasons force me to, quite apart from the fact that it would not be decent, in my position, to slate a young composer [Niedermeyer] who has for a long time been in the same situation vis-à-vis the theatre as I am. But I must warn you not to believe a word I say about the score.

In a letter to his father a couple of years later he bursts out in exasperation at the equivocations of the critic's life:

My old chest complaint has come back. What it is I don't really know. Alphonse [Robert] says it's simply nervous over-stimulation. I am forced so often to contain such tidal waves of anger that it's not surprising I feel my blood simmer or boil over. I detest the trade of critic – it makes me ill to have to handle all those platitudes with kid gloves. I am got at and imposed on on behalf of the most insignificant débutante, singer or pianist, the most miserable opéra-comique that is not worth a cigar-butt, all the nastiest sores that disfigure the art of music, in such a way as to give me a frightening idea of the power of the *Journal des débats* and also to intensify, if that is possible, my scorn of all these imbecilities. From time to time I lose patience and crush two or three mediocrities in my fist. Then, despair, lamentation, diplomatic missions suing for peace, letters from humble men bowing to the ground, letters full of *anonymous* abuse, visits by women armed with introductions from my best friends; next, acts of vengeance (anonymous, naturally) in the little journals; and then invitations to dinner, and evening parties given with the object of inveigling me. Witness the latest débutante, Mlle Nathan, for whom M. Crémieux the famous barrister and his wife have gone to incredible lengths to flatter and woo me. I declined to attend their dinner. They wouldn't admit defeat: they arranged an immense party at M. de

Custine's. Lamartine, Balzac, Hugo, Théophile Gautier, Chateaubriand, Mme Girardin were there. The whole of fashionable Paris literature, painting and music had been invited. This time I accepted, because the Bertin family was going and because I realized I would have to give in. And all this because Duprez is Mlle Nathan's teacher and he has got it into his dull head that I might take revenge on his pupil for the harm he has done me. The young woman makes her début next Wednesday. She is Jewish, all Jewry will be behind her,* she will have a great success, and she is very ordinary. Harriet thinks just as I do; Meyerbeer himself, Jewish as he is, doesn't dispute it, when you can get the truth out of him. They're going to hate me like poison if I say so much as the half of what I think. Perhaps I shall say it all. What a trade!

Right to the end of his career as critic – that "infernal chain which has links to every aspect of my existence" – he chafed against its shackles. "How rarely am I able to say exactly what I think!" Janin confirmed it when he remarked that though Berlioz said he found such and such a work "superb", "his friends, those who have an idea of what is going on in that capacious brain, are not deceived, and would like to know his final word on the masterpiece in question".

It was taken for granted that you wrote nice things about your friends. But Berlioz hated the compromise involved. "I am trying to support poor Gounod, who has just suffered an unparalleled *fiascone* at the Opéra" (with *La Reine de Saba*); but "how can one support something which has neither bone nor muscle? Yet I have to find something to praise."

He enlarges on the hazards of the *métier* in his *Memoirs*, where he speaks of the "misfortune of being both critic and creative artist", which exposes you to the flattery of people who need a good notice and who will sometimes "dig a tunnel fifty miles long" to get it ("until the critic, wearying of this mole-like burrowing, opens a sluice which inundates the mine, and sometimes the miner"). Worse still are the "laboured eulogies" he must force himself to write for reasons of prudence or friendship: "the manoeuvrings, the abject subterfuges I am

---

* This is a factual observation, not a racist sentiment. I have found no trace in Berlioz's writings of the anti-semitism or racial theories common in his lifetime. In a review of his friend Lenz's *Beethoven et ses trois styles* he disposes summarily of the author's notion that Mendelssohn's music will be prevented by its "Hebraic elements" from becoming generally accepted.

obliged to practise, the circumventions in order to avoid telling the truth, the concessions to society and even to public opinion, the rage repressed, the shame swallowed!" People (he adds) who find his criticisms excessively scathing would think differently if he really spoke his mind: "the nettles you complain of are a bed of roses compared to the gridiron on which I would roast you!"

All the same, his articles do not generally read like that. Berlioz nearly always seems himself in what he writes. By humour, by irony, by coded language, by a whole repertoire of diversionary tactics, he manages more often than not to extricate himself more or less gracefully. The methods devised by his predecessor Castil-Blaze for avoiding direct attack – praise of minor aspects of a work, digressions which leave no space for discussing the music – are developed and refined into a virtuoso technique. At the furthest extreme is what he called the "feuilleton du silence", which says nothing at all about the work under review, and – to quote Katherine Kolb – "thereby says it all". Time and again, after a few polite formulas, he will wave the ostensible subject to one side and raise the discussion to a more exalted level.

It is not often we catch him in obvious concessions to interests whose help, as a composer, he needs and whose hostility he cannot afford to incur. Even when we would expect to find him muzzled he is able to make his point. A piece on "M. Duponchel – the Opéra Chorus", written when that musically philistine but to Berlioz – with *Benvenuto Cellini* waiting to be staged – highly necessary functionary had just become director of the Opéra, shows him getting out of a potentially compromising position with ingenuity and honour:

M. Véron has finally relinquished the lyric sceptre into the hands of M. Duponchel. We see this as a good augury for music, precisely because M. Duponchel was accused, before his nomination, of caring only for staging and costumes, of basing his criteria of success solely on the spectacle and regarding the musical part of opera as a tiresome accessory. M. Duponchel may well have a pronounced bias in favour of the art at which he excels and which has won him his triumphs and the reputation that brought him to the Opéra; but he is too intelligent not to be aware of the ridicule his enemies would infallibly heap on his administration if he did not disprove, promptly and decisively, the intentions that have been imputed to him. There are grounds for hope that the art of music will on the contrary regain the position it should never have lost at the

Opéra. Already the new director, with the aim of making his choral forces the equal in power and richness of those of Vienna and Berlin, has announced auditions for twenty choristers who will be added to the Opéra's existing large chorus.

The article then addresses in detail the practical issues involved: the problem of where to find good voices, particularly now that Choron is dead and his school disbanded; the need to set up in Paris a singing academy on the lines of those in German cities; the thorough reform of the existing Opéra chorus that is long overdue, including an end to the current abuse whereby those furthest from the audience often do not bother to sing, and a new system of rehearsals in small groups which ensures that the weaker musicians are not carried by the stronger but learn the music properly; and, finally, much higher rates of pay, so that the choristers no longer have to earn their real living by singing in churches and are encouraged to take a pride in their work.

Berlioz concludes:

We make these simple observations to M. Duponchel in the hope of encouraging him to carry out the reforms required for this important branch of music. Remember that the German company kept going at the Théâtre Favart for two years, despite the extreme feebleness of its soloists, entirely through the vitality – to us so astonishing – of its chorus. But what was it, in fact? Really just a provincial chorus, made up of artists of the third rank, by German standards – good enough for Karlsruhe, perhaps, but certainly not for Berlin or Vienna. This being so, what results might not be obtained with the resources of the Opéra, efficiently employed? Spectacular décor and dance have become hackneyed, but the grand effects of vocal harmony have not. They are worth attention.

It is true that in the mid-1840s, by when his chances of gaining entry to the Opéra were pretty well nil, he no longer felt under any necessity to equivocate. The listless, rudderless career of the Académie Royale de Musique, and its dedication to the pursuit of mediocrity, called to his mind La Fontaine's fable "The Heron":

One day on its long legs the heron, with long beak
Fitted to a long neck, was going none knows where.

The Opéra, that great theatre with its great orchestra, its great chorus and its great subsidy, its long title and its immense scenery, resembles in more than one respect the pitiful bird of the fable. I left it six months ago "asleep on one foot"; and here it is in motion going none knows where, looking for nourishment in the meanest streamlets and not disdaining the very gudgeon it once scorned, the mere name of which used to revolt its fastidious stomach. But the poor bird is wounded in one wing, it walks and cannot fly, and its most convulsive strides bring it no nearer its goal, given that it doesn't itself know in what direction it is meant to be going.

Yet to read the review of the 1834 *Don Giovanni* revival in which Berlioz was so conscious of failing to say what he thought is to conclude that he was too hard on himself. The divine Cornélie Falcon at least is handled, though generously, by no means with kid gloves.

Mlle Falcon, so energetic in *Robert le diable*, was physically speaking, with her countenance "pale as a beautiful autumn evening", the ideal Donna Anna. She had fine moments in the accompanied recitative sung over her father's body. Why then did she all at once go off the boil in the great aria of the first act, "Tu sais quel infâme"? Oh! Mlle Falcon, with those black eyes of yours and the incisive voice you possess, there is no need to be afraid. Let your eyes flash and your voice ring out: you will be yourself, and you will be the incarnation of the vengeful Spanish noblewoman whose principal features your timidity veiled from us.

When it comes to reviewing the dreaded Mlle Nathan in Halévy's *La Juive*, what he writes has an air of fairness and, though hinting at pressures, of independence from them. You feel that the debutante herself, if not her eager backers, should have found it helpful.

Behind the balanced praise and blame, however, one can sense what labour it was to write such a notice. If Berlioz exaggerated the extent to which he was forced to compromise with the truth in his feuilletons, the reason was first that the truth as he saw it meant so much – meant everything – to him, and second that criticism, good though he was at it, really was felt by him as servitude. "To write nothing about nothing! To give tepid approval to insufferable inspidities! To speak one moment of a great master and the next of an idiot in the same language, with the same gravity of utterance! To expend your time, your intelligence, your spirit and patient endeavour on this drudgery!" His sense of disgust – it is not too strong a word – increased with the years. The combination of an idealistic, fastidious nature and the psychological burden of spending so much of his life on the triumphant trivia of the very operatic world from which he was excluded made him feel each concession as a culpable weakness, a betrayal of his ideals. Objectively, he may not have really had all that much to reproach himself with: as Tiersot says, "his chief failure in honesty consisted in nothing worse than not saying all the bad he thought of certain people and certain works". We are in a position to see how skilfully he acquitted himself, and how often his irony and humour came to his rescue and hinted, to the percipient, at the real meaning between the lines of his "tepid approval". But he himself was painfully aware how far it fell short of what it could have been.

It was by his own standards that Berlioz judged his lapses from integrity, not by the standards of contemporary reviewing. Those standards were not high. Not only did friendship, acquaintance, obligation, intrigue inevitably play their part: so did financial corruption. Balzac's *Illusions perdues* and also his *Monograph on the Paris Press* chronicle the power of money over the journalism of the day. Charles Maurice, of the *Courrier des théâtres*, made a favourable notice conditional on actors and dancers and singers subscribing to his journal and managements advertising in it; when Harriet Smithson's company omitted to do so he had his revenge: "they should take the channel ferry home while the weather is still fine". Louis Gouin, Meyerbeer's *homme d'affaires* in Paris, gives a glimpse of Véron, the director of the Opéra, buying Maurice's good opinion of Cherubini's *Ali Baba*: "Véron's greatest talent is to have the papers for him. Yesterday I heard a man say – talking to Carafa in the foyer of the Opéra – that the music of *Ali Baba* was even worse than it is generally considered to be; and this morning that same man who yesterday was saying it – M. Charles Maurice, who has probably been bought (he can be had cheap) – has written an article which says the exact opposite of what I heard him say."

Maurice, admittedly, was an extreme case. But others too could be bought. One of the best journalists of the age, Janin, was ready to exploit his position; a good review from him could cost a thousand francs. Meyerbeer was reckoned to have spent a large part of his fortune making sure that critics were on his side, by outright gifts of money as well as by his famous banquets for the press before first nights. Heine, himself venal, wrote – with malicious play on words – that "just as the apostle spares no pains to save a single lost soul, so Meyerbeer, on learning that someone denies his music, will work tirelessly on the renegade until he has converted him; and this single renegade, once saved, is *dearer* to him than the entire flock of the faithful who worship with undeviating orthodoxy". Fiorentino, who wrote criticism at different times in the *Constitutionnel*, the *Corsaire* and *La France* under his own name and in the *Moniteur* as A. de Rovray, made a profession of accepting money. One story which went the rounds in various forms had him declaring that Meyerbeer owed him 3,000 francs: he was supposed to have received 10,000 for his review of *L'étoile du nord* but had been given only 7,000. Scudo was another who got Meyerbeer to make him "loans". Gifts of money or objets d'art in return for good reviews were widely regarded as part of the natural order of things.

Berlioz, like others, would ask fellow-critics with whom he was on good terms to place puffs for his concerts in their papers so as to help drum up an audience. But there is no evidence that he ever took bribes. Nor that he offered them: he didn't have the money, but even if he had, it would have gone against his nature and character to do so. In this respect he could not have been more different from his *Débats* colleague Janin.

What also distinguished him from Janin was his seriousness and his consistency, and his conscientiousness: he would regularly prepare himself by attending rehearsals of a new opera and by studying the score. Even his most whimsical pieces illustrate his principles. Janin, in contrast, is capricious. Principles never stand in the way. He will take the first idea that comes into his head and run with it where it leads, trusting to his diabolical fluency and his natural exuberance of style and invention. His best reviews are tours de force; but with many of them you feel that they could as well have gone in another direction.

Berlioz, who could be as entertaining as Janin, never – whatever he would have said himself – gives one the sense of sacrificing his convictions. It was typically quixotic of him that he would praise – and take pleasure in praising – works or performances by people who were his opponents. He was aware of this "quirk" in himself, and in the *Memoirs* he cites it in mitigation, when admitting to sins of critical omission and commission – then punctures his own self-satisfaction:

> In justice to myself I can at least say that never for any consideration whatever have I been put off expressing, ungrudgingly, what I feel about works or artists I admire. I have warmly praised men who have done me a great deal of harm and with whom I am no longer on speaking

terms. Indeed, the sole compensation that journalism offers me for all its torments is the scope it gives my passion for the true, the great, the beautiful wherever they exist. It is sweet to me to praise an enemy who has merit – as well as being a duty which any honest man takes pride in fulfilling. On the other hand every untrue word on behalf of an untalented friend causes me acute unhappiness. But, as every critic knows, the result is the same in both cases. Your enemy, annoyed at the credit you acquire for your generous impartiality, dislikes you the more, while your friend, dissatisfied with the laboured eulogies which are the best you can do for him, likes you rather less in consequence.

As a good Dauphinois Berlioz stores up resentments; but revenge, when he takes it, is not mean or petty. The great Duprez, who had a good deal to answer for over the tribulations of *Benvenuto Cellini*, may have become the model – an anonymous model – for Berlioz's "astronomical study", the "Rise and Fall of the Famous Tenor"; but when from time to time during his decline he recaptured his voice for an evening and sang with his old eloquence, Berlioz responded with unqualified enthusiasm. In comparison with Fétis' root-and-branch dismissal of the Fantastic Symphony in the lead article in the *Révue musicale* of 1 February 1835, prompted by the publication of Liszt's piano transcription – a review which denied the composer the smallest melodic, harmonic or rhythmic invention and any skill whatever except in instrumentation – Berlioz's couple of paragraphs in the *Rénovateur* three months later exacted a temperate retribution:

The historical concert given by M. Fétis at the Théâtre-Italien drew a very small audience. He had announced a programme that was already familiar. Now the chief motive force of these concerts is curiosity; and M. Fétis had satisfied it last year, in such a way as not to inspire many with the desire to repeat the experience. In addition, he was known to be less than punctilious in keeping to the order of programme given on the poster. [. . .]

At the concert we attended recently a duet by Clari was offered as being by the Abbé Stefani, and several other parts of the programme were turned so topsy-turvy that no one knew where they were. It is undeniable that the aforementioned piece is delightful in its pithy original-ity, and M. Jansenne and Mlle Massi performed it very well. But, to those who did not know it, it was taken to be the work of the Abbé Stefani. This, it will be acknowledged, is an odd way to teach Parisians the history of music. Imagine if two centuries from now some professor presented a chorus of Rossini's or Meyerbeer's as being by M. Fétis. The conclusion would naturally be that M. Fétis was one of the great musicians of his time. You see where this kind of thing leads.

"The true, the great, the beautiful wherever they exist": that was his chief reason for being a critic. There were others of course, not least the opportunity to expound his views on vital general topics like the role of education in society, imitation in music, or rhythm. But above all – to quote Gérard Condé – there was his "sovereign need to share his enthusiasms, to analyse his sensations and fix them in writing". His "powerful capacity for wonder" must be expressed, communicated. He must convert others to the love and worship of his gods while at the same time, indirectly, guiding them perhaps to a greater understanding of, a closer contact with, his own music.

To do so he employed a style that was a blend of contemporary literature and speech and the writers of the Grand Siécle and the Enlightenment in whom he had been steeped since boyhood. Ultimately, he had no illusions about the ability of language to describe music: that was a will of the wisp. But what he could do, as Condé says, was "capture the attention of his readers by the shock of words and ideas, the rhythm and balance of the phrases, surprise them, make them smile, move them for a moment, and thus by a kind of complicity lead them into a state of sympathy with the work in question".

Often of course the sordid reality broke in on his visionary contemplations; the dwarfs of the musical world clamoured for attention. The defence of the beautiful necessarily involved "attacking whatever seems to me opposed to it". That was a war worth fighting, to begin with at least. But the price was eternal vigilance; the ideal was constantly under threat, and the enemy might lurk anywhere, even in the Société des Concerts:

> Why must this stately, sonorous chorus [from *Christ on the Mount of Olives*] be yoked to the sublime but sombre *Coriolan* overture? The practice has been in use at the Conservatoire for several years, the reason given being that the overture, finishing on a pianissimo, used never to be applauded. But is that really an adequate motive, to the artists who make up the Conservatoire committee, for creating a kind of monster out of two Beethoven scores which are different from one another in every respect? We cannot believe it. What does applause matter when

the genius of the composer is so vibrantly present in the work? Besides, admiration is not always indicated by the amount of noise, and we are quite certain that nothing in all the lofty conceptions of the giant of the symphony is more keenly felt and justly appreciated than the overture to *Coriolan*. These are the prejudices of our theatres that have intruded on the sanctuary of music; and we feel bound to protest against them, out of respect for Beethoven and for art itself.

The theme of Paris the city of extremes, where music is alternately godlike and ignominious, and the matchless resources which could make it the true mecca of the musical world are so often squandered and debauched, is central to Berlioz's criticism. There is a constant tension between what might be and what all too commonly is.

The contrast may sometimes be turned to fruitfully humorous ends, as in an article of 1841 where instead of writing yet another review of the Société des Concerts' Eroica he takes wing on an exalted flight of fancy, and then brings himself back to earth with an abrupt ironic fall and directs his spleen at the once-admired Conservatoire audience:

If I were rich, really rich, rich like those poor fools who give a singer five hundred francs for a cavatina worth five sous, and if I knew ancient Greek as Xenophon and Aristotle must have known it, I would seek out Mehemet Ali, or should it be the Sultan? (for I become confused when the Eastern Question comes up), and I would say to him: "Highness, sell me the island of Tenedos, sell me the Cape of Sigeum, and the Simois and the Scamander, and the plains *ubi Troja fuit*. Don't be alarmed: it won't interfere with your operations on the Hellespont, it has nothing to do with either war or commerce – it's a question of music and poetry, so it needn't concern you." Once I had become master of those sites hallowed by the muse of antiquity, the hills and woods where Andromache's tears and Briseis' and the blood of Hector and Patroclus flowed, where Achilles' great war cry and Stentor's rang out, and the Grecian army raged ten long years round the walls of Troy and the fiery Ajax's giant bones still lie entombed, I would fit out a vessel and embark an orchestra, composed as follows: sixty French violins, thirty French violas and thirty French cellos, twenty English double-basses, four flutes and four oboes from Paris, four German clarinets, eight German bassoons and four German trumpets, four horns from Paris and four from Vienna and two Paris timpanists. Then I would set sail for the Troiad.

On my arriving in that holy realm my first act would be to expel all those brutish Turks who know no poetry but the Koran and no music but the music of fifes and cymbals; I would get rid of all Greek pirates and fishermen, all bored and boring English tourists, all roving Frenchmen – sneering Voltairean sceptics with no imagination, no responsiveness, no enthusiasm, no heart – and all Italian dilettantes. In this way I should create a virtual solitude, its silence disturbed only by the plaintive sea and the ripple of the Xanthus and the wind's secret whispering among the ruins. I would construct a temple of music, bare of decoration except for two statues, and one evening, having read Homer and wandered through the places made deathless by his genius, would get my royal orchestra to recite me that other poem, by the king of musicians, Beethoven's Eroica symphony.[. . .]

Instead of which I must go to No. 2 Rue Bergère, to a damp and grimy little hall, where a few oily chandeliers define the murk and you find pale women raising their eyes heavenward in carefully studied poses, and rubescent men struggling not to fall asleep or nodding their heads out of time with the music and smiling as the anguished orchestra utters its great cries of pain, only to look serious again when it subsides, and demanding of their neighbours why the symphony is called "heroic" when there's no trace of a battle or fanfare or triumphal march in it, but adding that the first movement would make "a capital waltz", only the coda needs a "crack of the whip to liven it up a bit".

The war was not just against debased values, low standards of performance and the slapdash, inefficient organization of musical institutions: it was against the way Parisians thought about music, against received ideas, mindless generalizations, lazy thought.

Following our admirable custom in France, of allowing an artist one eminent skill and disparaging the rest, the mere announcement of a major composition by Liszt has provoked the inevitable outcry: he is too fine a pianist to be any good as a composer. In the same way, there being general agreement as to Beethoven's supremacy in instrumental music, very little attention is accorded to his solitary contribution to the lyric stage – although in our view, with five or six exceptions *Fidelio* leaves all the operas written in the past twenty years nowhere. It was the same with Gluck in the last century. As no one could challenge him in power, veracity, grandeur, energy, in the development of tragic passion, in the expression of grief or in scenes of terror, he was pronounced lacking in grace, freshness, melody – this for the man who wrote the scene in the Elysian Fields in *Orpheus*, the finale of *Echo and Narcissus*, the Thessalians' chorus in *Alceste* and the ballet music in *Armide*! One wonders where the pallid specimens that were preferred to him are now.

Only in later years did he begin to lose heart and doubt whether, after all, this ceaseless activity served "any useful artistic purpose", whether it did anything to "abolish a few abuses, eradicate prejudice, enlighten opinion, refine public taste and put men and things in their true place and perspective". By then the struggle had taken its toll. The Shakespearean and Virgilian epigraphs to his final volume of collected criticism, published in 1862, acknowledge defeat: "Love's labours lost"; "Hostis habet muros" ("the walls are in enemy hands"). Even then, though, it was still "good to be alive to worship the beautiful".

"To reveal the strokes of genius in a work", many of which were liable to have "escaped the notice of a public blinded by the prejudices of the moment": that was the critic's true role as formulated by Berlioz as early as 1825, when the twenty-one-year-old student took Castil-Blaze to task for his classicist strictures on Gluck's *Armide*; and that was what it remained. He saw his task as that of an educator, a persuader and cajoler, a teacher with certain basic unalterable convictions to inculcate; and all his talents as advocate and as writer were mobilized for it.

They were given in the service of all his admirations, but most of all in the service of Beethoven, because Beethoven was the crucial figure both as creator and as symbol: the incomparable master and the fountain-head of modern music, the representative of the new-found freedom of the composer to obey his own laws and remake musical form with each work.

Berlioz's criticism returned again and again to Beethoven's music, and especially the symphonies. His method of expounding them fused the two kinds of criticism identified by E. T. A. Hoffmann, father of Romantic writing about music: the poetic and the technical. By a mixture of literary analogy, evocative imagery, and technical example used not for its own sake but as outward manifestation of the inner idea, he sought to draw the reader into the composer's thought, into the music.

"Poetic" description was a feature of the new criticism in the period;

Schumann, whose *Neue Zeitschrift für Musik* was founded in the same year as the *Gazette musicale*, claimed that Jean-Paul could give a truer, more illuminating account of a Beethoven symphony than a dozen scribes who came with their ladders and measured the physical dimensions of the colossus. But though Berlioz made use of it, he nearly always included a pedagogic element as well, as though to involve his readers not only in the imaginative response but also, however momentarily, in the compositional process. His paragraphs on the slow movement of the Eroica, for instance, begin very personally, by likening it to the funeral cortège of the young Pallas in the *Aeneid*, but end with analysis which combines description and technical illustration:

> The theme of the march returns, but in fragments separated by silence and accompanied only by three pizzicato strokes on the double-basses; and when these bare bleak snatches of dolorous melody have collapsed one by one on to the tonic, shattered, obliterated, the wind instruments utter a cry and the whole orchestra dies away on a long pianissimo chord.

Even in the article on his beloved Pastoral Symphony, where the movement titles encourage impressionistic writing, an occasional analytic signpost defines the landscape:

> The musician-painter now takes us into a joyful peasant gathering. There is dancing and laughter, in moderation to begin with. The bagpipe plays a lively tune, accompanied by a bassoon which can manage two notes only. Beethoven no doubt wanted to evoke some genial old German peasant mounted on a barrel and armed with an ancient broken-down instrument from which he can barely extract the two principal notes of the key of F, the dominant and the tonic. Each time the oboe intones its bagpipe song (lively and artless as a young girl in her Sunday best), the old bassoon pumps out its two notes. If the melodic phrase modulates, the bassoon keeps quiet, calmly counting its rests until the return of the original key permits it to lay out its imperturbable F–C–F once again.

In general the two modes move hand in hand, as in this account of the second movement of the Seventh Symphony:

> Rhythm – a rhythm as simple as that of the first movement – is again the chief element in the incredible effect produced by the andante [allegretto]. It consists entirely of a dactyl followed by a spondee, repeated

uninterruptedly, now in three parts, now in one, now all together, sometimes as accompaniment, often focusing attention solely on itself, or providing the main subject of a brief double fugue in the stringed instruments. It is heard first on the lower strings of the violas, cellos and double-basses, played piano, then repeated shortly afterwards in a mysterious and melancholy pianissimo. From there it passes to the second violins, while the cellos utter a sort of sublime lament, in the minor mode. The rhythmic figure, rising from octave to octave, reaches the first violins which, while making a crescendo, hand it to the wind instruments at the top of the orchestra, where it bursts out with full force. The plaintive melody, now more energetic, becomes a convulsive wailing. Conflicting rhythms clash painfully against each other. We hear tears, sobs and suffering. But a ray of hope shines. The heart-rending strains give way to a vaporous melody, gentle, pure, sad yet resigned, "like patience smiling at grief". Only the cellos and basses persist with their inexorable rhythm beneath this rainbow-like melodic arc: to borrow once again from English poetry, "One fatal remembrance, one sorrow that throws / Its bleak shade alike o'er our joys and our woes." After further alternations of anguish and resignation the orchestra, as though exhausted by its struggle, can manage only fragments of the main phrase, before giving up the ghost. The flutes and oboes take up the theme with dying voice but lack the strength to go on; the violins complete it with a few barely audible pizzicato notes – after which, flaring up like the flame of a lamp about to go out, the wind instruments give a deep sigh on an incomplete harmony and . . . "the rest is silence". This plaintive exclamation, with which the andante opens and closes, is produced by a chord, that of the six-four, that normally resolves. In this case the placing of the tonic note in the middle of the chord, while the dominant is above and below it, is the only possible ending, leaving the listener with a sense of incompleteness and intensifying the dreamlike sadness of the rest of the movement.

Berlioz's Beethoven analyses were published serially in the specialist *Revue et gazette musicale* in 1838; but he wrote about the symphonies many times, and in other papers as well. One of his most explicitly technical passages, on the first movement of the Fourth and the way the timpani roll on A sharp (B flat) in the key of B leads back to the home key and unleashes one of the most prodigious crescendos in all music, first appeared in the *Débats*.

Of all the nine symphonies it was the Fifth that he discussed most often. Even if he loved the Pastoral more and placed the Ninth higher and thought of the Eroica in more mythic terms, the Fifth had a unique éclat. It was the one that Conservatoire audiences got most easily excited about; and in a sense, he said, you could understand why. Unlike the Eroica it came "uniquely and directly out of Beethoven's genius", unprompted by any external idea. In it were developed "his inmost thoughts"; its subject was "his secret dejections, his midnight visions, his brilliant and passionate enthusiasms", manifested in "melody, harmony, rhythm and orchestration as profoundly new and individual as they are endowed with nobility and power". Berlioz's feuilletons often return to the electrifying transition from the scherzo to the finale (a passage which, like the storm in the Pastoral, must have been overpowering in a hall as intimate as the Conservatoire's). In one he tells the story of the Grande Armée veteran rising to his feet and exclaiming, "L'Empereur!" In another he describes the seething excitement aroused in the audience by the whole work:

> At the first five or six performances of this masterpiece the public seemed relatively unmoved [by the first movement], not yet having grasped it. The latest test shows that their education has made notable progress. Everyone's emotional responses were at a high pitch. The pit even entreated the orchestra, in vain, to play the movement again. But it was in the finale that the Conservatoire Hall would have offered a curious spectacle to a disinterested observer. At the moment when the orchestra, leaving behind it the scherzo's grim harmonies for the dazzling march which follows, seems to be taking us suddenly from a cavern on the Blocksberg to a Temple of the Sun, the shouts of acclamation, the cries of "hush", the clapping and the convulsive laughter, restrained for a few seconds, exploded with such force that the orchestra was buried beneath the torrents of enthusiasm and disappeared completely. The entire audience was seized by a spasm of nervous excitement and not till it subsided were the players able to make themselves heard.

Sometimes he loses patience and turns on the Conservatoire audience for its failure to rise to Beethoven's lofty heights and for the element of fashion he increasingly detects in it. (The great institution founded in 1828 did in fact begin to run out of steam and lose its youthful élan in the middle years of the century.) Yet he continues to hope and to believe in the possibility of enlightenment. As late as 1860, when under the fresh impact of *Fidelio*, he writes a long two-part *critique admirative* in the *Débats*, describing the work in detail and defending it against those who would deny it the qualities that no one dared deny the symphonies, he will not give up hope that a more intelligent, educated public may arise:

> [*Fidelio*] belongs to that powerful race of maligned works which have the most inconceivable prejudices and the most blatant lies heaped upon them, but whose vitality is so intense that nothing can prevail against them – like those sturdy beeches born among rocks and ruins, which end by splitting the stone and breaking through the walls, and rise up proud and verdant, the more solidly rooted for the obstacles they have had to overcome in order to force their way out; whereas the willows that grow without effort on the banks of a river fall into the mud and rot, forgotten.

Its time will come:

> Who knows that light may not dawn sooner than one thinks, even for those whose spirits are closed at the moment to this beautiful work of Beethoven's, as they are to the marvels of the Ninth Symphony and the last quartets and the great piano sonatas of that same inspired, incomparable being? Sometimes, when one looks at a particular part of the heaven of art, a veil seems to cover "the mind's eye" and prevent it from seeing the stars that shine there. Then, all of a sudden, for no apparent reason, the veil is rent, and one sees, and blushes to have been blind so long.

There exists, as Condé says, so close a link between Berlioz's music and his writings, they seem so inextricably part of the single texture of his life and personality, and what he wrote, whether or not under duress, is generally of such a high standard, that it is tempting to see it as predestined and not as something which, halved in quantity, could have made room for a few more symphonies. But he himself leaves us in no possible doubt: it was a millstone, a self-perpetuating servitude, a calamity. Worse than the task itself was the psychological burden. Certainly, he craved an outlet and a platform. He would also make a distinction, sometimes, between "criticism", writing when you have something specific and potentially useful to say, and "feuilletonizing", writing even when you have nothing at all to say, because a regular column is required of you. But ultimately they came down to the same thing; and neither was what he wanted to spend his energies on. "May the fires of heaven and hell descend, rise up, and unite to consume those damnable feuilletons!" – the *Débats and* the *Gazette*. He is a journalist because he can't afford not to be, and because not to have the power it invests him with would leave him, as a composer, defenceless. The moment these two conditions no longer apply – when he has enough money from other sources and is about to stop composing – he gives it up. We can only regret that he couldn't have given it up sooner. The distraction from what he should be doing and longs to do is a constant heartache throughout most of his career.

It is expressed, unequivocally and with the true word spoken in jest, in an exchange of letters with Schlesinger which was published as part of "Tribulations of a musical critic" in the *Revue et gazette musicale* of 7 January 1838, where it neatly provided the review he said he couldn't write.

My dear friend
I absolutely must have, for tomorrow, a long article on the two albums which I am sending you herewith. The names Meyerbeer, Clapisson, Strunz, Panofka, Kalkbrenner, Liszt, Chopin and Thalberg figure prominently, and the edition is of an elegance surpassing that of any previous publication.

Maurice Schlesinger

My dear Maurice
I absolutely must have peace, and protection against albums. For the past two weeks I have been trying vainly to find three hours when I can think at leisure about the overture to my opera [*Benvenuto Cellini*]. Being unable to find them is a torture that you can have no idea of, and that is to me absolutely insupportable. I have to tell you that even at the cost of living on bread and water until my score is finished I do not wish to hear a word of reviews of any kind. Meyerbeer, Liszt, Chopin and Kalkbrenner have no need of praise from me. Your albums, I know, contain, beside theirs, several charming pieces which you don't speak of and whose authors you don't even name. But I am desperate. I need a little leisure and freedom in order to complete my work. I want to be an artist at last; I shall become a galley-slave again later. Until then, no more talk of reviews of any kind: it is killing me. So beware of starting your quarry from his lair; it would be absolutely inhuman of you. I have never been an apologist for suicide; but I have a pair of loaded pistols,

and in the state of exasperation to which you could reduce me I would be capable of blowing your brains out.

Yours ever

your good friend Hector Berlioz

The situation was fundamentally unchanged a quarter of a century later, as he told his son Louis:

Meanwhile I must go on writing, to earn my wretched hundred francs, and to maintain armed guard against all those clowns who would destroy me if it weren't that they are scared of me. And my head is full of projects, of real work, which I can't carry out, because of this slavery.

Berlioz put the whole thing in a nutshell near the beginning of his career as a full-time journalist:

Oh the brutal, brainless profession of reviewer! Then why do it, I will be asked. What a question. Why do you, sir, who are a banker, spend your day calculating figures, when you have a splendid horse, or horses, pawing your stable floor, and you could be pacing the woods and enjoying the last rays of the autumn sun? Why do you, doctor, who have artistic sensibility and taste, consume your existence in the infected air of the demonstration-room and amid the sufferings of a hospital, listening not to beautiful music but to cries of pain and as often as not, for all your skill, the rattle of the dying? For the same reason that I all complainingly write feuilletons which use up time that could be far, far better employed.

4

Art and Politics

By the time he wrote that rueful *cri du coeur* he had given up all thought of performing the *Fête musicale funèbre* at his winter concerts; most of it had still to be written, and the first concert was due in a few weeks' time. Two or three years later, when he revived the idea, he drew up a detailed plan for a performance. The plan, on four sheets of paper, gives the make-up of an orchestra of 111 and a choir of ninety-one, and a breakdown of expenses and receipts including performers' fees, printing, transport of instruments, cabs, hire, lighting and heating of the Conservatoire Hall, and the maximum possible yield of the hall section by section plus a probable donation of 200 francs by the Duc d'Orléans and another by the king, and minus the poor tax, the whole working out at an estimated profit of 1,500 francs. For the moment, however, the project was shelved. Composition must make way for immediately gainful employment. They were still camping out at 34 Rue de Londres and creditors were pressing (there was a doctor's bill outstanding from two years before). The lawsuit to recover Harriet's unpaid fees from the Théâtre Nautique had only added to their debts: they won, but there was nothing to pay her with – the impresario was bankrupt and in jail – and they ended up meeting the legal costs themselves.

Money was needed now. That year Berlioz wrote nineteen articles for the *Débats*, thirty-seven for the *Rénovateur*, a dozen for the *Gazette musicale* and four for the *Monde dramatique* – an average of three often very long pieces every two weeks. There was remarkably little duplication; notices of the same subject appearing in two different journals were nearly always separate reviews. The year 1835 was his most productive for journalism, as it was – until the 1840s – his least productive for music.

Harriet, who was used to being the breadwinner and could not bear contributing nothing, continued to make strenuous efforts to revive her career. The collapse of the Théâtre Nautique – which also put paid to the much heralded productions of Beethoven and Weber by the German company that Strunz and Girard had been assembling – forced her to look elsewhere. A letter of December 1834, written in English to an unknown person, solicits his help in arranging one or two benefit performances with amateur actors which if successful could lead, she says, to a professional tour of Germany, "where my husband is obliged to go shortly as a pensionnaire of the Conservatoire de Musique and where perhaps my school of acting might make a favourable impression". Nothing came of it. But soon afterwards a chance seemed to be offered her in Paris. The presence of two leading English actors inspired a plan to stage a short Shakespeare season at the Théâtre Ventadour, "confided" – the *Rénovateur* announced on 8 March 1835 – "to the talents of Mr Charles Kemble, Miss Smithson, Mr Abbott, etc. Each performance would be preceded by a grand instrumental concert", the musical items being chosen to link with the play in question. "Thus, to cite a name as great in music as Shakespeare is in poetry, Beethoven's *Coriolan* overture, followed by the same composer's marvellous Eroica symphony, would make an admirable introduction to the sublime Roman tragedy of *Coriolanus*, never performed in Paris." Though the project is not mentioned in the surviving Berlioz correspondence, the *Rénovateur*'s music critic was certainly behind it. The news item continued: "As the expense of these eight performances must be guaranteed in advance, subscriptions are being taken at M. Maurice Schlesinger's music shop, 97 Rue de Richelieu, where a detailed prospectus may be obtained. The minimum subscription is 100 francs. We trust there are still enough lovers of art in Paris to ensure that so eminently artistic an enterprise may not be stillborn for lack of encouragement."

That must have been what happened, however; or else it came up against the same bureaucratic reasoning as, a month later, made the Ministry of the Interior refuse Berlioz permission to put on a benefit evening at the Théâtre Ventadour, to replace the one that Miss Smithson had been promised by the management as part of her contract. "I regret to have to inform you that I cannot authorize a performance of the sort in an auditorium no longer operated by a responsible entrepreneur. Should your request be limited to giving a concert, you must address it to the Prefect of Police" (6 April 1835). Harriet had to abandon, for the moment, all idea of a return to the stage. She and Berlioz went to see Victor Hugo to ask him if he would write a play with a leading role that made a virtue of her imperfect French. And there the matter rested.

Berlioz was just as frustrated on his own account. A concert, following up his December successes, would have made money, especially as the orchestral material was paid for and Liszt and Chopin were ready to lend their aid; but where to give it at this time of year, with the Conservatoire Hall barred to outsiders from January to April? Everywhere else he tried he found only obstacles and monopolies. In any case, the Conservatoire was "the one hall in Paris where I can have my music performed properly". As a result, the best season of the year was unavailable. Liszt, who was planning a charity concert, had to give it in the 700-seat Salle St Jean at the Hôtel de Ville – "smoky and uncomfortable", Berlioz described it in the *Rénovateur* of 5 April, adding that "it will certainly not be big enough for all those who want to come; but there was nowhere else M. Liszt could have. The fact is that except for the Menus-Plaisirs, which is unobtainable during the Conservatoire season, our great city of Paris cannot provide its artists with a single concert hall suitable for large-scale instrumental music."

Liszt's programme, given by a scratch orchestra under Girard on 9 April, included two pieces by his friend – the Pilgrims' March from *Harold* and *Le pêcheur* – and the première of his own Grande fantaisie symphonique for piano and orchestra on two themes from *Lélio*, as well as a symphony by Ferdinand Hiller. To put on a concert himself Berlioz had to wait till the beginning of May; for although the Société des Concerts' season ended early that year, on 17 April, and he booked the Conservatoire Hall for the 26th, he had then to postpone it by a week when the society decided it wanted the hall after all for a benefit for its conductor, Habeneck.

The 3rd of May, as he knew well, was leaving it late; a fine Sunday afternoon could lure half his potential audience away to the fountains at Versailles or the horse-racing in the Champs de Mars. In the event the weather was splendid and the receipts came to 2,500 francs instead of the hoped-for 4,000. He probably made a small profit, but at the cost of holding only one rehearsal, which was not enough for the ambitious programme he had chosen: a revival of the popular "Episode in an Artist's Life" of 1832, the Fantastic Symphony followed by *Lélio*, with Liszt playing his variations on Moscheles' *Alexander March* as an entr'acte. The concert, he told his father, was "fairly satisfactory from the financial point of view", but "the musical performance was detestable".

Such experiences could only sharpen his interest in the new one-thousand-seat hall under construction that winter and spring in the Boulevard Bonne-Nouvelle, not far from the Conservatoire and opposite the Théâtre du Gymnase from which it took its name, Gymnase Musical. The director, Saly-Snerbe, hoped to found a permanent institution giving concerts all year round, with an orchestra of seventy-five made up of young players from the Opéra and the Théâtre-Italien (neither of which had performances on the evenings when the Gymnase planned to be in action), plus a few recruits from the provinces. Berlioz, after inspecting the hall during the first fortnight of May and hearing the orchestra rehearse under the violinist-conductor Tilmant *aîné*, pronounced himself on the whole well satisfied. Both before and after the opening, which took place on 23 May, with Liszt among the soloists and Meyerbeer and Rossini in the audience, he followed its progress closely, writing no fewer than eight critical but encouraging reports in the *Rénovateur* between May and October. Two of the June concerts, on the 4th and the 25th, included music of his: *Harold* (given at both of them) and the three overtures, *Francs-juges*, *Waverley* and *King Lear*. Though his reviews do not mention them, it looks as if he was unhappy with the way they were played; he talks of fluctuations in the standard and personnel of the orchestra; there are some first-rate wind-players – Berlioz is lyrical in his praise of the new clarinettist, Klosé – but the cellos and double-basses are weak compared with the violins. (In one article he criticizes the antiquated French practice of tuning the strings of the bass a fifth apart, not a fourth as in Germany and England.) Yet from both his point of view and that of Parisian musical life as a whole there was everything to be said for this new enterprise which proposed to defy the trend of the times and the popularity of Musard's café-concerts by offering programmes of serious music "from which the galop and the contredanse are formally excluded".

All depended on persuading the politicians and bureaucrats to make an exception and allow the Gymnase Musical to feature vocal music in its concerts – an essential element for any such organization hoping to attract a sizeable public. The Ministry of the Interior, however, sided with the Opéra-Comique, which felt threatened by the new venture, and it turned down the request. Lobbying continued. An anonymous article of 31 May in the *Gazette musicale*, possibly by Berlioz himself, asked how choruses by Handel, Bach, Gluck or Palestrina could conceivably pose a threat to the Opéra-Comique. "Its administrators can rest assured: no one has designs on the ensembles that are the glory of their repertoire." But the argument cut no ice. Towards the end of June the Ministry again said no. Despite the hope of liberalization which the July Revolution had held out five years before, rigid demarcation still hemmed in the performing arts. That same summer a production of *Othello* at the Porte St Martin with the great Frédéric Lemaître was halted by the police, minutes before the première, on the grounds that the play belonged to the Théâtre-Français. In music it remained as difficult as ever to do anything serious outside the established institutions. Yet what sense was there, asked the *Gazette*, in a system in which you had to get the government's permission in order to sing an oratorio or a mass?

Some time towards the end of 1835 Berlioz's interest in the Gymnase Musical took an actively personal turn, and the possibility of his becoming salaried musical director of the place, with official authorization to include vocal music, was mooted and then taken up at the highest level by his supporters, prominent among them the Bertins. Such a post was the answer to prayer. It would solve his permanent financial crisis at a stroke and give him unimagined freedom to compose music and have it performed. He would also have a chance to put into practice some of his ideas for the revitalizing of musical life, among them the creation of a school of choral singing such as Paris had lacked since the decline of Choron's and the death of its founder.

For the moment, the old struggle continued. To economize, and because they had been so happy there the year before, Berlioz and his wife decided to return to Montmartre. He announced the move in an affectionate letter to his father which shows how far they had put their former estrangement behind them:

6 May 1835

My dear Papa

I am just rid of my last concert, and seize the first moment of liberty to write to you. Adèle, in her last letter, gave me quite good news of your health, but without adding much detail about your daily life at La Côte. I fear it may be as sad and uneventful as ever. However, it appears that time hangs less heavily on you outside in the fields than in the solitude of your study. I should be only too happy if this taste for agriculture were to develop further; I could hope from it the physical results that we admire in my grandfather's constitution, joined to habits of mind that are less gloomy than you are inclined to.

What a long time since I saw you, father, and how often it strikes me as strange that we should be kept apart in this way! M. Robert's arrival in Paris has made me feel more keenly than ever the pain of our separation. Is it really impossible for you to follow his example some time? It seems a journey to Grenoble is enough to alarm you these days – I gather Mama went there on her own or at any rate without you. But why should this be? Change, movement, would I am convinced be the best thing for your complete recovery. I bet Mama agrees with me. What is she up to? How is she? Are you at all pleased with Prosper? His wayward moods are a thing of the past now, I think. Are his powers developing? I have never believed there was anything in the least ordinary about him, and I should be very surprised if my diagnosis in his favour turned out to be wrong.

As for my boy, he's as charming and healthy and good-humoured as ever, and he has just cut his first tooth. His mother is beside herself with joy at this momentous event. We shall shortly be going back up to Montmartre, to an enchanting place, and not at all costly. The garden is huge, there is a superb view over the plain of St Denis, and everything is less expensive than in Paris because of the exemption from import duty.

Berlioz then speaks of his concert of the previous Sunday, of the composition he hopes to work on during the summer – the *Fête musicale funèbre* – but which he fears will not be finished in time for his winter concerts, and of the bankruptcy of the Théâtre Nautique and the lawsuit.

But I should need a whole volume to give you all the details of my position as I would like to. I hope it will improve yearly. My wife grows ever more excellent, and I love her more than I can say. Probably it will be possible for me to leave Paris in eighteen months' time; we shall then make a big trip to England and Germany, and she will be able to take up her art again.

Last week, for the third time, I had a request from Vienna for a score of my symphonies, "at no matter what cost". I answered that, as I count on visiting Austria quite soon, it seems to me wiser to wait till then and have my works performed when I am there. I am convinced that in my absence it would be a disaster.

The day before yesterday a music-lover who had been at my concert presented me with the complete works of Shakespeare in English in one volume. The book is worth a hundred francs.

My paper's come to an end! I was chatting to you and didn't notice. Farewell, dear father. Hoping for news of you in the next fortnight. I embrace Mama and you and Prosper and Adèle with all my heart.

H. B.

They moved to Montmartre early in June, escaping the worst of an exceptionally hot month and leaving the gossip and turmoil of the city behind them. Liszt and the Comtesse d'Agoult had just eloped to Switzerland, replacing as topic of the moment Halévy's defeat in the election to the Academy of Fine Arts (rumoured to be due to anti-semitism) and the scandalous behaviour of Berlioz's one-time "Ariel". Meyerbeer reported it in a letter to his wife: "Your former piano teacher Camille Moke, the present Madame Pleyel, has been given a terrible beating, in her own house, by one of her lovers whose jealousy she aroused." The man dragged her by the hair out into the street. "Her husband, who until then had supposed her to be the most virtuous of wives, has had his eyes rudely opened. All Paris is talking about her infamy." In the autumn Pleyel obtained a judicial separation. Berlioz's domestic life had become conventional by comparison.

The new apartment was at 12 Rue St Vincent. It included a drawing-room that had once been a summerhouse built by Henri IV for his mistress "la charmante Gabrielle", and a little conservatory room which Berlioz could use as a study. As before, there was a big shady garden sloping down the hill away from Paris, ideal for entertaining friends on fine summer and autumn afternoons. On one such visit – a party in honour of Louis' first birthday, attended by "the élite of the young writers of the counter-revolution, that is those who have shaken off the yoke of Victor Hugo" (Gautier among them) – Berlioz and his friends amused themselves, "like schoolboys", playing prisoner's base.

But life was not the same as it had been the summer before, when he was completing *Harold* and working on other new pieces for his winter concerts. Then, though they were poor, money had not seemed quite the burden it had since become. Very soon they were going to be entirely dependent on his freelance earnings; the six-monthly instalment of his Prix de Rome stipend due on 1 July would be the last. The fears expressed in the letter to his father were well founded: the *Fête musicale funèbre* was not finished in time for his concerts. He managed to write at most two of the projected seven movements. Of one of them we have no details (it may well have been an early version of what became the first movement of the Symphonie funèbre). The other, *Le cinq mai*, a twelve-minute choral setting of Béranger's "Ode on the Death of Napoleon", had been at least partly drafted already.

Berlioz conceived the *Fête* as an aggregation of contrasting pieces on the theme of France's illustrious dead, in which an ode to Napoleon had a natural place. A review of the première of *Le cinq mai*, written by a colleague of Berlioz's on the *Gazette*, speaks of "a large composition of heterogeneous character" – of which the Napoleonic ode was part – designed for performance in the Panthéon. The idea of a musical happening on such a scale was not as utopian as we might think. Louis-Philippe, seeking to strengthen the sagging revolutionary credentials of his regime, had begun to revive the tradition of commemorating great events with grand public ceremonies. Berlioz obviously had such a celebration in mind when he thought of the Panthéon and – as he told Ferrand – a performing body of seven hundred. He had dreamed of such a thing ever since Le Sueur's stories of the great days of the Consulate rekindled his boyhood fascination with the musical rites of antiquity as evoked by Chateaubriand.

What the whole work would have been like there is no way of knowing. Music related to the Symphonie funèbre's imposing and tragic march might have sounded very fine in the Panthéon. So, at moments, would *Le cinq mai*. It has stirring things in it, including the refrain "Pauvre soldat" which came to Berlioz in Rome when he fell into the Tiber, and which appears each time in different orchestral form. The sober scoring is impressively sonorous, with – at one point – double-basses in four parts (and, like his arrangement of the *Marseillaise*, no oboes). *Le cinq mai* was, rather to his chagrin, one of the most popular works on his tour of Germany in the early 1840s. The end is powerful; but as a whole the piece remains competent but unmemorable. Béranger's obscure semi-narrative poem is no help. Berlioz acknowledged that the verses were poor; he chose them nevertheless because, he said, "the *feeling* of that quasi-poetry seemed to me musical". Yet the work gives the sense of creative powers leashed in, waiting for some grand call to mourning to release them.

While he was failing to complete his *Fête musicale funèbre*, an event of horrid appositeness occurred during the first of the national holidays that commemorated the Three Glorious Days of the 1830 Revolution. On the hot and cloudy afternoon of 28 July the King and his entourage, on their way to review the National Guard in the Place de la Bastille, were riding up the Boulevard du Temple – the "Boulevard du Crime" immortalized in *Les Enfants du paradis* – when gunfire from a first-floor window raked the royal party. The Corsican adventurer Fieschi, with two republican accomplices, had set up a kind of multiple cannon designed to destroy everything in its path in a single burst. Nearly twenty people were slain, including the commander-in-chief Marshal Mortier. But Louis-Philippe escaped with minor facial injuries; despite his wounded horse, he was able to react with proper dignity and call out, "Gentlemen, ride on."

There had been other attempts on his life, as well as a great deal of popular disturbance, and general agitation against the regime on the part of republican organizations and in protest at the increasingly terrible living conditions of the Paris poor; but the King had not come so near being killed before. Public outrage was used as a pretext for curbing the freedom of the press and the theatre; censorship was imposed, stricter than any since the decrees which provoked the July Revolution. The victims of Fieschi's "infernal machine", as the newspapers christened it, received a state funeral, with the cortège, accompanied by sixty thousand National Guardsmen ("heroic bulwarks of the throne"), processing across Paris from the Place de la Bastille to the Invalides, where Cherubini's C minor Requiem was performed. Next day in Notre-Dame Le Sueur's Te Deum was sung at a service of thanksgiving for the King's deliverance.

Berlioz's three-thousand-word article in the *Débats* a few days later, on "Le Requiem des Invalides et le Te Deum de Notre-Dame: MM. Cherubini et Lesueur", is a *critique admirative* which in its discussion of such things as musical style in the mass for the dead, music suitable for cathedrals and the proportion of performing forces to size of building, seems to be prophesying his own Grande messe des morts. He had been ruminating such a work, in one form or another, for years – the text of the Requiem, he wrote later, was a "quarry" that he had "long lain in wait for" – and it is impossible that the events of 28 July should not have prompted further thoughts on the subject. As he remarked in his article, "composers of funeral music can always count on opportunities to have their works performed". In fact it was "l'attentat Fieschi" that in due course brought the Grande messe into being. But in the late summer of 1835 that was still a mirage. "The whole thing [*Fête musicale funèbre*] would have been long finished if I had had one month to work exclusively on it; but I can't take so much as a day, on pain of being without the necessary soon afterwards." It is the newspapers that "give me my daily bread". Throughout the summer they kept him busy.

For Harriet, the seclusion of Montmartre helped to distance her a little from the frustrations of Paris, in whose teeming artistic life she could play no part. She shrank from accompanying her husband to the first night of Vigny's *Chatterton* the previous winter; Berlioz had to excuse her to his friend. "Many, many thanks for the complimentary tickets. My wife was for a moment in two minds whether to accept; but *everything* considered, the obscurity to which circumstances have temporarily condemned her talents is a source of such sadness to her that a great dramatic occasion of the sort that you have so kindly invited her to could only be a cruel experience, and one best avoided. So I shall come on my own to applaud *Chatterton*, with all the warm affection and enthusiasm that I feel for the poet and for the cause he pleads so well. I am therefore returning the box, which I beg him to exchange for a stall."

Berlioz was well aware how hard life was for someone in her circumstances, and how vulnerable she was, as he reminded Adèle.

> Harriet hates to see me so enslaved [to journalism], all the more as she herself can do nothing. For a moment we were on the point of leaving for North America, but uncertainty as to what she would be offered there, and Louis being so young, decided us against it. Truly it is she who needs courage, for after all I am occupied, I am producing something, I can drown my sorrows in activity of a sort, whereas she! Tormented all day by servants who rob us, driven almost mad with anxiety by the slightest illness of the child, surrounded by a world for which she is not cut out and which doesn't even speak her language, inactive yet conscious of an immense talent which could make us rich if circumstances were different – no wonder she has bouts of despair: they are justified. [. . .] Harriet and I often talk of you; she really loves you. By the way, never speak in your letters of "irritations which will abate" or "prejudices which time will efface", etc. As you can imagine, such expressions wound and upset her terribly, and when I fail to hide those passages from her it can make her cry for a couple of days. I don't care for such language either; those "irritations" which are abating *double or triple mine*.

In another letter, to Edouard Rocher, he asks him to address his reply to Schlesinger's, not to Montmartre, if it has anything to do with payment still due for the legal summonses before his marriage: it would simply "revive painful memories" in Harriet. She is "very easily upset, and I try to avoid any occasion for it".

Yet their troubles brought them closer together. "In spite of all the pains and griefs and worries that she and I have to put up with daily because of the difficulties we are in, it seems to me that our affection grows stronger. She keeps me going when the absurd obstacles I encounter at every step drive me to rage; I console her as best I can for the frustration of her talents and her wasted future [. . .] and from this exchange of loving care springs a still greater tenderness."

In the first half of September 1835 the baby became seriously ill. For a time they feared they would lose him. Both mother and father were kept up night after night. Going to him in the small hours, often in bare feet and scantily clad, brought on Berlioz's recurrent sore throat in virulent form, and Harriet too fell ill. Not till the end of the second week in October was Berlioz able to write to his mother that Louis was out of danger. "He's running about the garden with his maid. His progress is very slow. Despite the intelligence which shines from his little face, he can't yet say anything clearly."

Any mark of affection from the family at La Côte, or from Berlioz's friends, was sure to send Harriet's spirits soaring, especially if it was a gift for her son. She was "in seventh heaven" at some toys sent by Prosper, and the smock and bonnet made by Adèle "won her heart". The child was "growing and getting stronger all the time. He still can't say one word. Harriet, however, claims he pointed to his smock and said 'Aunt' quite distinctly, and I am deputed to tell you." "Harriet is very touched by the interest you [Ferrand] take in her; but what delights her still more is what you say about our little Louis." "The case arrived very late yesterday evening. Harriet was delighted at being shown so much attention by our excellent mother." Mme Berlioz sent them money and offered various items including a barrel of wine, some jam, a cloak for Hector, and other articles of clothing and linen. He declined the cloak ("I never wear one") and the wine – the cost of bottles and portage, not to mention the risk of theft, would cancel any advantage – but said yes to the jam, for which "Louis has a passion", and to a pair of sheets and some towels, and a few shirts for himself.

Regularly through the summer and autumn the need to keep in touch with the musical scene and get material for his articles took him down the hill into Paris. Though some of his dozen or so pieces for the *Gazette musicale* could be dealt with at home – the two on Meyerbeer's piano music, for example – those in the *Débats* and the *Rénovateur* were more often than not reviews of events. He was, too, a frequent caller at Schlesinger's office, opposite his old lodgings in the Rue de Richelieu, where the *Gazette musicale* was edited. Berlioz, if not from the founding of the journal in January 1834 then very soon afterwards, was a key member of the editorial board as well as a regular contributor – writing about twenty articles in 1834, about twelve in 1835, about thirty in 1836 and about forty in 1837 (the exact number is uncertain, since not all his pieces were signed). Several times he acted as editor when Schlesinger was absent. The labour the *Gazette* involved him in for small remuneration – Schlesinger was notorious for paying his contributors little and late – was partly compensated for by the freedom he enjoyed to write on subjects that excited him, without reference to what was going on at the time. Between June 1834 and January 1835, for instance, he devoted seven articles to Gluck, none of them related to an actual performance.

Equally valuable was the sense of being one of a band of musicians and littérateurs with shared feelings and thoughts about the great aesthetic questions of the day, who worked together to uphold the sanctity of high art and defend it against the commercialized values of the encroaching philistines and the abuses of the operatic establishment. In pursuit of this goal the *Gazette* quickly established a distinctive style, a blend of news, comment, fantasy, invective and praise. Romanticism was wholeheartedly embraced. From the first the Hoffmanesque short story or *conte* containing discussion of topical issues was a prominent feature. So was the championing of Beethoven, not least the much-derided later works. The Berlin critic Rellstab might be suffered to describe the Ninth Symphony as the "ruin" of the composer's once-noble beauty and the sad consequence of ill health and bitterness of spirit; but much more typical were Berlioz's *critiques admiratives* on all nine symphonies or Stoepel's eloquent account, in one of the first numbers, of how he was converted from his former conviction that Beethoven's music was all contrivance, bizarrerie and the wilful breaking of rules. The *Gazette* took the high-minded view that music of real quality – in which it included Berlioz's – did not reveal itself all at once but had to be worked at, and was correspondingly scornful of composers who instead of challenging the public pandered to it. It also prided itself on good writing, and went out of its way to get the leading authors of the day to contribute: Balzac, George Sand, Dumas, Janin all appeared in its columns.

Maurice Schlesinger – a "ruthless, manipulative businessman with a streak of idealism", as Katharine Ellis has called him, and the model for Jacques Arnoux in Flaubert's *L'Education sentimentale* – was an editor of genius. He succeeded in imposing on the *Gazette* a consistent character while giving his writers their head. Though the journal existed to advertise the products of his publishing house, and was sometimes accused of being that and nothing else, he had the combined altruism and shrewdness to permit a surprising degree of independent criticism – which of course, provided it did not get out of hand, was good for the journal's image as a forum for free discussion. Schlesinger's mixture of sharp business instinct and disinterested love of art was demonstrated, in different ways, both by the *Gazette*'s treatment of Berlioz and by the war it waged against the hated Henri Herz, pianist-composer, publisher of endless sets of variations on popular operatic arias, and despised symbol of the low state of Parisian piano music. Schlesinger was not alone in ridiculing Herz. The flooding of the German market by trashy imports from Paris was one of Schumann's reasons for creating the journal *Neue Zeitschrift für Musik*, which first appeared a few months after the *Gazette musicale*. Schlesinger had a particular interest in doing Herz down – not least when Herz pirated his rights to piano transcriptions from *The Huguenots* (Meyerbeer was a Schlesinger composer). But at the same time he was crusading for higher standards, and seeking to elevate public taste and wean it from Herz and his "machine à variation" by fostering the music of Chopin, Alkan, Stephen Heller and to a lesser extent Liszt. He also attacked the Opéra for the cuts it regularly inflicted on the works in its repertoire. The Romantics who wrote for the *Gazette* could only applaud campaigns so entirely in the spirit of the journal's declared aims.

Yet it is typical of the *Gazette*'s relative fair-mindedness that it was prepared to print a favourable notice of one of Herz's concertos. With Berlioz, it is notable how even-handedly it reviewed him. Effusive, uncritical notices were rare. Maybe Schlesinger did not have a strong commercial interest in him, to begin with at least; until 1838, when the Requiem and the overture to *Benvenuto Cellini* were issued, his only Berlioz publications were a handful of songs. But it is clear he believed in his talent and went out of his way to support it. No other contemporary composer was given so much coverage in the *Gazette*. It did not always praise him – Stoepel's review of the reissue of *Neuf mélodies* is quite severe – but it took him seriously, as an important figure worthy to be discussed at the highest level. For Berlioz it more than made up for the vulgar derisiveness of Fétis in the *Revue musicale*.

By its second year the *Gazette* had begun to eclipse the *Revue* altogether. It had been founded with the aim of combining the scholarly interests of the *Revue* with a much wider appeal and, in doing so, of attracting a larger readership than Fétis' journal had ever done – a readership that could enjoy the articles without having any specialist knowledge of music – and in this it was immediately successful. It soon began to swamp its rival. By early 1835 the *Revue* was floundering. Fétis had left in 1833 to become director of the Brussels Conservatoire, abandoning the-day-to-day direction to his son Edouard. In November the journal finally gave in and was absorbed by its competitor, which henceforth became the *Revue et gazette musicale*. Fétis' last editorial, on 1 November, was a characteristic piece of resentful condescension: "It is up to these young literary musicians, who have come together to produce the *Gazette musicale de Paris*, to continue what I began. I have left them with an easier road to follow than I found. There will not be the same obstacles to overcome". He was made a member of the editorial board of the amalgamated titles, where in later years he would become an influential voice, generally for the worse, setting the tone for the same kind of dismissive and personally abusive treatment of Wagner as he had accorded Berlioz, and debasing the *Gazette*'s once-proud standards of criticism. But, for the present, his physical departure and the demise of his journal meant, for Berlioz, one fewer active enemy of his music. It was a significant moment, emphasized soon after by his discovery that Fétis' most recent attack, in the *Revue musicale* of 1 February, had prompted a counter-attack by Schumann. After printing a translation of Fétis' article, Schumann had sent for Liszt's transcription of the Fantastic Symphony and published a long and detailed and mainly favourable analysis which put Fétis decisively in his place. The disappearance of the *Revue* would secure a breathing-space of a few years before the advent of Scudo.

By the time of the merger between the two journals Berlioz was in the thick of preparing for his concerts. He had created time and space for himself by writing most of his articles in advance: of the six that appeared in various journals in November and December no more than two, both of them in the *Rénovateur*, were notices of performances. Three concerts were planned (as is shown by the lists of orchestral musicians that have survived in his hand); but only two were given, probably because this time he had less than fifteen minutes' new music to offer. This time, too, it was a joint venture with Girard, with whom he was sharing the proceeds and the costs. Girard, as well as conducting the opening concert (postponed from 15 to 22 November), had two works in it, an overture on *Antigone* and his orchestral arrangement of Beethoven's Moonlight Sonata. Berlioz had *Le cinq mai*, *Le jeune pâtre breton* sung by Falcon (who also sang an aria from Meyerbeer's *Crociato*) and *Harold*, with Urhan as before the solo violist.

The concert added to the laurels the symphony had won the year before; but once again Girard made a bad mistake, this time in the Serenade. Whether or not that was the sole reason for the breach which now took place, the fact is that the second concert – three weeks later, on 13 December – contained no music by Girard and was conducted by Berlioz. The altered programme featured, in addition to a cello solo played by Batta and vocal music by Gluck and Meyerbeer, the *King Lear* overture, a repeat of *Le cinq mai*, the Pilgrims' March from *Harold* and – for the first time under the composer's baton – the Fantastic Symphony. There was only one rehearsal, starting at 8.30 in the morning the day before the concert; but that seems to have been sufficient. It was a crucial step. "From now on," he wrote to Adèle, "I need not have recourse to anyone to conduct my music"; and to Liszt: "I am now conducting my concerts myself, and the performance shows the effect of it. The tempos were never quite right."

It was inevitable that Berlioz would turn conductor sooner or later. The logical conclusion of his painstaking work as organizer and administrator was that the end-product, the performance of his music, should be in his hands, not in someone else's. Despite his unhappy memories of the benefit concert of November 1833 – when the *Journal de France* concluded that he was temperamentally too nervous and excitable to be a conductor – he knew that, with all his lack of experience, he could give a more faithful account of his music than Girard ever could, or than the old pro Habeneck. Watching them do it, a practical visionary like him could not but imagine how he would do it and do it better.

He had to learn by trial and error. There was no one to teach him. He had to be a new kind of conductor; it was a new discipline that music such as his demanded, almost a new profession. He mastered it by degrees. As late as 1852 he could say that it was rare for him to conduct without making a single mistake (though orchestral players might privately say the same of some eminent conductors even today).

Conducting, he wrote to Adolphe Samuel in 1856, was a very difficult art, and one had to "practice it over many years before one could be completely sure of oneself". As he did so his style changed. In 1843 Spontini chided him for using excessively large, expansive gestures. A year later his movements were precise and economical, according to Charles Hallé, who played the G major Beethoven concerto with him ("his beat was so decisive, his indication of all the nuances so clear"), and they seem to have remained so: the Russian composer César Cui, in 1868, was struck by his remarkably neat, exact beat. But master it he did, and became, in the opinion of Hallé, von Bülow and others, the finest conductor of the age. Everything conspired to make him so: his profound musicianship; his comprehensive knowledge of the orchestra and of orchestral players; his instinct for leadership; his fabulous rhythmic sense; his thoroughness, his understanding that good organization was an essential part of the conductor's job (which led him to introduce sectional rehearsals and numbered orchestral parts); not least, his temperament: as Louis Engel said, he was "in later days the greatest conductor known, not 'although' but 'because' his nerves were in such an overexcited state that he nearly heard the impossible". (Engel tells a story of Berlioz detecting a minute difference of pitch between two clarinets in the midst of an orchestral tutti.)

The consequences of his decision to conduct his concerts himself were both obvious and immeasurable. By the time he was able finally to take his music to Germany he had acquired the authority and skill to teach it to musicians who had not encountered anything like it before. His experiences as composer-conductor led naturally – given his scientific cast of mind – to the systematic study of the instruments of the orchestra which became, in the early 1840s, the enormously influential *Treatise on Modern Orchestration*. Exactly how conducting affected his compositions we cannot say; but we can apply to him Pierre Boulez's dicta that there is no better training for a composer than "to have to play or conduct one's own works and to face their difficulties of execution", and that conducting is crucial to "an understanding of how to write for large orchestra and bring acoustic perspective to orchestral composition". It was also an activity that he loved, and that kept him young. He speaks of the "uplifting fatigue" of long rehearsals. And the occasions when he brought off a really good performance were among the greatest joys of his life.

The tragedy is that these matchless talents were never harnessed to a permanent, established position. Yet they so nearly were. The Gymnase débâcle is in some ways the most poignant reverse of Berlioz's career and the most far-reaching in its consequences. When, towards the end of 1835, he was approached by the management of the new concert hall and asked to become its artistic director, it seemed a heaven-sent opportunity: a guaranteed annual salary of 6,000 francs, paid monthly in advance, plus author's royalties on performances of his works and two benefit concerts a year – a likely income of about 12,000 francs and a first-rate position from which to put some of his reformist ideas into effect. He accepted the offer, and the contract was drawn up and signed. Everything now rested on a ministerial decision to allow vocal music – oratorios, masses, cantatas – to be included in the programmes. The Bertins set seriously to work to obtain it; a departmental head at the Ministry of the Interior was in favour; and the result of intensive lobbying was a categorical refusal on the part of the current minister, Thiers. The project collapsed, the Gymnase became a dancehall, and Berlioz, knowing that the job could have changed his life and Harriet's, sank into the "profound dejection" (he told Liszt) "which always succeeds those violent inner rages that gnaw one's spirit without being able to provoke an explosion – you know them, unfortunately, as well as I do" (25 January 1836). He was left with the hope that there might be a change of minister – and "perhaps not every minister will take the same view".

There often was a change. Ministerial crises were a feature of the unstable political climate, in which the so-called Party of Movement agitated for greater freedom, in line with the ideals of July 1830, against the conservative Party of Resistance, concerned to reassure society, and Europe, that France had outgrown the follies of its revolutionary past. Berlioz did sometimes gain under one Minister of the Interior part of what he lost under another. But in the constant tussle of interests and trading of favours art was an essentially minor matter, to be espoused or sacrificed first and foremost for reasons of political calculation. The Bertins, with all their cultivated tastes, understood this as well as anyone. There were bigger issues at stake, which might well oblige them to concede defeat in their efforts on a protégé's behalf. In the real world, art was a bargaining counter and the artist a suppliant for the goodwill of an unpredictable tyrant.

It was a role the French Romantics found intolerable on both idealistic and practical grounds. They saw the artist as the regenerator of society

– the musician above all. Music was the great potential emancipator of the masses, the supreme civilizing agent. Musical education could transform the very soul of society. So far from being the monopoly of the privileged, music should be freely available to all; the government, instead of making life difficult for musicians, should assist them in every way to spread the light of their talents and popularize music among all sections of the community, not least the poor. "La haute popularisation", based on the ideas of Saint-Simon and Lammenais and Auguste Comte, became the burning conviction of socially progressive musicians. Hence the many amelioristic movements and initiatives of the 1830s: Maurice Schlesinger's Society for the Publication of Cheap Editions of Classical and Modern Music, founded in 1834, whose declared aim was to make France a musical nation; Adolphe Nourrit's ideal of "Art for the people and by the people"; Wilhem's Orphéon, the male-voice-choir movement founded in 1833; Abbé Mainzer's choral classes for workers and his teaching manual *Méthode de chant pour les enfants* (1835). Liszt voiced a common belief when in a series of articles in the *Gazette musicale* in 1835 on "The Position of Artists and Their Place in Society" he called – "in the name of all musicians, of art and of social progress" – for wholesale public investment in music, including musical instruction in primary schools, encouragement of local philharmonic societies and regular gatherings on the lines of the popular festivals of Germany and England, and government-sponsored performance and publication of the best new works in the fields of dramatic, symphonic and religious music.

Berlioz, in whom intense idealism coexisted with a deep natural scepticism, looked on all these aspirations, like King Claudius, with an auspicious and a dropping eye. He was sympathetic to the educational ideas of people like Nourrit and Wilhem, and saw what in good hands, properly carried out, they could lead to. All his life he dreamed of the musical city and the solemn celebration attended by whole populations of initiates. But he did not believe that music as he felt and knew and understood it could be "brought within the grasp of everybody", as Fétis preached: Fétis who was living, scathing disproof of the theory – Beethoven's greatest music being manifestly not within his grasp. The plains of Troy would have to be purged of English tourists, Italian dilettanti and the mocking French before the Eroica could be fittingly performed there. He was all too conscious that even at the Société des Concerts' high solemnities there were people who went only because it was the thing to do. As a freelance composer who tended to write for large forces he was particularly in need of the enlightened state patronage that Liszt's utopian manifesto prescribed, and particularly at risk from the way things were managed in reality.

For the opera that he longed to write and to which, with the collapse of the Gymnase scheme, he must now look to make his fortune, he had once again to wait upon what he called "that hellish ministerial world" and welter in its "bottomless pit". The history of *Benvenuto Cellini* taken only as far as the beginning of 1836 – that is, with a production still over two and a half years ahead – shows just how hard it was for a composer of Berlioz's reputation (good and bad) to reach the point of having an opera accepted for performance by a Paris theatre.

In the spring of 1834, at Montmartre, while waiting for news of a possible *Hamlet* commission, he had decided to base an opéra-comique on Cellini's *Memoirs*. He had recently read the book in a new French translation and been attracted by the boldness and energy of this "bandit of genius" and perhaps also by the parallels between the artist's material difficulties and his own. Having drafted a scenario he asked his friend Alfred de Vigny to write the libretto. It may have been Vigny who gave him the idea in the first place, perhaps in the winter of 1833–4 when they became friends, or conceivably at the party in the Montmartre garden when Chopin, Liszt, Hiller and Antoni Deschamps were the other guests; Vigny had known the *Memoirs* since 1832 (when the records show him borrowing a copy from the Bibliothèque Royale). But he was busy with *Chatterton* and with his novel *Servitude et grandeur militaires*, and suggested their mutual friend Léon de Wailly instead. Wailly had some experience of the theatre, as a playwright and from having been involved in an *Ivanhoe* at the Odéon (just when Berlioz and Léon Compaignon were grappling with their Scott opera on Richard Coeur de Lion). He chose as his collaborator Auguste Barbier, a poet whom Berlioz greatly admired. The libretto they wrote delighted Berlioz, but it was rejected when all three of them presented themselves in July 1834 at the Opéra-Comique and had it read in their presence – "simpletons that we were"; for "despite the protestations of M. Crosnier, we think it was rejected because of me. I am regarded at the Opéra-Comique as a subversive, an underminer of the national genre, and they want none of me. As a result they rejected the words so as not to have to admit the music of a madman."

Having failed at the Opéra-Comique they tried the Opéra, and the

Bertin influence was again brought to bear. ('As usual I count on your friendship in asking your support for Berlioz" ends an undated letter from Armand Bertin to the Opéra's director, Louis Véron, enclosing the libretto of a work which may have been *Benvenuto Cellini*.) Like Crosnier, Véron drew the line at Berlioz, however; Berlioz was forced to recognize that he would never be admitted so long as Véron was there. But Véron was leaving; and his likely successor, Duponchel, the famous stage designer, was a Bertin protégé and therefore under an obligation. Early in 1835 Armand Bertin and Meyerbeer extracted a formal promise, in the presence of Berlioz and Barbier, that his first action on becoming director would be to commission an opera from them.

Berlioz had no illusions. Though Duponchel "imagines he likes my music," he wrote to Adèle in August 1835, "he understands it no more than M. Véron does". In any case Duponchel's nomination was being delayed by ministerial manoeuvrings and by the repercussions of the Fieschi plot, which had set all Paris in turmoil. "We're waiting. But I know so well what kind of animal these directors are that I wouldn't give an écu for Duponchel's promise. I can't forget that Meyerbeer was only able to persuade them to put on *Robert le diable* – the work to which the Opéra has owed its entire prosperity during the past four years – by paying the administration sixty thousand francs of his own money when they wouldn't take on the expense of it themselves. To be approved of by those rogues you have to be as second-rate as they are."

Duponchel – "a thin, yellow man with a face like an undertaker" (Heine) – duly became director and at first was as good as his word, only demanding certain changes in the libretto, which Vigny took in hand. The work was done by the second half of September and the revised libretto accepted. Duponchel even professed himself delighted with it.

At that point obstacles arose which seemed to show the director trying to wriggle out of his verbal agreement. Berlioz was unable to secure a contract. The Bertin influence had apparently waned and been replaced by that of Rossini and his banker Aguado, who were thought to oppose the commission. Duponchel used the fact that his engagement was only for the remaining two years of Véron's term as a pretext for not signing a contract: it would "unfairly commit his successor".

The case is complicated, involving as it does the Commission Spéciale des Théâtres Royaux and the Minister of the Interior, the inevitable

Thiers. But the upshot was that by the end of January 1836 Berlioz was still without a formal commitment of any kind. "Meyerbeer and Bertin urge me to write my opera all the same, convinced that when the time comes to put it on, means will be found. That is what I am going to do."

5

A Summer of Composition

His ambitions for *Benvenuto Cellini* received fresh stimulus soon afterwards from the reception of Meyerbeer's long-awaited opera. Berlioz
went with Harriet and Félix Marmion to the first night, on 29 February,
and saw *The Huguenots* triumph before an audience of well-wishers,
professional and amateur. The runaway success of *Robert le diable* was
about to be repeated.

Meyerbeer had been in no hurry to have the work produced, and
had resisted the impatience of the Opéra's management and of his
librettist Eugène Scribe (at one point Scribe was in a state of high alarm
that its greatest selling-point, the scene of the bathing beauties at the
court of Queen Margaret of Navarre, would be pre-empted by a similar
scene in the Opéra's popular ballet *Revolt at the Harem*). They were
desperate for another *Robert* – the one opera in the years 1831 to 1835
to do consistently good, indeed sensational business – but he could
wait. He knew the value of well-publicized delay. Curiosity about
Robert's successor was fed by regular reports in the press. Expectations
grew during the long months of rehearsal – never had an opera been
so carefully prepared – and were at fever pitch by the time the work
was finally unveiled.

They were not disappointed. *The Huguenots* fulfilled the most wildly
optimistic predictions that had been made about it. All through the late
winter and the spring and summer of 1836 Paris flocked to see it.
Fashionable society put off its migration to the country so as to catch
one more performance. Two months after the first night it was still
selling out the house and taking huge sums. Malibran herself was moved
to mount the stage and embrace Falcon at the end of her love duet with
Nourrit's Raoul de Nangis, that crowning number of the magnificent
fourth act which Meyerbeer, replacing an earlier duet, had written, it
was said, at Nourrit's insistence, composing it, to words supplied by

Nourrit and Emile Deschamps, in only three hours, and which had taken everyone by storm at its first rehearsal with orchestra – the ecstatic composer stopped beating time with his famous umbrella and called out, in his heavy Germanic accent, "Suplime . . . mais gontinuez, c'est barfait!"

Berlioz was scornful of the "platitudes" that Véron had been putting on at the Opéra in recent years, not excluding Halévy's *La Juive* (for which Wagner had a soft spot); but like other musicians he was caught up in the excitement *The Huguenots* aroused. "I am very curious to get to know his new score", he had written the previous year, adding that "Meyerbeer is the one established composer who has shown me a real and lively interest." He said this knowing what a compulsive flatterer Meyerbeer was – this small, oddly shabby-looking man with what Louis Engel called his "clever head" and the "cunning expression" that showed through his habitual "humble mock-modesty". He was aware of the lengths Meyerbeer would go to in order to ingratiate himself with the least of the critics – how much more with a critic of his prominence – in his almost paranoid apprehension of failure. Berlioz acknowledged that it was always difficult to get Meyerbeer to say what he really thought. He was also conscious of all that had been done to ensure the success of this great "musical encyclopedia", as he called it, "in which so many interests, artistic and financial, are at stake". Yet his regard for the score was high and unfeigned. He knew too how wise it was – given the way the Opéra worked or rather didn't work – for even a Meyerbeer to ensure personally that his operas were throughly prepared. In the first of many articles on *The Huguenots*, he wrote approvingly of Meyerbeer "enduring the complaints and all the expressions of discontent he was beset with because of the protracted labours made necessary by the style of the work and because of the meticulous exactitude with which he supervised them. 'That's unperformable! This has no common sense!' many said, unjustly, wearied by the endless rehearsals. And the composer, bowing his head resignedly, let the wave of ill humour pass, then took a breath and went on, murmuring to himself: 'If it's unperformable today, we'll see if it is tomorrow; if my music has no common sense, that's because it has another sort.' Experience has proved how right he was."

Much later, Berlioz came to see Meyerbeer's domination and manipulation of Parisian grand opera as fatal to any attempt he himself might make; it created an attitude of mind and an accepted style in which a work like *The Trojans* had no chance of thriving. "The influence of Meyerbeer," he wrote, "and the pressure he exerts on managers, artists and critics and consequently on the Paris public, at least as much by his immense wealth as by his genuine eclectic talent, make all serious success at the Opéra virtually impossible. This baneful influence may well continue to be felt ten years after his death; Henri Heine maintains that he has 'paid in advance'."

Whether or not this assessment affected what Berlioz thought of the works themselves, it is a fact that his admiration for Meyerbeer's operas waned. Already in 1849 he had reservations about *Le Prophète*; seven years later, during the composition of *The Trojans*, he confessed to "detesting" it. In 1865, having attended the dress rehearsal of *L'Africaine*, he was only too glad not to have to write about it. But in 1836 *The Huguenots* was for him a major work – "encyclopedic" character and all – and it remained so for long afterwards. It is one of the select circle of masterpieces, along with *Der Freischütz*, *La Vestale*, *Fidelio*, *The Barber of Seville*, *Don Giovanni* and *Iphigénie en Tauride*, whose performance imposes a respectful silence on the normally talkative musicians in his book *Evenings in the Orchestra* (1852). There is a suggestion that they may have been talking during *Robert le diable* on an evening when the narrator (Berlioz) is absent – the text is ambiguous – but *The Huguenots* is sacred. A performance of the Blessing of the Daggers by massed choir and orchestra at the Palace of Industry in 1844 is among the great experiences of his conducting career.

This may strike us as odd, a century and a half later, when performances of Meyerbeer's operas are rare (and, if they do happen, given as often as not perfunctorily, without conviction). No composer once so famous has fallen so low. To the intelligentsia of his day the Michelangelo of music, he has shrunk to an almost forgotten mass entertainer, expert concocter of the nineteenth-century equivalent of the Hollywood epic, with its elaborate stage pageantry, showy roles for the great vocal stars, glamorous orchestration and illusion of grand passions and profound issues – the creator or developer of a genre that lives on only in works which, like *Don Carlos* and *Aida*, transcend it. His importance in the history of music – so the argument goes – cannot of course be gainsaid; both Verdi and Wagner learned a great deal from him and paid him the tribute of imitation; but that very fact could only work against him, since comparison with more elevated operas inevitably laid bare the shallowness of his own, leaving him impaled for ever on

Wagner's epigram, "effects without causes". Once Verdi had absorbed the Meyerbeerian style and re-created it on higher moral ground, endowing it with much greater melodic invention and dramatic pace, once Wagnerian music-drama had captured the allegiance of the intellectual élite, his eclipse was only a matter of time. Later, when the tidal wave of Wagnerism had receded and the reaction against Romanticism had run its course, Berlioz's music might rise again but not Meyerbeer's. The disappearance of singers able to meet his virtuoso demands – commonly cited as the reason for his neglect – was no more than an excuse, masking an irrevocable decline.

Yet if we with our superior perspective can "see through" Meyerbeer, few of his contemporaries did. Mendelssohn, though conceding that the music of *Robert* was very well put together, found it heartless; and Schumann, who had been impressed by the early *Crociato*, was disillusioned by *The Huguenots*, relegating its composer "to the level of one of Franconi's circus-riders". But Wagner, whatever he may later have decided about the "weathercock of European music", who veered "with every shift of the wind", was unequivocal in his praise under the first impact of Meyerbeerian grand opera. As late as 1841 he was calling Meyerbeer, without irony, the "German Messiah" who alone could revitalize the moribund Paris Opéra. "Only what is genuinely excellent can really hold its place, which is why we keep on seeing *Robert le diable* and *The Huguenots* when some second-rate piece has to be taken off." Liszt, back in Paris briefly from Geneva in May 1836, wrote to Marie d'Agoult of the new opera's "prodigious workmanship and orchestral detail". Verdi, with all his low opinion of the Opéra and his complaint that to be a success there one had to be a millionaire, never doubted "the power of Meyerbeer's genius". Berlioz was in respectable company.

The admiration of Wagner, Verdi, Berlioz and countless other musicians should not really surprise us. The impact of *The Huguenots* and of what Shaw, in the midst of his most impassioned campaigning for Wagner, acknowledged as "the electrical Meyerbeerian atmosphere", was understandably enormous. *Robert* created a novel kind of musical dramaturgy. Meyerbeer had devised an operatic theatre which combined all the elements aural and visual – music, words, scenery, costumes, lighting, action, movement – into a coherent whole, and in which the score was at once monumental and fluid, massively constructed and responsive at every moment to the varying demands of the drama; and the process was refined and deepened in *The Huguenots*. The effectiveness of its carefully planned act structures – seen at their most striking in the third and fourth acts – is naturally not detectable in heavily cut modern revivals (which often seek to justify themselves by the strange argument that these works were habitually cut in the nineteenth century); but it was not lost on his peers. And though, in retrospect, the imaginative evocation of the past in *Don Carlos* and *Die Meistersinger* exposes the comparative superficiality of what Shaw called "the historical impostures of Scribe and Meyerbeer" and their merely decorative pageantry and local colour, at the time it was something new and very exciting.

The sheer weight of sound of the Meyerbeerian ensemble and the cleverly contrasted vocal and orchestral textures seized the attention not only of the aristocratic and bourgeois audiences but, still more, of the musicians. Berlioz, like Liszt, like others, was fascinated by Meyerbeer's experiments in instrumental sonority as a means of dramatic expression. He dwelt on his use of unusual solo instruments, such as the new bass clarinet and the revived viola d'amore, and on his telling combinations and inventive choices of colour: the presence of the nasal cor anglais in the middle of flute and clarinet chords so as to suggest, as the oboe would have done less well, the sound of an organ, in the introduction to Act 1; the grotesque superimposition of piccolo and double-bass, with the rhythm marked by pianissimo bass drum, in the accompaniment to Marcel's song celebrating the Siege of La Rochelle, and the sober-suited cello chords which punctuated his recitatives, so perfectly attuned to the character of the Puritan rough diamond; the sinister rattle of combined timpani and tenor drum beneath the orchestral crescendo between each phrase of the unison chorus "A cette cause sainte" at the end of the conspiracy scene; the effect of the trumpets playing the major sixth in a minor key as the murdering Catholics rampaged through the streets in the final scene. Here was an innovator, if not to learn from, then to emulate.

The Huguenots could only sharpen Berlioz's sense of the absolute necessity of a success at the Opéra. But their respective positions were fundamentally different, and the contrast is poignant to contemplate. Meyerbeer's letters and diaries reveal a world utterly remote in material terms from the one Berlioz inhabited, a world of great riches and the power they conferred to do as you liked: to compose your operas at leisure; to withhold them till the time was ripe; to dictate the conditions under which they were performed, and assemble the ideal cast; to devise new scenic effects likely to impress the public (and if necessary pay for them); to bend the director and his potentially obstructive functionaries to your will; to get the critics on your side with flattering attentions and well-placed gifts; to have a band of claqueurs permanently on the payroll; to run the whole thing like a business; and by these methods to make your position virtually impregnable. Maybe by no means all of it was indispensable: Meyerbeer would no doubt have dominated the Opéra on his own very considerable merits, including the merit of satisfying the public's taste for grand musical spectacles and reconstructions of history. But it helped. The Opéra was a death-trap of conflicting interests and negative impulses; the most sure-fire success was dependent on your making certain they were all working for you, or at any rate not against you.

Berlioz, on the other hand, was an opera composer on sufferance, and one who composed on borrowed time paid for with money that was not his but lent by a wealthy friend. His decision, taken at the end of January 1836, to go ahead and write *Benvenuto Cellini* without a contract was brave but impractical: it could not be carried out, for the old reason – he "lacked metal".* The account he gives in the *Memoirs* of his difficulties and their resolution, though touched up a little, is accurate in essentials:

> One must be free of other work when writing an opera – that is, one's livelihood must be assured for a certain period. That was very far from being the case with me. I was living from hand to mouth on the proceeds of my articles. [...] Writing them was practically my sole occupation. In the first access of excitement over my score I did attempt to keep two months clear for working uninterruptedly at it. But brutal necessity soon forced me to stop playing the composer and turn critic again. It was an agonizing decision, but there was no alternative. I had a wife and child; how could I leave them with nothing to live on? Yet, in my dejection, harassed on one side by poverty and on the other by musical ideas I was obliged to repress, I no longer had the heart to do my usual scribbling, so abhorrent had it become.

---

* Cf. Britten's reply to Koussevitsky's question, why he had not written an opera: "I explained that the construction of a scenario, discussion with a librettist, planning the musical architecture, composing preliminary sketches, and writing nearly a thousand pages of orchestral score, demanded a freedom from other work which was an economic impossibility for most young composers."

I was plunged in gloomy thoughts, when Ernest Legouvé came to see me. "How are you getting on with your opera?" he asked

"I haven't finished the first act yet. I can't get time to work on it."

"Supposing you had time?"

"Don't – I would write from dawn till dusk."

"What would you need to make you independent?"

"Two thousand francs – which I haven't got."

"And if someone . . . supposing you were . . . come on, help me."

"What? What do you mean?"

"All right – supposing a friend of yours lent it to you?"

"What friend could I possibly ask to lend me such an amount?"

"You don't have to ask: I am offering it to you."

The sum was 1,000 francs, not 2,000 (the other 1,000 was lent two years later), but it was still equivalent to ten feuilletons in the *Débats* and enough to relieve the pressure. Berlioz sent Legouvé a signed IOU and thanked him for "having the best heart of anyone I have met in my whole life: if there is anything superior to your goodness it is your delicacy", and flung himself into his opera. Winter was over, and with it the muddy lanes which isolated them from their friends and the bitter winds that made it so hard to keep warm in their draughty apartment on the northern slope of the village. It was spring. A summer of composition lay before him.

What the money granted above all was the sense that he now had time to devote to sustained work. It is a fact that between 1 May and the beginning of July no feuilleton by him appeared in the *Journal des débats*, and only three or four in the *Gazette*. True, at intervals during the summer he spent part of each week supervising rehearsals for *Esmeralda*, the opera written by the crippled Louise Bertin to a libretto based on Victor Hugo's novel *Notre-Dame de Paris*: there was no declining such a request from the Bertins, and they paid him well for it. Most of June, however, was completely clear (two of the principal singers, Nourrit and Falcon, were on holiday). But what was crucial was the end, for the moment, of the oppressive dependence on journalism. Psychologically it liberated him. Whenever Berlioz *felt* free and able to give his mind and all his creative attention to composing, he wrote quickly, with concentrated intensity. By the beginning of July half the opera was done: the scene between Balducci the papal treasurer and the carnival maskers under his window; the first version of the aria for

Balducci's daughter Teresa; the duet with Cellini and the captivating trio in which their plan to elope during the revels in the Piazza Colonna is overheard by Fieramosca, official papal sculptor and rival for Teresa's hand; Fieramosca's drubbing by the female inhabitants of the quartier; the big choral scene in the tavern on the edge of the piazza, where Cellini and his metalworkers carouse and celebrate the glories of the goldsmith's art; and the huge carnival finale in which, as Liszt said, "for the first time in opera the crowd speaks with its great roaring voice". It was once again like their first Montmartre summer two years before, when he was completing *Harold*; indeed the goldsmiths' chorus, at that stage the opening scene of the opera, had been drafted immediately after *Harold*, in the flush of his enthusiasm for the new project, and in the same bright "Italian" G major which the opera shares with the symphony. But *Benvenuto* takes *Harold*'s already audacious rhythmic freedom and brilliance of colour much further.

The opera had been often in Berlioz's thoughts since then. We catch an oblique glimpse of it in the notorious *Débats* article of September 1835 on *Zampa*, when he contrasts what he considers Herold's mish-mash of an overture with Weber's overtures to *Freischütz* and the others. Weber (he says), like Herold, fashioned them out of themes taken from the opera; but unlike Herold he succeeded in shaping them into a unified whole. Then (in an allusion to the casting of Cellini's Perseus which forms the climax of Berlioz's opera): "He threw silver, copper and gold into the melting-pot but was able to combine them into a single alloy, and when the statue emerged from the mould its sombre hue displayed but one metal, bronze." Apart from the little *Chansonette de M. de Wailly*, however, written in August 1835 to words by one of the opera's librettists and used for the offstage serenade in Scene 1, no work on the composition seems to have been done during the twenty-odd months between autumn 1834 and spring 1836. But now that the signal was given the pent-up music poured out of him, as it had done two years before when his Italian experiences were transmuted into the music of *Harold*. Only, this was a different Italy: except for Crispino's rustic serenade, used for the foundry-workers' song in the final scene, not the "wild Italy" where he took refuge from the deadness of modern Rome but the eternal city in its burgeoning Renaissance heyday, an Italy where Art, no longer "Juliet stretched upon her bier", was once again vitally alive and an issue of public importance. The subject seized his imagination; and having exorcized, in an article for the *Gazette*, his memories of the present-day carnival time in Rome and its squalid barbarities, he turned to the task of re-creating its one-time counterpart with all the resources at his command. The work would be a historical opera with modern connotations, a passionate comedy designed both to evoke the exuberance of sixteenth-century Italy and to show the triumph of the unorthodox, innovatory artist over his sceptical conservative opponents.

The libretto Berlioz eventually set had gone through several stages, the exact sequence and history of which remain unclear. Starting as an opéra-comique – about which we know nothing for sure except that it began with the goldsmiths' chorus – it was upgraded, with the Opéra in mind, into a much grander work (which apparently included the Siege of Rome and the killing of the Constable of Bourbon, based on the account of them in Cellini's autobiography), before becoming the two-act, four-tableau "opera semi-seria" that Duponchel was finally induced, with Meyerbeer's aid, to accept. In this form it owed almost as much to E. T. A. Hoffmann's *conte* "Signor Formica" as it did to the autobiography. Cellini's *Memoirs* supplied the sculptor's battles with officialdom, many of the characters' names (though some of them were given different identities), the three cannon-shots from the Castel Sant'Angelo which mark the end of carnival, and the casting of the Perseus – in Rome instead of in Florence, and commissioned by Pope Clement VII, not by Cosimo de' Medici. Most of the personal drama, on the other hand, was derived from the Hoffmann story, in which Salvator Rosa (an artist-bandit in the Cellini mould, much admired by the Romantics) helped a fellow-painter serenade the niece of a Balducci-like miser with guitars beneath her window and then elope with her under cover of darkness during an open-air performance on the last night of the carnival.

The resulting text, criticized at the time and since, does not succeed in "combining into a single alloy" the disparate elements of the drama, the heterogeneous character of which was at least partly the consequence of the different stages the project had gone through. The would-be serious theme of the embattled artist-hero is fundamentally at odds, not with a comic context per se but with this particular one, in which farce keeps rearing its grinning head. It is like an *Ariadne auf Naxos* without the rationale for the juxtaposition of *commedia dell'arte* and high romance; or like *Don Giovanni*, as it appears to those numerous opera-lovers to whom the mixture of deadly seriousness with farce at its crudest has been a stumbling-block from 1787 to the present day. Rather as the super-hero of *Don Giovanni* is permitted to rise to his full stature only at the end – till then the situations have been constantly mocking him – so it is not until the final scene of Berlioz's opera that the focus is at last on Cellini the artist at grips, however melodramatically, with his art, and not on the operatic lover enmeshed in the conventional complications of an amorous intrigue. It is true that Cellini takes part, in the second tableau, in the goldsmiths' hymn to the mystery and greatness of their craft, which is the philosophical core of the work; but he does so as the leader of the guild, *primus inter pares*: the song is a collective utterance. It is also true that Berlioz treats the essentially Italian plot in a subversively un-Italian way. The fact remains that when the libretto (the 1836 version, that is) does eventually give Cellini a moment to himself for reflection, he uses it to fantasize about escaping from it all and embracing the shepherd's simple life – an understandable human reaction in someone about to face the supreme crisis of his existence, and the cue for a noble piece of pastoral music, but not quite what one was hoping for.

In both operas, however, the score transcends the limitations of the libretto when it doesn't also transform its character. The overmastering virility of Don Giovanni's music contradicts the literal fact that he fails, seemingly, to make any fresh conquests. Similarly, Cellini's creative energy and audacity are not demonstrated only in the casting scene but are incarnate in the music of the opera as a whole – music so exuberantly inventive that a good production can sweep away the best-founded objections, as happened at the Lyon Berlioz Festival in 1988, when you were made to forget that *Benvenuto Cellini* had ever been a problem opera.

The libretto gave Berlioz what he wanted, a subject he could identify with in a setting that offered an exceptionally wide range of moods and situations, serious and comic: love songs, guild hymns, crowd scenes, prayers, solitary communing with nature, massive choral ensembles, parody. It was the opportunity he had been waiting for. Cellini's challenge to the establishment would be matched by his own; he would show Paris what the typecast symphonist whose place was in the concert hall could do in the opera house. After the months of compositional fast, he gorged himself on music.

In a long score – at its full length, getting on for three hours of music – there are few failures. One is the Teresa/Cellini duet in Act 2, despite some attractive phrases in the first section. Another is Cellini's "La gloire était ma seule idole", written very late on so that Duprez could have another aria, and eminently removable (allowing the second tableau to begin, as planned, with the panache and high good humour of the goldsmiths' scene). Otherwise, the composer's verdict stands. Having read through the score twelve years later "with the strictest impartiality", he could not "help recognizing" that it contained "a variety of ideas, a vitality and zest and a brilliance of musical colour such as I shall perhaps not find again".

The Damnation of Faust, his only dramatic work of comparable brilliance (if you can compare two such different works and worlds), may be much more tautly constructed and have a surer sense of direction, a greater coherence and depth of idea and mastery of means and end; but Berlioz was right: the abundance, the zest of *Benvenuto* is unique in his output and in the music of his time – above all in terms of rhythm, including the rhythm of contrasting timbres. The constantly changing pulse, the continual syncopation of instrumental colour, the sheer pace at which things happen, make it still, after a century and a half, an extremely demanding score to play and sing, and an astonishing one for its date. Although the influence of Meyerbeer is negligible – and if anything it is *Robert*, not *The Huguenots*, that we catch echoes of, comic echoes – the work is also a kind of "encyclopedia", of the Berlioz style, excluding only the austere monumentalism of what he called his architectural works. That would soon be heard in the Grande messe des morts; but it had no place here. *Benvenuto* was a celebration of life; and to that end he summoned his utmost vitality and virtuosity.

Like the women in the carnival crowd with their compulsive chatter (whose babbling thirds make a ludicrous yet strangely beautiful accompaniment to Harlequin's song), he could not stop himself. He had to give everything, all his inventiveness as melodist and harmonist, all his rhythmic energy and high spirits and his sensitivity to orchestral colour. Nothing must escape commentary. Every detail must be registered, from the single coin which is Harlequin's derisory consolation prize in the singing contest or the lava torrent of woodwind semiquavers which streams out when Fieramosca compares his feelings to Vesuvius in eruption, to the heaving, clanking rhythm of the bellows in the foundry where the statue is about to be cast. *Benvenuto Cellini* is an opera of memorable sound vignettes: the innkeeper's whining recital of the bill, with its pungent Mussorgsky-like modal harmonies and droll offbeat chords for bassoons and horns; the lampoon on musical philistinism and platitude, as Midas–Balducci beats out of time to the ass-eared Pasquarello's parody cavatina for ophicleide and bass drum, whose grotesquely prolonged final cadence carries off the prize (a passage, as Robert Craft remarks, that "would have delighted the composer of the bombardon part in *Wozzeck* as well as softened the anti-Berlioz prejudice of the composer of the Bear's music in *Petrushka*"); the monks' procession chanting its "Rosa purpurea, Maria sancta mater ora pro nobis" in harsh fifths against the softly luminous sound of solo soprano and alto and their accompanying flutes and clarinets and cor anglais, joined by muted strings – a jewel of a duet, with its tender, rapt melodic line and its deftly managed yet seemingly natural series of modulations that make it cadence successively on D, G, E, C and F before finally returning to the home key of E major.

Harmony as well as rhythm plays a part, too, in the rapidity of motion which is such a feature of the score, as the music slips in and out of keys in its headlong course: a trait not uncommon in Berlioz's fast music, when one thinks of the Queen Mab scherzo and the Ride to the Abyss, two other movements, like the elopement trio in the opera, where quicksilver harmonic change contributes to the sense of speed.

Liszt characterized the music of *Benvenuto* as "at once gorgeous metalwork and vital and original sculpture". The charm of the vignettes is equalled by the power of the scenes that are constructed on a large scale: most obviously the carnival, but also the casting scene: Cellini's men, when the metal gives out, passing goblets and bowls and statuettes from hand to hand, the huge shining Perseus rising from the ground and the people of Rome pouring in to gape and cheer. When well performed they are as exhilarating as anything in opera. The goldsmiths' scene in Act 1 and (in its uncut form) the sextet in which Cellini confronts the Pope are further examples of the assured handling of varied vocal and choral ensemble, as well as of a gift for comedy that must have surprised anyone who listened with an open mind. The sextet is in its way as central to the spirit of the work as is the great sextet in *Don Giovanni* to that work's strange fusion of opposites. In its mixture of grandeur and levity the musical treatment of the Pope epitomizes the whole score. His grave, unctuous trombone theme with punctuating swish on the cymbals, to which he enters Cellini's studio dispensing indulgence with practised hand, befits the dignity of his great office yet is compromised by a barely concealed twinkle. This hint of complicity comes out fully in his second theme, the roguish, swinging 6/8 melody to which he inquires impatiently after his statue. He is an ambiguous figure, at once awesome and profoundly cynical, though with the redeeming grace that he places supreme value on art: a buffo character with the power of life and death. When he informs Cellini that if the statue is not cast that day he will hang, the horror-struck repeated "Pendu!" of the bystanders is undercut by Cellini's ironic "So that is your indulgence for my sins!", sung to the opening phrases of the first papal theme in the silences between each "Pendu" and echoed by the harp on the offbeat. The passage sums up Berlioz's "opera semi-seria".

Typical of the score, too, are the transformations which both papal themes undergo. The jovial second theme is slowed to a shocked pianissimo when Cellini threatens to smash the model if the guards lay a finger on him, and then galvanized into a galloping presto for the sextet's final ensemble (a movement of Rossinian effrontery further enlivened by bars in 3/4 and 4/4 which go off like firecrackers under its prevailing 6/8). *Benvenuto Cellini* abounds in such thematic alterations and allusions. The first papal theme is prefigured many scenes before, when Ascanio jogs his master's memory about the statue, commissioned by the Pope, which all Italy awaits. The goldsmiths' genial G major guild song prefaces the third tableau, but now in an ominous E minor, scored for brass alone, with soft insistent trumpet thirds in each pause in the tune, echoed by the same rhythm on the drums. The fourth tableau is introduced by a reminiscence of the mock-pompous E major music to which Ascanio exacted Cellini's promise to complete the Perseus, tune and accompaniment now hardly recognizable in a spectral D minor: the statue has still to be cast and time is running out. Fieramosca's fencing aria is recalled, no longer boastful and thrusting but limping, abject on Prokofiev-like solo bassoon accompanied by awkward staccato cellos, when the humiliated papal sculptor is forced to don a worker's apron and help in the foundry. A moment later another transformation occurs, when the angry vehement music of the workers' revolt, changed from duple to triple time and from allegro to allegretto, reappears in a veiled F minor, and a sudden hush descends as everyone awaits the supreme moment of the casting. And at intervals in the score a chromatic bass figure, heaving up sometimes comically, sometimes menacingly, serves as a recurring motif and heightens the tension: most obviously in the final section of the carnival music, where the dense crowd sways and struggles like a vast pulsating organism that is only half human – a scene which in its quite different way rivals the depiction of mob violence at the end of the second act of *Die Meistersinger*.

Not only in the carnival but in the opera as a whole, rhythm plays a role it will hardly play again until Stravinsky. As David Charlton remarks, "probably no score since the Renaissance" had been composed more determinedly against the bar-line. The principle is established at the very opening of the overture, where the alla breve of the time-signature is immediately subjected to metrical ambiguity: is this music in 2/2 or 3/4? The goldsmiths' hymn constantly cuts across the bar and the three beats of its notation. In Teresa's aria (second version) cross-rhythms enhance the insolent verve of a piece which without them and without its piquant orchestration might seem commonplace. Fieramosca practising his swordsmanship, and seeing Cellini already transfixed on his blade, is accompanied by orchestral phrases successively in seven, six and five beats.

Or take the very characteristic passage in the opening scene where Teresa comes upon a bouquet among the flowers that the maskers have thrown through her window, and concealed in the bouquet a letter. Her pleasure at the flowers, followed by her discovery of the note and her progressive alarm as she finds it is from Cellini and he is about to pay her a visit, are conveyed in a recitative as lifelike as it is unconventional: the sustained woodwind notes rising by semitones punctuated by breathless violin figures, the rests between the snatched vocal phrases getting shorter each time and the tempo quicker, and then, with the sudden realization that her father has gone out and the coast is clear, the music expanding into half ecstatic, half anxious arioso on Berlioz's favourite cellos (whose role throughout the opera as bearers of expressive melody amounts almost to that of an obbligato instrument). The passage catches perfectly the mood and actions of the character, but it is also, you feel, written out of an overflowing delight in the possibilities of music as a language of comedy. It is typical both of the score's realism and of the high degree of skill it expects of singers, orchestra and conductor.

In terms of orchestral forces *Benvenuto Cellini* is quite modest by the standards of the Opéra of the day. There are guitars in a couple of scenes – in one of them, contrasted with the tangy, juicy sound of trumpets – and tambourines for the carnival music (and in one scene the timpanist is directed to play a roll on a tambourine placed on one of the drumheads), but no stage band and apart from an offstage anvil in the final tableau no unusual instruments – nothing like the multiple bells and saxhorns in *Le Prophète*. Where its demands are exceptional and indeed unprecedented is in the dexterity and rhythmic alertness required of every section of the orchestra. They presuppose a conductor of the new type (such as Berlioz was in the process of becoming), not an old-style violinist-conductor like Habeneck, who would actually be in charge of the performance.

Even the numbers which do not make a special feature of cross-rhythm are far from playing themselves. Least of all the Act 1 trio "Ah! mourir, chère belle . . . Demain soir, mardi gras", where Cellini tells Teresa of his plan for their elopement and Fieramosca, hidden behind an armchair, strains to overhear their hurried exchange. Berlioz never wrote anything more scintillating than this gleeful piece, which goes like the wind yet finds room for some of the most beautiful music in the score. In the original version the reprise of the whole first section of the trio, flashing 9/8 and lyrical 3/4, is motivated dramatically as well as musically; only when Cellini goes over his instructions a second time does Fieramosca, who meanwhile has managed to creep closer, succeed in hearing what is being said; the first time round, he catches just the final syllable of each sotto voce phrase, which he repeats uncomprehendingly. This of course requires the singer of the role of Fieramosca to master two different forms of a part hard enough to get right once, while the other two singers must learn to accommodate to them, and all at a galloping tempo, mostly in offbeat interjections executed with the lightest possible touch while the pulse which gives them the beat is articulated pianissimo by an orchestra of woodwind and muted strings.

In the garden room at Montmartre that summer, intoxicated with the composition of his score, it was as if Berlioz had forgotten who he was writing it for. *Benvenuto Cellini* imagines a Paris Opéra as it might be in an ideal or at any rate a very different musical commonwealth, peopled with sympathetic, dedicated singers, with a chorus all of whose members sing all the time and spare no pains to learn the music and get their tongues round syllabic choral writing moving at the equivalent of four hundred quavers a minute, an eager, virtuoso orchestra, a conductor to marshal and inspire them and a management and backstage staff who give the work their unstinting support.

The Opéra as it was was another story. He had ample opportunity that year to see at first hand what it was like. Louise Bertin's *Esmeralda*

– to begin with entitled *Notre-Dame de Paris* like the novel on which Hugo based his libretto, later renamed after its gipsy heroine – went into rehearsal in May 1836. For much of the next five months Berlioz supervised and sometimes directed rehearsals, and generally represented the composer with conductor, singers, accompanists, copyists, chorus, orchestra and management – Mlle Bertin, physically handicapped from birth and largely chair-bound, being unable to do so herself. It was a task that he found "delicate and difficult": not because he considered it a poor work but because of the awkward role it placed him in, given his position as the Bertins' music critic and the prejudices inevitably aroused by such a work. Musicians laughed openly at him for taking it seriously, or drew their own conclusions about his integrity in accepting the job. The whole thing was a gift to Paris gossip, and the Bertins' enemies sharpened their knives: an opera written by a woman – a crippled woman at that – was by definition no good, even without her being the spoilt daughter of the proprietor of one of the leading government newspapers.

Berlioz conceded that the power of the *Journal des débats* was the sole reason behind the Opéra's agreeing to stage *Esmeralda*, but he persisted in believing that it was worth performing. He had found very little that needed correcting when he went through the score at the beginning of the year (the author "knew everything that could be learned"). Mlle Bertin's talent was, maybe, "more intellectual than instinctive", and with a few exceptions the solo numbers were not up to the choruses. It was nevertheless a genuine talent, deserving of respect and serious attention; there were "some really remarkable things in the score", and the impartial were in for a surprise.

The rehearsals were not an enjoyable experience. It was disillusioning even beyond what he already knew of the Opéra to witness the casualness and want of zeal. The soloists – Nourrit, Falcon, Levasseur, Massol – showed little enthusiasm for their roles. When a choral number made a good impression everyone hinted it had been written by Berlioz – a backhanded compliment about whose value he had no illusions. "What an inferno that whole world is," he wrote to Liszt; "an ice-cold inferno! They all sing out of tune, bellow and rasp and scrape out of tune – and so feebly, without any energy, without the smallest intelligence. It's horrible. What will become of me when I'm there on my own account?" Then, as though to reassure himself: "It's only when it gets in front of the public that all this mob subsides and becomes musical. Till then, I defy you to conceive the chaos; the string rehearsals in particular are unimaginably painful."

By the end of October things were falling into place. Opinion generally remained sceptical. A gesture of Rossini's at the dress rehearsal went the rounds. Sitting in an easy chair to one side of the stage, the great man gave no sign during the first act but, at a pause in the middle of the second, got up and walked slowly towards the conductor. "Rossini va parler," everyone whispered. "Monsieur Habeneck," he said, "haven't you noticed? One of the lamps is smoking." But there were also those who thought well of the work: the pianist Charles Hallé, recently arrived in Paris from Germany, who described Louise Bertin as "a very clever and serious musician", and the violinist Sauzay, one of the players at the string rehearsals, who spoke of its "real beauties". Berlioz, in box 81 in the first tier with Harriet on the opening night, could still hope that with such a starry cast, and given its modest but genuine virtues, *Esmeralda* might yet achieve the "result reasonably satisfying to the amour propre of the Bertin family" that he had predicted.

It failed, catastrophically. The work was simply too tempting a target – for Parisian malice but even more for the political and professional opponents of the *Débats*. There were too many people who were not impartial. At first the full force of the opposition was muted. The audience at the première on 14 November was largely made up of friends and known Bertin supporters – as the *Figaro* tactfully put it, a public that was "perhaps not altogether *the* public". Even so, some dissenting voices were heard. After Quasimodo's Bell Song in the fourth act – the one number that even the work's most dedicated detractors had to concede was a hit – Alexandre Dumas called out "with all the strength of his mulatto lungs, 'It's by Berlioz! It's by Berlioz!'" At the end of the performance, when the authors were named, there were loud protests from some of the boxes, "directed" (wrote Nourrit in a letter to his brother) "as much against the power of the *Journal des débats* as against the opera". The second performance on the 16th, whether or not also played to a chosen house, seems to have gone the same way. Janin, who had delayed publishing his review till after it, spoke of the work surviving this further test "no less happily and no less decisively than the first" – as the *Débats*' opera critic he could hardly do otherwise. In a subsequent article he recalled that the second night provoked "the same loud applause and the same underhand and deplorable outbursts" as the première had done. Two further performances, on the 18th and the 21st, apparently passed without sustained protest. Even so, opposition had been loud enough to decide the management to make the composer shorten the opera for the fifth performance a few weeks later, on 16 December, and to add a concluding ballet, with the popular Mlle Taglioni in the leading role. It was no use. The enemy had only been waiting, and they came in force. During the last act of the opera the pit rose and shouted, "A bas les Bertin! A bas le *Journal des débats!* Bring down the curtain!", and kept up the clamour with such ferocity that Falcon fled the scene and the curtain was hurriedly dropped, to be raised again only for the ballet. *Esmeralda* of ill omen never reappeared. It was written off, to widespread satisfaction, as a predestined disaster (an impression that seemed only confirmed, soon afterwards, when the Duc d'Orléans' expensive mare Esmeralda was killed colliding with another horse at a point-to-point, and a ship of the same name went down with all hands in the Irish Sea). Mlle Bertin returned to private life. Berlioz was left to draw what moral he could from the essentially political débâcle of a work which, whatever its faults, was "better than a lot of the ephemera tolerated at the Opéra", and to reflect on the attitude of a management and cast which made no serious attempt to prevent it – if indeed they hadn't actually planned to be rid of the piece after a few token performances.

Once *Esmeralda* reached its première, his work as adviser and monitor was almost done. He no doubt helped the composer decide what passages to cut for the fifth and, as it turned out, final performance. But in the weeks between mid-November and mid-December he was mainly occupied with his annual concerts at the Conservatoire.

No detailed lists of players with their addresses, fees and signatures survive this time to illustrate the labour involved in assembling an orchestra. What we have are, first, a note of the expense incurred for hire, transport and, where appropriate, tuning of the extra instruments required at the concert of 4 December (piano, tambourine, harp) and, second, a memorandum in his hand showing how he spent, or planned to spend, 28 November, six days before the first concert. They give an idea of some of the other things that putting on a concert entailed. The memorandum reads:

Today Monday 28
To Liszt's [Liszt was playing at one of the concerts]
Go to Schlesinger's to collect money

NB. To M. Mantoue's for poor tax

Take or send [concert announcements] to the rest of the papers

Go to *Débats* [possibly to take his second article on the score of *The Huguenots*, which appeared on 10 December]

Rue de la Victoire for the Urhan business [Urhan, in addition to playing the viola in *Harold*, had a song in the programme of the first concert]

Write to [?Ambroise] Thomas

Go to Pape's [piano manufacturer who supplied the piano for the bell notes in the Fantastic]

Take boxes [sc. tickets for] to Pacini

Go to Mlle Bertin's [because the Bell Song was being performed at the first concert, or more likely to advise her on cuts in her opera]

Send tickets to Ch. Maurice [*Courrier des théâtres*]

Get large programmes of the Symph. [Fantastique] printed

Send box [sc. tickets for] to Rue de Rohan

Send Barbier [?tickets, or possibly Vigny's revisions to the libretto of *Benvenuto Cellini*]

We can follow Berlioz on his progress on foot through Paris that warm, overcast winter day, from 35 Rue de Londres (he and Harriet were now back in the city) to the various addresses that he called at: 23 Rue Lafitte, near the Opéra, where Liszt and Marie d'Agoult and their eleven-month-old daughter Blandine were living at the well-appointed Hôtel de France (having lately returned from Geneva); Urhan's lodgings in the Rue de la Victoire, which crossed the Rue Lafitte; Schlesinger's editorial office and music shop at 97 Rue de Richelieu; the poor tax office in Rue Pontoise-St Victor; the *Débats* in the Rue des Prêtres St Germain l'Auxerrois, just east of the Louvre; Pape's piano store in the Rue de Valois; le Boulevard des Italiens, the address of Emilien Pacini (where, as another page of the same notebook shows, Berlioz left sixty-six tickets for him to dispose of); the Bertins' house in the Rue de Seine; the printer, probably Vinchon Ballard *fils* of 8 Rue Jean-Jacques Rousseau just behind St Eustache; and some of the newspaper offices on the list if they could conveniently be included in his route.

Complimentary seats for the press were a major preoccupation. They made a hole in the budget – a good hundred could be given away to journalists. He begrudged the loss of revenue but could not do much about it. "I was assassinated with demands for tickets by the forty or fifty journals large and small which pullulate in Paris," he wrote to Adèle after the second concert, "and was obliged to give them everything they asked, so as not to set off the avalanche of abuse by which these gentlemen like to avenge themselves when one turns them down. [. . .] Normally I don't take much notice of that kind of petty vengeance; but theatre directors are fearful of the least line of print, and my position with Duponchel, who is not one of the bolder ones in this respect, made me bow my head and pay the levy. And the press has treated me very well. It's been a concert of eulogies in every key." Even Edouard Monnais in the *Courrier français* was less dismissive than usual. The anonymous critic of the *Carrousel* went into ectasies about "this admirable music of Berlioz", a "mighty poem where all life's joys and sorrows, every sensation of the heart and shadowy fancy of the spirit, and Nature in all her gentleness and rages, find an interpretation as tender as the breath of divine love, as violent as the storms of human passion"; he also reported that the applause for the Pilgrims' March was led by Cherubini and Meyerbeer, and predicted that "Hector Berlioz will write fine operas when M. Duponchel extends him a hand and allows his original music to be heard in the theatre."

In the *Monde* Liszt, through the pen of Marie d'Agoult, used the performance of "those two large and splendid compositions", *Harold* and the Fantastic Symphony, to defend and exalt

an artist who in many people's eyes has the grave defect of being contemporary and of venturing to attempt in his own age what Haydn, Mozart and Beethoven attempted in theirs. Surely it has been a sight worthy of attention, and calculated to raise the drooping spirits and downcast will of composers whose beginnings have not been greeted with the applause of the crowd, to see Berlioz so to speak in hand-to-hand combat throughout his early youth with an uncomprehending public, responding to vulgar sarcasm, unintelligent prejudice and total condemnation with undaunted perseverance, going forward like the philosopher who was informed categorically that the earth did not move, and, for sole argument, confining himself to the performance, by an ever-more-practised orchestra, of his work, which the torrent of complaining criticism merely raised yet higher, like a noble three-master borne aloft by the tempest.

Berlioz had no difficulty agreeing that the orchestra was finer than it had ever been. He told Adèle that it was the greatest artistic success he had yet had, thanks to the far better performance he obtained by conducting the concerts himself. "But imagine – I had a moment of real panic at the thought that I had nothing new to offer the public and might not cover the costs. Happily Harriet had greater confidence than I and urged me to go ahead. So I announced my two big symphonies which had never been given together in their entirety, and the crowd came."

At the second concert two Sundays later (18 December) Liszt repeated his Grande fantaisie for piano and orchestra on *Le pêcheur* and *Scène de brigands* from *Lélio* and then played the Ball and the March to the Scaffold from his arrangement of the Fantastic and a divertimento on a theme of Piccini. Liszt had returned from Switzerland an even greater player than when he left Paris the year before, wrote Berlioz in the *Gazette* after hearing him perform Beethoven's Hammerklavier Sonata at Erard's salons in May: "that sublime poem which had been till now, for practically all pianists, the riddle of the Sphinx" but which Liszt, like a "new Oedipus", had solved, giving "the ideal performance of a work reputed to be unperformable" and, in so doing, proving himself "the pianist of the future". Liszt and Berlioz were "the two most striking figures of the current musical scene", wrote Heine, who regretted only that Berlioz had had his hair cut – "that monstrous prehistoric head of hair that reared above his brow like a primeval forest above a precipitous escarpment". In addition to the Liszt items the first two movements of *Harold* were given again, and Berlioz opened the concert with the *Francs-juges* overture, chosen perhaps to erase the painful impression caused by his discovery, the previous spring, that a German publisher, Hoffmeister of Leipzig, had issued a pirated four-hand arrangement of the work, so "truncated and hacked about in the manner perfected by Castil-Blaze" that he scarcely recognized it.

As for the financial success of the two concerts, even though the receipts of the second were split between him and Liszt, that still left a profit, without reckoning the 64 francs which the Comte de Gasparin, the new Minister of the Interior, owed him for a box at the first concert and which would almost certainly not be paid. "That being so, I shall have made in two weeks one thousand seven hundred and sixty francs, which I was furiously in need of to pay the furniture bills and various others about to fall due." It was a good thing that Harriet, with her usual boldness, had insisted on his taking the risk.

For her too it had been a less unproductive year than 1835. She had appeared in March before a select and fashionable audience at M. de

Castellane's private theatre in the Boulevard du Temple, where her performance of Ophelia's mad scenes moved the critic of the *Quotidienne* to claim that "never has the great tragedienne been more nobly inspired, never has truer sensibility been expressed more poetically, more originally; the emotion, the amazement of the audience at that harrowing display of madness, in which song, speech, mime, laughter and tears follow on each other so swiftly, is beyond description".

Everyone wondered that so fine and so influential an actress should be excluded from Paris theatrical life. It may have been this renewed success that induced Dumas to persuade Frédéric Lemaître to include the same scenes in his benefit performance at the Variétés on 17 December, the day before Berlioz's second concert. It was perhaps a doubtful kindness. *Hamlet*, Act 4, shovelled on to the stage immediately after *Scipio, or the Step-father* was an incongruity that Janin took flamboyant exception to in the *Débats* two days later: "The most beautiful and moving scene in *Hamlet* yoked brutally to a play devoid of all verisimilitude! Miss Smithson shedding tears at a given signal, without preparation, without the motive and the cue for grief! The whole thing is most bizarre, most wretched. No one has the right to abuse Shakespeare and his touching interpreter thus; no one has the right to mutilate a masterpiece, and a great artist. Respect them: they are, alas, rare." Miss Smithson was too compliant; she lacked the courage of her art. "Let her be shown complete in a full-length play – nothing better. But to mutilate her like that is an outrage. I beg Miss Smithson to give heed to what I say. I entreat her – not in her name but in the name of her master, Shakespeare!"

Such words, only too true, only underlined Harriet's cruel dilemma. He might well call for Miss Smithson's return to the serious professional stage: what prospect was there of that? Yet another attempt to set up an English company, at the Ventadour, had been made that autumn – there is a letter from Harriet to Butler, whose wife she had made friends with at Montmartre, reporting on the negotiations – and again it had come to nothing. But the tribute Janin paid in the same article, as he recalled all that she had given them in the days of her glory and how it was due to her, "to her first of all", that they understood Shakespeare, must have brought a moment of happiness.

She was completely unlike what we knew of tragedy; she resembled no one else. What an experience it was to behold her pale, white-clad figure glide into Shakespeare's dramas like a sad or laughing phantom, ill-fated child for ever destined for death, whether her name be Ophelia or Desdemona or Juliet. She was the shining point of light among Shakespeare's sombre characters; she illuminated that drama, in which all the passions and longings of men are incarnated, with tragic truthfulness. As long as we live, the memory of Miss Smithson will remain in our minds, linked for ever to that of Shakespeare.

This was lofty; but the elegiac note was unmistakable.

Berlioz wrote proudly to Adèle of Harriet's "superb performance", and mentioned Janin's review, though without comment. Relations with La Côte were close again and cordial on all sides. The parents wrote asking Hector's advice about schools in Paris for Prosper; he went to see one and to talk with the principal, and sent them the prospectus. Even the breach with Nancy was finally mended. Her brother had quite rightly pointed out that it was for her to make the first move. She did, and after a few days he answered. "Your letter gave me great pleasure. Let's think no more of our old arguments; here is my hand, give me yours, and let's be friends again as we used to be." He could not resist adding: "Our errors of judgement often spring from its being applied to matters we know little or nothing of because they are outside our understanding. Give that a thought"; but Nancy was a great moralizer herself, and it can have done her no harm. Though the old intimacy could never be re-established, there was as before a greater equality of minds than with his younger sister. It is notable that his account of Harriet is franker and, though loving, more critical than in his letters to Adèle:

As for me, here in four words is my life: I am very happy to have the best and most beloved wife in the world, but it pains me to see all the privations that she endures without complaining, her isolation, and above all the waste of her enormous talent (her forced inactivity is killing her). [. . .] She has an ever-present consolation in her son; but she won't take enough account of the work I am forced to do, in the house and away from it, which obliges me to leave her on her own. The servants drive her mad. She doesn't go to Paris above once in three months. However, we're going together the day after tomorrow, it's the first performance of *St Bartholomew* [*The Huguenots*]; Meyerbeer doesn't want her to miss it. It will distract her a little.

Servants were a persistent bane. Like David Copperfield and Dora, Berlioz and Harriet seemed beset with it, unable to find any that were not "lazy, insolent, and dishonest". Harriet, like any Parisian bourgeois housewife, claimed they had got much worse since the July Revolution; and Mme Berlioz was asked if she could find someone in La Côte who might do instead.

Notwithstanding all their troubles, the correspondence for this period still suggests a couple who find happiness in each other as well as being united in love and concern for, and fascination with, their son. Berlioz's letters are full of Louis and his progress and the pleasure mixed with anxiety that he gives them both. "The other day we went on foot, *en famille*, to St Ouen. Louis was beside himself with delight at the sight of that expanse of water." (Berlioz is moved to exclaim that there is nothing so fine in Dauphiné, "unless it is the view of the valley from the heights of the Savoy frontier".) In the big garden at Montmartre, on their secluded hillside, Louis can "run about and laugh and shout with all his might" and, during the spring and summer months, charm his mother "by his childlike joy in the midst of all that greenery", which he could not appreciate the year before, being too tiny.

Paris, where they returned that autumn, to an apartment a few doors from the old one, at 35 Rue de Londres, was by no means such a good place to bring up a boisterous two-year-old. Life was also more expensive there. But they decided, with regret, to move back in time to avoid another freezing, isolated winter in Montmartre. Pressure on the household had eased sufficiently for them to afford it, thanks to Berlioz's fee for his work on *Esmeralda* and the loan from Legouvé (partly offset though they were by his writing fewer articles for the *Débats*), and thanks also to one or two gifts of money from La Côte. The hazards of life in Paris, however, were dramatically illustrated when Louis' nursemaid, without permission, took him to a café in town and pinched his finger so badly in the door that the whole nail came off and the doctor had to cut away the flesh hanging beneath it. Luckily (Berlioz told Adèle) the joint had not been affected, the nail and finger were growing again, and the new servant seemed much more reliable. They had also had to dismiss another who, resentful of Harriet's supervision, had taught Louis to rebuff his mother.

> Since we got rid of her, Louis has become very attached to his mother once more. What he shows me is passion more than any other feeling.

He calls out to me in his dreams, he won't eat or stay still while I'm out, and when I come in – shouts of delight and gambolling without end. He kisses my hand in the most tender and at the same time elegant fashion. At dinner he has got to sit on my knee, and he gives me everything he has. He comes to look for me in my study to bring me to table, and in the evening he tells me, in his own tongue and with highly expressive pantomime, all that he has seen in the street during the day (he never stirs from the window). Yesterday it was a troupe of itinerant musicians; he imitated for me the clarinet and the tambourine and the barrel organ in the most original manner, singing and gesticulating till we collapsed with laughter. [. . .] How I wish our parents could see Louis! For Prosper, don't worry about him. He's not developed yet, far from it, and I bet he is going to be much more intelligent than any of you imagine. In any case, even if he were to be only a skilled artisan – "a manufacturer of sugar beet", as he himself said four years ago – he would be no more unhappy for that, if it were all he was ambitious to be. Louis imitates umbrella-sellers all day, from which his mother and I conclude that he has a strong predisposition for . . . umbrella-selling. (22 December 1836)

By now Berlioz had his written agreement with Duponchel. The libretto had been further revised – at the beginning of October Alfred de Vigny spent the day in Montmartre going through it with him and took it away to work on – and the score was now all but finished. Only the final scene remained to be composed, and that was done in January or February 1837 and the orchestration completed by the beginning of March. *Benvenuto Cellini* could have gone into rehearsal then and there: Niedermeyer's *Stradella*, which was next in the queue, was on the point of appearing. But under the contract there were two other operas due to come first, Halévy's *Guido et Ginevra* and Auber's *Lac des fées*. Though neither had yet been begun, both had precedence. Life in the Rue Le Pelletier moved slowly (after *Stradella* saw the light, briefly, in March, the next new production, of Halévy's work, was a whole year later). The Opéra was in no hurry for *Benvenuto*. Berlioz must simply bide his time.

Instead a totally different prospect opened up. We do not know to what extent the idea was fed into the mind of the government minister concerned, by Berlioz or by his friends and allies in high places, to what extent it was the minister's own. The thing had been set in motion by another turn of the wheel of fortune, which brought the Comte Adrien de Gasparin into Molé's government as Minister of the Interior in the cabinet reshuffle of September 1836. The Count, an authority on agriculture and veterinary questions, was also a music-lover. He seems to have taken his responsibilities as patron of music much more to heart than had his predecessor, Thiers. On 21 November Gasparin presided over the students' prizegiving at the Conservatoire and, in his speech, voiced concern at the lack of opportunities for young composers to get their music heard. The present provision, he said, was inadequate. Two opera houses were not enough for the purpose; young laureates on their return from Rome should not have to kick their heels until such time as the theatre opened its doors to them. Ideally, there should be some institution equivalent to what the Salon was for painters, where new music was regularly tried out. One field where something might be done was sacred music.

Both the journals that Berlioz was connected with reacted positively. The *Débats* of 29 November reproduced the speech, with favourable editorial comment, and on the 27th the *Gazette* caried a short note about the minister and the hopes he had aroused. A few days later Berlioz, in an article in the *Gazette*, commended the Count's "just and lofty" ideas, which had "touched a sympathetic chord" in the breast of every young composer. No flattery was involved: such ideas could have been dictated by Berlioz himself.

It is possible that they were. He had a personal connection with the minister; a friend of his was an intimate of Agénor de Gasparin, the Count's son and private secretary. The Count had, too, been Prefect of Isère and had lived in Grenoble for a year or more, during which he could easily have come in contact with people close to the Berlioz family. As we have seen, he was at the Conservatoire on 4 December for Berlioz's concert. Adolphe Boschot remarks that "nothing is more agreeable to men who are in power for a season or two, and to whom the chances of politics give control over artists, than to be taken for artists themselves". On the other hand the Count is credited in Berlioz's *Memoirs* with "belonging to the small minority of French politicians who are interested in music and to the still more select company who have a feeling for it", and with having his own clearly formed resolve to restore sacred music to its former prestige in France. Apart from the Comte de Montalembert, Gasparin is the one prominent statesman who figures in the list of subscribers to the Société des Concerts for the year 1837. At all events, early in March 1837 he made his move, as Berlioz reported to his father:

I have just come from the Minister of the Interior's; he wants to commission me to do a big composition for the anniversary of the death of
Marshal Mortier and the others [the victims of Fieschi's attempt on the
King's life in 1835], at the Invalides. I had gone to see him about something
else, and the news took me unawares. I asked for a certain scope with
the performing forces, which he seems disposed to grant me. In any case
the affair is to be settled forthwith – it must be, so that I have time to
write the work between now and 28 July. Only, I fear the fever that such
a subject, and the idea of having five or six hundred performers at my
command, will give me. What a Dies Irae!!

The quarry he had been lying in wait for was within his grasp at last.

6

The Visionary Gleam

Though we may not agree, we can understand why Berlioz declared, at the end of his life, that if he were threatened with the destruction of all his scores but one it would be the Messe des morts that he would save from the flames. From its first performance, and at all the later performances he gave, it was associated not with defeat or failure, as were one or two equally important works, but with success on the grandest scale and – hardly less memorably – with a rare victory in the war against Paris officialdom. Longer than any other composition of his, it remained a cherished project, and bringing it to life a consciously felt necessity. *Romeo and Juliet* had almost as protracted a gestation, but was not a constant preoccupation during those years. If *The Damnation of Faust* was always implicit in the *Eight Scenes* of 1828–9, for much of the intervening decade and a half the work lay dormant, not given sustained thought until the early 1840s. The grain that became *The Trojans* lay buried for more than thirty years before it germinated and took root. And though *Beatrice and Benedick*, his last composition, started life, as an idea, in the early 1830s, the scenario he later drafted had little in common with the opera that he eventually wrote in 1860–62.

The history of the Requiem is different. Its genesis begins thirteen years before, with the Mass which he composed in 1824 and which was performed in St Roch in 1825 and repeated two years later in St Eustache. The two works are directly linked. There is music in the Requiem that originated in the Mass: most obviously the multiple brass fanfares and timpani chords of the Tuba mirum (which in simpler and less extended form heralded the second coming of Christ – "Et iterum venturus est" – in the Resurrexit of the Mass), but also the Offertorium, the chorus of souls in Purgatory, whose sad sinuous theme, in a different time-signature but in the same key of D minor and already complete with its tolling octaves on the offbeat, was conceived in 1824 for the Kyrie, the prayer that begins the mass.

In one form or another the work that grew into the Requiem was a continuous presence during these thirteen years. By the end of the 1820s Berlioz had rejected the Mass as a whole; but the ideas that went into it were still active. When he left for Rome in 1831 he took the score of the revised Resurrexit with him; and though he used a copy of it to send to the Academy of Fine Arts in Paris as his obligatory envoi for the year, it is clear that he had brought it for a different purpose: its fanfares were intended to take their place in the apocalyptic oratorio which he was already planning before he went to Italy. *Le dernier jour du monde* is a recurring motif in the correspondence of the early 1830s, in Italy and after his return (when, as we have seen, he tried to interest the Opéra in a staged version). It is the kind of project that a young composer toys with and then thinks better of. We hear nothing more of it after 1834. But the obsession remained; the Day of Judgement would not be denied. Only, it required a different setting, less theatrical, equally dramatic.

By the mid-1830s the streams were beginning to converge. Even if the *Fête musicale funèbre* of 1835 contributed nothing directly to the Requiem (it was still a live issue after the Requiem was written), its concept is evidence of the hold that the Revolutionary and Napoleonic tradition of musical rites on a monumental scale, transmitted to him through Le Sueur, continued to exert on his imagination. He had heard and read so much about them, he was so steeped in the tradition, it was as if he had been there himself. When the arrangements for the performance of his Requiem were being discussed he was able to recall in detail how, under the Empire, the funeral of Marshal Lannes had been organized. Throughout these years the ambition to revive and revitalize the tradition with a work of his own is never far below the surface of his thoughts and often at the forefront – as in August 1835, when the experience of hearing Cherubini's Requiem at the funeral of Marshal Mortier sets him thinking what he would do if he had the chance. From that moment – if we are to believe the journalist who in December 1837 described it as "having been knocking for the past two years on all the tombs of the great" – the Grande messe des morts is already fully present in his mind. It wants only an occasion.

When the occasion comes and he is commissioned to provide a requiem for a grand state ceremony, his immediate reaction is "What a Dies irae!" Later he recalled the trouble he had controlling his emotions and dominating the subject, before the "eruption" was "regulated" and the "lava" had "dug its bed": "the poetry of the Prose des morts so intoxicated and exalted me that nothing presented itself to my mind with any clarity: my head was seething, I felt quite dizzy".

Berlioz was by no means the only composer to be fascinated by the imagery of the medieval Latin poem, which enshrines humanity's fear of death and judgement in the transcendent doggerel of its brief, harsh lines and relentless triple rhyming scheme. It is the heart, and more than half the substance, of the mass for the dead. The imagery is terrifying, and it appealed irresistibly to the dramatist in him (as it did to Verdi). But there is more to the conception of the Grande messe des morts than that, just as there is more to the music than a sensational rendering of the Last Day. Judgement, in the Grande messe, becomes one element in a threefold succession of visions corresponding to the threefold imagery of the text. It is no paradox to say that one of the most striking things about Berlioz's use of brass and percussion in the work is its restraint. Their function is not so much spectacular as architectural, clarifying and emphasizing the musical and dramatic structure, opening new perspectives and at the same time underlining the grandeur inherent in the whole style of the work, in its long arcs of melody and its still small voice of humility as much as in its cataclysms. The sensational effect of the brass is due above all to the contrast it makes with the music's predominantly austere texture; the four brass groups are prominent in two, at most three, of the ten movements, and are confined to the Prose des morts; for much of the time the horns of the main orchestra are the only brass instruments to offset the bleak, mourning sound of the large woodwind choir.

In any case we would not think of Berlioz's apocalyptic armoury as peculiar to him, let alone "characteristically" extravagant, if we were familar with the many similar works written a generation or two earlier by Gossec, Méhul, Le Sueur and others, of which the Requiem was a direct and conscious descendant. Le Sueur's *Chant du 1er Vendémiaire*, composed for the eighth anniversary of the Republic, employed four separate orchestras, each one stationed at a corner of the Invalides – the building where Berlioz's Requiem was first performed thirty-six years later. What is special about the Grande messe is, in Saint-Saëns' phrase, its "constant and extraordinary elevation of style", and its aura of measureless antiquity – the sense, as Paul Rosenfeld has said, that "some *vates* of a Mediterranean folk were come in a rapt and lofty mood to offer sacrifice, to pacify the living, to celebrate with fitting rites the unnumbered multitudes of the heroic dead". It universalizes the tradition: the Revolutionary community becomes the community of humankind throughout the ages, voicing its immemorial longings and its fears and frail hopes; confronting its own mortality.

Though it is not the work of an orthodox believer, it has Wordsworth's "visionary gleam". Berlioz spoke of himself as an atheist, at most as an agnostic. The passionate faith of his boyhood did not survive long into his adult years. (If he had a god it was Shakespeare: "It is thou that art our father, our father in heaven, if there is a heaven," he will cry out, in one of the most harrowing moments of his existence.) But the very loss left a permanent mark. The absence of God is the driving force behind the Requiem. That, deeper than all other motives, is why he had to write it. The work conveys a poignant regret for loss of faith, a profound awareness of the need, the desperate need, to believe and to worship. Through his understanding of the religious impulse and his own unsatisfied yearning he could catch the eternal note and echo it in his music.

Two or three movements set out to embody the idea of the immensity of God in objective terms. In the Tuba mirum the thunder of the drums and the brass fanfares answering and overlapping one another, in different metrical patterns, from the four corners of the main performing body – a blaze of sound in E flat major which is the antithesis of the naked textures and modally flavoured A minor of the opening Dies irae – depict the event itself, the inexorable upheaval of Judgement Day. The Sanctus, for solo tenor and women's voices accompanied by violins and violas and a single high flute, evokes a shimmering vision of the angelic host, enhanced at its reprise by a serene cello descant and by bass drum and three pairs of cymbals struck very softly, like an audible equivalent of the swinging censers round the throne of God, while the arching phrases and static harmony of its companion movement, the Hosanna, represent the seraphim's unending chorus of praise. But the main focus of the music is humanity and its weakness and vulnerability: humanity hoping against hope (Requiem and Kyrie); striving to keep judgement far off and impersonal (Dies irae); lost in the desolation of an empty universe (Quid sum miser); pleading for salvation before the majesty of God (Rex tremendae); humanity in the Dance of Death, the endless procession of the dead scourged towards judgement (Lacrymosa); humanity on the edge of eternity (Hostias, where trombone pedal notes, answered by flutes high above, suggest Hell and Heaven and the infinite pulsating space between); humanity striving out of its terror of extinction to create a meaningful universe and a merciful God.

From time to time there is a glimpse of hope, as in the radiant major chord breaking for an instant across the Requiem and Kyrie at its most forlorn point, or the light that falls like a benediction on the closing page of the Offertorium when the chant turns from its sad persistent minor and the whole movement, fugato and chant, resolves in a glowing D major. But the prevailing tone is tragic. Through all the work's contrasts of form and mood, the idea of humanity's wonder and bafflement before the enigma of death is central and constant, from the measured climb of the opening G minor phrases and the silences that surround them to the resignation of the final coda, where solemn Amens, circled by luminous string arpeggios that seem to survey the universe, swing slowly in and out of G major while the funeral drums beat out a long retreat.

Berlioz tells us that as soon as he was sure of his commission he fell upon it with a kind of fury. "I felt as if my brain would explode from the pressure of ideas. The outline of one piece was barely sketched before the next formed itself in my mind; it was impossible to write fast enough, and I devised a sort of musical shorthand which was of great help to me, especially in the Lacrymosa." It is a fact that the Requiem was composed quickly – as it had to be, for the chorus and orchestra parts to be copied in time for rehearsals in the second half of July. The order confirming the commission was finally signed on 28 March. Two months later the score was drafted; and the whole thing was complete by the end of June. Even if the three weeks between the minister's initial request and its confirmation were used for preparing the text he was to set – essential preliminary work, given his dramatist's approach to the mass – that is rapid going. What the *Memoirs'* account does not speak of is the discipline that controlled and directed the outpouring of ideas. With all its diversity – of scale, volume and density, texture – no score of his is more closely argued. Edward Cone's classic essay "Berlioz's Divine Comedy" (an analysis that epitomizes the new open-minded attitude to the composer) demonstrates first how the text of the liturgy is freely adapted to highlight the implicit tripartite division of the requiem mass, and then how the score is constructed, at the level of both long-range tonal and instrumental design and harmonic, rhythmic and motivic detail, so that its large-scale progressions "embrace not only the individual movements but the entire work as well".

The remodelled text becomes the "libretto" of "a special kind of music-drama", a commemorative service of the dead within whose ritual frame we are made to share "the emotional experiences of a contemplative auditor attending [the mass] – one who, allowing his imagination full play, visualizes himself as present at the wonderful and terrible scenes described, and who returns to reality at the conclusion of the service with a consequent sense of catharsis".

To consider only the main textual changes that Berlioz made, the depiction of Hell in the Rex tremendae is extended by bringing forward "Confutatis maledictis / Flammis acribus addictis" – the accursed delivered to the flames – from later in the Prose des morts, and by adding words taken from a different part of the mass, the Offertory: "from the bottomless lake, save them from the lion's mouth, let not Tartarus engulf them, let them not fall into darkness", with "them", the dead, changed to the personal "me" of the Prose. These phrases are then omitted from the Offertory, which in the tripartite scheme of the Grande messe is concerned not with Hell but with Purgatory. Second, the vision of Paradise which succeeds that of Purgatory is made more emphatic by the repetition of the Sanctus in place of the Benedictus, while the separation of Paradise from Purgatory is underlined by the omission from the latter of the words "to cross over from death to [eternal] life". Third, "Te decet hymnus" from the opening Requiem and Kyrie is repeated in the concluding movement, the Agnus Dei, so as to effect the return from the Dante-like experience to the here and now.

The effect of these and other changes is reinforced in the musical setting. In the Rex tremendae the chorus, terrified by the prospect of divine wrath, fail to complete the phrase "Voca me cum benedictis" (itself a transposition from later in the liturgy): their tongues cannot utter the final words, "among the blessed"; the voices break off and the struggling, shouting mob falls silent, as though staring into the bottomless lake, which they evoke in a stammering sotto voce over a long, still double-bass note – "et . . . de profundo lacu", emphasized on the last word by cavernous horn, bassoon and clarinet octaves. The truncated text of the Offertorium is further dismembered and sung disconnectedly, in fragments, to an unvarying chant round which the orchestral fugato moves in mysterious sympathy; it is, as it were, all we hear of a cry for mercy raised unceasingly throughout Time. And, in the final movement, as the (non-liturgical) "Te decet hymnus" re-enters, the last of the flute/trombone chords, repeated from the Hostias, is taken up by flutes and bassoons, B flat minor becomes major, and with a sense of emerging from a momentous "sleep of dreams" we are back where we began, though transformed by the visions lived through in between. The ending draws the work together; in Cone's words, it "furnishes a final response to the initial questioning gesture of the entire Requiem".

Not everything in Berlioz's Requiem is a breach of orthodoxy. The contrast, fundamental to the liturgical text, between the grandeur of God and the littleness of human beings is a constant principle governing the musical setting. So is the alternation of grand, powerfully scored movements with more intimate ones. Each of the three numbers in which all four groups of brass take part is followed by one that is devotional in character. At the same time the dynamic level is reduced at the end of the big movements so as to prepare for the contemplative music of the next. The tumult of the Tuba mirum sinks to a whisper, which is continued in the Quid sum miser, scored for a handful of instruments and suggesting sinful mankind in the stunned aftermath of judgement. The majesty of "Rex tremendae" is subdued to a soft pleading as "salva me" emerges three times from the full orchestra in a dramatic pianissimo, each time differently harmonized, more abject, and leading in turn to the unaccompanied Quaerens me. The Lacrymosa ends on a diminuendo, a "melancholy, long, withdrawing roar" as the procession of the lamenting dead sweeps onward out of view, to be succeeded by the ageless sadness of the Offertorium.

Though the Requiem belongs to what he called his architectural works, designed for large resonant buildings and marked not by the "Berliozian" characteristics of complex, unpredictable rhythms, lyrical intensity, swift changes of mood and mercurial variations of instrumental colour but by broad effects and slow-moving progressions, it too has its vividly scored imagery: the haunting sound of the chorus chanting their desolate "et lux perpetua . . . luceat . . . eis" against the violins' repeated falling chromatic phrase; the brutally syncopated ryhthmic pattern which propels the main theme of the Lacrymosa convulsively forward and the prodigious modulation into B flat at the end of the same movement as the rout from the grave pours past and all the trombones sound for them on the other side; the cathedral-shaking rumble of bassoons and ophicleides and lower strings sounding the heroic second theme of the Offertorium like the psalmist's "one deep calleth another, because of the noise of the water-pipes"; the Offertorium's shining close (for which Berlioz altered the order of the phrase so that "promisisti" – "Thou promised" – should be the final word sung); the sense of vertical space created by the flutes and trombones of the Hostias. Yet what a change of idiom and atmosphere from the previous composition, *Benvenuto Cellini*, all speed and light and movement in triple or compound time, to the hieratic gravity of the Requiem, which begins and ends in 3/4 but otherwise is predominantly in common time. The proximity of two such radically different compositions barely six months apart illustrates the Protean diversity of Berlioz's oeuvre, his faculty of immersing all his being in, of becoming, the subject of the work in hand.

Though he had got what he longed for, French bureaucracy would not have been true to itself if it had left matters there. His enemies might represent him as the pet of government (28,000 francs, protested Adolphe Adam, squandered on a work which with all its army of performers made no effect whatsoever!); yet from the first he found himself entangled in the toils of Parisian officialdom. It was touch-and-go whether the order commissioning the Requiem would be signed at all. Gasparin's underlings unaccountably failed to have it drawn up. By the time they were induced to do so the minister was on the point of leaving office as a result of the fall of the Guizot cabinet. A little more and it would have been too late. The head of the Department of Arts at the Ministry, Edmond Cavé, was a devoted admirer of Rossini and an equally devoted opponent of the avant-garde: Berlioz had heard him dismiss it out of hand, conceding only that Beethoven was "not devoid of talent". In this, the *Memoirs* add, he was typical of the civil service of that period: "hundreds of similar connoisseurs blocked the routes along which artists had to pass, and worked the cogs of the great governmental machine that drove the musical institutions of France". It looks as if Cavé employed the classic bureaucrat's tactic, delay, calculating that the terms of Gasparin's order could be changed under his successor and the commission transferred to Cherubini. The grand old man had a new requiem of his own waiting to be performed; it and not Berlioz's was the proper one for the July ceremony.

Gasparin, however, apprised by his son of what was happening, had the order prepared and it was signed late in March. Berlioz was sure of his commission now and, on paper at any rate, his fee of 4,000 francs and ministerial responsibility for the costs of copying, rehearsal and performance. By late May most of the score was drafted; he made a timetable of what remained to be done.

To orchestrate:	
Dies irae and Tuba mirum	3 days
Rex tremendae	3
Sanctus	4
Lacrymosa	4
Agnus	4
Offertory	3
	21 days
The Requiem and Introit, plus the Quid sum miser and Quaerens me	8 days
Total for all this	1 month (June)

The final page of the full score bears the date 29 June 1837. It had taken three months. By now, preparation of chorus and orchestra parts was already in progress. With forces amounting to more than four hundred it was an enormous operation. Berlioz and his copyist Rocquemont organized it together, contracting it out to the Opéra's copying department. The Requiem is the first of his large-scale works on which he is known to have employed the man who became the indispensable aide-de-camp in all his concert-giving, in France at least. From now on Rocquemont would be responsible for copying the masters from which the larger sets of parts were made, for engaging and supervising other copyists, seeing to the transport of music and instruments (and at one point mounting guard over them when Berlioz feared sabotage), setting the parts out on the stands and, later, when the composer was abroad, housing his library for him. When they first met is not known. It could have been as early as 1827, in the chorus of the Théâtre des Nouveautés: a Roquemont without the c is listed in that year by the *Almanac des spectacles* as a chorister at the Nouveautés, apparently a tenor, which was Rocquemont's voice (his name appears on a tenor part of the Requiem). In 1839 he is recorded as living in Montmartre, and he may have been a neighbour of Berlioz's three years before. Their relationship seems to have been very cordial (the *Memoirs* describe him as "a man of uncommon intelligence and a tireless worker, who out of regard for me – as sincere as mine is for him – has rendered me unforgettable services on numerous occasions"). It was based on mutual respect, sharpened by friendly competition as rival calligraphers: Berlioz's hand was the more elegant and individual, but Rocquemont's was equally clear and he was the more accurate proof-reader.

Next to see to was the constructing of a wooden amphitheatre for the performers at the east end of the Invalides, opposite the organ – which meant meetings with architects and carpenters and of course civil servants – and the assembling of an orchestra much larger than any he had had to engage before: the usual names and as many again as could be recruited from among the students of the Conservatoire and anywhere else where competent players were to be found (his former Prix de Rome colleague Montfort was enrolled, gratis, to play percussion). At the same time he began rehearsing the chorus, the nucleus of which was drawn from the Opéra, taking it in separate sections: women, plus boy sopranos from St Eustache and the Madeleine; tenors; basses.

He had held one rehearsal of each, and was beginning to feel optimistic about the outcome, when the blow fell. The government decided to curtail the July celebrations. There would be just one day instead of the usual three. Among the events cancelled was the memorial service for Marshal Mortier and with it the performance of the Requiem.

Berlioz heard the news by chance while engaged in his preparations: no one had thought to stop him. He took it with remarkable resilience. The letters written under its immediate impact breathe rage, righteous indignation, oaths, but neither dejection nor self-pity. The government was guilty of "an abuse of power, a confidence trick, a piece of dirt, an act of *theft*". But "no matter: the Requiem exists, and I swear to you, father, that it's something that will make its mark on the art of music". And to Liszt: "Fortunately I have a hard skull, and it would take a mighty tomahawk to split it." This was just the kind of thing art exposed itself to by accepting aid from a government as shaky as the present one. But what other aid was there? "Representative governments, and cut-price ones at that! What a farce. But let's not talk of that – you and I would not agree. Happily we're at one about everything else."

Given the known hostility of many people from Cavé and Cherubini downwards, Berlioz may be forgiven for wondering whether "la raison politique" was really the only reason for cancelling the performance, as Montalivet assured him it was. True, Louis-Philippe was rumoured to have been leaned on by foreign chancelleries intimating that it was time France gave up commemorating the July Days. For the regime, too, the festivities were a potential danger point, an occasion for outbreaks of republican violence (the *National* remarked that many people only celebrated the July Revolution because they wanted another one). Yet the King risked stimulating further opposition in seeming to repudiate the popular movement which had brought him to power. The cabinet debated the issue for three days before resolving it, and no doubt the fate of the Requiem was not high on the agenda. Yet Berlioz was logical in pointing out that since requiems for the July dead continued to be celebrated in churches all over Paris there was no political reason why this one shouldn't be. "The actual reasons are sordid cheese-paring and the shameless fashion for ignoring contracts. That way some fifteen thousand francs will be saved. God knows where they'll go."

Berlioz had put his finger on the deciding factor: money. Huge sums from the public purse were spent that May and June on the nuptials of the heir to the throne, the Duc d'Orléans, and his Belgian bride Princess Hélène of Mecklenburg – Paris was *en fête* for several weeks – and another royal wedding was due at the end of the year. There was urgent need to reduce expenditure, and though the government couldn't say so openly the 200,000 francs Parliament had voted for the July celebrations – an event of doubtful political wisdom in any case – were an obvious economy.

Armand Bertin wrote Montalivet a "stinging" letter, which Berlioz delivered personally to the Ministry; and prompted by Félix Marmion, who was a friend of his, the minister sent word asking how he could compensate him for his disappointment – to which the reply could only be that "in an affair of this nature there is no possible compensation except performance of the work". For that, however, he must wait on the changes and chances of politics. Till then it was "like Robinson Crusoe's canoe": too big for him to launch by himself.

His prediction that God alone knew where the money earmarked for the Invalides performance would go proved singularly accurate. No one else could say. It had simply disappeared, leaving bills for copying (3,800 francs) and chorus rehearsals (about 1,000) and the composer's fee (4,000) all unpaid, and nothing to pay them with. The funds had apparently been spent by another department – but which one, and on what, who could tell? Meanwhile, choristers and copyists were badgering him for what they were owed. He himself had been counting on his 4,000 francs to settle some long-standing personal debts, including one to Edouard Rocher that went back seven years. As it was, he had to beg his friend to wait a little longer: "I dare say I shall have to do a lot of running about before I get my hands on it."

He did. Much of August, September and October was wasted in trying to extract payment. Letters to heads of department ("it is with all possible insistence that I urge you to bring this matter to a speedy conclusion. The lawsuits with which I am threatened by the singers and copyists whom I was officially instructed to employ no longer permit me to remain in a position that is as unpleasant as it is unlooked for"), increasingly tense interviews at the Ministry and finally a six-hour vigil outside the minister's office were all necessary before money to pay the bills was handed over some time in the final weeks of 1837. For his fee he had to wait till the end of January, and even then he got it only after a particularly violent scene in Cavé's office. At one point, he later discovered, an attempt had been made to have Gasparin's original order annulled so that the Department of Arts would cease to be liable for any payment at all.

One consequence of having to wait six months to be paid his fee was that in the meantime new debts were contracted. Another was the end of any hope of composing something for his November and December concerts, and therefore of putting on concerts at all. It was the first time since he began that he had not given any. Work during the month of August meant, once again, journalism: he wrote eight articles – four in the *Débats* (he had written none in July, in the weeks leading up to the 28th) and four in the *Gazette*. In September he wrote another eight. He was also editing the *Gazette* in Schlesinger's absence in Germany. While doing so he relieved his feelings about the Requiem by writing a novella cast in the form of an exchange of letters between Benvenuto Cellini and his friend the Florentine composer Alfonso della Viola. "The First Opera" describes how della Viola (a historical personage though not in fact a great innovator, but here representing Berlioz in thinly disguised fictional form) composes a dramatic work in a new genre at the order of the Grand Duke, only for His Grace to change his mind and cancel the performance at the eleventh hour; whereupon the composer bides his time for the next two years and then exacts hideous revenge by absconding with the performing material minutes before the work's première in front of the Grand Duke's court and the élite of Italy.

As it happened, Berlioz did not have to wait two years, and the revenge he took was the less spectacular if effective one of having his work performed. This time events fought for him. On 13 October the city of Constantine in Algeria was captured from the Turks; but the governor-general of France's north African colonies, the Comte de Damrémont, was wounded in the assault and died soon afterwards. A state funeral was decreed; arrangements were made for his body and those of the other soldiers killed in the siege to be returned to Paris. Here suddenly was the perfect occasion for the Requiem, and for Cavé and his staff to get its troublesome composer off their backs, at least so far as concerned the performance of the work. The funeral, happily, was nothing to do with them: it was the preserve of the Ministry of War. On 16 October Berlioz was on his way home from a further interview with Cavé about the outstanding debts for rehearsals and copying when the boom of the Invalides cannon proclaimed the tragic news. A few hours later he was summoned back to the Ministry of the Interior (Quai Malaquais) and informed of the new plan.

The precise sequence of events in the next few weeks is uncertain. What is clear is that Berlioz, still not paid for the work he has done and the bills he has incurred, remains understandably wary. He writes to Dumas asking him to give him another leg-up – "encore un coup d'épaule" – by enlisting the support of the Duc d'Orléans (Dumas, though no longer the duke's librarian, was still in touch with him). He goes to see Montalivet to ask him to use his influence with General Bernard, the Minister of War. He has interviews at the Ministry in the Rue St Dominique with Bernard (a hero of Waterloo who went into exile during the Bourbon Restoration and became a general in the US army). He fends off another attempt to supplant his Requiem with Cherubini's, during which Halévy tries to get the Bertins to persuade him to stand down. He corresponds with Vatout, head of the Department of Public Monuments, about the special amphitheatre required for the performers. Finally, on 15 November, he receives official confirmation from Bernard which puts everything in writing: the Requiem will be given at the Invalides ceremony and the War Ministry will defray all the costs of the performance to the value of 10,000 francs (the fee for the composition and the anterior expenses remaining the responsibility of the Interior). Now all that has to be settled is the date, depending on when the telegraph announces that the coffins have reached Toulon; from then on, bonfire beacons will signal the progress of the cortège across France. At the Conservatoire's annual prizegiving on 19 November Montalivet salutes the unique power of music to lend grandeur and éclat to the nation's festive or solemn occasions – a power which will be called on to speak for France in its bereavement when the chapel of the Invalides receives the body of an illustrious commander beneath its bannered walls and "Conservatoire students perform the melodies written by a former student of the Conservatoire."

Berlioz had got a hearing for his work, and a grander occasion than even the July ceremony would have provided: the funeral of a hero of the state and his faithful followers, slain while achieving a glorious victory for French arms. Everybody who was anybody would be there – many of whom had not heard his music before or been aware of his existence.

He himself, in the first flush of his triumph, believed he had "not lost anything by waiting". But he had. One crucial member of his audience was missing, the teacher whose doctrines made articulate his own deepest instincts about expression and style in religious music. Le Sueur had been ailing for some time. He might perhaps have made one last effort in July to witness his pupil's coronation; at least he would have known of it. By October he was dead. Berlioz was a pall-bearer at his funeral in St Roch on the 10th, and with a great throng of academicians and artists followed his body to Père-Lachaise. "It was a very sad ceremony for all of us his pupils, who were much in evidence," he wrote to his mother. "I have often been at solemnities of the kind, but the poor man was so unfailingly kind to me that this time it was hard to remain self-possessed."

The delay also meant that the number of performers was reduced by at least a hundred on account of the smaller budget. Perhaps that did not matter so much. But because the occasion was a funeral, not (as in July) a commemoration, his score could not be heard on its own, creating its own ritual of the dead as he had conceived it, but must take place within an imposed order of service, with the result that instead of the movements leading into each other with the effect planned they were followed each time by intonings and responses; and at the end, where the beat of the retreating drums and the choir's Amens haloed by the circling strings would have been the last sounds heard, the silence was filled by the De profundis, chanted in faux-bourdon. And whereas he had been going to conduct the July performance himself, for a state occasion of this magnitude he had no choice but to make way for Habeneck: Bernard was quietly insistent on the point. He was able to make sure he took one full rehearsal, however, and no doubt was involved in others; and the job of assembling the chorus and orchestra, and agreeing their fees, was his.

We know very little about the performance, musically speaking. It seems to have satisfied him. He had been anxious about it two days before. But at the public dress rehearsal, held in the Invalides on the morning of 4 December and attended by many friends (among them Mme Vernet and her daughter Louise Vernet-Delaroche), it began to come together: this despite the momentary absent-mindedness – Berlioz could not believe it had not been deliberate – which caused Habeneck to lower his bow and take a pinch of snuff just as he should have been directing the brass at the new tempo of the Tuba mirum. Berlioz, who was in charge of the massed timpani, stepped forward and conducted the rest of the movement.* *Figaro*, reporting the rehearsal in next morning's issue, remarked that the performers didn't yet know the work thoroughly. It was good enough to make a deep impression, however. Vigny wrote in his journal: "the music was beautiful and strange, wild, convulsive, sorrowful"; and the three-year-old Louis was "enraptured by his father's 'big trumpets' ".

By next morning conductor, chorus and orchestra were more secure and all went without serious hitch. The Grande messe des morts is one of the composer's least difficult scores to perform (though chorus tenors will hardly thank me for saying so) and one of the easiest to get right if you are prepared to follow his instructions. Habeneck could rarely find the fire and animation Berlioz's quicker music demands, but in a broadly paced work like the Requiem his best qualities would have been to the fore, especially if he remembered to leave his snuffbox in his waistcoat pocket. The performers were the finest in Paris; the chorus, trained by Schneitzhoeffer, composer and former *chef de chant* at the Opéra, boasted distinguished artists and famous operatic names like Levasseur, Massol, Dupont, Alizard, Serda, Stoltz, not to mention Mme Lebrun, who twelve years before had expressed her approval of Berlioz's Mass in such gratifyingly salty language and who, though her voice

---

* For a discussion of this curious incident, which has often been denied but is attested by independent witnesses, see p.802.

was a shadow of what it had been, was still a redoubtable presence. Duprez was the voice of the archangel in the Sanctus, a part whose heroic style and exalted vocal line suited him to perfection. Though the black drapes on the walls of the church diminished its normal resonance, the flagstones would have acted as natural reflectors for the large force of strings, placed directly on the floor of the nave, in front of the chorus and the woodwind and French horns on their scaffolding. At about three hundred strong the great mass of performers, a group of brass instruments at each corner, made an imposing sight. So, even more, did the funeral panoply: the catafalque, surrounded by hundreds of candles and smoking incense-boats (and heralded at its entry by a salvo from the Invalides cannon, accompanied by innumerable side-drums), the ranks of uniformed National Guardsmen and old soldiers from the Invalides drawn up near it in the nave, the captured bullet-torn flags suspended row on row above, and the myriad points of flickering light all over the darkened church. What the performance lost aurally it made up visually and in dramatic atmosphere.

The event spread Berlioz's name to a much wider and more influential group of people than before: not only the royal princes – at least one of whom, the Duc d'Orléans, was already something of a patron – but aristocratic, political, legal, diplomatic and military Paris and its wives, as well as the fashionable world, "le tout Paris", as the *Siècle* reported next morning, "the Paris of the Opéra, of the Théâtre-Italien, of first nights and the races and M. de Rothschild's receptions and the balls at M. Dupin's". It didn't matter if few of them were as moved as the officiating priest, the Abbé Ancelin, curé of the Invalides, who burst into tears at the altar and was still weeping in the sacristy ten minutes later, or as the Duc d'Orléans, who sent Berlioz word that never had he been so deeply stirred by music. The success was incontestable – a "success immense and general, with the public and with the artists", he told his father: "the greatest and the most hard-won that I have yet achieved".

The papers confirmed it. Only two or three of the dozens that reported the performance were hostile, and their critics, from the sound of it, had not been there: the *Journal de Paris* said Lablache sang a solo, when the work contained no solo for bass and Lablache was not present, and the *Corsaire* mentioned with equal accuracy a solo by Mlle Falcon. When the *Constitutionnel* ascribed his triumph entirely to the "heavy artillery" of the *Journal des débats* (and compared Berlioz to Victor

Hugo without intending a compliment), it was the voice of a small minority. The *Monde dramatique* spoke for the consensus when it said that the Requiem placed him in the first rank of composers of religious music: "in face of such a work Berlioz's enemies must pipe down and admire". Nor was it only the journalists who praised it. Bottée de Toulmon's magisterial notice in the *Gazette* carried all the greater weight for being written by the Conservatoire librarian, an acknowledged expert on medieval music who yet recognized the validity and power of Berlioz's innovations in the field. Bottée's article moved d'Ortigue to thank him for having "put into words what all of us must feel, a sense of national pride in such a work, in such a genius. [. . .] How I should love to see the expression of old toad-face, our Brussels friend [Fétis], when he reads you." Legouvé, who had been at both rehearsal and performance, wrote to Berlioz: "Hé bien, êtes-vous content? I have met no one who doesn't put it above your previous works." General Bernard's letter of congratulation on his "splendid and austere composition" was reproduced widely in the press. And Liszt wrote from Milan rejoicing in his friend's success, of which he had read in letters from Paris and in the few French newspapers that penetrated the Austrian censorship: "Once and for all, full and complete justice has been rendered to you." It was "high time".

There was talk of the government's publishing the score at state expense. One or two papers might accuse him of being a pampered lackey of the powers that be, claiming that he was given thirty-six thousand francs for the Requiem (which prompted him to remark that they "merely added a nought to the sum I had not been paid"). But that kind of adverse publicity was itself a mark of having arrived. For the moment he was riding high. Thanks to the Requiem, too, his fame was spreading beyond France. The London *Musical World* of 15 December reported its "triumphant success" and appended a biography of the composer, wildly garbled but quite favourable, and the *Morning Post* reprinted the long review from the Parisian *Galignani's Messenger*.

In Germany he was already a name to conjure with; he was continually having to turn down requests for copies of his symphonies: they were "still too young to travel without him", as he explained to Schumann in an open letter published in the *Gazette* of 19 February 1837 in response to reports of a fine performance of the *Francs-juges* overture in Leipzig. This resolve (Berlioz wrote) had been only strengthened by accounts of a massacre of the same overture at a Philharmonic Society concert in the Argyll Rooms in Hanover Square, London, when the tempo of the adagio introduction was doubled and that of the allegro halved (but even then the violins couldn't play it), the trombones came in a dozen bars early, the timpanist got in a hopeless muddle, and everyone fell about with laughter. The French musicians playing in the orchestra "told me quite frankly that they joined in the hilarity of their English hosts, though they were not laughing for the same reason".

> I should be afraid of forfeiting for ever the esteem of all true friends of music if by publishing them prematurely I exposed my symphonies [. . .] to a mutilation crueller even than that of my old overture – a fate which, have no doubt, they would suffer everywhere except in two or three artistic and hospitable cities such as yours. You see, I love them, these poor children of mine, with a paternal love that has nothing Spartan about it, and I should infinitely rather know them obscure but intact than send them off in quest of glory or a brutal death. [. . .] The approbation of Germany, the fatherland of music, has too great a value in my eyes and will be too difficult to win – if I win it at all – for me not to wait until I can go there myself and, as a pilgrim, lay my modest offerings at its feet.

At home, the power and influence he derived, for better and worse, from the "heavy artillery" of the *Journal des débats* was all the greater now that Janin had handed over reviewing of the Opéra and the Opéra-Comique. It was Berlioz who chronicled the sad and inexplicable retirement of the much-loved Adolphe Nourrit, whose farewell performance on 1 April, in scenes from Gluck's *Armide* and *The Huguenots*, left many in the capacity audience in tears; and it was Berlioz who was at the Opéra a couple of weeks later to review the spectacular house début of his old acquaintance Gilbert Duprez, Nourrit's successor, in *William Tell*. The *Débats'* opera feuilletons acquired an authority they had never had in the capricious, musically semi-literate hands of Janin. They were more closely argued without being any less entertaining to read. Berlioz defended Duprez against the ignorance of critics who used reports that Meyerbeer had had to alter Raoul's music to suit the new man's voice as evidence that the role was beyond the singer's powers. Duprez hardly needed defending, his success was so great. But the error served as pretext for a disquisition on the tenor voice and the varieties of timbre and character it embraced; on the changes habitually made for (and by) tenors, Haitzinger and Nourrit no less than Duprez, to accommodate role to voice; on the difference between head and chest voice, which latter Duprez preferred and with whose thrilling ring he had electrified the Opéra;* and on the combination of the two voices, *voix mixte*, at which Nourrit excelled.

For the Opéra the advent of Duprez and his swiftly won popularity could not have been better timed. It filled the void left by Nourrit's departure and it helped to distract attention from the alarming and mysterious vocal problems (were they only vocal?) of the lovely Cornélie Falcon, the young dramatic soprano – she was still only twenty-three – who was Meyerbeer's favourite singer and whom serious connoisseurs regarded as the great hope of Paris grand opera, the new champion of dramatic values against the cult of the *décorateur*. At the second performance of *Stradella* Falcon was unable to answer Nourrit's "Demain nous partirons – voulez-vous?" with the expected "Je suis prête": no sound came from her, and she fainted and was borne from the stage in Nourrit's arms. Falcon never fully recovered her voice. And three weeks later Nourrit was gone. Many, including Duponchel, the director, tried to persuade him to stay; but he was going through some kind of personal crisis (which Duprez's impending arrival may have contributed to but did not cause) and he was not to be moved. Berlioz and the Irish composer George Osborne spent a long evening walking with him up and down the boulevards in an attempt to talk him out of his wilder resolutions.

Félix Marmion was at Duprez's début, with Berlioz and Harriet and Nancy's friend Louise Boutaud, née Veyron, and her husband, in Paris on a visit. Marmion had been made a full colonel a few months before and appointed to the 11th Dragoons. The regiment was stationed in Paris and he was living in a charming apartment across the river from the Tuileries. They saw a lot of him; the froideur between them was a thing of the past. It was he who told his nephew of the peaceful end of his grandfather, Félix's father Nicolas Marmion; the old troubadour died at Meylan in March, at the age of eighty-five.

Relations with La Côte continued close and cordial. Berlioz's parents took an active interest in the Requiem, a state commission which greatly

---

* Though not Rossini, who likened Duprez's chest-voice high C in *William Tell* to "the squawk of a capon having its throat cut" and who agreed to receive a call from the great Tamberlick only on condition that he "left his *ut de poitrine* outside on the hatstand".

impressed the whole family; they were very upset when it was postponed and correspondingly pleased when all ended well. They sent money twice during the year, the first gift enabling Berlioz to buy the uniform which his membership of the National Guard made obligatory, the second helping to relieve the hard-pressed household, fallen deeper into debt when the fee for the Requiem was not paid. Nancy endeared herself to her brother and his wife by sending Louis a silver knife, fork and spoon. Joséphine Berlioz, knowing her grandson's penchant, sent some more of her jam, and Adèle, his godmother, embroidered him a smart pair of trousers, which he referred to proudly as his "patapon" (*pantalon*). Louis was beginning to know his alphabet; and, the following January, Berlioz had the pleasure of informing the family that the three-and-a-half-year-old boy, handing him a letter, said "from Aunt Adèle – you know, your sister". "We're thinking of finding him a school in a few months' time, so as to begin to get him into a different environment, for between ourselves he is thoroughly spoilt and most of the time does only what he wants. Harriet, however, spoils him less than I do, I hardly have time to be strict with him." In late September 1837, or early October, they had moved apartments again, this time only a few doors away, to 31 Rue de Londres. The servant problem seems to have been solved; at any rate there is no further mention of it. There are also fewer references to Harriet. We can make what we may of that, and of a phrase in the report of the performance of the Requiem that he sent his father: "Harriet wept a lot yesterday, but tears of joy do no great harm." Almost the only other mention of any length occurs in a letter of 12 October to Joséphine Berlioz, in which, after sympathizing with his mother's solitude during his father's "long absences" in the fields, he goes on: "Harriet too complains a good deal about mine; for, whether I am out or in, in my study, she is equally alone for a large part of the day. Louis is a distraction: he is so sweet, and so intelligent; but his almost exclusive predilection for me often costs his mother tears."

Harriet still had not given up hope of being able to resume her career. In May 1837 she made another appearance at the Comte de Castellane's private theatre, where her performance in the fifth act of *Jane Shore* was applauded by an audience of the rich and famous. At about the same time she again sought the patronage of the Duc d'Orléans, perhaps using the evening at the Hôtel Castellane as a pretext. Her letter has not survived; but a memorandum from his financial secretary informed the duke that "I have just found a most interesting request from Mme Berlioz (Miss Smithson) which was addressed to Your Royal Highness a few days before Your Highness's marriage. Madame la Duchesse d'Orléans, to whom I presented the request, has given 200 francs to assist this extremely unfortunate woman, whose distress is so little deserved. I beg Your Highness to authorize me to add 300 francs to the Princess's gift." Five hundred francs were duly delivered to Harriet by one of the Duchesse d'Orléans' gentlemen in waiting, who called at the apartment on 29 June, the day Berlioz completed the Requiem.

The money, as always, was welcome. But more important schemes were afoot. All that spring and summer, while he was at work on the Requiem, Berlioz pursued a project hardly less dear to his heart, which he had first discussed with Liszt earlier in the year, during what Berlioz later recalled as their "hours of smoke-filled talk" over Liszt's "long pipes and Turkish tobacco". Liszt in addition to the notorious "duel" with his pianist rival Thalberg – successive concerts culminating in a trial of strength at the salon of Princess Belgiojoso – gave three recitals of Beethoven trios with Urhan and the cellist Alexandre Batta in Erard's showrooms, all of which Berlioz attended. At one of them an unannounced change caught the audience cruelly on the hop, as Berlioz noted in the *Gazette*, and as Liszt reported to Marie d'Agoult: "The programme showed the Beethoven [op.70, no.2] first and Pixis' trio last. On Pixis' begging me not to destroy him, we agreed to invert the order – and everyone applauded what they took to be the Beethoven trio, and said how pallid the other sounded beside it . . . Isn't that delightful?"

During one of their conversations Berlioz broached his idea.

Marie d'Agoult to George Sand

26 March 1837

Berlioz–Alcibiades (*he* had red hair and a big nose too!) is forming in his most secret heart a desire that he dare not tell you of – that you should write a play in which there would be a part, almost entirely in mime, for his Aspasia. If you're not opposed to the idea (which would be a stroke of fortune for Aspasia), let me know and I'll write to you at greater length about it; for the moment you're not supposed to know anything.

George Sand to Marie d'Agoult

6 April 1837

I will do what is wanted for Aspasia; but I've not got a moment free before the end of the summer. I'm weighed down with work and my strength is giving way under the burden of it.

Berlioz to Liszt

22 May 1837

[Liszt and Marie were staying with George Sand on their way to Italy.] I have just been reading *Mauprat* [a story by George Sand serialized in the *Revue des deux mondes*]. Please compliment the author from me. It's fascinating. And what a devilish vitality of style! If Mme Sand ever writes a play, it won't send one to sleep, that's for sure. By the way, tell me about the idea we spoke of. What does she really think of it? On this subject, I have to tell you that last week Harriet played the fifth act of *Jane Shore* at M. de Castellane's, and truly it was wonderful. I don't believe any actress has ever combined truthfulness and dramatic poetry to such a degree.

Berlioz to Marie d'Agoult

15 June 1837

My wife and I are most grateful for the interest you have kindly taken in the project which we are so keen about. Though with no lack of confidence in Mme Sand's goodness of heart and artistic feeling, I know that nothing less than the support of an intermediary like yourself would have made me decide to put such a request to her. As our idea does not strike her as out of the question, I shall write to thank her and talk directly to her about it.

Marie d'Agoult to George Sand

[*c*. late June 1837]

Berlioz is delighted by the ray of hope I've given him.

Berlioz to George Sand

20 June 1837

I can't thank you enough, Madam, for the kindly welcome you have given a project which is of the keenest concern to me. Harriet bids me tell you that by writing for her you will be giving her back the breath of life. As it is, her situation is of the cruellest. The forced inactivity to which she is condemned by the impossibility of finding a *literary* English theatre, whether in Paris or in London (where the art of drama is finished for ever), is all the more painful in that, modesty apart, she is conscious that her powers are greater than ever and, by the unkindest trick of fate, it is her own innovations that before her very eyes are making the fortune of any number of actors and actresses of the second rank.

I believe, Madam, that you never saw her in her heyday, and know neither her Juliet nor her Ophelia nor her Jane Shore; but I have no doubt you have divined what is new and poetic in her artistic sensibility, in which modern passion and truth are constantly allied to antique beauty. A play of yours, performed by her, would surely be therefore something quite remarkable and of irresistible interest. Mme d'Agoult has led me to hope that you may be thinking of it for this winter.

The proposal is new: to place in the context of a French drama an Englishwoman who speaks French with difficulty and with an accent which has to be justified, or who does not know it well enough to express certain ideas and, when that is so, speaks in her native tongue while invoking the aid of mime. There is certainly a powerful drama there, which hangs on a lack of understanding or on the wrong interpretation of language or a word. You will find it, I am sure, and in writing it you will be doing a great and good deed for which all lovers of art will be eternally grateful to you. Furthermore, you will be giving a helping hand to a great artist who is in despair, with only too much reason, and whose sufferings are worthy of your sympathy.

Berlioz to Liszt

20 July 1837

Thank Mme Sand a thousand times from Harriet and me for her gracious promise, until such time as we can talk to her in person about it. Is she coming to Paris soon?

Berlioz to George Sand

17 September 1837

Several newspapers these past few days have announced that you are writing a play called *Les Joies du coeur perdues*. This news, as you will imagine, is of the greatest possible interest to us. The agitation it has caused my wife makes me venture to bother you again, to find out how true the report is and whether the play in question is in fact the one in which you kindly promised her a part.

Be so good, Madam, as to write me a few lines on the subject, and forgive my impatience, for which the ever-increasing force and originality of your admirable talent must be my excuse.

No further correspondence survives. George Sand doubtless replied to his anxious inquiries. But that was the end of it. *Les Joies du coeur perdues* was never completed, and no subsequent play by George Sand contained a part for Harriet. Her role as an actress was over; her world had finally and irrevocably contracted, and within its narrow bounds her life from now on would revolve round two people, her husband and her son.

Yet Berlioz had not quite given up. On the night of 14–15 January 1838 the Théâtre-Italien burned down and the director, Severini, was killed jumping from the blazing building. Three weeks later Berlioz formally applied for a licence to manage a reborn Italian company in a new location, the Théâtre Ventadour.

On the face of it he was not the most obvious person to be involved in the administration of a company dedicated to an art form of which he had so low an opinion. It was, however, the abuses of Italian opera that he objected to more than the genre itself, and they could be remedied. Quite apart from the argument of a regular salary, there were real attractions. There was the challenge – as he put it in his submission to the minister – of "achieving a marked improvement in the standard of choral and orchestral performance" (no one was better qualified to do that) and of working with some of the finest singers in Paris or anywhere else. And there was one other motive. While assuring the minister that the company would put on only "works already successfully produced in Italy or written for Paris by leading Italian composers", he added a further stipulation: that in the summer months he be authorized to perform "German opera and English tragedy". It was one last attempt to save his wife from the miseries of her frustration and from all that would follow from it for them both.

7

Malvenuto Cellini

Four months after the passing of Le Sueur came a sharper loss: Joséphine Berlioz died on 18 February 1838, aged fifty-three. She had been ill since December; but her letters had maintained almost to the last their native verve. "I am too weak to write to you at any length," she tells Nancy, and then flows on over several sides. "I can't eat a thing, although your father isn't stopping me, quite the contrary, but I've no appetite for anything and besides I'm so afraid of getting those painful swellings which I had for three weeks and which have been much less bad since I dieted and applied thirty leeches and took long baths and also hip-baths, so don't worry, I am being looked after well, Monique sleeps in our room, what with your father and me the poor thing has plenty to do, oh! how lucky to have so intelligent and affectionate a servant, as for the other [the cook] she's totally stupid, and Adèle isn't eating, I tell you, go on sending her long letters, it's her only distraction, when I am up to it she reads aloud to me", etc., etc. Berlioz and his mother had never had the conscious affinity that bound him to his father even during their worst misunderstandings; but in the last two years there had been a deepening of sympathy between them. The success of the Requiem had pleased her greatly and perhaps redeemed him a little in her eyes. As though he sensed time was short, he began writing to her more often. The last surviving letter, written a month before, ends: "Goodbye, dear Mama; I'm tied hand and foot here, otherwise you may well believe I would come and see you, even if it were only for four or five days – I really need it, and I am sure too that my visit would do you good. But later on we'll be freer, and then . . . Meanwhile, take good care of yourself, dear Mother, and don't neglect anything that helps dispel those melancholy thoughts you are so prone to. I embrace you tenderly."

What passed between Paris and La Côte immediately after her death is not known: there is a gap in the correspondence. Berlioz's letter to his father, a month later, took up the question of the inheritance.

> Your letter, Adèle's and the one from Camille, all arriving at about the same time, distressed me in a quite unexpected way. Adèle mentions certain arrangements, made in her favour by our excellent mother, with an air that makes me believe she fears the effect this slight advantage will have on her brothers and her sister. You add details about your intentions towards us that show the profound dejection with which you regard your own future. In the name of all that is most dear to you, don't talk like that – nothing is more unprofitable. According to my sister's letters you have borne our great loss with your usual courage. Are they mistaken? We'll talk later, much later, about those questions of bequest which you propose to me with such sad composure. In any case, so far as I'm concerned, whatever you do will always be right. I am grateful to Mlle Clappier for coming with my sister to spend time with you; her company is surely the best and most consoling you could have in such cruel circumstances; I had hoped she would not fail you. What's Prosper doing? No one tells me anything about him. And Nanci – how is she? You've no plans to travel, I fear; yet there's nothing in the world that would do you more good, in every way.
>
> As for me, my servitude continues, or rather gets worse day by day. But I have a reasonable expectation, though there's no certainty, of being nominated director of the Théâtre-Italien. The businessmen who chose me and got me to apply for the privilege in my name guarantee me a salary of ten thousand francs plus a fifth of the profits from the exploitation of the theatre. [. . .] Farewell, dear Father, don't worry about my future and think more about yourself. Of all the marks of affection you can give your children, the care of your health and of your peace of mind is the one they need most.

Berlioz threw himself into the Théâtre-Italien project with characteristic energy. His detailed submissions to the minister are impressive documents, cogently argued and demonstrating a grasp both of the Paris opera scene (which he knew inside out) and of the practical details involved, including redecoration, heating and lighting of the theatre (the Salle Ventadour), accessibility to the public, picking up and setting down of audience, parking of carriages in side streets adjacent to the theatre (Rues Ventadour, Thérèse, Des Moulins, Argenteuil, etc.), and the effect on local inhabitants. There is nothing half-hearted about them. Reading them, one can believe that he would have made a good job of it.

His prospects, in the spring of 1838, were not unpromising. The consortium, which included the chemist and amateur composer Henri de Ruolz, who had made a fortune from his patent silver-plating process, was solidly based. It was supported by the minister, Montalivet, himself. The Bertins too were behind it. That was as always a two-edged weapon. The anti-government press made much of the fact, accusing them of wanting to have Berlioz appointed director so that he could put on the operas of Louise Bertin, which no other theatre would touch. As a native French composer Mlle Bertin was automatically excluded from the repertoire of the Théâtre-Italien; but the *canard* was too good to pass up. A counter-bid was entered on behalf of Rossini's friend the ex-director Robert by the Isère deputy Félix Réal, a practised lobbyist, whose children, as it happened, were Robert's heirs. In the end Berlioz and company were defeated. He was actually nominated and signed a contract; but Montalivet had failed to secure the necessary political support. The parliamentary commission turned down the proposal and on 19 June the Chamber voted overwhelmingly against it.

Berlioz was not altogether sorry. The project finally voted on was not the one he had first presented but another, which laid on the successful bidder the obligation to rebuild the Théâtre-Italien on its existing site; the Salle Ventadour – to him the ideal location – had been rejected. "The whole thing has caused me so much bother, and such extraordinary tedium, that I am resolved not to chase that particular hare again next year. I was not born to get involved in money matters." It cannot have surprised him greatly when three years later the Italian opera was re-established along the lines he himself had proposed. That was politics, and life.

But the degree of hostility the affair confirmed, to the *Débats* and to him, was not a good omen for *Benvenuto Cellini*. And he was in dire need of money. His fee for the Requiem had come through finally at the end of January but three quarters of it had gone at once on paying the most urgent of his debts. In March a more modest hare, worth an annual 2,000 francs, had offered itself for chasing: a professorship of harmony at the Conservatoire. He put in for it but was persuaded by Cherubini to withdraw, on the grounds that being no pianist he was not fully qualified to teach harmony – only to find that the successful candidate, Bienaimé, was not a pianist either. The irony was completed by the fact that the dead incumbent, Rifaut, was the pianist who broke down while attempting to accompany Berlioz's Prix de Rome cantata *Orphée* ten years before.

Such reverses are typical of Berlioz's career, part of the unchanging pattern laid down in the 1820s when he was still a student, doing things no respectable student was supposed to do. Now, ten years later, he is a public figure and his activities are news. He is the composer of the Requiem for General Damrémont and the other heroes of Constantine. The subscription list for the full score published by Schlesinger is headed by the Duc d'Orléans. He is tipped for the Légion d'honneur (and will soon get it). Habeneck conducts the Lacrymosa before an audience of five thousand at a festival in Lille and writes him a congratulatory letter which is published in the *Gazette* (to the annoyance of Cherubini, who has had a Credo performed at the same concert but gets no letter). Danton *jeune*, the fashionable sculptor, adds him to his gallery of caricature portrait-busts, giving due prominence to the great beak and the shock of hair. But he is also, to the musical establishment, the same object of mistrust and disapproval that he always was. His position at the *Débats*, though it makes him more powerful in some respects, does not make him any more acceptable. And his very successes – ascribed, naturally, to influence and not to talent – only incite greater hostility.

In the second half of 1838 the opposing forces met on the battlefield of the Opéra. Berlioz recognized the supreme importance of it. "I am at the crisis point of my career and of my life."

Benvenuto Cellini was finally passed for production in January of that year. The music had long been complete except for the overture (which he composed in late January and early February, using the first of the Pope's two themes, Harlequin's song, and a lighter, high-stepping version of Teresa's lyrical melody from the trio, and combining them with an ebullient, metrically ambiguous new G major theme to create the most brilliant overture he had yet written). The work could have been staged much earlier, and it might have been a good thing if it had, before the success of the Requiem angered his enemies and before the well-publicized defeat of his Théâtre-Italien bid gave them fresh heart. But Halévy, a member of the Opéra staff and since *La Juive* a star, held Duponchel to the letter of their agreement and, though *Guido et Ginevra* was hardly begun, had it put into slow, protracted rehearsal as he composed it, thus blocking any other new production. After that it was Auber's turn. He had not started his *Lac des fées*, however, and had no objection to Berlioz's going first – according to Adolphe Adam, a clever move on Auber's part: "it can only make his own work shine the brighter after the inevitable fiasco of the other".

By the end of January the score was at the copyists'. The first chorus rehearsal was held on 15 March; it was taken by Halévy, the Opéra's chorus master, but the composer was present: he must "keep an eye on everything and be afraid of nothing". Already he could feel the Opéra's atmosphere of gossip and intrigue closing round him. By early May the costumes had been commissioned. From now on he was at the theatre every other day – "on the days in between I have to go and call on those of my singers who *don't know music* and din their roles into them so that they're ready for the next day's rehearsal". In June Duprez was away, in Lyon (Berlioz urged Adèle to go and hear him in *William Tell*), and the composer took his role at the soloists' rehearsals. The first stage run-through, with piano, was held on 26 June, and in mid-July the orchestra began its formidable task. The première, originally scheduled for July ("the worst moment of the year, but what could I do? I had no choice"), was put off till August, and then postponed again. Meanwhile the censors had drawn the line at the Pope, insisting on his being replaced by a cardinal; they also had doubts about the liturgical chanting of the offstage monks in Act 2, though they were persuaded to wait and judge its effect.

Berlioz was taken up almost exclusively with his opera in the six and a half months from mid-March to late September (so much so that he wrote only five feuilletons for the *Débats* during that time and had to appeal to Legouvé for another loan). It was both an exciting and a nerve-lacerating experience. The *Memoirs'* account of that long rehearsal period is coloured by the bitterness of hindsight – the singers already convinced it would be a flop, Habeneck surly, two orchestral musicians caught playing "J'ai du bon tabac" during the big finale, the dancers everlastingly complaining at the slow tempo of the saltarello but themselves playing the fool on the darkened stage at the end of the carnival scene, and everyone making fun of the colloquial style of the libretto ("'The cocks were crowing' – the cocks! It'll be the hens next"). His letters, however, paint a more positive picture. With all allowance made for his native optimism and his tendency to put a good face on things when reporting to his family, it is clear that he enjoyed seeing his score come slowly to life and begin to overcome hostility and incomprehension, and relished the challenge of taking on the chaotic maelstrom of conflicting interests and amours propres that was the Académie Royale de Musique. At that stage, how could he possibly acknowledge that it was beyond him?

The Paris Opéra was a famous death-trap. Berlioz was by no means the only composer who found it a "nest of adders", round which one trod with extreme wariness. France's premier subsidized theatre suffered in advanced form from the national delusion of knowing everything there was to be known about art. Verdi said that within a quarter of an hour of a composer's arriving with a new score everybody including the usherettes and the stage-door man could tell it was no good. He also said that out of hundreds of performances he had attended there not one was musically satisfactory; and Berlioz would come to agree with him, calling the house "the enemy of music". Two years after *Benvenuto*, when he was already waging his "all-out war of ridicule" against the place, he satirized the complacently negligent process by which highly paid singers condescended to think about learning their roles. The absurdities of theatre directors, with (in Edmond Gosse's phrase) "their customary loitering and fluctuating attention", would become a favourite target. But in the spring and summer of 1838 he was still hopeful. Though it was "pack-horse work" and the chorus began by saying his music was unperformable, things were moving. By the second week in May they had learned more than half the opera. Ten days later, the performers were warming up and were even breaking into applause; he was pleased with their progress, while "keeping an eye on the venomous insects" that surrounded him. At the end of June, though the rehearsals were "killing" him it was turning out better than he had dared hope. A fortnight later, "Duprez–Cellini is superb, you have no idea of the energy and beauty of his singing." There was still "the ordeal by fire of the orchestral rehearsals" to face, after which would come "the fusillade from the newspapers and from my special enemies concealed in corners of the pit. But I am armed against them *cap à pié*". At the end of July, with the première in sight, he told Legouvé that

> we are beginning to sort out the orchestra, despite the whining of the
> older players, who say they have never had to perform anything like it.
> The millions of wrong notes, tempos wrongly judged, and most of all
> the bungled rhythms, have so tortured me and set my nerves on edge
> that this torment is the sole cause of my illness, from which I've still not

fully recovered. Patience! We shall arrive at the first performance about
the 21st or 25th August. Duprez will be superb, the choruses are going
very well, Mme Dorus-Gras [Teresa] is not at all bad, and there is a
certain entry of the Prince-Cardinal which you are going to like. Apropos,
I wager you will be pleased with the overture. You will think I am
counting my chickens; but if my score is published, you will do me the
pleasure of accepting the dedication, won't you? After all, it was you
that gave me the *metal* to cast Perseus, and poor Benvenuto owes his
work, such as it is, to you.

Berlioz had always known it would be a close-run thing. "Although
all my friends believe we will have a success," he wrote in May, "I
believe it will be a stormy first night; if I have a success it will be a
violent and scandalous one." He felt he could survive the worst the
hostile critics might fling at him. But "the public is what counts – the
neutral, impartial public: that's what I aim to win".

Though it was a big step from his faithful phalanx of admirers in
the Conservatoire Hall or from the captive thousands at the Invalides
to the multitudinous, floating, heterogeneous public of the Opéra, he
might just have done it if *Benvenuto* had been given a chance to establish
itself. The hostile critics duly did their worst, some of them with a
depth of *mauvaise volonté* and dishonesty embarrassing to witness. But
others were enthusiastic, some quite perceptively so. And the pamphlet
war the work provoked did it no harm. In any case the score was its
own best defence. It simply needed hearing.

Circumstances and two or three individuals combined to deny it that
chance. *Benvenuto Cellini* had four performances in all, followed by
three more of the first act coupled with a ballet, and then disappeared
from the billboards of the Opéra for the next 135 years. The première,
put off again from late August to 3 September and then once more
when Duprez went down with a sore throat – "slight" (*Presse*), "severe"
(*Débats*) – finally took place on the 10th, five days before the Teresa,
Dorus-Gras, was due to go on leave. It was, as the composer predicted,
stormy. "From the first note of the opera to the last," wrote the *Artiste*,
certain people "in various corners of the theatre" kept up a commentary
of "groans, shrieks, prolonged whistling and ventriloquist's patter, the
whole seasoned with gross laughter". The hostility was directed partly
at the libretto's colloquial language and the farcical aspects of the action:
Balducci's "my stick, my gloves" in the opening scene; the innkeeper

reading out the bill for wine; the parody of King Midas with the ass's ears – a "piece of buffoonery", opined *Galignani's Messenger*, that was so drawn out "as to call down a general expression of displeasure"; the dressing up of Fieramosca in foundry-worker's leather apron, an "ignoble buffoonery" which "raised shouts of derision"; and Balducci's "Il réussit, j'en étais sûr! / Ma fille, embrasse ton futur", an "unaccountable change of opinion which was received with another roar of laughter by the auditory". Some were shocked by the levity of the Cardinal; his promise of pardon "sans confession" caused deep offence.

Berlioz's supporters, in their reviews, made much of what they considered the serious flaws of the text, while insisting that the music transcended them. This was not just a tactic. They were as affronted as the booers by its homely, casual tone and by its burlesque touches, so ill-suited to the dignity of the Opéra. Janin devoted most of his feuilleton to attacking the libretto's vulgarity (though he also took the line that a comic subject was alien *per se* to the passionate, essentially melancholy nature of Berlioz's genius). Such reactions were thoroughly in the French theatrical tradition, in which the libretto was of supreme importance as well as lending itself much more readily than music to critical discussion. Méhul remarked that an operatic score might contain very fine things and still make little impression: "in our unhappy country music cannot support a weak poem"; and Reicha noted that the essentials for an opera were a strong libretto and a good cast: "possessed of these a composer may produce an inferior work and yet it will be successful, especially in Paris. Without these crucial factors the contrary may befall a work of genius."

All this goes some way to explaining why *Benvenuto Cellini* aroused so much opposition. The fact remains that many in the first-night audience were out to get Berlioz, not his librettists: he was their quarry, as he well knew. "The rabid enemies that my feuilletons, the *Débats*' protection, my musical tendencies, and professional jealousy have between them earned me over the years all converged on the Opéra that day." Even before the performance began the critic of the *Artiste* heard people saying that "the music of *Benvenuto Cellini* was quite absurd – learned if you like, but learned to the point of being unintelligible; the author of such a work was doomed, he would never recover from the fiasco, and it would be a just punishment for his arrogance in presuming to be an innovator in music". The opera (the critic continued) was "condemned to the flames before a note was heard". At the other extreme, less numerous, were the composer's sympathizers, bent on making it a triumphant success. Others, without being partisan, had come to listen to the music and perhaps applaud it. And in the middle were the representatives of what Boschot calls "l'esprit français, l'esprit parisien et boulevardier", which "claimed its rights, especially the right not to listen to the music". They noted that the décor was less than lavish, that the drama seemed unexpectedly vulgar, that Duprez the reigning star was below his best, and that the house was not nearly as full as it was for Meyerbeer, which meant that the piece probably wouldn't last long.

It remained an open question which side would finally win. Would Berlioz's partisans succeed in carrying the indifferent majority with them? Over the next two days composer and librettists worked at altering and trimming the text and adjusting the score to fit the changes. The innkeeper's scene disappeared; so did Balducci's "Il réussit, j'en étais sûr"; the carnival pantomime was curtailed, as was the sextet. It was a shorter, less burlesque *Benvenuto* that was given on the second and third nights (12 and 14 September), and it went more smoothly, with the opposition much quieter and the applause less contested. But the receipts were lower still – half what they had been at the première.

The satirical journals, as expected, went to town, celebrating the richly merited downfall of "Malvenuto Cellini"; the audience, said the *Charivari*, "went to sleep and woke up hissing". But the press as a whole was more favourable than not. For every critic who derided "M. Berlioz's system" (without specifying what it was) there were two who welcomed the work and said it should be given an opportunity to make its mark. *La France musicale* – the Escudier brothers' house journal, rival to Schlesinger's – thought the opera both difficult enough and good enough to deserve "ten first performances", and had particular praise for the "unequalled power and energy" of Berlioz's orchestra. The performers too were now mostly on his side: the orchestra had been won round before the first night, and the chorus, though sluggish, were willing. Mme Dorus-Gras agreed to postpone her tour of the provinces till the beginning of October. Another half dozen performances and *Benvenuto* would be over the worst.

He reckoned without the management, and without his friend Duprez. The great tenor's triumphs of the previous season had gone to his head. Duprez was offended that his two female colleagues received a bigger share of the applause (Stoltz especially – Ascanio's second-act aria was the hit of the opera). The role, he decided, gave him too little chance to shine. The last straw was a mishap which occurred at the third performance, as he recalled many years later in his autobiography:

> We know that Berlioz's talent, fine musician though he was, was not exactly a melodic one. *Cellini*, like his other works, was written in a style which to my Italian-trained ears sounded very strange. When this opera appeared I was on the point of becoming a father for the third time. On the evening of the third performance I set out from home, leaving Mme Duprez in imminent expectation of the happy event – a fact which, as may be imagined, put me in some degree of agitation. Having had two daughters I particularly wanted a son; and as I left the house I begged Dr Gasnault [. . .] to come and inform me if my wife was brought to bed of a boy. While I was on stage in the last act I perceived my faithful doctor in the wings, his face radiant. My delight caused me to forget myself. When one loses one's place in music as learned and complicated as Berlioz's it is not easy to find it again. I came out of the business none too well.

Next day he announced that he was standing down.

He was roughly handled by the press. Even journals which had not liked the work deplored his "mauvaise action". "Duprez has just indulged in a coup d'état at the Opéra", wrote the *Monde dramatique*. "Why so, you will ask. Because our tenor was not applauded and encored and called back after the performance and crowned like a Roman gladiator. His vainglorious caprice is an open insult to Berlioz, a serious affront to the public and an act of rebellion against the director. If everyone had not gone mad and treated Duprez like a grand seigneur when he 'condescended' to succeed Nourrit, none of this would have happened." *Benvenuto Cellini* was stopped in its tracks. There was no understudy. Alexis Dupont, Duprez's replacement, had to learn the part from scratch.

Berlioz, resilient as ever, contrived to remain hopeful. Hostile critics might demonstrate his disregard of "the fundamental laws of art", but his peers believed in him: Paganini, who was at the first night, leading the applause; Hugo, who wrote, "You have done a fine and noble thing. I am still full of all that I have heard. Sing, you who were made to sing, and let them shout who were made to shout"; Liszt who, in Florence, ruminating on the steps of the Loggia dei Lanzi before the moonlit statue of Perseus, wrote in the *Gazette*, "Honour to you, Berlioz, for you too fight with invincible courage, and if you have yet to tame the Gorgon, if the snakes still hiss round your feet and threaten you with their hideous forked tongues, if envy, stupidity, malignity, treachery seem only to crowd more densely about you, fear not – the gods are with you; they gave you, as they gave Perseus, helmet, wings, shield and blade: that is, energy, swiftness, wisdom and strength."

After everything that the opposition could do, the work still stood its ground. "Impossible to tell you," Berlioz wrote to his father, "all the plots and cabals, the arguments, the duels my work has given rise to." It was a free-for-all, in which his defenders talked almost as much nonsense as his detractors. "The French have a mania for arguing about music, without having the first idea, or any feeling for it. That was so in the last century, it is so now and always will be. The important thing is that I should be heard frequently, very frequently; I count on my score to set me to rights more than on anything that may be said in its favour." The performances were being interrupted while Dupont learned his part. "But after that, the Opéra's repertoire is arranged in such a way that I shall be played much more often with Dupont than I would have been with Duprez."

But he deluded himself. Even when Dupont knew the role (which took longer than expected) there were further delays. The director, who had not even bothered to come to the first performance, was in no hurry for the fourth. It was not billed until 21 November, nine weeks after the third, and was cancelled at the last minute when one of the singers was indisposed. There was talk of giving the work on the 28th, and again on 2 December, but no performance. After that, silence till 7 January, then again a postponement, and finally on the 11th a performance, well enough received but taking only about 3,000 francs; and after that the fate reserved for the more interesting of the operas that had not caught on: an isolated act followed by a ballet. Act 1 was heard in February and March, twice with *The Gipsy* and once with *Le diable boiteux*. Another performance was spoken of, but nothing came of it. Then silence once more, this time for good.

The performance of single acts was, of course, a long-unhallowed custom of the Paris Opéra. No one but Meyerbeer was too grand to be subjected to it (even he could not prevent cuts being made when he was not there). Hence the story of Rossini accosted on the boulevard by the beaming director – "Maestro, we are performing the fourth act of your *William Tell* tonight" – and making his famous riposte, "What! All of it?" But *William Tell* was an established work which, whatever the indignity of such treatment, was not ultimately harmed by it. *Benvenuto Cellini* still needed nurturing by a committed director who was prepared to take a risk at the box office. Duponchel was not committed, nor resolute enough to stand by any commitment he might have felt. The picture of him given in the *Memoirs* and *Evenings in the Orchestra* is of the archetypally ignorant, infatuated opera director, the director who in Barzun's phrase "knows nothing about music but can smell out his natural enemy": a man at once indecisive and full of self-esteem, and in any case much more interested in the décor. He evidently regarded *Benvenuto*, like *Esmeralda*, as the price that had to be paid for the good will of the Bertins, a price which he kept as low as he prudently could. He liked the libretto – which suggests an unconventional streak – but had no time for the score, and complained in his languid way, when the musicians began to come round to it, "We're now told Berlioz's music is charming – it appears our ridiculous orchestra is lauding it to the skies." Berlioz seems to have been slow to grasp the fundamental fact, crucial to the future of his opera, that the director would do nothing to prolong its life, if indeed he was not actively hastening its end. Not unnaturally, he needed to believe that it had a future, that the work which was the most advanced and brilliant he had yet written would catch on, given a chance. It took him a long time to accept that his hopes for a success at the Opéra, the goal of his greatest ambitions, lay in the dust, with all that that meant for his career and for the long-awaited upturn in his material fortunes.

By November 1838 his health had given way, and he went down with acute bronchitis, his resistance sapped by the accumulated strain of the past seven or eight months – the strain, for someone of his temperament, of so much suppressed anger, of having to listen to the director lecture him on the art of music, of having to tolerate the Opéra's lackadaisical manner of work and appear not to mind the usual whispering campaign or "the *bons mots* of the tenor and the prima donna (at which the wretched composer is obliged to laugh heartily, with death in his heart)", and the necessity of keeping a good front as disaster loomed. He was ill on and off throughout the winter. Money problems which he had hoped his opera would relieve were so bad that he again had to resort to borrowing. Auguste Morel, his friend on the *Journal de Paris*, was asked to see if he could arrange a loan with their mutual friend Lecourt, the Marseille lawyer, and for the second time that year Berlioz sought the good offices of his brother-in-law Camille Pal.

There remained the resource of concerts. Nothing had come of the St Cecilia's Day performance of the *Fête musicale funèbre* apparently planned for that year – the whole project remains a mystery – but two other concerts were organized at the Conservatoire, scheduled for 18 November and 2 December, then put off till the 25th and the 16th on account of his illness.

Because Berlioz was confined to the house during the weeks leading up to both events, all the usual ticket arrangements with the Conservatoire accountant François Réty had to be transacted by letter. As a result we have a glimpse of one more side of the business of freelance concert-giving:

23 November [1838]

This is my final request for tickets [for the concert of 25 November]. Please send me two 1st-tier boxes with four places, or one with six, two 2nd-tier with 4, one ground-floor box, 2 stalls and two pit seats. In addition Alizard [bass] and Desmarest [cellist] will be coming to ask you for tickets for themselves.

30 November [1838]

If you have received the tickets for my second concert, please have sent on to me by messenger:

12 seats, 1st-tier boxes
12 2nd-tier
12 ground floor

They are for selling and are wanted as soon as possible. I would also like you to send Schlesinger his whole bundle of tickets, as you did the first time.

8 December [1838]

Please, dear M. Réty, have the three enclosed posters displayed at Mme Klotz's concert tomorrow. I've given instructions not to have the concert billed in Paris until Monday because of tomorrow's performance at the Opéra. I also need, for the newspapers:

2 1st-tier boxes
4 2nd-tier
3 ground-floor

5 gallery seats
5 orchestra
and 10 pit
Affectionately,

H. Berlioz

I'm altogether better, I shall be going out any moment now.

It wouldn't be a bad idea, as well, to distribute a few programmes in the boxes tomorrow.

He had recovered enough to conduct the second concert, on 16 December. At the first, on 25 November, his place was taken by Habeneck, who conducted a revised programme including the Fantastic Symphony and two of the most successful numbers from *Benvenuto Cellini*, Teresa's aria and Ascanio's from Act 2 – sung, as at the Opéra, by Mmes Dorus-Gras (back from the provinces) and Stoltz – but excluding the planned extracts from Gluck's *Alceste*, which Berlioz was determined to conduct himself. Afterwards his friends came to the house in force to congratulate him, and stayed till late. Despite his absence the concert had been a success. It brought three benefits in addition: a gift of 500 francs from the Duc d'Orléans; a new friend and kindred spirit in the Hungarian pianist and composer Stephen Heller, lately arrived in Paris, who wrote enthusiastically in the *Gazette* of his first encounter with Berlioz's strange, thrilling music; and an invitation from the president of the Philharmonic Society of London, Lord Burghersh, who was at the concert, to spend two months in London putting on both his symphonies. The money was tempting; but after what his Paris friends had told him of the massacre of the *Francs-juges* overture at the Argyll Rooms he was wary. The English were "execrable musicians, who refuse to rehearse, yet like the Italians take it for granted that they are the world's premier virtuosi". Berlioz's prejudice was not entirely unfounded; and it would be nearly ten years before he was induced to test its accuracy for himself.

The Duc d'Orléans had not attended the concert nor apparently been invited; but his gift was a not unexpected bonus, since Berlioz had been to see him shortly before to present him with the full score of the Requiem, published that autumn. He reported to Adèle on 9 October that though priced rather high the work was selling well.

The same letter told of the excitement of everyone at 31 Rue de Londres at the impending arrival of Prosper Berlioz – for he was coming at last. "Harriet is greatly looking forward to having him as her squire and showing him Paris, and Louis asks every day if he's come and whether he'll be going hunting with him." Prosper, aged eighteen, arrived in mid-October, with a younger companion, the fourteen-year-old Alexandre Rocher. The two boys were installed at the Pension Babil, a private boarding-school in the Rue Notre-Dame-des-Champs, in the south-west of Paris between the Boulevard Montparnasse and the Jardin du Luxembourg.

So little was remembered about the shadowy young man whose entry in his father's Livre de Raison has an enigmatic question-mark beside it, and whose life belied his name, that legend took the place of fact. It was said, much later, that Prosper was given the piano lessons denied his brother, that he had ambitions of becoming a composer, that he taught himself the harp; that on his return to La Côte St André for the Christmas holidays he reproduced from memory whole passages from his brother's opera; that after being assumed to be backward he was found to have an exceptional gift for mathematics.

His complete absence from the *Memoirs* led the early biographers who passed on these legends to accuse Berlioz of cold-hearted indifference to Prosper's fate – an example of the danger of making deductions from negative evidence; for it is clear from the many letters not available to Hippeau and others in the 1870s and 1880s that Berlioz was fond of his brother and took his interests to heart. The correspondence of the 1830s, beginning with the long letter to his father from Rome about Prosper's problems and about provincial education in general,* speaks of him quite often and always sympathetically. Nothing survives from Prosper's first five weeks in Paris; but on 26 November Berlioz wrote to tell his father that his brother was

> working hard; the man in charge of his studies told me several times that he was very pleased with him. You know we've always got on extremely well, my brother and I; I can assure you that I have his complete trust, and that the best way to obtain it is to show that one trusts him. He complains of being surrounded exclusively by small boys. I don't know if it was expressly for that reason that you placed him in this institution. He needs blankets; he freezes in bed. He would also like to have a room of his own to work in, as one or two others do. I find him more advanced

---

* See Vol. 1, pp. 530–32.

than I expected. His mind is quite well stocked. I think my sisters judged him too severely. His is not a quick wit, but it's one that is going to develop sooner or later in a really remarkable way. He's beside himself with delight when I take him out, and it's a joy for me to see him.

Ten days later, "Prosper, I repeat, is in need of blankets. You imagine that boarding-school directors do what they're supposed to; but in fact those poor children have to fight every evening over a single *mattress-cover*, which they take it in turns to have on their beds."

There is no further mention of blankets, so presumably they were supplied. What remains obscure is how and when Prosper heard *Benvenuto Cellini*. An oral tradition still alive at La Côte St André in the early 1900s maintained that he and Alexandre Rocher were given tickets for the revival on 11 January 1839, from which the older boy came back in a state of feverish excitement, and spent the night pacing up and down the room (which he shared with Alexandre), singing passages from the opera. He could not subsequently have played them on a piano at La Côte – four days after the performance he was dead. The recollections of his brother's score must have been picked out on a piano at the school, the incident being reported by Alexandre Rocher and later transposed to La Côte. One way or another, it remains possible that Prosper was the first member of the Berlioz family to hear Hector's music.

He may well have been at the Conservatoire on Sunday afternoon, 16 December for his brother's concert – the culmination of all those that Berlioz had put on in the hall in the past few seasons. Together with some smaller pieces, it comprised his two symphonies and, between them, music by the great forebear who had revealed to him his vocation: the scene between Alceste and the High Priest from Gluck's opera (with Mme Stoltz and Alizard) and the grand aria for Alceste from the end of Act 1.

If Prosper was there, it is not difficult to imagine why Berlioz should have failed to mention it in his letters. Everything was eclipsed by the extraordinary incident which occurred immediately after the concert, and by its even more sensational sequel.

Paganini was in the audience. It was the first time he had heard *Harold*, the symphony with viola obbligato that he had called into being. At the conclusion he came up on to the platform with his twelve-year-old son Achille, his interpreter (for cancer of the throat had made his voice almost inaudible), and, gesticulating wildly, accosted Berlioz at the orchestra door as he was going backstage. Motioning to Achille to climb on a chair, he spoke into his ear. The boy turned to Berlioz: "My father says he is so moved and overwhelmed, he could go down on his knees to you." On Berlioz's protesting, Paganini whispered "Yes, yes!" and clutching his arm drew him back to the platform where, amid the musicians gathering up their instruments, he knelt and kissed his hand.

What followed was stranger still. Standing talking to Armand Bertin in the cold, damp air of the street Berlioz caught a chill and was still in bed two mornings later, when Achille Paganini put his head round the door. The boy handed him a note, then went out again immediately. Thinking it a simple letter of congratulation, he opened it and read: "*Beethoven spento, non c'era che Berlioz che potesse farlo revivere*: Beethoven being dead, only Berlioz could make him live again; and I, who have enjoyed your divine compositions, worthy of the genius that you are, beg you to accept as token of my homage 20,000 francs, which will be remitted to you by Baron Rothschild on your presenting the enclosed. Ever your affectionate friend Nicolò Paganini."*

> Imagine what I felt on reading the opening phrase – and then the cheque for twenty thousand francs, offered like that! Harriet, coming into the room just at that moment and seeing me in tears with a letter in my hand, supposed I had had bad news. "What is it? Has something gone wrong? Don't despair." "No – quite the opposite . . . Paganini –" "Yes?" "He's written to me . . . Do you realize what he's sent? Twenty thousand francs!" "My God! is it possible?" She got me to translate the letter, then ran to fetch our son who was playing in the next room, calling out, "Louis, come here, come, come and thank God for what He has done for your father." And mother and child both knelt by the bed.

News of Paganini's homage spread through musical and literary Paris like fire. The Théâtre de la Renaissance promptly staged a reconstruction of the already celebrated scene at the Conservatoire. Messages of felicitation poured in, and a few abusive letters (one of them begging Berlioz to blow his brains out: if it had been Rome, he told Liszt, he would have been assassinated). His room was never empty of visitors, including some who had not favoured him with a word before but

---

* 20,000 francs = about £10,000 or $16,000 today.

were now to be counted among his oldest supporters. Friends were "re-emerging from under the paving-stones"; enemies "bite their lips" and "try, vainly, to devalue the great artist's noble action, which they either will not or cannot comprehend". The *Gazette* reproduced Paganini's letter and Berlioz's reply in facsimile, together with one from Janin to Berlioz lauding the generosity of the incomparable violinist – a generosity "greater than that of any king or minister or even of any other European artists, the world's true kings". Janin had enjoyed himself savaging Paganini in the past. But "from now on" he was "inviolable"; he had given Berlioz "three years of leisure, and the time to make a masterpiece".

The weather was still so cold and foggy that Berlioz was forced to stay indoors on the 18th and 19th. On the 20th he deposited the cheque at Rothschild's bank in the Rue Lafitte. His first call, however, was at the Néothermes in the nearby Rue de la Victoire, where Paganini was staying. He found him alone in the billiard room, and they hugged each other in silence, their eyes overflowing with tears.

> He wept, this man-eater, this murderer of women, this ex-convict, as he's always being called – he shed hot tears as he embraced me. "Not a word", he said, stopping me; "no merit of mine: I have had the most profound satisfaction of my life – you have given me emotions that I never imagined – you have carried further the great art of Beethoven." Then, wiping his eyes and striking the table, he gave a strange laugh and began talking volubly, but as I couldn't follow what he was saying he fetched his son to act as his interpreter, and then with the help of little Achille I understood him. "I am so happy, so happy, when I think that all those vermin who wrote and spoke against you won't be so bold now. For no one can say that I don't know what's what, or that I am an easy touch."

"Many people still refuse to believe it." Berlioz himself was certainly well aware of the gossip, innocent and otherwise, that soon began to circulate, casting doubt on the truth of the incident. The story told by Liszt many years later – that Paganini made the gesture, which he could easily afford, on the advice of Janin, in order to reinstate himself in the good graces of the Paris public, which had taken to boycotting his concerts, whereupon he played eight times to full houses – refutes itself: Paganini had long given up playing in public. But it is symptomatic of a deep-seated reluctance, from whatever motive, to accept such an improbable and even irritating event at face value. The man's reputation for miserliness was a natural pretext for Parisian scepticism.

Less obviously concocted is the story Hallé claimed to have had from Mme Bertin: that the actual donor was Armand Bertin, and Paganini merely lent his name. "What would have been a simple *gracieuseté* from a rich and powerful editor to one of his staff became a significant tribute from one genius to another, and had a colossal *retentissement*." This version is, at any rate, feasible. Armand Bertin was undoubtedly concerned at his protégé's financial difficulties and on many occasions tried to use his influence on his behalf. During his conversation with Berlioz in the street after the concert, the idea could have occurred to him – to enlist Paganini's aid in a benevolent fiction which the violinist's fame would make doubly beneficial to Berlioz. But it seems unlikely, to say the least, that such a man as Paganini should agree to act as front for another's philanthropy, and far less out of character that he should be stirred to a sudden act of generosity by the music of a fellow-artist whose work he already admired and whose position had been further weakened by the reception of his opera, which Paganini had witnessed at first hand. His own explanation, given to Morel in an interview published in the *Journal de Paris* a few weeks later, has the ring of sincerity:

> I did it for Berlioz and for myself. For Berlioz because I saw a young man of genius whose courage and strength might in the end have broken in the daily unremitting struggle against jealous mediocrity, ignorance and indifference, and I thought: I can help him. For myself because one day I shall be given credit for it, and when my claims to musical glory are reckoned up it will not be the smallest of them that I was the first who recognized a man of genius and pointed him out to the admiration of all.

For Berlioz the gesture was a godsend of inestimable value. Coming at the end of a year of successive reverses, and so soon after the bruising campaign for *Benvenuto Cellini*, it lifted his morale and his sense of his own worth to the heights and gave him hope. The money brought benefits as great and more tangible: if not the "three years of leisure" that Janin grandly invoked, then the means to throw off the entire burden of debt which had weighed on him and Harriet since their wedding, the possibility to plan and carry out the long-desired visit to Germany, and the time to make a masterpiece.

8

"Speak, My Orchestra"

How great a godsend is easily demonstrated. Of Paganini's 20,000 francs, half went instantly on overdue bills and loans. They had been that deeply in debt: not simply to friends like Legouvé and Edouard Rocher, who, though Berlioz disliked being unable to repay them, were not demanding creditors, but to the moneylenders he had resorted to in the five years since his marriage. That constant nightmare was now banished. He had the inestimable pleasure of settling every one of them; he could also tell those with whom he had been negotiating for loans that there was no need after all.

Of the 10,000 francs left, a thousand or so went on rounding off the accounts of his two concerts and making a few much needed domestic purchases, among them "a new dress and hat for Harriet, a suit of clothes for Louis, and for myself two cravats, repair of my black suit, a work-table and cardboard files, and a bookcase for my scores". The rest was deposited at Rothschild's at 4 per cent interest.

It was not only sorrows, he told Adèle, that came "not single spies" as Shakespeare said, but blessings as well. Paganini's gift was followed a day or two later by the news of his appointment as deputy curator of the Conservatoire Library, the curator of which, his friend Bottée de Toulmon, held his post unpaid. This was the library where, sixteen years before, he had discovered the secrets of music and where, as he pored over *Alceste*, he was accosted by Cherubini and chased round the table by the Conservatoire porter Hottin – now his faithful orchestral attendant and a devoted fan.

We do not know who was instrumental in getting him the job – Bottée, the Bertins, Montalivet, or a combination of them – nor what went on behind the scenes during the seven weeks that elapsed before the appointment was made official, on 9 February 1839. The salary, which he had been led to believe would be 2,000, turned out to be 500 less (Tiersot remarks, "Thus at the age of thirty-six [thirty-five] Berlioz has an assured income of 1,500 francs"). It was, however, backdated to the beginning of the year.

Cherubini, or whoever it was (Berton, Berlioz's ancient adversary, was also a member of the appointments panel), made sure it was not he that succeeded to the chair of composition left vacant by the death of Paër in May, but Carafa. Paër, however, had been a member of the Institute and director of the king's private music, and Berlioz, ever-hopeful, thought he might still get something from the resulting flux. Auber was favourite to inherit the royal office but might in consequence resign the similar position he held with the Duc d'Orléans, who could well give it to him instead. He also put his name down for the Institute, though without much expectation – his main rivals, Onslow and Adam, had been candidates twice before – but withdrew on learning that Spontini had applied. It was Spontini who was elected. And nothing came of the other possibility: Auber stayed and occupied both posts. What he did get was the Légion d'honneur. In May, in the same batch as Duponchel, the director of the Opéra – bizarre juxtaposition – he was made Chevalier: a "banal honour" which had no value in his eyes (he told his father) except that he had "never done anything to solicit it", and which he owed to the begetter and dedicatee of the Requiem, the Comte de Gasparin, once again briefly at the Ministry of the Interior. It was probably around this time, in the winter of 1838–9, that Armand Bertin and Montalivet devised the plan mentioned in the *Memoirs*, to override Cherubini's opposition and secure him a professorship of composition plus a pension from the ministerial fund for the encouragement of the arts, the two making an income of 6,000 francs: a plan duly frustrated by bureaucratic delays and Montalivet's subsequent departure from the Ministry. As such démarches show, Berlioz and his supporters were well aware that Paganini's munificence had fundamentally altered nothing. He was still in need of a regular settled income that did not come from journalism and that gave him the security to be a composer and to compose.*

For the moment, however, he had what he needed: release from the fragmenting pressure of material anxieties, liberty, unimpeded scope for the imagination, freedom to create a major work – Paganini's work.

---

* Another salaried position he had hoped he might get, but didn't, was that of inspector-general of music education in primary schools.

The two men discussed the project while Paganini was still in Paris, and then corresponded about it after he left for Marseille in the last week of December with the parting words, "Adieu . . . aimez-moi!" Berlioz submitted various ideas (one of them, perhaps, for the symphony on Schiller's *Maid of Orleans* that we know of from a later source); but, as he must have expected, Paganini declined to make the choice for him. "You know best what will suit you."

He chose a symphony on *Romeo and Juliet*. "Symphonie dramatique" the title-page of the full score designates it, "with chorus, soloists, and prologue in choral recitative, dedicated to Nicolò Paganini and composed after Shakespeare's tragedy". Such a work had been lurking in his imagination for many years: if not since the first night of the English company's production in September 1827, then certainly since a year or two later, after Beethoven had revealed to him the dramatic potential of the symphonic medium and especially after he had got to know the Ninth from the full score in the Conservatoire Library. Emile Deschamps, who wrote the verses for the vocal movements in *Romeo*, recalled their discussing the project together in the late 1820s. By the time Berlioz inscribed Juliet's "How if, when I am laid into the tomb" above Cleopatra's "Grands Pharaons" in the Prix de Rome cantata of July 1829, he had, he said, "often imagined a musical setting" of that awestruck monologue. And even if the two themes in the symphony's second movement which come from the *Sardanapale* cantata of 1830 – the larghetto for solo oboe and the main dance melody – were not first conceived for a *Romeo and Juliet* work and then made use of for the Prix de Rome score (as I think they were), the idea of a large-scale composition on the play was certainly not forgotten during the next few years. Seeing Bellini's *Montecchi e Capuleti* in Florence on the way to Rome, in late February 1831, and noting what he felt it lacked – the whole Shakespearean atmosphere and so many essential features of the play – helped define for him what a true *Romeo* score should be like.*
His ideas veered towards opera, but not for long. The following June he was thinking of an orchestral scherzo on Mercutio's Queen Mab speech and mentioning the idea to Mendelssohn as they rode in the Campagna. The whole work ripened (in the words of the *Memoirs*) under "the blue Italian sky". According to Auguste Barbier, Berlioz discussed some kind of musical *Romeo and Juliet* with him when they

* See Vol. 1, pp. 446–7.

met at the Villa Medici in 1832. Even the possibility of using the antique cymbals discovered at Pompeii, which add an extra glitter to the scherzo, may have occurred to him before he left Italy.

Thus when, in January 1839, he settled on a symphonic treatment of the play, it sealed the direction his thoughts had long taken. The choice was not influenced by the fate of *Benvenuto Cellini*, nor would it have gone the other way if the opera had been a success. Even if things had been quite different and Berlioz free to fulfil his ambitions as an opera composer, he would still have devoted creative energy to the development of the dramatic concert work; that was always going to be a central preoccupation from the moment he discovered Beethoven. Casting *Romeo and Juliet* as a symphony – a symphony of a new kind – was in no sense a *pis aller*. It was the way he wanted it. What happened to *Benvenuto* only confirmed a decision already taken. The Opéra as it was, with the attitudes it enshrined and the singers it had, was no place for so sacred a theme. His view of the place was summed up in a letter of April 1839 written in reply to a fellow Gluck enthusiast about the possibility of the Opéra's putting on one of Gluck's works. "Given the state of the performing forces at that bazaar which goes by the name of theatre, it would be a profanation. You have no idea what atrocities are committed there. Music and drama are dragged through the mud." Perhaps if Nourrit and Falcon had still been in the company, an operatic *Romeo and Juliet* might not have been totally out of the question. Even then it would have required an ethos, and a management, utterly unlike the reality. The choice, in any case, was a positive one. By its "very sublimity" (he would later write) the passion of the two lovers and their utterances – the heart and *raison d'être* of the work – had to be expressed in "the language of instruments, a language richer, more varied, less restricted and by its very vagueness incomparably more potent" in such a context. "Speak then, my orchestra!"

He drew up a plan, and wrote out in prose the text of the music to be sung and gave it to Deschamps to put into verse. Deschamps had been involved in the project from its inception, and was at work on a French translation of the play; he was the obvious collaborator (given that Berlioz, distrustful of his own literary ability, still felt he needed one). The verse text seems to have evolved gradually over the first six months of 1839. While it was taking shape, Berlioz began with the first of the orchestral movements, "Roméo seul – Tristesse – Bruit lointain de concert et de bal – Grande Fête chez Capulet"; the manuscript is inscribed "begun 24 January [1839]". By 8 September, seven and a half months later, the score was complete.

In the *Memoirs* he recalled those months as a time virtually free of journalism – "no more newspaper articles, or very few" – during which he could give himself undistracted to his score and live the "ardent existence" of its full-time composer. That was how he remembered it. It was his first large-scale Shakespearean composition, the fruit of many years' reading and reliving the play. He was re-creating in music the impressions of that ineffaceable evening at the Odéon when for the second time he was branded by the flame of Shakespeare's genius, and his eyes, "of a pale intense grey" (as Armand de Pontmartin observed them), were "fixed on Juliet" with an "expression of ecstasy" into which "body and soul were entirely absorbed".

In prosaic actuality he did not renounce journalism while he was writing *Romeo and Juliet*. What gave him the sense of liberation that he remembered was – as always, on the rare occasions when it occurred – the fact of not being tied to it for a living. The tally of articles is actually larger than for 1840, though smaller than for 1838. What we find, however, when looking at the incidence of feuilletons during the months of the symphony's composition, are long periods of relative or almost total inactivity which would have made it possible for him (as he said) "not to break off for more than three or four days in thirty". March and April were busy months for the music critic of the *Journal des débats* and even more for the regular contributor to the *Gazette*, but February and May were nearly clear, as was August, and in the ten weeks from late May to early August he wrote only one article; between 19 June and 9 August there was nothing by him in any journal. The critic was active again in September and October, by which time the score was finished and work on it had shifted to the preparation of chorus and orchestra parts. November, the month of rehearsals and première, was again completely free.

It is likely that the most concentrated creative work, or at any rate the first rush of ideas, occurred in February. By May the "fever of my choral symphony on Shakespeare's *Romeo*", he told his father, had passed; by then everything was "so precisely mapped" that he was writing with a kind of objectivity, "like a copyist". The adagio, the Scène d'amour, demanded patient, laborious working out, not only because of its importance, placed structurally and spiritually at the centre of the work, and because the emotions it expressed "moved him too much", but also because of its novelty of form, an introduction-cum-exposition leading to a rondo (the theme of which is made from phrases of Juliet's and Romeo's themes combined, symbolizing their union). The Queen Mab scherzo, on the other hand, I imagine coming into being in a flash and, for all its originality of conception and sound and its delicate brilliance – its subtle equivalence of Mercutio's fantasy (what Kemp has called "the lightness, the exquisite pictures, the quicksilver changes, the spirit of delight and of threatened violence") – being composed at a gallop.

The fifth movement, the Convoi funèbre, was written in late June; a draft of it is dated the 25th. At the end of July he was once again in a state of "exaltation", this time over the finale. Its composition, like the adagio's, involved protracted labour. By contrast, the Tomb Scene, the last movement to be written, in some ways the most startling and prophetic music he ever wrote, was surely composed at white heat in a burst of sustained compositional excitement. It is the direct reliving in music of what he saw on the stage of the Odéon twelve years before, when Kemble and Harriet Smithson played the star-crossed lovers and the production ended with their deaths – in the Garrick version (in which Juliet wakes from her drugged sleep before the poison has killed Romeo). He had never forgotten it.

> At the name of "Romeo", breathed out faintly from the lips of the reviving Juliet, the young Montague stands motionless, riveted. As the voice calls a second time, more tenderly, he turns towards the tomb. He gazes at her: there is movement. He can no longer doubt it – she is living. He flings himself on the funeral couch, snatches up the beloved body, tearing away veils and shrouds, carries it to the front of the stage and holds it upright in his arms. Juliet looks dully about her from sleep-drugged eyes. Romeo calls her name; he clasps her in a desperate embrace, parts the hair hiding her pale forehead, covers her face with kisses, laughing convulsively. In his heart-rending delight he has forgotten that he is dying. Juliet breathes deeply. Juliet! Juliet! But a stab of agony recalls him: the poison is at work, devouring his vitals. "O potent poison! Capulet, Capulet, forbear!" He crawls on his knees. Delirious, he imagines he sees Juliet's father come once more to take her from him.

In reliving it Berlioz was again the "real Romeo" of his letter to Albert Du Boys written near the beginning of his courtship of Miss Smithson. Romeo is the dominant figure in the symphony. The music of the Tomb Scene is, while he still lives, much more his than Juliet's; even when the lovers are, briefly, reunited it is his emotions and his physical exaltations and agonies that the hectic, garish texture and frantic love themes, and their subsequent collapse, express rather than hers. And in the Scène d'amour's rondo theme, created jointly from the music of their separate avowals, his melody with its passionate concluding phrases (Wagner called it the melody of the nineteenth century) is the leading voice.

No music that he had yet written, not even the Fantastic Symphony, had sprung from so deep within his innermost soul and drawn so fully on his "heart's book inscribed on every page" (to borrow one of the lines by Victor Hugo that he added as epigraph to the Fantastic). Did this intense identification with his score make the vexations and difficulties of living more difficult and more vexing whenever he emerged from the all-consuming world of *Romeo* into "the light of common day"?

It is possible to pick out spasms of exasperation from his letters. He writes with uncharacteristic sharpness to his sister Adèle, who was insisting that there was no good reason why he shouldn't absent himself from Paris in order to attend her wedding; though he waits a day or two to give his anger time to cool, he still takes heated exception to her homilies. In a letter to his father he speaks of the frequent rages he is obliged to contain. In another, to Nancy, "Harriet is ill again, I've just sent the doctor a note; I've no idea what it is. Louis has been pretty unbearable these last few days." A couple of weeks later he cannot conceal his irritation at what he considers Harriet's overreaction to the presence in the next apartment of a madwoman who keeps banging on the wall and inveighing against "that wicked Englishwoman". "It is exceedingly tiresome; but it's a waste of time to try reasoning with my wife about it; she was becoming quite hysterical and going into really alarming palpitations." So Harriet and Louis have gone to stay at the Hôtel Bedford with their friend Mme Lawson. "For me, coming and going all day [preparing for the performance of *Romeo*], this fresh distraction is just what I don't need."

We should not make too much of all this, however. The last two outbursts date from after the completion of the symphony. And once fully launched on a major composition Berlioz could detach himself from his surroundings and let his inner mechanism take over, and, equally, come back to earth and take up everyday affairs when he had to. These texts can be balanced by others that show him in excellent spirits.

Grave events in 1839 marked his life outside *Romeo*. Prosper died on 15 January and was buried in the Montparnasse cemetery.

The circumstances of his death, apparently from typhoid, are tenuous. There are no letters from Berlioz to his family between 20 December and 1 March, and only two to La Côte, both to Edouard Rocher, the first written on 9 January, which ends: "I leave you, to go and see my brother, who is still ill", the second, a couple of weeks later, mentioning his end. But for a letter from Nancy Clappier and one six months later from Adèle in Paris, sent after she had visited the Pension Babil and been to see Prosper's grave, there would be no record of the family's reaction to his death. Shortly after Prosper died Harriet went down with acute pneumonia and was so ill he feared she too would not survive. In March Adolphe Nourrit committed suicide, jumping from the balcony of his hotel in Naples after a successful performance at the opera. His body, brought back to Paris, was buried in Montmartre on 11 May. No one had been delegated by the Opéra or by the Conservatoire to pronounce his funeral oration. But Chopin played the organ at the service and there was an enormous gathering of artists, friends and admirers, overflowing the church on to the porch and the street outside. Berlioz described it to his father in a letter written immediately after his return from the cemetery. "Oh what a sad, sad ceremony! The church of St Roch crammed, on all sides people unable to restrain their sobs, women fainting, his brothers, brothers-in-law and friends choking with grief, Dérivis *père* quite overcome – old Orestes has lost his Pylades. The clergy had been very accommodating, out of regard for poor Adolphe's well-known religious convictions. His humanitarian dreams made him popular with the workers, and there were a lot of them at the graveside. All that farrago of theatre, theology, republicanism and love of absolute dominion in art is to my mind quite extraordinarily absurd. But it interests and excites many who knew the unfortunate man intimately; I am one of those who did."

In April Adèle, aged twenty-four, married a local notary, Marc Suat, a friend of Berlioz's friend Alexandre Figuet-Dufeuillant. The wedding was celebrated in the church at La Côte by the same M. Petit, almoner of the Convent of the Visitation, who had taken Berlioz to his first communion, and where Adèle, like Nancy, had been a boarder. Dr Berlioz and his elder daughter thought she could have done better; and

Nancy's and Camille's supposedly low opinion of M. Suat would be the cause of friction between the two sisters – the elder inclined to be bossy and the younger quick to take offence – for many years to come. But it was a happy marriage, the happiest of any member of the family.

The coolness between Adèle and her brother was only momentary. He and Harriet sent her (she told Nancy) "an elegant casket full of everything you can imagine that is most fashionable and complete in the way of pens, paper, seal, paper-knife, ruler, and all with my monogram on, and under the work-tray a drawer with a charming blotter in it. [. . .] This keepsake from Hector has delighted me, though I can't help thinking his wife had a lot to do with the details of the present; in the midst of his preoccupations Hector wouldn't have had a mind for all that – impossible!" Adèle had meanwhile sent him and Harriet a present of a complete teaset, which could not have been more welcome: when Ferrand and his brother had been in Paris recently they had to borrow cups and spoons to serve tea to them. She had also spoken of a possible visit by her husband and herself to Paris, and of a return visit by Louis, rising five, to his grandfather at La Côte. Harriet's first reaction was one of

> pride at sending my poor father so handsome a boy; then tears came at the inconceivable idea of their being separated, and finally, as it's a long time ahead and he'll be bigger then, she's more or less decided in favour. But you will come and fetch him. He's the most charming and the most appallingly badly brought up child I know. He threatens everybody with his sabre and calls them rude names when he's checked; he swears like – like his father. The day before yesterday he cut open my mattress with a bayonet stroke – he got hold of my National Guard equipment. And with it all he is charming. He's enchanted at the notion of picking strawberries and peaches with his grandfather, but I don't know how he would take his parents' absence: he can't be parted from them for an evening without crying.

Family visits were in the air. While Adèle hesitated before the momentous step of a trip to the capital and begged Nancy and Dr Berlioz to decide for her, Hector wrote to his father to ask "what solid reason" he could have for not coming to Paris. "At the beginning of winter your presence is no longer required at La Côte, the wine harvest is done by then and you are free. Louis talks about you all the time and asks why he can't see you. I think you would be delighted with the child; but as for sending him to you, as my sister asked me the other day, I fear many things make it impossible, most of them to do with him. He doesn't want to lose sight of us, and when his mother and I have to go out without him he gets in such a frantic state that one almost fears for his life." If only his father would make the journey! If he came in November he would hear *Romeo and Juliet "under my direction* – for there's really no alternative to conducting the orchestra myself": under another conductor, no matter how intelligent and dedicated, it was not the same thing at all.

It may have been partly this consideration that led him, some time in the spring, to take the drastic step of himself removing *Benvenuto Cellini* from the repertoire of the Opéra: he could not bear it to be performed any longer in that "approximate" fashion which, for him, was tantamount to "totally wrong". He wrote to Duponchel: "I have the honour to inform you that I am *withdrawing my opera Benvenuto*. This will, I am persuaded, give you pleasure." Yet it is by no means certain that the work was by then condemned beyond reprieve, nor that in the eyes of the operatic authorities Berlioz was a composer with no future. The revival on 11 January was a modest success – the takings below average but better than for some operas. Similarly, the issue by Schlesinger of nine "morceaux détachés", some quite substantial, beginning with the offstage serenade and ending with "Sur les monts", though no substitute for the publication of the complete vocal score was a lot better than nothing. Another performance was announced for the 23rd, and then cancelled because Dupont was ill. A month later (when Ferrand was in the audience) it was – as we have noted – cut down to the first act followed by a ballet. The formula was a commonplace of the time. One can see, however, that it was not for Berlioz, and that withdrawing the work was the only reasonable option. He had finally accepted defeat. As he said to Legouvé, when offering him the dedication of the overture, "I have not been able to inscribe on my work, as Benvenuto did on his, 'If anyone dishonour thee, I shall be thy avenger.' Such an undertaking would have been too much for me – Cellini himself would not have been equal to it." Yet operatic projects were still being dangled before him. Even Duponchel, ever indecisive, does not seem to have written him off. Swayed perhaps by the pamphlet – it was more like a book, all of 350 pages – which d'Ortigue had written in support of *Benvenuto* and in criticism of the Opéra's artistic policy, he was again making approaches. There was talk of another opera, this time to a libretto by Scribe himself; only (Berlioz reported), Duponchel insisted he should "write music that is less difficult to perform and easier for the mixed audience of the Opéra to understand; and I completely agree with him". Other directors were showing signs of interest. Crosnier, of the Opéra-Comique, was even considering putting on *Benvenuto Cellini*, whose libretto he had turned down five years before, and was also talking of a new work. So was Anténor Joly, director of the new Théâtre de la Renaissance (the company located at the Salle Ventadour which had opened with Hugo's *Ruy Blas* a few months before, and where Berlioz had at one point been planning to give a big retrospective concert of his works). It looks as if the talent for operatic comedy revealed in the trio and the sextet had not gone unnoticed. That *Benvenuto*'s failure was the death blow to his operatic ambitions – the commonly held view – may have been true in the long run, but it was far from obvious at the time. Though the work itself was *malvenuto*, that need not mean the composer was barred from the opera house, especially if he learnt his lesson well, composed less technically demanding music and provided himself with a decent libretto.

Berlioz does not give the impression, in this immediate post-*Benvenuto* period, of a man half crushed by the disappointment of the hopes he had placed in his opera. Antoni Deschamps, in a poem entitled "To Hector Berlioz, on the death of Adolphe Nourrit", calls him a "dauntless fighter", a "sturdy oak" whose fortitude defies the storm and whose protective branches shelter those less strong than he. To Liszt, Berlioz speaks of loving to "swim in the sea and tumble in the breakers, just as you do". To Schumann, who he wishes would come to Paris, he describes the "continual feverish agitation" in which they live, and which, though it can be cruel, has its charm. "I am sure the roar of our artistic ocean would please you. Oh, how we would dream and sing together if you came. Ours is a motley world, with few honest young men worthy of the name of artist, and many *animals* and an enormous number of FOOLS and a prodigious quantity of *SCOUN-DRELS* (you see I observe the law of crescendo) and many other names in ls and els to the purpose." Yet "there are blessings in Parisian life that are beyond description and that you would appreciate".

The pianist Clara Wieck, whom Schumann married the following year, came to Paris in February 1839 and was the lioness of the season, as the *Gazette* called her. She met Berlioz at a soirée at the Bertins'. A stranger came up to her. "He at once began talking of you," she wrote to Schumann. "He is quite taciturn, with extraordinarily bushy hair, and keeps his eyes lowered, staring at the floor. He's coming to see me tomorrow. At the beginning I didn't know who he was, and wondered at his speaking of you all the time. In the end I asked him his name; when he told me I gave a start of pleasure which must have flattered him."

No more than the letters do the newspaper articles of these months convey any sense of deep discouragement. The open letter to Liszt published in the *Gazette* of 6 August, a racy account of the Paris musical scene, is not the writing of someone who has lost his sense of the ridiculous, or his enthusiasm, beginning as it does with a plea to Liszt to come back and play for them again:

> Do you remember our soirée at Legouvé's and the sonata in C sharp minor [the Moonlight] and the lamp put out and the five of us stretched out on the rug in the darkness, listening mesmerized, and Legouvé's tears, and mine, and Schoelcher's respectful silence, and the astonishment of M. Goubeaux?

and ending with the latest from the world of opera:

> Apropos of money, they've found a way of making it, by not building a theatre for the Italiens. The singers of our great Opéra are to be pitted in combat with those from beyond the Alps: there is a plan to combine the two troupes in the Rue Le Pelletier. It will be a rude confrontation: Lablache against Levasseur, Rubini against Duprez, Tamburini against Dérivis, Grisi against Mlle Nathan, and all against the bass drum. We shall be there to pick up the dead and dying.

At the Opéra, he continues,

> they won't hear of reviving Spontini's masterpiece. Ambroise Thomas, Morel and I were saying the other day that we would give five hundred francs for a good performance of *La Vestale*. As we know it by heart we sang it till midnight; we missed you as accompanist. Spontini's cause has been defended in a pamphlet by one of our friends, Emile D[eschamps]. A few papers followed his lead, and the cause was being won, when Spontini took it into his head to publish a letter, which had already appeared two or three years ago, on modern music and musicians. His enemies would have paid several thousand for its publication. He has

given it them for nothing. That doesn't prevent *La Vestale* from being a masterpiece; but it does mean that we won't see it again.

Finally,

Ruolz's opera has been in rehearsal for the past two and a half months. In consequence the singers don't know a note of it, but the costumes are ready, and Duponchel intends to have it performed next Friday.

A similar zest informs the homily that he delivered in the *Débats* of 22 September in the manner of Don Quixote's advice to Sancho Panza on the latter's becoming governor of Barataria. The occasion was the début of a new singer, Masset; but it was Duprez, at the outset of his fame, who was intended and clearly understood. Considering how Duprez had left him stranded only a year before, Berlioz was conspicuously fair-minded in his subsequent references to the great tenor (giving high praise, for example, to his singing in the duet for Orpheus and Eurydice from Act 3 of Gluck's opera at a concert in March of this year). The homily, though based on bitter experience, utters its home truths without rancour.

You have now arrived. In a few months you will be famous, you will receive constant applause and your salary will be beyond computation. Authors will woo you, directors will no longer keep you waiting in their anterooms and when you write to them they will reply. Women who are unknown to you will speak of you as their protégé or their dearest friend. Books will be dedicated to you, prose and verse. Instead of the hundred sous you have been giving your porter on New Year's Day you will have to make it a hundred francs. You will be excused National Guard duty. You will have periods of leave during which the provinces will compete for your performances; flowers and sonnets will rain at your feet; you will sing at the préfet's soirées and the mayor's wife will send you apricots. You stand at last on the threshold of Olympus; for if the Italians speak of *dive* – goddesses – it is undeniable that the great male singers are gods. Very well: since you are now become a god, be a good devil in spite of it and don't disdain those who offer you sound advice. Remember that the voice is a fragile instrument and can break or deteriorate in a moment, often without known cause, and that an accident of that sort is enough to hurl the greatest of the gods headlong from his exalted throne and reduce him to the condition of men, or lower. Don't be too hard on the poor composer. When from the elevation of your elegant barouche you catch sight of Meyerbeer or Spontini or Halévy or Auber on the pavement, do not nod to them with a gesture of friendly protectiveness: they will smile pityingly, and the indignant passer-by will regard it as the height of impertinence. Do not forget that some of their works will be admired long after the memory of your *ut de poitrine* has vanished from the earth.

When Berlioz's sister Adèle and her husband Marc came to Paris at the end of May she found him (she told her father) "in very good health, very fashionable, he looks younger". She thought he had "an air of contentment".

Adèle had finally nerved herself to make the journey. Her brother received the news with delight. "Wonderful! So you alone of all the family have decided to undertake this epic voyage. My dearest sister, I thank you. Harriet is overjoyed and Louis runs about the house shouting like a madman that he is going to see his aunt Adèle". They must stay near them, in the Rue du Mont Blanc, where there were furnished apartments to let. "I don't know who can have told you that we lived at the other end of Paris. Paris is the Chaussée d'Antin, it's the Boulevard des Italiens, and we're near all that. The fine weather has returned today – it came with your letter."

The Suats duly stayed in the Rue de la Chaussée d'Antin (the renamed Rue du Mont Blanc), at No. 20, the Hôtel d'Antin. They were in Paris for about three weeks, during which they saw their relatives every day. Adèle sat for her portrait; and her brother took her to call on Alfred de Vigny. On 29 May they all went to the Opéra to see Auber's *Lac des fées*, with Duprez singing the leading role (the work had been running for a couple of months, but he was still in it). During the entr'actes they strolled about the foyer and Adèle was introduced to the celebrities who were there, including Dumas. "Harriet, who is looking after my amusements in the kindest way, asked him for tickets for the Comédie-Française on Saturday, they're doing one of his recent plays, *Mademoiselle de Belle-Isle* – another enjoyable evening in prospect!" They also saw the young prodigy Rachel in Racine's *Iphigénie*; they visited the Panthéon, Notre-Dame, the Arc de Triomphe, the Madeleine, the Jardin des Plantes, the Gobelins and the park at Vincennes; and Adèle went to see Mme Babil at the boarding-school where Prosper died, and planted two rose-trees on his grave.

It was an opportunity, too, to get to know her nephew and, as she told her father, she seized it gratefully. "This morning [30 May] Hector brought Louis, and I kept the dear child all day till the evening, when I gave him back to his mother. I took him with me to see Mme Augustin Blanchet, who was enchanted with him. The fact is, I can't say which is the nicest between him and Mathilde [Nancy's six-year old daughter]: I was proud to be in charge of such a lovely child. We stayed two hours at the Tuileries, and he entertained all the people near us, he has such engaging and original ways. We already get on perfectly together, he tells everybody about his Aunt Adèle, he caresses me a great deal, and Mathilde has found a formidable rival. How I wish I could get you to know him, dear Papa." Above all, Adèle was able to give the anxious family in Dauphiné a reassuring first-hand account of her brother and his ménage:

> I repeat what I said to Nancy: everything I have seen of his domestic life has entirely satisfied me. His wife loves him passionately, he is extremely attentive and considerate to her. He has calmed down and acquired the assurance of a householder and a father; he looks happy. So we can set our minds at rest, dear Papa.

A week later, on 8 June, she returned to it:

> I can't describe to you, Father, all the trouble he is taking and the kindness he shows me. I am amazed, considering his usual state of preoccupation. He's working hard just now at a new symphony, on *Romeo and Juliet*. It's apparently an immense work; he hopes to finish it before the winter. His wife has high hopes . . . Altogether, they are relaxed, happy and *very united*. Hector is now a real family man, concerned about the future of his son. Harriet too has very simple tastes, looks after the household with great zeal, and hardly ever goes out. But tomorrow we're going together to Versailles to dine with an immensely rich friend of Hector's [Georges Kastner] who has been so obliging as to invite us.

Dr Berlioz, though not to be tempted on any account to make such a journey (Grenoble being his absolute limit), took a keen vicarious pleasure in his daughter's, and her reports gladdened his heart: "What you tell me of the harmony that reigns between Hector and his wife, as well as of their child's charming ways, has caused me the liveliest satisfaction. The happiness of all my children today can almost make me forget the tribulations with which my life has been so long beset."

All in all, the visit was such a success that Nancy announced she was coming to Paris next year. Several weeks later, on 29 July, Harriet plucked up courage and wrote in French to her new friend.

At last, my dear Adèle, I take the resolution and the pen in an attempt to express my heartfelt contentment on learning that you and my brother-in-law have arrived safe and sound in your peaceful home. You tell me that you hope you have found a new friend in me. Yes, my dear Adèle, I have a sincere friendship for you, and I believe you have perceived that I cannot flatter or pay compliments. Hector will want to correct my letter, but no – it is beyond correction so let it go as it is; if it makes you laugh, so much the better.

I trust you and your dear husband will be happy until I learn to write the French language well – in other words, till eternity. God bless you both.

H. Berlioz

Hector has been *very ill* and I just now am rather poorly, with an inflammation caused by toothache.

I went to see your portrait with Louis and M. Dufeuillant. Louis examined certain pictures which we said were your portrait; he shook his head and said NO; but then letting him look by himself, he found the real one under a chair, and clapped his hands and cried, "It's her! it's her!" I could not help shedding a few tears when I saw the portrait, because *God alone knows if we will meet again in this world*. But you will ever have my best wishes for you and yours. *God bless you* [in English].

Adèle was impressed with her sister-in-law's performance; she told Nancy she hadn't thought Hector's "good and excellent wife" could write French so well.

In the same envelope as Harriet's letter came one from Berlioz: "You can imagine how delighted we shall be to do [Nancy] the honours of the capital. Harriet is absolutely counting on Mathilde. I am up to my eyes, finishing my symphony. In eight or ten days, I hope, it will be done. It intoxicates me; working on it puts me in a state of exaltation which you will understand, knowing me as you do. Yesterday I was radiant, effervescent with joy. Today I am taking a rest. I have not slept since I saw this great machine taking the shape and the physiognomy that I intended. Anyway, I trust that all will go well."

In the event the eight or ten days stretched into six weeks. The choral finale gave him as much trouble as the adagio and for similar reasons – its complexity of structure, its crucial importance, and the emotions it aroused in him. Its content and form had evolved gradually over the summer in conversations and correspondence with Deschamps.

Deschamps to Berlioz

Friday, 21 June [1839]

My dear collaborator

Here is another bit of the finale. Forgive me for sending it to you piecemeal like this, but that is how it's coming to my inspiration (if that's the word). If you have kept my notes could you let me have all my verses back, from the beginning till now? I need them to coordinate the whole thing and go over it in detail – I've not kept anything. When I've made a copy I can then send it all to you, if you like.

Come on, take heart! I am counting on you so much! This is going to be something unique. A libretto for a symphony! An orchestra representing an opera! And thanks to you it will all become something enchanting, while remaining utterly original. We'll meet soon. Thank you as always, and my homage at the feet of Mme Berlioz, who was your first and veritable muse. As for me, I'm merely a musette.

Yours
Emile Deschamps

After the finale came the Tomb Scene (quite possibly an afterthought). *Romeo and Juliet* was completed on 8 September. "I have finished the symphony," he wrote to Kastner, "finished, totally finished, which is to say – finished. Not another note to write. Amen, amen, amenissimen."

The date of the première – 24 November – was still eleven weeks off, but there was much to do. How much, the surviving documents give us some idea. *Romeo and Juliet* was his biggest venture so far in the concert hall, the culmination of nearly a decade of concert promotion and management. The preparing of orchestra and chorus parts was an operation almost on the scale of the Requiem. Throughout the rest of September and part of October, in the intervals of attending rehearsals and performances for his newspaper articles (now back with a vengeance), he was kept busy supervising and checking, with Rocquemont, the work of copyists and lithographers, as well as seeing to the translation of the sung text for the tour of Germany he hoped to be making the next year; all this in blustery winds and torrential rain which turned the streets into a morass of mud.

But the Requiem had been not nearly so difficult to perform. *Romeo* was the most exacting concert work he had written. Ensuring an adequate performance required not only energy but ingenuity, so that the time and resources available were used to maximum advantage. "It will wear me out," he wrote to Lecourt in late September, "but there's no alternative. Unless I take the greatest pains, a machine of this magnitude would never move or wouldn't function properly."

By mid-October he had chosen the fourteen voices from the Opéra for the small prologue chorus and was rehearsing them in the green room during intervals in the performances. He was also coaching his favourite bass, young Alizard, in the role of Friar Laurence, which suited "his deep, smooth voice to perfection". The Ministry of the Interior had finally granted him the Conservatoire Hall for three Sundays (he had applied in August), accepting his argument that the performers would "only agree to do the necessary number of rehearsals for the modest fee I am offering on condition that the work is given several times, which will assure them a slightly more substantial profit". With the Opéra's chorus-master, Pierre Dietsch, he began knocking his choristers into shape. He had also to give thought to dressing them in such a way that the Montagues and the Capulets were differentiated: the women perhaps in white in both choirs but with sashes of contrasting colour; he told Nancy that he was going to call on Duponchel and flatter him by asking his advice. "The important thing, however, is to get them to sing in tune and come to life a bit." On 28 October he sent Rocquemont a note requesting him to see that all the parts and extra instruments were ready by the afternoon of 13 November for the first orchestral run-through the following morning.

After that came the sectional rehearsals: first and second violins by themselves, then violas, cellos and basses, then wind instruments, and finally percussion (for though he does not say so, he must surely have taken the timpani, triangles, tambourines, cymbals, bass drum and antique cymbals separately, given the unprecedentedly demanding parts for percussion in the Fête and the scherzo). Then, one more full rehearsal, followed by a public dress rehearsal on the 23rd. No wonder Hottin had to add to his duties as orchestral attendant the provision of several glasses of mulled wine for the conductor.

On top of all this there were the legion complimentary tickets to allocate and distribute. The Bibliothèque Nationale's Berlioz papers include a double-sided list of "Billets à donner" for the première of

Romeo and Juliet, densely covered with names and figures in the composer's hand; in many cases the actual seat numbers are noted. Among the recipients are Heine, Gautier ("Stalls, nos. 42 & 43"), Hallé, Liszt's mother (her son was in Vienna), Beethoven's amanuensis Anton Schindler, Laurent-Jean, Francis Wey, Habeneck. Six tickets were reserved for the Berliozes' servants and their friends, and one for "le maître de Louis" – the boy had begun going to a local kindergarten run by the educationist and playwright Prosper Goubeaux. And near the bottom on the left of the reverse page we find one in the name of "R. Wagner". Other writers and musicians we know were there include Balzac, Alfred de Vigny, Sainte-Beuve, Legouvé, Eugène Sue, Schoelcher, Marie d'Agoult, Kalkbrenner and Cherubini.

Gounod, then a precocious ex-student of twenty-one about to leave for Italy as the current Prix de Rome, recalled forty years later the excitement of the preparations for the symphony in the Conservatoire Hall (where often before, hurrying out of Halévy's composition class, he had slipped in unnoticed and "listened intoxicated to [Berlioz rehearsing] his strange, impassioned music, which opened up new and exotic horizons"). "I was so struck by the sweep of the great finale, the Reconciliation of the Montagues and Capulets, that when I left the hall I had the whole of Friar Laurence's superb 'Jurez tous par l'auguste symbole' in my head. Calling on Berlioz a day or two later, I sat down at the piano and played it to him in its entirety, at which he stared at me in astonishment. 'Where the devil did you get that?' 'At one of your rehearsals.'"

As the rehearsals gathered momentum a sense of anticipation, a conviction of being part of something historic, spread through the performers. Yet in planning three consecutive performances of a new symphony Berlioz was taking an enormous financial risk. The result at any rate would show him how much real interest there was in his music. It was a test case. Harriet, as before, encouraged him and predicted that his gamble would come off.

It looked as if she was right. On the day of the first performance there was such a crowd at the box office that scores of people were turned away; they could have taken another 1,500 francs. All the same – he had written that morning to his friend Jules David, critic of the *Commerce*, who had just published a sympathetic article about him – he had need of all the courage he could find. How would the crowded hall, full to the rafters with music-lovers and musicians, dandies, famous artists, royalty, government officials, journalists by no means all sympathetic, and the intellectual élite of Paris – how would it react to a symphony of such unprecedented length, so unlike any symphony it had heard before even from him? It was the most drastic trial of strength he had ever faced in the concert hall. Even the first night of his opera was not the same; for, here, he was directly in the firing line, at the head of his two hundred performers – the hundred-strong orchestra ranged in front of him, the choral forces and their sub-conductor behind him on the forestage. It depended on him.

The introductory movement, with its instrumental, then choral recitative interrupted by solos for contralto and tenor, clearly puzzled the audience and was followed by a profound silence. It was not until the music of the ball in the second movement that he knew he was all right: during the long crescendo over descending bass which succeeds the grand "réunion des thèmes" the audience caught fire, and the end of the movement was drowned in an avalanche of clapping and bravos. After that, the Scène d'amour was received with respect rather than enthusiasm, but the scherzo provoked wonder and astonishment; and if the second Prologue, the Convoi funèbre and the Tomb Scene were no more than *succès d'estime*, the finale took the hall by storm and brought the afternoon to a triumphant end. As Marie d'Agoult said in her letter to Liszt next day, it was "one of those battles after which one sings the Te Deum". Berlioz reported to his father that the performance was a "tour de force such as only my system of sectional rehearsals could have achieved. The artists themselves are amazed at what they did." He had "nearly succumbed to the fatigue of the rehearsals", but the outcome had revived him. "Uncle Auguste will give you a full account of it, he was there with my cousins." All in all, it was "probably the greatest success" he had yet obtained.

The hint of reserve is understandable. It had worked, almost against the odds; but several movements could have gone better – among them the Scène d'amour, already his "morceau de prédilection". The second performance would be "still more satisfying".

It was. This time the Scène d'amour made a deep impression and the Convoi funèbre was enthusiastically received. At the end the reconciliation scene brought the house down, and the entire orchestra and chorus rose to their feet and cheered. No one had heard an orchestra play with such power and precision. Never had he had such a victory. It was repeated a fortnight later at the third performance, when the first two movements of *Harold* and Teresa's cavatina, sung by Dorus-Gras, were given as added attractions and there was another good house. Among the many letters of congratulation was one from a member of the staff of the Opéra, the head librarian Gentil, who thanked him for the "exquisite delicacy of this great composition and the sheer abundance of a genius so rich that it shines with its own brilliance, borrowing none from others"; the scherzo took "the art and science of music further than I had believed possible". Rosine Stoltz, his Ascanio, wrote saying how moved she had been; and an English visitor bought his baton for 120 francs. Though the hard core of hostility remained, some doubters had been converted to his music by the symphony.

The papers were in the main very favourable. As he knew they would, his opponents, who had come with "evil intentions" but had been "forced for appearance's sake to be all smiles", made up for it afterwards in the *sans-culotte* press. One of them compared the Queen Mab scherzo to the squeak of a badly oiled syringe. Alphonse Karr (whose recently founded magazine *Les Guêpes* – "The Wasps" – had as its declared aim "to laugh at a lot of people who would like to be taken seriously") jeered that "music without melody", which Berlioz's was, was like partridge and sauerkraut without the partridge, and claimed that the "strident noise in the violins" which represented what the programme called "Romeo feeling the first effects of the poison" had prompted a member of the audience to exclaim, "Yes, it's just like the colic." These were expected irritants. The *Presse*, the *Quotidienne*, the *Temps*, the *Débats*, the *Artiste*, *Galignani's Messenger*, the *Nouvelliste*, all welcomed the new work. Stephen de La Madelaine predicted that it would stand as a monument to human genius: "That is what we say of this score, which we have heard twice and carefully pondered, while sharing the enthusiasm that, at each moment, seized hold of the most imposing audience an artist could dream of."* Bowes, in *Galignani's*, looked forward to its performance in England and Germany, "where Shakespeare is better understood" and where, "notwithstanding its Parisian triumph", its "definitive success" awaited it. Gautier praised Berlioz for his "unshakeable will and pertinacity" (as well as for having "given a soul to each instrument of the orchestra"); "for in these days of polemics and publicity it is not enough to be exceptionally talented,

---

* Balzac likened the audience to a "brain": "C'était un cerveau que votre salle de concert."

one must also be exceptionally courageous"; the French public feared originality, which to them "is like a red rag to a bull". But Berlioz, "like Mucius Scaevola, would rather burn his hand than lay a single grain of incense on the altars of banality and commonplace". Janin's review recalled the composer's student days, when the idea of the symphony first came to him, at a time when he was so poor he had hardly the wherewithal to replace one of the two (*sic*) strings of his guitar if it broke, and when he was forced to sing in the chorus of the Opéra-Comique, from which he arrived at the Odéon one evening with the remains of make-up still on his cheek and, seeing Miss Smithson, exclaimed, "That woman will be my wife" – the same who was in one of the stage boxes at the Conservatoire for the performance of the *Romeo and Juliet* she had inspired, and next to her a fair-haired boy, listening to his father's symphony. After that Janin did not have a great deal to say about the music; but he concluded with a flourish, though he seemed to have quite forgotten his own negative review of *Benvenuto Cellini*:

> The success was great, as it had to be. He took a terrifying gamble, and won hands down. Those who deserted him, who betrayed him, those who treated his opera like the work of a child, those who were lacking in intelligence and in gratitude towards him, the great singer who did not have the courage to fight for such a genius and left him high and dry – what will they say, what can they be thinking, at the sight of him gloriously risen from defeat? There is only one thing they can say: "I bite my thumb," as the Capulets say to the Montagues. Then bite your thumbs, bite them to the bone, thankless wretches that you are! I will not stop you. But, for us – let us clap hands and cry Vivat to our hero and escort him on his triumphal way, and once more give thanks to Nicolò Paganini, who paid for this score as no king in Europe today would have done. Share our happiness with us, Nicolò Paganini, you who kissed Berlioz's hand. May his triumph, half of which belongs to you, restore a little strength and life to your body worn out by genius! May the good news reach you on the mild shores of the Genoese sea, dazzling in the pure sunlight of Italy, so that you know how much we, who blasphemed you in a moment of anger, are your grateful devotees.

This was all very fine. But rather more helpful was the long and detailed analysis by Stephen Heller which appeared, in the form of a letter to Schumann, in two successive issues of the *Gazette* shortly after the final performance of *Romeo*. By the time Heller wrote his essay he had heard the symphony five times – three rehearsals and two performances (a postcript was added after the third) – and had studied the manuscript full score; and he began by chiding the inconsistency of the musical public, which demanded novelty and originality and, when it got it, was put out at not being able to take it in at one hearing and blamed the author, when it had no one to blame but itself. It behaved, said Heller, like the Viennese bookseller Trattner in Jean-Paul's novel, who boasted that he printed nothing that had not been printed already. Many people wanted to hear only the music they had already heard. But all music that was new, original, bold needed to be heard repeatedly until no one found it new, bold and original. This was not a paradox. How many people, musicians of integrity among them, had not reacted with alarm to Beethoven's Choral Symphony when it first appeared and, where Beethoven displayed greater independence and inspiration than ever, saw only oddity and obscurity and dismissed it as chaotic and barbarous – containing admittedly some beautiful things, but at what a price! An effort was required to grasp new forms and understand the ideas behind them – as in fact had happened with the wild and fantastical finale of Beethoven's Eighth Symphony, which no one now took exception to, and with the adagio of the Ninth, which people were moved by without bothering to ask whether it was innovatory or not. Yet the same people asked just this question when they listened to Berlioz, and shook their heads over innovations which they said could come to no good: symphonies, they said, had managed perfectly well so far without prologues or librettos; why shouldn't they go on in the same way to the end of time?

Heller also nailed the persistent fallacy (which we find constantly aired by scribes like Fétis, Blaze de Bury and Karr) of the composer's "system" of descriptive music. "Berlioz, to my mind, by no means asks of music more in the way of effects than it is able to provide. Music has always been granted the faculty of expressing pleasure, pain, love, grief, fear, grandeur. Why make an exception of him and refuse him the right to translate the same emotions into sound?"

Having vindicated the composer's right to produce such a symphony, Heller proceeded to discuss it as a whole and then movement by movement, concluding that the work was a masterpiece but drawing attention to a few weaknesses. Two of those singled out in the article, a chanted "Requiem aeternam" in the Convoi funèbre and a passage near the end of the finale, were removed by Berlioz round about this time.*

Other alterations followed, prompted as always by the experience of judging the effect in performance. Berlioz habitually went on testing and revising up to the moment of publication of a work, sometimes beyond. But no score of his for the concert hall, not even the Fantastic Symphony, was subjected to so much revision as *Romeo and Juliet*. By the time he published it, eight years later, he had made many changes, in detail and structure.

Even then he spoke of possible "blemishes" that he "may have missed", and of a composer having, in such a case, to "resign himself to the work's imperfections". Berlioz in the *Memoirs* treats *Romeo* with a special passionately protective love. "Oh, the ardent existence I lived [during its composition]! I struck out boldly across the great ocean of poetry, caressed by the wild sweet breeze of fancy, under the fiery sun of love that Shakespeare kindled. I felt within me the strength to reach the enchanted isle where the temple of pure art stands serene under a cloudless sky"; but in the very next sentence it is "not for him" to determine whether he succeeded.

When he wondered whether Paganini would have been pleased with the work, undertaken "with the object of justifying in his eyes what he had done for me", did he also wonder whether after all he had been right to cast it in this form?

It is possible; but I don't think he did. The opening words of the preface to the 1858 vocal score are ironic in tone but firm and unequivocal in intention: "There will doubtless be no mistake as to the genre of this work. Although voices are frequently employed, it is neither a concert opera nor a cantata but a choral symphony." Each of Berlioz's large-scale concert works adopts a different solution to the problem of communicating dramatic content. In the Fantastic it is a written programme. In *Harold*, movement titles are considered sufficient, as in the Pastoral Symphony. In *The Childhood of Christ* a tenor narrator sets the scenes. In *The Damnation of Faust* the genre, this time, is concert opera. In *Romeo* the solution is the entirely novel one of choral recitative – a device mentioned a few years earlier (perhaps with a *Romeo* symphony already in mind) in a note which he added on the occasion of a

---

* Regrettably in the case of the ten-bar chanted "Requiem", as John Eliot Gardiner has demonstrated in his recording of the work, which restores the passage.

performance of the Fantastic, to the effect that the written programme might not have given rise to so much misunderstanding if it had been possible to "recite or sing it between the movements of the symphony, like the choruses of ancient tragedy".

None of these works copies any of the others. Berlioz does not care to repeat himself – or rather, he cannot. The particular poetic world requires, each time, its own unique guise. This continual reinvention of form in response to the poetic *donnée* has always been disconcerting to commentators who feel the need to classify. But every work, and every movement in it, had to find the shape and means of expression appropriate to them. For *Romeo* it was the dramatic symphony – the realm, higher than that of opera, which Beethoven's music had revealed, and where Shakespeare belonged. The fundamental artistic choice was never in doubt.

What matter that the genre was new? Like the early Romantics in general, he saw "genre" as something not set but having to be created afresh. Beethoven had shown the way. *Romeo*, however unprecedented its multi-movement scheme and its mélange of elements, was for Berlioz a legitimate, a natural consequence of the Ninth Symphony, that true beginning of modern music whose final movement brought the implicit drama of the previous three into the open. To Wagner – lately arrived in Paris and listening to *Romeo and Juliet* in the Conservatoire Hall – Berlioz's formal solution was as wrong as his music was revelatory; the Ninth suggested quite other conclusions, which he set out not long after in a brilliant novella, "A Pilgrimage to Beethoven", published in the *Gazette*. Beethoven, by calling on voices and words to resolve the mighty conflicts he had generated, had in effect acknowledged that the symphony as an art form could go no further and must merge into a new kind of drama. But to Berlioz the Ninth marked the final stage in the emancipation of the symphony from its eighteenth-century restrictions. The genre of *Romeo* was not one of his worries – any more than it was a problem for Heller or d'Ortigue or Stephen de La Madelaine or Léon Kreutzer, to name only his more intelligent critics, or to the Marquis de Custine, for whom Berlioz was at once poet and musician, "your two natures aiding each other marvellously, as your two arts are complementary".

Among his first listeners, of course, there were those who found the mixed form too foreign to accept. Marie d'Agoult, in a letter to Liszt, described a visit from Sainte-Beuve, who "spent a long time talking about Berlioz's symphony. He inclines to the conventional common-sense view: why not make it an opera?" (Marie d'Agoult herself, when not writing for Liszt's eyes, was critical of the work.) But many other music-lovers, in that age when the concept of "absolute music" was not the power it would be later in the century, simply took it as it came.

Certainly, Berlioz was attempting something he had never attempted before: instrumental, non-verbal music which enacted not a programme, as the Fantastic Symphony did, so much as a dramatic text. Ian Kemp's essay "*Romeo and Juliet* and *Roméo et Juliette*", shows how closely the events of the orchestral movements follow the play, while not ceasing to be music. The work exemplified Berlioz's belief that "music is free and does what it wants"; programmatic content, no matter how specific, is subservient to musical logic. What exercised him was not the principle embodied in the orchestral movements but finding a precise balance, in the structure of the work as a whole, between dramatic narration and symphonic design. It preoccupied him for a long time and, as the *Memoirs* imply, he was never completely satisfied.

His doubts focused on the Tomb Scene. The second Prologue, a strikingly vivid piece which originally – in emulation of Shakespeare – introduced the later movements, was in due course removed in the interests of tauter construction and continuous musical flow. But its absence created a difficulty for the uninstructed listener. Without the explanation it provided, the action depicted by the music of the Tomb Scene was not strictly intelligible. This was especially so if one didn't know that the Tomb Scene was based on the Garrick version, as performed by Kemble and Harriet Smithson in 1827 – a version which once Berlioz had seen it could only be for him thereafter, despite his rooted objection to such alterations, the definitive form of the lovers' last moments. The question of intelligibility continued to worry him, and in the end he added the famous note calling for the suppression of the movement at all performances not given before an audience endowed with exceptional sensitivity and familiar with the fifth act of the play as emended by Garrick – that is, at "ninety-nine performances out of a hundred". You can understand how he felt. With or without Garrick, the piece stood at the furthest limits of tone painting. And it was too important, too sacred to be listened to uncomprehendingly or with an ear only for its startlingly modernistic gestures and sounds, not for their agonizing meaning. That was more than he could bear. Yet his injunction, taken literally, would deprive the work of one of the most remarkable things in it.

Perhaps in today's more enlightened climate the problem has lost its sting. It does not require a vast expenditure of effort to acquaint ourselves with the action of the Tomb Scene's musical narrative so that we follow its supremely graphic embodiment of events to their heart-rending conclusion. The music speaks. The controlled ferocity of the opening "allegro agitato e desperato", as Romeo bursts into the tomb; the solemn chords, separated by silence, as he surveys the cavernous vaulted space and the corpses laid on their biers; the long, grieving melody of his Invocation, over shuddering syncopated bass and intermittent drum rolls; the descending chromatic scale of tremolo cellos as he drinks the "mortelle liqueur" (a sound Wagner remembered when he composed the potion scene in the first act of *Tristan*); Romeo's amazed reaction as Juliet stirs, returning to life to the melody, now on solo clarinet, of her soliloquy in the balcony scene; the nightmarishly bright, "baseless" orchestral textures and distorted love themes which depict their wild embraces; then the collapse as Romeo is overcome by the poison, the bass slipping lower as he lurches and falls, the trombones crying out as he tries to speak, the twisting bass dwindling into silence; frenzied violin phrases, then trenchant string chords and rapid scales as Juliet makes her decision and finds Romeo's dagger; finally two dissonant fortissimo chords, a tremor in the strings, and a barely audible oboe phrase ebbing to nothing – all this is at once dramatically specific and riveting musical discourse. It is also essential to a work at whose heart is the vision of young love, complete, all-embracing, but tragic because the world can only destroy it. In the radiant light of the Scène d'amour the physical disintegration of that love becomes as poignant as anything in the music of the nineteenth century.

There have always been those for whom the violence of Berlioz's images in the Tomb Scene, and his whole use of the language of music to present the drama's harrowing reality, is shocking and unacceptable – just as the more classically minded members of the audience at the Odéon in September 1827 found the realism of the lovers' deaths too much to stomach. To such objections his answer could only be the same as it was when Boieldieu objected to his treatment of the death of Cleopatra: the extreme nature of the subject demanded nothing less.

Commentators have tended to see the formal plan of *Romeo and Juliet* as a rather awkward compromise between symphony and opera or oratorio (as the Ninth itself is still sometimes said to be); and until recently it was more common to extract the three central movements and play them on their own than to perform the whole symphony. Yet they have their true being in the context of the work. The different movements and sub-movements are interdependent. The more one studies Berlioz's *Romeo and Juliet*, the stronger its compositional grasp appears. So far from being arbitrary, the scheme is logical and the mixture of genres – the inheritance of Shakespeare and Beethoven – precisely gauged. The introduction, depicting the feud of the two families, establishes from the start the principle of dramatically explicit orchestral music and then, by means of the bridge of instrumental recitative (as in the finale of the Ninth Symphony), crosses over into vocal music. Choral prologue now states the argument of the symphony, which choral finale will resolve; the Prologue, in chant-like recitative suggestive of ancient tragedy, prepares the listener for the various themes, dramatic and musical, that will be treated in the core of the work. In addition, the two least overtly dramatic movements, the adagio and the scherzo, are prefigured and emphasized, the one in a contralto solo celebrating the rapture of first love, the other in a nimble scherzetto for tenor and semi-chorus which introduces the mischievous Mab. At the end the finale brings the drama fully into the open. It does so in the form of an extended choral movement which culminates in the abjuring of the hatreds depicted orchestrally at the outset of the work.

Though the heart of the symphonic drama is with the orchestra, voices are not forgotten; they are used sparingly yet enough to keep them before the listeners' attention, in preparation for their full deployment in the finale. At the beginning of the Scène d'amour the songs of revellers on their way home from the ball float across the stillness of Capulet's garden, intensifying the silence that ensues when the voices have gone. Two movements later, in the Convoi funèbre, the Capulet chorus sings a single-note chant against the orchestral fugato. Halfway through, the roles are exchanged: the chant is now in the orchestra while the voices take over the fugal music, so that the Convoi becomes a choral move-ment, in preparation for the finale. In this way the employment of the chorus follows what Berlioz called (in an essay on the Ninth Symphony) the "law of crescendo". The crescendo operates not only in terms of texture and volume but also emotionally; for the voices, having begun as onlookers (in the form of a small flexible group, lightly accompanied), become full-scale participants in the tragedy, just as the anonymous contralto and the unnamed Mercutio-like tenor of the introduction give way in the finale to an actual person, the saintly Friar Laurence, developed into a much more commanding figure than he is in the play.

At the same time the two movements preceding the finale take on an increasingly descriptive character. The funeral dirge merges into a bell-like tolling, hypnotic in its insistence; and the orchestral Tomb Scene carries the work nearer still to overt narrative. In this way, again, an abrupt transition is avoided; the quasi-operatic or oratorio-like finale is heard to evolve out of what has gone before.

The same care is devoted to the details as it is to the structure. A single note may be rich with meaning (listen, for example, to the double-basses' ominous G natural just before the adagio, a sudden dissonance akin to the premonitions of disaster which occur periodically in the play). Throughout, thematic resemblances and echoes help to link the different sections and lend unity to the diversity of musical imagery created in response to Shakespeare's poetry. The "réunion des thèmes" in the Fête, whereby the tune of the preceding larghetto is superimposed on the music of the dance (anticipated by the appearance of its first six notes twice in the previous bars), is only the most obvious example of the process. In the introduction the theme of the trombone recitative representing the Prince's rebuke to the warring families is formed from the opening notes of their angry fugato, which is literally mastered, tamed, by being stretched into notes three times as long. A transformation of the ball music provides the departing guests with their dreamlike song. The Queen Mab trio is based directly on the scherzo theme (which itself recurs during the trio as a buzzing viola counterpoint to its quivering stillness, cutting metrically across it). In the Tomb Scene the clarinet's melodic line, which suggests Juliet waking from her "death-counterfeiting sleep", uses note for note the rising cor anglais phrases of the opening (adagio) section of the Scène d'amour. As in the Scène d'amour, it is followed by the love music, but now fragmented, torn apart, as though Romeo were reliving the course of his love in blurred, distorted flashback. And in the finale, as the families' vendetta breaks out again over the bodies of their children, the return of the opening fugato, in the same key of B minor, unites the two extremes of the vast score.

The work is also honeycombed with smaller thematic references. The solo oboe's lingering notes which hang in the air after Juliet's suicide echo a phrase from the funeral procession that bore her, supposedly dead, to the tomb. The angular phrases of Romeo's unfocused longing, at the opening of the second movement, recur in various guises in what follows, as subsidiary figures or as elements in leading melodies. This principle is active to the end: the theme of Friar Laurence's oath of reconciliation which closes the symphony takes as its point of departure the introduction's angry "feud" theme in B minor, reborn in a broad magnanimous B major.

With all its riches, Berlioz's Dramatic Symphony remains one of his least performed works, a favourite more of musicians than of the public. Because its form still challenges our habits of listening, its genius is peculiarly dependent on idiomatic performance and sympathetic atmosphere. It makes exceptional demands on our imaginations and on our concentration. Yet when performance and atmosphere are right and our imaginations engaged, problems of genre evaporate. That it had a special place in its creator's affections is easy to understand. No score of his is more abundant in lyric poetry, in a sense of the magic and brevity of love, in "sounds and sweet airs" of so many kinds: the flickering, fantastical scherzo, which stands not only for Mercutio's Queen Mab speech but for the whole nimble-witted, comic-fantastical, fatally irrational element in the play, and in which strings and wind seem caught up in some gleeful yet menacing game; the noble swell and curve of the great extended melody which grows out of the questioning phrases of "Roméo seul"; the awesome unison of cor anglais and horn and four bassoons in Romeo's invocation in the tomb of the Capulets; the sadness, the haunting beauty of Juliet's funeral procession; the adagio's deep-toned harmonies and spellbound melodic arcs, conjuring the moonlit night and the wonder and intensity of the passion that flowers beneath it.

Romeo and Juliet, in Boschot's phrase, "opened up to music an unknown future". Its effect on the young Wagner was, by his own confession, overwhelming, revealing till then unimagined possibilities of musical poetry and at the same time driving him deep within himself, to protect and assert his creative identity. What he received he would give back in *Tristan and Isolde*.

For Berlioz, the symphony was a repayment of debt to Shakespeare and Beethoven, the two supreme creators who had shown him the way. It was a gesture of gratitude to the benefactor to whom it owed its existence, a tribute to the woman whom Deschamps called his muse, a joint act of homage to his "two wings of the soul", music and love. It summed up all he had yet attempted in the field of symphonic music; and it crowned a decade of endeavour and achievement. No one, he told Adèle, had ever before dared put on one and the same symphony three times in succession. But it also marks a turning-point. *Romeo* is the culmination of the specifically French period of Berlioz's career, its zenith both in composition and in performance. From now on his career will begin to turn in a new direction; and from the point of view of Paris and his life there the direction, however concealed at first, will be downhill.

9

Lost Illusions

Berlioz's enemies could be forgiven for not seeing it that way. The commission he received in the spring of 1840 to compose a work for the tenth anniversary of the 1830 Revolution, and the allocation of 10,000 francs of public money for the purpose, were to them yet more evidence of the special status he enjoyed; as Adolphe Adam complained, it was "really shameful for the rest of us French composers to see government favours lavished on a man whose character and talents are so contemptible". This was the first time since 1835 that the authorities had ventured to commemorate Les Trois Glorieuses on a grand scale – and it was Berlioz they were turning to, yet again, to provide the music.

The motive for the celebrations was transparent: to recapture lost popularity and divert attention from France's recent humiliation at the hands of England in the Middle East; and it was natural that the protégé of the *Journal des débats* should be associated, in the minds of the regime's increasingly vocal republican and liberal opponents, with what they could only regard as an expensive fraud. The anti-government *Charivari*'s issue for 28 July, the day of the ceremony, lumped him with the suppressors of liberty. "During the burial, which will take place in a large hole in the square of the defunct revolution, M. Emberlificoz will perform his defunct funeral march. A few creaking carts will enhance the picturesque qualities of the composition."

No doubt the commission had been lobbied for by the protégé's well-connected supporters. The new Minister of the Interior, the Dauphinois Charles de Rémusat, knew the Bertins well and, as a journalist, had been involved like them in the newspaper agitation which led directly to the revolution he was now in charge of celebrating. No doubt, too, Berlioz felt that after the last-minute cancellation of the Requiem in 1837 the government owed him a crack at the July ceremonies. He had some suitable music ready: at least one movement from the *Fête musicale funèbre*, which he had begun in 1835 but had never brought to fruition. It had been meant to commemorate the great men of France, not what the *Memoirs* call the "more or less heroic" victims of the Three Days. This was none the less an occasion that called for grand music. The July dead were to be honoured by being buried at the base of a two-hundred-foot column erected on the site of the Bastille and designed by his old friend of Villa Medici days, the architect Joseph-Louis Duc. Berlioz was asked to provide a funeral march for the procession and another movement for the entombment. He decided, however, on a three-part scheme: first a slow march, "bleak but awe-inspiring", then a "kind of funeral oration", delivered while the bodies were laid in their new resting-place, and finally a "hymn of praise" at the moment when, the tomb being sealed, all eyes were raised to the column crowned by the golden figure of Liberty. Since the work was to be heard, to begin with at least, in the open, he scored it for wind instruments and percussion, without strings.

Even with two hundred instrumentalists the chances of its actually being heard were not good. In the most favourable circumstances open-air music was a lottery, and these were not favourable. For most of the four hours and five and a half miles, as the procession made its slow way from the church of St Germain l'Auxerrois by the Louvre, past the quays and the Place de la Concorde, along the Rue Royale and the boulevards to the Place de la Bastille, the music was barely audible above the noise of the shouting, seething crowd. Berlioz, marching – often backwards – in full National Guard uniform, beat time till his arm ached. He had placed the trumpets and muffled side-drums, which set the tempo, in the front ranks so that they could receive the pulse directly and, with luck, transmit it to the rest of the band behind; but he might as well not have done, for all that was audible. Only when the procession came to a temporary halt or when, quite far along the route, the large plane trees of the Boulevard Poissonnière served as reflectors, could the music begin to make an effect. In any case it was the vast catafalque and its fifty coffins draped in funeral velvet, drawn by twenty-four horses caparisoned to the hooves in mourning black, that Paris had come to see, not the rows of red-faced sweating bandsmen pumping out a march no one could catch anyway.

At the Place de la Bastille – where the band took its place on a special platform designed for it by Duc – the second movement, the funeral oration, could at least be heard; but just as a rustle of snare-drums and a summons of trumpets announced the Apotheosis – music designed to turn mourning to triumph – the drums of the Ninth Legion of the National Guard struck up. The men had been standing since morning in the blazing sun; the show was running late, and the appointed time for starting the manoeuvre had come. Perhaps too there had been a failure of communication, and the officer in charge assumed that with the sealing of the tomb the ceremony was over. The order was duly given; the drums maintained a steady barrage; and the Apotheosis sank without trace.

Fortunately there had been a large audience for the public dress rehearsal in the Salle Vivienne two mornings before. It was so successful that the manager engaged Berlioz on the spot to give two further performances in August, at which the work was again an immediate hit.

The Symphonie militaire (later renamed Symphonie funèbre et triomphale), far from being a successor to *Romeo and Juliet* and the other two symphonies, represents a reversion to an earlier, pre-Beethovenian style, the monumental French tradition of public ceremonial music. The first movement was almost certainly composed before *Romeo*; the second movement went back much further, being adapted from a scene in *Les francs-juges*. What was new was the resourceful and imaginative handling of the sonorities of the wind band, which Wagner so admired. In the first movement especially, the variety of colour achieved within the natural limitations of the medium and the deliberately massive style of the music is remarkable. This is the best of the three movements: a funeral march relentless in its rhythmic tension and its slowly gathering crescendos, majestic in its breadth of melodic span and its harsh grandeur of sound. In the second movement a striking idea – the solo trombone as priestly orator, to whose simple, lofty utterance the congregation responds with increasing fervour – is let down by the thinness of the musical ideas. The exuberant finale is also on a lower level: it is the apotheosis not so much of the ransomed souls as of the archetypal French triumphal march for military band. Yet it was just this accessibility compared with his other symphonic works, the "normality" and forthrightness of the music's idiom, that the public and the more conservative musicians found appealing. Adolphe Adam himself swallowed his scorn so far as to consider the last movement "really very good"; with its "regular four-bar phrases" which could be "easily understood" it was a "great advance", superior to anything he had done before. Habeneck was heard to remark, on the way out of one of the indoor performances, that "the fellow has some damn fine ideas". Even Mainzer reviewed the work favourably. Cavé, Berlioz's old adversary at the Ministry of the Interior, could hardly contain his enthusiasm. And Wagner, his admiration untempered by the excrescences which spoiled *Romeo and Juliet*, praised it wholeheartedly in a long and generally critical essay on Berlioz in the Dresden *Abendzeitung*: it was "grand and noble from first note to last" and, unlike the rest of the composer's output, destined to "live and be an inspiration as long as there is a nation called France".

Whatever Berlioz himself really thought of it – this time he had "written so big that the myopic could read me" – there was no question but that his military symphony was the most popular of his compositions to date; the finale in particular electrified listeners. Four months later, when Napoleon's remains were brought back from St Helena by a government eager to show itself as Bonapartist as the next, and the monstrous bier processed through Paris before being placed in a marble tomb under the dome of the Invalides, the symphony dazzled by its absence. Berlioz was asked to add a triumphal march to the funeral marches already composed by Auber, Adam and Halévy but, given too little time, declined. Instead he stood by and watched his colleagues "break their backs against my July Apotheosis". At the public dress rehearsal in the Opéra on 13 December the three marches fell flat, only Halévy's raising some tepid applause. He had the satisfaction of being accosted afterwards on the main staircase by one of the orchestra, a man unknown to him, who grasped his hand and exclaimed, "M. Berlioz, here is a day that puts you on top of the Vendôme Column."* "Everyone missed him," said the *Ménestrel* – "friends and unbelievers."

The finale of the *Symphonie militaire* figured in a mammoth concert that he gave at the Opéra shortly before, on Sunday 1 November, with more than four hundred performers – the Opéra orchestra augmented by the extra woodwind, brass and percussion required for the big movements of the Requiem as well as for the Apotheosis, and a large chorus. The concert was intended as a retrospective of his most recent work (including movements from *Romeo*). He had been planning such a project at least since the previous March, when he applied to the

---

* The column commemorating Napoleon in the Place Vendôme.

Ministry for permission to give a similar concert in the Panthéon and was turned down. Berlioz was not invariably successful in his approaches to the authorities: Louis-Philippe, about this time, refused the proffered dedication of the Napoleonic cantata *Le cinq mai* (it was dedicated, much more appropriately, to Horace Vernet). But, to the opposition satirists, his pretensions were asking to be attacked. The "Festival de M. Berlioz" at the Opéra roused *Charivari* to fresh flights of inventive sarcasm: the concert, "grandiloquently announced under the title of festival", was, it said, merely the means of satisfying the self-esteem of the critic of the *Journal des débats*. It would be followed – "in response to universal demand" – by "the ascension of M. Hector Berlioz in a bass drum", from which, when it reached the flies, the composer would address the audience: "I am the famous Hercules of music of whom you have no doubt heard. France, my ungrateful country, has denied my genius. What have I done to it, ladies and gentlemen, that it should not appreciate me? I have written music!", etc., etc. At the end the drum's skin would split and deposit M. Berlioz with a crash on to the stage. *Charivari* also seized on rumours of opposition to Berlioz among Habeneck's henchmen to claim that the musicians had sent a petition to the minister registering their unwillingness to perform under his direction (a favourite journalistic ploy, used in our own time against Pierre Boulez); they would rather be sent to work on the fortifications that Louis-Philippe was building on the outskirts of Paris.

The concert provoked from Paul Scudo a review which achieved new depths. Blaze de Bury, Karr, Azevedo, Fétis himself, were far surpassed. The review, given here in full, is a sample of the work of the man whom his teacher Choron described as "a blackguard and a confidence trickster", but who, from 1840, when he became music critic of the *Revue des deux mondes*, till 1864, when he died in a lunatic asylum, was a dedicated thorn in Berlioz's side.

> Rossini wrote from Italy after the first performance of *Puritani*: "I do not speak of the famous duet between Lablache and Tamburini – you must have heard it from Bologna." What would the great man have said if he had been at M. Berlioz's festival? We believe he would still be laughing. Never was a more comical affair presented before an assembled group of friends (the word public is not applicable here). Everyone was laughing, the violins and oboes and trumpets behind their stands and the spectators in their stalls. The music for the dead can at least boast that it made the living laugh till they cried.

How is one to render account of such a spree? What can one say of the posters six feet high, of the musicians stacked to the flies, of the mountains of ophicleides and trombones vomiting their ghastly cataracts of sound? Of that musical mish-mash, that chaos which the audience received with a mocking smile and saluted, on leaving, with an Olympian yawn? At bottom, it is quite simply Hoffmann taken literally. People reproach M. Berlioz for his extravagant lucubrations; but M. Berlioz could perfectly well reply that music has nothing to do with what he is up to. When M. Berlioz splashes his posters on every wall, when M. Berlioz erects his scaffolding, he is engaged in bringing to life the weird and wonderful tales of Hoffmann. If he piles the double-basses and ophicleides, the cymbals and side-drums and Turkish crescents sky-high, it's to give substance to the fantasies of the sublime storyteller of Berlin. The music of M. Berlioz is critic's music; to take it at its apparent face value would be the height of absurdity – you might as well look for reality in "The Golden Pot" or "The Life of Kreisler" or "Murr the Cat". The public does not appear to us to have understood the full irony of those trombones which roar at the slightest provocation or the subtle, teasing mockery behind those eternally thudding bass drums. Here, in our view, is the reason why the public does not appreciate M. Berlioz and persists in refusing him an honoured place among the great masters. Once it has understood that what the author of all those fantastic symphonies and operas is trying to do is not to establish a genre but to criticize it for the disastrous thing it is – once it has become clear that M. Berlioz is presenting his lucubrations as Hoffmann did his fantastic tales, not for them to be taken seriously but so as to demonstrate to one and all that art would be on the verge of ruin if it ever took such a wrong direction, then the public which today rejects him will receive him with applause and raise triumphal arches in his name; for it will realize just how well this musician has deserved of art in offering a warning example of unrestrained excess and thus steering the general taste away from the dead-end it was straying into and towards the serene and harmonious worship of the ideal and the beautiful.

However, there are certain actions, wanting in respect, which M. Berlioz should have abjured with regard to two of the greatest masters that music has ever known. One should not presume to deal on equal terms with men of the stamp of Gluck and Palestrina, and we do not think their masterpieces are free to be treated just as if it were a question of the *Francs-juges* overture or the *Sardanapale* cantata. M. Berlioz has enough at his disposal to provide his musico-satirical entertainments on his own.

There is every reason to protest against the deplorable behaviour of those who make a point of altering the text instead of transmitting it honestly. If there is one thing that is holy and may not be meddled with without a kind of sacrilege it is surely the mind of a genius. Performing a score means transmitting it; and to presume to give to a work of Gluck or Palestrina something extraneous which could not have been part of the composer's intentions is quite simply to travesty it in a monstrous manner, to profane it. One would suppose M. Berlioz had taken it on himself to demonstrate to the universe that no music can exist without the formidable apparatus of which he has constituted himself the disposer supreme. The music of the future is not enough – he must have the music of the past as well; he must reinforce Palestrina and run amok among the works of Gluck. Old Gluck, the master of the terrible, the poet of *Armide* and *Iphigénie*, is not sufficiently highly coloured for his taste. Poor Gluck! You never imagined, when your orchestra called up "the spirits of hatred and rage" to the sound of trombones, that the day would come when M. Berlioz would help you out with a few ophicleides. Or Palestrina, serene master of religious inspiration – wrenched from the Sistine Chapel (where a few soprani suffice for his fugal melodies) and crushed beneath a vain display of voices and instruments. If the public had not shown, by its indifference, what it thought of such a parody, we should run the risk of soon seeing the masterpieces of Paisiello and Cimarosa performed in our theatres behind ranks of ophicleides and double-basses and trombones. All this is no doubt most entertaining, and the aim of it is comedy; but the great composers should not be involved in it, for then what was amusing becomes a scandal. Let M. Berlioz be the architect of his own reputation and recruit as much brass for his symphonies as he pleases, and even add a few marine trumpets to his regular artillery if he thinks it a good idea. But in God's name let him at least respect the masterpieces that time has hallowed; let him leave in peace those noble works that the world has embraced once and for all in their unvarnished simplicity, and let him in future abstain from invoking the royal shades of Palestrina and Gluck and making them the fawning lackeys of his own arrogance.

Berlioz had a rule, never to reply to hostile criticism; and it would have been better if he had left this confused heap of malice unanswered.

But the slur about Gluck and Palestrina was not to be endured. He wrote to the editor of the *Revue des deux mondes*, François Buloz, demanding rectification:

> The act from *Iphigénie* [*en Tauride* – Act 1] was performed exactly as the composer wrote it; no ophicleides, in consequence, were heard. As for Palestrina, a few sopranos were so far from sufficing him that his madrigal "Alla riva del Tebro" – a secular piece, by the way, which could never have been heard in the Sistine Chapel – was written in four parts, sopranos, contraltos, tenors and basses. It must have required a strange state of distraction to find that a choral piece, performed as the composer wrote it, *without* accompaniment, was "crushed beneath a vain display of instruments". These are the sole errors that I am concerned to point out. They wrong me in my role as interpreter of the masters I admire.

He might have saved his ink. Buloz did not get round to answering. The letter was printed a week or two later in the *Gazette* and the *Débats* and one or two other papers. But it never appeared in the *Deux mondes*. Instead, Scudo, without reproducing the letter, seized on it as a pretext for returning to the attack:

> We wish we did not always have to occupy our readers with the indiscretions, musical or otherwise, of the author of the Fantastic Symphony; but what can we do? When M. Berlioz is not giving a festival he writes us letters; when his baton leaves our ears in peace, his epistolary verve importunes us. Since the document is familiar – it has already appeared in any number of journals, "at the earnest request" of M. Berlioz, as each paper made clear – we will refrain from printing a fifteenth edition, believing that it is quite enough if we reply to it. It will perhaps be remembered that in our last review, while protesting against the air of familiarity and condescension which the fantastic musican assumed towards the great masters, we were rash enough to speak of ophicleides. M. Berlioz, pretending to take us literally, claims that there were no ophicleides in the piece and goes on to belabour us with his unanswerable argument, as if a material fact was all that was involved. We spoke of profanation, and we stand by it. Did M. Berlioz or did he not uproot an act, a scene, a gobbet from Gluck's score, so as to sandwich it between the ridiculous witches' sabbath that he put on under the name of "festival" – yes or no? That is the entire question. What has one ophicleide, or

twelve, more or less, to do with it? On such a subject one does not reckon with M. Berlioz, and we have no wish to argue with him about something of so little importance. The author of the Fantastic Symphony knows that very well; but he writes all the same. To write is to attract the public's attention to oneself. When one cannot give a "festival" or a concert one drafts a letter and hawks it round. It's publicity, and publicity that costs nothing. M. Berlioz thumps it as one thumps a bass drum to bring in the passers-by. He is right – the method works, sometimes. Sometimes, unfortunately, the opposite happens. Witness this episode in Vienna. By dint of hearing M. Berlioz publicize himself at all hours of the day, by dint of seeing his name blazoned from enormous posters amid the radiance of four hundred musicians, the Viennese were persuaded to take his reputation seriously and regard this singular beneficiary of Paganini's whimsical irony as the greatest composer who ever lived – all this without having heard a note of his music, or rather by virtue of the fact. Such is the continued power of charlatanism (whatever people may say); so true is it that a reputation can be forged by hitting hard enough, and a name worked up by round-the-clock publicity can for an instant stand in place of actual work. However, they are not countrymen of Mozart and Beethoven for nothing. The Viennese wished to find out for themselves. The overture to *Les francs-juges* was sent for from Paris. They performed it, or rather they attempted to perform it, for after the twentieth bar laughter broke up the performance, uncontrollable laughter from the orchestra and the audience, wholehearted unanimous laughter such as M. Berlioz's music alone has had the secret of since the time of Homer's Olympus, and which will ensure him fame in years to come; for, seen in their true light, as the Viennese saw them, M. Berlioz's lucubrations have more comedy in them than Rabelais put into *Pantagruel*. However, since not everyone believes that the art of sounds was invented to provoke mirth, the Viennese dilettantes soon laid the ill-omened *Francs-juges* overture aside and went back with all speed to the overture to *Coriolan*, to the C minor symphony, to Strauss' waltzes or whatever – anything, serious or not, that has the right to call itself music.

All this is fact. M. Berlioz can write to us to his heart's content. We shall not reply further. Only, if he succeeds in showing us to be inaccurate on this point as triumphantly as he has shown us to be on the other, we shall be happy to announce that Queen Mab (his, of course) is a master-piece of clarity and tunefulness, and that the four or five hundred musicians in his "festival" were wanting in common sense when they refused unanimously to disentangle this gibberish.

The critic had picked up a true fact and garbled it to his own ends. Berlioz himself withdrew the Queen Mab scherzo from the programme when it proved impossible to achieve an adequate performance in the rehearsal time available. The episode of the *Francs-juges* overture – the replica of the one in the Argyll Rooms in London – merely confirmed him in regretting that he had published the work. Schumann, commenting on the incident in the *Neue Zeitschrift für Musik*, had an answer: Viennese audiences were the most reactionary, the most impervious to the new, in all Europe. As for the barefaced distortion of Paganini's gift, Paganini might have given it its quietus; but he was not there to do so, having died the previous spring. In any case Berlioz knew better than to waste emotional energy on such crude personal attacks. Gluck was another matter. But the rest was the common currency of boulevard journalism, albeit a particularly nasty example and given a specious authority by the journal it appeared in. The attacks on Liszt in the Paris press after his triumphal reception in his native Hungary in 1839 make just as sad reading. Berlioz was by no means exceptional in this respect. Equally unpleasant things were written about Balzac (a target of systematic abuse in the same *Revue des deux mondes* throughout the 1840s), about Delacroix, about any artist who presumed to do something different and challenge the sacred norms of bourgeois culture. It was just malign bad luck that the *Revue des deux mondes* happened to be one of the papers Dr Berlioz saw. But I doubt if the sneers of Scudo and his kind made as strong an impression on their victim as they do on us, reading them today, or if they contributed much to the sense of growing disillusionment that can be detected in him around this time.

Disillusionment first and foremost as to the possibility of establishing anything serious in Paris, of making sustained headway against the obstacles in his path. There is nothing new about such obstacles: he knows them of old; but they are becoming, psychologically speaking, more formidable; he is losing patience with the intricate manoeuvring required in order to get things done in France; he is beginning to have moments when he wonders if the game is worth the candle, in terms of either nervous energy or – more immediately to the point – cash.

His concert at the Conservatoire on 13 December – the first four movements of *Romeo*, *Sara la baigneuse*, *Le cinq mai* (sung by Alizard) and the Fantastic Symphony – earned him a note from Balzac expressing "profound admiration" and wishing he were "as rich as the late Paganini – I would do better than merely writing to you; as it is I can only tell you what he proved to not a few imbeciles, that you are a great musician and a fine genius". But it also earned him a deficit of twelve hundred francs.

It was the same with his "festival" at the Opéra. On balance it seems to have been an artistic success. Reviews were mainly favourable. His friend Dufeuillant, who accompanied Harriet to the concert and who saw Adèle and Marc Suat a few days later, told them that (as Adèle reported to Nancy) "Hector's festival was pretty successful. The Opéra was full and there was a brilliant society audience. Certain passages were greeted with loud applause. There was one solitary boo, which made poor Harriet burst into tears." The system of sectional rehearsals devised for *Romeo and Juliet*, though so taxing to the stamina and concentration of the conductor – going from the Opéra to the Théâtre-Italien to the Conservatoire and back, and on his feet for hours at a stretch – again proved its worth, and the long and demanding programme was brought off with only a single general rehearsal. The Opéra orchestra seems to have come round to being directed by him instead of by Habeneck; and in the end all the talk of sabotage, the greasing of double-bass bows, slitting of timpani heads, "accidental" miscrooking of trumpets, which the press made much of and which caused Berlioz a panicky twenty-four hours, turned out to be groundless. The reception was good; the solitary boo at the end of the Dies irae prompted such a heartening demonstration from spectators and performers that he would have "paid a thousand francs if it had been for sale".

Even the disruptions to the concert, though he could have done without them, helped to make it a talking-point, the condition of true success in Paris. The first, when the pit called for the Marseillaise (either as a counter-attraction to Berlioz's music or as a gesture against the government ministers and members of the royal family present, or both), was soon over. The second was more eventful. Just as the interval began, Bergeron, editor of the *Charivari* and a member of the staff of the republican *Siècle*, entered Emile de Girardin's box and slapped his face. It was a riposte to Girardin for insinuating, in the pro-government *Presse*, that Bergeron had been involved in the attempts on the King's life. Mme de Girardin – the writer Delphine Gay – screamed "Help!

murder!", and the whole house rose in alarm. The two men were forcibly separated and the aggressor was led away still shouting his name. In the foyer there was more politics: a man came up to Montalivet and attacked him verbally in violent terms (Thiers, standing near by, prudently made his escape). Many left before the final item in the programme, the Apotheosis. Despite all this, Berlioz could count the evening a major achievement, except in one particular: he did not make a sou from it, in fact was left 130 francs out of pocket.

This is a constant refrain of 1840 and the years that followed. After all his efforts over the past six seasons he was as far as ever from subsisting on the proceeds of his music – further, in fact: for now he lost on it. "Music on a large scale ('la grande musique') is ruining me". That there were special factors involved in the last two instances – a public rehearsal for the Napoleonic ceremony a few hours after his Conservatoire concert, which cut the potential audience, and the unexpected necessity of paying the Opéra musicians as well as the additional players in order to keep them happy, which swallowed up his fee for the festival concert – did not alter the fundamental truth. He was forced to face it squarely. Paganini's generosity had saved him but ultimately had changed nothing. How could it? The situation remained much as it had always been; in fact it had got worse. It is notable that when the winter season came round again at the end of 1841 Berlioz gave no concert, at the Conservatoire or anywhere else; for the first November and December since 1831 (when he was in Rome) there was no musical event given by or associated with him. Two years before, he had performed *Romeo and Juliet* three times in succession in less than a month. But *Romeo* itself had helped to educate him and strip away the illusion which Paganini had fostered. All the months of work that went into it, and the splendid box-office receipts (13,200 francs), had yielded a profit of precisely 1,100 francs. "Is it not sad to have to recognize that so fine a result – given the smallness of the hall and the habits of the public – is insignificant if I look to it as a means of existence? Serious art simply does not nourish the individual."

This new mood of discouragement, only temporarily deflected by the popularity of the Symphonie militaire, is discernible in Berlioz from the beginning of the year 1840, in the immediate aftermath of *Romeo and Juliet*. Partly it was a natural reaction to all the tension and exhaustion and exhilaration, a reaction more acute even than normally followed the conclusion of great enterprises. Like Sherlock Holmes in

"The Reigate Squires", after the case of Baron Maupertuis and the Netherland-Sumatra Company, he was a prey to the blackest depression. Two months later he was still in a state of nervous prostration; his spleen was such that he "could have massacred the Eternal Father and His Son". Nothing had savour any more. He felt "a hundred and ten years old".

His irritation, exacerbated by the high winds in Paris that January, had other causes too. One was the extreme response of his relatives to Janin's review of *Romeo*. Janin had spoken of the tribulations of the young Berlioz, too poor to replace a broken guitar string and forced to take a job in the chorus line of the Opéra-Comique (*sic*). Both Nancy, the first to see the article, and Dr Berlioz ("my old blood rose to my head when I read the opening lines of your letter") took it as a grave slur on the family's dignity and social position. Dr Berlioz sent his son a deeply reproachful letter; and Nancy, working herself into a fine fury (who would have thought, she told Félix Marmion, that she and not Adèle would be the *exaltée* of the family?) penned the critic a vigorous missive. In it she refuted the implication that Berlioz's father had not supported him in Paris, pointed out that it was his father who gave him his liberal education, and would leave him a hundred and forty thousand francs when he died, and urged Janin to publish a retraction. The reply was prompt but coolly impenitent: Janin stood by everything he said. Nancy copied both letters and sent them to her uncle, complaining that Janin, quite apart from his lack of courtesy to a woman, had "failed to understand that it was my parents, my gentle, honorable father, that I was defending and not my brother's reputation as a rich man or a poor man". Marmion could only console her with the reflection that even the finest feuilletons were ephemeral; an "insolent hack", a "spurious and mendacious mind" like Janin, "however fluent and brilliant", would not survive into posterity if that was the best he could offer. "Sooner or later I shall have occasion to meet him; when I do I shall compliment him on his gallantry and his respect for the truth." Adèle alone, for once, took a relaxed view.

> It seems clear that Jeanin [*sic*] was determined to write his little romance at whatever cost – what matter whether it was true or not? Those gentlemen are not very particular. [. . .] Here I interrupted my letter to listen to what an artist said about [Hector] in the *Temps*, Marc brought it home from the club and read it aloud; it's extremely laudatory. So,

dear sister, we should let ourselves enjoy [his success] unreservedly. Do the journalist's absurd stories matter? What strangers and the indifferent think is of little concern to us, and our relations and friends know perfectly well how things stand.

Berlioz's reply to his father has not survived. The letter he wrote to Nancy can hardly have satisfied her and did not put an end to the animated family debate.

Friday evening   [13 December 1839]
I've hardly time to reply, dear sister, but tomorrow I shall have none at all. It was not from my father but from my uncle that I learned of the upsetting effect of Janin's article on you all. I myself was annoyed by it for a thousand reasons, the least of which concerned me. Above all I thought of how it would make people attribute to my excellent father a character and social position that are not his. But what false notions you form, from a distance, of the press and the way it functions! It's entirely fluid and unpredictable. I hadn't seen Janin for a fortnight when his article appeared, I had no idea when he was going to do it, and before he published it it never entered his head, any more than it did mine, that he should submit it to me for censorship. If I had known he would raise that ancient history I should certainly have begged him not to, but I had no reason to suppose he would. I have just seen him; when I explained things, he said that of course he wouldn't have.

As for the facts, it's pointless to contest them: too many artists knew me and saw me at the Théâtre des Nouveautés for the thing to have been kept secret. Besides, I was then so desperate, so incensed at the opposition I was encountering that, rather than return to La Côte as they wanted to force me to, I was attempting to go to East Africa or America. I failed to find an opportunity to do so, and it was then that I went to the Nouveautés. I need not remind you that short of dying of hunger [the letter stops there: the rest has been torn off].

Another irritant – one he could not avoid – concerned Paganini's affairs. The ailing violinist wrote from Nice on 20 January 1840 asking his friend to help his Paris lawyer assemble the papers required for settling a case arising out of the activities of the casino and pleasure gardens which had been set up in his name in the Rue de la Chaussée d'Antin two years before. Berlioz was still involved with it in March, to judge by a letter from Paganini to his Genoese lawyer: "You may freely write to this same friend Berlioz, whom you should not confuse with the common riff-raff but should look on as a transcendent genius such as arises but once every three or four hundred years and as a man of the utmost probity, worthy of our trust."

Paganini died on 27 May 1840, in Nice, never having heard the work he had made possible. His passing left Berlioz feeling yet more isolated. It underlined the uniqueness of the great act of philanthropy which had brought *Romeo and Juliet* into being but which had otherwise changed nothing. He could echo only too fervently the sentiments of Gautier's friend the violinist-composer Allyre Bureau, who wrote in the socialist newspaper the *Phalange* that Berlioz was "a composer whom France would do better to take pride in than amuse itself by disparaging and belittling all it can. No doubt they are waiting till he is dead to discover that quite possibly he was something of a genius." Such testimonies, however pleasing, needed translating into material terms. The July symphony, after all the costs had been paid, cleared him a little under 3,000 francs, which relieved the pressure for a while. But there was no security in such occasional windfalls, and no certainty that there would be any more. The lucrative official position he had sought for years still eluded him; his post as deputy librarian of the Conservatoire, at 1,500 francs a year less tax, only nibbled at the problem. With about 1,500 from the *Débats* it gave him an income of 3,000; and he needed well over twice that to live in Paris. Meanwhile, the capital from the remains of Paganini's money, which he had invested at Rothschild's Bank, was diminishing fast. He was back almost where he had been before Paganini's gift, a slave to journalism, with all the psychological consequences that followed – more and more dependent on it, less and less able to stand it. The account in the *Memoirs* of the three days he spent in his room vainly trying to write a review, while his thoughts flew off "a thousand miles from that accursed opéra-comique", belongs to this year.

Paganini's death was for Berlioz the symbolic end of an era. Audiences were actually getting smaller; the public was losing interest. The trend which culminated three years later in the fiasco of Victor Hugo's play *Les Burgraves* was under way. With the advent of the capitalist-industrialist decade – the railway decade (the Paris–Versailles line had recently opened), the decade of Guizot's slogan "Enrichissez-vous!" – Romanticism was being seen as a spent force, a nuisance: it no longer possessed either the sensation value or the genuine appeal it had had in the 1830s;

it was barely tolerated. From now on, as Barzun remarks, "the careers of Hugo, Vigny, Delacroix and Berlioz become a ceaseless guerrilla".

It was not only Berlioz's music that felt the effects. A subscription, opened in France in 1839 to help pay for a statue to Beethoven in his birthplace, Bonn – an initiative of Liszt's – closed twelve months later at the grand total of 438 francs. Reviewing the final Conservatoire concert of the 1840 season, Berlioz noted that the audience for a programme which included the Seventh Symphony was so small that it could easily have been counted. "Yes, it was a warm sunny day, yes the great fountains were playing at Versailles, yes the races were on, yes there had already been ten other fine concerts this year in the same hall, supplied by the same celebrated composers, performed by the same virtuosos, and paid for at the same prices; and yes, one gets tired of everything, even of paying". Two or three years before, the hall would have been full.

Paris was becoming less and less likely, in his eyes, as a place where great things could be achieved in music – least of all in the theatre, which at the advent of Donizetti, the conqueror from Italy, had simply rolled over and was waving its paws in helpless surrender. Berlioz knew that he could have revolutionized performing standards at the Théâtre-Italien – not to mention his own bank balance – if he had been given the job. For the same reasons he actively sought the succession to Habeneck at the Opéra, when in 1841 the ageing conductor was widely rumoured to be going to replace the even older Cherubini as director of the Conservatoire. The Opéra was in dire need of a firm artistic hand (a Berlioz feuilleton, about this time, speaks of the dreadful languor and casualness of the ensembles in a revival of The Huguenots). In its present state there was nothing to be done there. The discussions with Scribe in 1840 about a possible opera were pursued with no more sense of urgency on the composer's side than on the librettist's. When they did finally agree on a project Berlioz felt in no hurry. Who would play the male lead now that Duprez was losing his voice? As for poor Falcon, she had lost hers. The great soprano, still only twenty-five, made her long-awaited come-back on 14 March 1840 in a benefit performance which included three acts of La Juive and the love duet from The Huguenots. After eighteen months' rest and study the singer believed she was cured. So did everybody. But the evening was one long agony. In the Débats three days later Berlioz mourned the destruction of a voice that "by its range, its force, the beauty of its accents, the infinite gradations of its timbre, its dramatic expression and unblemished purity" had been "a marvel".

With Falcon went any hope of dramatic values regaining their primacy at the Opéra. The rumour going round that spring, that they were thinking of putting on Weber's masterpiece, filled him with alarm, as he wrote in the *Gazette*. "There was talk recently of dismembering the *Freischütz* and serving it up, dressed after the approved manner of Parisian cuisine, to the gluttonous appetites of the Opéra pit." Happily the threat had been lifted and Weber, for the moment, had escaped.

Music's low status in Paris was bizarrely exemplified by the summons he received that September, condemning him to two days' detention for failing to turn up for National Guard duty on 29 July, the day after the celebrations in the Place de la Bastille. When he pointed out that his guard duty the day before, directing two hundred musicians for five hours at a state ceremony, surely earned him an exemption, his sentence was reduced; but he still had to spend twenty-four hours in the "Hôtel des Haricots", as the prison on the Quai d'Austerlitz was known. The punishment, commonplace though it might be, was in its absurd way symptomatic.

All this led to one conclusion. The time had come to do what he had long been thinking of doing: travel, take his music to other countries than France, above all to Germany where – as Liszt kept reminding him – it was eagerly awaited. "Aren't you going to introduce your symphonies to Germany, which will understand them and love them?" wrote Liszt in the *Gazette*; "Germany is their true fatherland." Since Schumann's long article on the Fantastic Symphony in 1835, Berlioz had been steadily attracting notice as a musical phenomenon worth investigating; the first astonishment that France should have anything to export beyond opéra-comique had given way to curiosity and interest. From early in 1840 his name became more familiar still through the reprinting of his *Débats* articles in Schumann's *Neue Zeitschrift für Musik*; by the end of the year they had appeared in twenty issues of the journal. His overtures were becoming well known. The *Francs-juges* in particular had been heard all over the place – in Leipzig several times, in Berlin, in Weimar, Bremen, Mainz, Cologne – and had inspired the composer and conductor Johann Christian Lobe, friend of Liszt and of Goethe, to publish an open letter in the *Neue Zeitschrift*. "During your overture, which is unquestionably the expression of a great and rare musical talent, the Weimar audience was not for one second brought

up short, still less baffled by the work, but on the contrary transfixed.
Your overture was like a shock, a flash of lightning, and it drew an
answering glow of enthusiasm. The success it obtained was not mere
goodwill, such as is accorded to an established figure or to an acquaintance, a friend, a compatriot. The audience had no choice: it conquered
them irresistibly."

Clearly, it was time for the bigger works. They were increasingly in
demand. For several years he had been turning down requests for his
symphonies, waiting till he could perform them in Germany himself.
Now was the moment. By rights, 1840 should have been the year. All
through 1839 and in the last days of 1838 his letters spoke of the
impending tour. Immediately after Paganini's gift: "I can now make a
trip to Germany. Chance has brought to Paris this winter a whole crowd
of German artists who show the most encouraging zeal for my music."
In February 1839, to Schumann: "I mean to come and see you in Leipzig
next year." In March he told Adèle he had to undertake "a big journey
next year in Germany, and I'm preparing for it in all sorts of ways, by
my work and by taking steps to safeguard my position in France before
I leave". Six months later, in November 1839, he regretted not being
able to consider visiting Ferrand in Sardinia: "I must cross the Rhine
and not the Mediterranean. The German tour is indispensable, and
everything has been prepared perfectly for me, so I am assured." Shortly
afterwards, he was "more intent than ever on this far-flung musical
tour".

And then nothing. In April 1840 he makes inquiries about the possibility of giving a concert in Munich or Speyer around the time of a Bavarian
festival at which his Requiem is to be performed ("the concert would
pay my travelling expenses"). But of the tour of Germany there is not
another word. Silence descends on the whole ambitious project. What
occurred to alter his resolve and put off, for so long, something on
which he had set his heart, something so clearly indicated and in his
best, most pressing interests?

He could have been delayed at various times by events in the French
capital. The composition of the July symphony and the lobbying
required kept him in Paris throughout the spring and summer of 1840
(he did not get confirmation of the commission till the second week of
July). It is possible, too, that the festival concert at the Opéra on 1
November had priority over everything else, being designed not only
to remind Paris of the Dies irae and the Lacrymosa – twice in the

previous eighteen months he had tried unsuccessfully to have them performed – but also to demonstrate his powers as a conductor in the citadel of Paris musical life and show what he could do at the helm of the Opéra's orchestra and chorus. (That would explain too why he sacrificed his fee to allay the dissatisfaction of the orchestra at not getting paid as the auxiliary musicians were.) In April 1841 he "daren't leave Paris" for the same reason: the post of musical director may be about to become vacant, so he must be on hand in case that happens.

These are details, however, arguably not enough in themselves to account for the German tour being postponed so long. There was still room for a trip of a month or two. The overriding reason was something else. It was Harriet who stopped him.

"On one pretext or another my wife had always opposed my plans for travelling." So Berlioz in the *Memoirs*, attributing it to an "insane jealousy" for which he had given "absolutely no grounds" but which "in the end had cause". The sense of shame and guilt and regret behind those last words is undisguised. No matter that he had been driven to it by the nagging accusations which finally precipitated the thing she dreaded, no matter that he continued to support and care for her: he had done exactly what his parents had said he would when they opposed his marriage. He had left her for another.

To begin with it was not so much jealousy as utter dependency. The thought of separation was too much for her. She had grown too reliant on him to bear his absence; she could not cope without him.

Harriet's demoralization had happened very gradually. There were many contributory and interacting causes, but one fundamental cause from which most of the others derived. She who had worked for as long as she could remember, and been accustomed to support others and provide for the household, was condemned to complete professional inactivity and to earning not one penny. Instead she had to stand by and watch, with a mixture of distress and injured pride, while her husband slaved to pay off debts which had been largely hers in the first place. She was conscious too of powers as great as ever and longing to be used but which she could do nothing about; she had become, in Raby's phrase, "a resonant memory". The total lack of artistic fulfilment on her side created a gulf between their experiences. If she had been able to go on working, the inherent stresses of living with a creative artist might have been less intense. Harriet loyally supported Berlioz in his career, sometimes persuading him to take risks that he himself hesitated to take. But the daily contrast between his activity and her enforced idleness gnawed at her self-esteem. When he went to his study to work, she had nothing comparable to go to. She felt useless.

For the first five years of their marriage he as loyally strove for her return to the stage, believing passionately in her genius and feeling for her in her frustration, and only giving up when she herself finally lost heart. Exactly when the tensions undermining the relationship forced their way to the surface and began to dominate daily life is a question we cannot answer. When Adèle and her husband came to Paris at the end of May 1839, Berlioz and Harriet obviously put their best foot forward; but Adèle was in their company every day for three weeks and would hardly have missed signs of serious disharmony. Her verdict on her brother's ménage is categorical: Hector and his wife are happy and very united.

What her more sharp-eyed sister Nancy Pal thought when she came to Paris thirteen months later is not known. Nancy must have written to Adèle and to her father but her letters have not survived. The evidence for the visit is indirect: a note from Félix Marmion written in late March 1840, urging Nancy to hurry and pack her bags so as to be in time to attend Hector's "grande fête musicale" (the projected Panthéon concert); an undated letter from Berlioz to Alfred de Vigny inviting him to come and take an evening cup of tea with them – "last year I presented my young sister, now it's the turn of the elder"; a later remark of Berlioz's, recalling the summer evening when he and Nancy called on Félix Marmion at his apartment on the Quai d'Orsay; and two letters to Nancy from Nancy Clappier which show that the visit took place some time in June 1840. Her account of the trip delighted her old friend but left her wanting more. Had she nothing to tell about her brother? What famous people did she see? "Was M. Janin one of them? An encounter with him under the auspices of Hector would have been interesting." Nancy's reply made her godmother commiserate with her on the "impressions you received in Paris"; but her dissatisfaction seems to have had nothing to do with her brother's marriage and everything to do with ancient frustrations and sibling rivalries. "I suffered for you," Mlle Clappier continues.

> What true things you say, well observed and well expressed, and, later,
> about artists and men of letters. They live in another world; they no
> longer know how to sympathize or speak with us. That is hard, and it

upsets me. One has to think of them as beings apart; but a brother, to whom one goes open-heartedly – that is a blow. I trust at least he doesn't share the idiotic arrogance of our little authors (for I feel the need to cut them down to size) and that he'll resist such infatuation. It seems to me he is in a high enough position to escape that idiocy. He has so fine a tact, he is so quick to perceive the absurdity of things, that he must have laughed at it more than once. My poor child, perhaps you find a great man in your brother instead of the friend of earlier days.

Yet I have the feeling that if Nancy had let herself speak freely she would have declared that all was not well in the Berlioz household. This, of course, is speculation. The inferences from what is known could be drawn differently. Thus the dejection he confesses to in a letter of January 1840 to Ferrand – "If you knew how sad I feel within! Horribly sad. What will become of me?" – could be simply the physical and psychological reaction after *Romeo and Juliet*. Again, though it is possible that the composition of *Les nuits d'été*, apparently begun in the spring of 1840, came out of a profound sense of emotional disillusionment and loss – the cycle starting with a springtime idyll but passing through the death of the lover to reach the conclusion that the "faithful shore" where love "lasts for ever" is only a dream – it cannot stand as sure evidence of his private life or even of his state of mind at the time he composed it. That was not how his creative processes functioned.

Equally, his going to visit his father for a week or two in September 1840 on his own, without taking his wife and his son with him, does not necessarily carry ominous implications. Perhaps, when he saw his father, he hinted that there was trouble at home. It was during this visit that Dr Berlioz spoke of his own deep depression and of the overdose of opium he had taken a few months before in the hope of ending it. But all we know is what Berlioz wrote on his return to Paris. "I arrived dead-beat at four in the morning. Impossible to describe the delight of Harriet and Louis: I might have been coming back from New Holland at the very least. We talked a lot of La Côte and especially of you, dear father. Harriet is deeply touched by the desire you expressed to get to know her. You need not doubt that the moment there is a chance for all three of us to come and spend a month with you we shall seize it. The presents I brought for Louis made him jump for joy; but I have to tell you that, pleased as he was with the letter and the slippers from

Mathilde, Monique's brioches and jams were a much more sensational success." It is not hard to imagine what happened: Berlioz wanting Harriet, and Louis, to come with him, she unwilling, and he, not having seen his father for eight years and perhaps having already roused the old man's expectations, deciding to go all the same, by himself. Her reluctance is entirely understandable, given the early history of her relations, or rather non-relations, with her husband's family and given what we know of her extreme sensitivity to slights – a sensitivity which their belated friendliness soothed but did not heal. She needed more wooing, she needed more positive gestures of goodwill from the man whom her husband loved above all other men but who had at first disdained to consider her his daughter-in-law. Perhaps she had got them now. But by the time Berlioz was free to go to La Côte again it was too late.

All the same I do not see Harriet as the shrinking, passive, timorous character we meet in so many biographies of Berlioz. The actress who worked out her own innovatory conception of Ophelia in secret and imposed it on the Odéon public was not shrinking. The woman who, though prostrate with a broken leg and in severe pain, protested when her company tried to exclude two of their number from a share in the proceeds of a benefit performance and urged Mlle Mars to refuse to take part unless the two actors were reinstated, was not passive. The wife who encouraged her husband to have his music performed even if it meant losing money they could not afford was not timorous. To the charge often made against her that she was a chronically bad manager and a spendthrift – a charge based on an inadequate notion of the couple's debts, and valid only for the years of her decline – there is an answer in the testimony of Adèle: that, in June 1839, Harriet was "looking after the household with the greatest zeal". To the equally common and censorious complaint that she never took the trouble to learn French, there is an answer in her extant letters, written without her husband's help. There are very few of them; they contain mistakes; spelling is eccentric; infinitives and participles are apt to be interchanged. But she can get along in it. When Félix Marmion visited her during Berlioz's absence in Germany, she harangued him about her grievances for an hour – in French. If, later, she confessed apologetically that she could not write to her sister-in-law, it was not because she was unable to express herself in the language but because her morale had sunk too low. She was ashamed. She had lost belief in herself.

Harriet in 1827, when the "celestial Smithson" was at the height of her fame.

Liszt (1811–86) at about the age of 30. The friendship between him and Berlioz, which for twenty-five years was very close, enriched both their lives.

Paganini (1782–1840). The great violinist's admiration had an important influence on Berlioz's early career.

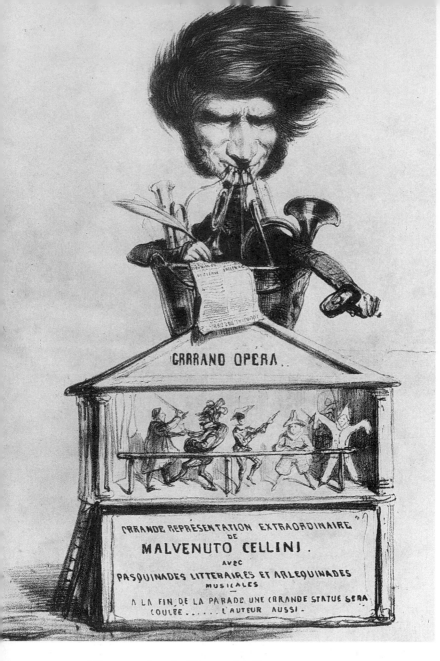

"L'homme orchestre" – "One-man band".

Above, left: Giacomo Meyerbeer (1791–1864).
Above, right: François-Antoine Habeneck (1781–1849), with snuff-box.
Below, left: Jules Janin (1804–74), drama critic of the Journal des Débats *and colleague and friend of Berlioz.*
Below, right: Armand Bertin (1801–54), chief editor of the Débats *during most of the period when Berlioz was the paper's music critic.*

GRANDE SALLE DES MENUS-PLAISIRS.

(GARDE-MEUBLE DE LA COURONNE),

Rue Bergère, N° 2.

Dimanche 16 Décembre 1838, à deux heures précises,

DEUXIÈME ET DERNIER

GRAND CONCERT VOCAL ET INSTRUMENTAL,

donné

Par M. Hector BERLIOZ,

Dans lequel on entendra M. Alexandre BATTA.

Programme.

1° **Harold**, symphonie en quatre parties, avec un alto principal, de
M. Berlioz. L'alto solo sera joué par M. Urhan.
>   1re partie : *Harold aux montagnes, scènes de mélancolie, de bonheur et de joie.*
>   2e partie : *Marche de pélerins chantant la prière du soir.*
>   3e partie : *Sénérade d'un montagnard des Abruzzes à sa maîtresse.*
>   4e partie : *Orgie de Brigands, souvenirs des scènes précédentes.*

2° **Grand air** de *Marie Stuart*, paroles de M. de Jouy, musique de
M. Giulio Alari, chanté par Mme Laty.

3° **Le Jeune Pâtre Breton**, romance tirée du poëme de *Marie* de
M. Brizeux, musique de M. Berlioz, chantée par Mme Stoltz.

4° **Cantando un di**, madrigal à deux voix, de l'abbé Clari (ancienne
école d'Italie), chanté par M. Boulanger et Mlle Bodin.

5° **Solo de violoncelle**, par M. Alexandre Batta.

6° **Grande scène** du troisième acte d'*Alceste* de Gluck, chantée par
M. Alizard et Mme Stoltz, terminée par l'air final du premier acte
du même opéra.

>   RÉCITATIF :
>   Air : *Qui me parle? Que répondre?*
>   (Ce morceau appartient à l'*Alceste italienne*, il n'a jamais été exécuté à Paris.)
>   Chœur : *Malheureuse! où vas-tu?*
>   Air : *Ah! divinités implacables!*
>   Air : *Caron t'appelle!*
>   Air : *Ombres! Larves!*
>   — NOTA. Cet air est celui dont les paroles françaises chantées à la représentation, sont :
>   *Divinités du Styx.* Le traducteur ayant mutilé et défiguré la phrase du début, le premier
>   vers a été changé pour pouvoir reproduire la partie de chant telle que Gluck l'avait conçue
>   dans l'origine.

7° **Symphonie fantastique** en 5 parties, de M. Berlioz (*redemandée*).
>   1re partie : *Rêveries, passions.*
>   2e partie : *Un bal.*
>   3e partie : *Scène aux champs.*
>   4e partie : *Marche du supplice.*
>   5e partie : *Songe d'une nuit du sabbat, Dies irœ burlesque, Ronde du sabbat.*
>   La *Ronde du sabbat* et le *Dies irœ* ensemble.

L'Orchestre, composé de 100 musiciens, sera conduit par M. H. BERLIOZ.

Prix des places : 1res loges, 8 fr.; Secondes, 6 fr.; Loges de rez-de-chaussée 5 fr.; Stalles de
galerie, 8 fr.; Stalles d'orchestre, 5 fr.; Parterre, 3 fr.; Amphithéâtre, 2 fr.

On trouve des Billets chez M. Retty, au conservatoire, et chez M. Schlesinger, rue de
Richelieu, n 97.

Vinchon, Imprimeur du Conservatoire de Musique, rue J.-J. Rousseau, 8.

*Handbill of the concert of 16 December 1838, at the end of which Paganini came
up on the platform and knelt before Berlioz.*

One of two pages, in Berlioz's hand, showing some of the recipients of complimentary tickets (more than two hundred) for the first performance of his symphony
Romeo and Juliet, *the work whose composition Paganini's gift of 20,000 francs had
made possible. Over thirty journals are listed. Among the individuals named are
Heine and Wagner.*

Marie Recio (1814–62), Berlioz's mistress, later his wife.

Her decline was slow but cumulative and irreversible. We can trace it in Berlioz's letters, sometimes between the lines, sometimes openly. It came to affect everything – not only her marital life and her social relations but her management of the household, her demeanour, her dress. Many things conspired, some that are obvious, like the sacrifice of her career as an artist and the permanent frustration it caused, others that can only be conjectured. Persistent illness took its toll of her vigour and energy – not only pneumonia and pleurisy but also tonsillitis, influenza, toothache and inflammation of the gums, and a stream of heavy colds. Though she supported her husband to the hilt in all the manifold activity of his career, she would not have been human if she had not resented it and had not brooded on the contrast between his busy involvement in the artistic world and her exclusion from it. Inevitably she was left for long hours on her own, with her child and the servants. Her sense of isolation could only deepen and with it her loss of the will or the power to mitigate it. ("Harriet hardly ever goes out" is a refrain of the correspondence.) And when friends came to the house and the discussion grew animated, and Gautier and Liszt and the Deschamps brothers and Legouvé and Alfred de Vigny talked poetry and music and drama – "everything" (in Berlioz's words) "that constitutes life" – and Harriet's French, good enough for normal conversation, was unable to keep up, I don't doubt she could feel terribly out of it. As anyone knows who has had the experience, there is nothing that arouses feelings of insecurity and jealousy more quickly, even in those of sanguine temperament, than looking on while your nearest and dearest gabble away in a language you can't follow.

For a long time Berlioz did everything he could to reassure her, associating her as much as possible with his career, protecting her as much as possible from wounds to her sensibilities, even agreeing to put off his foreign travels, and striving to find work for her while there was any hope of it – but, as time went on, with a sense of helplessness before her increasing inability to help herself. The slight exasperation that occasionally shows itself in his letters in the first years of their marriage – as when he described Harriet's solitariness in Montmartre during the winter of 1835–6, which she might have lessened by visiting her neighbour Mme Blanche, wife of the director of the local asylum, if she had not been so frightened of the odd-looking inmates roaming the rooms and gardens of the place – had grown greater by the late 1830s, by which time her nervousness had become more acute and her tears ever more abundant.

She could still rouse herself. Adèle's visit in May–June 1839 acted as a tonic to her confidence. We catch a glimpse of the other Harriet as she accosts Dumas in the foyer of the Opéra and makes him promise to provide her sister-in-law with tickets for his latest play. It may be that her freshly stimulated spirits revived the flagging fortunes of their marriage and it was this momentarily recovered happiness that impressed Adèle.

Even when it had faded again, Berlioz continued to love Harriet, but with feelings in which passion, increasingly, was replaced by pity. To the end he did not cease to love her; but he pitied her more. Adèle noted that "[Hector's] wife loves him passionately; he is extremely attentive and considerate to her." Though Adèle seems to have accepted the distinction quite complacently, as if it were only natural, it speaks volumes.

The sexual relations even of people we know well are generally their own secret. Nothing can be proved about Berlioz's and Harriet's at this stage of their life together, any more than anything can be deduced from the fact that Harriet had only the one child. Legouvé's statement that her ardour grew as his cooled may or may not be true. But it seems very likely that physically they became less intimate. In that case no amount of attentiveness and consideration on his part could have made up for it: her frustration and sense of inadequacy as she reached forty were complete. Except for Louis, he was her whole life – and he was turning away from her; she no longer attracted him. The jealousy already active in her could only spread like a malignant disease.

Clearly, there was no precise moment when the Harriet of the first years of their marriage turned into the pathologically suspicious wife or, later, the secret drinker that Berlioz's letters to his sisters admitted she had become. It was a long-drawn-out, painful metamorphosis. But 1840 was, I believe, the crucial year. It was as if Paganini's 20,000 francs, instead of making things easier between them, had paradoxically made them more difficult by the very fact of relaxing the pressures under which they had been living their straitened but united life. And for Berlioz it was as if by the act of giving form and substance to Romeo's passion a chasm had finally been opened between the vision of what love might be and the reality of what it was, and he now found himself on the wrong side of it with no way of crossing back. From 1840 we have Legouvé's story of Louis being woken in the middle of the night by the noise of his mother berating his father, and the boy running to her and crying, "Mama! Mama! don't be like Madame Lafarge" – the murderess whose trial in the second half of the year fascinated the whole of France. The period of "bitter domestic strife" (the *Memoirs*' words) could have occurred in 1840, before what Berlioz had been accused of became, in 1841, fact.

There is one more piece of evidence – in Berlioz's music. If the *Nuits d'été*, however suggestive, cannot be used to prove anything, another song can. The composition of *La mort d'Ophélie* – his setting of Legouvé's paraphrase of the Queen's speech in *Hamlet* – marks, if not the actual, then the symbolic end of their marriage. The elegiac significance of this infinitely sad *mélodie* would be hard to miss even without the unmistakable reference in the voice part's first nine notes to the *idée fixe* of the Fantastic Symphony – Harriet's theme, now heard in the context of the drowning Ophelia. Its meaning is as clear as if he had told us. The manuscript of the song is dated 7 May 1842. By then Harriet's nightmare had come true.

IO

Marie

The circumstances in which Marie-Geneviève Martin alias Marie Recio entered Berlioz's life and took root there will probably never be known. His *Memoirs* give nothing away. She is introduced briefly and anonymously in connection with his "first musical expedition outside France", as the travelling companion who went with him and who since then has accompanied him on his various journeys. He adds that "by dint of being accused and tormented in countless ways, always unjustly, till I could find no peace or rest at home, in the end I came, by accident, to take the smooth with the rough, and my life was transformed".

There is practically no evidence from other sources either. (A Martin is listed among the female members of the chorus at the première of the Requiem in 1837; but the name was a common one.) For all we know, Marie could have been the unnamed young woman, the "fugitive", like her a singer, with whom Berlioz so nearly went to Berlin in 1833, and the "accident" their meeting again some years later. Their ages fit exactly – though in that case, for the idea to be feasible, the story of her being sold into servitude and kept captive would have to have been pure invention on the part of Janin and the others, devised in order to appeal to their friend's exaggerated sense of chivalry.

Very few biographers have had a good word for Berlioz's slim, voluptuous dark lady, daughter of a Grande Armée officer and of a Spanish woman, Sotera de Villas, whom Major Martin met (though he never married her) during the Peninsular War at about the time Berlioz's uncle, Second-Lieutenant Marmion, was distinguishing himself at Uclès and Santa Cruz de la Mudela. Henry Barraud accuses Marie of having "poisoned the remainder of Berlioz's existence". Not all accounts are hostile. When she died, the writer of her obituary in *La France musicale*, as if aware of the antagonism she aroused, was warm in his praise of "this devoted and intelligent woman". Evidently she had her admirers.

But the weight of contemporary witness is against her: she was of a jealous temperament; she had a sharp tongue and made trouble; she alienated many of Berlioz's friends; she was arrogant and given to bossing people about, not least her unfortunate lover. Adèle and Nancy referred to her as "la Princesse". Wagner asked Liszt whether "the Almighty would not have done better to leave women out of the scheme of creation. Berlioz has enabled me once again to observe with the precision of an anatomist how an unpleasant woman can wantonly ruin an altogether exceptional man." Louis Engel said that she "positively ill-treated" her husband. "In the midst of a rehearsal at Baden-Baden, she shouted 'Ector!' with a six-yards accent on the second syllable, simply to tell him there was a draught from an open window." Hanslick recalled her demanding imperiously, after a rehearsal in Prague, "Hector – my cape! Hector – my gloves!" Morel complained to Lecourt that their friend was "totally subjugated by a woman unworthy of him – this Recio who is mentioned here and there in his letters, a singer without talent who sings out of tune, who did him a great deal of harm in Germany, and, here, causes him to waste his time and his money (of which he never had that much) and to neglect his friends somewhat and his interests almost entirely".

In Legouvé's reminiscences there is an appalling story about Marie calling at 31 Rue de Londres and asking for Madame Berlioz and, on her appearing, repeating the request several times to a puzzled and flustered Harriet, before saying triumphantly, "No – you're the old Madame Berlioz, the one who's been discarded. I mean the young, the pretty, the real Madame Berlioz. I am she!" When Legouvé, having heard it from Berlioz himself, exclaimed in horror that he must break with her at once, Berlioz agreed that he should – but he could not: "I love her." Can we believe the story? Old men forget. They also, as Henry V remarked, "remember with advantages". Louis Schloesser, who had been a student in Le Sueur's class, concocted in old age a strange tale whereby Berlioz encountered Harriet Smithson and the other English actors, newly arrived from London, on a pleasure-boat on the Seine and immediately formed a friendship with her which on her side blossomed into deep affection, though not into love – all this at a time when Berlioz and Harriet had not even met. The story, with its echoes of Flaubert's *Education sentimentale*, is recounted in good faith and great circumstantial detail. Legouvé himself was no mean romancer. Yet his anecdotes, even when factually wrong, often seem right in emphasis. Though the tale of the two Madame Berliozes may be an invention, the Marie Recio we meet in eyewitness accounts and in her surviving letters might just, you feel, be capable of it.

If she subjugated him during her lifetime, you could say he took posthumous revenge. The intention declared in the Preface to the *Memoirs* – to refrain from "confessions" (in contrast to Rousseau) and to "admit none but venial sins" – is applied with rigour in her case. She makes barely an appearance, and never by name. Marie is no more than a footnote. Having referred in passing to the "travelling companion", the narrative returns to Harriet, whom he still "sees often" and for whom his "affection is in no way diminished; the wretched state of her health only makes her more dear to me". Marie isn't even granted an initial. Camille Moke is at least "Mlle M—". Marie Recio, in Berlioz's life, is like a minor Camille – a young woman of great physical charm who "set his senses on fire", a musician of far smaller gifts but who, having captivated him, did not let go.

Nowhere is there any hint that he felt for her the exalted type of love that Estelle, Harriet, Camille herself and, during his long liaison with Marie, several other women too in different ways inspired in him. Her hold on him appears to have been primarily sexual. In his letters from Germany to people in the know, she is "black eyes". One of his friends, at the time of *The Childhood of Christ*, refers to her with a wink as "Marie non vierge".

Yet she may at first have meant more to Berlioz than we imagine, offering not only the excitements his private life had been for some time without (and a household where he could find a break from the turmoil at home, and where Mme Martin, whom he liked despite her villainous Spanish accent, made a welcome fuss of him) but something more besides: a musician's feeling for and understanding of his art. Marie may have first endeared herself to him as an admirer of his music. Berlioz on his side may have been impressed, to begin with at least, by her potential as a singer. Though critics generally concentrated on her graceful figure and dark, lustrous eyes, others as well as he described her voice as "pure and fresh". He may have encouraged her to take lessons – which she did – from the celebrated teacher Banderali (who had taught his favourite singer, Alizard). He may even have coached her himself – until, by the classic progression, the relationship of professor and pupil grew into something else and she became his mistress. But though all this is possible, there is no way of knowing it.

The years 1841 and 1842 are altogether among the least well documented of his career. Adolphe Boschot called them "the mystery years", "les années mystérieuses". Boschot insinuated that in locating his first foreign journey in late 1840 instead of in late 1842 the author of the *Memoirs* was deliberately muddying his tracks. Since he admits on the same page to having taken a mistress it is hard to see what motive he could have had for that. More likely, his memory confused 1842 with 1840 (the year, incidentally, when he had hoped to set out on his travels), because of the similarity of the gala concerts given in November of each year, both of them at the Opéra: the one already described, at which the Apotheosis was performed, and the other two years later, which included the whole Symphonie funèbre et triomphale.

Boschot, by selective quotation from the feuilletons, also postulated a state of melancolia and disorientation in which Berlioz, disheartened with everything in his public and private existence, no longer had the will to compose: no large-scale work came into being in the twenty months from January 1841 to September 1842, when Berlioz left for Brussels. True; but there were compelling financial reasons for that: "La grande musique me ruine." Largely for the same reason, he gave no concert in Paris during the winter season of 1841–2. But a composer who in this period completes *Les nuits d'été* and publishes it, writes the violin-and-orchestra piece *Rêverie et caprice*, *La mort d'Ophélie*, an act of a grand opera for Scribe and the recitatives for a production of *Der Freischütz*, orchestrates Weber's *Invitation to the Dance* for the same purpose, adds string parts and a chorus to the Symphonie funèbre and arranges for the work's publication, and researches and writes a comprehensive series of essays which he then collects and revises to form the monumental *Treatise on Modern Instrumentation and Orchestration*, can hardly be said to be dragging his heels.

As for the feuilletons, the sixty-three he wrote – twenty-five in the *Débats*, thirty-seven in the *Gazette* and one in the *Sylphide* – are neither more nor less high-spirited, scathing, enthusiastic, caustic, quixotic, despairing than any other set taken at random from his long journalistic career – what he called his "Thirty Years' War against the academics, the routineers and the deaf". Thanks to recently discovered documents, including twenty-six letters, ten to members of the family, these two years have become less mysterious. It is still possible that Berlioz, for whatever reason (shame at the double life he was leading?), wrote less often to his friends and relatives than in other years; but we should be wary of assuming so. What Mr Justice Swallow calls "accidental circumstances" play a bigger role in such matters than scholars generally allow for; a letter which has not come down to us and therefore "does not exist" may none the less have been written. We happen to know, from a reference in another letter, of one such from this period, written to Adèle in the spring or summer of 1841 and apparently enclosing various autographs – Adèle had recently become a collector – including one of Eugène Sue's (both Berlioz's sisters were avid readers of the popular novelist, whose latest work, *Mathilde*, was being serialized in the *Presse*). There were certainly others. Much has been made of the gap in Berlioz's correspondence with his close friend Humbert Ferrand between October 1841 and September 1847 – surely a clear indication of something. As it happens, he went on sending Ferrand letters – they were simply not published. When he did not write, often it was because Ferrand was in Paris.

In fact, 1841 and 1842 repeat many of the patterns of previous years: lobbying for an official position which would provide him with a salary he could live on; continuing, though equivocal, relations with the Opéra; persistent anxieties about money. These last were more than usually pressing. They forced him to swallow his pride and appeal to his family in Dauphiné to arrange for him to have the 6,000 francs left under his mother's will. "Two months from now at the very latest," he told Nancy in March 1841, "I shall be absolutely in need of it, but if possible please let me have it sooner and I will deposit it at Rothschild's at 4 per cent, as I have been doing up to now with my money. The fact is, I can't make ends meet, and I'm gradually spending my modest capital. In two months it will have run out." Berlioz was well aware how such a confession would be received. His sisters were unable to understand that a musician of his eminence should not be comfortably off; it made them question the eminence ("it's no longer possible for us to participate in our poor brother's dreams of fame and fortune"). He had to submit to an inquisition from the sceptical Nancy, which he answered in a letter dated 29 March 1841.

You would be right to be astonished if I had indeed spent as much as you say, but your calculations are wide of the mark. To begin with you are wrong about what I could have told you as to the money on deposit at Rothschild's. I could not possibly still have had 10,000 francs there last spring, since that was all I put there in the first place at the time of

Paganini's gift, the rest having been spent on paying my debts. And as you can imagine, I have made quite a hole in it since then. I made a profit only on my concerts in the Rue Vivienne [August 1840]. On the three first performances of *Romeo and Juliet*, all told, I lost 1,600 francs.*
I am presenting you with the facts, since you have to have them. Then, this season I felt I ought to give a concert at the Conservatoire, with chorus. I consulted Harriet, who said I absolutely must, even if I was certain to lose on it. I lost 1,230 fr. Even the festival cost me money. [Berlioz proceeds to describe how he gave up his fee of 500 francs, and some of his own money, to keep the musicians happy.] The *Gazette musicale* isn't bringing me in a sou: everything I do for it goes to make up the number of articles overdue from before Paganini's gift. At the *Journal des débats* I earn about 1,600 fr.; it's very rare for me to do more than sixteen articles a year.

This is not to mention the expenses of my copyist. For the festival, the parts had to be doubled because of the large number of performers; since they were my property it was I who had to pay. Large-scale music is what is ruining me, until such time as it pays me back in jobs what it costs me in toil, trouble and cash.

You see that I am in real need, in the near future, of the sum that my mother left me. The thought of starting all over again on that frightful existence of debts, loans and privations from which I emerged two years and four months ago fills me with dread. I still have a thousand francs at Rothschild's, on which I am obliged to draw each month in order to make up the amount I lack – and it's a large amount – for my normal expenses. So there is every reason why I must insist that you take the steps required to procure me my mother's legacy. You may well imagine that I should never have asked for it but for the most dire necessity.

What he did not admit, to Nancy or to himself, was the possibility that his investment in large-scale music would never be paid back in official positions.

The concert he conducted at the Conservatoire the following month (25 April) did not make him any money but did not lose him any either. It was organized by Liszt – back in Paris from a tour of England and Scotland – in aid of the Bonn monument which France had been so

---

* Either he is garbling the figures, or some unforeseen costs cropped up after he had calculated a profit of 1,100 francs. See p. 218.

reluctant to support. The all-Beethoven programme consisted of the overture *The Consecration of the House*, the Emperor concerto, the Kreutzer sonata (with Liszt and Lambert Massart) and the Pastoral – the first Beethoven symphony that Berlioz had conducted. Wagner, who was still scraping a living in Paris, described the event in a report to the Dresden *Abendzeitung*:

> Liszt and Berlioz are friends and brothers, both of them know and revere Beethoven, both draw vigour from his miraculous abundance, and both know they can perform no better deed than to give a concert for Beethoven's memorial. But there is a difference: Liszt earns money without expenses, whereas Berlioz has expenses but earns nothing. [. . .] How willingly would we all give concerts for Beethoven! But Liszt can actually do it, and at the same time supply proof of the paradox that it is wonderful to be a famous man. Yet how many things would and could Liszt not do if he were not a famous man – or rather if people had not made him famous! He would and could be a free artist, a little god, instead of being what he now is, the slave of a tasteless, virtuoso-worshipping public. All that this particular public demands from him is tricks and meretricious rubbish. He gives it what it wants, basks in its favour and plays – in a concert for Beethoven's memorial – a fantasy on *Robert le diable*! [Liszt had produced his new composition with sensational effect at the Salle Erard the previous month.] It was done, however, with some reluctance. The programme consisted exclusively of Beethoven's works, but that did not prevent a raving audience from calling thunderously for the fantasy, Liszt's most popular showpiece. It was a point in favour of this very talented man that he threw out a few angry words – "Je suis le serviteur du public; cela va sans dire" – before sitting down at the piano and rattling the favoured piece contemptuously off. Thus one is punished for one's sins. One day Liszt will be called on in heaven to play his fantasy on the devil before the assembled company of angels – though perhaps that will be for the last time!

Berlioz's account in the *Débats* (which praised the orchestra but did not mention the conductor) merely remarked that the fantasy was "demanded with such insistence that, despite the strict intention to confine the concert exclusively to Beethoven's music, [Liszt] was obliged to yield". The review was largely given up to a *critique admirative* of the Emperor concerto. But the main part of the feuilleton was an attack on the latest negligent and lacklustre revival of *Don Juan* (*Don Giovanni*) at the Opéra.

It was thanks to the Opéra that Berlioz's finances now took a slight turn for the better, through his involvement in a project which he had fervently hoped would never materialize and about which he had at best very mixed feelings: the long-threatened production of *Der Freischütz*. After several flops, and with Meyerbeer still sitting on *Le Prophète*, the Opéra was looking for a money-spinner. Castil-Blaze had made a mint in the 1820s with his *Freischütz* adaptation, *Robin des bois*. Why not revive the work and get Berlioz, the leading French champion of Weber, to supervise the musical side and tailor the score to the needs of the house, thus lending the affair respectability and at the same time spiking the guns of the critic of the *Journal des débats*? Since the spoken word was by sacred tradition as outlawed at the Opéra as it was at the Funambules, the dialogue would have to be recast as recitative. Berlioz was the man to do it.

He did it – with the greatest reluctance, but he was left with no choice, as his letter to Léon Pillet, the director, made clear. "I do not think one ought to add to *Freischütz* the recitatives you ask me for; however, since without that condition it can't be put on at the Opéra, and if I didn't write them you would entrust their composition to someone perhaps less familiar with Weber than I am and certainly less dedicated to the glorification of his masterpiece, I accept your offer on one condition: *Freischütz* will be performed exactly as it is, with nothing changed in the libretto or the music." Though Pillet was indignant that he should suspect otherwise, it transpired that, like a true Opéra director, he had been intending to make cuts and to remove the entire role of the Hermit. Berlioz was able to put a stop to that. He also blocked Pillet's proposal that, for the obligatory ballet, in addition to orchestrating Weber's "Invitation to the Dance" he should adapt the ball music from the Fantastic Symphony and the Fête from *Romeo* and "work them into the score of the opera". After some terse exchanges it was agreed to use dance music from two other Weber operas, *Oberon* and *Preciosa*.

The result could only be a compromise. As Wagner complained in a long article on Weber and his opera in the *Gazette* shortly before the first night and again afterwards in the Dresden *Abendzeitung*, recitatives and ballets upset the balance of the work and distorted its character.

In particular, the often quite brief musical numbers and, even more, the vivid little tone paintings in the Wolf's Glen scene could not but suffer when interlarded with musical declamation. Having feared that Berlioz's recitatives would be too idiosyncratic, Wagner found them anonymous. They sent the audience to sleep. Berlioz agreed, though for a different reason. Much more of a purist than Wagner, he felt he was right to suppress his own personality. The fault lay in the heavy, rhetorical way the singers delivered them. Try as he would, he could not persuade the Max and the Caspar to let their conversations flow: "obtaining a light, easy gait from our operatic cantors" was like "getting an elephant to move like an Arab steed". The emphatic style of grand opéra was ingrained in them. The orchestra and chorus, under the Opéra's second conductor, Battu (Habeneck was unwell, though in his zeal for the work he insisted on joining the ranks of the violins), were adequate, the singers less so. Berlioz had to agree to the Agathe, Mme Stoltz, transposing her first aria down a tone and her second a minor third, though she sang the high notes in the final sextet at pitch and brought the house down. He was, however, able to prevent Duprez taking the role of Max, a part which was too low for him but which the great tenor intended to accommodate to what was left of his voice by means of some hair-raising modulations. But Duprez's replacement, Marie, though a good musician, was a dull singer. Despite all this, Berlioz could not help feeling elated with the success of the work and the effort he had put into it, not to mention the 230 francs he received for each performance.

After an uncertain first night (7 June) *Freischütz* was catching on. His feuilleton in the *Débats* six days later, though offering a few detailed criticisms of the singers, concentrated on the positive aspects of the event: the first complete performances in Paris, and the first time the Hermit's music had ever been heard there; the growing response of the public; the demonstration that the Opéra could obtain decent results in a relatively short time when it gave its mind to it (M. Pillet had not taken the decision to put on *Freischütz* till the beginning of March); and the fresh revelation of the beauty and mastery of Weber's score. The review said nothing of Berlioz's part in it, nor of the *Invitation*, and of the recitatives only that Germany could rest assured that their author (unnamed) had at least refrained from making Samiel the black huntsman sing.

Wagner himself, in a second article in the *Abendzeitung*, reported that the public was flocking to it in ever-increasing numbers, and acknowledged that "they have not been able to kill it – our dear and glorious *Freischütz*". Later, of course, that was just what they were able to do. Under Pillet's successors, Nestor Roqueplan and Duponchel, bits started to fall off – part of the finale with the Hermit and then the entire opening scene of Act 3 – until the opera was sufficiently cut down to size to fulfil its function as curtain-raiser to a ballet.

The tribulations of *Freischütz* in the late 1840s and early 1850s roused Berlioz to passionate protest in the *Memoirs*. "The way they perform what is left of it! The singers! The conductor! The indolence and sluggishness of the tempos and the helpless incoherence of the ensembles, the appalling inanity and insipidity pervading every aspect of the interpretation! If you want to be smirched, reviled, persecuted, be an innovator, a standard-bearer, a poet, a man of genius. Pedlars, money-changers: pending the advent of a new Christ to scourge you from the Temple, be assured that everyone in Europe with the slightest feeling for art holds you in bottomless contempt."

By the time he wrote that, more than ten years later, the Opéra had become for him "musically speaking a house of ill fame". For the moment, however, he was still on tolerably good terms with it, despite, even perhaps because of, his exacting criticisms. Pillet looked up to him, and his relations with Pillet's mistress, the formidable Rosine Stoltz, were cordial. There had been talk of Berlioz's conducting the *Freischütz* performances himself, and the possibility of his succeeding the sixty-year-old Habeneck as musical director was being actively considered. He had an agreement with Pillet and Scribe for another opera; and *La nonne sanglante* – "The Bleeding Nun" – was pursuing its unhurried course.

Over the next few years Berlioz composed the best part of two acts of this gothic grand opera which Scribe took from *The Monk*, a horror novel by the English writer Matthew ("Monk") Lewis, recently translated into French by Berlioz's friend Léon de Wailly. He received the libretto of the first act (versified by Germain Delavigne) some time in June 1841, and by late August the music for it was almost done. Most of the second act seems to have been written by February the following year. Scribe, who had kept him waiting, was slow in producing the rest: clearly he did not see the collaboration as a priority. His lack of urgency was shared by the composer. The *Nun* crops up fairly often in Berlioz's correspondence of 1841 and 1842. You can feel him convincing himself that this "secret, black and midnight" tale of ghosts and daggers and castle doors that open mysteriously, heartless dynastic marriages, benign hermits, elopements, Bohemian peasants, and heroines who share the same name and (as in *The Woman in White*, though much less effectively) look alike, is an exciting piece of work. In December 1840 he reads the scenario to Harriet, who is "enthusiastic about it". Nine months later, he believes that "this time no one will complain the play lacks interest. Scribe, it seems to me, has made very good use of the famous legend; and in addition he has concluded the drama with a tremendous dénouement, borrowed from a work of M. de Kératry's, scenically spectacular" (an explosion which destroys the castle). If Scribe, who is supposed to have his finger on the public pulse, thinks there is still a market for this kind of thing – and the success of the not entirely dissimilar *Freischütz* and the continued popularity of *Robert le diable* suggest he may be right – then he is prepared to go along with it. The surviving music, all from Act 2, shows Berlioz bowing his neck to the yoke and placing himself patiently in the shafts of the Paris Opéra, dully conventional verse and all (for Scribe and his associates, however skilful at crafting a well-made drama, were no poets). Its relation to the brilliant but demanding *Benvenuto Cellini* is like that of Schubert's draft of a symphony in D to the Great C major (his attempt at something less ambitious and more manageable after the Musikverein had declared the Great C major unplayable). The ballad-like account of the Nun and her legend achieves a certain frisson. It and the hermit Hubert's aria, with its regular four-bar phrases, short, easily assimilable motif and dark, rich orchestral sonorities which anticipate some of the music Verdi wrote for Paris, give an idea of the kind of opera composer Berlioz might have become if he had taken that road. The idea sounds far-fetched. But at the time he was half in earnest. If he felt in no more of a hurry than did Scribe, that was at least partly because the Opéra did not have the voices he needed. "Duprez has only six or seven notes and the others have too many." He would be mad to have the work performed unless there was a different leading tenor.

Hence his great interest in a tenor called Delahaye with a strikingly beautiful voice and a natural gift for singing, whom he heard, perhaps at a private gathering, some time in 1841. Delahaye was studying medicine, but Berlioz persuaded him that his future lay in music, not in "travelling about the Normandy countryside on a grey horse, trying to heal the sick for 1,500 francs a year"; and he and Auguste Morel took the young man under their wing and gave him coaching – though in the event Delahaye's operatic career would be confined mainly to the provinces.

By this time another newcomer with an attractive voice and the ambition to shine as an opera singer was on the scene. Marie Recio's engagement at the Opéra, very possibly with Berlioz's help, took place in October 1841. An album-leaf dated 11 June 1841, inscribed "à Marie" and bearing the words "Nessun maggior dolore", Dante's "There is no greater pain than to remember happiness in a time of misery" (allusion to a period of enforced absence?), was seen briefly in Paris in the early 1960s. It has since disappeared, so there is no way of telling whether it is authentic: at that time many forged Berlioz documents were circulating. If genuine, it points to the affair being already well established by the summer of 1841. Some writers have concluded that Berlioz's letter of 3 October 1841 to Humbert Ferrand shows him on the verge of a confession to his old and trusted friend: "If you come [to Paris] this winter we will have endless talks on a thousand matters which can't be properly explained in writing. How I should like to see you! I feel as if I am descending the mountain at alarming speed; life is so brief! I realize that for some time now I have been often thinking of its end. So I find myself greedily snatching up, rather than picking, the flowers my hand can reach as I slide down the rough pathway."

Whatever the truth of such surmises, Boschot is surely right when he says that "in the autumn of 1841 it was obvious to anyone who was involved with the theatre or journalism, or who simply frequented the boulevards and exchanged gossip, that Berlioz was very interested in Mlle Recio".

Because of all that followed, and because her operatic career was still-born, it is commonly assumed that she was without talent. Wrongly, I think: for whatever Berlioz's standing at the Opéra in the months immediately after *Freischütz*, the management would hardly have engaged her if she had not shown some promise. It looks as if stage fright, more than lack of talent, was her downfall. The reviews speak of her nervousness as well as of her inexperience (a nervousness that was presumably responsible for the "bad habit she has of bending her knees every time the note is at all high"). The sketchbook which Berlioz kept on his first tour of Germany contains an entry made at Leipzig on 3 February 1843, where below the refrain of his song *Absence* is written: "after the rehearsal at which Marie sang really well". "Après la répétition" has been added above some word or words heavily crossed out. I take it that at the performance Marie did not sing so well.

Nerves did not lessen her determination to sing. Berlioz's biographers have not forgiven Marie Recio the humiliations she subjected him to and the weaknesses she exposed in that proud character. Because of her, it is said, he compromised his integrity and debased his standards by praising her insignificant débuts in his feuilletons. In fact his sins in this regard do not amount to all that much. During the eleven months of her engagement at the Opéra – October 1841 to September 1842 – she played two roles, Ines in *La favorita* and the page Isolier in *Le comte Ory*. Berlioz reviewed both débuts in the *Journal des débats* and probably was also responsible for the three brief, mildly encouraging references included in the news section of the *Gazette*. The praise he bestowed on her in the *Débats* is restrained, and concerned more with promise – with "intentions" – than achievement. In going out of his way to compare her trim and fetching appearance in *Ory* with that of the over-mature ladies who insisted on playing the role when they should rather be "donning the pilgrim's coat and cape" than the page's treacherously revealing costume – in which their bodies and legs resembled nothing so much as "a sack of nuts on a trestle" – he was certainly guilty of malice, as well as of ingratitude towards the singer who normally played Isolier, Mme Stoltz, his faithful Ascanio in *Benvenuto Cellini* three years before and an admirer and supporter of his music. By that one spiteful, imprudent phrase, written to please his lover, was he not throwing away all the gains he had made at the Opéra over the past year and forfeiting a real chance of succeeding to Habeneck's position? – for la Stoltz was Pillet's mistress and, increasingly, the power of the place: "la directrice du directeur", as Berlioz would later call her.

It could be said that the dig at Stoltz's Isolier shows a kind of integrity: it was high time she gave up such roles and someone had the courage to say so; Berlioz, however ungallantly, was fulfilling that necessary office. Singers in those days were well accustomed to personal criticism; and Berlioz's was not especially cruel by the standards of the time. In any case I doubt if he lost the job because of it. He was not passed over for someone else. The job did not become vacant; Habeneck stayed where he was. For the moment, no one succeeded him.

As for Marie Recio's insisting on singing at Berlioz's concerts, it was painful while it lasted but it did not last long. Already by the spring of

1843 it was almost over. She appeared twice more in early 1844 but then agreed to stop and, although she continued occasionally to sing in public, never reappeared at a concert conducted by him. Yet that he should have given in at all, and should have allowed her, no matter how good her intentions, to sing his songs in public, at best no more than moderately well, and not once but at one concert after another, argues a degree of weakness which on his own terms was criminal. He knew it himself. The conversation Legouvé reports as taking place under the colonnade of the Palais-Royal, one day when they were sheltering from a spring shower, has the ring of truth, in spirit if not in literal fact:

> "You see," he added, after having enumerated his torments, "it's diaboli-
> cal, isn't it? – I mean, it's at once tragic and grotesque. I said I deserved
> to go to hell . . . but I'm there! And that frightful joker Mephisto laughs,
> I swear, to crucify me by torturing my musician's nerve ends. To tell
> you the truth, I'm tempted sometimes to laugh myself." And, in fact,
> while tears of rage brimmed his eyes, his face twisted in an indescribable
> expression of mockery.

He felt it acutely, but was helpless to act. Her grip on him was too tight.

A stronger person, or one more ruthless, would have extricated himself, if only by following Napoleon's dictum that in love the sole victory lies in flight. But in love Berlioz rarely showed the boldness and decisiveness that marked his career as musician and as composer, promoter and performer of his music. It was as if, fighting on so many other fronts, he had too little energy or moral courage left for the home front. He was easily manipulated. You could call it weakness or at least lack of ruthlessness (goodness of heart played a part in it) that he deferred to Harriet's wishes and put off the German tour so long. To be able finally to make it required "nothing short of a coup d'état in my domestic life". He used exactly the same expression when, five years later, he succeeded in travelling to London without Marie: to recover his liberty, there had to be "not one coup d'état but a whole succession of them". A clean break, a decisive no, was beyond him.

He tried more than once to get free of Marie – but ineffectively, with nothing like the determination she showed to keep hold of him. Once, during the first tour of Germany, exasperated by her singing, he gave her the slip; but she found out where he had gone and caught him up

– and went on singing. There were no doubt other occasions. His friend the Irish musician George Osborne described one such incident, one evening when they dined together in Paris. "We conversed on the usual painful subject [Marie Recio's "uncontrollable jealousy"] and, as I saw but one remedy, I frankly told him of it. Much to my surprise, he sat down and wrote a charming letter of adieu to the lady, which he left at her lodgings when walking out with me. Next day he told me that he had gone back to the house, took the letter from the servant and tore it up, his courage having failed him."

Though Marie Recio was the most frequent performer of *Absence*, it is hard to believe she was in any sense the source of *Les nuits d'été*. Quite apart from the fact that one would rather not think of her as the inspiratrix of those wonderful love songs, the theme of the cycle – loss – and the tragic intensity of its two central numbers surely rule out any such connection. If the setting of Gautier's poems was prompted by anything specific in the composer's life it must have been the end of an old love, not the start of a new one. But we can only conjecture what stimulated him to compose the work. It is possible that he wanted to show, after the Requiem and the Symphonie funèbre, that he was more than the noise-maker of the cartoonists' stereotype and could do just as striking things on the scale of the voice-and-piano *mélodie*. That was precisely the response of Stephen Heller in the *Gazette*. His review made the point that, contrary to the rooted opinion, held by "a multitude of old fogeys of every stripe", that Berlioz composed "with the fixed intention of subverting the fundamental elements of music", he felt and heard and wrote like anyone else, as he showed in this new collection of songs, in which the sacred flame burned as brightly as in *Romeo and Juliet*. But I doubt if Berlioz was greatly concerned to correct the popular prejudice against him; however much he would have liked to, he knew it was not susceptible to argument. All through his career he wrote songs because he wanted to. They provided contrasting smaller items for his concert programmes. They were also a natural form of expression for him; they satisfied a need. This time, for reasons that are both undefined and unmistakable, the need was exceptionally strong.

We know less about *Les nuits d'été* and its genesis than about almost any other major work of his. It is the one genuine mystery of Boschot's "années mystérieuses". The songs are not mentioned in the correspondence of 1840–41, the presumed period of their composition. All we have are the date "23 March 1840" on a manuscript fair copy of *Villanelle*, the approximate date of the cycle's publication – mid-to-late summer 1841 – and the fact that two of the songs, *Absence* and *Le spectre de la rose*, were announced for a concert sponsored by the *Gazette* in November 1840, though in the event they were not performed.

By the time he came to compose the songs, Berlioz knew Théophile Gautier well. There is no written record of their having discussed the project – there was no cause for one. They saw each other often, both socially and as fellow-journalists, and they lived quite near each other; Gautier's street, the Rue Navarin, was in the same arrondissement (the modern 9th) as the Rue de Londres. Berlioz had also had ample opportunity to get to know Gautier's verse: the collected poems from which all six songs came were published in 1838 as *La Comédie de la mort* (a title that must have appealed to him). Gautier was pleased when composers set his poems to music, and sometimes wrote them with that purpose in mind. One such, *Barcarolle*, renamed *L'île inconnue*, became the sixth song of the cycle.

The scheme of the work seems to have come to Berlioz only gradually; he may even have started with individual songs. At one point the cycle consisted of four, not six, with the same beginning and end as in the final version but with *Absence* preceding *Le spectre de la rose*, and *Sur les lagunes* and *Au cimetière* still to come. It could have been then that the circumstances of his personal life moved him to add them – both of them concerned with loss and death, the one a seascape like the final song but a tragic one, with the bereaved lover doomed to travel alone over the empty sea, the other the evocation of a moonlit graveyard where the dead still have power to possess the living – with the result that the cycle became an anatomy of romantic love and acquired its definitive structure and its dramatic and emotional progression.

Thus *Villanelle*, the simplest of the six in both tune and accompaniment, already carries a hint of melancholy beneath the skittish surface, conveying it by variations of harmony which heighten the tension from verse to verse and imply that the idyll in the woods and the lover's whispered "toujours" are not all they seem. The much grander *Spectre de la rose*, with its long, seductive melodic spans and its textures at once rich and sparkling, still retains something of the playfulness of *Villanelle*, as well as having a delicate fragrance appropriate to its poetic "conceit": the ghost of a rose which returns to haunt the dreams of the young girl who wore it at her first ball. At the same time, the music's largeness of style anticipates the third song. *Sur les lagunes* is constructed round a characteristic Berlioz rhythmic and melodic ostinato, a rocking three-note figure (D–E flat–D) which, recurring almost invariably at the same pitch, suggests both the boat's movement across the calm water and the obsessive grief of the lover who must set out on his journey bereft of love. The loneliness of the end, after the last passionate climax, is palpable, as the sea swell of the bass subsides and the harmony hangs suspended, unresolved. This "lament" (the song's subtitle), the most dramatic number in the cycle, is also the only one in a minor key. But Berlioz was just as likely to express loss by means of the major mode, as *Absence*, the fourth song, shows. Here it is separation from a living but distant beloved that is evoked in a major-key refrain of the barest simplicity, enclosing two minor-key verses in which the sense of unbridgeable apartness rises each time to a cry of pain. After that, down a major third to *Au cimetière*, where stepwise movement in the voice part combines with the accompaniment's shifting, somnambulistic chords to create a sense of morbid fascination. Like the second song, *Le spectre de la rose*, it is haunted by a ghostly presence. The poet lingers at dusk in the graveyard, held against his will, hearing in the moaning of the dove the lament of the dead beneath his feet, while the Berliozian flattened sixth grates against the prevailing D-major harmonies. This claustrophobic atmosphere is abruptly dispelled by the bright sounds and sea rhythms of the final song. *L'île inconnue* looks back to the mood of the opening, and mocks the Romantic assumptions and gestures of the intervening four. Yet there is a difference, reflecting all that has been lived through in between. In the end the music half-succumbs to the same illusion: that the enchanted shore where one loves for ever is there, just over the horizon, and, though it will never be found, must be for ever sought.

The original voice-and-piano cycle (which was published by Catelin and dedicated to Louise Bertin) has long been eclipsed by the popularity of the later chamber-orchestra version, with the help of the conventional wisdom that, since Berlioz's songs do not sound well with piano accompaniment, the work can only be incomplete in that form: it lives and has its being in the iridescent colours of the orchestral incarnation for which it was always waiting. Yet even in this halfway state, when sung by an interpreter with the skill and subtlety to exploit the enhanced primacy of the vocal line, and played by a pianist who understands the music, *Nuits d'été* remains one of the jewels of Berlioz's oeuvre, justifying

Heller's claim that it is as rich and characteristic as the composer's grandest orchestral works.

Whatever its origins, by the time it was published, some time in the summer of 1841, Marie Recio was entrenched in his life. How soon Harriet found out we do not know. Berlioz continued to live with his wife and son, but in an atmosphere far removed from the mutual tenderness and supportiveness of earlier times. If she did not know it yet for certain, she suspected. She had long suspected, searching his correspondence, his feuilletons, his belongings, for tell-tale signs. Though her suspicions had been groundless then, the gradual cessation of physical intimacy between them had naturally aroused them. It cannot have come as a surprise.

Even if the rest of the world romanticizes the French when it assumes that every Frenchman of a certain age takes a mistress as a matter of course and his wife accepts it with a reasonably good grace and arranges her life accordingly, what Berlioz was doing was far from unusual. His friends and peers – Hugo, Alfred de Vigny and others – had long known similar situations. But Harriet was not a Frenchwoman, schooled to make the best of it. If for Berlioz what had happened between them was a permanent sadness (whatever the immediate stimulus of his new relationship), for Harriet it was an irredeemable disaster. It left her bereft, without anything she could rely on: a son to whom she could only cling more closely but who she had always imagined loved his father more than he loved her, and a husband who had turned away from her and whom she must alternately scream at and implore to forgive her, to her ever deeper degradation. She felt alone in the world, with nothing to live for and nothing to look forward to.

The effect on Louis – eight in August 1842 – can only be guessed. For a while, though the state of the ménage was gradually becoming known to Nancy and Adèle (by common consent their father was kept in ignorance of it), references to him in Berlioz's letters remained cheerful and positive. "Louis is beginning to read; he 'sings from dawn to dusk' like La Fontaine's shoemaker, and it is indeed 'a marvel to behold him'" (December 1840). "Louis is making great progress; he has a teacher for piano and drawing, and is beginning to write" (July 1841). "Louis is working at the piano. His mother finds that he is making progress" (October 1841). In 1842 the tone shifts. "Louis is growing and developing pretty slowly. Harriet loudly bewails his lack of progress" (June). "Louis often suffers from headaches, which rather worries us"

(July). To Nancy the previous February Berlioz confided that "Harriet never goes out, and I am hounded by her because I go out all the time – but I have to see my world and get on with my affairs." In the same letter, however, he spoke of both Harriet and Louis attending his recent concert in the Salle Vivienne, "radiant" at its success, and he made much of a fan letter about the concert, addressed to Harriet by a young cabinet-maker who gave it to their cook to pass on to them. Berlioz conducted with a raging sore throat, and with cramp in his right arm which forced him to use his left instead, and a buzzing in his head "which prevented me from hearing anything – it was like what I imagine it must be for the sailors on the gun-deck of a frigate during a battle, less the dead bodies".

Whatever the stress at home and the difficulties and embarrassments of a double existence, his public life went on much as before. The first of the two Salle Vivienne concerts in February 1842 (the third for which he had been contracted by the manager of the hall after the success of the public dress rehearsal of the July symphony in 1840) was a triumph: the house full to overflowing, with people sitting on the steps leading to the inner doors of the hall; a decent profit despite the cost of copying parts for the strings which he had added to the symphony, and despite giving away more than 250 tickets out of a seating capacity of 1,000; and in the peroration of the Apotheosis such an uproar from the excited audience that the huge orchestra was inaudible. "If my father had been there, with you all and my uncle and the memories of the Empire and the still more active thoughts of the Three Days, when there was all that brave slaughter in the streets of Paris (for that lies behind the work), he would I am sure have had an experience unlike any he has known before." The cabinet-maker's letter was one of several that told of listeners carried away by the finale of the symphony: "One gentleman couldn't keep still on his chair, another kept saying, in a voice stifled by emotion, 'It's wonderful, it's wonderful, it's Michelangelo in music', and a third said to me, weeping, 'Ah, sir, they are entering paradise.'"

At the second concert a fortnight later the symphony was repeated before another large audience. So was *Rêverie et caprice* (premièred at the first, with the violinist Alard). *Harold* was replaced by the Fantastic, though the Pilgrims' March was again played and rapturously received. Instead of Beethoven's Triple Concerto, performed by Alard, Desmarest and Hallé at the first concert, Hallé gave the première of a "Grande Caprice Symphonique" for solo piano by Stephen Heller, which the whimsical but nervous composer listened to in the cramped orchestra room under the hall, through the din of assembling bass drum, side-drum and piccolo players. Heller's account, in a letter to a friend, gives a glimpse of concert life from the other side. On entering the room just before the concert was due to begin, he found two men "furieusement agités": "one was Berlioz, enveloped in his great carbonaro coat, the other the unfortunate Hallé, victim of my *Caprice*, both of them pale, tense, and absorbed in gloomy thoughts. They were chattering with cold and their noses were sharp and pinched. I, alas, added my nose to theirs. Berlioz exclaimed, 'Sacré nom de Dieu' (I beg pardon, Madam, in the name of historical truth) – 'Forestier the first flute is missing, and a horn and double-bass haven't arrived.' "

Instruments and instrumentation were much in Berlioz's mind at that moment: he was in the middle of writing a series of articles for the *Gazette* which before long, collected in book form, was to establish him as a world authority on the subject. The *Grand Traité d'instrument-ation et d'orchestration modernes* would alone make this an important and productive period in his career. Its immediate stimulus seems to have been the publication of two manuals by his friend Georges Kastner, the second of which – *Cours d'instrumentation considérée sous les rapports poétiques et philosophiques de l'art* – he reviewed in the *Débats* in October 1839. Welcome as Kastner's books were – nothing like them had appeared before – he clearly felt there was scope for another, more comprehensive and up to date. Kastner's *Traité*, for example, said nothing about the pedal notes of the tenor trombone, which had figured as long ago as the March to the Scaffold, and whose majestic, baleful tones had been a feature of the Requiem's Hostias, as they would be of the Judex crederis in the Te Deum and the first act of *The Trojans*.

Berlioz would surely have undertaken his own treatise even without the spur of Kastner's. The work was the outcome of nearly twenty years' experience as listener, composer, critic and conductor; it was the logical culmination of the self-imposed course in orchestration which had begun almost from his earliest evenings at the Opéra and the sessions in the Conservatoire Library that followed, as, with the scientific curiosity he had inherited from his father, he first set himself to penetrate the secrets of the art and discover how the colours and textures he heard had been created. The systematic examination of the orchestra and its component elements was a conscious part of his mastering the composer's craft during the years with Le Sueur and Reicha. It was not on the official syllabus but it was on his. In pursuit of it he had countless discussions about technique and expression with those musicians who were interested and willing to experiment, and in the process found out just what the instruments could and could not do, and what they had never done but might do if pushed beyond accepted norms; he got to know each of them individually, what kinds of role suited it best, its personality, its soul. We can see the first fruits in the *Eight Scenes from Faust* of 1828–9. The virtuoso string writing of Mephisto's debonair Song of the Flea, the Rat Song's lewd bassoons, the sylphs' gossamer violins, the choice of the viola's dusky timbre for Marguerite's ballad and of the darker cor anglais for the heartbreak of her Romance, show an inventive ear for orchestral colour already founded on practical knowledge. Throughout the 1830s he continued to explore and learn, both from experience (at one point we hear of him sitting in on the trombone class which Dieppo started at the Conservatoire in 1836) and by consulting instrumental *méthodes*. Once he began to conduct, he became even more closely involved.

A potent reason for imparting what he had learned was, as he saw it, the common misuse of the orchestra: so many of the new works he encountered as a critic betrayed their composers' ignorance. The *Treatise* among other things was intended to serve as a manual for those who were unfamiliar even with such basic facts as the range of a particular instrument, and who as a result either gave it notes it could not play or, fearful of doing so, confined it to the cautious safety of the middle register. The book, in addition, set out to correct abuses – abuses due not only to ignorance and poor taste but also to the spirit of routine which ruled in music conservatoires. Why, for example, tell composition students that "you must never employ such and such an instrumental layout", asked Berlioz in his review of Kastner's *Cours*. Why be the slave of the so-called hierarchy of instruments? Why not have the cellos at the top playing the tune and the clarinets in the bass, as Weber did with such happy effect in the introduction to his *Oberon* overture?

Behind the *Treatise*'s didactic purpose lay contemporary Parisian practice and malpractice. A performance of *Don Juan* at the Opéra in May 1841 – by which time the project was in preparation – aroused his wrath, among other reasons because trombones were added to scenes where they didn't belong and the accompaniment to the serenade was played on a couple of guitars instead of the mandolin for which Mozart wrote it. The *Treatise* aimed to teach respect for the orchestral genius of the masters and understanding of the poetic character and range of expression proper to each instrument.

The degradation of the trombone was a particular grievance. He enlarged on it in a review in the *Débats* of 14 December 1841, written shortly after "De l'instrumentation" began appearing serially in the *Gazette*. "The craze for the bass drum seems to have abated in recent months, but the craze for the trombone is growing." It was being used indiscriminately to reinforce the orchestra without regard to the special qualities of its timbre, and in dramatic contexts which made nonsense of its imposing character. "At the Opéra-Comique an old buffer is in despair at losing his snuffbox – three trombones! He's happy again because he's found it – three trombones!" In due course the *Treatise* attacked the use of the trombone's "Olympian tones" to accompany a comic song or to "solemnize a dancer's pirouette as though it were Alexander entering Babylon". It gave examples from composers who understood how to write for that grave, resplendent instrument. The trombone was illustrated by pages in full score from Gluck (Alceste's "Divinités du Styx" and the apparition scene in *Iphigénie en Tauride*), Mozart in *The Magic Flute* (the chorus "O Isis und Osiris"), Spontini in *La Vestale*, Beethoven in *Fidelio* (the gravedigging duet), and his own Requiem and Apotheosis. He made no bones about citing his works: no one could gainsay his standing as a pioneer of the modern orchestra. The quotations from the Fantastic Symphony, *Romeo and Juliet*, the Symphonie funèbre, and *Lélio* (the muted clarinet in the penultimate movement and the piano trills and arpeggios in the *Tempest* fantasy) mark the first printed appearance of any part of them in full score. Works by other living composers were quoted: Meyerbeer, Halévy and Rossini, and among their forebears Weber and Méhul. Beethoven was represented by substantial excerpts from five of the symphonies – nos. 3–7 – as well as from *Fidelio* and the Emperor Concerto. The greatest number of musical examples, however, came from the works of Gluck. How could it be otherwise? It was from Gluck that, as a boy of seventeen, he had had his revelation of the orchestra, the modern medium of dramatic expression par excellence.

The *Treatise* is deliberately Janus-faced. It points to the future and to all that waits to be done; it draws attention to newcomers to the symphony orchestra like the harp, the valved horn and valved trumpet, the E flat clarinet which he had been the first to introduce, and the saxophone and the numerous family of saxhorns, inventions of Adolphe

Sax (the Belgian genius who had just settled in Paris and whom Berlioz encouraged and befriended). The opening chapter starts with the ringingly avant-garde declaration that "any sound-producing body utilized by the composer is a musical instrument". Yet it is Gluck that is given pride of place. He inspires its most lyrical flights – as in this account of the flute in the chapter "Wind Instruments without Reeds". Berlioz has been speaking of its neutral tone-colour in the middle and upper registers compared with that of the oboe and the clarinet, and the general rather than specific role it is usually given.

> Yet when you study it closely you realize that it has its own expressiveness and an aptness for rendering certain feelings in which no other instrument can challenge it. For example, if it is a question of giving a sad melody a desolate yet at the same time resigned character, the soft notes of the flute's middle register, especially in the keys of C minor and D minor, will produce just the nuance required. To my mind only one composer has taken full advantage of this pale colouring, and that is Gluck. When you listen to the pantomime music in D minor which he wrote for the scene in the Elysian Fields in *Orphée* you see at once that only the flute could have played the melody. An oboe would have been too childlike and its tone would not have sounded pure enough; a clarinet would have been less inappropriate but some of its notes would have been too loud and none of its softest notes could fine themselves down to the thin, veiled sonority of the F natural in the middle register or the B flat above the stave which lends the flute its profound sense of sadness in this key of D minor, where they frequently occur. Nor would the violin, the viola or the cello, solo or as a section, have been able to convey the incomparably sublime lament of a suffering, despairing shade. It required the instrument Gluck chose. And Gluck's melody is so conceived that the flute lends itself to every troubled movement of that timeless grief, still instinct with the passions of earthly life.

The fusion of the two modes, the subjective-evocative and the technical, is a feature of the *Treatise* (as it was of the analyses of the Beethoven symphonies a few years earlier). In the chapter on the viola, the famous passage in *Iphigénie en Tauride* where Orestes' "Peace returns to my heart" is contradicted in the orchestra – a passage which caught Berlioz's imagination before he had ever heard it, from reading the account in Michaud's *Biographie universelle*, and which remained for him a touchstone of dramatic expression – is similarly evoked and analysed.

"The scene in which Orestes, exhausted, gasping, devoured by remorse, falls into a doze as he repeats to himself 'Le calme rentre dans mon coeur', while the restless orchestra groans and sobs", owes its unfailing fascination "chiefly to the viola part, to the tone quality of its third string and the syncopated rhythm, and to the strange kind of unison that results from the syncopated A being brusquely cut across, amidships, by the A of the double-bass in a different rhythm." Once again, though "the old composers only rarely gave the viola prominence", Gluck provides the *Treatise*'s main example, being given precedence over Beethoven, whose use of the violas doubling the cellos in the theme of the slow movement of the Fifth Symphony is cited as showing how "the cello sonority can thereby acquire greater roundness and purity while remaining the predominant tone-colour".

The chapter on the clarinet has the same dual character. It contains, among other things, a table of trills throughout the three-and-a-half octaves of the instrument's range (divided into easily practicable, difficult, very difficult and impossible); an admonition to clarinettists to play their part on the instrument specified by the composer and not simply accommodate everything to the B flat clarinet; an evocation of the tone qualities of the different registers, with particular emphasis on the sinister effect, discovered by Weber, of the low notes when sustained, and also with a warning to composers who wish to employ its piercing top register to cover the attack of the first notes by the forte of the whole orchestra so as to allow the player to establish a clean, steady tone before launching into his solo; a tribute to the instrument's unequalled capacity for dynamic nuance, for imperceptibly starting and swelling a note or making it diminish and dwindle to nothing ("whence its precious ability to suggest distance, echoes, echoes of echoes, a twilit sound"); and the characterization of the clarinet as an epic instrument, the voice of heroic love – a quality *The Trojans* will abundantly demonstrate when he comes to compose the work fifteen years later.

The articles began coming out, weekly with some gaps, in late November 1841. Throughout the winter he was busy getting them ready. Last-minute details were checked with friendly players (e.g., "My dear Coche, can I count on you tomorrow evening at a quarter to eight for the *flûte tierce*, or the piccolo?"). By the time of the last of the Salle Vivienne concerts, on 15 February 1842, nine articles had appeared and serialization was also in progress in an Italian periodical, the *Gazetta musicale di Milano*.

Despite Berlioz's gloom in the orchestra room, the concert, according to Maurice Bourges' review in the *Gazette*, was another great success. Bourges was ecstatic, claiming that "justice" had "dawned for M. Berlioz at last"; the second concert, like the first, showed that the composer was unappreciated no longer, and that no matter how unbelievers might contort themselves to prove this or that proposition against him, he had an unanswerable riposte in the "profound impression his music produces, at each fresh encounter, on an immense audience".

If the audience really was immense, the evening must have made a profit, the cost of copying being already covered. Yet, as before, such ad hoc gains were no solution: they could not be relied on. He was in as great a need of a settled income as ever. "Everyone thinks I am rich, or at least very comfortably off – and, except after Paganini's gift, I have never had a moment's peace, but have been in constant embarrassment." All the avenues and places were earmarked in advance or occupied by "idiotic old men" ("viellards stupides", a much-quoted phrase from *Hernani*), and the government's arts administration, in its weakness, allowed it.

Two possibilities, however, presented themselves in the first half of 1842 and he pursued them energetically. The first was the Opéra post. There had been talk of it for some time. In May 1841, in the Dresden *Abendzeitung*, Wagner reported the "strong rumours that [Berlioz] is to be made chief conductor of the Opéra, while Habeneck, the present conductor, will take over Cherubini's position as director of the Conservatoire". At one point Cherubini was said to be at the point of death, and Berlioz nominated in his place. "But the grand old man came back to life with a vengeance – furious with me, who in fact am not after his job. He says he'll 'stick a knife in me'. He believes his wife is trying to poison him. He's in his second childhood. And he's running the Conservatoire! The minister can't bring himself to pension him off."

Whether Berlioz's efforts on behalf of Marie Recio compromised his chances at the Opéra is an academic question. There was no vacancy after all. Cherubini was at last persuaded to resign, in February 1842, but Habeneck was not chosen to succeed him: Auber got the job, and Habeneck stayed put. A month later the grand old man died, leaving a *fauteuil* vacant at the Academy of Fine Arts. It was worth only 1,500; but, for Berlioz, that was good money and, hopeful as ever, he joined the scramble. Auber and Carafa, he knew, would oppose him, and he had dangerous rivals in Adam and Onslow, but he thought he could count on the support of a fair number of academicians, including Spontini, Horace Vernet, Ingres and Halévy, and possibly the archaeologist Raoul Rochette (with whom his fellow-Dauphinois Champollion had promised to arrange him an interview). There is no need to suppose that the admiring tone of Berlioz's obituary of Cherubini in the *Débats*, or of his article on the revival of the master's *Les deux journées* in the same paper a few weeks later, was motivated by the Institute election. For one thing, as Barzun remarks, he "knew better than to think that justice to the dead would flatter the survivors". For another, his disagreements with Cherubini the man, their duel of wits and ideas and personalities, going back to the day of their chase round the library table, had never prevented him appreciating the works of the composer or recognizing what his own music owed to it – just as, for Berlioz, the greatness of *La Vestale* and *Fernand Cortez* existed quite independently of the personal asperities and absurdities, the often insufferable arrogance, of Spontini himself. The domain of music lived by completely separate laws and standards, and the character of the creative artist did not come into it. (As he said of Spontini, "the temple may be unworthy of the spirit that dwells in it, but the god is still a god".) Boschot may be right in finding Adam's obituary of Cherubini "vibrant with the emotion of the candidate"; but Berlioz's admiration for a good deal of Cherubini's music (whatever his pedantry as a teacher and whatever he thought of Berlioz's music) was unfeigned and long-lasting, and he had always been prepared to say so.

Not that it would have made any difference. He did not even reach the short list. Onslow was elected (19 November), beating Adam by two votes. It was a kind of consolation that Alfred de Vigny had failed twice that year to win election to the French Academy, on the second occasion being passed over for a classical scholar called Patin, whom Berlioz, in a letter to Nancy, rechristened "Potin" ("pinchbeck"). But the 1,500 francs would have come in handy. By that time his hopes of a second salaried post had crumbled too. The death in April 1842 of Guillaume-Louis Wilhem, the great pioneer of amateur choral singing, had left vacant the job of inspector of singing in primary schools. The salary would solve his money problems and the work appealed to him (that he was interested in amateur and school music and believed in its importance is attested by many feuilletons). When he told the Comte de Rambuteau, Prefect of the Seine, whose appointment it was, that if he got the job he would take it seriously, he meant what he said. But though he had powerful backers and though, as was de rigueur in France when applying for such positions, he paid interminable visits to members of the municipal council to argue his case, and did all he could to counter the inevitable salon intrigues and the "high-society ladies who make up to the Préfet on behalf of their lovers", the job went to Wilhem's deputy. After all, it would not have been right for Berlioz, would it? – he was too grand for such a modest post, beside having no need of it, being rich.

He had never felt more discouraged. A letter from Adèle to Nancy, written a month earlier, on 23 May 1842, bears witness to his state of mind:

> I heard from M. Dufeuillant that Hector is actively canvassing for a position as Inspector of Singing, worth 4,000–6,000 francs. It would be a great resource for him, but although well supported he has little hope of getting it; as usual he is encountering fierce opposition. What a life! My heart bleeds at the thought of it. From what M. Alexandre [Dufeuillant] wrote to us, Hector is in a state of profound dejection at the moment, his health is affected, and his wife is beside herself with worry. Some of the 6,000 lent by my husband is still left at Rothschild's, but once it is used up what then? He told M. Alexandre, who questioned him closely, that his expenses are about 7,500, and all told he earns hardly more than 5,000!

The time was out of joint. His prospects had if anything worsened. The Bertins were losing influence, weakened by the death of Bertin de Vaux, kingmaker of so many governments in the past ten years. The swing to the left at the elections in early July created a mood of instability and apprehension, which was intensified a few days later by a national catastrophe. On the morning of 13 July the Duc d'Orléans, heir apparent and most popular member of the royal family, fell to his death when the horses bolted as he drove by the half-built fortifications near Porte Maillot. It was a disaster for the regime, a shock for the country as a whole, and a personal blow for Berlioz, as for the many artists whom this liberal prince had befriended.

But, more than politics and the political situation, the whole drift of modern society had become inimical. France was simply not organized for, was not interested in, support of the arts. Berlioz does not seem to have thought of his fellow-Dauphinois Stendhal as much more than the author of an ill-considered biography of Rossini. If he had he could have drawn appropriate conclusions from the fact that the funeral of the great writer, who died on the same day as Bertin de Vaux, was attended by three people. But there was Balzac, that "innocent galley-slave" who had the misfortune to be a man of talent, writing desperately through the night; and cretins with sixty millions in the bank couldn't give two sous (which 200,000 francs would be to them) to assist such a man.

> For that reason, for all his love of painting I couldn't help laughing defiantly when I heard that the banker Aguado was dead! A poor troupe of German artists here have been left in the gutter by the bankruptcy of their director. A benefit concert was put on for them the day before yesterday. All the expenses were paid by *Liszt*. It had to be an artist who came to their rescue – under the "patronage" of five ancient hags, all millionairesses, who were "so upset" at all the trouble they were having placing the tickets, and one of whom was absolutely broken-hearted because her husband wouldn't allow her to spend more than 100,000 francs on the redecoration of her bedroom.

All this was entirely typical. Anything he tried to do was a waste of effort. Music as he understood it was "a ruinous art for whoever practises it, and will be until it is suitably rewarded by a monarch or at least by a minister. If Napoleon were alive . . ." He must have realized he was echoing what his poor dead teacher Le Sueur used to say, centuries ago.

It was time finally to be gone. Abroad was where his future lay. While he sweated not to make a loss on concerts in Paris, the German conductor Heinrich Romberg had put on the Grande messe des morts in St Petersburg, with hundreds of performers, and made a personal profit of 5,000 francs. He could do the same. He would begin with a sortie to Brussels, and then head east across the Rhine. Snel, the Belgian conductor, director of the Société Royale de la Grande Harmonie, whom he met in Paris that summer, suggested he should come to Brussels and conduct the Symphonie funèbre et triomphale during the festivities commemorating the Revolution of September 1830. The work was thoroughly apropos; and the chorus part recently added at the climax of the Apotheosis, to a text by Antoni Deschamps beginning "Gloire et triomphe à ces héros", would be no less suitable for Brussels than for Paris. At the end of August Berlioz wrote Snel a long letter with details of the programme, the instruments required, the price of tickets, and the artists taking part: Ernst, the brilliant young Bohemian violinist (who would also play solo viola in the Pilgrims' March), and two singers from the Opéra, the contralto Mme Widemann and the soprano Mlle Recio. It would be a good idea, he added, to get one of the newspapers to publish the text of the chorus as well as the programme – but not the names of the singers: "I have strong reasons for not doing so. Just say 'Mmes xxx of the Académie Royale de Musique de Paris'." A few days later, on 3 September, he sent word to Rocquemont: "I have work for you!" The orchestral parts were made ready in secret. Nothing was said at home. His friend Morel, who lived a few streets away in the Rue de Provence, was deputed to keep a friendly eye on Harriet during his absence. On the 19th he dined with Meyerbeer, who was writing on his behalf to Frankfurt to prepare the way. Early next morning he slipped out of the house, leaving a note for Harriet with the maid, and, accompanied by Marie, took the coach to Brussels.

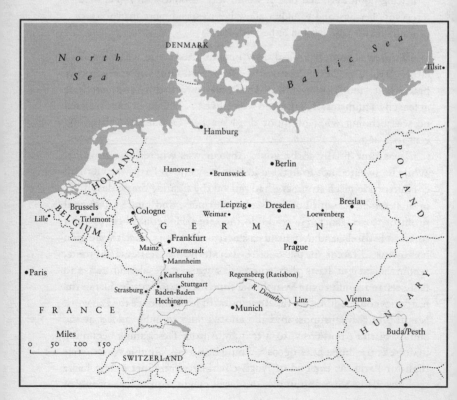

II

Germany at Last

Considering how large a part foreign tours played in Berlioz's life during the next fifteen years and what a stir he created almost everywhere he went, the beginning could hardly have been less auspicious. No one was expecting him at Frankfurt, the second stop on his itinerary: Meyerbeer's letters had gone astray. And Brussels turned out to be like Paris, only worse: little if any money to be made; a crippling poor tax which the authorities chose that moment to reintroduce; critical opinion as deeply divided, but with the doubters if anything in the majority; a general public whose indifference or incomprehension was not leavened, as it was in Paris, by a corps d'élite of faithful admirers; and, unlike the Salle du Conservatoire, halls far too reverberant to allow unfamiliar music a proper hearing. In the acoustical confusion the Apotheosis itself made little impression on Brussels' phlegmatic music-lovers; only the Pilgrims' March was applauded. And at the first of the two concerts there was the toad-like Fétis, denouncing the music to a group of acolytes as "hideously ugly" and "mad".

Not for the first time Berlioz must console himself with the approval of the orchestral musicians – on several occasions during the final rehearsal they broke into applause – and with the interest of the handful of critics who responded to his music positively. One of them, the Italian-born Marcus Aurelius Zani de Ferranti, enthusiast, man of parts, accomplished guitarist, who wrote for several Brussels journals and taught Italian declamation at the Conservatoire of which Fétis was head, delighted Berlioz by taking issue with his boss over the Pilgrims' March and the harmonic propriety of its recurring bell-like C natural and B. When Fétis asked how one could be expected to condone a piece in which one kept hearing two "wrong notes", Zani retorted that Berlioz must be an even finer composer than he had supposed, since he could apparently break the rules and still produce a movement which was a masterpiece of conception and workmanship and a continual pleasure to the ear. Even he, however, conceded that it would be a long time before such music became really popular – not in fact till the man-in-the-street was a poet.

Berlioz and Marie Recio spent about three weeks in Brussels, arriving on 21 September and putting up at the Hôtel du Domino, Place de la Monnaie, in the centre of town. On the face of it the visit was well timed. The city was *en fête*, celebrating, though in heavy rain, its "September Days" with artillery salutes, archery contests, horse-racing, open-air concerts and a choral competition. Berlioz's concert of the 26th, organized by Snel at the Royal Military Band's newly acquired auditorium, the Salle Cluysenaer in the Rue de la Madeleine, was the main musical event of the fourth day. As director of the band and maître de chapelle at the collegiate church of St Gudula, Snel was a powerful ally. A requiem of his composition featured at the opening service in honour of "the citizens who gave their lives for national independence" (and was reviewed by Berlioz next day in the *Emancipation*). While Snel's band provided the wind and percussion for the symphony, the main body of the orchestra was supplied by the opera house and by the Conservatoire, where Fétis, whatever he might be doing behind the scenes (Berlioz was told that he was trying to influence some of the critics against his music), made no difficulty about his students' taking part. Most of the musicians, being students, played for nothing. The press, if in many cases unconvinced or even hostile, discussed him seriously. They were also quite kind to Marie: though, according to the *Observateur*, there was "not much to say about the voice or the singing of Mlle Recio", *La Belgique musicale* found that despite a soprano voice that was "a little thin and still deficient in technique" she sang *Le jeune pâtre breton* "with just the right feeling, and deserved her applause". Nor could he complain of any lack of devotion on the part of the local musicians; Snel, Victor Hanssens, Mertz, Wéry, Zani de Ferranti were full of zeal. He was persuaded to give another concert, on 9 October in the Temple des Augustins. By then he had had an audience with the King, Leopold I, and presented him with a manuscript of the Pilgrims' March, a fact duly noted in the newspapers. But the official festivities were now over; and the second concert, which included the Fantastic Symphony, attracted only a few hundred people. It was better received than the first. Once again, however, he was disappointed in the acoustics; and the takings, even before the poor tax relieved him of a quarter of them, were meagre in the extreme. All in all Brussels was too reminiscent of Paris, without the advantages or the style. It could only seem a curtain-raiser, an antechamber to the courts and cities of Germany.

On the morning of 12 October Berlioz wrote Snel a farewell letter of thanks, to which Marie added her own postscript, and the two travellers set off for Frankfurt. Part of the journey was by steamboat down the Rhine, and his spirits rose with the grandeur of the passing landscape. He gazed at the wooded hills and the dark swift stream and the crags topped with ancient towers, his head full of Goethe and Hoffmann; he was in Germany at last. In the saloon he heard himself discussed at a nearby table by a party of Englishmen who had been at his concerts in Brussels. Was it a good omen? A morning or two later, on encountering some young men with instrument cases crossing the square outside the Frankfurt opera house, and asking them to present his card to their director, he was struck by the look of keen respect their faces took on at the sight of his name. The next moment all expectation was dashed. Guhr the director had not received Meyerbeer's letters – knew nothing of his coming to Frankfurt – had made no preparations – could not do anything just now – the theatre was busy, the company deep in rehearsals for Lachner's *Catarina Cornaro* – in short, sorry, no time.

The lack of planning, the casualness this suggests on Berlioz's part can only seem shocking in our international age, when visiting celebrities or rather their agents commonly fix their appearances years in advance. But there were practically no agents then. Liszt the travelling virtuoso par excellence had one, the invaluable Belloni, but that was still exceptional. There being far fewer concerts than now, it was easier to fit one in at the last minute. That was how things were done. Berlioz's first tour of Germany proceeded ad hoc. From one town he might write to the next and arrange a concert only a couple of weeks ahead. One or two of the most successful stops were afterthoughts. (Contrariwise, concerts set up well in advance could fail to materialize.) In towns ruled by a prince or a duke the orchestra could be commandeered at short notice. And in many of the places he planned to visit there were influential friends or acquaintances whose help he could count on: Meyerbeer in Berlin, Ferdinand Hiller in Frankfurt, Karol Lipinski and Wagner in Dresden, the French violinist and composer Chelard in Weimar, Louis Schloesser in Darmstadt, Anton Bohrer in Hanover, Mendelssohn in Leipzig, and in Brunswick the Müller brothers whom he had heard in Paris in the 1830s, when their incomparable string quartet played Beethoven better than anyone imagined possible. He could count, too, on a general interest in new music, and a particular curiosity about his, such as France or even Paris did not begin to match. The attitude of Lindpaintner, the kapellmeister at Stuttgart, was widely shared: "Since you are here it's certainly not going to be said we let you leave without performing some of your works, which we are so curious to know." The welcome he received shows how much his reputation had preceded him, spread by performances of his overtures, by Schumann's articles in the *Neue Zeitschrift*, by the translations of his own feuilletons regularly appearing in the same journal, and by the propaganda of a small but growing body of admirers. His advent, long heralded, was eagerly expected. Germany was waiting for him. Here and there he might draw a blank; but in centre after centre he found musicians who, like Mendelssohn, were happy to "shake him by the hand and say 'Willkommen' to Germany".

It was none the less an epic undertaking. Berlioz's Napoleonic comparisons – he liked to describe the reports of his progress as "dispatches from the Grande Armée" – were not so very far-fetched. It was one thing for a pianist or a violinist to travel the length and breadth of Europe: that had become almost commonplace. But no composer had attempted a journey – a campaign – on such a scale before. To have to drag heavy trunkfuls of music about with you, mostly by coach or boat (railway lines were still few and far between), to be dependent each time on the goodwill and administrative ability of a different director or intendant, to arrive each time in a strange place and face a strange orchestra, to start each time from scratch with a new set of players mostly unfamiliar with your music and bewildered by its style, required feats of organization, personality and nerve for which, though his experiences of concert promotion in Paris were some preparation, there was really no precedent. The degree of success achieved on his first German tour, though surpassed on later visits, is a tribute among other things to diligent staff work.

The "Letter from Weimar" addressed to Liszt in the *Journal des débats*, highly coloured as it is and drawing on many different encounters, both the best and the worst, gives an idea of the difficulties that beset the travelling composer, in contrast to the relatively smooth progress of his pianist counterpart. It also shows why, with all the difficulties, he enjoyed it so much.

To all questions about my plans and about the next stage of this journey barely begun, I could have truthfully answered like the character in Molière:

No, I am not returning for I never went,
Nor go I hence, for I am here detained,
But stay here neither, since 'tis my intent
At every moment to be gone . . .

To be gone – where? I hardly knew. True, I had written to Weimar, but the answer had not come and until it did I could reach no decision. You, my dear Liszt, know nothing of such perplexities. It is of small interest to you whether the town you propose to pass through has a decent musical establishment, let alone whether the theatre is available, the intendant willing to let you use it and so on. How should such information concern you? You can confidently say, adapting Louis XIV, "I am the orchestra! I am the chorus and the conductor as well. [. . .] I need no theatre, no special carpentry, no elaborate construction of ramps and tiers. I don't have to wear myself out taking interminable rehearsals. I don't require a hundred musicians or even twenty – I require none at all. I don't even require any music. A large room with a grand piano in it, and I have a great audience at my command. [. . .]

For the composer who would attempt, as I have, to travel in order to perform his works, how different. The never-ending toil he must endure, the torture that rehearsals can be – no one who has not experienced it can have an idea what it is like. To begin with he has to face the cold gaze of the whole orchestra, who resent being put to this unexpected inconvenience and extra work on his account. Their looks say plainly, "What does he want, this Frenchman? Why can't he stay where he belongs?" However, each man takes his place. But the moment the composer glances round the assembled company he is aware of alarming gaps. He asks the kapellmeister to explain. "The first clarinet is ill, the oboe's wife is in labour, the first violin's child has the croup, the trombones are on parade, they forgot to ask for exemption from their military duties, the timpanist has sprained his wrist, the harpist isn't coming, he needs time to study his part", etc., etc. Nevertheless one begins. The notes are read after a fashion, at a tempo more than twice too slow (nothing is so dreadful as this devitalizing of the rhythm!). Gradually your instinct gets the better of you, your blood begins to glow, you get carried away and involuntarily quicken the beat until you are giving the correct tempo. The result: chaos, a raucous confusion to split your ears and break your spirit. You have to stop and resume the original pace, and work your way laboriously, piecemeal, through the long phrases which so often before, with other orchestras, you were wont to sail through swiftly, without hindrance. Even then it is not enough; despite the slow tempo, strange discords are discernible among the wind instruments. You try to discover the reason. "Let me hear the trumpets by themselves . . . What are you doing? I should be hearing a third, you're playing a second. The second trumpet in C has a D: give me your D . . . Good. Now, the first trumpet has a C which sounds F. Let me hear it . . . Hey! What the devil? You've given me an E flat."

"Excuse me, I'm playing what's written."

"You're not, you're a tone out."

"I'm sorry, I'm playing a C."

"What key is your trumpet in?"

"E flat."

"That's what it is – you should be playing an F trumpet."

"Oh yes – I hadn't looked properly. Sorry, you're quite right."

"Timpani, why are you making such a frightful din over there?"

"I have fortissimo, sir."

"You haven't – it's mezo forte – mf, not ff. In any case you're playing with wooden sticks when you should be using sponge-headed ones. It's the difference between black and white."

"We don't know them," the kapellmeister interposes. "What do you mean by sponge-headed sticks? We only know the one kind." "I suspected as much, so I brought some with me from Paris. Take the pair on the table there. Now, are we all ready? . . . For Heaven's sake – it's ten times too loud. And why aren't you using mutes?" "The orchestral attendant forgot to put them out on the desks. We will have them tomorrow", etc., etc.

After three or four hours of this anti-musical tug of war they have not been able to make sense of a single piece. Everything is fragmentary, disjointed, out of tune, cold, dull, loud, discordant, detestable. And this is the impression you leave on sixty or eighty musicians, who finish the rehearsal exhausted and disgruntled and go around saying they have no idea what it's all about, it's a chaotic, heathenish music, they have never had to put up with anything like it before. Next day little progress is visible. It is only on the third day that the thing takes shape. Only then does the poor composer begin to breathe. The harmonies, correctly pitched, become clear, the rhythms leap to life, the melodies sigh and smile; the whole ensemble acquires confidence, cohesion, attack. The stumbling and stammering are forgotten: the orchestra has grown up, it can walk and talk, it has become a man. With comprehension, courage returns to the astonished players. The composer asks for a fourth trial of skill, and his interpreters – who when all is said are the best fellows in the world – grant it with alacrity. This time, *fiat lux*! "Watch out for the expression. You're not afraid now?"

"No – give us the right tempo."

Via! And there is light! Art is born, the whole conception becomes manifest; the work is understood. And the orchestra rises to its feet, applauding and acclaiming the composer, the kapellmeister congratulates him, the inquisitive people lurking in the hall emerge and come up on to the platform and exchange exclamations of pleasure and surprise with the players, with many a wondering glance at the foreign maestro whom at first they took for a madman or a barbarian. At this point you would like to relax. Do no such thing! It is now that you must intensify your vigilance. You must return before the concert to supervise the arrangement of the desks and inspect the orchestral parts to make sure none of them have got misplaced. You must go meticulously along the ranks, red pencil in hand, writing German key-indications for French in the wind parts, altering ut, ré, ré bémol, fa dièse to C, D, Des, Fis. You have to transpose a cor anglais solo for the oboe; the orchestra does not possess the instrument in question and the oboist is inclined to be nervous about transposing it himself. If the chorus or the soloists are still unsure of themselves, you must rehearse them separately. But the audience is arriving, it is time; and you stagger to the conductor's desk, a physical and mental wreck, weary, stale, flat and unprofitable, scarcely able to stand – until that magical moment when the applause of the audience, the zest of the players, and your own love for the work transform you in an instant into a dynamo of energy, radiating invisible, irresistible rays of light and power. And then the recompense begins. Then, I grant you, the composer-conductor lives on a plane of existence unknown to the virtuoso.[. . .]

When the concert is over and he has triumphed, his joy is multiplied a hundred times, shared as it is with the gratified pride of every member of his army. You, the great virtuosos, are princes and kings by the grace of God; you are born on the steps of the throne. We composers must fight and overcome and conquer to reign. But the very dangers and hardships of the struggle make our victories the more intoxicating, and we would perhaps be more fortunate than you – if we always had soldiers.

Soldiers were just what were lacking in Frankfurt. But he took the opportunity to arrange a return visit for late November. He and Guhr agreed provisionally on two concerts of his works in the local theatre, to include the first two symphonies – *Harold* and the Fantastic – and the big movements from the Requiem, at a fee of 1,200 florins. It remained to settle the dates: Guhr would write to him as soon as they could be determined. On 17 October Berlioz deposited the orchestral parts of the two symphonies at the opera house – rehearsals were to start in his absence – and added a plea to Guhr to guard them with his life, as they were manuscript parts and the only ones he had. A week later he dispatched all the Requiem music – full score by post, orchestra and chorus parts, plus a vocal score for the accompanist, by coach. "There are many more parts than are needed for the number of performers that we will have in Frankfurt, however I'm sending it all because I plan a full-scale performance in Berlin. Please make a note of the carriage dues."

By then he was in Paris again, in the throes of preparations for a gala concert at the Opéra on 7 November in which the Symphonie funèbre figured in its final version, with strings and – for the first time in Paris – chorus, between the second act of Auber's *Gustave III* and Adam's ballet *Giselle*, Berlioz conducting the wind band and the chorus on stage, Habeneck the strings in the pit. He was also busy putting the finishing touches to the *Treatise*, for which Schonenberger, whose premises were in the Boulevard Poissonnière, was paying him an advance of 2,500 francs.

It was Germany that dominated his thoughts and energies, however; the *Treatise* itself was a vital part of his plans, since the advance was providing financial security for the trip. He also contrived to obtain paid leave of absence from the Conservatoire Library. It looks as if Auber, the new Conservatoire director, opposed it. At any rate, ten days after Berlioz wrote to his immediate superior, Bottée de Toulmon, asking him to obtain it from the director, the Minister of the Interior informed Auber that he was granting the assistant librarian leave of absence: "M. Berlioz being entrusted with collecting information useful to the government, I have decided that he shall continue to draw his emoluments." Berlioz had not lost his aptitude for diplomatic manoeuvring.

The information he was deputed to collect concerned nothing less than the musical institutions of Germany: he was to examine them, assess their quality, and report on the way they were organized and the lessons France could usefully draw from them. At the same time the Foreign Minister, Guizot, sent a circular letter to French consuls and agents in Germany, enjoining them to "grant this distinguished composer all the facilities which may be of service to him, and assist him to fulfil his mission in a manner honourable to France and profitable to art".

Other influential contacts were set to work. Meyerbeer wrote to the Munich clarinettist Heinrich Baermann enlisting his aid:

> Our brilliant Berlioz, whose new and bold compositions have won your respect, as you often told me during your stay in Paris, is about to begin a concert tour of Germany. I helped convince him he should do this because his music is far more suited to a German audience than to the public here, although it is gaining in popularity here as well. [. . .] In Frankfurt on Main, where he will give concerts on the 25th and 29th [December], the theatre management has placed all orchestral and singing personnel at his disposal. [. . .] Given that Munich's population is so much larger than Frankfurt's and its theatre seats so many more people, I believe you would make a very advantageous arrangement for him and perhaps organize a larger number of concerts.

A few days before Berlioz left Paris Meyerbeer introduced him to Alexander von Humboldt, the great German geographer and explorer whose *Tableaux de la Nature* had been a favourite book of his boyhood. As counsellor at the Prussian court in Berlin he would be a useful link with the King.

Berlioz's intention had been to go straight to Frankfurt, arriving there in the last week of November; but Guhr wrote to say that Christmas would be better; and Snel persuaded him to try a third concert in Brussels, tempting the public with the bait of the soprano Mme Nathan-Treillet – the same Mlle Nathan about whose début three years before he had been dubious, but who had since made a career for herself and become a favourite with the Belgians. The concert was scheduled for 10 December, then postponed till the 17th; the two Frankfurt evenings were finally fixed for successive Sundays, 25 December and 1 January.

Officially he had leave for three months from the beginning of December; but he told Dufeuillant that he might be away twice as long. This time his departure was not being kept secret from Harriet. During his absence she had felt "quite desperate" (he told Nancy); but he had made his point and need no longer steal out of the house like a thief. How much she knew or guessed about Marie we cannot tell. She must have had suspicions at least; Mlle Recio's name had been mentioned in more than one report from Brussels. Three days before he left, Berlioz told Nancy that "Harriet is finding it very hard to accept; all the same I hope to leave her in a more reasonable state than I found her in when I got back from my first journey. When you write to her, next month, sending my pension, explain to her again (I have done it already) that she must go to the Banque de France on the exact day indicated on the note; tell Camille to make it out in the name of Mme Berlioz and not in mine." He promised to send her money from Germany and to arrange for her to have the royalties due on forthcoming performances of *Freischütz*. Short of giving up Marie, short of renouncing Germany and staying in Paris, he would do all he could to make her life bearable.

Nothing could do that. Berlioz's sisters exchanged anxieties about their sister-in-law. "What will become of Harriet during this long absence?" cried Adèle, adding sententiously, "If she were like any other woman she and Louis could have come and stayed with us. Unhappily, she's not." Adèle did in fact invite them to St Chamond, but Harriet refused. The effort, and the humiliation, would have been too great. Nancy sent her a cheerfully consoling letter, saying how pleased she was that they were in correspondence. "Tell me about your dear boy, he too can write to his Aunt Nancy, who loves him very much and would like to hear that he hasn't forgotten her. You mustn't be embarrassed by your French – use a dictionary. I don't want to lose any of it. We still await my father, who hasn't been able to tear himself away from his fields in this unexpectedly fine weather." But Berlioz, though his heart bled for her, could not look back. He had waited too long for this moment.

Ever since Mme de Staël's *De l'Allemagne*, the French imagination had nourished itself on the loftiest ideas of German culture and enlightenment; but, for Berlioz, it was especially sacred. Germany was the home of music, the cradle of Beethoven and Gluck and Mozart and

Weber. In the event his expectations were not disappointed. He might be surprised to find the standard of theatre choruses much lower than he had supposed; and nowhere that he visited came anywhere near Paris as a centre of fine singing. The general level of orchestral skill at that time – before the demands of Berlioz's and Wagner's scores, and later Liszt's, helped to raise it – was not high. But as a genuinely musical environment, as a country responsive to music and organized for it and alive to the possibilities of the new, Germany was immeasurably superior to France – as serious as France was, except intermittently, frivolous. Individual deficiencies like the rarity of competent harpists, the almost universal neglect of the cor anglais, the often poor state of the bassoonist's instrument even when the player was good, the cracked and chipped cymbals, were balanced by the excellent clarinets, the prevalence of the valve trumpet (almost unknown in France), the power of the bass tuba – the basso profundo of the brass, which he had not come across before – and the general superiority of the brass instruments in workmanship and tone quality. Above all, it was an atmosphere "far removed from the squalid intrigues and platitudes of Paris", an atmosphere in which he could thrive and feel at home despite his ignorance of German. They spoke the same language. Almost everywhere he went his music was treated as important enough to merit investigation. All over Germany he encountered musicians who, like the Stuttgarters, were "curious to know it". Only at the outset of his tour did he find himself obstructed by uncooperative kapellmeisters.

Like the one in September, the journey began badly. Berlioz, with Marie Recio, reached Brussels on 14 December, staying this time at the Hôtel de l'Europe, and started rehearsing immediately – only for news to come from Paris that Mme Nathan-Treillet was ill and would not be appearing. As no comparable attraction could be found at such short notice, the event was called off. He cast round for alternatives to Snel's concert society, then realized there was no time: with his first Frankfurt concert scheduled for the 25th he should be there no later than the 19th. He must simply cut his losses.

As before, the sight of the Rhine restored him. At Mainz he inquired about putting on a performance of the Symphonie funèbre with the Austrian military band which was quartered there and which had performed one or two of his overtures. But the band had left. And old Schott, "the patriarch of music publishers", squashed flat any suggestion of an orchestral concert instead. "The worthy man gives the impression of having been, like the Sleeping Beauty, in a coma for the past hundred years. To all my questions he answered very slowly, interspersing his words with profound silences: 'I do not think . . . you can . . . give a concert . . . here . . . there is no . . . orchestra . . . there is no . . . audience . . . we haven't any . . . money.' "

In Frankfurt, to which they travelled by slow train, a greater disillusionment was in store. No concert there either: Guhr was desolate, but there was nothing he could do; the violin prodigies from Lombardy, Teresa and Maria Milanollo, were monopolizing the theatre – the public had gone quite wild about them.

Berlioz had heard them in Paris and knew the furore they could create. But was Germany to be no better than France?

According to Ferdinand Hiller, Guhr had "seen to it" that no evening was free for the marauding Frenchman. Presumably he had tried rehearsing some of the music Berlioz left with him and had decided it was not something to be encouraged; Guhr was fond of the extra-musical – in Haydn's *Creation*, at "Let there be light", he had the theatre's gas lamps turned up – but he drew the line at the Fantastic Symphony. Hiller may be right. It would be another ten years before Berlioz finally performed his music in Frankfurt, by which time Guhr was no more. On the other hand Guhr had a good excuse in the profit the Milanollos were making for his theatre. The possibility of a Berlioz evening remained alive for a few more weeks. When he met Guhr in Mannheim in January a Frankfurt concert was still on the cards; Guhr talked of providing him with twenty-four violins, eight more than the theatre's normal complement. Berlioz remained on friendly terms with him. He used Frankfurt as a base throughout the tour and, for part of it, left the chorus and orchestra parts of the Requiem in Guhr's keeping. But his comment that "one way or another he seemed destined to find my music a source of embarrassment" suggests that he had a shrewd idea what Guhr thought of it. Hence the way he pictures him in the first of the *Débats*' Letters from Germany; he works off his frustration at what he privately called "that bloody town of Frankfurt" by having some fun at the expense of its irascible kapellmeister:

Guhr is a small man with a rather mischievous face and bright, piercing eyes, his movements rapid and his speech curt and incisive. It is clear he does not err on the side of indulgence when he directs his orchestra. Everything about him suggests musical intelligence and purpose: he is a leader. He speaks French, but not quick enough for his natural impatience, and he interlards each sentence with great oaths pronounced with a German accent, the effect of which is most curious. I shall indicate them by their initials.

The moment he saw me:

"Ah! SNTT ('Sacré nom te Tieu!') – it's you, my dear. Then you didn't get my letter?"

"What letter?"

"I wrote to Brussels to tell you – SNTT – wait, I don't speak properly – a misfortune, a great misfortune – Ah, here is our stage manager, he will act as my interpreter." And continuing to speak in French:

"Tell M. Berlioz how upset I am, that I wrote to tell him not to come yet, that the little Milanollo girls are filling the theatre every evening, that we've never known the public get so excited about anything, SNTT, and that serious music and concerts on a large scale will have to wait till some other time."

The stage manager: "Mr Guhr wishes me to tell you, sir, that –"

I: "Please don't bother to repeat it. I understood all too well; you see, he didn't speak in German."

Guhr: "Ah! ah! I spoke French, SNTT, without knowing it."

I: "You know it very well, and I know that I shall have to go back, or else take a chance and go on with my journey at the risk of being checkmated by infant prodigies somewhere else."

Guhr: "What can one do, my dear, the infants make money, SNTT, French romances make money, French vaudeville draws the crowds. What would you have me do? SNTT, I am director, I cannot refuse money. But stay till tomorrow at any rate, and you can hear *Fidelio* with Pischek and Mlle Capitaine and, SNTT, you shall tell me what you think of our artists."

I: "I am sure they are excellent, especially when you conduct them. But my dear Guhr, why do you swear so much? Do you think it consoles me?"

Guhr: "Ah! ah! SNTT, that's just speaking in the family way" (he meant to say "familiarly"). At that I was seized with uncontrollable laughter, my ill-humour vanished and, taking his hand I said, "All right, since I am one of the family, come and drink some Rhine wine with me. I'll forgive you your little Milanollo girls and stay to hear *Fidelio* and Mlle Capitaine, whose lieutenant you seem to want to be."

As much as his music it was Berlioz's personality, his humour (disconcerting though it could be) and, when he was in the mood, his charm, as well as his authority as a musician, that won him friends in Germany and made his journey, once it had got under way, the success it was. Even when people disliked his music they responded to something exceptional in the man. The orchestras felt the power of a maestro who was nearer to our idea of a conductor than any they had yet worked with. Language was not often a barrier. Quite a few had studied at the Paris Conservatoire (the acknowledged centre of instrumental teaching); French was widely understood; and to those who did not speak it he was generally able to make himself clear – if not directly, then through the "concert-master", the leader of the orchestra whose role, he discovered, was so much more important than the first violin's in France. Not all the players succumbed to his spell: in Stuttgart, illness, which he could not help suspecting was diplomatic, deprived him of eight of the sixteen violins on the day of the concert. But most of the time, whatever their immediate resistance, he carried them with him through the hazardous but increasingly rewarding challenges he placed before them.

The Stuttgart concert was the first that Berlioz gave on German soil. He and Marie travelled by coach from Frankfurt to the capital of the kingdom of Württemberg, a hundred miles to the south, on about 26 December. This time he knew no one, though he had a letter of introduction from Kastner to Gustav Schilling, the music historian. Schilling was friendly but there were serious language difficulties; the two men were reduced to conversing in Latin, "Dr Schilling's French being rather like my German". Lindpaintner, the kapellmeister, made him feel at home, however, and a concert was fixed for the 29th in the Redoutensaal.

Several friends, among them the violinist Ernst, had advised him to concentrate on the large centres and not to bother with towns of second rank, where the musical forces would be inadequate to his needs. But with Berlin not ready to receive him and Munich and Vienna uncertain he had no choice but to start small and leave the largest compositions till later – the "forte to his crescendo". The great thing, after Frankfurt, was to have an orchestra. At Stuttgart it numbered the standard forty-six players, and included some fine woodwind, good horns (though, as at Frankfurt, their high notes were too brassy for his taste), excellent trombones and – almost unheard of in Germany, he was to discover –

a first-rate harpist. The strings, if too few (and fewer still at the concert), were young and energetic. He felt able to offer the Fantastic Symphony, a movement or two from *Harold*, and the *Francs-juges* overture. During the interval at the opera (*Freischütz*) Lindpaintner introduced him to the band, Berlioz made a short speech which Lindpaintner translated, and next day they began. To his surprise he found them brilliant sight-readers, who coped with the music's rhythmic intricacies quicker, it later transpired, than almost any orchestra in Germany. The two rehearsals which were all he could be given produced perfomances that "if not very powerful – that was impossible – were at least intelligent, precise and vital". At the end the King sent his grand marshal and intendant, Baron von Topenhaim, to convey his congratulations and those of the court, Prince Jerome Bonaparte among them. The meagre receipts – the hall held only four hundred people, and tickets were priced very low – took some of the shine off. But he felt he had created an impression and made a few converts, even if Schilling was not among them: the good doctor, he was sure, was wondering what on earth he had done, letting such a brigand loose on Stuttgart.

It was Schilling, however – perhaps he had a sense of humour – who recommended him to the Prince of Hohenzollern-Hechingen; and on New Year's Eve, two days after the Stuttgart concert, Berlioz and Marie travelled by coach through the Black Forest to the little kingdom sixty miles to the south. Hechingen was the diminuendo and pianissimo of the tour. The Prince's diminutive hilltop palace maintained a musical establishment of under thirty players, some of whom would have done better not playing. Yet Berlioz never forgot the three days he spent there and the welcome he received. The Prince's passion for music was genuine and all-consuming. It and the fact that he could indulge it as he did made Hechingen a collector's piece, a phenomenon so peculiarly German that it would have been a shame to have missed it.

His orchestra, directed by the composer-violinist Thomas Täglichs-beck, whom Berlioz had known in Paris a few years before (when, unlike Berlioz, he had symphonies of his performed on two occasions by the Société des Concerts), contained five decent violinists, a good cellist, a skilful double-bass – the Hechingen chaplain and archivist – and one or two fine wind players. This was the nucleus. The more important notes for third and fourth horn were pencilled in to the viola parts, the harp part was rewritten for piano, the trumpet parts drastically simplified for the benefit of the two very uncertain trumpeters, the solitary trombonist confined himself to the three or four notes he was sure of, the Prince stood next to the timpanist to count his rests; and by dint of other suppressions and rearrangements and after holding five rehearsals in three days they brought off a short programme consisting of the Pilgrim's March, the Ball from the Fantastic, the *King Lear* overture and *Le jeune pâtre breton*, to widespread satisfaction, if not the composer's. Even Marie Recio was encored. Afterwards, at a supper party in the Villa Eugenia, Berlioz sang the cello part in a riotous performance of a trio of the prince's composition.

When they got back to Stuttgart next day (3 January) there was a letter from Baermann, forwarded by Meyerbeer, informing him that nothing could be done in Munich at the moment. Fortunately there was also one from Johann Christian Lobe, Weimar violinist, composer and critic, to whom Berlioz had written on the strength of his open letter on the *Francs-juges* overture published in the *Neue Zeitschrift* four years before.* Lobe's answer did strange things with French language and spelling but was hearteningly positive: "Mon avis sur votre voyage et: Venez! Venez! Venez!" Though February (he said) was not the ideal time to come, once he secured the support of the court there would be no problem. The Grand Duchess was a keen music-lover and actually owned a score of the *Francs-juges* overture; a letter from the King of Württemberg would not be a bad thing; and he should write to the Weimar kapellmeister, Chelard, who, though not particularly influential, could be obstructive: if his vanity were offended, "his friendship for you could go to the devil – a spirit whom you may believe in a little, no? Yes sir, there is a devil, especially in the world of music! He is called envy, you know him well, that is so? You will find him in Germany also. Be on your guard! Come, and find an artist who love his art, who love all true artist and who love you above all, you who is an artist who go his road by all the obstacles which genius must pass."

Lobe's enthusiasm persuaded Berlioz to give up Vienna for the moment and go north, advancing his visit to Weimar by several weeks and taking in Mannheim and Karlsruhe on the way. He wrote to both Chelard and Lobe and then stayed on at the Hôtel du Roi de Württemberg for a few more days to await their replies. While doing so he heard Lindpaintner and the Stuttgart orchestra give a brilliant

* See pp. 223–4.

account of Beethoven's overture *Leonore no. 3*, only for the audience to receive it with indifference. At dinner afterwards he had the melancholy satisfaction of overhearing a neighbour ask indignantly why they didn't play Haydn's symphonies "instead of this uncivilized music with no tunes in it". He also attended performances of *Freischütz* and Auber's *La muette*, and was surprised – not for the last time in Germany – by the conductor's rapid tempos. And the Germans were supposed to take everything too slowly!

At Karlsruhe the theatre was being monopolized by a flautist from Piedmont, and they continued up the Rhine to Mannheim. Berlioz did not enjoy Mannheim. The rain was relentless, the inhabitants more interested in commerce than in art, the trombones of the otherwise quite lively little orchestra unequal to the Brigands' Orgy in *Harold* (which had to be given without it), and Marie's contribution – three numbers in a programme of no great length – embarrassing. "The first two times [at Stuttgart and Hechingen] it was not too bad," he wrote to Morel, "but the last! . . . And at the very idea of another singer she was up in arms." Till now he had borne it, relieving his feelings by making a wry reference to her in his album opposite the tune and text of *Le jeune pâtre breton*, alongside the lines that speak of the "soft, frail voice" which "is like a sigh half pleasurable, half irritating". But now, back in Frankfurt again preparatory to moving north, he was goaded to action. It would mean missing Hiller's oratorio *The Fall of Jerusalem* next day (18 January), but he had decided to give Marie the slip. "She insists on singing at my concerts," he told Hiller; and "she sings like a cat." His luggage was smuggled out and deposited at the coach station. That evening he left Marie behind at the hotel (the Russischer Hof) – ostensibly in order to attend a reception at Baron Rothschild's to which she had not been invited – and, dressed incongruously in his most formal clothes, took the coach to Weimar. Marie, like Harriet, was handed a note. It contained money for the journey back to Paris, and gave no address.

No wonder his account of Weimar strikes a new tone. He was free. "Yes! this is different. Here I can breathe. I feel something in the very air that proclaims a cultivated, artistic town." It was just as he had imagined it: calm, luminous, airy, in a landscape of streams and wooded hills and charming valleys. "So that was Goethe's summer-house, where the late Grand Duke liked to go and take part in the learned discussions of Schiller and Herder and Wieland. This Latin inscription was carved in the rock by the author of *Faust*. And those two little windows, did they really light the garret where Schiller lived? Was it there in that humble abode that the poet of the noblest passions of the human heart wrote *Don Carlos*, *Mary Stuart*, *The Robbers*, *Wallenstein*?" Even the weather had changed and now smiled on his new-found liberty.

It was short-lived. Marie was more determined and more resourceful than he. She ignored the note and used the money to buy herself a ticket to Weimar, a destination she could guess easily enough since it had been more or less settled as the next stop on the itinerary: she hardly needed the evidence of the passenger list, which the clerk was persuaded to let her examine. Nor did she have much trouble tracing him in Weimar. He had checked in at the Hôtel du Prince Héréditaire (Hotel Erbprinz), and it was there that she found him a day or two later. Hiller, meanwhile, had learned the course of events from the porter at the Russischer Hof. His letter commiserating with his friend for being caught was answered not by Berlioz but by Marie, in tones of high indignation; at the bottom were two lines in her lover's hand to effect that he had *not* been "caught" – they were "reunited". Berlioz, writing to Morel soon afterwards, was obliged to ask him "not to say a word about M." in his reply, "for she came after me and rejoined me at Weimar – I'll tell you about it. Write to me as if I hadn't written you this letter. All your information will be deemed to have come spontaneously from you." As the information requested related to Harriet, about whom he had anxiously asked for news, it is clear that his escape had led only to his falling more helplessly in thrall to "black eyes" and her charms: he could not even inquire openly after his wife. At the Weimar concert a week later (25 January) Marie sang three of his songs, including, for the first time, *Absence* (with piano) and the even more suggestively named *La belle voyageuse* which he orchestrated for the occasion, perhaps as a symbolic gesture of apology and reconciliation. Marie had got her way, and Berlioz must make the best of it. She was there. Vocal numbers were more or less de rigueur at all orchestral concerts. If she sang, at least it gave her presence a veneer of respectability. And there was always the hope that her singing would get better.

None the less the visit to Weimar marks the turning-point of the tour. It would be a few more years before the town, under the aegis of Liszt and the young Crown Prince Carl Alexander, aspired to rival the great centre of arts and sciences it had been under the old Grand Duke

– a renaissance in which Berlioz's music would play an important part. Even so, Weimar was the most responsive place he had yet been to. He had his partisans there already. The orchestra might not be all that much to write home about but it was willing; it knew the *Francs-juges* overture well and could not wait to tackle the Fantastic Symphony. At last he had a good number of strings – forty-three (including twenty-two violins): Lobe and Chelard between them had nearly doubled the theatre's twenty-four. As always, there had to be compromises: the cor anglais part in the Fantastic taken by the first clarinet (an especially fine player), the harp replaced by a piano, and a bombardon standing in for the missing ophicleides. One can imagine too what simplifications had to be practised, in all these smaller German musical establishments, in the passage for multiple timpani at the end of the Scène aux champs. But the movement, for the first time on the tour, clarinet and all, made a deep impression on both the orchestra and the audience. The theatre was full, and Berlioz, who conducted in a dark-red waistcoat (which he subsequently left behind in his room at the hotel), was recalled several times and surrounded at the stage door by admirers old and new who kept him up till three in the morning. To crown it, the theatre gave him all the receipts. He took the opportunity to send Harriet 200 francs.

The obvious next stop was Leipzig, only fifty miles away to the north-east, where Mendelssohn directed the already famous Gewandhaus concerts; but he hesitated. He remembered how little if at all Mendelssohn, friendly though he was, had reciprocated his admiration for his music during their time together in Rome – an admiration all the greater since Berlioz had heard the *Hebrides* overture in Paris the year before – and he suspected that what he himself had done in the years since they last met could only have deepened the gulf separating them as composers. Would Mendelssohn wish to help him put on performances of his music in Leipzig? But Chelard told him not to be so diffident; and, having sent letters to Dresden about a possible visit in February and enlisted Meyerbeer's aid to the same end, Berlioz wrote to Mendelssohn on 23 January and a few days later received a most cordial reply, assuring him that it would be "both a duty and a pleasure for me to do all I can to make your stay in Leipzig agreeable and profitable" and urging him to come as soon as he could leave Weimar. A concert was fixed for Saturday 4 February, ten days hence; it was also agreed that he should take part in a charity evening in aid of the

Leipzig poor on the 22nd, perhaps after the visit to Dresden. Berlioz, still on the defensive, apologized for being able to offer only "old stuff" – his latest scores were in Frankfurt. However, for the charity concert he suggested the finale of *Romeo and Juliet*, provided they could be sure of a first-rate bass as Friar Laurence.

Arriving in Leipzig on the evening of 28 January and depositing Marie and the baggage at the Bayerische Hof, he went straight to the Gewandhaus, where Mendelssohn was rehearsing his latest work, the cantata *Die erste Walpurgisnacht*. Berlioz's subsequent Letter in the *Débats* described their meeting:

As Mendelssohn stepped down from the rostrum, radiant with the sense of achievement, I came forward, thrilled at having just heard the work. The moment could not have been better chosen; yet, after the first exchange of greetings, the same melancholy thought struck us both.

"What! Twelve years? Can it really be as long as that since we daydreamed together in the Campagna?"

"And in the Baths of Caracalla."

"Ah, still the same scoffer, I see, always ready to mock me!"

"No, no, my mocking days are over. I said it to test your memory and to see whether you had forgiven me for my irreverence.* In fact I mock so little that I am going to ask you on the spot, in all seriousness, to make me a present of something of great value to me."

"What is that?"

"The baton with which you have just been rehearsing your new work."

"With the greatest pleasure, on condition that you let me have yours."

"It will be copper for gold. Still, it's a bargain." And Mendelssohn's sceptre was brought to me forthwith.

On the day of the performance Berlioz sent him his own "heavy oak cudgel", with a note which he hoped "the last of the Mohicans would not have disowned":

To Chief Mendelssohn.

Great Chief! We are pledged to exchange tomahawks. Here is mine. It is rough-hewn. Yours is plain. Only squaws and palefaces like ornate

---

* Berlioz was alluding to an occasion when, during a heated religious discussion in the Baths of Caracalla, Mendelssohn missed his footing and fell down a ruined stairway, whereupon his companion, helping him to his feet, said, "Look at that for divine justice: I blaspheme, you fall."

weapons. Be my brother; and when the Great Spirit sends us to hunt in
the land of souls, may our warriors hang our tomahawks together at the
entrance to the council chamber.

The incident apparently caused disapproval, though the nature of it
remains obscure. According to Mendelssohn's sister Fanny Hensel, who
lived in Berlin, Berlioz arranged for the phrase "Mine is rough-hewn,
yours is plain" to be inscribed on his baton, but the German translator
rendered it as "I am coarse, you are simple." It seems unlikely. Berlioz's
biographer Edmond Hippeau thought that Mendelssohn's Lutheran
piety was offended by the invocation to "the Great Spirit"; yet considering how familiar and well-loved Cooper's novels were to that whole
generation of artists (Schubert had a copy of *The Last of the Mohicans*
beside him during his final illness), that too is a little hard to credit.

The fact remains that Leipzig was much more uneasy about Berlioz
than Weimar had been. Though individual musicians and music-lovers
might be attracted by these strange new compositions, there was no
Johann Christian Lobe or Grand Duchess Maria Pavlovna to set the
tone by their enthusiasm. The merchant city of Leipzig was already
the bastion of conservatism that it remained under Mendelssohn's
successors, in conscious opposition to Liszt's Weimar, champion of the
new and "progressive" in art. Leipzig was the centre of the great Bach
revival, which was gathering momentum all the time – thirteen years
had passed since Mendelssohn's performance of the *St Matthew Passion*
brought the work back from oblivion – but which would leave Berlioz
unmoved until Saint-Saëns converted him to Bach near the end of his
life. (With all his admiration for Mendelssohn, he thought him still "a
little too fond of the dead".) Critical comment on Berlioz's music in
Leipzig was, predictably, more hostile than not. A German, one critic
wrote, could not regard the way he handled his material as either artistic
or natural; Berlioz "does not wish to please us, he wishes to be original";
compared with the Witches' Sabbath, Weber's Wolf's Glen was a
lullaby; and so on. Even his taking advantage of the resources of
the place to increase the violins to twenty-four – sixteen was the
Gewandhaus' number – was considered presumptuous. As for Mendelssohn, nothing that he heard either as listener or as participant (he played
the harp parts in the Fantastic on the piano and rehearsed the chorus
for the finale of *Romeo*) disposed him to revise his opinion: it still
"grieved" him that a man so "intelligent, balanced and sensible in his

judgement" composed as he did. Berlioz wrote ruefully on the subject of Mendelssohn to his friend d'Ortigue: "He's a very great master – I say this in spite of his enthusiastic compliments on my *romances*. Of the symphonies, the overtures, the Requiem, he has not said one word to me."

Whatever he thought, he could not have been more helpful. He and the concert-master Ferdinand David – his "fidus Achates", as he introduced him to Berlioz – did everything to make the concert a success, musically if not commercially (the "little Leipzigers", as Liszt called them, seem to have been less curious to hear the Frenchman's works than were the citizens of other German towns, and the hall was not full). Owing to the performance of Mendelssohn's cantata, due on the 2nd, there was time for only two rehearsals, but the orchestra was so skilled and disciplined that that was just about enough; the difficult finale of the Fantastic, in particular, was brought off "with a precision and demonic fury without parallel", though he had to recognize that the audience was "more astonished than touched" by the work.

One musician who, though ambivalent about him, continued to find evidence of a "divine spark" in Berlioz was Robert Schumann. Schumann was in Leipzig, about to take up a post at the new Conservatoire, when Berlioz arrived. They met, for the first time, on 30 January, and next day Schumann attended Berlioz's first rehearsal of a programme which included the Fantastic Symphony and the *King Lear* overture. He noted his contradictory impressions in the diary which he kept jointly with Clara. "A friendly encounter." "Unfortunately he does not speak German at all, so we didn't speak much. I had imagined him to be a livelier, more temperamental person. There is something hearty in his laughter." Schumann found "a trace of weakness" round the mouth and chin in his "otherwise distinguished face": Paris and "the dissolute life of young people there" had "spoiled him". "He now travels with a Mlle Recio who apparently is more than his concert singer." "He often strikes me as like the powerless King Lear himself." "Conducts extremely well. Much that is unbearable in his music, but extraordinarily imaginative, even full of genius."

As there could be no rehearsal on 2 February, Berlioz went to Dresden to make final arrangements for two concerts (the 10th and 17th). The round trip was 142 miles but thanks to the recently opened railway line it could be done in a day: he was back in time for Mendelssohn's concert.

The Dresden visit had been set up only two weeks before, by letters from Berlioz to his old Paris acquaintance, the concert-master Karol Lipinski, and from Meyerbeer to Reissiger, the kapellmeister, and to the intendant, Baron von Lüttichau. Meyerbeer's to Reissiger is a characteristic mixture of flattery, hyperbole and gentle insistence: "You are too much *au courant* with the world of contemporary art – to which indeed your own great works belong – not to have heard of Berlioz's imposing symphonies and the immense sensation they have produced. Berlioz is at present engaged on an artistic tour of Germany with the object of making his splendid musical poems known to us as well. [. . .] I have done everything in my power to secure him favourable conditions in Berlin, and I very much hope that Dresden will not be slow to do the same."

Dresden was not. Though quite a small city with a population of only seventy thousand – about a sixth the size of Berlin's – the capital of the kingdom of Saxony had the largest musical resources he had yet encountered in Germany. From the moment of his arrival, on 6 February, they were placed royally at his disposal. Baron von Lüttichau laid on the excellent military band as well as the orchestra, and for the first time he was able to programme the Apotheosis from the Symphonie funèbre. The Dresdeners heard a wider cross-section of his work than any other town: not only the first two symphonies but the Fête and Scène d'amour from *Romeo* and the Apotheosis and its preceding Hymne d'adieu; not only *King Lear* but also the overture to *Benvenuto Cellini* and Teresa's cavatina; the Sanctus, Offertorium and Quaerens me from the Requiem; the Napoleonic cantata *Le cinq mai*; *Rêverie et caprice* for violin and orchestra which, though a rather poor piece, was useful as a sop to the local concert-master (it was played in Leipzig, Brunswick and Hamburg as well); and *Le jeune pâtre breton*, *La belle voyageuse* and *Absence*, the latter for the first time in its orchestral guise, having been scored – "for Marie", the autograph says – on 12 February, a few days before the second concert.

The Dresden orchestra, in contrast to the military band, was not accorded as much praise in the *Débats*' Letters as the orchestras of Berlin and Bruswick: we read of – for once – a good cor anglais player but also of an oboist who insisted on embellishing his part at the beginning of the Scène aux champs, of trombones that sounded too "well-bred" for the Brigands' Orgy, and of an ancient double-bass player "barely able to support the weight of his instrument". (Berlioz found several instances in Germany of this "mistaken regard for the old", a view he shared with Wagner, who in *Mein Leben* speaks of two antiquated violists in the Dresden orchestra who "to my sorrow stuck tenaciously to their jobs, notwithstanding their right to a pension".) But Lipinski and his men were determined to better their Leipzig rivals and worked long and strenuously. Berlioz was given eight three-and-a-half-hour sessions as well as additional rehearsals with chorus, and he seems to have been tolerably satisfied with the results. On the morning after the first concert his grateful bandsmen blew him an aubade under the windows of the Hôtel de France and, though suffering from a headache and a sore throat, he helped them empty a vat of punch. People were in a state of great enthusiasm, he wrote to Morel, "which they can only express by squeezing my hand or by bows and hugs, as I don't know a word of German". The normal theatre prices had been raised by a third, so that there was handsome profit. After the second concert he sent 500 francs to Harriet.

As visitors would be for the next hundred years, he was struck by the extraordinary beauty of the place. Dresden was also a very friendly city. Everyone offered hospitality. In the royal library he was shown some scores by Hasse, the eighteenth-century Dresden master, among them a Te Deum whose bell-like sonorities probably helped to inspire his own Te Deum. And he met some of the leading musicians of the day: the tenor Joseph Tichatschek, Wagner's Rienzi and first Tannhäuser; the great Wilhelmine Schröder-Devrient, whom he had thought a superb artist when he heard her in *Fidelio* twelve years before but whose voice had coarsened and whose fondness for spoken inflexions in her singing he now found obnoxious (whereas for Wagner she remained the supreme exemplar, rather as Berlioz would never hear a word against Mme Branchu, his ideal of the dramatic soprano); Elias Parish-Alvars, the "Liszt of the harp", whose playing astonished him and with whom he discussed technical points for last-minute inclusion in the *Treatise*; and Wagner himself.

Berlioz arrived in Dresden at the very moment Wagner took up the post of assistant kapellmeister. The two men had been acquaintances in Paris a few years before, when the *Gazette* published ten articles and short stories by Wagner between July 1840 and May 1842. Since then Wagner's life had been transformed by the triumph of *Rienzi*, which had led to the present appointment. One of his first tasks was to assist at the rehearsals of the composer whose *Romeo and Juliet* had come to him as the revelation of a new world of music but about whom he felt uncomfortably ambivalent.

Their relationship, probably, could never have been other than difficult. But already, in Dresden, the fatality which pursued it ensured that dismissive remarks about Berlioz's music from Wagner's pen saw the light just when they met. The second part of Wagner's *Autobiographical Sketch*, which pictured Berlioz as a composer lacking any sense of beauty and shunned by all but a small clique of admirers, appeared in the *Zeitung für die elegante Welt* two days after Berlioz's arrival. No doubt a friend took care to draw his attention to the passage. (Lipinksi may well have, for one: he told Berlioz that he suspected Wagner of scheming against him.) If so, Berlioz refrained from reacting. The sentiments contained in the "Letter from Dresden", published in the *Débats* that September and reproduced in German periodicals two months later, are irreproachable. (As he told Lipinski, he had "decided not to voice the suspicion which you raised with regard to Wagner".) Wagner, the article says, assisted him "with energy and goodwill". *The Flying Dutchman* (performed on the second evening of his stay) is praised for "the sombre colouring of the music" and for the "remarkable effects of storm and wind which are an integral part of the dramatic character of the work"; he criticizes only what he finds an excessive use of tremolo both in it and in *Rienzi*. You have the feeling that in his general remarks he is bending over backwards not to be influenced by anything Wagner may have said about him; but only with the hindsight of the Wagnerian hegemony to come could his sympathetic assessment of a composer still near the beginning of his career be found wanting:

Having endured in France untold hardship and all the frustrations and mortifications that come when one is obscure, he returned to his native Saxony and had the audacity to embark on the composition of words and music of a five-act opera, *Rienzi*, and the good fortune to accomplish it. The work had a brilliant success in Dresden. It was soon followed by *The Flying Dutchman*, a three-act opera for which he again wrote both words and music. Whatever one's opinion of these works, it will be conceded that there are not many men who could twice bring off a double feat of this kind, and that at the very least it reveals him as a figure of unusual ability and interest. That is what the King of Saxony clearly appreciated. When he guaranteed Richard Wagner a livelihood by making him assistant to his senior kapellmeister, lovers of art could have echoed the words with which Jean Bart replied to Louis XIV when the King informed the intrepid sea-dog that he had appointed him commodore: "Sire, you have done well." [The article then discusses the two operas, before concluding:] I repeat, all honour to the enlightened King who, by taking him so decisively under his protection, has in effect saved a young artist of rare talents.

Berlioz's thoughts on the comparative roles of princely patronage in Germany and France do not have to be guessed.

A day or two after the second Dresden concert he was back in Leipzig to prepare for the charity evening due on 22 February. There he discovered that, though the chorus, rehearsed by Mendelssohn, knew its part in the finale of *Romeo and Juliet*, the bass chosen to sing Friar Laurence had made no headway with his. They struggled on; but at the final rehearsal, as the orchestra kept having to be stopped on the soloist's account, Berlioz thanked the choir and orchestra for their efforts and brought the proceedings to a halt. The finale was abandoned and replaced by three shorter pieces: *King Lear* (already performed at the first Leipzig concert), *Absence* and the Offertorium, whose simple choral chant could be mastered quickly. To his chagrin, Lipinski turned up at the concert, having come from Dresden to hear the *Romeo* finale. But the revised programme earned Berlioz a special suffrage. At the rehearsal hastily organized on the morning of the concert, the normally taciturn Schumann "opened his mouth, to the astonishment of those who know him, and grasping my hand said, 'This Offertorium surpasses everything.'" Clara Schumann, who to her regret missed the concert ("the Offertorium is said to make an extraordinary impression"), confided to the Schumann diary that though Berlioz's music was "full of interest and imagination . . . it gave her no pleasure", and she thought him cold and offhand when he came to their house on 27 February and heard Robert's piano quintet and two of his string quartets. "He was unwell, nevertheless he could have behaved in a more friendly and sincere manner if his soul were truly inspired by art"; but "Robert is of a different opinion, and has taken him to his heart, which I cannot understand."

Though Mendelssohn said nothing about the Offertorium (remarking only on a well-placed double-bass entry in the newly orchestrated *Absence*), others beside Schumann were impressed, and there were calls in one or two Leipzig papers for a complete performance of the Requiem.

That would have to wait for Berlin, however; the big movements demanded larger forces than Leipzig could provide, and in any case he was feeling too ill to do anything. The past three weeks had taken their toll; he was forced to stay indoors, looked after by Dr J. C. A. Carus (medical assessor in the case of the Leipzig soldier Woyzeck on which Büchner based his play and Berg his opera). Dr Carus absolutely refused payment, producing instead of a bill a blank sheet of paper on which he asked him to inscribe the theme of the Offertorium. Such personal responses were some compensation for the disapproval of the critics. Berlioz left Leipzig with mixed feelings, though none about the Gewandhaus and its marvellous acoustics. With a hall like that, he exclaimed to d'Ortigue, and an amateur choir of that quality, what couldn't he do in Paris!

Berlin was to have been next; but, just as he was preparing to leave, a letter came from Meyerbeer urging him to postpone his arrival by ten days – the musicians were busy with command performances for the King – and use the time gained to visit Brunswick before Berlin instead of after. On a morning early in March the travellers reached Brunswick, 120 miles north-east of Leipzig, Berlioz having spent the night in the open compartment of the coach so as to "escape the smoke and stench of six abominable pipes going full blast inside". The experience cannot have done his health any good – he fell sick in Brunswick too – but the warmth of his reception by the Müllers and the other musicians made up for all his ills.

In some ways Brunswick, not Berlin, was the high point of the tour. Meyerbeer told him he would find a "vintage orchestra", and he did. The section leaders of the strings were the four members of the Müller Quartet (the Busch Quartet of its day) and there were three other members of the clan in the orchestra, not counting the kapellmeister Georg Müller. Having asked Berlioz what forces he would like, Carl Müller the concert-master and his brother Georg went round recruiting the best additional players in Brunswick and assembled an orchestra more than eighty strong, better than any he conducted except in Berlin, and ready for anything: Berlioz commented in the *Débats* that he had never met one like it for "passionate dedication to the task in hand". One of the violinists, Zinkeisen, who had heard *Romeo* in Paris, begged him to let them play the Queen Mab scherzo, and for the first time in Germany he decided to risk it. After the opening rehearsal, at which *Harold* and the overture to *Benvenuto Cellini* were brought off in cracking style but the scherzo was a shambles, the players agreed to meet secretly each day an hour in advance of the scheduled time, so as to work on all the most difficult passages before the unsuspecting conductor arrived.

Meanwhile the presence of some of Brunswick's leading music-lovers, invited to the rehearsals at Georg Müller's suggestion, helped spread the word, so that by the day of the concert (9 March) the town was buzzing. Long before the start, the Ducal Theatre was full. On coming on to the platform Berlioz found the conductor's desk swathed in greenery as though for a triumph already won, and had a moment of panic ("in Paris a demonstration like that would doom an artist twenty times over"). But the audience was conquered from the beginning; the whole programme, one of the longest he gave in Germany, was received with acclamation. Even Marie's *Absence* had to be repeated. So did the Pilgrim's March; and the finale was played with such ferocity and élan that at the end he was moved to cry out, "in French, it is true, but the tone of my voice must have made my meaning clear, 'Stupendous! Thank you, gentlemen, I congratulate you; you are perfect brigands.'" The calm and gravity of the March and of the opening fugato were equally finely rendered. The Queen Mab scherzo went as well as it had ever done in Paris, if not better. And at the conclusion of the final work, the Fête, the hall erupted, the wind blew fanfares and the strings rattled their bows, and Georg Müller, advancing with armfuls of flowers, laid them on the composer's scores "in the name of the entire ducal establishment".

Brunswick, 14 March 1843

Dear Father

I have been wanting to write to you for ages, but I don't know what instinct made me wait till I had a great success to announce to you, greater than all the others. [...] To begin with, the performance was marvellous, and the enthusiasm of the public and the artists surpassed anything I could have dreamed of. [...] After the concert the orchestra invited me to a grand supper which they had planned in association with the chief amateurs of the town. It was a brilliant party; I was covered afresh with choral hurrahs (as is the harmonious custom in Germany), with poems, vivats, toasts and wreaths. The theatre was full and the receipts larger by 48 thalers than they had been before. But the price of tickets is so modest, and on no account to be raised, that all I got – I was dividing them with the director – was 750 francs. The cost of transporting my music is ruinous – it weighs 500 lb. Without that my voyage would be quite lucrative. Tomorrow I go to Hamburg – I'm expected there – and from there to Berlin where two concerts have been billed, for which I will have no expenses and half the gross receipts guaranteed. The trip is very important to me, I have to see the King of Prussia to offer him the dedication of the *Treatise on Instrumentation*. M. de Humboldt is going to introduce me. But the concerts will be on a huge scale, and I fear the fatigue. I was absolutely knocked out by the ones in Dresden, where they also fêted and serenaded me. One day I went from Leipzig to Dresden in the morning, to make preparations for my two concerts, left again at one o'clock in the afternoon and was back in Leipzig for Mendelssohn's concert, having done 160 miles in a few hours. The power of the railways!

There has practically not been a winter in Germany this year; I've seen snow only once, in the Black Forest, on my way back from the Prince of Hechingen's. I hope this strange temperature suits you: in Germany there are an enormous number of people ill. I've paid my tribute, with sore throats, upset stomachs and persistent headaches, everything you can think of, and I'm not yet over it; I've been through the hands of the doctors of Dresden, Leipzig and Brunswick. Whichever of my sisters writes to me should send her letter to Berlin, poste restante, as I shall stay only six or seven days in Hamburg.

Farewell, dear father, I trust this "dispatch from the Grande Armée" will give you pleasure – it's that more than anything that will make it precious for me. I embrace you with all my heart.

H. Berlioz*

He had not foreseen how expensive the portage of manuscript material would be. Next time he went to Germany, two years later, he took far less bulky, printed parts, for the Fantastic and the Symphonie funèbre at least (*Harold* and *Romeo* were not published till the late 1840s). But the gains from the visit to Brunswick – the joy of working with such musicians, the admirers and friends he made there – were not to be measured in cash. And one tangible and highly cheering result was the pamphlet produced by the local playwright, professor of German

---

* A week later Dr Berlioz wrote to Nancy, enclosing the "letter from Hector, who is getting more applause in Germany than thalers or ducats – as always, alas . . ."

language and literature and writer on musical subjects, Robert Griepenkerl, who was inspired by the Brunswick rehearsals and concert to spring to his defence against his Leipzig detractors. *Ritter Berlioz in Braunschweig* – "Sir Berlioz in Brunswick" – was a trenchant rebuttal of critics who found the French composer wanting in the qualities a German had come to value and expect. Such people, in Griepenkerl's opinion, failed both to appreciate what was best and most characteristic in German music and to realize how Berlioz, transcending his nationality, had penetrated "the depths of the German spirit". His music's gift for expressing humour, by the juxtaposition of dramatically opposing moods, linked him with Shakespeare and Beethoven, especially the Beethoven of the later works, which many German critics had yet to come to terms with and which they rejected because of that very quality. The composer's Romantic, "German" affiliations were reflected in the choice of subject-matter for his next symphony, which he intended to base on Schiller's *Maid of Orleans*. In sum, Berlioz represented "an advance in the development of instrumental music" greater than anything since Beethoven, to whom he stood in an organic relationship such as no contemporary German composer had achieved; the public understood this, but its instinctive enthusiasm was dashed by the carping of the critics, who came "hobbling after".

Griepenkerl, with Johann Christian Lobe, is the first of a line of German nineteenth-century artists – Hans von Bülow, Hallé, Felix Mottl, Mahler, Hans Richter, Weingartner – for whom Berlioz is not a French composer so much as a great composer. Their support, their faith, armed him against the unbelief of Mendelssohn and of the scribes, and after his death kept his name alive in Germany.

Even without Griepenkerl's pamphlet, which was published the following month, he was in high spirits when he left Brunswick, about the middle of March, for Hamburg (Berlin being still not ready to receive him). Before leaving he sent three large parcels by mail coach to Heinrich Schlesinger, Maurice's publisher brother, in Berlin: they contained music he would not need till he got there. With him he took *Harold*, *Le cinq mai*, the *Francs-juges* overture, *Rêverie et caprice*, *Invitation to the Waltz*, the Offertorium and Quaerens me, the cavatina from *Benvenuto* and Marie's songs.

Hamburg, the great Baltic port a hundred miles to the north, had not been on his itinerary and he knew nobody there, but it maintained the impetus of the tour; the concert in the municipal theatre on 22

March was "one of the best I gave in Germany", with a fine orchestra augmented for the occasion and thoroughly rehearsed, a bass, Joseph Reichel, who had a splendid deep voice (he could sing comfortably down to B below the stave) and who was one of the handful of first-rate singers that he came across on his travels, and a large and attentive audience. Only Krebs the kapellmeister, after being cooperative and helpful during the preparations, struck a dissonant note, making it clear, when the concert was over, what he really thought: "My dear fellow, in a few years your music will be all over Germany – it will become popular, and that will be a disaster. Think how it will be imitated! Only think of the style it will breed, the extravagances! It would be better for art if you had never been born."

The month Berlioz spent in Berlin (staying, with Marie, at the Hôtel de Petersbourg) summed up what for a French musician was excitingly but humiliatingly different about Germany. It was not just that Berlin had a "magnificent", nearly ninety-strong, opera orchestra of exceptional "precision, ensemble, vigour and refinement" and the finest opera chorus he had ever heard; nor that the company's standard of performance in both *The Huguenots* and Gluck's *Armide* was far superior to the Opéra's of recent years (though, as the Letter in the *Débats* was addressed to Habeneck, he could hardly say so openly); nor that both the (amateur) choral society and the (professional) military bands were "of such splendour, beside anything France could boast in the same line, that French national pride could only feel chastened by the comparison". It was the atmosphere of the place: Berlin was, simply, a musical city; music was everywhere, part of the air you breathed; it was honoured and enjoyed by everyone whatever their class or occupation. The King, Frederick William IV, had a passion for it, and was as interested in contemporary music as he was in the works from the time of his great-uncle Frederick the Great, which he was for ever asking his kapellmeisters to dig up and perform for him. He agreed to the dedication of the *Treatise* and, on learning that movements from *Romeo and Juliet* were on the programme of Berlioz's second concert, altered his plans to make sure he was back in Berlin in time, and afterwards demanded a full score of the Fête for his library (a copyist manuscript was hastily prepared, with the title-page in Berlioz's hand). The Crown Princess asked intelligent questions about the orchestration of Queen Mab; the Crown Prince arranged a matinée at the palace at which more than three hundred musicians from the Berlin and Potsdam military bands under their director Wiprecht played an arrangement of the *Francs-juges* overture and pieces by Meyerbeer, Wiprecht and the English ambassador, the Earl of Westmorland.* At a court concert given midway through Berlioz's stay the head chamberlain, Count Redern, who was a very capable pianist, accompanied Schubert's *Erlkönig*. When the musical part of the evening was over, Berlioz was able to converse with Humboldt, who, though looking "singularly awkward in his courtier's harness", was charming company and took an active interest in his doings. The court of Louis-Philippe must have seemed very far away.

Though the visit to Berlin had been postponed until a more convenient time, it still proved difficult to fit his requirements – including an amphitheatre for the large chorus, erected on stage – into the theatre's busy schedule; but two evening concerts were arranged, at the first of which, in addition to some of the standard pieces, two hundred performers gave the Dies irae and Lacrymosa amid loud applause (8 April). Berlioz had come near to cancelling the whole thing: the chorus, by an oversight, had learned the music at the wrong tempos, and at the final rehearsal on the evening of the 7th, finding itself at grips with the orchestra and the brass choirs playing at the right tempos, went to pieces. Chaos reigned. For a moment he lost heart completely. After an emergency chorus rehearsal next morning, confidence was restored. But the concert left him "stupid" with fatigue; at the end he shook the hands of the people pressing round him and listened to their congratulations in a daze. "Only Wiprecht managed to bring me to myself with a hug like a cuirassier's: the good man made my ribs crack, interspersing his exclamations with Teutonic oaths beside which Guhr's were Ave Marias." Worn out by his exertions, he took to his bed, and thus missed the Choral Society's annual Holy Week performance of *The Death of Jesus* by Graun, Frederick the Great's kapellmeister, which everyone had been urging him to attend. But he heard Bach's *St Matthew Passion*, and was more impressed than he cared to admit.

His second concert, postponed till the 23rd, included the first four movements of *Romeo*. He thought the performance of Queen Mab almost as good as the one at Brunswick. That had been special. But the Berlin orchestra was technically the best he had encountered in Germany,

---

* Westmorland (Lord Burghersh) was a prolific composer. He founded the Royal Academy of Music.

and he was full of admiration for its efforts. He put it in a letter addressed to the "Artists of the Royal Chapel", written on the 24th, the day before his departure: "Gentlemen, I cannot resist expressing, before I leave, my gratitude for the welcome I received from you. Loaded with work as you were, you nevertheless brought all possible patience and zeal to rehearsing my compositions and performed them with an understanding and vitality beyond praise. Be assured that I shall never forget my debt to you, and that I take with me the liveliest appreciation of your skills."

With the coming of spring he began the long trek home. Breslau, like Vienna and Munich, would have to wait until next time. But he could make one or two stops on the way; it would help pay the cost of the journey back to Paris. The first was at Hanover, where he gave a concert on 6 May. After Berlin, the atmosphere and conditions took him back to the early days of the tour. In his album he noted: "Depressing concert. Orchestra wretchedly short of strings – three double-basses! The players inclined to put on airs, and not prepared to rehearse more than twice. They dispatched *Harold* in really priceless style; the excellent Bohrer ashamed for his orchestra. The audience not bad." Several Brunswick-ers, including Griepenkerl, travelled the fifty miles to Hanover to hear the concert, and poor Bohrer had to listen to their gloating accounts of the musical feast they had had two months before. Marie, who had been rather in the shade in Berlin, where she took part only in the second concert, contributed three numbers, including the difficult cavatina from *Benvenuto Cellini*. There is no mention of her having sung "really well", as she is reported by Berlioz to have done at Leipzig and Hamburg. Hanover, with Mannheim, was the low point of the tour. Despite the friendliness of the Crown Prince and the interest he showed, Berlioz can have had no inkling of the pleasure his visits would give him in the years ahead.

Darmstadt was another matter. It must have been decided late on – a letter written on 26 April from Magdeburg outlining his plans makes no mention of it – but it brought the tour to a rousing conclusion. After passing through Kassel ("seven in the morning: Spohr is asleep and not to be disturbed") and stopping a day or two in Frankfurt, the travellers reached the town on about 15 May and put up at the Darmstadter Hof. Berlioz had friends and contacts in Darmstadt. The concert-master was Louis Schloesser, his fellow pupil in Le Sueur's class in the early 1820s;

the kapellmeister, Johann Wilhelm Mangold, had studied at the Paris Conservatoire under Reicha, as had his younger brother Karl Amand. Berlioz also came armed with a letter from the Frankfurt Rothschild for Prince Emile, who in turn introduced him to the Grand Duke, and all was soon arranged. The orchestra had a few more strings than the Hanover band, and its spirit could not have been more different. Everyone was eager to rehearse: five sessions were allocated. He was encouraged to offer a longer programme than at Hanover, with some movements from *Romeo* in addition to *Harold* (the viola part played by Schloesser), *Le cinq mai* (Reichel) and the rest. The Letter in the *Débats* does not go into great detail about the concert (23 May) – no doubt he felt his readers had had enough – but it is clear he was pleased with it (except for a disaster in the offstage choral music at the beginning of the Love Scene) and delighted with his reception in Darmstadt, where local musicians and music-lovers invited him and Marie into their homes. (Schloesser's son Adolph remembered him often visiting the house, "where in my mind's eye I see him now, sitting on the sofa in the drawing-room drinking cup after cup of tea".) The entire receipts of the concert were made over to him and he did not have to pay any of the costs. All in all it was a bright note to finish on.

Berlioz's journey had achieved its object. For an exploratory tour unprecedented in character and scope – eleven different places, fourteen concerts and more than forty rehearsals – it had been a remarkable success, and it prepared the ground for later visits that were even more prestigious as well as more lucrative. He left behind partisans and a healthy interest in his music. Some people, critics especially, were both mystified and alarmed by it; like Krebs, the Hamburg kapellmeister, they wished he had never been born. But for every one that rejected it there was another for whom his advent, both as composer and conductor, was like an act of providence: he had revealed a new realm of musical expression and made them play better than they knew they could. Even Hanslick, who later as high priest of "absolute music" turned against Berlioz's (as he turned against Wagner's), bore witness that "whoever lived and cheered, as I did, at the time of Berlioz's concerts in Germany can testify that never was any dazzling musical phenomenon greeted with such excitement". By likening it to "a fiery meteor passing overhead" Hanslick implies it was a phenomenon of brief duration. But if other critics, like Hanslick, drew back from their first enthusiasm, many musicians remained faithful. From now until the end of the century and beyond, he would have German disciples who kept the flame alive.

For Berlioz himself, however, the effect of those five arduous months was cruelly two-edged, exhilarating but also deeply depressing. The experience could not but leave him yet more dissatisfied with a state of affairs at home that gave his creative genius and his powers of leadership only sporadic outlet and which he had gone to Germany to escape – dissatisfied not only for himself but for the society and musical culture of which he was part. The contrast struck him like a slap in the face the moment he resumed his career in Paris at the beginning of June 1843. He had come back an even better conductor than he was when he went. But where was the orchestra, assembled and tuned, waiting for him to give the signal? Where was the organization ready to under-write the cost of the concert? Where was the public curious to hear what he had to offer? As he told his father a few days after his return, "If I had been born in Saxony or Prussia I should now have a salary of ten or twelve thousand francs for life, with a guaranteed pension for my family after my death. In France I have . . . a liberal constitution, the liberality of which does not extend to bothering about the men who could bring honour to their country."

Germany had shown him a tantalizingly different and in general far superior way of doing things. He put his findings and his conclusions in writing in his report to the Minister of the Interior. The report is even-handed. Berlioz admits that he went to Germany very much prejudiced in its favour by its fame as "the classic home of music" and by the "deplorable state of some of our own establishments", but that this was not always borne out by what he found. He makes no bones about the deficiencies: the low standard and inadequate size of many opera choruses; the poor state of some of the wind instruments and the scarcity of others; the rarity of good new works; the fact that out of all the companies he heard, performing a wide variety of operas (*Armide*, *Figaro*, *The Magic Flute*, *Fidelio*, *La Vestale*, *Freischütz*, *Moïse*, *La muette*, *The Vampire*, *Norma*, *The Huguenots*, *Rienzi*, *Linda di Chamounix* and *The Flying Dutchman* are mentioned in his *Débats* Letters), only seven singers – three basses, two baritones and two sopranos – can be considered really first-rate. Such weaknesses, however, pale beside the fundamental strengths: the widespread diffusion of basic musical education, the feeling for music throughout the population, and music's central role in church and state, embodied in institutions solidly based, with a clearly established hierarchy. Germany, in point of fact, is remarkable more for the number than for the quality of its musicians. Amid the multitude of good orchestras there is not one as good as the Paris Conservatoire. Indeed, better results can be obtained in Paris than anywhere else in the world – or could be, if the knowledge and the will to make intelligent use of resources were not so often lacking. And France has only Paris to set against Germany's wealth of capitals, the consequence of the division of the country into princi-palities, each with its own "chapel" or musical corps directed by a competent musician who is nearly always a composer of repute: Meyer-beer in Berlin (where Spontini was before him), Marschner in Hanover, Chelard in Weimar, Reissiger and Wagner in Dresden.

No less important is the institution of concert-master, invariably a distinguished violinist, whose job is to direct the light operas and ballets and who, when the kapellmeister is conducting, sits at the first desk and transmits his instructions to the players. The concert-master is also responsible for seeing that the orchestral material and all other physical requirements are up to the mark. "We have no comparable position in Paris. When the assistant is not conducting he has no obligation to play and is not expected to do anything to help his superior." Berlioz then discusses the formation and the standards of the normal theatre orchestra, and finds some things better than in France, some less good: nowhere are the flute and the horn so well played as in Paris, and no woodwind group in the theatre orchestras that he heard is as good as those of the Opéra and the Théâtre-Italien. The military bands, on the other hand, are incomparably superior. "Even those in the towns of second rank – for example, Darmstadt – surpass most of ours; and we have no conception of the marvels that the Crown Prince of Prussia has achieved in Berlin," making use of a single director-inspector. He, Wiprecht, is in sole charge of everything from the training of the musicians and the purchase and maintenance of instruments (including the newest and most up-to-date) to the balance and ensemble of each separate band and the surveillance of the repertoire. "His choice of music is nearly always judicious. As a result they are saved from performing the wretchedly trite medleys which too often degrade our military bands in France, dragging them down to the level of the dives on the outskirts of Paris." (Shades of the band at the Rouge-gorge in *Les Enfants du paradis*.) "This is a more important matter than may be supposed: it plays a large part in holding back the musical progress of our population, by accustoming them to the trivial and the vulgar."

Contrast Germany, which possesses a much finer feeling for harmony and melodic style, in consequence of Luther's introducing part-singing by the whole congregation at divine service and himself writing so many excellent chorales for the purpose. The taste for singing that Luther fostered, and the wish to do it well, led to music being studied in school. In consequence, "a large majority of the men and women of all classes who come to church have in their hands books containing, along with the words of the service, canticles and chorales in several parts, which each one reads and sings according to their type of voice. The effect of these immense choirs, formed spontaneously by the assembling of several thousand singers in the larger churches, is unbelievably majestic." Germans get such pleasure from joining their voices together in song that everywhere, even in remote villages, you find so-called Lieder-Tafel, groups of men who meet in the evening and, seated at long tables, sing four-part choruses, while in the towns there are flourishing choral societies, made up mostly of well-to-do men and women who attend rehearsals regularly and punctually, study their part at home beforehand and contribute to the cost of their meetings. No wonder, he adds, that the festivals held annually all over Germany can call on such large and well-ordered choral forces.

You can feel his heart go out to the dedication, the seriousness of it all, just as you can when he turns to the economic basis of the professional musician's career:

A pensions system is in force for all artists in all German courts; hence the zeal and conscientiousness with which the chapels are served. Instrumentalists and choristers derive their livelihood from their salaries; they enjoy a security for the future which ours do not. The composer-kapellmeister can produce or ponder his works undistracted. He does not compose in order to live: the sovereign on whom he depends has put him in a position to live in order to compose.

By the time he submitted his report, on 28 December, Paris had reasserted its realities. The difference was neatly epitomized by the fate of the benefit concert for Baron Taylor's new musicians' cooperative, the Association des Artistes Musiciens, which Berlioz had agreed to conduct, the programme comprising Beethoven's Fifth, Act 2 of *La Vestale* and the *King Lear* overture. Planned for 14 September at the Théâtre-Italien, it was postponed until 19 November and moved to the

Opéra, then put off again till December; after which, too many interests being opposed to it and the obstacles proving insurmountable, the project ran into the ground and was heard of no more.

Though he had kept his journalistic friends supplied with accounts of his progress and from time to time the press took note – a lithograph of the twelve "Principal Composers in 1843" shows him, quill pen in hand, leaning out of the window of a stagecoach crowned with laurels – it left no lasting impression. Paris musical life went on as before. The effect on his reputation at home was certainly less than he imagined it would be and much less than he had hoped. His supporters apart, nobody wanted to hear about it. In so far as they believed it, it annoyed them. They were happier denying that he had had any success at all. The "Letters" published in the *Débats* between August 1843 and the following January were read only to be mocked; Paris was not concerned to know how music was organized in Germany.

In one respect, however, the effect of the tour on his Parisian existence was crucial. Griepenkerl mentioned a symphony on Schiller's *Maid of Orleans*. But it was another idea, long dormant, that had worked its way to the surface under the prompting of north Germany and its scenes and associations. *The Damnation of Faust*, the great representative score of Berlioz's middle years, was already active in his imagination, and it was now only a matter of time before he wrote it.

12

Ophelia Drowning

In Berlioz's autobiography the two and a half years between his return from Germany in the early summer of 1843 and his departure for Vienna in the autumn of 1845 are dealt with very summarily. They form an interlude during which nothing of significance happened, while he waited till he could be on the road again, once more breathing a genuinely artistic atmosphere. In fact a good deal happened that was of significance, in his career and his domestic life. You can see why he linked the two long narratives of his travels in Austro-Germany with so brief a bridge passage and why he reserved the watershed in his relationship with musical Paris for the performances of *The Damnation of Faust* in December 1846. But those years witnessed events that had the closest bearing on the crisis to come and on his whole future existence.

Berlioz during that time was much more than the reluctant feuilleton-ist and organizer of monster concerts pictured in his *Memoirs*. If in terms of music composed it was one of his less productive periods, he nevertheless wrote the *Roman Carnival* overture and the first versions of *The Corsair* and the *Funeral March for the Last Scene of Hamlet*, as well as a number of lesser pieces: the rousing *Hymne à la France*, to a text by Auguste Barbier; three songs, *La belle Isabeau*, *Le chasseur danois* and the charming *Zaïde*; three little movements for his friends Jacob and Edouard Alexandre's newly patented harmonium; and an arrangement of the *Chant sacré* for six of Adolphe Sax's instruments (the first known use of the saxophone). He also saw two of his symphonies, the Fantastic and the Funèbre, through the press.

In terms of journalism and authorship the years 1843–5 yielded more than just the usual crop of feuilletons – some of them of unusual interest or amusement, like the account of the revenge exacted on the grocer's assistant who hissed *Freischütz* at the Odéon and whose skull, twenty

years later, adorns the Wolf's Glen in the Opéra's production of the
work, or the plan for a reform of French military bands on the German
model, or – again inspired by Germany – the utopian novella *Euphonia,
the Musical City*, serialized in the *Gazette*. The *Treatise*, to which
he had made last-minute revisions in proof in the light of the latest
developments in instrumental technique and manufacture, was not the
only book of his to be published in this period. So was *Voyage musical
en Allemagne et en Italie*, which he was busy working on in the
autumn of 1843 and which appeared the following summer in two finely
produced octavo volumes of about four hundred pages each. *Voyage
musical*, after selling well, soon went out of print, and virtually all its
material was reproduced either in the *Memoirs* or in later collections
of his journalism; but in some ways it is his most complete and characteristic work. The "Letters from Germany" written for the *Débats* were
the main item in the first volume. In the second it was the experience
of an aspirant and subsequently successful Prix de Rome in Paris and
then in Italy, here brought together for the first time from different
sources and collated and augmented to make a continuous sequence.
But there was room for a lot more besides, taken from ten years of
feuilletonizing: *Freischütz*, the Beethoven symphonies, evenings at the
Opéra in the early 1820s, the tribulations of a music critic, the rise and
fall of the great tenor. The book is an anatomy of Berlioz's personality
and musical beliefs and a homage to his gods, made up of *critique
admirative*, personal reminiscence, theorizing, satire and short story.

Nor was his concert-giving activity confined to the gigantic agglomer-
ations of performers in the Palace of Industry and the Cirque Olympique
which thenceforward fixed him in the popular mind – like Wagner and
Mahler after him – as the apostle of noise. The first four concerts of
the period were given with normal forces, and two of them were among
the most successful he ever put on in Paris. At the first, played to a
large audience in the Conservatoire Hall on 19 November 1843 (a few
weeks before his fortieth birthday), Queen Mab was heard again after
an interval of four years, Duprez sang the Paris première of *Absence*
and, with Dorus-Gras and Massol, the trio from *Benvenuto Cellini*,
and the end of the Symphonie funèbre, as the nine-year-old Louis told
his Aunt Nancy, was drowned by clapping and stamping ("Papa a
gagner assé dargent dans ce concer"). Spontini – reported as being,
with Meyerbeer, one of the notabilities present – was moved to write
Berlioz a resounding letter beginning "Vivat! terque quaterque vivat!"

At the fourth concert (4 May 1844), a Berlioz—Liszt evening at the Théâtre-Italien, Liszt gave his services, playing – in addition to music by Weber and himself – his piano reduction of the second movement of the Fantastic Symphony immediately after the orchestra had played it. The receipts were a staggering 12,000 francs, and Berlioz made a profit of over 6,000. His "great beast of an orchestra", he told Nancy, "left most German orchestras standing". The *Roman Carnival* overture, composed in the second half of 1843 out of music from *Benvenuto*, Act I, and published soon after, was one of the hits of the winter and spring concert season. It won the ultimate accolade of an arrangement for two pianos and eight hands, and was performed by Liszt, Pixis (the arranger), Hallé and Ferdinand Hiller.

As for the first of the monster concerts – given on 1 August 1844 at the close of the international exhibition of the Products of Industry, in one of the exhibition's temporary pavilions in the Champs-Elysées – the labour of it nearly killed him and, because of his obligation to split the profit with the bandmaster Isaac Strauss, whose concert of dance music next day was poorly attended, he was left with only 860 francs for all his pains; but the event itself was a huge success: an audience of seven or eight thousand, a programme of good music mostly well chosen for performance by a massive orchestra and a chorus of four hundred and fifty (including some famous operatic names), and a precision of ensemble which amazed everybody. Berlioz was acknowledged by enemies as well as friends to have brought off a triumph of organization and conducting skill. Once again Germany was the inspiration – the summer festivals which united professionals and amateurs in grand acts of communal music-making. His 1,022 performers at the Palace of Industry contained deputations from Rouens, Orléans and Lille, and representatives of philharmonic societies from further afield, as well as every Parisian singer and instrumentalist he could lay his hands on.

As before, his system of sectional rehearsals proved its worth. Without it – to take only one example – he could never have got the double-basses, thirty-six of them, to play the famous passage in the scherzo of Beethoven's Fifth together: when they first tried it the sound reminded him of "a herd of stampeding hogs", but they were able to go on working at it until it was right. With the aid of two assistants, Tilmant of the Opéra-Comique and Morel, in charge of wind instruments and percussion respectively, plus five chorus-masters located at strategic points in and around the chorus – which, being in front of the orchestra (the normal practice then), had to have the conductor's beat relayed to it – he achieved the unanimity that so impressed the critics.

Not everything turned out to be well suited to the conditions – the March to the Scaffold was one of the pieces that made the least effect – but to his great satisfaction the scene in the Garden of Delights from Gluck's *Armide* was listened to with religious attention, as were the *Freischütz* overture (with twenty-four horns playing the introduction) and the prayers from *Moïse* and *La muette*. The Blessing of the Daggers from the fourth act of *The Huguenots* – the solo lines of Saint-Bris and the three monks each intoned by twenty basses – electrified performers and audience alike; Berlioz's new *Hymne à la France* was cheered to the rafters; and in the chorus from Halévy's *Charles VI*, added to the advertised programme at the request of Schlesinger (who had just published a cheap edition), the patriotic refrain "Never shall the Englishman be lord in France" was seized on by a large section of the audience and roared out in unison with the choir. The ministers present were not amused, it being government policy to pursue a closer entente with England, and Berlioz had a tricky interview afterwards with the commissioner of police. But in the public gaze his star had never stood higher. The Parisian imagination was fascinated by the whole operation: the nationwide character of the event, the scale of the publicity for it, the sight of the approaches to the Champs-Elysées jammed with carriages a good hour before the concert, the exhibition space banked at one end with tier on tier of performers ranged in perfect order under eight conductors whose arms moved as one, and the vast seething audience. Everyone from the Duc de Montpensier downward seemed to be there. (A few days before, Berlioz had received an urgent note from the duke's secretary and tutor, Cuvillier-Fleury: "His Highness wishing to attend your festival on 1 August, he has instructed me to settle the arrangements with you. Where can I find you? If you care to come to the Tuileries between eight and nine this evening, you can watch the fireworks from the windows of the Duc d'Aumale and we can talk.") The very failure of Strauss's dance concert next day – a failure which the commissioner had more or less guaranteed by refusing to allow dancing – underlined Berlioz's ascendancy.

A few weeks later *Voyage musical* was published, to excellent reviews, with a dedication to the same Duc de Montpensier and, for frontispiece, a lithographed portrait of the composer in serenely masterful pose, arms folded, baton lightly but firmly grasped in one hand. Berlioz was the man of the hour; and the satirists, in complaining that the portrait stared at one from every shop window, were merely confirming the fact. "M. Hector Berlioz may now walk along the boulevard contemplated by himself. What an icon! Such melody in the curve of the nose! Such *furia francese* in the recess of the chin! As for the hair, how it curls in the key of F! Oh great man, it is time to bring Napoleon down from his column and put your statue in rosin in his place."

This being France, however, and not Germany, it was a Pyrrhic victory. In Germany he would not have been solely responsible, with Strauss, for the organization of the festival; would not have wasted time and energy countering the opposition of the commissioner; would not have been obliged to hold the festival in a temporary structure which the contractors had to be bribed not to pull down on the day appointed for the concert; would not have had to recruit the thousand-odd performers himself or see personally to the construction of an amphitheatre for them, or gamble his money on the receipts exceeding the costs; would not have conducted the final rehearsal to the din of bawling carters, cracking whips and neighing horses as the heavy machines left over from the exhibition were dragged, somewhat late, away or, when the rehearsal was over, have had to find carpenters for the emergency lowering of the chorus platform, so that the orchestra, behind it, could be clearly heard; would not have finished the concert in such a feverish sweat that he had to change into dry clothes on the spot, behind a barrier of harps with their covers replaced, before venturing into the open air; would not have had to watch while the poor-tax inspectors counted the takings and relieved him of an eighth of them; and would not have had to pay the commissioner 1,231 francs for a posse of special constables whose services he had not asked for in the first place. Euphonia, the musical city, centre of monumental performances of great works given under true festival conditions, was not located outside France for nothing.

Yet with all its manifest and fundamental disadvantages Paris still worked its spell. The correspondence of these two and a half years, full as it is of projects for visits abroad – to London, The Hague, Milan, Copenhagen, Baden-Baden – and even to other parts of France such as Rouen, Châlons sur Saône, Bordeaux and Lille, shows just how addicted he was to the stimulus of his home town and to what George Eliot called "that rapid concentrated life which is known only in Paris". Paris, to him, was still the "electrifying city" to which one must "constantly return once one has lived there, above all if one is French". There could be no question of living anywhere else. Paris meant not only friends but all "the intelligent people who are to be found there, the whirl of ideas in which one lives and moves", the verbal antics, the sheer wit and savoir faire and irrepressible creative malice of its inhabitants.

Not long back from Germany, and though only too conscious of what he has left behind, he cannot wait to share with his sister Nancy his pleasure at the latest skirmish in the eternal war of words: Janin's demolition of Dumas' play *Les Demoiselles de Saint-Cyr*, the playwright's long and eloquent defence in Girardin's paper *La Presse* (where the play was being serialized), and Janin's riposte, written with murderous élan:

> There should have been a duel; but the only wounds have been to Mme Girardin's amour propre, which Janin reduced to a bleeding carcass. In fact it was she who suggested to Dumas that he write the article, so the national muse has only got what she deserved. I myself haven't seen *Les Demoiselles de Saint-Cyr*. Dumas had already nearly fallen out, a few weeks ago, with his namesake Adolphe Dumas, author of *Mlle de la Vallière*. It was being put about – and the story was repeated to Adolphe – that Alexandre, meeting him outside the Odéon after the performance of *Mlle de la Vallière*, said, "Hello, Thomas". Do you get it? There were two Corneilles, Pierre the great Corneille and his brother Thomas, the unfortunate author of *Ariane*. That would make Alexandre Dumas Pierre and Adolphe the other. "The other" was horribly upset by the sally. Dumas, who insisted that he never said it nor even repeated it as an anecdote, was furious at its being attributed to him: he claimed he had enough good manners to have said, on the contrary, "Hello, Pierre". Ten of us were talking about it on the boulevard one evening with Dumas (Alexandre or Pierre) when "Thomas" came by, and we found a way of making them shake hands by assuring Thomas that Pierre had just that moment been praising *Mlle de la Vallière* in the most eloquent terms. If you have read the polemic between Janin and Dumas you cannot have understood the half of it, it contained a mass of treacherous allusions which only those in the know could catch.
>
> Since my return I've seen neither Janin nor de Vigny nor Hugo nor Balzac nor Sue nor Legouvé, nor Scribe either [. . .] I must tell you that in Germany fashionable ladies can't bring themselves to refer to "Sue"

["sweat"], which they find coarse: they call him by the purer name of M. Eugène Perspire. [Sue's] *Les Mystères de Paris*, by the way, is a European success, everybody in Berlin is desperate to get hold of the *Journal des débats* solely in order to read it.

His next letter to Nancy, a few weeks later, was interrupted in the writing by the visit of a man from Dresden bringing news of friends left behind in Saxony, "which makes me ill, I so long to go back there and so dislike being in Paris"; but the flow of gossip continued unabated:

The Queen of England has happily spared us her visit to Paris. I was deeply alarmed at the thought of the absurdities about to be perpetrated on the subject of that brood mare. [Victoria was staying with Louis-Philippe in Normandy, at the Château d'Eu.] An idiot of a poet called on me only a couple of days ago with a cantata in honour of Her Britannic Majesty which he wanted me to set to music . . . He came to the right person!

From another side, here is Brizeux who sends me from Brittany the text of a song devoted to O'Connell. But I've lost faith in O'Connell since I saw him persist with his passive agitation, telling the Irish, "You've got no bread, you've no shirts on your backs, let's agitate and agitate, snap our fingers at that swine Peel and that wretch Wellington, and all will be well. Now all of you, give me a shilling, go back to your homes, those of you that have one, and keep the peace." Is he really nothing but a gigantic Robert Macaire?

Apropos that prodigious creation, I talked with Frédéric [Lemaître] in Brussels. He's depressed at the enormous success of his most celebrated role, no one wants to see him as anything except Robert, which he finds a real bore. In point of fact, nothing so audaciously original and true has been seen on any stage for a very long time. It's the drama of the century, and I bear Mme de Girardin a serious grudge for getting the performances stopped in Paris because of the immortal scene of the shareholders, in which certain allusions were detected. "Oh – if I'm to be asked to produce accounts, you must see that business is no longer possible." What a line, and how sublime Frédéric was in his indignation, weeping with anguish at being suspected, fainting, then coming to himself again to say, "I give you notice, gentlemen, that tomorrow the till will be open – for receiving".

We may ask what need there was to live anywhere else, given the successes just described, given the reputation he was enjoying. Why not stay and consolidate his position? For the simple reason that there was no real position to consolidate. It was built on sand. The successes were ephemeral. They were ad hoc achievements, victories won outside the system, at a cost in physical and nervous energy that was wearing him down. The newspapers, genuinely admiring, might salute the unprecedented grandeur of the Festival of Industry, and the Duc de Montpensier send a magnificent porcelain vase as token of his "high satisfaction": there was no security in that. Berlioz exaggerated only slightly when he likened his Parisian struggles to the ordeal of Sisyphus. He must start from the bottom again each time, pushing his rock up the mountain by sweat of brow and spirit. Each enterprise was a fresh gamble. Some made money, some lost it. Some, like the concerts he gave in Franconi's Cirque Olympique, the hippodrome on the north-east side of the present Rond-Point des Champs-Elysées, left him, though not out of pocket, with discouragingly little to show for his exertions.

The director, Gallois, had been impressed by the size of the receipts at the Festival of Industry and hoped, by redecorating the hall and installing heating, to make it a fashionable winter venue for music on the grandest scale. He undertook all financial responsibilities. Berlioz's contract required him to assemble the chorus and orchestra, choose the programmes and prepare and conduct the performances, which were planned for Sunday afternoons when there were none at the Conservatoire. The concerts, when they eventually got under way in January 1845, offered varied and unusual programmes, including extracts from *Ruslan and Ludmila* and *A Life for the Tsar*, the operas of the Russian nationalist composer Mikhail Glinka who had come to Paris that winter (and whom Berlioz also championed in the *Débats*), Beethoven's Emperor Concerto played by Hallé, Berlioz's new overture *La tour de Nice* (the later *Corsair*), and music by Félicien David, whose symphonic ode *Le désert* was the sensation of the season. *Le désert* and David's Janissaries' Chorus were part of a "séance orientale" (16 February) which also included the popular *Marche marocaine*, subtitled "Turkish war-song", by the latest keyboard lion, Léopold de Meyer. The concert was topical, in view of the Moorish flavour of the hall's architecture and the vogue for things Middle Eastern which had hit Paris with the arrival of six Algerian chiefs and their picturesque retinues on an official visit. A bearded Bedouin appeared in the foreground of the *Illustration*'s engraving of the first concert, and the *Charivari*'s series "The Arabs in

Paris" showed a group of turbaned and kaftaned men twisting and yelling in agony while a Berlioz-like conductor unleashed his orchestra at them.

Berlioz was put to enormous effort, first to collect his outsize forces – the Société des Concerts, whose players he normally recruited, forbade them to take part, though there was no clash of dates – and then to prepare them. A letter of late February 1845 gives details of sectional rehearsals for the concert of 16 March:

Wednesday 12 March 9.30	violins and violas
1	cellos and basses
3	harps
Thursday 13 March 9.30	chorus men
12.30	chorus women
3	wind instruments, timpani, bass drum, cymbals, triangle

Another letter, to Michel-Maurice Lévy, who was supplying a hundred voices from his singing school for the finale of *Romeo* and the Dies irae/Tuba mirum at the same concert, is concerned with both rehearsing and seating arrangements:

We will rehearse next Saturday at ten o'clock at the Circus. Please remember the layout of the chorus, which will be as follows. On entering the hall your pupils will turn to the right and go and sit in the tiers next to the other choir, with the tenors in front in rows one to four or five and the basses in rows five to eight. In consequence your hundred pupils will have the chorus of Capulet men on their left, arranged in the same order:

Orpheonist Basses	Capulet Basses	Montague Basses	Capulet Sopranos
Tenors	Tenors	Tenors	Montague Sopranos

These were for him routine procedures, if on a much larger scale than his concerts at the Conservatoire. But the quality and discipline of the orchestra seems to have been lower than usual – Glinka describes the musicians as "not very good at paying attention" and "preferring to chat with their neighbours"; and it was all finally to no great purpose. Though the first two concerts may have done good business (the *Illustration*'s engraving suggests a full house), the novelty soon wore off, public interest waned, and the season closed after only four. Berlioz had hoped to found an annual series; but too much was against it. The Cirque was on the edge of town. In bad weather the mud discouraged attendance. And the acoustic turned out to be too reverberant for all but music of broad tempo and slow harmonic movement; only the Dies irae, repeated at every concert, sounded well in the "heartbreaking rotunda".

Berlioz was at fault in not ascertaining this beforehand. The whole enterprise, however, demonstrated yet again the difficulty – in the long run the impossibility – of getting anywhere as a freelance composer-conductor. You had to be inside the system. But the system didn't want him. One by one the avenues were blocked. During these two years he made a further sustained attempt to achieve a secure position in Paris musical life. Every time, the authorities responded with indifference or outright hostility. As before, the obstacles were partly personal, partly institutional and bureaucratic, often a mixture of the two. A feature of Berlioz's life in Paris is his capacity to win and keep the friendship and support of individuals even when they belong to organizations hostile to him. One could cite dozens of examples (Glinka remarked on the contrast between Berlioz's helpful, positive attitude and the "intolerable arrogance and superciliousness" that he generally encountered in Paris). The musicians who played for the Société des Concerts were mostly for him. Unfortunately, Habeneck and the committee were against. The record – not a note of his programmed by them between 1833 (*Rob Roy*) and 1849 (two pieces from *The Damnation of Faust*) – speaks for itself. It was not as if contemporary music was never played there during those years. More than one substantial work by such luminaries as Dancla, Masset, Rousselot, Ruolz and Schwenk figured in the repertoire. Stephen Heller was moved to protest in the *Gazette*: "Why does one never hear anything by Hector Berlioz at the Conservatoire concerts?" – he was, after all, the leading French composer. "Must he resign himself to sleeping the long sleep that transforms the most rabid enemies into zealous panegyrists? Once dead, he will live for a long time, of that I am certain. The cry, 'Berlioz is dead', will rouse a thousand voices to cry, 'Three cheers for Berlioz.'"

At least he had been allowed to put on his own concerts in the Conservatoire Hall, outside the society's season. That too was now stopped. The concert of 19 November 1843 proved to be the last. Shortly afterwards the Minister of the Interior announced a ban on anyone's using the hall except the society. Since for the past twenty years Berlioz had been almost the sole user (giving twenty-three concerts there between 1830 and 1843), it is hard not to conclude that the ban was aimed at him – the more so as it did not prevent Félicien David putting on Le désert there a year later and his Christophe Colomb three years after that. It could have been Habeneck's doing, but I suspect it was Auber's; the prohibition was introduced not long after he became director. You can imagine Auber and his close friend Adolphe Adam thinking it up as a simple and devastatingly effective way of getting at him. Berlioz was the natural enemy of both of them. His reviews of Auber's operas, if usually polite, made it pretty clear what he thought of them. Adam, on his side, had ample reasons to feel vindictive: the government commissions lavished on him in 1837 and 1840, his evident refusal to take Adam seriously as a composer (though he was never as rude as Adam was about him), and his failure to recognize Auber for what he was, the leading composer of the century after Rossini, Beethoven being too flawed to rank on the same level.

The full consequences of Berlioz's exclusion from the Conservatoire Hall did not register immediately; in November and December 1844 his energies were taken up with the Cirque Olympique concerts, and the following year he was in Vienna. When they did, the blow to his career was crippling. The hall was the only good one for orchestral music in Paris. Most of his important premières had taken place there. He would know soon enough what it meant to be deprived of it.

It was Habeneck no doubt who frustrated the projected gala concert of Baron Taylor's Association des Artistes Musiciens described in the previous chapter. His relations with Berlioz had long been at best ambiguous. Quite apart from any mutual abrasiveness of character, they could only worsen as Habeneck's powers declined with age and illness, and Berlioz's reputation as a conductor, and a conductor of the new school, increased. They were not improved when after conducting the first performance of the Roman Carnival overture, in February 1844, with the saltarello played up to speed – the same music which Habeneck had maddened him by taking too slowly at the Opéra – Berlioz encountered the old man in the green room and said, "That's how it goes." But it was circumstances as much as personality that made them adversaries. Habeneck felt threatened by his younger rival, who was still being spoken of as his successor at the Opéra, a job

Habeneck had no intention of giving up, and he fought to preserve his position.

We cannot say how close Berlioz came to getting it. In August 1843 he described Pillet as very much on his side: "I shall never find a better disposed director." But Pillet was director in name only; his mistress Mme Stoltz ruled the roost. Berlioz's influence seems to have waned. Two years later, in 1845, his efforts on behalf of his friend the bass Alizard were a failure. "I'm on bad terms with the administration," he told the singer. "I did see Perrot, who is still a good friend of mine; so far the only answer he has had (from Gentil) is, 'Alizard has greatly displeased Mme Stoltz.'" The Opéra was "sunk in oafish, mindless stupidity to the tip of its long ears". By then he had given up all thought of a position there and had declared open war in his feuilletons. Two years before, though it was "tottering", he could still hope it might yet "recover its strength and its nerve". By 1845 he felt that there was nothing to be done. The musical standards of the place had slipped beyond recovery; it was working "on the principle of the Gospels", exalting the mediocre and humbling the first-rate. A fine work performed there was reduced to the state of "strawberry beds ravaged by turkeys". When Habeneck finally retired in 1846 he was succeeded by Girard.

In the meantime Berlioz made two other attempts to obtain an established position. One was a plan for a second opéra-comique theatre which would concentrate on performing works by young native composers, while serving as a training-ground – at present lacking – for both composers and singers. The need for such a company had been recognized as long ago as the 1820s, when musicians, Berlioz among them, campaigned for the Odéon to be allowed to perform new French works (a privilege restricted to the Opéra and the Opéra-Comique).* The campaign failed, and soon afterwards the Odéon ceased to be an operatic house. Since then there had been frequent talk of creating a third lyric theatre, but no action. In July 1844 Berlioz and the impresario and dramatist Armand Dartois sent the minister a project for a theatre about the size of the Variétés or the Vaudeville (1,200 seats) devoted to putting on twenty new operas a year (none, they were careful to add, written by either of the proposed directors). Though it is not clear where the money was coming from, they must have been sure of it, since they were prepared to open within three months in the event of

* See Vol. 1, p. 205.

the licence being granted. The draft proposal is a persuasive document, explaining in convincing terms why the new theatre was needed and answering every possible objection. But it was not taken up.

Nor was the petition which Berlioz addressed to the Minister of the Interior, Duchâtel, four months earlier:

26 February 1844

Dear Minister

Pardon this direct appeal to your goodwill, which the extreme difficulty of my position obliges me to make. That position, which is exceptional (though no one believes it), attracted the interest of one of your predecessors. M. le Comte de Montalivet, on learning how far I was from being able to make use of the knowledge and powers he was so good as to recognize in me, and aware how impossible I found it to commit myself to compositions of any great extent for want of an assured livelihood even for as little as a few months, undertook to rescue me from this plight. M. Armand Bertin and M. Cavé both, successively, informed me of his intentions and of the means by which he proposed to carry them out, namely a chair at the Conservatoire and a grant, which would enable me to work in peace and in a manner beneficial to art. However, M. de Montalivet left the Ministry of the Interior soon afterwards, and all that came of his undertaking was my nomination to the post of curator of the Conservatoire Library at a salary of one hundred and eighteen francs a month. That is my sole assured income. As a result I have constantly to write useless articles and devote myself, against the grain, to vapid critical work of no lasting value – lacking independence as it does – yet which is my sole means of existence. I am a composer but I have no time to compose – so much so that I cannot continue with the large-scale work [*La nonne sanglante*] which I began two years ago for the Opéra. When its turn comes, as it will quite soon, I shall not be able to find the time to complete it and supervise its production.

In France and in Germany I have had much experience directing large bodies of performers; yet I have neither chorus nor orchestra to conduct.

It is not a mark of excessive self-esteem to believe that I am much more capable of teaching harmony, orchestration and general composition than certain obscure professors at the Conservatoire; yet I have never succeeded in obtaining so much as a class in *solfège* at that establishment.

On the rare occasions when I manage to write some musical work of middling length it is normally enough to guarantee the financial success of the concert in spite of the very large costs of performance, thanks to the curiosity which new compositions of mine stimulate in the public. But, constantly interrupted and distracted by occupations alien and abhorrent to the artist and to art, it can sometimes take me a year to produce a work which in more normal and fortunate circumstances I should complete in two months. It is hard to have to confess that I *do not have time to work* and that I do almost nothing of what I can do best.

Forgive me, Minister, for acquainting you with the bizarre difficulties of my life, in the process of begging you to help me overcome them – difficulties all the crueller in that no one believes them, and throughout Europe, wherever my name is known, I am considered well off.

Perhaps you will see fit to carry through what M. de Montalivet began, by enabling me to direct my energies where they belong instead of deflecting them from their true course, dishonorably and without profit to art.

The creation for me of a class in instrumentation at the Conservatoire would help me to achieve this aim. Is it presumptuous of me to hope that you will?

The minister responded with a single cash payment from the fund for the encouragement of the arts, but declined to make any permanent provision. When Berlioz wrote a month later asking to be put on the small list of annual payments, he was turned down. Such begging letters were de rigueur in a centralized state. But there is a note of desperation about this one.

At the end of his démarches he was where he had been before. The strain was telling. After the concerts at the Cirque Olympique Dr Amussat, his anatomy professor at the Ecole de Médecine more than twenty years before, who had since become a friend, told him he was ill from anger even more than from fatigue and urged him to take a relaxing holiday on the Mediterranean.

Amussat had given him the same advice after the concert in the Palace of Industry the previous August: "Go south, get some sea air, forget all about the things that overheat your blood and overstimulate your nervous system, which is highly enough strung as it is. Goodbye, and go – you really mustn't hesitate." Berlioz took the advice, needing a change even more than Amussat may have realized. The stress of putting on such an event might have been sufficient to precipitate nervous exhaustion without any additional cause. But the weeks leading to the Palace of Industry concert coincided with the crisis that had long been gathering in his domestic life. Harriet had reached the end of the line.

She had taken his five months' absence in Germany very badly. He wrote to her several times; but it was not enough. Whether it was then that she began drinking heavily or whether the habit was already ingrained is impossible to say. Berlioz did not mention it in his letters to Nancy till the summer of 1844, but his silence could have been due to a natural reserve: as Adèle remarked to her sister in July of that year, their brother "must be suffering cruelly to complain to *you*".

A letter from the eight-year-old Louis to Nancy, written on 21 February 1843, gives a pathetic picture of Harriet's state during her husband's absence:

Good-day, my dear Aunt, how are you, I am very anxious to know if you have had news of my Papa. Mama is very sad because she has not had any letters for a month. Since September 20th when my Papa left for Brussels without saying anything to us my poor Mama hasn't been able to sleep, every day she waits for a letter which never comes. I don't know where my Papa is. M. Berton Mama's doctor wrote to him the day before yesterday to ask why he doesn't send us his news, he addressed the letter to Leipzig where we think he is at the moment. [. . .] Mama really wanted to write to you, only she is so sad that she can't find the words to express her thoughts.

Berlioz's letter of 17 February from Dresden, enclosing 500 francs, presumably arrived a few days later. What happened then is not clear, though Harriet apparently went away; for the next we hear of her, in a letter of 26 May from Félix Marmion to Nancy, she was "back in the Rue de Londres, more or less cured physically but still suffering a good deal in her mind and even more in her feelings".

Yesterday I spent an hour listening to her grievances – but with great interest, I assure you; she has never been more original. What a strange and, you could say, gifted person she is! It was a mixture of jests, tears, sarcasms, reminiscences, what have you – it was at once comical and very touching. But poor woman: her youth and beauty have gone beyond recall, she knows it, she has no illusions on that score, although I believe she still has a great need of *love*.

On his return from Germany a week later Berlioz picked up the tangled threads of his affairs where he had left them. But life at 31 Rue de Londres could never be the same again. By now Harriet can hardly have been ignorant of the presence of a mistress in her husband's life. Marie could not remain unacknowledged. Though he had stopped mentioning her in his feuilletons he continued to be involved in her attempts at a career. On 18 August 1843 she appeared at the Opéra-Comique as Charlotte in Auber's *L'ambassadrice*. *La France musicale* reported it as a success; but, whether by malign accident or deliberate mischief-making, gave her role as that of the heroine of the work, Harriet, not of Charlotte (a correction was published next day). Berlioz told his Dresden friend Lipinski that the début had been "very success-ful". The *Corsaire* thought otherwise. "Mlle Recio – is that her real name? – who passed like a shadow in *Le comte Ory*, on another stage, has made an ill-advised appearance in the role of Harriet [again!] in *L'ambassadrice*. After *Le comte Ory*, alas! After *L'ambassadrice*, holà!* It is said that the débutante presented herself at the Théâtre Favart with the air of a conqueror. Self-assurance is one thing, but there are limits. They say she is a pupil of M. Berlioz. Well – yes, he is certainly capable of it." The following January, in a letter to Louis Schloesser, Berlioz described Marie as "engaged at the Opéra-Comique" and as having just "played with great success at another theatre in two benefit perform-ances". At about the same time he asked Saint-Georges to let her take the title role in Flotow's one-act *L'esclave de Camoëns* at the Opéra-Comique. There is no evidence that she did. But she sang *Absence* at Berlioz's February concert in the Salle Herz and, with Gustave Roger, an arrangement for tenor and soprano of the Sanctus from the Grande messe des morts at the following concert, given at the Opéra-Comique on 6 April. In June she took part in an evening at the Odéon in aid of the fund for restoring Mount Carmel monastery in Jerusalem, of which Berlioz wrote a brief anonymous news item in the *Ménestrel*. There are also echoes here and there of her singing Spanish songs – with "an Andalusian grace", as one newspaper reported.

Such promotional activities cannot have been unnoticed by Harriet. Berlioz, however, clearly hoped that things could go on as before. He could not give up his mistress, but he could not abandon his wife. Throughout the second half of 1843 and the first six or seven months

---

* Adaptation of Boileau's famous epigram against Corneille: "Après *Agésilas*, / Hélas! / Mais après *Attila*, / Holà!"

of 1844 he continued to live with her in the apartment in the Rue de Londres. From the autumn of 1843 Louis was a boarder at his school in Paris, but he was at home at weekends and in the holidays.

At first the family correspondence for this period contained few references to Harriet. In July 1843 Dr Berlioz wrote to Nancy that he had had M. and Mme Amédée Faure to lunch: "They told me that our poor Hector had become terribly thin; he is preparing none the less to leave for England, despite the strenuous and pig-headed opposition of his wife." At the end of December Berlioz told Adèle that "Harriet has been ill, she is better now but her morale gets worse all the time; her jealousies and emotional outbursts are beyond belief. I can tell you, I need an enormous dose of patience. Don't say anything about it when you reply." A few days later she was "not yet fully recovered, and as tempestuous as the weather". Berlioz was still at home in February 1844 – when Félix Marmion reported him writing on behalf of his cook's son, corporal in an infantry regiment – and he lived there through the spring and early summer.

In the summer of 1844 the storm broke. A letter of 19 May to Nancy spoke of "torments every day, every night". Five weeks later he could no longer gloss over the truth: there was "not a single instant of respite".

I rented an apartment for her in the country; she stayed there a fortnight, and on her return my punishment began again. It's an impossible existence – screams, insults, denunciations, curses, recriminations, so sickening that they would drive me into a fury if I didn't know what to attribute this madness to: a habit, now deeply rooted, of drinking eau-de-vie (since I must tell you everything). It fills me with an insurmountable disgust, as you may imagine. If you could see the disorder, the way she dresses, the abandonment of all care for her person. She cannot even keep our household accounts. She gets up in the middle of the night when she knows I am asleep, comes into my room, closes the door and launches into tirades which go on for three hours at a stretch, sometimes till dawn. Next day she begs me to forgive her, swears she loves me and I could trample her underfoot and her affection would not change. And then at night it begins again. Oh, it's unbearable. [. . .]

I am obliged to tell all my friends to stop coming to see us. If I have the luck to make a profit on the festival I shall leave as soon as possible.

Louis, when he is home from school, calls out that he wants to sleep, but it is no good – her fury rages unchecked. The poor child grows more and more affectionate. His mother loves him deeply, in fact is absolutely devoted to him; but the infernal habit is too strong. I could hardly believe what the servants told me when I questioned them. She herself doesn't deny it; only, she claims that I am the cause and that she has to, as a "consolation".

Pity me; I don't know how it will end; but end it must. Say nothing about it to my father – pointless to upset him with such sad revelations. My life is turned upside down.

The torment continued. During the rehearsals for the festival concert he would return exhausted to the house in the evening, desperate for rest but unable to get any. In the end he moved out and took a room in a hotel. After the concert, on the eve of his departure (for Baden-Baden, he had planned, but actually for Nice), he persuaded Harriet to return to the country, to Sceaux, and he gave up the apartment in the Rue de Londres; he hoped she could be made to see that it would be better for them to separate and for her to live outside Paris. "I felt my heart break when I left her," he told Adèle, after his return in mid-October. "While I was away I wrote her loving letters, urging her to make new efforts to uproot the terrible habit, which is degrading and destroying her little by little. She replied that I was wrong to doubt that her attempt would succeed, and that by the time I was back this ghastly failing would have vanished for ever. Yesterday I went to Sceaux without telling her I was coming. I entered the room and found her in the most appalling state, hardly able to speak, a glass on the table and the apartment reeking of eau-de-vie. I cannot tell you what I felt. It's horrible. She has become enormous."

Harriet, when she recovered herself, would not hear of their living apart; she insisted on returning to Paris and being with him. "She swears by all the gods that she will not torment me nor disturb my days or nights. But is it possible? Then, again – but, oh, I should pain you too much if I told you all . . ." He would make one more effort. "I shall take an apartment with her, though God knows what it will be like for me. She is so unhappy, one must excuse her and not crush her with the ultimate despair, that of being abandoned by me." In November he found a new apartment, at 43 Rue Blanche, on the slopes of the Montmartre hill, a couple of streets north of the Rue de Londres. For the moment, Harriet stayed in Sceaux.

Memories almost too painful to bear crowded upon him. That autumn he was working on incidental music for a production of *Hamlet* at the Odéon, in a translation by Léon de Wailly. The production did not materialize; but the death-haunted *Funeral March* (revised four years later) was written for it. Perhaps too the poignant *Death of Ophelia*, composed two years before, was to have played a part.

Shortly afterwards, as though by fatality, a company from England came to Paris with *Hamlet* in its repertory. Berlioz could not wait to see it, he told Nancy, yet dreaded the emotional upheaval it would cause. "I cried this morning – cried in the streets as I went about my affairs, thinking of Hamlet, of Ophelia, of all that is no more, of all that has become like poor Yorick, or near enough ... Forgive me. Farewell, my heart is breaking. If I have been the cause of suffering, I have suffered myself – and it is not over. Farewell, farewell, dear Nancy. It's only sisters that remain the same, and for whom one doesn't change."

His sisters, though shocked, did not desert him. But their deepest concern was for their nephew. Adèle wanted Louis to come to a boarding-school in Lyon (everyone agreed he must be sent away). "It would be a relief to me to know the little fellow was near me." If Hector went to Germany, what would become of Louis if he wasn't sent to them? Berlioz had been trying, with the aid of Armand Bertin, to get him into a college at Versailles. In late 1844, however, the Education Minister Villemain awarded him an exhibition, covering half the fees, at the Royal College in Rouen (where Flaubert had been a pupil in the 1830s), and he was dispatched there. On balance, lonely as his life at school would be, he was best off away from the terrible scenes at home and the emotional dependency of an alcoholic mother: they were more than a sensitive child of ten could cope with. A friend of Adèle's, visiting them in August 1844, told her (as Adèle reported) that "Hector had grieved him dreadfully but still more little Louis, there was such an air of sadness about the boy."

Harriet no doubt, by her addiction, had put herself beyond their sympathy.

Louis' letters to his Aunt Nancy certainly give a sad impression. In his bewilderment the child seized on the distant figure of his grandfather, Dr Berlioz, and made him into an image of all that was beneficent and dependable.

> I am going to give my grandfather a surprise. Please don't tell him. You will say to him that I can't write because I am ill, and then what will be

his surprise, on August 18th I would set off for La Côte. I would tell Monique to say to my grandfather that there is a little boy who wants to talk to him, when my grandfather came I would say to him, I am your grandson Louis Berlioz. Tell Monique if you want but don't let her tell my grandfather. (20 November 1843)

Dear Aunt, Papa has made me very sad because he doesn't write me a word. He wrote to us that he was at Nice [. . .] and would return at the earliest on October 15th. Dear Aunt, write to my grandfather that I wrote him about ten letters and that Papa did not post a single one, for I found them all in the [unintelligible word] where we always put letters and cards. Dear Aunt, Mama and I thank you very much for the letter you wrote us, and I even more than Mama because you thought a little of Mama and me. [. . .] Dear Aunt, you must ask my grandfather if it is true that he has given me a white horse that he has. Dear Aunt, Mama has told me to write to you that she was very sad because of Papa. (2 October 1844)

My very dear Aunt, forgive me for not writing to you for so long. Dear Aunt, Mama is sad because Papa no longer comes to see her, he doesn't write to her, and he has left her in the country where her lodgings are very bad, and Mama would like to go back to Paris but she can't. Dear Aunt, I will soon go to a college in Rouen, which Mama is very sad about. I should have gone on December 2nd but the date has been put back. Dear Aunt, tell my grandfather to write to Papa so that I can go and spend a few days with him. (3 December 1844)

It was a mercy Louis did not know what his grandfather was saying on the subject. Dr Berlioz (Adèle reported to Nancy) would not hear of his grandson's coming to stay: it would be far too much of a strain and a worry. He was even put out at the idea of Louis' writing to him. "If I don't reply he will be cut up; if I do, it will fatigue me and I won't know what to say to him." "I can't tell you [Adèle goes on] how surprised and upset I was at my father expressing himself like that. So the poor child is destined to be spurned by those closest to him. If our poor mother were alive, how different it would be! [. . .] I replied with a few hurried lines, thanking him for the large consignment of wine he had sent us and assuring him that I had never encouraged Louis to write and would on the contrary dissuade him from doing so."

Berlioz had not forsaken his wife altogether; he continued to provide for her, while doing everything possible to promote the "amicable separation" which, according to him, was eventually agreed between them. But though his mail went to the apartment at 43 Rue Blanche – to which Harriet moved some time that winter – he was much more often to be found at 41 Rue de Provence, the apartment of Marie Recio and her mother a few streets away (a block north of the present Boulevard Haussmann): it was, he said, not his official address but it was his real one. Marie had got what she wanted, in all but name.

That too she would appropriate before long. When she accompanied Berlioz to Austro-Hungary in the winter of 1845–6 she went as his wife. She was in Lyon with him when he gave two concerts in the summer of 1845, and was seen by his sisters: the liaison, which he had kept from them, was out at last. By now, however, certain ground rules had been laid down, not all of them in her favour. She renounced any further ambition to sing at his concerts and allowed that he was free to engage any soprano he wished (though it is significant that *Absence*, "her" song, did not figure again in his programmes for another eight years). His continued affection for Harriet aroused Marie's jealousy, but his obligation to support and, up to a point, care for her was not challenged. And he retained, in his mind at least, the freedom to travel without Marie if he thought it necessary.

Very likely Marie had been going to go to Baden-Baden with him – the trip he was planning for the end of August 1844 (and which he was still intending to make when he wrote to Nancy on the 24th). But, probably on the advice of Dr Amussat, who feared that Germany would not provide the complete break his system craved, the destination was changed at the last minute to Nice, and he went on his own.

It was thirteen years since he was last there, "on the occasion of another convalescence", as the *Memoirs* put it. Then he had come back to life from the painful death of his love for Camille Moke. Now his need for the balm of sun and sea had a different source but was in its way as great. Exhausted by the concert in the Palace of Industry, on the verge of typhoid fever if he didn't take a holiday, he fled from Harriet's scenes (like Aeneas from Dido's anguish), from Marie's demands, from the heartbreak and bad conscience and hopeless entanglement of his emotional existence.

The room he had in 1831 was occupied by an English family, but he found another on the same Ponchettes rock, higher up, in an old tower (still standing today) from which he could look out as before across the blue Mediterranean and watch the fishing-boats and the vaguer shapes of far-off ships, and at night the moon "opening its silver fan" over the wide expanse of sea.

Little is known of the month or six weeks that Berlioz spent in Nice. No letters survive from that time. We may guess from its title – *La tour de Nice* – that it was there that he drafted the new overture which he tried out at his next concert a few months later before setting it aside for revision, and there that its images of the sea in gentle and in boisterous mood came to him. Fifteen years on, in the *Débats*, Napoleon III's annexation of Nice prompted him to imagine the joy of his "chère tour des Ponchettes" on finding itself French – that tower "where I spent so many peaceful hours and from whose summit so often, before sunrise, I made my morning salutation to the sleeping sea". The brief paragraph in the *Memoirs* speaks of long swims, renewed exploration of the rocks and bays and inlets of the place, expeditions down the coast, and of "enjoying, with delight, a calm whose worth I appreciated more than ever".

He must have been reminded of more from his previous visit than the scenery, or the rocks where he found his "old friends", the ancient cannon from some long-forgotten siege, "still slumbering in the sun". The memory of Camille and her treachery had been active again earlier in the year when he wrote the chapter in *Voyage musical* on the escapade that landed him in Nice, more dead than alive, at the outset of "the happiest weeks of his life" – one of two passages in the "Italian Journey" that still remained to be done (the other being the famous description of the spleen or *mal de l'isolement*). Reliving the pain of his rejection had reanimated the desire for revenge, and he added to the utopian tale of "Euphonia the musical city", which he was writing for the *Gazette*, a fantasy love-plot drawn from life, whose characters wore the thinnest of token disguises: Camille turned into Ellimac, a fascinating woman and a brilliant talent, but brittle, heartless and self-seeking; her hippo-potamus-like mother Ellianac – *canaille* ("scum") backwards – and Ellimac's betrayed composer-lover Rotch who, discovering her turpitude, has her and her entourage crushed to death in a dénouement of Edgar Allen Poe-like horror and grotesqueness.

But 1831, even if the wound never completely healed, was a clean break and a new beginning; he had only his own salvation to work out and his own fortunes to make or mar. In 1844 life's complexities could be evaded no more than momentarily. They were waiting for him when he returned, some time in mid-October.

He had hoped his absence would help accustom Harriet to the idea of their living apart; but she was still passionately unreconciled to it, and the misery continued into the new year. On 22 May 1845 she sent Félix Marmion a plaintive note begging him to come to lunch in the Rue Blanche. "You will be doing me a great service, because it will give me an opportunity to see Hector, who has almost abandoned me, and to tell you once again how much I respect and esteem you. My husband is leaving for a long journey, and you are too, I am not well and, God knows, life is so uncertain, it could be the last [time] we meet together."

The journey was to the south of France, and Marie Recio went with him.

The notion of a Berliozian *voyage musical en France* is on the face of it surprising, given his opinion of the level of musical culture in the French provinces (the inhabitants of Dauphiné, for example, being "entirely innocent in all matters pertaining to the art of music"); and, from what little we know of the four concerts he gave in Marseille and Lyon in June and July 1845 and their reception by the public, he had no great cause to alter it. Trying to din his music into the orchestra in Marseille made him feel more like a "sergeant-instructor" than a musician. Finding even mediocre trumpet-players in Lyon proved an almost insuperable task. The heat of high summer, too, was hardly the season for getting an audience. Yet it was a challenge that he must face. More and more offers had been coming in as his fame grew. For some months he had been in negotiation with the philharmonic society of Châlons sur Saône for a concert. Bordeaux also was showing interest. A summer tour of France had its attractions. It meant a change from Paris, at a time when there was nothing much doing. His next important commitment, the Beethoven Festival in Bonn, was not till August. That spring, Félicien David had given his *Désert* with great success in both Lyon and Marseille (Adèle Suat wrote rapturously about it, though in some alarm that her brother's star was being eclipsed). In Marseille there was Alizard, his favourite singer, and there was the delightful Méry, and Morel's great friend Lecourt, barrister, amateur cellist, keen Beethovenian, a man with a healthy admiration for his music (he had come all the way to Paris to hear the Symphonie funèbre). In Lyon the musical director of the opera was François Georges-Hainl, fellow-student at the Paris Conservatoire in the late 1820s. The painter Isidore

Flacheron and his Abruzzian wife Mariucia, companions in the old days in Subiaco, lived there. And within a few hours' coach ride would be Nancy in Grenoble, Adèle in Vienne (the Suat family had just moved there) and his father at La Côte: at last he would be able to hear his son's music. Dr Amussat had recommended another visit to the south as remedy for the fatigue and stress of the Cirque Olympique concerts; so that, when a reasonably good offer arrived from Marseille at the end of May, he decided to accept.

Not a great deal is known about the two concerts he gave in the Grand Theatre on 19 and 25 June. More than half the account that he published much later in the *Gazette* concerned his conversation with the driver of the omnibus which conveyed bathers from the sea to the centre of town, who told him of the famous passengers he had had over the years and who is represented whimsically as a fan of his music. A contemporary news item in the *Débats* reported that among the works performed were *Le cinq mai* (with Alizard), the Apotheosis, and *Hymne à la France*. Some movements from the Requiem may also have been given. Berlioz was so impressed with the oboe and cor anglais player, a German called Wacker or Walcker, that he wrote to both Liszt and Mendelssohn recommending him (the man wanted to return to Germany); but he was less than enchanted with the orchestra as a whole. He was careful to cultivate the local critics and was rewarded with good notices. The public seems to have been lukewarm; but members of the male-voice choir, the Société Trotebas, serenaded him afterwards.

About the two concerts in Lyon a month later, on 20 and 24 July, there are more details. From Avignon, on his way by steamboat up the Rhône at the beginning of July, Berlioz wrote to Hainl specifying the choral and orchestral forces he needed – over two hundred, including the extra wind and percussion for the Apotheosis – and the publicity required to achieve receipts of nine or ten thousand francs. By recruiting professional musicians from Châlons, Vienne, Dijon and Grenoble, as well as the best local amateurs, he got his forces or as many as the scenery in position on the stage of the Grand Théâtre allowed room for, but it is doubtful if he got his ten thousand francs. It was hot summer weather, and the new star of the Paris stage, Rachel, was in Lyon. Berlioz's success, such as it was, was nothing like Félicien David's. As he wrote in the *Gazette*, his friend Hainl "would have liked people to be trampled to death in the rush to get in; but notwithstanding the music-lovers who came from Grenoble and Vienne and Nantua and even from Lyon, no one was killed. Now if his Grace the Bishop had declared from the pulpit that my music made them 'better men' . . .*But he didn't; and, without it, there was no way people were going to be crushed in the entrance to a concert hall in the provinces in August [July] – though I did get a serenade, like the one in Marseille." The press, however, was again very favourable; one critic described the Apotheosis as "*SUBLIME, trois fois SUBLIME*", and a long article in the *Clochette* claimed him as "one of our glories".

The article was probably the work of Georges-Hainl himself. George, as Berlioz called him, was a tower of strength. He directed the chorus, played cello in most of the orchestral pieces and timpani in the slow movement of the Fantastic, and taught himself to play the harp in the Pilgrims' March by the simple expedient of removing the strings adjacent to its two recurring notes, C natural and B. Berlioz formed a good opinion of the abilities, musical and organizational, of this exuberant lion-maned musician.

He also had the unexpected satisfaction of welcoming his old music-master Dorant into the orchestra. Berlioz encountered him in the street.

He had just arrived from Vienne, and his first words on seeing me were: "I'm playing for you. What shall it be – violin, cello, clarinet, ophicleide?" "Ah my dear master, I see you don't know me. Violin – can I ever have too many? Does one ever have enough?" "Good. But I'm going to feel lost in the middle of your great orchestra, not knowing a soul." "Don't worry, I'll introduce you."

And next day, as the rehearsal began, I pointed him out to the assembled musicians. "Gentlemen, I have the honour to present a very able teacher from Vienne. There's a grateful pupil of his among us. That pupil is me. In a moment you may decide I don't do him any great credit. All the same please receive M. Dorant as if you thought otherwise, and as he deserves." You can imagine the surprise and the applause. Dorant was more uneasy than ever. But once launched on the symphony, the demon of music took possession of him. Before long I saw his face flushed and his bow bounding. I on my side felt a strange emotion conducting the March to the Scaffold and the Scene in the Fields, played by my old teacher of *guitar* whom I hadn't seen for twenty years.

---

* The Bishop of Norwich had been reported as saying so of Jenny Lind's singing.

There were two general rehearsals plus the now usual sectionals, some held at the theatre, some at the premises of the Cercle Musical (an amateur society), some at the barracks. They may not have been entirely free from friction, to judge by a note he received from one of the amateur performers, most likely a chorister, which he quoted in the *Gazette*: "It is possible to be a great artist and polite." (Berlioz admitted to having a very short fuse where choruses were concerned. "Before rehearsals have even started a sort of anticipatory rage seizes me, my throat tightens and although nothing has yet occurred to make me lose my temper I glare at the singers in a manner reminiscent of the Gascon who kicked an inoffensive little boy passing near him, and on the latter's protesting that he had 'not done anything', replied, 'Just think if you had!'")

Marshalling and preparing his performers took time. He stayed in Lyon nearly four weeks. Lyon was the biggest city in France after Paris, and he was offering his near-compatriots a demanding cross-section of his work – movements from the first two symphonies, the *Roman Carnival, Le cinq mai*, the Apotheosis, and *Hymne à la France* – as well as music by Gluck, Weber and Grétry. And some at least of his family would be in the audience, hearing his music for the first time.

On the 9th – the weather still blisteringly hot – he took leave of his rehearsals and spent the day with his father at La Côte St André. They had not seen each other for five years, during which time both of them had aged more than in years. What passed between them on that blazing July day in the cool house on the main street of La Côte? Was it a happy encounter? How much did the son tell his father about his life? Did he speak of Harriet? What account did he give of Louis? What did he say about his continuing struggle in Paris, about his plans for future compositions, about his rehearsals in Lyon and the prospect for the two concerts? We have no idea. Nor do we know why in the end, whether from ill health or for some inner, more complex reason, when there was a chance at last to hear his beloved son's music – the cause, the dream for which Hector had renounced his heritage and abandoned the family home – Dr Berlioz failed to make the thirty-mile journey to Lyon, and so never heard it.

Nor, when the time came, was Camille Pal able to attend. But Nancy and her daughter were at the first concert, with Adèle and her husband. They all drove over from Vienne, where Nancy and Mathilde were staying. What the sisters thought of their brother's music is not recorded.

We have only a letter from Adèle to Nancy written ten days before.

I'm writing this without knowing if you were at the rendezvous at La Côte [Berlioz had tried, unsuccessfully, to arrange a family reunion]. Anyway you'll be here on the 15th or 16th, won't you – all the more reason now! We'll be going together to Lyon to hear Hector's music, *at last*. I feel moved in advance. Will it be the success we wish? I wonder – I'm anxious: it's a bad moment, everyone's in the country or taking the waters. I was amazed when I received our brother's letter telling of his arrival in Lyons. My husband was going there on business that very evening. I had just time to put on my hat, and went with him. We had no trouble finding Hector; but we had an adventure on his account which I'll tell you about later and which disturbed me a good deal – you will judge whether wrongly or not. [. . .] Our reunion here and in Lyon is going to be lovely. We shall be there in force to applaud. Bring your best clothes for this great event. It's now or never!

Did the adventure Adèle referred to involve Marie? She was in Lyon with Berlioz, at the Hôtel du Parc (he wrote to Hainl afterwards to ask about a cameo brooch she left at the hotel, and in the same letter sent "greetings from Marie and me to Mme George and a kiss for your two charming little girls"). That his sisters saw Marie and were told, or divined, the truth is surely clear from the note in which, shortly before leaving Lyon, Berlioz did his best to explain and justify the situation to Nancy and at the same time to forestall further discussion:

26 July

Dear Sister

I have time to write only a couple of lines. The second concert was much less well attended than the first, as we foresaw on finding that Rachel was playing *Andromaque* the day before and *Virginie* the day after. Happily the audience was much more enthusiastic and their applause made up for the poor receipts.

I leave this evening for Paris. Your letter is written with as much warmth of heart as reserve and good sense; but it would take too long and serve no purpose to reply. It's a whole history, whose events I cannot change . . . It is my fate to be constantly, and in spite of myself, outside the path normally followed. The impossibility of my home life, and Harriet's *monomania* or *illness*, brought all this to pass. Nothing could be proof against such a calamity, not even the deep affection I still have for her. As to the person you speak of, her name is not the one I mentioned in your presence. That lady is a friend of Méry's, not of mine.

Farewell. Don't raise the subject with me again – there's no point. Above all I don't want my father upset, and I trust that no one in our foolish town will be so stupid as to tell him.

Within ten days of his return to Paris he was off again, this time alone, to Bonn for the Beethoven Festival organized by Liszt: three days of performances, on the second of which Hähnel's monument to the town's most celebrated son was to be unveiled in the main square.

Earlier that summer Liszt had talked of including the Grande messe des morts in the programme and also of putting on a few of those Berlioz–Liszt concerts for which the two of them were famous (one of which had raised money in Paris for the Beethoven statue four years before). In the event Berlioz went as an observer, one of the throng of journalists and celebrities from many countries who flocked in swelter-ing August heat to the little town. "Where are they going to put us all?" he wrote to Hainl a few days before leaving Paris. "I can see us having to erect tents on the banks of the Rhine or sleep on the barges."

He found somewhere to stay; but the organization proved appalling. The committee supposed to be running the festival was inept and petty-minded in equal measure (at one point it suggested saving money by not engaging any wind instruments), and Liszt had his work cut out to "establish a bit of order amid the chaos" (as Léon Kreutzer noted in the *Gazette*), for which he was in turn accused of courting the limelight. "He was beset with a swarm of envious little cabals," wrote Berlioz to Nancy. "Bonn is a provincial town and, as such, a hotbed of those mean and foolish notions which spring up the moment local or national self-esteem is involved."

Berlioz's long report in the *Débats* was divided between praise and blame. He could not ignore the confusion and the missed opportunities, and as a good journalist he made the most of them. The invitation he received from the committee in charge of the festivities had "not actually prevented" him from attending them (he wrote); but he had to use his fists and vault over a barrier to get anywhere near the statue for its ceremonial unveiling, and heard the Mass in C only by slipping in at the artists' entrance and finding a seat near the altar (while from the other end of the cathedral came an uproar "like a town being sacked"). As for the performances, how much better they could have been, with a little foresight and imagination! It would have been perfectly feasible – and here was the occasion if there ever was one – to create a crack orchestra worthy of "the father and supreme master of modern instrumental music", made up of the leading players of Europe north of the Alps chosen without regard for narrow nationalistic ideas, instead of the rather ordinary band that had been assembled from local resources. Berlioz amused himself listing some of those who could have figured in it: Baermann and Blaës among the clarinets, Hainl among the cellos, Dieppo leading the trombones, Barret the English oboist (instead of the feeble player they had to listen to), the competent double-basses raised to greater heights by Schmidt of Brunswick, Müller of Darmstadt and, from London, the great Dragonetti, and his friends Massart, Seghers, Cuvillon and Very adding much needed strength to the violin section. Many of these people were there – in the audience. The organizers might even have found a harpist to play the harp part in Liszt's cantata instead of resorting to a piano, like any minor German chapel.

Nor could he refrain from castigating the Paris Conservatoire for failing to send an official deputation. As for the Société des Concerts, which owed its fame and very existence to Beethoven's works but stood aloof exactly as it had done a few years ago when Liszt tried to persuade it to give a solitary benefit concert in aid of the project: well, if gratitude and admiration were more than mere words, its conduct was outrageous.

Yet the fact of the festival (he argued) outweighed anything that could be said against it. It had happened: that was the great thing; Liszt's years of dedication had borne fruit. Despite some notable absences (no Mendelssohn, no Schumann, no Wagner, no Spontini, no Auber) a huge spontaneous gathering of musicians and music-lovers, perhaps all the more animated for containing so few official delegates, had been there to share in it and pay their tribute. Berlioz's article evoked the sheer excitement of it: the emotions of the first evening when, arriving by train from Paris with a group of colleagues, he found himself in a large hall decorated with greenery and glowing with the light of a thousand candles, which lit up Beethoven's portrait high above the platform and the heraldic shields bearing the names of his works; the buzz of conversation as friends greeted each other after years of absence, and among them all the ardent, youthful Liszt, "the heart and soul of the festival"; the grand and solemn impression made at the opening concert by the Ninth Symphony, conducted by old Spohr (at tempos similar to

Habeneck's except for a much quicker double-bass recitative at the beginning of the finale); the magnificent young sopranos from the choral societies of Bonn and Cologne, dazzling in their white dresses, who attacked the most difficult passages in the Missa Solemnis fearlessly and sang the cruelly demanding Ode to Joy with a beauty of tone and a clarity unheard of in Paris; the overwhelming power of the great unison, "Bow down, ye millions", like the voice of a vast cathedral congregation; Liszt playing the Emperor Concerto as only he could; the Fifth Symphony given, under Liszt's direction, without the cuts and alterations still practised at the Conservatoire, and being revealed as "an even finer work when performed complete than when corrected" (Berlioz was discreetly silent on the subject of Liszt's conducting, which he described to Nancy as really a species of non-conducting); the high quality of Liszt's cantata, a work – culminating in a hymn to Beethoven based on the slow-movement theme of the Archduke Trio – which "immediately places him in the top rank of composers" and which, he told Nancy, deserved "all the good things I wrote about it".

Whatever its faults, he concluded, the festival gave the musical world an opportunity to express what countless men and women felt in their heart of hearts about Beethoven: the enthusiasts whom his music exalted almost to frenzy, the humorists it delighted with its jests and sudden quirks, the thinkers to whom it disclosed boundless horizons, the outcasts who heard in it an answering cry of protest and defiance, the religious to whom it spoke of God, the lovers of nature – all who turned to him as to a benefactor and a friend. Only, it was a little late: "the bronze Beethoven is insensible to all this homage; and it is sad to think that the living Beethoven, whose memory we thus honour, would not perhaps have obtained from his native town in the times of want and suffering, so numerous in his arduous career, one ten thousandth of the sums lavished on him after his death. None the less it is good to glorify in this way the demi-gods who are no more. It is also good not to make them wait too long. The town of Bonn, and Liszt most of all, should be thanked for having understood that posterity had long pronounced its verdict on Beethoven."

Berlioz's account did not mention the ceremonial lunch given at the Goldener Stern on the final day, at which the half-suppressed rivalries and frustrations of the festival erupted and guests fought each other for seats, Liszt was publicly upbraided by Chelard for failing to refer to France in his speech, a drunken Lola Montez, who had gatecrashed the feast, made an embarrassing scene, and a spectacular thunderstorm inundated the town, bringing the heatwave to an end not a moment too soon and silencing the squabbling banqueteers.

Perhaps he decided to skip it. But he was one of the select company who, along with Queen Victoria and Prince Albert, attended a musical party given that evening ten miles down the Rhine at the castle of Bruhl by the King of Prussia. Frederick William had invited some of the finest singers of the day to entertain his guests: Jenny Lind, the new reigning star of Berlin (Berlioz was bowled over by her voice and artistry), Pauline Viardot, Staudigl, Pischek. Meyerbeer was at the piano. Liszt also played. It was a memorable end to the festival. The King greeted Berlioz most amiably, but the Princess failed to recognize him ("not very flattering for my physical attractions – we had a long conversation in Berlin – and the funny part is that at the end of the evening she scolded Meyerbeer for not introducing me to her"). At midnight the party broke up. By now the storm had passed, "and the sinking stars invited sleep".* He caught the last train back to Bonn "dead-drunk with music, exhausted with admiring", and slept till noon. Next day he crossed the river and took lodgings in the village of Königswinter, where he wrote his report for the *Journal des débats*, relaxed after the turmoil of the past three days, and gathered himself for the next stage of his life.

The Bonn Beethoven Festival gave him something beside the joy of participating in an act of homage, however imperfect, and the stimulus of meeting old friends and making new ones: a pressing invitation to visit Vienna without delay. The Viennese delegation – Josef Fischoff, professor of piano at the Hochschule, Dr Bacher, rich lawyer and patron of music, Johann Wesque von Puttlingen, diplomat, composer and important figure on the Viennese scene – sought him out and insisted that he come. Berlioz had been considering a trip to St Petersburg, perhaps in November or December, encouraged by a letter from General Lvov, director of the Imperial Chapel, which he found at Schlesinger's on his return from Lyon. But Russia would have to wait. His goal for the first part of the winter was now Vienna.

Having written and dispatched his articles he stayed on in the village, absorbing the peaceful landscape where Beethoven – the oldest locals

---

* "suadentque cadentia sidera somnos" (*Aeneid*, ii, 9, quoted in Berlioz's second *Débats* article).

remembered it – would come as a young man, crossing the turbid river to wander and compose in its woods and pastures. Berlioz's thoughts were of the "benefactor", the "friend" whose works he had listened to and read and meditated, analysed, proselytized until they had become almost part of himself. He thought too of what he might still do under their inspiring influence but had not done, the scores that existed in his imagination and clamoured to be born. It was high time he gave one of them the breath of life.

Adolphe Boschot, in his biography, evokes Berlioz, alone in Königs-winter in mid-August 1845, possessed by the Beethovenian presence, conversing with his mighty mentor and, spurred by his example, commit-ting himself to the composition of the great work that was waiting to take shape and form. It is a seductive idea and a plausible one. *The Damnation of Faust* had been a reality since his return from Germany in 1843 – of that there can be no question. One of the *Eight Scenes from Faust*, Marguerite's Romance and Soldiers' Chorus, was on the programme announced for 3 February 1844 (the concert at which the *Roman Carnival* overture had its première). It was not performed – the chosen singer was indisposed – but there are indications in the choral and orchestral material of the *Damnation* that the piece was revised for the occasion. The score of the *Eight Scenes* was on his desk again – that much is clear. But the final, crucial step – the formal act of commitment, the decision to write the work whatever the consequences – was surely taken at Königswinter. In the previous two years he had composed a fair amount of music but nothing of any great extent: he was too conscious of the arguments against doing so. Once written such a work would want to be performed and would therefore have to be copied, an outlay which in the current climate of Paris he could easily not recoup. I have no doubt that he mentioned both the project and the serious objections to Liszt, during or just after the festival, and that Liszt (to whom the work was subsequently dedicated) told him he must go ahead and write it all the same. The solitary communings at Königswinter did the rest. Though the opening number, Faust's "Le vieil hiver", was written down a couple of months later, in an inn on the Bavarian frontier, I see its conception as the immediate consequence of the decision reached in the numinous tranquillity of his rural retreat. It is, at the least, symbolic that the "pastoral symphony" with which the work begins should have more than a touch of Beethoven, in the melody's serene stepwise ascent to the keynote followed by its characteristic falling sixth (reminiscent of the opening of Beethoven's *An die ferne Geliebte*), as well as in the pantheistic nature-worship of the statement in F major on full orchestra.

The decision must have seemed, in retrospect, inevitable. Once it was taken, the music forced itself out of him with an urgency and certainty and a disregard of convenience or physical circumstance that surprised Berlioz himself, used as he was to rapid composition. He wrote the score, he said, "with an ease such as I have very rarely experienced".

By late August, after spending a few days sampling the summer festivals in Cologne, Coblenz and Stolzenfelds, and then pausing briefly at Frankfurt, he was in Paris. Presumably he was in touch soon afterwards with his librettist, Almire Gandonnière, for in a letter of 3 October he speaks of their "business" having "begun well" – they should only "reduce the length of the recitatives" as much as they can – and asks him to look in one morning around eleven or twelve when he is in Paris so that they can discuss it: Gandonnière lived in Montmartre.

It is possible that Berlioz asked one of his more eminent literary friends before settling on this relatively obscure journalist. Gandonnière had written pieces for Villemessant's periodical, the *Sylphide*, to which Berlioz contributed occasionally. Until a few months before, he had been editor of the *Chronique* but the review had closed down. Gandonnière's friendship with Gérard de Nerval may have suggested the idea of employing him on *The Damnation of Faust*: Nerval was by definition a co-author of the libretto, since the text of the *Eight Scenes*, which were being incorporated in the work, came from his celebrated translation of Goethe's *Faust*. Berlioz may actually have approached Nerval first and then turned to Gandonnière.

As it happened, it was not a bad choice. Following his usual practice he would have given him very precise instructions as to what he wanted done; Gandonnière's task was to versify a text drafted in detail. He performed it efficiently enough, so far as it went. Only, the impetus of the composition left him behind. When Berlioz took the coach from Paris, with Marie Recio, on 22 October, he had with him the text of much of the first two parts and the opening scene of the third. After that, at large in central Europe, with the musical ideas outrunning the words, he must perforce and at long last become his own librettist.

13

The Damnation of Faust

Berlioz's second tour of German-speaking lands reaped what the first had sown. This time he came as a sought-after guest. It was no longer a question of persuading the authorities to put their musical resources at his disposal: they wanted him; he had become a name. The cities of central Europe competed for the kudos of his presence. He visited only five – fewer than half the number before – but gave almost as many concerts, including six in Vienna (where he also took part in a seventh) and six in Prague. The stir he caused was that much greater than in 1843; only the Berlioz-fever of Brunswick was a foretaste of what he experienced now in Prague and Pesth and even in Vienna – Vienna where five years before (as Scudo had taken pleasure in reporting) an attempt to perform the *Francs-juges* overture ended in laughter. From the first, Vienna greeted him with open arms. The very customs officer who checked the baggage as he and Marie disembarked on 2 November from the Linz steamboat, several days later than expected, struck the proper note by exclaiming, in French: "Thank heavens you're here, M. Berlioz! What in the world can have happened to you? We've been waiting for the past week. All the papers said you had left Paris and were shortly to give concerts in Vienna. We were getting quite anxious about you." It wouldn't have happened in Paris.

Vienna, like Berlin, was a capital city dedicated to music. Within a few days of his arrival there he attended one of the annual concerts of the Gesellschaft der Musikfreunde, given in aid of the Vienna Conservatoire in the huge Riding School, and was astonished by the quality of the four-hundred-strong orchestra and chorus of six hundred, practically all of them amateurs and chosen by audition from the even greater number – half as many again – who applied. The same superiority was evident in professional music-making. Otto Nicolai's Kärntnerthor orchestra was simply the finest in Austro-Germany. Berlioz heard them in Beethoven's Fourth, a symphony by Nicolai and the great soprano scena from Weber's *Oberon* (superbly sung by Mme Barthe-Hasselt), and their "passionate fidelity, disciplined force and refinement of detail" moved him to declare "such an orchestra, directed like this, the highest achievement of modern art and the most complete manifestation of what we mean by music today". His own orchestra, the Theater an der Wien's, was not in that class, but it was young and keen and he had the satisfaction of training it over a period of two months. By the end of November, by which time he had given three concerts, it was "going like a lion".

Berlioz's concerts at the Theater an der Wien – directed, he was thrilled to hear, from the same rostrum on which Beethoven had stood, forty years before – were musical and social events of some magnitude. It became fashionable to wear Berlioz cameos as earrings and bracelets. Pies were named after him. He sat for two leading Viennese portraitists, Prinzhofer and Kriehuber, and their handsome lithographs were on display all over town. The Pilgrims' March, the March to the Scaffold and the Scene in the Fields were popular numbers, and the *Roman Carnival* overture was played continually, not only at all his concerts but at many others, including those of the two Strausses, father and son, and of their rival, Adams, and was invariably encored. "We should never have predicted," wrote a local critic, "that compositions so bold and so unlike what we are used to would have such immediate success." The fine playing at Berlioz's first three concerts had made the reputation of the new orchestra of the Theater an der Wien, "which till now had not created much of an impression. It is true that Berlioz's conducting, especially at the rehearsals, is as exact as it is uncompromising, and that all those young men, Austrians and Bohemians, are totally devoted to him". He had to extend his stay and put off going to Prague till January. In the meantime a further concert was planned for the end of December.

Two months later, when the Swiss composer Joseph Weigl, director of the imperial chapel, died, there was a move to appoint Berlioz in his place. It failed, not for lack of powerful backing but because he could not bear the thought of being permanently exiled from Paris. Meanwhile a banquet given on the eve of his forty-second birthday by a hundred and fifty musicians, music-lovers and men of letters raised his fame still higher. Kriehuber's portrait, set in a forest of flowers and greenery, dominated the room; and at the end of dinner Baron Lannoy, president of the Musikfreunde, presented him with a ceremonial silver-gilt baton engraved with the names of the forty principal subscribers and wound round with a sprig of silver laurel leaves on which were inscribed the titles of his works – a gift which Lannoy hoped would remind him "of the town where Gluck, Haydn, Mozart and Beethoven lived, and of the friends of music who join me in crying, 'Long live Berlioz!' " Berlioz's reply – "wonderful in style and language", Louis Engel recalled – was quoted only in very shortened form in the Viennese press report reproduced in the *Gazette* in Paris; but the report shows him associating Félicien David with the honour paid to him: it was "proof of fraternity between the artists of Vienna and those of Paris, whom Félicien David, here with us today, and I are both doing our best to represent among you".

David had arrived in Vienna not long after Berlioz. He was touring Europe with *Le désert* and other works, partly with the object of raising support for le Père Enfantin's project for a Suez canal; but to Marie Recio his presence was an affront to Berlioz, as she wrote to Desmarest in Paris:

I am adding these few lines without saying anything to Hector, but I want you to know how David has behaved by way of thanking him. When he was still in Munich he was written to twice and advised not to come so long as Berlioz was giving concerts here. His answer was that "he was very sorry but he had no time to wait and would come all the same". However, when he got here it seems that everybody told him he was very much in the way, and he was urged to go to Pesth and Prague. He promptly arranged to give a concert in the same theatre, booking it for the first available day after Hector's second concert. Ever since then he's been doing all he can to tread in his footsteps. [. . .] I would never have expected such behaviour from David; but at this moment money is all he thinks of. Hector is being friendly towards him, but I, who do not have the same reasons, am only too glad that you should know about it and tell Morel and others of our friends, and I should be very happy if Morel published a few words on the subject. I dare say the Escudiers have made much of the success of *Le désert*, but I assure you it has been nothing of the sort, I expected it to do much better than it has. I wish you had been here a moment ago to witness Hector's success at Dreyshock's concert and the expression on David's face.* Can you believe

* 17 December 1845. Berlioz conducted the *Roman Carnival* overture, *Le jeune pâtre breton*, and *Zaïde*. The overture, brilliantly played by the Kärntnerthor orchestra,

it, he's been to see us only once, and then only because a gentleman we know pointed out that it was rude not to, when Hector had visited him on several occasions when he was ill. I have to say it, gratitude is a rare thing.

Marie Recio was now the official consort, signing herself "Marie Berlioz", introduced everywhere as the composer's wife and, increasingly, manager, throwing herself into the role with meddling alacrity, yet accepted as a necessary inconvenience who in the end was powerless to dim the éclat of Berlioz's personality. His charisma, his confidence, conquered almost everyone. There were hostile critics, of course; and there were frivolous music-lovers, as elsewhere. (Joseph Fischoff reported in the *Musical World* a couple of years later that some Viennese were saying Mendelssohn's *Elijah* would be acceptable "if cut by two thirds". "We have thus before us the legitimate descendants of that accursed race whose forefathers hissed the *Don Giovanni* and scoffed at *Fidelio*.") But even when it found against him, discussion was generally conducted in a civilized tone. His impact was incontestable; he was, said the critic of the *Theaterzeitung*, "a sort of spiritual yeast which sets all minds in fermentation". Others welcomed his advent unreservedly.

Berlioz basked in the warmth of his reception. The Prinzhofer portrait shows him at his most serenely commanding. Though the elegant rings and jewel-topped cane invented by the artist drew from him the protesting inscription, "H. Berlioz *non dandy*", there is no mistaking the well-being of the sitter. (He himself thought it and its companion picture, with hand thrust Napoleonically in waistcoat, the best likenesses that had yet been made.) He was enjoying himself, revelling in the riches of Vienna's musical life, the fine singers to be heard there, Staudigl, Barthe-Hasselt, and Pischek, whose musicianship he admired as much as his "incomparable voice and thrilling vehemence" ("Don Juan, Romeo and Cortez rolled into one"), the brilliant violinists, young Joachim among them, and the high quality of the music-making at the imperial chapel; returning again and again to the winter balls given in the Redoutensaal, at which the youth of Vienna were raising ballroom dancing to an art and Strauss's syncopations were teaching Europe the

---

brought the house down, and made up for a funereal performance by four pianists which he had had to endure at a soirée given shortly before by the music publisher Haslinger.

meaning of rhythm; using the notoriety of his name to ignore protocol and call unannounced on Metternich (who questioned him about his music, "of which it seemed His Highness, without having heard any of it, had formed a rather strange impression, whereupon I endeavoured to give him a different one"); and tasting a popularity that could only do him good. In Vienna, that December, he had everything he lacked in his home town: a public curious to hear his music, a musical establishment attentive and cooperative, a general belief in the importance of what he was doing, material success, favourable conditions in which to prepare the performance of a major work, *Romeo and Juliet* (which he had not been able to give in its entirety since the premières six years before) and, in between, the leisure and peace of mind to compose.

The first sustained work on *The Damnation of Faust* dates from these weeks in Vienna, in the suburb of Fischofstadt where he and Marie were staying. Here it was that he revised, quite radically, the existing choral movement by the banks of the Elbe, expanded its final D major chord into the Dance of the Sylphs, and drafted – I don't doubt with Pischek's voice and personality in mind – Mephistopheles' lullaby, "Voici des roses", making of the scene a double theme-and-variations in which variations and themes were fused into a single whole and no one could tell from the score which came first.

Romeo was got ready with unhurried thoroughness during the last fortnight of December. There were daily chorus rehearsals and five orchestral sessions, not counting sectionals, and much painful wrestling with Queen Mab. When the time came – or perhaps he had always intended it – Berlioz stepped down, handed the performance to the Theater an der Wien's concert-master, Groidl, and heard the symphony from the audience. Whether or not it lost something in consequence – it could hardly have failed to – he took advantage of the experience to sit in judgement on the work and assess it in detail and as a whole. Over the next few weeks he carried out a wholesale revision. The end of the scherzo was shortened and made more telling: Mab now really vanished "into thin air". The succeeding second prologue was removed altogether, and the first prologue altered so as to include the thematic anticipations which, in the final version, prepare the listener for the two instrumental movements that follow. Cuts were made in the finale, both in the friar's narrative and in the culminating oath of reconciliation. And the sixth movement, the Tomb Scene, was sacrificed – surely to the composer's regret, for he retained it in the full score published not long afterwards; but so many people agreed with d'Ortigue in finding it baffling that he decided for the moment to set it aside; the Vienna performance of 2 January 1846 seems to have been the last associated with Berlioz that included this controversial but, once known, indispensable movement.

Despite the warm applause for the composer and for his Friar Laurence, Staudigl, *Romeo* did not enjoy the popular and critical success of the three earlier concerts: the work bewildered as much as it pleased. None the less a fifth concert was demanded and given two Sundays later, on 11 January, this time in the Redoutensaal, including the inevitable *Roman Carnival*, *Harold* with Ernst as soloist, the Love Scene and Queen Mab, and a ballad by Esser sung by Pischek. Berlioz was also contracted to return from Bohemia for a sixth and final concert, in aid of the Empress' hospitals fund, at the beginning of February.

Vienna's accolades, splendid as they had been, were surpassed by those of Prague – "the city", he later wrote, "that was most passionate about my music". He had been in two minds about going there, his Viennese friends assuring him that it was a hotbed of antiquarians, buried in the past, living on its reputation as the city which "understood Mozart", and impervious to anything new. So till lately it had been; but a new spirit was stirring. The crucial event was the appointment, a couple of years before, of a young director of the Prague Conservatoire, Johann Friedrich Kittl. His predecessor had admitted nothing more recent than early Beethoven. Kittl changed all that. He dragged the repertoire into the modern era, introducing Beethoven's later works and music by Schumann, Mendelssohn, Hiller and even Berlioz, whose *King Lear* overture he conducted in March 1845 before a half-horrified, half-fascinated audience. Kittl's modernizing campaign was supported by a band of radical young musicians and writers who modelled themselves on the "Davidsbündler", Schumann's League against the Philistines. As one of them, Eduard Hanslick, put it, Schumann's articles in the *Neue Zeitschrift* were their Bible. Berlioz became a symbol for the group, a fabulous creature whom they longed to see and hear in person. They pounded Liszt's transcription of the Fantastic on their pianos and steeped themselves in Griepenkerl's pamphlet, Lobe's open letter in the *Neue Zeitschrift* and anything else that gave information about this extraordinary figure, "a Frenchman" (in Hanslick's words) "who wrote symphonies and whose gods were Beethoven and Shakespeare!" In the spring of 1843 he had been reported in nearby Dresden and they waited breathlessly; but he did not come. Now, two and a half years later, he was in Vienna. This time he came, and took Prague by storm.

The timing could not have been better. Kittl's reforms were gathering pace. The *King Lear* performance the previous March generated a vigorous controversy in the local press in which the nature and propriety of Berlioz's music were treated in the wider context of the then central issue of "pure" music versus tone painting. The level of debate was high; even those like Bernard Gutt, editor of *Bohemia*, who deplored what he was doing, wrote responsibly about it. On their side his partisans, by their praise, prepared the ground. Berlioz was a public figure before he set foot in Prague. It was a long and enthusiastic article by the Prague lawyer and musicologist August Wilhelm Ambros that made him think again and, after corresponding with the writer and with a senior Conservatoire official, Count Nostitz, arrange to come there as soon as his Viennese commitments allowed. This was exactly what Ambros and the Davidsbündler had planned.

The railway line to Prague had been completed a few weeks before; and on 13 January, having dispatched scores and parts by mail coach, Berlioz, with Marie, left Vienna from the Kaiser Ferdinands Nordbahnhof at Praterstern. The scheduled time for the three hundred miles of the circuitous route was fifteen hours; but halfway through the journey they found that flooding had made part of the track impassable, and the passengers had to debouch and make a long detour by road to the point where the line resumed, and there wait two hours for the next train. For Berlioz the delay was beguiled by an encounter with an itinerant musician, a Styrian harpist whom he caught sight of in the station waiting-room staring intently at him and, while he did so, picking out the first few bars of the Queen Mab theme on his harp. It transpired that the man had witnessed a heated argument about him in a Viennese café and had vowed that if he made enough money next day from his playing he would buy a ticket for the coming concert – which he did, and thus found himself an intrigued if puzzled listener to *Romeo and Juliet*, whose scherzo – "what a queer piece" ("quel drôle de morceau") – he could not get out of his head. Their conversation over lunch in the buffet (described in the *Gazette* and subsequently in *Evenings in the Orchestra*) whiled away the two hours' wait very pleasantly. His last sight of his friend, glimpsed from the window of the compartment as the train gathered speed, was of the man leaning on his harp, his left hand plucking the motif while his lips mouthed the words "quel drôle de morceau" just as Berlioz was murmuring "quel drôle d'homme".

The travellers were in Prague by the afternoon of the 14th. Dr Ambros came to the station to meet them and installed them in comfortable rooms at the Blue Star Hotel (Zum blauen Stern) in the Old Town, across the square from the Pulverthum. Hanslick was enrolled as interpreter; and, next day, work began. They assembled an orchestra of eighty, made up of the two dozen resident players of the nearby Estates Theatre, plus a large contingent chosen from among the students and professors of the Conservatoire, a few good amateurs, and some bandsmen from the local barracks. Every day, called for at his hotel by Ambros and Kittl, with Hanslick in attendance, and escorted by them to the hall, Berlioz rehearsed his forces for anything up to four hours at a time, while the Conservatoire students not playing in the orchestra came in a body, a hundred strong, to absorb his music and study his style of conducting.

Time was also made for some serious sightseeing, including a climb up Hradčany to admire the churches and battlements and the magnificent view from the top of the hill, across the Vltava (Moldau), to the towers and palaces of the Old Town. And one morning he was prevailed on to pay a call on the grand old man of Czech music, Tomaschek, a visit to whom was de rigueur for all foreign musicians. Hanslick, as a former Tomaschek pupil, was deputed to accompany him, and years later recalled "as if it were yesterday" their crossing, "on a bright wintry morning, the Moldau bridge beyond which lived the great Figured Bass himself".

Just as we neared the contrapuntal residence, Berlioz with charming insouciance revealed that he had never heard of him, let alone knowing any of his works. I had almost no time to bring my companion up to date on the missing chapter of music history, "Tomaschek". So as not to confuse him with too many different titles, I laid stress on one work which Tomaschek set particular store by, a requiem (actually a fine composition). We entered, and there followed the kind of half-comical, half-painful scene known as Interpreting. The haphazard, piecemeal exchange of banal yet not readily translatable phrases was made no easier by the natural tension between the revolutionary artist and the arch-conservative. Fortunately Berlioz remembered his cue and said how gratified he was to meet the composer of "that splendid Requiem". The old man, who was inclined to be crusty from living so much on his own, accepted this homage with a slight movement of the head and the announcement that he would like to attend Berlioz's next concert.

On the way back, Hanslick adds, " 'Il a l'air bien enchanté de lui-même' was all the comment that Berlioz, after a moment's reflection, would make on his new acquaintance."

"Tomaschek has spoken," wrote Berlioz to Wesque von Puttlingen a few days later: "one third for, two thirds against. He says that I am not completely mad but not far off it." But it did not matter. Musical Prague had gone mad too; they were treating him "like a Grand Lama, a Fetish, a Manitou". At the first concert, given on 19 January in the hall of the Sophieninsel, the wooded island upstream from the Charles Bridge, three pieces were encored, and at the second concert, the following Sunday, five: the *Roman Carnival* overture, Pilgrims' March, March to the Scaffold, and Ball Scene and Scherzo from *Romeo and Juliet*. Several critics testified to the extraordinary attentiveness and responsiveness of the packed houses. Hanslick spoke of the "total absorption and stillness during the playing". "We expected a partly bewildered, partly scandalized audience," wrote another. "Instead, people listened to the music with an almost breathless concentration and at the end of every piece the applause was like thunder." From what they had read beforehand in certain journals, said the same critic, they "expected to find in Berlioz's music a mixture of contrived *coups de théâtre* and tiresome distractions, an incomprehensible jumble of sounds interspersed with occasional lucid passages. Instead, one musical glory after another soared before us in luminous magnificence."

Ambros and his friends had worked hard for this result, filling the press with news of his doings for weeks before his arrival in Prague. Even so, the scale and intensity of it took them by surprise. No one, wrote an English critic, J. Lander (whose notice was reproduced in the Paris *Gazette*), could have predicted that the Bohemian public, "attached as it is to the old masters", would react in such a way to the "innovations and audacities of this musical revolutionary". The second concert, said Lander, was "a triumph without precedent in Prague". Berlioz's success was "spontaneous, general and, if I may use the word, more violent even than in Vienna".

The Praguers had no objection to coming back to hear the same pieces: they could not have enough of them. There was another capacity audience for the concert which Berlioz, postponing his return to Vienna, was persuaded to give two evenings after the second, this time at the Estates Theatre (where *Don Giovanni* had its première). The long programme was a recapitulation of the other two: *Roman Carnival*, the two songs *Zaïde* and *Le chasseur danois*, the Pilgrims' March, the first four movements of the Fantastic, the three central orchestral numbers from *Romeo*.

Berlioz fever was not confined to the musically sophisticated and the fashionable. All classes in this amazingly musical society, working men, peasants from the surrounding countryside included, were caught up in it. And with it went a loftiness of discussion in the press which must have gladdened his heart. How gratifying to find at last a critic pointing out, as Hanslick did in his review of the first concert in *Ost und West*, that the reviewer must "*examine* the work before he passes judgement on it", and answering the accusation of "lack of melody" by demanding in what way the themes of the Pilgrims' March and the *Roman Carnival* were not melodies, or "that pale, wonderful theme of the Symphonie fantastique". Berlioz's themes had "something astringent about them, something out of the common run"; yet they were "noble, pure and of the loftiest spiritual expression". Only, he disdained to advertise them, to "post in front of every theme a diminished seventh chord or the dominant cadence with fermatas, as guard of honour, or to dispatch a few staccato chords or arpeggiated triads two beats ahead as outriders". "I beseech you," Hanslick continued, "study Berlioz's scores, and you will see that there is in them, along with the spontaneity, an admirable intellectual coherence and, along with all the passion, a solid, orderly design at the core." Even Gutt expressed regret at not being able to comprehend the music. Notwithstanding his own negative reviews, he gave space in the journal for several eulogistic articles, and at the end of Berlioz's stay concluded that "Prague will hold him in affectionate memory, as he will Prague." As for Hanslick, the city's rapturous response – he said – was proof that its reputation was no idle legend. "Praguers, you rightly boast that Mozart recognized your musical insight. You are no less entitled to boast that you recognized Berlioz's genius!" Berlioz was simply "the sublimest manifestation in the realm of musical poetry since Beethoven".

Within a year Hanslick, under the influence of none other than Gutt, would have shifted his ground dramatically, repudiated his enthusiasm for the works of both Berlioz and Wagner, and taken up the entrenched position with which he was ever after associated: that musical sounds express nothing beyond themselves. "Though still responsive to the greatness and boldness of [Berlioz's] conceptions," wrote Hanslick, by then half a century older and wiser, "and to individual passages of the highest beauty in his music, yet over the years I have moved a long way from the boundless admiration of that youthful time in Prague." In the winter and early spring of 1846 he was still in thrall to the music and to the man. "Our enthusiasm for Berlioz's music," he later recalled, "was reinforced and intensified by our personal contact with him and the impression his noble and attractive personality made on us. [. . .] In his art – make of it now what we will – there was a shining integrity. All self-seeking and smallness of mind was foreign to this man with the head of a Jupiter."

To Hanslick's reminiscences we also owe some precious glimpses of Marie – even if Hanslick exaggerated the "impracticality" of Berlioz, who had, after all, been organizing concerts quite competently for years before she came on the scene.

Berlioz arrived in the company of a beautiful fiery-eyed Spanish lady, Mariquita Rezio [sic]. He passed her off as his wife; it was therefore understandable that we took her for the famous former actress Miss Smithson, well known and dear to us from Heine's reports. But when Ambros, at our first encounter, expressed his delight at seeing next to Berlioz the original of the Fantastic Symphony's "double idée fixe", he was met with a glare and the reply, "This is my second wife. Miss Smithson is dead." In fact his wife was still alive, and continued to live for quite a time while Berlioz and his beautiful Spaniard travelled through Germany and Austria. The man with the lion's mane and the commanding eagle glance was helpless beneath the slippered heel of the señora. With all our deep respect for Berlioz, it verged on the comical when with an imperious toss of the head she commanded him, "Hector, my cape, Hector, my gloves!"; at which Hector, submissive as a bashful suitor, would hasten to lay the cape on her shoulders and hand her her gloves.

Hanslick, however, considered that her thrifty way with money was "extremely useful to her impractical Hector". She would take her pen to the estimates for his concerts and afterwards check the accounts, "inexorably beating down the cost of cymbals or triangle", and in this sense if in not many others he thought her justified in her boast, whispered to him "after the painstaking settlement of some account or other, 'It's lucky for Hector that I am his wife'"; for "without his dark-eyed finance minister, 'Hector', ingenuous and open-handed as a crown prince", would have been a lot worse off. He might have been; but two years later, when planning a visit to Prague, he was emphatic that "this time I shall go *alone*".

Berlioz, with Marie, made arrangements to return to Vienna in time to prepare one final concert ("assuming the carriages don't jump the rails") before moving on to Pesth, Breslau and Brunswick. But his renewed triumph at the third Prague concert on 27 January made it clear to all that he must come back for another visit before he left Austria: as one of the Prague Conservatoire professors, Gordigiani, put it in a letter to Marie, they had to see him again soon, "to quench the longing he has left behind in the hearts of all musicians; for his music has awoken passions and stirred excitements till now unknown to poor mortals". Accordingly, while in Vienna, Berlioz sent detailed instructions to Kittl and Ambros for two further concerts in March, one of them to consist of the complete and newly revised *Romeo and Juliet*, of which Prague had so far heard only three movements.

On 1 February, in the Vienna Redoutensaal, he conducted his ardent young orchestra for the last time, and afterwards bade an emotional farewell, thanking them in Italian, which the concert-master Groidl translated sentence by sentence into German. The Emperor sent a servant with the gift of a hundred ducats, together with the curiously phrased message, "Tell Berlioz I found it most entertaining." It may have been during this visit that Kriehuber made the celebrated drawing of Liszt seated at the piano before the score of a Beethoven sonata, eyes turned transcendently upward while Ernst, violin in hand, sits on his right and Kriehuber himself on his left and Berlioz and Czerny stand beside the piano gazing at him.

A few days after the final concert the travellers left Vienna for Pesth. It was an expedition into unknown territory. Different as Vienna and Prague were from each other – Vienna altogether grander and more elegant and, since well before the days of Mozart, looking down on its provincial rival – they had close links and, for a musician, many features in common. But Hungary was a land apart. The very journey there was a step back into a wilder, more primitive age; for, the Danube being wrapped in dense fog ("like Homer's gods when dirty work is afoot"), the steamboat service was suspended and the heavy four-wheeler to which the passengers were transferred ploughed laboriously through mud and floodwater, several times nearly depositing them in the river.

When he eventually reached Pesth he found a city seething with nationalist fervour and discontent – "devoted to the Austrian Empire", he wrote in the *Débats*, "much as Ireland is devoted to England, or Poland to Russia, or Algeria to France". The strength of anti-Austrian feeling was borne in on him repeatedly during the fortnight he spent in the Hungarian capital. It was apparent from the start in the regulation he came up against which prohibited the employment at the National Theatre not only of the German language but of musicians from the German Theatre. The National, where the concerts were being held, had far too few strings for his purpose. Fortunately one of his Viennese friends, the publisher Heinrich Müller, had given him a letter of introduction to the violinist Treichlinger, who recruited extra players from the Pesth Philharmonic, and an adequate orchestra was assembled. Several numbers were encored at the first concert, given on Sunday morning 15 February and including the *Roman Carnival* and movements from the first two symphonies; but one piece dominated the concert and the second given five days later, and Berlioz's whole visit to Pesth: the march based on the old Hungarian air known as Rákóczy. He had drafted it the night before he left Vienna, after the intendant of the National Theatre, Count Ráday, who was in Vienna, advised him, "if he wanted the Hungarians to like him", to "write a piece on one of their national tunes", and lent him a collection of them to choose from. The March was completed and scored as soon as Berlioz reached Pesth, and immediately given to be copied. Six years earlier when Liszt played his arrangement of the melody as an encore at a concert in Pressburg it brought the house down – the tune was banned at the time – and the secret police reported the incident to Vienna. Yet, rousing as Berlioz's *Marche hongroise* is, I doubt if he was quite prepared for the sensation it caused and the deep vein of patriotic sentiment it touched. It was like a spring released. His surprise is still evident in the account written the following year:

> No sooner had the announcement of a new piece of *hony* [national] music gone up all over Pesth than the national imagination began to seethe. People speculated as to how I had treated the famous, nay the sacred melody which for so long had set the hearts of Hungarians aflame with a holy passion for glory and liberty. There was even some anxiety about it, a fear of profanation – an attitude which, far from being

offended by, I respected. [. . .] At length one of them, a M. Horváth, editor of a Hungarian newspaper, unable to contain his curiosity, called on the publisher who was dealing with the arrangements for my concert, found out from him the address of the copyist responsible for making the orchestral parts, went straight there, asked to see the manuscript, and examined it attentively. He was not reassured by this inspection, and next day could not disguise his apprehensiveness.

"I have seen your score of the Rákóczy March," he said uneasily.

"Well?"

"Well – I'm nervous."

"Nonsense!"

"You state the theme piano. We, on the contrary, are accustomed to hearing it played fortissimo."

"Yes, by the gipsies. In any case, is that all? Don't worry, you shall have such a forte as you never heard in your life. You haven't read it properly. One must always consider the *end*."

All the same, on the day of the concert I felt a tightening in my throat when the moment came for this devil of a piece to be performed. After a trumpet fanfare based on the rhythm of the opening bars, the theme, you will recall, is announced piano by flutes and clarinets accompanied by pizzicato strings. During this unexpected exposition the audience remained calm and silent. But when a long crescendo ensued, with fragments of the theme reintroduced fugally, broken by the dull thud of the bass drum, like the thump of distant cannon, the whole place began to hum with excitement; and, as the orchestra unleashed its full fury and the long-delayed fortissimo burst forth, a tumult of shouting and stamping convulsed the theatre: the accumulated pressure of that boiling mass of emotion exploded with a violence that sent a thrill of fear through me; I felt as if my hair were standing on end. From that fatal bar I had to give up all thought of my peroration. The thunders of the orchestra were powerless against that erupting volcano; nothing could stop it. We had to repeat the piece, of course. The second time, the audience could scarcely restrain itself a few seconds longer to hear a bar or two of the coda. Horváth in his box was throwing himself about like a man possessed. I could not help laughing as I shot him a glance, as if to say, "Well – are you still nervous, or are you satisfied with your forte?" It was a good thing I had placed "Rákóczy-induló" (the Hungarian title of the work) last in the programme: anything we had tried to play after that would have been lost.

These stirring events [. . .] had a curious sequel. I was mopping my
face in a little room behind the stage when a shabbily dressed man entered
without warning, his face glistening and working strangely. On seeing
me he fell on my neck and, embracing me passionately, his eyes filling with
tears, barely managed to stammer out: "Ah, monsieur – me Hungarian –
sorry fellow – no speak French – *un poco italiano* – forgive – my ecstasy
– ah! understand your cannon – yes – big battle – German dogs – I keep
you" (striking his chest emphatically) "in heart of me – ah! Frenchman
– republican – know to make music of revolution!"

Berlioz had to donate the manuscript to the city of Pesth, making do
with a copy, in which he revised and lengthened the piece by about
thirty bars soon afterwards. The original lacked the extended coda
which, when Bernard Shaw heard it played under Hans Richter at the
right steady tempo, made him feel that "if it were to last another minute
I must charge out and capture Trafalgar Square single-handed"; but
with its proud, high-stepping treatment of the theme in the opening
bars (whose piano marking misled Horváth), its royal trombones, and
the sizzling violin tremolo which runs like a lighted fuse towards the
explosion, it was still music to uplift the Hungarian spirit. For the rest
of his stay he was fêted like a national hero. Though prices were raised
for the second concert, given on 20 February, the theatre sold out. The
German-language papers were inclined to be critical but the Hungarian
ones were ecstatic. *Honderü* hailed him as one of the greatest of living
composers.

The tide of national feeling was rising fast. He saw it on all sides: at
the balls, given with unexampled luxury and brilliance by the Hungarian
nobility, at which native Magyar dress was worn and the csárdás reigned
supreme; at the National Theatre where Ferenc Erkel's *Hunyady*, an
opera on a heroic episode from the country's past, was the hit of the
season; and at a political banquet where toasts and speeches and gipsy
music and the fiery wines of Hungary "combined to rouse the company
to a yet higher pitch of revolutionary fervour". The well-known orator
Déak, who spoke at the dinner, still counselled gradualism and constitutional change (while a neighbour of Berlioz's growled, "Fabius cunct-
ator!"). It did not look as if he would be able to hold back his troops
much longer.

In the last week of February Berlioz and Marie returned to Vienna,
this time by steamboat up a now peaceable Danube, and after a few

days set out by coach to Breslau, two hundred miles to the north. The original plan had been to give three concerts there; but after Prague and Pesth he found the musical atmosphere of the Silesian capital cold and uninspiring. One or two of the older musicians warned him that he would not cover his expenses – the inhabitants of Breslau were not interested in music; and the apathy of the audience at a concert he attended soon after his arrival was distinctly unencouraging. Beethoven's Fifth Symphony was received in total silence and there was no applause at the end – out of "respect", he was told. He was mortally afraid of being respected too. In fact the single concert he gave there, on 20 March in the hall of the university, was a success, financially as well as artistically. In its more formal way the town did him proud. The concert at which, on 14 March, he heard for the first time Mendelssohn's complete *Midsummer Night's Dream* music (it impressed him profoundly) was put on by the kapellmeister expressly "in honour of M. le chevalier Berlioz of Paris", and at his own concert he was applauded quite disrespectfully.

The reason for his uncharacteristic aloofness in Breslau – for once he delegated many of the preliminaries to others – was, more than anything, *The Damnation of Faust*. "It is preoccupying me to the point of my almost forgetting the concert I am preparing here – or rather that is being prepared for me," he wrote to d'Ortigue on 13 March. He was composing, or sketching, in every spare moment. Even in the hectic days at Pesth it had insisted on his attention; one night when he was trying to find his way back to the hotel, perhaps after attending one of the Hungarian balls he speaks of, he stopped under the light of a shop's gas jet to note down the presto 2/4 refrain of the Peasants' Dance. He worked at the score on the Danube steamer on the return to Vienna, and on the slower journey from Vienna to Breslau. By then he had set all that existed of Gandonnière's verses, and knew he would have to dispense with his help for the rest of the text if the impetus was not to be lost. It was in the Breslau coach that he wrote the words for Faust's invocation, "Nature immense, impénétrable et fière", and realized that he could do it. The music of the invocation was presumably sketched soon afterwards in Breslau, on the two sheets of manuscript paper (later used on the blank side for revisions to the Serenade in *Harold* and pasted into the autograph score of the symphony) which show his creative imagination at work as step by step the form and the tonal structure of the piece took shape. In Breslau too he noted down the students' Latin song, "Jam nox stellata", and probably sketched other scenes: for the same letter to d'Ortigue speaks of his working at the score "avec fureur".

Whether he was able to continue during the next three and a half weeks in Prague is doubtful (though at least one idea dates from then – the melody of Marguerite's apotheosis, "Remonte au ciel, âme naïve, que l'amour égara", which he got up in the middle of the night to put on paper while it was fresh in his mind). Berlioz was welcomed back to Prague with the old fervour when he reappeared in the city on 25 March. Ambros had made sure public interest was kept alive during the two months' absence; the newspapers had been full of the composer's triumph in Pesth and his impending return. The two concerts originally planned became three, an extra one being added on 7 April, in aid of Mount Carmel monastery in Jerusalem, while *Romeo and Juliet* was still in preparation. On 31 March, in the Estates Theatre, the Fantastic Symphony was given complete, the finale included, for the first time on the whole tour. Berlioz's reasons for omitting it hitherto seem to have been purely practical; good as the Austrian and Bohemian orchestras were, he doubted if they could perform it with the *diable au corps* it required and which only his Paris orchestra, that "Young Guard of the Grande Armée", was fully equal to. In the event the Prague performance did not entirely dispose of his fears, to judge by the letter he wrote after the concert to Hanslick in Vienna. Hanslick had passed up the chance of getting to know the movement in favour of a trip to the imperial capital. He took with him a letter of introduction from Berlioz to Liszt: "M. Hanslick, who will be delivering this note, is a charming young man, full of enthusiasm for the great things of music, and writing about it as one writes when one has soul, heart and intelligence." A week later Hanslick received a note from Prague: "Henri IV wrote, 'Hang yourself, Crillon: we were victorious at Arques and you were not there.' Our Witches' Sabbath was performed last Tuesday. However, I don't invite you to hang yourself, for it can go a lot better. Warmest regards, and come back to us soon." A letter from Berlioz to Griepenkerl, asking for the Brunswick concert to be postponed a few days, and for two trombones capable of playing the pedal notes in the March to the Scaffold, also mentions the "extreme feebleness" of the four Prague timpanists which spoiled the end of the Scène aux champs. But the audience encored the Ball Scene and the March and tried to encore the *Roman Carnival*. Prague had not wearied of Berlioz and his music. The

Fantastic in particular (he told d'Ortigue) had passed into the popular language. People were even singing the tunes in the street, and using them as a kind of musical argot: you hummed the *idée fixe* melody when you met a woman you thought charming; the debased version of the theme in the Witches' Sabbath meant that she looked vulgar and bold; the oboe solo near the end of the first movement signified feeling sad and anxious. After the concert of 7 April a review in *Ost und West*, signed "M" (possibly the poet Alfred Meissner), again compared Berlioz to Beethoven and declared that he was not a French Romantic but a universal genius in the lineage of Shakespeare, Goethe and Schiller. "If he belongs to any people, he belongs to Germany, the land of serious spirits, those whose weapon is the mind; it should claim him as its son."

The performance of *Romeo and Juliet* on the 17th was the crowning triumph of the second visit to Prague. Vienna's reservations were largely superseded. If one or two critics retained doubts (Gutt especially), the audience seemingly had none; the applause, said the anonymous review in *Ost und West*, was tumultuous and prolonged even by the standards of the Praguers' response to Berlioz's music; the composer had to take several bows after each movement. The reviewer had gone to the concert with misgivings, expecting some kind of bizarre hybrid, only to find his preconceptions "totally overcome: we have to acknowledge it as altogether a well-organized masterpiece". That the Viennese critics had failed to rise to the challenge of the work was an added satisfaction. "From now on we shall not pay the slightest attention to critical pronouncements from Vienna."

Berlioz seems to have been really pleased with the performance. He had a superb Friar Laurence, Strakaty, and the choral parts of the work had never been so well sung as they were by the amateurs of the Prague Choral Society, impeccably trained by their director J. N. Skroup. The sole mishap occurred when the contralto, Mlle Rzepka, an inexperienced singer with a splendid voice whom he had picked out at an audition in the Sophiensaal in January, went so flat on the unaccompanied "Le jeune Roméo, plaignant sa destinée" that the ensuing E major chord on the harp (played by the brilliant young harpist Anna Claudius) "hissed and shuddered like a spoonful of molten lead in cold water". But the singer recovered her nerve and her sense of pitch in time for the Strophes. All in all, he felt, the concert was one of the most satisfying of his career.

It was made more memorable still by the presence of Liszt, who had arrived in Prague from Vienna, via Brno, the previous week. Liszt had not yet heard a note of *Romeo*, and it was a joy to see him, at the final rehearsal, "frequently astonished and moved by it". At the rehearsal, and after the concert when a delegation from the choir came to thank the composer for the pleasure he had given them, Liszt acted as interpreter – Berlioz's knowledge of foreign languages, some English and Italian apart, being still that of a thorough Frenchman. As he wrote to Nancy, "the inhabitants show such delight at having me back and such a desire to hear me again that I find myself charmed even by the Bohemian language, of which I know not a word. I do have two or three words of Hungarian, though no more than that. As for German, I can say 'Yes! No! Once again, gentlemen, one, two, three, four, five, six, a pause, what the hell, all the timpani, one desk, more light, a package of music', and that is about it."

Liszt was chosen by acclamation to be the principal speaker at a grand supper, given for Berlioz in the Three Lindens Hotel after the final rehearsal on the 15th and attended by the musical community and the nobility of Prague. He presented the guest of honour with a silver-gilt chalice and, in what *Bohemia* called a "glowing testimonial address" punctuated by repeated cheers, praised his courageous and unwearying struggles against all obstacles and, heedless of the scorn of bigots and mediocrities, his pursuit and eventual attainment of his steadily perceived artistic goals. "The public for which Mozart wrote *Don Giovanni* could not fail to appreciate Berlioz." There were speeches by Kittl, Dreyschock, the brothers Skroup and the leading critics. Berlioz, in reply, drank a special health to the press which had treated him, he said, more kindly than he deserved, since he had rudely neglected to make the usual courtesy visits; but he meant by his impoliteness to pay them a compliment ("when this was translated for them they laughed uproariously"). He was made to promise he would return next year to perform *The Damnation of Faust*. "This splendid evening," *Bohemia* concluded, "demonstrated to Berlioz just how much Prague understands and loves and admires him." It ended with Liszt the worse for champagne and Berlioz and Belloni, in the street at two in the morning, urging him to wait till daylight before fighting a duel with a Bohemian who had drunk even more deeply.

Immediately after the concert Berlioz and Marie set out on the long train-cum-coach journey via Dresden, Leipzig and Berlin to Brunswick. (Marie again left a valuable article behind, this time a fur muff worth

400 francs.) It is possible that after Prague even his beloved Brunswick was an anticlimax; but the lost letter from Berlioz to Ambros, written while he was there, might tell us otherwise. Assuming that the Müllers had assembled the same orchestra as in 1843 (he had asked Griepenkerl to make sure they did), he may have had no reason to feel dissatisfied. The skill and zeal of his players were not in doubt; the only question was whether the postponement of the final Prague concert, from the 14th to the 17th, left enough time to rehearse a programme which included only one piece from the previous visit, the Pilgrims' March: the others – the Fantastic Symphony, Zaïde, Le chasseur danois and the Roman Carnival – were new to the orchestra. However, the planned date, 24 April, was kept to, so perhaps all was well.

In any case the true anticlimax was not Brunswick but Paris, which the travellers reached in late April or early May. Berlioz had felt his heart miss a beat at the thought of having to give it up for a post in Vienna; but he must have wondered why, now that he was back to the old demoralizing round: the feuilletons from which he had been blessedly immune the past six months, the positions that were always about to fall into his lap and never did, the haphazard, wastefully disorganized character of the whole musical scene, the enmity he faced for saying so and for being the composer he was, an enmity "all the greater since my German tour, the reports of which exacerbated it". At least he had no more illusions on that score; success abroad was not going to make any difference in Paris, except for the worse. Success at home was achieved laboriously and riskily, when it was achieved. In Paris he was obliged to make his way "like a red-hot cannon ball, hissing and smashing and burning". Yet he must continue to speak his mind, the more so as he had again seen what other countries could do.

A monster concert given at the end of July in aid of Baron Taylor's Association des Artistes Musiciens in the Hippodrome on the Place de l'Etoile – forty bands, under the baton of Tilmant, playing arrangements of Spontini, Auber, Rossini, Gluck and Handel, and his own Apotheosis – prompted the same melancholy reflections. The marches from Fernand Cortez gladdened his heart ("Spontini," he wrote in the Débats, "is the father of warlike music. Cortez would have had no need to burn his ships if such strains had summoned his soldiers to the conquest of Mexico"); but the concert was a fresh demonstration of the old eternal truths. "Open-air music is a delusion"; the massed sonority of eighteen hundred wind instruments dispersed to the four winds. The French, who fought the campaigns of the Revolution and the Empire and brought off the Trois Glorieuses, were powerless to build a concert hall. "We lack seriousness, weight, calm", qualities which made the adolescent superior to the child and the man to the youth. "We lack the ability to rise above petty passions, petty ideas, petty things", above the cult of malice. "We lack the belief, the unwavering belief, that the spirit that creates is superior to the spirit that destroys".

The lack of a hall was only one of many frustrations. Everything worthwhile was a gamble in Paris, won, if at all, in the face of official indifference or active discouragement. The performance of the Grande messe des morts which he conducted in St Eustache that August, at the request of Baron Taylor and his association and in memory of Gluck, was a success but could easily not have been. For it to happen at all, influence had first to be exerted in high places to induce the archbishop to sanction the participation of women in a religious ceremony. After that there were the opponents within the musical establishment to circumvent. We have no evidence that Habeneck made trouble this time (though he could have done – after all, the Requiem was his work), but Pillet did, scheduling an Opéra rehearsal for the same day as Berlioz's – "out of the kindness of his heart", as Léon Kreutzer wrote to d'Ortigue (away on holiday in his native Provence): "You can imagine the rage and despair of Berlioz. In the end we went in a body to see M. Pillet and got him to agree that another rehearsal which he had planned for the day before the performance would not take place and he would allow all his people to turn up." The association had money for only one rehearsal with orchestra. It was, said Kreutzer, "disastrous". "After such an awful rehearsal," Kreutzer continued, "you will be astonished to hear that on the day of the performance everything went perfectly. It was a great and practically unanimous success. As for me, I find this Requiem [he had been too young to hear it in 1837] a very fine thing, I put it a hundred times above the Symphony [?funèbre]. I find the music powerful, majestic and, though many people would stone me for saying so, profoundly logical. I was filled with enthusiasm! And I can only pity the unhappy man who is off shooting at ortolans (and I may add not killing any) when there was an unused pair of cymbals next to me which he could have been playing. I must tell you that I fulfilled my role in the orchestra very well. It was, as you know, on that daintiest of instruments, the tam-tam."

Once again Paris had shown that it had the resources (Berlioz never put on a performance of the complete Requiem anywhere else, even in Russia). Five hundred singers and players took part. But to mobilize such resources required an unremitting, exhausting struggle which could well come to nothing, or leave you penniless. Yet Paris, despite everything, was where he must still strive to establish himself. The potential of Paris remained unequalled. Paris, and not Prague (as *Ost und West* had reported), was where he would give the première of *The Damnation of Faust*, on which he was working every free hour he had.

There were any number of interruptions: newspaper articles (eight between the end of May and the end of July), a concert at the Théâtre-Italien in May in honour of the governor of Syria, Ibrahim Pasha, at which he conducted David's *Le désert* and his own arrangement of Léopold de Meyer's *Marche marocaine*, and the preparations for the Requiem at St Eustache. In the second half of June he went to Rouen to see Louis, who had recently taken his first communion. They dined together and Berlioz produced the presents he had bought for him in Prague and Paris. The headmaster gave the boy an excellent report; though not a quick learner he was a diligent pupil. His father, for the moment, was reassured.

The first half of June was dominated by a last-minute commission from the city of Lille – not to be refused despite the absurdly short notice – for a cantata celebrating the opening of the French section of the railway line from Paris (Gare du Nord) to Brussels. The *Chant des chemins de fer*, or *Railway Cantata*, cost him three nights' work. It has its stirring moments; but, though he published it later, I doubt if he would have been inconsolable if the theft of the score and all the performing material, which happened while he was receiving the compliments of the Ducs de Nemours and Montpensier in an adjoining room, had proved permanent. (The music was recovered, but not his hat, stolen at the same time.) To judge from his letters and from the account he wrote for the *Gazette* more than two years later, he rather enjoyed himself in Lille, and was reasonably pleased with the performance, especially with "the fresh-sounding voices such as we can never find for our choruses in Paris", not to mention the serenades – no fewer than four – that he was treated to outside his lodgings and the gold medal sent him by the mayor a few weeks later, inscribed "from the city of Lille to M. Berlioz". But the organization of the festival was chaotic, and the town council was rent by factions. There was nowhere for the throng of late arrivals to stay, thieves were everywhere (Janin, author of the cantata's text celebrating Peace and National Unity and the Workers, had his diamond-studded Turkish decoration stolen at the ball), a marquee caught fire, the supply of refreshing drink gave out and the crowds gasped in the blazing heat, and the salvo of cannon which the organizers insisted must follow the final chord of the Apotheosis – performed on the promenade by 150 bandsmen from neighbouring regiments under the composer – failed to ignite, the lighters having been left in the depot. At least this last débâcle spared Berlioz the inevitable mirth of the caricaturists; they had to make do with the disappearance of his hat. But it is understandable that his account of the occasion should find a home among *Les Grotesques de la musique*.

Nothing distracted him for long from his *Faust* score. He had returned from Germany with several scenes drafted, others sketched, the movements from 1828–9 revised and their place in the scheme of the work established, and the decision taken to include the Hungarian March (thus increasing the number of acts or parts from the projected three to four, the march becoming the finale of Part 1). Now, in springtime Paris, the composition flowed on. Just as, eighteen years before, he had read and reread Nerval's translation at all hours, wherever he happened to be, so now ideas flooded into his mind anywhere and everywhere as though by their own volition – in cafés, in the Tuileries Gardens, on a milestone in the Boulevard du Temple, on the Boulevard Poissonnière one warm Sunday when, on his way to call on Heine, he followed an infantry troop marching down the road and, lost in the music of his chorus of soldiers and students, was carried along by the crowd and found himself on a train bound for Enghien. Sometimes the music was worked out in preliminary sketches and then copied afresh. More often he composed straight on to full score, subsequently inking over and filling out the pencilled notation. He had never written more fluently.

The love duet and trio-finale of Part 3 were composed in late June, after the visit to Louis, during a stay of a few days at the Baron de Monville's château just north of Rouen. This was presumably one of the "four large pieces" referred to two months before, in mid-April, as being all that were needed to complete the work. Yet at the beginning of July it was "still far from being finished"; the last page of the autograph full score is dated 19 October, four and a half months later. If the inspiration for *The Damnation of Faust* came swiftly, almost unbidden, the work of mastering it, of shaping the multitudinous scenes and images and atmospheres into a coherent whole, was necessarily long drawn out. He had (in his own words) to "polish the different sections and join and fuse them together with all the tenacity and patience I am capable of, and complete the orchestration, which had only been roughly indicated here and there". It was not merely the piecemeal progress of the composition – Berlioz on tour, cut off from his librettist, writing the required verses as the musical ideas presented themselves – that involved so much subsequent organization, but the whole character of the work. Quite apart from incorporating the *Eight Scenes* (which, contrary to what commentators used to state, amount to at most a third of the score), he had to find a way of combining a mass of material as disparate as that of Goethe's superficially loose-knit drama from which it was taken. That was what he was doing all through the late summer and autumn. Every detail counted; every fleck of instrumental colour, every subliminal motivic reminiscence, mattered to the musical structure and the dramatic meaning. Legouvé describes listening to him expound *The Damnation of Faust* while the young Théodore Ritter played from the piano-vocal score, and realizing that for Berlioz "no thought was so hidden, no sensation so fleeting but that he would render it in the language of sound".

To take one example, the change in the key of Marguerite's "King of Thulé" ballad from G in the *Eight Scenes* to F was pregnant with significance for both meaning and structure; F is one of the two keys through which we see Mephistopheles manipulate his creatures (though Marguerite's soul escapes his grasp at the end, as Goethe's Part 1 hints that it will). In F the song's characteristic rising augmented fourth, previously G–C sharp, became the tritone F–B – the Middle Ages' forbidden interval, the *diabolus in musica*; B and F are the grim, lopsided pillars through which Mephisto makes his first, spectacular entrance and his final exit. Faust's "Heaven has won me back", cadencing in F, is followed by a rasping fortissimo in B as the devil materializes in a flash before him – a dramatic contrast of a kind beloved by the composer, but also fulfilling a symbolic and structural function. Similarly, the scene in Pandaemonium near the end of the work, having opened with a triumphant statement of the B–F tritone (hissing with tam-tam and cymbals), closes with the same flamboyant juxtaposition. Mephistopheles' summoning of the will o' the wisps, which comes straight after "The King of Thulé", begins with the two notes F and B before arriving at D major for the diabolical minuet which, together with Mephisto's serenade (transposed from the E of the *Eight Scenes* to B), will conjure

Marguerite into the arms of Faust. D, the key not only of the minuet but also of the scene on the banks of the Elbe, Faust's "Le vieil hiver", Brander's song and the Amen fugue, is the other tonality – midway between B and F – in which the devil's influence is felt, even when the music seems innocent of it.

Because it is so diverse a score, so concise in style, so sardonic in humour and dazzling in contrast, we can easily miss the logic that binds it and the deadly seriousness underlying its brilliance. But Berlioz could not have devised a mere kaleidoscope of picturesque and fabulous scenes: it was too personal to him to be only that. As the Prague journalist who first wrote of the work remarked, he was "himself a Faust". The sufferings of the central character echoed his own. He had been there, he knew it all: the disillusioned idealism, the attachment to an idea of love that never found fulfilment, the wanderings, the thirst, like Byron's, for sensation, the pantheistic worship of nature, the longing to be united with all existence, the terrible sense of alienation, the self-questioning that turned beauty to ashes, the black depressions which precipitated from the depths of the psyche the demon of eternal denial. The *mal de l'isolement* that is at the heart of the work went back to that first devastating onslaught of spleen in the fields at La Côte St André as he listened to the distant voices of the Rogation procession – the same chant that the women and children sing at the wayside cross in the Ride to the Abyss, the last stage of Faust's path to hell. No less autobiographical, in their nostalgic recall of his first communion and the days of his boyhood faith, were the words added for Faust in the Easter Hymn. It was his own experience that he was dramatizing.

Even if he had not grown used to the unredeemed protagonist of *Faust*, Part 1, he cannot have felt any inclination to soften his hero's fate in the light of the radically different Part 2. He had other intentions. There could be no salvation for this Faust: he was much further along the road to ruin than Goethe's. The adventures of the mind, the continual striving, had lost their savour. He was doomed from the start; Mephistopheles, his shadow – a more Satanic figure than in Goethe – had him in his grasp. Even from *Faust*, Part 1, Berlioz took only what was strictly relevant for him. He used and developed ideas in the poem – for instance the fire motif associated with Mephistopheles – but he also altered it for his own darker purpose. (Only compare the "Forests and Caverns" scene in Goethe – ironic, sexually suggestive, and placed earlier in the action – with the unambiguously tragic interpretation of it in the

Damnation.) The hint of Faust's fate in Part 1 was seized on and made the motive force of the whole drama.

Likewise the appeal of the cathedral and prison scenes – obvious material for musical setting – was ignored: they were more concerned with Marguerite than with Faust. They belonged, besides, to the operatic stage, for which *The Damnation of Faust* was not conceived. From the beginning it was a concert work – nearer to opera than *Romeo and Juliet*, yet still not aimed at the theatre. The first surviving reference, in an album leaf of the opening bars of Marguerite's Romance dated "Vienna, 12 January 1846", is to a "drame de concert en 3 actes".

Two months later it is "mon grand opéra de *Faust* – opéra de concert en 4 actes". Is there an ambiguity in this form of words? Not long afterwards the *Damnation* came near to being adapted by the composer himself for the London opera season of 1847–8. Even in its unadapted, non-operatic form its colour and animation have often seduced directors into putting it on the stage. You can understand why; but like a will o' the wisp, while luring them on it mocks their best efforts. If Berlioz had been able to be a full-time theatre composer he might have cast it in operatic form, though even then I doubt it. To quote Katherine Kolb, "closed doors at the Opéra merely opened those of his deeper inclinations". The *Damnation* as we have it, and as Berlioz himself described it, is "an opera without décor or costumes". It is an opera of the mind's eye performed on an ideal stage of the imagination, hardly realizable within a framework of live drama. We see it more vividly than any external visual medium could possibly depict it, except the cinema (which Berlioz seems at times to be anticipating). As John Warrack has said, "the pace is different, the arena impalpable and too varied, the dramatic logic not that of the theatre but of an imagination able to free itself from physical surroundings and to course with the composer in a flash of thought from scene to scene or dwell upon a held mood of hilarity or tenderness or terror". In its fluidity and swift succession of moods, in the abruptness of its transitions from light to dark, from earthy brutality to the most translucent beauty, in its sense of heightened reality, it has the character of a dream.

The details leap out at us from the music: the din and reek of Auerbach's cellar and the straddled drinkers bawling through the smoke, the silence of Faust's study at dead of night, the lulling airs of the Elbe valley, the long column of soldiers and students marching into the distance on its way to the ancient town where Marguerite lives, the stillness of her room. But such things are more than a picturesque background: they are the drama itself, projections of the imaginings of its chief actors. The stealthy fugato "burrowing like a mole" in the dim light of Faust's study, then petering out, is suggestive not only of the solitariness of the small hours but of the weariness of a frustrated soul, the restless workings of an unsatisfied mind. When Marguerite enters her room, still oppressed by her vision of Faust, the flute melody, at once languorous and tense, evokes both physical atmosphere and psychological state. The recall, far off but nightmarishly vivid, of the soldiers' and students' songs, with all their lewd suggestiveness, breaking in on the Romance, is an epitome of her fate, like the images of sexuality and death in the account of Ophelia's end in *Hamlet*.

Berlioz conveys his meaning with an economy and a brevity unique in the music of its time, his own other works included. The deceitfulness of the sylphs' dance round the sleeping Faust is registered by the almost imperceptible pianissimo of the cellos' and basses' pedal note, reminding us that Mephistopheles holds the threads. In the opening scene of the work the flattened sixth in the melody's sixth bar (B flat in the key of D major) reveals the tiny worm of consciousness eating away Faust's imagined felicity from within. The hunting horns, which, by an inspired touch, are the sole accompaniment to the scene of Faust's final subjugation, seem merely an ironic juxtaposition – an energetic activity indifferent to the tragedy being enacted before us – until we realize that the quarry the huntsmen are pursuing is Faust.

Instrumental timbre is as integral to the characterization as are melody, harmony and rhythm. Faust the austere sensualist and insatiable dreamer has his grave string chords, his modally flavoured harmonies, his proudly arching phrases, Marguerite her demure flutes and clarinets, her naïvely angular, aspiring themes, her passionate heartbeat, Mephistopheles his diminished chords, his dry pizzicato, his sneering trombones eloquent of more than human power.

In three rending chords and a flash of cymbals and piccolo Mephisto stands before us. But he is no mere demon king of pantomime, for all that he displays an almost human weakness for the histrionic. He is a grand seigneur, a master spirit. There is evil behind his lightest mockery and behind that a hint of the regret of the fallen angel, griped by the pain of immortal fires. His caressing lullaby, "Voici des roses", is itself the voice of the supernatural being with dominion over nature; the tenderness of the melody suggests the perverse affection of the tormentor for his victim, even while it is contradicted by the softly snarling brass. To create his fiend the composer sometimes undermines the conventional or natural order of music. The introduction to each verse of his nonsense song in the Leipzig cellar cuts increasingly across rhythm and tonality (both this and the violins' flea-like hoppings were already present in the *Eight Scenes*). In the Ride to the Abyss the wailing oboe tune, above the galloping strings, is dragged through a wild gyration of keys, and the disjunct metrical patterns pile up as the riders approach Pandaemonium. And in the scene where Mephistopheles summons the will o' the wisps – where for the first time we see the devil plain, not playing a part for the benefit of humans but alone with his kind – the unison woodwind and horns sound eight of the twelve notes of the chromatic scale: for the evocation of Goethe's Spirit of Eternal Negation all sense of key is suspended. When the will o' the wisps appear, the darting, flickering piccolos that represent them can scarcely heed his command to restrain their natural "zig-zag" movements – an example of the composer adapting Goethe and Nerval to his musical purposes.

In such ways as this the meaning of *Faust*, Part 1, is expressed, or those aspects of it that Berlioz chose for his purpose. The philosophy is not stated but, rather, absorbed and embodied in the language of music. It is central to that purpose that each part of the work, for Faust, begins in aspiration and ends in dust. As Barzun says, "each opening is individual and characteristic and marks a leap forward in the drama, just as each closing is collective, anonymous and, except for the last one, tragically soulless". The Hungarian March is part of that scheme; performed at the moderate and unvarying speed indicated, it acquires the relentless momentum of a war machine, the disciplined frenzy of regimented man in which Faust the Romantic individualist can have no part. The same terrible anonymity – in every sense soul-destroying – finally engulfs him in the scene in Pandaemonium, where Berlioz borrowed from Swedenborg the idea of a "language of the damned", a nightmarish babel of syllables.

The philosophic core of the work is the Invocation, "Nature immense", which precedes Faust's fall, and the contrast between it and that other scene of Faust's communion with nature, the pastoral symphony which opens the work – a contrast pointed by the identical musical phrase and pitch of the first words in both movements. In the earlier scene there was still hope, or so it seemed; the ecstasy of contemplation was such that he could for an instant believe his ennui cured. In the Invocation we see him, near his end, alone with another nature, of untamed energy and vast indifference: only amid the grandeur of the forests, the howling winds, the boom of cataracts and the cold gleam of the stars can he find an echo of his solitary self. These are the first lines Berlioz wrote after he had taken the decision to be his own librettist:

> Nature, vast, unfathomable and proud,
> Thou alone givest pause to my unending ennui;
> on thy omnipotent breast I feel my misery less,
> I regain my strength and believe in life at last.
> Yes, blow, hurricanes! Roar, you mighty forests,
> crash down, you rocks, torrents, hurl headlong your waters!
> My voice delights to mingle with your majestic sounds.
> Forests, rocks, torrents, I worship you!
> Glittering worlds above, to you the longing
> of a heart too big and a soul insatiable cries out
> for the happiness it cannot seize.

This is familiar Romantic sentiment; but it prompted the composer to a timeless statement of human isolation. He never wrote a grander or subtler movement. The brooding, latent power of the introductory bars, moving down from C sharp minor through B flat minor (a sound, as Julian Rushton says, "chilling in its tonal remoteness") and passing through a cavernous F minor to arrive at F sharp minor for Faust's first utterance, the strength and heroic energy of the vocal line (achieved, the sketches show, after much experimentation), the command of long-range tonality, the magnificently expressive chord progressions and modulations, the great rolling, rumbling bass which rises and descends beneath the surge of tremolo strings like a natural force, the darkly resplendent orchestral colour moving "in perfect cadence" with the words, make the piece a landmark in the experience of many a Berlioz-lover. The final phrases, flung into space, give the climax a superb defiance. Then the unison strings play a long, winding melodic line which strains upward only to fall back on itself in a modal close of desolate inconclusiveness.

The appearance of Mephistopheles at that instant is logical and inevitable, as was his first apparition at the moment of Faust's sentimental recovery of faith and his abrupt intrusion upon his lovemaking. To quote Warrack, it is Faust's "own devouring solitude that precipitates the characters and events of the *Damnation*, so that these come to seem not a string of lurid or touching vignettes but a dramatization of the soul's condition, a nightmare progress from frustration at the failure of learning, of easy companionship, of God, of nature, of love, into an ever more terrible isolation, whipped by the devil who cannot be escaped because he is within, until journey's end is reached in the total dullness, the numbing of all sensation and the exclusion from any hope, that is hell." With all its teeming movement, its wit and zest for life, the subject of the work is loneliness: the loneliness of Marguerite, whose awakened passions are deprived of their object, the loneliness of Mephistopheles, the being who cannot love or die, the loneliness of Faust, whose too hotly questing soul gets the dusty answer of the universe and in whom Berlioz has traced the defeat of the Romantic Dream.

The defeat of *The Damnation of Faust* was, in retrospect, predictable. For several years Romanticism had been recognized to be in retreat. It corresponded less and less to the mood of the public, even the public which had a taste for the unusual and which had followed Berlioz's concerts in the 1830s. Gautier might proclaim that "Hector Berlioz, in our view, forms together with Hugo and Eugène Delacroix the Trinity of Romantic art": how many really cared one way or the other? Berlioz was naïve to suppose that the success of *Romeo and Juliet* seven years before – large houses, three successive performances – set a precedent for the new work.

Yet *Faust*, less problematic in formal structure than *Romeo*, containing far more vocal music and what Sir Thomas Beecham called "a bunch of the loveliest tunes in existence", could well have been expected to have greater immediate appeal. One did not need to grasp its full meaning or subtlety in order to appreciate it. Less than ten years after the composer's death it became a hugely popular work in Paris; the Colonne Concerts alone gave it five or six times a season. No one was bothered then by lack of scenery and costumes. But in 1846 the problem was not primarily one of appreciation: it was to get people to come and listen to it. For all his apparent optimism Berlioz seems to have sensed this in advance; the correspondence for October and November is exceptionally full of requests to journalistic colleagues to insert puffs – some drafted by himself – in their newspapers. Every stop of the experienced publicist was played on to stimulate interest in the work and persuade people that it was the focus of lively curiosity. "The opera-legend conceived during M. Berlioz's recent and brilliant travels in Germany" was said to "present a variety of incident and a splendour of colour likely to justify the extraordinary degree of interest which it is exciting in the musical public". The concert would "undoubtedly attract a large audience", and "the élite of the artistic and elegant worlds" would be there. Much was made of the fact that the Duc and Duchesse de Montpensier had agreed to attend.

It was all in vain. When Berlioz stepped on to the rostrum at the Opéra-Comique on Sunday afternoon, 6 December, he confronted a half-empty theatre. Despite further energetic publicity in the interim, it was worse still at the second performance a fortnight later. The public, musical and otherwise, was not interested.

To some extent this indifference – of which he later wrote that "nothing in my career wounded me more deeply" – was due to special causes. But that merely underlined the vulnerability of his position. The unstable political and economic climate in Paris that autumn and winter – the government losses in local elections, Louis-Napoleon's escape from Ham, the fall in business confidence, the rise in prices and the consequent social unrest – was no doubt against him, though it did not prevent *Gibby la cornemuse*, Clapisson's new work, from playing to full houses. Berlioz would certainly have attracted a bigger audience if he had not been debarred from the Conservatoire Hall, scene of all his major symphonic premières in the 1830s and his natural home in the eyes of those who frequented his concerts. This was a crucial factor. Recession or not, the Opéra-Comique was not a place one went to in the afternoon, even on a Sunday. The Opéra or even the Théâtre-Italien would have been better. But the Opéra was out of the question; he had been writing too openly about its artistic degradation to be able or to wish to have any dealings with it (in a recent review he had likened the hit-or-miss character of Mme Stoltz's vocal line to "the necklaces worn by savages, made up at random of pieces of coral, large beans, fishbones, teeth, bits of wood and sheeps' knuckles"). Any idea of his succeeding to the conductorship had long been abandoned. Habeneck, besides, was hanging on to the job, and "in any case" (Berlioz told Hainl, who was thinking of putting in for it) "they don't want a conductor but a kind of steward who carries out the will of the directress". As for the Théâtre-Italien, Pillet had enough influence there to make it unavailable as well. The Salle Herz was too small. That left only the Opéra-Comique, with whose director, Basset, he was on good terms.

The singers he engaged – Roger (Faust), Hermann-Léon (Mephistopheles), Dufflot-Maillard (Marguerite), Henri (Brander) – were all members of the company. None of them was a great draw, however, though Roger soon would be. And that Berlioz was on sufferance even at the Opéra-Comique is shown by the postponement of the performance at the eleventh hour owing to the theatre's being required unexpectedly on the day when his general rehearsal was scheduled. The première was put off by a week, till 6 December. It now clashed with the annual prizegiving at the Conservatoire (itself postponed till that date so that pupils could give a benefit performance in aid of the victims of the recent Loire floods); but he had got his forces more or less ready and did not dare wait any longer.

The rainy weather and the state of the streets, slushy with melting snow, was only the coup de grâce.

The reaction of those who did come is hard to gauge. There was evidently some bewilderment. Maurice Bourges, in the *Gazette*, complained that the audience failed to respond to Marguerite's Romance, though the singer gave a faithful account of the scene, "one of the most powerful in the score". On the other hand the scene by the Elbe, according to Marie Escudier, gave general pleasure; the Dance of the Sylphs was encored. So was the Hungarian March.

If the public was in two minds, the press was predominantly favourable. In terms of critical reception *The Damnation of Faust* was one of Berlioz's most successful premières. Scudo for once was silent; his routine demolition did not appear till the following May. Azevedo stuck his usual pins into the music and the man, and the *Siècle*, true to form, thought it "one of the author's feeblest compositions, if not the feeblest of all"; but critic after critic, while observing that so rich a score was not to be understood at a single hearing, praised its many beauties, its inventive sounds, unheard before, and its abundant vein of fantasy: Berlioz, they said, was the one composer capable of tackling such a subject. "The extraordinary character of Faust," wrote Bourges, "that strange mixture of reverie and fiery passion, of unappeasable ardour and languorous despair, could not but enchant the man who has already given us *Harold*, the *Episode in an Artist's Life* and *The Return to Life*, and who has long meditated a *Hamlet*." Even Adolphe Adam, though continuing to regard Berlioz as everything but a musician, paid tribute to his convictions (however misguided) and found, along with "unspeakable aberrations", some "remarkable flights, and effects of sonority that are quite new", not least the "ravishing" Dance of the Sylphs. (Adam also liked the Hungarian March, whose "tune – not by Berlioz – has forced him into a regularity of phrase and rhythm which he usually neglects".) But the notices struck an ominous note, absent from reviews of his concerts in the past – the recognition that, in d'Ortigue's words, there was an unbridgeable gulf between his conception of art and the public's. D'Ortigue, his most consistent champion, had never conceded that before. Now, though Berlioz possessed melodic genius, his melody was "not the Italian melody which we have made our standard and with which our ears have grown familiar"; and, preoccupied with his innovations, he had lost sight of his audience and gone beyond the point at which their perceptions stopped. Gautier emphasized the artist's heroic refusal to sacrifice to the gods of commercial success or to make the slightest concession to the Philistines; but this was "a flabby age, in which the fashion is all for the commonplace, under the name of good sense". Janin, who had kept his feuilleton open for a final paragraph recording the work's success, had instead to speak of the cruel struggle, the endless combat of one who would rather die than yield an inch to the habits and base instincts of the crowd. "Happy, thrice happy, he who can win applause like M. Scribe! Alas, how I pity and how I envy the unfortunate man who compels praise in the way Berlioz does."

Janin expressed the feelings of many – musicians, friends, music-lovers, admirers: *Faust* had fallen but it remained a magnificent achievement. Their pity and their admiration prompted them to give a dinner in his honour, on 29 December, presided over by Baron Taylor, at which Roger spoke on behalf of the singers, Offenbach on behalf of Germany and Osborne of England, and the guests subscribed to a gold medal to commemorate the new work. In the meantime the second performance had come and gone. By all accounts it was more confident than the first, though Roger, barely recovered from a heavy cold, omitted "Nature immense". Hermann-Léon, the Mephistopheles, was less hesitant, as was the chorus, whose uncertainty had forced Berlioz to cut the Pandaemonium scene at the première. Three numbers were encored. But the audience was even smaller; the theatre was hardly more than a third full.

Berlioz was left with debts of five or six thousand francs and no means of repaying them. The copying bill alone was enormous, bigger than any he had had before: *Faust* was the largest score for whose performance he was personally responsible (the copying of *Benvenuto Cellini* and *The Trojans*, the only larger works, was undertaken by the theatres concerned). Even if, as is possible, he skimped a little on rehearsals, two hundred performers meant a massive outlay in fees. His plan for a third, evening performance at which some of the loss might be recouped – for surely all those good notices would have their effect and the public would come – had to be given up. It was hopeless. The Opéra-Comique was busy with two new works and did not have a single evening free, and there was nowhere else to be had. "I am checked for want of a hall. *There is no concert hall in Paris*," he wrote to Nancy. Never again, he vowed, would he stake so much as twenty francs on a performance of his music. "There's nothing to be done in this ghastly country, and I can't leave it quickly enough. I'm waiting till the German translation of *Faust* is finished before setting forth to find cities more hospitable than our rascally Paris." Like a bird of prey he must seek his living far and wide: "only barnyard fowls live happily on their dung-heaps".

One place above all offered a way out of the crisis. A winter journey across snowbound northern Europe was not an enticing prospect. But in Russia if anywhere he might rebuild his shattered fortunes.

14

To Russia

For some time now a visit to St Petersburg had been on the cards. Glinka had encouraged him, at the time of the Cirque-Olympique concerts; so had Léopold de Meyer. He was already in correspondence with the director of the Imperial Chapel, General Lvov; and he had prepared the ground by dedicating the score of the Fantastic Symphony, published in the spring of 1845, to Tsar Nicholas I (receiving a diamond ring in return). He would have gone in the winter of 1845–6 had Prague not intervened (his request for leave of absence from the Conservatoire Library in October 1845 gave as the reason "to go to Austria and Russia"). Now he hastened to make the necessary arrangements. Letters asking for concert dates during the Lent season were dispatched to Lvov, to Guedenov, intendant of the Imperial Theatre, and to Count Michael Vielhorsky, the influential St Petersburg music-lover and amateur composer whom he had met in Vienna the previous winter. He remained in Paris only while the text of the *Damnation* was hurriedly and expensively translated into German, and while he raised enough money to settle his debts and pay for the journey.

Friends came to his aid, prompted by the same pity and admiration, and the same feelings of responsibility as Parisians, that had moved them to salve his wounded spirit by giving him a banquet. Adolphe Sax lent 1,200 francs. So did Ferdinand Friedland, the young Breslau music-lover who had been a keen supporter on the most recent tour of Germany. Others lent five or six hundred. Armand Bertin had the *Débats* cashier advance him a thousand. Hetzel, the publisher, whom he barely knew, insisted on his accepting a thousand-franc note when they met by chance in a café ("it's a very costly journey, especially in winter"), and when he demurred, agreed to regard it as advance on an article. The simplicity and good grace with which the offer was made touched him deeply; he felt that in Hetzel he had acquired a friend for life. In this sense *Faust*, his greatest public disaster, was his greatest personal vindication. His peers at any rate believed in him.

None the less there was no solid reason to keep him in Paris. More and more artists, Berlioz wrote in the *Débats* – Meyerbeer, Liszt, Thalberg, Rossini himself – were keeping aloof, forced by the "petty turmoil and perpetual intrigues of our miserable little musical world to accept the hospitality of foreign cities where art is alive and honourable and held in honour". Should he not do the same? What was there for him to stay for? True, the Duc de Montpensier had been excited at the idea of getting him to compose a symphony for chorus and military band on the return of Napoleon's Army of Italy after its brilliant campaign, a subject that the duke knew – perhaps from his late brother the Duc d'Orléans – Berlioz was interested in, and had had a word with the Minister of War about commissioning it. Berlioz got as far as going to see the minister, only to find him, as he expected, "less inflammable" than the prince. At the Opéra big changes were impending (on paper at least), which might benefit him; but it was far too uncertain to count on.

Pillet's days were numbered. Mme Stoltz's paranoid behaviour was one of the winter's talking points. The diva was so desperate for applause of any sort that she scheduled one general rehearsal after another in the vain hope of a "succès d'orchestre"; when the musicians, on Habeneck's advice, did eventually applaud her she declared that the opera in question was ready for performance, and the first night was announced. It was an open secret that Meyerbeer was sitting on three completed scores, *Le Prophète*, *L'Africaine* and *Le camp de Silésie*; the last named had been performed in Berlin, but none of them would he let the Opéra get its hands on, knowing well what their fate would be. For want of decent singers and strong musical direction, recent revivals of *The Huguenots*, *Robert* and Halévy's *La Juive*, the theatre's three mainstays, had been travesties.

In these straits, stuck for a novelty by an established composer, Pillet persuaded Rossini to allow one to be carved from his existing scores. Nierdermeyer performed the necessary surgery, Vaëz and Alphonse Royer ran up a libretto, and *Robert Bruce* was billed as a "new opera by the great Rossini". There was a long tradition of such pasticcios in the Paris theatre. But, as Berlioz pointed out in the *Débats*, quite apart from the dramatic monstrosity of the thing, a score consisting of famous numbers from *La donna del lago*, *Zelmira*, and *Bianca e Faliero*, written as showpieces for the finest singers of their day, might have been designed to measure the vocal poverty of Pillet's company – the very defect whose consequences had driven him to this bizarre expedient. Berlioz even wondered whether Rossini, the supreme hoaxer, hadn't chosen the music expressly so as to exact a stinging revenge on the house that had been casually mutilating his works for years: "in her best days" Mme Stoltz could never have sung O *mattutini albori* with anywhere near the poetic charm of the prima donnas who were still remembered – and on the opening night (30 December 1846) she sang it so flat that "for five minutes we writhed in an agony made the crueller by the entry of the horn, playing the tune in unison with the voice but at the correct pitch while the singer went her separate way".

Despite it, the audience remained quiet (the royal princes were present, and the décor was sumptuous). But in the second act an incident occurred which in retrospect was seen to herald the final downfall of Pillet and his froward *directrice*. During another aria, sung flatter than ever, the *claque* injudiciously applauded. Cries of protest rang out from many parts of the house. The *claque* redoubled their efforts. So did the protesters. Mme Stoltz stopped singing and, in the words of Stephen Heller (whose caustic review of *Robert Bruce* for the London *Musical World* was reprinted in the *Critique musicale*), "rage in her countenance, began to tear into pieces a very handsome lace handkerchief". Someone shouted something abusive, at which she advanced to the footlights and loudly demanded "how a woman could be insulted in this fashion". The theatre was in uproar. When Mlle Nau, taking her bow at the end of the act, received rapturous applause, Stoltz was seen to stride towards her, arm raised as if to strike. In a letter to the *Débats*, pleading indisposition after an attack of pleurisy, she explained that she did it to protect Mlle Nau from the sudden fall of the curtain. Not many chose to believe her.

Thanks to Rossini's name and to some spectacular scenery, however, *Robert Bruce* defied critical scorn and ran throughout the winter and spring, with Stoltz still in the cast. Mme Rossini sprang to the defence of her husband's opera, sending a box containing two asses' ears to the office of the *Débats*, one addressed to Armand Bertin, the other for Berlioz to pass to his friend Heller. But the episode was recognized as having sealed the fate of the Pillet regime, and lobbying for the succession began. Among the most fancied bidders was a two-man team consisting of Nestor Roqueplan – a writer of small distinction and a known philistine, but a formidable operator and polemicist – and the inevitable Duponchel. Anxious for the support of the *Débats*, they wooed Berlioz, undertaking if appointed to make him musical director and to throw in the post of co-principal conductor, to be shared with his former friend Girard, who had recently taken over from Habeneck.

Berlioz knew what such promises were worth. In any case he had no time to wait. Events must be left to take their course. He went for a brief shooting holiday on the estate of his dentist near Beauvais, and then made ready to depart.

Some time towards the end of January he wrote to his copyist-librarian Rocquemont. The letter is known only from an auctioneer's résumé which indicates gaps in the text and does not name the works referred to; but the main drift is clear.

> My dear Roquemont
> Diligence and silence! I wish to leave for Russia *alone*. To do so I need your help. That being so, please go tomorrow first thing to Sax's [where his music was kept] and parcel up the following works I want to take with me. [. . .] Have all the rest taken to 43 Rue Blanche [. . .] Make up a package wrapped in oilcloth, marked "M. H. Berlioz, via Cologne" and having done so leave it with the concierge at Desmarest's, 13 Rue Joubert, with a note saying I shall come and collect it. Don't come to the house [sc. 41 Rue de Provence]. I'll make a rendezvous with you for settling your account. You will understand that not a word is to be said to a soul about any of this, and you yourself know nothing.

Did he go to Russia alone? One would like to think so – it is bad enough imagining him reduced once again to such subterfuge, let alone foiled in the attempt – and I am inclined to believe that he did. He certainly meant to. Marie, however, was made of sterner stuff than Harriet. There was no way he could have slipped off undetected, as he had in 1842. No doubt his aim was to present Marie with a fait accompli, so that by the time she found out it would be too late for her to obtain the necessary visas and other documents. In this he may have been successful. When she did find out, the extra expense of a travelling companion could be adduced as an argument against her going with him. But it looks as if his intentions went much further and he came near to a complete break – near enough for him to tell his sisters about it or for them to hear of it from mutual friends. A letter from Adèle to Nancy, written not long after their brother's departure, is quite explicit:

"Like you I think that the affectionate tone of his letter, at the moment of leaving the country, was due to his rupture with his princess. I should like to be certain that is so."

If the rupture did take place, it was quickly healed. When Berlioz sent Balzac a note at the beginning of February, taking him up on the offered loan of his fur-lined greatcoat ("the one I was counting on looks far too short and I'm particularly afraid of having cold legs"), he asked him to have it delivered to 41 Rue de Provence, Marie's address.

He had met the novelist late one night on the corner of the street and they had stopped to chat. Balzac was enthusiastic about his chances of making a fortune in Russia, and adamant that he would "not be able" to bring back less than 150,000 francs; he also insisted that on his way through Tilsit he looked up the postmaster, Nernst, an interesting and cultivated man whom Balzac had got to know during his visits to the Countess Hanska in Galicia.

With or without Marie Recio, Berlioz left Paris on 14 February, St Valentine's Day – in a bass drum (said one paper) which was waiting for him at the entrance to the Rue Blanche, drawn by four horses with cymbals on their hooves. The *Charivari* suggested that M. Berliozkov should settle in Russia: polar bears were clearly audible in his symphonies, and he could make a splendid living by exhibiting his music-loving flea.

As if to celebrate the event, the weather had turned glacial. Paris itself was under six inches of snow, and on the way through Belgium the train stopped for several hours while workmen cleared the track of a fresh fall. In Berlin he stayed long enough to get the letter of recommendation from the King to his sister the Tsarina which he had asked Alexander von Humboldt a few weeks earlier to obtain for him. The letter, written in French, shows Frederick William IV addressing Alexandra Federovna in skittish vein:

> Dearest Empress and Sister
> Humboldt is pressing me to write you a line which Berlioz (the z is aspirated in French) can take with him to Petersburg. As the said musician, about whom I spoke in my last humble and obedient communication, is a sort of prodigy on the little Kilikeya and the great Gumbgum, but most of all with the Boumboum, I shall not disappoint the joy of the aforesaid Alexander and of this Boumboum Berlioz, and I write you this note which will serve the great pupil of the supreme Apollo Musagetes Delios

Delphicus Dreifussicus as a key to all positions of power and honour in the Russian portion of the globe. Much good may his music do your ears, without deafening you to the expressions of purest fraternal love from your fat, faithful

Fritz

On the evening of the 19th, at a performance of Adam's *Giselle* at the Opéra, Berlioz ran into Schumann. Next morning he set out across the snows of Prussia to Tilsit, half amused, half maddened by the courier of his postchaise, an amateur composer of dance music who whistled incessantly through his teeth and, after each stop, insisted on getting his captive passenger to harmonize the polka or waltz which he had written down while the horses were changed. Mercifully the man was replaced at Tilsit, which they reached after two days' travelling. Berlioz also had the pleasure of discovering that Nernst, the Tilsit postmaster, was every bit as interesting as Balzac had said. On entering his office he found "a large man in a cloth cap, severe of countenance yet with an air which suggested both wit and benevolence. He was seated on a high stool and remained there when I came in. 'M. Nernst,' I inquired, with a bow. 'Yes. May I ask who I have the honour of speaking to?' 'Hector Berlioz'. 'You don't mean it!' he exclaimed, bounding off the stool and landing in front of me, cap in hand." Over an excellent curaçao they discussed Balzac, "the incomparable anatomist who has probed to the very heart of contemporary French society" – Nernst was "one of the small number of foreigners who know French well enough to be able to admire him with true passion" – until it was time to continue the journey. From Tilsit another day across snow-bound plains took him to the frontier town of Taurogen, where postchaise gave way to covered sledge. Now not Balzac's voluminous coat nor the straw packed close round the passengers could keep out the cold during the four interminable days and nights that followed; and the uneven movement of the sledge over the frozen rutted surface threw him about "like shot shaken in a bottle". He could only reflect, as he gazed out over the white wastes, that he was better off than the soldiers of Napoleon's army on their calamitous retreat, which his uncle had described so long ago.

The contrast when at last he reached St Petersburg and was installed in a warm room on the Nevsky Prospect could not have been more dramatic. Within an hour or two State-Councillor Wilhelm von Lenz, an acquaintance of his in Paris (famous later as the author of *Beethoven and his Three Styles*), had called for him and borne him off to a party at the house of Count Michael Vielhorsky and his cello-playing brother Matthew. Though the Russian imperial family was German in origin, French was the language of polite society, and he was made to feel immediately at home. Count Michael introduced him to all the bigwigs of the city's musical life: General Lvov, General Guedonov, Heinrich Romberg, Prince Vladimir Odoyevsky, Prince Emmanuel Galitsin – for the Vielhorsky salon, he realized, was a kind of "little Ministry of Fine Arts" – and arrangements for his first concert, to be given two weeks from then in the Assembly Hall of the Nobility, were agreed on the spot; even the price of the tickets was settled, being fixed, after discussion, at three silver roubles (12 francs). Here he was, in the thick of things after only a few hours in St Petersburg.

Next morning Romberg, conductor of the Italian opera, took him under his wing and they set about collecting an orchestra. It turned out to consist entirely of German musicians except for a handful of Russians, one Englishman and a French cellist, his old Paris acquaintance and one-time fellow-Saint-Simonian, Dominique Tajan-Rogé. Lvov, musical director and aide-de-camp to the emperor (and composer of the Russian national anthem), performed a similar service by putting together a chorus formed of members of the two opera companies and the Imperial Chapel. Over the next fortnight they rehearsed in unhurried fashion a programme made up of *The Damnation of Faust*, sung in German – the first two parts only, no adequate Marguerite being available – plus the Fête and scherzo from *Romeo and Juliet*, the *Roman Carnival* overture and the Apotheosis. Romberg and Ludwig Maurer, conductor at the German theatre, were recruited to play the antique cymbals in Queen Mab. The only problems encountered concerned the German text of *Faust*. For the non-German-speaking choristers it had to be copied into the parts in Russian characters. This was done; but at the end of the first rehearsal Romberg revealed that the translation was so bad as to be in places virtually unusable. A new one was commissioned from another German littérateur, Münzlaff. In the meantime Romberg corrected the worst excesses and they soldiered on.

On 15 March (3 March, Russian calendar) the programme was rousingly applauded by an audience described by Odoyevsky as "filling the enormous Assembly Hall of the Nobility to overflowing". *Faust* in particular astonished everybody. Its multilingual listeners did not seem greatly bothered when Mephistopheles (Versing), addressing his master in German, was answered by Faust (Ricciardi) in French. The whole sylphs' scene – sung in a manner which "left our French choristers far behind" – had to be repeated. At the end of Part 2 the orchestra rose and acclaimed him as one man; and he was summoned straight from the rostrum to the imperial box, where the Tsarina, with her sons the Grand Dukes Alexander and Constantine, kept him talking for a quarter of an hour, following up her compliments next day with the gift of a diamond ring "worth 400 roubles – 1,600 francs" (he told Morel). Prince Galitsin sent him a twenty-nine-stanza ode in French. Berlioz, like Liszt five years before, was the toast of Petersburg, fêted in all the aristocratic salons and entertained in the dazzling apartments of the Grand Duchess Marie, the Tsar's daughter, at the Winter Palace. And he was rich: if not as rich as Balzac predicted, rich beyond the dreams of a Parisian composer-conductor. The profit on the first two concerts – the second being given ten days later, with the same programme – amounted to 15,000 francs. At a stroke his debts were wiped out. He had the satisfaction of sending his new friend Hetzel a banker's draft which rendered him his 1,000 francs only four months after he had lent it; and doubtless the other loans were repaid in similar fashion. "Russia, which saved me" was his succinct tribute when, seven years later, he wrote his farewells in the final chapter of his *Memoirs*. It had.

The impact of Berlioz's music on the Petersburg musical public is harder to measure. Though some took to it instantly, others did not know what to think. His immense vogue was due partly to snobbery, partly to the force of his personality, partly to the standard of perform- ance he achieved, which genuinely amazed his listeners. The writer Vladimir Stasov, recalling it many years later, described the Russian nobility as "friendly, sympathetic and respectful" to Berlioz. "They may not have grasped the essence of his music, they may have found little in it that suited their taste, especially now that the Italians were the rage, but they gave heed to their aristocratic arbiters in matters musical [the Vielhorskys, Odoyevsky and Lvov]. The arbiters gave the pitch, and the rest, in chorus, sustained the note. Thus the fashionable world made a fuss over Berlioz."

Stasov's contemporary review, published in *Otechestvenniye Zapiski*, paints a fuller, more complex picture. Everything else in the season, he says, was overshadowed by these concerts; they were the most magnificent, most brilliant (in terms of both orchestra and applause), most deafening concerts that were presented this year. Everyone flocked to them; how could they do otherwise when Berlioz has such a colossal reputation throughout all Europe? The truth must be told, however: probably nowhere else has Berlioz's arrival been preceded by such widespread prejudice as it was in our country. No sooner did it become known that he was coming than the public began to receive reports through letters from abroad, and in other ways, that Berlioz is utterly worthless, that he composes in the manner of a washerwoman wringing out her laundry, that he is a noise-maker, a *tapoteur*, etc. Even after attending his concerts, some people continued to say such things. Others added that Berlioz belongs to that young generation which "has sown its wild oats, spent itself, and become staid and respectable"; that, of course, Berlioz has very lofty ideas, but none of them has been embodied in melody.

The young Polish princess, Carolyne Sayn-Wittgenstein, after hearing *Romeo and Juliet* that spring, wrote to Liszt in indignation at the many in St Petersburg high society who had failed to respond to the work. "The elegant women were there in force, but it bored them." The Love Scene, "that divine adagio", left them cold. "All around me people were saying, 'Is that all it is?'" Yet Odoyevsky was struck by the enthusiasm with which the audience at the opening concert responded to music that for most of them was utterly new; not only (he wrote) did they encore the March and the Dance of the Sylphs, but they listened attentively to the Easter Hymn and had no trouble following the difficult double chorus. "There must be a special affinity between his music and our innate musical sense: only this could account for such a response." Stasov himself argued that "the reputation he enjoys and the extraordinary impression he makes on everyone cannot possibly be ascribed to fashion alone": there was something inexplicably yet incontrovertibly prodigious about this strange figure, this portent.

Many of Berlioz's Russian listeners must have felt the same confusion of mind as was reflected in Stasov's review. Stasov would soon become a whole-hearted admirer; but his 1847 article was a maze of contradictory reactions. Berlioz "has no gift for musical composition"; like Liszt he has "not composed anything that could be considered music". The two men are none the less "the most brilliant heralds of the future". There is "no knowing what new wonders can be expected of him". The Dance of the Sylphs, that "transparent, microscopic paradise", is a marvel; "never before has his orchestral treatment of such scenes been so charming and delightful". One leaves his concerts "shaken, uplifted, as if we had been in the presence of something great, even though we cannot account for its greatness".

One thing was unequivocally clear: his supremacy as a conductor.

> Probably no one else has ever delved so deeply into the art of musical performance as he has; no one else has ever experienced the joy he does when "playing the orchestra" (as he himself puts it). His amazing ear catches every nuance, even the most elusive. He never permits a single one to slip by; he brings each one out through the thunder of the entire orchestra. Under Berlioz's direction the orchestra is like a steed that feels the full power of its rider. Leading it, Berlioz is a veritable general, adored by all his forces, inspiring them by some kind of extraordinary power to accomplish unprecedented feats. Under him, they do things it would have seemed no one on earth could have made them do.

After only two general rehearsals (preceded, we may be sure, by sectionals), the ad hoc band of musicians is transformed: it "becomes one man, one instrument, and plays as though all its members were finished artists. Berlioz's concerts end. He leaves. And everything is as it was before – each man for himself. The mighty spirit that had inspired everyone for a moment is gone."

Stasov thought that in contrast to the seminal visit of twenty years later – by which time the nationalist group of composers was active – Berlioz's advent in 1847 had no immediate effect on native Russian musical life, or what there was of it. (His orchestra, remember, was almost exclusively German.) "Everything remained exactly as before." The sole Russian musician of that period on whom he had a profound effect (Stasov continues) was Glinka, who had already come under his influence two years earlier; but Glinka was still an almost solitary pioneer. At the house of the corpulent, pop-eyed Count Michael Vielhorsky and in the other salons where Berlioz was received, Russian music was not mentioned. With the public it was the same. "They enjoyed listening to and reading and talking about Berlioz's innovations in this, that and the other thing. They willingly called him a genius, a giant and so on, who had introduced 'new elements', but their musical tastes did not change a hair's breadth, and they remained quite happy with the 'old elements'."

For the moment, however, St Petersburg gave itself wholeheartedly to this phenomenon, and the roubles flowed. Even the French ambassador was attentive. Everyone vied to have him as guest of honour. (What he liked best, though, were the games of billiards at Vielhorsky's with Lenz and others, accompanied by beer and cigars.) On 15/27 March the Apotheosis was repeated at a charity concert. And though Lent would be over by then and the opera in action again, General Guedenov was happy to rearrange the Imperial Theatre's schedule to make room for a performance of the complete *Romeo and Juliet* in late April/early May.

While the *Romeo* choruses worked at their music, Berlioz went to Moscow, travelling another four days and nights, this time through a landscape beginning to shed its winter carapace. Moscow, which he reached on about 24 March/5 April, was another world. Here, though he liked the tea, he felt an alien (an impression intensified by the melancholy sight of the captured French cannon encircling the Kremlin). Use of the Hall of the Nobility was granted him only with the greatest reluctance; the snowy-haired Grand Marshal in charge of it was quite unable to grasp that his visitor was not an instrumentalist but merely a conductor, and insisted on applying the local rule whereby every artist that borrowed the hall had in return to perform at a private gathering of the nobles. (On the guitar, Berlioz suggested.) In the end the rule was waived, but for one concert only. In other ways too Moscow was more than a thousand miles from Petersburg. Its musical resources were a fraction of its rival's. The performance of Glinka's *A Life for the Tsar* which he attended at the Bolshoi was so poor that the music was almost unrecognizable; and the choral and orchestral forces he was given to work with were of a depressingly low standard, the former especially. The Moscow choristers, he found, were in the habit of learning their music without any accompaniment, by trial and error; he had to insist on a piano and a pianist being fetched. As a further irritant, the censor, after examining the libretto of *Faust*, decided that the final lines of the students' Latin song – "Per urbem quarentes puellas eamus", etc. ("Let's roam the town looking for girls") – were a threat to public morals (the Petersburg censor had raised no objection) and struck them out.

Despite all this the concert was well received, and netted him another 8,000 francs, which but for the Grand Marshal's regulation might have been doubled: for, at the end, members of the audience jumped on to the platform and begged him to give another concert – he simply could not leave after only one – and he received letters to the same effect. In one respect the performance of the *Damnation*, Parts 1 and 2, was an advance on St Petersburg's: Faust and Mephistopheles conversed in the same language – French, "Baltic style". The chorus, as before, sang in German.

The frustrations of Moscow were strangely underlined by two meetings with a young Russian, a self-taught composer, who came to him for advice as to whether he had a true aptitude for composition. A Muscovite nobleman, he said, was prepared to pay for him to study with the best teachers in Germany or France if a musician of repute would vouch for him. Berlioz was intrigued and attracted by this tall, pale young man speaking impeccable French, who was almost literally consumed by his passion for music and who had moments, he said, when he "heard a whole world of glorious, enchanted sound ringing and vibrating about him" but at other times (like a character in a Turgenev story) lapsed into paralysing self-doubt. The man agreed to bring some samples of his work, but next day turned up empty-handed, having spent the night going through his manuscripts and finding nothing worth submitting. He promised to set to work on something new. When a letter eventually came, it contained no music. "The young Russian apologized again for not sending me any. To his despair (he wrote) and in spite of all his efforts, inspiration had failed him utterly."

By then Berlioz was back in Petersburg and spring was in spate. En route they had crossed the immense Volga, waiting for several hours until the cracking ice floes separated sufficiently for the boat to force a passage. On arriving he found that though the chorus had been busy preparing *Romeo* there was still much to do. The week or ten days between his return and the concert on 23 April/5 May was spent in intensive rehearsal of the work which, even after *Faust*, he seems to have regarded as the most difficult of all his concert pieces – requiring to be prepared "with as much care as a new opera is prepared in a good opera house".

For that reason he was particularly pleased with the resulting performance of what he called, in a letter to Adèle two days later, his favourite work ("mon ouvrage de prédilection"). The Imperial Theatre was crammed, the audience – a sea of diamonds, tiaras, splendid uniforms and flashing epaulettes – the most brilliant that had ever come to hear his music, and the reception so tumultuous that a second performance was arranged on the spot. Yet though he was given a royal welcome when he came out at the beginning to conduct the first two movements of *Harold* (with Ernst as soloist), and was recalled repeatedly throughout the evening, he sensed that *Romeo* was not as much to the general taste as *Faust* (a view confirmed by the box-office manager, who thought it prudent to add some scenes from the latter work at the next concert). It did not matter, however: he felt he was performing *Romeo* for himself, for his own delight. "I was in just the right vein," he wrote to Adèle, "really suffering, as one has to be to catch its spirit; and how well I conducted, how well I played the orchestra! Only the author can know how well the conductor has served him." But it was at a cost. By the end he could not contain his feelings. Ernst found him in his dressing-room backstage in floods of tears, and taking his head on his shoulder let him cry for a quarter of an hour.

A few days later Berlioz unburdened himself to Liszt. His friend's relationship with Princess Sayn-Wittgenstein had just begun. Berlioz himself had met her at Vielhorsky's and had called on her two days before the concert; he too was at the beginning of a friendship which would play a crucial part in his life before he was many years older.

An extremely amiable and intelligent princess, who knows better than any of us where you are and what you are doing, has kindly agreed to take these few lines under her protection and deliver them to you. Good-day, dear, marvellous pilgrim; I think of you a great deal. There are plenty of opportunities to talk about you here, where everyone loves and admires you almost as much as I do. What tremendous wanderers we two are, don't you think?

Just now I feel sad enough to die. I'm in the grip of one my attacks of *isolation*. It was the performance of *Romeo* at the Grand Theatre that brought it on. In the middle of the adagio I felt my heart contract, and now that's it, I'm in its power for God knows how long.

What deplorable temperaments! . . .

[. . .] The King of Prussia has just let me know, in a letter from Count Redern, that the Berlin Opera is at my disposal to perform *Faust* in its entirety, so I am going to Prussia. But my heart isn't in it . . . Will I feel differently? There I go with my lamentations again! What a misfortune it is to be so electrifiable an electric machine . . . The Princess tells me you're composing a lot. When is the Vienna performance of [your opera] *Sardanapale*? [. . .]

Goodbye, my dear friend, I can't write any more, my nervous trembling has started again, my heart's beating this rhythm

and I must stop. Goodbye, I embrace you; I wish I could see you. The sun's as hot as Italy – 34 degrees, what agony. Come back cold, ice, fog, insensibility! . . . Goodbye once more. Don't laugh at me: however far away you may be I shall feel it if you do.

In this hypersensitive state Berlioz had been overwhelmed, the day after *Romeo*, by a visit to the Imperial Chapel, arranged by the Tsar's daughter-in-law, the Grand Duchess of Leuchtenberg, so that he could experience the incomparable choir in a liturgical setting, performing an unaccompanied mass of Bortniansky's. He had already heard them in rehearsal and knew them for the best in Europe: eighty voices – tenors, basses, boy trebles and altos – of wonderful purity, delicacy and power, the basses capable (like the man in *The Seagull*) of going far below the stave. A day later, he told Adèle, he was still trembling. "I would not advise anyone gifted with a certain sensibility and with a deep sorrow in their heart to expose themselves to such an experience."

There was something he did not tell Liszt or Adèle: he was in love. She was a member of his chorus, who perhaps had caught his eye during a rehearsal for *Faust* or *Romeo*. He seems to have told no one until he wrote five months later, half self-mockingly but still grieving, to Tajan-Rogé, enclosing a letter for him to deliver to her. We do not even know her name.

Since I am telling you confidences, would you believe it – I let myself be snared in Petersburg by a passion, as genuine as it was grotesque, for one of your choristers! (Here I will allow you to laugh, in the major mode for full orchestra – go on, don't hold back.) To continue, by a passion most poetic, heart-rending and totally innocent (with or without double meaning [i.e. "harmless" and "stupid"]), for a young girl – but not too young – who said she would "writ" to me and who, speaking of her mother's obsession with getting her married, added, "What a nuisance".

How often we walked together, on the outskirts of Petersburg and sometimes beyond into the country, from nine in the evening till eleven. What bitter tears I wept when she said, like Marguerite in *Faust*, "My God, I don't understand what you see in me . . . I am just a poor girl, far below you . . . You can't possibly love me like that," etc., etc. But it's so possible that it's true, and I thought I should die of despair, passing the Grand Theatre as the coach left Petersburg. And I felt really ill in Berlin when I found no letter from her. She had so often promised to "writ". And in Paris too, no news. I wrote, but had no reply. That *is* a nuisance. It's not fair! Come now, my friend, you are a good fellow, don't laugh any more, for even as I tell you about it I weep hot tears. Be really kind and give her the enclosed note and, if you can, tell her how unhappy she is making me by not letting me hear from her. No doubt she's married by now. Her fiancé, who left for Sweden the evening of my first concert, has certainly been back a long time. She works her fingers to the bone making corsets in her sister's factory – yet not so much that she can't write to me. She knows how to write, she knows five languages, Russian, French (apart from "minor" faults like the ones I've mentioned), German, Danish and Swedish.

God! I can see us now, by the Neva one evening as the sun was setting. What a whirlwind of passion! I crushed her arm to my breast and sang the great phrase in the adagio of *Romeo and Juliet.* You can see if I love her! [Berlioz then quotes Romeo's love theme.] I promised her, I offered her, all I could promise and offer . . . and I have not had so much as two lines since I left. I am not even sure it was she who waved goodbye from far off just as I was getting into the coach at the post-station. Farewell. You at least will "writ" to me.

PS As it's very probable that one way or another she is now married, try not to let anyone know about your message, so as not to compromise her. And when you answer, don't mock me too much.

It is hard to see how such a relationship could have been carried on if Marie Recio had accompanied Berlioz to Russia: she must surely have been, and seemed, thousands of miles away. Whatever Marie may once have meant to him, he hungered for a different, a more exalted kind of love such as she had perhaps never aroused in him or at least aroused no longer; he had felt starved of it and of the heightened consciousness it brought, the sense of vibrant life, even the suffering. When he did finally get a letter – one in which she apparently accepted that she must marry her fiancé, though she would "rather it was him" – he told Tajan-Rogé that he felt "gratitude to her for reviving the pain he had been trying to forget". It showed him that he could still love.

With the coming of spring and the impending migration of Petersburg society to its country estates, the season was almost over. On 8/20 May he appeared for the fifth and last time, conducting the Fantastic Symphony at a farewell concert for the German bass Versing, his Friar Laurence and Mephistopheles, who was leaving the Imperial Theatre. A few days later he said goodbye to friends old and new and set out for Germany.

In Riga, armed with letters of introduction from General Lvov, he inquired about putting on a concert. The auguries were not good. Riga (where Wagner had been kapellmeister ten years before), was very much a port, crowded with ships and busy buying and selling grain – the theatre orchestra barely thirty strong. The postmaster, a less sanguine character than his counterpart in Tilsit, warned Berlioz that he would have an audience of a hundred if he was lucky, and not a man among them. In this he was wrong: seven men turned up and a hundred and thirty-two women, and Berlioz made all of three silver roubles' or twelve francs' profit. Yet (he told Count Michael Vielhorsky) it had been worth the time and effort for the enthusiasm shown him by the players, "whom I didn't know and whom I believe I can now count among my friends". The ad hoc orchestra of about fifty, assembled by Kapellmeister Schrameck and made up of local professionals and amateurs and a few musicians from nearby Mitau (Yelgava), gave a lively account of itself. At least 139 of Riga's 80,000 inhabitants were introduced to a cross-section of the composer's work and seemed to like what they heard: *Harold*, with a fine solo violist, Löhmann, and the difficult finale brought off in cracking style, the *Roman Carnival*, the Hungarian March, the sylphs' scene ("without chorus!!") and two orchestral songs, tolerably well sung by a member of the Riga opera company, Mlle Bamberg (17/29 May). On top of that there was the bonus of a performance of *Hamlet* at the local theatre with a first-rate actor, Baumeister. "As always I was turned upside down by that marvel of the greatest of all human geniuses. The English are quite right to say that, after God, it is Shakespeare who created the most."

Berlioz reached Berlin on 3 June (Gregorian calendar). There he was joined by Marie Recio – at any rate she is mentioned, for the first time, in a letter to Morel written on 20 June, the day after the performance of *The Damnation of Faust*.

Faust had mixed fortunes in Berlin. The royal invitation promised Berlioz half the gross receipts, but von Küstner, the intendant, insisted on subtracting the costs first, which left him a profit of little over 400 francs. On the eve of the concert the King asked for the starting-time to be advanced to six o'clock, with the result that many of the audience arrived in the middle of the second part. Of the singers, Boeticher, whom he had admired and worked with four years before, was a splendid Mephistopheles, but the Faust, Krause, and the Marguerite, Brexendorff, were worse than useless.

To be torn to pieces by the great Rellstab in the *Vossischer Zeitung* was routine and indeed honourable; the same had happened to Meyerbeer and Spontini (and, if Berlioz had known, to Chopin). But, for the first time in Germany, he had to contend with an actively hostile group in the orchestra, fomented by the first flute, who took offence at the statement in the "Letters from Germany" that Paris, inferior to Germany in clarinettists and brass-players, excelled it in flautists. The man persuaded some of his colleagues that the whole orchestra had been insulted (though Berlioz had described it as "magnificent" and "outstanding for its precision, ensemble, vigour and refinement", as he reminded the concert-master Leopold Ganz in a letter written just before his departure). The intendant had to call the band to order, and some of the musicians were fined. After that things began to improve. At the concert the playing was as good as he had known in *Faust*, and the singing of the choir, trained by Essler, better: the sylphs' scene in particular had a quality of sound that not even the Petersburg chorus could equal.

It is doubtful if a less inadequate Faust and Marguerite would have made much difference to the reception of the work. His anxiety lest Germany "bear him a grudge for having musicalized her great poem" was well founded. When Brexendorff got the bird for "The King of Thulé", Berlioz had more than a suspicion that the composer was included in the boos, and that it was not merely the partisans of Prince Radziwill, composer of his own setting of *Faust*, who were indignant at a Frenchman laying hands on a sacred German masterpiece and mangling it for his own immoral purposes.

If they had stopped to think, they might have acknowledged that the text of any literary work, however eminent, is necessarily adapted when set to music. But to recognize that the music of the *Damnation* was respectful of Goethe would have required them to approach it without prejudice and to listen to it with understanding. Berlioz, being both an intelligent person and no nationalist, could only respond with the scornful declension, "Patriotism – Fetishism – Cretinism", while wondering "why those same carpers have never lectured me about the libretto of my *Romeo and Juliet* symphony, which differs considerably from the immortal tragedy. No doubt it is because Shakespeare *was not a German*."

The King, however, appeared well satisfied, and decorated his visitor with the Cross of the Red Eagle. Earlier he invited him to dinner at Sans Souci and, in the garden after dessert, singled him out among the guests, calling out "Hey, Berlioz! Come and give me news of my sister and tell me about your Russian trip", and engaging him in conversation for so long and with such good humour that the watching courtiers could not wait to be presented to him: "a man who makes the King laugh and laughs with him!" It reminded Berlioz of the scene in *The Huguenots* where Raoul de Nangis receives the Queen's letter and is immediately surrounded by people exclaiming, "Vous savez si je suis un ami sûr et tendre". Next evening he and Meyerbeer took tea at the Crown Princess's salon, and he was invited back the day after for a more intimate chat. The Crown Princess was in the theatre early in the morning for the two final rehearsals. Whatever his critics might say about the profanation of Goethe, he was a celebrity. Only the French ambassador ignored him. Meyerbeer, visiting him at the Hôtel du Nord, was accosted on the stairs by the proprietor, who clutched him by the sleeve and cried, "Oh, Herr Generaldirektor, what a man this Berlioz is – and how unfortunate for me that I put him on the third floor!"

Berlioz's plan had been to make several stops on the way home. As late as 22 June, three days before his departure from Berlin, he was still intending to give concerts in Hamburg and Bremen, and was talking of not returning to Paris for a month or longer. He was in no hurry to be back. Paris was the place that had "punished him for writing" *The Damnation of Faust*, and where Félicien David's new symphonic ode *Christopher Columbus*, unlike *Faust*, had been given its première in the Conservatoire Hall and, again unlike *Faust*, was making a mint of money. (Its success, wrote Roger to Berlioz, made one despair of Parisian taste; the work was simply *Le désert* recycled, "the same old camel with its legs cut off to make a ship".) What caused Berlioz to change his plans and go straight back, stopping only in Cologne, was no doubt the news that Pillet had gone at last and Roqueplan and Duponchel were the chosen successors. He was in Paris early in July.

He would have done better to stay in Germany. After all, he knew his men and knew how much reliance to place on them. As he realized only too soon, he ought never to have listened to them, and in any case should not have helped two such anti-musical mediocrities become directors of the Opéra. His duty, he admitted, lay not in smoothing their path to power but in stopping them by all possible means. But their promise to make him musical director "dazzled" him. "I immediately thought of the great things that might be achieved with such an instrument by someone who knew how to use it."

It did not him take long to discover how matters stood. Every time he tried to see Roqueplan and Duponchel, either they failed to keep the appointment or one of them would turn up a couple of hours late and apologize for not being able to have any useful discussion in the "unavoidable absence" of the other. By the time he contrived to meet them, the post of musical director had disappeared from the agenda. The co-principal conductorship, unfortunately, was not available either – Girard would not hear of dividing the position. But they might perhaps make Berlioz *chef du chant* (head of singing) instead.

For a while it seemed they actually might. Early in August he cancelled a long-planned visit to La Côte St André with Louis on the grounds that he would be taking up his new duties on 1 September and there was too much to do in the meantime. As late as 15 August the *Gazette* announced that the directors of the Opéra had "just recruited our collaborator Berlioz, putting him in charge of vocal and choral preparation". From the directors' point of view, having him on the staff, however undesirable in other respects, meant that they would be spared the usual attacks in the *Débats*. They would also be safe from any danger of having to put on *La nonne sanglante* or any other work of his: a ministerial rule prohibited employees of the house from writing for it. It had not stopped Halévy having three works given there while he was *chef du chant*. But the rule was still technically in force, and could be invoked for Berlioz.

There followed a fortnight of bureaucratic delays and haggling over the salary – after which, wearying of the whole business, he accepted a much more lucrative engagement in London, the conductorship of Adolphe Jullien's Grand English Opera at the Theatre Royal, Drury Lane.

Berlioz had already been approached by Jullien with a view to adapting *The Damnation of Faust* for the Drury Lane stage, and was in correspondence with Scribe about the necessary changes and enlargement to the libretto. On the heels of that came an offer which there was no resisting: to take charge of the musical side of an annual winter season at a salary of £400 (10,000 francs) and, in addition, to compose an opera for 1848–9 and, for another 10,000 francs, to give four concerts of his own music during a further four-week period. The appointment (apparently brokered by the Escudier brothers) was to be for six years. Berlioz promptly wrote to Rocqueplan and Duponchel releasing them from their promises, while offering, diplomatically, to remain at their service in any way that suited them. Their reply, published in the *Gazette* and the *Monde musical*, was a model of its kind.

> My dear Berlioz
> Your letter came as a surprise and a disappointment; but the friendly terms in which it was conceived encourage us to believe that you harbour no resentment at the unintended delay in the concluding of our arrangements. We like to think that you decided you would prefer not to stifle your musical genius by confining it in a position which is partly an administrative one, and that at your age, at the height of your powers, you would rather be free to pursue an unhampered career of noble artistic experiment. As for our regrets, they are sincere. It enhanced our prestige to have a name so closely associated with the advancement and rejuvenation of music at the head of such an important department. We are losing one of our most glorious banners in the campaign we have undertaken. It remains for us to count on the kind undertakings with which your letter ends, and to hope that they will not be in vain.
> Be assured, my dear Berlioz, of our regard and our devotion.
>
> Nestor Roqueplan, Duponchel

Berlioz was free to go on holiday: Drury Lane did not require him till the beginning of November. The last ten days of August were spent writing his second "Letter from Vienna" for the *Débats*, preparing for a concert promoted by Baron Taylor's Association des Artistes Musiciens (in the end not given), and getting ready for the London trip. Early in September he set out with Louis for Dauphiné.

The railway line from Paris to Lyon was not yet complete, and they went by coach, as Louis' father had done in the days when he travelled home to face the parental wrath over his vocation. For Louis, aged thirteen, it was the fulfilment of a dream. His father had so often talked of taking him to see Dr Berlioz and failed to do so that he had almost stopped believing in it. (A letter of the previous June thanked his Aunt Nancy for arranging for him "to spend the holidays with my grandfather who I love so much, for it's sure I shall go, for if it had been Papa or Mama I wouldn't have taken any notice, because two years ago Papa promised to send me there but didn't, and last year Mama and Papa promised I would go to England and I haven't.") This time it was really happening. What he felt on seeing at last the relative who had loomed so largely and beneficently in his imagination is not recorded. Louis had come to accept that his grandfather was not equal to answering his letters – the task was delegated to Nancy – so perhaps he was partly prepared for the shock of finding a frail, deaf old man with the shakes, living on opium and obsessed with his bowels ("talking about them in the street, with full details", Adèle complained). We get a happier glimpse of Dr Berlioz in the *Memoirs*' account of the visit, laughing with pleasure at Hector's description of the Tilsit postmaster springing to his feet on hearing his name and exclaiming, "You don't mean it!" Berlioz recalled "the naïve pride he took, in spite of all his philosophy, in this unusual evidence of his son's celebrity. 'You don't mean it!' he would repeat, with renewed laughter. 'In Tilsit, did you say?' 'Yes, on the Niemen, the eastern frontier of Prussia.' 'You don't mean it!', and he would laugh again."

Berlioz must have realized that very possibly they would never see each other again. They spoke at length of his career, and were reconciled. The old man kept returning to the Requiem and his wish that he could get to know it. "Yes, I should like to hear that tremendous Dies irae that I have been told so much about. After that I would gladly say, like Simeon, 'Nunc dimittis servum tuum, Domine.'"

The coming of Hector and Louis brought the whole family to La Côte: Nancy with Camille and Mathilde, Adèle with her husband Marc and their two daughters, Joséphine and Nancy, perhaps Félix Marmion too – at sixty now a retired colonel – and his wife; for though Marmion had failed in his attempt to persuade the King to let him stay on in the army – he was still, his petition pointed out, in the prime of life – he had finally succeeded in marrying a wealthy widow.

It was not an altogether happy reunion. Adèle's old grievance against her brother-in-law Camille Pal, in whose slightest gesture she saw a veiled insult to her socially inferior husband, flared up again. Berlioz, accompanying her back to Vienne on the way to Lyon at the end of the holiday, reasoned with her in vain. For Louis, however, the two weeks spent in the family house were like paradise. He had his father's company and active affection for longer than at any time since he was a little boy. They went shooting together, Louis with his own gun which his father had bought him. Monique, the housekeeper, made a great fuss of him; he saw his aunts, who loved him, and met his cousins; and his grandfather presented him with a watch. He would look back on it as the happiest time of his life.

It was a life admittedly not over-rich in happiness. The effect of his broken home and his lonely exile at boarding-school was becoming more apparent. Louis' letters from this period show a child full of natural affection but painfully conscious of his day-to-day isolation from those dearest to him. This one, written to Nancy, dates from the previous spring, when Berlioz was in Russia.

Dear Aunt

I have written a letter to my grandfather who I love a lot, and Papa told me it would make him happy. Please I beg you reply to me each time I write to my grandfather, as I will be happy. Dear Aunt, I have just taken communion for the fourth time, last Sunday. I am not so high in my class as last year but I am working better, which gives me hope for next year. Mama is feeling better than two months ago when she was ill, and if I go to Paris, as I hope, she will be pleased, but I am not sure of going, for Mama does not have enough money, but the headmaster still has twenty francs of mine and perhaps he will let me have it. Talking of twenty francs, the little gold piece you gave me is lost in spite of the care Mama took to keep it for me. Please, dear Aunt, tell me the address of my good Uncle Marmion, as I would very much like to write to him. Dear Aunt, I'm getting cleverer every day at drawing and singing, in June I am going to sing the psalms of David, done by the son of a friend of Papa whose house I go to, called M. Berdealleains. You'll see, one of these days I will be a singer.* Dear Aunt, if I go to Paris at Easter I promise to tell Mama to write to you – it's that Mama doesn't dare because she doesn't write good spelling and she is afraid her letter won't get there, but that's all right, I will beg her to write as soon as possible, and will show her your letter. Dear Aunt, give my love to my uncle, my grandfather, my Aunt Adèle and my two uncles and give them a thousand kisses from me. I on my side will embrace Mama for you. Dear Aunt, tell me if you know where my cousin François and my cousin Pauline

---

* The previous October Louis wrote: "Everybody says I will be a great tenor when I am grown up, and that I will be a painter, because I have lots of feeling in the two arts."

are, as I would like very much to write to them too. As I am writing to you I take this opportunity to ask for their addresses, it is such a long time since I wrote to any relations except Papa and Mama. Dear Aunt, Papa gave a requiem at St Eustache which was a success and an opera at the Opéra-Comique, *The Damnation of Faust*, which was also such a success that Papa was given a medal. Dear Aunt, tell me when you can come to Paris to see Mama and Papa, as that will give them great pleasure and me too. Farewell, dear and good Aunt, I send my love to you and all the family and to good Monique.

> Your nephew Louis

The contrast between the days at La Côte and the reality of the Lycée, to which he returned from Paris early in October, was too much, and a violent reaction followed. He had been badgering his father to take him away from Rouen and send him to a college in Paris or Versailles, but Berlioz refused, presumably pointing out that his grant would be forfeit if he did, and encouraging him to work harder and augment it by winning prizes (a system still known in France today). The response this prompted was written with a disregard of the rules of spelling quite untypical of Louis and obviously intended to provoke:

Dear Father

It is true, I can win prizes if I want but I don't want, not at all, you will see if I don't stick to my word. I swear to you that I won't, because *I don't want to*. I've already begun on my plan – I'm 45th out of 45 pupils in the sixth grade, and have to go back two classes, so at 14 [13] years of age I am still at the seventh after 7 years of Latin, and I shall do so well that you will be really pleased with what I have said. You can't agree to me changing colleges, well I can't agree to staying, so whatever you do you can't make me do it. My letter was all right because a master corrected it for me. You say a fine boy like me shouldn't talk like that. Well, I will talk like that. M. Bérat charges 100 fr. for two lessons a week, two hours each. If I'm sent away from the college you know I can't get in to any other college. You don't want me to lose half my scholarship, you want me to stay and win prizes, well I will lose it all just to please myself and even more so as not to go to college at Rouen any more.

> Farewell.   L. Berlioz

11 October 1847

At least say *if you can agree* to tell me how Mama is.

There is no record of how the father answered the son's show of defiance. Louis stayed on in Rouen, and Berlioz made ready to depart for London. He could not wait to get away. It was a break from everything and everybody. After "a whole series of coups d'état" (he told Tajan-Rogé) his right to go on his own, without Marie, had been conceded. As for Harriet, who was still drinking, he supported her and her household but saw little of her. For the moment, he was free. There were no ties to keep him in Paris – no public avid for his music, no established position to call forth his powers. The third opera house for which he had campaigned had come into being at last, but without him: Adolphe Adam had secured the privilege and was busy transforming the Cirque-Olympique into the Opéra-National.

It was as if all his work for higher standards over the past fifteen years had achieved nothing. His old adversaries Castil-Blaze and Fétis were still at it. Castil-Blaze had just made a new version of *Fidelio* which incorporated the Seventh Symphony, in a vocal arrangement. Fétis was now an influential voice on the *Gazette*. The journal that summer gave prominent billing to a three-part essay on "Recent Transformations in the Symphony", in which, just as in the old days, the Brussels sage wrote about Beethoven with ineffable condescension, dismissing the Ninth as a dead end and rebuking its errors and general lack of artistic vitality, and the aberrations for which it had been responsible in modern music. Such an article would not have appeared under Schlesinger's editorship. But Schlesinger had sold his business to Gemmy Brandus, and Fétis was solidly entrenched. The much-talked-of alterations at the Opéra would, Berlioz knew, be strictly cosmetic. Foyers and auditorium had been lavishly redecorated, and people were flocking to the place once more; but though some better singers had joined the company and the chorus had taken advantage of the closure to rehearse, he could not believe any lasting good would come of it, given that Nestor Roqueplan and Duponchel were as ignorant as Pillet and much less interested in music. (A year later, he was reporting that the "Nestoration" of the Opéra had finished it off altogether.) Berlioz's disenchantment was complete. His friends might say what they liked; but he was "renouncing *la belle France* for perfidious Albion". Though he longed for it to be otherwise, it was so. In a letter written from London not long afterwards he tried to sum up for one of them, Morel, the reasons that had led him inescapably to this decision:

As for France, I've given up thinking about it. God keep me from yielding to temptations such as you put forward in your last letter, that I come and give a concert in Paris in April. If ever I am rich enough to *give* concerts for my Paris friends I will do so; but don't imagine that I am any longer so naïve as to rely on the public to cover the costs. I shall make no further appeals to its attention, simply to be rewarded with indifference and lose the money I gain with such effort from my travels. It will be for me a great sadness, for the sympathies of my friends in France are still those that are dearest to me. But facts are facts. Having compared the impression produced by my music on all the audiences in Europe that have heard it, I am forced to conclude that it is Paris that understands it least. Have I ever seen at my Paris concerts *members of society*, men and women, *moved* as I have in Germany and Russia? Have I seen princes of the blood interested in my compositions to the point of getting up at eight in the morning in order to come and sit in a dark cold hall and listen to them being rehearsed, as the Princess of Prussia did in Berlin? Have I ever been invited to take the smallest part in a concert at court? Does the Conservatoire Society, or at least the people who run it, show anything but hostility to me? Is it not grotesque that they perform works by everyone who has the slightest name in music but not by me? Is it not wounding to me to see the Opéra constantly having recourse to musical bunglers, and its directors armed at all points against me with prejudices which I should be ashamed to have to combat if their hands were ever forced? Does the press not grow daily more vile, do we find anything in it (with rare exceptions) but intrigue, skulduggery and idiocy?

Even the people I have so often helped and supported by my articles – have they ever shown the slightest real recognition of it? And do you imagine that I am taken in by all those smiling people who conceal their nails and teeth only because they know that I have claws and can defend myself? To witness on all sides nothing but imbecility, indifference, ingratitude, threats – that is my lot in Paris. If at least my friends were happy there! But far from it: nearly all of you are slaves to disagreeable, thankless positions; I can do nothing for you, and your efforts on my behalf are of no avail. For these reasons, France is wiped from my musical map, and I have made up my mind as far as possible not to look to it, and not to think of it, any more. I am not in the least in a gloomy frame of mind to day; I don't have the spleen; I speak to you with the greatest sang-froid, and with complete lucidity of mind. I see things as they are.

15

An Exile in London

If only he had! If only the expectations he took with him to London at the beginning of November 1847 had been half, even a quarter fulfilled!

Berlioz had great hopes of England. He thought seriously of settling there. There would no doubt be prejudice to overcome, but so there was everywhere, and it had not stopped him in Germany, or Austria, or Russia. The death of Mendelssohn at the age of thirty-eight, on the very day he arrived, though a grievous loss to music and a shock to him personally, could be seen as leaving the English in want of a foreign celebrity to take to their hearts. Eternally optimistic, he imagined that he might be the one.

Not all his hopes were disappointed. He found audiences capable of rising to the challenge of the new, musicians who responded, and critics willing to swallow their preconceptions and think again. He left good friends there and keen supporters. The visit led to further engagements in the 1850s. It began what was to be in years to come a close relationship between England and his music, sustained by a succession of conductors with a marked affinity for it: Ganz, Hallé, Richter, Harty, Beecham, and in our own time Colin Davis, Roger Norrington, John Eliot Gardiner, Simon Rattle, to name only the most obvious. But in terms of his immediate career and the bright financial prospects that had been held out to him, it was – in the words of the *Memoirs* – "the old familiar story".

He had not been totally unprepared. Before he left Paris the Escudiers signed a counter-deed releasing him from the agent's commission "in the event of Jullien's failing to carry out his agreement in full". A week after he arrived in London he told Tajan-Rogé that Jullien, having "made his own fortune", had "got it into his head that he is going to construct mine"; but "I have my doubts." He cannot have been unaware of the scepticism surrounding this latest gamble. ("So Jullien is trying opera," observed Lumley, the manager of Her Majesty's Theatre; "I believed him in better circumstances.") But taking risks was part of the impresario's game. To succeed at it required courage, a quality in which Jullien, who as a boy had distinguished himself for bravery at the battle of Navarino and later had been one of the most noted duellists in Paris, was by no means lacking. And, lunatic though he might be, the man's optimism was infectious. Besides, he had, manifestly, made a great deal of money. He knew the English scene. As a contemporary remarked, "the world laughed at him but applauded too, and paid him handsomely for the entertainment he afforded". He had a flair not only for publicity but also, between whiles, for serious music-making. Louis Engel, looking back on Jullien's career, was in no doubt that "this country thirty years ago owed [him] much with regard to orchestral music". He was (Engel continued) "certainly by all outward signs a charlatan. The grimaces which he made when conducting, the studied preparation of his appearance, his over-embroidered French cambric shirt-front and, to put it mildly, the exaggeration of the stories he used to tell, misled a number of people into thinking he was nothing but a humbug. But it happens very often that in external habits and manner a man may be a humbug, yet seriously and profoundly able where his proper work is concerned."

Jullien's famous Promenade Concerts – of which though not the originator he was the acknowledged king – shrewdly mixed the popular and the classical. If people came for the glamorous dance numbers, played by an exceptionally large and capable orchestra (augmented by, among other things, a garden-roller dragged over sheets of iron in simulation of "the roar of heaven's artillery"), or for the spectacle – not only such effects as the lighting of pans of red fire and the detonation of maroons at the psychological moment in the *Huguenots* quadrille but the moustachioed maestro himself ("the Mons." as *Punch* called him), dressed to the nines, rebuking the audience for its inattention and conducting Beethoven in white gloves and with a jewelled baton which a footman handed him on a silver salver – they stayed for the symphonies. Whatever the means, Berlioz had no quarrel with the end. And Jullien had taken an obvious shine to him and sincerely meant to make him rich. He could only let him try. In any event, he was committed to the enterprise.

The omens at first seemed good. Berlioz travelled to London some time in the first week of November, in the company of an English journalist, Charles Gruneisen, an acquaintance from Gruneisen's years

as Paris correspondent of the *Morning Post* and a staunch advocate of
his music. The Channel was smooth as a lake; and on their arrival at
Folkestone Gruneisen sprang on to the quay ahead of him and, turning
round, shook his hand and bade him "welcome to British soil" – a
gesture of national pride (Berlioz remarked to his father) "such as would
never occur to a continental". The sheer size of the great city astonished
him as the train drew in to London Bridge station – he would have
agreed with Mr Podsnap's Foreign Gentleman that "London, Londres,
London" was indeed Very Large – and the impression deepened as the
cab rattled along broad thoroughfares and through spacious squares
to Jullien's residence at the southern end of Harley Street. Though at
that date London had spread westward no further than Bayswater, and
Notting Hill was still covered with fields and woods, and Kensington
and Chelsea were distinct villages, the scale of the place was daunting
after Paris; robust walker as he was, he found it rather more than the
mere "step" he had been assured was all that separated Harley Street
from the Theatre Royal at the bottom of Drury Lane. Jullien took him
there immediately after his arrival and showed him round the theatre
– the same in which Harriet Smithson had made her London début
thirty years before.

His quarters too were lavish, as well as rent-free. Jullien and his
English wife Susan, a former flower-seller, lived in style. (Maretzek,
chorus-master at Drury Lane and arranger-in-chief for the Promenade
Concerts, recalled being shown in by "a footman in a blue-velvet,
gold-buttoned dress coat, satin knee-breeches, silk stockings and
buckled shoes" and, when he asked Jullien "why this ceremony?", being
told "C'est la mise-en-scène! Absolutely necessary in this country.") On
the 8th Jullien paid the first instalment of his salary – £100 (2,500 francs)
– and took him to Coutts' Bank in the Strand, where he opened an
account. Berlioz discovered he knew more English than he had supposed.
Though he understood less than half of what people were saying
("there's a lot of hard work to be done there"), he could say almost
everything he needed to and with surprisingly little accent. Soon afterwards he heard the orchestra – his orchestra – in action at a Promenade
Concert and was impressed by its quality. Made up of players from
Covent Garden and Her Majesty's (whose seasons were not due to
begin for several months) and typically international in character,
it contained many friends and acquaintances of his – the violinists
Auguste-Joseph Tolbecque and Prosper Sainton, the cellists Alfredo

Piatti and Scipion Rousselot, and Baumann the bassoonist among others. They gave him an ovation after the Weber–Berlioz *Invitation to the Waltz* and were obviously pleased to see him. Jullien was certainly doing things on the grand scale. He had engaged a chorus of over a hundred, and had had the theatre lavishly refurbished for the opening of what was claimed to be the first truly national English-language opera house of modern times. "The new drop scene," reported one newspaper, "painted to imitate white satin, surmounted by blue hangings, well accords with the general light effect of the beautifully decorated *salle*."

In the matter of casts, not to mention repertoire and performing material, the company was admittedly on weaker ground. Mme Jullien went to Paris in October to recruit Pauline Viardot, Mlle Nau and Duprez, but none of them took the bait, though Viardot, according to the *Musical World*, was offered the enormous fee of 100 guineas a night for forty performances. It had been left somewhat late to engage top-class singers, especially top-class singers who were willing to relearn their roles in English. In the end she secured the services of Dorus-Gras, who was popular with the London public as a concert artist and whose English pronunciation was said to be acceptable; the soprano was signed up for the whole three-month season at a fee of 50,000 francs, and was to open it with Donizetti's *Bride of Lammermuir*. Much was expected of Jullien's protégé, the young tenor Sims Reeves, fresh from several years' study in Italy and a successful début at La Scala. He would sing Edgar opposite Dorus-Gras' Lucy and also the male lead in a new opera, *The Maid of Honour*, by Balfe, in which the popular Miss Birch would sing the titular heroine. But they were still short in several departments. Berlioz found himself negotiating in the director's name. He exchanged letters with the Viennese soprano Barthe-Hasselt, but nothing came of it. Pischek was secured; then his wife died, and he cancelled. Staudigl, another London favourite, agreed to take part; in the end he did not come either.

As to repertoire and material, here too Jullien showed himself unversed in opera management. He had hopes of putting on one of Halévy's recent works, though it might have to wait till the following season. He was also very keen to do *Robert le diable* but appeared to have no idea of the planning and preparation involved – quite apart from the little matter of an English translation – nor of the voices they would need. *Iphigénie en Tauride* was talked of, and Jullien got very excited at the thought of the pearl-encrusted gold helmet and plume of ostrich feathers Pylades would wear in the fifth act. Though the newly formed company had no scores or chorus and orchestra parts of its own, except for Balfe's opera, Jullien was quite unperturbed: he had an arrangement with the people at Her Majesty's, they would lend him everything he needed.

Jullien, Berlioz had to admit, was a master of improvisation and an ingenious, audacious fellow. He was responsive to every new idea, abounded in projects, and was forever picking his conductor's brains. At his behest Berlioz wrote to Paris on one errand after another: to commission the scenario of a two-act ballet from Théophile Gautier in time for production not later than the beginning of February; to find out how successful Verdi's new opera *Jérusalem* had really been ("this is a director's question, and is not concerned with merit"); to order twenty copies of his *Voyage musical* from Delahaye the bookseller in the Rue Voltaire, for Jullien had a notion he could interest a London publisher in bringing out an English edition. Some of his schemes died a natural death. A few days after arriving in London Berlioz told his father that he was going to write a piece on the theme of *God Save the Queen* for the theatre's opening night. "I hadn't thought of it but Jullien who has his eyes and ears everywhere would like me to repeat what I did to the Hungarians in Pesth and make the English native lyre twang." Not surprisingly, nothing came of it. We have to wait till *The Trojans*, Acts 1 and 3 – the Trojan March and "Gloire à Didon" – for another Berliozian national anthem.

Jullien freely conceded that the company was short of star singers but said he was willing and able to treat this first season as a long-term investment and wait till the second to recoup on it; the début of the great Pischek in *Mephistopheles*, the stage version of *The Damnation of Faust* with which he intended to open the second season, would be all the more sensational for Pischek's not being heard in London this winter. After that would come the new opera with libretto by Royer and Vaëz. Berlioz exchanged letters with Scribe about *Mephistopheles* and also about the possibility, suggested by Scribe, of their doing another opera for Jullien which incorporated some of the existing music of *La nonne sanglante* – the *Nun* herself now having to be considered a dead duck, since Roqueplan and Duponchel, knowing how much had still to be written, accepted it only on condition that it went into rehearsal immediately.

For the four concerts for which Berlioz was contracted (and for which Henry Chorley, the critic, was already busy making an English version of *Faust*), Jullien was of the firm opinion that rather than start at once they should wait till the end of January, by which time the Queen would be back in town and Drury Lane in full swing. Berlioz agreed and got on with preparing *Lucia*. The start of full rehearsals in the second half of November was a welcome distraction from the bouts of ennui which attacked him in his first weeks in London. Despite the dinners and suppers he attended he felt lonely, and found himself missing Marie. A friend of Morel's, a secretary at the French embassy called Grimblot, was a frequent and stimulating visitor and helped to keep the spleen at bay. Grimblot made him an honorary member of his club, the Athenaeum ("God knows what entertainment is to be found in an English club," he wrote to Morel). On 17 November at Exeter Hall (today the Strand Palace Hotel) he heard Mendelssohn's *Elijah* – "a magnificent work, of indescribable richness of harmony". On the 23rd Macready, who had acted with Harriet in *Macbeth* and *Jane Shore* in Paris twenty years before, gave a dinner party in his honour at his house in Clarence Terrace, just north of Baker Street, by the park, and Berlioz met Thackeray, Morris Barnett the critic, the playwright Tom Taylor, the mesmerist Elliotson, Dickens's wife (a nearish neighbour, in Devonshire Terrace), Julius Benedict the composer – an old friend from Paris days, who lived in Manchester Square – and Adelaide Procter the poetess, author of "The Lost Chord". A few days later he saw Macready in Henry Taylor's historical drama *Philip van Artefelde* at the Princess Theatre in Oxford Street.

By now Dorus-Gras had arrived, Sims Reeves was proving to be a charming and stylish singer not unreminiscent of Rubini, and rehearsals were intensifying. It was Berlioz's first experience of conducting opera in the opera house, a dream he had long cherished. He surely wished it had been with something more to his taste than *Lucia*; but he must have been delighted to be working in a theatre at last. During rehearsals he re-seated the orchestra, separating the cellos and double-basses into two groups and placing the horns with the other brass instruments, not on the opposite side of the pit.

The Bride of Lammermuir opened the season on Monday 6 December amid scenes of gratifying enthusiasm. Dorus-Gras, an expert Lucy, was recalled several times, and Reeves created – in the words of the *Illustrated London News* – "the greatest sensation of any tenor since the days of

Braham"; his final curtain was the signal for such "tumultuous cheering" that the ensemble at the end of Act 2 was performed again as an encore. No one had heard so fine an opera chorus before; and the precision, power and delicacy of the orchestral playing were much remarked on. *Lucia* having no overture, Berlioz, who wanted his musicians to have something they could get their teeth into, made it a pretext for starting the season with some Beethoven, and *Leonore no. 2* brought the house down. At the end of the opera Jullien appeared, bowing repeatedly, to loud acclamation, the national anthem was sung by audience and performers "in grand chorus", and the evening closed with a ballet, conducted by Maretzek. The press was in the main warmly encouraging. Reeves was hailed as a major discovery, and Berlioz as "one of the greatest living *chefs d'orchestre*"; Mme Dorus-Gras' vocal agility was judged to be as remarkable as ever and her accent treated indulgently; and it was recognized that the décor and the costumes, which made the actors look like real Scotchmen of the period, not like "characters in a masked ball", represented a welcome break with Italian operatic tradition, and that the careful preparation of the whole performance set new standards of excellence. The *Morning Post* spoke for many when it hoped that "the new effort made last night to establish an English lyrical establishment will succeed", the lack of one having been till then "a national reproach". J. W. Davison in the *Musical World* concluded that "M. Jullien has fulfilled the promises of his prospectus in every item. He has provided one of the very finest bands in the world; a complete and powerful chorus; the best performers he could possibly obtain, and a conductor whose name is European. That M. Jullien may succeed to his utmost expectations this year is our earnest wish; his outlay has been enormous." And the review in the *Times* (Davison again) ended with "All's well that *begins* well."

Davison, who had been in Paris, had arrived just in time for the performance, bringing Marie Recio with him. They took the steam-packet from Boulogne but in mid-Channel hit a westerly so strong that the boat was forced to put in at Ramsgate. Berlioz was at London Bridge to meet them before hurrying off to the theatre. Marie seems to have stayed about a fortnight. On 18 December she signed a receipt at Coutts' Bank for the substantial sum of £39.7.6, presumably on the eve of her return to Paris.

The first hint that all might not end well comes in a letter from Berlioz to Belloni, Liszt's agent, written on the 19th: "I have a superb orchestra and a chorus of 120 first-rate voices. However, I fancy all this musical abundance will be reduced later to a decent minimum." *Lucia* was doing respectable business and the reputation of the company stood high; but Jullien was already beginning to run out of options. He had the ideal tenor but a less than ideal prima donna, for Dorus-Gras, as the *Musical World* later put it, "either could not or would not learn the English words of a second opera" – she refused both Amina in *Sonnambula* and Susanna in *Figaro* – "so that the *Lucy of Lammermoor*, worn to a thread at the Italian theatres, was obliged to be played night after night", with inevitably declining receipts.

In the meantime Balfe's *The Maid of Honour*, the season's second offering, had opened (20 December), with Sims Reeves and Charlotte Birch in the leading roles and the composer conducting, and was drawing good houses, partly on the strength of the ballad sung by Reeves in the last act, "In this old chair my father sat", which was invariably encored.

It was still not enough. Jullien, living far beyond his means, had spent with a magnificence that presupposed full houses at every performance, and had reached the end of his resources. Berlioz was due for his second £100 at the end of the first week of December, but pay-day came and went; all he received was assurances. Early in January he discovered the dismal truth. It was not the Drury Lane affair that had done for Jullien: he was done for already. The opera company, if not (as the cynical Lumley assumed) a pretext to get himself declared bankrupt, was at best the throw of a gambler, an adventurer whose image was inseparable from the flamboyance which periodically ruined him. The full extent of his plight was revealed when the sale of his Regent Street music shop for nearly £8,000 left him still heavily in debt. Somehow fresh credit was arranged – though Berlioz prudently removed his scores and musical material from Harley Street to Grimblot's lodgings to forestall seizure by the bailiffs – and the season continued. But it did so by dint of the conductor, the chief singers, the chorus-master, the ballet-master and the stage-manager all agreeing to a cut of a third in their salaries, on Jullien's promising to make up the money later. The irrepressible impresario then set off on a concert tour of the British Isles, taking half the orchestra with him, including some of the best players.

Before he left, a meeting of the English Grand Opera's committee was summoned to decide what to put on next. Berlioz pushed the claims of *Iphigénie en Tauride*, Sir Henry Bishop hinted that a revival of one of his operas would meet the case, and Planché thought they could not do better than give Planché's, and Weber's, *Oberon*. In the end they settled on another Donizetti, *Linda di Chamounix*. An English translation was commissioned in haste, and "after sundry announcements and postponements from day to day" (*Musical World*) the work was put on with a cast which apart from Willoughby Weiss and the contralto Miss Miran (Lady Alison in Balfe's opera, and like Reeves a Jullien discovery) was made up of English singers new to the operatic stage. Not surprisingly it was the weakest of the company's productions. The *Musical World* attributed the continued good houses not to *Linda* but to the popular French ballerina Mlle Sophie Fuoco, who was on the bill most nights. The press, however, was generally sympathetic, the *Illustrated London News* regretting the débutants' lack of success despite Jullien's "untiring and praiseworthy" efforts to establish a native English opera: "he has already made us acquainted with a magnificent tenor and contralto, and given certain representations with a completeness never before known on our boards".

By mid-January Berlioz, with the rump of the orchestra and a reduced chorus, was conducting *The Maid of Honour*, *Linda* and *Lucia*, all without payment: the 33⅓ per cent cut had turned out to mean no salary at all. He was also suffering from a fluey cold and cough which was not responding to "treatment by fatigue and theatre draughts" and which towards the end of the month became bronchitis. The winter was mild and infections were rife. On the 29th, the *Musical World* reported, "medical certificates certified that neither Miss Birch nor Mr Whitworth could appear" in *The Maid of Honour*, and as Dorus-Gras refused to sing two nights running, the theatre was left "to get on as glibly as it could with *Linda di Chamounix*, a last resource!" Berlioz was in bed for nearly a week and Tolbecque the concert-master directed several performances in his place. His illness, he admitted, had been exacerbated by anger and sheer frustration. The trumpeted "English Grand Opera", he told General Lvov, had resolved itself into two Donizettis and a Balfe, and as for some of the *chanteuses anglaises* that he had to put up with, "they would make the hairs on your violin bow twist and snap". Maretzek, the chorus master, in his reminiscences, describes Berlioz's mood – so optimistic when he first arrived – as gloomy in the extreme: he never referred to Jullien except as "My Salary", while Balfe became "My Old Armchair". Thus, "My Old Armchair is getting played out, it needs a new frame, new springs and new coverings"; or "Have you heard any news of My Salary?"; or "I see by the papers that My Salary has had a big success in Leeds."

Jullien, whom the *Musical World* reported as "making a mint of money" in the provinces, was still insisting in his letters that they would all be paid; and the Drury Lane season staggered on. *Iphigénie* was announced as being in preparation. It failed to materialize (not altogether to Berlioz's regret, given Miss Birch's doubtful intonation). The same happened with *Haydée*, Auber's latest hit at the Opéra-Comique, which was advertised but not performed. In the end, with two weeks of the season to go, *Figaro* was added to the repertory. In spite of a less than brilliant cast it restored something of the company's first lustre, winning the conductor fresh laurels and raising his spirits. He had taken the opportunity to restore most of the cuts and expunge the spurious orchestration in use at Covent Garden, and the Mozartians in the press were duly grateful.

On 7 February, four days before *Figaro* opened, Berlioz gave his first concert. Jullien had been adamant that nothing should be allowed to stand in its way (it was in any case in the contract, for what that was now worth); and in the second half of January Berlioz began preparing a varied and exacting programme of his works: *Harold*, the first two parts of *Faust*, with Sims Reeves and Weiss, the last two movements of the Symphonie funèbre, *Le jeune pâtre breton* (translated into English for Miss Miran), the *Roman Carnival* overture, the cavatina from *Benvenuto* (Dorus-Gras) and the Offertorium. It was not easy going, in the atmosphere of crisis which involved everything connected with Jullien. Attendance at rehearsals, by what was left of the orchestra, was erratic. The chorus were slow to adapt from Balfe and Donizetti to *The Damnation of Faust*. And so much hung on this first trial of strength – perhaps his whole future in a country where, many were saying, a fine position awaited him. In the end he was able to hold five rehearsals with an orchestra of fluctuating size and eighteen with the chorus; Jullien brought the flower of the band back to London in time; and the concert, performed by combined forces of nearly 250 arrayed on the Drury Lane stage, was a triumph. Julius Benedict, writing to a friend in Paris, called it "the musical event of the winter", a success, "as conductor and composer, all the more brilliant in that there had been no lack of cabals and intrigues bent on damaging him in the eyes of the London public". Four pieces were encored. At the end Berlioz was greeted with tremendous applause, "the orchestra and chorus

joining heartily in the demonstration". The success was general. Everyone, Charles Godfrey, Prince Albert's bandmaster, told him – everyone
"except our composers" – was delighted with it. The response of the
press surpassed anything that Benedict had ever seen on a first visit.
Though the *Morning Herald* grumbled about lack of counterpoint and
Chorley's review in the *Athenaeum* was at best ambiguous, the rest
was a chorus of wonder and approval. The musician whose *Francs-juges*
overture had been laughed off the platform of the Argyll Rooms ten
years before, whose music had been likened to Turner's paintings (the
touchstone of madness), whom the *Dramatic and Musical Review* had
written off as "a kind of orchestral Liszt, than which I could name
nothing more intensely disagreeable", whose *Faust* the *Times* (Davison
himself) dismissed only a year before as having "scarcely any melody
and no decided rhythm", was a composer after all.

As Morris Barnett observed in the *Morning Post*, "those who had
come to blame remained to praise; those who had heard that the music
of Berlioz was characterized by its want of invention, as well as by its
lack of science, were astonished to find new effects, learned combinations, and poetical feeling – in a word, all the attributes necessary
to constitute the great musical writer". Barnett had been at several
rehearsals, and argued that though "want of continuity" was often said
to be "the ruling sin" of Berlioz's works, once one had grasped the
composer's design one realized that "each passage illustrates the passing
thought, and each instrument forms a link in the poetical chain".

Edward Holmes, critic of the *Atlas* and friend of Keats, had been
one of those who expected not to like it:

> We the more cordially acknowledge the powerful impression made upon
> us by this first hearing of the compositions of M. Berlioz, because we
> were among the most mistrusting and infidel of the audience. Detraction
> and false criticism in professional whispers and newspaper paragraphs
> had predisposed us to expect a critical penance on the occasion; and this,
> coupled with a somewhat pardonable unwillingness hastily to believe in
> original genius, or that the implements of the great German masters had
> passed in reversion to a Frenchman, rendered us anticipative of anything
> but pleasure. Surprise and gratification were complete, as all these preju-
> dices were dispersed before the beautiful, the original and poetical effects
> of the music; and we can only say that, if Berlioz is not Beethoven, he
> who can maintain such an activity of attention during four hours, by the

frequency of original and interesting compositions, must be a worthy follower of that master, and a poet musician of no common stamp.

Holmes considered the charge that "Berlioz has no melody", and asked:

How then does he contrive to fix the attention of his hearers for hours? The fact is that he has melody – though not of the conventional standard – and he knows how to set it off, too, by exquisite harmonizing and effects of instrumentation. We confess that, to our taste, some of the most beautiful things of the evening were the choruses from *Faust*, in the second part. The Easter Hymn is a noble composition [. . .] with a long and masterly pedal point well worth hearing. There was also in this part another beautiful and melodious chorus, succeeded by a sylph dance so exceedingly fanciful and pretty that the audience could not fail of encoring it. The chorus of Souls in Purgatory, in which the voices in octaves keep up a little plaintive monotonous phrase on the dominant of D minor while the instruments continue, in the fugued style, a stream of severe counterpoint, is highly interesting and effective. The word original is too feeble and conventional to describe the effect of these works, which are pure creations.

Holmes "left the house with an earnest desire to hear the whole of the music again, and as soon as possible".

Berlioz had made his mark; and he could be forgiven for boasting, in his letters to Morel and Alfred de Vigny, that his music "took with that English audience like a match with a train of powder". However disastrous the losses he had incurred through Jullien's débâcle, he said, they faded before the joy of being able to present his music in reasonably faithful form to the London public. His appearance each evening at Drury Lane was now the signal for loud applause. At Sims Reeves's benefit on 9 February the *Roman Carnival* and Pilgrims' March were received with acclamation. As for the newspapers, he had never had such reviews. Over the next days he made a dossier of them; and he could only exclaim, in a grateful letter to Charles Gruneisen (one of many he wrote to journalists), "Long live the English critics! *There* are people who listen and don't fence with fine phrases like so many of our dear colleagues in Paris." Gruneisen's notice in the *Illustrated London News*, he added, was the only one to point out that the soloists in *Faust* didn't know their roles. "Despite that, the performance as a whole was good, I thought, though we should improve on it anon."

He desired nothing better than to repeat the concert – as soon as possible, as Holmes had said. In the event he would have to wait nearly five months for the chance to do so.

Writing in *Fraser's Magazine* that autumn Holmes concluded that "the most disastrous contingent of the failure of Jullien in his late operatic scheme at Drury Lane was the disappointment which it involved to the distinguished composer Berlioz", for whom lasting success was "just within his grasp – a success which only wanted time to confirm and repetition to popularize it".

It had been assumed that the concert would be repeated forthwith; 17 February was actually named as the date. This time, rumour had it, the Queen and the Prince Consort were coming.

The announcement was premature, as Berlioz knew only too well. "Now that Jullien is no longer paying the orchestra or the chorus, I daren't run the risk of their failing me at the last minute. Yesterday evening [11 February], after *Figaro*, the defection began. The horns told me they wouldn't be coming." There had been a near-disaster at Sims Reeves's benefit two nights before when, after the *Roman Carnival* overture, such a long delay ensued before *The Bride of Lammermuir* that the audience protested noisily, stamping their feet and shouting for Jullien. "Just as the storm seemed to have gathered to its utmost height," reported the *Musical World*, "M. Hector Berlioz walked into the orchestra, and his presence turned the tide immediately from exasperation to commendation. The band commenced the *sinfonia* to the *Lucia*, and all seemed going smooth and easy, when, just as the curtain should have gone up, out stole from the side wings a gentleman in mourning, portentously clad, and ominously affected as to his aspect, and announced 'that Madame Dorus-Gras refused to appear', whereupon there ensued such an uproar as would be difficult to describe." It transpired that the diva was in her dressing-room, fully costumed, but was waiting for an assurance that she would be paid. No such assurance being forthcoming, the part was read at sight by Miss Miran from the orchestra, a "female attendant" holding the score in front of her. "Miss Miran was greatly applauded, and acquitted herself astonishingly well when it is considered that the music of Lucy lies entirely out of the register of her voice." Happily she was relieved at the end of Act 1 by Miss Messent, who having meanwhile arrived at the theatre sang the rest of the part from the stage, and the evening was saved.

Three days later Berlioz wrote to Kittl in Prague, proposing some performances of the complete *Damnation* at the Estates Theatre. He had been thinking of staying in London till July; now, he said, he would be ready to leave for Prague at the end of the first week in March.

Jullien must have contrived to raise more money, for the season went on till its appointed close (25 February), continuing to draw good houses. On the 16th there was a command performance of *The Maid of Honour*, conducted by Berlioz; the opera was watched by the Queen and Prince Consort and the Duke and Duchess of Saxe-Coburg from a royal box done up in pink and white gauze striped with gold and with copious floral decorations to the borders and cornices. Afterwards Jullien, magnificently attired, attended them to their carriages. Bankrupt he might be, but he owed it to his public to go out in style. In the published exchange of letters with Dorus-Gras' husband which followed her defection, he made no bones about his embarrassments ("I have certainly not been able to pay Madame Dorus-Gras with the regularity which, until I entered this speculation, has characterized my money transactions in this country"). Yet at his benefit night before "a bumper house" on 23 February "his entrance into the orchestra was hailed with immense cheers from all parts of the house". Such was the affection in which he was held that no one seemed disposed to blame him. Berlioz himself, who had most reason to, could not bring himself to treat him, in his *Memoirs*, with anything worse than humorous exasperation.

Euphoric to the last, Jullien announced Berlioz's second concert for the 24th. It was a gallant gesture to his long-suffering conductor, but it was no more than that. The money he had raised was required, inexorably, elsewhere. So were the proceeds of the first concert, which were absorbed by Jullien, not by Berlioz. The fee of £100 that was owed for conducting it, together with the salary due for December, January and February – £300 – remained unpaid. It had vanished, like the further concerts he was contracted to give, like the season which was to have followed next December and the staged *Damnation* and the other projects planned for it.

Even without his second concert Berlioz was still a celebrity. The Apotheosis figured prominently in a recital at Buckingham Palace given by Godfrey and the Band of the Coldstream Guards in the presence of the Queen and Prince Albert. A few days later, on 22 February, he was a guest at the Royal Society of Musicians' annual banquet-cum-concert, held at the Freemasons' Tavern in Great Queen Street, Covent Garden (today the Connaught Rooms). The famous Braham, Weber's Sir Huon in the original *Oberon*, accompanied himself at the piano as he delivered Dibdin's "Stand to your guns, my Hearts of Oak" with a vigour that belied his seventy-four years. Charlotte Dolby, for whom Mendelssohn wrote the contralto part in *Elijah*, was encored for her charming rendering of Hatton's "Day and Night", and various madrigals, including Wilbye's "Flora gave me fairest flowers", were performed by a group of gleemen and choristers from Westminster Abbey. Berlioz was obliged to listen yet again to "In this old chair" – Sims Reeves sang it twice – but he had the satisfaction of being toasted during dessert by the acting president of the society and the six hundred male and female fellow-guests, and of being able formally to express his thanks (in French) to the public, his performers and his colleagues of the press for all they had done for him.

While they dined, the February Revolution broke out in Paris. Three days later Louis-Philippe abdicated and the Second Republic was proclaimed. Within a month the political life of the continent of Europe was transformed, with revolutionary uprisings in the Austro-Hungarian Empire and elsewhere. On Berlioz, the immediate effect was twofold: everything he heard of conditions in Paris inclined him less than ever to return; and the disturbances in Prague put an end to any immediate idea of giving concerts there – at any rate we hear no more of it. He fired off anxious letters to his friends, asking what had become of them; and, concerned about his post as Conservatoire librarian, he wrote to the new Citizen-Minister of the Interior, but received no reply.

All things considered, it would be better to stay on in London. London was safer than Paris, and cheaper: he was still living free at 76 Harley Street (Jullien had at least done that for him), he still had sixty pounds in the bank and the prospects of doing something and earning a bit of money were by no means hopeless. Frederick Beale, of Cramer and Beale, 201 Regent Street, talked seriously of putting on a grand evening of his music at Exeter Hall. The concert did not happen, but Beale agreed to publish piano-duet editions of the three orchestral movements from *Faust*, and Benedict was commissioned to do the reductions. Beale was also keen to exploit the topicality of France and revolutions by bringing out a group of patriotic pieces arranged by Berlioz for voices and piano: the Apotheosis, the Hungarian March, two Rouget de Lisle songs – the *Marseillaise* and *Mourons pour la patrie* – and Méhul's *Chant du départ*. It is not clear whether all seven works saw the light, but three certainly did: the Apotheosis, the *Marseillaise* and the Hungarian March, and Beale gave him a good price for them.

From London too dates the version of *La mort d'Ophélie* for two-part chorus and chamber orchestra which, with its diffused colours and textures – muted strings, woodwind without oboes and bassoons, concerted women's voices, including the low contralto voices he encountered there for the first time – softens and distances the sharpness of the solo voice-and-piano original to a gentler elegy. The manuscript fair copy is inscribed 6 July, but the arrangement was prompted by the idea of a Berlioz–Shakespeare evening at Covent Garden which was being discussed much earlier, in February and March, possibly as a follow-up to a performance of Shakespearean scenes given by Macready and other leading actors in aid of the fund for the purchase of the poet's house in Stratford-upon-Avon. Berlioz's insistence on a fortnight of chorus rehearsals and four full sessions with the orchestra, for a programme which included his *Romeo and Juliet* symphony, probably helped cool the directors' enthusiasm for the project; but it was the opposition of Michael Costa that finished it off. The Italian-born Costa was the Habeneck of London: musical director at Covent Garden and conductor of the Philharmonic Society, the committee of which was run by many of the composers, Costa included, whom Godfrey described as less than delighted at Berlioz's arrival on the scene. Costa's opposition, unlike Habeneck's, sprang more from dislike of his music than from jealousy of a potentially rival conductor (who was older than himself). Renowned for the discipline he exacted from his players, he was too highly regarded and well entrenched to be afraid of competition. Berlioz thought Costa conducted admirably when he heard him in Exeter Hall, on 13 March, at the Philharmonic Society's opening concert of the season in a programme which included the London première of Mendelssohn's Italian Symphony ("magnificent, far superior in my opinion to the other one in A [the Scottish] which is done in Paris"). The opposition went deeper. It was an incompatibility of musical outlook and taste. Costa was a composer of middle-of-the-road operatic and sacred works – on one of which Rossini commented: "Kind Costa sent me the score of an oratorio and a Stilton cheese. The cheese was excellent" – and an incorrigible arranger of the works of others, Mozart not excepted (a practice Berlioz likened to "slapping a trowelful of mortar on a Raphael painting"). He could only deplore Berlioz's music and take good care not to encourage it. The musicians Berlioz talked to at the Philharmonic concert could not believe the society hadn't offered to perform anything of his; and Beale, with Davison and the writer Charles Rosenberg, mounted a campaign, both privately and in print, to force the committee to invite him; but Costa and Anderson, the treasurer, were not to be moved. Berlioz was irresistibly reminded of the committee of the Société des Concerts.

He determined none the less to stay and wait his time. The Philharmonic notwithstanding, he was now a familiar and respected figure in the musical life of the capital, invited to receptions and parties and events of all sorts. His presence added distinction to a gathering. Despite occasional fits of spleen he was, too, a lively and sought-after companion. Many musicians admired and liked him. The *Musical World* spoke of his "polished and courteous manners; no conductor that ever entered an orchestra was more affable in his demeanour, or more gentlemanly in his conduct" towards the players; and Holmes described him as having "the art of conciliating" them and "of engaging their best efforts in his behalf, perhaps beyond any composer of our time, his demeanour being perfectly simple, free from airs of superiority, or any assumption of the great man".*

Now that the Drury Lane season was over, the pace of life grew less hectic – quite apart from the stress of working for Jullien, he had often had to rehearse from midday to 4 and then perform the same evening from 7 till 10 or 11. A letter of mid-March, to d'Ortigue, sets out a more leisurely timetable: "Get up at 12; 1 o'clock, arrival of visitors – friends, new acquaintances, artists with letters of introduction; work from 4 till 6; if no invitation, go and have dinner quite a way from where I live; after that it's time for the theatre or a concert; I stay listening to music, of sorts, till 11.30, then off with two or three artists to have supper together in some tavern, and smoke till 2 in the morning."

We catch glimpses of him in the documents from the spring and summer of 1848. He is reported conducting the Hungarian March, first at the annual morning concert given at Covent Garden by the pianist Louise Dulcken (sister of the Leipzig concert-master Ferdinand David),

---

* Holmes also praised his "admirable temper" which, no less than "his very gentlemanly address and great promptitude, admirably adapts him for a position at the head of an orchestra. We have seen him, on occasions that would, in one of the irritable race, have almost justified a fit of anger – mild, considerate and good-humoured."

then at a concert by the recently founded Amateur Musical Society, whose high-born members include the Duke of Leinster among the double-basses, the Marquis of Kildare and Lord G. Fitzgerald (cellos), Lord Arundel on the trumpet and an Honourable bassoon. ("When is the Philharmonic Society going to follow an example so worthy to be followed" and perform one of his works, asks the *Musical World*.) He is to be found of a Sunday evening at Mme Dulcken's, four doors up the street from Jullien's ("a fine house", with "a good piano in every room", notes the fourteen-year-old Wilhelm Ganz in his diary, which remarks on Berlioz's "fine big head, eagle nose, high forehead and piercing eyes").* Also in Harley Street, at the Beethoven Rooms, he attends concerts by the Beethoven Quartet Society, where instrumentalists of the calibre of Molique, Sainton, Hill and Rousselot perform three quartets an evening on Mondays during the spring (including those late works, for which Berlioz's "too partial delight", in Chorley's view, is to blame for the "obscurities" of his music). He hears Jenny Lind in *Sonnambula* at Covent Garden from Morris Barnett's box. (London is agog at the duel of the prima donnas, Lind versus Pauline Viardot, the reigning star at Her Majesty's.) He spends evenings with Barnett – a man of parts, who lived for some years in Paris and trained as a musician before becoming a playwright and an actor well known for impersonating Frenchmen – and the two of them talk far into the night over cigars and good wines at Barnett's lodgings in Southampton Street, off the Strand. He frequents other journalists: Holmes; Chorley; Gruneisen, who has led an adventurous life as a foreign correspondent and only just escaped being shot as a spy while reporting the Carlist wars in Spain; and the raffish but amusing Jim Davison, pontiff of the *Times* and the *Musical World*, infallible dismisser of everything good in contemporary music that is not by his adored Mendelssohn (Wagner "hideous", Schubert "an overrated bungler", Chopin "a morbidly sensitive flea", Verdi "the greatest impostor that ever took pen in hand to write rubbish"), yet whose company Berlioz can't help enjoying even though his criticism is worthless. He visits Maretzek at his rooms off Golden Square on a morning of Dickensian fog and, summoning red

---

* The Ganzes, father (Adolf) and son, had just left Mainz, where Adolf was kapellmeister, and settled in London, at Brydges Street, Drury Lane. Berlioz already knew Adolf's brothers, Leopold and Moritz, respectively concert-master and first cello of the Berlin orchestra.

wine, sugar, cloves and cinnamon, re-enacts the Wolf's Glen scene in *Freischütz* while demonstrating the correct preparation of Burgundy punch ("Probatum est!"). Introduced by a letter from Alfred de Vigny to the celebrated London dandy the Comte d'Orsay, he is hospitably received at the house of the count's mistress Lady Blessington in Kensington Gore. He is seen at Willis's Rooms in King Street, St James's, at a matinée of the Musical Union, the principal chamber music society, where he hears string quartets by Haydn and Mendelssohn and Schumann's piano quartet (a work of "great pretensions" but "devoid of any particular merit" – *Musical World*); he gets to know the Union's founder and director John Ella, violinist, pioneer of explanatory programme notes, consistent champion of Berlioz's music and the first to publicize it in England, at the time of the Grande messe des morts in 1837 (their friendship will ripen in the coming years, and Berlioz will dedicate *The Flight into Egypt* to him). He takes the opportunity of being in London to inquire what lay behind Moore's "When he who adores thee", the lines which made so deep an impression on him at the time of his setting them to music twenty years before (and later will learn from the poet Leigh Hunt the true story of the Irish patriot Robert Emmett). He sits up late several evenings over bowls of punch with the composer Vincent Wallace, recently returned from the Viennese triumph of his opera *Maritana*, and warms to the man's eccentric character – "outwardly phlegmatic, as the English often are, fundamentally reckless and violent like an American" – and to his amazing traveller's tales. He is the first person that Charles Hallé visits on his arrival from Paris after the February Revolution; the pianist's description of the state of Paris and the breakdown of its musical life, recounted over cigars in his rooms in Maddox Street the same evening, strengthens his own resolve to stay as long as he can.

Berlioz liked London; he enjoyed the London whirl and its sociabilities. Yet we have a clear sense that his existence had reached a crisis. It was not only that his career there had turned out so differently from what he expected – that London had the richest, most varied concert life in the world and he no real part in it; not only that unrest spreading from the continent was beginning to affect England as well ("everyone is terrified of undertaking anything that costs money") or that the growing flood of refugee artists threatened to restrict the opportunities open to him; not only that the collapse of the Paris banks had probably cost him several thousand francs, and if he returned there he would have no choice but to "sit on the street corner and die of hunger like a stray dog"; not only that, from what Hallé told him, Germany too (in Hallé's words) was "in hateful disorder". Where was he not an exile? He was at home nowhere.

His failure to make a living in London, just as in Paris, left him in a state of profound discouragement: the difficulties in the way of a composer – a composer of his kind at any rate – were simply too great. His letters over the next few years keep coming back to the same point: the "certainty of being de trop in this world", and the wish to have done with art, to be finished with grand musical projects and the frustrations they entail. Fortunately he will not do so; the grandest project is yet to come. But the mood is strong, and it first overtakes him in London, in the wreck of expectations which he recognizes he should never have let himself be seduced into believing in – a mood of disgust with what he sees as the complexity and compromise, the sordidness, inseparable from the dealings of civilization. He gives vent to it in reply to a letter of Nancy's describing their father's worrying physical and mental state. "Poor father, he sees the affairs of this ridiculous world of ours with too clear an eye to have the least illusion about anything – hence the incurable ennui. I realize that if my life continues I shall soon be prey to the same malady. Only physical activity, only distant voyages could make me support life patiently." He fancies taking ship with Rajah Brooke, the "intrepid and intelligent Englishman", who is visiting London, and sailing to Sarawak on the coast of Borneo, "the most beautiful island in the world" – the region which all his life has been the magnetic pole of his imagination. "Oh, if I were not held by so many ties in Europe, what a perfect opportunity to leave it floundering in its own morass and hear no more of it!"

The longing is like a refrain. A few weeks later (1 May): "We have a mere four or five thousand top-class pianists in London at the moment ... God, how I wish I could travel seriously, that is do eight or ten thousand miles without stopping, and see something new and less ugly." Eighteen months later it is the same "maladie de voyager", a yearning, like a sickness, fostered by his tours of Europe but instinct in him and never far below the surface. "Shall I tell you? I dream of nothing but ships, the sea, far-off islands, perilous explorations." And again: "The sea! The sea! A good ship and a favourable wind! Fly the old continent, go among simple, primordial savages, and hear no more of our own systematically brutal, corrupt savages." As so often with him, the conventional poetic stance – the idealization of the savage in symbiotic relationship with unpolluted nature – is felt with peculiar intensity. Where others play with the idea, he clasps it to his soul. He really is, for the moment, the Indian he likens himself to, moving homeless over the earth.

The urge must have been precipitated into conscious thought during the evenings spent yarning with Wallace, who had done what Berlioz dreamed of doing – had travelled the globe, knew the South Seas, and once for six months on end lived the life of the Maoris, the Polynesians of New Zealand. It had been alive in him from the earliest days, when he pored over his father's atlas, "studying the intricate pattern of islands and straits and promontories in the South Seas and the Indian Archipelago, pondering the origins of those remote regions, their inhabitants and climate and vegetation, and filled with an intense desire to visit them".

The words are from the second chapter of the *Memoirs*, and were written at his lodgings in Harley Street. By the end of March he was immersed in it. The preface – concluding with the image of the Niagara Indian in his canoe, submitting to the superior force of the current but continuing to sing till the very instant the cataract seizes him and hurls him into the abyss – is inscribed "London, 21 March 1848".

Nothing more natural than that he should choose this moment to begin. Autobiography was integral to all his published writings – criticism, with him, had always been an individual, personal testimony – but several things now conspired to spur him to more sustained utterance. For one thing, the idea of an artist setting down the intimate record of his struggles was in people's minds, with the impending publication of the *Mémoires d'outre-tombe* of Chateaubriand, the great founder of French Romantic literature, who was one of the presiding geniuses of the young Berlioz's imaginative awakening and whose shadow, as Pierre Citron observes, passes across the opening pages of the book. For another, Jullien's project for an English edition of *Voyage musical*, revised and enlarged by the addition of further articles on Mendelssohn and Gluck, though it had not materialized had helped cast his mind back over the past. His friends had been saying for some while that he ought to extract the autobiographical chapters and develop them into a complete book, especially since the two volumes had gone out of print. Now if ever was the time – when his world was falling apart and his career seemingly in ruins, and his life (more even than he realized) had reached a turning-point – to set things straight, explain himself to the few among his contemporaries who could be presumed curious to know, and vindicate his name before the judgement of posterity. It would give him an occupation, which otherwise his life at the moment was lacking. He had leisure to devote to it. Apart from a visit to the Strand on 22 March to transfer £20 from his account to Harriet's in Paris, the aforementioned engagement with the Amateur Musical Society on 7 April, and dinner with Hallé and Barnett at Benedict's house in Manchester Square on the 10th, the record for those weeks is blank.

The preface and chapters 1 to 4 – La Côte St André, his first communion, Dr Berlioz, dreams of travel, Virgil, Félix Marmion and the Grande Armée, Estelle, early compositions, first medical studies – were written between 21 March and 10 April, by when he had brought the narrative to the autumn of 1821 and his departure, at the age of seventeen, for Paris. On the 10th he broke off, noting that he was going out to watch the Chartists' meeting on Kennington Common – was England too about to be engulfed? – but adding a relieved, ironical paragraph the same evening. "Your Chartist is a very decent sort of revolutionary. Everything went off satisfactorily. The cannon, those eloquent orators and formidable logicians whose arguments appeal so powerfully to the masses, were in the chair. They were not required to utter a word, their presence being enough to persuade everyone of the inexpediency of revolution, and the Chartists dispersed in perfect order. My poor friends, you know as much about starting a riot as the Italians about writing a symphony."

Two hundred thousand had been expected – and nearly as many special constables sworn in, armed with rifles and staves, among them Louis-Napoleon, who was living in London, in King Street, biding his time till France should be ready for him – but barely a tenth of that number turned up; the rally produced nothing more subversive than a petition for reform, which was dispatched to the House of Commons in a hansom cab, and the threat to public safety receded. In the event Berlioz's life was disturbed not by political upheaval but by the bailiffs, who arrived at 76 Harley Street early on 20 April while he slept and took possession of the house; they were with difficulty persuaded not to impound his clothes. He was forced to move out, and took a cheap set of rooms at 26 Osnaburgh Street, on the south-east side of Regent's

Park, where Marie joined him a few days later.* On the 22nd the newspapers announced that Jullien had been declared bankrupt. Relieved of all legal obligations, he was free to start again and was soon raising fresh credit and collecting the orchestra for a summer season of promenade concerts in Surrey Gardens.

By now France was in the throes of its first elections held under universal (male) suffrage. Berlioz watched events with mixed feelings. Paris seemed to be quieting down a little, he wrote to Morel. "God grant it lasts, and the Assembly is a true representation of the country – then one might actually hope for something important to come out of it." Yet he had few hopes for music: men like Lamartine, Victor Hugo and Schoelcher might be deputies, but what could they really do? "It's a question of money: since people lack it for the necessities of life, the Republic has other things to do than spend it on the luxury of art. That is painfully obvious." And a few days later, to the architect Joseph-Louis Duc: "One must have a tricolour flag over one's eyes not to see that music is dead in France now, and that it's the last art our rulers will want to be bothered with."

The letter to Duc sums up Berlioz's state of mind so well that it is worth quoting at length:

26 May [1848]

My dear Duc

Our piece, the Apotheosis, has come out at last. It was thought necessary to mutilate the title-page. I had put: "*Composed for the inauguration of the Bastille Column*", and further on, "Dedicated to M. Duc, architect of the *Bastille* Column". They then realized what the column had to do with it and the point of the dedication. Since the recent Chartist agitation the London bourgeois have had a profound horror of anything remotely connected with revolutions. In consequence my publisher did not wish the title of the piece to make any mention of your monument or of those it was put up to commemorate.

His Paris friends (he goes on) reproach him for his absence, but they are wrong if they think it is against his interests.

A long time now, I've stifled my love of France and uprooted from my heart the foolish habit of relating all my thoughts to it. For the last seven

* Claire Clairmont, Byron's and Shelley's friend, was a lodger in the same house; but she seems to have been out of London during the whole time that Berlioz stayed there.

years I've lived solely on what my works and my concerts earn me abroad. Without Germany, Bohemia, Hungary and above all Russia, I should have starved many times over in France. People talk to me of "positions" to get, of "jobs" to apply for. What positions? What jobs? There is nothing vacant. Isn't Auber at the Conservatoire, Carafa at the Gymnase, Girard at the Opéra? Apart from that, what is there? Nothing. Has the French mind abandoned its love of mediocrities since the Revolution? Maybe; but in that case it will have been replaced by the love of worse men and things (if anything can be said to be worse than the mediocre). No, I have nothing to do in France except cultivate the friendships that are dear to me. For my career, I have attempted enough, suffered enough, waited enough; it will not happen there. In France I have received nothing but snubs and insults more or less ill disguised. I have found only stupid opposition, the national mind being stupid where high matters of art and literature are concerned.

One day perhaps they will ask for him – when he is old and worn out and no longer good for anything.

In short, I have nothing better to do than what I am doing now: I am a savage, I hold on to my liberty, I keep moving so long as the earth carries me and there are deer and moose in the woods; and if I suffer often from cold and hunger, exhaustion, sleepless nights and the ravages of the paleface, at least I am free to dream beside the waterfalls and in the silent forests, and to worship great Nature and thank God for still granting me a feeling for her beauties.

I saw *Hamlet* a few days ago. Marie and I came out at the end literally shattered by it, trembling all over, drunk with admiration and the sadness of it. The new actor Brooke is wonderful, far superior to Macready and Kemble – he is Hamlet. What's more he is very handsome and distinguished-looking. Three other parts were very well done: the Ghost, Polonius and the first Gravedigger. What a world a masterpiece like that is! And how this one above all harrows you, heart and soul! Shakespeare wanted to depict the nothingness of life, the vanity of human designs, the despotism of chance, the indifference of Fate or God to what we call virtue, crime, beauty, ugliness, love, hate, genius, stupidity. And he cruelly succeeded. They had condescended to give us *Hamlet* as written, practically complete, a rare thing in this country, where there are so many people superior to Shakespeare that most of his plays are corrected and augmented by the Cibbers and the Drydens and other rogues who should have their bottoms publicly spanked. For that matter, they do the same to music. Costa has "corrected" and "re-scored" Rossini's *Barber* and Mozart's *Don Juan* and *Figaro* for Covent Garden. The bass drum runs riot.

The opening paragraph, indeed the letter as a whole, tells us what we would expect about his attitude to politics and society. He is forced to accept the publisher's act of censorship, but he sees the absurdity and ignobility, the vanity, of it. The Apotheosis was written to celebrate the Bastille Column and the July Days; and the fears of the English propertied classes ought not to be suffered to suppress the fact.

The often scornful criticism of the Second Republic revealed during the revival of his fame which began under the Third, when his letters were first published, caused pain to republican admirers like Tiersot, Romain Rolland and Redon. Some tried to explain it away. Others could not forgive him for failing to side with the forces of democracy and for playing into the hands of the reactionaries – some of whom, Stasov complained, were able, thanks to his jibes, to "make their peace with Berlioz the reformer, Berlioz the bold Titan, who all his life toppled lies and falsehoods from their age-old pedestals. He stumbled – they instantly applauded him and burst into song."

Berlioz might have replied that the lies and falsehoods on their pedestals were not the monopoly of a single ideological group. In fact the correspondence of this period shows greater ambivalence than his disapproving champions supposed, an ambivalence which modifies his ideas according to who he is writing to. To Nancy, by adoption if not by nature a proponent of Law and Order, he will refer to the "pretentious idiocy" of the ceremony of the public reading of the new constitution on the Place de la Concorde, and joke, rather feebly, that the "constitution of the ceremony" will need to be robust to resist the effects of the extremely cold weather they are having. To Lenz, in St Petersburg, he writes that the Russians must be "making fun of us, we who style ourselves 'advanced' peoples. You know what they call woodcock that are high? It's the same word, '*avancés*'. [. . .] And you're still thinking about music, barbarians that you are. What a pity! Instead of working for the great cause, the root and branch abolition of family, property, intelligence, civilization, life, humanity, you busy yourself with the works of Beethoven! You dream of sonatas, you write a book about art." To Liszt, on the other hand, he remarks that men like the current directors of the Opéra are "a thousand times more our enemies than the unhappy people who kill on the barricades". Even to Nancy he will speak, apropos the Chartists, of "the insolent English aristocracy" who refuse to "yield an inch of their territory and think it perfectly natural that they should have everything and the poor nothing"; and he quotes Beaumarchais' Don Basilio in *The Barber of Seville*: "What's worth taking is worth hanging on to."

Such contradictions reflect the classic dilemma of the reformer who abhors violence and recoils from the destruction that drastic change involves – who would abolish privilege but not what has been achieved by means of it. In his case, the once-active desire for social justice came up against the imperatives of the creative ego and lost. It was more than the revulsion of the performing artist whom social unrest robbed of his livelihood – the anger that made Hallé cry "O damnable Revolution!" when it destroyed the life he had built in Paris and forced him to begin again in another country. Berlioz's works show marked populist leanings and hostility to oppression in their choice of subject, during the first part of his career especially. Their composer, however, remained a natural aristocrat. He was increasingly sceptical as to the benefits of radical political action for any but a minority. He saw what it did to the lives of friends and fellow-musicians, and how destructive it was in general of musical life – how many leading European musical periodicals, for example, were forced by the revolutions of 1848 to close. Inevitably, over the years, as a creative artist striving to have his works properly performed, he came to prefer political systems which offered the best conditions for it, whatever their other drawbacks. They were generally neither democratic republics nor constitutional monarchies but despotisms. It was a natural declension. Even Wagner, having risked everything for the revolutionary cause, ended up depending on the patronage of a far-from-constitutional monarch; the vision of a popular theatre where the People could see *The Ring* free, without paying, gave way to the exclusivities of Bayreuth. Berlioz's position is encapsulated in the letter he wrote to General Lvov during the preparations for his first London concert. At the time he had yet to have a full complement of players at a single rehearsal; the musicians came and went as they pleased. "That is how discipline is understood in this country." Only the choristers showed him a dedication almost as great as in Petersburg. "Oh, Russia!" he exclaims, remembering "the organization of its theatres and its chapel – the clear, exact, unyielding organization without which, in music as in many other things, nothing good, nothing beautiful is attainable".

Near the end of his eight-month stay he was finally able to put on a second concert, on Thursday 29 June in the Hanover Square Rooms. The recognition that with Jullien's bankruptcy he had lost all hope of recovering the large sums he was owed seems to have prompted the musicians to treat the concert as a testimonial. According to Albert Ganz, whose father and grandfather both took part, the leading players from Her Majesty's and Covent Garden (the members of the Beethoven Quartet Society included) "joined in fraternal rivalry to do him honour". "One and all," adds Ganz, "declined to hear of any pay." Two invitations to the rehearsal survive; they are in French, and engraved, with a facsimile of the composer's signature. But he also wrote a note in English to the Covent Garden violist Henry Hill, soloist in *Harold*, for Hill to read out to members of the orchestra. It shows what his English was like at this stage: "Mr H. Berlioz has the intention to give at Hanovre Square room a concert, Wednesday the 28 Juin [later changed to the 29th] at half past two, there will be a rehearsal the 27 at ten o'clock. Mr Berlioz will be most happy to excite as much interest to the Gentlemen whose names follow, as to receive their assistance at this occasion, and he takes the liberty to ask them for it."

With one rehearsal only, attended by fewer than half the players, the programme wisely included a good deal of music that had been performed before: *Harold* (but without the difficult finale), *Roman Carnival*, the Hungarian March, the Song of the Flea and the Elbe scene from *Faust*, *Invitation to the Waltz*, two movements from Mendelssohn's G minor piano concerto with Mme Dulcken, "Ah, non giunge" from *Sonnambula* sung by Pauline Viardot, and Alfonso's big number from *La favorita* (Massol). To it were added four Berlioz songs: *Zaïde*, *Le chasseur danois*, an unnamed "romance française" and, for the first time in its fully developed form, *La captive*, with Viardot. The concert was an artistic triumph for the composer-conductor, only marred by the absence of cymbals (some accounts say drums as well), which, as he explained to the audience before the March, were "in the room, but their use is prohibited by the proprietors of the hall", apparently at the insistence of the neighbours. Four pieces were encored and more asked for but not granted – the musicians had to have time to get to their theatres for the evening performance. Berlioz was greeted at the end "with tumults of applause".

Financially, however, the concert was a fresh disappointment. Though the hall was "attended by almost every musical man of eminence in the metropolis" (the *Morning Post*) it was "not crowded". News of further violence in Paris seems to have alarmed many and kept them at home. Instead of the £500 profit the *Musical World* fondly imagined, or even the £50 Berlioz hoped to make, there was the tiniest margin, perhaps even a loss (the evidence is contradictory). Gustave Roger noted in his diary the presence of many French – "artistic France in exile assembled to applaud that wild and too long misunderstood genius Berlioz, to whom justice will be done when he finally blows his brains out" – but described the concert as "magnificent for the enthusiasm it aroused, not for the money it made. Berlioz is an eagle who inhabits the mountain-tops and the clouds; the gold-mines don't have seams up there."

While the concert was taking place, civil war raged in Paris. The diverse forces whose temporary alliance had brought down the monarchy – moderate and radical republicans, legitimists, socialists, building workers, intellectuals and the mainly petit-bourgeois National Guard – had fallen apart and were at each others' throats. When on 21 June the government closed the National Workshops – opened in March for the unemployed, in recognition of the universal right to work – the populous eastern districts of Paris, swollen by immigration from the countryside, rose in their wrath. Barricades were thrown up from the Faubourg St Denis to the Left Bank. After three days of bitter fighting the insurrection was bloodily put down by troops armed with artillery, and thousands of the survivors were deported to Algeria or New Caledonia without trial.

Berlioz felt "ashamed to be making music at such a moment". A few days later a letter came from Harriet, describing the near escape she had had, fired on at close range while she was walking one evening in the garden at Montmartre: the bullet hit a tree an inch from where she was standing. He must go back. Now that the concert had been achieved there were no immediate prospects to keep him in London. Beale and others spoke of getting him over again soon; Rosenberg attacked the "culpable negligence" of the Philharmonic Society, whose "treatment of so eminent a man" was a "stain" on the organization; and the *Musical World* declared that he was leaving behind him "many many friends" who would "look forward with sincere pleasure to his next appearance in London". But that must all be for later. His long stay had come to an end, and he got ready to leave. He saw Jullien, who promised to send him some at least of the money he had lost. On behalf of Gautier (who had not been paid either) he tried to reclaim the manuscript of his unperformed ballet scenario on Goethe's *Wilhelm Meister*, but it had been mislaid and no one had any idea where it might be. On 3 July he dined again at Macready's. His farewell letter to the press, thanking London for its generous welcome and the critics for their open-mindedness, was published in the *Musical World* on the 8th and reproduced in the *Morning Post* and the *Athenaeum*. On the 8th he and Roger called on Barnett in Southampton Street and spent part of the day (in Roger's words) "drinking, smoking and laughing in a variety of tongues". On the 11th he withdrew the remaining £20 12s. 6d. from his account at Coutts'. On the 12th he noted in the manuscript of his *Memoirs* that he was leaving England. Next day he took the boat train to Folkestone, en route for Paris.

Paris, when he arrived, was "completing the burial of its dead". The paving-stones torn up to make barricades had been replaced; but there were many marks of devastation (Duc's statue of Liberty on the Bastille Column had been damaged by gunfire) and an evil stench hung over the narrow streets. Berlioz saw a pianist playing for pennies in the Place St Germain l'Auxerrois, and heard of architects mixing mortar on building sites and painters scratching a living as street-sweepers. It was a particularly bad time for orchestral musicians: their salaries were low enough in normal circumstances and they lived mainly from teaching, but there were no pupils. He himself, he told Camille Pal, had gone back to living as he had done a quarter of a century ago when he was a medical student in the Latin Quarter, getting by on eighty or a hundred francs a month. An advance from Pal gave him breathing-space; but he was still alarmingly short of money. Fortunately the *Gazette* published his first two articles on Prague (including the Tale of the Wandering Harpist); and the rest of *Voyage musical en Bohème* and the articles on Marseille, Lyon and Lille were issued over the next four months. Brandus paid his contributors better than Schlesinger had ever done; he also agreed to publish the four-hand arrangement of the Hungarian March. All this was just as well, for the beleaguered *Journal des débats* had put its journalists on half-rates. Berlioz reviewed the first night of the erstwhile Royal Academy of Music in the *Débats* on 26 July; the feuilleton, headlined "Opening of the Théâtre de la Nation, alias Théâtre-National, alias Opéra (old style)", began by treating "opening" in the sense of autopsy. It was, he told Liszt, the first shot in an "all-out war by ridicule".

More than ever he must depend on journalism. A commission appointed by the government to reform the Conservatoire was said to be recommending, among other things, the abolition of the librarian's stipend, Berlioz's one regular source of income. He wrote again to the latest Minister of the Interior, begging him to safeguard his position or, failing that, to create for him a chair in orchestration; and he sent another request for payment of the eight hundred-odd francs of his salary still owed him from the beginning of the year. His friend Stephen de La Madelaine, now an employee in the Ministry, might perhaps be able to see to it. But he was not sanguine on either count.

This was the situation at the beginning of August 1848, when all such considerations were put out of mind by a letter from La Côte St André. It brought news that his father was dead.

Above: watercolour of the Lorelei Rock by Turner.
Below: The Rhine near Coblenz, with the Schloss Stolzenfels. Berlioz made his long-delayed tour of Germany in 1842–3, and on several occasions travelled by boat up the Rhine.

Above: Liszt playing Beethoven, with the violinist Ernst on his right, Kriehuber (the artist who drew the picture) on his left, and Berlioz and Czerny standing facing him. Below: One of Prinzhofer's two lithograph portraits of Berlioz, made in Vienna in 1845. Berlioz thought it a good likeness, but said he never wore a ring or carried a cane, and inscribed a copy "H. Berlioz – non dandy".

*Above: Prague, where Berlioz conducted six
concerts in 1846 and achieved some of the
greatest successes of his career.
Below: Weimar, and inset, Princess Carolyne
Sayn-Wittgenstein (1819–87).*

Berlioz conducting the chorus of the Société Philarmonique, engraved from a drawing by Gustave Doré

Above: L'Institut de France, where Berlioz competed for the Prix de Rome as a student between 1826 and 1830, and where he was elected a member of the Académie des Beaux-Arts in 1856.
Below: the Crystal Palace on the south side of Hyde Park, where he represented France on the international jury on musical instruments at the Great Exhibition of 1851.

Photographs (from top to bottom) of
Berlioz's sister Adèle (1814–60), his uncle
Colonel Marmion (1787–1869), and the
Berlioz family's much-loved housekeeper
Monique Nety (1792–1857).

Berlioz pictured by an anonymous citizen of his home town on his visit there in 1845.

Pauline Viardot (1821–1910) as Orphée in Gluck's opera, which Berlioz edited for the famous revival in 1859.

16

Return Journey

Dr Berlioz died at noon on 28 July 1848. The old man (seventy-two in June) had been failing for some time. During the final weeks his two daughters were with him constantly. On the 18th the lifelong freethinker took the sacraments "in a state of calm acceptance, his mind perfectly lucid", Nancy noted with approval. By the 23rd it was obvious that the end was near. His head and arms shook convulsively (the effect of continued doses of opium), his voice had sunk to a whisper, and he stared hollow-eyed, unseeing. Much of the time he slept. When awake, he was delirious and had only brief moments of awareness. Once, when Adèle, responding to his more than usual restlessness, asked what he wanted, he moved her inexpressibly by answering, "Nothing, my child – I am looking for your eyes." Once, Nancy heard him ask if there was any news of Hector and Louis. And once, on Monique's showing him a picture of his son, he spoke his name clearly and called for pen and paper: "I shall write presently," he said. But he never did.

His funeral on the 31st filled the church. Afterwards all La Côte followed his body to the cemetery on the western edge of the town. At the graveside Dr Robin spoke of his medical achievements and his dedication to the art of healing, and M. Prud'homme gave thanks in the name of the poor and the destitute whom, time out of mind and almost to the end, he had helped unstintingly with food, counsel and money.

One mourner was not there. Berlioz found out too late. Why neither of his sisters alerted him in time is not clear. He wrote in bitter reproach to Nancy: "Two lines from you or Camille, and I'd have come and would have seen him again. That I should seemingly have been left in the dark at such a moment breaks my heart and exacerbates my grief to an unbearable pitch. There were so many links between my father and me, we loved each other for so many different reasons. For so many years I had seen him very rarely and, as you know, had not even had letters from him." He had to be satisfied with Nancy's explanation – that the letter he had written announcing his return to Paris had been inadvertently left unopened at the Pals' Grenoble address. But the thought that he had missed taking a last farewell of his beloved father – beloved throughout all the vicissitudes that divided them – sharpened his bereavement. It may have been then that he began revising the harsh and tragic *Funeral March for the Last Scene of Hamlet*, first drafted in 1844 at the time of the breakdown of his marriage but now associated, in its sense of annihilation and finality, with a new loss. "Oh, if I had at least been there," he wrote to Adèle, "to share in your pain if not to alleviate his! I cannot believe he would not have recognized me. I am now in a state of utter dejection. It is as if my life no longer had an object. Instinctively, all my efforts were directed towards my father, I wanted him to show he approved of them, I hoped he would be proud of what I did . . . and now . . ."

Memories of the distant past possessed him. He had relived them in London earlier in the year when writing the opening chapters of his *Memoirs*. Now they flooded back of their own volition and bore him on a tide of nostalgia to his boyhood. He must go to Dauphiné.

He was wanted there in any case, to settle the inheritance: Dr Berlioz had died intestate.* Adèle and Nancy would rather not have returned to the deserted house so soon, and he apologized for making them: being so seldom at liberty he had to take what spare time there was. His departure was set for 21 August and then, at his sisters' request, postponed a week. Louis, who was in Paris for the holidays, would have liked to go with him; but Berlioz needed to be free for what he had in mind: more than a family reunion, a journey to the sources of his being.

He took the coach to Lyon and from there to Vienne, where he stayed with Adèle and her family a few days. Then brother and sister went on together to La Côte. Nancy was in the house waiting for them. He went straight up to his father's study and the three of them embraced. The sight and touch of the objects that had belonged to his father – the copy of Plutarch, the notebook and pens, the stick he walked with, the watch he consulted obsessively during his last illness and which Nancy took

---

* The will made by him in 1815, shortly after Napoleon's fall, had been revoked seven years later, and he had never made another.

from a drawer and gave to her brother – moved him to fresh tears. In this small, quiet room above the sunny courtyard he had had musical notation explained to him, had been shown how to play the flageolet and later the flute, had construed Virgil and felt Dido's anguish in his inmost heart, had received his whole education, been handed the key to a fabulous kingdom of knowledge and imagination, and had acquired for his teacher an admiration compounded of awe and the profoundest sympathy.

Yet this could be no more than the first stage in the search for lost time. The goal was Meylan and the sacred mountainside and the goddess who had inhabited it and whose numinous presence must surely – must it not? – inhabit it still. A day or two later, at dawn on the 5th, he caught the mail coach to Grenoble. He was there by eight o'clock. With the sunlight already hot on his cheek he walked out of the town and up the valley. It was a perfect September morning such as he had known so often in his boyhood, crystalline, still, the sun glinting from the great rock-face before him.

In Meylan he went first to his grandfather's house, recently sold to a tenant farmer who had built a new house at the other end of the garden. There was no one there. He looked in at the long drawing-room where the family used to gather in the old days, and found nothing changed: the same multicoloured paper birds stuck on the walls, the little wicker cage he had made as a child, his grandfather's backgammon set and the chair where he slept in the afternoon, the dance floor where Estelle in her pink satin shoes waltzed in his uncle's arms. Outside, everything was different. Half the orchard had been ploughed up; the field of maize where he hid himself and his sorrows from prying eyes was gone; the bench on which his father sat for hours on end staring up at St Eynard had rotted away.

Leaving the village below him, he climbed the steep hillside towards the white house where he had first seen Estelle. It was thirty years since he had been there. "I am like a man who in the meantime has died and is returning to life. And in returning I rediscover all the feelings of my former existence, as fresh and intense as before." His heart beat fast from more than the effort of the ascent; in his anxiety he mistook the way and had to ask some threshers at work in a barn to put him on the right path. It led past the little stone fountain he had been looking for, and soon he reached the drive leading to the house, the new owner of which was standing by the gate lighting a cigar. He did not stop but went straight on, not once looking round, waiting till he came to an old tower at the top of a hill, from which he knew he could see it all in a single glance. At last he was at the tower.

Over there, where those young beech trees are shooting up, my father and I sat, and I played him "Nina's Musette" on the flute. Estelle must have come here. Perhaps I stand in the very same portion of space where her enchanting form once stood. Now – look! I turn and my gaze takes in the entire picture: the blessed house, its garden, its trees, below it the valley and the winding Isère and, beyond, the Alps, the glaciers, the far-off gleaming snow – everything her eyes looked on. I breathe in the blue air she breathed . . . Ah! A cry such as no human language can convey re-echoes from St Eynard. Yes, I see, I see again, I worship. The past is before me. I am a boy of twelve. Life, beauty, first love, poetry without end! I throw myself on my knees and shout, "Estelle! Estelle! Estelle!" to the valley and the hills and the sky. I clasp the earth in a convulsive embrace and bury my teeth in the grass. And it begins: an access of loneliness, indescribable, appalling.

When the fit had run its course he got up and began walking avidly over the nearby hillside – "like a dog in search of its master's scent" – identifying every remembered landmark made holy by association with her, tasting, repossessing the past. It was now afternoon. He took a long ritual farewell of the sacred place and turned to go.

And desolate as a ghost returning to its grave, I descended the mountain. I passed the drive that led to Estelle's house. The man with the cigar had disappeared; he no longer defiled the peristyle of my temple. Yet I could not bring myself to enter, eager though I was. I walked on slowly, so slowly, stopping at every moment, tearing my gaze agonizingly from each cherished object. I no longer needed to control my heart; it seemed to have stopped beating. I was becoming dead once more. And over all a stillness and solitariness, and the sun's soft glow.

Just before dusk he was at Murianette on the opposite bank of the Isère, where he spent the night with his cousins and his Aunt Félicia.

I had, it may be imagined, a strange abstracted air. My cousin Victor, when we were alone for a moment, could not resist asking me:

"What is the matter with you? I've never seen you like this."

"The matter with me? Well – you'll jeer, but as you ask me I'll tell you. Anyway, it will be a relief to talk, I'm suffocating. I was at Meylan yesterday."

"I know. What is there?"

"Among other things, the house of Mme Gautier. Do you know her niece [grand-daughter] Mme F[ornier]?"

"Yes – the one they used to call the beautiful Estelle D[ubeuf]."

"Well, when I was twelve I was madly in love with her – and I love her still."

Victor burst out laughing. "You idiot, she's fifty-one, her eldest son is twenty-two – we read law together."

He laughed louder than ever, and I joined in, but mine was a bleak, nervous laugh, like the glint of an April sun through rain.

"Yes, I see that it's ridiculous, yet at the same time – it's ridiculous and it's true; it's childish and immense. Don't laugh – or rather, laugh if you like, it won't make any difference. Where is she now? You must know."

"Since her husband died she's been living at Vif."

"Vif? Is that far from here?"

"Seven or eight miles."

"I shall go there. I want to see her."

"Are you mad?"

"I shall find some excuse for calling on her."

"Hector, I beg you not to. It would be extremely foolish."

"I want to see her."

"You'll never have the self-control to manage such an encounter properly."

"I want to see her."

"If you do, you'll merely make an ass of yourself and compromise her."

"I want to see her."

"But just consider –"

"I want to see her."

"Fifty-one years old – more than half a century. What do you suppose you'll find? Much better preserve your youthful memories – keep your ideal unsullied."

"Oh God! The whips and scorns of time! All right. At least let me write to her."

"Write by all means. Ye gods, what a lunatic!"

He handed me a pen and subsided into an armchair, where he gave way to a fresh burst of hilarity, in which I joined in fits and starts; and between sunshine and shower I wrote the letter, which had to be copied out again because of the raindrops that blurred every line.

The letter, without naming the writer (it was signed, in English, "Despis'd love"), told of his first sight of Mlle Estelle, at the age of twelve, of her being so "pardonably cruel" as to smile at his infatuation, of his glimpse of the house as he came down the valley on his way home from Italy, of his encounter with Mme F— at the coach stop, and of his return, only the day before, in defiance of time, to the scenes of his first and unchanging love. Sixteen years would pass before he knew whether it had been received.

Next day he visited his uncle and aunt, Victor and Laure Berlioz, who lived in the country south of Grenoble, by the swift-flowing Drac.

I imagine Berlioz writing the account of his pilgrimage in the family house at La Côte immediately after his return from Grenoble. Though the final section of what was to be the first completed version of the *Memoirs* mostly belongs to the early 1850s, the immediacy and detail of this chapter suggest an earlier date. He could well have felt the need to put his experience on paper at once; and where better to do it?

In the second week of September the two brothers-in-law arrived and a family conference was held. Its conclusion was that in the uncertain political and economic state of the country they should wait before valuing the estate. Meanwhile Hector would receive an advance on his share. The three siblings went through their father's library and divided it between them. The document recording these decisions was signed by all five parties and dated 12 September. A separate deed formalized certain legacies promised verbally to Dr Berlioz's housekeeper Monique Nety: an annuity of 200 francs, free use during her lifetime of "the small house in the street that runs up from the large garden to the market-place" (at present leased to her brother Claude, a veteran of the Napoleonic Wars), and various items of furniture from the big house. Arrangements were made to send Hector his share of the library and of the wine cellar. But he took his father's book, *Mémoires sur les maladies chroniques*, with him when, a day or two later, he returned to Paris.

In his letter to Estelle, Berlioz spoke of "going back to the vortex". Outwardly it would not be so different. He put on no concerts of his own in Paris, but that had been so ever since *The Damnation of Faust* two years before; otherwise, Parisian life seized him and spun him round just as it had always done. Yet an epoch in his life had ended. Influences already in operation now accelerated and intensified. Many things – the act of writing his autobiography, begun six months before in a mood of disillusionment and regret, the ever-deepening conviction that there was no settled place for him in French musical life except as a journalist and that the Romantic ideals and energies of the 1830s had finally been defeated by forces utterly alien to them, his father's death, his experiences at Meylan – united to produce a change, turning him in on himself and on his memories. We see it in the grimly resigned face that looks out obliquely from Courbet's portrait, painted in 1850; we hear it in the fundamental difference – despite the similarities that link the two works – between the Requiem of 1837 and the Te Deum of 1848–9, not to mention the other fundamental difference, that the Te Deum will wait six years before it gets a performance. The work inaugurates the so-called classical period of his career which later French commentators, fixated on the "wild" Berlioz of the Fantastic Symphony, will equate with declining creativity. In fact the flame burns as intensely. At forty-four he is at the height of his powers. But henceforth his art will turn increasingly to the past.

17

The Call of the Past

The past: most obviously, *The Flight into Egypt*, composed in 1850, music whose archaic modal touches and simplicity of utterance look back not only to his teacher Le Sueur but, beyond, to the chants and noëls heard during his boyhood, in the church and in the fields of La Côte St André. The solo tenor's "Les pèlerins étant venus" has the same first six notes as the ancient liturgical chant "O filii, o filiae", the Shepherds' Farewell is a carol in the old triple-time, one-in-the-bar French tradition (as French conductors of the piece, unlike their English counterparts, have generally understood), and the overture, with its circling melodic lines, rustic woodwind and prominent flattened seventh, breathes the air of a far-off age. But the Te Deum too is suffused with a sense of the past. The sweet insistent sound of women's voices which had been a feature of his choral writing from the Messe solennelle of 1824–5, is more pervasive here than at any time since the Mass, appearing at regular intervals throughout the work. We hear it in the modally inflected melody of the Tibi omnes (nearly forty moderately paced bars for sopranos and altos before the first entry of the men's voices), in the Dignare Domine and in the Te ergo quaesumus, and at "Salvum fac populum", the central section of the Judex crederis. Its source, I have no doubt, was the experience – never forgotten but now vividly relived – of the sound of young girls singing the eucharistic hymn at the eleven-year-old Berlioz's first communion, an epiphany which had opened before his marvelling gaze "a Heaven of love and pure delight, a thousand times more beautiful than the one I had so often been told about".

Since then, Heaven had become a progressively less probable place. The hardening of outlook is reflected in his music. The Requiem's harsh but cathartic visions give way, in the Te Deum, to remote, impersonal ritual. Despite richer textures and fuller sonorities than the Requiem's

– with the trumpets, trombones and ophicleides/tubas part of the orchestral sound, not separate from it – the work is more forbidding, more ancient. The God to whom it prays, whose infinite majesty it hymns, is yet more distant, the judgement evoked more implacable still. Yet the child's glimpse of the blessed country survives, unharmed, unsullied.

What prompted him to compose a Te Deum at this particular point in his life? Certainly not (as has been suggested) so that Louis-Napoleon, who was already being spoken of as future emperor, might be induced to choose it for his coronation. The composer would in due course lobby for just such an honour. But the work's Napoleonic associations belong entirely to the uncle; the nephew is nowhere to be found. Its origins lie far back, in the project for a military symphony celebrating the deeds of the First Consul and his troops – "Le retour de l'armée de l'Italie" – which Berlioz conceived in Italy as he travelled over the sites of their famous victories. Some of the ideas that collected round the project went into the abortive *Fête musicale funèbre* begun in 1835, and thence into the Symphonie funèbre et triomphale; but it left traces in the Te Deum as well. Maurice Bourges, reviewing the first performance in 1855, stated that "The Return from the Italian Campaign" was the work's point of origin: Berlioz had imagined "General Bonaparte making his entry beneath the cathedral vaults", whereupon "the sacred canticle would resound on all sides, the banners wave, the side-drums roll, the cannon boom and the bells ring out in great peals". Though Bourges exaggerated what he called the "war-like physiognomy of the work", the information can only have come from the composer himself. And though the concept changed over the years, the bell motif remained central: the descending three-note figure which peals out in the first movement is developed into a kind of motto for the whole score.

How and when Napoleon's entry into Notre-Dame took on a universal character and the military symphony became a more or less orthodox setting of the Te Deum, we cannot say; but there are one or two clues. One is Berlioz's account of being shown some music by Hasse in the Dresden library in 1843 and remarking among it a Te Deum which had "the ceremonial brilliance of a great peal of bells", though in his view little else. If he was not already thinking of writing a Te Deum of his own, the idea may have come to him at that moment – to match and outdo Hasse in sheer sound and at the same time add expressive and dramatic qualities that he felt were wanting. Evidence, of his intention at least, is found in the catalogue which appeared as an appendix to the printed text of *The Damnation of Faust* in November 1846, where among "unpublished works" is a "Te Deum for double chorus and large orchestra". At that stage he may have done no more than plan the main outlines; but the decision was taken.

One stimulus to commit himself could well have been the experience of conducting his Requiem in St Eustache shortly before, in August 1846 – the first time he had directed a performance of the whole work himself and the first time he had heard it in its entirety since the première nine years before. It reminded him that he had further things to say on the subject, and other ways of saying them. Though essentially different, the two scores are linked by many common features – features so numerous, in fact, that Berlioz could announce to Liszt after the première of the Te Deum that "the Requiem has a brother". To begin with, the liturgical text was as drastically reordered as that of the requiem mass had been. The first two movements observed the correct sequence but, after that, three verses were brought forward so that a contrasting movement, the gentle, entreating Dignare, could separate the brilliant Christe, rex gloriae from the splendours of the Tibi omnes. Similarly, the Te ergo quaesumus was made to interpose its quiet prayer between the Christe and the final movement, the Judex crederis. "Judex crederis esse venturus" – "We believe that Thou shalt come to be our Judge" – is only the nineteenth of the canticle's twenty-eight verses. But here it was held back so that the work could culminate in a panorama of humanity awestruck before the terrible grandeur of God, the music swaying between fear and hope like the swing of a gigantic bell as the endless generations repeat their "non – non – non confundar in aeternum" – a movement which Berlioz justly described as "without doubt the most imposing thing I have produced", and whose text is a mosaic of verses assembled from different parts of the canticle.

Again as in the Requiem, the musical expression throughout aimed to emphasize what was a constant theme of the text even before it was rearranged: the littleness of human beings in face of the Creator. Thus, to take one example, the jubilant polyphony of "Te Deum laudamus, te Dominum confitemur" twice gives way, at "Te omnis terra venera-tur", to a multitudinous pianissimo in contrasting homophonic style, as though indeed the whole earth were prostrated in worship.

At particular moments, too, the Te Deum echoes its predecessor. The Judex crederis is in the same surging 9/8 metre, majestic and mcnacing, as the Lacrymosa, its "first cousin" (Berlioz's term for it). Near the end of the Dignare the cries of "Have mercy upon us", in a soft pleading F sharp minor, resolve magically into an even quieter D major (the last of the ascending and descending pedals on which the movement is constructed) with an effect of benediction that recalls the final bars of the Offertorium. The composer's favourite device of harmonic variation for cumulative expressive effect – as at the threefold "Salva me" in the Requiem's Rex tremendae – is even more strikingly exemplified by the Te Deum, both in the Judex crederis, where successive reharmonizations of the main theme, enhanced by brass writing of apocalyptic grandeur, tighten the screw, and in the Tibi omnes, whose opening phrase is differently harmonized at each of its nine repetitions, in tribute to the unity-in-diversity of the heavenly host. In the same spirit the sustained cries of "Sanctus" converging as though from every corner of the universe are given new orchestral colour at each reappearance.

Nine months after the St Eustache performance of the Requiem a note written by Berlioz to Stasov just as he was leaving St Petersburg gives a fresh hint of the Te Deum: "As to your question about the organ, it can on occasion be employed successfully in religious music, in dialogue with the orchestra, but I do not think it is effective when used simultaneously." The score which saw the light a year or two later allots an important role to the organ in four of its seven (eventually eight) movements. Occasionally, organ is combined with orchestra, usually to expand the sonority spatially, to add a further colour or to highlight an important structural point; but mostly they play in dialogue: organ and orchestra are conceived as conversing from opposite ends of the church, "like Pope and Emperor".

In the months following his visit to Russia Berlioz had little leisure to turn his idea into reality. Then London intervened. But by the autumn of 1848, a month or two after his return to Paris, he was at work. It was more than two years since his last big score, *The Damnation of Faust* – years far from inactive but filled with everything except large-scale composition. It was also time, in the alternating pattern of his oeuvre, for another ceremonial piece of populist character. About a year and many interruptions later the seven movements – one of which, the Te ergo, was a revision and extension of the Agnus Dei from the Messe solennelle – were complete. On 1 September 1849 he wrote to Nancy apologizing for his silence: he had been "pinned down by a great devil of a finale, double chorus, call it what you will, which prevented me from sleeping and absorbed me totally. That is why I didn't write. Now that the finale is pinned down in its turn, i.e. sketched in such a way that it can't get away from me, I return to the real world, and here I am." By the end of the month the Judex crederis was done.

In the event it would be nearly five years before he succeeded in having the Te Deum performed. Several of his letters talked of the possibility and of his hope that the Minister of the Interior would defray the heavy cost of copying. Imperial ceremonies came and went. But the work that might have added lustre to them remained unheard and unheeded. Berlioz welcomed Louis-Napoleon's accession to power on both general and personal grounds: it must surely be to his advantage as well as to the country's. He would have been well advised to learn from his abortive encounter with the Prince-President in December 1849. Invited to a private audience at the palace, he arrived to find sixty provincial deputies there before him, and an hour and a half later was informed that the audience would not take place after all. Instead, against all the evidence of the man's monumental philistinism he continued to nurture the illusion that Napoleon III would be to him what Napoleon I had been to Le Sueur, a patron, a benefactor, an enlightened authority overriding jealous opposition and cutting through petty obstacles – for example, making him director of a revived Imperial Chapel as Napoleon had made Le Sueur, and ordering the Opéra to put on The Trojans, in emulation of Napoleon and The Bards. Berlioz submitted detailed plans for reform of the chapel; but it was Auber who was appointed. There was to be no imperial intervention in favour of The Trojans either.

If anything he was worse off under the Second Empire than under the Republic from whose "pretentious stupidities" he regarded Louis-Napoleon as having "rescued" France. The despised Republic not only safeguarded his position as Conservatoire librarian – the chamber rejected the commission's proposal to abolish it – but also accorded him, early in 1849, a grant of 500 francs from the fund for encouragement of the arts. Nor were the slovenly standards of the Opéra the consequence of 1848; the sins castigated in his reviews during these years – the orchestra's careless intonation, the lacklustre work of the chorus, the poor quality of much of the solo singing, the common neglect of nuances, the general lack of energy and discipline for want of determined leadership – were precisely those he had been pointing out before the

Revolution. The effort lavished on *Le Prophète*, which finally came to production in April 1849, and the sumptuous performance that resulted, merely set the day-to-day mediocrity of the place in sharper relief. It took all Meyerbeer's enormous prestige and fortune to achieve such a result, but there was nothing new in that: so it had when *The Huguenots* was first produced, thirteen years before.

The deficiencies in French musical life which Berlioz stigmatized in his report of the speech by the Republic's Arts Director, Charles Blanc, at the Conservatoire prizegiving in December 1848 were, as he admitted, what they had always been: low public taste; no generally available hall in Paris suitable for symphonic music and oratorio; military bands not to be compared with those of Prussia, Austria and Russia; the clergy's rooted prejudice against music; the bad old tradition that banned young women from choral singing not only in churches but even in the Orphéon movement (the justification for which could hardly be that of moral propriety, when the English and the Germans, who were at least as moralistic as the French, were able to boast many similar organizations which admitted women); and, underlying everything, the absence of sustained, intelligent state support for serious music, under a succession of governments consistently lacking in any real regard for it.

Berlioz was agreeably surprised that Charles Blanc, brother of Louis Blanc "the workers' friend", should have such enlightened ideas. But the ills were not to be remedied by one right-minded bureaucrat, least of all when money was short. They went too deep. The Republic had, briefly, abolished the poor tax on concerts but it was soon restored and, though constantly attacked in the press, continued to act as a check on freelance promotion.

For him therefore there was no real prospect of change. The occasional concert might come his way, like the huge festivity of 29 October 1848 organized for the Association des Artistes-Musiciens and held, republicanly and at republicanly low prices, in Louis XIV's private theatre at Versailles; Berlioz conducted an orchestra and chorus over four hundred strong in music by Beethoven (*Leonore no. 2*), Mozart (*Ave verum*), Gluck (excerpts from *Armide*), Rossini (overture to *La gazza ladra*), Weber (*Invitation*) and his own Fête chez Capulet, Hungarian March and *Captive*, and, by doing so, briefly endeared himself to the government. Such glamorous events, however, were never going to occur very often. Yet when in the spring of 1849 Girard and the committee of the Société des Concerts, possibly prompted by Meyerbeer, asked him for something for one of their Sunday afternoon solemnities, he could imagine momentarily that a barrier had been overturned. The sylphs' scene and Hungarian March, though flanked by Beethoven's Seventh Symphony and the second act of *La Vestale*, were received enthusiastically by the society's conservative public, while the composer waited backstage among the firemen, nervous as a débutant ("delivered into the hands of Girard – who, however, did well – I was rather like a hen which, having hatched duck's eggs, sees its little charges jump into the water and daren't follow them"). If the other "great walls of China" that still hemmed him in in France were to fall (he told Janin), "perhaps what I have done would have the same welcome as in the rest of Europe and I could be forgiven for being alive and a Frenchman. Then, perhaps, I should be able to produce new things more important than those I have been concerned with up to now." That he had managed to survive during the past six years was due to Germany and Russia. "You can't think how it saddens me to set to work knowing that I can expect approval for my labours only from foreigners." But though Janin's brief notice in the *Débats* was headlined "Berlioz at the Conservatoire – at last!" the event proved a solitary exception. Another twelve years would pass before the society programmed his music again. As for putting on his own concerts, that was a gamble he could no longer take: the risk was too great. The resolution he had made after *The Damnation of Faust*, not to "stake twenty francs on the popularity of my music with the Paris public", remained rigorously in force.

Why, then, did he stay in Paris instead of going where his music was profitable? What kept him there so long – three years all but two months between his coming back from London in July 1848 and his returning there in May 1851? Why so little mention even of the possibility of foreign travel – yet after that a whole succession of journeys, with sometimes only a brief interval in Paris before setting out again?

There was, I think, no single reason for his on-the-face-of-it puzzling decision, if decision it was, to stay put. Rather, it was a combination of separate factors. One was the continuing unsettled state of continental Europe. The deaths of several friends made him acutely aware of it: Becher, the radical journalist who had been one of his most enthusiastic advocates in Vienna in 1845–6, shot by firing squad for his part in the uprising of 1848; Prince Lichnowsky, Prussian right-wing deputy to the new German National Assembly, lynched by a mob; Count Batthyány,

Hungarian patriot, arrested after the Austrian army's capture of Pesth and executed. As we have seen, his plan to perform the *Damnation* in Prague vanished in the political and social upheavals of the time. It was no longer the Europe that had welcomed him before the revolutions. As for England, though plans were afoot for another visit – his London friends, Edward Holmes and Adolphe Duchêne de Vère among them, were trying to get up a performance of the Te Deum at Exeter Hall (the Sacred Music Society had, independently, asked for the score, which Berlioz however had no intention of releasing before he himself had conducted it), and Beale was working to set up a new orchestra – all this took time. And before he could accept, he would have to be absolutely sure of the financial arrangements. Meanwhile it was wisest to hold on to what he had: his post at the Conservatoire Library, potentially at risk whenever he was not there to defend it, and his other regular source of income, the music feuilleton of the *Journal des débats*, now appearing as frequently as in the most prolific days of the 1830s and early 1840s – sixteen articles in 1849, thirteen in 1850, twenty in 1851 – and anything up to five thousand words long, spread over ten columns of varying depth, paid once again at the pre-Revolution rate of 10 francs a column.

He might still hope, incorrigibly, for a breakthrough in his career as a musician in France. Writing to Liszt to tell him of the Société des Concerts' unexpected approach, he remarked that "perhaps, in the end, the mountain will get up and march towards me". But his resolve remained to do nothing further to make it happen – to give up marching towards the mountain. And the mountain stayed put. In the eighteen months from July 1848 to January 1850 Berlioz was first and foremost a critic, and more or less resigned to being so, despite his complaint that it was "a dog of a trade and a trade for dogs – always biting or licking", and that it got in the way of composing the Te Deum.

Even now he did not feel free to speak his mind. Whereas in praising Halévy's new opéra-comique *Le val d'Andorre* "I said what I thought", with Clapisson's *Jeanne la folle* "the opposite" was the case. Yet to see through his already qualified eulogies required no great clairvoyance. Clapisson's score might have some attractive things in it: "the introduction is colourful, Philippe's song beneath the castle walls is in a fresh and original style, the finale of the third act is full of the sort of harmonious buzz and bustle that excites applause, the orchestration is in general nicely handled". But that was all. His feuilleton employed the familiar tactic of devoting nearly half its space to a different, only distantly related topic. When at last it reached the work under review it spent another column squaring up to it:

Once upon a time a first night at the Opéra was an event in the life of the little town of two thousand souls called Paris. People would talk about it in advance and would scheme to gain entry to the dress rehearsal, and take up positions for and against the authors. The ladies wore their best and sparkled from the dress-circle boxes. Everyone argued about the work during the entr'actes; and music publishers went around like journeying ants from one critic to another, assuring the *Constitutionnel* that the *Débats* thought it superb and the *Débats* that the *Constitutionnel* was in raptures. In those days Habeneck put on a white tie and the orchestra tuned up. Today, what happens? Around seven in the evening you run into a friend in the Rue Le Pelletier. "Where are you off to?" he asks. "To the Opéra." "Good Lord! What's on? *Le comte Ory? La vivandière?*" "Where have you been? It's the first night of *Jeanne la folle*." "Well I'm blessed. I hadn't heard about it. Who's it by?" "Scribe and Clapisson. I have a spare ticket – would you like it?" "Thank you, no, I have an important party to go to. Goodbye." The fine ladies are no longer in their most sparkling attire; they put on paste, sometimes nothing, not even rouge, and the men wear old gloves that have done duty on other similar occasions. Everyone looks old, and anxious, preoccupied, unoccupied, run down. The music publishers no longer come. What would be the use? Since they don't sell anything they can't buy anything. The critics breathe again; they're at liberty to rave in moderation. We're all of us in accord except the orchestra. Seven o'clock strikes. The theatre's half empty. Three loud knocks signal the commencement of hostilities. The semi-audience goes on discussing the presidential candidates and their chances. In the midst of this hum of conversation a trombone chord rings out and the curtain rises. There's no overture: the composer didn't have time to write one. No matter – we come straight to the point, which is that the scene represents a gorge in the Alpuxares, not far from Grenada; to the spectator's left, the towers and drawbridge of a medieval castle. Aben-Hassan, a Moorish conspirator, and his companions, sworn enemies of the Spaniards, emerge from different parts of the forest, singing a chorus the gist of which is: "Keep quiet, let's hide, be careful, wait and see, when you're a Moor you've all the time in the world."

As a whole, the fifty-five *Débats* articles of 1848-51 do not read like the forced labour of a man imprisoned in his *métier*. He has not gone stale. Generally, you feel, he speaks his mind – or near enough. When diplomatic considerations oblige him to be less than candid, his skill at writing between the lines enables him to convey his meaning. The perennial shortcomings of the Opéra receive no quarter; but on the rare occasions when "la grande boutique" (as Verdi called it) concentrates its energies and produces something worthy of its resources and subsidy – as it does with *Le Prophète* – he praises ungrudgingly. Only too aware what lies behind the metamorphosis, and personally sickened by the manoeuvring, the dinners and the "flattering unction" that are now required to make an opera a critical success, and by Meyerbeer's assiduous courting of him in a series of letters beginning "Cher et illustre maître" and ending "I fear you tonight even more than I love you", he none the less does justice to the magnitude of the composer's achievement. Although refusing to attend any except the final rehearsal, he makes a thorough study of the score, hears two performances before reviewing the work and, in his notice, goes through it in often admiring detail. He delights in the triumphs of Roger and Pauline Viardot (the ideal interpreters for whom Meyerbeer had held back the work so long). He even has a good word for Girard's conducting. At the same time he has no hesitation in criticizing what he considers Meyerbeer's pandering to the lowest tastes of the public, exemplified among other things by the bravura style of Fidès' second cavatina in Act 5, for which "there can be no excuse in the role of an old woman worn out by age and grief". Reporting on the revival of *Le Prophète* six months later he addresses his reproaches directly to the composer: "I must confess to you that such vocal contortions make me feel ill, quite apart from the violence they do to dramatic appropriateness and expression. The sound irritates my nerve ends as though I were listening to the rending of a piece of calico or a diamond scratching on a window-pane. You know how I love and admire you. But I have to say that at such moments, if you were near me and the puissant hand that has written such grand and lofty things were within reach, I should be capable of biting it to the bone."

Berlioz writes as an independent spirit. The cynicisms and atrocities of the Paris musical scene have not ground him down; they provoke him to rage, to scorn, but not yet to despair. In the face of every discouragement the philistines can offer he cleaves, like Hoffmann's hero, to his ideals. He still believes that art (as he writes to Nancy) "is just about the only thing in this world that lasts and that one will be sorry to lose. To feel its power and worship its beauty, it is worth submitting to the confidence trick called life." And he has not yet lost his appetite for the oddities and curious corners of musical life.

If you liked the fantastical Hoffmann, if you followed him to Kapellmeis-ter Kreisler's or to that mysterious mansion where Gluck takes him one night to play him *Armide* in his own special way, or into the smoky cellar lit only by the blueish flicker of a bowl of punch and the bloodshot eyes of those two unfortunates, one of whom has lost his reflection and the other his shadow, then you like music and are not afraid of the smell of tobacco or the stimulus of alcohol. If so, go to the Passage Jouffroy. There you will find an enormous tap-room where, every evening, two hundred pipes are at it full blast while at one end of the room, dimly visible through the cloud and stench, six or seven vocalists on a little stage, accompanied by a tinkling piano, hoarsely dispense comic songs, nocturnes, romances and character ballads. The roar of conversation, rattle of glasses and click of heels makes them practically inaudible, but it covers up the wrong notes. At about ten, however, when the crush and smoke are at their densest, if you've managed to find a place near the stage you'll see a strange figure emerge. At the sight of him there's a profound hush; the most fanatical pipe stops puffing, the cigars go out, the waiter stands stock still, clutching his bottles, like a Sisyphus who has forgotten to push his rock; the Proserpine of the cash desk utters one word, and the strolling multitudes feel their legs struck motionless and their feet nailed to the floor. It's Darcier! Already his face has assumed the personality of the character whose dark or guileless or lamentable story he is about to sing you; he is in the part, acting, gesturing. He speaks as much as sings, but with such verve and depth of feeling and such incontestable power, larding his chant with ornaments so extraordinary and notes so unexpected, along with wild cries and shouts of laughter but also with stifled or tender or delicate sounds and phrases of profound sadness, that you are utterly captivated and can only weep or laugh unrestrainedly. Darcier is an artist. You have to see him and hear him to know what an artist he is. His style is pure Bohemian, in voice and in movement. After electrifying the room with the legend of the "Louis d'or" and moving it to tears with "The Departure of the Conscript" he will sit at one of the tables and drink a tankard of beer and smoke a pipe like any ordinary mortal. Yet none of your gods of the Opéra is more acclaimed and petted and deafened with bravos than he. Darcier is actually a good musician, despite the habit he's got into of kicking rhythm and metre to kingdom come; you realize it the moment he begins to play the piano, you see it even in the brazen way he dismembers a melody. When he was twelve he was in a church one day – why or how I have no idea – where the choir was directed by Delsarte. Moved by the force and quality of one or two of the great man's notes, he waited for him at the church door and, still in a daze, accosted him with, "Sir, I don't have a voice, but if you – if you would give me lessons I think that all the same I could sing." He had in fact a most attractive voice but thought that to sing well it was better not to. "Very well, my friend," replied the shrewd and knowing professor, "come and see me. I'll take you as a pupil. I have a feeling you're right." Delsarte duly taught him music and singing. When puberty came he told him not to sing until his voice had finished breaking. Darcier ignored the prohibition and, probably as a result, spoiled a vocal organ which, as it is, still has power and charm even if it lacks freshness. After that he took off for the provinces and, putting Scarron's comic novel into practice, became an expert swordsman, giving lessons in cutlass, two-handed, infantry sword, rapier, quarter-staff, kick-boxing and piano. Now, back in Paris, he is making his fortune by augmenting the fortune of the proprietor of this *estaminet-lyrique*, who pays through the nose to have him. Darcier is brother of the charming actress of the Opéra-Comique. Duprez, Roger and all the great artists go to hear him; poets and composers brave the fumes every evening to sit at his feet. Before long he would have an audience of kings if we still had any.

By the time he wrote that, in the spring of 1849, his reasons for staying in Paris had become more compelling and more personal. In October 1848 Harriet had the first of a series of strokes. A second followed in mid-February, a third, the most violent, in July, a fourth soon afterwards, and a fifth early in October. On that occasion Louis was home from boarding-school, and father and son scoured the *quartier* adjoining Montmartre in frantic search of a doctor. (Some time in the spring of 1848 Harriet had moved out of the city to the Rue St Vincent, Montmartre, round the corner from where she and Berlioz had lived in the mid-1830s in the time of their happiness.) Copious bleedings and mustard baths were still the prescribed medical response. They did not actually kill her. But though the attacks became less frequent she was left paralysed on the right side, able to speak only with difficulty and in need of two full-time female attendants. "Harriet is no worse" was the best he was able to report. There could be no significant improvement in her condition. At times she had so little power of speech that he could only guess what she was trying to say, ask, "Is it such and such?", and wait for her yes or no.

An unpublished letter dated "Montmartre, 19 October [1849]" shows Berlioz at her bedside.

> (I am writing to you, my dear Louis, on behalf of your mother and at her dictation.)
>
> My dear Louis
> I am not too bad at the moment, the fine weather is doing me good, but I don't find it easy to speak, which very often gives me trouble making myself understood.
>
> I hope you are working hard; your father tells me you are content, and that he is content with you. Write to me next week and give me detailed news of what you are doing. Your letters do me so much good! They console me in my sad state. I embrace you with all my heart, my dear child.
>
> Your affectionate mother
H. Berlioz+
>
> +Your mother's signature, written with her own hand.
> P.S I too embrace you, my good Louis, and will write soon. Hector B.

In the four years from their separation in 1844 to her first stroke Harriet had receded towards the fringes of her husband's life. She was, at first, living a few streets away from the Berlioz/Recio ménage in the Rue de la Rochefoucauld; but though he continued to support her and certainly saw her from time to time, the correspondence of the period mentions her only rarely. Now all that was changed. She was once again near the centre of his existence. If Marie objected, *tant pis*. Harriet's sufferings made her "only more dear", as he wrote in his *Memoirs* (work on which was proceeding out of reach of Marie's eye, in his librarian's office at the Conservatoire); "I see her often." In the summer of 1849 he and Marie and her mother moved house, but only to the next street, to a fourth-floor apartment at 19 Rue de Boursault (the western end of the present Rue de la Bruyère). It remained a trek to Montmartre, though after the construction in late 1849 of a flight of steps direct to the top of the hill the journey was shorter. Sometimes he went there twice in a day. His letters were full of her.

20 July [1849]

It appears, my dear sister [Nancy], that the family is highly aquatic at the moment. You are drinking the waters of La Mothe; my uncle is doing the same at Uriage, and Suat is going to take them at Plombières; I, for my part, smelled the Enghien variety while strolling in the woods at Montmorency last week. If Camille is sent off to swim in them at Aix the party will be complete. God grant that at least your orgy of drinking at La Mothe will have a good effect on your health. How is it that you didn't take Mathilde with you? Or did the cares of government prevent her from getting away? [The sixteen-year-old Mathilde was passionately interested in politics.] She is not like Voltaire's Orosmane who was content to "give an hour to the cares of his empire". Apropos of empire, there's a vague rumour going round in its favour. We shall see. I met the president on the boulevard yesterday; we recognized each other and exchanged cordial greetings. I was extremely gracious with him, which will surely have given him hope.

I'm in quite a cheerful mood today, thanks to a considerable lessening of anxiety and grief. Four days ago Harriet had a third attack, worse than the previous ones – I thought she was dying. Nothing is so dreadful as these convulsions, caused by pressure on the brain: the gurgling, the darkening of the face . . . Fortunately she was bled in time, liberally, and the worst of the symptoms were relieved almost at once; she gave a deep sigh, and the convulsions ceased. But for two days the poor thing knew nobody; she stared fixedly at me but her eyes were blank, with no spark of understanding. Since yesterday she has been better. She knows who I am. She remembers nothing of the appalling crisis she has just been through; she realized they had bled her only when she saw her arm. I'm just leaving her now. She's almost gay. She conveyed to me that she wanted to know your news and I gave her those I had just received. What a strange and terrible thing, this overlaying of the whole frightful experience, so that the patient has no recollection of it.

Caring for Harriet took money as well as time. In response to some probing questions from Adèle he admitted that the Montmartre establishment cost a good 3,500 francs a year. "The two maids economize as much as possible, except for laundry, which is ruinous." But he was adamant that Harriet's comfort and peace of mind came first.

Yes, without doubt poor Harriet's house causes me serious financial embarrassment; but in all conscience should not the expense have priority over all others? What Louis told you may have been sensible from the point of view of economy, but he was very wrong to speak about it to his mother without telling me, and I had all the trouble in the world ridding her invalid's mind of the impression his thoughtless words had left. I daresay she would resign herself to going into a nursing home; but the mere idea of leaving her room, her garden and flowers and sunshine and her green shady walk and the view of the St Denis plain, the open sky, and her two maids (who I am sure are honest), has upset her terribly. She wouldn't last two months in one of those cold, gloomy places. [. . .] I managed to persuade her eventually that I had nothing to do with the suggestion which Louis made to her. And that's the truth. I would resign myself to anything, to living in students' lodgings and surviving on crusts of bread rather than give Harriet such heartbreak.

To the expense of Harriet's ménage was added, in the autumn of 1850, a sharp increase in the cost of maintaining Louis. The sixteen-year-old boy embarked as apprentice on a frigate bound from Le Havre for Guadeloupe and New Orleans.

Not surprisingly his progress at school had been erratic and generally very slow. Berlioz had more than one awkward interview with the headmaster. Louis' problems were exacerbated by lack of money, as he explained to his Aunt Nancy: he was competing with boys who paid to have private coaching, "while I don't have any because Papa says he can't afford it". He excelled only at drawing. Nancy, writing to her brother in October 1848, might well congratulate him on his son's excellent disposition, in her view worth more than many more brilliant attributes – "he has rare and most attractive qualities of heart, and you're lucky that you will have such a treasure of affection in your old age"; but, as she also pointed out, he must decide on a career soon or it would be too late. For a moment there was talk of his following his great-uncle Marmion and becoming a soldier. The choice, however, was not long in doubt. He would be a sailor.

Berlioz was torn between vicarious excitement at the thought of his travelling the wide world and distress at being separated from him just as they were growing close. He fretted about Louis' hyper-emotional temperament, and "shuddered" to think that he was developing "a double-barrelled imagination like his parents'". A year later, in September 1849, the boy was still doing badly at school, and remained "very much a child". And that December he was again "not getting on in his studies; the headmaster is highly dissatisfied". Louis, however, persisted in his determination to be a sailor; and Berlioz threw himself into making the necessary arrangements and finding the means to pay for them.

The publication of various scores brought in some extra money: *Harold in Italy* (1848) was followed in the next two years by several collections of smaller pieces – *Feuillets d'album*, *Fleurs des landes* and *Vox populi* (combining two patriotic choruses, *Le menace des Francs* and *Hymne à la France*) – and Covent Garden bought his *Freischütz* recitatives. It was not enough, however. The idea of a volume of stories – germ of the later *Evenings in the Orchestra* – failed for lack of a publisher: "the times, they say, are 'so hard for the book trade'," he wrote to Nancy, "that George Sand herself told me she had spent a year looking for a publisher for her charming idyll *Le Champi*" (the novel had been serialized in the *Débats*). Berlioz was reduced to raising further loans from his brothers-in-law on the security of his share of the estate. Meanwhile a naval friend of the Bertins, a Captain Page, commander of a frigate lately arrived from Bombay whom government economies had deprived of his ship and turned ashore, was proving a useful contact, though talking to him revived Berlioz's longing for travel. "He thoroughly approved of [Louis'] plans and assured me he took a keen interest in them. He said that whether he is at sea or not I can count on his help and that of his friends. And he declared the profession of sailor the finest in the world and that never for one minute has he been bored at sea, and that he found little to amuse him on shore." By March 1850 Louis was "working hard for his naval exams". In February the alarmed father had rushed to Rouen on learning that the boy had fractured his collar-bone, but the break soon mended. Louis, having talked to one of his older schoolmates, now a midshipman and just back from Brazil, was even more set on a career in the navy.

Berlioz had much greater cause for anxiety in the winter of 1850 than Louis' health. Nancy was dying. She had been ailing for more than a year. The visit to the springs at La Mothe was an attempt to find some new remedy. It had aroused her brother's suspicions – as he wrote to Adèle, "when doctors send their patients to spas it's generally because they don't know what else to prescribe them" – but the family, Nancy included, seem to have agreed to keep him in ignorance; or perhaps they all deceived themselves as to the real nature of the disease. For over a year he had no inkling of the truth.

Though he loved Adèle more intensely, Berlioz was conscious of the affinities that bound him to Nancy at a level deeper than the differences in their circumstances. Rereading his father's *Mémoires sur les maladies chroniques* in the late summer of 1849 and thinking over the events of twelve months before, as the first anniversary of the old man's death came round, had brought both his sisters very close to him.

> The traces of his pen in the margin showed him meditating on his book and correcting it with care, and reminded me of all that was fine and lofty in his practice of medicine and astute in his talent, which was made to shine on a larger stage; but his unutterable kindness and the loving care he devoted to our childhood are, for us, quite other reasons for a sense of loss. Above all, at the period of life I have reached, time, as it ushers in our declining years, seems to lend us a keener gaze with which to see the distant objects of our first affections, and make us regret them more bitterly. I wish I could see you both. Give me at least, immediately, some truthful news of Nanci, from her herself.

Not till the following March did he learn how serious it was. Even then Adèle did not name it; but she revealed that her sister was in unremitting agony, and had been, day and night, for several months. It was rampant breast cancer, with all that it involved in excruciating pain and general physical disintegration.

Adèle nursed her to the end. She died on 4 May 1850, without benefit of morphine. Four years later, recalling the horror of it as he wrote the final chapter of his *Memoirs*, Berlioz inveighed against the barbarity of modern conventions about dying.

> No doctor dared be so humane as to put an end to my sister's martyrdom by making her breathe a flask of chloroform. They do it to spare patients the pain of an operation that lasts a few seconds yet will not consider using it to save them six months of torment, when it is known for certain that no remedy, not even time, will cure the disease, and death is clearly their sole deliverance, their supreme happiness.
>
> The law, however, forbids it, and the doctrines of religion are no less rigidly opposed. And my sister herself would have no doubt rejected that way of escape had it been offered her. "God's will be done" – as if everything that happened did not happen because of God's will, and as

if God's will would not have been as well manifested in the release of the patient by a swift and peaceful death as in the prolonging of her pointless and abominable torture.

How senseless, how infinitely absurd are all these questions of fate, the existence of God, free will and the rest of it – an endless maze where human understanding wanders helplessly lost.

In any case, inexorable pain of that degree of intensity, with no possibility of remission, is of all things in this world the most hideous for us conscious, sentient beings; and it is sheer barbarity or stupidity, or both, not to make use of the sure and painless means available nowadays for ending it. Savages are more intelligent and more humane.

For the present, his greatest concern was for his surviving sister, after what she had lived through. "At least let me have news of you – your silence worries me. I'm afraid of your grief. And yet you must have suffered a thousand times more cruelly in witnessing the agony of our poor one now set free. I wrote five days ago to Camille, and to Odile. She said I would get a letter from you any day. Are you ill? Please have Suat send me word. Farewell, I embrace you. Poor sister! Now there are only two of us."

A day or two later the letter came. It showed him that all reticences between the sisters had been resolved and that in her final weeks the dying woman had unburdened herself of her most secret thoughts.

15 May

My dear, dear sister

Your letter, which I was begging for the day before yesterday, has shattered me. I had guessed all too well all the details of our unhappy Nanci's physical torments, but what you tell me of her mental suffering breaks my heart. Added to them, it must have made her torture unbearable. You may be sure that she had long made up her mind about the two members of her intimate family. I too had long divined her efforts to delude us as to her private sorrows, her disillusionment, all her disappointed hopes. But of course one had to pretend to be taken in. At least poor Mathilde with her vulgar and frivolous nature will, as you say, suffer less than those differently constituted. [...] Thank Mlle Clappier, Mme Charmeil and our aunts most warmly from me for all the love and care they gave Nanci during her long agony.

As for you, my poor sister, I can only adore, with tears, the gentle, noble and forceful qualities of your heart. I know you . . . what more is there to say?

Please tell our excellent Monique how grateful I am for the unfailing affection she showed our sister; it touches me deeply. In a little while, when it won't look like a merely formal gift, which might hurt her, I should like to give her something useful or agreeable. Would you do it and tell her it's from me? You can let me know how much you have spent; twenty francs more or less is neither here nor there.

On hearing of Nanci's death Harriet was terribly upset. She moaned and wept, raising her hands but unable to utter a word. I daresay she also drew melancholy parallels between their two fates.

Chance willed that the day before our sister died I was engaged in conducting my Requiem at St Eustache. A sad and strange coincidence, was it not?

The performance of the Requiem was the work of a new organization, in existence only since the winter – the Grande Société Philharmonique de Paris. It represents Berlioz's final attempt to establish himself as composer-conductor and concert promoter in France. While it lasted, it was a further reason for his staying in Paris. The idea had come to him the previous year, prompted by the appearance of a new auditorium, the Salle Ste Cécile, the former gymnasium of the riding school at 49 *bis* Rue de la Chaussée d'Antin. The place still smelled of horses – throughout the fifteen years of its life as a concert hall people would complain of having to take their music with a whiff of the stables – but it was a fine hall in other respects, large but not too large, with good acoustics and in a fashionable part of Paris. Berlioz hailed its advent at the beginning of 1849, on the occasion of the début of a new orchestra, the Société de l'Union Musicale: "We must begin by announcing the great news. Paris has a concert hall!" The Union was the creation of the violinist Manéra, a Habeneck pupil and former leader of the Société des Concerts du Conservatoire. His programmes, modelled on those of the Conservatoire – Beethoven, Rossini, Weber and the occasional new work – only whetted Berlioz's desire to do the same and do it better; and Manéra's premature death in August 1849 appeared to leave the field wide open. The Union rallied and, a few months later, re-formed under the Belgian violinist-conductor François Seghers; but he was not deterred. By the end of the year the Société Philharmonique had been formally constituted, with Berlioz as founder-director, president and chief conductor and Pierre Dietsch, the Opéra's chorus-master, in charge of the choir; a prospectus invoking the examples of similar societies in London, Vienna, Brussels and St Petersburg had been drafted, and the first of a season of monthly Tuesday evening subscription concerts was in preparation.

The society was a cooperative, modelled on that of the Conservatoire concerts, with a similarly worded constitution and the profits divided among the members – orchestral players (ninety), choristers (110) and committee of fifteen – on the basis of number of attendances, for which, just as with the Société des Concerts, tokens or *jetons* were issued (or forfeited, in the case of non-attendance). At the same time care was evidently taken not to make too obvious a challenge to Girard and the Conservatoire Orchestra. Of the dozen or so programmes offered by the Philharmonique during its one and a half seasons of active life, only three contained music by Beethoven, the prop and stay of the Société des Concerts. The membership of the two orchestras, too, was almost totally different, to judge by a handwritten list of the personnel and by the names given in a letter of Berlioz's written on Société Philharmonique headed paper to the secretary, the cellist Seligmann (Offenbach's desk-partner at the Opéra-Comique). The letter names forty-three string players, whom Seligmann is asked to "convene, for the rehearsal *next Friday, noon, at Sax's*", and then continues:

Write, in the letters to the horns and the trumpets, "bring all keys", and in the cornets', "bring A and B flat and E flat".

And don't forget to cross out "Salle Ste Cécile" and underline "Salle Sax, 10 Rue Neuve St Georges".

All this as soon as possible – the porter has only just time to take them round; he'll come to collect them on Tuesday morning.

Yours ever

H. Berlioz

Let me know when we're going back to see M. Chassiron, whose address I can never remember.

In the letter to the first oboe, Cras, write: "Bring the COR ANGLAIS."

Ten years later, Cras will be the Société des Concerts' first oboe, and Lalo, the last of the violins listed, a well-known composer. Only one of the string players named, Léon Gastinel – violinist and recent Prix de Rome – figures in a roughly contemporary list of the Société des Concerts. Berlioz seems to have recruited his orchestra from among the younger theatre musicians and freelance players in Paris (some of them newly arrived from the provinces), leavened with older, more experienced hands like Lambert Massart, who was concert-master, and Tajan-Rogé, his friend of St Petersburg days. It is clear that though he had a committee in support the main burden fell on him before even a note was heard. It was he who, together with his journalist colleague and fellow-committee-member, Léon Kreutzer, took on the job of drumming up publicity in the press, and he who lobbied the great and the good to lend their names as patrons to the new enterprise. (Among those he netted were Spontini, Liszt, Halévy, Ambroise Thomas, Adam, Félicien David, Baron Taylor, Armand Bertin, the Comtes de Gasparin and de Castellane, a clutch of countesses, duchesses and princesses, and in England Sterndale Bennett, George Alexander Macfarren and Davison.) The minutes, too, were generally written by him.

After years of taking the artistic decisions himself, rule by committee was irksome and added to his labours. "We have meetings and discussions without end," he told Liszt. "I have the greatest difficulty in conforming to the niceties of representative government, thanks to which we spend a week doing what I could do in one hour." On the other hand, the great thing about the Société Philharmonique, as he acknowledged, was that he could give concerts – well-prepared concerts – without being solely responsible and solely at risk. With the proceeds divided among so many, he was unlikely to make much money out of it, but he wouldn't lose any either. He had his own orchestra and chorus, and at last could make a sustained impact on the musical life of Paris – and do something for young composers: Article 36 of the constitution required the society to perform each year a work, up to thirty minutes long, by the returning Prix de Rome. And though Berlioz was careful, in this inaugural season, not to give too blatant pride of place to his own music, he made no secret of his hope that it would be the means of having the Te Deum performed. The society also had ambitions beyond Paris: once the season was over, there were plans to take the whole company to Rouen and Amiens, and to perform a mass by Dietsch in Versailles.

At first the prospects seemed good. According to Paul Smith's "Review of 1850" in the *Gazette*, everyone had wanted to be involved in it, so great was Berlioz's prestige as conductor. The opening concert, on 19 February 1850, was suitably starry: Roger and Levasseur in the first two parts of the *Damnation*, young Joachim playing Ernst's fantasy on

Rossini's *Otello*, Pauline Viardot and Mlle Dobré singing Gluck, Roger again in an aria from Méhul's *Joseph* and, to end, the Blessing of the Daggers from *The Huguenots*. There were getting on for three thousand francs' profit and encouragingly positive reviews. The three subsequent concerts, however, though well supported in the press, boasted fewer glamorous soloists and did much less good business. Arnoldi and Mme Julienne were unimpressive in the first act of *Alceste*; the charming and fashionable soprano Mme Ugalde cancelled because of ill health; the antics of the Polish violinist Apollinaire de Kontski, combining pizzicato and arco in the same piece and then removing all but a single string so as to perform "Grâce pour moi" from *Robert le diable* on the "monochord", only made the audience laugh. Roger and Félicien David were on the bill at the fourth concert and Wieniawski at the second, and there were artistic rewards in Mme Massart's fine performance of the Weber Concertstück and Massart's of *Harold*, and in the Paris première of Mendelssohn's overture to *Athalia*; but at the society's general meeting, held in Sax's Rooms on 27 April, the treasurer could only announce a profit of 4,370 fr. 25c. – 1,000 of which represented a government subsidy – to be shared among a membership of over two hundred. True, Berlioz had been able occasionally to procure additional engagements for his players (there were always rich amateurs looking for an orchestra to perform for them). But even allowing that the society had not got going till mid-season, 20 francs a head was meagre recompense for four concerts and nearly a dozen rehearsals. The faithful Léon Kreutzer, welcoming the society's second season in the *Gazette* that autumn, could not conceal the fact that the inaugural concerts, so rich in plaudits, had been poor in receipts, though he was confident that this time the takings would match the applause.

At the general meeting there had been even more urgent matters to discuss than the remuneration of the members. The whole assembly had been in turmoil as the society split into two factions: the chorus, which supported Dietsch, and the orchestra, solidly for Berlioz. What had brought to the surface the latent conflict between the two men was a catastrophic accident at Angers ten days before. On 16 April, as the third battalion of the 11th Light Infantry marched in full battledress across the suspension bridge over the Maine, someone forgot to give the order to break step, the bridge collapsed, and more than two hundred officers and men were drowned. All France was shocked by the disaster.

The committee, which had been planning to give Berlioz's Te Deum in St Eustache, turned its attention to a performance of his Requiem in aid of the victims' families. But Dietsch, the society's chorus master, was himself the author of several masses (the Credo from one of them had figured at the society's *concert spirituel* the previous month). Was he not just as entitled to have his music chosen for the charity performance? So his supporters argued. A chorister, claiming to speak for all his colleagues, complained that "M. Berlioz's music is tiring for us artists." This drew angry protests from the orchestra, answered by counter-protests from the chorus. Berlioz offered to resign and let a new committee be elected. There were calls for Dietsch's resignation instead. The meeting broke up in disorder. But the upshot was that on 3 May the Requiem was performed at St Eustache, and Dietsch held aloof. In the *Gazette* Kreutzer noted that there was "no occasion to regret the absence of the chorus-master, M. Dietsch; orchestra and chorus matched each other in skill under the sole direction of M. Berlioz". The committee was re-formed and the disaffected choristers replaced. No one was appointed in Dietsch's place. In the revised statutes, dated 16 July 1850, "power to regulate the inner organization of orchestra and chorus" was vested solely in the *chef d'orchestre-président*. There was now no overall *chef de chant* but instead two deputy chorus-masters, Justin Cadaux for the women and Alexander Leprevost for the men, and, above them both, the begetter, animator, artistic director and heart and soul of the organization, whose heart was still in it but whose soul was beginning to weary of the struggle. (His request, in May, to the Minister of the Interior, for the Society to be allowed to hold its concerts in the Conservatoire Hall had been rejected.)

Such crises, of course, were not peculiar to the Philharmonique. Its rival at the Salle Ste Cécile, the Union Musicale, was so disunited that not long after the row at the Philharmonique a faction broke off and, taking the conductor Seghers with it, founded the Société Ste Cécile. The Union was left to regroup under Félicien David. That winter there would be three separate bodies competing for public attention in the Rue de la Chaussée d'Antin.

The Philharmonique, having started late the previous season, was determined to be ready in good time. Throughout much of the summer there were weekly meetings of the orchestra, by no means always fully attended but at which a quorum of musicians worked at the music planned for the following season: Beethoven (the Fifth Symphony), Weber, Gluck, an overture by the 1848 Prix de Rome Gastinel (two movements of a symphony of his had been performed the previous season), but also rather more Berlioz than before, including the first four movements of *Romeo and Juliet*, the Fantastic Symphony and the *Francs-juges* overture.

The seven concerts which the Philharmonique gave in the Salle Ste Cécile between October 1850 and April 1851 contained fine things and interesting novelties: the première of *Sara la baigneuse* in the version for triple choir, several of those deep-toned monumental Bortniansky pieces which had so impressed Berlioz in the Imperial Chapel in St Petersburg, more of his beloved Gluck and Weber, the revival of some virtually forgotten pieces by Le Sueur, and the new keyboard prodigy from Bohemia, Liszt's pupil Wilhelmine Clauss, playing Beethoven's Appassionata. At the end of the Fantastic Symphony, at the second concert (12 November), the ladies of the chorus presented Berlioz with an enormous crown of oak, laurel and privet leaves, and at the fifth (25 February), after the Scène d'amour, two young women dressed in white stepped from the audience and placed before him a white satin cushion bearing a coronet of gold. He also had the pleasure of passing off his Shepherds' Farewell as the work of a certain Pierre Ducré, seventeenth-century choirmaster at the Ste Chapelle (named in honour of his friend the architect Duc, in whose album he had first jotted the thing down), and hearing from Duc that a society lady of his acquaintance, a connoisseur of ancient music, had declared that "Berlioz would never be able to write a tune as simple and charming as this little piece by old Ducré." The programmes, too, offered no lack of vocal glamour. Viardot sang her Spanish songs, Roger was once again to the fore, Mlle Frezzolini the new star sang Schubert's *Serenade* and an aria from Bellini's *Beatrice di Tenda*, and there were items by Rossini, Donizetti and Auber.

Despite all this the season had to be reckoned a failure. The paying audience was simply too small. Much of the time half the house, sometimes more, was papered. An occasional windfall might help to keep things going: the rich Mlle de Reiset paid for a movement of her Symphony in C to be included in the concert of 25 February, the Société des Crèches de Chaillot engaged the orchestra at 1,000 francs to play in the Jardin d'Hiver, and M. Henry Cohen gave the same for a performance of his dramatic oratorio *The Monk* (based on Lewis's famous novel). But this was hardly what the society had been created for; and, even so, the musicians (as Berlioz told General Lvov) earned "practically nothing. Hence their heartbreakingly irregular attendance at rehearsals." Not even his prestige and personality could keep the enterprise alive on promise alone. So, though the Philharmonique was not formally disbanded at the end of the season, and hope of being able to resume operations lingered on into the winter of 1851–2, its appearance at the inauguration of a new hall in the Marais, the short-lived Salle Barthélemy, on 24 June 1851 – when the young composer Ernest Reyer hired it for 1,500 francs and, in Berlioz's absence, conducted it himself – proved to be its last.

The Union Musicale was no more fortunate. It too failed to prolong its existence into the new season. Only Seghers' Société Ste Cécile survived and flourished. Exactly why that should have been is hard to determine. Seghers was a fraction of the conductor Berlioz was. Admittedly Berlioz himself had trouble at times raising his players to a satisfactory level of performance – he told Morel in November 1850 that after seven rehearsals of the Fantastic Symphony he had nearly given up – but we have no reason to suppose that Seghers' orchestra played better. At this distance there is no way of knowing just how well or badly either of them played. The review of Cohen's *The Monk* in *La France musicale* accused the orchestra of culpable negligence. On the other hand, when the Philharmonique gave a mass by Niedermeyer at the Church of St Thomas Aquinas, on the left bank, a couple of months earlier, the composer wrote Berlioz a rapturous letter thanking him and his chorus and orchestra for a "magnificent performance" which had brought him "the joy such as rarely happens in the life of an artist, that of hearing his work as he conceived it".

The Société Ste Cécile, however, had certain advantages, and in the end they were crucial. Its concerts were held fortnightly, not monthly, and not on weekday evenings but on Sunday afternoons (in alternation with the Conservatoire's fortnightly concerts during the latter's spring season). In consequence it could more easily build up a regular following and, not having to reckon with the prior demands of the theatre orchestras' evening shows, more easily recruit players. The Ste Cécile had strong financial backing and was therefore less dependent than the Philharmonique on good receipts. Furthermore, again unlike the Philharmonique, it was directed by a man whose position was clearly defined and unambiguous. Whereas Berlioz was at one and the same time conductor, dedicated to improving the standard of orchestral concerts, and composer, looking for opportunities to perform his works,

Seghers was simply conductor. His activities were coloured by no such conflict of interests as prompted a journalist to nickname the Société Philharmonique "Ste Cécile, Berlioz & compagnie". In fact, Seghers' programmes, though not unlike Berlioz's, were, objectively considered, both better balanced and more wide-ranging: Haydn and Mozart as well as Gluck and Spontini; Mendelssohn; quite a lot of Weber, much more Beethoven, more "early music" but also some Schubert (and fewer of those would-be crowd-pulling vocal items which were so compromising to the Philharmonique's ideals). It even played Berlioz – the *King Lear* overture in November 1851 and, later, the first two performances in France of *The Flight into Egypt*. But at the Ste Cécile Berlioz was one composer among many, whereas the Philharmonique's public was sometimes asked to attend concerts dominated by music which, since the failure of *The Damnation of Faust*, was recognized in knowledgeable circles as not worth listening to. Perhaps because it could afford to be, the Société Ste Cécile was more adventurous. Berlioz told Liszt that he hoped the Philharmonique would perform some of his friend's recent compositions, but nothing had come of it by the time the society disbanded. The Ste Cécile, on the other hand, gave the Paris première of the overture to *Tannhäuser* at its inaugural concert, and a year later, in December 1851, the Great C major Symphony. Berlioz was profoundly impressed by the Schubert, describing it as "worthy of a place among the lofty achievements of our art", and the second movement in particular as "an absolute marvel". It was just the kind of work he should have performed. He might have, if he had still had an orchestra at his disposal; but by then his career as conductor of symphonic concerts in Paris was practically over. As champion of young French composers, too, it was the Ste Cécile that took the palm, developing what the Philharmonique had only begun. Berlioz's attempts to include new music – a declared intention of the Philharmonique's – were often frustrated by the committee. He was never the free agent he had hoped to be. Almost everything the Philharmonique set out to do would be achieved, on paper at least, by the Ste Cécile. Compared with such disappointments it hardly mattered that he made next to nothing out of the venture (84 francs on the opening season, he told Adèle); he had not really expected to.

Yet anxiety about money was a continued and constant fact of life in these years. He was chronically hard up. A projected visit to Dauphiné in the late summer of 1850 had to be abandoned: he could not afford the two hundred francs it would have cost. He must also decline an invitation to visit the writer Armand de Pontmartin at his country house in Provence: he was "stuck in Paris" and wouldn't be going south that year.

How I should have liked to come! I can picture myself, from here, sailing down the Rhône at twenty-five miles an hour, arriving at Avignon and, after an ecstatic dinner at Mme Pierron's magnificent table d'hôte, being introduced to your amiable donkey and negotiating with her to take me to the house of M. Pontmartin. Then the delightful talk, the flights of fancy, the smoking, the time-wasting, all the pleasures of Horace's villa at Tivoli plus, of course, cigars. (Horace never allowed one to smoke at his place – Virgil said the smell of tobacco disagreed with him. I had this at Tivoli itself, from a waiter at the Hotel Regina, so it must be true.)

But I shall console myself this winter, when I join you at d'Ortigue's fireside or at mine or even at yours (if you will allow me), when I shall say: do you remember those five lovely days we might have spent together at your villa, and the larks we might have trapped? Do you remember the swims we might have had in the Rhône? (I presume the Rhône has the grace to flow past your door.) Do you remember the noble ham and the miraculous Cavaillon melon you were going to offer us? And it will be lovely. Are not the joys of the mind and the imagination sweetest? You are condemned to the dull actuality; truly, I pity you. However, if you will kindly tell your slave one evening to fetch an amphora of that famous Falernian wine, which no well-bred Horace is without, and will drink half a dozen bowls in my honour, I shall feel much less concerned about you, and will return the compliment in modern wine at the first opportunity.

Warm regards to d'Ortigue, whom I thought still prosaically ensconced in his square off the Rue St Lazare.

Yours regretfully
Hector Berlioz

Apart from Harriet's ménage, Louis had become the biggest drain on his resources. The cost of his board on a training vessel, Berlioz calculated, would be three or four times that of the college. Louis, having seen the ocean at Le Havre, thought of "nothing but ships and voyages". A place on a merchant ship was secured with the aid of an influential naval acquaintance, Admiral Cécille, and in September father and son, just turned sixteen, travelled to Le Havre, as Berlioz told Adèle:

Paris, Tuesday 24 September 1850

Dear sister

I was on the point of answering your first letter today when the second arrived. After my return from Le Havre I hadn't felt equal to describing that upsetting journey. Louis wrote to tell you he was leaving, and in fact we left in a rush because I got word that the ship on which I was seeking a passage for him was about to sail. The owner told me we must be in Le Havre on Thursday 12 September at the latest, so there was not a moment to lose. But when we arrived we found the ship not yet loaded; and as two passengers had been granted a delay of embarkation we had to wait six days in the hotel. During all this time my poor boy was in high spirits and keen as mustard. He listened avidly at mealtimes to the talk of travellers arrived from New Orleans or from Mexico and others who were leaving for Valparaiso or California. One day he heard a naval officer tell me that "out of every ten young people who take up our career at least eight give up after their first voyage". That evening when we were alone Louis said: "He thinks I'll get tired of sailing, well you'll see, in spite of sea-sickness, which they say is so awful, in spite of exhaustion and everything, I shall stick to it."

We found several friends of mine at Le Havre, and Louis even ran into two of his comrades from the Lycée in Rouen. They all congratulated him on embracing so fine a career. I hope to God they're right . . . At last, at six in the morning on the Tuesday I took him to the ship and at seven, in superb weather and a light westerly wind (the best), the *Félix* set sail. Despite all our efforts, and our promises to each other that we would take our parting calmly, you can imagine what we were both feeling . . . I caught the train back to Paris, having embraced Louis – I couldn't even bring myself to follow him as far as the lighthouse, from which I could have seen the *Félix* stand out towards the open sea. What harrows me is the thought not so much of the perils of navigation as those of manoeuvring: I'm haunted by fear of an accident on board, I dread the dejection that can come from solitude, I dread the fever of the Antilles, and who knows what else. The *Félix* is commanded by M. Duhait, a very well-spoken young captain. He promised not to ask too much of our poor apprentice during the first days. The boatswain's mate and an old sailor also promised me they would keep an eye on him and help him along. The *Félix* goes first to Guadeloupe (a French colony in

455

the Antilles) and stays there a week, then makes for Haiti (Santo Dom-
ingo), where it will be for a month. [. . .] At Pointe à Pitre (Guadeloupe)
I've an old comrade from the Academy in Rome [Gibert], Louis has
taken a letter for him, and I've another in New Orleans [Guiraud]. All
the same I was nervous about Louis going ashore, until the captain
reassured me: he'll be allowed off only occasionally and then only with
the captain himself or the first officer. I hope to have news of the *Félix*
in *two months*. As the Southampton steam-packet leaves for the Antilles
every three weeks and takes nineteen days, Louis will find a letter from
me at Port au Prince (Haiti) when he gets there. He'll be back in Le
Havre in February or March. [. . .]

The six months he spends on the *Félix* are costing me six hundred
francs, five hundred of which I've paid in advance. I also had to buy him
a whole sailor's outfit in Le Havre – woollen shirts, linen shirts, woollen
coat, oilskins, boots, and even a mattress and blankets, etc. – and give
him some money, even though he'll have little chance of spending it. In
all, and including the journey and our stay in Le Havre, I spent nearly
nine hundred francs, which I didn't have and therefore had to borrow.

Harriet was terribly affected by this parting, though less perhaps than
I: her illness has greatly diminished all her faculties. The day before
yesterday she complained of "not being able to cry". It's true; since her
paralysis, when she's upset she sobs but there are no tears.

In the same letter Berlioz listed his current debts as

900 fr. borrowed for Louis' departure
about 300 fr. to the Montmartre doctor
350 fr. to my tailor
180 fr. still due my copyist
32 fr. to my hatter

1,762 fr.

and begged Adèle and Marc and Camille between them to help by
trying to sell part of his inheritance for him.

Two months later, to his joy, a letter came from Guadeloupe. Louis
had been sick only once, on the second day out, and was enjoying
everything (Berlioz told Adèle) except having to scrub the bridge every
morning. "He finds the heat a bit much in the roads – the captain hardly
ever lets him go ashore, which doesn't prevent him gorging on coconuts,
avocados, bananas, oranges, sweet lemons, sugar cane and all the other

fruits of the Antilles." A second letter, from Port au Prince, arrived in January. And in the last week of March 1851 Louis himself docked at Le Havre. Berlioz, who had been waiting with barely containable impatience, hurried there by the night train. He found him taller, stronger and more handsome: the sea air had "got rid of the red patches he used to have on his face", though his hands were all "rough and calloused". The captain praised his courage and steadfastness. Louis, on his side, had been proud to discover that his father's was a name to conjure with even in Central America. Berlioz spent over a thousand francs kitting him out for his leave in Paris and for his return to Guadeloupe, due in the third week of April.

Thanks to a further advance from Marc Suat against the inheritance, the financial position had, temporarily, eased. Nevertheless he was still living on the edge. The post of chief Conservatoire librarian, to which he succeeded in March 1850 on the death of Bottée, brought no increase in stipend. I don't doubt that an important motive in his applying, "reluctantly" as he said, for the vacant chair at the Academy of Fine Arts in March 1851 was the 1,500 francs it would add to his regular income. He was reluctant because he knew that a music section with Auber, Adam and Carafa in it was unlikely even to include his name on the short list forwarded to the full session of the Academy – in which case the candidate's obligatory round of courtesy calls on all academicians would be so much time and energy wasted. But he had promised Spontini he would.

It was Spontini's death that created the vacancy. For years he had been obsessed with death, believing that his end was imminent and getting his wife to give him daily readings of the prayer for the dying. He had not even been able to enjoy the tumultuous applause he received at a Conservatoire concert in February 1849, when part of La Vestale was performed. At dinner with Spontini and his wife a few days later (he told Nancy), Berlioz "spent the evening trying to reason with him, demonstrating to him that he was in good health – to no purpose. He clutched me to him with a kind of frenzy and said: 'Ah, my dear Berlioz, I have such a horror of death. It is so terrible to die! And my hour is come, I feel it. You will replace me at the Institute. Be sure to see that there is no music at my funeral, I want none . . .'"

And now, two years later, Spontini, like Nancy, was dead. Berlioz felt his world contracting. He had been among the handful of musicians who was on good terms with the old curmudgeon and who against the tide of fashion remained faithful to his genius. "Though his death had been long expected, it affected me deeply all the same. I loved him, that not very lovable man, by dint of having admired him. And then, the very asperities of his character attracted me – no doubt they meshed with mine." He vented his love and admiration in a long article – fifteen columns, nearly eight thousand words – for the *Débats*, half biographical, wholly personal and appreciative. "I think it's one of the best things I have written," he told Adèle; "but then I felt at ease in it – heart and imagination were able to speak their own language. And how I relieved my feelings with the help of my great whip, which I laid across the shoulders of the great artist's puny enemies! Ah!, it did me good!"

Such outspokenness cannot have done him much good with the Academy. It can have made no significant difference, however. Though the music section surprised Berlioz by short-listing him after all (no doubt they argued that they couldn't very well not do so, and there was no danger of his being elected), it was Ambroise Thomas who won. Niedermeyer came second, with five votes, Batton, professor of voice at the Conservatoire, third with three, and Berlioz last, with none.

Whatever Adam and the others might think of him, and however little the Paris public yearned to hear his music, he was still a figure to be reckoned with. That spring the Festival du Nord approached him with a view to getting him to Lille to conduct some of his music, in a new hall specially built to accommodate the forces gathered from all over northern France. When the time came he was elsewhere; but the Lacrymosa was given, under Girard, and was received with immense applause. There was also official recognition, of a kind. The Minister of Trade invited him to represent France on the international jury examining musical instruments at the Great Exhibition in London. Berlioz thought it "a singular idea for a Frenchman to have"; but he was the obvious choice. He had in any case been hoping he might go to London that spring to conduct some concerts. On 7 and 8 May the twelve French delegates met and were briefed, and on the evening of the 9th Berlioz took the train to Calais from the Gare du Nord and next morning crossed to Folkestone in halcyon weather. The *Félix*, with Louis on board, had set sail for Guadeloupe a few weeks before.

Berlioz's second visit to England is much less well documented than the first, when as befitted the conductor of the Grand English Opera his doings were widely reported. The surviving correspondence for these eleven weeks is sparse and tells us little about his personal life. We do not even know whether Marie Recio was with him when he arrived in London and took rooms on one of the upper storeys of the home of his friend Adolphe Duchêne, 27 (the present 58) Queen Anne Street, near his former lodgings in Harley Street and one block north of where the Wigmore Hall now stands. The handsome late-Regency terraced house was only twenty-five minutes' brisk walk from the Crystal Palace. Another asset was that its double drawing-room on the first floor served as rehearsal room and concert hall for the Beethoven Quartet Society, which he had admired three years before and which now had his great friend Ernst as leader. With his door ajar the sound came clearly up the stairwell as he worked.

His duties as juryman kept him pretty busy throughout his stay; but between whiles and all day on Sunday he was free to explore London and admire its parks and leafy squares, see old friends – Morris Barnett, Beale, Ella, Davison, Gruneisen – and make new ones, rest his English in the company of compatriots like Gautier, Janin and Sax who had come over for the exhibition, sit for Baugniet's handsome portrait engraving, and enjoy the surrounding country, marvellously green and lush after a rainy March and April. Without the stress of an opera company to direct, he could begin to relax. Not that he was anonymous. Even in a London thronged with visitors from the known world, invitations to public and private functions rained down. The Royal Commissioners in charge of events asked him to draw up plans for a series of concerts in the Eastern Gallery of the Crystal Palace, to mark the conclusion of the exhibition. There seemed a real prospect of music-making on the grandest scale, and Berlioz was soon happily making lists of performers, calculating costs and devising a programme to be repeated four times at weekly intervals throughout August and to include the Te Deum.

For his own curiosity and to gather material for his feuilletons – this time there was no respite as there had been in 1847–8: Armand Bertin was insisting on regular reports – he sampled the teeming musical life of the capital. Purcell's anthems at the Abbey left him cold, alas. Beethoven's chamber music and Ella's Musical Union were much more to his taste. And at a Philharmonic concert in Hanover Square Rooms on 9 June he heard the great scena from *Freischütz* delivered with superb fire and fidelity by a young French dramatic soprano in the making, Mme Charton-Demeur. Hers was a name he would have cause to remember in the years to come.

Half a dozen evenings were spent at the two Italian opera houses. He saw *Fidelio* – in Italian – at both Her Majesty's and Covent Garden (where Tamberlick was a wonderful Florestan and *Leonore no. 3* was given as an entr'acte before, not after, the dungeon scene), and also *Figaro*, *Don Giovanni*, *Il flauto magico* and *Il franco arciero* alias *Der Freischütz*. The latter, according to the programme, was being given "with recitatives by Hector Berlioz", but there was no sign of them; and he had, too, the indignity of being refused entry to the stalls and redirected to the gallery on the grounds that the trousers of his evening dress were not black. Correctness evidently mattered more in the auditorium than in the orchestra pit. Once again Costa was bent on "giving the great masters lessons in instrumentation": he enriched the *Freischütz* overture with bass drum, cymbals and ophicleide and tampered freely with Beethoven and Mozart. Berlioz told Armand Bertin that he had "toned down" his criticism, but in reality the shoddiness of London opera "disgusted" him. Costa's example was followed by Balfe in *Don Giovanni* at Her Majesty's, where an ophicleide solo added its "bovine snorts" to the tune from *Una cosa rara* played by the Don's private band during supper – an effect (wrote Berlioz) as ugly as it was implausible. "In the Devil's name, Don Juan was a man of taste, was he not? If one of his people had taken it on himself to perform Martin y Soler's music on the ophicleide, the cultured Spaniard would certainly have made Leporello show the numskull the door." There was some compensation in the celestial Sontag. Her Zerlina had "everything one looks for, everything one has dreamed of for that delicious *bricconcella*, united with singing of sheer perfection".

At the opposite extreme he liked, when he had an hour or two free, to wander the crowded streets absorbing the sights and sounds and smells of a city crammed with the peoples of the world, and listening to the itinerant musicians, who did a roaring trade. Their music – if one excepted that of the Chinese sailors whose performance, given on a junk moored in the Thames, Berlioz analysed with horrified fascination – was by no means always the worst to be heard, being often given by talented performers who had found they could earn in a couple of hours in the open air twice what a theatre musician was paid working much longer hours in a stifling pit. Some were capable English musicians who blacked themselves to attract more attention and, accompanied by violin, guitar and assorted percussion, sang lively, tuneful five-part songs which soon prompted a shower of coins. Some were genuinely exotic, like the two rather depressed Indians who sang a sad, sweet song in E minor to the accompaniment of small drums played with the fingers, or like the ferocious-looking Scotsman "clad in the curious costume of the Highlands" who, with two children in plaid and kilt at his side, played the air of the clan Macgregor on the bagpipes and, inflamed by the instrument's droning and squealing, seemed "about to conquer England single-handed".

Far and away the most extraordinary example of popular music-making that he encountered was the annual Charity Children's service in St Paul's, held that year on Sunday 8 June. Berlioz had read what Fétis wrote about it and was determined to be there. In the end he got in thanks only to a pass from the organist, John Goss, and by pretending to be a member of the cathedral choir and ascending to the organ loft, where he was given a surplice to put on and a bass part to sing. The reality surpassed all expectation. "What a scene, what a sight!", his English neighbours kept exclaiming as they looked down on the immense multitude below. The spectacle of 6,500 children massed under the dome on row upon steeply rising row of benches, the girls all in white with coloured ribbons, the boys in dark blue with metal discs glinting on their jackets, was stirring enough. But when that host of voices struck up the Old Hundredth – "All people that on earth do dwell" – and when, later, they added their "Long live the king" and "May the king live for ever" to the tuttis in Handel's *Zadok the Priest*, and the whole company with trumpets, drums and organ performed Ganthony's psalm, the overwhelming volume of sound perfectly proportioned to the huge reverberating space moved him to tears – and not him alone, for Duprez, on the way out, was still blubbering unrestrainedly and "old Cramer, in his rapture forgetting that he speaks French, cried out to me 'Cosa stupenda! stupenda! la gloria dell'Inghilterra!'"

Even as he hid his tears behind his copy of the music, "like Racine's Agamemnon behind his toga", Berlioz was analysing the experience – "the realization of part of my dreams, and proof that the power of musical forces on a vast scale is absolutely unknown, on the continent at least" – and wondering if something similar might not be done on a smaller scale but with a comparable ratio of mass to density at the Panthéon in Paris (only, the children of the poor in London looked so much more robust and well nourished, compared to "the peaky, sickly

air of the young working-class population of Paris, worn out by poor
diet, overwork and general privation"). At least he would add a chorus
of children's voices to the Te Deum.

Coming out of St Paul's half dazed, he followed the crowd down the
hill and found himself, he hardly knew how, aboard a Thames river-
boat, where it came on to rain in torrents. By the time he landed at
Chelsea the rain had stopped but he was soaked to the skin. In his wet
clothes he walked back through Chelsea and Kensington to Queen
Anne's Street, where he went to bed.

But the nights following days like that know no sleep. The resounding
clamour of "All people that on earth do dwell" revolved endlessly in my
head, and St Paul's whirled before me. Once again I was there, in
the cathedral. But now by a strange transformation it had become
Pandaemonium; it was the scene of Martin's famous picture. Instead of
the archbishop, there was Satan enthroned, and grouped round him,
instead of the thousands of worshippers and children, the fiery eyes of
unnumbered demons and the damned gleamed from the heart of the
visible darkness, and the whole iron amphitheatre on which the millions
sat vibrated terrifyingly and gave forth ghastly harmonies.

At last, tired of these unremitting hallucinations, I decided, though it
was scarcely dawn, to get up and make my way to the exhibition palace,
where I was due in a few hours' time for jury duty.

London still slept; none of the Sarahs and Marys and Kates who wash
the doorsteps every morning was to be seen, sponge in hand. An old
gin-fuddled Irishwoman smoked her pipe, crouching alone in a corner
of Manchester Square. In Hyde Park the cows lay on the thick turf
chewing unconcernedly. The little three-master, plaything of a seafaring
nation, rode idly at anchor on the Serpentine. By now the first shafts of
light were slanting down from the high glass panels of the palace open
to "all people that on earth do dwell".

The watchman on guard at the entrance to this Louvre, accustomed
to seeing me at all sorts of odd hours, let me through and I went in. The
deserted interior of the exhibition palace at seven in the morning was
another scene of peculiar grandeur: the all-embracing solitude, the silence
of the place, the soft light from the transparent roof, all the fountains
stilled, the organs dumb, the trees motionless, and the rich abundance
of products brought there from every corner of the earth by a hundred rival
nations. The ingenious works of peace, the instruments of destruction that

speak of war, all the things that create activity and noise, seemed now in man's absence to be holding mysterious converse in the unknown tongue that one hears with "the mind's ear". I was preparing to listen to their secret talk, thinking I was alone in the palace, when I saw that there were three of us – a Chinaman, a sparrow and I. The slit eyes of the oriental had opened before their time, so it appeared, or perhaps like mine had never closed. With a little feather whisk he was carefully dusting his beautiful porcelain vases, his hideous grotesques, his lacquer-ware and silks. Then I saw him take a watering-can, draw water from the basin of the glass fountain and, coming back, lovingly water a poor flower, Chinese no doubt, which was wilting in a vulgar European pot. After which he sat down a few yards from his shop, looked up at the gongs hanging there and moved as if to strike them, then, remembering he had neither brothers nor friends to wake, let drop his hand, in which the hammer was ready grasped, and sighed. "Dulces reminiscitur Argos", I murmured to myself. Putting on my most affable manner, I went up to him and, supposing him to understand English, wished him a "Good morning, sir" of unmistakably friendly curiosity. His only response was to get up, turn his back, open a cupboard, and take out some sandwiches, which he set about eating without giving me a glance and with an air of some scorn for what the barbarians call food. He was evidently thinking of the succulent shark's fins fried in castor oil that he feasts on in his own country, and of the soup made of swallows' nests and the famous woodlouse jam which they do so well in Canton. Faugh! The thought of his unmannerly gastronomy turned my stomach, and I walked on.

Passing a great 48 cannon, cast in copper at Seville, which seemed as it faced Sax's nearby shop to challenge him to make an instrument of equal calibre and volume, I startled a sparrow in the maw of the Spanish monster. "Poor survivor of the massacre of the innocents, fear not, I shan't denounce you. On the contrary – here!" And, taking from my pocket a biscuit which the master of ceremonies had pressed on me at St Paul's the day before, I crumbled it on to the ground. At the time of the construction of the exhibition palace a tribe of sparrows had made their home in one of the big trees that now adorn the transept. The creatures insisted on staying there even as the building work closed round them; they could hardly be expected to realize they were trapped, in so vast a cage of glass and metal. When they did they were astonished. The sparrows flew hither and thither, searching for a way out. For fear of the damage they could do to the more fragile exhibits, the decision was

taken to exterminate them, and it was carried out with a mixture of
blow-pipes, different kinds of trap and the treacherous *nux vomica*.*

My sparrow, whose hiding place I had discovered but whom I was
certainly not going to betray, was the sole survivor. He is the Joash of
his race, I thought. "I'll save him from the wrath of Athalia." As I uttered
this remarkable line, improvised that moment, a noise like rain flooded
the vast galleries. It was the fountains and water-jets, which their keepers
had just released. The crystal towers and artificial rocks were vibrating
under their streams of liquid pearls; the policemen – kindly, unarmed
gendarmes rightly respected by one and all – were arriving at their posts;
M. Ducroquet's young apprentice was advancing towards his master's
organ, pondering the new polka he was about to delight us with; the
ingenious silk manufacturers from Lyon were putting the finishing
touches to their splendid displays; the diamonds, prudently locked away
overnight, were sparkling in their showcases; and the great Irish clock
in D flat minor, in its place of honour in the Eastern Gallery, was
relentlessly beating one, two, three, four, five, six, seven, eight, determined
to show its independence from its sister in Albany Street, which has a
resonance of a major third. The silence had kept me awake; these sounds
made me feel sleepy. I sat down in front of the Erard grand piano, that
musical marvel of the exhibition, and, leaning my elbows on the richly
decorated lid, was falling asleep, when Thalberg tapped me on the
shoulder: "Hey! colleague – the jury's assembling. Look alive – we
have thirty-two musical boxes, twenty-four accordions and thirteen
bombardons to examine today."

Berlioz found his duties as member of the jury for Class Xa, Musical
Instruments, both wearisome and rewarding. The building itself, and
the concept of a "Great Exhibition of the Works of Industry of All
Nations", was the wonder of the modern world. As an idea it was soon
to be taken up by other countries, France not least, and the building
has long since vanished; but this was the first such exhibition and it
remains the most legendary. Joseph Paxton's gigantic cathedral of glass
and steel, erected on the south side of Hyde Park, was in scale as well
as material a revolutionary construction, five hundred yards long and
nearly a hundred and fifty across. (Think of the biggest of Paxton's

* The advice given by the Duke of Wellington to Queen Victoria – "Try sparrowhawks,
Ma'am" – had not been followed.

greenhouses at Kew and multiply a hundred times.) And the variety, the sheer quantity of the products arrayed in the endless galleries staggered the imagination. On the other hand, by no means all of them, in music at least, were a tribute to the skill of their makers. There were days when he felt that if he were to listen to one more out-of-tune brass or wind instrument his head would split; and he regularly cursed Ducroquet's young assistant and his polkas. But the poor quality of so many of the other exhibits had at least the merit that the best of France shone all the more brightly. There could be no question – Erard, Sax, Vuillaume, Ducroquet outclassed nearly all their competitors. Berlioz's task as French delegate was to look after his compatriots' interests so far as was compatible with maintaining, as he said, the impartiality of "a Minos or a Radamanthes". No doubt he argued their claims forcefully in the discussions with his fellow-jurors, among them Sterndale Bennett, Cipriani Potter, Dr Henry Wylde, the Chevalier Neukomm from Germany, Thalberg, Dr Black of Kentucky, Sir George Smart and the chairman, Sir Henry Bishop, whom he had got to know in 1847–8, when Bishop was on the committee of Jullien's Grand English Opera. In the end, of the eight exhibition medals awarded three went to English organ builders and one to Boehm of Munich for flute and woodwinds generally, but the other four were won by France: Sax for clarinet and brass instruments, Ducroquet for organ, Vuillaume for violin, viola, cello and double-bass, and Erard for piano.

For the last fortnight of July Berlioz was living in London at his own expense. The Minister of Trade in Paris, impatient at the length and cost of the proceedings, stopped paying the jurors after the 15th and ordered them all home, but he and a few others stayed on; he was the last French delegate to leave. Despite the manifest quality of the French entries he thought it best to see the thing through; and the result, he felt, vindicated his decision. Duty, however, would have to be its own reward. He lost 420 francs by it; and though he publicized the fact in the *Débats* that November, the jurors who stayed remained unpaid. In due course he discovered that he had forfeited a further 335 francs by the docking of his librarian's salary for the three months May–July: that he was absent on government business was considered no extenuation.

Nor, in the end, did the project for a Crystal Palace festival materialize. The plan had been, by bringing together choral societies from Liverpool, Manchester and London, to crown the Great Exhibition on a scale and with an éclat appropriate to the occasion. It would also, naturally, provide an opportunity of performing his Te Deum. Somewhere along the way the idea foundered. All he did obtain was Prince Albert's permission to dedicate the score to him.

Likewise, the various schemes he was involved in for performing the Te Deum in Paris that autumn got only so far before they were dropped. All attempts to resuscitate the Société Philharmonique proved equally unavailing. Nothing came, either, of the job of director of music education in Paris schools, which he had been offered by the Préfet de la Seine at a salary of 4,000 francs. "Nothing is possible in this damned country of ours," he told Adèle; any thought of his putting on concerts was out of the question: he could not even pay the interest due on loans from his brothers-in-law. "You can imagine what this does to my morale, the faculties within me that it paralyses, the inactivity as an artist to which I am condemned." It must have been the ultimate humiliation when, about this time, he felt forced to ignore the urgent promptings of a new composition. He dreamed one night that he was composing a symphony; in his dream he heard the first movement, an allegro in A minor and 2/4 time. Next night the same thing happened; he heard the music again, and saw the score. On waking in the middle of the night he could recall the movement almost in its entirety. But what was the use? To have composed such a work would have involved an expense he could not possibly afford. So he lay there, steeling himself against the temptation to get up and set it on paper. When next he woke, it had gone.

Yet had he but known it, his life was about to change. At its lowest point his career was entering on its period of greatest fulfilment.

While in London he had discussed with Beale the possibility of founding an orchestra with the aim of doing what the Philharmonic failed to do: perform works by modern composers other than Mendelssohn, popularize Berlioz's music, and at the same time outclass the Philharmonic in standard of performance, all at lower-than-normal prices. Such a plan had long been talked of. Now it was coming to fruition. Discussions continued after his return to Paris; and early in the new year an agreement was concluded and a contract signed for six concerts at a refurbished Exeter Hall in the spring. That was not all. Meanwhile, from beyond the Rhine there was light. A day or two after Berlioz got back from London a note from Belloni informed him that Liszt was planning to stage *Benvenuto Cellini* in Weimar.

18

Prospero's Wand

The seven years that followed were the apogee of Berlioz's musical life. His career as composer reached its culmination with *The Trojans*, completed in the spring of 1858; as conductor and proselytizer with the performances of Beethoven's Ninth Symphony in London in 1852 and the concerts of his own music that he gave in Leipzig, Hanover and Dresden in 1853–4. *Benvenuto Cellini* was staged in Weimar, where Liszt also put on several "Berlioz weeks". Even in France there were victories, and a degree of official recognition, to set against the perennial defeats. The Te Deum was heard at last, with the help of friends who agreed to cover part of the costs. *The Childhood of Christ*, composed with Germany in mind, triumphed in Paris, conferring an unwonted respectability which led to his being elected to the Institute (at the fifth attempt). As writer too he had his greatest success with *Evenings in the Orchestra*: no book of his published during his lifetime did so well. To this period also belongs one of his most beautiful and quintessential scores, the orchestral version of *Les nuits d'été*.

Composition was the last thing he had thought of. If we except a few additions to *Benvenuto Cellini*, he wrote nothing between *The Flight into Egypt* of autumn 1850 and its sequel *The Arrival at Sais* which dates from more than three years later. It was not that the impulse had died – his brain teemed with ideas. What he had lost was the will to set them down on paper. As we have seen, a symphony dreamed two nights in succession was suppressed without mercy. Once written, such a work would insist on being performed, and therefore copied, rehearsed, put on, at a cost and at a risk which given his financial responsibilities for Harriet and Louis he dared not contemplate. A bitter decision; but was it not wiser in every way to hold on to what he had, to consolidate? He tried to explain it to his Detmold friend Baron von Donop, who had talked reproachfully of works which he "ought" to undertake. The obstacles were simply too great. He could not face beginning again the old struggle. "Little by little there has been a kind of crystallization of mediocrities which blocks the avenues and walls up all the doors. They whisper in the ear of the powers that be, and render all means of producing my works out of the question. It's like those oceanic insects, the corals and madrepores, which construct barriers of rock round the beautiful Polynesian islands, on which ships are dashed to pieces." Better to "devote what energies I have to making my existing scores as well known as possible than to abandon them to the changes and chances of musical life and give them sisters whose first steps I should not be able to watch over."

In the same spirit, the list of his complete works which he published early in 1852 – the so-called Richault catalogue – has, in its explanatory introduction, a valedictory air. He has (it seems to be saying) produced everything he intends to; he has established a tradition for correct performance of his works; it remains only to publish those few that have yet to appear.

Within weeks of writing to Donop, in November 1853, Berlioz had begun composing. But the preceding two years saw the fulfilment of that resolve: to devote his energies to his existing scores, in London, and still more in Germany, where he had partisans eager to further his cause and in a position to do so – the King of Hanover, Baron von Lüttichau, Griepenkerl, Donop and the Prince of Lippe-Detmold. Above all, Liszt.

On 14 January 1852 Liszt wrote to Belloni in Paris. Though "Bell" was no longer his full-time secretary (now that Liszt had renounced the career of travelling virtuoso and settled in Weimar), he still worked for him. Liszt mentioned various artistic and business errands for Belloni to perform on his behalf. A large part of the letter, however, concerned Berlioz.

> Tomorrow I begin [orchestral] rehearsals for *Cellini*. The scenery and costumes are in train, and I trust that nothing will occur to prevent the work from being given on *16 February*. After the success of *Cellini* – of which I have no doubt – I shall take steps to have the dramatic symphony *Romeo and Juliet*, the Fantastic, etc., performed here in a fitting manner; and I hope it will not be more than a year before I succeed in giving, either in Leipzig or elsewhere in the neighbourhood (for here, unfortunately, we lack a space large enough for so grand an affair, not to speak of all the

difficulties in the way of assembling a force of three or four hundred singers and instrumentalists), Berlioz's Requiem *in its entirety*. When you see him you may tell him that, friendship quite apart, I consider myself honour bound to create for his works, one by one, the position they deserve in Germany. It is, for me, a matter of art and of personal conviction; in consequence it has to be dealt with seriously, worthily, without the least trifling. As you know, my dear Belloni, I lack neither persistence nor, perhaps, savoir-faire, and if the required circumstances and opportunities are not always at my disposal I nevertheless try to arrange things so that time is on my side. There are a very small number of men and works that cannot be understood and admired by halves. They have to be treated differently from the others. Berlioz is of that number; and I like to believe that he will not misjudge the motives which up till now have put me off actively involving myself in the performance of his works in Germany. For one thing, I did not have the material means to hand (he will not have forgotten the worse than mediocre state in which he found the Weimar orchestra under Chelard's direction!) and, for another, I have needed the last two years in order to achieve the *moral credit* required to impose a degree of silence on the mob of fogeys, fools and knaves.

Liszt's generosity to his fellow-composers is one of the shining lights of nineteenth-century music history. Attempts have been made to minimize it, but the facts confound all such envious small-mindedness. It was typical of the man that when the Schumanns turned against him his response was to promote Robert's music in Weimar – he conducted *Genoveva*, the complete *Manfred* music and Part Three of *Scenes from Faust*. And he echoed Schumann's dedicating the Fantasy to him fifteen years before, in the period of their friendship, by making Schumann the dedicatee of the B minor Sonata. By now the German Romantic movement had already suffered the split between the rival camps of Leipzig and Weimar which was to widen into the all-out war of the Brahmins and the Wagnerites. But Liszt's instinct and ideal was always to include, not exclude, to reconcile, to champion without regard to ideology or friendship: the Music of the Future would come not in one form but in many.

It takes nothing from his generosity that in Berlioz's case it was activated partly by an intense consciousness of what he owed him. The debt went back to his first encounter with the older man's music, at the première of the Fantastic Symphony.* Liszt's deep involvement, from the mid-1840s, with Wagner's music and ideas has tended to overlay the importance of that earlier revelation of a new expressive force in music, a new way of writing for the orchestra. It was one of the formative experiences in his life as an artist. On that December afternoon in 1830 Berlioz became for Liszt not only a kindred spirit but a composer to investigate and learn from, a leading force in the campaign for what Liszt called "the renewal of music through its closer union with poetry". He was an exemplar whose influence Liszt's own music would reflect in many ways, great and small: in the development of cyclic form, and in a host of orchestral touches which testify to his knowledge of his friend's scores, like the bass-drum roll at the opening of *Ce qu'on entend sur la montagne* or the timpani chords and the combination of harp and cor anglais in the *Dante* symphony. It was only natural that such a composer should play a prominent part in Liszt's plan to make Weimar the centre of progressive music, and that, having put on *Tannhäuser* in 1849 and *Lohengrin* in 1850, he should turn to *Benvenuto Cellini*: Berlioz was second only to Wagner as an artist to be cherished and encouraged by every means possible.

Therein lay the seed of future discord. For the moment, all was well. Wagner might scold Liszt for squandering time and energy and money on so obviously unredeemable an opera; but the composer was only too happy. He had never thought to see his "Lazarus" rise again.

Most of August 1851, following his return from London, was spent repairing the damage inflicted by the Opéra and, with Rocquemont's help, putting the manuscript in order. Several passages cut in 1838 were restored, including the innkeeper scene and the pantomime at Cassandro's travelling theatre in the Piazza Colonna – neither of which had been thought consonant with the dignity of the Académie Royale de Musique – and a section of the prayer in Act 2. On the 29th Belloni dispatched a large parcel to Weimar and Berlioz wrote to Liszt announcing that it was on its way. His letter is compounded of gratitude, excitement, appeals for caution, and practical advice. He could guess the limitations of the Weimar company, even after three years of Liszt's reforms. He also knew his friend's determination.

* See Vol. 1, pp. 426–7.

I've not wasted time and yet it's only today that I've completed the reparations to *Benvenuto*. I can assure you that the copyist's task won't be complicated now. So I suggest you start by having a vocal score made, for the benefit of the translator, who wouldn't be able to write on my manuscript without wrecking it; in any case there's practically no room left anywhere for the German words. There will be time to make the orchestral parts and copy the full score while the solos and the choruses are being learnt. But I beg you to make sure the copyists don't dissect my score, which I have taken so much trouble to put back into shape. In fact it's bound in four volumes, so can occupy four people at once.

You'll receive at the same time the seven or eight numbers which were published with piano accompaniment, and the [printed] libretto, corrected to conform with the present state of the score.

I fear you are short of some wind instruments at Weimar, so you'll have to be so good as to adapt certain passages. For instance, I've often employed four bassoons. When they have exposed chords to play, replace the first and second with two clarinets if they've not got anything important to do at the time. I have a bass clarinet in the Septet and in the overture. If one can't be found, best to have its part played most of the time by an ordinary clarinet in B flat. Do you have two harps? Two piston cornets? They can be replaced by two valve trumpets, in low A and low B flat. As for the three timpani, one can be omitted; it will be easy to find a second timpanist, of a sort, for the places where there are simultaneous rolls on two drums.

I say nothing to you of the singers, I don't know the Weimar personnel, nor how the chorus is constituted now. Only, it's more than probable that *acts of will* on your part will be required to obtain a true performance of many of the numbers whose complex rhythms must be brought off with verve, not approached hesitantly, gropingly. It's virtually a matter of educating them.

As for the overture or overtures (including the *Roman Carnival*), they're available in score and parts from Brandus.

Now, however childish my joy may seem, I will not hide it from you. Yes, I am overjoyed to have this work presented before an unprejudiced public, and presented by you. I have just examined it in earnest after thirteen years of oblivion and I swear that never again shall I find this Cellinian verve and impetus, nor such a variety of ideas. But that only makes it more difficult to perform; theatre people, singers especially, are so devoid of *humour*! Still, I count on you and your fire to Pygmalionize all those statues.

Farewell, write to me on receipt of the parcel, and let me have a few details of your operatic family.

Your grateful and devoted friend

Liszt needed all his fire, first to overcome opposition in the company to his putting on the work – it was said that it would ruin their voices – and then to galvanize his performers. The young tenor Karl Beck, who had been an inadequate Lohengrin eighteen months before, proved equally resistant to the new role that was thrust upon him. He could not refuse it; but he insisted that he was not going to sing the big aria in the second act, "Sur les monts les plus sauvages", and the piece was omitted from the German libretto published at the time. But Liszt had patience as well as fire (*Beck et ongles* – "beak and nails" – as Berlioz remarked). For *Lohengrin* he had held dozens of orchestral rehearsals, full and sectional, and he worked with similar care and pertinacity on *Benvenuto Cellini*. As with Wagner's opera, additional instruments were brought in from other German cities to augment the Weimar band (including third and fourth bassoons – a bass clarinet had already been acquired for *Lohengrin*), and except for the sacrifice of "Sur les monts" it was done with a completeness that astonished the composer when Liszt sent him his report of the three performances given in late March 1852. "How did you manage to have all the instrumental paraphernalia that is in my score? You must have the power of a Moses – you strike the walls of the theatre with your baton and draw forth torrents of instrumentalists, as his staff made water flow from the rock."

Berlioz had not been there to witness his opera's resurrection. He had planned to arrive in Weimar in time for the première on 16 February, stay to hear at least one further performance and, at Liszt's suggestion, give a concert the proceeds of which would pay for the journey, before returning to Paris so as to be in London at the beginning of March. To his acute disappointment *Benvenuto* was delayed by the illness of two of the singers: diplomatic, perhaps, in Beck's case, real in that of the Ascanio, Rosa von Milde. By the time the postponed first night could take place, on 20 March, he was deep in preparations for the launching of the New Philharmonic Society and must be content with enjoying its success at second hand. Despite fears of a fresh cabal, the work had succeeded. Berlioz urged his friend to tell him "the truth and only the truth" whatever it might be ("you are the only one I trust to give it to me"). But Liszt had brought it off; and his bulletin to the French and English press could truthfully report the fact:

> Honour to the master metalworkers! Make way for the beautiful things! *Benvenuto Cellini*, performed yesterday, is on its feet again and will stand at its full stature. It is "sans puff" that the news of its success can be given to London and Paris. I thank Berlioz most sincerely for the noble pleasure accorded me by the close study of his *Cellini*, which is one of the most powerful works that I know. It is at once gorgeous metalwork and vital and original sculpture. The performance, notwithstanding a few deficiencies of detail and the too small chorus at my disposal, would not have displeased the composer. The orchestra as a whole behaved perfectly and the majority of its members openly showed their respect and admiration for this magnificent score, the performing of which a hidebound opposition had been resolved to prevent, and which will now be part of our repertoire.

A letter from Princess Carolyne confirmed Liszt's bulletin – at the same time giving details of the obstacles he had to overcome – and advised Berlioz to write thanking the Grand Duchess Marie Pavlovna for her support, which he duly did. The review in the *Neue Zeitschrift* (reproduced in the London *Musical World*) was no less emphatic. "First nights are generally like final rehearsals. But already at the première of *Benvenuto Cellini* we missed none of that precision, accuracy and nuance which is so essential in Berlioz's music. The occasionally complicated choruses went remarkably well. Especially, however, must we praise our orchestra, which has achieved a collective virtuosity under Liszt's guidance." The work was given for the second time on 24 March and again three nights later. Soon after, returning to his London lodgings from a six-hour rehearsal "dripping like a water-rat", Berlioz found a letter from Liszt on the hall table. It contained, along with news of the performances, an invitation to come to Weimar for a revival of the opera towards the end of the year.

Though it had prevented him from seeing *Benvenuto* rise from the dead, in other respects the visit to London could not have been better timed. He was seriously short of the money needed to keep Harriet in her Montmartre apartment and to pay for Louis' latest voyage, his third, with a merchant ship of a new company. The boy – he was still only seventeen – set sail for Havana, via Plymouth, at the beginning of

December 1852. Till then he had to be supported in Paris and, while he waited to embark, in Le Havre.

For a moment Berlioz had thought of accepting a conducting engagement in St Petersburg, but the fee offered was too low, given the expense of the journey and the loss of his Conservatoire salary while he was away. He would lose it while he was in London – after many démarches, leave of absence without pay was the best he could obtain – but the terms of the engagement were so good that he could afford to. The chance too of making music under decent conditions and for a public which had at least "a genuine *desire* to like music" was not to be missed. Beale was offering a choice chorus, an élite orchestra, and whatever rehearsal was necessary, and unlike Jullien he seemed in a position to deliver. In Paris there was nothing like that. Out of gratitude and admiration Berlioz helped his friend Ernst to organize, and himself directed, two concerts which the great violinist put on at the Salle Herz early in 1852, and at the first of which he had the pleasure of conducting Mendelssohn's *Hebrides* overture. But that was all. No other musical reasons could be adduced for staying, and plenty for not doing so.

The coup d'état of the night of 1–2 December 1851, which overthrew the Second Republic by force and involved the arrest of many officers and over two hundred deputies, and a fine crop of executions and exiles (among the latter Victor Hugo), left him, as it did many once liberal artists, almost indifferent. Like Delacroix, Berlioz had feared the effect of the egalitarian republic on the arts, and thought a stable regime would benefit them. He even imagined that the New Year's Day service of thanksgiving in Notre-Dame for the plebiscite confirming Louis-Napoleon as president for the next ten years could prove the occasion his Te Deum had been waiting for. The hope, however, was short-lived. The five hundred choristers and instrumentalists assembled under Girard's direction performed a hotch-potch of music by Le Sueur and Adolphe Adam, and he had to console himself with the news that at the dress rehearsal Adam, while walking among the workmen and scaffolding with his friend Auber, had been knocked senseless by a falling canopy. Though, "thanks to Louis-Napoleon and the army", they all slept peacefully in their beds, he could not deny that "we artists live in a state of death – if you will pardon the antithesis".

Politics, under the new government, crossed over into the realm of art, however much one might pretend it didn't. As protégé and employee of an opposition, Orleanist newspaper Berlioz was suspect to the authorities and therefore inherently unlikely to have his Te Deum chosen for an official ceremony. Worse, political comment being largely out of bounds, the editor was looking to his columnists for more frequent, up-to-the-minute reports on the arts. The *Débats'* music critic found himself writing every week; and because Bertin wanted to be first with the news, Berlioz would set straight to work on returning from the opera and sit up with a jug of coffee till dawn.

There was a further twist. His feuilleton of 3 February on the revival of *William Tell* at the Opéra, though confined to musical and dramatic matters, was considered too critical by the censor and banned. But Armand Bertin, inadvertently, allowed it to be printed and it appeared on the front and second pages "with all its imperfections on its head". Berlioz had decided to be frank just when frankness was actively discouraged. The article was a reasoned root-and-branch catalogue of missed opportunities, congenitally lax standards and directorial complacency. It exposed the eternal approximation of the Opéra, for all its pretensions to European pre-eminence – something to be expected no doubt in run-of-the-mill repertoire, where disorder had become a tradition, but unacceptable in a masterpiece like *William Tell*, the performers clearly taking as their motto Rossini's famous mot, *E troppo buono per questi* ("It's too good for them"). It instanced the shoddy ensemble, the poor intonation, the excessive din of the drums, due chiefly to their being placed against a reflecting wall (a matter long overdue for attention by musicians and architects), the disagreeably intrusive rap of the conductor's bow on the roof of the prompt box – a method of alerting those on stage to an important entry or nuance, in use at the Opéra but at no other major house in the world. Worst of all was the drastic miscasting of most of the leading roles: Mme Laborde (Mathilde) a light coloratura soprano whose lack of firmness and purity of tone was betrayed every time she had to sing a legato phrase, Mlle Dussy barely audible as Jemmy, Morelli a Tell chiefly notable for his artistic indiscipline and his execrable French, and poor Gueymard, who should never have taken on the part of Arnold at this early stage of his career and whose attempts to force out the high notes, at severe risk to his health and vocal safety, ended more often than not in disaster, to the distress of all save the groundlings, who came in a strictly sporting spirit for the high chest Cs (*uts de poitrine*), which they found all over the score, including places where there weren't any ("the actual *ut* in the final aria is for them only an *ut de poitrine* slightly higher than the others"). In short, at the Opéra everything was approximate, and everybody did as they pleased. "They pronounce at will, sing at will, move and dance at will. It's only the *ut de poitrine* that doesn't happen at will." However, as the house was full every evening, from the administration's point of view what need was there to do better? *E troppo buono per questi.* "In conclusion I shall add only two words: in God's name get a French coach for Morelli, and let Gueymard live."

All this was no doubt no more than the plain truth. But, apart from the fact that the plain truth was not what was required from journalists by Louis-Napoleon's nascent dictatorship, the Opéra was once again, as in the time of Louis-Philippe, an extension of governmental power. The Prince-President, though congenitally bored by the kind of music heard at the Opéra, had taken it and the egregious Nestor Roqueplan under his protection. He was there for the gala performance of *Le Prophète* given on 6 January 1852 in celebration of the plebiscite, when it was remarked that he frequently gave the signal for applause. The *William Tell* feuilleton, appearing a few weeks later, caused a minor uproar. Armand Bertin was summoned to the censorship office and carpeted. Berlioz's outspoken criticism prompted congratulatory letters and visits from fellow-musicians but was not viewed favourably in the Elysée Palace, and he judged it prudent to write to the President's private secretary, whom he had met at a convivial dinner a few months before, to protest his loyalty, though without retracting the criticism. His two succeeding reviews were, however, less outspoken; and he was not sorry when the time came to leave for London, with the prospect of four feuilleton-free months of serious music-making.

Berlioz travelled to London on 3 March 1852 with high hopes. This time most of them, in the short term, were fulfilled. In the barrister-musician Frederick Beale he was dealing with an able and punctilious administrator. The New Philharmonic Society was solidly founded, with rich backers including the engineer Sir Charles Fox (knighted for his part in the Great Exhibition) and the railway magnates Thomas Brassy and Sir Morton Peto. Henry Jarrett, horn player and noted orchestral fixer, in charge of assembling the band, did his work efficiently. The prospectus named most of the best instrumentalists in London, English and foreign. The New Philharmonic, it stated, would seek to "extend a knowledge of the productions of the greatest masters by a more perfect performance of their works than has hitherto been attained" and at the same time "give to modern and native composers a favourable opportunity for establishing the worth of their claims upon the attention and esteem of a discerning public". It added that "exclusiveness, the baneful hindrance to all progress of art, will not be tolerated in this society". All this would be made more widely available than before: "As the directors are desirous that these performances should be open to all lovers of art, the prices of admission will be fixed at the lowest rate compatible with a just estimate of receipt and expenditure."

Here was an undisguised challenge to the monopoly of the old Philharmonic, whose ultra-cautious choice of works and soloists and rough and ready performances were notorious but had remained largely impervious to change. It was no accident that two of the three symphonies identified by the *Musical World* as the "stock favourites" of the old society, Mozart's Jupiter and Beethoven's Fifth (the third being the Pastoral), figured on the prospectus, nor that Mendelssohn, the one modern master the old society recognized, was prominent in the programmes of the new. So too was a lot of other contemporary music, which the Philharmonic neglected seemingly on principle. The declared aim of presenting everything well rehearsed was, again, a deliberate rebuke to the rich but stingy Philharmonic, where the policy of one rehearsal a concert was a permanent stumbling-block to higher standards of orchestral playing in London. As the *Musical World* observed sarcastically, "At some period, not far off, Mr Costa will possibly be able to make the orchestra play *piano*, or even *pianissimo*, when the directions of the score suggest the aid of those gradations of sound to which our English orchestras seem perversely hostile."

Rehearsal was the one thing about which Berlioz felt apprehensive. Beale paid him his first month's salary of £50 (1,250 francs) promptly on his arriving in London, with Marie, on 4 March, and presented him with a first-rate orchestra, including nearly seventy strings led by the eminent violinist Sivori, with the great Bottesini at the head of twelve double-basses, and a chorus of upwards of two hundred voices, directed by the young composer Frank Mori, which promised equally well. But would the orchestra rehearse? "The whole success or failure of the enterprise depends on how many I can obtain"; the society's ambitious repertoire presupposed the most thorough preparation. He knew the English reluctance. It was a hallowed tradition, partly economic in origin, and one that would survive Berlioz's brief reforms – ten years later Joachim was complaining that there was never time to achieve anything really good: "our Hanoverian orchestra could not sight-read better, but it remains at that" – and that would last well into the next century.

On the whole Beale was as good as his word, and the orchestra lived up to its exciting promise. For Beethoven's Ninth Symphony, previously always thrown on with a single rehearsal, there were half a dozen. The chorus proved eager and responsive, with splendid sopranos and altos ("in Paris we have no conception of the women's voices in England, still less of the intelligence of these choristers, who in three sessions have the most complicated works by heart"). Before the opening concert the first four movements of *Romeo and Juliet* – music ultra-resistant to being thrown on – had four full orchestral rehearsals, and were so successful that they were repeated at the third concert. Not only the Ninth but Mendelssohn's Italian Symphony and Violin Concerto were given performances which it was generally agreed surpassed any heard before in London. The performance of Beethoven's Fifth at the second concert on 17 April, said the *Times*, "but for one unfortunate slip of the second violins, might with justice have been pronounced unprecedented in this country".

As always, Berlioz held sectional rehearsals, not only for strings and wind but also – a rarity then as now – for percussion. (The young Wilhelm Ganz, in addition to being one of the sixteen-strong second violins, was deputed with Eduard Silas, the Dutch composer and pianist, to play antique cymbals in Queen Mab. When they got to Addison the publisher's premises at 47 King Street, Golden Square (the modern Kingly Street), they found that the tambourine, triangle, timpani and bass drum players had been invited as well.) Inevitably, the habits of generations were not to be lightly overturned, and corners were cut. By no means everyone always turned up. A letter from Berlioz to Jarrett written on "Monday evening the 20th [April]" begins: "I have your attendance list. But Mr Winterbottom signed, and he wasn't there";* and among the players to be convoked "for next Thursday" (for the finale of Act 2 of *La Vestale*) are "the horn and trumpet who didn't come today". Another letter to Jarrett insists on eight harps (for the Weber–Berlioz *Invitation*) "at Blagrove Rooms [in Mortimer Street] next Monday", and adds that "we absolutely must have two rehearsals – it's agreed with Beale".

---

* There was both a bass player and a trombonist of that name.

A few works were singled out by critics as not having been adequately prepared: the *Francs-juges* overture, at the fifth concert, and even more, at the second, the new cantata *The Isle of Calypso* by Henry Loder, about which Berlioz felt obliged to publish a letter of apology (in which, however, he blamed the singers for not having attended the preliminary rehearsals, provoking a spirited retort from Sims Reeves, who blamed Berlioz for not having let him and his wife know where the rehearsals were being held). But the press was almost unanimous in proclaiming it the finest series of concerts and the best orchestra ever heard in London, at least when its chief conductor and not his assistant Dr Henry Wylde was at the helm.

The opening concert in Exeter Hall on Wednesday 24 March was immediately seen by every critic except Hogarth of the *Daily News* (he was secretary of the old Philharmonic Society) to have set totally new standards. One or two notices criticized Berlioz for not making the repeats in the Jupiter and for giving Thoas' solo in the *Iphigénie en Tauride* excerpts to a dozen choral basses. The extraordinary animation of both performances, however, was not denied (the Gluck was encored). For the first time real pianissimos were heard. Weber's *Oberon* overture was played "with a fire, impetuosity and *finesse* which we have never heard surpassed by any body of instrumentalists". And the panache and delicacy of the *Romeo* movements roused the audience of fifteen hundred to amazement and prolonged cheering. Berlioz, declared the *Times*, was "a musical colourist whose most vivid scenes will recall to the ardent observer some of the later pictures that came from the golden brush of Turner" – a comparison which was intended as high praise and not, as Chorley had meant it ten years before, as a damning indictment. The overture to *William Tell*, Beethoven's Triple Concerto with Silas and the section leaders Sivori and Piatti, plus a fantasy for double-bass by Bottesini, made up the rest of a long but exhilarating and historic evening.

The New Philharmonic Society kept Berlioz busy during most of the fifteen weeks he spent in London. This time we hear little of his social life: a call at Chorley's house in Eaton Place early in his stay; an evening or two at the famous salon of Harriet Grote, wife of the historian, in Savile Row; and a reference to late-night suppers washed down with iced champagne and rum. He must have passed convivial hours with old friends and fellow-musicians and journalists like Ella, Howard Glover, Barnett, Gruneisen, Davison, Edward Holmes, the Duchêne de

Vères and others. How often Marie accompanied him we cannot say.
I have the impression that she had settled for a less interfering role than
she had played in Prague six years before, and led a more independent
life. But that could be wishful thinking. The only record of her on this
trip, a note to Mme Charton-Demeur written shortly before she and
Berlioz left London, does not suggest that she had been relegated entirely
to the background:

> Dear Lady!
> Come on *Thursday*, so that we can say hello and goodbye. I have an
> errand for your husband's stout legs, to take this note for my mother to
> the house, at the earliest possible moment, there's something I need her
> to do for us.
> [in English] Good by my dear
>
>   Marie

On 1 June Berlioz went back for another taste of the Charity Chil-
dren's service at St Paul's, where he was spotted in a surplice among
the combined choirs of St Paul's, the Abbey, St George's Windsor, the
Temple and the Chapel Royal, singing alongside Joachim and George
Osborne, whom he brought with him.* On 29 April, the day after his
third concert, he took part in a morning concert at Hanover Square
Rooms given by the French pianist Emile Prudent, when he conducted
Beethoven's *Prometheus* and Auber's *Zanetta* overtures, Mendelssohn's
Wedding March and his own *Absence* (sung by the German tenor
Alexander Reichardt). The composer John Francis Barnett, many years
later, recalled seeing him walking down Regent Street the morning after
one of the *Romeo and Juliet* performances, and being struck by "how
deep and poetical was the expression of his features. There was also a
look of pleasure on his face such as one might expect after his artistic
triumphs the previous night."

As before, his main activities were in an area of a few square miles,
bounded on the north by Marylebone Road and the south by the Strand,
on the west by Cavendish Square and St James's Street and the east by
Dean Street, Soho, where his first encounter with his orchestra took
place at Caldwell's Rooms (No. 20) a few days after his arrival in

---

* George Eliot was at the service. "Berlioz says it is the finest thing he has heard in
England, and this persuaded us to go. I was not disappointed – it is worth doing once,
especially as we got out before the sermon."

London. From his and Marie's lodgings at 10 Old Cavendish Street (above the premises of Nurse the carver and gilder) Blagrove Rooms in Mortimer Street was only a few minutes' walk away, and Beale's office at 200 Regent Street not much more. From there to Exeter Hall in the Strand was another half an hour on foot. Ella's Musical Union matinées at Willis's Rooms in King Street, St James's, were certainly another haunt, at least on afternoons when Marie Pleyel, née Camille Moke, was not playing (the pianist, now one of the great European names, was making her first visit to London in several years and gave two recitals for the Union). The New Philharmonic Society was borrowing a leaf from Ella's book by circulating descriptive programme notes at its concerts. Ella, one of Berlioz's leading champions in London, had pleased him by reproducing Richault's list of his complete works in the Union's *Monthly Record*; and it was in response to a question about the most recent item in the catalogue, *The Flight into Egypt*, that Berlioz sent his friend the celebrated open letter which recounted the origin of the work in the Shepherds' Farewell, sketched one evening at the corner of a card table while friends were playing écarté and passed off as a piece of music from the seventeenth century discovered in an old cupboard during the recent restoration of the Sainte-Chapelle.

The letter to Ella, published in French in the Union's bulletin and in the *Musical World*, was not Berlioz's only exercise in satire. He found time to pursue a project which he had toyed with a few years before but dropped for want of a Paris publisher interested in taking it: a new selection of his feuilletons. The idea had grown from that of a miscellaneous bundle of pieces to a collection with a shape and, beneath its veneer of fantasy and humour, a serious theme or rather three main themes, forged in the heat of the action and only too relevant to his situation: in Barzun's words, "How is art to be financially supported in the modern world? How do music and its devotees actually live and behave in a commercial society? How should they? And what light do the lives of the great composers throw on these interrelated problems?" Berlioz brought with him from Paris a portfolio of mainly recent newspaper cuttings already chosen or thought likely to figure in the book. On 10 May he asked Rocquemont to chase up a couple of *Débats* pieces which he had decided to add – they had been requested but the paper had failed to send them. A few days earlier, he gave d'Ortigue an account of the project:

Will you do me another service? Go and see Amyot the publisher in the Rue de la Paix, or Charpentier, Rue de Lille, and see if one of them would like to publish a large octavo volume, 450 or 500 pages, by me, very droll and caustic and with a lot of variety, entitled *Tales of the Orchestra*. They comprise short stories, anecdotes, novellas, cracks of the whip, critiques and arguments (in which music is treated only incidentally and not theoretically), biographical sketches, conversations, carried on or read or recounted by the musicians of an unnamed orchestra *during the performance of bad operas*. They attend seriously to their part only when a masterpiece is being played. The work is accordingly divided into "evenings". Most of them are literary and begin with the words: "A very dull French or Italian or German opera is being given. While the side-drum and the bass drum get on with it, the rest of the orchestra listens to such and such a reader or speaker," etc. When an evening begins with the words: "*Don Juan* is being performed" or *Iphigénie en Tauride*, or the *Barber*, or *La Vestale* or *Fidelio*, the orchestra bends with zeal to its task and no one reads or speaks; the evening consists just of a few words on the performance of the masterpiece. As you will imagine, such evenings are rare. The others give rise to endless scathing ironies and jests, in addition to stories whose interest is purely in the romance of the tale. I'm just finishing it.

A couple of weeks later he spoke of having been "totally absorbed, these last few days, completing my book".*

Though *La Vestale* is among the masterpieces performed with devotion in the book, that was not how it was received by the London press when he conducted the second act at the concert of 28 April. There was a good cast of singers, including Clara Novello, Reichardt and Staudigl, and Spontini's widow arrived from Paris that morning with the baton with which the composer had been wont to conduct the works of Gluck, Mozart and himself; but, as Berlioz told d'Ortigue, almost all the critics found against the work. "I had the weakness to feel quite heartbroken at this *lapsus judicii* – as if I didn't know that nothing is beautiful or ugly or true or false for everyone, and as if the understanding of certain works of genius were not inevitably denied to entire peoples ... I am almost ashamed to have had such a success [with the *Romeo and Juliet* pieces at the same concert]."

---

* Coinciding with a break in rehearsals between the fourth and fifth concerts.

The concert was also notable for bringing Berlioz and Marie Pleyel together, in public, for the first time since they were engaged in a more personal sense. (She had been at the Bonn Beethoven festival, but there is no record of any contact between them.) The diva pianist played Weber's Concertstück with the orchestra in the second half, for which – according to the *Illustrated London News* – she was given a tumultuous ovation only equalled by the ovation Berlioz received in the first half for *Romeo and Juliet*. Next morning Mme Pleyel complained about him to the committee of the New Philharmonic Society. Chorley, with whom she was on friendly terms, backed her up a few days later in the *Athenaeum*, accusing him of conducting the Concertstück badly. Berlioz's comment, in a letter to Gounod, was that there were "two thousand people who could attest to the exactitude, verve and finesse" of the performance. The *Musical World* reported that "M. Berlioz conducted the concerto with the greatest judgement and the orchestra accompanied it to perfection", while the *Morning Post* said nothing about the orchestral playing but thought the pianist, though brilliant and graceful, "deficient in power and deep passion" – precisely the criticism that Berlioz made some years before in the *Débats*.

The whole concert was rich in ironic resonances. *La Vestale*, which followed the Concertstück, was the work through which Adolphe D., hero of the short story "Suicide through Enthusiasm", found out the shallowness and brittleness of his lover Hortense, alias Camille/Marie. Berlioz had just been editing it for inclusion in his book. Even if the victim had not seen the story when it appeared in the *Gazette* nearly twenty years before, she must have been aware of the far more blatant and brutal portrait of herself – Camille barely disguised as "Ellimac" – in the novella *Euphonia*, and must too have read what he had to say about her in the *Débats* and more recently about her rival the seventeen-year-old Wilhelmine Clauss – "among women pianists, the first". Mlle Clauss was in London that season and played Mendelssohn's G minor concerto at the New Philharmonic's fourth concert. If Berlioz was driven by a persistent and still smarting desire for revenge, Marie Pleyel on her side could feel she had plenty to complain of – whether or not he conducted badly. But there is nothing about the incident in either of the letters she wrote to her close friend Liszt soon afterwards, nor in the reminiscences of Eduard Silas, whose concerto she had recently performed in Brussels, and who was at the concert, playing antique cymbals in Queen Mab. Silas did leave an account of a visit he paid her in her rooms at 175 Regent Street about this time:

> When I got there, she came in and said: "I must take off my bonnet, it interferes with my smoking." I thought I had misunderstood her; but when she presently brought out a box of big strong cigars, her meaning became clear. She offered me one, took one herself, lay down on the sofa and exclaimed: "Now play me something." I soon saw that I had found more than my match in the consumption of big and strong cigars. Mme Pleyel is a fine woman, an excellent pianiste, has led rather a wild life and has all sorts of scandals attached to her name, but – I liked her nevertheless.

We shall probably never know what really happened at the concert. The charge has to be considered unproven. As Barzun remarks, "although Berlioz might at one time have shot or strangled her, at no time would he commit a crime against Weber". Wittingly, at least. But there remains the possibility that one or both of them was thrown off balance by the encounter – their first, face to face, since before the breach, twenty-two years ago, and the first time she had heard his music since the première of the Fantastic Symphony in December 1830, when she cried out "Superb, superb, prodigious!" after the March to the Scaffold.* In any case he had the best possible distraction. Within days he was plunged in preparations for the most important trial of strength he and his musicians had yet faced, the ultimate test of the new society's intentions: Beethoven's Ninth Symphony.

The performance, on 12 May, took the crowded hall by storm, as the *Times* testified. Thanks to "the liberality of the managers", who would have no truck with "the time-honoured 'one'" rehearsal, "the orchestral masterpiece of the greatest composer for the orchestra, which, too long a sealed book to the world, was pronounced by those who should have taken pains to know better, a rambling and unintelligible production, the offspring of a morbid and decayed intellect – the Ninth Symphony of Beethoven, 'caviar' once even to the initiated", was given "in such a manner as to create an excitement almost unparalleled within the walls of a concert room". The critic, Davison, went on to describe the performance in admiring detail.

* See Vol. 1, p. 429.

The time of the *allegro* was indicated to a nicety, and amidst all its extraordinary combinations, its exciting *crescendos* and overwhelming climaxes, the majesty which is the prevailing characteristic of the move-ment was never once lost sight of. The *scherzo* was equally well-timed, and the *trio*, for the first time in our remembrance, played as fast as it should be. Long as is this extraordinary movement (nearly twice the length of any other of the same character), it was felt to be brief by the audience, who, charmed by its originality and the admirable decision with which it was executed, burst into an absolute uproar of cheers at the conclusion, and it was some time before M. Berlioz could proceed with the *adagio*, the more tranquil beauty of which, however, soon created a different kind of feeling, and substituted a pleasing repose for an unbearable excitement.

Davison was critical of certain details in the finale but had nothing but praise for the choir. "Even in the two final choruses, where the orchestral accompaniments reach the last degree of force and fullness, they sang with a vigour that nothing could abate. The enormous rapidity with which the concluding movements were taken did not once endanger the steadiness and precision of the execution."

The *Morning Post* called it "the most worthy execution of Beethoven's magnificent symphony, and at the same time the best orchestral perform-ance, ever heard in this country. [. . .] We never before heard so much accent and true expression from an English orchestra." The choir too was exemplary, though the critic (Barnett) disliked the "wishy-washy 'Ladies Magazine' verses" of the English translation in which the finale was sung. Gruneisen in the *Illustrated London News*, recalling that at the Paris Conservatoire the choral part of the work was always "very deficiently done", hailed it as "the greatest victory ever yet attained in the development of Beethoven's intentions. [. . .] We heard on Wednesday night professors of no little note, whose sneers and scoffs at the Ninth Symphony years back we had not forgotten, make avowal that it was incomparably the grandest emanation of Beethoven's genius." Gruneisen found Sims Reeves, in the tenor part, disappointing, but the other soloists, Clara Novello, Miss Williams and Staudigl, admirable. "Above all, honour and glory to the gifted conductor, who wielded *Prospero*'s wand and subdued all the combined elements to one harmonious whole. Well did Berlioz earn the ovation bestowed by the moved thousands who filled the hall on this memorable occasion, one to be for ever treasured in our musical annals." The critic regretted only that the rest of the programme, after the symphony, should have been placed in the inadequate hands of Dr Wylde. Was the New Philharmonic Society intended "to become a school for conductors"?

Perhaps the directors took the hint. The fifth concert, two weeks later on 28 May, was conducted entirely by Berlioz. Davison, in the *Musical World*, went into ecstasies over the performance of Mendelssohn's Italian Symphony. "For the first time in England the times of every movement were correctly taken. The *allegro vivace* was really 'vivace', and the saltarello was given in *presto* time, as its character demands and as the author has written in the score. In the first movement the fugue, which commences the second part, was begun *pianissimo*, and the gradual *crescendo* beautifully managed. The *andante* in D minor was played to perfection, and unanimously encored. Equally faultless in its way was the *minuetto*, where the *trio* for horns and bassoons was given with that softness and delicacy upon which its effect chiefly depends." As for the finale, "greater delicacy, precision, and more thorough attention to light and shade, have rarely been noticed in an instrumental performance". The same was remarked of Mendelssohn's violin concerto, played by Sivori, in the second half – "accompanied by the orchestra with a delicacy and correctness of which we can remember no parallel in this country". Gruneisen thought the vocal items by Smart and Mercadante very poor, but he, like Davison, praised Silas' D minor piano concerto (with the composer as soloist), Beethoven's overture *Leonore no. 2*, and Berlioz's arrangement of the *Invitation*, in which the eight harps produced a fabulous glitter; and he reminded the purists who objected "to the introduction of a dance in a classic programme" that the finale of the Italian Symphony is one: a programme which "began with a tarantella" might "consistently end with a waltz".

The sixth and final concert on 6 June clinched the success of the series. Admittedly Dr Wylde was back; but the Ninth Symphony was given again, with if possible even greater éclat (and with Sims Reeves replaced by Reichardt). Marie Pleyel reappeared, this time on her own, playing Liszt's arrangement of the skating scene from *Le Prophète* and the tarantella from Rossini's *Soirées musicales*; Reichardt, Staudigl and the chorus sang substantial excerpts from the first two parts of *The Damnation of Faust*; and at the end, in the words of the *Illustrated London News*, "the ovations bestowed on Berlioz, by the band as well as by the immense auditory, went beyond the bounds of a *furore* in Italy". "The greetings when he left the orchestra seemed fairly to overwhelm him," reported the *Literary Gazette*.

The new society had had its sins of omission and commission, as Gruneisen pointed out: several works promised in the prospectus but not given, including Berlioz's Requiem, Mendelssohn's *Loreley* and *Walpurgisnacht* and a new cantata by Macfarren; too many duds among the new works that were performed; and, worst of all, "the investing with power as an occasional conductor a professor" who was manifestly unequal to it. "Before Costa's nomination to the sole sovereignty of the orchestra, a standing evil at the old Philharmonic Society was in having so many conductors; and how the directors of the new undertaking could fall into such a glaring error as that of permitting Dr Wylde to direct on several occasions, when in Berlioz there was a master spirit to command, having the imaginative glow of the poet as well as the thorough knowledge and experience of the working of large orchestras – an artist who commanded the respect of the players by his genius – is utterly inconceivable." But that the society and its chief conductor had succeeded, triumphantly, and introduced a different conception of orchestral performance, was generally recognized. In what had been, said Davison, the busiest season for years, their achievement stood out from all others.

As a composer Berlioz was considered to have established himself beyond serious dispute, thanks to the extraordinary impact of his *Faust* and *Romeo* music. "His genius," declared Gruneisen, "has overcome prejudice and bigotry, and his fame is now a fait accompli in this country." Chorley might still huff and carp; but that (Berlioz told Gounod) was "a misfortune for which I console myself with the reflection that it is one I share with every artist of any originality and worth". Shortly before returning to France he was treated to a banquet attended by most of the leading musicians and critics of the capital. Toasts were drunk to his speedy return.

There is no doubt that Beale had every intention of inviting him back next season, and Berlioz believed that he would be; he turned down an offer from a New York impresario who had been at the final concert – a five-month engagement at 25,000 francs – because of it. True, the society, despite the large audiences, had ended with a loss, chiefly due to the enormous cost of putting on the Ninth Symphony, but that had been expected in the first year: it was an investment. Beale (wrote Berlioz to d'Ortigue) was determined to go on, "while ridding himself of an individual who has an interest in the enterprise but who is an embarrassment to us".

The author of *Evenings in the Orchestra* should have needed no reminding that (in Barzun's words) "conditions are never right for art – they can only be more or less unfavourable". He was too sanguine. The individual was not so easily got rid of. Dr Wylde with his "spasmodic gyrations" and "tremulous stick" (Gruneisen) might be an embarrassing conductor and a composer distinctly over-represented on the society's programmes, but off the rostrum he was an effective operator, and he was strongly entrenched: it was he who had secured the society its sponsors. That, in a nutshell, was how the directors had come to commit the "glaring error" of letting their professor loose. Beale had been unable to prevent it. The New Philharmonic was saddled with a musician who, young as he was, embodied the ancient abuses of amateurishness, complacency and inadequate preparation which it had come into existence to supersede. But Beale's and Berlioz's way was expensive; the sponsors had to dig deeper into their pockets than they had supposed would be necessary. Dr Wylde came a lot cheaper. Berlioz had by no means heard the last of him. This year, 1852, would remain the high point of his successes in England, and a glorious exception. Henceforth his greatest triumphs as conductor-composer would be in Germany.

Back in Paris in the third week of June, other cares awaited him. The three-month reprieve from criticism was over and he must again grind out his feuilleton: no longer weekly, as in January and February, and not always on subjects antipathetic to him – Lenz's book *Beethoven and His Three Styles*, Gounod's choruses for Ponsard's drama *Ulysses*, and the unveiling of a statue to Le Sueur in his native Abbeville were all worth writing about – but none the less a rude comedown after the passionate activity of London.

During his absence Harriet's condition had, he found, remained outwardly unchanged. "She is perhaps less unhappy than we think," he wrote to Adèle in August. "In the summer months it's peaceful for her with her garden and the fine prospect of the Plain of St Denis and the Montmorency hills; she has two very attentive maids who are attuned to her habits, and women friends, not too demanding, who come and see her from time to time, and her newspaper which she reads two or three times in the morning, and my visits, and . . . hope." Disappointingly, the electric-shock treatment her doctor was trying in order to restore sensation to the paralysed right arm was having no effect. Despite that, Berlioz could report in late October that she was "quite cheerful". They had just had a letter from Louis, who was on his way back from Havana and expecting to see them in about a month's time.

Louis' relations with his father had gone through a bad patch. A plan for him to come to England that spring with a view to a reunion in London or Folkestone was abandoned when Louis, in one of those violent swings of mood to which he was not surprisingly prone, wrote twice to say that he wanted to give up the sea. Berlioz, fresh from the encounter with Marie Pleyel and up to his eyes in the Ninth Symphony, responded with maximum irritation:

London, Monday 3 May

You say you're going mad. You are!

You must be mad or plain stupid to write me such letters. It was all I needed, in the midst of the exhausting life I'm having to lead here. In your last letter from Havana you told me you would arrive with a hundred francs, and now you *owe* forty! Who told you to pay 15 francs' duty on a packet of cigars? Couldn't you have thrown them into the sea?

Here is *half* a bank-bill for a hundred francs; you'll get the other half when you have acknowledged receipt of this one. Then you can stick them together and a money-changer will give you your cash.

It's a normal precaution when sending money by post. I'm writing to M. Cor [head of the company that owned Louis' ship] and M. Fournet to find out where matters stand with your next voyage. You may be sure I set no store by the wild and absurd things you tell me. You embarked on a career which you chose yourself. It's very hard, I know, but the hardest part is over. You have only one more voyage of five months to accomplish, after which you will spend six months taking your hydrography course in a French port, and will then be able to earn your living.

I'm working to put aside the money necessary for your expenses during those six months. I have no other means of helping you out.

What is this you tell me about your torn clothes? You mean that in a month and a half in Havana you've worn out your things? Your shirts are frayed. So you need dozens of new shirts every five months? Are you making fun of me?

I strongly advise you to weigh your words when you write; I don't care for this style of yours. If you thought life a bed of roses, it's time

you began to see otherwise. In any case, and in a word, there is no way
I can give you a profession different from the one *you chose*. It's too
late. At your age one should have enough practical sense not to behave
as you seem to want to.

When you have sent me a reasonable letter, acknowledging receipt of
this half-note, you'll get the rest and my directions. Till then, stay in Le
Havre.

Farewell.

When Berlioz returned from London Louis was already in Paris. Face
to face with his son, he could only love and tend him, while wishing
he would not spend so much of his father's money "on nothing". "The
dear child knows the trouble I have making it," he told Adèle, "yet he
indulges in every sort of extravagant childishness – only to regret it
afterwards." By the first week of August he was safely at sea, once
again well pleased with his profession, delighted with the new captain,
Liebert, and – to his anxious father's relief – out of reach of the
unseasonable gales that were making the Normandy coast a danger to
shipping.

Berlioz himself spent ten restorative days by the sea in Normandy
later that month, at St Valery en Caux, ordered there by his friend and
medical adviser Amussat after an illness accompanied by headaches,
vomiting and extreme exhaustion. He could afford the expense of a
holiday, thanks to extra money earned from publications. Richault
bought both the *Corsair* overture and *The Flight into Egypt*, and
Evenings in the Orchestra finally found a publisher in Michel Lévy.
The man was a notoriously hard bargainer (Edmond Goncourt called
him "that legal robber"), but at least he paid something. Berlioz's
Parisian career was enjoying one of its temporary upturns. Long extracts
from the book appeared that autumn in the *Gazette* and the *Débats*,
giving readers a taste of the character and scope of the collection: the
Prologue, setting the scene – the orchestra pit of an unidentified opera
house; the tale of the Wandering Harpist encountered in the waiting-
room of a wayside station on the line between Vienna and Prague; the
Rise and Fall of the Tenor; the history of the claque, from Nero to the
present day; the nights when a masterpiece like *Don Giovanni* or the
Barber imposes a reverential silence on the talkative musicians; Vincent
Wallace among the Maoris; and the farewell banquet at which the
narrator analyses the conditions that habitually keep music captive,

like Virgil's Cassandra "raising her eyes to heaven, her eyes alone, for chains bind her hands", and the occasions when, exceptionally, it is set free and everything conspires to let it give of its best. The *Evenings* came out in late November and by the end of the year had sold so well that Lévy was talking of a reprint.

The other stroke of good fortune was the decision by Baron Taylor and the Association des Artistes Musiciens to mount a large-scale performance of the Grande messe des morts in honour of the Baron de Trémont, who had died leaving part of his wealth to the five affiliated associations. The baron, a senior figure of government and society under both the Empire and the July Monarchy, and a noted patron of the arts, had a low opinion of Berlioz's music; but if the composer knew this it can only have added piquancy to the success of what was practically a state occasion. "Grand, if lacking in finesse" (he told Liszt), the memorial performance of 22 October was the most impressive the work had yet received. Nearly six hundred performers in the lofty, reverberant space of St Eustache, the choir raised – for the first time – on a specially constructed amphitheatre, the church full, with social and political France there in force: this was the performance which so moved the seventeen-year-old Saint-Saëns that long afterwards he still vividly recalled how, in the Tuba mirum, it was "as if each slender column of each pillar in the church became an organ pipe and the whole edifice a vast organ".

The event was also a triumph of organization and of goodwill harnessed to a clearly defined artistic end – musical Paris united under his baton, "gods and demigods" singing alongside "ordinary mortals" ("one or two of them less well than ordinary mortals"). If not the disciplined, dedicated choral and orchestral community of *Euphonia*, the science-fiction fable which comprised the twenty-fifth "Evening" of Berlioz's book, it was a step towards it. The occasion would not have been truly Parisian without an attempt by officialdom in the shape of the director of the Opéra to spoil the performance at the eleventh hour by forbidding the Opéra chorus to take part (Roqueplan told Baron Taylor he was out to "crush" Berlioz). But the Minister of the Interior overruled him and Roqueplan was forced to rescind the order, which made victory all the sweeter – though he was able to prevent Roger, his leading tenor, from taking part and singing the Sanctus.

The minister, Comte Fialin de Persigny, one of the architects of Louis-Napoleon's coup d'état, was an ally perhaps worth cultivating in the campaign to get the still unperformed Te Deum chosen for the impending coronation of the Emperor. His intervention on behalf of the Requiem could be a sign that the Te Deum's hour had come. Berlioz was divided between hope and scepticism. In late October, amid rumours that the coronation would be held on 4 December and energetic lobbying by his influential friends, he was even ready to forgo the trip to Weimar and stay in Paris in case he was needed. In the end it was the scepticism that was right. The coronation was postponed till an indefinite date; and when Napoleon III married Eugènie de Montijo in Notre-Dame at the end of January he managed without the Te Deum, notwithstanding the assurances the composer received from the Emperor's secretary that it would certainly be given. While London still pended – the contract with the New Philharmonic for next season had not yet arrived – the visit to Weimar was hastily reinstated. He could look forward to hearing *Benvenuto Cellini* after all.

It was going to be a different *Benvenuto*. Since the March performances there had been unexpected developments. Soon after his return from London a long communication arrived from Liszt. The letter – its contents can be inferred from Berlioz's reply of 2 July – spoke of the two-day festival Liszt had just conducted at Ballenstedt, a small town fifty miles north of Weimar, at which two movements of *Harold* were given. It asked the price of a set of orchestral parts of each of the three symphonies, the Fantastic, *Harold* and *Romeo*, and of chorus parts of the latter (Liszt was pursuing his plan of performing all his friend's major works in Weimar). The most important part of the letter, however, concerned the drastic changes Liszt proposed making to the final tableau of the opera: nothing less than cutting nearly the whole of it so that the action could move straight from the sextet and the Cardinal's ultimatum to the finale and the casting of the statue. The cut would mean losing not only Cellini's pastoral aria "Sur les monts" – which in a sense was not being sacrificed, since the tenor, Beck, had never sung it anyway – and the chorus of striking foundrymen, with its strange, shadowy pendant, "Peuple ouvrier, rentre à pas leste", but also the spectral D minor entr'acte, Ascanio's comic number, "Tra-la-la, mais qu'ai-je donc?" and the evocative Abruzzian song with guitar and anvil accompaniment, "Bienheureux les matelots"; but (Liszt argued) the work would be strengthened.

What Liszt didn't tell him (or, if he did, Berlioz's letter passed over it in remarkable silence) was that his opera had already been given in cut form in a version devised, without the composer's knowledge, by Liszt and his pupil Hans von Bülow. The young prodigy, who arrived at the Villa Altenburg the previous summer, had quickly become Liszt's most valued disciple, entrusted with important tasks that Liszt himself was too busy to undertake: copying out Liszt's two-piano arrangement of the Ninth Symphony, corresponding with Wagner (still exiled in Zurich after his part in the Dresden uprising of 1849), taking rehearsals, translating Liszt's article on *Tannhäuser* into German for publication in the *Illustrierte Zeitung*, and himself writing propagandist articles for the *Neue Zeitschrift*. One of the latter was a long and eulogistic essay on *Benvenuto Cellini* which appeared in two instalments, on 2 and 30 April 1852.

Bülow had first come across Berlioz's music nine years before when, a boy of thirteen and already a fine pianist, he was taken to see him conduct in Dresden in the winter of 1843. Since then he had had few if any chances to get to know it better, and was still ambivalent about it when he began working on the opera. "Although I don't at all care for the course which Berlioz pursues" (he told his father in January 1852) "– anti-Wagnerian, pseudo-imitation of Beethoven – yet his genius, which is manifested in so many aspects of his art, interests me a lot." Two months later, having absorbed the score, he had changed his mind. The essay in the *Neue Zeitschrift*, though written at Liszt's prompting, expressed genuine enthusiasm on his own account. Berlioz, he wrote, was a spearhead of modern music – Beethoven's immediate, most vigorous successor; disdained in France (though his music contained more originality and more nobility of spirit than all the combined productions of the three-headed Cerberus [Auber, Meyerbeer and Halévy] which barred the Opéra to him), but a major force for progress in Germany.

Bülow's delight in the music of *Cellini* did not prevent him criticizing what he identified as a flaw in the structure of the opera, namely the fourth tableau, which the librettist had "tried to enliven with a series of varying situations and little incidents" but which he had succeeded only in making "a patchwork so wearisome for the purely musical listener" that one couldn't enjoy the beauties of the final scene. "If we may be so bold as to suggest a partial restructuring in the interest of enhancing the work's stature and making it more widely appreciated, we would propose omitting the whole fourth tableau and moving the ending, the casting of the statue, to the third tableau, where it would have considerable effect." In this Bülow certainly had the backing of Liszt. Indeed it is clear that the wholesale cut was Liszt's idea in the first place. Only, he left it to his brilliant assistant to carry out. Bülow told his mother that as he "agreed with Liszt's opinion as to the uselessness of the last act [tableau], which only wearies people and sends them to sleep, Liszt proposed that I should make the relevant cuts, as well as the slight alterations in music and text necessitated by them. I discharged the task to his satisfaction, though it was my first appearance as a versifier." In its new, truncated form the opera was given its fourth performance on 17 April.

Before we throw up our hands we should remember three things: first, the musical mores of a period when that kind of thing was accepted as normal and when Berlioz himself, a twentieth-century purist at large in the nineteenth, a musician quite untypical in his belief in the sanctity of the composer's intentions, was prepared to have the solo in an excerpt from his revered Gluck sung by several voices in unison; second, that the idea that there could be such a thing as a definitive text of an opera was of quite recent date; and, third, the adaptability of composers in all ages, an adaptability often deeply disconcerting to their adoring and protective admirers (e.g. Beethoven suggesting cuts in the slow movement of the Hammerklavier sonata, or Elgar agreeing to record his violin concerto in a version reduced to a third of its length.) In this case, admittedly, the robust pragmatism that was being applied was not the composer's but his interpreter's. But Liszt, exceptional as he was, was the child of his age. Not for nothing was he the supreme improviser, arranger and paraphraser. He was interested above all in making what he did as effective as possible. Since the later scenes of *Cellini* had been found ineffective, something obviously had to be done, and he did it.

If Berlioz was taken aback on reading Liszt's suggestion, he did not let on. Indeed, on reflection he found that he largely agreed with it. His friend's observations, he replied, were "perfectly fair"; he himself had always found the scenes in question "frigid and intolerable" (*glaciale et insupportable*), but no one before Liszt had pointed out the very simple method of dispensing with them. "It's a matter of not making the Cardinal exit after the [sextet], and of going straight on to the dénouement". The dramatic interest of the final scenes, he acknowledged, sagged badly "amid Fieramosca's entrances, exits, challenges, etc., Teresa's alarm and the bribing of the workmen", and the opera would be better without them. Some of it, though, was worth saving. "I've found a way of preserving the workmen's chorus ('Bienheureux les matelots'), which will begin the last act, the solos being given to Francesco and Bernardino, and Ascanio's aria (with a change of words), and Cellini's 'Sur les monts'. These three numbers must, I think, be kept, despite the somewhat low style of the second of them. If Cellini's aria is unsingable by your tenor (something that to me is incomprehensible), it would always be possible to leave it out in the scenario which I shall be letting you have."

A day or two later he sent Liszt a long letter containing the necessary musical and textual alterations. The opera "thus shortened", he concluded, "will not exceed the duration of a normal show *in Germany* [his italics], especially now that there are only two changes of scene".

The resulting score underwent further detailed changes over the next few years, the most important being the omission of the Andante section of the Teresa/Cellini duet, the restoring of "Sur les monts" to its original position between the sextet and the finale, and the resuscitation of the second "Peuple ouvrier" ensemble, in modified form and now placed at the beginning of the act. This, the so-called Weimar version, was how the work was known, and championed by conductors of the eminence of Bülow, Mottl and Weingartner, right up to the middle of the next century – in fact until 1957, when Arthur Hammond produced a version for the Carl Rosa company which went back to the Paris sequence and, beyond, to the work as it was first planned, as an opéra-comique with spoken dialogue. The Covent Garden performances of 1966 and 1969, based on research by Maurits Sillem and Hugh Macdonald in the Opéra's archives, followed Hammond's lead and took the reconstruction much further, and a recording, conducted by Colin Davis, was issued by Philips in 1972.*

Strictly speaking, to mix distinct sources – in effect, to make one's own version – is a dubious course. But there are works about which their composers cannot be considered to have said the last word, and *Benvenuto Cellini* is one of them. Scholars may deplore what Robert Haas did with the adagio of Bruckner's Eighth Symphony when he

---

* Productions of *Benvenuto Cellini* are now much more likely to reject the Weimar version and take the entire material, Paris and Weimar, as their starting-point – a preference made easier since the publication of Macdonald's ingeniously comprehensive edition of the opera in its various incarnations.

came to the rescue of the composer, beset by advisers who knew better, and combined two separate versions of the score; but many musicians have no doubt that he was right and that the ten bars that Haas restored are necessary. Berlioz's opera is a different case. Nothing can make it a masterpiece – it was too deeply scarred by that first fateful decision to enlarge it from opéra-comique to grand opera. None of those involved, neither the composer nor his librettists, was experienced enough to avoid the attendant dangers. The Opéra's ban on spoken dialogue meant that scenes of an essentially non-lyrical character – the ones that Liszt later took exception to – had to be forced into music against the grain. Rendered entirely in music, with long stretches of recitative, the whole section chopped and changed, never settling down and in the end dragging, as the composer said, "intolerably", while its fine ensembles were lost in the general scrappiness. Yet the scenes had a clear narrative function, that of piling up obstacles in the hero's path so that his victory would be the more dramatic. The order of events in the Paris tableaux 3 and 4 is, potentially, neater and more logical than in the shorter, amalgamated Weimar scheme.

This is the main argument for turning the recitative back into speech and thus giving the final numbers the pace they otherwise lack – a not unjustifiable liberty, given that Berlioz himself planned to perform his opera in precisely that form at the Théâtre-Lyrique a few years later. We can accept the Weimar cuts and reshapings, or we can make a composite version, recast the work in the genre that suits it best – opéra-comique – and restore some striking music which, once known, it is a pity to lose.

One can understand why Liszt wanted to cut all the Fieramosca scenes at the end, and why Berlioz saw the sense of doing so. Liszt had two reasons. First, the scenes, as set, dissipated the dramatic momentum just when it should have been accelerating to its climax, the casting of the statue of Perseus. Second, they emphasized the comic element in the opera, whereas Liszt wanted not only a shorter but a more serious *Cellini*, one which emphasized the embattled artist-hero (identified in Liszt's mind with Berlioz ever since the opera's débâcle in 1838) and which made the triumph of the *Perseus* a clear parable of the opera Liszt had helped overcome its enemies. The Weimar *Cellini* as revised by Berlioz and Liszt was a much less burlesque work – the purely comic scenes drastically curtailed, the role of Balducci the bumbling papal treasurer reduced in size and importance, the pantomime of Midas and the ass's ears pared to half its original length, many humorous exchanges in the sextet removed or shortened, the Pope/Cardinal deprived of his opera buffa presto (for which there was no longer a place), and Fieramosca's role in the final tableau cut almost to nothing.

One can also understand why Berlioz insisted on making an exception for the three above-mentioned numbers. But retaining them created fresh problems. Both Ascanio's aria and the Abruzzian song are much more effective in the Paris sequence; and "Sur les monts", whose paean to the virtues of the simple life is just about acceptable when Cellini has a day to cast the statue, becomes, with all its beauties, an absurdity when the time is reduced to an hour.

Should he have accepted Liszt's fait accompli? Ideally, perhaps not. But I think we can see why he did – why he went along with it and then continued to prune the score right up to the moment of its publication in vocal score in the summer of 1856. Some of his changes were designed to make the music less difficult to play and sing. But above all he felt an intense gratitude to Liszt for breathing unlooked-for life into his long-buried opera. He was, besides, only too willing to adapt it to German taste and to "la durée d'un spectacle ordinaire d'*Allemagne*": Germany was where its immediate future appeared to lie, not France. The old version had been a failure in the best Parisian style, effectively killing any chance of his building a career as an opera composer in France; the new was, increasingly, a success and a vindication of his belief in the vitality of one of his most adventurous scores.

All the same, I doubt whether Berlioz ever considered the case closed. If he had he would hardly have sanctioned a second publication of the vocal score, seven years after the first, which contained spoken-dialogue cues (on the lines of the projected production at the Théâtre-Lyrique). The publication, issued in Paris in 1863, reveals the curious fact that after all its vicissitudes *Benvenuto Cellini* ended as it began, as an opéra-comique.*

For the moment, in the autumn of 1852, he was content with what he and Liszt had worked out together. He was going to hear his beloved score again – that was what mattered. Marie would be hearing it for the first time. The visit must be short, ten days at most, so that he could

---

* A news item in the *Ménestrel* of 2 August 1863 announced that the work "is to be transformed into an opera with spoken dialogue".

sign on at the Conservatoire at the appropriate time and not have to apply for official leave. But he would see two performances of the opera and give a concert of his works; and, thanks to Liszt, the intendant was paying his travel and hotel costs. On the evening of 12 November he set off with Marie for Weimar in a mood of high anticipation.

19

Liszt

He was not disappointed. November 1852 surpassed all his previous visits to Germany. Only in Brunswick ten years before had he had such a welcome. Liszt had set the greatest store by his "Berlioz Week" – "an important week for art" – and the little town was full of musicians and critics come from other German cities and from abroad, making, in Gruneisen's phrase, "a kind of musical congress". The court itself seemed eager to pay tribute to its famous visitor. The orchestra was augmented for the occasion and the theatre chorus, for the first time, was joined by the local choral society to form a choir of over a hundred so that *Romeo and Juliet* could be given complete.

Not least, there was the unique atmosphere Liszt had created among the family of young musicians whom his reputation, personal magnetism and openness to the new had drawn to the Villa Altenburg, the large mansion on its hill above the town, given him by the Grand Duchess Maria Pavlovna to use as he pleased – an atmosphere of generosity and belief in the future, in which Liszt's pupils, treated by him more as friends and colleagues than as students, laboured under his guidance in the common cause of art. There was nowhere in Europe like the Altenburg. The house was a world, with its spacious salons, one of them containing the original death-mask of Beethoven, its endless bedrooms, many occupied rent-free by resident pupils, its fabulous collection of keyboards, including Beethoven's Broadwood piano and a spinet that had belonged to Mozart, its exuberant music-making, its sense of being the headquarters and nerve-centre of a campaign to change the face of music, its ease and conviviality, and its late-night parties at which the cigar-smoking Princess Carolyne presided and radical ideas in politics and art were the norm.

Berlioz was received there as an honoured guest. And, on top of the musical feast that Liszt was laying on for him, to be able to spend so much time in the company of the man, whom he had not seen properly for years, to rediscover their ancient affinities and common enthusiasms (not yet soured by the question of Wagner) and their shared humour – Liszt was almost as compulsive a punster as he was; to be the recipient of so much selfless kindness and devotion; to find that his brilliant, charismatic friend still believed in him and was making a public declaration of his faith – these were inexpressible joys.

That his new young admirers – Bülow (twenty-two), Bernhard Cossmann (thirty), Karl Klindworth (twenty-two), Raff (thirty), Dionys Pruckner (eighteen) – were also devoted Wagnerians to a man would in time cause problems but was as yet no more than a distant cloud. They were at one with Liszt and gave themselves body and soul to the festival, helping at rehearsals, looking after visiting musicians, running errands of all kinds, and standing in as percussionists at Berlioz's concert, Bülow on the bass drum, Pruckner on the triangle and Klindworth on the antique cymbals. In the background – and not always in the background – might lurk the hostility of the old Weimar to the pretensions of the new, the scarcely veiled social insults to the Princess, the fact that Liszt so rarely succeeded in carrying the general public with him in his adventurous repertory, the rooted opposition that would eventually force him to abandon his attempt to recreate the city of Goethe and Schiller and Herder, "the Athens on the Ilm". For Berlioz, fêted as he had never been, these could not be immediate issues.

The Weimar writer Adelheid von Schorn, then a girl of eleven, remembered studying his "remarkable head" while he and Liszt talked to her mother in the street, and thinking that "his handsome face would have been quite captivating if its expression had been gentler", especially "next to Liszt, whose physiognomy had such exceptional charm". But he was happy. It was as if he was being received into his kingdom.

He and Marie arrived early on Sunday morning, 14 November, and were given rooms at the Erbprinz Hotel (Hôtel du Prince Héréditaire) on Marktplatz. For the next week he lived his music. *Benvenuto* was being performed on the Wednesday evening, so there was time to sit in on more than one rehearsal. He had been curious to know whether Liszt felt the tempos as he did. In several places, he discovered, he didn't, as we can see from the notes in Berlioz's hand jotted down at the time and preserved in the Weimar archives:

> Keep the tempo steady in the solos at Balducci's entry at the
> beginning of the finale [Carnival scene].

Cut the Andante of the duet.

The prayer and the [monks'] chanting *not so slow*.

The Andante of the duet *not so slow*.

The Cardinal's entry *not so slow*.

Ask the bass drum to play less loud.

Fieramosca's aria quicker.

Whether or not Liszt took the composer's advice on tempo, Berlioz seems to have been generally satisfied. Liszt was by now a much more experienced conductor than when Berlioz had heard him last, at the Beethoven Festival in Bonn seven years before. Above all he was thorough, and he had faith in the opera. (A year later he told Fischer, the chorus-master at Dresden, that "*Cellini*, with the exception of Wagner's operas – and they should never be put into comparison with each other", was "the most important, most original music-dramatic work of art that the last twenty years have produced".) The response of the audience, too, was warmer than in March and April – an advance which Bülow, writing in the local periodical *Deutschland*, attributed to greater familiarity with a work so different from anything encountered before, but also to the beneficial effect of the cuts and changes in the final scenes. Bülow reported that the "charming duet" for Teresa and Cellini (the Andante marked in Berlioz's rehearsal notes for sacrifice) was removed before the second performance, the composer having decided that it "held up the action". Clearly, the new *Benvenuto* had Berlioz's approval. The contrast between a performance animated by goodwill and one ruined by "sordid cabals" made him shed a few tears as he recalled "the heartbreak this same *Benvenuto* caused me in Paris"; but they were tears of gratitude as well. And now that he had heard it again after all these years – "from the back of a box, like an ordinary listener" – he knew that his score was alive and vital, and he was sure it had a future.

Immediately after the first night the theatre was put at his disposal, and *Romeo and Juliet* and the first two parts of *Faust* were rehearsed over the next few days. The concert, on the evening of Saturday the 20th, was a further triumph. The composer and pianist Ignaz Moscheles, who had come from Leipzig to attend the festival, was in two minds about Berlioz's music but was bowled over by his conducting, which inspired the orchestra (he noted in his diary) "with fire and enthusiasm" and "carried everything as it were by storm". Despite the long programme and the lateness of the hour, several movements in *Faust*, including the double chorus, had to be repeated. Afterwards Berlioz was invested with the grand-ducal Order of the White Falcon and there was a joyous gathering at the Altenburg. Next day, having dined with the Grand Duke, he attended the second performance of his opera. And on 22 November, his last evening, the *Berliozwoche* closed with a dinner and ball at the town hall (*Stadthaus*), given in his honour by the entire Weimar company. From letters and notes written by the participants, from newspaper reports, from biographies or memoirs like those of the critic Richard Pohl and his wife the harpist Jeanne Eyth, we can re-create "the swelling scene": the long candle-lit tables of the banqueting hall, a plaster cast of the composer's new portrait bust by von Hoyer in a prominent position; the toasts raised to Berlioz and Liszt by Bülow, Griepenkerl from Brunswick, Marr the stage manager and the actor-singer Eduard Genast among others; Liszt enlarging on his plans for the city; at the final toast to the hero of the feast, the presentation by Cossmann, leader of the cellos, of a silver baton on behalf of the orchestra; the request by many of them for a signed copy of his lithographed portrait, and the deputing of the trombonist Moritz Nebich (one of the outstanding players whom Liszt had attracted to Weimar) to collect their names and send them on to Paris; Berlioz trying to get Liszt to take the Order of the Falcon, and then writing: "Dear friend, I'm keeping the white bird since you wish me to have it. My affection for you has wings like yours, to *soar*, but not to fly at random. Farewell!! . . . *For ever il tuo*"; Marie "radiant with pleasure and dancing like a willis"; Liszt towards the end of the evening scribbling a note for the Princess at the Altenburg: "The company at the *Stadhaus* is in the best of humours, and a perfect decorum still reigns. Berlioz is deeply touched, and is behaving admirably. Incidentally, he has not drunk a drop of brandy! I can't really leave yet; but be calm and set your mind entirely at rest"; and Berlioz – unable ever to stop thinking of Paris – reflecting that "all this orchestra, all these singers, actors comical and tragical, directors, intendant", gathered to fête him, represented "a category of ideas, an attitude, such as they have no conception of in France".

It was late when the party broke up; but not everyone went to bed. On the travellers' arriving at the station at three in the morning they found that a crowd from the theatre had come to see them off, and they steamed out of the Weimar station to the sound of renewed hurrahs.

The next twelve months were again dominated by foreign trips. Berlioz spent about half the time, all told, in Paris but it was in Germany that his career continued to flourish and put down roots. At home, where concert promoters now had two new taxes to contend with in addition to the eternal *droit des pauvres*, his achievements were confined to the reprinting of *Evenings in the Orchestra* and a contract with Richault to publish *The Damnation of Faust* for 700 francs. To secure a second edition of the Requiem, made necessary by several small but important changes, he had to go abroad, to Ricordi (who pleased him by producing a more finely engraved score than any he had ever had from his French publishers). In Weimar Liszt was still adding to his Berlioz repertory: having already given several performances of *Harold*, he conducted parts of *Romeo* and the *Damnation* at an all-Berlioz concert in February and had hopes of being able to put on the Te Deum. In Paris . . . "As for Paris", Berlioz told Gruneisen,

> everything is just as it was – that is, impossible for me. Everything's closed to me, the theatre, the Conservatoire, even the church. The business of the Te Deum, which was going to be performed at the ceremony of the Emperor's marriage and then wasn't, would be too long to describe here. They preferred to do bits of a Le Sueur oratorio and of a Cherubini mass, a sanctus by Adam, a march from an old Opéra ballet, *Les filets de Vulcain* [by Schneitzhoeffer] and some plainchant orchestrated by Auber. The director of the Opéra has given Gounod my *Nonne sanglante* libretto, of which I'd already written two acts; the Opéra-Comique has little appeal for me, and as for the third so-called Lyric Theatre, it's nothing but a musical jakes where every donkey in Paris comes to piss. The Conservatoire is a club which blackballs me – the committee of the Société des Concerts would take good care not to ask me for so much as an overture. So you see I have plenty of time, musically speaking. I can't have my works performed any more except in foreign countries.

In Germany the demand for his services as composer-conductor was still growing. Bénazet, the new manager of the casino in Baden-Baden, engaged him for a gala concert in August, when the season would be at its height, at the handsome fee of 2,000 francs; and Frankfurt, where he had never yet succeeded in appearing, invited him to come and give two concerts immediately afterwards. Meanwhile another visit to London was under active discussion.

As he half-expected would happen, the New Philharmonic Society had not asked him back. Beale, who at one point was confident they would, was outmanoeuvred by Dr Wylde and resigned from the committee. Lindpaintner was summoned from Stuttgart for the first part of the season and, for the second part, Spohr, with the worthy doctor in attendance. Berlioz could only agree that he was not the one to help "Dr W. acquire the reputation of composer and conductor of the first rank that he absolutely has to have". He had found it impossible, the previous season, "just to please the man Wylde, to conduct in defiance of common sense, as he did. He wants only a blind or one-eyed man for partner, and I wasn't even wearing spectacles."

The New Philharmonic's decision dismayed subscribers and provoked strong criticism in the press: the *Musical Times* said it would be "felt as a serious drawback", and the *Illustrated London News* posed the question – "asked again and again, in places where musicians and amateurs most do congregate" – "how is it that Berlioz, who, as a composer and conductor, achieved such wondrous triumphs last season, and who in Weimar recently created such an immense sensation", had not been re-engaged? At first Beale had hopes of reversing the decision or even of raising his own orchestra and putting on a few concerts in the spring – a complete performance of *The Damnation of Faust* was spoken of – and there was much manoeuvring behind the scenes. (Berlioz commented that it was "like Paris".) In the end it was the old Philharmonic that bit the bullet and engaged him, taking advantage of his presence to offer him half the programme at one of its Hanover Square sessions. For though Beale failed with his concert plans he succeeded in having him invited to London to conduct *Benvenuto Cellini* at Covent Garden. After weeks of negotiation Berlioz was contracted to direct the first three performances of an Italian-language version of the work, with a first-rate cast headed by the great tenor Enrico Tamberlick. It followed an attempt to have the opera produced at Her Majesty's, a plan overtaken by the bankruptcy of Lumley the manager and, after a lawsuit, the ceding of the theatre to Frederick Gye, the manager of Covent Garden. Gye promptly closed Her Majesty's for the foreseeable future and sacked the staff – an event that would have important consequences for the fortunes of *Benvenuto Cellini* at the Royal Italian Opera.

During the five and a half months that Berlioz spent in Paris between returning from Weimar in the last week of November 1852 and leaving for London on 14 May 1853 he continued to write feuilletons on the novelties of the day, but his chief musical activity was preparing his opera for London. Changes decided on in the light of the Weimar performances – adding an evocative orchestral preview of the Carnival, before the rise of the curtain, and a new version of the workmen's "Peuple ouvrier" to open the final act – had to be entered in the score and an Italian translation commissioned and then vetted. He was also making his own piano reduction for Covent Garden, and there was the copying of chorus and orchestra parts to supervise and check – he had insisted on its being done in Paris, where he could keep an eye on it. Liszt was informed of the changes, including a new dénouement in which, instead of the casting being reported from offstage, the Perseus would be shown emerging "red and incandescent" from the shattered mould – a metallurgically impossible feat but a coup de théâtre of which the composer entertained high hopes.

As soon as he returned from Germany Berlioz was busy as go-between, on Liszt's behalf, with Charles Dietz the instrument-maker. Liszt was keen to acquire a clavi-harp, an instrument patented by Dietz's father and perfected by the son, and he also had his sights on a still more ambitious and compendious affair, a piano-organ whose pipes would reproduce wind-instrumental sounds and be in effect a one-man orchestra. Berlioz paid many calls at the workshop in the Rue Fontaine St Georges but soon came to the conclusion that Dietz was not seriously interested in the project, and turned his attention to the young organ- and harmonium-builder Edouard Alexandre, who was. The three-keyboard monster, shaped like a grand piano but extending right to the floor, was completed and delivered to Weimar the following year.

Berlioz did not grudge running errands for the friend to whom he owed so much. It brought them, besides, into closer contact. His visit to Weimar, he told Liszt, had had the additional happy result of renewing their correspondence. "It's a real joy for me when, coming in from my muddy or exhausting treks through Paris, I see on my table an envelope streaked with the flashes of your pen; your zigzags console me for the foursquare, all too legible letters I am obliged so often, to my cost, to answer". He reported his latest conversation with Alexandre, then added: "I should also like the instrument, if possible, not to have an ugly shape. That is not unimportant. I am overcome with repulsion at the sight of certain musical machines such as melodiums and small organs, which resemble linen-presses or commodes. And if I love the harp so much, the way it looks has perhaps something to do with it. I should like to see you govern a handsome slave."

Otherwise the winter and spring brought few satisfactions. Early in December he had Meyerbeer to dinner, with Barbier, Chorley (the curmudgeonly critic had somewhat come round to his music after hearing *Cellini* in Weimar, "the excitement" of which "was remarkable, almost amounting to a contagion not to be resisted"), Jules Lecomte from Brussels, the Duchêne de Vères, and Feuillet de Conches, the master of ceremonies at the Elysées Palace – the latter no doubt with the Te Deum in mind. One evening later in the month Vieuxtemps, Mlle Clauss and the Weimar cellist Bernhard Cossmann came to the apartment and played "Schubert trios" – presumably both the B flat and the E flat – of which Berlioz remarked that they contained "des choses admirables et neuves" (not quite what one might have hoped from him, after his enthusiastic response to the Great C major Symphony). In February a new orchestra made up of current Conservatoire students gave its début concert at the Salle Herz under Jules Pasdeloup, the former timpanist of the Société Philharmonique, a musician of limited ability but great persistence who in the sixties and seventies would become the most celebrated symphonic conductor in Paris, until out-classed by Edouard Colonne. The concert began with the *Roman Carnival* overture. Berlioz was there; but it is impossible to tell from his brief report in the *Débats* what he thought.

Louis spent four days in Paris in December 1852 before returning to Le Havre for his hydrography course. Father and son were now rec-onciled and the best of friends. "The poor dear child has not the faintest idea of economy," wrote Berlioz to Adèle. "For him, as for M. Scribe, 'gold is a chimera' [*Robert le diable*] which he 'handles' very maladroitly. But I beg you never to reproach him for it. His is not the gentlest of professions, and when he is on land I don't want him to go too much without. And then we are such boon companions that, three quarters of the time, when he presents me with a thumping great bill I burst out laughing, as if I were half in the joke. In fact I am, more than half. He is still in need of 'influence', so that he can pass this famous exam and be admitted as a volunteer. Fortunately I've obtained for him the patronage of Admiral Cécille, who sent me word this morning that he would take charge of everything." Berlioz soon had cause to repent his indulgence. Ashore in Le Havre, Louis went to pieces. He skipped his lessons and took to gambling, with calamitous results. By the beginning of March he had seen his tutor only five times, had spent all his money, and still owed for lodging, meals and tuition. If he failed his exam, Admiral Cécille said, the best thing would be to pack him off for three years on a frigate. After a first angry outburst Louis sent his father a deeply contrite letter. He had "none the less scattered my money to the winds and spent three months learning absolutely nothing". Berlioz was so upset that he told Harriet, and then tried to salve his conscience with the thought that she hardly understood what he said. It was indisputable that her illness had begun to affect her mind. She was weaker, too, and now had to be lifted in and out of bed; a third nurse was needed in addition to the devoted pair, Joséphine and Madeleine.

Berlioz himself spent part of March and April in bed with one of his bouts of bronchitis. By the time he left for London in May he was better, and Louis had actually passed his exam and been posted to the *Corse*, a steam-sloop in the service of the French navy. His father had chosen him a good patron. The young man – he would be nineteen next birthday – seemed really to have turned over a new leaf. In June the *Corse* sailed for Scottish waters, putting in at Edinburgh and other ports including Lerwick in the Shetlands. Three months later a report by his commanding officer Captain Maucroix described Midshipman Berlioz as "showing zeal and a ready will"; both his conduct and his morale were declared to be good. The crisis, for the moment, was past.

The eight weeks that Berlioz spent in London that summer, though they could hardly live up to the excitements of the previous year, were far from uneventful. To breach the fortress of the Philharmonic even for half a concert and a fee of ten guineas was no mean achievement. The committee, however, drew the line at the "two strenuous rehearsals with the complete orchestra" which he said were the minimum required for the Fantastic: one rehearsal was the rule. They settled instead on *Harold* – a score many of the players were familiar with – plus the *Roman Carnival* overture and The Repose of the Holy Family from *The Flight into Egypt*, with Gardoni, a star of the former Her Majesty's company, as tenor soloist. The date of the concert, the society's sixth of the season, was fixed for 30 May.

Even such a programme – to which Costa added Beethoven's Fifth and shorter pieces by Spohr, Bottesini, Donizetti and Weber in the second half – drew deeply on the London players' notorious sight-reading skills. But from the moment Berlioz appeared, to hearty and prolonged applause, he and the orchestra carried everything off with aplomb and panache. It could "only be regarded", wrote Gruneisen in the *Illustrated London News*, "as a rehearsal of the two works" (the symphony and the overture), wanting as it did "the light and shade so necessary to develop the subtle thoughts of Berlioz"; but "the spirit of the execution was good". The concert was a notable victory. "Professional prejudices and artistic antipathies received a deathblow", Gruneisen claimed; "the most bitter adversaries of his system were heard to exclaim, 'He is, indeed, a wonderful man!'" The Repose of the Holy Family (the première of the piece), charmingly sung by Gardoni, had to be repeated; and the *Roman Carnival* brought the session to a rousing finish. Was it an omen for his opera?

Benvenuto Cellini was awaited with keen interest. As Davison reminded readers of the *Musical World*, the opera had recently triumphed in Weimar, where "Franz Liszt (as though to redeem his Wagner–Schumann heresies) had the courage to bring it out" and "the Saxe-Weimarians – of quicker apprehension than the Parisians, whose conceit is only surpassed by their musical ignorance – at once plunged into the depths of Berlioz's reveries and followed his imagination throughout its wayward, flickering and eccentric course", to such an extent that "the approval of the public declared itself in shoutings. Joseph Joachim was present, and can verify what we say". Now (Davison said) it was London's turn to give its verdict; Berlioz's triumph at the Philharmonic had made it all the more timely.

Gye needed a critical success. The first production of the Covent Garden season, Auber's *Muette de Portici*, had been coldly received, and *Rigoletto*, the next, though it drew good houses, had a bad press. Spohr's *Jessonda* was sure to be a hit, but *Benvenuto* too, given the composer's standing in London, might do well. Berlioz himself was optimistic. He had feared the customary haste of the English; but in the event he had no complaints. The cast was strong, headed by a really musical and intelligent Cellini, Tamberlick – a tenor with the voice he had "dreamed of when writing the part". Costa was cooperative, the orchestra excellent, the chorus able and willing, the chorus-master, Smythson, the best he had ever worked with; and Augustus Harris's staging promised well.

During the three and a half weeks between the Philharmonic concert and the première he was kept busy rehearsing orchestra, chorus and soloists (the latter with the help of young Wilhelm Ganz's piano accompaniment), and there is little trace of where he went or what he did when he was not working. Once again he and Marie were lodged in Old Cavendish Street, this time at No. 17, the house of Mrs Elizabeth Turnour the dressmaker. One evening he took a cab up to Haverstock Hill in Hampstead for a sumptuous dinner given by Tamberlick for the entire cast ("he can – he earns 125,000 francs a year. Forgive him: he's a fine, thoroughly decent man, unaffected as you or me, it's not his fault if he has a voice of gold"). As before, he presumably attended concerts and operas and observed the London musical scene at first hand, though this time he gave only the briefest and most general account of it in the Paris press:

> After the French Season, "the London Season! the London Season!" is the rejoicing cry of every Italian, French, Belgian, German, Bohemian, Hungarian, Swedish and English singer; and the virtuosos of the nations reiterate it with enthusiasm as they step on to the steam-boat, like Aeneas' soldiers repeating "Italiam! Italiam!" as they boarded their vessels.

Nowhere in the world was so much music consumed during a season.

> Thanks to this colossal consumption all artists of genuine talent, after a few months spent getting themselves known, may be sure of finding work there. Once they have become known and been taken up they are awaited every year; their reappearance is as dependable as the migration of pigeons in North America. And never for the rest of their lives are they known to deceive the expectations of the English public, that paragon of fidelity ever ready to welcome and admire and applaud them, unheeding of "th'irreparable ravages of time".* One has to have witnessed the turmoil of a favourite artist's life in London to have any conception of it. More curious still is the life of the long established professors like Mr Davison, or his admirable pupil Miss Goddard, or Messrs Macfarren, Ella, Benedict, Osborne, Frank Mori, Sainton, Piatti. They are always rushing hither and thither, playing, conducting, at a public concert or a private soirée, with barely time to greet their friends through the window of their cab as they cross Piccadilly or the Strand.

---

* Racine, *Athalie*.

He took pleasure introducing Adolph, son of his old Paris and Darmstadt friend Louis Schloesser, to London musical circles, beginning with Beale. Doubtless he and Marie went to one of the regular Sunday evening gatherings at Beale's house in Finchley Road frequented by foreign artists of which Schloesser speaks. The young man must have seen Berlioz rehearsing, for – in addition to the usual description of his "aquiline nose" and the "shock of hair in which" (a new touch) "he frequently buried his fingers" – he mentions his "somewhat melancholy expression, unless excited by the subject of conversation or when conducting his orchestra. During rehearsals," Schloesser goes on, "he would stop his instrumentalists when occasion required, and would sing (without a real voice) a few notes to the bassoon, the oboe or any other instrument at fault, irrespective of pitch."

On 22 June, three days before the première of his opera, Berlioz cashed the Philharmonic's cheque at the Union Bank in Princes Street. By then he was confident of success, as he told Barbier: everyone at the opera-house was on his side; the Philharmonic concert had raised public expectation still higher. "You can't imagine what a difference there is going to be between the *Malvenuto* of Paris and the *Benvenuto* of London. Come!"

He reckoned without the Italian opposition. Gye had already roused its wrath by closing Her Majesty's; but with the invasion of the Royal Italian Opera by a French composer and conductor and a largely non-Italian cast he had gone too far. Tamberlick alone was Italian. Mme Jullienne (Teresa) and Mme Nantier-Didiée (Ascanio) were French, Tagliafico (Fieramosca) Italian by origin but born and brought up in France, Zelger (Balducci) Belgian, and Formès (Cardinal) and Stigelli (Francesco) German.

As well as the admirers or well-wishers in the audience – Pauline Viardot, George Eliot, Edward Holmes, the King and Queen of Hanover, Crown-Prince Carl Alexander from Weimar, Ferdinand Hiller, New Philharmonic subscribers and the rest – there were certainly people who genuinely took against the libretto or the music or both. Queen Victoria noted in her diary that "we saw and heard produced one of the most absurd and unattractive operas I suppose anyone could have composed". For Spohr, the fine things in the score were far out-numbered by passages "so eccentric and harsh that all one's pleasure was destroyed". They would none the less have suffered it to be heard, and heard again. That was exactly what the Italian faction was determined to prevent. It had men posted throughout the house and even in the wings, and (in the words of the *Morning Post*) they "hissed throughout with a determination which the vigorous efforts of the major portion of the audience failed to overpower", the "sibillations" being "delivered with a simultaneousness, precision and perfectness of *ensemble*" which there was no mistaking. According to the *Times*, some of the demonstrators had penny whistles and door keys. The editorial in the *Musical World* a week later declared that "the demonstrations of Saturday night" could not possibly be seen as "significant of anything that regards the merits and demerits of *Benvenuto Cellini* as a work of art" and had everything to do with matters of musical politics, among them the fact that "Meyerbeer, Auber, Halévy, are gradually taking possession of the Italian stage in London", that "Jullien has had an opera produced at Covent Garden", that "Her Majesty's Theatre is shut up", and that "the Italians begin to tremble for their supremacy". The only question in many people's minds was whether Costa knew about it in advance and let it happen, in revenge for Berlioz's criticizing the liberties he took with Mozart, Beethoven and Weber.

Certainly some opposition could have been predicted. Hostile demonstrations were by no means unknown in the West End. Five years before, a dramatization of *The Count of Monte-Cristo* given at Drury Lane by actors from Paris had to be taken off and transferred to another theatre because members of the English acting profession (in the words of Wilhelm Ganz, who was playing in the orchestra) were "so jealous that a French company should play at the English National Theatre" that they "hissed, shouted and whistled the whole evening". But though the existence of a cabal against Berlioz's opera had leaked out – Marie Recio told Silas, before the curtain went up, that there would be trouble – no one was prepared for its scale and persistence. The "cat-calls and howls", reported Chorley, were "louder even than the thunderstorm which was raging outside"; and, despite the presence of the Queen and Prince Albert in the royal box with the King and Queen of Hanover, they continued throughout the performance. The singers, Tamberlick apart, were heckled even before they opened their mouths; the *Roman Carnival* overture, which introduced the second of the three acts, was booed while it was going on. One or two numbers were encored, but the performance as a whole, though apparently a good one, was turned into a rout. At the height of the uproar Pauline Viardot turned to Edward Holmes: "Don't you think, Sir, it is very wrong to hiss an opera like this?" "I could hardly reply to her, from vexation," wrote Holmes to Clara Novello. "To see the generous work of Berlioz so crushed – the labour of months and years destroyed in a few hours – quite overpowered me." At the end the house rallied and with cheers demanded the composer. But he would not appear. Before leaving the theatre that night he withdrew the work.

Perhaps if he had been twenty years younger and in his own country he might have stuck it out and fought back with counter-demonstrations organized in the manner of Victor Hugo's at the battle of *Hernani*. As it was, with the prospect of the cabal continuing operations at every performance, he felt he could neither sustain the struggle nor expose his singers to such treatment. He must simply put the best face on it. "I'm certain there is a serious future for this score, in Germany and later in France," he told Brandus, "whatever its present fate and the ill luck the libretto brings upon it; in my view the music is new and of unquenchable vitality"; and to Liszt: "I assure you that *Cellini* is worthier than ever of your protection and sooner or later, I trust, will do its patron honour." Meanwhile he could only accept defeat philosophically. "Life is conflict, and I walked into an ambush."

He was helped in his philosophy by the reaction of sympathy and solidarity in his favour on the part of musical London, the non-Italian element at least. The day after the débâcle more than two hundred orchestral players from Covent Garden and the New Philharmonic, and the Covent Garden chorus, offered their services for a testimonial in Exeter Hall, and a committee including Beale, Ella, Osborne, Benedict, Henry Smart, Sainton, Frank Mori, Davison, Gruneisen and Chorley was set up to arrange the concert. Within a few days the subscription list for tickets, collected by Broadwood, stood at nearly £200, even before the concert had been advertised. In the event it proved impossible to arrange: by the time the hall could be made available, too many of the musicians would be in Norwich for the festival. The subscribers, however, refused to take their money back, and it was agreed to use it to sponsor an English edition of *The Damnation of Faust*. Berlioz, thanking everyone concerned in an open letter to the *Musical World*, could almost feel (as he said) that the Covent Garden experience had been worth it for the kindness and friendliness it had earned him.

Back in Paris on 10 July he was at once caught up in preparations for more German concerts, and within three weeks he and Marie were on the road. Just before setting out he wrote to Liszt to thank him for the sympathetic messages from the Grand Duke about *Benvenuto Cellini* – "so he was in London that day, *Dies irae, dies illa*?" (Liszt, we learn from a letter of his to the Princess, had read Berlioz's account of the débâcle aloud to the Grand Duke while they sat on a bench under an oak tree in the park at Weimar) – and to bring him up to date on his various activities, including publications:

The engraving of *Faust*, with German and French text and in full score and vocal score, is proceeding, and the English edition will soon be in train. So I have only three scores still to publish, including the Te Deum. After that God knows what I'll decide. There's a full-scale conflict going on in my mind between love of art and repugnance, between weariness with the known and desire for the unknown, between a dogged tenacity and Reason which cries "Impossible!" Our art, as we conceive it, is a millionaire's art – it needs millions. With millions, every difficulty disappears, every darkened understanding sees the light, the moles and foxes are driven back underground, the block of marble becomes a god, the public becomes a man. Without millions, after thirty years of effort Hodge is where he began.* And not a monarch, not a Rothschild or whoever, that comprehends this!! Could it be that we are quite simply fools and insolent rogues, we with our private pretensions?

I am as convinced as you of the ease with which Wagner and I can mesh our gears together, if he will only put a little oil on his wheels. As for the few lines you speak of [in *Opera and Drama*], I've never read them and do not have the slightest resentment on their account; and I've fired enough pistol shots at the legs of the passing throng not to be surprised at being peppered with buckshot in my turn.

[. . .] I shall profit by your advice for Frankfurt, if I decide to go there; I already suspected the existence of those highway critics and the necessity of dropping a coin in their hats as they wait there with their blunderbusses. All the same, what a humiliation.

You write me twelve-page letters so as to talk of me and my affairs, and I have the simplicity to answer you *on the same subject*. But it is only simplicity, combined with a slight fear of venturing tactlessly on subjects you don't wish to raise. Never forget, dearest Liszt, that no one – I mean it, no one – feels a keener interest in all that matters to you,

---

* Hodge ("Gros-Jean") and the block of marble becoming a god are allusions to two of La Fontaine's fables, "The Milkmaid and the Jug of Milk" and "The Sculptor and the Statue of Jupiter."

and none will be happier than I when the problems that still stand between you and a peaceful life are resolved.*

I had indirect news of your children recently. My son is now launched; he's a midshipman [*aspirant de marine*] on a French naval vessel.

We are all aspirants.

What is to become of so many aspirations?

One of them – carte blanche to organize concerts and put on well-rehearsed programmes without regard to expense – came nearer to being realized at Baden-Baden than he can have imagined would be possible. The fashionable spa town in the south-west corner of Germany had its reigning grand duke, but the uncrowned "King of Baden" was the holder of the gambling concession, the forty-six-year-old Edouard Bénazet. Under his shrewdly beneficent rule it had become the favourite high-summer resort of Europe's rich and would-be rich, the haunt of German and Russian royalty and nobility and well-to-do bourgeois, of Parisian notables, diplomats, bankers, generals, artists, adventurers and demi-mondaines. They came to drink the waters and play the tables or just to see and be seen and grasp whatever pleasure fate cast in their way. But Bénazet had other tastes as well and money to indulge them. He had studied briefly at the Paris Conservatoire before embracing his father's profession of croupier and thriving mightily in it, and he reckoned that a gala concert directed by the leading conductor of the day would be an agreeable way of investing a little of his profit and making the place even more fashionable. It would mean closing the casino on the day of the concert but that would only whet the appetite for gambling. In 1853 and then every year from 1856 to 1863 Berlioz spent several weeks making music under unusually civilized conditions. Though he shared the revulsion of Turgenev (who lived in Baden in the 1860s and set his novel *Smoke* there) at the people Turgenev described as "crowded round the green tables with the same dull, greedy, half-stupefied, half-exasperated, wholly rapacious expression which gambling fever lends to even the most aristocratic features", he liked the summer gaiety and brilliance of the town and the fantastically varied society, in which he was always sure of finding friends; and he delighted in the charm of the surroundings, the bosky parks, the old

* A reference to the Princess's dispute with the Wittgenstein family and her protracted attempt to have her union with Prince Nicholas dissolved so that she and Liszt could marry.

castle, the balmy air that made him feel so well, the brooks and waterfalls and aromatic pine forests, and the rampart of mountains which formed so grand a setting for this "pearl of the Black Forest". The audience that gathered in the Salle de la Conversation, and that overflowed on to the terrace outside, might not be an élite in anything except rank, and the circumstances of the concert might oblige him to include more display pieces than he would have wished; but such limitations were outweighed by the satisfaction of working with sympathetic musicians – among them several of his favourite French artists like Arban the cornettist and the horn player Baneux – for an impresario who paid, and paid liberally, for however many rehearsals were judged necessary.

Every morning for a week Berlioz and his orchestra caught the seven o'clock train to nearby Karlsruhe and rehearsed with the musicians of the local company till half-past twelve, when it was time to eat the sumptuous alfresco lunch laid on by Bénazet, after which they took the train back to Baden. On the morning of 11 August the Karlsruhe contingent made the journey in the opposite direction for the final rehearsal in the Salle de la Conversation, converted into a concert hall and festooned with flowers and greenery. That evening a glittering if less than fully attentive audience was treated to the first two parts of *Faust*, uncut, followed by two duets from *Semiramide* sung by the famous Sophie Cruvelli and her sister Marie, Ernst improvising new variations on his *Carnaval de Venise* (the violinist had arrived in Baden just in time to take part), a clarinet solo by Cavallini, and to round it off the *Roman Carnival* overture. Berlioz was pleased with his chorus and orchestra and with his three German soloists (Eberius, Oberhoffer and Bregenzer) and felt that *Faust* had caused quite a number of musicians and amateurs to revise the wild ideas they had fastened on his music. Strauss the Karlsruhe kapellmeister, a puzzled listener at the rehearsals, shook him warmly by the hand afterwards, confessing that at first he had found it all "so new" that he could make no sense of it – "but this time light has dawned, I see it all, I understand it, and I give you my word of honour it's a masterpiece".

It was the same in Frankfurt, where Berlioz and Marie travelled a day or two later and where with the cordial support of the conductor Gustav Schmidt he gave two concerts in the theatre, the programme of the first being repeated at the second: *Faust*, Parts 1 and 2, again, *Harold* (Ernst), the Repose of the Holy Family (sung by Caspari, the Faust) and *Invitation to the Waltz*. The public, he admitted to Liszt, was "sparser than in Baden" but it was more cultivated; the courtesy visits to local critics which Liszt recommended reaped their reward; there was a splendid supper afterwards; a local poet addressed a twenty-eight-line ode to the Maestro Français on behalf of all the "sympathies allemandes"; the military band played the *Francs-juges* overture beneath the windows of his hotel; and altogether the Frankfurters behaved unlike normal inhabitants of a commercial town. Only, as in Baden, "a good half of the audience" took the Amen fugue seriously; and one of the players, "with a knowing look", said "Is it ironical? I'm afraid it is." "In truth" (Berlioz's letter to Liszt goes on) "the fugue is not unpleasant enough: it has an organ-like sonority and a vibrancy of harmony which spoil it all – so that when Mephistopheles says to the drunkards, 'By heaven, gentlemen, your fugue is very fine', there are bourgeois who, while agreeing with him, must find me highly immodest – I pay myself compliments in public! In a sense, though, that only makes the joke better."

Back in Paris on 1 September his other life took over: two feuilletons "sprang" at him and seized him "by the throat", and he had to devote his creative energies to telling the yet unknowing world about Vogel's *La moissonneuse* at the Lyrique and Halévy's *Nabob* at the Opéra-Comique. But almost at once fresh proposals arrived from Germany: in the second week of September both Hanover and Brunswick wrote inviting him, Hanover for one concert, Brunswick for two. At the same time plans were set afoot for Prague and Munich.

Hanover was to have come first, but the King stayed in England longer than expected and the concert was postponed till the beginning of November. Berlioz did not leave Paris for Brunswick till the evening of 12 October. He was thus still there when Liszt arrived on a visit to his three children, whom he had not seen for eight years, and took up temporary residence at the Hôtel des Princes in the Rue de Richelieu. With him were the Princess, her daughter Marie, her cousin Eugène and Wagner. They had all met at the Drei Königen in Basel, where Liszt, with his disciples Bülow, Peter Cornelius, Pruckner, Pohl and Joachim, had travelled from the Karlsruhe Festival to see Wagner, who, in exile, had gathered round him in spirit a band of devotees bent on disseminating his music throughout Germany. After spending a few convivial days together – Liszt playing the Hammerklavier Sonata, Wagner reading aloud part of his *Ring* poem – they separated. While the young men returned to Germany (on the way, getting into trouble with the Baden police by singing the trumpet fanfare from the second act of *Lohengrin* in the street), the others took the train to Paris, where they arrived late on 8 October. There, in the spare moments left by socializing, sightseeing and musical events (including *Robert le diable* at the Opéra), Wagner went on with his reading ("I had a great weakness for it at the time"); and he was in the middle of *Götterdämmerung*, Act 3, one evening at the house of Liszt's children in the Rue Casimir-Périer when Berlioz walked in. He behaved (wrote Wagner) "with admirable forbearance in the face of this misfortune". It was the first time the twin objects of Liszt's proselytizing enthusiasm had met since Dresden in 1843. Next morning the visitors were entertained by Berlioz to breakfast. Liszt played excerpts from *Benvenuto Cellini*, the composer accompanying "by singing in his rather dry way". This was Wagner's first encounter with the work he had advised Liszt not to perform. That evening (11 October) Berlioz was at the Café de Paris with Janin, Victor Cousin, and Armand and Edouard Bertin for a select dinner given by Meyerbeer to smooth the way for his new opera *L'étoile du nord*. On the 12th he and Marie took the night train from the Gare de l'Est, en route for Brunswick.

The two concerts given in the Ducal Theatre on the 22nd and 25th, to capacity houses, garnered a fresh harvest of applause and golden opinions. Brunswick once again rose to its opportunity. The playing of the "incomparable" orchestra, in *Harold* and in excerpts from *Romeo* and from all four parts of *Faust*, delighted him; The Repose of the Holy Family, sung by the local tenor Friedrich Schmezer, "conquered all the pious spirits"; Joachim – a last-minute addition to the programme of the second concert – was a dazzling soloist in his own violin concerto and in a Paganini caprice; the Minuet of the Will o' the Wisps, which Berlioz had not heard since 1847, glittered sensationally (in contrast to Mephistopheles' serenade, delivered by an unnamed baritone with all the devilry of a churchwarden); the *King Lear* overture, which he directed from the full score belonging to Griepenkerl, was given the best performance of all the many he had conducted; and the public once again showed its special affinity for his music. Women kissed his hand in the street as he left the theatre – "one of them said, with a candour not very flattering for the man (if he had had extra-musical ideas), 'It's not love, it's admiration.'" His hotel room was full of flowers sent anonymously or left on the conductor's desk and taken there by the orchestral attendant. A supper for a hundred guests followed the first concert; and before the second the kapellmeister Georg Müller, on behalf of all the performers, presented him with a silver-gilt baton inlaid with garnets. A new pension fund for the widows of local musicians was named after him. And at a concert in the public gardens he had the pleasure of hearing the *Roman Carnival* overture brought off in lively style by a military band of fifty, and encored; on being recognized in his balcony seat, he had to stand up and acknowledge the applause while the band blew fanfares and the women waved their handkerchiefs. Amid all the festivities and the hard work he found time for an excursion on foot into the Harz Mountains, scene of the witches' sabbath in Goethe. And he met a man who was to be one of his most devoted partisans in Germany, the chamberlain to the Prince of Lippe-Detmold, Baron von Donop. Von Donop, who had become enamoured of Berlioz's *Romeo and Juliet*, travelled from Detmold to hear the three movements given at the first concert. Over lunch he urged him to write an opera on the play. Berlioz replied that even if he could find adequate actor-singers for the two main parts, the values of Parisian operatic life were so debased that he would "certainly be dead before the first night". That evening, in an entr'acte, von Donop repeated the conversation to his neighbour. The man was silent for a moment, then struck the edge of the box and exclaimed, "All right – let him die, but let him write the opera."

The remark typified the excitement his music and personality generated in Germany. They felt he was one of them. Even the hostile critics, and the nationalists, affronted that a German pension fund should be named after a foreigner, conceded that his progress through the land was a triumph. At Bremen, as he was boarding the train, an old man grabbed him by the shoulder and, raising his hat, shouted, "Monsieur! Monsieur! Grand Komponist, Monsieur, grand Komponist!" At Leipzig, while he was writing letters in the hotel the evening before his first concert, a young man, blind, was led in: he had just got off the train from Dresden and come straight to the Bayerische Hof. "I speak French so bad, forgive, sir. Your hand – you allow – I know by heart the scores of you – the concert tomorrow – *Harold*, Queen Mab, the sylphs of *Faust* – I am so happy – Goodbye, sir – excuse."

Never had he been so entirely in his element. "You were right to say I would soon forget my ennui once I had come *in medias res*," he told Janin. "I don't give a thought to the fatigue of it any more, even the prodigious sweat I work up at rehearsals does me good, as well as entitling me all the more to say I'm like a fish in water." Paris seemed very far away. He hardly minded when the main purpose of his writing to Janin – to ask him to forward a letter of application to the music section of the Academy, a chair having become vacant through the death of Onslow – was frustrated by the section's speeding up the normally sedate process of nomination, so that the list of candidates was submitted to the Institute before Berlioz could formally apply. "Much good may it do them. My thoughts were elsewhere – I was making music, and that doesn't tend to direct one's mind towards academies and academicians."

In nearby Hanover, where Berlioz and Marie arrived about 28 October, the audience at the opening concert on 8 November was smaller than in Brunswick (though swelled by a group of Brunswickers eager for another taste of *Faust*) but scarcely less warm. This was a dramatic change from the indifferent public and unwilling orchestra of ten years before. The blind King of Hanover may have set the tone – he and the Queen sat through all four hours of Berlioz's final morning rehearsal – but the transformation was due more than anything to the large number of young players who had recently joined the orchestra, Joachim at their head, and to the vivid performance of parts of *Faust* which resulted. The whole atmosphere was different. On his appearing in the theatre for the first rehearsal he was greeted by fanfares from the brass and woodwind and clapping from all the strings, and found the scores on his desk garlanded with laurels "like prize hams" (he told Ferrand). When the orchestra learned that he would probably be out of pocket because of a misunderstanding with the management over his share of the receipts, it promptly waived its fees. Berlioz accepted for the first concert but declined for the second, which the King invited him to give a week later, on the 15th. In Hanover he discovered, at last, a good Marguerite, Mme Nottès (to whom he later dedicated *Absence*), and was able to programme Parts 3 and 4 of *Faust*. The aged Bettina von Arnim, Goethe's and Beethoven's friend, paid him a call: she came, she said, not to "see" him but to "look at" him. And during a break in one of his rehearsals Joachim introduced him to Brahms.

From Hanover (which he left with an engagement to return in the spring) he and Marie took the train ninety miles north-west to Bremen, where on 22 November he conducted *Harold* (Joachim), the Repose and the *Roman Carnival* to loud applause at a subscription evening of the local concert society. Next day, escorted to the train by a deputation from the society, they set off on the long journey back across Germany to Leipzig.

The visit to Mendelssohn's old city had been a late idea, set up between Ferdinand David and the faithful Griepenkerl while Berlioz was in Hanover; but in some ways it was the most remarkable achievement of the tour. Leipzig was a conservative place, soon to harden into the role of bastion of traditional verities against the subversive activities of Liszt and the Weimar School. Yet Berlioz, in two concerts at the Gewandhaus, won it over to an extent he had not dreamed possible. Though the *Neue Zeitschrift* had been spreading news of his progress, the Leipzigers were quite capable of proving the exception; which made their partial conversion all the sweeter. The first concert – given on 1 December as part of the Gewandhaus subscription series, and offering, in addition to Beethoven's Eighth Symphony, the first three movements of *Harold* (with David), Queen Mab, the Elbe scene from *Faust*, the *Jeune pâtre*, the *Roman Carnival* overture and, for the first time, the complete *Flight into Egypt* – was judged by one and all a great success. Berlioz could not help finding the demeanour of the audience somewhat "cool compared with the ardour of Brunswick, Hanover and Bremen" – he was glad of the comforting presence of Liszt and his entire entourage, who had got up early on an icy-cold morning to come over from Weimar and cheer him on. Coolness was the Leipzig way, of course. But at the second concert, on 10 December, it thawed dramatically and he was given an almost Brunswick-style ovation for a programme consisting of *Faust*, Parts 1 and 2, the first four movements of *Romeo* and, for the second time, *The Flight into Egypt*.

Berlioz, to begin with, had thought so little of his "Fragment of a mystery play in antique style" that its success took him unawares. Having performed the Shepherds' Farewell twice at the Société Philharmonique in 1850 – passed off as the music of an unknown seventeenth-century choirmaster – he had had parts copied for the other two movements with a view to giving the whole work in a later season; but the society collapsed and there were no further concerts. After that, though published in mid-1852 it was seemingly forgotten till the spring of 1853, when he gave the third movement, the Repose of the Holy Family, in London. Its warm reception by the Philharmonic Society audience made him include the piece in all his subsequent programmes in Germany. But the Leipzig performance was the première of the complete score. Everyone was delighted with it, Berlioz included.

Brahms, who had meanwhile arrived in Leipzig, fell in love with the work, which remained thereafter his favourite among Berlioz's oeuvre. Cornelius wrote lyrically to his sister, urging her to recommend it to Schott for performance in Mainz: "Each of the three pieces is beautiful, but the third, a tenor solo with a final Alleluia of angels, the most beautiful. It is a composition that will live for ever."

That such ostensibly backward-looking music should particularly appeal to Leipzig was perhaps not surprising. What was extraordinary was the degree to which his music as a whole found acceptance. The *Signale*, reviewing the first concert, contrasted the audience's respectful response with the harsh judgements previously pronounced on it: people were coming to terms with the complexity of a musical idiom and melodic style which, like that of Beethoven in his final period, was fundamentally polyphonic and in which each and every orchestral voice was an animate being – an idiom which, of necessity, could not be grasped all at once. They were beginning to recognize (the article continued) what had so often been denied: that his works, though conforming to no predetermined rules, had their own organic unity. "This time he has overcome more than one prejudice. The conviction has grown that he possesses not only intelligence and artistic seriousness but heart as well – that he can say a great deal very simply and is not constantly striving to bring the walls crashing down with tumult of brass but uses force where it is appropriate, and also likes to express, by gentle means, the subtlest, most tender feelings of the human breast."

There were still pockets of resistance. Anton Schindler, in a Frankfurt journal, poured scorn on the idea of Berlioz as "Beethoven's successor". But though one or two other critics might continue to attack him in the old dismissive terms, the press as a whole took his music seriously and saw much to praise; and his performers rose to the challenge. The chorus – the Singakademie plus the Pauliner Sängverein and the boys of the Thomaskirche – gave of their considerable best (a compliment he would return by dedicating Part 3 of *The Childhood of Christ* jointly to the Singakademie and the Pauliner Sängverein), and the orchestra refused all payment for the second concert. Afterwards a band of students from the Pauliner choir came to the Bayerische Hof and serenaded him. David held a brilliant soirée in his honour, at which Liszt performed his fantasy on two themes from *Benvenuto Cellini* and Liszt and Bülow played the latter's four-hand transcription of the opera's overture. And at another soirée, on the evening of his fiftieth birthday (11 December), there were fresh demonstrations of esteem. His only fault, it seemed, was that he was French and not German. The ladies of the Singakademie berated him for it – he even lapsed into English at rehearsals! "Why don't you speak German, M. Berlioz? It should be your language – you *are German*."

All in all, against expectation, Berlioz found himself the talk of Leipzig, his music admired and discussed, his company sought and his opinions deferred to – as Brahms reported to Joachim in a letter describing an evening of chamber music at Brendel's at which he played his Scherzo op.4 and the slow movement of his F minor sonata: "Pohl, Berlioz, etc., were there and, before I forget it, Schloenbach, Giesecke and all the literary notabilities (or nonentities?) of Leipzig. Berlioz's praise was so exceedingly warm and hearty that the rest meekly followed suit. He was just as cordial yesterday evening at Moscheles'. I have much to thank him for." The twenty-year-old composer-pianist had made a name for himself on a tour of Germany with the exiled Hungarian violinist Ede Reményi earlier that year and had arrived with the accolade of Schumann's recent article, "New Paths", in the *Neue Zeitschrift* (Schumann, no longer the journal's editor nor even a contributor, broke a long silence to salute this young "master" who had "sprung fully armed like Minerva from the head of Jove"). Berlioz wrote to tell Joachim of Brahms's success, adding that "he made a great impression on me the other day at Brindel's [*sic*] with his Scherzo and his Adagio. Thank you for introducing me to this shy, audacious young man who has taken it into his head to write new music. He will have much to endure."

There is an ironic aptness in the friendly encounter in Leipzig between one of the most feared composers of the "new order" and the musician who in a few years' time would be being hailed by the Leipzig camp as the apostolic leader destined to save music from the Weimar heresies and restore it to the truth of the old beliefs. It shows Berlioz in the position which, given his temperament and principles, was the only one that could be his, that of an independent spirit owing allegiance to no one group, master of no one but himself – an artist for whom schools, exclusive sects, national partisanship were a tyranny and an irrelevance and an obstacle to music's essential freedom. Although to find his music accepted in Germany was an honour he could never prize too highly, what could it matter to him that he was of a different nationality? Such a concept, in the sphere of modern music, had no meaning.

Certainly it would have been to his advantage to learn to speak German. One can say that he should have, and that it was very "French" of him not to. Quite apart from that, his determinedly independent stance – he was well aware – made him vulnerable: it risked isolating him from the main musical currents of the day. But, holding the views he held, he could not do otherwise.

His refusal (in Barzun's words) to "bind himself or anyone else" to a single artistic creed or programme is the underlying message of an article, half humorous, that he wrote while in Leipzig in response to a commission from his friend J. C. Lobe, editor of the local *Fliegende Blätter für Musik*. Lobe invited him to give his thoughts on the current state of music and on its future, excusing him only from speaking about its past. Berlioz thanked him "for that dispensation". Even so it would take "a great big doctoral tome" to contain such a summary, and the *Fliegende Blätter* ("Flying Leaves") would be dragged down by the weight and unable to fly. Besides, "what the art of music is today you know, nor can you suppose that I don't. What it will be, neither of us knows." Berlioz, sidestepping Lobe's request, concludes that what he is being asked for is his "certified profession of faith", such as conscientious voters ask of candidates canvassing for the honour of representing them in the National Assembly. "Only, I have not the least ambition to represent anybody, to be deputy, senator, consul or even burgomaster. And if I were aspiring to consular rank I think that to win the votes, not of the People but of my fellow-practitioners, I could not do better than emulate Marcus Coriolanus, make my way to the Forum and, baring my breast, show the wounds I received defending the fatherland." As for the things he loves and those he hates or despises, Lobe knows what they are and no doubt feels the same, so what need of spelling them out? He goes on: "Music is the most poetic, the most powerful, the most vital of all the arts. It should also be the freest, but it is not yet so. Hence our artistic tribulations, our despairing sacrifices, our weariness unto death."

Berlioz then develops the parable of modern music as Andromeda chained to her rock, waiting for Perseus to deliver her from the monster. The monster is Routine. His days are numbered; he is getting old, his teeth are a wreck, his nails blunted, and his heavy paws slip as he tries to clamber up the rock. Perseus, when he rescues the maiden, restores her unravished to Greece, ignoring the jeers of the satyrs in their caves who point out that in chains she is easier to possess. The true lover of music has no wish to possess her: he will receive, not take. If he could he would give her wings to make her freer still.

> That, sir, is all the profession of faith I can make, and I make it solely to prove that I have a faith. So many professors have none! I have one, unfortunately, which I have too long proclaimed from the housetops in pious obedience to the gospels. How wrong the proverb is which says "Faith is the only salvation." On the contrary, faith is the only perdition, and by faith I shall be damned. I will merely add what my Galilean friend Griepenkerl puts at the bottom of all his letters to me: "E pur si muove."* Don't denounce me to the Inquisition!

He made a related point in a letter sent from Bremen to Adolphe Duchêne, apropos of the complaint in a Hanover journal that Weber, Beethoven and Mozart – German masters gifted with qualities lacking in Berlioz – never obtained such triumphs in Germany. "It's no longer musical *routine* that I'm up against but *Teutonism*."

For the time being, German or French, he could only enjoy the luxury of his success and look forward to more of the same in the spring, when engagements beckoned in Dresden, Hanover, Oldenburg and Eberfeld. David spoke of putting on *Benvenuto Cellini* in Leipzig. And preparations were set in hand to give both the Requiem and the Te Deum at a festival in Brunswick, with forces assembled from choruses and orchestras in the region.

The most important immediate and long-term result of the Leipzig visit, however, was Berlioz's decision to write a sequel to *The Flight into Egypt*. Only a month before, he had told von Donop in so many words that his composing days were over. Now he was in full flow again. A month after his return to Paris in mid-December he was able to report to Liszt that *The Arrival at Sais* (as it came to be called) was three quarters done and, but for the proofs of *Faust*, would be already finished.

The Flight into Egypt was, suddenly, the talk of the moment. Berlioz arrived in Paris to find, to his alarm, that the Société Ste Cécile had announced it for its concert on 18 December, under the uncertain bow of Seghers. Thanks to a hurriedly convened rehearsal at his apartment with conductor and singer (Chaperon of the Opéra-Comique) and the loan of his own set of parts, the work was performed adequately and

---

* "Yet it does move": Galileo's aside after his recantation.

actually encored. The *Ménestrel* reported it as carrying off the honours of the evening. Had Paris suffered a change of heart?

Paris had not. Not content with being congenitally sceptical about his vaunted successes beyond the Rhine, it was now conspiring to undermine them. During Berlioz's absence in Germany a Polish count, Tadeusz Tyzkiewicz, brought an action against the Opéra for mutilation of *Der Freischütz*. The Count claimed that the performance for which he had bought a ticket did not correspond to the work of that name and constituted a breach of faith, and he sought to force the director, Roqueplan, to give an uncut performance of the work and to incur a fine for every day he failed to do so. The case was dismissed – as Roqueplan's counsel observed, how could one seriously bring an action for musical malfeasance with a name like Tyzkiewicz? – and costs were awarded against the Count, who was merely reimbursed 7 francs for his ticket. But while it lasted the French press was full of it; and Berlioz, with a mixture of amusement, fury and incredulity, found himself named by counsel for the Opéra as the person responsible for the cuts. He, who had "spent fifteen years" of his life as a critic "combating correctors, curtailers and mutilators, and when *Freischütz* was staged at the Opéra twelve years ago prevented its being shorn of a single note and had it performed in full for the first time in France", was now accused of having mutilated it – "when the cuts being complained of were made while I was out of the country, without my being notified and by a director with whom I was not on speaking terms!"

Even so, knowing the Parisian public's profound lack of interest in all such matters, he might have let it pass but for the fact that musical journals in Germany had picked up reports of the trial and were treating him as a brigand and a profaner of the German heritage. Though their indignation did them honour, this was not to be endured. He promptly wrote a detailed disavowal, explaining that he was "as little implicated in the indecent assault on Weber's score" as were the editors of the musical journals or M. Tyzkiewicz himself, and got it printed in the *Débats*, the *Gazette* and the *Siècle*; he then fired off letters to German friends and colleagues, enclosing a copy and begging them to have it reproduced as widely as possible. The *Neue Zeitschrift* duly published it on 1 January 1854; but on the 6th he had the mortification of receiving a letter from a Leipzig student who accused him of sacrilege against the great German masters, and who followed it up with another purporting to come from the entire student body – the same people who had treated him as a hero only a month before. Berlioz had enemies enough among the old guard of Germany without having them added to unnecessarily. He riposted with a letter written in both sorrow and anger. His correspondent, it seemed, read the libels but not their refutation. "I would have you know that I am as innocent of all this as you are. I would also have you know that I have given more proof of my religious respect for the great German masters than you could in your entire life, and that on this score I am beyond the reach of such false accusations and superficial judgements. You held it to be your duty to write me your second letter in the name of your colleagues, the students of Leipzig. I trust you will also consider it a duty to communicate to them my reply. As for my works and your musical opinions, I have nothing to say. It is not for me to argue their value."

Germany, since his return, continued to preoccupy him in other ways. He was busy collecting all the chorus parts of the Requiem that he could lay hands on, including those belonging to Baron Taylor's Association des Artistes Musiciens, for the forthcoming Brunswick performance. In the end it did not take place; but meanwhile the large parcel he sent Griepenkerl had managed to get lost in the post: a month later there was still no trace of it. He was also sending copies of his scores to various German friends and admirers: the Requiem and *Sara la baigneuse* to David (who, however, reported that the ladies of his choir drew the line at singing about a young girl's "lovely neck and foot"); and *La captive* and one of the *Nuits d'été* songs to Nieper, to translate into German for Mme Nottès to sing. Liszt was once again active on behalf of *Benvenuto Cellini*, investigating possible German publishers and performances (Dresden seemed the likeliest place), and drawing from his friend a fresh effusion of gratitude: "You are in every way a man apart. I have known it for a long time, but such prodigies are so rare that one cannot help being amazed."

Dresden, where he was due in April, was the indirect cause of further vexation in the Paris press. *La France musicale* printed a report that he was soon to be appointed kapellmeister to the Saxon court, and it was repeated in other papers. Berlioz rebutted it in a sardonic letter to the *Gazette* in which he let it be known that he would leave his beloved France only in order to take up the post of director of music to the Queen of the Hovas in Madagascar. The squib, aimed at Paris, misfired: he was accused by the Berlin *Stadtzeitung* of insulting Germany.

Happily, many in Germany were still vigorously promoting his cause.

Cornelius, who had translated *The Flight into Egypt*, published a long and flattering article about him in the *Neue Berliner Musikzeitung*. ("He overwhelms me," Berlioz told Liszt. "You transmit your bad qualities to everyone around you.") It was thanks to such encouragement that he was composing again. In contrast, his position in Paris remained precarious. The sudden death of his old friend and employer Armand Bertin, on 14 January, was a professional as well as a personal blow. It removed one of his most loyal supporters. Until Armand's landscape-painter brother Edouard agreed to take over as director of the *Débats* the future of the paper, and therefore of its chief music critic, was in doubt.

Up in Montmartre Harriet's grip on life was weakening. To her other disabilities were added failing vision and a painful eye infection. Berlioz himself was ill for most of February and part of March with vomiting, persistent diarrhoea and kidney infection. He kept to the house, correcting the *Faust* proofs and struggling out only for the premières of Meyerbeer's *L'étoile du nord* and Adrien Boieldieu's *La fille invisible*. Never (he told d'Ortigue a few weeks before) had he felt less disposed to write feuilletons. "Life is slipping away . . . I long to *work* – and I am forced to *toil* in order to live." Yet the review of *L'étoile du nord* is one of his most amusing. The Opéra-Comique not being under the direct protection of the Emperor, he was freer to say what he really thought. But though the underlined "un bel *opéra nouveau*" is ironic, he seems to have been genuinely impressed by the score, and not merely admiring of Meyerbeer's adroitness in fashioning the stock ingredients of the genre into a work guaranteed to make its publisher's fortune, or the patient determination with which the composer devoted months of rehearsal to securing a first-rate performance from a second-rate company. To the expert fatuities of Scribe's libretto, on the other hand, he gave no quarter; or rather, he demolished them with the deadlier weapon of laughter. His blow-by-blow account of the plot – Peter the Great living incognito as a drunken, quarrelsome carpenter among the schnapps-happy peasants and gipsies of Finland and Russia – is a masterpiece of facetious humour.

Ill as he was, he prepared for the forthcoming visit to Germany. His first engagement was in Hanover, where he was due towards the end of March. He was thus still in Paris at the beginning of the month when Harriet died.

Berlioz to Adèle

Montmartre, Monday 6 March 1854

Dear Sister

Harriet died last Friday 4th [3rd] March. Louis had spent four days with us and left for Calais on the Wednesday, so happily she saw him again. I had just left her a few hours before her death, and I returned ten minutes after she expired, without pain, without the least movement.

The last rites were yesterday.

I had to arrange everything myself – the town hall, the burial. I feel wretched today. Her state was appalling; the paralysis was complicated by erysipelas; she breathed only with great difficulty. She had become a formless mass of flesh . . . and beside her the radiant portrait I had given her last year, where she looks as she was, with her great inspired eyes. And now no more.

My friends have come to my aid. A large number of men of letters and artists with Baron Taylor at their head escorted her to Montmartre cemetery, near to the sad house, in dazzling sunshine, with the view over the Plain of St Denis.

I didn't go with the procession – I stayed in the garden. I had gone through too much the evening before, looking for the pastor, M. Haussmann, who lives in the Faubourg St Germain. By one of those brutal chances that often happen, the cab had to go past the Odéon Theatre where I saw her for the first time, twenty-seven years before, when the élite of the intelligentsia of Paris, that is of the world, was at her feet – the Odéon where I suffered so much. We could neither live together nor part; we worked out this agonizing problem over the last ten years. We caused each other so much suffering.

I have just come from the cemetery again, I am alone; she rests on the side of the hill, facing north, towards England, to which she never wanted to go back.

I wrote to poor Louis yesterday, and am going to write to him again.

How horrible life is! Everything comes back to me all at once, the sweet memories and the bitter. Her great qualities, her cruel demands, her injustice, but also her genius and her misfortunes. I can only cry horrible, appalling! She made me understand Shakespeare and great dramatic art, she endured hardship with me, she never hesitated when our livelihood had to be risked on some musical enterprise – but then, in complete contrast to her courage, she always opposed my leaving Paris, she wouldn't let me travel: if I had not resorted to extreme measures I should still be almost unknown in Europe. And her *motiveless* jealousy, which ended by being the cause of all that has changed my life.

My dear sister, I wish I could see you. But it's impossible. And I'm leaving for Germany again in a month's time; I've an engagement in Dresden, the King of Saxony's intendant wrote to me yesterday – I'm expected. I've no stomach for anything, I care about music and the rest about as little as . . .

I've kept her hair. I'm alone here in the big drawing-room next to her deserted room. The garden's beginning to break into bud. Oh, to forget, to forget! What can relieve me of memory, blot out all those pages from the book and volume of my heart? We live so long! And there is Louis, so tall he no longer resembles the dear child I used to watch running about these garden paths. The daguerrotype portrait of him aged twelve is here. I feel as if I have lost the child, and the tall young man I kissed six days ago cannot console me for the loss of the other.

Don't be surprised if I sound strange – I could give you many other instances of the same kind. Oh fatal faculty to call back the past! That is the reason why I have so cruelly succeeded in arousing similar impressions through some of my works.

And yet everyone says we must be thankful to see her sufferings come to an end; it was a dreadful existence. I have nothing but praise for the three women who looked after her.

Farewell, dear sister. I congratulate you on having been able to save Mathilde.* I send you my love. Be careful how you write to me: your letter can help me bear up or cast me down the more. Farewell.

Fortunately, there is Time, which never stops and which crushes and kills everything, sorrows and all.

Berlioz to Louis

Monday 6 March 1854

My poor dear Louis, you will have received my letter of yesterday, by now you know everything. I'm here all alone in the big drawing-room at Montmartre, next to her deserted room. I've just come again from the cemetery, where I laid two wreaths on her grave, one for you and one for me. I don't know what I'm doing – why I've come back here.

---

* Mathilde, Adèle's niece, had been seriously ill with typhoid.

The servants are staying for a few days. They're putting everything in order, and I shall try to see that what there is yields the maximum for you. I've kept her hair. Don't lose this little pin that I gave her. You will never know how much each of us suffered at the other's hands, your mother and I, yet it was those very sufferings which bound us so closely to one another. At least she saw you before she died. I had been there the evening before, the day after your departure, and I came back ten minutes after she breathed her last, gently and without pain. She has been set free. I love you, dear son. Yesterday evening we talked for a long time about you, in this sad garden, Alexis Bertchtold and I. How I long to see you become a reasonable man! How happy I should be to know that you were sure of yourself.

I shall now be able to help you more than in the past, but must still take precautions so that you don't squander the money. Alexis himself thinks the same. At the moment I have no resources. My difficulties will last for at least another six months, for I have to pay the doctor, and the sale of the furniture will produce practically nothing. [. . .] I shall have to borrow money for the trip to Germany.

Berlioz to Adèle

Saturday 11 March [1854]

Dear, wonderful Sister

Impossible to go even as far as Châlons. I have to work every evening till midnight correcting a mountain of proofs [of *The Damnation of Faust*] which piled up during the few days last week when I didn't work. It all has to be ready in time for my departure, and I have only three weeks left.

Yes, you are so right to say I must be thankful that I was here. I cannot bear to think of her dying far from me. It would have been too dreadful. At least she saw her son, who perhaps might not have come had I been away. She saw me a few hours before she died; she knew I was there near her. Thank you for your letter and all the marks of affection it contains. Instead of shunning the place that brings back such cruel memories, I go there daily. Every morning I go to the cemetery, and I suffer less than if I didn't. It's as if I'm going to see her in her own home once more – only, now she's more peaceful.

Louis to Adèle

[March 1854]

My dear Aunt

Several times since the death of my poor mother I've taken up my pen to write to you; but the harrowing memories it would have aroused always held me back. Poor mother! What a sad existence she had! Oh no, we must not be sorry she is no more. Now that she sleeps in the tomb she no longer suffers. I've always lived far from her. While still a child I went away to Rouen. From that time on I saw her only at long intervals, and during the brief times I spent with her I had to hide my heartbreak behind a smiling face. Sometimes my courage failed me, and then I left abruptly, which in the eyes of some people made me pass for a bad son. Poor fools, you had no idea what I was going through. After that, I went away to sea, and saw her only two or three times. What joy for her when I came back, but how sad it was for me! She had to breathe her last far from me, nor could I follow her to her last resting-place, any more than I could ever support her on my arm, any more than I could ever admire her on the stage.

At last, all is over. I have only my father left, poor kind father. I could not love him more than I did before. I love him just as he does me, and God alone knows the depth of affection there is between us. I know I have sometimes been a trial to him; but I am very young, dear Aunt, and young people go through terrible times. Since my loss I have felt a new strength, and I am going to use it to avoid causing any kind of distress to him who is dearest to me in all the world; and, God willing, he will be proud of his son. I cannot think of the day when he has to leave this earth. Since I reached the age of reason I have known that that day will be my last. The thread of my life is but the extension of my father's. If it is cut, the two lives will end.

Berlioz to Louis

Paris, Thursday 23 March 1854

Dear friend

Your letter has brought me an unexpected joy. So there you are with 70 francs a month. If you manage to change your practice with money you can surely save a little. Let me know if you think that sooner or later you can redeem your watch, which I'm afraid you pawned in Le Havre in the days of your folly. It was given you by my father. If you can't get it back I will buy you another out of the money I have for you. I've just had a watch-chain made for you with your mother's hair, I should like you to look after it with the greatest care. I have also had a bracelet made for my sister, and I'm keeping the rest. I won't be able to send your linen till Saturday the 25th, because of the formalities which have to be gone through and which the feuilleton that I'm doing today and tomorrow obliges me to postpone till the end of the week. I imagine you have seen the charming things Janin said about your poor mother in his feuilleton last Monday, and the sensitive way he alluded to my *Romeo and Juliet*, quoting the words of the funeral march, "Strew flowers."

Journal des débats

Monday 20 March 1854

How sadly, how swiftly they pass, those legendary divinities, frail children of Shakespeare and Corneille. Alas, it was not so very long ago – we were young then, filled with the thoughtless pride of youth – that Juliet, one summer evening on her balcony above the Verona road, with Romeo at her side, trembling with rapture, listened and heard the nightingale, and the lark, the herald of the morn. She listened with a pale, dreamy intensity, a bewitching fire in her half-averted eyes. And her voice! a golden voice, pure and vibrant, a voice through which the language and genius of Shakespeare in all their rich, perennial vitality and force found superb utterance. When she moved, when she spoke, her charm mastered us. A whole society stirred to the magic of this woman.

She was barely twenty, she was called Miss Smithson, and she conquered as of right the hearts and minds of that audience on whom the light of the new truth shone. All unknowingly she became a new passion, a poem unheard till then, an embodied revolution. She pointed the way for Madame Dorval, Frédéric Lemaître, Malibran, Victor Hugo, Berlioz. She was called Juliet; she was called Ophelia, and was the inspiration for Delacroix himself when he drew his touching picture – Ophelia shown in the act of falling, one hand slipping from the branch to which it still clings, while the other clutches to her fair bosom the last sad garland, the hem of her robe about to meet the rising waters, around her a weeping landscape and far off, hastening towards her, the wave that will engulf her in her sodden clothes and "pull the poor wretch from her melodious lay to muddy death".

She was called, lastly, this admirable and touching Miss Smithson, by another name (Malibran bore it too): Desdemona, and the Moor, as he embraced her, called her his "fair warrior". I see her now just as she was then, white-faced as the Venetian woman in [Hugo's] *Angelo, Tyrant of Padua*. She is alone, listening to the rain and the moaning of the wind, the beautiful lass, enchanting and doomed, whom Shakespeare out of love and respect lapped round with his noblest poetry. She is alone, and afraid; an unutterable unease troubles the depths of her soul. Her arms are bare, a corner of her white shoulder is visible. The bareness had something pure and sanctified about it, the holiness of the sacrificial victim, the woman about to die. Miss Smithson was marvellous in this scene. She was more like a vision from on high than a creature of our clay. And now she is dead. She died a week ago, still dreaming of the glory that comes so swiftly and so swiftly fades. What images lie there, what worlds of poignant regret! In my youth they sang a chorus in homage to Juliet Capulet, a sad funeral march, with the same cry going through it, repeated again and again: "Strew flowers, strew flowers!" So they passed into the gloomy crypt where Juliet slept, and the dark melody ran its course, telling of the chill and terror of those mortuary vaults. "Strew flowers, strew flowers, she is dead", the dirge sang, like an Aeschylean hymn. "Juliet is dead (strew flowers). Death lies on her like an untimely frost (strew flowers). Our instruments to melancholy bells are turned, our wedding cheer to a sad burial feast, our bridal flowers serve for a buried corpse!"   (J. J.)

Liszt to Berlioz

[March 1854]

She inspired you, you loved her, you sang of her, her task was done.

20

The Childhood of Christ

Harriet's long martyrdom was at an end.

What Peter Raby calls Liszt's "sensitive compliment, since it implies an enduring value and significance for her life as an artist" has not been viewed with universal favour – one commentator estimates that "romantic egotism could go no further" – but Berlioz was grateful for it, on his behalf and on hers. A strength of their relationship had always been their respect for one another as artists. Whatever differences separated them they were united in that, and in their conviction that if life was to be lived for the highest ends then there was none higher than art. The corollary, that the true artist must expect to suffer, was for the Romantics an article of faith. Suffering was "the badge of all their tribe"; it was a source of their being as artists. "Who going through the vale of misery use it for a well," the psalmist said. Or, to quote one of their favourite texts, Goethe's "Wer nie sein Brot mit Thränen ass": "They who never ate their bread with tears, never lay weeping through a night's long agony – they know ye not, ye Heavenly Powers." But Harriet had been excluded from art, except by proxy through his music. His sense of the heartbreaking waste sharpened as he remembered how in the privacy of their home she would enthral him by reciting passages from roles – Cordelia, Desdemona – that he had not seen her play and she would never play again. It added to the overmastering pity which in the midst of his sorrow and guilt swept over him at the fresh recognition of all she had had to endure. In the turmoil of his feelings he turned to Shakespeare – Shakespeare whom Harriet Smithson had first revealed to him, thereby changing his life. Shakespeare is the all-knowing, all-compassionate deity – "our father which art in heaven, if there is a heaven" – to whose hands he commends her spirit and his in the anguished, exalted passage of the *Memoirs* which recounts her death. "Feux et tonnerres!": the exclamation that bursts from him as he contemplates the tragedy of her life is, surely not coincidentally, the same as Faust's when he hears of the catastrophe that through him has fallen on Marguerite. Wittingly or not, by marrying her – so that she settled in France – he had brought it about.

At least he was now released from having to watch her slow decline into speechlessness and immobility – though that itself left a hole in his existence. The regular visits to Montmartre had ceased; he no longer had her to care for. At least too there was no more necessity to live a double life: the fiction, kept up in Germany and England, that Harriet was dead and Marie his sole consort was now fact. And with the expenses of the apartment in the Rue St Vincent off his back – once the lease was disposed of and all the legal formalities satisfied – he could look forward to greater freedom of action. It is no accident that the following winter would see him putting on concerts in Paris on his own account for the first time in eight years. But, for the present, such considerations could have little meaning.

Though he had been afraid he would have no stomach for a tour of Germany, he knew it was what he needed. Arriving in Hanover, with Marie, on the morning of 28 March, he began rehearsing next day and at once came to life. He had been engaged to conduct a few pieces at the final subscription concert of the season, but the King overruled the committee and insisted on the whole programme's being devoted to his music. Some of the local press grumbled at the music of the masters being ousted in favour of a "note-spinner", and the response of the audience to the Fantastic Symphony and the Love Scene and Scherzo from *Romeo* was much less positive than it had been to *Faust* the previous autumn. Joachim, writing to Liszt, complained that the public – "more materialistic" in Hanover than anywhere else – were "as slow and cautious as snails": confronted with Berlioz's "energy" they could only "draw in their horns". But Berlioz was so delighted with the playing and with the enthusiasm of the King and Queen (the Queen, who had asked for the Love Scene, announced proudly at the final rehearsal that she now knew it by heart) that he hardly minded. Having such a large number of society ladies occupying the centre of the stalls "always made for a cold audience". What was important was that he was among artists who were with him in what he did. "It's a marvellous orchestra," he told Liszt on the eve of the concert, "except for lacking timpanists who can play and can count their rests. We have two harps, exquisite wind players, and a superb string section – they sing with such *soul!*" Rose, the first oboe, played the cor anglais "like an archangel". To Baron Donop he confessed that hearing the adagio from *Romeo* and "its elder brother" the Scène aux champs in the same concert had been an overwhelming experience; and in a long letter to his uncle Félix Marmion a few days later he spoke of Harriet's death and of the feelings the concert had brought flooding back:

> Expected though it was, the separation has been terrible. We had remained friends; and then, the bonds of artistic sympathy had always united us in spite of everything. She had such an intelligent understanding of the poetic world, poor Harriet. She divined what she had never learned. And she revealed Shakespeare to me – and God knows how great an influence such a revelation has had and will continue to have on my career. It's incalculable – infinite.
>
> Hence the impossibility – at once cruel and cherished – of forgetting. Everything reminds me of her. Last Saturday again, conducting a scene from my *Romeo and Juliet* symphony in Hanover, I was shattered by the mixture of lovely and harrowing memories the music recalled. And my Fantastic Symphony, which figured on the same programme, and which was the cause of our marriage. I could apply Dante's words to it: "Galeotto fù il libro."*

On 2 April the travellers went east to Brunswick, where on the 8th Berlioz conducted three works (including, for the first time, the revised *Corsair* overture) at a concert directed by the kapellmeister Karl Müller. From there he had intended to make a detour to Weimar and pay a courtesy call on the new Grand Duke, the young Carl Friedrich, who had succeeded his father Carl Alexander the year before; but he found he was wanted at once in Dresden, to prepare the performances of *Faust* and *Romeo* planned for the 22nd and 29th.

Dresden was in many ways the greatest of all his successes in Germany. It had by no means been the artistic high point of the 1843 tour; and his hopes cannot have been raised by the discovery that Krebs, the Hamburg kapellmeister who told him ten years before that it would have been better for art if he had never been born, was now installed there. But he must have heard that the orchestra had improved thanks to a new generation of players: his letter to Lipinski, after listing the

---

* "The book was our Gallehault" – the intermediary between Launcelot and Guinevere, over whose story Paolo and Francesca first fell in love.

forces required, ended, "I am immensely keen that we should do something altogether exceptional in Dresden." They did. He had a moment of panic that *The Damnation of Faust* would not be ready in time (the chorus-master, Fischer, was incompetent and the newly engraved parts were full of mistakes). It passed, however, and the performance four days later, on 22 April, was by a long way the best the work had yet received.

Not for the first time in Germany there were complaints that he had vandalized a national monument. The critic of the *Sächsische Constitutionelle Zeitung* accused him of slandering Mephistopheles by making him trick Faust (Mephistopheles, Berlioz informed Griepenkerl, was "an honest and upright devil who keeps his word"); and the same reviewer protested at the slur on the morals of German students, depicted as "roaming the town looking for girls", which they never did. Karl Banck, in the *Dresdener Journal*, though admitting Berlioz's exceptional prowess as a conductor, denounced the work as "a mutilation and a disgrace". "He allowed me a few pieces like the Ride to the Abyss, the Sylphs' Chorus and the March," wrote Berlioz to Liszt, but found the music as a whole "totally lacking in ideas". "I am tempted to emulate Mlle Clauss, who asked Davison for piano lessons so as to have the support of the *Times* and the *Musical World*. Perhaps those gentlemen will be so good as to give me a few lessons in composition."

Other journals were loud in their praise. In any case, as he well knew, such disparagements were normal irritants, if not indeed a measure of his growing popularity in progressive circles in Germany, inevitably stimulating greater opposition. What mattered was the wholehearted response of the audience, the skill and power of the young orchestra – he had "never seen one like it" – and the approval of the Dresden management. Baron von Lüttichau, the intendant, came on stage at the end of *Faust* and asked him to give a repeat performance, which took place three days later, on the 25th. His second programme, given on the 29th and consisting of *Romeo*, *The Flight into Egypt*, and the *Roman Carnival* and *Benvenuto Cellini* overtures, was also repeated. The day after the first *Faust*, Lüttichau called on him at the Gold'ner Engel and (Berlioz told Liszt), "having showered me with compliments, said quite explicitly – words which coincide with your predictions – 'It's really first-rate, our company, isn't it? A pity it's not directed as it ought to be. You would be the man to give it life'." Lüttichau returned to the subject more than once during the visit. Between them, he said, they could make Dresden the musical centre of Germany. When Berlioz objected that the post was not vacant, he replied: "It could become so."

The excitement aroused by Berlioz and his music among all but the most conservative Dresdeners is captured in the account which Hans von Bülow, who was there visiting his mother, sent to Liszt:

I am delighted to be able to give you the best possible news of an event which you cannot have closer to your heart than I, who have felt my enthusiasm for Berlioz grow at every concert. Last night's [29 April] was one of the most dazzling triumphs that he has enjoyed in Germany. A packed house, full to overflowing with all that is most artistically elegant in Germany, received the composer with the greatest warmth on his entry. The audience punctuated every piece on the programme with sustained applause, with *rinforzandos* not heard in Dresden since Wagner's flight; they encored the third movement of the Sacred Mystery, and clapped with frenzy when a laurel wreath thrown from one of the upper circle boxes landed at the composer's feet. In spite of their exhaustion the orchestra surpassed themselves in the last piece, the overture to *Cellini*. A special ovation, prepared in secret by the younger members of the orchestra, brought this memorable evening to a close amid wild applause from the audience. [. . .] M. de Lüttichau immediately begged him to favour them with a repeat of the last concert, and it will take place tomorrow, Monday. So – four concerts instead of two, and the almost certain prospect of the production of *Cellini*, to which the performance of the opera's two overtures will have contributed not a little. Mr Banck's perfidious critique had an adverse effect on the repeat of *Faust*; at the second concert the audience was not large. On the other hand those who were there were the élite of the public, musically speaking, and they were very demonstrative. The remarkable crescendo in the numbers of the audience, which gave the lie so strikingly yesterday to the press, would have been evident at the repeat of *Faust* but for those insects, the critics. The whole orchestra and the singers are head over ears with enthusiasm. They are delighted that they can now rate their talents and capabilities as they deserve, thanks to this incomparable conductor who has made them feel the shame and sterility of the last five or six years. Beginning with M. de Lüttichau, who is positively beaming, to an extent I should never have believed him capable of, they would all like to keep Berlioz in Dresden as their conductor. Everyone has played his part and there is an excellent spirit everywhere. By the end of the first rehearsal M. Berlioz had destroyed every vestige of opposition and won round the most refractory (and God only knows how many there were!). In sum, the predictions you made when you were in Dresden last year might very well be soon fulfilled. M. de Lüttichau has already offered more than hints to M. Berlioz. Among other things, he's asked him to prepare and conduct Gluck's *Orpheus*, which M. de L. intends to stage next season. And on M. Berlioz's remarking that there was no spare place in Dresden, everything being well filled, he answered in these pretty clear words: "Who knows?"

Can you believe it? A week ago Krebs, at the Catholic Church, bitterly reproached the orchestra, actually reprimanded them, for having played so magnificently under the baton of a "foreigner"! What a public humiliation for the local conductors, under whose direction the orchestra had never managed to show such zeal and ardour. [. . .] At some point it would perhaps be as well to remind M. Berlioz that the earliest and warmest allies he has found in Dresden, among the orchestra and the public, belong to the Wagner party and have long belonged to it. These words – pointless, perhaps – are prompted by the memory of some of Mme Berlioz's chatter on the subject of Richard Wagner, which has irritated me considerably. But she is, on the whole, an admirable woman, with just the weakness of being a bit of a chatterbox and of telling a lot of tales which it would be a mistake to pay any attention to.

[6 May] At present I am enjoying to the full the echoes of Berlioz's intoxicating music, with which I spent three weeks that I should be very sorry to see erased from the programme of my life. I can gauge the depth of my admiration and sympathy for the works of this master now that I really grasp them; I understand and appreciate his music in all the consistency of its individuality, and his flights of genius, which struck me from the first, no longer shine in the darkness, for that is now dispersed. You don't yet know the last two parts of *Faust*. How I envy you! The fourth in particular is magnificent in inspiration, sublime in originality.

Berlioz, with Marie, left Dresden on 2 May, escorted to the train by a deputation from the company, and arrived at Weimar station at one o'clock on the morning of the 3rd to find a similar contingent waiting for him. The four-day visit to Weimar has not left much trace, but it had important consequences. Plans were laid for concerts the following winter, by when his oratorio – now expanding to a tripartite work – should be finished and ready for performance. He talked much with Princess Carolyne and strengthened a friendship which would have a profound influence on his future as a composer. He was certainly received by the new grand duke – Liszt had been insistent on the point – and wore the handsome Cross of the White Falcon which the grand duke's father had bestowed on him eighteen months before but which he had had to have sent on from Paris, having forgotten to bring it. He saw Cornelius, who on the 4th wrote to tell his mother that he was richer by 25 thalers, which "good old Berlioz has given me, in five shining gold pieces, for the translation of his *Flight into Egypt*". Cornelius added that he was now to translate its sequel (*The Arrival at Sais*, completed in Dresden), and then went on: "I'll tell you a secret, only don't breathe a word about it: there is a chance that Berlioz will be appointed *Hofkapellmeister* in Dresden, where he has just given four brilliant concerts. This is of great significance for our entire party."

Berlioz returned to Paris exhilarated by the experience, full of plans for fresh tours of Germany, and already dreaming of a complete German edition of his works. He had actually made a fair amount of money. It was, once again, thanks to "cette chère Allemagne" that he lived. Early in June he told Morel that if he finished his sacred trilogy in time he would perform it later that summer in Munich and then in Dresden. A return visit to Brunswick in September was also being discussed.

The question of his appointment to the Dresden chapel was still a live issue in October – at any rate he believed it was – as he completed the final chapter of his *Memoirs*, where it is mentioned: though his Paris friends were opposed to it (he wrote) he might well end up settling there. Yet in the event the previous nine months, from August 1853 to April 1854, would prove to have been the high-water mark of his presence in Germany. The Dresden idea came to nothing; already by November, when Lüttichau wrote to him about a possible production of *Cellini* the following year he made no reference to it, and Berlioz's sense of propriety did not allow him to raise it himself. Reissiger, the incumbent, who had talked of retiring (he had held the post since 1828), stayed on. All in all, in the second half of the 1850s the number of Berlioz's German engagements fell off steeply. He did not return to Hanover for the complete *Romeo and Juliet* which the King wanted him to give in the spring of 1855. He never went back to Dresden, to conduct *Orpheus* or *The Childhood of Christ* or *Cellini* (which was not given there till the 1880s), nor to Leipzig, nor even to Brunswick. There were two further "Berlioz Weeks" in Weimar in 1855 and 1856. But by 1857 only the annual concert in Baden remained.

For this, I think, there was no single reason – certainly not any lessening of interest and commitment among his partisans (Cornelius' diaries and letters, for instance, are unswerving in the belief that "Wagner and Berlioz are the main representatives of modern music") – but, rather, several separate, mainly unconnected factors. One was the gradual undermining of Liszt's position in Weimar, culminating in his resignation as director of the theatre in 1858, and more generally the declining impetus of the whole avant-garde movement associated with him. We should never forget the passionate antagonism Liszt's ideas and activities, and anyone identified with them, aroused among what was after all the majority of prominent German musicians. That his influence had increased, was increasing and ought to be diminished – that, in Alan Walker's words, "the man had to be stopped" – was an article of faith with the old guard: the devilish trinity – Liszt, Wagner, Berlioz – was threatening to destroy music as they knew and loved it; the Weimar menace was spreading its tentacles: Liszt's disciple Bülow had a foothold in Berlin, and the Leipzig journal *Neue Zeitschrift für Musik*, Schumann's child, was in the hands of a paid-up Lisztian, Franz Brendel. For Dresden to fall to one of the most notorious non-musicians of the gang, and a foreigner, a Frenchman at that, was unthinkable.

As Cornelius said, it would have indeed been a victory for Liszt's party to have Berlioz established there – which is, very likely, why it didn't happen. We can easily imagine the manoeuvring that went on behind the scenes to prevent his being appointed. The critic Karl Banck for one would have been dead against it. So would Wagner's successor, assistant kapellmeister Krebs (who was conspicuously absent from the dinner Lüttichau gave in Berlioz's honour after the second performance of *Faust*). And Reissiger, though he had been aimiability itself and had done everything in his power to help the visiting conductor, can hardly have been keen to make way for a rival for whom the orchestra played so much better than it played for him. Lüttichau may simply have come to the conclusion that his plan was too fraught with difficulties to succeed.

In short, Berlioz's very successes only stimulated the opposition – opposition which, given the natural conservatism of musicians and by virtue of Germany's being the most musically articulate and organized of all countries, was particularly resistant to innovation. Think of the long-lasting hatred of Wagner's music in official circles. Think of Hanslick declaring, of Mahler's Second Symphony, "One of us is mad, and it isn't me."

It is notable that nearly a year elapsed between Berlioz's being informed, in April 1854, that the King of Hanover had conferred on him the Order of the Guelphs and his receiving it. (Only one musician had been so honoured before – Marschner, who was the Hanover kapellmeister.) All the same he would certainly have continued to make regular visits to Germany but for two other reasons. One – easily overlooked but of perhaps crucial importance – was the breakdown of his health, which made him less and less able to face the strain of touring, even for the satisfactions and rewards it brought. The other was his decision – itself the offspring of Germany – to consecrate his remaining strength to composing a work, bigger than anything he had yet produced, which should be his musical testament.

By the summer of 1854 the centre of gravity of his life was shifting back to Paris. He was persuaded by his friends to cancel a planned trip to Munich, very much at the last minute, so that he could apply for the vacancy that had occurred in the music section of the Academy of Fine Arts (through Halévy's being appointed permanent secretary). He did so although not going to Munich meant forfeiting, among other things, a handsome fee, and with the virtual certainty that he would not be elected. There could be, for him, no question of honour either, given the sort of people who were elected and those, like Balzac, who weren't; but the money – 1,500 francs a year – was worth getting hold of, the prestige could be useful, and not to stand would jeopardize his long-term chances. In consequence, instead of conducting his music in south Germany he spent a hot and fruitless week mobilizing people to canvass for him, writing endless letters, rushing about Paris paying the obligatory courtesy calls on a regiment of academicians, and soliciting votes from composers whom he trusted as he would "adders fanged"; at the end of which Clapisson was elected. "So – till the next vacancy. I am resolved to go on with the same patience as Eugène Delacroix, or as M. Abel de Pujol who applied ten times. [Ambroise] Thomas' play-acting was pitiful and did not deceive me for a second. Reber showed me every mark of genuine sympathy, and the three other musicians [Auber, Adam and Carafa] every mark of genuine dislike. Halévy campaigned for me with one hand; I don't know what he did with the other."

The summer also saw him dabbling in the mire of imperial artistic politics – for how else is one to characterize *L'impériale*, the cantata which he interrupted his oratorio to compose, to a text of abject sycophancy and "absurd pomp" even by the normal standards of such offerings? Berlioz persisted in admiring Louis-Napoleon (and never lost his fascination with Bonaparte), but hardly, surely, to the point of swallowing the poet's comparing the resurgence of the Napoleonic dynasty to the birth of the Messiah. Perhaps he was moved to accept the text by the fact that its author, Captain Achille Lafon, was on active service in the Crimea – Louis Berlioz's new ship, the *Phlégéton*, was involved in the war (to his father's intense anxiety), having been assigned to the Baltic as part of a diversionary attack just about the time Lafon read "L'impériale" to an approving Emperor. Perhaps the Emperor himself suggested that he set it to music. The resulting score, resounding if commonplace, does something to dignify the words. There is some fine sonorous writing for the brass, and the cumulative treatment of the double chorus and large orchestra culminates in a stirring conclusion in which repeated shouts of "Vive l'Empéreur" alternate with wind triplets above a torrent of tremolo strings, while timpàni and side-drums thunder out the French army tattoo known as "Aux champs". But the 1844 *Hymne à la France* revives the Revolutionary tradition of large-scale public music more convincingly. *L'impériale*, despite its more ambitious structure, bears the marks of haste. Berlioz dashed it off with a view to performance at a ceremonial concert on 15 August, the "fête de l'Empéreur" (Napoleon I's birthday, a day of national thanksgiving under the First Empire, had been adopted by the Second). Twelve thousand musicians were to be assembled in the Palais de l'Industrie, the new "Crystal Palace" being constructed at the southern end of the Champs-Elysées for the Great Exhibition which Napoleon III was planning for the following year – France's answer to England. As the time for the concert approached, the building was still without its glass roof, however, and the performance was switched to the Tuileries Gardens, where it was given by a military band of two hundred, without *L'impériale*, and in the absence of the Emperor, who was visiting Queen Victoria.

Berlioz was not there either. One real benefit of not going to Munich was that it left him free to take a holiday. He had again been suffering from diarrhoea and vomiting, which looked like the first symptoms of cholera, and he was worrying himself to distraction about Louis. So, having completed his round of academic visits, he took the train from the Gare St Lazare to Motteville and from there a carriage to St Valery en Caux, the fishing village on the Normandy coast west of Dieppe, where the narrow-mouthed harbour runs deep inland between wooded cliffs, and where he had been two summers before. He stayed a week, and would have stayed longer but for reading in a local paper that the *Phlégéton* was taking part in the bombardment of the fortress of Bomarsund – news which brought him hurrying back to Paris in quest of further information. To his infinite relief there was a letter waiting for him, part of it written after the capture of the fort. Louis was safe and well. ("God keep you, my dear Morel, from ever experiencing such emotions.") Berlioz could well imagine "what the poor child must have felt – he who has never been in so much as a skirmish – finding himself for the first time in that hell that is called a naval battle."

A fortnight later he travelled to Dauphiné for the long-delayed division of the estate. On 13 September Joséphine Suat wrote to her cousin Mathilde Pal: "Uncle Hector arrived today. You can imagine how happy we were to see him after six years' absence. This morning we went to meet him at the station [Vienne] because he had written to Mama to warn her of his arrival, but he wasn't there – he arrived by the 11 o'clock boat. The journey had given him a migraine, but I hope a good night's rest will cure that. [. . .] We are very happy, dear Mathilde, because my uncle has kept his promise and dedicated one of his recent works to us [Part 1 of *The Childhood of Christ*]. Today he tried to get me to play him something, but as you can well imagine I refused – I merely showed him my music, so at least his ears were spared."

He was in Dauphiné for about two weeks. A letter from Mathilde to an unnamed aunt describes the family reunion as less than animated. "We're none of us in much of a state to enjoy ourselves. Uncle Suat is not very well, Uncle Hector has rheumatism which gives him a lot of pain, Aunt Marmion is prostrated by her fear of cholera, and my father [Camille Pal] as cross-grained as can be. Only Uncle Marmion is in better health than ever." "The pleasure of being all together" (she adds, apparently without irony) "makes us put up with this depressing place. The weather is lovely and sunny." A few days later the succession was settled. Berlioz's portion was the Ferme du Nant at Le Chuzeau, on the outskirts of La Côte, and Le Jacques at Murianette, the property on the green hillside far above the Isère, facing Mont St Eynard, which had belonged to Grandfather Marmion: on the 24th he wrote out and signed a document empowering Camille Pal to administer it for him. From now on, despite low rents, the income from the two properties would ease the financial pressures of his life.

When the family was not in council he spent as much time as he could with his sister. It was his first visit to La Côte since his father's death, and with Adèle, amid the "millions of things" they had saved up to say to one another, he relived those harrowing days and found, as he had expected, an irresistible charm even in their saddest evocations of the past. He certainly went to Murianette to look over the farm and refresh the memories that rooted him in that "incomparable landscape", for in a letter to Adèle a year later he spoke of his "incurable passion for the Isère valley" and of his longing to be "this very moment in the woods of Le Jacques" instead of stuck in Paris examining musical instruments for the Exhibition. He renewed contact with his boyhood friend Casimir Faure, and found that they felt the same mutual affection and regard as in the old days.

> La Côte, Tuesday evening
>
> My dear Casimir
>
> Our conversation of this morning is still going on in my head, or rather my heart. I was delighted, though not surprised, to discover in you once again that warmth of spirit which used to exert so strong but gentle a hold on me. You attracted me as electrified substances attract iron filings – I could have said, as the magnet [*aimant*] attracts, but I was afraid of a pun, though you are really and fundamentally loving [*aimant*]. Thank you for the affectionate feelings you still have for me, which not even your afflictions have cooled.

One other subject that was discussed with Adèle was the advisability of his remarrying. Félix Marmion had raised it with his nephew on a visit to Paris earlier that summer. Like him, Adèle was in favour of it, provided Louis' interests were safeguarded. So were his Paris friends. Few of them particularly liked Marie Recio; but it was better that he should regularize his position now that the traditional period of mourning was over. On 19 October, a couple of weeks after his return to Paris, they were married in the Eglise de la Trinité, not far from their apartment, and then in a civil ceremony at a notary's in the Rue St Anne, the street where Le Sueur had lived, long ago. John Ella, in Paris after a walking tour in France and Switzerland, wrote to tell Hallé in Manchester about it: "I was one of the four *témoins* at the wedding of Berlioz, and I am happy to say that he is in better spirits, with only one wife to provide for."

A week later Berlioz wrote to Louis, in Cherbourg:

> Paris, 26 October 1854
>
> I was so sad this morning, my dear Louis. I dreamed last night that we were at La Côte together, walking in the little garden. Not knowing where you were, the dream affected me painfully. Your note, which the porter gave me as I was going out, set my heart at rest. I'm writing to you in the midst of my errands, in my room at the Conservatoire, in the hope that this letter will be more fortunate than the last three, which apparently – from your last but one sent from Kiel – never reached you. I wrote to Kiel on receipt of your letter. Anyway, I hope we'll see you, if only for a few days. I have some news to give you which probably won't surprise you, and which I told my sister and my uncle of in advance, on my recent visit to La Côte. I have remarried. This relationship, as you will realize, had by its duration become indissoluble; I could neither live alone nor abandon the person who had been living with me for fourteen years. [...] Your interests, you may be sure, have been taken care of. If I die first, my wife inherits no more than a quarter of my meagre fortune, and I know she intends to make it revert to you in her will. She brought me her furniture as dowry; its value is greater than we thought, but it will return to her if I die before she does. All this has been settled in accordance with my brother-in-law's [Suat's] instructions. I don't doubt that if you retain any animosity towards Mlle Recio or any disagreeable memories, you will hide them in the depths of your soul for love of me. The wedding took place quietly, without either fuss or secrecy. If you write to me about it, don't say anything I can't show my wife – I want there to be no dark places in my domestic life. [...]
>
> Farewell, dear son and friend, dear Louis. Love me as I love you.

Louis answered "with warmth of heart and good sense", his father told Adèle. What he really thought is conveyed perhaps more accurately by a letter from Félix Marmion's wife to Mathilde. Louis, on a visit to the south, spoke of "his many grievances against her ladyship. But he has forgiven her everything. He understands that the marriage was necessary. Hector needs someone to watch over his health and his purse, and that woman performs the double role perfectly."

On the eve of the wedding, in his office at the Conservatoire, Berlioz wrote what at that stage he intended to be the last pages of his *Memoirs*. Ella may have thought him in better spirits. But the mood of these final paragraphs is scornful and sweepingly dismissive. The writer has given up all illusions about his native city, yet remains defiantly unreconciled to his lot. Though he touches on his recent successes abroad and utters "fervent thanks to holy Germany where the worship of art still burns pure and strong, to generous England, to Russia which saved me, to my good friends in France, to all the rare spirits and noble hearts, of whatever nation, that I have known and have been blessed in knowing", the main thrust is a sustained attack on Paris and its philistinism, its commercialism, its anti-musical opera-houses, its lack of a single good public concert hall, its dedication to the sort of trash "for which Rabelais had a name",* and its supreme indifference to his music. He mentions the symphony dreamed and suppressed and the idea for a big opera which has been haunting him for the past three years but which he hopes, as with the symphony, he will have the strength to resist writing. Paris is a city where he can "do nothing", where he is considered lucky to be a feuilletonist – "the only task, many would say, that I was sent into the world to fulfil".

He was busy enough as feuilletonist that autumn, finding his "ten columns harder to tackle than the Russian columns on the banks of the Alma", though the effort hardly shows. His five *Débats* articles include a tribute to Sontag, dead of cholera in Mexico City, a critique of Gounod's *La nonne sanglante*, searching but sympathetic (earlier, in response to an embarrassed letter from Gounod about the *Nun*, he had begged him not to feel any awkwardness on his account, and reminded him how much pleasure his *Sapho* had given him), and a description of his holiday at St Valery. The pretext for the latter was the decision by the leading critics not to review the opening of the Opéra season, after the new administration announced it was suspending free passes. "All the most powerful (goose) quills held counsel in the foyer," Berlioz told Bülow, "and we resolved unanimously to declare a 'war of silence' on the Opéra", and hence to ignore the trumpeted return of Mme Stoltz

---

* "torcheculatif" – "arse-wiper".

to the Paris stage. After discussing the Escudiers' new life of Rossini (with a side-swipe at Stendhal) and a performance of Palestrina's Missa Papae Marcelli by the Choeurs Niedermeyer, the article ended, "The rest is silence."

Such writing shows no decline in vigour nor, one would think, in spirits. Yet the same mood of angry defiance as in the *Memoirs* fuels the letter he wrote Adèle on 27 August, just after his failure in the Institute election:

> My passion for music, or rather for Art, grows beyond all bounds. I am conscious of faculties greater than ever – to which material obstacles prevent my giving outlet. At this moment I actually feel ill from the inability to satisfy my love of art. How otherwise? In France? Nothing – nothing. Among the governing classes indifference and idiocy, crude industrialism, barbarism, among the rich ignorance and brutality, and vulgar preoccupations everywhere. [. . .] And then my damnable feuilleton, which obliges me to busy myself with so many villainous commonplaces, and even to speak of them often with a kind of deference!
>
> Oh how I breathed with delight, a week ago, stretched out on the high cliffs of St Valery with the calm sea lapping three hundred feet below my grassy couch! What marvellous sunsets, what peace, what pure air up there on those lofty heights!

Only that kind of passionate intercourse with Nature can make him forget for an instant his love of art and the sorrows it causes him. But the effect is always to revive them more intensely.

> I am obsessed by plans for compositions, grand, bold plans which I am certain I could bring off. Then, on the point of beginning, I stop: "Why undertake such a work," I think, "and become fatally attached to it, only to create more anguish for myself when it's finished (if I think it beautiful), and see it given over to infants or beasts, or buried alive? The mightiest productions of the human spirit can find neither hearth nor home, at the present time. The English talk of raising a statue four hundred feet high to Shakespeare – and they don't have a single theatre where the masterpieces of this demigod are worthily performed. It's a belated impulse of vanity on their part – the sense of admiration is neither general nor real.
>
> I recently finished my sacred trilogy on *The Childhood of Christ*. I don't know when I shall be able to hear it, nor whether I shall be able

to introduce it to those few people of intelligence in Paris who are well disposed towards me. Most of it is so simple, so restrained in colour and form, that I don't see how I could find singers here capable of performing it faithfully – they're all more or less infected with the false and trivial taste that's admired in the opera houses. Can you imagine the part of the Virgin Mary sung by a virtuoso with a throat thirsting for roulades, or by a prima donna dressed to kill who must have 'effective' cavatinas which allow her to let herself go and shake her locks and show off her fine arms? Fortunately I shall find what I need in Germany.

But he found it in Paris.

Much as Berlioz longed for recognition at home he had no great hope of getting it. He had learned to be sceptical of the fair prospects his friends were forever dangling in front of him. The latest – a performance of the Te Deum in St Eustache in May 1855, as a kind of unofficial launching of the coming Exhibition – looked promising, but he was not banking on it: "I know my Paris too well." The success of *The Childhood of Christ* in Paris was the last thing he expected. The very existence of the work was a kind of accident: beginning with the little organ piece written at the corner of a card-table for his friend Duc's album, and then growing slowly, almost haphazardly, as if it knew, itself, that it could come into the world only by stealth. When systematic composition was finally undertaken, after a long period of self-imposed dearth, it was with the certainty that in Germany at any rate it would be given a sympathetic hearing and, besides, would not lose him money. Paris had not even been in question; he was still resolved never again to put on a major work at his own risk. The sequel to *The Flight into Egypt*, *The Arrival at Sais*, which he wrote in response to the former's reception in Leipzig, was intended for German audiences. So was *Herod's Dream*, the last composed but the first in the sequence of the triptych, added at the request of Beale, who came over from London to urge him to do it. (Chorley had also taken an interest and suggested one or two ideas.) London indeed was another place where the work might have a future. But Paris – the disaster of *The Damnation of Faust* was still too painful, and the unavailability of the Conservatoire Hall (which had contributed to it) too serious a stumbling-block. Not until quite late on did the notion come to him that after all it would be nice to give it in Paris, even to gamble some money on it, so that he could introduce his "petite sainteté" to the few hundred supporters who still believed in him.

The letter of 27 August to Adèle, just quoted, is the first inkling of a change of heart. By the second half of October he had begun to organize a performance – on which, however, he had "no intention of risking any money". A week later he could no longer "resist the temptation *whatever it costs me* to perform it for my Paris friends before leaving for Germany". Two weeks after that he was resigned to "losing eight or nine hundred francs", but told himself that the experience of trying the work out would be "*useful for Germany*".

In fact he made a profit of nearly 500. The house, that Sunday afternoon, 10 December, was full to overflowing (many were turned away), making a repeat a foregone conclusion. After the second performance, on Christmas Eve, he was 1,100 francs to the good. In numbers, maybe, it didn't equal what he had achieved in the past – the Salle Herz held only six hundred, so that even three capacity audiences (the third performance, given for charity, took place on 28 January) amounted to barely two thirds of those that had heard *Romeo and Juliet* fifteen years before. But what audiences! No one had seen such emotion at a concert. "The whole hall," wrote Cosima Liszt to her father, "was stirred to the depths"; Berlioz's work had "a gigantic success". On his first entry, after the Mendelssohn piano trio which opened the concert, he was applauded for several minutes. At the end – reported Léon Gatayès in Dumas' journal the *Mousquetaire* – he had to come back twenty times. Clapping and cheering broke out during many of the movements. At the second performance the enthusiasm was at least as great. The final bars of The Repose of the Holy Family were drowned in loud cries of *bis*; he had to come to the front of the platform and call out, "We're going to play the piece again, but this time please allow it to finish." And, contrary to what he had feared, his Opéra-Comique soloists – Jourdan (Narrator), Depassio (Herod), Mme Meillet (Marie), Meillet (Joseph), Battaille (Père de famille) – entered fully into the spirit of the work. The orchestra and choir were equally devoted: they offered to do the second performance for nothing, though he did not feel able to accept.

Never, not even for *Romeo*, had he had so many congratulatory letters: from Gounod ("it's full of an angelic purity and unction that recall what the blessed Fra Angelico dreamed and painted. [. . .] May God's holy angels give you all that you have imagined for them"); from Auguste Barbier, from a deeply moved Rosine Stoltz who insisted on singing *La captive* gratis at the second and third performances, from

Alphonse Robert, from d'Ortigue ("I'm still in tears, yesterday I wept like a child – Barbier will tell you, we were sitting together"); from Count Tyzkiewicz, the young Pole who had unwittingly caused him so much vexation over the Opéra's mutilated *Freischütz*; from Humbert Ferrand, who thought it "a celestial work, above everything else that you have done"; from the bedridden Heine ("I may soon have to quit the Champs-Elysées for the other, mythological ones, which will probably be less amusing") – Heine's wife Mathilde had come back in a rapturous state and wanted to hear it again; from Duc, who reported that the connoisseur of ancient music had quite forgotten her annoyance at the Ducré hoax* and had "applauded the modern composer whole-heartedly"; from Ambroise Thomas; from Adolphe Adam himself. Even his opponents, it seemed, were coming round. "Berlioz," said the *Moniteur officiel*, "has harvested in one day the fruit of many years of struggle and patient hard work." The newspaper reports were rapturous, with the sole exceptions of Scudo in the *Revue des deux mondes* ("chaotic, impotent") and Jouvin in *Figaro*. But a scathing review from Scudo was the touchstone of artistic achievement. "An enemy like that," Lecourt said, was "a gift from the gods." More curious to read (Lecourt added) were his new friends, who imagined that he had moved towards them, when it was they that had moved. "Without realizing it they have laid down their arms."

Immensely gratifying as it was, Berlioz could not help finding his triumph two-edged. It stirred the mocker, the Mephistopheles in him. So he had finally become respectable, had he? He was judged to have made progress, was extolled for the very qualities he had always been told he lacked: charm, gentleness, economy of means, simplicity, melodiousness – all this thanks to a work which, fond though he was of it, was in his view not in the same class as *Romeo* or *Faust*. It had been well received because it was easier, less developed and the subject more immediately accessible – that was all. "What a lot of people there will be in the kingdom of heaven if all the poor in spirit are there," he jested to Adolphe Samuel after reading the reviews. The success of his "little oratorio", he told the Princess, was "insulting to its older brothers". Though he could not deny that "really" he was "overjoyed", he understood the irritation the painter Salvator Rosa felt when people kept praising his smaller landscapes: "sempre piccoli paesi!" *The Childhood*

* See above, p. 451.

of Christ was a "piccolo paese" compared to *The Damnation of Faust*, which Paris had rejected, or the still unperformed Te Deum.

Even more galling was the suggestion that he, of all people, had "changed" or had adapted his style to suit the taste of the public. All that had changed was the subject – as Gautier, no doubt prompted by the composer, argued in an article which appeared after most of the other reviews, and in which he asked rhetorically, "Has the composer radically altered his manner, as they are saying in explanation of his success? Not at all. Hector Berlioz is the same as he was. Only, having to depict a series of simple religious scenes, he has employed the quiet colours and gentle, transparent tones of his musical palette. It is the difference between the styles of Dante's *Inferno* and of his *Paradiso*."

To Berlioz this was axiomatic. The identical preoccupation dictated *The Childhood of Christ* as dictated his *grandi paesi*: "passionate expression", which he defined as "expression bent on reproducing the essence of its subject, even when that subject is the opposite of passion, and tender feelings are being expressed or the most profound calm". He remained, as always, a dramatist. Though not conceived for the stage, and tending to portray its characters in the stylized manner (as he put it) "of the old illuminated missals", the work was structured as a series of tableaux, presenting the human elements of the story – the uneasy might of Rome, the world-weariness of Herod, the fanaticism of the soothsayers, the joys and griefs of Jesus' parents, the busy welcome of the Ishmaelite household – and juxtaposing them, like the scenes in the *Damnation*, in a way that looks forward to cinema.

An example is the transition from Herod's rage to the calm of the Bethlehem stable. We see as though in angry close-up the fear-distorted faces of Herod and the soothsayers, like faces in a Bosch or Brueghel crucifixion. Then the nightmare fades and the manger comes into focus. In the epilogue it is again as though the glowing family circle of the Ishmaelites were growing faint and blurring before our eyes. The moment has come for the narrator to draw the timeless moral; and the composer, having shown us the loving-kindness of his good Samaritans, tracks away from the scene, causes it to fade by means of a series of quiet, still unisons surrounded by silence. Their purpose is to separate us from the scenes we have been witnessing, to make them recede across the centuries and return to the ancient past from which he called them up. The distancing process, by removing the audience from the dramatic action, achieves the necessary transition to the final meditation on the meaning of the Christmas story.

Everything is visualized. When the Holy Family, having trudged across the desert, reach Egypt hungry and exhausted and beg for shelter, the musical imagery brings the scene palpably before us. The plaintive viola motif, the wailing oboe and cor anglais (an instrument whose "ancient" sound colours much of the score), the fragmentary violins, the tremor of cellos and basses, Mary's panting utterances, Joseph's long, swaying melody constantly returning, Gluck-like, on itself, the tap of the drums as he timidly knocks, the shouts of "Get away, filthy Jews!" which interrupt the prevailing 3/8 metre – all this combines to make a vivid and poignant "expression of the subject". Nor is it only the refugees from intolerance and persecution that arouse the composer's compassionate understanding. He illuminates the loneliness of the tormented Herod and the forlornness of the soothsayers, whose gloomy choruses and weird cabbalistic dance in 7/4 time embody the sense that superstition is at once sinister and ridiculous, to be pitied.

Such music was not unfamiliar to those who had followed Berlioz over the years. What surprised them, though it shouldn't have done (they had heard the Pilgrims' March and the Offertorium), were the Shepherds' Farewell and the trio for two flutes and harp (an idea borrowed from Gounod's *Sapho*), the little overture representing the shepherds gathering at the manger, the purity of the scene at the oasis, the hushed beauty and intricate workmanship of the unaccompanied chorus which closed the work, the far-off angelic voices heard at the end of each part. How did they fit with the accepted image of Berlioz? Here was the well-known apostle of the grandiose and the grotesque using a handful of instruments to the manner born: Part 2 was written for chamber orchestra with half a dozen woodwind (no bassoons, and no horns); Part 3 required only slightly bigger forces; and even Part 1, in which trombones appeared, was sparingly scored.

Though the public was wrong in believing all this to be uncharacteristic of him, it was right in sensing something special about the achievement. In composing the work he may not have repudiated his past methods and principles; but they would not have been enough to carry him successfully though the hazardous task he had set himself. The subject was full of pitfalls; it bristled with occasions for false sentiment and refined vulgarity (as so much nineteenth-century religious art exemplifies). *The Childhood of Christ*, miraculously, is free of such defects. Maybe something of the beautiful austerity of the first inspiration was sacrificed when the original three-movement piece was expanded into a full-length oratorio. Even so, the music avoids taking the short step into sentimentality, and in the most perilous places, like the scene in the stable, never seems in danger of doing so. Its naïvety is unforced, spontaneous.

The explanation lies in the nature of Berlioz's style. The purity the subject demanded did not have to be sought; the archaic flavour that permeates much of the score came naturally to him. It was in his musical blood, nourished by the folk music of his native Dauphiné, the noëls and other popular chants he heard in his boyhood, and by the biblical oratorios of Le Sueur, his teacher. Le Sueur's interest in modal music – uncommon in that period – was passed on to his pupil. Berlioz had often resorted to modal inflexions for particular expressive effect; so that when the subject suggested a more systematic use of them he could meet the need without falling into pastiche: it was an extension of his style. By the time *The Flight into Egypt* was composed the development of music had left such things so far behind that he thought it prudent to guard against misrepresentation by printing an asterisk alongside the theme of the overture, with a warning that the seventh of the scale was to be read as a natural, not as the usual sharp. The piece is certainly untypical of its time. But it is pure Berlioz, as are the long, chaste lines and sweet serenity of the scene where the Holy Family rests in the shade of three palm trees, while the child sleeps surrounded by angels.

How are we to account for the sharpness of vision and the unclouded truthfulness of feeling that made the music of this scene as fresh as the spring water gushing up out of the desert? Beyond the possession of a style able to encompass such simple sublimities lay something else: the memory of childhood beliefs once central to his life, and of music experienced as drama in the context of religious ceremony. By now he had long ceased to be a Christian in any conventional sense of the word. But he could recall that time as though it were yesterday. More and more he was returning to his roots. "I am beginning to live only in the past," he told Adèle not long after completing the work. The intensity of recollected emotion was such that in composing it he could momentarily re-enter a world in which the events and personages of the Christmas story, as they stamped themselves on a hypersensitive child, were once again vibrantly alive. The pang of regret gave an added sharpness to the retelling. No sentimental recovery of belief (like Faust's) was involved. It

was an act of piety in the Roman sense. His mind remained sceptical.
But his imagination believed. He remembered what it was like to have
faith. And at the end, having re-enacted the age-old myth and stepped
out of the magic circle, he could only pay tribute to the power of the
Christian message and, agnostic that he was, bow before the mystery
of Christ's birth and death.

The success of *The Childhood of Christ* had immediate repercussions
– most immediately an engagement for three concerts at the Brussels
Opera. Offers also came from England and Germany as well as from
Paris, where both the Opéra-Comique and the Théâtre-Italien wanted
to give it. In all, the work had eight performances in its first four months
– far more than any other of his major compositions. From Brunswick
his friend Gustave Roger, the tenor, wrote to tell him of the excitement
the news had aroused in Germany.

Dear Berlioz

Bravo, bravo, bravo!
Bravo, bravissimo!
Ssimo, ssimo, mo, mo!
Mo, mo, mo, mo, mo, more

as long as Cherubini's Amens and in every rhythm and tone, from the
jew's harp and the piccolo to the gunboat: that is the symphony our
hearts have been performing since the birth of Christ! It's the Te Deum
of all Germany, and of your friends whose congratulations I've undertaken to convey to you. They're hoping, they're waiting for you. The
King of Hanover told me so the day before yesterday. And since you've
taken it on yourself to bring the Christ back to life, you will be "crucified",
and by the Gentiles: in the best sense of the word your Cross awaits you
[the Order of the Guelphs].

Everything about it is allegorical and heaven-sent. The Christ is Art,
so old, so enslaved that you have had to regenerate it. The Holy Spirit?
Well, that's your prerogative. Is there not someone in your house called
Marie? Ave Maria – I hail you, you are full of grace, though you can
make no claim to the title of Virgin – the Holy Spirit has seen to that;
he has many sacrileges to lay to his charge!

Who takes the role of the Ass? The public, that worthy beast, delighted
to have fresh sweet hay instead of those grubby Italian leftovers, those

musical thistles, in its manger. And tell me, who is the Ox? It's the *servum pecus* [Horace's "slavish herd"] of enemies and eunuchs, the hostile critics; it's the Academy, shoving its pale muzzle and great vacant eye over the crib. The Magi? That's us, it's England, Germany, placing gifts of gold, myrrh and frankincense at your feet.

To round it off: they say you've come down a little from Mount Sinai. No longer in the burning bush of Horeb, amid lightning and thunder, but with unclouded clarity has Genius, the Unknown, revealed itself. In a word, God is made Man.

So, thank you – though I shall "hang myself for not being there". St Jourdan is indeed fortunate. But it had to be: did they not always tell me that Christ was baptized in the Jourdan?

Good-bye, dear friend, and *laus in aeternum*. For you and for Madame my most reverential Alleluias.

More important were the long-term consequences. *The Childhood of Christ* got Berlioz back into the way of composing. It made him realize that he was not done with writing music – that the arguments against doing so were not overwhelming after all. Even if the project which had been gathering in his imagination since the early 1850s posed other and incomparably more formidable problems, it could not but find encouragement in the resounding success of the trilogy and above all in the fact that it had happened in France. By his own confession he was turning more and more to the past, reliving his boyhood and the ancient worlds he had inhabited – there where lay the springs of his being and the experiences that determined the course his existence as an artist would take. How could *The Childhood of Christ* not be followed by *The Trojans*? Already we hear unconscious anticipations of the opera. The dim fabric of divided lower strings descending chromatically through almost an octave as Herod recounts his dream clearly prefigures the music of the scene where the shade of Hector appears to Aeneas during the sack of Troy. The torrent of chromatic chords which evokes the massacre of the innocents will be heard again when Cassandra foresees the "river of blood" engulfing the city. And I shall never forget my surprise, when rehearsing *The Childhood of Christ* with orchestra alone, at hearing for a second the pulsating octave Cs of the *Trojans* Septet in the final ensemble before the epilogue (a sound normally covered by the voices). Such repetitions are rare with Berlioz, for whom each work normally marks a new beginning. It is as though the opera were insisting on making him aware of its presence.

At the Villa Altenburg in the new year he discussed the idea with Liszt and the Princess. He may well have hinted at it during his brief visit in May of the previous year. This time, however, it was in the open. When he spoke of the powerful objections to composing a work of that kind, they insisted he must ignore them: Paris might be hopeless, but there was always Weimar; Liszt would be more than happy, would be delighted to produce it there. The Princess gave notice that she would return to the attack. "I am being encouraged, urged, bullied even," wrote Berlioz in February 1855 to his fellow-critic Fiorentino the day after leaving Weimar, "to write a great theatrical machine. I need to consult you about it; we must go on with the conversation we began in the Rue St Georges about the material impossibility of such an undertaking, given the habits of the Paris Opéra." As yet he was still not persuaded. But the seed had been planted.

2 1

Private Passions

For the moment, he could do nothing about it. In 1855 Berlioz was exceptionally busy: visits not only to Weimar and Gotha but to Brussels and London as well, concerts in Paris, and work as an assessor at the Exhibition (having been a member of the English jury on musical instruments he could hardly refuse to serve on the French). There was also the labour of seeing his remaining scores – *The Childhood of Christ*, *Lélio*, the Te Deum, *L'impériale* – through the press, and a revised edition of the *Treatise* to prepare, including a chapter on new instruments, prompted by what he heard at the Exhibition, and a section on "The Art of the Conductor", commissioned by the London publisher Novello.

In the end Berlioz did not give a concert in Gotha (it was put off till February 1856) nor in Hanover either. But the fortnight he and Marie spent in Weimar fully maintained the excitement of the visit two years before. As before, the orchestra was augmented by players from nearby Erfurt and Gotha and the opera chorus joined by the local amateur society to make a choir of more than a hundred voices. At the court concert which he conducted in the sumptuous hall of the Ducal Palace on 17 February Liszt played his E flat piano concerto – the work's première – in a programme otherwise devoted to Berlioz's music: the Fête from *Romeo*, *La captive* sung by Emilie Genast, the sylphs' scene from *Faust* and, from *Benvenuto Cellini*, the goldsmiths' hymn to their craft. Four nights later, after two rehearsals a day, Berlioz gave a monster concert in the theatre: *The Childhood of Christ*, in Cornelius' translation (with Liszt playing the melodium part on the piano), followed by the Fantastic Symphony and its sequel *The Return to Life*, also translated by Cornelius.

It was Berlioz who suggested they add the monodrama to the programme already planned. His reawakened interest in the complete

Episode in the Life of an Artist, not heard since the mid-1830s, surely originated in a wish to pay tribute to the memory of Harriet Smithson, whose work it had pre-eminently been. The monodrama, revised for this performance, now contained not only a modified and slightly shorter spoken text but also a new ending which, after the concluding *Tempest* music, reintroduced the symphony's *idée fixe*, Harriet's theme, on pianissimo violins against the Artist's murmured "once more", before closing on a soft chord for flutes and clarinets and the words "encore, et pour toujours". The intimate family associations were emphasized by the dedication of the published score to Louis.

For the first time the work was performed as he had conceived it, as a music-theatre piece, with the Artist (played by the young Weimar actor Grans) on a forestage built over the orchestra pit, and musicians and conductor invisible on a special rostrum behind the lowered curtain, the veiled sound giving the effect of the music's taking place in the mind of the Artist, and the curtain rising only for the final number, the *Tempest* Fantasy – at which point the Artist was represented as emerging from his dreams and nightmares and directing his students in a rehearsal of his new composition. Berlioz wrote him a speech to deliver to the assembled and now visible chorus and orchestra, in the manner of Hamlet's homily to the actors. At the end the curtain was lowered again, the Artist was given over once more to "sweet silent thought", and from the hidden orchestra came the last faint echoes of the *idée fixe*.

Lélio, ou le retour à la vie (its title in the published score) may well strike us, despite the interesting things in it, as Berlioz's most *outré* and least convincing work. For him, though, on stage behind the curtain with so many friends and well-wishers – Liszt playing the piano part and the tam-tam in the Chorus of Shades and Madame Pohl the harp – he could only give himself to it uncritically and relive all that had once gone to creating it; the Aeolian Harp in particular, that strange, potent frisson of authentic early Berlioz, moved him inexpressibly. The audience, seemingly untroubled by fastidious doubts, loved it all too. At the end he was given a tumultuous reception, redoubled when Emilie Genast, who had sung Mary in the oratorio, presented him with a crown of laurels in the name of the whole company.

Once again Liszt's Weimar took him to its heart. The New Weimar Association, founded a few months earlier under Liszt's presidency to give formal embodiment to the futurists and their struggle for the soul of Germany, had elected him one of its half-dozen out-of-town members.* It held a banquet for him – also attended by Brendel, Griepenkerl and one or two visiting kapellmeisters – at which Joachim Raff pronounced a eulogy in Latin and the politically radical guitar-playing poet Hoffmann von Fallersleben ("homonym of the great Fantastical", as Berlioz called him) improvised Latin verses in his honour, ending

> Vivas, crescas, floreas
> Hospes germanorum,
> Et amicus maneas
> Neo-Wimarorum.†

Raff set the ode to music then and there, and having been copied on scraps of paper it was performed at sight by the guests. The evening concluded with Cornelius reciting a comic poem in imitation of a Russian speaking bad German, each verse ending with the line "Hats off to Berlioz". Next night, despite twenty-two degrees of frost and a foot and a half of snow, Raff's chorus was sung beneath Berlioz's window by members of the club. The day before he left Weimar he thanked Hoffmann in a note adapted from the opening lines of Book 2 of the *Aeneid*, where Aeneas at the court of Dido begins his account of the fall of Troy:

> The hall fell silent and all eyes were on him
> As from his lofty couch Father Hoffmann began:
> "At last you have fulfilled our desire".‡ And many other things that have
>   touched me
> deeply and that I shall never forget.

The two-week stay passed in a whirl of music-making and sociability. On the day after the court concert – the eighteenth birthday of the Princess's daughter Marie – the visitors attended a convivial gathering at the Altenburg, at which lunch was followed by an informal evening concert. Liszt played his transcendental study *Mazeppa*. Berlioz inscribed in Princess Marie's album a fifty-bar "Waltz sung by the wind

---

* The other five were Bülow, Joachim, Klindworth, Rudolph Viole and Wagner.
† "May you live, grow, flourish, / Guest of the Germans, / And remain the friend / Of the New-Weimarians."
‡ "Nostrum desiderium / Tandem implevisti": the opening lines of Hoffmann's ode.

in the chimneys of one of my castles in Spain"; the piece was entirely in chromatic notes, and in a friendly dig at Liszt's harmonic style he added a postscript asking him to be so good as to write the bass. He dined five times at court and was invited back by the Grand Duchess Sophie for a revival of *Benvenuto Cellini* next year; and he had his portrait painted by a local artist, Lauchert. Luck was on his side too. If Nicholas I of Russia had died ten days earlier the concerts would have been cancelled because of official court mourning: the Dowager Grand Duchess was the Tsar's sister.

His star was at its zenith; he was among kindred spirits, the friend of the New-Weimarians, progressive Germany's honoured guest. In an article published in the *Revue et gazette musicale* Cornelius called him a German in all but name and said that Weimar was now his home town (and *La captive* worth a whole opera). Cornelius told his mother that even if he became a successful opera composer he would continue to work for Berlioz, "because he is an exceptional spirit, whose friendship means more to me than winning the lottery, which any ass can do. Moreover, he is generous, like all true artists. He had hardly arrived here when he was handing me 30 bright thalers in payment of my latest translation, adding 'avec mille amitiés reconnaissantes' – whereas I got Rubinstein's 30 thalers only after a lot of trouble and anxious waiting and as if it were a special favour on his part."

New Weimar could not have enough of his music. A third concert was offered. It had to be declined, however: by the time it could take place he would be back in Paris. His admirers must be content with his promise to return in 1856. They were at the station to see him off and, as the train began to move, flung armfuls of flowers through the window of the compartment.

Brussels, to which Berlioz and Marie travelled from Paris on 12 March, was a different story. By contrast with Weimar, where he made a good profit, the three performances of *The Childhood of Christ* were poorly attended: well-to-do Belgians, disapproving of a sacred work being given in a theatre during Lent, stayed away. Those who came – "artists and foreigners", Berlioz reported – seem in the main to have liked the work; but the performances, except for the last, were wretched affairs. At the first, only two of the soloists, Joseph (Carman) and the Narrator (Audran), knew their roles: the rest blundered badly. Mlle Dobré (Mary) went wrong in the second duet, and at one point the Père de famille, Barielle, dried up completely: Berlioz had to sing the part from the conductor's rostrum, to the puzzlement of the audience who couldn't make out where the sound was coming from. The orchestra, though friendly and willing, inflicted "Huron-like tortures" on the composer; everything not on the down-beat threw them into confusion. The two flutes in the trio played "like Spanish cowherds", and the horns were so feeble that he had to boost them with cornets and trumpets at the climax of the Massacre of the Innocents chorus (an addition which he retained when the full score and parts were published that autumn, though he does not seem to have included them in subsequent Parisian and German performances). His chief musical satisfaction was the successful use of an electric metronome to keep the distant angelic choir in time with the main body of the performers – a mechanism patented by a Belgian inventor called Verbrugghen, useful in a period when offstage bands and choruses were a commonplace. Berlioz who had long been imagining such a device – it figured prominently in the massed choral performances described in his futuristic novella *Euphonia* – was enthusiastic about it (despite the disadvantage of an audible click, which he persuaded Verbrugghen to eliminate) and wrote to Belloni recommending it to Verdi for his *Sicilian Vespers*, due to be produced at the Opéra that summer.

Otherwise the pleasures of the two weeks in Brussels were social and personal. One was his growing intimacy with the young composer and critic Adolphe Samuel, who was a devoted admirer. Another was the friendship of the French historian and philosopher Edgar Quinet, in exile since Louis-Napoléon's coup, who wrote to a friend a few weeks later to describe their meeting:

> The other day, to my joy, I received a visit from Berlioz, whom I didn't know but whom I have always admired in the teeth of the ungodly. I admire and love this artist who follows his muse without worrying about flattering the public. I love the disinterested single combat against easy success. Berlioz himself attracts me as much as his music; his strength of will, his energy, his pride, are to me the finest of symphonies. He had my admiration, he leaves with my friendship. What a fine work the life of a true artist is! But it wasn't all just conversation. I twice heard his oratorio *The Childhood of Christ*, with full orchestra. There are songs in it such as Raphael might have created.

Another famous nineteenth-century writer crossed his path again in Brussels. On his first evening at the Hôtel de Saxe he sat opposite

George Eliot, who noted in her diary: "As we took our supper we had the pleasure of looking at Berlioz's fine head and face, he being engaged in the same way on the other side of the table."

This time there was no avoiding Fétis. They dined with him the day after the opening concert. Berlioz had no doubt that the sage of Brussels, though outwardly cordial, was still fundamentally opposed to his music and horrified that so many of the staff and students at the Conservatoire should think well of it. In fact the old "toad's" opinion had shifted quite a long way, to judge both by the latest edition of his biographical dictionary – a lot less dismissive than before – and by the letter he wrote to Liszt to inform him about the new work (which Liszt already knew, having heard it the previous month). "I had Berlioz here. His *Childhood of Christ* was a success. The work is simple and naïve, but there's feeling in it. It shows a marked modification of his original crude talent." Fétis found him "much changed and aged". "He's a man of spirit and great intelligence, both musical and general. Unhappily the richness of his imagination is not the equal of the technical skill he has acquired." This is a curious reversal of the old days, when Fétis allowed him imagination but refused him any skill except in instrumentation. At least he now acknowledged that the poor man knew how to write music.

What impression Berlioz's wife made on Fétis, on Samuel, on the many other people she encountered on this and other journeys we do not know. Hanslick's picture of her, and Louis Engel's, have been cited. But in general Marie left tantalizingly little trace. She was evidently a vigilant defender of her husband's interests, as she saw them. She took an active part in his business negotiations; in a letter to Richault, with whom there had been some tough bargaining over the publication of his latest scores, Berlioz referred to her as his "homme d'affaires" (though how "perfectly" she "performed her role" of "watching over Hector's purse" – to quote Mme Marmion – may be doubted in view of a note from Berlioz to an unnamed agent warning him that should she persist in gambling on the stock market he will "not recognize any debts she may incur"). Clearly she was a woman of energy and determination. Herself unwell at the time, she insisted on arranging for the physically handicapped Ferrand to be comfortably seated at the second Paris performance of *The Childhood of Christ*. But though Roger reminds her that, full of grace as she is, she can lay no claim to the title of the Virgin Mary, the record as a whole is barren of the kind of personal allusion that would bring her before us "in her habit as she lived". Considering that she accompanied Berlioz on all his visits to Weimar and, presumably, participated in the long discussions about a possible Virgilian opera and, being the person she was, did not sit silent while others talked, references to her in the letters to and from Liszt and the Princess are surprisingly formal, as well as infrequent. There is no sense of closeness, of warmth. One concludes that she was accepted by them but not loved.

Whether she was able to watch over his health, given her own ailments, is by no means certain either. When he does mention her, as often as not it is to speak of her being ill. She had a weak heart and suffered from painful skin complaints.

From our health-obsessed perspective it can sometimes seem as if hardly anyone in that age of bad drains and insufficient personal hygiene was ever really well. Berlioz lived in a world accustomed to illness. His circle was full of invalids: Ferrand partially paralysed, the Princess plagued with abcesses and boils, Meyerbeer often ill with diarrhoea and his wife practically living at spas, Heine pinned to his "mattress grave", dying by slow degrees ("at death's door", wrote Berlioz in 1851, "but still mentally alive" and "giving the impression of standing at the window of his tomb so that he can continue to look out on this world of which he is no longer part, and jeer at it"). For Berlioz himself it was a time of increasingly poor health. The inflammation of the intestines which would later have so devastating an effect on his bodily and mental well-being began to be chronic about then. In part no doubt, like the sore throats and headaches he had long been prone to, it was occupational. The pace at which he lived, the stresses both inner and external, would have undermined the strongest constitution sooner or later. But the low spirits and ill humour that afflicted the final years of his life are at least partly accounted for by his being, by then, in frequent and often excruciating pain.

He was ill in April 1855 during rehearsals for the Te Deum, which was coming to fruition at last after nearly six years of waiting. Organizing a performance on that scale – selecting and engaging his huge forces (an orchestra of a hundred and fifty, a double chorus of two hundred, and six hundred children for the third choir), holding meetings with the Archbishop of Paris, the clergy of St Eustache and the mayor of the third arrondissement, lobbying the press to publicize the event, fighting off the usual attempts to obstruct it (the archbishop had last-minute doubts, even though half the proceeds were going to the local poor), conducting two choral rehearsals a day, and finding a replacement organist when Henry Smart, who was coming from London to inaugurate Ducroquet's new instrument, cancelled at two days' notice – all took toll of his weakened health, though he rallied on the day.

That spring, too, it looked as if Louis had inherited his father's physical predisposition as well as his nervous temperament. The young man spent two months in hospital in the naval base at Toulon with persistent diarrhoea. By then relations between father and son had rallied after going through a time of further estrangement. The previous November, to Berlioz's joy, Louis had been in Paris for two periods of leave. After a cordial interview with his protector Admiral Cécille he left for Cherbourg by night train on the 13th but, in circumstances that are obscure, missed his ship, the *Laplace* – it sailed without him – and went instead to Le Havre, where in five days he got through all the money he had been given by his father, by his great-uncle Félix Marmion and by his mother's friend Mme Lawson. Though Admiral Cécille recommended severe punishment for the breach of discipline, he got off with a short detention on the guardship and obtained an appointment on another vessel, the *Fleurus*. But the experience left him with bitter resentment against both the Admiral and his father. After an exchange of reproachful letters Berlioz was without contact with him for nearly four months, apart from a single, cold note in which Louis informed him that he was "withdrawing his affection, though not his respect" and that he "had no obligations at all" to his benefactor. For news, Berlioz had to depend on Louis' occasional letters to Adèle and Marc Suat plus what he could glean from the papers and any information his Marseille friends Morel and Lecourt could give him. The war with Russia was still raging, and the names of the French dead were posted daily in the streets. He felt crushed with anxiety and guilt. What kind of son had he brought up, or failed to bring up – "unhappy, badly formed, monstrously formed"? Worse than his hopeless extravagance with money was his ingratitude to Admiral Cécille. Yet (Berlioz told Adèle, "trembling" as he wrote), "I love him in spite of everything. If something terrible were to happen to him it would kill me or send me mad."

Louis' behaviour was a hardly surprising reaction to all that had happened and not happened in the past ten years, culminating in his mother's death and his father's marriage. But there was something else which may explain why he went to Le Havre and spent all his money, something his father did not find out till long afterwards. When Louis was at Le Havre in the winter and spring of 1853 he had a liaison with a young woman called Zélie Mallett, daughter of a laundress, which led to the birth of a baby girl, christened Clémentine (the name of the training vessel he had served on in Le Havre). We know about it from a letter written ten years later to Louis by Zélie's mother. Louis had evidently lost touch with them in the meantime. But it looks as if some of the money he annoyed his father by getting through so fast ("how can one spend 150 francs a month in the provinces?") was going to support mother and child.

By April 1855 the breach had healed and Louis was once again "ce cher enfant". At the end of July he was in Paris convalescing from his illness. A month later he sailed from Toulon for the Crimea in the *Navareins*. Berlioz heard about it from Adèle: by ill chance the letter Louis wrote him just before embarking was entrusted to a friend who instead of posting it delivered it by hand four weeks later. Meanwhile Louis again drew heavily on the money – his mother's legacy – deposited for him with Marc Suat. Berlioz wrote an agitated and contradictory letter to Adèle. He could not know that Sebastopol, besieged for nearly a year in conditions appalling for both sides, would fall while Louis' ship was still at a safe distance.

It's quite impossible to make the poor child understand the necessity of *anything*. He has never been able to accept that the world might be any different from the way he presumes to see it. It's a failure of intelligence. I learn from you that he left yesterday, and the grief and anxiety this news causes me is, I admit, stronger than all the other feelings his conduct arouses. It's a hard, horrible business, being a father that loves his son! If one had neither heart nor pity it might just be bearable. But neither is it all roses in the life of a young man who needs to spread his wings but who, at the age of twenty, experiences the harsh constraints society imposes on anyone not born rich or lucky. One could say much on the subject. The world is vile and abominably organized. But as each one is obliged to take it as it is, it's clearly an error to behave as if it were any different. Forgive me, dear sister, for telling you my secret thoughts. I shall play the role of ordinary father as *I have to*.

The world's a stage (as Shakespeare and Cervantes said), but it's a tragic rather than a comic one.

I've not told my wife anything about your letter – I'd rather keep these details to myself.

The performance of the Te Deum in St Eustache on 30 April, though on the grandest scale and marked by excellent ensemble between the widely spaced groups (his Brussels friend Adolphe Samuel was stationed in the organ loft to transmit the beat to the local organist Edouard Batiste), does not seem to have made as great and lasting an impression as those of *The Childhood of Christ*, or as that of the Grande messe des morts eighteen years before and its more recent revivals. The press was good rather than brilliant. One critic thought the work too concerned with worldly pomp and circumstance – an odd judgement, given the humble, pleading Dignare, the female voices raised in gentle supplication in the Te ergo, and the apocalyptic Judex crederis. Though the great church was packed the receipts failed to come up to expectations; there were suspicions of malpractice at the box office, and both Belloni, in charge of tickets, and Marie were furious, calling it "daylight robbery". But Berlioz was content. What did the money matter? "The Judex surpasses all the enormities I have been guilty of up to now," he wrote to Liszt, a few hours after the concert. "Yes, the Requiem has a brother, a brother born with teeth like Richard III (minus the hump)." This time, "no *piccoli paesi* – it's a scene from Revelation". He was besieged by admirers who thronged round him the moment it was over – among them, he told the Princess, none other than the ex-director of the Opéra, Nestor Roqueplan: "the end of the world is nigh".

At any rate, the event had made a stir. It seemed to confirm the upturn of his Paris fortunes – the more so when, within a few days, there was talk of his being put in charge of the musical celebrations planned for the new hall under construction in the Champs-Elysées, opposite the Exhibition Palace. Perhaps there *was* a future for him in France.

Yet with a slightly different twist of fate his career could easily have found its fulfilment in London. Late in 1854 Costa resigned from the Philharmonic Society. The committee, mindful of Berlioz's reputation with musicians and public, offered him the entire season of eight concerts, on condition only of his giving no others.

Had he been free to accept there is little doubt, given his record, that he would have made a success of it, would then have been asked back the following year and might even have established himself permanently in London, as he had often thought of doing; in which case *The Trojans* would probably have been seen at Covent Garden nearly a hundred years sooner than it was, with who knows what consequences. For the frustration of this eminently possible dream he had his old enemy Dr Henry Wylde to thank. A fortnight before receiving the Philharmonic's offer Berlioz had signed an agreement with Wylde to conduct two concerts with the New Philharmonic. He promptly appealed to Wylde, "not as a concert manager but as an artist", to release him. "I can't go back on the word I have given you. But consider the immense harm you will be doing my career if you compel me to refuse what I am being offered."

It is as easy to see why the last thing Wylde wanted was to have his hated rival at the old Philharmonic as it is difficult to see why he engaged him for two concerts at the New – unless he did so knowing the other offer was imminent and reckoning that it was the least painful way of stopping it. At any rate he ignored the appeal. We are left wishing Berlioz could have been more ruthless. The Philharmonic, balked of its first choice, tried Spohr, and finally turned to Wagner. By the time Berlioz and Marie arrived in London on the evening of 8 June – travelling in the company of their friend Toussaint Bennet and his son, the pianist-prodigy Théodore Ritter who had come to hear *Romeo and Juliet* – one of the stormiest seasons in the history of the Philharmonic Society was drawing to a close and Wagner had the English press at his throat.

In retrospect, Berlioz's encounter with his embattled colleague was the main event of the month he spent in London. With all their differences of character, personality, and artistic beliefs and methods, and their differences of situation too – Wagner's conducting attacked by the critics, Berlioz's praised – they were for a brief moment united, and discovered a mutual regard and a pleasure in each other's company that neither can have expected.

Both were suffering under the English aversion to rehearsing and the English addiction to long programmes; both hated the "approximation" that resulted. Berlioz put a more diplomatic face on it; Wagner railed openly against it – "You are the famous Philharmonic orchestra. Raise yourselves, gentlemen, be *artists*!" – and, according to Klindworth,

Liszt's pupil, who had recently settled in London (and would later be famous for his piano reduction of *The Ring*), "waged war with the Directors for doing such absurd things as putting down an operatic air quite unsuitable to the artistic standard which the Philharmonic Society should follow and to the singer to whom it was assigned. '*Where are the directors?*' he furiously asked at the rehearsal." But Berlioz's experiences were not dissimilar. Though, unlike Wagner, *persona grata*, he had to make do with the same conditions. He was forced to omit the first movement of *Romeo* and the choral introduction to the third when it transpired that a high soprano and a baritone – both French – had been engaged for the contralto and tenor solos, and that the off-stage Capulets would not have a single rehearsal with the orchestra. Dr Wylde in that ineffably English way assured him that the chorus sounded splendid; and Berlioz had to defend his decision in a letter to the *Musical World* in which he set out the whole sorry sequence of events, concluding that "for my part I am opposed to making such experiments in public". True, the second movement, the Fête, was brought off with a verve and energy that drove the audience wild – the walls of Exeter Hall shook, an eyewitness recalled, and the piece had to be repeated. But it was very much against the odds; some of the best players were engaged elsewhere and replaced by inferior deputies, and other gaps in the orchestra remained unfilled. The performance of Queen Mab was full of mistakes. It is clear that he was far from satisfied with the concert as a whole. (A year later, speaking of a projected performance of *The Childhood of Christ* in London, he hopes that "we can do better than last time at Exeter Hall".) Even with three movements from *Romeo* instead of four it was too long a programme to prepare adequately: the *Romeo* pieces, Mozart's G minor symphony and *Magic Flute* overture, Beethoven's Emperor concerto (with Mme Oury), an overture by Henry Leslie and vocal items by Mozart, Rossini and Venzano. Wagner had good reason to see the two of them as brothers in adversity.

Not surprisingly, neither admired the other's conducting: Berlioz a Toscanini to Wagner's Furtwängler. Wagner heard the first of Berlioz's New Philharmonic concerts (on 13 June) and found him, in the Mozart symphony especially, rigid and unfeeling, with no depth. Berlioz, though missing Wagner's penultimate concert on the 11th (having to rehearse his chorus in a vain attempt to get it to relearn the *Romeo* music in English), attended the last on the 25th, when the main works were Beethoven's Fourth Symphony and Spohr's Third, and thought him unclear in his beat and self-indulgent in his changes of tempo. As men, however, they warmed to each other. Both of them were conscious of the opportunity presented by their being in London together, and of their obligation to the watching Liszt to make the most of it. They were living within twenty minutes' walk of each other – Wagner at 22 Portland Terrace near the north gate of Regent's Park (the street no longer exists), Berlioz at 43 Margaret Street in rooms rented from Mary Pannier the dressmaker.

The first meeting of which there is any record took place at Wagner's lodgings. Berlioz "was expected", Klindworth recalled (in his tantalizingly brief account); "Wagner said to me, 'When Berlioz comes into the room play something from his *Romeo and Juliet*', which I did." On about the 16th they dined at Sainton's house, 8 Hinde Street, Manchester Square (Sainton was leader of the Philharmonic) and after dinner had a long tête-à-tête. They dined together again before Wagner's final concert on 25 June, on the eve of his departure, and at Portland Terrace afterwards sat up drinking punch and talking till three in the morning.

The day before, the 24th, Berlioz sent Liszt a report of his doings in London.

Dearest friend,

Till now I've not had a second to write, so frantic has been the London whirl for me this year. Today being Sunday I've been left a little more to myself and am taking advantage of it. We've talked often about you with Wagner these past days and you can imagine with how much affection, for on my honour I believe he loves you as much as I do. No doubt he'll tell you himself about his time in London and all he has had to suffer from hostility born of prejudice. His ardour and warmth and courage are superb, and I confess that even his violence delights me. Fate seems to prevent my hearing any of his recent compositions. On the day when at Prince Albert's request he conducted his *Tannhäuser* overture at Hanover Square Rooms I was compelled, at the same hour, to attend a dreadful chorus rehearsal for the New Philharmonic concert I was conducting two days later. [. . .] Tomorrow, Monday, Wagner finishes with his Hanover Square concerts and will be leaving promptly the day after.

There's something remarkably attractive about him, and if we both have our rough edges at least they dovetail:

explain this to Cornelius [. . .] Goodbye – they're coming to collect me to go to Champion Hill [Camberwell], where I've promised to spend part of the day.

Monday morning. I'm back from my country expedition – that is, I got back yesterday evening. Klindworth was there; he played a delicious, melancholy piece of yours. Then we sang – he, the two daughters of the house [the Benecke family], a young German painter and I – some five-part pieces of Purcell, which these ladies seem to know like their Bible but which Klindworth and I found of somewhat limited charm. The others drank it up like consecrated milk. All the same there is a fundamental feeling for music in these English natures; but it's a conservative feeling, first and foremost religious, and anti-passionate. Wagner did for himself in the eyes of the English public by appearing to think little of Mendelssohn. Mendelssohn, for a good many people, is Handel and a half! And for my part, if I didn't have the same deficiency where certain other masters are concerned, whom I detest with the force of a hundred-and-twenty pounder, I would say that Wagner is wrong not to regard the puritan Mendelssohn as a real, richly individual talent. When a master is a master and when that master has invariably honoured and respected art, one must honour and respect him too, however different from ours the line he follows. But Wagner could turn the argument against me if he knew who I abominate so heartily; only, I shall take care not to tell him. When I hear or read certain pieces by that gross master [Handel] I clench my teeth and wait till I'm at home, at which point I relieve my feelings by hurling curses at him. No one is perfect.

Ten days later Wagner wrote to Liszt from Zurich:

I bring back from London one real gain, the cordial and profound friendship I have conceived for Berlioz, which he reciprocates. I was at a concert of the New Philharmonic conducted by him, and must confess I was scarcely edified by the way he performed Mozart's G minor symphony. The execution of his *Romeo and Juliet* symphony was most inadequate and filled me with pity for him. But a few days later we were

alone together at dinner at Sainton's. He was in very good form, and I
had made so much progress with French since I came to London that I
was able to have a lively discussion with him on all kinds of matters
relating to art, philosophy and life during the five hours we spent in each
other's company.

This meeting filled me with deep sympathy for my new friend. He
appeared to me in a quite different light from before. Each suddenly
recognized in the other a companion in misfortune, and it seemed to me
I was luckier than Berlioz. After my last concert he came to see me with
my few other London friends. His wife accompanied him. We remained
together till three in the morning and embraced when we parted.

Liszt, in his reply, quoted part of Berlioz's letter, then added: "Of
all present-day composers, I regard him as the one with whom you will
be able to have the most direct and frank and interesting relationship.
All things considered he is an honest, generous and tremendous fellow."

That the two should be friends was naturally Liszt's dearest wish.
They were the spearheads of the progressive movement which he was
devoting his energy and genius to fostering. It was unthinkable that
they should be enemies.

For a while the London momentum was maintained. At the beginning
of September Wagner wrote "a very cordial and charming letter"
(Berlioz told Liszt), repeating his invitation to come and see him in
Zurich, asking if he could let him have copies of his full scores, and
giving an account of his work on *The Ring*. The letter has not survived
but part of its contents may be inferred from Berlioz's reply:

So you are at work on your *Nibelungen*, and melting the glaciers in the
process! It must be wonderful, writing in the presence of the splendours
of nature. That is another joy that is denied to me [i.e. in addition to his
inability to speak German]. Beautiful landscapes, high peaks, the sea in
its grandeur absorb me completely instead of stimulating ideas and
thought: I feel but cannot express. I can only draw the moon by looking
at its reflection at the bottom of a well.

I wish I could send you the scores which you do me the pleasure of
asking for. Unfortunately my publisher has long since ceased to give me
any. But there are two or rather three that are coming out in a few
weeks' time – the Te Deum, *The Childhood of Christ* and *Lélio* (a lyric
monodrama) – and these at least I can send you. I have your *Lohengrin*.
If you could let me have your *Tannhäuser* I should be very pleased. The

meeting you propose would be a real treat for me; but I dare not think
of it.

Soon afterwards Wagner wrote again to Liszt: "It would, I confess,
be of great interest to me to make a careful study of his symphonies in
full score. Do you have them, and will you lend them to me – or would
you in fact care to make me a present of them? I should be very grateful.
But I should like to have them soon."

The vehemence of Wagner and the slight reserve that held Berlioz
back had as much to do with circumstances as with temperament.
Wagner had more ground to make up. Whereas Berlioz had always
refrained from attacking him (and had given a warm welcome in the
Débats to an article by Liszt in praise of *Tannhäuser*), he had described
Berlioz, in print, as being, with all his high-mindedness, a rather disagreeable character. He had informed the world that, though in his way a
genius, Berlioz had no sense of real beauty and was going artistically
in the wrong direction. To Liszt he had made no bones about disapproving of his friend's misguided devotion to *Benvenuto Cellini*, and pronounced disparagingly on works which, though he rightly sensed that
their whole dramatic bent and method were alien to his, he had neither
heard nor seen. Now he found himself face to face with a different
Berlioz. He might be as fundamentally ambivalent about the composer
as he had been ever since the revelation of *Romeo and Juliet* fifteen
years before: Berlioz still had "no depth"; and, as he told Liszt, he was
"amazed" by the same "grotesque" quirks of taste in *Evenings in the
Orchestra* (a copy of which Berlioz sent him about this time) as in his
musical compositions. Yet those compositions, wrongheaded as they
were, continued to fascinate him. And now the man had presented
himself in an altogether more favourable light. His wife was a menace,
with her envious tittle-tattle, but that only cast her husband's superiority
into greater relief. However strong Wagner's desire to please Liszt, the
attraction he told him he had conceived for Berlioz was, I am sure,
genuine. He felt he had made an important new friend. Notwithstanding
the superficial unpleasantness of his London existence, Wagner was in
a confident, expansive state of mind. He was working on the second
act of *Die Walküre*, with a wonderful consciousness of powers at full
stretch, far above the puny vexations of the Philharmonic. "They say
Wagner remains calm," Berlioz had written to Morel from Paris a few
weeks before, "certain as he is that in fifty years he will be master of

the musical world" – a boast that was both magnificent and, as it happened, true. Berlioz seemed more of a wanderer on the face of the earth even than he.

Berlioz on his side also meant what he said to Liszt: he liked Wagner. He was understandably a little more wary. Even without being constantly reminded by the suspicious Marie, he was aware of Wagner's public attacks, as well as of the exclusive position that was being claimed for him, that of the sole true future for dramatic music. By one of those malign chances which recurred throughout their relationship, the excerpts from *Opera and Drama* that Davison was serializing in the *Musical World* (partly with the intention of damning Wagner out of his own mouth) reached the passage on Berlioz in the very next issue after Wagner's departure. But Berlioz had a fairly robust attitude to criticism of his music; he was surely sincere in what he had said to Liszt a year or two before, apropos of himself and Wagner and what the latter wrote about him: that, as a critic, he had thrown too many brickbats, over the years, to object when he received some in his turn. As for Wagner's music, I imagine he saw himself adopting an intermediate position, and being ready to admire it without accepting – how could he? – the more messianic claims advanced on its behalf.

Berlioz, more tactful than Wagner, did not tell Liszt what he thought of their friend's conducting. But he mentioned it in an exuberant letter to Théodore Ritter, who, after playing the antique cymbals in Queen Mab, had returned to Paris with his father:

If I'm a little late in answering your letter it's because since you left I've been in the thick of it: visits, dinners, piano trios without end – correspondence in the *Musical World* with the amateur choristers I wouldn't allow to sing in *Romeo and Juliet* – lunch at Beale's – piano rehearsals at Glover's [Southampton Street] – riots in Regent's Park, a hundred men arrested, the workmen trying to rescue their "brothers", several wounded, my wife coming back in a state – onset of migraine – reading Handel's *Samson* – return of migraine – yesterday a frightful rehearsal at Exeter Hall – Glover's cantata, style very piquant but difficult, making me sweat till the gutters in the Strand overflow – then the finale of *Harold* and a ferocious concerto by Henselt played by M. Klindworth in free style, me dancing for an hour on a slack wire, Cooper our first violin unable to contain himself any longer and calling out "Sempre tempo rubato!" – the cornets not turning up because the military "bank" in *L'étoile du nord* has kept them at Covent Garden – once more *L'étoile du nord* and a soirée at Glover's where Meyerbeer is expected – excuses from the great man on grounds of awful gripes – someone quoting Heine's book *Le Marquis de la diharrée* [a satire on the thirteen-year blockage of *Le Prophète*] – or rather *diarrhée* (do I know how to spell it!) – Meyerbeer arriving just when everyone has finished bewailing his absence – congratulations on end of the gripes – moonlight stroll through the streets of London – go and rejoin my wife at Ernst's – Mme Ernst asking me if I like Molière – *do I like Molière*?! – the next second me offering to give them something – scene from the *Misanthrope* – after which the chessboard, and Ernst and M. Louis Blanc sitting down grimly to their stupid strategies till three in the morning – Ella's matinée – the said Ella presenting Meyerbeer to "his public" between two bishops – Wagner's departure after worthy Mr Hogarth has presented him in his turn to Meyerbeer, asking the two celebrities whether they "know each other" – joy of Wagner at quitting London – renewal of all the critics' fury against him after his final Hanover Square concert – he conducts, in fact, *in free style* like Klindworth playing the piano, but is very engaging in his ideas and conversation – we go and drink punch at his place after the concert – he repeats his vows of friendship, embraces me passionately, says he used to be full of prejudice against me, weeps and jumps up and down – no sooner has he gone than the *Musical World* publishes the passage in his book where he tears me to pieces in the most witty and amusing fashion – frantic joy of Davison as he translates it for me – "All the world's a stage", as Shakespeare and Cervantes say – Ella presenting me with a superb edition of the complete works of this same Shakespeare – "poet", as they are careful to inform visitors to the Crystal Palace: "W. Shakespeare, poet" – so good of you to tell us – and I shake you all by the hand and *sign myself* (as the Germans say), "H. Berlioz, non-stop man of letters".*

In the ten days of his stay that remained after Wagner's departure he continued to be as busy as before. He made several visits to the offices of Novello's at 69 Dean Street, during one of which he signed an agreement for an English edition of his *Treatise*, revised and with new material, for a lump-sum payment of £40. He spent time with old friends like Holmes, Osborne, Chorley and Silas (who helped him check

* The letter culminates in a welter of untranslatable puns.

a proof copy of the vocal score of *The Childhood of Christ* for misprints),
did his best to argue Glover out of dismissing Verdi's music as worthless
(a prejudice shared by most of the London critics), and took Marie to
see the Crystal Palace, dismantled the previous year and re-erected on
Sydenham Hill. His second and final New Philharmonic programme,
on 4 July – attended by Meyerbeer, who sat in the front row – was
another mammoth miscellany: in addition to *Harold* (with Ernst) and
the Glover and Henselt works, there was music by Mendelssohn,
Mozart, Beethoven, Meyerbeer, Rossini, Benedict and Praeger. Apart
from Ernst's playing it seems to have been the singing of the Gotha
contralto Anna-Rose Falconi that pleased him most (an admiration that
would shortly have a significant sequel). Two mornings later he directed
the annual royal gala concert given at Covent Garden by Mrs Anderson,
one-time piano teacher of the young Victoria and now in charge of the
musical education of the princes and princesses. Marie told her friend
Mme Duchêne that apart from Pauline Viardot singing *La captive* the
occasion wouldn't amount to much – "the usual exhibition". But what
an exhibition – in A. W. Ganz's words, "every star of the operatic
firmament there in full blaze". Grisi, Bosio, Mario, Tamburini, Lablache
– no less – sang the second quintet from *Così fan tutte*, and Ernst gave
his *Carnaval de Venise* and Mme Nantier-Didiée Ascanio's air from
Cellini. Room was found amid the glitter for Beethoven's Choral Fantasy
(with Mrs Anderson), the overture to *Euryanthe* and, as a grand climax,
Rossini's Stabat Mater. That Berlioz was engaged to conduct the concert
– and had been first choice to take over the old Philharmonic for the
season – is indicative of the high regard of the London musical authorities. Three years before, at the time of the inauguration of the New
Philharmonic, the Andersons were, with Costa, the enemy.

After the Wagner experience (Grove's *Dictionary* called the year 1855
one of the Philharmonic Society's "most disastrous on record") the
committee decided it was time they had a native English conductor,
and Sterndale Bennett was appointed. But Berlioz, as he left on 7 July,
had every reason to believe there was a future for him in London. He
had just been offered the musical directorship of a new series of concerts
to be held at the Crystal Palace – though he was uncertain whether to
accept (and in the end decided against it) – and Beale was negotiating
to bring him over to conduct *The Childhood of Christ* and the Te Deum
at St Martin's Hall in Long Acre during the winter/spring season. Beale,
Ella and others were also keen to have him inaugurate the new St James's

Hall when it was complete. His many London friends would have been as astonished as he to know that he had given his last concert in England.

It is tempting to treat the next seven months as an interlude before the visit to Weimar in 1856 and the crucial consequences that flowed from it. But though his head was full of thoughts of a Virgilian opera he had by no means committed himself to writing it, and there were more immediate things on his mind: the pamphlet on *The Conductor's Art* (*L'Art du chef d'orchestre*) which he had undertaken to deliver to Novello's in September, along with the revisions to the *Treatise*; the publication of his last major works and the hours of proof-reading involved; the concerts in the Palais de l'Industrie for the closure of the Exhibition, which he had every hope he would be in charge of; and, in the coming winter, possible visits to Vienna and Prague in addition to the planned concerts in Gotha and Weimar and the expected return to London. He had no idea that quite soon the pattern and focus of his life would alter decisively.

July was occupied with checking the scores of *The Childhood of Christ*, *Lélio* and the Te Deum, and with sessions of the jury on musical instruments, which lasted right through to late September and proved even more fractious than those at the Great Exhibition in London four years before. He had the novel experience of finding himself supported by Fétis against the other jurors, who objected to the names of the manufacturers being concealed, which obliged them to vote on the identification-numbers alone and, as Halévy naïvely complained, "listen to the instruments without knowing who they were by".

L'Art du chef d'orchestre was written in odd days snatched from jury duty and sent in mid-September, with the revisions and additions, to London, where Alfred Novello's sister Mary Cowden Clarke was engaged to translate it. The manual was serialized in the *Gazette* in the new year and in the *Musical Times* the following spring, and incorporated in the revised French edition of the *Treatise* issued by Schonenberger. It was not the first of its kind – Kastner had produced one ten years before – but it was the first to treat the subject analytically and technically in a way we would recognize as modern. Kastner championed the violinist-conductor of the old school, the maestro who came up through the ranks. This method remained in fashion in Paris longer than in most other places – it was still being advocated there as late as the 1870s. Holoman even argues that Berlioz's using a baton, not a violin bow, was the main reason why he was never seriously considered for a conducting post in France. Certainly Kastner's treatises were the ones officially recognized by the Institute and adopted at the Conservatoire. But it was Berlioz's that went round the world and his *L'Art du chef d'orchestre*, as well as his practical demonstration of the craft and art of the virtuoso maestro, that influenced the European development of conducting.

Princess Wittgenstein was in Paris for five weeks in August and September with her daughter Marie. She brought a long essay by Liszt on "Berlioz and his Harold Symphony" (which she attempted, unsuccessfully, to interest the *Revue contemporaine* in publishing). Immersed through he was in Wagner's writings and doctrines, Liszt had not renounced his belief in Berlioz. Like many of its early readers, he was in two minds about his friend's *Memoirs* (Berlioz had sent him the manuscript the previous spring, with a view to its possible publication in Germany after the author's death). "Berlioz's passion for Estrella [*sic*] has something symbolic about it," he told the Princess. "There is in his musical style, so tender, at times so tormented, something of the ardour of a lad of twelve for a sweetheart of eighteen." The warfare with Cherubini, on the other hand, he found "puerile" and "in very bad taste". But he was promoting his music as actively as ever: a performance of either the Requiem or the Te Deum was being planned for the forthcoming Thuringia Festival. And he and the New-Weimarians were delighted with the letter that Berlioz addressed to the Dowager Grand Duchess on the subject of his opera, the vocal score of which Litolff was publishing in Brunswick.

> My *Benvenuto Cellini*, assassinated in France some years ago, has recovered a spark of life thanks to the care of a celebrated doctor, your kapellmeister at Weimar. A German publisher has now been found who is prepared to take it into the fresh air and launch it on the world, and I venture to beg Your Royal Highness to continue your protection of the convalescent by accepting the dedication of the work.

The letter "enjoyed a great success", Liszt reported to Marie Wittgenstein. "The Grand Duchess was much amused by its style, not customary on such occasions; and tomorrow Vitzthum will reply to Berlioz that she accepts the homage rendered her by this score."

The last ten days of October and the whole of November were consumed by the organization of the series of gargantuan concerts marking the close of the Universal Exhibition and the distribution of the prizes. Prince Napoleon, the Emperor's cousin and the person responsible for the whole event, had an unusually high opinion of Berlioz and entrusted him with the musical side of things. He could not understand why someone of his ability and distinction should have no commensurate position in Paris musical life; and as soon as the concerts were over he tried to have him promoted from Chevalier de la Légion d'honneur to Officier. The bureaucrats had other ideas, and the decoration, awarded to Verdi that summer, was not vouchsafed to Berlioz till nearly nine years later. For the moment, however, he was the man in control. To a great extent he could decide who was to take part. Though the personnel of the contingents coming from London, Brussels, Cologne and Vienna were not subject to his choice and would have only one rehearsal under his baton, the rest of the combined choir and orchestra of 1,250 were his to select or reject from among the many hundreds who answered his call, and to drill into shape. The leading institutions supplied the most; but all were eager to be represented. Duprez sent four of his best pupils; Masson, who had commissioned the Messe solennelle thirty years before, offered two basses from his choir at St Roch ("they have fine voices and are musicians. If you can use them for your concerts you will have two good artists the more"); Ancessy, conductor at the Comédie-Française, contributed four violins and a double-bass: "Their small number will show you how careful I have been to choose only those who are capable of giving a good account of your splendid works."

Little by little the army was assembled and taught the music assigned to it. Here too his word went. It was the first time for ten years that he had had the chance to stage one of those popular festivals such as had been a dream of his ever since Le Sueur's descriptions of the massed gatherings of the Revolution had crystallized his boyhood visions of the ancient world and its monumental rites. He put together a programme consisting of music of his own written expressly to renew the old French tradition, and of works by Gluck and Weber and Beethoven, and others which he thought lent themselves to performance on a massive scale: three movements from the Te Deum (Te Deum laudamus, Tibi omnes and the March for the Presentation of the Colours, with thirty harps), the Apotheosis and the Napoleonic cantata L'impériale, a scene from Armide, the Freischütz overture, the last three movements of the Fifth Symphony, the prayer from Moïse, the Blessing of the Daggers from The Huguenots, Mozart's Ave verum, and "See the conquering hero comes" from Handel's *Judas Maccabaeus*. There were ten days of rehearsals, from nine till four each day. No doubt for the trio of Beethoven's Fifth he took the double-basses separately, as he had done in 1844. All this was normal. So were the interminable meetings with architects and carpenters about the placing and construction of the special stand for the performers. What was not normal was his total exemption from financial responsibility – for the huge copying bill, for the payment of the musicians and the removal men and the rest – nor the fee of 8,000 francs that he received afterwards from Ernest Ber, the impresario engaged by the government to put on the concerts.

When it came to marshalling and directing his forces in the hall – built on the site today occupied by the Petit Palais – Verbrugghen's electric metronome proved a godsend (the man had come with it specially from Brussels). With his left hand Berlioz simply activated a mechanism which transmitted the beat instantly to five sub-conductors – Tilman, Bottesini, Hellmesberger, Vauthrot, Hurand – stationed at intervals through the vast assembly. The cartoonists, for whom he had failed for some time to provide much of a target, were roused to action, and both the megalomaniac proportions of the chorus and orchestra and the evident absurdity of the new-fangled machine were seized on and ridiculed. That was, as so often, a measure of one's prominence, and he cannot have minded. The size of the performing body was proportionate to the size of the hall; and thanks to the metronome the whole thing held together and went without serious mistake. Before long the device would be in use in most lyric theatres except the Opéra.

One thing his authority did not extend to was the protocol of the opening concert, on 15 November, at which the Emperor, "high on a throne of royal state" (the performers partly concealed behind it), delivered a formal address, and trophies were handed out to the prize-winners in front of an international invited audience, many in resplendent uniforms, arrayed on a huge three-sided amphitheatre. Berlioz had feared that opposition from the likes of Auber and Girard would recall the days of the première of the Requiem. In the event it was more like the première of the Symphonie funèbre et triomphale, with music, in that "Aladdin's palace of a hall", coming a poor second to spectacle. Halfway through the cantata – the work written in praise of him – the Emperor fingered his speech, and an official motioned to the conductor to stop. It was, in a way, a poetic judgement on Berlioz for having composed the piece. But the musicians made up for it by themselves breaking into applause and throwing their hats in the air at the end of the Apotheosis, in defiance of etiquette. His real compensation, however, came next day when, in the absence of the Emperor, the performers were placed further forward and the programme was heard complete by a paying audience of thousands. The concert was repeated on the 24th. Though Gounod and Félicien David also directed their own events it was Berlioz's that captured the public imagination and dominated the press.

For the rest, Paris went its way. "That great imbecile of a theatre", the Opéra, was sunk in immemorial sloth; only by making a tremendous scene at the dress rehearsal had Verdi managed to secure a halfway passable performance of *The Sicilian Vespers*. Berlioz, who was in London by the time it finally reached its première, caught up with it in the autumn and wrote a notice which reads like genuine praise. For himself, the situation was as before; the Exhibition concerts had changed nothing. Félicien David was able to hire the Conservatoire Hall twice for performances of his *Désert* and *Christophe Colomb* (and lose nearly 2,000 francs: the march of time had not been kind to them, and Berlioz, quoting Racine, doubted if the composer's partisans could do anything to arrest it "et de David éteint rallumer le flambeau"*). He on the other hand could hire only the Salle Herz – half the Conservatoire's size – which in effect confined him to *The Childhood of Christ*, and even then not on any of the Sundays when the Société des Concerts was not performing: Pasdeloup's orchestra had booked them for the entire season. He would have to be content with a Friday, and give the work on one rehearsal.

Pasdeloup himself had personal experience of the imperial passion for music, while conducting a concert at court in an antechamber adjoining the main room where the audience was sitting. He had just begun a symphony when the Emperor entered the room and, hearing a noise, abruptly closed the communicating doors. "But he'll end up being the Emperor's head of music, you'll see," wrote Berlioz to Morel. "Apart from the little Bennet – Théodore Ritter, a splendid child whose future I really believe in – and Camille Saint-Saëns, another real musician, aged nineteen, and Gounod, who has just produced a very fine mass, I see only ephemera swarming above this stinking swamp called Paris. But enough – in fact too much. What's the use of com-

---

* "and rekindle the snuffed-out David's flame".

plaining? Cholera exists. Why shouldn't Parisian music as well?"

His chief musical joys were necessarily private. If he were to succumb and compose the work his imagination was goading him to, it would be strictly for himself: no one should hear it. In the intimacy of his home or at his friends', he could live his feelings to the full, listening to music that moved him, discussing, giving vent to his impulse to proselytize, to share and communicate his dearest enthusiasms. There must have been many such sessions that left no record, but we know of several, two from this period. Early in 1855 he went with Théodore Ritter to Legouvé's house in the Rue St Marc and together they took him through *The Damnation of Faust*, Berlioz explaining the meaning of every turn and nuance in the score, till Legouvé realized how much the music was intended to convey "not only in the domain of external nature but also and especially in the domain of the human spirit".

Twelve months later Berlioz invited Ritter round to 19 Rue Boursault and had the inexpressible pleasure of introducing him to Gluck's music.

My dear, very dear Théodore

Remember this day, 12 January 1856: the day when, for the first time, you entered on the study of the marvels of great dramatic music – when you glimpsed the sublimities of Gluck. As for me, I shall never forget how your artist's instinct recognized unhesitatingly and adored wholeheartedly that genius then new to you. Yes, be sure of it: whatever the semi-knowledgeable and semi-feeling may say – those with only half a heart and one lobe to their brain – our art has two supreme gods, Beethoven and Gluck. One reigns over the infinite realm of thought, the other over that of passion; and though the first is far above the second as a musician, there is none the less so much of the one in the other that these two Jupiters make one god, in whom our admiration and veneration can but lose themselves.

Your brother and devoted friend
Hector Berlioz

Legouvé too found Berlioz's analyses of Gluck, to which he willingly subjected himself, unforgettable. But even more evocative, Legouvé recalled, was to hear him expounding the Ninth Symphony.

His articles, admirable as they are, give an imperfect idea of it, for they contain only his opinions. When he spoke, the whole of him was in it. The eloquence of his words was enhanced by his expression, his gestures, tone of voice, tears, exclamations of enthusiasm, and those sudden flashes of inspired imagery which are sparked by the stimulus of a listener hanging on every word. An hour spent in this way taught me more about instrumental music than a whole concert at the Conservatoire – or rather, when I went to the Conservatoire the following Sunday, my mind full of Berlioz's commentaries, Beethoven's work suddenly opened before me like a great cathedral flooded with light, the whole design of which I took in at a glance and in which I walked about as though it were familar ground, confidently exploring every recess and corner. Berlioz had given me the key to the sanctuary.

For public musical satisfactions he looked, as before, to Germany. The hoped-for visits to Vienna and Prague did not materialize, but both Gotha and Weimar confirmed that they were expecting him for concerts in February. He exchanged regular letters with the Princess, and he remained in close touch with Liszt. The news of the Berlin critics' attacks on Liszt's *Thirteenth Psalm*, which the composer had conducted there (together with *Tasso*, *Les préludes*, and the E flat piano concerto with Bülow as soloist), roused him to indignation. "So the learned men of Berlin are back astride their Rosinantes of so-called religious paradox," he wrote to the Princess. "They want the Christian to pray as a statue would if it could speak." The Princess (he went on) had no doubt heard of the sensational events provoked by Thalberg's presence in Buenos Aires – women fainting, and one carried home dead, though she was now said to be better.

> Honestly, one would rather not see one's name in the newspapers now, so gross has the puffery become. Or perhaps one should go one better and announce that at such and such a concert one saw men slaying each other, and women delivered who weren't pregnant, and that at a certain point the whole audience went down as if struck by a gigantic galvanic pile – and more of the same. For several weeks Meyerbeer has let it be known that he is "having trouble with his teeth". Would you like me to announce that Liszt is "not having trouble with his teeth"? It will impress a lot of people who are afraid of being bitten. There I go, Princess, abusing the permission you gave me to talk wildly (more puffery – you never gave it to me!). But this business of "worldly" religious music gets on my nerves.

Berlioz's interest in performing Liszt's works has been doubted; but

I think that, though it sprang chiefly from friendship and a sense of obligation, it was genuine. We cannot tell how much he really liked Liszt's concerto which he conducted at Weimar in February 1855 and which he described as "your magnificent composition, so vigorous, so new, so brilliant and fresh and glowing"; but he would have included it in his concert at the Opéra-Comique two months later if the one pianist available, Liszt's pupil Fumagalli, had not required too much time to learn it. Later there was a question of his doing the symphonic poem *Orpheus* at the Salle Herz in March 1856, but in the end the concert did not take place. And, though one cannot imagine Berlioz caring greatly for the Faust Symphony, which Liszt dedicated to him (in return for the dedication of the *Damnation*), that would hardly have stopped him performing it if he had had the chance. Writers on Liszt who complain that the favours were all in one direction have omitted to observe the chronology. By the time Liszt's orchestral works became available Berlioz's conducting career was in decline. He could no doubt have performed some of them at Baden in the late 1850s and early 1860s; but by then the old entente was over and they had taken divergent paths. His one remaining major series of concerts, in Russia in 1867–8, came long after Wagnerism and the development of Liszt's harmonic style had driven them irrevocably apart. Certainly, before that happened, Berlioz was conscious of a one-way traffic. "When will your Berlin plans come to fruition?" he wrote in November 1855, shortly before Liszt's concert there. "What pieces will you be performing? Your laconicism on the subject of your works causes me suppressed humiliation – I am shamefully expansive when it's a question of mine. If you go on like this, in future I shall restrict my letters to politics, morals, and conchology." A couple of weeks earlier he told the Princess that though Liszt's letter did him a power of good "it would have done even more if it had contained more details of the performance of *Prometheus* and *Orpheus*" at Brunswick.

It is possible that when it came to his own music Liszt experienced a kind of awkwardness towards his friend, an apprehensiveness, which made him hold back. He seems not to have taken up Berlioz's suggestion that the Société Philharmonique might programme something of his; and in general, though we have almost none of his replies to Berlioz's letters, they do not appear to have shown any eagerness on his part to respond to such inquiries.

What the correspondence makes clear is how often Berlioz carried out commissions for Liszt in Paris and how little he begrudged doing so. The picture of someone egocentrically and cynically obsessed with his own concerns to the exclusion of everyone else's, his friends' included, which some writers have tried to pin on him, is simply not borne out by the evidence, in fact is contradicted by it. Liszt for one would not have recognized it. Berlioz may have drawn the line at the request of Cousin Raymond to find him a better seat just as the second Palais de l'Industrie concert was about to begin; but in general he was courteous and conscientious to a fault. Many are the letters in which he undertakes to help or advise a friend, an acquaintance, a stranger, about giving concerts in Paris. In the midst of the exhausting preparations for the Exhibition, he took time to chase up Adolphe Sax, who had failed to send a promised case of saxophones to Liszt; and he returned later to check that they really had been dispatched. At the same time, he went to see Brandus and Dufour about the publication of Liszt's scores in France and to ask why the royalties due had not been paid.

In January 1856, shortly before his concert at the Salle Herz, he twice wrote to Sainton in London in response to an inquiry about the possibility of the contralto Miss Dolby putting on a concert in Paris, and booked the hall provisionally for her. The first letter gave a detailed inventory of the costs involved: hire of hall and lighting, orchestra plus one rehearsal, printing of tickets, poor tax, hire of instruments, fee for promoter (Belloni or Gouffier); also what price to charge for tickets and how many would have to be given to newspapers for publicity and the critics, the other artists likely to be available to take part in the concert, the desirability of giving it during the daytime – in the evening they would get only "un orchestre à bric-à-brac" – and the best conductor to engage – Tilmant – in the event of Berlioz himself not being in Paris in March (he was expecting to go to Belgium). He followed it up with a second letter giving the smaller number of strings (twenty-eight) he thought sufficient for the hall, how to get in touch with Tilmant and with Belloni, which critics it was advisable to visit before the concert, and finally the necessity, if some Handel was included in the programme, of bringing the orchestral parts from London, as they could be difficult to find in Paris. In all this Berlioz did not see himself as going out of his way to do Sainton a favour: it was part of the natural quid pro quo of a musician's life. As it happened, he did not go to Belgium, but Miss Dolby decided not to give a concert in Paris. Had she done so he would happily have organized it for her and conducted it gratis, having "received many marks of fraternal courtesy and good fellowship from English artists".

His own concert, consisting of *The Childhood of Christ*, took place on 25 January 1856 at 1.30 p.m., shortly before his departure for Germany. Despite the single rehearsal he was pleased with his performers: a hand-picked orchestra of fifty-two players, an excellent choir of forty-eight taken mostly from the best of the Opéra and the Opéra-Comique, and principal singers "in every way right for the characters". Thanks to a notebook in his hand giving a detailed record of the event, we know the names of everyone in the chorus and the orchestra, and what they were paid (the soloists seem to have sung for nothing), and who came to the concert. Most of the music section of the Academy were there, including Ambroise Thomas, Adam, Clapisson and Reber (no doubt invited with an eye to the next Institute election), as well as a host of colleagues, friends and acquaintances, among them Ernst, Sax, Gounod, Félicien David, Vincent Wallace, the Viardots, Edouard Alexandre, d'Ortigue, the Escudier brothers, Louis Engel, Michel Lévy, Delacroix, Chenavard, Amussat, Charles Blanc, and Alphonse Robert and his wife. Though held in the Salle Herz, not the Conservatoire, and on a Friday, not a Sunday, it was the crowning concert of his Paris career. He gave only one more on his own initiative.

The Childhood of Christ was the main work at the concert in Gotha, to which Berlioz and his wife travelled at the end of January. Wangenheim, the intendant, allowed him four rehearsals, and he thought the performance (on 6 February) "quite good" and the soloists not ill-suited to their roles. He pleased Duke Ernest by opening the programme with the overture to the Duke's *Santa Chiara* (Berlioz had heard the work at the Opéra the previous autumn and reviewed it in a feuilleton which, he said, mixed truth and falsehood so intricately that you couldn't tell them apart). The Duke decorated him with the cross of the Knightly Order of the Ernestines, he received a fee of 200 thalers, and he and Marie were guests of the court at the annual Shrove Tuesday ball and the supper afterwards. But the most significant event was the performance of *Le spectre de la rose*, the second song of the *Nuits d'été*, sung by the local contralto Anna-Rose Falconi. Hearing her in London had prompted him to orchestrate it for her in time for the Gotha concert, transposing it down from D to the richer key of B major and adding an eight-bar introduction in which flute and clarinet in octaves intoned the wide-spanned melody while muted violins spun round it their silken arpeggios. For the exalted central passage – "This gentle perfume is my soul, and it's from Paradise I come" – he enhanced the delicate scoring with the sparkle of a harp; the part was played by the Weimar harpist Jeanne Pohl, whom he had invited to Gotha for the trio in *The Childhood of Christ*. Berlioz had scored the fourth *Nuits d'été* song, *Absence*, twelve years before, and possibly one other since then. Even so he might not have thought of orchestrating the rest but for the presence in the audience of the young Swiss publisher Jakob Melchior Rieter-Biedermann from Winterthur who, using Cornelius as intermediary, persuaded him to do an orchestral version of the whole cycle. Cornelius was commissioned to make the German translation, and Berlioz left Germany with an agreement to supply the manuscript of *Les nuits d'été* as soon as convenient after his return to Paris.

The travellers made the short journey to Weimar in the company of Liszt who, though unwell, had come to Gotha for the concert. He had been himself preparing the large local amateur chorus for *The Damnation of Faust* – which was being given in its entirety for the first time in Weimar – and doing it so well that Berlioz found they had learned it thoroughly; and he was also conducting rehearsals of *Benvenuto Cellini* for a gala revival on 15 February, the Dowager Grand Duchess's birthday, with a new tenor, Caspari, a refurbished staging and the score (in Berlioz's words) "shining like a newly polished sword". Liszt's goodwill to his friend (the latter ruefully remarked to Adèle) did not quite extend to "letting me *just once* conduct my opera"; he was too attached to the work he called "a second *Fidelio*" to bear relinquishing it even to its composer. He remained, though, as devoted as he had always been. Outwardly the three-week stay was like the previous two. It was a third "Berlioz Week" in all but name: a concert at court the day after *Cellini*, with extracts from *The Damnation of Faust*, the *Corsair* overture and Litolff's piano concerto (Théodore Ritter the soloist); a brilliant account of *Faust*; a dinner held in his honour by the New Weimar Association, complete with apostrophizing in verse by Hoffmann von Fallersleben; and a pressing invitation from the Grand Duke to come back as soon as possible.

In reality it was different. The visit marked a watershed in relations between Berlioz and Liszt. Though they remained friends it would never be quite the same.

In an entirely amicable spirit, Liszt had sought to further the rapprochement between Berlioz and Wagner which, to his enormous satisfaction, had taken place in London that summer. To consolidate the alliance between the three of them that Liszt had set his heart on, Berlioz must be converted to Wagner's music. It is likely that during his stay Liszt played him passages from the operas on the piano, at the Altenburg; and *Lohengrin*, conducted by Liszt – the opera he had pioneered in 1850 and considered a work of transcendent genius – was given two performances at the ducal theatre.

To Liszt's annoyance, at the first of them Berlioz and Marie got up and left in the middle of Act 2. At the second, on 24 February, he "stuck it out this time' (Liszt wrote to his friend Agnes Street) "and heard *Lohengrin* from one end to the other", but – Liszt told Bülow – "didn't enjoy it much. We hardly spoke about it, but he expressed himself pretty freely to other people, which has upset me." The *Dresdener Journal* printed a story, picked up by *La France musicale*, about an argument over Wagner's music between Berlioz and Litolff on one side and Liszt on the other during which, "in response to some sharp words from Liszt, Litolff took a very valuable cane, which he had intended as a present for Liszt, and broke it in two, saying 'I am breaking with your party just as I'm breaking this cane.'" Berlioz's reaction was not so violent. But no more than Litolff could he subscribe to "Liszt's party".

Writing many years later to Berlioz's biographer Hippeau, Liszt put his finger on what went wrong. "Without any personal quarrel, the burning question of Wagner (now much reduced) led to a coolness between Berlioz and myself. He did not think that Wagner was the destiny of German musical drama, surpassing Beethoven and Weber." Thus it was not so much Wagner's music that Berlioz rebelled against as the Wagnerian theory of musical evolution, then being aired and discussed and (he felt) thrust down his throat, to be swallowed or rejected. In fact, neither of the works that exemplified "Wagnerism" had yet been heard; *Rheingold* and *Walküre* were still on their composer's desk. The dispute had lifted off the ground and acquired a propulsion of its own. Wagnerism was devouring Wagner, or at least making it difficult to listen to the music without preconception one way or the other. Berlioz (and not he alone) was driven by antipathy to the doctrine – antipathy to the very idea of a doctrine – into conceiving notions about the music that bore little relation to reality, in fact into misrepresenting it in precisely the way his own compositions had so often been misrepresented: as "music without melody". When he heard *Tannhäuser* again, in 1864, three years after its Paris première and in less fraught circumstances, he confessed to finding much of it very moving, especially the final act. Only, he couldn't see why there had to be so much fuss. For him, Wagner, though of great interest, was not a burning question, and certainly not the one way forward for music.

No doubt Marie poured oil on the flames (she was heard to say disparaging things about Johanna Wagner, the composer's niece, who sang Elsa in *Lohengrin*). It is possible that till now Berlioz had not realized just how deeply committed Liszt was to Wagner and Wagner's ideas. But I doubt if resentment at Liszt's devoting himself so passionately to the Wagnerian cause – and therefore by inference less to the Berliozian – was a significant part of his attitude. I don't believe he felt "betrayed". Liszt after all was still doing wonders for him too. It was, simply, that the subject in itself drove an ineluctable wedge between them.

While in Weimar, Berlioz received a letter from Bülow in Berlin, asking in the name of his colleagues and fellow-enthusiasts if he would let them have the full score of *Faust* at a reduced price for the library of "masterpieces of modern music" that they were aiming to create – a request he responded to with alacrity. Weimar and all it stood for in his life, the encouragement, the active support and promotion, the warmth of hospitality – he could not prize it too highly. To be a member of the New Weimar Association was an honour and a pleasure. But he did not believe in "parties" and could not belong to one, even – especially – when it was his friends'. If he "expressed himself pretty freely" about it, that was surely due not to jealousy, as Liszt half thought, but to being in his turn "upset" that after twenty-five years of close and inspiring comradeship a matter of musical ideology could cause a coolness between them.

What part the Princess played in this drama, what she thought of the passions that fired it, is unclear. Liszt, writing to her a few months later, spoke of Berlioz's "less than friendly attitude to my activity and my tendencies". But there is evidence that she herself was concerned at the hold Wagner's genius exerted over Liszt. Perhaps, even, it was with that in mind that she cultivated Berlioz as a potential counterweight and now once again urged him to write the epic opera she believed he had it in him to write. At any rate there was no coolness between them, but on the contrary a strengthening of friendship. And this time, when she looked him in the eye and told him that if he shrank from the tribulations such a work was bound to cause him – if he was "so weak as to be afraid to face everything for Dido and Cassandra" – she would never see him again, her words answered his deepest desires and melted his last resistance. It was all he needed. When, two hours after the performance of *Faust*, Berlioz left Weimar with Marie – seen off at the station with a chorus from *Cellini* – he took with him a solemn undertaking, made to the Princess and to himself.

22

The Trojans

"For the last three years I have been tormented by the idea for an immense opera, for which I would write the words and the music, as I have just done for my sacred trilogy *The Childhood of Christ*. I am resisting the temptation to carry out this project and shall, I trust, resist to the end. To me the subject seems magnificent and deeply moving – guarantee that Parisians would think it flat and tedious."

Thus Berlioz in October 1854. "Three years" would place its inception in 1851. In a real sense, the history of *The Trojans* goes back much further, thirty years and more, to the Latin lessons in his father's study, the tears shed for Dido, the epiphany at Vespers in the church at La Côte St André. It continues with the epic guitar improvisations in the Roman Campagna and the vision, from the heights of Posilippo, of the whole coast swarming with his Virgilian heroes. Seven years later, in 1839, discussing the scene in the Elysian Fields in *Orphée* he remarks that "but for the anachronism one could believe Gluck meant to portray the still-suffering shade of the Queen of Carthage, the Dido whom Virgil shows us as *indignata sub umbras* and who, on seeing the Trojan warrior, the source of all her grief, flees deep into the shadowy wood to hide her wounds and lamentations". Other references could be cited. There is never a time when Virgil is not his companion and the work is not present by implication like an underground river running beneath the external reality of his life. And in the early 1850s it comes up into the light of day.

In April 1851 Gounod's *Sapho* was produced at the Opéra. It was not very well received, and its lack of success was blamed partly on its classical subject; but Berlioz, as well as having a good deal to say in favour of the music, found the subject profoundly appealing.

It seems I have the misfortune to be neither of my time nor of my country.

For me, Sapho's unhappy love and that other obsessive love of Glycera's, and Phaon's error, Alcaeus' unavailing enthusiasm, the dreams of liberty that culminate in exile, the Olympic festival and the worship of art by an entire people, the admirable final scene in which the dying Sapho returns for a moment to life and hears on one side the last distant farewell of Phaon to the Lesbian shore and on another the joyous song of a shepherd awaiting his young mistress, and the bleak wilderness, the deep sea, moaning for its prey, in which that immense love will find a worthy tomb, and then the beautiful Greek scenery, the fine costumes and elegant buildings, the noble ceremonies combining gravity and grace – all this, I confess, touches me to the heart, exalts my mind, excites and disturbs and enchants me more than I can say.

Eight months later, in January 1852, when *Sapho* was revived, he used the occasion to reaffirm his faith in "the beautiful", in "unadorned truth, grandeur without grandiloquence, force without brutality", and in works "dictated by the heart in an age of machinism, mannequinism (neologism too), and industrialism more or less disguised under a veneer of art".

"You are the Catos of a vanquished cause," we shall be told. So be it. But the cause is immortal – whereas the triumph of yours is for a brief hour only. Sooner or later the support of your gods will be denied it, and your gods themselves will disappear.

His own opera on an antique subject had come a step nearer.

A year later, in *Evenings in the Orchestra*, the narrator, asked by the musicians to tell them about the Paris Opéra, quotes Aeneas' opening words on the fall of Troy: *si tantus amor casus cognoscere nostros* – "If you are so eager to know of our calamities"; and, in the same book, modern music rent by rival doctrines is likened to Cassandra, "prophetic virgin fought over by Greeks and Trojans, whose inspired words go unheeded and who 'lifts her brilliant eyes to heaven – her eyes alone, for her hands are chained'". This had been one of the passages set for his baccalauréat, thirty years before.

By 1854, though still resisted, the idea was in the open, acknowledged; against his will he had begun turning it over in his mind (the libretto, he told Félix Marmion, had been pondered for two years before he began to write it in May 1856). Allusions now grow more frequent. In August 1854 the deep wooded inlet of St Valery en Caux makes him

think of the natural harbour where Aeneas' fleet anchors on the north
African coast; he quotes the Latin words in the feuilleton that describes
his visit to the little seaside town. A week or two later, in a letter to
Bülow, he half-jocularly likens the misfortunes of *Benvenuto Cellini* to
the *fatum* ("Fate") of the ancient world (the King of Saxony had
managed to get himself killed just as the Dresden theatre was about to
begin rehearsing the work) and adds that one could say of it as Virgil
says of the dying Dido, *Ter sese attollens cubitoque adnixa levavit /
Ter revoluta toro est* ("thrice raising herself on her elbow, thrice falling
back on the bed"). Then, unable to contain his admiration: "What a
great composer Virgil is! What a melodist, what a harmonist! *He* could
have made the deathbed remark *Qualis artifex pereo* ['What an artist
dies in me!'], not that humbug Nero, who had only one inspired idea
in his life, the night he set Rome on fire." In October, writing of Sontag's
death and praising her great qualities as singer and artist, he concludes
that she "would have been worthy to sing the incomparable love duet
in the last act of *The Merchant of Venice*: 'In such a night the young
Cressida, quitting the Grecian tents, rejoined her lover beneath the
walls of Troy'." Berlioz, quoting from memory, recalls it wrongly: in
the play Troilus is described as "sighing his soul toward the Grecian
tents / Where Cressid lay that night". But the allusion suggests he has
already thought of finding the text of the love scene between Aeneas
and Dido – obligatory for an operatic setting but missing in Virgil – in
Shakespeare; the Shakespearean lines, with their reference both to Troy
and to Dido wafting "her love to come again to Carthage", could
almost be said to have demanded it. The following April he quotes the
passage again, working it, with sublime inconsequence, into a review
of the latest offering at the Opéra-Comique, and adding that it was "in
such a night", too, that Jessica "slandered her love, and he forgave it
her" – a conceit which will also find its place in the love duet (as will
Portia's "the moon sleeps with Endymion").

Meanwhile, in February, he has had his long discussions with Liszt
and the Princess in Weimar. And a year later, when he is again in
Weimar, the Princess returns to the attack. Her friendly threats and his
own sense that the moment has come for a supreme effort, and that
whatever the almost certain consequences (Second Empire Paris being
what it is) he must seize it before it is too late, conspire to break down
his last resistance. He recognizes that he has, finally, no choice.

Berlioz was back in Paris on 3 March. The weeks immediately

following were spent clearing the decks. By the middle of the month the remaining songs of *Les nuits d'été* were orchestrated; and on April 1, having been copied by Rocquemont, they were dispatched to Rieter-Biedermann (together with the revised vocal score). *Le spectre de la rose* carried a dedication to Anna-Rose Falconi, for whom it had first been scored, and *Absence* to the Hanover mezzo-soprano Madeleine Nottès; the other four songs were inscribed to the Weimar artists who had performed his music over the past few years: Feodor and Rosa von Milde, Caspari, Louise Wolf.

In mid-April he suffered the disruption of an enforced move: the landlord of the apartment in the Rue Boursault raised the rent by a prohibitive two thirds (Paris was going through a period of sharp inflation). Berlioz would have liked to buy an apartment with money raised from the sale of one or more of his Dauphiné properties (they yielded an uneconomically low rent), but no purchaser could be found. He and Marie and her mother, Mme Martin, moved temporarily to a cramped flat in a recently built house in the nearby Rue de Vintimille, till they could find something better. By now the outline of the opera was taking shape; and it was there, on 5 May – anniversary of Napoleon's death, "an epic date if ever there was one" (as he wrote to Félix Marmion) – that he began writing the text. The room was tiny but he could manage, he told Adèle, because he was "only doing the words. When it comes to the score it will be torture for me, not being able to move about and work at a large table and make a noise without being heard." Odd (he went on) that he had never yet had a proper independent workroom but had always written more or less on the edge of things, while "hankering after the sort of studio painters and sculptors have, untidy but large, echoing, and isolated. What I do have that is good is a terrace, with air and sky and a view over all Paris and towards Montmartre." In October they found an apartment – though only to rent – on the fourth and fifth floors at 4 Rue de Calais, the short street running at right angles to the Rue de Vintimille. It was not the most luxurious of addresses. (The English pianist Alice Mangold, calling on him some years later, was struck by the desolate appearance of the inner courtyard, "the square of cobbles strewn with straw, cabbage leaves and what not, where a few sickly looking fowls were seeking food".) But he had, if not a studio, room to spread himself and work on his score undisturbed. The months stretched ahead, waiting to be filled by composition.

Partly by chance, partly by design, the two years in which Berlioz wrote *The Trojans* – spring 1856 to spring 1858 – were almost entirely free of conducting engagements. The concerts planned for London in 1856 failed to materialize; Jenny Lind had come out of retirement, and the London season was so dominated by her recitals and other appearances – an average of one a week – that the idea had to be dropped. Beale had, in addition, intended to bring him over in the autumn of 1857 to conduct *The Childhood of Christ* for the opening of St James's Hall, the new auditorium going up on the east side of Vine St, between Regent St and Piccadilly; but when the time came the hall was still unfinished. He also received a very lucrative offer from America, and there were invitations from Stockholm and Toulouse; but he turned them all down. During these two years he directed only three concerts, two in Baden and one in Paris (a Niedermeyer mass at St Eustache in July 1856), and appeared at one other, conducting *Le spectre de la rose* (with Falconi) in a programme given by Théodore Ritter in April 1857 at the Salle Herz.

The loss in earnings was partly made up by the windfall of his election, on 21 June 1856, to the Institute, membership of which carried a maximum stipend – depending on frequency of attendance at official meetings – of 1,500 francs a year. By an irony that he must have appreciated he was elected to the chair vacated by Adolphe Adam, who died suddenly during the night of 3 May. Berlioz won on the fourth ballot, scoring nineteen votes against six each for Gounod and Félicien David and two for Panseron. Azevedo, furious at David's defeat, ridiculed the result, and Scudo delivered his immortal thrust about choosing a journalist instead of a composer. But Berlioz's friends and admirers were overjoyed, some of the younger composers hailing it as a victory for them, and congratulatory letters poured in, from Legouvé, John Ella, Beale, Baron von Donop, the Princess, the widows Spontini and Le Sueur, Arban the cornet-player, the painter Chenavard, Balzac's step-daughter the Comtesse de Mniszech and many others, strangers included – letters whose most formal phrases are fired by genuine pleasure and affection. His *Débats* colleague Joseph-Esprit Duchesne wrote from Vervins:

> Can I believe my eyes? Have I read the newspaper aright? M. Berlioz elected a member of the Académie des Beaux-Arts? The Ronde des fraises replaced by the Valse des sylphes? Providence works in a mysterious

way. So, unconditional amnesty has been granted to the *vague des passions*, to the great Harold, to Romeo, to Queen Mab, Faust and King Herod. Will future generations credit it? And to think that you have not atoned for any of those sins by so much as an opéra-comique. Spontini at least wrote *Julie, ou le pot de fleurs*, not to mention *La petite maison*. But you, dear master – how have you managed to have your Last Judgement forgiven? I see none but your Virgin Mary and your Infant Jesus who could plausibly be thanked for this miracle. We must just accept it, uncomprehendingly, and bless God for His strength.

Now don't go falling asleep at the Academy, and don't disown any of your past. I had rather see Shakespeare confessing his faults to Boileau. You belong to those who understand you and love you. You are one of their most glorious memories, one of the most radiant reflections of their youth. Stay true to us and to yourself.

There was no danger of his failing to. But the acquisition of academic respectability – confirmed soon afterwards by a letter from the imperial household accepting the dedication of his cantata, accompanied by a specially inscribed gold medal with the Emperor's effigy on it – could only be welcome. However little he thought of the "honour", it gave him access to circles and individuals who could well be useful if and when it came to having his opera performed. As he put it to his uncle, "I was sitting on a bayonet, but now I have a chair. My musical value is acknowledged in the market-place, since three days ago."

Further fame arrived that autumn in the shape of a short biography in the series "Contemporains" which the journalist Charles Jacquot had begun bringing out a couple of years before under the pseudonym Eugène de Mirecourt. Jacquot/Mirecourt got some of his facts wrong and garbled the information Berlioz sent him, but his pamphlets were widely read and this one was a great deal more favourable than many in the series. (Janin, for example, was viciously attacked.) Apart from criticizing the composer's feuilletons for "unnecessary vehemence and acerbity, and humour in poor taste" it was broadly sympathetic. Berlioz may have been irritated by the book's errors, but it enhanced his growing prestige. The following January he was photographed by Nadar in the great artist's studio in the Rue St Lazare, a session which produced the noble, tormented image with the eagle head and the hands thrust into the sleeves of a capacious greatcoat – one of the finest of all the pictures that were made of him and an authentic portrait of the composer at the time when he was composing the first act of his crowning work.

In this period, too, he was relatively free of anxiety about his son. The war with Russia ended in March 1856. Shortly afterwards Louis entered the merchant navy. Great-Uncle Félix and Aunt Adèle had been opposed to his leaving the navy, and Berlioz was inclined to agree with them, but in the end the young man had his way. To begin with he worked for companies based in Marseille, and his father had the satisfaction of knowing that between ships he was cared for by his friends Morel (now director of the Marseille conservatoire) and Hippo-lyte Lecourt, who had contacts in the local shipping world. In October 1856 Louis sailed for India as lieutenant on the *Belle Assise*, a vessel belonging to Baron Rothschild. (Berlioz had gone to see him on Louis' behalf.) He was away for nearly a year, and subsequently from December 1857 to July 1859 on the *Reine des Clippers*. During these absences he wrote fairly regularly. Berlioz could worry now in moderation. His son was evidently doing all right and, in his early twenties, had finally decided to grow up.

There remained his own health. The intestinal disorder which had been plaguing him for more than a year worsened about this time. After the fatigue and tension of the Exhibition Concerts in November 1855 he was prostrated by it, and from then on it recurred with increasing frequency. He tried various doctors, including his cousin Alphonse Robert. They all diagnosed "intestinal neuralgia", or a general neuro-pathy located specifically in the intestines or the bladder, without however being able to treat it. During the composition of *The Trojans* the pain and debilitation were sometimes so bad that he would spend several days in bed dosed with laudanum, which did something to relieve it, though it dulled his brain and the accompanying internal trembling was unpleasant.

The steep decline in Berlioz's physical state contributed to the idea – common at a time when the work was still waiting to be discovered (in Dent's phrase) "like some buried city of the ancient world", and very few people had more than a nodding acquaintance with it – that *The Trojans* was the product of an artist past his peak, composed laboriously and fitfully over a period of many years, and fatally uneven. This strange notion is difficult to credit now that the opera is widely known and we are in a position to recognize the justice of Tovey's verdict: "one of the most gigantic and convincing masterpieces of music-drama". The notion was based – to quote the French critic Claude

Rostand – "not simply on incomprehension but first and foremost on a liberal measure of pure ignorance": ignorance compounded by an error of Berlioz's biographer Boschot, who supposed that work on the opera began not in the summer of 1856 but nearly eighteen months earlier, in February 1855, in which misdating he was followed by Barzun and other writers.

In any case, the old dichotomy, beloved of French commentators, between the "Romantic" and the "Classical" Berlioz – between the wild, "passionate" early works and the poised, "serene" later ones – was a figment of their imaginations. *The Trojans* needed only to be known to expose the fallacy. It needed to be performed properly, and published. Its revelation at Covent Garden in 1957 – notwithstanding earlier performances, that is what it amounted to – showed that far from being in decline the composer was at the height of his powers. The backward glances to classical French opera, in particular the Gluckian cast of certain passages in Acts 1 and 5, signal no denial of innovation, no retreat into musical conservatism. Gluck, for Berlioz, was not a figure from a vanished century: he was a living presence. Conceiving a work in his spirit did not mean turning back to the past. "Gluck," as he said, "was a Romantic." Gluck equalled not limitation but possibility, infinite possibility. Spontini too. *Tragédie-lyrique* and its successor, Spontinian proto-grand opera, expanded and enriched by the expressive force of Berliozian Romanticism at its most highly charged, were absorbed into his personal style. *The Trojans* is the summa of his output. (Only *The Damnation of Faust* is absent – Mephisto and his spirit of eternal denial had no place in the ancient world.) As Kemp says, "everything making up Berlioz's musical personality is fused in this one work". It unites the electric energy of the Fantastic, the tragic visions of the Requiem, the sadness and sensuous beauty of *Romeo and Juliet*, the massive grandeur of the Te Deum, the archaic simplicity and sweetness of *The Childhood of Christ*, the refinement of *Les nuits d'été*. It is his greatest score and his most daring and eventful – a conscious summing-up and a reaching out into new regions.

His first task, when he finally set to work that spring, was to reduce the huge scope and outwardly discursive method of the *Aeneid* to the scale and conditions of opera. Even though he was restricting himself to two, at most two and a half, of the poem's twelve books and had five acts to do it in, the task was formidable. He was writing for the finite dimensions of the stage – an ideal theatre, maybe, but a theatre none the less. Yet he must keep faith with Virgil, with the Virgilian world that had been his home since childhood. The richness of the poem's episodic detail must not be sacrificed to the claims of dramatic coherence. Those claims, however, remained paramount.

The key lay in Shakespeare – in his open form and mixing of genres and his making coherent by means far transcending the unities of time, place and action. Shakespeare, in *The Trojans*, is the inspiration for much more than the text of the love duet. His influence is manifest in the far-flung topography of the action, in the elements of the homely and the grotesque and the supernatural which are allowed their part, in the closely woven web of poetic, psychological correspondences and resonances, and in the juxtaposing of sharply contrasted scenes which – and this is Virgilian too – create new perspectives and at the same time anchor the drama's epic preoccupations in human reality. All this had long been Berlioz's intention. A Virgilian opera "on the Shake-spearean plan" was how he first spoke of it to Liszt and the Princess.

The shaping of the poem to make what Donald Grout has called "the unique opera in which the epic has been successfully dramatized" involved systematic condensing, expanding, transposing, reinventing. (To cite one small example, the text of Dido's monologues in the fifth act is a mosaic of lines taken from many different points in Book IV.) Though the action is confined to Troy's fall and the Trojans' sojourn at Carthage, running through it explicitly and implicitly is the *Aeneid*'s main theme, the founding of a new Troy in Italy – necessarily made more emphatic than it is in the early books of the poem, given the demands of stage drama. (Thus in the opera Hector's ghost, appearing not in a dream but to a fully awake Aeneas, identifies the hero's destined goal, and the Trojan women as they die reiterate the cry "Italie!".) With all its wealth of varied incident and atmosphere *The Trojans* has a sweep and momentum appropriate to a story of the destruction of cities and the migration of peoples.

The libretto draws on Berlioz's intimate knowledge of all twelve books of the poem; the material he added nearly all comes from within the *Aeneid*: Andromache's ritual mourning (borrowed from Book III), the comic duet for the sentries (derived from the episode in Book V where the women rebel at the prospect of further voyaging), Aeneas' farewell to his son on the eve of battle (Book XII). Both the elevation of Cassandra into protagonist of Acts 1 and 2 and the invasion of Iarbas which provides the climax of Act 3 are a development of suggestions in the poem. Much of the opera's text is direct translation or paraphrase of the Latin.

Once he had reworked the epic as a medium for musical drama Berlioz could recreate it in his own language. The musical rendering of the characters and their passions, he told the Princess, was the easiest part: he had "spent his life with that race of demigods". But not that alone is reborn in music: it is the whole Virgilian ambience, it is the colours and textures and rhythms of the verse, the mixture of monumentality and pictorial vividness, the structural balance of violence and calm, the symbolic linking of widely separate events and emotional states, the sense of fatality, of the power of unreason in human affairs, the sympathy with suffering; it is Virgil himself. Time and again the music *is* the verse.

We hear it in Cassandra's anguish at the impending annihilation of Troy (echoing Aeneas' *O patria o divum domus Ilium*) and in the slowly gathering horror of the ensemble in which, at the news of Laocoön's death, a new fear "insinuates itself" into the hearts of the Trojan people; we hear it in the entry of the Wooden Horse through the torchlit darkness, and in the veiled sonority of muted horns and divided lower strings as Hector, "recalled to life by the will of the gods", lays on the staring, transfixed Aeneas his divinely decreed mission, then gradually fades from sight, "becoming dead again"; we hear it in the change from the sound of Acts 1 and 2, harsh, possessed, rhythmically on a knife-edge, to the warm, expansive Act 3, paralleling the effect in the *Aeneid* when Virgil cuts from the frescoes of the Trojan War in the Carthaginian temple of Juno to the vision of the enchanting Dido moving among the throng; in the strange, antique sadness of the music for the farmworkers, like "the melancholy voice of Virgil" as Berlioz had often imagined it "reading from the *Georgics*"; in the glowing moment, mirroring the poem, when Aeneas strips off his disguise and utters his orchestra-silencing "Reine – je suis Enée"; more indirectly but with no less authentic touch, in the Palinurus-like figure of the young sailor Hylas consumed with longing for his lost homeland and rocked by the sea to a death-like sleep; and in the terrible stillness and finality of Dido's farewell to life. He did not have to search for it: it had been his kingdom for almost as long as he could remember. The act of realizing it in music was a final entering into his own. Through Virgil he could become most fully himself.

The Trojans shows the influence of the theatre where Berlioz had passed so much of his artistic existence, the Opéra, and of the kind of works he had seen and heard there: *tragédie-lyrique*, and grand opera as anticipated by Spontini and developed by Auber, Rossini, Meyerbeer and Verdi. From grand opera (itself a development from the baroque) came the five-act form, the central role of the chorus, the big crowd scenes, the stage bands, the processions and ballets, the struggles between private desire and public duty, even the key of the love duet, G flat major, for which Meyerbeer had set the fashion with his "Tu l'as dit: oui, tu m'aimes!" in *The Huguenots*. Like any other composer, Berlioz borrowed ideas from anywhere and everywhere. Two details in the Septet, the sound of waves breaking on a warm, flowery shore and the rapt, enchanted melismas added for Dido, came from music he heard about this time, Gounod's *Sapho* and the sextet in *Figaro*.

These are outward resemblances. Quite apart from the unfashionable ancient-world subject, the conception and the whole feel and climate of the work are peculiar to Berlioz and light years away from what his contemporaries, the great and the less than great, were doing. Even when he works within the tradition he goes further than anyone else. In no other opera in the repertory does the chorus play so large a part; it is on stage and actively contributing for three quarters of the three and a half hours the score lasts. The symphonic interlude Royal Hunt and Storm, though it harks back to the ballet-pantomimes of French eighteenth-century opera, is without precedent in its scope and grandeur, and in the sheer power of its evocation of Nature, a primeval forest at the dawn of the ages, convulsed by a torrential rainstorm that is almost palpable. As for the conventional conflict of love and duty, nothing I know comes near the agony of Aeneas' "Ah! quand viendra l'instant des suprêmes adieux" – music from which all superfluous gesture has been cut away. Verdi and Wagner *express*, unforgettably, the pain of loss and grief. With Berlioz, in a passage such as this or in Dido's "inutile prière d'un coeur qui se déchire", it is the pain itself, direct, unmediated. From the beginning of the opera – from the hectic babble of woodwind, literally baseless, as the inhabitants of Troy rush outside the walls to celebrate their supposed deliverance – he responds to the passions of the epic tale with an intensity and momentousness of feeling (varied occasionally and Shakespeareanly by its opposite) that few operas can match.

He is, naturally, at pains to forge into a coherent whole the wide

diversity of scenes inherent in his subject and articulated in separate
though often linked musical numbers. The means are, first, large-scale
tonal design and, second, recurring motifs – melodic, harmonic, rhythmic, sonic – of which the Trojan March, the fateful hymn stated in
Acts 1, 3 and 5, and echoed subliminally at other points, is only the
most obvious.* Third, he patterns the acts in related ways; Acts 1 and
3, for example, both contain opening chorus followed by aria for
mezzo-soprano soloist, procession, ceremonial anthem, pantomime,
duet, late entry for tenor, and fast-moving finale on a grand scale. He
also sets up parallels between ideas or incidents, as when the musical
rendering of Dido's first words in the final tableau ("Plûton semble
m'être propice") ironically recalls, in its broken phrases and slow
descent through a chromatic octave, the music of Hector's prophecy,
three acts earlier, which was to be the cause of her abandonment.

Finally, contrast is made a structural principle. Most strikingly,
contrast between the musical idioms of Acts 1 and 2 (Troy) and Acts
3 and 4 (the first two Carthage acts), and then between the scale and
character of one act and the next: Act 1 spacious and, for much of its
course, static, followed by the dynamic, highly compressed Act 2 –
Troy on its last night; Act 2 giving way to the Arcadian picture of
peaceful, industrious Carthage in Act 3, which, however, like Act 1,
ends with a highly dramatic, martial finale; Act 4, both dynamic (Royal
Hunt) and static (Dido's garden by the sea), a time out of war, but
framed by the word "Italie" and ending with a grim reminder of the
issues of fate and war which will come to a head in Act 5, the act
that draws together and completes the preceding four. Then, frequent
smaller-scale contrasts of musical character and dramatic perspective:
the Trojans' celebration cut across by the entry of the grieving Andromache (ultimate image of the misery of war, not forgotten in the ensuing
catastrophe), itself succeeded by Aeneas' horrified narration of the death
of Laocoön; sudden, Virgilian shifts of focus from high romance and
affairs of state to the experience of ordinary people swept along by the
tides of epic events – the sentries' grumbling about "Italy" yielding in

---

* Another is the rising chromatic figure which punctuates the refrain of the love duet
in Act 4, echoing the moment in the previous act where Aeneas tells his son that he can
teach him only the virtues of a fighting man and respect for the gods – how to be happy
he will have to learn from others. The recurrence of the figure in the duet, contradicting
the lovers' felicity at its height, signals what will happen: Aeneas will place duty to his
god-given mission before his happiness, and Dido's.

turn to the anguished, exalted mood of Aeneas' monologue, with its panting rhythms, long arcs of melody and heroic orchestration.

The central theme of *The Trojans* is embodied in music of truly heroic temper. Nothing in the work is more magnificent than the passage where Aeneas, his decision made, already part of history, turns shoreward and utters his "A toi, mon âme, adieu", while beneath pulsating woodwind chords the unison strings add a curving, swelling melodic line that could have been written by no one else. Yet the author of *The Trojans* has no illusions about great causes and their effect on the individuals caught up in them. The juggernaut of Roman destiny rolls ruthlessly across the lives of his two contrasted but complementary tragic heroines: the inspired prophetess whom no one will believe (and whose heartache is like a projection of the unheeded Berlioz himself), and the injured queen whose tragedy was the origin of it all. The role of Dido is the composer's tribute – a tribute of extraordinary radiance and tenderness – to the mythical but to him totally real being who first possessed his boyhood imagination forty years before.

Just what it meant to him to be making it come alive at last in music is revealed by his correspondence. While he worked on the opera his creative exuberance overflowed into his letters. They are the log of its progress; they convey a unique sense of excitement, a conviction that this was what all his past life had been preparing for. Though they mention other things he did during that time – conducting at Baden, visiting Plombières, seeing friends and colleagues, attending a family reunion at La Côte, going to receptions at the Tuileries, writing feuilletons – they show us that the opera was the centre of his being. Better than other words could, they describe the "ardent existence" he lived in those two years when *The Trojans* ruled over his thoughts and actions.

To Liszt   12 April 1856
  I've started roughing out the plan of the great dramatic machine which
  the Princess is kindly taking an interest in. It's beginning to become clear;
  but it's enormous and consequently dangerous. I need plenty of peace
  of mind, which is precisely what I haven't got. It will come, perhaps.
  Meanwhile I ruminate, and gather myself like a cat before a desperate
  spring. I am trying above all to resign myself to the sorrows this work
  is bound to cause me . . . Anyway, whether I succeed or not, I shan't
  talk to you about it till it's done.

To Princess Carolyne Sayn-Wittgenstein   17 May 1856

I'm ashamed not to have replied to your fine encouraging letter before. Please excuse me. I wanted to be able to give you positive news of the great enterprise which you have brought into being. I finished the poem of the first act only the day before yesterday. It will be the longest, and it took me ten days to write – the 5th May to the 15th, the first I have had entirely to myself since I got back from Weimar. I will not tell you what stages of discouragement, delight, disgust, pleasure and rage I passed through during those ten days. A dozen times I was on the point of throwing the whole thing into the fire and giving myself up for ever to the contemplative life. But now I'm certain I shan't lack courage to go on to the end – the work has got hold of me. Generally it was in the evening that I felt discouraged; in the morning, in the youth of the day, I returned to the attack. Now I hardly sleep, I think of nothing else; and, if I had the time to work at it, in two months the whole mosaic would be finished. But how can I? I've now got to immerse myself in my candidature for the Institute and rush about Paris from morning till night, seeing all and sundry (mostly sundry). And every so often those eternal, infernal feuilletons to write, on débutants male and female, revivals of antiquated operas, first performances of antiquated operas, end-of-season concerts which go off between my legs like forgotten squibs at the end of a firework display that singe the beards of the passers-by.

For the music, a good year and a half will be needed to construct it, I guess (as the Americans say). It will be a big construction. May it be built of bricks well baked in the fire, and not of unbaked, like the palaces of Nineveh. Without firing, bricks soon turn to sand and dust.

I am sick with sadness today. I've just lost one of my dearest friends, the great surgeon Amussat, my old anatomy teacher. He died worn out with toil – after thirty years of unrelenting struggle and hard work. Poor young Fumagalli, whom Liszt thought highly of, has also died, a few days after Adam. Yet another of my friends is dead – Dr Vidal, the medical specialist of the Opéra (which is terminally ill). I'm never out of the cemetery. The Good Lord is gunning us down. I hope he's missing you all at Weimar. How is Liszt?

I receive letters from no one. [. . .] Couldn't Pohl bring himself to be so kind as to have the goodness to send me six lines in answer?

Farewell, Princess, you too will have to answer, some night, to the shade of Virgil for the crimes I am committing against his beautiful verse

– especially if my palace is built of unfired bricks and my hanging gardens are planted only with willows and wild plum trees.

To Théodore Ritter   23 May 1856

I've finished the second act (poem) of my great beast of an opera. I'm thoroughly ill – I go to sleep in the street; I don't know what it is. [Grétry's] *Richard Coeur-de-Lion* has been given at the Opéra-Comique, and is being given this evening in a rival production at the Théâtre-Lyrique. It's delicious. The romance galvanizes the entire house. The whole thing has a fineness, a truthfulness, an inventiveness and good sense that are captivating. And none of your coarse orchestration. I so much prefer those simple unassuming orchestral scores with holes in the elbows of their coats, and even in the seat of their pants, to those great loud-mouthed mountebanks covered in cheap brass finery who bawl from the height of their soapboxes, "Roll up, gentlemen, every place is taken!", etc. [. . .]

Louis is back in Toulon. He went to Athens, and put in at Tenedos. Tenedos! Queer for me to hear that island mentioned, having written its name several times in my first act.

To Toussaint Bennet and Théodore Ritter   late May 1856

I'm going to spend the day touring the academic shrines. Believe it or not, M. Ingres himself has unbent and promised me his vote – on the second ballot, if his Benjamin, Gounod, isn't elected on the first. The musicians in the section are very much for me, including Halévy, despite my recent article on his *Valentine*. Auber is as always relaxed, determined to side with the big battalions, like the Good Lord and other rogues. As for Carafa: blinkered and unshiftable.

[. . .] Between ourselves, now that I've two acts written the music's driving me mad with wanting to come out. But I'm resisting it; I must finish the poem first. But I'm making notes.

To Bennet   11 June 1856

I have just finished the third act of my poem, and yesterday, as well, I wrote both words and music of the big duet in Act 4, a scene stolen from Shakespeare and Virgilianized which reduces me to the most absurd state. I've had to do no more than transcribe that immortal love babble which makes the last act of *The Merchant of Venice* a worthy pendant of *Romeo and Juliet*. Shakespeare is the real author of the words and the music. Strange that he should intervene – he, the poet of the north – in the great work of the poet of Rome. Virgil left out the scene. What singers, those two!

To his sister Adèle Suat   14 June 1856

I'm well ahead with my great poem. The third act was finished yesterday and, in addition, I've written the words and music of a scene in the fourth; the music settled on it like a bird on ripe fruit. It's a scene from Shakespeare introduced into the Virgilian subject. Working at my opera intoxicates me, as the composition of *Romeo and Juliet* did, ten years ago. I swim with strong strokes in this lake of antique poetry. What gratitude we owe those great spirits, those mighty hearts, who give us such noble emotions as they speak to us across the centuries. It seems to me that I've known Virgil and Shakespeare, that I can see them.

To Adèle   22 June 1856

No doubt you know already that I was elected a member of the Institute yesterday. This coup d'état by the *youthful* party in the Academy of Fine-Arts is making a stir in our world which I didn't foresee. I can't describe the joy, the rapture. My apartment is never empty of well-wishers. Congratulatory letters have been pouring in since this morning. Yesterday evening, when I came back, I found the staircase covered in flowers and greenery, left by I don't yet know which friend. The whole music section was perfect for me. As for Horace Vernet and his fellow-supporters, it's a triumph for them. Farewell. No news [of Louis] from Marseille. Let me know if you have any. I embrace your husband and your dear daughters – and you too! I've been doing nothing but embrace people since yesterday. Marie came to the Institute to await the result in the studio of a sculptor. She nearly fainted when they came and announced victory.

To the Princess   24 June 1856

A thousand apologies, Princess, for not replying till today to your last two letters. As you will have guessed, the *Aeneid* and the Academy were the cause of the delay – but the *Aeneid* much more than the Academy. Every morning as I got into a cab and went on my pilgrimage I thought not of what I was going to say to the Immortal I was visiting but of what I was going to make my characters say. But now this double preoccupation is at an end. The Academy has elected me, as you know, and the opera is virtually complete – I'm at the final scene of the fifth act. I get more impassioned about the subject than I should, but am resisting the appeals for attention that the music makes from time to time. I want to get everything finished before starting on the score. Yet last week it simply wasn't possible not to write the Shakespearean duet "In such a night as this / When the sweet wind did gently kiss the trees", etc. And the music of this litany of love is done. [. . .] I still have twenty-two colleagues to see and thank. I saw fifteen this morning and submitted to being embraced by a lot of people who voted against me. So here I am, a respectable person, no longer a vagrant or a gipsy; the gutter is forsworn for ever. What a comedy. I don't despair of being Pope one day.

To Baron von Donop   26 June 1856

I have finally followed your advice; I'm at present busy with the composition of a five-act opera on a subject very close to my heart. I've just finished the poem. I shall polish and correct and refine it as best I can for another week, and then start on the score. It's a sea of music. God grant I don't drown in it.

To the Princess   late June 1856

Certainly, yes, it's possible – and I should already have sent you the manuscript but for the fear of seeing you disappointed. However, sooner or later you'll have to know what you think of this amateur poetry, and I shall do as you say. In two or three days *The Trojans* will leave here by train. Will you be kind enough to let me have it back as soon as possible and show it only to close friends whose discretion can be counted on? [. . .] The thing now is the music; and you'll see what an enormous score this libretto presupposes.

You laugh at my plans for withdrawing from the world, my longing for deserts, and so on. All the same it's a fact that for the past week I've not been able to find one hour's freedom for thinking over my project, and the whole of next month is going to be torn from me bit by bit by all kinds of tiresome affairs that I can't escape. And then . . . and then . . . and then – would you believe it, I've fallen in love, but utterly in love, with my Carthaginian queen! I love her to distraction, this beautiful Dido. You will find many borrowings from Shakespeare in the midst of the Virgilian poetry. I've laced my Cyprus wine with eau-de-vie. I wish Mlle Rachel would do me the favour, one of these days, of reading the fifth act and the scenes with Cassandra in the first and second. There are accents there that must be found, silences to gauge, inflections to catch. But she is too much the diva, and just now especially too *diva furens*. La Ristori's success has put her into a state of rage that makes her unapproachable. Liszt should by now have received Gounod's mass. I thank him warmly for his letter and for sending the parcel to Litolff, and even for his puns – in future I shan't be so ashamed of my own.

So you will, won't you, keep my manuscript for three or four days at the most? Many apologies for sending you such a scribble. I'm at the Institute, writing in haste between two sessions.

Your very devoted, grateful toiler, for all that the task you've laid on him is such an arduous one

H. Berlioz

To the Princess

Baden, 12 August 1856

I cannot thank you enough, Princess, for your adorable goodness in writing me so helpful a letter. That is a real analysis! That is what is meant by entering into the spirit of the thing!

You were keen to encourage me. I don't overestimate the value of what you say. You go so far as to credit me with the beauties of Virgil's poetry and praise me for my thefts from Shakespeare. Don't worry, I have the courage to carry it through to the end; it wasn't necessary to lure me on with eulogies which belong to others. It's beautiful because it's Virgil, it's striking because it's Shakespeare – I know it. I am only a pilferer. I've foraged in the garden of two geniuses and cut a swathe of flowers to make a couch for music, where God grant it doesn't perish, asphyxiated by the fragrance.

Liszt is quite right about the word *Italie*, which sounds so poor compared to *Italiam* with its accent on the second syllable. But I'm writing in French. I had actually used two Latin words, *votum* and *peplum*,* but was advised to replace them by equivalent French expressions.

Yes, I shall arrange the Ascanius scene so that it's not he who says, "Oh Queen, our path was stained with blood." That's not the way a child would answer. But he'll take up the story again to say, "I am his son", his childlike pride unable to contain itself when Panthus says "Our chief is Aeneas." [. . .]†

---

* Respectively: vow, and the robe of state which clothed Athene's statue.
† In the end the passage was given to Ascanius.

Thank you, then, for everything your exquisite kindness prompted you to say to me by way of encouragement. When I am back in Paris I shall try to rid myself of all other business and embark on my musical task. It will be hard. May all Virgil's gods come to my aid, or I am lost. What is immensely difficult about it is finding the musical *form* – that form without which music does not exist or is merely the lowly slave of the text. That is Wagner's crime: he wants to dethrone music, to reduce it to "expressive accents", thus exaggerating the system of Gluck (who happily did not succeed in keeping to his ungodly theory). I am for the kind of music you yourself call free. Yes, free, and proud, sovereign, conquering. I want it to grasp, to assimilate, everything, I want there to be, for it, no more Alps or Pyrenees. But to achieve its conquests it must fight in person and not through its lieutenants. I certainly wish it to have, if possible, fine verses drawn up in battle array, but it must itself advance into the line of fire, like Napoleon, and march in the front rank of the phalanx as Alexander did. Music is so powerful that in given cases it could conquer on its own; again and again it has had the right to say, like [Corneille's] Medea, "Myself – that is enough." To want to take it back to the old recitation of the antique Chorus is the most unbelievable, but happily the most unavailing, folly in the history of art.

To find the means to be *expressive*, *truthful*, without ceasing to be a musician, to endow music, on the contrary, with new means of action – there is the problem. And then, as Béranger says, "That one can even go to mass – that is what Freedom means." Oh, the droll effect of Béranger's name in this context! Never mind – you understand.

Yet another danger for me in composing the music of this drama is that the feelings that have to be expressed move me too much. That's no good. One must strive to do the most fiery things coolly. It was that that held me up so long when I was writing the adagio of *Romeo and Juliet* and the final scene of reconciliation. I thought I should never find my way out of it.

Time, Time! He is the great master. Unfortunately, like Ugolino he eats his children.* Bülow is here, and so is Pohl. The [Baden] concert takes place next Saturday. I imagine Liszt is at this moment at grips with his "good friends" in Hungary. I trust he'll give me news of the battle, for he still has his *bataille d'Arbelles (d'art belle)* to fight.†

---

* Thirteenth-century tyrant who figures in Dante's *Inferno*.
† Alexander's victory over Darius in 331 BC.

I finish on this punning alexandrine, so as to stop thinking of Dido and Cassandra, and to provoke you a little – if that's possible.

Your devoted and grateful Iopas

To the Princess   Paris, 3 September 1856

Your letters give me courage. As the soldier said of Napoleon, they put fire in my belly. I'm working. Musing in the woods at Plombières I did two important pieces: the first chorus of the Trojan mob and Cassandra's aria. Then, I've added two scenes – short but useful and curious – to the opening of the fifth act. One of them offers a musical proposition full of interest. Two Trojan soldiers are on guard at night before the tents, one marching from right to left, the other from left to right, and chatting when they meet in the middle of the stage, about their leaders' insistence on going to conquer this accursed Italy, when they're doing so nicely in Carthage, well fed, well lodged and the rest. [. . .] The contrast between the base instincts of the soldiery and the heroic aspirations of the royal characters is, perhaps, a happy one. It's a march in triple time, over which the soldiers talk. It's half written. [. . .]

I am quite transported by some words of Father Nestor's in Shakespeare's *Troilus and Cressida*. I've just reread that amazing parody of the *Iliad*, where Shakespeare none the less made Hector greater even than Homer did. Nestor, paying tribute to the sublime generosity of Troy's defender, says he has seen him many times in the midst of battle thunder past in his chariot with his sword uplifted, so as to spare the trembling ranks of Greeks. "Lo, Jupiter is yonder, dealing life." What a picture I should make of that, were I a great painter. God in heaven, but it's beautiful. Nestor: "Lo, Jupiter is yonder, dealing life." I feel as if my heart will burst when I come upon phrases like that.

You tell me splendid things about Liszt's visit to Hungary; but when and how his mass was performed you don't say. His noble profile, hanging above my piano, seemed to be smiling at me when I got home yesterday from Plombières. So all is well! I like to think so.

Farewell, Princess, please don't mock me too much for taking advantage of the permission you gave me to tell you about my work. You let me believe that you were interested, like Dido, *Trojae supremam audire laborem.**

The Baden concert was brilliant. Bülow will tell you about it.

* "to hear of Troy's last agony".

To Auguste Morel   9 September 1856

Is your opera well advanced?

I'm working exclusively on mine – without so much as mentioning it to Royer, who's the same as all the other Opéra directors were, a musical Hottentot. He regards me as a great symphonist who can and should do only symphonies and who doesn't know how to write for voices. He's heard neither *Faust* nor *The Childhood of Christ* and knows nothing about such matters, nevertheless it's his rooted opinion. He was saying so to a friend of mine just the other day. I was quite sure in advance that it would be so – I know his ideas on music. I go on with my score all the same, with a vague hope of getting into the place later from the top, I mean by the will of the Emperor.

To Adèle   26 October 1856

I'm in a state of inner agitation – and I feel the fever will calm if I talk to you for a moment. Thinking of you refreshes me. You don't know that another link has been forged between us since you seemed to take an interest in this thing that excites and disturbs me, that eats into me, that kills me and that makes me live. I've always suffered a lot, in silence, from seeing all of you (your husband excepted) consider only the final result of my efforts and my artistic dreams. This non-sympathy, non-comprehension, this isolation which cuts you off from the intellectual world I live in, has been a cause of great unhappiness to me. Unfortunately you don't know music; but at least, now, the literary side of my work (don't laugh at this pretentious word) gives you a means of communication and opens a window through which you can look out on my garden. The idea that you watch me working there is a quite new and delightful sensation.* And can you believe it? (you must forgive me) – I love you the more for it.

So, you see why I had to write to you today. I'm trembling from head to foot, from heart to brain – with impatience, pain, enthusiasm, superabundance of life. I can't write my score fast enough. It needs a large, a disastrous amount of time. I'm anxious about its future. There's no one to perform it. The Opéra is in the hands of the greatest enemies of my art. The Emperor knows nothing, understands nothing. [. . .]

Yesterday evening I had the misfortune to open a volume – I've three editions of Shakespeare, two in English, one in French, a *translation*. I

---

* Berlioz had shown her the libretto when she came to Paris not long before.

chanced on *Hamlet*, and couldn't put it down. I reread it from end to end. I'm knocked out by it – it's as if my heart is alternately contracting and dilating, at that prodigious and devastating picture of human life, at the awe caused by the contemplation of so gigantic a genius, at thinking of the causes that still prevent so many people from understanding him, at the crimes of his interpreters and translators – and the poet's indifference to the effect he'll produce, like the sun which pours its light on the earth without troubling itself whether the clouds of this puny planet get in the way.

To the Princess   14 November 1856

I've not ceased a single day from my Phrygian task, in spite of the moods of disgust, inspired by my illness, when I found everything I had done cold, flat, insipid, absurd, and wanted to burn it all. The human mechanism is really bizarre and unpredictable. Now that I'm better I reread my score and it seems to me not as stupid as I thought. I'm still only at the big ensemble "Châtiment effroyable! mystérieuse horreur!", after Aeneas has recounted the Laocoön catastrophe. I compose a piece in two days, sometimes one, then spend three weeks thinking it over, polishing it and instrumenting it.

I also continue to make small changes to the poem. I've just added a scene to the first act. It won't make it any longer – it will be instead of some ballet music, during the popular rejoicing which, if you remember, takes place on the plain before Troy. The whole Trojan population, the army led by Aeneas, Priam, the queen, Helen, the princes and princesses, the people, the priests, come in procession to make thank-offerings to Jupiter and Neptune for the deliverance of Troy. I thought that one of the most touching figures in the story ought also to appear at the ceremony. So, after the various arms of state have laid their gifts at the field altar and just as the festive games are at their height, the musical style changes abruptly and, to the sound of mime music, desolate, haunting, (if possible) heartbreaking, Andromache comes forward, holding by the hand Astyanax who carries a wreath of flowers. They are in white (the mourning colour of the ancient world), and they kneel silently before the altar. The child places the wreath, the mother prays, then presents her son to Priam, who blesses him. Overcome by tears, she lowers her veil, takes Astyanax by the hand again, and the two go slowly out without saying a word and return within Troy. Cassandra, pacing like a wounded lioness, sees Andromache as she goes past at the back of the stage and says, "Keep back your tears, widow of Hector, do not exhaust the spring. Disasters soon to come, alas, will make you weep long and bitterly." And the Trojan women in chorus: "Andromache and her son! Wives, mothers weep to see them [etc.]" These eight lines will be sung or rather chanted in an aside during the playing of the mime music. Then the celebrations begin again.

To Adolphe Samuel   25 November 1856
I'm not sure the false prophets of our art are worth the trouble we take to oppose them. Besides, whenever art mixes with commerce (as is the case with works written for the theatre) it always has fifty justifications for its misdeeds to throw at our heads, and its commercial success confounds its accusers. Still, in the long run some good comes of our protesting. The general common sense absorbs it and benefits from it. But how long it takes! If you could see what goes on, and doesn't go on, at our great Opéra! [. . .]

    As you guessed, I'm absorbed in my great musical and dramatic machine. It advances slowly, very slowly. I shall have scarcely finished the first act a month from now. It will take eighteen months of work. I'm beginning not to let myself be moved any more by the subject – an important stage in mastering it.

    God knows what will become of the work. It would need a theatre directed by people devoted to our ideas and an attentive public that had shaken off Parisian habits. What's more it needs two women of exalted talent – and I don't know of any. Those two antique beings, represented by the average modern singer, would be travesties.

To Camille Pal   5 December 1856
So as not to be distracted I'm giving no concerts in Paris this winter, and I won't go to Germany; I'm restricting myself to a journey to London in May – I've promised to go there to inaugurate a new hall with the first performance (in England) of my oratorio *The Childhood of Christ*. And I'd give a lot not to have to go there either.

To the Princess   25 or 26 December 1856
You ask me for news of Troy. I only got back there tonight. Yesterday I was at Carthage, completing the scoring of the finale of Act 4 and the great duet for the lovers (which doesn't mean that the preceding pieces are done). I'm working now on the finale of Act 1, the scene of the entry

of the Wooden Horse – all the rest of the act is done. I'm still continually improving the poem. Recently I realized that the dying Dido's allusion to French domination in Africa was pure puerile chauvinism and that it was far fitter and grander to stay with Virgil's own idea [the prophecy of Hannibal]. [. . .] Then, a host of words changed, lines rewritten. In fact I keep polishing and pruning. But when I think of what is to become of it my heart grows cold. The taste of the vast majority is so different from ours. What moves us leaves the general public so cold, what delights it repels us. And where shall I find my *Priameia virgo*, Cassandra? and Dido? [. . .]

At the Institute we're about to elect a successor to Paul Delaroche. I think and hope that Delacroix will succeed this time. Have you read the tedious inaugural address of Ponsard? Is it conceivable – a Voltairean provincial who for no rhyme or reason sets up a hullabaloo against Shakespeare's fame? Noodle! Overripe cucumber! Recently, in bed, I reread *King Lear*: "I am a foolish fond old man . . . I think this lady to be my child Cordelia". "And so I am, I am."

To Bennet   14 January 1857

I would have finished instrumenting the big finale of Act 1 of *The Trojans* but for the sickness which curdles the blood in my veins. After half an hour the pen falls from my hand. But what matter if it's done or not done, well done or badly done?

Last week Prince Napoleon gave a charming dinner for artists and scholars. We came in pairs from the Institute: two musicians, Halévy and I, two painters, Ingres and Flandrin, two from the moral sciences, Michel Chevalier and M. Walowski, two from the French Adademy, de Vigny and Ponsard, then Dumas the chemist, and A. Dumas *fils*, who would be a member of the Institute if he weren't so intelligent; then Disraeli the English orator, Lord Holland, and a few unknowns who could also be members but who are not, though for a different reason from the one mentioned above for young Dumas. There was no engraver, sculptor nor architect. A sole astronomer, M. Babinet, shone by his presence.

I'm worn out giving you these details. The same day we had elected Eugène Delacroix, to replace Paul Delaroche. M. Ingres had to swallow that insult too, but in spite of it he couldn't have been more gracious that evening. For the first time he sought me out and positively courted me, urging me to chastise without mercy those wretched singers who destroy great works. He paid me glowing compliments. One would have sworn he voted for me at my election. As Shakespeare says, "All the world's a stage."

To Bennet   29 January 1857

Thank you for your kind and comforting letter. But I don't need to be encouraged to continue with my work so much as you believe. Ill as I am, I go on. My score grows, as stalactites form in damp caves, and almost without my being aware of it. At the moment I'm completing the scoring of the monster finale of Act 1. Till yesterday it made me very anxious because of its size. But I sent Rocquemont to the Conservatoire to look out the score of Spontini's *Olympie*, which has a triumphal march with the same tempo and the same length of bar as mine. I counted the bars: he has 347, I have only 244. What's more there's no action during the immense processional development of the *Olympie* march, whereas I have Cassandra on stage while the cortège of the Wooden Horse passes in the distance. So I think it will do. I've also entirely finished the duet and finale of Act 4. See how easily you lure me on to talk of my work. Ah – I've no illusions, no, and you make me laugh with these old clichés about a "mission to fulfil". What a missionary! But there's an inexplicable mechanism in me which functions despite all arguments, and I let it because I can't stop it functioning. [. . .] So here I am with an act and a half of the score behind me. In time perhaps the rest of the stalactite will form, if the roof of the cave doesn't collapse first. [. . .]

It's a good thing my letter's coming to an end. The pale rays of the sun which lit up my window when I started writing to you have gone and I feel chilled to the marrow; all I see is dim half-light, and I'm going to stretch myself out on my sofa and shut my eyes, physically and mentally, so that I see nothing and stay there vacant as a leafless tree with the rain streaming down it.

To Bennet   5 or 6 February 1857

Five days ago I was on the point of writing you a long letter, which luckily I postponed. I was in a state of ecstasy – I had played my first act through mentally from beginning to end. There's nothing so absurd as an author who, imitating the Good Lord, considers his work on the seventh day and "finds it good". But imagine: apart from two or three passages I had forgotten the whole thing; hence my delight. The result was that in reading it I made real discoveries. The only part I hadn't written was the mime scene for Andromache. Its importance daunted me. Now it too is done, and of the whole act I think it's the piece that comes off best. I shall get Leroy to try it soon (it's a clarinet solo with chorus). I wept buckets over it. Imitating the Good Lord again, you see – though a lively sensibility was not his strong point, if one is to believe that appalling old rogue Moses.

For the past few days, on the other hand, I have been on tenterhooks. Legouvé had kindly given half a day to going through my poem in detail. He was enthusiastic about it as a whole but made four important criticisms on dramatic – dramaturgical – grounds, and I realized that he was right. The first three corrections were quickly done; the last, on the contrary, which concerned the opening of the fifth act, made me sweat. I've now finally dealt with it. But, as it involves another change in the finale of the fourth act, I shall have a few pages of the score to rewrite.

To the Princess 13 February 1857

I've nearly finished the fourth act. It's coming in floods, but disorganized floods. The end and the middle are written and I'm about to begin the beginning.

The first act is entirely done. It's the longest – it will last an hour and ten minutes. So the other acts must be as condensed as possible, to keep the whole within reasonable proportions. The second and fourth will be short. As to the impressions this music makes on me, they vary with my mood, according to whether it's sunny or raining and I have or haven't got a headache. The same piece that gave me paroxysms of delight the day before when I read it can leave me cold and disgusted today. I console myself for these swings of mood by reflecting that it's been the same all my life with everything I have ever done.

The other day I was finishing the instrumental piece with chorus for Andromache's mime. In came the cornet-player Arban, who has a keen sense of melodic expression. He began singing the clarinet solo, perfectly, and there I was in seventh heaven. Two days later I got the Opéra clarinettist to come – Leroy, a first-rate virtuoso, but cold. He tried the solo. My piano was a little flat, so the two instruments weren't in tune, the virtuoso phrased it "approximately"; he found it very "pretty" – and I was in hell, fed up with Andromache and Astyanax, ready to throw it all on the fire. What a frightful thing is this *approximately* in musical performance! However, I think the young man will end by understanding his solo if I make him study it bar by bar. For the moment, though, there's no point.

The last piece I've written, which I hope you will like, is the ensemble that comes before the lovers' duet in the fourth act: "Tout n'est que paix" [etc]. It seems to me that there is something new in the expression of this happiness at "seeing the night" and "hearing the silence", and giving sublime utterance to the sound of the sleeping sea. What is more, this ensemble links on to the duet in a quite unexpected way; it came about by chance, for I was not aware of it when I was writing the two pieces separately.

The Théâtre-Lyrique is nearing the end of its rehearsals for *Oberon*. I can't imagine what they'll make of Weber's score. It's after that that the director wants to put on *Cellini*. However, the season is getting on, the public's mania for [Masset's] *La Reine Topaze* is still raging, the theatre finishes its performances in May and, as I see it, it would hardly be prudent to risk this revival in the middle or at the end of April, only to have it cut short so soon. What is more, the tenor [Tamberlick] I was counting on has just broken [*brésilié*] his contract and gone off to Rio da Janeiro. Forgive the pun.

Did I tell you of the parody that's been made on La Fontaine's fable, apropos the murder of our poor good archbishop?

> Sur un arbre Verger (perché)
> Il ouvre un archevèque (large bec), etc.

It's revolting; but everyone's killing themselves laughing. Last week, when they were taking the poor wretch to execution, some workmen called out, "Hey, Verger, you've got yourself guillotined on a Friday! That'll bring you bad luck."

To Adèle   25 February 1857

I'm still tormented by my intestinal pains, which had left me in peace for a couple of weeks. All the same I'm forging ahead. At the moment I am writing the score of the fourth act, the act of love, of tenderness, of fêtes and hunts and the starlit African night. [. . .]

The other day I had a great joy. Baron Taylor – president of the Artists' Associations, who used to be director of the Théâtre-Français – had often asked me, at the Institute, to read him my poem. I was really scared of doing so, but finally I gave in – and I can hardly bring myself to tell you what he said. "There has been no comparable opera poem since Quinault's *Armide*. It's superb. If I became director of the Opéra I'd put it on tomorrow and spend a hundred thousand francs on it." It's true that since I read it to you it's been changed and improved a lot. The reactions and suggestions of my friends – Legouvé especially – have not fallen on deaf ears. But what a long task! I shall be very happy if I can have finished it a year from now.

I'm going to work on the ballet. I want to do an almehs' dance, just like the music and dancing of the Indians I saw here sixteen or seventeen years ago. My colleague at the *Débats*, Casimirski, is going to give me a verse from the Persian poet Hafiz which I shall have sung in Persian by the singing almehs, as the Indian girls did. There's nothing anachronistic about that. I've gone into the question. Dido could easily have had Egyptian dancers at her court who'd come earlier from India.

Talking of India, Louis should have just arrived there; but it will be two months at least before I can get news from him. I'm not going to London this year; the hall I was to inaugurate won't be finished. That's fine with me – my work won't be interrupted. I shan't give any concerts here either.

In this connection I have an enormous project, to be carried out – if possible – when *The Trojans* is finished. It's a retrospective of my complete oeuvre, in ten concerts. The great difficulty will be the hall I shall need for it. [. . .]

If only I were well! I have nervous torments that would discourage Job on his dunghill, violent spasms of enthusiasm and disgust, which I can make no one understand and for which no one feels nearly as sorry as they would if I had arthritis or a sprained ankle – yet it's far more painful.

How I wish I could see you, dear sister, and talk to you a little. I'm not absolutely an Orestes pursued by the furies, but you would be an excellent Electra . . . If the Emperor were prepared to help me, even just a little, I feel I could move mountains. His abhorrence of music, and even more the Empress's, grows from day to day. You won't believe it, this harmoniophobia. Still, the Minister of State has just subscribed for ten copies of the Te Deum. The King of Prussia and the Kings of Saxony and Hanover have also subscribed. I hope the Russian court won't lag behind; but I have no hopes of Prince Albert, to whom the work is dedicated. He's capable of sending me what he sent Meyerbeer on a similar occasion – his own *complete musical works*.

To Adèle   12 March 1857

What luck! a letter from you this morning, dear Adèle. I'm so ill, I needed it to restore me a little. My neuralgia pains are worse than ever. I think the cause is the agony I've been in for the past eleven days at not being able to work at my score. I'm in a veritable wasps' nest of concert givers. They expect me to get up when I'm fast asleep and listen to their masterpieces in my house, others come to bear me off to their place, and all of them insist that I go to their performances and puff them and talk about them in my column – it's enough to drive me mad. In addition, we've had the first performance of a genuine masterpiece, poor inspired Weber's *Oberon*, at the Théâtre-Lyrique. I saw it three times, and also had to be at the general rehearsal, to give a hand to the conductor who didn't have all that much idea what he was about. It's had a splendid success. All Paris is talking of *Oberon* – this marvellous opera that's been vilified for the last thirty-two years. [. . .]

I recently gave a formal reading of *The Trojans* at the home of Edouard Bertin, the proprietor of the *Journal des débats*. Most of my colleagues on the paper were there and several others not on the staff. It was a great success. Everyone seemed struck, almost frightened, by the size of the musical undertaking, and by the force of those epic passions and the grandeur of the whole Virgilian–Shakespearean setting. They urged me to give up everything, forget everything, and just work on my score. You can see how easy it is to follow that advice. Still, if I'm better when the warm weather comes then perhaps the end will be in sight. I'm back on it again today – I'm going to attack the great scene (without words) of the Royal Hunt in Act 4, where Dido and Aeneas are overtaken by a storm in the forest. I've finished the scene of the ring – do you remember it? – the one where Ascanius playfully draws the ring of Sichaeus, her first husband, from the queen's finger. The idea comes from a picture by Guérin. It's a finely proportioned quartet [later a quintet]. There's one particular phrase of Dido's – "Tout conspire à vaincre mes remords et mon coeur est absous" – which seems to me very moving . . . for those capable of being moved. I have got to find a way of speaking to the Emperor – for a time well ahead: the Opéra at the moment is in total disarray, and nothing would be more out of the question than to put on *The Trojans* there with the ramshackle means available. I went to the Tuileries last Monday – the Emperor receives the Institute, the deputies and the army every Monday. I wasn't able to address a word to him: he spoke only to the *useful*. The bore of these evenings is having to wear one's uniform and sword and all one's medals, big as your hand, which make a noise like an ironmonger's stall in a high wind.

To the Princess   24 March 1857

I leave Ascanius and the Tyrians roaming the African forest, with the trumpets sounding and the thunder rolling, to give myself the pleasure of talking to you. [. . .] I've added a tirade for Cassandra *during* the finale of the first act, at the moment when the procession is going off after crossing the back of the stage: "Stop! stop! yes, fire . . . an axe! / Search the monstrous horse! / Laocoön . . . the Greeks . . . it hides / a deadly trap, etc." It gives a vibrancy to the scene, and is declaimed (in music, I mean) over the march, as the sound of the cortège fades into the distance.

To Adèle   9 April 1857

The day before yesterday I finished the devilish scene of the storm during the Royal Hunt, where there are many different stage pictures that the music absolutely must render: naiads bathing amid the calm of the forest, distant fanfares, huntsmen alarmed at the approach of the storm, streams transformed into torrents, cries of ill omen from the rampaging nymphs at the moment when Dido follows Aeneas into the cave, grotesque dances by the satyrs and fauns brandishing, like torches, the branches of a tree struck by lightning, etc., etc. I must now tackle the second act, which I'd left behind.

From time to time I go to the Monday soirées at the Tuileries. The last time Marie and I went the Empress asked for me and I had a long conversation with her about my opera; she wanted an account of the subject of each act. Her "gracious" Majesty (she really is) is very well versed in Virgilian literature, and I was astonished at her detailed remarks about the *Aeneid*. God, she's beautiful! There's the Dido I need – or rather, no, her radiant beauty would be the ruin of the piece: they'd throw the book at an Aeneas who could think for an instant of leaving her. I seized the opportunity, as I was taking my leave, to ask her permission to read her my poem, later on when the score is further advanced. The idea seemed to appeal to her, at any rate she granted it readily. It's a question now of arranging it with the Duc de Bassano, who will find an evening when the Emperor is free and disposed to listen to me. [. . .]

I've recently had a very serious proposal from the Americans: to go there in October and spend five months in New York, Philadelphia and

Boston, performing my works. They offered me twenty thousand dollars (105,000 francs) and the cost of the journey, the money to be paid me in Paris. After long reflection I turned it down for this year but said I would accept for 1858. I want to finish my score before taking on anything else.

To Adèle   26 June 1857

At the moment I'm finishing the music of the second act (Acts 1 and 4 have been complete for a long time now). It is, I think, the hardest part of my task. The scene with Cassandra and the Trojan women presented great difficulties. But I hope I've achieved my object and managed to express the mounting enthusiasm, the passion for death which the inspired virgin communicates to the Trojan women and which at the end draws from the Greek soldiers a cry of appalled admiration. I've also done, in the third act, the Carthaginian national anthem which is to greet Dido several times at her entrance. It's the God Save the Queen of Carthage. As you see, I'm getting on, and by this time next year it will all certainly be finished.

To Adèle   Plombières, 4 August 1857

My mother-in-law returned to Paris two days ago, and Marie and I are going to Baden next Monday. The waters are doing both of us a power of good. The tremendous heat you complain of suits us very well. I find the weather admirable. The climate's tropical; I look in the woods to see if there aren't pineapples already growing, as in Guyana and the Antilles. You can't imagine how beautiful our woods are when the sun rises, or the moon. Three days ago, when Marie was taking her bath, I went out alone early to the Fountain of Stanislas. I had with me my *Trojans* manuscript, some music paper and a pencil. The lodge-keeper arranged a table in the shade, and a bowl of milk, some kirsch and sugar, and I worked there peacefully, with the splendid landscape before me, till nine in the evening. I happened to be writing a chorus with very apt words: "Has such a day ever been seen?" [. . .] Our Baden concert is being prepared and promises well. I want to take special trouble with it; it has to be splendid. Among other things I've included the Judex from my Te Deum in the programme, and I shan't have any peace until I've heard a rehearsal of my chorus. I've no anxieties about the orchestra in this immense movement, without doubt the most tremendous that I've written, but the vocal part has got to be grandly performed. I'm thirsty for music; when I get to Baden I'm going to bathe in it, drink it in through every pore. [. . .] Bénazet wants to do everything *royally* for the concert (I don't say imperially – our Emperor's love of music is well known). It's going to cost him an arm and a leg, and it's going to be good. And you won't be there, neither you nor your family nor my uncle. It's always thus.

A few days ago, dozing in a field under a beech tree (like Virgil's shepherd) I had a marvellous idea for the staging and the versification of my finale with Cassandra and the Trojan women. A few extra lines had to be written, but it will involve almost no change in the music. I have to tell you there is an antique, a radiant beauty about it. What agonies I am preparing for myself by becoming so passionate about this work, by lavishing so much love on it!

To Adèle   7 September 1857

I share wholeheartedly in your loss; I regret and grieve for that excellent woman [Monique Nety], even more for the loving care she gave our father than for what she did for us in our childhood. I had been thinking of her a lot recently. Louis having told me how touched she was by the collective letter he and my nieces wrote her, I had thought a letter from me would give her pleasure. Consequently, in bed one morning I wrote to her mentally and memorized my letter, and was about to send it to her when I got the sad news. In the letter I attempted to cheer her up a little by giving her a few details of my trip to Baden. It was probably just at the time she was dying.

To Emile Deschamps   31 October 1857

At the moment I'm with friends at St Germain [en Laye]. They have installed me in a sitting-room open to the sun, with a view over the Vale of Marly, the aqueduct, the woods and vineyards and the Seine. The house is set apart, with silence and peace all round, and I work at my score with a happiness I can't describe, without a thought of the sorrows it can't fail to cause me later on. The sight of the countryside seems to make my Virgilian passion more intense than ever. I feel as if I knew Virgil, as if he knew how much I love him. Don't you find yourself, too, having the same charming illusion? Yesterday I was finishing an air for Dido which is simply a paraphrase of the famous line *Haud ignara mali miseris succurrere disco.** After I'd sung it through once I was naïve

---

* "My own troubles have taught me to help the unfortunate." The air is "Errante sur les mers" in Act 3.

enough to say, out loud, "That's it, isn't it, dear Master? *Sunt lacrymae rerum** – just as if Virgil had been there.

To Adèle   27 November 1857

I am still ill and filled with an unconquerable sadness. I forget myself only in working. We've been back ten days from St Germain. It wasn't easy, adjusting to my little workroom, used as I had become to the big salon surrounded by a garden and looking out on the hillside of Marly. I don't go out; nothing can tear me away from my score. Thank goodness, the opéras-comiques have left me a little breathing-space this month. [. . .] I leave you, good, dear sister, I've not two ideas. I have but one, to complete my finale [Act 3], an overwhelming piece full of fury and warlike enthusiasm, which I'm sure no one would think had come from the pen of a sick man beset with sadness. The musician "I" is very different from the "I" that you know; the one would love to be able to rid himself of the other.

To the Princess   30 November 1857

No great credit to me that I turned down the American offer you mention. Was I not bound to stick to my task? And it would have been the height of inconsequence, would it not, to interrupt it for another in which art had no great interest? [. . .] I should be in a fine mess now if I had accepted. The talk in America is of nothing but bankruptcies; their theatres and concerts are heading for the Niagara Falls. Ours are in no such danger. There's no cataract here – there's no current. We paddle about on a motionless swamp full of frogs and toads, enlivened by the quacking and flapping of a few ducks, and where shipwreck is only to be feared when the boats are completely rotted. But I live in my score, like La Fontaine's rat in his cheese, if you'll pardon the comparison. I'm about to begin the fifth act, and in a few months everything will be done. The poem has again been changed quite a lot since we last spoke of it. There is a new and grander end; I've removed a good deal and added a bit. I've not read it to the Empress; the Marquis de Belmont, who was going to fix an evening for me at St Cloud, died while I was in Baden, and I've not yet thought of looking for another go-between to her "gracious" Majesty. My one idea is to finish the score. [. . .] I go at it with a concentrated passion which seems to grow the more it is satisfied.

* "grief at the heart of things".

What value will it have in the end? God knows. In any case I experience
real happiness in digging out and fashioning and equipping this great
Robinson Crusoe's canoe – which I shan't be able to launch unless the
sea itself comes for it; and I shall never forget, Princess, that it is thanks
to you and you alone that I gave myself to this luxury of composition.
No indeed, without your encouragements and your tender reproaches I
should never have undertaken such a thing. Let me thank you for the
one and the other – whatever griefs the work causes me later.

To the Princess   27 December 1857
Forgive me, Princess, for not replying to your last letter till now. I was
in the grip of Aeneas' final monologue and could not have put two ideas
together until it was entirely written. At such times I am like one of those
bulldogs which let themselves be cut in pieces rather than leave go what
they have between their teeth.

To Adèle   16 January 1858
This evening I shall go on with my wretched feuilleton, and tomorrow
as well, and then, the moment it's done, back to my score, which I've
not touched for twelve days and which is like the building work at
Carthage during Dido's great love-affair, *pendent opera interrupta*. Then,
no more letters from me.

To Louis Berlioz   9 February 1858
The Indian mail leaves tomorrow, and today I've a few moments for
chatting briefly with you. I'm impatient to hear your news. How was
the long crossing? How are you? How did you find it on board? Don't
forget any of these details.

     [. . .] I'm working as hard as I can to finish my score. At the moment
I'm at Dido's final monologue, "Je vais mourir dans ma douleur immense
submergée." I am more content with what I have just written than with
anything else so far. I believe that these terrible scenes of the fifth act
will carry in their music heart-rending conviction. Once again I have
made changes to this act: I've made a large cut and I've added a character
piece, designed to contrast with the epic, passionate style of the rest. It's
a sailor's song; I thought of you, dear Louis, as I wrote it, and I'm sending
you the words. It's night; the Trojan fleet's at anchor in the port; Hylas,
a young Phrygian sailor, sings as he rocks at the masthead of one of the
ships: "Vallon sonore / Où dès l'aurore" [etc.] Farewell, dear Indian, I

embrace you with all my heart. Come back to me soon, fit and wise and rich, and all will be well.

To the Princess   20 February 1858

What you tell me of the revival of *Alceste* at Weimar doesn't surprise me. The only thing that does is that the bourgeois are allowed into the theatre when such works are being performed. If I were the Grand Duke I should send each of these fine fellows a ham and two bottles of beer, with a request that they spend the evening at home. [. . .] Would Liszt be so good as to congratulate Mme Milde on my behalf for the way she played Alceste? I believe what you say about her. She must have been a charming Queen of Thessaly. "Mourir pour ce qu'on aime" [etc.]: if Mme Milde sang that immortal phrase well she can boast she is an artist. Oh the bourgeois! the beer-drinkers, the eaters of ham! Who allowed them to come and hear, or rather listen to, that? You must have suffered. There are things the mob should not be allowed to see. The three goddesses may have unveiled before Paris on Mount Ida, but Paris was a handsome young prince. I don't suppose the immortal trio would have revealed themselves to Thersites. [. . .]

Recently a chamberlain of the Emperor – the very one who has replaced the poor Marquis de Belmont – offered to ask the Empress's permission for me to read her *The Trojans*. "He was sure of success", etc. And here comes a letter, in which my mahout apologizes and says that no one dared to ask HM, that I must solicit this favour directly, that it's the prerogative of M. Bacciocchi, etc., etc. Tell me that I'm wrong not to believe in anything!

To Adolphe Samuel   26 February 1858

Yes, *The Trojans* is almost done; I have only the final scene to write. Tomorrow I have to give a reading of the poem to about twenty people. Last month I gave another at a gathering of Institute colleagues. It had a great effect. They say it's very fine. I wish it were possible for you to get to know it. I've worked at this poem with the utmost patience, and I'm not going to change anything more now. But how should one not be patient? I was reading yesterday, in a life of Virgil, that he spent eleven years writing the *Aeneid*; and this miracle of poetry seemed to him still so incomplete that before he died he ordered his heirs to burn it. Shakespeare rewrote *Hamlet* three times. Only by working in that way can one do great things, things that last.

I think you will be happy with my *Trojans* score. You will easily
imagine what the passionate scenes are like, the scenes of tenderness, the
portrayals of Nature, but there are others that you can't possibly have
any idea of – among them the ensemble in which all the characters and
the chorus voice the horror and fear they feel at the account of the
appalling death of Laocoön, devoured by serpents, and the finale of the
third act, and Aeneas' final scene in the fifth. I've resolved to make a
piano arrangement of the whole work. It will involve a critical study of
the full score which I think will be useful, making me scrutinize its hidden
corners.

It matters little what becomes of the work after that – whether it's
performed or not. My Virgilian and musical passion will have been
satisfied, and at least I shall have shown what I believe can be done with
an antique subject treated on a large scale.

To Théophile Gautier   2 March 1858
Excuse me, my dear Gautier: yesterday I was so preoccupied with the
last piece of my score that I forgot our rendezvous. If they'd been waiting
for me somewhere to guillotine me I'd have been capable of not turning
up, and keeping M. Samson waiting.

To Emile Deschamps   3 March 1858
What will become of this enormity? God knows – though it's not even
certain He does. But in writing it I yielded to an irresistible urge; I've
satisfied a fierce passion which flamed up in my childhood and which
has grown continually since then. Why should I complain if the work is
never performed? All those creatures in the ancient poems are so beautiful!
All that world driven by epic passions speaks so harmonious a language!
Music is in its element there. But where to find a Cassandra? It is very
certain that the sublime *Priameia virgo* is not at the Opéra. Where find
a Dido? Where an Aeneas? Which of our tenors could bear his shield
like a hero and nobly declaim, as he embraced Ascanius, "Others, my
child, will instruct you in the art of happiness. I shall teach you only the
courage of a fighting man, and respect for the gods."

To Adèle   11 March 1858
The Emperor wants an economical Opéra, he has little interest in putting
on new works which cost a hundred thousand francs to stage. They're
about to do Halévy's *La magicienne*; it's the first time for three years

that a work of that size has been produced. A semi-flop is predicted; it's said to be cold and empty. I shall have to say the opposite.

In short, my time is not yet come. I am quite resigned to its never coming, rather than see my work profaned or have it outraged by the simpletons who are at the Opéra at the moment.

I assure you, dear little sister, that the music of *The Trojans* is something grand and noble; what's more, it has a poignant truthfulness, and there are inventions in it that, unless I am pathetically mistaken, will make the musicians of all Europe prick up their ears, and perhaps make their hair stand on end. I feel that if Gluck returned to earth he would say of me, when he heard it, "Truly, this is my son." That's not exactly modest of me, is it? But at least I have the modesty to admit that lack of modesty is one of my failings.

On 12 April he completed and dated the final scene of the opera, the extended finale (later replaced) in which Scipio Africanus, Julius Caesar and groups of poets and artists pass in front of the Capitol, a scene inspired by Anchises' review in Book VI of the souls of future Roman worthies. Alongside the date he added an exhortation from Virgil: *Quidquid erit, superanda omnis fortuna ferendo est* – "Whatever will be, all fortune may be mastered by endurance."

He was going to need a great deal of it in the months to come.

23

Lobbying

Throughout the next five years the opera continued to dominate Berlioz's life. These were the years when he composed *Beatrice and Benedick* and had it performed, when he contemplated writing an opera on *Antony and Cleopatra*, when he published two further collections of his writings to much acclaim, when excerpts from his *Memoirs*, serialized weekly over a period of ten months, kept his name in the public eye, and his revival of Gluck's *Orphée* made theatrical history; but it was *The Trojans*, as in the months of its composition, that remained the urgent preoccupation. Only, happiness now turned to frustration.

He had known it would. The probable fate of the work had all along been the strongest argument against being lured into composing it, and even as he did so and experienced the greatest satisfaction of his life he had no illusions. But though he might still protest that whether performed or not the score existed, and in any case there was no one at the Opéra capable of taking the leading roles (he had only to spend an evening there to thank his stars he wasn't being dragged through that mire), the situation had moved on, out of reach of philosophy. The work had acquired a momentum of its own. It was there, waiting, demanding to be put on, and he was there, compelled to lobby for it and to be on the alert for the advent of any new singer with the voice and dramatic talent required.

In this his case was significantly different from Wagner's, superficially similar though they were. Whereas for Wagner, exiled in Switzerland, cut off from the world of the opera house, with the manuscript of *The Ring* piling up on his desk, there was for the moment no practical possibility of any part of his magnum opus being performed, Berlioz was actively involved in the arena, a leading if controversial player, in regular contact with the Opéra – the obvious and only suitable theatre for his work – and with access (as member of the Institute) to the

ultimate arbiter of what went on there, the Emperor. He could not put
the score on one side and forget about it: it insisted on his attention.
The moment it was finished he had started work on the piano-vocal
reduction, a chore which occupied him on and off for the next eighteen
months. Nor could he simply bide his time and wait. He was too ill for
that: he might wait too long. "Come a Cassandra, come a Dido, come
an order from the Emperor, and I can produce the thing. But there's
someone else who could easily come first, and that is Death." He had
to continue to hope, to campaign. *The Trojans* must come before
everything. That meant being available at all times, staying in Paris,
turning down invitations to conduct in Europe – Prague, Cologne,
Stockholm – and in America. Dislike it as he might, he was committed
to soliciting – a repugnant but also delicate task, for one had to take
care at all times not to overplay one's hand. Hence his alarm when his
Strasbourg friend Schwab, in a review of the 1858 Baden concert in the
Courrier du Rhin, referred to the Emperor as having "taken *The Trojans*
under his protection".

In April 1858 Berlioz had written an appeal to the Emperor to read
the libretto and, if he liked it, to override the opposition of Royer,
director of the Opéra. The work, he said, "is grand and powerful
and, for all its apparent complexity of means, quite straightforward.
Unhappily it is not commonplace (*pas vulgaire*), but that is a fault
which Your Majesty will pardon." The letter was never sent; the Duc
de Morny, the Emperor's half-brother, persuaded him that it would
not be politic. Morny (whom Alphonse Daudet would later describe as
"an absolute idiot" but "no fool when it came to administrative matters") did however offer to smooth the way. That was something.

At the beginning of May Berlioz was at the Monday reception in the
Tuileries. The Emperor came up and asked him for news of his opera,
questioned him about it, and actually agreed to look at the libretto: the
Duc de Bassano would arrange an audience. Berlioz told the Princess
that he was "on the verge of an important démarche". But when the
day came there were forty-two people present, and the composer was
vouchsafed only the briefest exchange: the Emperor would read it if he
could find the time, and if not would get it studied by somebody. "But
who that somebody is I've not yet been able to discover. They think
he's taken my poem to Fontainebleau, where he has gone for a fortnight's
rest. If that's the case, perhaps he'll read it himself." Four months later
there was still no word, and his first optimism had evaporated. The

Emperor had "had his twenty-five degrees below zero look", he told Liszt. "He took my manuscript, assuring me that he would read it 'if he could find a moment's leisure'. The technique is as old as the hills. I am sure King Priam did it in just the same way."

In the end he had to accept that "the Greeks, Trojans, Carthaginians and Numidians" could not be expected to rank high on the Emperor's agenda and that, however well disposed in theory, Napoleon III would never do for him what his uncle did for Le Sueur when he ordered the Opéra to put on *The Bards*. To the Emperor their relationship was of no consequence. It was symbolized by an incident at one of the imperial house parties at Compiègne, reported by Berlioz to the Goncourt brothers, who recorded it in their *Journal*:

> The Emperor complained that his sight was failing. "The queer thing is, I can't tell the difference any more between black and blue. Who is that over there?" "Sire, it is Monsieur Berlioz." He raised his voice. "Monsieur Berlioz, is your tail-coat blue or black?" "Sire," Berlioz hastened to reply, "I should never take the liberty of appearing before Your Majesty in a blue tail-coat. It is black." "Good", said the Emperor. And that is all the Emperor said to him in four days.

In any case Napoleon III regarded the Opéra as a kind of plaything, useful more than anything for giving pleasure to his friends. The next large-scale work scheduled for production after Félicien David's *Herculaneum* was by Prince Poniatowsky, nephew of one of Bonaparte's marshals, and the one after that was by the Duke of Gotha. Besides, the Emperor left the practical decisions to his bureaucrats. Though some of them, like Morny and Fould, the Minister of State, seemed well-disposed to Berlioz, for them *The Trojans* was not an important issue; and there were plenty of others in that paradise of intrigue and delay who could be depended on to obstruct and to put it about that the libretto was a bore and the music would last eight hours.

His other strategy was to exert pressure on the authorities by mobilizing public opinion in his favour. To this end he continued throughout 1858 and 1859 to distribute copies of the poem and hold readings for officials and influential friends and artists. Blanche, secretary to the Minister of State, and Mercey, Director of Fine Arts, were present at a reading given at the architect Hittorf's house in January 1858. Baroche, president of the Council of State, having studied the libretto, pronounced it "fort beau" and promised to speak up for the composer. Like Morny he was a member of the Opéra board. Véron, former director of the Opéra, couldn't stop talking about it; he declared that if he were still in charge there he would spend 150,000 francs on producing the work. Such an accolade, however, was two-edged. Even Berlioz's sympathizers hesitated before so large a sum. They were disconcerted, too, when he told them what he thought of the present condition of the Opéra – as he reported to Humbert Ferrand the day after a meeting with the minister in November 1858:

> "Indeed . . . your great reputation . . . gives you the right . . . thoroughly entitles you . . . to expect . . . But a grand opera in five acts . . . tremendous responsibility for a director . . . I shall see what can be done . . . had already heard tell of your work . . ." "But Minister, it's not a question of putting on *The Trojans* this year or next year either. The Opéra is in no state to bring off such an enterprise. You don't have the necessary singers. The present Opéra is incapable of the effort required." "As a rule one should surely write for the resources available . . . Well, I shall see what can be done."

If composers had always written for the resources available, some of the greatest works would never have come into existence. But his candour did not exactly help promote his cause. It left even well-wishers wondering just what he did want. The trouble was, his work was not "vulgaire" and he gloried in the fact. Not for nothing did Berlioz admire Coriolanus and what he called "that great-hearted patrician's ferocious contempt for the multitude", and revel in quoting, to the Princess, the great speech beginning "You common cry of curs!" and ending "Despising, for you, the city, thus I turn my back. There is a world elsewhere." But where was it for *The Trojans*?

Till now all that anyone knew of the work was its libretto. But early in August 1859, shortly before leaving Paris for the annual gala concert in Baden, he invited a dozen or so people to the Salle Beethoven, in the Passage de l'Opéra, to hear excerpts from the score – Cassandra's aria and the scene with Coroebus, and the duet "Nuit d'ivresse" – sung by Mme Charton-Demeur and Jules Lefort, with Théodore Ritter accompanying. The music made a deep impression on the little audience but more so still on the composer. That may be why he had waited so long before risking an experiment which could only be another nail in his philosophy of resignation. It committed him more irrevocably, more perilously than ever, to the quest for a performance. Two months before, he told Princess Carolyne that "whatever fate awaits it, I feel nothing but happiness at having completed the work", and spoke of his sense of a lifetime's fulfilment. Now such stoicism was no longer possible. The music had taken matters into its own hands. He was forced to confess to her that

> the thought of the quarantine that is being imposed on the work (if indeed it ever gets out of it) tortures me day and night. I had not heard any of it before, and those great phrases brought to life by Mme Charton-Demeur's splendid voice intoxicated me. I now imagine its effect in the theatre; and against my will the stupid opposition of those idiots in charge of the Opéra is breaking my heart. I know I promised you I would steel myself against every ordeal, and here I am completely failing to keep my promise. I feel an intense bitterness.

But there was no turning back. The Baden programme was altered to include the same *Trojans* pieces, sung – this time with orchestra – by Lefort and Pauline Viardot. Berlioz wrote to Adèle, three days before the concert, that "the joy I feel at the effect of my *Trojans* scenes lifts my spirits to the skies. The artists are beside themselves." Mme Viardot was going to be "an admirable Cassandra".

She more than lived up to his expectations. At the concert her Cassandra was "magnificent and moving" (he told Morel), and the duet between Dido and Aeneas was encored. He was full of it when he got back, and talked excitedly about it to Adèle (she had brought her sickly daughter Joséphine to Paris to see a specialist). It would be a recurring motif in the coming months: Pauline Viardot as his heaven-sent Cassandra, or Dido, or even both. If the project for a production in German in Vienna came to fruition – he wrote to her shortly after the Baden concert – would she take part? He must have her. Alternatively, might she persuade the director of the St Petersburg opera to put on the work, in Italian? Countess Kalergis, niece of the Tsar's chancellor, who was so moved by the Love Scene from *Romeo* at Baden the year before, could help get it accepted.

The Baden concert was glowingly reviewed in several French papers. Ernest Reyer in the *Courrier de Paris* pronounced the whole *Trojans* a masterpiece. Marie Escudier in *La France musicale* called for a production without delay. But the immediate aftermath had nothing directly to do with the opera. By the time Berlioz returned to Paris in the first week of September his life had been marked profoundly by two events. He had been asked to supervise a revival of Gluck's *Orphée* at the Théâtre-Lyrique; and he had fallen in love with his Orpheus, Pauline Viardot.

Berlioz had long liked and admired the Spanish mezzo-soprano, daughter of Manuel García and scarcely less famous sister of the great Malibran. For several years he had been on affectionate terms with her and her much older husband, the writer and prominent republican Louis Viardot. Their town house, 28 Rue de Douai, was a couple of streets away from the Rue de Calais, and he often attended her Thursday afternoon salon, where serious music could be expected – for she was a fluent pianist and as captivating a singer of lieder and Spanish and Russian folk-songs as she was of opera, and also a talented composer, who liked to discuss her songs with him (one of them, *En mer*, was dedicated to Berlioz). Their professional association went back many years. It was she who gave the first performance of the orchestral version of *La captive*, in London in 1848. She sang for him several times during the two seasons of the Société Philharmonique (1850–51), and in 1856 she took part in the annual concert at Baden, singing arias by Graun and Bellini. He did not share her taste for bel canto opera, but he considered her none the less – at least from her Fidès in *Le Prophète* onwards – a superb vocalist and, more important still, a singer of rare soul and intelligence.

Pauline Viardot, on her side, thought highly of Berlioz as man and artist. By the mid-1850s she could refer to him as one of her four "true friends" (the others being Turgenev, George Sand and the painter Ary Scheffer). He was, she told Julius Rietz, "the best symphonic conductor *after someone else*" (i.e. after Rietz). About his music she was ambivalent. But that, like other things, changed dramatically during the week or ten days they spent working together at Baden. She told her husband that she could not get *Romeo and Juliet* out of her head, and she became passionate about Cassandra's recitative and aria ("Les Grecs ont disparu . . . Malheureux roi") and the long scene with Coroebus; she urged both Rietz and Liszt to come to Baden to hear them. Neither was able to; but after the concert she continued to write enthusiastically to Rietz about it. Two weeks later, by which time she had had a chance to study the whole of the first two acts, her early impressions were confirmed: with one or two exceptions it was all on the same exalted plane, and there were passages of "incredible élan". Next day Berlioz reported to Louis that Mme Viardot had exclaimed, "Oh, if only I could play Cassandra at once instead of Orpheus!"

New-found enthusiasm for his music, the sense of participating in the birth of a masterpiece, and at the same time the shared pleasure of restoring Gluck, all played a part in the deepening of her affection. With him it was that and much more. Love, for her an emotion that must always be subdued to career and family whatever the cost – and there was a cost – was for him the purpose and justification of existence. "One loves because one loves," he would write soon afterwards in a review of *Orphée*, "without the least consideration of the more or less fatal consequences of loving." She was attracted by his genius, his personality, his warmth, the quickness of mind and playfulness of spirit which rarely deserted him even during his worst bodily and mental torments; but those torments moved her above all to pity, to a healing compassion, whereas her goodness inspired him to adoration. He felt he had found in her at last – too late – the woman of his dreams; and during a two-day visit that September to the Viardots' château at Courtavenel, twenty miles south-east of Paris, to work on *Orphée*, he poured out his heart to her, as she reported to Rietz:

> The sight of this man in so much physical and psychological pain, so unhappy in his home life, so touched by the welcome we gave him, a prey to such agonies of heart, the violence of his efforts to conceal them – that ardent soul which is bursting its case, that life which so to speak hangs only by a thread, the immense tenderness overflowing in his glance, in his least word – all this, I tell you, shattered me. We went a long walk together, during which he became a little calmer, less agitated. "My whole life," he said, "has been one long ardent pursuit of an ideal which I myself created. As soon as it found a single quality, a single charm belonging to that ideal, my heart, avid for love, attached itself to it. Alas, disillusionment soon proved that I was mistaken. My life has passed in this way; but now, just as I feel it near its end, this ideal, which I had had to give up as the fantastic figment of an insane imagination, has suddenly materialized to my dying heart. How can you expect me not to adore it? Let me spend the last days that remain to me in blessing you, in thanking you for proving that I was not mad." Then he entreated me, with tears, to grant him one favour: not to refuse to go and see him if he is seriously ill and sends for me, and to come to his room whatever obstacles are put in my way. I promised I would, and I will.

Doubts have been cast on the accuracy of this account. Berlioz's numerous letters to her, that autumn and winter, are full of affection and gratitude for his ministering angel but contain no declarations of love. How could they? He was an intimate of the whole Viardot family and not just of Pauline. (For the same reason, their relationship could only be platonic.) When, that weekend, illness forced him to retreat to his bed, Louis Viardot came to his room to sit with him and keep him company and to reassure him that he was not being a nuisance to his friends. Berlioz was well aware that, for her, family ties came before everything except her art. The description quoted above has the ring of truth. It chimes with everything we know of him. That he should, as she said, "after a long and warm friendship have the misfortune suddenly to fall in love" is no more nor less explicable than such emotional revolutions ever are. She was a fascinating woman – not beautiful, certainly (many thought her ugly) but, at thirty-eight, extremely striking, with dark Iberian eyes overarched by magnificent eyebrows, great personal magnetism, and what Turgenev's friend Polonsky called "a wonderful, infectious laugh". She was the first woman to capture his heart with whom he was on completely equal terms – a musical intelligence as exalted and keen as his own, a mind that placed the artist's calling and the artist's sensibility as high as his did, a devotee of Shakespeare, Goethe, Homer, Cervantes to satisfy his most exacting requirements; a woman, moreover, who had conceived a passion for his opera, his ewe lamb. No wonder he fell in love with her. They were in almost daily contact, working together as kindred spirits in that musical Babylon to re-establish Gluck, the composer who more than ever, since *The Trojans*, was like a father to him – all this at a time when ill health and nervous debility made him peculiarly vulnerable and hyper-responsive to displays of affection. It was an escape from his unhappy home life, into something radiant and real. Her presence, after Marie's, liberated and fulfilled him. "I could talk to you till kingdom come. In your fresh and poetic company I feel in my element. Everywhere else I'm like a fish out of water." With the prolonged absence of his son and the slight loosening of the links with Liszt, his stored affections were running over. He was "avid for love".

Their collaboration on *Orphée* seems, with hindsight, both surprising and predestined. In the general Parisian consciousness Gluck no longer meant anything. Though individual musicians and music-lovers still swore by him, for the public at large he was an almost forgotten figure, heard occasionally at the Conservatoire concerts but ignored in the opera house.

Berlioz himself had often conducted scenes, but by now his only regular concerts were in Baden. In Paris Gluck survived only as parodied in Offenbach's hugely successful *Orphée aux enfers* (*Orpheus in the Underworld*), which opened at the Bouffes the year before and was still running. If its satire was aimed principally at bourgeois hypocrisy and the imperial regime and not at Gluck, it none the less devalued him. He was assumed to be irretrievably of the past. When Carvalho announced that the Théâtre-Lyrique was going to stage *Orphée*, Royer, the director of the Opéra, claimed it couldn't be done: "There's no music in it. The thing's absurd." "What do you think of Gluck's critic? Pretentious ass!" was Berlioz's comment. But that was after the work had opened and was filling the house at every performance.

Orphée aux enfers had only sharpened his desire to see *Orphée* brought back to life. Ever since the 1830s if not earlier he had dreamed of a worthy revival of the work which in the form of the extracts with guitar accompaniment in his father's library first made him aware of Gluck's music, and which he encountered in the flesh at the Opéra in 1824, sung (he soon discovered) with alterations made for the tenor, Nourrit, and in a staging that he remembered as deeply inadequate. The idea of such a revival keeps recurring in his feuilletons. In more than one he drew a detailed comparison between the Paris (French) adaptation that Gluck made in 1774 for *haute-contre* or high tenor and the original Vienna (Italian) score of 1762, in which the title role was written for castrato voice in the contralto range. As we have seen, excerpts from *Orphée* sometimes figured in his concert programmes. By the 1850s there was no one in France with his authority as a Gluckian scholar-performer,* and no one so conscious of the need for a correct edition of Gluck's operas, without which those "incomparable examples of expressive music", preserved only in corrupt texts, were in danger of becoming so many mute Memnons, "colossal sphinxes guarding their secrets for all eternity". The feuilleton of 3 July 1857 which voiced these fears was reprinted in his new collection of pieces published in March 1859, a couple of months before Carvalho heard Pauline Viardot sing at a benefit concert for his wife, Caroline Miolan-Carvalho, and

---

* See for example the exchange of letters in April 1857 with the singer and early-music editor François Delsarte over a disputed trombone harmony in *Alceste*.

decided that he must revive *Orphée* and put Berlioz in charge of it.

Berlioz's interests and Viardot's converged. He knew the largely forgotten Italian original as thoroughly as he knew the French (in one or two respects he preferred it). He also recognized that the rise in standard pitch over the years had made the French, tenor version impractical. She on her side had been singing extracts from the Italian, contralto *Orpheus* for the last fifteen years – on one occasion under Berlioz's baton, when she and Mlle Dobré performed the duet from Act 3 at the Société Philharmonique's inaugural concert in February 1850. It was natural that they should work together on a full-scale revival. All that separated them was a certain disagreement over fidelity to the text: Berlioz's scrupulousness was more literal and, as we would consider, modern; Viardot, brought up in the bel canto tradition, and with the imperatives of the prima donna, took a more latitudinarian view. This was no small difference, and in the long run it would drive a wedge between the two friends and fellow-artists. For the moment they were virtually as one.

The documents show Berlioz at work throughout September and October, preparing the score and performing material – in essence, adjusting the (longer) Paris version to the alto pitch of the original – and coaching the protagonist in her role, teaching the conductor, Deloffre, the tempos as they had been preserved at the Opéra in the 1820s, watching over the orchestra (and complimenting the timpanist, the seventeen-year-old Massenet, on his unusually exact intonation), insisting on décor and costumes of suitable beauty and simplicity (Delacroix's help was sought), and preventing Carvalho from indulging his impresario's prerogative and pepping up the piece with the overture to *Iphigénie en Aulide*, a chorus from *Armide* and other "improvements".

Berlioz had at first been sceptical about the young ex-Opéra-Comique baritone when he became a theatre director in 1856. "You say support Carvalho and the Th. Lyrique," he wrote to the Princess. "Yes, it's what I'm doing – but so as to give this director the notion that he is what we wish he were. There's nothing genuine about his so-called 'feeling for high-class music'. 'Vanity, frailty and lies', the song says. To that I add 'and stupidity'. Carvalho is merely a little less stupid than his colleagues." The man's record, however, argued undeniably in his favour. It showed him to be a theatre director with a difference, one prepared to take risks, have intelligent hunches and back them and, in addition to the obligatory ephemera, promote interesting work both new and old. *Oberon*, staged in 1857, was followed by revivals of Weber's *Euryanthe*, *Preciosa* and *Abu Hassan*, Mozart's *Figaro* and *Seraglio* and, in March 1859, the première of Gounod's *Faust*. Carvalho also explored the possibility of staging *Tannhäuser*. Immediately after *Orphée* he announced *Fidelio*, not seen in Paris for years; and he would be responsible, years later, for producing the Daudet/Bizet *L'Arlésienne*, the score with which the composer found himself as a dramatist.

Orphée itself was a gamble. Royer was by no means the only person to believe the work beyond resurrection. Berlioz, for a moment, wondered whether the director's "good intentions" might not "pave the way to hell" when he chose for the role of Eurydice a singer "from a café chantant in the other Champs-Elysées". But Carvalho let himself be persuaded not to add music from *Armide* and *Iphigénie*, agreed when Berlioz told him he must engage two skilled mimes for the chief demon and the suffering soul, and generally allowed him his way.

He also showed uncommon interest in Berlioz the composer. He had come near to reviving *Benvenuto Cellini* in 1856; and he now told him that he was delighted by the libretto of *The Trojans* and would like the work to open the new Lyrique which the government planned to build in the Place du Châtelet to replace the theatre in the Boulevard du Temple, due for demolition in Haussmann's reconstruction of central Paris.

The proposal had Berlioz in two minds. Here, in glaring contrast to Royer, was an opera director who believed in him. Spurred by the possibility of a production, he composed the missing Act 4 ballets in a fever of excitement. ("I'm writing ballet music all over the place," he told the Princess in December 1859 – "in the street, in the café, at my friends'"). His friends were in no doubt that he should close with Carvalho, and Edouard Alexandre offered to put up 50,000 francs for a production. On the other side, though, was the question of artistic resources. Quite apart from the danger that Carvalho would want his wife to take the role of Dido (as Delacroix said, "Dido sung by a titmouse!"), the company had no suitable tenor (neither, for that matter, did the Opéra). The new theatre would also have to be a good deal larger than the old if it was to be big enough for a work on this scale, and therefore have more land allocated to it than seemed likely – the present Lyrique was an intimate house, perfect for *Orphée* but far too small for *The Trojans*. To complicate matters further, the Opéra was rumoured to be about to get a new director: Royer was to be replaced by Prince Poniatowsky. The Prince was saying – "too loudly" – that if he got the job he would stage Berlioz's opera. "The Prince has a work in rehearsal, and the author of *The Trojans* will shortly have a feuilleton to write on it, and . . . you know the rest."

For the moment Berlioz had every reason to go along with Carvalho, and to feel grateful to him for the joy of steeping himself week after week in his beloved Gluck, of helping to create what it was becoming clear would be one of the supreme singing and acting performances of the age, and of seeing *Orphée* achieve popular success of a magnitude undreamed of.

Not since the days of Mme Branchu had a singer brought to the noble plainness of Gluck's music the answering fire, the genius it presupposed. "If you could see how little she resembles a woman in male costume," wrote Berlioz to Louis on the day of the first performance. She suggested "a young poet of the ancient world" – and with "accents, poses, facial expressions to make the heart turn over".

The theatre was full every night, and the "Poloniuses" who complained that it was "one long recitative" were heavily outnumbered. People came back a second, a third time. Writers and painters as well as musicians flocked to the Lyrique. Flaubert went repeatedly. Dickens, in floods of tears, was taken backstage by Mme Viardot's husband and presented to her (he wrote) "still disfigured with crying".

The supporting cast received little notice in the reviews. (Berlioz thought Marie Sax, the Eurydice, "ignorant as a carp of everything to do with art"; Pauline Viardot's verdict was "une belle voix sans art".)* It was Mme Viardot's triumph. She had not sung on the Paris stage since Gounod's *Sapho*, seven years before. At many of the early performances she was far from well; but she carried all before her. Every evening, Berlioz told the Princess, she would arrive in her dressing-room coughing and sneezing and in a terrible state of nerves; and every evening, called on to fear nothing and forget her cold, she went on like a lioness, more uplifted and uplifting than ever, and held the audience spellbound by singing and gesture and movement which combined the studied and the natural and spontaneous in perfect harmony.

---

* Sax was famous for the question she asked Viardot at one of the early rehearsals, when Berlioz kept stopping the orchestra to criticize the chorus. "That's Monsieur Gluck, isn't it?" "No, it's one of his friends." "Well, he's got a nerve – *in his absence!*"

Berlioz, ill as he was too, was at most performances. He went on advising his "cher Orphée" and where necessary admonishing her. Thus, after the tenth performance: "The other evening I forgot to say two things. First, the phrase 'La mort est tout ce qui me reste' now goes very well; the timbre of the adopted notes is excellent – don't change it. Second, in the name of your father the god of day, who is also the god of poetry, don't say 'je te suis, tendre-hobjet de ma foi'. If you absolutely must breathe before 'objet', say 'cher-objet' and so avoid making an appalling line of eleven feet and an abominable hiatus. That will leave only one h too many. But no one's perfect." His admiration for her genius did not prevent him criticizing her, in the *Débats*, for embellishing Gluck's vocal line in one of the recitatives and for changes she made to the musical text in the final phrases of "J'ai perdu mon Eurydice" and in one or two other places. Such details apart, however, her Orpheus had him, like everyone else, under its spell.

His two feuilletons said nothing of his own part in the proceedings (a part which included editing a new vocal score and seeing it through the press). It was widely recognized, however, and acknowledged by the reviewers. He felt that this was only just, though he would have liked greater emphasis on the triumph of Gluck and less on that of himself or the prima donna. But the runaway success of *Orphée*, surely, could only be good for his own chances: it showed that classical subjects could still appeal to the public and do thriving business at the box office.

Orphée undoubtedly enhanced his standing – as an arbiter of musical opinion, as an authority on Gluck, even as a professional man of the theatre, all these things; but not as a composer. Carvalho might be as keen as ever to put on *The Trojans*: at the Opéra everything was as before. Royer kept the job, and nothing happened. All Berlioz's diplomacy, the soliciting he so hated, had seemingly been to no purpose. Meanwhile his music maintained a half-life in Paris. That April, in Holy Week, he had conducted *The Childhood of Christ* at the Opéra-Comique, with most of his faithful singers and a chorus which, he felt, for the first time sang the final unaccompanied "O mon âme" with the right expression. The audience, however, was disappointingly small – war with Austria had been declared the night before – and an expected profit of 2,000 francs was reduced to 400. In June 1859 he had a success in Bordeaux, conducting the *Roman Carnival* overture and excerpts from *Romeo* and the *Childhood*. But the retrospective of his output in a series of ten concerts, which he had projected while composing *The Trojans* and which was intended to lead up to a grand production of the opera, had come to nothing, for lack of money but also, crucially, because there was no decent hall available in Paris. This had been borne in on him again in the spring of 1858 when, at the intercession of the Duke of Gotha, the Conservatoire Hall was obtained for a concert put on by the duke's kapellmeister, the composer and virtuoso pianist Henri Litolff, directed by Berlioz – the first he had conducted there for fifteen years. In a programme consisting largely of Litolff's music, his own main contribution, the Fête from *Romeo*, superbly played by an orchestra made up of most of the Société des Concerts' members, brought the house down; the composer was recalled again and again. He was left with the thought that if he could "perform the whole of his repertoire like that", Paris would understand his music. But, of course, he couldn't. The government gladly made use of his expertise: he was the moving spirit on a committee set up by the minister in July 1858 under Halévy's chairmanship to establish a universal pitch for France and its dominions (it was Berlioz who assembled tuning-forks from all over Europe and had them measured and classified). But it did not order *The Trojans* to be produced, or authorize him to use the Conservatoire Hall.

He remained more celebrated as a writer on music than as a musician. That was no doubt partly his fault for writing so well. His brilliant demolition of the various operatic settings of *Romeo and Juliet*, on the occasion of an ill-fated revival of Bellini's *Capulets and Montagues* at the Opéra, was held to have dealt the production its death-blow. *La France musicale* declared that "the most merciless of all the criticism was that of the man whose opinion has the greatest weight in Paris journalism, M. H. Berlioz".

It was symbolic that he should be occupied reviewing other people's *Romeo and Juliets* and *Fausts* rather than performing his own. More than ever he was before the public as a writer. From September 1858 to July 1859 the *Monde illustré* printed regular extracts from his *Memoirs*, edited so as to exclude intimate details of his personal life but with enough left to cause quite a stir. The chapters published included his first communion, the audition for the chorus of the Nouveautés, Shakespeare at the Odéon, Beethoven and the Conservatoire professors, the July Revolution, Habeneck and the pinch of snuff, and *Benvenuto Cellini* at the Opéra. Early in 1859 the Librairie Nouvelle, a publishing house in the Boulevard des Italiens, approached Berlioz for another collection of his journalism – a lighter sequel to *Evenings in the Orchestra*. A few weeks before, the *Chronique parisienne* had featured a dozen or so anecdotes of his – "The right to play in F in a symphony in D", the Dresden music-lover who wondered whether the Amen fugue mightn't be meant ironically, the amateur cellist who hadn't washed his face since Rossini kissed him on the forehead, the dancer who refused to dance in the key of E major – and it was no doubt this that gave the Nouvelle Librairie's proprietor, Achille Bourdilliat, the idea of getting him to make a whole book out of these and similar pieces.

Les Grotesques de la musique, published at the beginning of March 1859, was the result: brief squibs celebrating the bizarreries of the musical world or exploding the vanity and pretensions of performers great and small, varied by higher flights of fancy like the paean to the skylark or the meditation on the inevitable passing of all things, and by a few longer items such as the letters from Plombières and Baden, the account of the concerts given by the author in the French provinces in 1845 and 1846, and reflections on the thirst for gold that drove famous singers to the ends of the earth at the risk of their health and even of their lives. The collection (he told Pohl) was intended to "amuse while saying things that are deadly serious"; and the press, generally, thought that it did just that. Reviewers vied with each other to praise it – the *Ménestrel*, for example, finding "behind its hearty laughter and its wry enthusiasms" satire that was all too accurate. Like its predecessor, it sold well and provided some of the money needed, among other things, to finance the course that Louis would soon be taking in Dieppe to qualify as master mariner. But it did not advance the cause of *The Trojans*. The epigrammatic humour and learned fooling of the *Grotesques* sorted oddly with the idea of a five-act grand opera on the *Aeneid*. In so far as Berlioz was a composer he was what the critic of the *Ménestrel* called him: "our eminent symphonist".

Yet *The Trojans* remained the great issue. He was still living in the score. The work of reducing it for piano went on that autumn. Pauline Viardot, in the midst of studying the role of Orpheus, willingly lent a hand. The young Saint-Saëns, who was helping with the preparations for *Orphée*, remembered ever afterwards the sight of "Mme Viardot, pen in hand, eyes alight, the manuscript of *The Trojans* on her piano, doing the accompaniment of the Royal Hunt". Berlioz continued to lobby for the work's acceptance at the Opéra, encouraged by the success of the two scenes at Baden. In mid-October 1859 he went to see General

Mellinet, head of military bands, who had the ear of the Emperor. The general promised to speak to His Majesty. But Berlioz was not sanguine. What if he did? Even if the Emperor's response were favourable, his officials could obstruct it. "I am like Brunel after the construction of the *Great Eastern*. Everyone swore, and *proved*, that the Thames was not deep enough for so gigantic a ship. If Brunel's fate had depended on the secretaries at the Admiralty, the *Great Eastern* would still be on the slipway, written off as pure madness."

A week later, on 24 October, there was another private run-through of movements from the opera, this time in the salon of the Viardots' house in the Rue de Douai, to honour Princess Carolyne, who was in Paris for a few days, staying at the Hôtel du Rhin, Place des Vosges. Five scenes were sung, including Dido's final recitative and aria and one or possibly both of the duets heard at Baden (Lefort was present) and perhaps also the duet with Anna, "Reine d'un jeune empire", for we hear of Moscheles' daughter Clara, who was a Viardot pupil, taking part. Berlioz was beside himself with delight, as he told his brother-in-law Marc Suat:

> I heard Dido's farewell for the first time – "Adieu, fière cité" [etc.]. I was terribly moved. This is it, it really is. Oh, there are accents there that break your heart –
>
> > Vénus, rends-moi ton fils! Inutile prière
> > D'un coeur qui se déchire. A la mort tout entière
> > Didon n'attend plus rien que de la mort.
>
> How childish I am to tell you this. But how can I help it? I'm so happy not to have fallen too far below my subject.
>
> Mme Viardot shook like a leaf as she sang the scene.
>
> The Princess kept exclaiming; she pressed my hands in hers and embraced the singer. Whatever happens the opera exists. I work daily to perfect it; I must have the right to inscribe on the title-page of the score the words that Clio sings in the Epilogue: *Stat Roma!*

After the Princess's departure on 28 October the two friends continued to write to each other. She poured on him the balm of her praise and admiration, tending his wounds and at the same time encouraging him to fresh projects; he responded gratefully while scolding her for what he called her illusions, and gave her news of the various activities which despite his ill health kept him busy.

One of them was to lobby on behalf of Liszt, who had applied for the position of Corresponding Member of the Institute left vacant by the death of Spohr. Berlioz threw himself into the cause, mobilizing support among his colleagues: Halévy, Delacroix, Baron Taylor, Kastner, Thomas, Auber, even "ce bon gros Clapisson", and many others, were pressed for their vote. "I was asked this curious question: 'Is it as composer or as virtuoso that M. Liszt is being presented?' 'As everything,' I replied. 'Will that do?'" But his efforts came to nothing. The commission appointed to short-list the candidates ignored Liszt altogether. It elected Verdi and Carafa's protégé Carlo Conti, permanent secretary of the Naples Academy, who had already applied on eight previous occasions. "Wagner was not even considered," Berlioz told the Princess. "Such are academic bodies."

Flattering for Verdi, isn't it? But he had nothing to do with it, and is no doubt surprised to receive so signal a distinction. I have to say that Verdi is a man of honour, proud, unyielding, who knows how to put the little curs and great donkeys in their place when they get above themselves. He's as far from the mocking play-acting and jesting – sometimes stupid jesting – of Rossini as he is from Meyerbeer's snake-like slipperiness. Many a time he has jolted the people at the Opéra and the Arts Ministry out of their culpable torpor. You should at least grant him your approval for that.*

We'll do better for Liszt next time there's a vacancy. Delacroix and one or two others are pretty well up in arms about it. As for Liszt, I was rather sorry to see him attribute to this election the kind of importance it can't possibly have for him – it was important only for us. The Institute should do all it can to acquire people of stature, instead of taking to its bosom, with a protective air, so many midgets scarcely worth drowning in the irrigations of Gulliver. [...] I had been going to answer you yesterday, I was boiling with ideas, but was laid low by my damnable neuralgia at its most violent, and spent sixteen hours in bed. Today I'm still writhing but my arms aren't, unlike yesterday, so I am able to write to you.

* Verdi was of very little account in Weimar circles, but he and Berlioz were on friendly terms. A couple of months later, in a letter from Genoa to Léon Escudier, Verdi wrote: "Give my warmest greetings to Berlioz, whom I esteem as a composer and love as a man."

No one would have imagined, from reading Berlioz's feuilletons or the pieces in *Grotesques* (most of which were of recent date), what a sick man he was. The energy of his writing was unimpaired, the ardour of response to sympathetic ideas as great as ever (one has only to read his article on the operatic *Romeos*, and in particular the magnificent counterblast which the evasions and approximations of their librettists and composers inspired him to, to see that). But his intimates knew how much pain he was in. Some of them doubted he had more than a short time left. Pauline Viardot wondered whether, even if his opera did inaugurate the rebuilt Théâtre-Lyrique, he would be there to see it. The Princess, when she saw him that October, was shocked at the change since his last visit to Weimar three and a half years before. From the report she sent home, Liszt supposed that his old friend was "not long for this sad world".

She nevertheless tried to set him going on something new, knowing that his spirits lifted when he had a project, and knowing too that the opera he was contracted to write for Baden, on an episode of the Thirty Years' War, did not appeal to him. While they dined together the possibility of an opera on *Antony and Cleopatra* was touched on. Berlioz took the bait. "Yes, one could do something great but very harsh on that subject. I can't think of an example of love more poisoned than Antony's for the Queen of Egypt; I don't believe any man was unhappier than that unhappy man after he'd lost the battle of Actium, and his infernal mistress, his 'Serpent of old Nile', had fled like a coward and abandoned him. I can't contemplate without a shudder that ocean of grief. No matter: if I recover some of my strength I'll try it." Within ten days he returned to Cleopatra. In the meantime he had reread the play and was full of it. True,

the subject, of all those that could inspire me, is the least accessible to French taste and therefore the most dangerous. You can't suppose I would have the impertinence to distort Shakespeare's creation by making an academic Cleopatra, a Spanish queen, speaking in correct, measured terms and deferring to court etiquette? No, it's precisely because the fiery and capricious Egyptian is the very opposite of such dolts that she bewitches me. I adore that mad creature who wanted Julius Caesar to sleep with her with his sword at his side, who plagues the wretched Antony in every vilest way, yet has no desire to survive him and doesn't – a jade who hops on one foot through the streets of Alexandria, and has a salt-fish hung on Antony's hook one day when he's fishing in the Nile, whose fantasy changes twenty times in a quarter of an hour – a brazen hussy who questions Mardian the eunuch about his affections, and finally the idiotic, cowardly woman who flees the battle of Actium without knowing why she's doing it. What a character for a musical fantasy! But who would I write such a work for? For you of course. It's true – forgive me. But, dear Princess, one has to shut one's eyes to the fact that the future is a mirage. That is the important thing, for me and for our projects. Unfortunately I know quite well that what I see on the horizon is not a lake but a burning desert. What are you going to do about that? One can't will oneself into believing.

A month later: "Yes, I shall do *Cleopatra*, if I have time. But you know what Hamlet says: 'Had I but time . . . Death is strict in his arrest.'" In the following ten days he thought further about it, and his ideas began to develop.

Your letters agitate me terribly, Princess; your dreams, your schemes fall on me like gunpowder on fire. If I were twenty years younger you would make something of me. [. . .] Recently, as I was entering Mme Viardot's salon (where music was going on), the distant hum of harmony gave me a shock accompanied by a series of flashes, and I thought I saw Cleopatra aureoled in a strange radiance. Yes, I think I would make a seductive creature of that torpedo. It would be so different from everything I've done. There would be so much scope for the unexpected, the strange, the excessive. I think I'd restrict myself to borrowing only certain details from Shakespeare, and would do better to give my fancy free rein. To begin with I must have the interior of a pyramid, and priests of Isis with their mysteries and their juggleries. For Cleopatra I must have audacities on a grander scale; I must have the scene on the Cydnus,* I must have a secret orgy for the women with the eunuch Mardian, counterpart of the triumvirs' public orgy on young Pompey's galley. Perhaps there'll be a way of presenting the cold sagacious Octavius and the Egyptian madcap at the same time. What a contrast that will be! Yes, it would be curious.

But it requires time and life. I consider myself very lucky to have had a year for completing and correcting my Trojan score; it's been a priceless gift of fortune. And then, as the proverb says: "Grasp all, lose all." Besides, it's so discouraging, seeing the likely fate of these great musical

---

* "The barge she sat in . . .", *Antony and Cleopatra*, II, ii.

machines. On all sides great donkeys and little curs, not to mention the hogs that come and rootle with their snouts in artists' plantations. Why bother growing pineapples and sugar cane and the noble palm tree?

After that there is no further mention of *Cleopatra*, except for an inquiry two years later from the Princess, who would still not hear of his "task being now accomplished" and was anxious to "talk to you again of Cleopatra – the Pyramids – Mark Antony!" But by then the time for striking sparks had passed.

You can say, like Boschot and Barzun, that something of these ideas was channelled into *Beatrice and Benedick*, the "caprice written with the point of a needle" which he composed for Baden in place of the work originally commissioned. The fact remains that *Cleopatra* would have been totally different from anything he had done, *Beatrice* included – harsher, darker, crueller.

More than all the discouragements Paris could put in his path it was ill health, the progressive, compound debilitation and demoralization caused by almost constant pain, that made him stop composing once the Baden opera was done. The Princess was right to try to get him working again. (He had felt quite disoriented and at a loss when the final scene of *The Trojans* was completed and his "Penelope's robe" no longer awaited him each morning in his study.) His brain still seethed, his creative energies were alive and champing to be off. It was only that the flesh was too weak.

Berlioz's pathology has yet to be diagnosed. No doubt it had powerful psychosomatic elements. The state of anger he was so often in was clearly an important cause. He suffered much less in the weeks following his decision to throw off, at long last, the burden of criticism – only for the attacks to be precipitated afresh by the rage that seized him when Choudens published a cut version of *The Trojans at Carthage*. Rewarding musical activity, equally, could alleviate the pain or even banish it for a while. He usually felt better at Baden, not only from taking the waters but because he was leading the active performer's life normally denied him. Writing from there in August 1859 he told Adèle that his "névralgie" had practically gone – the life there suited him "so much better than inaction". (At the start of the Litolff concert which he conducted at the Conservatoire in May 1858 he felt so groggy – in this case with flu – that he could hardly stand; but the moment "the miraculous orchestra spoke" his strength came back: he "could have carried Mount Athos".) Sometimes, when he began a new treatment, his symptoms disappeared so rapidly that he imagined himself cured. The nervous attacks, accompanied by uncontrollable weeping, which his letters refer to in these years, seem not to have been directly connected with his intestinal condition. But the latter must have been at least partly nervous in origin. It was a condition which could have been inherited from either or both of his parents. Quite apart from that, the state of tension, physical and mental, in which he had lived for so long – beginning with the tension of pursuing a career against the wishes of a beloved and respected father – could well have produced internal disorders of one kind or another, even if he had not been predisposed to them.

Whatever its cause, the pain was real enough. It was located mainly in the intestines and to a lesser extent in the bladder, but could also affect the eyes and the head. Sometimes it was manageable (in September 1858 he reports that "the Good Lord is making me suffer just enough to keep his hand in"). More often it was excruciating; and its cumulative effect, over the years, was to drain his strength and wear down his spirit.

Saint-Saëns, who saw a good deal of him in his final years, said that occasionally he would abandon his diet and go on a spree – as when, one evening, they dined very late on oysters and white wine, and smoked many strong cigars and drank black coffee, with inevitable retribution for the sick man next day. Most of the time he did what he was told, without deriving any long-term benefit. He consulted a whole string of doctors. His friend Amussat might have helped him, but he died before the malady fully declared itself. Of the others – Alphonse Robert, Sichelatire, Huguier, Cabarrus, an unnamed Englishman, and a homoeo-path recommended by Legouvé – one or two gave him momentary relief but none knew how to treat it. Ironically, the least unsuccessful was J. H. Vries, a Eurasian practitioner known as "the black doctor" who claimed to be able to cure cancers with Malayan herbal remedies passed to him by his mother. His special ointment was applied to a malignant growth on Adolphe Sax's upper lip which doctors had declared inoper-able, and the tumour disappeared; and he was credited with other spectacular healings. After consulting him Berlioz enjoyed several entirely pain-free weeks in February 1859 and felt a different man. He went so far as to compose a short hymn for the tabernacle which Vries was proposing to construct in the Champs-Elysées in obedience to the prophecies of Solomon and Ezekiel and as harbinger of the coming era of universal peace; and he conducted the *Roman Carnival* overture at a dinner held in Vries' honour by Sax's friends at the Hôtel de Ville. The medical establishment branded "le docteur noir" a quack, though not itself notably successful in the treatment of cancer. The fact is that Sax lived for another thirty-five years; and Berlioz had his longest period of remission.

After that the pain returned, if anything worse than before. In September 1859 he began a course of treatment with Huguier the famous surgeon, whom he met by chance when calling on Roger the tenor, victim of a shooting accident in which he had lost an arm. Huguier, after examining Berlioz, told him he was suffering from a neurosis of the sympathetic nerve; but neither the diagnosis nor the treatment did him any good. A month later he was seeing an English doctor and being subjected to electrotherapy. The doctor, he told Pauline Viardot, "placed me between the pads of his machine, and the positive and negative poles waged a battle royal on my sympathetic nerve. No detectable result as yet. But I warn you all that at our next encounter, if you give me your hand in the usual cordial way you will receive a shock and see sparks coming out of mine. That will be the electrical fluid being released – the positive fluid, of course, for nothing in the world is more positive than my affection for you. I'm punning again. Is that a good sign? Let's hope so". But it proved no more effective than the other treatments. "What humbugs these doctors are. They're just as they were in Molière's day."

On 23 October Berlioz was returning from the doctor's when Wagner accosted him in the street. He was, wrote Wagner to Mathilde Wesendonck, "in a pitiable state of health. He had just had electrical treatment – a last attempt to alleviate his dreadful nervous condition. He described to me his pain: it begins when he wakes up, and then goes on, getting worse all the time. I recognized my own complaints."

Wagner had been in Paris since the middle of September, but the two men had not succeeded in meeting. From now on they saw one another quite often. A couple of weeks after the encounter in the street they sat together at a private evening of late Beethoven sonatas and chamber music, and Berlioz introduced Wagner to Gounod, who was sitting on the other side of him. On 18 November he sent Wagner a ticket for the first night of *Orphée*. They met again soon afterwards: Berlioz spent the evening, with Liszt's daughter Blandine and her husband Emile

Ollivier, at Wagner's lodgings at 16 Rue Newton, just south of the Etoile. On 12 January, having mislaid the details of Wagner's forthcoming concert, he wrote asking him to let him have them again: "It's time we announced it in the *Journal des débats*". The paper carried the announcement on the 15th, repeating it on the 24th, the day before the concert.

On the 21st a bulky package was delivered at 4 Rue de Calais.

> Dear Berlioz
>
> I am delighted to be able to offer you the first copy of my *Tristan*. Accept it and keep it out of friendship for me.
>
> Richard Wagner

The score was inscribed "To the dear and great author of *Romeo and Juliet*, from the grateful author of *Tristan and Isolde*".

Wagner's immediate reason for being in Paris was to give a series of concerts of his music at the Théâtre-Italien. But he had taken out a long lease on the apartment; the concerts were a means to a much more important end. He had set his heart on getting a Paris production of one of his operas, and he meant to have it.

24

Wagner

History is written by the victors; or, to quote W. H. Auden, "History to the defeated / May say Alas but cannot help or pardon."

For the best part of a century the Berlioz–Wagner issue was judged from the perspective of Wagner's triumph and Berlioz's defeat. "His first name, Hector, did not bring him good fortune," wrote Liszt; "Achilles–Wagner appeared, dominator of contemporary musical drama." Berlioz's article on Wagner's Paris concerts, in the *Débats* of 9 February 1860, was routinely thought of – when it was thought of at all – as an act of betrayal; together with his comments on the downfall of *Tannhäuser* at the Opéra in March 1861, his failure to come to its aid with a sympathetic review and his dissenting annotations in the score of *Tristan*, it was considered clear evidence of an overmastering jealousy and vindictiveness. He knew – everyone did – that Wagner was in Paris for more than concerts and had his sights on the Opéra, and that he had influential backing, more influential than Berlioz was ever able to muster; the very manner of *Tannhäuser*'s entry to the Opéra – a wager between Napoleon III and the Austrian ambassador's wife Princess Metternich which obliged the loser (the Emperor) to agree to whatever the winner asked – underlined the futility of Berlioz's years of lobbying on behalf of *The Trojans*. It was no secret, either, that waiting behind *Tannhäuser* – in the event of its success – was *Tristan*. When *Tannhäuser* failed, what was Berlioz's reaction? "I am cruelly avenged."

It did not matter that *The Trojans* was the apple of his eye no less than *Tristan* was of Wagner's. In the messianic climate of late-nineteenth-century Wagnerism there could be no comparison between the two works. One represented the vibrant, victorious future, the other the buried past. What if Wagner did attack Berlioz more fiercely in public than Berlioz ever attacked Wagner? It was only natural. He was in the right.

All this happened in another age. The history these ancient quarrels enacted has run its course; Wagnerism, the cult, has ebbed – with no diminution in the magnitude of Wagner's achievement – and we are free to admire and love the work of both composers, to believe in both of them.

It was possible even then: just possible. Pohl managed it. Though Bülow found the strain too great, Cornelius could describe himself as "A pale young Lisztian / To his last breath and tone, / A Wagner–Berlioz Weimarian, / Cornelian too in mind and bone". He did not see why one had to choose. Liszt himself longed for his two friends to be united; their skirmish was a distraction from the real fight which was for the soul of musical Germany, and which ranged his futurist party against the reactionaries of Leipzig, whose hostile manifesto, signed by Brahms and the renegade Joachim, was published that same spring of 1860. But Wagner's theories – the music which embodied them was still largely unknown – were too drastic, too imperious and insistent to be ignored. They were the question of the hour, and everyone in artistic and intellectual Paris must necessarily respond, with revulsion or fascination – Berlioz among them, all the more as he was widely assumed to belong to the Wagner camp. And being the musician and the man he was, he could only respond as he did: with fascination, yes, but with revulsion. The reasons were at once local and personal, and deep-seated and general.

For one thing, the situations of the two composers made conflict inevitable: on one side Wagner, filled with the conviction that he had given birth to an epoch-making score for which (like Stravinsky and *The Rite of Spring*) he was the chosen vessel, and seeing a production of *Tannhäuser* as making the way straight for *Tristan*, whose success could in turn lead to the staging of *The Ring*; on the other side Berlioz, knowing that he had written a great work and struggling to get it accepted in his native city, only to find that Wagner had "popped in between the election and his hopes". How could he not feel jealous? But the antagonism went deeper than a temporary, tactical rivalry. Given their antithetical characters and beliefs, we can see that the two men could hardly have acted or spoken otherwise. With such profound differences, we may wonder that they got on even as well as they did – though at the moment of their closest rapport, in London in 1855, they were about to diverge furthest as creative artists.

The differences were legion, beginning with the nine and a half years between their ages: already, when Wagner first came into contact with Berlioz's music, the older composer had completed half his output and the younger had written, of his acknowledged works, only *Rienzi* and *The Flying Dutchman*; by the time of their confrontation in 1860–61 Berlioz was near the end of his career and Wagner on the crest of his. They differed, fundamentally, in so many vital ways, over so many things. First, over the role of music in drama, a disagreement no less radical for each having misrepresented the other's position. Then, over the kind of subjects they were drawn to (there is little trace in Berlioz's operas of the psychological depths and complexities of *The Ring* and none of the Wagnerian preoccupation with Judaeo-Christian ideas of redemption: the tragic figures of *The Trojans* live in the shadow of their fate and go down uncomplainingly to eternal night). Over their view of their place in the development of music, Berlioz seeing his work as, with all its innovations, a continuing, Wagner believing himself to be the culmination of what had gone before. Over the lengths to which they were prepared to go, at their own and others' expense, to serve the demands of their genius (Wagner would never have suppressed a symphony that was struggling to come into the world, as Berlioz did). And, finally, in their music's methods of construction and the whole sound of their orchestra.

Yet I doubt if Berlioz, in London with Wagner in 1855, thought at that stage in terms of an inherent rivalry between them (not till six months later, in Weimar, did he realize the extent of Liszt's dedication to Wagner's ideas). With Wagner's arrival in Paris in the autumn of 1859, however, their innate and acquired differences came inexorably to a head. There could be no question now of the meshing of gears of which Berlioz had written to Liszt four years before: their needs were in direct conflict. The conflict was merely exacerbated by Wagner's proselytizing and Berlioz's resistance to it.

What remains remarkable is that at the moment when he knew he had written the music of the future and was the heir of the ages, Wagner should continue to regard Berlioz as one of the élite and to attach such importance to converting him to the right path. Notwithstanding his often swingeing criticism of him – notably in *Opera and Drama* – Berlioz was the one contemporary composer he took really seriously. He brushed the others aside, Meyerbeer, Verdi and the rest; but Berlioz, wrong-headed though he might be, was a colleague whose creative force and energy were so worthy of respect that his insistence on following an independent and diametrically opposite course was a continual irritant. What was Berlioz doing trying to patch up the unredeemable *Benvenuto Cellini*? What was he doing writing a *Faust* symphony, he asked Liszt indignantly. "Only one thing can save him: the drama" – the drama as Wagner conceived it. When Berlioz read him the poem of *The Trojans* in February 1858 he could hardly bear it. His exasperation boiled over in a letter to the unfortunate Bülow. He confessed that he dreaded meeting him again and having to say something about it. "The sight of him, pondering the destiny of that nameless absurdity as if the salvation of the world and of his own soul depended on it, was more than I could stomach." Yet two years later, in May 1860 – several months after Berlioz's review of his concerts – his sense that when all was said he was of the true lineage revived all over again when he read the long *critique admirative* of *Fidelio* in the *Débats*. They were brothers after all. He wrote to Liszt the same day, reaffirming that the three of them formed a unique triad of equals. Why couldn't Berlioz see it? It could only be because the influences he was subjected to – chief among them Marie Recio's – made him a stranger to his real nature. Late in life, with Berlioz long gone, Wagner would not hear of his being criticized; he was "the saviour of our musical world". Cosima, in her diary, describes him going for a walk in the country on a serene autumn afternoon and uttering the one word, "Berlioz!" But while Berlioz was alive his attitude could only be profoundly ambivalent. For Wagner, he that was not with him was against him. And Berlioz mattered more than anyone. He must constantly try to get him on his side, and feel rebuffed when he failed to. The gift of the full score of *Tristan*, with its flattering inscription, was both a sincere homage to the man, and to the work that had revealed "a new world of music", and a bid for his support. Surely it would be forthcoming.

Undoubtedly Marie "made trouble". Unable to grasp the larger context, she could only see him as a threat to her man – how much more, now that he was manoeuvring his way into the Opéra ahead of *The Trojans* and (as she told Berlioz's nieces) exploiting the authority of the Emperor "to climb over the backs of everyone else"! Reyer describes Marie, on the way out of Wagner's first concert, covering herself and Berlioz with ridicule by exclaiming loudly, "What a triumph for Hector!" To Wagner it was the classic example of the man of godlike talent brought low by a mediocre, mean-spirited woman. But, even without Marie, Berlioz could not have acted differently.

We may think: how could the composer of *Sur les lagunes*, of Dido's "Errante sur les mers" and Hylas' song and the *Trojans* septet, not be stirred to admiring recognition by the magnificent seascape that is the prelude to the third act of *Tristan*? How for that matter could the tenderness of Brangaene's music, the magic of the hunting horns melting into the babble of the brook – how could such things not strike echoes in his imagination? How, knowing the story of Tristram and Iseult, could he fail to understand the meaning of the never-resolved harmonies of the prelude to Act 1 (in the opening phrase of which Wagner made the most direct of all the score's many allusions to Berlioz's *Romeo*)? How was it that the two tragic masterpieces of the nineteenth century (if we except *Otello* – and Verdi, for Wagner, was a figure of no importance) could have missed their historic conjunction, passing like ships in the night?

For two interconnected reasons, one musical and technical, the other ideological. At least Berlioz declared himself baffled by *Tristan* after he had examined the full score and listened to the prelude at the first of Wagner's concerts (whereas a hearing of the libretto of *The Trojans* was enough for Wagner to dismiss it as a "nameless absurdity"). He also studied Pauline Viardot's vocal scores of *The Flying Dutchman*, *Tannhäuser* and *Lohengrin*, excerpts from which formed the bulk of Wagner's programme. When he returned them a few weeks later he warned her to take care that the diminished sevenths didn't escape and gnaw her furniture. There are quite a number of diminished sevenths in *The Trojans*. But more than anything it was the frequency of dissonance in Wagner's music that he objected to. "Wagner has just given a concert," he told Adolphe Samuel, "which exasperated three quarters of the audience and roused the other quarter to enthusiasm. For me, I found it a painful experience, even while admiring the vehemence of his musical feeling in particular instances. But the diminished sevenths, the dissonances, the brutal modulations, threw me into a fever, and I have to say I hate that style of music – it revolts me."

If, on the contrary, he was charmed by the prelude to *Lohengrin* and singled it out in his review as "admirable in every respect" and "un chef-d'oeuvre", that was because, as well as being the finest of the early Wagner pieces in the programme, this "beau morceau" had in it "no harshness (*duretés*) of any kind". In contrast, the "superb" and "magisterially orchestrated" march and chorus from the second act of *Tannhäuser* contained "a few rather harsh modulations, which follow one another too closely", though the music "imposed them with such vigour and authority" that "the ear accepted them without resistance". But both the *Flying Dutchman* and *Tannhäuser* overtures were, in his opinion, marred: the former – after its explosive opening based on an electrifying open fifth – by the incessant repetition of chromatic scales leading only to further chromatic scales, the allegro of the latter by its development of an in itself not very interesting two-bar theme which was "bristling with chromatic sequences, modulations and harmonies of extreme harshness". Even the theme for unison brass in the prelude to Act 3 of *Lohengrin* – a piece "to which one can scarcely find anything comparable for grand, unstoppable force and brilliance" – would, he thought, have been better still without the harmonic clashes. In other words Berlioz responded like the harmonic conservative he had by that time become (and in a certain sense had always been). No wonder that in the *Tristan* prelude – "a sort of chromatic moan", the only theme "full of dissonant chords made still more painful by prolonged appoggiaturas which replace the true note" – harmony was the insurmountable stumbling-block. It was not dissonance per se that he was opposed to; as he was careful to explain, what he minded in the *Lohengrin* Act 3 prelude was its presence *there*. What he could not bear was its being used systematically, instead of being reserved for moments of special expression.

Berlioz was not the first ageing composer to find the newest music beyond him. Though, as Wagner complained, he was handicapped by his ignorance of the German language ("to which my dramatic conceptions are linked in so close a connection"), that was not the real obstacle. He could understand the early operas clearly enough, while disliking certain aspects of them. One would love to know what he would have thought of the predominantly diatonic *Meistersinger* or the first act of *Walküre*. But the latest advances in harmonic vocabulary and syntax that were pioneered by Liszt and had now burst forth with shattering effect in *Tristan* inevitably left him stranded, uncomprehending. The idiom was simply too alien.

Nevertheless the tenor of his review of Wagner's music in the *Débats* remained balanced between praise and criticism. The criticism, too, concerned details; the praise was for the composer's "great musical qualities". Even in the passage on the *Tristan* prelude the emphasis was almost as much on the critic's failure to discern its meaning as on the music's strangeness. The notice of the concert concluded that Wagner "possesses that rare intensity of feeling, that inner fire, strength of will and faith in himself which move and compel and captivate; but these qualities would shine more brightly still if they were combined with more invention and less striving and with a juster appreciation of the constituent elements of the art of music".

Though a conservative assessment, it was not a hostile one. Only in the light of Wagner's later deification could it have seemed culpably inadequate. Unfortunately it did not stop there. The article ended with an examination of "the Music of the Future" and the critic's own relation to it. Here we come to the crux. Berlioz would much rather not have been caught up in an ideological dispute that to him was both distasteful and, in a sense, irrelevant; but he had to make his position clear: he was forever seeing himself ranked among the futurists – more than ever now Wagner was in Paris – and it irked him. He didn't belong to them; or, if he had once belonged as a kind of associate member, he could no longer. He believed in the future of music, not in the Music of the Future.

Like others, he had formed an inaccurate picture of Wagner's theory; but even if he had liked the practice better the idea of a doctrine would not have been acceptable. He might be prepared to admire *Tannhäuser* for itself, when he heard it under more favourable conditions three years later at Weimar, but not for a priori reasons, and certainly not – *Tristan* still less! – as the one way forward for dramatic music. Such doctrines went against everything he believed. They did not open up the future: by definition, they obstructed it. His whole life was against so confining a notion. If he was for any -ism, it was pluralism – for accepting that Mendelssohn, for instance, could be a master even though he followed a fundamentally different path. Aged nearly sixty, with his work all but done, he did not have the overwhelming imperative that drove Wagner – the need to give form to the vast new worlds of music-drama within him and to convince the outside world of the rightness and inevitability of his mission.

In so far as Berlioz had a musical creed it consisted simply (as he told Lobe in 1853) of "what I have done and what I have not done". His thoughts on the new ideology had been hardening over the past few years, ever since he and Liszt had words about it at Weimar early in 1856, shortly before he began work on *The Trojans*. In a letter to the Princess a year later he spoke of the painful impression made on him by certain passages in a piano trio by Liszt's pupil Bronsart which the Weimar musician had had performed in Paris and which, by its apparent "belief in ugliness", its "cultivation of the horrible", seemed actually to be saying that "fair is foul". "Can you imagine such a doctrine? Making dissonance into a *system*! And in so doing supplying a weapon for the dullards, the reactionaries of art to attack and destroy the pioneers who, as it is, hack out a path with so much difficulty." The experience had upset him deeply; he would sooner go back to the early sonatas of Mozart and Pleyel. "And then the rogues who come up to me afterwards and say, 'You must like that stuff, you.' Flattering, isn't it? Yes, I like it, as one likes drinking vitriol or eating arsenic."

The final section of the *Débats* article took the form of a catechism, for and against: if the Music of the Future meant this, it commanded his support; if that, he could have none of it.

Perhaps inevitably, he loaded the dice. Worse, he did it in a way that made him appear both disingenuous and fuddy-duddy. His positive catechism was a very mild affair. It presented modern music as an emancipated art, free to do as it wished in response to the new needs of the spirit even if that meant breaking the old rules; but his specific propositions offered nothing that an enlightened musician could disagree with and little that was interesting, apart from "sound ranks below idea, idea ranks below feeling and passion". For the rest, he rode his ancient hobby-horses, like a nodding, rambling Don Quixote, across ground long fought over and peripheral to the debate: vocal decoration as the enemy of dramatic expression, singers' licence, the absurdity of Kyrie eleison bawled out as by a chorus of drunkards in a tavern, Gluck's bold use of upper pedal-notes and the sublime effects he produced with them. For the first time Berlioz begins to sound like an old man.

The negative section, on the other hand, was a passionate tirade in which his pent-up feelings poured out pell-mell in an angry flood.

But if the Futurists tell us: "One must do the opposite of what the rules prescribe; we are tired of melody, tired of melodic patterns, tired of arias, duets, trios and movements whose themes are developed regularly; we are surfeited with consonant harmonies, with simple dissonances prepared and resolved, with natural modulations skilfully contrived; one must take account only of the idea and forget about sensation; one must scorn the ear, strumpet that it is, one must brutalize it in order to master it; it is not the purpose of music to be pleasing to it; music must be made accustomed to anything and everything, to strings of ascending and descending diminished sevenths which resemble a knot of hissing serpents writhing and tearing each other, to triple dissonances which are neither prepared nor resolved, to inner parts forcibly combined without agreeing harmonically or rhythmically and rasping painfully against one another, to ugly modulations entering in one part of the orchestra before the previous key has made its exit; one should show no regard to the art of singing and give no thought to its nature or its requirements; in opera one must confine oneself to setting down the declamation, even if it means writing intervals that are outlandish, nasty and unsingable" . . .

And so on in similar vein until:

"The witches in *Macbeth* are right: 'Fair is foul and foul is fair.' " If that is the new religion, I am very far from professing it; I have never been part of it, I am not now and I never shall be. I raise my hand and swear *Non credo*. On the contrary, I firmly believe that fair is not foul and foul is not fair. Certainly, it is not music's sole purpose to be pleasing to the ear. But music's purpose is a thousand times less to be unpleasing to it, to torture and destroy it.

The outburst, however exaggerated, was sincere and deeply felt. But it was a serious error. A caricature of futurist music, it satisfied few people apart from those who already felt as he did. It left him more isolated than ever, separating him from the Wagner–Liszt camp and from the Parisian progressives who were drawn to Wagner and his far-ranging, audacious ideas, but without really reconciling him with the establishment. It turned him into, of all things, the ally of Fétis – Fétis who had been busy demolishing Wagner in the press for the past ten years, just as, before, he had demolished Berlioz. It gave a veneer of truth to Scudo's epigram, invented in an uncharacteristic moment of partial insight: Berlioz and Wagner as "enemy brothers", two *enfants terribles* sprung from Beethoven's demented old age. And it consigned him to the limbo which he was to occupy for many years to come, that of the eternal outsider on the margin of musical history.

The immediate consequence was that his non-credo provided Wagner with an opportunity which he seized gratefully. On 15 February, six days after Berlioz's review, the *Débats* published his reply. The fourteen-hundred-word open letter set out to put Berlioz right about "the Music of the Future", a phrase which Wagner, disingenuously in his turn, claimed was used only by his enemies (in fact it was in daily use in Liszt's circle, as a glance at their correspondence will show). He was saddened, he said, that a musician of Berlioz's intelligence, and a friend, should sink to the level of the prejudiced and the vulgar by attributing to him such grotesque doctrines; but at least in countering these erroneous notions he, Wagner, could try to explain his real theory, that of the *Work of Art* of the Future, a union of all the arts inspired by the example of ancient Greek tragedy; and this he proceeded to do. The letter ended by asking Berlioz to "let hospitable France give sanctuary to my lyric dramas. I on my side await with impatience the production of *The Trojans* – an impatience justly and trebly motivated, by the affection I have for you, by the significance your work cannot fail to have in the present state of music and still more by reason of the special importance I attach to it in relation to my own guiding ideas and principles."

Berlioz told Hallé that this "confused and turgid" letter did Wagner more harm than good. But he deluded himself. The casual reader was left with the impression that Berlioz was failing to use his authority to help a fellow-artist get his operas put on in Paris; worse still, jealously protective of *The Trojans* (a work which apparently derived from Wagner's ideas), he had turned against his former friend and was stirring up opposition to him, using as pretext the non-existent threat of "the Music of the Future". The letter also gave Wagner a platform from which to publicize his revolutionary ideas about music-drama, thereby sowing the seeds of the cult which would take so strong a hold on the French imagination in the last decades of the nineteenth century.

The irony of being asked to "let" Paris stage Wagner's operas must have brought a bitter smile to those fine-drawn lips. His own opera was aground like Robinson Crusoe's canoe, miles from the sea. It was still projected for the new Théâtre-Lyrique, going up slowly in the Place du Châtelet; and, though Carvalho resigned at the beginning of April 1860 and went to the Opéra-Comique, the contract he had signed was honoured by his successor Charles Réty – in July Berlioz told Camille Pal that rehearsals were due to begin the following January. But Réty had no experience of directing an opera house, and the company was losing money. *Fidelio*, with Pauline Viardot, was not the commercial success that had been hoped for. By the end of the year bankruptcy threatened. Berlioz wished it would happen, so that a less incompetent

Wagner (1813–83), in 1860, during his eighteen-month stay in Paris.

Berlioz attended Nadar's studio in January 1857, when he inscribed the visitor's book with a quotation from the love scene of his Romeo and Juliet, *and this iconic photograph was taken.*

Part of the Dido–Anna duet (from the autograph score of Act 3 of The Trojans), composed later the same year.

The Trojans at Carthage *as seen by Cham and Grévin*: "Troy relieved, or If only they had had the score of The Trojans..."; "New method of killing cattle soon to be introduced at slaughterhouses"; "the Devil takes to his heels"; "Petit Cancan Carthaginois".

Above: design for the final scene
of The Trojans at Carthage at
the Théâtre-Lyrique.
Below: Louis Berlioz (1834–67).

Estelle Fornier (1797–1876): the photograph she sent Berlioz in 1864, to "remind you of present realities and to destroy the illusions of the past".

Berlioz in St Petersburg, where his career as conductor reached its culmination in the winter of 1867–8.

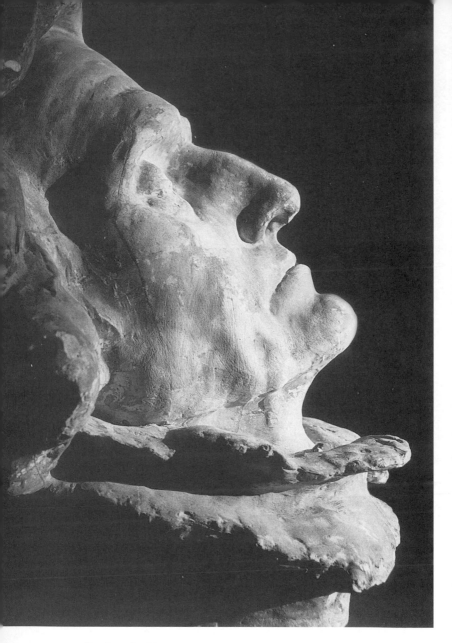

Death-mask, 1869.

management could take over. Besides, where was their Cassandra, where their tenor? "Find me a tenor who knows how to sing 'Viens embrasser ton père,'" he wrote to Cornelius in November.

Meanwhile, it had been announced in mid-March that *Tannhäuser*, by order of the Emperor, was to be given at the Opéra. Wagner was busy rewriting the first act, though he was adamant that he would not pander to local taste by adding a second-act ballet for the Jockey Club and the other posh subscribers who never arrived before ten o'clock. In May he responded enthusiastically to Berlioz's *Fidelio* articles and there was a cordial exchange of letters. Some time that summer Berlioz attended a soirée at the Viardots' house in Paris at which the diva and Wagner sang through the second act of *Tristan* with Klindworth accompanying. The evening has left no trace in the Berlioz correspondence. According to Wagner's *Mein Leben* Berlioz congratulated him on the warmth of his performance but said nothing about the music. We may assume that he remained unconverted.

Rehearsals for *Tannhäuser* began in October. By the time it received its première five months later on 13 March 1861, after delays due among other things to opposition by the tenor, Niemann, and to the extreme feebleness of the conductor, Dietsch – by the iron rule of the Opéra, the composer was not allowed to conduct even the dress rehearsal – 160,000 francs had been spent on it. The staging, by general consent, was sumptuous. But the enemies of the work were out to destroy it: on the one hand the Jockey Club, which issued its members with whistles "pour siffler *Tannhäuser*", and on the other a cabal of soi-disant serious musicians and critics – led by Héquet of the once high-minded *Gazette musicale* and (according to Baudelaire) Scudo – who felt it their sacred duty to expel the new Antichrist. From the final scene of Act 1 onward, there were frequent noisy interruptions, compounded by indignant appeals for quiet. At the second performance on the 18th it was worse, and fighting broke out among the audience. The third (24 March) was so tumultuous that, according to Wilhelm Ganz, "no member of the audience could hear a note of the music the whole evening" and the sole success were the hunting dogs – lent personally by the Emperor – who were greeted with cries of "Bis les chiens!" and repeated requests for their return. Next day Wagner withdrew the work.

Berlioz held aloof. He may or may not have expressed his malicious delight to Gautier, meeting him in the street after the first night or after the dress rehearsal (Judith Gautier, the source of the story, was eleven at the time and her accounts of the incident, written much later, are conflicting). In any case he refused to do the *Débats* notice, and delegated it to d'Ortigue: his protest would be made silently. (D'Ortigue's notice was studiously even-handed.) He must have realized that, in his state of continued and unconcealed anger at the ease with which Princess Metternich had secured Wagner's entry to the Opéra when he himself was excluded, he could not conscientiously do it.

His crime against Wagner was thus confined to not reviewing *Tannhäuser* and to rejoicing over its downfall in two private letters. The first, to his close friend the pianist Mme Massart, a dedicated anti-Wagnerian, was written the day after the première:

> God in heaven, what a performance! Everyone was laughing. The Parisians were revealed yesterday in a totally new light. They laughed at the bad musical style, they laughed at the depravities of the farcical orchestration, they laughed at the silliness of an oboe. They finally understand that there is such a thing as style in music. As for the horrors, they were hissed splendidly.

The other, a week later, was to Louis:

> The second performance of *Tannhäuser* was noisier than the first. There was less laughter – it was fury. They brought the house down hissing and booing, this in spite of the presence of the Emperor and Empress, who were in their box. The Emperor is having a good time. On the way out, on the staircase, people were openly calling the unfortunate Wagner a scoundrel, an impertinent, a lunatic. At this rate, one of these days the performance will be brought to a halt and that will be that. The press is unanimous in wiping him out. As for me, I am cruelly avenged.

These private letters have been used to prove Berlioz guilty of betraying Wagner. But he had sworn him no oath of allegiance. He betrayed only himself. In a less angry, embittered state he could never have seen the booing of *Tannhäuser* as a mark of discernment on the part of the Opéra audience – that public that he had studied and anatomized and judged at its true worth time out of mind and at whose hands he had suffered similar treatment twenty years before. To recall an identical massacre his memory need only go back as far as *Benvenuto Cellini* at Covent Garden in 1853. These thoughts, I am sure, passed through his mind in the interim, for the second letter no longer gloats: there is a gleam of fellow-feeling for a colleague in the same adversity as he has been in himself, and he expresses no satisfaction in the failure of Wagner's opera. He may still see it as his "revenge": he would not have been human if he had felt otherwise, with *The Trojans* spurned by the same theatre. But – as he said – what a cruel revenge!

The fourteen months between Wagner's first concert and the première of *Tannhäuser* had not been the happiest of times for Berlioz. His health was if anything worse. Remissions were rare. He felt better only when his creative juices were flowing, or when he was free to make music as he was in Baden, where his niece Nancy Suat, who went there with her father and her sister Joséphine in August 1861, reported to her cousin Mathilde that they found their uncle "in a better state than we dared hope; his health in fact has improved", though he was "still often in pain". Inevitably the pain dragged his spirits down. He wondered how much longer he had to live – and what there was to live for. "I desire nothing but sleep, while waiting for something more permanent." Hanslick, visiting him in the summer of 1860, and not having seen him for fourteen years, hardly recognized him. "However much the pallor of his sunken face and the completely white hair set off more vividly the fineness of his features, the strength and freshness of former times had vanished. The eyes were dull and sickly, reminding me only at moments of the old fire."

Life with Marie gave him little if any pleasure. He felt trapped; he even had murderous thoughts, to judge by the letter to Adolphe Samuel written just after the first Wagner concert: "I write to you seldom and then laconically, because I am continually ill; my neuralgia increases and allows me neither peace nor truce. And then, my mind is unquiet, troubled . . . My life is outside; my life at home is exhausting, exasperating, almost impossible – quite the opposite of yours. There is not a day, not an hour when I'm not ready to risk my life, to take the most drastic and violent measures. I say again, I live in my thoughts, in immense affections, far from home . . . I can't tell you more." Reyer speaks of evenings when, after music with Théodore Ritter at Bennet's house, he and Berlioz would cross and recross the distance between their two front doors – "he smoking countless cigars which he never finished" – retracing their steps again and again so that the moment of having to go inside could be put off as long as possible. When it came, "he hesitated a moment as his hand touched the bell-pull, then murmured a cold chilly adieu in a suppressed voice".

The friendship with Pauline Viardot seems to have declined in the summer of 1860. Her Fidelio a few months earlier had made it clear to him that she was losing her voice; she had ceased to be his ideal Dido. A coolness sprang up. His letters grew less frequent. She sang for him in Baden in August. But it was no longer the same.

A worse blow had struck at the beginning of March. Out of the blue a telegram announced that Adèle was seriously ill. He took the next train to Vienne and sat with her until the heart specialist from Lyon assured them that the patient would recover, and then returned overnight to Paris. She died next day, aged forty-five. Louis, to his father's gratitude, went straight from Dieppe to be with his uncle and cousins. Berlioz was shattered. "We loved each other like two twins," he told Morel; "she was a really close friend." And a few weeks later: "I feel everything splitting apart around me, almost nothing has any interest for me any more."

From this slough of despond he was lifted by the challenge of the Théâtre-Lyrique's Fidelio. The production took the customary Parisian liberties, including moving the action to the fourteenth century, before the invention of handguns, so that Leonore had to threaten Pizarro not with a pistol but with an iron bar; but his double feuilleton, an essay of seven thousand words, concentrated on the work. It was a *critique admirative* as in the old days, when he expounded Beethoven to his fellow-countrymen and could still believe that what he was doing served a purpose. Now he no longer believed. He wrote for himself. But the effort did him good.

His spirits were not always down. The thought of his Suat nieces, to whom he took it on himself to write more often, could raise them.

If only I felt better, if my mind were free and my chain longer, oh then wouldn't I come and see you! What parties we'd have, how happy and gay we'd be! For it appears – I'm often told – that on the rare occasions when I'm light-hearted I can be very agreeable to those I love. We'd read wonderful things together, we'd go together and see wonderful things and I'd make you hear wonderful things, and they would reveal countless aspects of the world of the spirit and the soul that would enchant you; and Joséphine would be cured, and your father would be pleased seeing you both soar with your young wings in the land of the imagination. For you have wings – the two of you are angels, my dear little nieces. [. . .] On Sunday we spent the day at St Germain. The sun was *almost* shining. But the forest is already leafless, and they're building everywhere. They are ruining the wild tracks where I used to love walking last year, the quarries are being filled in and the rocks levelled. Soon it'll be like Paris. All the same the view from the top of the hill is still splendid – the plain, the Seine, the Marley aqueduct, the castle of Montecristo, the woods, the vines, the plumes of smoke from the locomotives as they hurry to the horizon: all this makes the walk worth while. If the two of you were here – the three of you – we'd go and dine with the forest warden, who really knows how to do fricassee of rabbit, or in a shack down by the river where you can get excellent fish.

His real life was outside in more senses than one – not only away from the apartment in the Rue de Calais but away from Paris. Paris – the *Débats*, the Conservatoire Library, the Academy – gave him much of his livelihood, but except as a journalist he remained tangential to the musical scene. He was seen essentially as a non-practitioner. In March 1861 General Mellinet made him a member of the commission appointed by the Minister of War to examine candidates for the top musical jobs in the armed forces. But his only conducting engagement was in Baden. He was appointed to none of the posts made vacant by the death of Girard, who on 16 January 1860 had a fatal heart attack while conducting *The Huguenots*: not the Opéra, not the Société des Concerts, not even – though he had influential backing – the court concerts (Auber saw to that). Berlioz the composer was held equally at arm's length. *The Trojans* still waited in the wings. Anything he composed now was for abroad. Even *Le temple universel*, the stirring anthem for double male chorus and organ which the Paris Orphéonists rehearsed with such enthusiasm in February 1861, was written for performance not in France but at an Anglo-French jamboree at Crystal Palace on Sydenham Hill, planned for the following June but in the end postponed and then cancelled.

It was abroad that he continued to exist as a musician, in actuality and vicariously. In January 1861 "The Youth of Györ", a society in the town of Györ in Hungary who had been fired by a performance of his Hungarian March, sent him a silver wreath of exquisite workmanship accompanied by a letter of such glowing thanks that for an instant he felt young again. From time to time Cornelius wrote from Vienna, ardent, respectful, affectionate letters reporting on performances of *Harold* and the Fantastic, expressing his longing to hear *The Trojans*, giving news of the operas he was doing or had done (*Le Cid*, and *The Barber of Baghdad* which "would show you that you have a disciple in Germany and that *Cellini* has offspring!"), and warming Berlioz's heart by speaking of "the tears that come into my eyes now as I think of you and of the many moments of enthusiasm and happiness we shared". The only orchestral score Berlioz put on paper in the two years between completing *The Trojans* and beginning to write *Beatrice and Benedick*, his arrangement of Schubert's *Erlkönig*, was made for Baden.

It is symbolic that a German spa town, and not Paris, should be the cause of his last major work. Symbolic too that his response to the advent of Wagnerism and to his own growing isolation should be not a final summoning of his greatest powers, not a *Cleopatra*, but something altogether slighter, offhand, inconsequential, cast in the form of a one-act opéra-comique: a celebration of love not as grand all-consuming passion but as "a torch, a flame, a will o'the wisp, coming from no one knows where, gleaming then vanishing from sight, to the distraction of our souls" – "a caprice written with the point of a needle", whose conclusion was that "madness is better than stupidity".

Beatrice and Benedick – to restore the Shakespearean form of the hero's name (in French rendered as "Bénédict") – seems to have become a definite project during the visit to Baden in August 1860. Berlioz had already persuaded Bénazet to release him from his contract to write an opera to Edouard Plouvier's somewhat gothic drama set in the Thirty Years' War. But Bénazet was still hoping to have something of his for the opening of his theatre, which was expected to be ready in time for the holiday season two years hence; and Berlioz, conscious of how much he owed to his munificence and as always rejuvenated by the stimulus of sustained music-making and the improved health and spirits it brought, agreed. He left at the end of the month with a contract for a one-act opera on *Much Ado about Nothing*, for which he would compose both score and libretto at a fee of 2,000 francs each plus a further 1,000 for conducting the work.

He had arrived in Baden on 11 August, after spending a week taking the waters with Marie at Luxueil. The concert, on the 27th, was one of the most glittering he had ever given there: a much bittier programme than he would have wished, with a dozen separate items (the overtures to *Les francs-juges* and *Euryanthe* at either end), but offering five of the brightest lights of the day. Pauline Viardot sang excerpts from *Orphée* and Caroline Miolan-Carvalho the Bach–Gounod *Ave Maria* and the cavatina from *Benvenuto Cellini*, Vieuxtemps was heard in his D minor violin concerto, the great cellist Léon Jacquard played a concerto by Molique, and Roger, still a mesmerizing performer despite his artifical arm, gave his famous rendering of *Erlkönig*, with the orchestration that Berlioz had written for him.*

The travellers were back in Paris by the beginning of September. In the first flush of his new-found energy Berlioz sent the vocal score of *The Trojans* to be engraved, at his expense, and then set to work on the new project. An opera on *Much Ado* was something he had thought of nearly thirty years before, when the Théâtre-Italien had briefly shown an interest in it. He had taken up the idea again in the early 1850s and, with Legouvé in mind as librettist, had sketched an outline of a plot which transplanted Benedick and Beatrice and their mutual disdain to the Boccaccio-like scenario of a villa in the hills of Sicily in time of plague, where the Count and Countess of Palermo scheme to make the two enemies fall in love. Now, while cutting the action to a minimum, he decided to keep much closer to the play. The draft of the text was completed towards the end of October. A month later he was deep in composition: the pieces were coming in such a rush, he told Louis, that he could hardly get them down on paper fast enough. "I'm really enjoying myself and composing my score *con furia*," he wrote to Cornelius the following week. "It's gay, caustic, occasionally poetic; it brings a smile to the eye and to the lips." To Ferrand he reported that he was working again with fervour, though only on a small scale: it was "a relaxation from *The Trojans*".

At first he planned nine numbers (not counting the overture). By the end of November it had risen to a dozen, the extra pieces probably

* We get a curious glimpse of Berlioz and Marie in Baden from the reminiscences of the pianist Alphonse Duvernoy, who was Miolan-Carvalho's accompanist in the *Ave Maria*. Berlioz apparently disliked the piece intensely and "forgot" to include it when he sent the programme to the printer. The diva found out just before the posters were due to be pulled, and, though it was already late in the evening, Duvernoy – then just out of the Conservatoire – was dispatched to confront the *Maître* with her ultimatum. The young man knocked on the door, a woman's voice called "Who's there?" He answered, "M. Duvernoy, with an urgent message for M. Berlioz", the door opened revealing Madame in her nightdress, and the next moment he was standing by the bed and telling the recumbent composer that "Mme Carvalho has asked me to say, if the *Ave Maria* is not on the poster she won't sing." This provoked a stream of imprecations from Marie; but the *Ave Maria* was restored.

being the Sicilienne and its reprise, and the Enseigne, "Benedick the
married man", originally intended to be spoken, then made into a
separate number referring back to the music of the trio. At that stage
what was to be the most celebrated piece in the score, the Duo-
Nocturne for Hero and Ursula, "Nuit paisible et sereine", had
apparently not been thought of; the idea – following Shakespeare – of
developing Hero's conventionally romantic love for Claudio into an
explicit foil for the more tortuous feelings of the two main characters
came later.

After the rapid progress of the first few numbers, composition slowed
as illness, feuilletons and other preoccupations reasserted their claims.
The words of the Nocturne were not written till the following August
in Baden, one evening on the battlements of the old castle; the music
was sketched soon afterwards at the Institute during a speech by a
fellow-academician. At about the same time the drinking scene (no. 9)
was added, and Benedick's and Beatrice's "L'amour est un flambeau,
l'amour est une flamme", sung to the angular, glancing music later used
for the overture, replaced the original finale, which had been simply a
reprise of the opening chorus.

Not till early in November 1861 does Berlioz's correspondence speak
of an opera in two acts. Even in its two-act, fifteen-number form,
including the women's trio and the distant chorus which he added soon
after the Baden première, it remains a divertissement, mercurial and
fleeting as the love which the protagonists celebrate in the final number.
In a small theatre with a good production it can be a delight. In a
grand-opera setting, spread thin, it seems insubstantial, its lack of
dramatic or musical ambition laid bare. Berlioz called it "one of the
liveliest and most original things I have done". At first sight this is a
surprising judgement. Formally the work breaks no new ground, being
content to stay within the unexacting conventions of opéra-comique;
most of the numbers do not develop the action but dilate on situations
created by the spoken dialogue. The originality is, rather, in its attitudes
and in the delicacy with which, at its best, it depicts them, catching the
conversational quality of Shakespeare's dialogue as though "with the
point of a needle" indeed. The tender yet sparkling woodwind writing
and the teasing, fine-spun lines of the first-violin part are marvels of
orchestral imagination and craftsmanship.

Though much of the dialogue and some of the lyrics come directly
from Shakespeare, there was never any question of a full-scale setting

of *Much Ado*: no Don John, no sinister intrigue, no Dogberry and the watch, and Claudio himself a shadow. "I have taken as my text part of Shakespeare's tragi-comedy," he told the Princess; it is simply a matter of "persuading Beatrice and Benedick that they love each other" and of throwing their abrasive relationship into relief by contrasting them with "the sentimental couple". Berlioz does not use the starry-eyed Hero merely as a pretext for some beautiful love music. The moonlit murmurings of the Nocturne – Tiersot called it a musical paraphrase of Virgil's *Per amica silentia lunae* – are as necessary to the work as are the proud ardour of Beatrice's aria and the cut-and-thrust of the final duettino in which she and Benedick play at hiding their recognition of twin natures. Hero's straightforward feelings are set against those of the two main characters, who exemplify the heretical suggestion that the obstacles to the fulfilment of operatic love may lie not in fate or dynastic or social pressures but in the two people themselves. Romantic love which lasts for ever is an illusion: hence the parody cadenza in Hero's aria. But it is a beautiful illusion, with continual power over the imagination: hence the Nocturne. Light-hearted as it is, the work is a statement about love.

In this, for all its drastic simplifications, it is faithful to Shakespeare, who in *Much Ado* abandoned the dream world and the stereotyped attitudes and romanticizing of sexual attraction of his earlier comedies in favour of a realism which calls the whole conventional pattern of institutionalized romance into question and exposes the discrepancy between complex, ambiguous private feeling and the social rituals which are supposed to embody it.

Where the opera adds material it takes its cue from the play. Beatrice's protest at the banal rhymes in the chorus's rejoicing – *gloire/victoire*, *guerriers/lauriers* – derives from Benedick's wry admission, in the play, that when he tries to fashion a sonnet in praise of Beatrice he cannot rhyme as a poet should. In the avowal of deep feeling that Berlioz's Beatrice makes during their courtship – a more open avowal than Benedick's – she parallels Shakespeare's. Even the one major addition to *Much Ado*, the foolish, fond old *maître de chapelle* Somarone (literally "great donkey" – hence the braying motif in the Sicilienne) has its source in the play, in the very precise musician Balthazar. Somarone's "grotesque epithalamium" comes at the same point in the action as Balthazar's "Sigh no more, ladies" (prompting Benedick to the almost identical comment that "if my dogs had howled thus, I would have hanged them"). He has usually been taken as a satire on the pedants of the Paris Conservatoire with whom Berlioz clashed in his student days – this despite his being given well-known sayings of two of Berlioz's heroes, Gluck and Spontini, as well as a phrase of Thomas Moore's in the text of the epithalamium. The portrait is, rather, that of a court musician of the old school, vainglorious (which Berlioz knew both Spontini and Gluck could be), fussy, intent on his painstaking fugues, devoid of all sense of dramatic and expressive aptness, but conscientious, energetic, convivial and capable in his cups of singing a jovial song in honour of the fiery wines of Sicily.

The peculiar glow of the scoring of this number, for two trumpets, cornet, tambourine and guitar, like sunlight after an evening shower, is characteristic of the sound world of the work. In *Beatrice* the noonday Italian brilliance of *Benvenuto* is subdued to a softer light, yet still sharp-edged, glinting with unexpected juxtapositions and wrong-footing rhythms. Listen to the third and fourth bars of the main (4/4) section of the overture: the dancing triplets (piano) stopped short by a pizzicato chord, mezzo forte on the offbeat, itself followed without a break by a dotted phrase on clarinets and horns – an almost Stravinskian effect of rhythmically articulated contrasting timbres. The overture, which was composed last, sums up the work. Racy, headlong yet ironically poised, brilliant but touched with warmth of heart and a delicate spirit of fantasy, it breathes a single atmosphere while drawing on half a dozen different numbers which we recognize retrospectively: the wide melodic span of Beatrice's aria, the pianissimo conclusion of the Nocturne, the triumphant but rather empty tuttis of Hero's aria, the long descending and ascending melody of the Wedding March, an allusion to the men's trio and its conspiratorial humour, above all the motif of the final Scherzo-Duettino, whose nimble triplet rhythm and angular dotted phrase work their way in everywhere and spread their gleeful mirth across the whole texture of the orchestra.

Listening to the score's exuberant gaiety, only momentarily touched by sadness, one would never guess that its composer was in pain when he wrote it and impatient for death. *Beatrice and Benedick* accepts the world as surely as Berlioz railed against it. It is not a young man's work. There is none of the prodigality of ideas found in his earlier Italian comedy but, on the contrary, an extreme economy and a demonstration of the melodic possibilities in the basic means of music, notably the scale. It comes, manifestly, at the close of a career – a career seemingly ending in disappointment and isolation – but it is without either bitterness or illusion. In this unlooked-for epilogue to his oeuvre Berlioz repays a little of his lifelong debt to Shakespeare, reminds those with ears to hear that he is not always a noisy composer and can be a witty one, and finds for a moment in art the felicity that life denied him.

In the men's trio, "Me marier? Dieu me pardonne" ("Me get married? God forgive me"), Benedick punctures each recommendation of Claudio and Don Pedro in favour of matrimony with its deftly rhyming opposite: "Une douce compagne . . . Que la ruse accompagne . . . Qui berce vos ennuis . . . Et qui trouble vos nuits . . . Une constante amie . . . Une intime ennemie [. . .] Un trésor d'amour . . . Qu'épuise un seul jour . . . Source de vie . . . Caquet de pie", etc.*

It is hard to believe Marie was entirely absent from Berlioz's mind when he wrote those lines, which are his own, not translated from the play. Or that Benedick's words in the same number were not being echoed when in a letter of February 1861 he commented unfavourably on his son Louis' "matrimoniomania". Louis had talked, not for the first time, of marriage. It provoked a savage homily on the stupidity of aspiring to "that heaviest of all chains" and to "the difficulties and unpleasantnesses of married life", than which there was "nothing more heartbreaking, more maddening".

Relations between father and son were going through one of their most fraught but also most obscure periods. Louis' movements are unclear – as they were, much of the time, to his father. He had passed his master mariner's exams the previous summer (1860). But not till November of the following year, nearly eighteen months later, does he seem to have found, temporarily, a position; and not till a year after that, in November 1862, was he finally placed to his satisfaction, with the help of his father's friends, as first lieutenant on the *Vera Cruz*, a merchantman of the Compagnie Transatlantique, and was able to resume his seafaring career. In the meantime he sent Berlioz disgruntled letters from Marseille and other ports, or came to Paris in vague quest of a position there and then did nothing much except spend his father's money.

---

* "A sweet companion . . . And a cunning one . . . Who soothes your cares . . . And disturbs your nights . . . A constant friend . . . An intimate enemy [. . .] A treasure of love . . . Spent in a day . . . Fountain of life . . . Chattering like a magpie," etc.

Berlioz was reaping the harvest of his son's disturbed childhood. The young man's mood fluctuated violently. He felt that his father failed to grasp his problems: he was loving, perhaps, but uncomprehending. Louis' letters veered between angry reproaches and passionate dependence. In one he demanded to know why if his father was a famous man the newspapers didn't mention him more often, provoking the irritable reply that Louis was a child and a provincial to be surprised at it. ("What do you want them to say? Do you think the world cares about what I do?") In another, while hinting that he had a wife and child, he blamed his father for not doing more for him and for not really loving him. Berlioz was stung to a defensive reply:

Anyone reading your letter without knowing anything of our respective situations would believe that I have "no real affection" for you, that the world says "you are not my son", that "if I wanted to" I could find you a "better position", that I am wrong not to urge you to "come to Paris" and solicit for a POST here, and leave the one you have; that I "humiliated" you by comparing you to whichever Béranger character it was you referred to. Frankly, though I don't want to indulge in recriminations, you have gone too far, and it has grieved me in a way that I've not experienced before. Honestly, is it my fault if I'm not rich and don't have the wherewithal for you to live a comfortable life in Paris with your wife and child, or children if you have more than one? Is there a shred of justice in reproaching me for that? You wrote to me at Baden in the middle of August, since when not one word: you left me two and a half months with no idea what had become of you. Alexis [Bertchtold] didn't know either. And now you write in this sarcastic way. My poor dear Louis, it's not good.

Don't worry about what you owe your tailor; the bill will be settled on demand. If you want me to get this debt off your back sooner, send me the tailor's address and I will go and pay it. It's true I thought you younger than you are; but do you have to add my poor memory for dates to my other crimes? Do I know what age my father was when he died, or my mother and my sisters and my brother? Should one conclude from this that I didn't love them? No, really – but I sound as if I'm justifying myself.

The answer, three weeks later, was devastating. In it Louis revealed details of his life which till then had been kept hidden, and at the same time laid bare the lacerations of his most secret heart:

24 November 1861

Dear Father

More than ever I am sad and discouraged. I wrote you two letters this week, two harrowing letters which I'm preserving carefully as lessons. The total isolation I'm in was the reason for these abominations of desolation which I couldn't keep to myself. Alone (I've kept my word) I reviewed the various faults I've committed in this world. I recalled your reproaches, then I reread your counsels. Nine years ago, when I was a navigator and just a youngster, I went gadding about like an absolute scoundrel. You told me then that a boy of my age and looks and intelligence shouldn't lead such a life, shouldn't sponge on others, etc.

Since then, I've spoken of marriage. I had one in mind. I can't reproach you for having made it come to nothing because the family of the desired object had neither seen you nor heard you nor read you. But sore, disgusted at my lack of success thanks to the family I then had – M. and Mme Suat, Caffarel, Burdet, Marmion (of whom I've heard nothing more), and spurred by one of your letters in which you told me that marriage was the heaviest chain a man has to bear, I thought I should live differently. So I abducted a young girl from her family and lived with her for fourteen months. In reply to my confession of this latter fault you judged it proper to torture me. My heart, my amour propre – you squeezed them dry.

I promptly sent my companion back to her family; I looked after her interests and took all the appropriate measures to restore her fortune. Now the lawyer has gone bankrupt, the brother-in-law has stolen all that's left, and the family will have nothing more to do with their shamed and shaming child: my poor companion has only *five francs* to her name. Her child is going to the foundling hospital on the 17th of next month. So here I am, the woman in the gutter, the child in care, and this because all I can do is commit one fault after another. A third of my existence is spent on land, and I shall have to spend it alone. I see Joseph Lecourt, who is the same age as me, living happily in the family home, and Léon Morel petted by his excellent uncle and by his grandmother. My colleagues, who are almost all married, hurry home as soon as they return, to rest and relax in the bosom of their families. But I alone, a pariah abandoned by his family, by his closest friend (Alexis doesn't write any more) – I can count only on the charity of a foreigner, Mme Lawson. She is the only one that writes to me and is genuinely fond of me. I'm waiting for her now – as she will be waiting for me when I get back, if I'm at sea.*

But all this is of no importance. Why should I care what my family thinks? In their eyes I'm damned. It's all over.

Rereading your letters, I wept.

My two documents of desolation I've put back in their folder. And I've finally understood this: you love me, but in a strange fashion. I'm quite certain you would suffer appallingly if tomorrow they told you I was dead; but I'm also certain that if you have a festival to direct the day after, I shall be forgotten. I see that your children are called Romeo and Juliet, Faust, etc. I understand that your masterpieces, which represent years of delight and which are later to make your name famous, have to come well ahead of me, who merely represent a second or two of abandonment or oversight and twenty-seven years of burden.

You are a man of genius, you love and suffer and live as a man of genius can love and suffer and live.

I understand everything, I ask nothing; I'm just telling you my impressions and ideas. Forgive me if I upset or annoy you.

You haven't answered my last letter, in which I believe I gave you news of my change of job. I hoped that by telling you the result of the services I had rendered I would be giving you pleasure. Perhaps you didn't read my letter, or if you read it you've forgotten about it. No doubt it's been put with the other worthless papers, the self-seeking invitations, the requests for money – in short it's ceased to exist. If in ten minutes' time your glance falls on the score of The Trojans, this letter will join the other. All this is very sad, yet I mustn't complain, for fear of being tiresome, like a discarded mistress whom one no longer loves but whom one did love. So I shall say good night, and go to bed and brood with dried-up but heavy heart, until fatigue plunges me into the deep sleep that brings nightmares with it.

Good night, Father, allow me to embrace you, let me love you as you love your scores. Love me a little, me who like them bear your name, me whom you created unintentionally.

Your son L. Berlioz

---

* Mrs Lawson, widow of Kemble's stage manager, was an English friend of Harriet Smithson's, and took an active interest in Louis' welfare.

We do not know how Berlioz reacted – his next surviving letter to Louis dates from March 1862, nearly four months later. In any case the immediate crisis passed. Louis came to Paris in December 1861 for a few days' leave, having just obtained a lieutenant's post "not through influence" (Berlioz reported to Marc Suat) "but entirely because his superiors are satisfied with him". A brief note to his father in January ends "I adore you." But it is clear that, ill, preoccupied with his Baden opera and the eternal non-performance of *The Trojans*, Berlioz neither would nor could comprehend what his son was going through. The time of their close and loving intimacy was yet to come.

The newspapers *were* talking of Berlioz, more than Louis supposed if less than he expected. In April 1861 the Société des Concerts under Girard's altogether more sympathetic successor Tilmant had pro- grammed the Elbe scene from *The Damnation of Faust*, complete, and the ensuing double chorus, "Villes entourées de remparts", and the composer received an ovation, as several journals reported. "They must think I'm dead," he wrote to Janin. As if to balance it – Paris being Paris – the inaugural concert of Pasdeloup's new venture at the Cirque- Napoléon – Concerts Populaires de Musique Classique – featured the *Invitation to the Dance* minus the quiet concluding andante, which the conductor cut "in order", he explained, "to allow the piece to be properly applauded". Three weeks later, on 23 November, the Fête from *Romeo* was played at a gala concert at the Opéra.

By then things had begun to stir in that venerable institution and Berlioz's star had risen a few degrees. The removal of *Tannhäuser* had left a hole to be filled, and encouraged his supporters to press the claims of *The Trojans*. The management, moving carefully, invited him to supervise a revival of *Der Freischütz*. Rehearsals began; but after a month they stopped. Instead a new idea was broached, prompted by Pauline Viardot's recent success in excerpts from Gluck's *Alceste* at the Société des Concerts: to repeat the triumph of her Orphée in a second, hardly less glamorous role, and to put Berlioz in charge of it. To Royer's surprise and dismay, Berlioz declined the honour (and the very considerable fee). Alceste was not Orphée: it was a soprano, not a mezzo/contralto role, and the transpositions Mme Viardot would be obliged to make and the added notes and altered cadences she would not be able to resist making – the equivalent (he told Royer) of adding words and altering the rhymes in Corneille's verse – would amount to a desecration that he could not possibly be party to. He even tried, unsuccessfully, to persuade the Opéra not to do *Alceste*. If they wanted something by Gluck, why not *Iphigénie en Tauride*, with Mlle Sax? At the same time he wrote to Pauline Viardot, explaining his position in an outspoken letter which cannot have enhanced their friendship but in which the artistic disagreements largely suppressed at the time of *Orphée* burst out uncontrollably:

> Nothing happened, and I did not seek to dissuade Royer from engaging you, but from putting on *Alceste*. I know all the havoc they will wreak when they edit that poor sublime score and I can foresee what will be done without being written down. I know that you can't decide to refrain from making changes in the final cadences of the arias and that you will introduce others in the recitatives, and then perhaps will believe, later, that you've done nothing special, when you publish the variants, as you did for Orpheus' aria. These are the sole reasons that led me to refuse, three times, to take on the restaging of *Alceste*. There is nothing in the least personal in my opposition, and I am astonished you can have thought so. I am only too delighted at your engagement by the Opéra, which happened a few days after Royer told me *The Trojans* had been accepted. Sorry – I am resigned to being considered a fool and a fanatic. But I love *Music* more than *my* music, and every outrage inflicted on great men of genius wounds me a thousand times more than any I can be subjected to myself.
>
> Yours as ever, and without variants
H. Berlioz

The Trojans had been accepted. That was the extraordinary news announced at the beginning of June 1861. A soirée at Edouard Bertin's on 2 May, at which Charton-Demeur and Lefort sang their customary excerpts from the work and a distinguished audience was in attendance, had led to renewed calls for its production. The private secretary of Count Walewski, the newly appointed Minister of State, was present at the soirée. So was Royer himself. The feeling was growing that the Opéra must do it. Berlioz's opposition to *Alceste*, very bold in the circumstances, many would have said very foolish, had annoyed the minister but had not harmed him with the management; perhaps, paradoxically, it had even raised his standing. Royer, reporting to the minister, set out the arguments: a great work by a gifted man of high reputation, a member of the Institute, with public opinion and the European press behind him, which only the Opéra was capable of putting on properly. Réty, director of the ailing Théâtre-Lyrique, was prepared to give up all claim to it.

This was a big step forward but not a decisive one, as Berlioz well knew. It would certainly not do to get too excited about it. The minister still had to give final authorization. And *The Trojans* was only third in line, behind a five-act opera which Gounod had yet to complete and one by the Belgian composer Gevaert. At that rate it would be another two years. He must, he told Ferrand, fold his arms and wait till his rivals had had their say; he was resolved not to torture himself any more about it. "I've stopped running after Fortune – I wait for her in my bed." All the same (he added) he couldn't help "answering the Empress a little too frankly when she asked me a few weeks ago at the Tuileries when she would be able to hear *The Trojans*. 'I hardly know, Ma'am, but I begin to think one must live to a hundred to be performed at the Opéra.'" Besides, what sort of condition would the old place be in when it came to put on the work? It didn't know "what saint to invoke". Three times the previous month it had nearly had to close.

Meanwhile, to show willing, he complied with Royer's request that he shorten the work, and made a cut of six minutes in Act 1, the longest act.* (Royer informed the minister's secretary-general that there was now "only about half an hour's music to cut to bring it down to reasonable proportions".) Berlioz also agreed to attend the rehearsals of *Alceste* – on the understanding that he was not responsible for all the modifications imposed but also on the principle that it would turn out worse if he didn't – and, as he told the minister, to transmit to all concerned everything he knew about the work and the composer's style. He was at the Opéra in June and July, and again in September and October and, when *Alceste* with Pauline Viardot finally saw the light on 21 October 1861, could feel that but for him it would not have been possible. "I had to direct the director, the conductors, the coaches, the stage manager – the whole thing." (The quality of the ensemble was also vindication of the electric metronome, which the Opéra had finally agreed to instal.) The gratified minister arranged for him to receive composer's royalties. Once again success at the Opéra had been achieved

---

* This was the scene with Sinon the Greek spy. Removed from the autograph, it was never replaced, and survives, except for a few bars of orchestral score at the beginning and end, only in an early version of the piano-vocal score.

by him against his will and in someone else's work. But surely it would stand him in good stead for the future.

For the present there was his Baden opera to complete for the opening of the new theatre next year. In Baden that August he worked on it in his spare moments, while he rehearsed a programme which included, among the longer items, two movements from the Requiem (Dies irae–Tuba mirum and Offertorium), Beethoven's Choral Fantasy, the andante and finale of Mendelssohn's violin concerto with Sivori, Méhul's overture *La chasse du jeune Henri*, and *Harold*, with the Strasbourg violinist Grodvolle – "performed for the first time as I want it to be". Bénazet had allowed him eight full rehearsals for the concert. The excellence of the arrangements even extended to a brand new triangle, of Sax's manufacture, for *Harold*'s adagio introduction. Berlioz sent it a few days later to Richard Pohl (Liszt needed one for performances of the work in Germany): "It's in the image of God, like all triangles, but unlike other triangles, and certainly unlike God, it is well tuned."

That autumn *Beatrice and Benedick* continued to progress. Except for the overture it was finished and orchestrated by the beginning of December. Meanwhile he had secured his ideal Beatrice, Mme Charton-Demeur, released from an engagement in America by the outbreak of the Civil War. The rest of the cast was recruited from the Opéra-Comique. There was talk of staging it there too, after Baden – the director, Perrin, was interested. Berlioz, however, did not "dare risk anything in the theatre [in Paris] until my great ship is launched". His faithful booers were capable of getting up a demonstration against it which could alarm the minister "and put *The Trojans* off till the Greek Kalends"; they had booed the Fête chez Capulet at the Opéra's gala concert (provoking thunderous counter-applause). Baden, however, was all set; and in February 1862 he began holding regular rehearsals at his apartment, with Saint-Saëns accompanying.

First he had to wean his singers from their stilted, over-solemn delivery of the Shakespearean dialogue and persuade them to "speak like human beings", then slowly teach them the notes. In April 1862 two numbers, Beatrice's aria and the Nocturne, were sung at a private concert at Marie Escudier's and warmly applauded.

As the opera gradually came to life he felt pleased with what he had done, but also more and more conscious that that was it: he had, he told Louis, finished everything he had to do and would not compose anything else. In the same valedictory spirit he prepared one more volume of his writings, for publication by Michel Lévy in the autumn, under the title *A travers chants: études musicales, adorations, boutades* ["sallies"] *et critiques*. The book, dedicated to Legouvé, was a summing-up of his career as a writer on music – a resigned summing-up, as the two epigraphs emphasized: "Love's Labours Lost (Shakespeare); *Hostis habet muros* (Virgil)." The enemy held the walls; yet, like Aeneas, he must fight on. The analyses of Beethoven's symphonies (reproduced from the long-out-of-print *Voyage musical*) and the essay on the nature of music which preceded them, the recent pieces on *Orphée* and *Alceste*, the passionate pages, also of recent date, which set Shakespeare's *Romeo and Juliet* against the operas that failed so miserably to measure up to it, the various articles on Weber, the review of Wagner's concerts, the homily on the injurious effect of large theatres on singers and listeners alike, comprised his weightiest statement of musical beliefs, his testament – all rounded off, with a stroke of calulated bathos, by a few lines from a feuilleton of March 1862 on "L'école du petit chien": the singers whose extended upper octave enabled them to produce high Es and Fs which, in terms of their character and the gratification they gave, resembled the yelp of a King Charles spaniel whose paw has been trodden on. The title's (untranslatable) pun – "Over the fields of song" – exactly hit off a creative artist who had always made his way *à travers champs*, across country, not by recognized paths. One of the longer pieces was the letter on the Baden festival which he had addressed to his fellow-academicians the year before for reading out at their public session, but which had been rejected as "unsuitable in form": the Institute's committee, Halévy reported, "found it very witty, but too eccentric".

Berlioz nevertheless came within a few votes of being appointed Permanent Secretary of the Academy of Fine Arts six months later, in April 1862, when the post fell vacant on the death of Halévy. He had been persuaded against his will to stand, and could not help giving a sigh of relief when Beulé the archaeologist was elected instead. The prospect of a spacious rent-free apartment at the Institute, not to mention the Permanent Secretary's salary, must have appealed to him, especially as 4 Rue de Calais had recently been discovered to be so badly built that the house was falling apart and they were having to move to another floor while theirs was repaired. But the job would have tied him down too much, and he suspected that its demands were beyond him. He preferred to be free; and he needed his energies for his Baden opera.

Rehearsals continued throughout the spring and early summer, on the whole to his satisfaction. Mlle Monrose, the Hero, might be "entirely devoid of musical instincts" (he told Liszt) but her "fresh and natural voice" was just right for the part, and in the end she learnt it. As for Charton-Demeur – "the best female singer we have in France at the moment" – she was simply Beatrice personified. And though the men were no more than average, they were keen and conscientious and refrained from altering their music.

Early on the morning of Friday 13 June he left Marie with their friends the Delaroches at St Germain to return to Paris, and had just begun rehearsing some of the cast at the apartment when a telegram informed him that she was dangerously ill, and he hurried back. In fact she was already dead. She had gone to bed the night before apparently in good health, but suffered a massive heart attack next morning while getting dressed. When she failed to appear, Mme Delaroche went up to her room and discovered her lying dead on the floor. Berlioz got there to find it was all over. He had left his singers rehearsing, with instructions to give Mme Martin some pretext for his absence. But when at eight o'clock that evening he had still not returned she questioned the maid more closely and, learning that an urgent message had come from St Germain, set off at once. Soon afterwards Berlioz, accompanied by the Delaroches, started back to Paris to arrange the formalities and prepare the funeral; the two trains crossed en route. Mme Martin arrived to an apparently empty house, opened a door and came upon the corpse of her daughter, attended by a priest, and fainted away. For two days she hovered between life and death.

Marie was buried on the 16th, in the larger Montmartre cemetery. Berlioz wrote to Louis, in Marseille, next day, telling him that it wasn't necessary to come. "My nieces also offered. But I feel it is better for the moment if I am left to myself." His friends were taking turns to sleep at the apartment so that he should not be alone at night. But Louis came, and stayed ten days. When he left, on the 29th, he took with him a copy of the recently printed vocal score of The Trojans, inscribed: "My dear Louis, keep this score safe; and in recalling to you the harshness of my career may it make the difficulties of your own seem more bearable. Your loving father, H. Berlioz. Paris, 29 June 1862."

In terms of their relationship, this was a good time for father and son. The experience brought them closer together.

Paris, 12 July [1862]

I'm writing to you in a moment of exhaustion; I find such a great comfort in chatting a little with you. Yes, I was happy, during the night, knowing you were close by . . . But I don't want to sadden you – I prefer to think of the new position you have and the rise in your fortunes that is in prospect. You won't be making those interminable voyages that would have taken you so far away from me. In a few years you will have a fine salary and will be profiting from maritime enterprises. And we'll see each other more often. That is my dearest wish.

We do not have the letter Berlioz wrote to Louis immediately after Marie's death. Perhaps it would have afforded a clearer idea of what he really felt. In the letters that have survived he spoke of the cruel blow, of his isolation now that Marie was gone, of the tears he shared with his mother-in-law when she returned a few days later, and of her being a lot calmer than he, once she had recovered from the immediate shock. His feelings may well have been agitated. He had had murderous thoughts about Marie, had described his home life, only a couple of years before, as virtually impossible (Liszt, dining with them the previous year, said it "weighed on [Berlioz] like a nightmare"). The will Marie made ten months earlier does not suggest the most harmonious union. It named not her husband but her mother as residuary legatee and requested that her portrait, if it was not going to be kept, should not be sold but given to her friend Anna Banderali-Barthe.

On the other hand she was the woman he had lived with for the better or worse part of twenty years, who in more youthful times had been his desired sexual partner, who had stood up for him well if not wisely and by her lights had done her best for him. The notice of her death in *La France musicale*, signed by the editor Marie Escudier, described Berlioz as "plunged into the most profound affliction by this unexpected loss". As if going out of its way to correct any unfavourable impressions that might have been formed, it called the deceased an "intelligent and devoted woman, unstinting in the loving and sensitive care she lavished on her husband".

Whatever his feelings, he had no choice but to bury them in work. The première of *Beatrice and Benedick* was due in just over six weeks' time. Rehearsals resumed a week after the funeral. A fortnight later the whole cast assembled at the Opéra-Comique (Rue Favart) for the first production rehearsal. (At the same time the stage manager reported from Baden that the Strasbourg chorus knew their music.) On Saturday 26 July there was a complete run-through with soloists and piano on the stage of the Théâtre-Lyrique in front of a small invited audience; it was the last event in the theatre's home in the Boulevard du Temple before the demolition men moved in. Two days later Berlioz, with friends and musicians and a flock of journalists, took the train from the Gare de l'Est to Strasbourg. From there another train brought them to Baden, where they put up at the Hôtel de Darmstadt. Louis had not been able to get leave, but Legouvé was there, and Reyer, and Gounod. Pauline Viardot, who had written a sympathetic letter about his bereavement (they were friends again), was in residence at Baden for the summer and sat in on the orchestral rehearsals, of which – according to Richard Pohl, who had come from Weimar to hear the new work – there were half a dozen. The theatre, which held a thousand, was pronounced charming, until it was discovered that the orchestra pit was too small. "Can you believe it," wrote Reyer to Bizet. "Berlioz is furious. Monstrous negligence by the architect. When they pointed out his error to him, he replied that the important thing was for the public to be comfortable. The fellow doesn't bother about musicians. But you'll see how I shall make him move the barrier back."

Teaching the orchestra to master the delicate score was not an easy task. We hear of particular problems with the flutes. In the end he seems to have been tolerably well satisfied. Pohl, arriving a few hours after the dress rehearsal, found him in the Salle de la Conversation, in excellent humour and "dining in the best French style with his leading tenor", Montaubry. The orchestra, Berlioz wrote a few days later, delighted him with its agility and refinement. As it happened, he was in such pain on the day of the première (Saturday 9 August) that he conducted all the better – he felt for once emotionally detached from it all and as a result "did not make a single mistake": he was "much more excitable" at the second performance, which took place two days later. Some of the smart Russian and German and French visitors seem to have been less than rapturous in their response. Though several newspapers described the reception as brilliant, Reyer, writing to Bizet, spoke of "a *succès d'estime* for the music, for the poem a *succès d'ennui*", and went on: "What an audience! I had to stop myself bursting into the Princess Battera's box like an enraged bull – they were making

jokes in loud voices throughout both acts." But the artists in the house
were enchanted by the work. Reyer thought it "a marvel of art and
artifice". Berlioz's genius, wrote Gounod, "combines the innocence of
a child and an extraordinary complexity of spirit"; the Nocturne was
"absolutely beautiful, perfect – immortal like the sweetest and most
profound things the greatest masters have written".

Bénazet, though he had spent a great deal of money on the production,
had scheduled only two performances – *Beatrice* was the first of several
operas commissioned for the theatre's opening season – but he was
well pleased, and engaged the composer and the prima donna to come
back and repeat it next year. Perhaps it was he, as well as one or two
of the reviews in what was generally a favourable press, who suggested
that the very short second act could with advantage be made longer.
Within a few days of returning to Paris Berlioz was writing an ensemble
for the three women to balance the men's trio in Act I and, immediately
following it, a distant chorus with solitary guitar accompaniment summoning the bride to her wedding. The chorus – gentle, shadowy,
attenuated – closes with the last of the minor sixths in a major key
which are a fingerprint of his style and a messenger of angst throughout
his music. The trio contains some of the tenderest music he ever wrote.

Tenderness had re-entered Berlioz's life. He had fallen in love with
a woman less than half his age who loved him in return. She was called
Amélie, but otherwise almost nothing is known about her. If Legouvé's
memory is to be trusted, she was married. Berlioz had apparently got
to know her soon after Marie's death. Though it is only conjecture,
biographers have generally assumed that they first met in the Montmartre cemetery: seeing him in tears, she came up to him and they got into
conversation and agreed to meet there again. Maybe they did. It would
lend to the history of their tragic idyll an aptness, and a shape such as
is sometimes found in life as well as in art.

Berlioz talked to Legouvé one morning in Baden, in the woods below
the old castle.

> We sat down on a bench, for the climb had tired him. He was holding
> a letter, which he clutched convulsively. "Another letter?" I said with a
> laugh, trying to cheer him up.
> "As always."
> "Oh – is she young?"
> "Alas, yes."

"Attractive?"

"Too attractive – and with a mind, a soul."

"And she loves you?"

"She says so, and writes it."

"Then, surely, if she also gives you proof of it – "

"All right – she gives me proof of it. But what do such 'proofs' prove?"[. . .]

When I had read it I couldn't help saying, "Come on now, what on earth can you find to get so upset about? It's a letter written by a superior woman, and full of warmth and tenderness. What's the trouble?"

He interrupted me desperately: "I'm sixty."

"What does that matter if she sees you as thirty?"

"Look at me – look at my sunken cheeks and grey hair, look at these wrinkles."

"Wrinkles don't count in a great man. Women are quite different from us. We can hardly separate love from beauty, but they fall for all kinds of things in a man."

"That's what she says when she sees me in my moments of despair. Sometimes, for no reason, I sit down suddenly and begin sobbing. The terrible thought strikes me that she guesses! And then with an angelic tenderness she asks me what she can do to convince me. 'Have I not forgotten everything for you? Am I not running countless risks for your sake?' She takes my head in her hands and I feel her tears fall on my neck. And yet, in spite of it, I hear the dread message in the depths of my heart: 'I am sixty, she cannot love me, she does not.' Oh my friend, what torture – to turn a heaven into a hell!"

I left, without having been able to console him and, I own, deeply moved, not by his grief alone but by his humility. How far from the pathetic arrogance of Chateaubriand and Goethe, who fondly supposed that their genius endowed them with eternal youth, so that no amount of adoration surprised them. I prefer Berlioz – he is so much more human. How touching I find it that this allegedly arrogant man should have so far forgotten that he was a great artist and remembered only that he was an old man.

Perhaps Legouvé's famously romancing imagination is at work here; or perhaps Berlioz succeeded in persuading himself that his new friend loved him after all. When, later, he told Ferrand about the affair, he described it as "a love which came to me smiling, which I did not seek and even resisted for a time". Berlioz and Amélie were in contact throughout the autumn of 1862 and the first part of the winter. How close the contact, how often they met, in secret or not, and whether they were lovers, we cannot say. Certainly there is a new vigour in Berlioz's letters to the Princess, to Ferrand, to Pauline Viardot that autumn. He may still think of his work as finished (he has written the last note of orchestral music he will ever blot a sheet of paper with – "Othello's occupation's gone"), his one remaining ambition may be to be rich enough to resign from the *Journal des débats*, and he may be impatient to cut the last threads that bind him to art so that he can look death in the face and say, "Whenever you want"; offering Stasov the autograph of the Te Deum (the patriarch of Russian music, on a visit to Paris, had asked him for one of his scores for the library in St Petersburg), he may tell him that when he composed it he still had faith and hope but the only virtue left him now is resignation. But the energy with which he writes contradicts the confession of indifference.

The account of the Opéra which he sends to Pauline Viardot in Baden has a touch of the old zest:

> The Opéra still does nothing, apart from good business, and to tell you how low the vocal part of its performances has sunk is beyond my powers. They yell and bray, *largo assai*, without remission. From a distance you would think the women were having their throats cut and the men were in convulsions. The public utters not a word and returns home at the end of the evening shaking its ears and saying that that must be the way grand opera has to be sung. The minister is delighted, the Emperor doesn't give a damn, Royer is ill, M. Martin is taking charge of everything, the orchestra roars, and M. Cormon [the stage manager] blushes. They're reviving *La muette*, for which there is felt an imperious need. But Michot [the Masaniello] is no good, Emma Livry is not much of a mime, and the whole thing has ground to a halt.

This was the theatre that was supposed to be going to stage *The Trojans*. In February 1862 the Minister of State, Count Walewski, had ordered Royer to put the work into rehearsal as soon as Gevaert's opera, due in September, reached performance. In the event Gevaert's opera failed to materialize but the poor reception of Gounod's *Queen of Sheba* in March, coming only a year after *Tannhäuser*, made the minister wary of new five-act operas. The talk was now all of economies – Charton-Demeur, whom they had been going to engage, was said to be too expensive – and the count, whenever he met Berlioz, shook hands with him (Berlioz told his nieces) "in the manner of the man who said, 'Put it there! You won't have my daughter.'"

Except for mention of the vocal score, copies of which were sent to Liszt and Kastner, *The Trojans* practically disappears from the correspondence in the second half of 1862. We hear of discussions with Perrin about a possible production of *Beatrice and Benedick* at the Opéra-Comique; Galli-Marié (the future Carmen), was considered as an alternative to Charton-Demeur, who was now in Havana. Of *The Trojans*, no word. His "big ship" seemed as far as ever from launching.

Then, suddenly, events took a new turn. There was movement in the stagnant world of Parisian opera. Réty resigned from the Théâtre-Lyrique in October, shortly before the building on the Place du Châtelet opened. He was replaced by his predecessor Léon Carvalho – the same Carvalho who, when he was at the Lyrique before, had contracted to open the new theatre with *The Trojans* and who now made it clear that he was still very interested. Two months later the ineffectual Royer resigned as director of the Opéra, and Perrin succeeded him.

The Opéra's new boss was not bound by his predecessor's undertakings, which in the case of *The Trojans* had stopped short of a formal commitment. Carvalho, on his side, wanted the work and was pressing for it. Berlioz clung to the hope that it might yet be put on at the theatre for which it had been intended. On 10 January 1863 he wrote to Perrin.

> Will you allow me to draw your attention to a work of which you may perhaps retain a vague idea and in which you appeared to take some interest at a time when you were free of the cares that beset a theatre director? I shall not add to the number of petitioners who must be particularly importuning you just now. May I merely beg you not to ignore a work which by its nature is eminently suited to the Opéra, which would give an unexpected éclat to its repertoire, and which would have a great impact on the audience, if only by the splendid variety of its staging, in which your special talents would have great scope.
>
> Would you reread the poem of *The Trojans*? Unhappily I have no way of letting you hear the music; but I am convinced that this score contains a good number of pieces very likely to become popular, in the good sense of the word, within a week of the first performance. There is absolutely no musical trickery in it. It is daring, it's true, but it is also grand and simple and clear as day.

He was also at pains to put Perrin right about other aspects of the work, to nail the rumours that were circulating. "It's been said there are twenty-two roles in it: there are nine. It's said to last eight hours – which no one can tell: it's the music and not the drama that determines the length of an opera, and nobody knows it. In fact, timed exactly, and including sixty-six minutes for intervals, the score lasts no longer than *The Huguenots*."

When no response came he wrote again, giving the Opéra till 15 February to decide. The 15th came and went. A few days later he burned his boats and signed with Carvalho.

25

Beneath the Walls of Troy

1863, his sixtieth year, might have been an *annus mirabilis* for Berlioz, the fulfilment of three decades of promise and achievement. Progressive Germany welcomed and fêted him as it had in Liszt's time. It was France or rather Paris that still held out. But even Paris seemed to be relenting. Nothing dramatic; but straws in the wind, perhaps. In February, at a concert given in the Salle Martinet by Félicien David's Orchestre de la Société des Beaux-Arts, Berlioz conducted *The Flight into Egypt*, the *Roman Carnival* overture and *Invitation to the Waltz* (complete with the quiet epilogue that Pasdeloup cut), and with such success that they were repeated two weeks later. Not long afterwards, on 22 March, the Nocturne from *Beatrice*, sung by Viardot and Vandenheuvel-Duprez, was encored at the Société des Concerts. Berlioz was moved to write offering the society his collection of scores and performing material, "engraved and manuscript, representing practically the totality of my works". For most of his career the committee had been hostile, performing his music only twice in twenty-eight years when Habeneck and Girard were in charge. But it was time to forget the past. "I have often thought with anxiety," he wrote, "of what is to become of this costly collection when I am dead." The Société des Concerts was "the sole musical institution in France in whose future a composer can have confidence. I should be happy if, as from today, it would accept this music as a gift and grant it the hospitality of its library. One day perhaps these works will be of some value to the society." He would ask only that, in the event of its accepting his offer, he be permitted to make use of the material for any concerts he might give. Within a week of receiving the letter the committee had met and voted in favour. The gift was announced at the general meeting on 17 May, amid "numerous expressions of approval".

In the last week of March Louis arrived in Paris for a few days' leave

– just too late to attend the Conservatoire concert, but he was planning to come to Baden for the revival of *Beatrice* in August. Berlioz delighted in his company; it made him feel young again. Their troubles too seemed consigned to the past. Louis entered enthusiastically into the negotations for *The Trojans* and wrote out a draft contract. The contract laid on the director of the Théâtre-Lyrique the obligation to produce the opera "*as it is*" and not to "impose any cut, addition or change". Once rehearsals began (the document continued), the author would "remain sole judge of whatever modifications to his work" might be required. The theatre was "never to perform *The Trojans* other than complete, that is in five acts" and with musical resources which included an orchestra of sixty-eight (strings 10–10-7–7-6, the necessary woodwind, brass and percussion, and two harps), an onstage and offstage brass group of twenty (mostly saxhorns of various types) and an augmented chorus of seventy-four. The première was to take place in December. On his side Berlioz undertook to devote all his time and energy, from 1 September, to supervising the preparations. He would conduct two general rehearsals, and the first three performances as well "if M. Carvalho considers it appropriate".

In retrospect, this repeated insistence on *The Trojans*' being given complete strikes a grimly ironic note. For the moment, hopes were high.

On 30 March Berlioz set out for Weimar, entrusting Louis, whose leave had been extended, to the loving care of Mme Martin. The next few weeks belonged to Germany. It was his first visit to Weimar for nearly seven years. Much had changed. The Dowager Duchess Maria Pavlovna was dead. Liszt was gone, and the Princess. With the appointment of Franz Dingelstedt as intendant in 1857 Liszt had gradually lost his supremacy in the Weimar theatre. Dingelstedt was bent on reasserting the claims of drama. Opera no longer came first. The failure of Cornelius' *Barber of Baghdad*, given a single, noisily contested performance the following year, led Liszt to resign. He stayed on in Weimar for another two years. Then, in August 1861, he sealed the door of the Altenburg and moved to Rome.

Dingelstedt had been less than welcoming when Richard Pohl, fresh from the Baden première, recommended *Beatrice and Benedick*; but he was prevailed on by the combined efforts of Pohl (author of the German translation), Liszt's successor Lassen, and the Grand Duchess Sophie, who commanded a performance of the work for her birthday on 8 April. Even without Liszt and the dynamo of the Villa Altenburg it was a rewarding two weeks. Liszt's absence at least meant that Berlioz was free to conduct his opera himself. It also meant no awkward conversations about Wagner. But even on that subject a spirit of reconciliation ruled. On 6 April he heard *Tannhäuser* at the Weimar theatre and found that it contained "some really beautiful things, the last act especially, which is profoundly sad yet also grand. Why then," his letter to Lecourt continues, "must one, etc. etc.? But there would be too much to say." (Presumably what he didn't add was, "why must one conclude that Wagner is the future of music? Why does there have to be Wagnerism as well as Wagner?") Rosa von Milde, a favourite singer of Berlioz's and the dedicatee of *L'île inconnue*, struck him as "ideal, the personification of Elisabeth" and "adorable in her dove-like beauty". She was less than ideal in his own opera – "Mme Milde is enchanting," he told Pauline Viardot, "but she made the Sicilian lioness a very German Beatrice" – yet, after all, it was "another sort of truth"; and the performance as a whole, with the new trio making almost as great an effect as the Nocturne, went "much better than at Baden". Unlike his Baden counterpart Montaubry, the Weimar Benedick, Knop, didn't stumble in the final duet. "These Germans are true musicians." Making music with them was a joy.

The première being a court gala, etiquette forbade applause, but the atmosphere in the house was brilliant, the Grand Duke and Duchess entertained him after the performance in their box where his old admirer Crown Princess Augusta, now Queen of Prussia, charmed him by her intelligent response to the score, and a banquet given in his honour kept him up half the night. Two evenings later at the second performance (10 April) the applause more than made up for its absence at the first. People had come from as far afield as Berlin to be there. After that there were further banquets and suppers at court (at one of which the three hundred guests were regaled with the Hungarian March played by a military band in the gallery, while the Grand Duke raised his champagne glass in toast to Berlioz). He had private conversations with the Grand Duke, who questioned him about the Nocturne and was surprised to learn that the music for it was sketched at the Institute during a fellow-academician's speech ("some orator!"). At a soirée in the palace, attended by a select company that understood French, Berlioz read aloud the libretto of *The Trojans*. Carl Alexander was so taken with it that he wrote off then and there to his cousin the Duchess of Hamilton, instructing her to show the letter to her cousin Napoleon III. "Poor Grand Duke," was Berlioz's comment; "he can't believe it possible that a sovereign should not be interested in the arts."

Pohl's daughter Louise, writing more than thirty years later, gives a much darker picture of the composer during these two weeks. She found him admirable – "a man of refinement and distinction, French in the best sense of the word, with nothing in the least affected about him" – but the impression that stayed with her was of someone "deeply melancholic, taciturn and uncommunicative" despite "the great success he was having in Weimar and the honours heaped upon him":

> The only creature that could draw a smile from him was a large and magnificent Newfoundland dog belonging to one of his friends, whom he enjoyed visiting. The hound adored him too and liked to lay its splendid head on Berlioz's knee. He stroked it, and said that the dog had "loving eyes". Berlioz was sometimes in such frightful pain that he would lie motionless on his bed. The doctor thought that, unlike other people's, his nerves had no protection – they were too near the surface.

Certainly he arrived in Weimar in a bad state. But plunging into music again wrought a magical change: the pain all but disappeared. In the letters he wrote from Germany there was suddenly no mention of it. For a short time after his return he actually believed himself cured, such was the effect of "this month of pure musical intoxication".

He had planned to spend no more than two weeks in Germany; but the visit was extended, thanks to an invitation waiting for him when he reached Weimar. The invitation, brought by an old acquaintance, the violinist and composer Max Seifriz, was from his liberal host of 1842, the Prince of Hohenzollern-Hechingen; it asked him to come to Silesia and give a concert. The Prince's lands in Württemberg now belonged to Prussia and he was living four hundred miles to the east at Loewenberg, between Dresden and Breslau. In the meantime, however, he had maintained and strengthened his orchestra; and the Berlioz connection begun twenty-one years before was actively in force. (Seifriz, the present kapellmeister, had been a member of the orchestra in 1842.) When Berlioz arrived on about 15 April, with Pohl and his harpist wife Johanna, he found the Prince physically decrepit but as high-spirited as before and more in love with music than ever, and fifty "*musical* musicians" who knew his scores inside out. His host had chosen the programme himself: *King Lear*, the Fête and Love Scene from *Romeo*, the *Roman Carnival*, and *Harold*. Berlioz's letter to the Massarts overflowed with the wonder of it.

> The Prince has had a delightful concert hall constructed in his castle at Loewenberg, with perfect acoustics, and a green room behind the orchestra which houses his music library – everything that's required. He's given me an apartment next to this jewel of a hall; and every day at four o'clock they come to my sitting-room to tell me that the orchestra is assembled. I open double doors and find fifty artists at their posts, seated silently, *already tuned up*. They rise politely as I mount the rostrum; I take my baton and give the first beat, and off we go. And how they go, these fine fellows! Can you imagine it – they played the finale of *Harold* at the first rehearsal without a mistake and the adagio of *Romeo and Juliet* without missing a single accent! The kapellmeister Seifriz said to me after this adagio: "Ah sir, when we listen this piece, we – always – have tears."
>
> Do you know, dear friends, what touches me most in the marks of affection I am shown? It's realizing that I must be dead. So much has happened in twenty years which I have the impertinence to call progress. I'm played almost everywhere. A music director from Breslau who has just arrived informs me that his society performed the Queen Mab scherzo last month and it was encored. The Dresden director, who came to Weimar last week, told me similar news. A month ago movements from the Requiem were given in Leipzig. My *Corsair* overture is played all over the place – and I myself have heard it only once. The other overtures, especially *King Lear* and *Benvenuto Cellini*, are often performed, and they are precisely the ones least known in Paris. The day before yesterday (laugh or smile if you wish, Madam) I surprised myself when conducting *King Lear*: I couldn't repress a few tears. I thought that perhaps Father Shakespeare would not condemn me for having made his old British king and his sweet Cordelia speak in this language. I'd forgotten the overture, which I wrote in Nice in 1831.
>
> There's no harp in Loewenberg. The Prince has brought the Weimar harpist here – 250 miles!
>
> I've been interrupted *five times* while writing this. The Prince is forced by his gout to stay in bed; he's furious at having to miss our rehearsals. During dinner – to which he generally invites the visiting artists who've come here for tomorrow's concert – he writes me pencilled notes which

a great flunkey in gold braid brings on a silver salver, and I answer them between the pears and the rum baba (there's no cheese here). [. . .] Then I go and spend half an hour at his bedside, and he tells me – oh, what things! He knows everything I have written in prose and music. This morning he said, "Come, let me embrace you – I've just read your analysis of the Pastoral Symphony." [. . .] Can you believe it: the four rehearsals and two performances of *Beatrice* that I conducted at Weimar tired me nowhere near as much as the rehearsals for the Loewenberg concert. I'm quite done in. That's because a theatre orchestra is a slave, and a slave placed in a cave, whereas a concert orchestra is a king on his throne. And then these grand symphonic passions agitate me rather more violently than a character opera like *Beatrice*.

Why aren't you here? What pleasure it would give the intelligent listeners that surround me to hear you! And, my dear Jacquard, there's a young man of seventeen here who is worthy to be your pupil – only, he doesn't have an instrument like your beloved cello. I'm off: they've come to collect me, the orchestra is at its post, *tuned*. I'm going to sing myself the scene from *Romeo and Juliet*. I shall think of you. Oh, how well they speak the phrase

On the day of the concert (19 April) messages reported its progress to the still-bedridden Prince. The six-hundred-seat hall was full, most of the audience seemed to know the music well, and they raised the roof when, after the Pilgrims' March, the Prince's chamberlain, Colonel Brodorotti, came up on to the stage and pinned the Cross of the Order of Hohenzollern on the composer-conductor's lapel. Next evening there was a grand dinner followed by a ball. Pohl said he had never known Berlioz so gay and talkative.

He stayed on a few days in the hope that his host would recover sufficiently to demand a second concert; but the Prince remained a prisoner to his bed. Instead a reading of *The Trojans* was held in his salon, with the doors of the bedchamber open so that he could hear. On the evening of Berlioz's departure he summoned him for the last time and, kissing him, said: "You are going back to France, where there are people who love you. Tell them I love them."

The contrast between Germany, where rulers fostered music as a matter of course and orchestras were familiar with his works and needed no urging to play them, and Paris, where every move had to be fought and intrigued for, was as lowering as ever. Berlioz returned on about 25 April to find *The Trojans* as he had left it. Negotiations between Carvalho and Mme Charton-Demeur over the latter's fee were still not resolved; the whole project hung suspended. He returned too to the tawdry world of the feuilleton and the awkward business of avoiding saying exactly what he thought about the new opéras-comiques that were coming on at Carvalho's theatre – a task, he told the Prince, as tedious as that of the two sentries who stood guard at the gates of his castle. But "whereas those gallant soldiers carry out their duties fittingly, I who as a critic am supposed to guard the temple of art cannot even prevent the riff-raff from dumping their music against the walls".

Happily he had also the theatre's revival of Weber's *Oberon* to write about. More happily still, there was another big event to call him away from Paris: an invitation, arranged by the young Alsatian composer and critic François Schwab, to conduct *The Childhood of Christ* at the Festival of the Lower Rhine in Strasbourg. He had intended to stop in Strasbourg on his way back from Germany to rehearse the chorus but had stayed too long in Loewenberg. There was no cause for regret, however. Schwab had done his work. Preparations were well advanced by the time Berlioz arrived from Paris on the morning of 11 June and installed himself at 103 Grande Rue, home of the violinist Jean Becker, in the centre of town.

The Strasbourg *Childhood of Christ* was his one great triumph in France outside Paris. Admittedly there was a strong German contingent from the other side of the Rhine, as well as among the members of the local orchestra: Baden was only thirty miles to the east and Karlsruhe not much further. He knew many of them already and could count on a friendly welcome. But it was France none the less.

Berlioz was the toast of the festival. On 20 June, after the general rehearsal of his oratorio, he and his fellow-guests of honour, the kapellmeisters of Schwerin and Brunswick, crossed the Rhine by the new iron bridge to the town of Kehl on the opposite bank and were received by the societies of the region with banners and fanfares accompanied by cannon fire from the fortress. When the entire assembly had processed to the church, and massed choirs had sung Kalliwoda's *Chant allemand*, Berlioz thanked his hosts in a speech that Kücken, the Schwerin kapellmeister, translated sentence by sentence – to which (the *Courrier du Bas-Rhin* reported), "notwithstanding the sanctity of the surroundings, all the singers responded with acclamations and prolonged applause".

He gave a version of the same speech at the Préfet's banquet on the 21st, after attending a competition for all the brass and wind bands of the district:

> You have rightly said, sir, that under music's influence the soul is uplifted, the mind broadened, civilization advanced and national hatreds effaced. Today we see France and Germany join hands. Love of art has brought them together. This noble love will do more to unite them completely than the marvellous Rhine bridge and all the other modes of rapid communication that have been established between the two countries. The great poet has said: "The man that hath no music in himself / Is fit for treasons, stratagems and spoils – / Let no such man be trusted." No doubt Shakespeare availed himself of the freedom to exaggerate, which is the prerogative of poets. Yet observation proves that if his principle is extreme as applied to individuals it is much less so for nations, and it will surely be recognized today that where music stops barbarism begins. I give you the civilized city of Strasbourg and the civilized cities of France and Germany which have united with it with so much ardour to achieve its magnificent festival.

In another seven years the cannon of Kehl would be employed in shelling their French neighbours into submission.

On the morning of the 22nd the choral societies of the region had their turn, Berlioz presiding over the panel of judges, and in the afternoon everyone gathered for the grand event which formed the climax of the festival: Beethoven's Seventh Symphony, a cantata composed for the occasion by Schwab to a text by Méry, excerpts from an opera by Elbel, Weber's overture to *Euryanthe* and, after an interval, *The Childhood of Christ* conducted by the composer. A huge temporary structure of steel and glass, seating more than eight thousand people, had been erected in the Place Kléber. Berlioz was afraid that his *petite sainteté* would be lost in the immensity. But the correspondingly ample forces – chorus of 450 (reduced for certain parts of the score) and orchestra of ninety – carried the music to every corner. The final chorus, "O mon âme", crowned the work with a finality and beauty he had not known before. "It was truly the holy ecstasy I dreamed of and felt when writing it," he told Ferrand. "An unaccompanied choir of two hundred men and two hundred and fifty young women, rehearsed for three months: they didn't drop an eighth of a tone. Such things are unknown in Paris. After the last Amen – that pianissimo that seems to vanish into a mysterious distance – there was an explosion of clapping like nothing I have ever heard. Sixteen thousand hands applauding. Then a rain of flowers, and all sorts of other demonstrations of enthusiasm. I looked for you in the crowds." He wrote to his uncle Félix Marmion the same day to tell him about it: "My Austerlitz sun seems about to rise." The letter to Ferrand concluded: "This has been a brilliant year for me from the start. Will it end that way? Wish me luck!"

But it had already started to go wrong. The consequences of the decision to give his opera to the Théâtre-Lyrique were closing in inexorably.

After protracted negotiations, Carvalho and Charton-Demeur reached agreement by the beginning of June. Berlioz had the Dido he had insisted on, but at her fee of 6,000 francs a month, not the 4,000 the director had tried to reduce her to. He would pay for it with his life's blood. Though the fee was less than the singer was offered by other houses eager to have her, it swallowed up a dangerously high proportion of the budget. Carvalho now made it clear that something must give; his company was not rich enough to put on so large a work uncut, and his stage – it had turned out to be smaller than the old Lyrique's – was not big enough for the grand-opera scene of the Wooden Horse. He told the composer that part of the work would have to go and it had better be Acts 1 and 2, the Troy acts. They would then be able to do the Carthage acts in style.

Berlioz might have responded by withdrawing the work altogether. Had he done so, it would have waited even longer to be discovered but would have preserved its identity as one unified, long but not exceptionally long epic opera. The factitious notion of "Part One" and "Part Two", of complementary but separate works, would not have implanted itself, to bedevil and confuse the history of *The Trojans* for a century. With hindsight we can see that he would have done better to stand firm and cut his losses.

Only, he was too far in to draw back. Unlike Wagner, he could not wait. Death could summon him at any time. He must hear some at least of his score before that happened. There was nothing for it but to bury his disappointment (tempered by the lack of a suitable Cassandra – Mlle Morio, whom he and Bizet coached in the spring, had proved inadequate), and comfort himself with the promise that the full score, when it appeared, would restore the work to its pristine five-act state. Perhaps meanwhile the Opéra might even be induced to put on *The Capture of Troy*.

What he felt in his heart comes out in a letter written in July to Ferrand, to whom he had announced Carvalho's coup d'état a month before: "Don't give me even more regrets. I have had to resign myself. Cassandra is no more. *The Capture of Troy* will not be performed. The first two acts are omitted for the moment. I've had to replace them by a prologue; we begin only at Carthage."

Yet, despite the blow, his morale at first remained high. He was still in a positive frame of mind as he composed the replacement scene: new verses about the fall of Troy declaimed by a rhapsode in front of the curtain, adaptation of the Trojan March, and grand, sombre orchestral Lamento which set the theme of the Cassandra–Coroebus duet "Quitte-nous dès ce soir", intoned slowly by brass and woodwind, against mourning violin phrases and sudden surges in the lower strings.

The contrast between Berlioz's optimistic mood up to and including the early performances of *The Trojans at Carthage* and his consuming bitterness afterwards has been thought odd, if not a little perverse. But there is nothing surprising about it. That his first excitement did not last was only natural: the facts could not be ignored indefinitely. Long before he wrote the scathing account in his *Memoirs* a profound disillusionment had set in. Equally, his delight at becoming physically involved with the work at last, at hearing the score come even partially to life, could only be profound. The Théâtre-Lyrique was not the Opéra; but in some ways that was a blessing. He did not have to contend with the indifference, the lethargy, the patronizing superiority that greeted composers who braved the premier opera house of France and which he had experienced twenty-five years before with *Benvenuto Cellini*. Carvalho was that rare beast among managers, an enthusiast (even if in a crisis the enthusiast would always yield to the manager). Whatever his faults – and they certainly revealed themselves – he believed in Berlioz and in his work. The singers likewise, whatever their faults, were on his side. Later, even at his most disillusioned, he was at pains to emphasize how cooperative they had been, how they had never, any of them, behaved condescendingly or badgered him to alter their music, as their counterparts at the Opéra would infallibly have done. And "from the lowliest member of the orchestra" he had received "nothing but devotion". The failings of the performance were not due to lack of goodwill.

Above all, his Dido lived up to expectations. He went through the whole part with her in the first week of June and was moved to the depths. Coaching her was a joy; over the succeeding weeks and months she showed the willingness to learn and the desire to master the heights of the role such as distinguish the great singer from the mere diva.

At the beginning of June he read the libretto to the cast. Chorus rehearsals began soon afterwards. They were taken by the company's chorus-master, Léo Delibes, but the composer was in frequent attendance. In the second half of June he was away in Strasbourg. On his return he resumed his sessions with the singers. There was work to be done. The Anna, Marie Dubois, had a fine voice but (he told Ferrand) was "anti-music incarnate": he had to teach her the part note by note and go back over it again and again, then try to "lay a bit of style on her": she was coming to the apartment to rehearse with Mme Charton. "Dido would be put out if her *soror* didn't know her duet 'Reine d'un jeune empire' which she herself sings so admirably." A week later, on 15 July, he reported to Carvalho that the two ladies' voices sounded marvellous together. "I was quite surprised at the progress Mlle Dubois has made; she even knows her duet with Narbal, which she found so difficult. I've no more anxieties about her." To Morel, the same day, he was rather less sanguine: she "has a magnificent contralto voice but doesn't know how to sing".

Berlioz, by his own wish, was involving himself closely in the production. Carvalho had decided to direct it himself; but some of the ideas adopted were the composer's, among them the tableau of Dido and Ascanius and the ring, taken from Guérin's painting in the Louvre, which he had in mind as he composed the quintet "Tout conspire à vaincre mes remords". (Several reviews referred to the picture when speaking of the garden scene.) It was Berlioz too who suggested seeking the advice of Flaubert, whose novel, *Salammbô*, set in ancient Carthage, he had read the previous winter. "Here is the note I've had from M. Flaubert: see if you can make use of it," began the letter to Carvalho just quoted. The letter, after mentioning Mlle Dubois and her two duets, continued: "All these effects will be new to the audience at the Théâtre-Lyrique. Have confidence in me, give me my head, support me, and we will take Latium. Talk to our painters and try to see that what they do doesn't smother me in conventionalities. No threadbare old tricks! We're staging Virgil, not the Abbé Delille."* To friends and relations he continued to speak of Carvalho's infectious enthusiasm for the whole project.

From time to time other activities and commitments intruded. At the beginning of July he spent several days at the Institute judging the candidates for the music Prix de Rome and arguing the case for the eventual winner, the twenty-one-year-old Massenet. In the same month he signed a contract with Choudens for the publication of the two parts of *The Trojans* in full score and in vocal score, and of *Benvenuto Cellini* in vocal score; and at about this time he collected most of his small-scale compositions for voice and piano into a single volume for Richault to issue later in the year under the title *32 Mélodies*. In August he went to Baden for the revival of *Beatrice*, taking his son with him. (It was the first time Louis had heard his father's music since the performance of the Requiem at St Eustache in 1846, seventeen years before.) Berlioz fell ill with an infected throat and had to hand over the first general rehearsal to the local conductor, Koenemann. It went so badly that the cast told him it would be better not to give the opera at all, and he dragged himself from his bed to direct the second; he was at his post when the work was performed, on the 14th and 18th. Though Mme Charton was in lovelier voice than ever and her aria was a triumph, the performance as a whole was worse than the previous year's and much less good than in Weimar. The new Hero and Ursula sang the Nocturne vulgarly, and in the first act the Benedick, the usually reliable Jourdan, kept losing his place. Berlioz had the pleasure of Pohl's company and of further conversation with the Queen of Prussia. At the theatre he saw Reyer's *Maître Wolfram*, *Orphée* with Pauline Viardot, and *Le chevalier Nahel*, Litolff's setting of the Plouvier libretto which he had turned down in order to write *Beatrice*; and in a nearby meadow he watched Nadar make several ascents in a hot-air balloon. As always, Baden did him good. Yet he cannot have been sorry to get back to Paris, where the great business of his life awaited him.

* Eighteenth-century translator of Virgil.

The Théâtre-Lyrique's season opened on 1 September with *Figaro*. During September Berlioz continued to coach his singers. The designers were well advanced with their work; but the orchestra and its conductor, Deloffre, were busy with the next show, Bizet's *Pearl Fishers*, and the chorus was making slow progress. This was a long way from the conditions of the contract written out by Louis six months before: "From 15 September the Théâtre-Lyrique will devote its entire time to the preparation of *The Trojans*." It was not till October that things really began to move. By the middle of the month he was half living at the theatre. On the 24th he reported to Louis (just back from Mexico) that the première, originally planned for the end of November, would take place between the 15th and the 20th. "Everything's going well, apart from a few minor accidents in the singing of the chorus. The décor and costumes will be splendid. Mme Charton and Monjauze [Aeneas] are superb. Come soon." A day later he told Ferrand that the rehearsals were having "a tremendous success. Yesterday I came out of the theatre so overcome that I could hardly speak or walk."

What did he feel during these final weeks as the great day, the *summa dies*, drew near? For one thing, frustration at being prevented by the iron and idiotic rule of French opera-houses from conducting the work himself; but surely, too, a sense of emotional fulfilment at hearing whatever was well done: young Cabel singing Hylas' "Vallon sonore", Monjauze half covering the charming Ascanius (Mlle Estagel) with his shield at "D'autres t'enseigneront, enfant", and his expressive singing of Aeneas' "Ah! quand viendra l'instant des suprêmes adieux", Mme Charton's "Je vais mourir" and the wonderful way, Aeschylean in its antique power, she uttered the last words of her aria – "Je ne vous verrai plus, ma carrière est finie" – as she left the stage, still sustaining the final E flat and not looking into the theatre. (After one rehearsal Mme d'Ortigue was surprised to see him enter her house in tears and collapse into a chair. "What happened? Did the rehearsal go badly?" "No – no. It's so beautiful!") And finally the recognition, no longer to be denied, that even what was left, the performance of the three Carthaginian acts (now divided into five), was no more than an approximation.

Notwithstanding the subsidy of 100,000 francs, which after protracted campaigning had been agreed in July, the company's resources were simply not equal to it. They were further stretched by poor houses in the early part of the season. *Figaro*, though it picked up later, did not begin well. Receipts for Bizet's opera averaged less than 1,000 francs. Berlioz gave it an encouraging notice but it did not catch on.

Little by little *The Trojans at Carthage* began to feel the pinch. The orchestra, though supplemented by several players whom Berlioz paid for, was smaller than he had stipulated. He had to reduce some of the orchestration, most notably in the Royal Hunt and Storm: the full force of brass which would have been assembled for the entry of the Wooden Horse in the complete *Trojans* was no longer available. The staging too suffered reductions. It was not merely that Carvalho's audacious plan to create real cataracts in the Royal Hunt by diverting water from the nearby Seine had to be abandoned when a switch failed and serious flooding was only narrowly averted, so they made do with a painted waterfall instead: the whole elaborate scene, conceived for the stage and the stage techniques of the Opéra, inevitably made a feeble effect, given that (in Berlioz's words) "the leaping satyrs were represented by a troupe of twelve-year-old-girls who brandished no flaming branches, the firemen having forbidden it", and given that "there were no nymphs flying through the forest crying 'Italie!', the female choristers being stationed in the wings and their cries too weak to penetrate to the auditorium".

Worse, as the première approached, Carvalho insisted on making the already truncated opera shorter. Berlioz tried to oppose him but his resistance was ground down. Though he was not averse to omitting the confrontation of Aeneas and Dido at the harbour (realizing that the music's vehemence risked leaving Mme Charton without the necessary vocal power for "Dieux immortels! il part" in the following scene), he fought hard to prevent further cuts, but in vain. In due course the Anna–Narbal duet disappeared. So did the second ballet and, between the public dress rehearsal and the first night, the sentries' scene, which the director – in the spirit of the Abbé Delille, not of Shakespeare – thought "out of place in an epic work". What made it worse still was that Carvalho, not having the face to approach Berlioz himself, got mutual friends to do so instead.

It was not that he had lost his enthusiasm for the piece. Two crucial factors, however, were at work. The downside of his enthusiasm was a tendency to regard himself as the collaborator of the composer-dramatist, not the servant. Saint-Saëns called it a "mania for leaving his mark on everything he produced". He admired Berlioz's opera; but he felt he could make it still better. His views, too, about staging it differed in many particulars from the composer's. And he pestered him with niggling points of detail, as the *Memoirs* exasperatedly recalled:

"Look, will you do me a favour?"

"What is it now?"

"Leave out Mercury. The wings on his head and heels will make people laugh. No one has ever seen wings except on the shoulders."

"So human beings have been seen with wings on their shoulders? But you're right: wings on the heels will make people laugh, and wings on the head even more so. Ha! ha! ha! Since one doesn't often run into Mercury in the streets of Paris, we'll leave him out."

"Aeneas mustn't come on in a helmet".

"Why not?"

"Because Mangin, who sells pencils at the street corner, wears one – a medieval helmet, it's true, but a helmet none the less – and the wags in the gallery will laugh and call out, 'Hey, there's Mangin!' "

From the notices it appears that Mercury, with or without wings on heels and head, survived. But Aeneas was docked of his helmet. ("Why," asked the *Constitutionnel*, "did M. Monjauze, who at the final rehearsal was fully armed for his first appearance before Dido, judge it becoming to present himself to the Queen of Carthage at the première looking as if he had just got out of bed?") All to no avail, however: a cartoon by Cham showed "M. Mangin lending his helmet to Aeneas in return for the latter's undertaking to sell some pencils for him at Dido's court".

The other factor was outside Carvalho's control: money. He had become dangerously short of it. *Oberon* and *The Pearl Fishers* were not attracting an audience; the house was three quarters empty. He had to fill it. The government's subsidy was not due to be paid till January. Only one course of action was open to him: *The Trojans at Carthage* must be brought forward. When Berlioz wrote to Louis on 24 October he believed that the first night was more than three weeks ahead. Abruptly, the date was changed; the public dress rehearsal was called for 2 November; the première, scheduled for the 18th, was given on the 4th. Though "nothing was running smoothly, least of all on stage", and the work was "still in need of three or four strenuous general rehearsals", it was pointless to protest. "In such cases, as is well known, directors become very fierce."

The Trojans at Carthage did what was required: it saved Carvalho's bacon. It also enhanced his reputation as an enlightened impresario with the courage to back his hunches. For a work that in subject and treatment went so counter to the taste of Second Empire Paris it fared better than could have been predicted. Throughout November, during which it was given three times a week, receipts were surprisingly good. The Théâtre-Lyrique was not a fashionable house. (Neither the Emperor nor the Empress nor, apparently, any senior member of their households condescended to attend the show – nor did either Pauline Viardot or Rosine Stoltz, both at one-time pretenders to the throne of Carthage.) But Berlioz was a public figure, hated by some maybe but generally considered worthy of respect, all the more now that with the recent deaths of Delacroix and Alfred de Vigny, and with Hugo in exile, he was almost the last survivor of the men of 1830. More than this, the work was widely admired. Some returned several times. Meyerbeer was there night after night, "for my pleasure and my instruction". So was Corot, who knew the score almost by heart and sang it at his easel when he couldn't get his neighbour Mme Charton-Demeur to come and sing it for him. On all sides Berlioz saw spectators moved to tears. If Louis overheard two young men exclaiming that "such music should not be *allowed*", he also reported seeing a woman so overcome that her companion had to remind her to restrain herself: "Yes, I know, it's beautiful, I'm not saying it isn't, but that is no reason to get in such a state." Marie d'Agoult wrote hailing the genius which had stirred her in her youth and which she had rediscovered in the "masterly utterances of a poet's and an artist's soul such as one encounters rarely and is honoured to have known", and wrote again after the third performance to tell him that "Dido's despair pierced me to the marrow of my bones." The friends who were with her, she added, "were astonished, in view of your reputation, to find you so classical, and to experience such charm and tenderness where they had expected only force". She ended by hoping Berlioz would "let us hear your Cassandra soon". The one-armed Roger, who had been disappointed not to be given the part of Aeneas, nevertheless sent a glowing note; and among other congratulations was one from the poet Auguste Barbier, librettist of *Benvenuto Cellini*, beginning "Well roared, lion!"

As it happened, the first night had come near disaster owing to what several critics recognized as the unpreparedness of the production. When the curtain fell at the end of the Royal Hunt – all of nine minutes of music – the audience naturally expected it to go up again after only

a short delay. In fact it took the scene-shifters more than three quarters
of an hour to strike the set and replace it with what Fiorentino in *La
France* described as a "Babylonian construction" of "columns, pillars,
gardens stretching into the distance, avenues of sphinxes and lions, and
galleries and terraces". Long before the garden scene began, the gods
were in full cry, chanting *Le pied qui r'mue* and calling for *The Trojans*
to the tune of *Lampions*. Even if they did not also sing the soldiers'
chorus from Gounod's *Faust* (as one witness recalled many years later),
the mood of the house when the curtain finally rose was, as one reviewer
remarked, "peu sympathique". In the event the garden scene enchanted
almost everybody and saved the day. The septet was greeted by such
torrential applause that even Berlioz's enemies, it was noted, had to
join in, and the piece was repeated. A dozen numbers were acclaimed
from all parts of the theatre. In sum, the evening was adjudged a success
– a success not simply due to the vigorous demonstrations of the
composer's admirers.

Between the first performance and the second two nights later, steps
were taken to reduce the running time. The processions of the builders,
sailors and farmworkers vanished. So did Iopas' stanzas (poorly sung
by de Quercy). And so did the Royal Hunt – a fact commented on
sarcastically in a cartoon by Grévin headed "Non-symphonic interlude",
which showed a bemused Berlioz, in antique tunic, with a large pair of
scissors and a bulging waste-paper basket, over the caption: "Well,
where's this Royal Hunt? And the virgin forest? And the cave? The
stream? The naiads, the satyrs, the nymphs? The storm, etc., etc., etc.?"
"In the bin." "Oh, M. Berlioz – but that was why I came. Didn't the
public like it? Dangerous admission! On that principle your bin would
very soon be full." From now on, however, the production flowed more
smoothly.

The large number of cartoons stimulated by Berlioz's opera – *Le
Journal amusant* devoted a whole number to it – was a kind of tribute
to its impact. The work was important enough to merit attacking and
pulling down: to be pictured felling an enormous ox in an abattoir with
notes blasted from a tuba ("New method of killing cattle to be introduced
at all slaughterhouses"), causing the Devil to flee in alarm from the
Théâtre-Lyrique, and relieving the siege of Troy, as the Greeks scatter
with their hands over their ears before an army of brass instruments
bellowing from the ramparts. ("If only they had had the score of *The
Trojans* . . .") The press treated *The Trojans at Carthage* as a major

event, with long articles and sometimes quite serious discussion of the issues it raised. Louis, collecting the cuttings for his father, claimed to have amassed more than sixty that were positive, against many fewer that were not. True, Bernard Jouvin in the *Figaro* spent three thousand words roasting the work, concluding that Carvalho would have done better to replace the ghosts of the Trojan dead with the ghosts of Gluck, Spontini, Beethoven and Weber, and have them denounce Berlioz to a text supplied by the critic, after which the opera could have terminated without the remaining numbers and to the relief of one and all. Scudo declared number after number to be quite worthless (the duet for Dido and Anna was "so vulgar, so badly designed and so distorted with impossible modulations that one would take it for the music of a deaf man"), then ended by fatuously assuring Berlioz that "if he has fallen, he has fallen from a lofty height and his disaster will not weaken the esteem owed to a man who has devoted ten years of his life to the realization of his dream". *Le Nain jaune* – "The Yellow Dwarf" – printed columns of witticisms on the lines of "M. Hector Berlioz, who for the past fifteen years has been demolishing musicians, has now succeeded in demolishing music." But they were a minority. Though such attacks – Berlioz felt ashamed to confess it – caused him real distress, he could not complain at the reception he was given by the press as a whole. Critic after critic responded to the music with admiration and love. He had not written it in vain.

Some were idiots – the *Mémorial diplomatique* lumped *Tannhäuser*, Gounod's *Queen of Sheba* and *The Trojans* together as examples of the same "school" and argued that the Opéra had done more than enough by staging two of them, and the *Siècle* cheerfully confessed that "Wagner and Berlioz, a few minor differences apart, are for me the same thing" – but far more showed knowledge and deep appreciation of the work. Kreutzer, Gasperini, Fiorentino, d'Ortigue, Johannes Weber, Prosper Pascal, Marie Escudier, Auguste Durand and many others wrote with understanding. Almost everyone praised Carvalho for daring to take it on where others hesitated. But several notices made it clear that dramatically as well as musically the performance was flawed.

At this distance it is impossible to say how good or bad it was. Writing to the Princess two weeks after the first night Berlioz reported that the orchestra "goes confidently", adding, "but I needed the Opéra orchestra: the wind instruments lack sufficient virtuosity". Six months later, in the Postface to the *Memoirs*, the orchestra and the chorus were both described as "small and weak" and the sound of the orchestra in the Royal Hunt as "thin and lacking in vigour". As was customary, few critics mentioned the conductor, Deloffre. Those who did praised him, if in rather unspecific terms. According to the Supplement to Fétis' *Dictionary* published in the late 1870s, Deloffre was a good musician but his beat was unclear. Adolphe Jullien called him "experienced but rather feeble". Monjauze, the Aeneas, got a mixed press – and Berlioz, in the same letter to the Princess, reported him as "fine and stirring one day out of two" (in the *Memoirs* this dwindled to "there were days when he showed warmth and animation") – but for Mme Charton-Demeur there was almost universal admiration. The hapless Mlle Dubois seems to have been a real turkey ("if Mme Dubois' twittering were the equal of her blond plumage she would be an accomplished *Anna soror*"); Georges de Massougnes, the young journalist who became a champion of Berlioz, thought she ruined the Anna–Dido duet. Yet according to several reviews the duet was one of the numbers most admired as the run continued. Again, whereas Carvalho was generally considered to have staged the opera splendidly, reading between the lines one finds enough to explain the dissatisfaction with the production that Berlioz expressed in his *Memoirs*.

By that time his attitude had hardened. Carvalho talked of reviving *The Trojans at Carthage* and was even thinking of doing *The Capture of Troy*, but he would have none of it: the Théâtre-Lyrique was "impossible", and its director, "who continues to pose as collaborator, more impossible still". The dream was over.

Perhaps if his health had not broken down and he had been able to go on attending and supervising the performances, things might have been different. As it was, in the second week of November he developed acute bronchitis, brought on by the weeks of tension and the hours spent in the draughty, dusty theatre. He was in bed for more than three weeks and missed ten consecutive performances. Happily Louis was at them all and would come straight to his father's room on getting in and give him an account of it. But Louis, though his delight in the music was a deep satisfaction to Berlioz, could not tell him all he needed to know. It was a shock when, still not fully recovered, he attended the fourteenth performance, on 4 December, and discovered what had happened to the already mutilated work in his absence. Hylas, for one, was no more – Cabel had been removed from the cast. His contract was for fifteen appearances a month; as he was now in *La perle de*

Brésil, which joined the repertory at the end of November, he would have had to be paid extra if he had continued in *The Trojans at Carthage*. It had been the obvious course to drop him. That was a clean cut if a barbarous one. Worse, to save time, short passages had disappeared from many parts of the score – the beginning of that death by a thousand cuts which would be the destiny of *The Trojans* in France for the next hundred years.

Audiences too had fallen off; the interest aroused when the work was new had subsided. In any case Mme Charton was leaving to go to the Théâtre-Italien, for a higher fee. *The Trojans at Carthage* closed on 20 December, two performances earlier than planned.

Berlioz consoled himself as best he could with the thought that at any rate the work was now known (he might have added, "some of it"). "Never mind," he wrote to the Princess on 23 December, "these twenty-two performances have sown an enthusiasm in the musical world that I only wish I could have given you proof of." The work was "worthy to be offered" to her.

It was a brave show of spirit; but he could no longer conceal the truth. Though Carvalho might still have plans, Berlioz himself had none. For him it was the end of *The Trojans*. Not just because Mme Charton was no longer available and there was no other Dido in France: he had had enough.

The Postface which Berlioz added to his *Memoirs* the following summer is dominated by a mood of "to hell with everything". Increasingly worn down by ill health and physical pain, he had neither the strength nor the will to resist when Choudens insisted on issuing a vocal score of *The Trojans at Carthage* which conformed to the production at the Théâtre-Lyrique, cuts and all. Nor could he do more than rage helplessly when the publisher began to make difficulties over the full score of the complete opera which he was contracted to bring out and by which Berlioz set so much store. The whole experience was symbolic. His chief joy had become his bitterest disillusionment. The work that summed up all he stood for had suffered "a damn'd defeat". Paris had won. It had wanted his opera, if at all, only in truncated form, reduced to acceptable dimensions. The words of the *Memoirs* are a stinging indictment of failure. "The agony of seeing a work of this kind laid out for sale with the scars of the publisher's surgery upon it!" And "Oh my noble Cassandra, my heroic virgin, I must then resign myself: I shall never hear you – and I am like young Coroebus, *Insano Cassandrae incensus amore*": on fire with wild love for Cassandra. Gounod scarcely exaggerated when he said of Berlioz that, "like his great namesake Hector, he died beneath the walls of Troy".

26

Evening Star

The deepening gloom of Berlioz's final years has been so dwelt on by biographers that we need to be reminded that it is not the whole picture. To every two or three testimonies to his consuming bitterness at least one contemporary impression can be opposed, sometimes from the same time. Where Gounod, at Baden in 1862, thought he was cracking up, Richard Pohl found him in unusually good form. Louise Pohl's memory of him in Weimar in 1863, roused from profound depression only by a friend's dog, is mitigated by that of her father, who had never seen him in such spirits. Though in Verdi's subsequent memory Berlioz was "a poor sick man who railed at everyone", and Liszt, as early as 1861, described him as declining towards his grave, isolated, deprived of both "the warm sun of popularity and the sweet intimacy of private life", other friends saw him differently. The man portrayed in Saint-Saëns' reminiscences is a much livelier, more mercurial figure.

He would hardly have won the admiration and loyalty of so many of the younger Paris musicians if he had not been – if he had spent his time complaining and presenting a scowling countenance to the world. Their devotion was stirred by much more than a sense of the wrongs he had had to endure. He was a neglected genius: he was also a magnetic personality, interested in their problems and their hopes as well as in his own sufferings. His empathy with the young drew them to him.

Something of what attracted them comes out in a little known memoir by Louis Bourgault-Ducoudray, a pupil of Ambroise Thomas who competed for the Prix de Rome in 1862 and who later became a professor at the Conservatoire and a specialist in ethnic music.

"Well, who won?"
"I did."
"Excellent! I'm very pleased. What are you doing this evening?"

"Nothing."

"Let's walk."

This dialogue took place at the corner of the Chaussée d'Antin and the boulevard in the month of June 1862, the day after the judgement passed by the Académie des Beaux-Arts – judgement which had awarded me first prize. My interlocutor was Hector Berlioz; a recent bereavement [Marie's death] had prevented him from attending the Institute the day before and taking part in the vote.

Berlioz, at the time, was fifty-nine [fifty-eight]. His intellectual powers were still at their height and his inspiration in full flow. The composer of the Fantastic Symphony thoroughly looked the part. A mane of grey, almost white, elegantly wavy hair, an eagle's beak of a nose, fine-drawn powerfully arched brows beneath which glittered two penetrating eyes, a tragic forehead, more broad than high, a thin-lipped mouth at once mocking and proud, a delicately sculpted chin, gave his face an expression of bravery and incomparable poetry. His body, in appearance frail, indicated nerves of steel, with the power to multiply its muscular energy tenfold and make it endure the most extreme fatigue. His voice with its strange timbre and abrupt, pungent delivery, the fire of his glance and his sparing but electrifying gestures, completed an exterior from which an extraordinary personality projected, both engaging and aggressive, seductive and formidable. This incorrigible idealist and inveterate dreamer truly seemed like a *revenant* from the fantastic realm of ghosts and genies. The contrast between that higher world where his mind soared and the world of reality was for him a constant source of irritation, and these endless wounds, aggravated by his hypersensitive nature, provoked his caustic intelligence to sarcasms and jests which he gave vent to, on his good days, with naïve delight and diabolical high spirits.

I was twenty-two years old and I loved Berlioz with passion. The spell of his magic eye had me in thrall. At the preliminary exam, which precedes the actual competition and the candidates' entry *en loge*, I studied, for the first time close to, and not without keen emotion, that exceptional physiognomy. During the session at which the text that was to test the competitors' talents was dictated to them, Berlioz had several times transgressed the behaviour proper to an Immortal to deliver some quip or startle us with a pun.

The glamour of his person magnetized my whole generation of composers. I can see him still, when we came out of the exam, recrossing the Pont des Arts escorted by a crowd of disciples dogging his footsteps and hanging on his words. Although his music was more or less ostracized and his finest works had not succeeded in winning the recognition of the public at large, his influence as musician and poet on the young of that time was none the less considerable. This influence, augmented by the external appearance of the man, had something mysterious, almost occult about it. In Berlioz we felt a force whose starting-point and mechanism were clear but whose outcome had still to be grasped. The extracts from his works which we heard performed now and then revealed to us undoubted power and audacity of conception; yet with the great majority of the public his works did not "take". In our eyes the unjust banishment which Berlioz suffered at the hands of the mob made him all the greater. To the prestige of the great musician was added that of the persecuted artist, the heroic fighter, I will almost say the martyr.

To meet Berlioz the day after my departure from the schoolroom, to walk *arm in arm* with him and talk on familiar terms like an old friend was an unimagined godsend, an unheard-of piece of luck. You can imagine how I savoured it. That evening Berlioz was in the vein – you could say, "in eruption"; his liveliness had something volcanic, his energy overflowed as though from a crater. His mind didn't merely flash, it blazed. What a walk we had! If I lived to be a thousand I could never forget it. His dazzling improvisations were in every key, broached every subject: memories of his youth, intimate outpourings, theories of art, grand musical conflicts, favourite books, historical figures exalted or brought low. Meanwhile we elbowed passers-by, turned round abruptly and retraced our steps, threaded our way through, as if the whirlwind where his thoughts revolved had created a torrential current that swept us along. All the great personages of history and art were evoked and judged, from Cleopatra, "that prostitute" as he called her, to Savonarola, whose sublime inspirations elated him. Before long, amid this swarm of ideas and characters, Shakespeare inevitably made his appearance – Shakespeare his favourite poet, his worship of whom verged on fanaticism, and whose plays were the Bible by which this votary of poetry and art lived. Berlioz admired all Shakespeare but I think he had a special predilection for *Hamlet*. He had made a written translation of long passages and dreamed of translating the whole play. "Have you thought of doing an opera on *Hamlet*?" – "I would never dare. I did compose three entr'actes for the play, which I called *Tristia* – 'sad things'. I've never had them performed. When I am consumed with melancholy I perform my music mentally and listen to it within myself."

We spoke of the best conditions for creating music. "Everything I've composed," he said, "I undertook spontaneously, almost by accident. Even for the works which I carried in my head a long time, some chance circumstance was necessary to induce me to write them. It was my intense dislike of cards in general and of whist in particular that made me compose *The Childhood of Christ*." – "How was that? I see no connection." – "It's quite simple. I was at the house of friends. Cards were being played. According to my wont, I turned my back on the game and amused myself rousing the flames which flickered in the grate. As I was poking the fire I heard a tune take shape in my brain. It was a gentle, graceful melody, pastoral and primitive in colour, rather like an old carol, mingled with a harmony of flutes and oboes. There was nothing boring about my social life that evening! By the time the game of whist was over I had finished my chorus, which I named 'The Shepherds' Farewell to the Holy Family'. A few days afterwards I added two more movements, and later my 'game of cards' was joined by two other parts: hence *The Childhood of Christ*." – "But it didn't reconcile you to whist?" – "I dislike it more than ever!"

[Berlioz goes on to talk about the Princess's threats and encouragements which induced him to begin work on *The Trojans*.]

"Once my poem was done I had to write the music too, for I felt totally obsessed by the need to compose." – "When will you have your opera performed? I'm longing to hear it and applaud it. The evening of the première you'll have no more ardent proselyte or more determined defender than me." – "For that, I should need a singer who is also a great tragedienne. I'm looking for one – but the pavements of Paris hardly nurture such a seed."

As we emerged on to the boulevard, carried along by the momentum of our inexhaustible talk, we ran into a tall, slightly stooping figure who was ambling past, lost in thought, and whose melancholy appearance was in such marked contrast to our exuberant mood that I stopped short. I gave a cry as I recognized the solitary walker. It was Berlioz's colleague and friend, my revered teacher, Ambroise Thomas! We shook hands. At once, by one of those sudden transformations characteristic of him alone, the sombre features of Ambroise Thomas relaxed and a smile lit up his face. Like an instrument tuned instantly by a practised hand he adapted himself to our spirited conversation; and he too, the great melancholic, kindled by the volcanic Berlioz, himself caught fire as he recalled old memories and the experiences of far-off times. The two of them outdid each other as they ardently relived their first deep musical emotions, in particular those aroused by Spontini's *La Vestale*. I cannot describe the youthfulness, the enthusiasm that overflowed from the very souls of those two great artists in that hour of mutual confidences. All I can say is that a moment came when Berlioz, possessed by the double daemon of artistic inspiration and rediscovered youth, and unable to contain himself an instant longer, then and there struck up at the top of his voice, in the middle of the boulevard, one of the motifs from *La Vestale*. Total stupefaction of the passing crowds – everyone was turning round and whispering. "Be quiet, Berlioz," said Ambroise Thomas, seizing his arm. "If you go on like that we'll be arrested!"

How late our walk went on I do not remember. But during the few hours it lasted I lived ten years.

As Reyer remarks, Berlioz did not produce pupils but he had disciples; "if he gave us no lessons, he taught us a great deal". On his side, these contacts with the young were of crucial importance, not simply for their rejuvenating effect but for the hope they gave him that his music might not be forgotten after his death, might yet survive the opposition that it continued to provoke and that, against his will, cut him to the quick (Bourgault-Ducoudray recounts how a loud catcall amid the cheers after a performance of the Fête from *Romeo* reduced him to the state of "a wounded lion".) In Tiersot's words, "he realized that they had come at last, those who were to understand him; he sensed that it was their generation that would bring about his rehabilitation". He sensed it, but he did not know. In his darkest hours he could not be sure it had not all been an illusion. Their belief helped his unbelief.

Their company, too, was a precious means of keeping the spectre of loneliness at bay. Liszt rightly divined how much his old friend dreaded isolation. Where he was wrong was in concluding, from a lifestyle woefully lacking in lustre, that Berlioz no longer had "any friends or partisans".

What is true is that the sphere of his activities, from the beginning of 1864, contracted sharply. Once *The Trojans at Carthage* disappeared from the billboards, his life as an important public figure was virtually over; he became a private person. In January, most of which he spent in bed, he arranged the Trojan March as a concert piece; but after that he composed nothing, if we except the two little motets for women's voices, *Veni creator* and *Tantum ergo* – pieces of such uncertain date that they cannot be considered definitely his last compositions, nice though it would be to think of him ending with a symbolic gesture to his first musical experience fifty years before, the eucharistic hymn sung by the girls at the Convent of the Visitation in La Côte St André.

His career as conductor, so far as Paris was concerned, was effectively over. In December 1863 he had put himself forward to succeed Tilmant at the Société de Concerts. Whether because of his poor health or because unlike nearly all nineteenth-century Parisian maestros he was not a string player or because a composer-conductor was suspect, or for all these reasons combined, he was barely considered, coming a poor third to Deldevez, a violinist, and the cellist Georges-Hainl (who got the job). He appeared only once more on the rostrum in Paris, conducting his friend Léon Kreutzer's Concerto symphonique in the Salle Erard in March 1866. Most Saturdays he was to be found at the Institute; but the doings of the Academy of Fine Arts were rarely news.

His unimportance was underlined, in May 1864, by the prodigious obsequies laid on at the Gare du Nord on the 14th for Meyerbeer's coffin – the Michelangelo of music had died twelve days before – on the first stage of its triumphal journey home to Berlin. Berlioz was made Officier of the Légion d'honneur in August (in the same batch as his friends Legouvé and the pianist Aglaé Massart). The award obviously gave Marshal Vaillant pleasure – his note informing him of it went well beyond the requirements of protocol. But it was nearly thirty years since he had been appointed to the junior grade, Chevalier, and – unlike Félix Marmion – he was never made Commandeur. As Prosper Mérimée told him at the ceremony on 15 August, "They should have made you Officier long ago – which proves I have never been minister."

Reports continued to reach him of performances abroad – in St Petersburg, Moscow, New York, Copenhagen, Prague (where Smetana conducted Romeo and Juliet), and at festivals in Germany: performances not merely of extracts but of complete works. In Paris they made do with extracts. From time to time the Société des Concerts or Pasdeloup's orchestra would include one in their programmes (not always letting him know). At the Conservatoire The Flight into Egypt was becoming almost a popular item. That was as far as it went. Months after The Trojans at Carthage, strangers might still come up to him in the street and thank him; but, officially, he was a marginal figure. It would be many years before his partisans were able to carry the majority with them and impose his major scores, and by then the composer would be long dead. For now, they could work only in a small way, heartening as their tributes were. On 4 November 1864, the anniversary of the première of the opera, Dr Blanche the director of the asylum at Passy gave a surprise dinner party in his honour. After the meal Gounod, "with his weak voice but profound feeling", sang Hylas' song and, with Mme Banderali-Barthe (Marie's friend), "Nuit d'ivresse"; a pianist played some of the ballet music; and Berlioz spoke the scene in Act 5 beginning "Va, ma soeur, l'implorer". Many of the guests – doctors, scientists, scholars, artists – knew the work well, having seen it anything up to half a dozen times. "They professed a most respectable partisanship – appropriate in a madhouse." Two months later, in January 1865, Gasperini gave a public lecture on *The Trojans*. To the musical world as a whole, however, Berlioz had ceased to be a force. He no longer counted.

More than anything it was because there was no longer any reason to fear or court him: he had ceased to be music critic of the *Journal des débats*. At least *The Trojans at Carthage* had achieved that. The sale of vocal score and full score to Choudens, together with the royalties from the performances at the Théâtre-Lyrique, finally made him sufficiently well off to do without the income from journalism which he had depended on for the past thirty years. In February 1864 he asked Edouard Bertin for an unspecified period of leave. At first there was talk of his continuing to contribute articles on general topics that interested him. But, though he wrote at least once more, anonymously, in the *Gazette*, he had done his last feuilleton – to the chagrin of musicians who had been wooing him for a favourable notice ("they've lost their deposit") and of managers like Carvalho who had come to take his encouraging words for granted. His retirement was announced in *La France musicale* on 20 March. D'Ortigue, who had been filling in for him since October, was appointed music critic of the *Débats* in April.

Berlioz could hardly believe his deliverance. He was free at last. "No more platitudes to condone, no more mediocrities to praise, no more rage to repress, no more lies, no more make-believe, no more shameful time-serving." He "need never set foot in an opera house again, never speak of an opera house or listen to anyone speak of an opera house, nor ever have to laugh at the messes they concoct in those great stew-pots. *Gloria in excelsis Deo, et in terra pax hominibus bonae voluntatis.*" He could indulge in the pleasure of walking past the façade of the Opéra or the Italiens or the Lyrique and not going in. On the rare occasions when he went to anything, he could do so as a private citizen. In March 1864 he saw the première of Gounod's *Mireille* at the Lyrique (though he left at 12.30 a.m., exhausted, before the fifth act had begun). In April and May his young friend Théodore Ritter played the five Beethoven piano concertos at the Salon Pleyel and he was there to hear and delight in them. The following spring he heard Joachim and various colleagues play Beethoven – the Archduke trio, the Kreutzer sonata, the E minor Rasumovsky quartet, "music of the starry spheres; you will understand that after experiencing such miracles of inspiration it's impossible to endure commonplace music, manufactured goods and works recommended by the Mayor and the Minister of Public Instruction".* He did go to a general rehearsal of Meyerbeer's post-humous *L'Africaine* at the Opéra. But he attended as an amateur.

The consequence of all this was a drastic alteration in his daily life. Till now it had been a life of action, combat, physical exertion and constant mental stimulus, the continual generating and expending of nervous energy. Now that was changed, radically. When he got up in the morning – more often than not after a night of pain and fitful sleep – there was nothing demanding attention: no score to work on, no festival or concert to plan, no tour to prepare, no minister to lobby, not even a feuilleton to write.

It was fortunate that so many of his friends were near neighbours. Berthold Damcke and his wife Louise were a few doors away at 11 Rue Mansart (where their salon was a gathering place for musicians), Léon Kreutzer lived round the corner in the Rue de Douai, the Massarts at 58 Rue de la Chaussée d'Antin, within walking distance, Gasperini in the Rue St Lazare – streets all belonging to what is now the 9th arrondissement. They saw to his needs, bore with his asperities and indulged his obsessions. It was understood he could drop in any time he liked and join in the talk or else stretch out on the sofa, muddy boots and all (Damcke, though a stickler for order, managed not to say anything), or warm himself silently by the fire. With Stephen Heller, Ritter and the d'Ortigues, they formed a close-knit group and were

* Stephen Heller describes himself and Berlioz walking in silence back to the Rue de Calais after one of the concerts, their heads full of the E minor quartet's adagio and its "sublime prayer", then Berlioz, at his door, seizing Heller's hand and exclaiming: "That man had everything – and we have nothing!"

often in each other's company. Berlioz was free to get up and leave without a word if the conversation bored him. But often there was music – Mme Massart might play a Beethoven sonata or accompany a visiting musician-friend such as Wieniawski – and then there was no talk. When Louis or Félix Marmion were in town he would bring them with him. He took to reading Shakespeare aloud, in French, sometimes whole plays at a time: *Hamlet* and *Coriolanus* chez Massart, *Othello* at the Château de la Muette in Passy, where Spontini's widow and her sister-in-law Mme Erard and the widow of the painter Ary Scheffer lived, all of them "excellent hearts". It became, Heller said, a passion with him. "In general he read well, though often he let himself be carried away by his feelings. At the finest moments tears flowed down his cheeks; but he went on, hastily brushing them aside so as not to interrupt the reading."

From time to time other friends reappeared briefly in his life. In October 1864 Liszt came to Paris, and Berlioz invited him and his daughter Cosima von Bülow to dine at the Café Anglais, with a fourth, "provided he doesn't make an F sharp in our C major chord" (the young Gasperini, "one of the rare critics with brains", was chosen). One evening, at the Café Cardinal, he was hailed by Balfe, and they dined together and afterwards, at the Grand Hôtel where Balfe was staying, smoked a particularly fine cigar and talked and talked of Shakespeare.

The violinist Benoit Hollander, then a boy of twelve who had come to Paris to have lessons with Lambert Massart, met Berlioz at dinner in his teacher's house in 1865.

I can see him now, very aristocratic, like an old émigré. Of medium height, his body was very emaciated. Thin-lipped, with a Roman nose, his long hair was white. It had been a reddish blond colour and he had the white skin of that type. If he had had his hair short he would have resembled a Roman emperor. He wore a black satin tie well up the collar. His trousers were white and black check. They told him who I was. He was very kind and gentle in his manner. I remember as he sat there he made me sit on a footstool and began plaiting my hair (I wore it long) at the back of my head, and talking about Shakespeare. Of course I did not know what it was all about. When he left, he put on a light grey overcoat with a fawn collar. This much impressed me and later on when I had the money I had one made of the same colours.

Occasionally he went further afield, to dine with the Charton-Demeurs at Ville d'Avray, north of Paris. Mme Charton remained devoted to him – a devotion she expressed, among other things, by agreeing to make herself unavailable for the revival of his opera which Carvalho was threatening to put on. In July 1866 he was persuaded to serve on the international jury of a choral-music competition at Louvain in Belgium, and after studying seventy-three anonymous masses and nearly two hundred motets was pleased to find that the winning score was the work of his London friend Eduard Silas.

Essentially, however, his existence was one of "retiréd leisure". He had the trim gardens of the Parc Monceau a half hour's walk from the Rue de Calais, and the Cimetière Montmartre a few hundred yards away. The park was a favourite haunt. "I own a fine garden," he told Pauline Viardot, "which costs me nothing, despite the two or three gardeners who are kept busy constantly tidying it and raking it and varying its adornments." He liked going there very early and enjoying it in the first light of dawn, spending a solitary hour or two drinking in its peace and freshness and richness of colour. "Then at ten – as I am a good prince – I let the public in, and I slip away so as not to overawe them by my presence."

More and more, he was thrown back on his physical symptoms, and on his books, his fears for Louis' safety, his invasive ennui. In the circumstances his health, and with it his spirits, could only worsen. There was not enough to occupy his latent, still vital energies. On the rare occasions when there was – when he was involved in rehearsing Gluck, for instance, or organizing a series of concerts – the transformation was dramatic. Most of the time he lived in his memories, and in the letters he exchanged – with Louis, with the Princess, and with Ferrand, now as ill as he, but who, because he no longer came to Paris as he had in the forties and fifties, wrote much more often and with whom the old shared affection grew stronger still.

To Ferrand he writes, in May 1864: "If we could talk, I feel that sitting by your chair I could make you forget your sufferings. Voice and look have a power that paper lacks. Have you at least flowers and new foliage in front of your windows? I've nothing but walls in front of mine. On the street side of the house a dog has been barking a good hour, a parrot squawks, a parakeet imitates the chirping of sparrows. From the direction of the courtyard the washerwomen are singing and

another parrot calls out incessantly, 'Slope . . . arrrms!'* What is there
to do? The days are so long." In July he closes his *Memoirs* with: "I
say hourly to Death, 'When you will.' What is he waiting for?" In
August he tells the Princess that he is "almost always in bed, my
neuralgia has got worse and has moved to my head. At times I totter
like a drunken man, and I daren't go out alone." He thanks her for her
affectionate sermons and consolations – "When the sound of the bells
has passed one looks up at the sky and sighs and feels calmer for a
moment" – but he is "as incapable of finding a medicine in faith as of
having faith in medicine".† Meanwhile he must tell her, and she will
not be surprised to hear it,

> the population of Paris has been struck by an inexplicable craze. Everyone,
> men, women and children, are shouting at the tops of their voices, in
> the street and the public gardens, on foot, on horseback, in vehicles,
> "Heh! Lambert! Hi! Lambert! Have you seen Lambert?" No one knows
> what it means and everyone is saying it. Last night as late as midnight
> the whole of Paris resounded with "Hi! Lambert!" The craze is con-
> tagious. Now I too want to shout "Hi! Lambert!" It's fun, it's charming.
> Try it – you'll see, it will give you pleasure. I'm told that "Lambert" is
> already all the rage in Le Havre, Rouen and Versailles. The whole of
> France will be saying it. Good God! The human brain is liquefying.

His own was kept active by the renewed correspondence with the
Princess, who challenged him with ideas which, as she perhaps intended,
stirred his old combativeness.

> I confess it saddens me to see how easily you allow the personal to
> influence you in matters of art. You find it natural that we shouldn't
> admire someone who doesn't admire us, and vice versa. That's appalling;
> it represents the negation of art. I can no more not adore a sublime work
> by my worst enemy than not abominate a frightful nonsense by my
> closest friend. I swear that for me it's the truth – because I am an artist,

---

* Elsewhere Berlioz writes of a parrot he had, a large grey bird whose answer to every
question was "cochon".
† Cf. his letter to the Princess of two years earlier: "Like you I have one of the theological
virtues, Charity, but I don't have as you do the other two. The enigma of the world,
the existence of evil and pain, the raving madness of the human race, its stupid savagery
which it sates on the most inoffensive creatures and on itself, reduce me to the hopeless
resignation of the scorpion surrounded by red-hot coals. All I can do is not poison
myself with my own sting."

and whoever doubts it insults me. [. . .] I read lots of travel books, I keep up (why?) with all the doings of the disagreeable insects that infest this great head, the earth. If I wasn't so ill and didn't hate sea-sickness so much, I'd travel, I'd go to Tahiti. There's a small population of charming children there, Nature at its most celestial, a perfect climate, French is spoken (and Kanak, the gentlest of tongues), and they don't make bad music.

One of the great attractions of the correspondence you permit me to carry on with you, Princess, is digression. You let me digress, I'm not required to hold my thoughts or my feelings on a leash. You know so well how to make allowances for the grievous impulses of a poor spirit who spins like a planet that has lost its sun. I've said it before: you are good! Thank you. But when you write to me don't say *flattering* things – I have so little belief in them. When you do it's as if you were humouring me, as one humours halfwits, and that makes me sad. There are passages in my scores where I think I have indeed expressed certain feelings in a wholly exceptional way, but they are precisely those that you know little or not at all. As for my literary style, in so far as I have one, it's that of a writer who searches for the word that will convey what he feels, without ever finding it. I write with too much violence. I want to calm down but can't. This lends the movement of my prose an uneven, lurching gait, like the steps of a drunken man.

When I write to you as I do now I give you as complete a proof as I can of affection and trust, of a childlike lack of reserve. I am at your feet, I listen to my dreams and fall asleep weeping, and I am conscious that you do not laugh at my tears. So I shall not say: Forgive me, excuse me, etc. You have nothing to forgive, I have no excuses to give you . . . because you understand.

"O God! O God! How weary, stale, flat and unprofitable seem to me all the uses of this world!"*

A slight improvement in both health and spirits seems to have occurred that August. Though the Damckes and the Massarts were away and Mme Martin was taking the waters at Luxueil, Louis arrived from Mexico in the first few days of the month and stayed a fortnight. Heller was still in Paris, and the three of them took to dining together on the outskirts, away from the August heat of the city, and walking afterwards

---

* Quoted in English.

in the glow of the evening, enjoying the sight of the swallows as they skimmed low over the shining Seine, and talking of Shakespeare and Beethoven and the worship of great art: it was that, they agreed, that made life, with all its disillusion and heartbreak, worth living. But in the third week Louis returned to St Nazaire and Berlioz returned to his solitude.

Earlier that year his sense of isolation had been intensified by a harrowing episode which seemed in retrospect fated, as though pre-destined to figure as the final mortuary tale in the curious story of his life. He received word that the smaller Montmartre cemetery where Harriet was buried was due to be demolished as part of the extension and modernization of the city. Unlike many lovers of Paris, who disliked what Henry James called "the deadly monotony" of Haussmann's work, with its "miles of architectural commonplace" and "its huge, bleak, pompous, featureless sameness", Berlioz approved of the changes and had no objection to the broad new boulevards and streets which to the Goncourts had "nothing of Balzac's world about them but make one think of London or of some Babylon of the future". It was still his Paris, and it was looking more splendid every day. Unfortunately one of the new streets was set to obliterate the graveyard; Harriet's remains, if he wanted to preserve them, would have to be moved. Not long before, he had had Marie's moved to the larger cemetery where Edouard Alexandre had bought him a plot of ground in perpetuity, and he now arranged for his first wife to be exhumed and reburied with her. On an overcast morning in late winter he walked up the hill to the sloping ground where Harriet's body had been laid ten years before and, from a distance, leaning against the trunk of a cypress tree, watched the gravedigger jump into the grave and wrench off, with a crack, the coffin's rotting lid. The man bent down and took the head, and put it in a temporary coffin beside the grave. Then he gathered what was left of the body, still wrapped in its damp and blackened shroud, and deposited it likewise. The municipal officer in charge called out to Berlioz to come nearer. "And as if the grotesque must also have its part in that grim scene, he added, with a slip of the tongue, 'Ah, poor inhumanity!'" The new coffin was placed on a cart, and the hearse trundled down the hill to where the vault stood ready for it. "The two dead women lie there now in peace, waiting for me to bring my share of corruption to the same charnel-house."

In the meantime he was frequently there. The day Louis left Paris in

August he slept for two hours stretched on a tomb. There was besides, as he told the Princess, a fresh reason for going: the presence of another person who had been dear to him – Amélie.

> My favourite walk, especially when it rains, when the heavens open, is the Montmartre cemetery near where I live. I go there often, I have many connections there. Recently I discovered a grave which I was quite unaware had been opened or closed. She had been dead six months, and no one had thought or been able to tell me she was dying. She was twenty-six years old, she was beautiful, and she wrote like an angel. I, we, had agreed it was wiser to stop seeing, to stop writing to each other, to live totally separate lives. It was an effort. We caught sight of each other in the distance one evening at the theatre – a nod, nothing more. She was already dying, and I didn't know it. Six weeks later she was dead – I didn't know that either. Not till six months later. Enough.

It is possible that the theatre was the Lyrique, and she had come to hear *The Trojans at Carthage*.

In the same letter he spoke of the emptiness of his heart. It was surely the discovery of Amélie's death that precipitated the last act in what Etienne Rey calls "la vie amoureuse de Berlioz". Within a week of his letter to the Princess he had set in train the final return to Estelle.

Even though he may have contemplated it many times since the pilgrimage to Meylan in 1848 after his father's death, I have no doubt that finding the new grave was the catalyst. There was no one left now; they were all dead – Harriet, Adèle, Marie, Amélie. Only Estelle Dubeuf remained – the first, the last. She must end the story, as she had begun it, the "tale told by an idiot, signifying nothing", but which after all would have meaning. She must close the book. His *Memoirs* would have one more chapter.

The strange idyll that Berlioz ventured on in the late summer of 1864, and that forms the epilogue of his autobiography, has excited in some readers a mixture of embarrassment and scorn. "Stupide Roméo", Offenbach noted in the margin of his copy. As a character in one of Jeanette Winterson's novels remarks, "we fear passion and laugh at too much love and those who love too much". If the love is only too clearly the work of the imagination, what more absurd? Yet Berlioz's action is typical in its combination of romance and logic. It was his final return to the past, to his imaginative and creative roots. What more natural? It was she who had shown the way. She had given him his vocation: to be the voice of ideal love, radiant visions, unfulfilled longings, loss. He had completed his task. It was time to render account.

In the first week of September he took the night train to Dauphiné. His nieces and their father were waiting on the station platform at Vienne. He spent most of the next two weeks with them at their country house outside Vienne, at Estressin. By the 21st he was in Grenoble, where he saw various people: his other brother-in-law Camille Pal, his cousin Benjamin Berlioz, priest at the church of St André, and his old friend Auguste who, though no relation, bore the same name.

The fortnight with the Suats was peaceful; but it began the journey back towards lost time when, on seeing Adèle's portrait in the living-room at Vienne on the morning of his arrival, he broke down and wept. To Joséphine and Nancy the loss of their mother four years before was an accepted fact; habit had dulled the pain. To him it was as yesterday. The reawakened memory brought back all she had been for him, her indulgence, her patience with his whims, her loyalty, her unexacting love. It was a preparation for what he was about to face.

Marc Suat made inquiries and discovered Estelle's address in Lyon. As soon as Berlioz had it he hurried to Grenoble and from there to Meylan – for the ritual of return must begin in the kingdom where she had first become known to him; he must trace, more painfully still, the footsteps of sixteen years before and of thirty years before that; he must confront the past, which had his heart in its grip and was tearing it out by the roots as it receded further and further from him. The quest could be disastrous. It would take him down into the depths. But he was committed to it. And at the end there might be a kind of peace.

On the morning of 22 September he climbed the hillside as far as the old tower, saw the rock he had searched for in vain in 1848, stood on it as she had, descended the hill and went into the grounds of the house, with the owner's permission walked round the garden and looked indoors, where the rooms were just as they had been. That evening he was in Lyon. He took a room at the Grand Hôtel but did not sleep. In the morning he wrote a note begging her to grant him a few minutes of her time. His intention had been to present it before his name was announced, in case her first impulse on being shown his card were to refuse to receive him; but when he reached her apartment in the Avenue de Noailles he was so nervous that he forgot, and gave the maid the note and the card together. But she did receive him and he stayed for half an hour. "I saw her," he told the Princess. "Impossible to describe our meeting – what time has done to her, my reconstructing her beauty, her sad dignity, my almost fainting as she held out her hand when I asked." They talked about their lives. She told him she would soon be going to live in Geneva, with one of her sons who was getting married. "I am deeply touched by the feelings you still have for me," she said. He had passed the first ordeal.

Wandering the streets in a turmoil of conflicting thoughts, he ran into Maurice Strakosch, brother-in-law and agent of Adelina Patti. The brilliant young soprano was a favourite of Berlioz's. They had become friends soon after she made her Paris début, at the age of nineteen, in November 1862.* Patti was in Lyon for *The Barber of Seville*. Strakosch extorted a half-promise that Berlioz would dine with them that evening at the Grand, where they were all staying, and offered him a box for the following day. He had been going to leave that night, but here was a heaven-sent pretext for seeing Estelle once more. Would she agree to let him take her to the opera? He rushed back to the Avenue de Noailles. She was out, and he left a message with the maid, and then tormented himself in his hotel room with the thought that she had given orders not to admit him again. In the end, after a further fruitless call at the apartment, he went back a third time and met her coming down the stairs, en route for his hotel with a note to let him know that unfortunately she was not free – she was going to the country the next day. She was putting the note back in her pocket when he almost snatched it from her. He had a letter, written to him in her hand!

The evening with Patti passed like a dream. The bewitching creature made a great fuss of him, kept asking why he was sad ("I won't have you unhappy"), insisted on coming to the station to see him off, and flung her arms round him one last time as the train began to move. The contrast haunted him all the way to Paris.

> What would I not have given for such marks of warmth and affection from Mme F—, and from Mlle Patti the gestures of a conventional politeness! When that delicious Hebe pampered and petted me it was as if a marvellous glittering bird with eyes like diamonds were humming round me, alighting on my shoulder, pecking at my hair and, with a flutter of brilliant wings, whistling me its sweetest, gayest tunes. I was

---

* He was soon happily punning on her name: "*Oportet pati*. The Latinists translate this by 'suffering is our lot', the monks by 'Bring the pâte', the lovers of music by 'We must have Patti'."

enchanted, but not stirred – because this girl, young, beautiful, entrancing, famous, who at twenty-two has conquered the musical public of Europe and America: I do not *love* her; whereas the aged, saddened, obscure woman, who knows nothing of art – my soul is hers, as it once was, as it will be to my dying day.

The return was desolate indeed.

Estelle replied to his first, long, emotional letter with one that (he told her) was "a masterpiece of grim reason". He had asked for the chance to become her friend: to write to her from time to time, to be answered, and to visit her once a year and see her alone, not in company; and, as a first step in their acquaintance and "as a pretext on the author's part for getting you to think of him a little", had sent her his three books. Her reply was not what he had hoped, though he could hardly have expected otherwise. She was touched by his memories and their persistence; but she was now an old woman – too old and too wedded to the emotional seclusion of her life to form a new relationship such as he desired. Did he seriously believe it possible? She scarcely knew him, had no way of judging his "tastes, character, qualities – those things which are the only foundation of friendship. When two people have the same way of feeling and of looking at things, an affinity may spring up between them. But when they are not thus alike, correspondence cannot suffice to bring about the kind of thing you look for from me. For my part, I think it is impossible." She would keep a place for him in her memory, and hear of his doings with pleasure. He could write; but she did not promise to be prompt with her replies. And she could not guarantee to be alone if he came to see her: her son and his wife might well be with her when he called, in which case he would "have to endure their presence, for I would think it highly irregular that it should be otherwise".

The next two weeks were a torment. In a letter that crossed with hers he had suggested paying her another visit in Lyon before she moved to Geneva. There was no response. Twice he begged her to send him her new address. For fourteen long days he was in the depths, as no answer and no address came. "I was born to trouble. Everything is crumbling around me," he told the Princess. "The nights are terrible." Then in the middle of October she wrote. "When I am settled in my new home I will let you have my address. I cannot do so at the moment, I do not know it myself. I would have waited till my son arrived and could tell it me, had I not feared you might misinterpret my long silence." Ten days later, notification of her son's wedding arrived, addressed in her hand. Then, again, silence.

He made inquiries in Lyon and found that she had been gone several weeks. Did she mean after all to conceal her whereabouts? His spirits were at their lowest, when one morning in November, sitting by the fire, he was handed a card, and a moment later Estelle's son, Charles Fornier, and his wife were ushered in. They were in Paris and at *her* behest had called on him.

After the first shock of finding him the living image of Estelle at eighteen, Berlioz rose to the occasion and the conversation took wing. Suzanne Fornier was a Creole from the Dutch East Indies, the favourite region of his boyhood's imaginary travels, which made another link. He saw them several times during their stay, arranged treats for them, and charmed them into accepting him as a friend, until Mme Charles felt free to scold him for the way he wrote to her mother-in-law. "You frighten her," she said. "I can well understand her saying to me sometimes, in a sad voice, as she shows me one of your letters: 'What am I to answer to this?' You must learn to be calmer, then your visits to Geneva will be delightful and we shall have a lovely time doing you the honours of the town. You will come, won't you?"

Little by little the relationship Estelle had recoiled from took root and grew. She began to feel interested in spite of herself, flattered, intrigued. While he strove to restrain himself, the tone of her letters relaxed and became friendlier, at times quite playful. He sensed – he told the Princess – that though she had no active recollection, and thought it mostly imagination on his part, "the other" – the boy who had fallen in love with her fifty years before – was beginning to influence her without her realizing it. He took the opportunity of the coming Conservatoire concert at which Act 4 of *The Trojans* was to be performed to send her a copy of the libretto, marked at the right place by some oak leaves from the hill above Meylan. In the event the committee asked for so many cuts that he withdrew it and there was no performance. But Estelle had agreed to be there in spirit, and he responded with his longest and most outgoing letter. Within a week she had answered it.

You must not think I have no compassion for "unreasonable children". I always found that the best way to quiet them and make them sensible was to distract their attention by giving them pictures to look at. I am taking the liberty of sending you one. It will serve to remind you of present realities and to destroy the illusions of the past.

Yet you feel that she did not altogether mean it, and that (as he told the Princess) she might even be beginning to say to herself in the secret recesses of her heart: "It would be a pity not to have been loved like that." When he told her about his *Memoirs* she urged him to complete the book and publish it. "I am a real daughter of Eve and I should love to read your life before I die."

He had come a long way in only five months.

The *Memoirs* were completed on New Year's Day 1865. By then he had his final chapter. It brought the book full circle. "Already I am conscious that my life has changed for the better. The past is not wholly and irrevocably past. My sky is blank no longer. Through tears I look towards my star – distant but bright, soft, seeming to smile on me from afar. True, she does not love me. Why should she? But she might have remained for ever oblivious of me, and she knows that I adore her."

The relationship deepened in the months that followed, especially after the first of his visits to Geneva. He began to write to her with something of the freedom and liveliness that close friends like the Damckes or the Massarts inspired in him.

First of all, don't imagine I'm writing to you in order to prompt a reply. Truly, that's not it; it's simply that this evening I feel an irresistible desire to talk with you a little. You are not to write to me any sooner because of it – otherwise I shouldn't dream of yielding to the imperious need of sending you the smallest note, no matter how laconic. All you have to do is read me, and then tell me once again: "This child is unreasonable."

As I told you the other day, you're my millions, and miser that I am I can't prevent myself from counting them up. What a misfortune for me that you don't know music: I could send you some of the speaking phrases that your memory dictated to me, many years ago, at a time when you were certainly far from thinking of me.

What are you up to in Geneva? I can see you from here, silently embroidering in your little drawing-room. Madame Suzanne rocks the baby in her arms, M. Charles is playing chess with that pretty, spirited girl whose name I forget. Then some visitors arrive, wanted or not, tea is brought in and conversation begins: "I hear the cholera in Paris is over." – "Yes, but it's broken out at the foot of the Alps. You heard about the panic among the workmen who are digging the Mont Cenis tunnel? Luckily we haven't got it in Geneva." "No, God be praised." – "That was a splendid letter the Emperor wrote to the Duke of Magenta about Algiers. Now there's a monarch who works all right, and who knows his job." Or maybe quite the opposite is said, depending on your visitors' political opinions.

But forgive me, it looks as if I'm *criticizing* the conversation in your drawing-room. It's an inveterate habit – like freed convicts who drag their left leg as if the chain were still attached to it. That alone would be enough to identify me as someone escaped from the hulks – and I hardly deserved them! Justice is often very unjust.

Talking of chains, my son in his turn still wears his aboard the *Nouveau Monde*. He left the day before yesterday for Mexico, carrying eight hundred men, the fine flower of the riff-raff of Europe, who are on their way to get themselves killed. There's some good in the Emperor Maximilian: he's ridding us of a lot of rascals.

Sorry – my left leg is playing up again.

All my friends are now back in Paris. None the less my evenings are terribly monotonous. For almost three years now we've been going round and round the same topics. Our stories have become musty, our arguments moth-eaten, our enthusiasms threadbare. Yesterday, at my neighbour D[amcke]'s, I pointed out that we had just said the same thing for the eleventh time. "It's you who are always repeating the same thing," he said. I replied by quoting Molière: "Gad, sir, I'm always saying the same thing because you're always saying the same thing to me. If you didn't always say the same thing I wouldn't always say the same thing."

Still, it's sad. Oh, if you were there! Well – I should "always say the same thing" to you too.

What a driveller I am. And yet I'm not like the Englishman who cuts his throat so as not to suffer the boredom of seeing the sun rise every morning in the same place. On the contrary, I could wish my sun were fixed on the horizon; I should never tire of watching it.

Farewell, dear Madam, farewell. Good night!

Only occasionally did he lose heart ("I tire you with my adoration, which you tolerate only out of kindness") or she have to chide him for going too far. He delighted both in her replies and, almost more, in having her to write to. "Oh what a happy evening spent here by the fire," one letter ends. "My pain is almost gone. You have lifted a mountain of affliction from me." It was an unbelievable happiness –

"as if Virgil, Shakespeare, and Gluck and Beethoven returned to this world, all four of them, to say, 'You understood us and loved us. Come here so that we may bless you!'" He might have died without seeing her again, without ever having been able to open his heart to her.

There were even moments when he thought of composing her a great orchestral poem (just as he had dreamed in boyhood of writing an opera in her honour):

> But it wouldn't be worthy of its subject. My physical sufferings would paralyse me, and I don't want to risk writing a mediocre work. And then you wouldn't hear it; it would remain a closed book for you. Madness! It's too late. Besides, many passages in my old works, in *Harold in Italy* and the Fantastic Symphony, were in reality dictated by my memories of the star, the soft blue star that illumined the morning of my life. I should repeat myself – and God preserve me from such musical ramblings. Singing to *you* I would have to be totally inspired. And then, music lives by contrast, and I can see none possible in a musical epic inspired by such a muse. You have never done me harm, nor did I experience the slightest bitterness of heart on your account. And when I had sung in every tone and with every inflection imaginable my boundless adoration and enthusiasm for the Stella, and painted in the most vivid colours that part of the sky where she shone, and the splendid landscape graced by your footsteps and lit up by your eyes (to quote La Fontaine), I could only begin again, and so on for ever.

He would like one day to be "immensely famous and admired, so as to make you dear to my admirers. Oh, you will be dear to the Germans especially: in their country they still live the life of the spirit."

Mostly he sent her a letter once a month, as he had promised; but sometimes he could not resist writing ahead of time: the act of writing made her for the moment a larger part of his existence. His letters kept her up to date with his doings as well as with his thoughts: the long process of proof-reading and correcting the *Memoirs*, which were finally printed in July, for posthumous publication; his Monday evening soirées at the Tuileries; his fluctuating health; reports of his music from abroad; the stir made by the *Francs-juges* overture at one of Pasdeloup's concerts in the Cirque Napoléon, cheered by everyone in the vast auditorium except his three faithful booers; the telegram from Vienna announcing that the Männergesangverein had performed the soldiers' and students' chorus from the *Damnation* on his sixty-first birthday; Carvalho's attempt to revive *The Trojans at Carthage*, "a fresh butchery" which "I shall oppose with all my strength"; and details of his everyday life.

In mid-August 1865 came the long-planned visit. He travelled to Geneva, arriving on the 18th and putting up at the Metropole, by the lake. Estelle had already received, two weeks before, a bound copy of the *Memoirs* with – as bookmark – a ribbon attached to a flake of granite chipped by him, the year before, from the rock where once he had seen her stand looking down into the valley, in the days of her beauty.

It was their first meeting since the encounter in Lyon the previous September – since the first tentative flowering of the relationship-by-correspondence which she had declared impossible. At once he felt miraculously better. His "cher médecin" had wrought a wonderful cure. "My visit to Mme F.," he told Louis, "has done me an immense amount of good. This morning, at the time when the pains usually arrive they found the door shut." From the first he was received like one of the family. It seemed everyone had looked at the *Memoirs* and read the passages about Estelle – and they did not mind, they were pleased. His photograph, which he had feared would have been shoved in a drawer, was on display in the living-room. If, to begin with, Estelle, not surprisingly, was constrained with him, encouraged by her daughter-in-law she grew less timid and more at ease. Mme Charles – Suzanne – had just presented her with a granddaughter. Berlioz was invited to the christening, and gave the baby "a two-minute music lesson". He was there for hours at a time and was scolded when he didn't come – his hotel was only a step from the Quai des Eaux-Vives where the Forniers lived, and they wanted him with them. The youngest son arrived, and they all went for walks by the lake and drives further afield. At first Berlioz chafed terribly at not being able to see Estelle by herself, even while he told himself how unjust he was and how stupid his "senseless struggle against the impossible". In the end, whether by accident or design, they found themselves alone together long enough for the conversation to develop along lines which she, if not he, cannot have wished – as the letter he wrote a few days later in Vienne makes clear:

> My dear doctor,
> This time you have ventured into the field of surgery and have carried out an operation which, unhappily, succeeded. You have eradicated for

ever a notion which I had not even expressed but which you must have
guessed. During the operation you looked stern and displeased. Yet I
was not to blame if the chaste ambition of spending the rest of my days
with you stole into my heart. It was because of the intoxication of your
presence. I am not yet used to seeing you; and I thought ahead to the
grievous moment of saying goodbye: it made me lose my head. But it's
at an end. Reread the final pages of my *Memoirs* – you will see that my
most cherished hopes had long been confined within the bounds which
you yourself laid down the other day: in your own words, to see you
from time to time, correspond with you a little, maintain your interest,
your goodwill – that's all. I shall not stray beyond the circle. Two or
three times a year I shall come and adore you in person, see you for
twenty-four hours, hear your voice, breathe your air; then I shall hasten
back to Paris, proud and happy as a bee returning with its spoils and,
unlike the bee, full of tender gratitude.

On balance, though his intestinal neuralgia resumed in full force, the
visit could be accounted a success. He was a friend of the family; his
obsession, which might have been regarded as an intolerable intrusion,
was accepted; he had established the right to address her, for the first
time, as his *chère amie* – all this in a year. His act of faith – what Barzun
calls the "pragmatic testing of his love-illusion" – had justified itself.
He might have found a dull old woman devoid of distinction. But she
was no lifeless icon. She had a mind and spirit, and a power of expression,
of her own: qualities that are evident from the few of her letters which
survive – those that had been safely printed in the *Memoirs* before she
insisted on his burning the rest. These qualities, of course, only made
him regret more passionately that he had not known her earlier. He
continued to long for so much more than he could have. But what he
had could easily not have been his at all. And even at its most heartbreaking (he told the Princess), it was a pain he needed: "I have no other
interest in my life." It gave what was left a kind of vindication, and a
reason for still loving.

27

Louis

There was one other interest: Louis. Berlioz's love for his son had survived the periods of estrangement, the feelings of anger and guilt on both sides, the recurring parental anxieties fed by the young man's impulsive character and spendthrift ways, and had grown stronger; and it was matched on Louis' part by an ever-deepening adoration of his father. By the mid-1860s they had become very close.

Berlioz could still be irascible with him. As late as June 1865, when Louis confided his momentary hesitations at the prospect of being promoted captain and the burden of responsibility it would bring, his father responded with a testy, uncomprehending letter full of irrelevant references to his own career; he appeared to think Louis was asking for money. Louis, shocked and wounded, tore up four different answers before sending a placatory but firmly argued reply which ended: "Rest assured that I am *not waiting for you to die!*"

That was a rare discord, however, attributable perhaps to the irritability of a chronically sick man on a bad day. Little by little Berlioz's worries about his son diminished until they were concentrated on fear for his safety in the Gulf of Mexico, where his duties took him for part of each year.

Louis' abilities, his mastery of his job, were no longer in doubt. Depressive though he might often be, given to extreme swings of mood and moments of self-disgust, naturally solitary yet chafing at his single state and his want of a settled home, he was clearly – his father was delighted to acknowledge – a brilliant sailor, regarded very highly by the Compagnie Générale Transatlantique for which he worked: a cool hand in a crisis, a skilled and dedicated officer who ran an efficient ship and took an exemplary pride in his work.

The admiration between father and son was mutual. One of the things which had brought them together was that Louis had come to know and love his father's music, first by hearing *Beatrice and Benedick* in Baden and then by being actively present throughout the seven-week run of *The Trojans at Carthage* and living the bitter-sweet experience at his side. Everything had become much clearer. He could now better understand his father, put his life in context and enter into his enthusiasms and disappointments with all the indignant ardour of his own exalted nature. There were, he recognized, deep affinities between them. Increasingly he looked at the world through his father's eyes and rejoiced and suffered with him. From St Nazaire, where the company was based and where he lived when not at sea, he followed the doings of his great but misunderstood creator, as reported in the newspapers or as his letters recounted them.

Thus he revelled in an article by Reyer in the *Moniteur* which spoke in glowing terms of *Beatrice* (and criticized Wagner for his "corrections" to Beethoven's Fifth Symphony), and in one by Gasperini, a stinging attack on the Conservatoire for its disapproving attitude to his father's music. He quoted with relish how a critic called Jonas had "crushed the memory of Scudo" and his dismissal of *The Trojans*: when one had spent one's life as that man had, Jonas observed, one could not expect any mercy after one's death (Scudo had recently died, shortly after being certified insane). And he was roused to rage by the enormous success of *Roland à Roncevaux*, a five-act opera by the amateur composer Auguste Mermet, son of an officer in the Grande Armée. Napoleon III had given the work his blessing. Mermet, received by the Emperor in his box, was the object of universal wonderment for having written the words as well as the music – as if *The Trojans* and its poet-composer had never existed!

Above all, the fate of that great work haunted Louis. He railed against the "gangrenous" society that had rejected it. "Oh! I would sacrifice ten years of my youth to have *The Trojans* put on complete and fittingly at a rejuvenated Opéra and given fifty performances. After that, things could happen as they would. Once the work was understood it would be taken up with tears and rapture. But no – never, never, never . . . no tenor, no leading lady, no intelligent chorus, only a splendid orchestra (poor M. Desmarest!), and no money." A few months later: "Alexis writes enthusiastically of Pasdeloup's concert [at which the Septet was performed]. It revives our dreams: a superb orchestra, a theatre given over to you, masterpieces worthily represented, the intelligent world electrified, the base multitude banished from the temples of art." Writing in his cabin on the *Louisiana* going to the Antilles and recalling his recent reading of *A travers chants*, he regretted "not knowing the masterpieces that you admire, the Choral Symphony, *Alceste* and so many others". How happy he was to share his father's opinions on "the daubers of art" and his sadness at the spectacle of all those worshippers of the Golden Calf. "Like Christ, only more harshly, you have chastised the temple moneylenders, though unlike him you have not been able to drive out more than a few. But the day will come when justice is done, and then they will say: 'He was a man, we shall not look upon his like again.'" On another occasion he reread the eleventh and twelfth books of the *Aeneid*, then went back to Book 4 and, "stirred to the depths of my being", got out the score of *The Trojans*. After that, sleep was impossible.

> I spent the night in extravagant fantasies: I restored the great opera, I found outstanding artists, I had the work put on under your direction, then little by little I saw the audience moved to tears. You were understood . . . you triumphed.
>
> When I reach that state, I need to be alone; the sailor ceases to exist. And I must have the open air and the spectacle of nature. Yesterday I went in search of both. I jumped fences and climbed along the cliffs, risking my neck, browsed on ripe blackberries and rolled on the grass, free and alone. The expedition did me so much good that I intend to set off tomorrow morning, taking with me the first volume of Shakespeare. Dressed like a huntsman I shall roam far and wide, eat at farms, sleep on clean straw and, in sight of the sea, breathe from the cliff-tops the great sky and the great poetry of Shakespeare, weep tears to my heart's content, and return the following evening exhausted but having lived.

Both in his love of walking and in his cult of Shakespeare Louis was his father's son. At first all he had was *Othello* translated by "a noisome night-soil man who has prudently chosen to remain anonymous". In time he acquired all the plays, in Guizot's translation, and buried himself in them when his duties allowed. Sometimes it was too much. "To say my prayers every night, that is, to open a work by Shakespeare – I can't any more. To be uplifted to such a height, only to fall head first into the mire of material concerns, deprives one's mind of the strength one requires to do one's job." He "defied any intelligent man, even if he knew the complete works of Shakespeare by heart, in English and French, not to feel a strange thrill on starting to read one of them".

Reading *Henry IV, Part 1*, he was struck by "the passage, very powerful for me, where the king reproaches his son. You too have had the same fears, and have had to reproach me, you too have suffered from the heedless, rash, violent, exasperated character of your adored son. As for me, I know now what Henry V felt, but unlike him I have no power or ambition to leave my rut and like a meteor astonish the world, which means so little to me – though I should like to astonish my father!"

He became a voracious reader, like his father. At various times, in addition to Shakespeare, we hear of Goethe's *Hermann and Dorothea*, Victor Hugo's *La Légende des siècles*, the Greek classics, Chateaubriand's translation of *Paradise Lost*, Jules Verne's *Voyage to the Centre of the Earth*, Louis Figuier's *La Terre et les mers*, Nadar's *The Right of Theft*, and *Faust*. *Hamlet* he had read so often that he knew it practically by heart. When his favourite books were at the binder's he felt bereft – and correspondingly restored when they came back.

It's midnight. I've been eating like a wolf. Everything I had left over this evening has been devoured, in company with half a pound of bread. My friends are back: Aeschylus, Sophocles, Euripides, Aristophanes, Shakespeare, nicely bound, are here. I can see them; it seems to me they're looking at me. Tomorrow I shall meet them again.

If you come, bring *Faust* in the translation by Gérard de Nerval.

Good night. Till tomorrow.

*Nuit splendide et sereine**

I love you.

It's one in the morning. The moon's rising, I'm going to bed. The ships, those great skeletons, are at rest. Only the seamen, their masters, yell and vomit beneath my windows, lurching and falling over. Now they're singing *The Sapper*. I'm tempted to get dressed and go and sleep on the beach.

The contrast between his secret inner life and the banal existence of a sailor in port drove him to distraction. If only (he cried) he could see a few performances of *Don Giovanni* or of a Shakespeare play (his father had recently been doing both), it might set him up again. Instead:

Yesterday evening I asked the ship's library clerk if he had Goethe's *Faust* on board. After pronouncing it "Goethe" I thought the poor chap

---

* From the Duo-Nocturne in *Beatrice and Benedick*.

mightn't understand, so I said "*Faust* by Go-eth". While this was going
on the officer of the watch, who was passing, joined in, and assured me
that he hadn't granted shore leave to those two sailors. "Which sailors?",
I said. – "Faust and Goeth." – "Merde!" – "I beg your pardon, sir?"

Yet, though he hated the squalor, the petty jealousies, the constant
jockeying for position, the money-grubbing mentality of the bosses who
gambled with sailors' lives and the philistinism of so many of those he
consorted with, which made him long to have cultivated people to talk
to, he loved his work. He loved "playing with this immense machine,
this *city* called a ship"; he loved seeing to everything, directing everything
and making it function smoothly. Above all,

> I adore the sea, the naval existence, the grandeur of this life of action
> which pits me against the elements so that I conquer them, or at least
> am not conquered by them. When everything is in turmoil, I breathe, I
> admire, I am afraid, I hope, and I take hold of my world, which is my
> entire world, I do battle, and I admire the horror – but the grand,
> awe-inspiring horror of it all, the horror of the second Walpurgis Night
> of Goethe.
>
> Till we meet again.
>
> L. Berlioz
>
> Father, I love you.

As he gained in confidence and authority, the balance of their relationship shifted. Berlioz was conscious of it. "Louis and I have become like
brothers," he told his niece Mathilde, "and it's he that is the older
brother." It was now Louis who fretted protectively over his father's
well-being: who said he was not to be alarmed if he heard his ship was
lost but should wait patiently, since false rumours were always going
round; who dissuaded him from sending money, as he had plenty of
his own – "I would be easier in my mind if I could be sure you took a
cab whenever you need one, and didn't go short of anything in the
house" – and begged him not to economize with an eye to his son's
future, for "who knows which of us will survive the other? If it is to
be I, why not make use of the time that is left us on this earth for loving
one another?"; who sent regular sums to Paris for his father to invest
for him; and invited him to come and stay in St Nazaire: he'd fetch him
from Nantes and instal him in

> a nice warm room. We'll eat together, alone, like two friends. You'll

come on board. Ah, but to come on board *my* ship one must wade through mud above the ankles. Do you have a good pair of boots that you can tuck your trousers in? We'll walk on the beach, you'll see our little ocean trying to work itself up into a fury, and laugh with me at the wavelets as they rage. We'll be happy in each other's company, you'll forget your ennuis and I my fatigue. You'll come with me when I have to go on board to give orders, you'll see something of your sailor son whom you don't know, carrying out his functions.

A few days later he wrote to say that there was a room with a comfortable bed waiting for him, and the kind of food he liked, "and my grandfather's hooded cloak to put on when you come on board".

The visit took place at the beginning of April 1865. Berlioz was taken violently ill in the train at Nantes and spent the first three days in bed; but he rallied, and the rest of the stay passed well enough. He dined with Louis' commander M. de Valency and his wife, and made his son prouder than ever. "Everyone here is talking of you," Louis wrote, a few days after his father's departure. " 'What a handsome, noble head he has'; and the captain adds, 'M. Berlioz can certainly not disown his son.' Apparently I grow more like you the older I get."

Theirs was not a simple relationship, however. With such a history, and given their natures, it hardly could be. Louis, taciturn, expressing himself face to face with difficulty, could be tongue-tied in his father's presence. In the north Atlantic, driving before the gale, he might dream of their spending their lives side by side "between sky and sea", in the mutual worship of Nature. "Your character is young, your heart is young, your body is not old"; on board a yacht commanded by his son, his friend, free to go where he wished, Berlioz would forget his troubles. But when they were together, in the flesh, Louis recognized that it would not work. There was a magnetic current running from one to the other which galvanized but which could also oppress. When it did, he had to go out; he had to get away and breathe a different air, a different world of ideas. Often he was conscious of constraints, of his inability to voice his thoughts and put into words the intensity of his love.

In a sense there was no need to, for either of them. They knew it. But in his letters Louis gave his adoration full scope. His father was the centre of his universe. When on shore, he would write two or three times a week – and wish he had time to write more often. "I love you so much that I fret every day I can't write and tell you so." When he wasn't writing he was in imagination talking to him. "If you could read what I say to you, every day, every night, you would see that I think of nothing without speaking to you about it, without asking your advice." There was "no circumstance, happy or miserable" in which he did not call him to witness. He had had "many mistresses, many friends, and one real friend, Alexis – but writing those words has never brought tears to my eyes". With his father it was different. Their two existences were the strands of one rope: "if one strand breaks, the other will too; neither of them can exist without the other, for they form a single whole". "I don't know what they mean by worshipping God; but *they* don't know what I mean by loving my father!"

His tenderness flowed out to embrace him.

> Poor father! I now feel something of the turmoil of your heart, I understand you, for I know the power of memory. You are alone now, you revisit your past, all that you loved reappears, your heart, still young, is on fire within you, you can make no one understand what you are going through. I alone could be your confidant, to me alone, your beloved brother, your friend, your adored son, you could impart a little of that fire which consumes you, I am at your side – but I am thousands of miles away. Oh the horror, the fatality, the injustice of it!

About three times a year Louis came to Paris on leave and stayed a few weeks. His bed was kept ready for him in the study and he was welcomed with open arms. They walked in the Parc Monceau, or sat on a bench talking of Shakespeare, went to the theatre, spent evenings with the Damckes and the Massarts, where Louis heard Ritter play the Love Scene from *Romeo and Juliet*. He was in Paris in February and March 1866 and again in late July and early August, when Berlioz no doubt had the pleasure of taking him to a rehearsal or two of *Alceste* – the Opéra had engaged him to supervise a revival – and of introducing him to the sublimities of the work, which Louis had regretted not knowing.

More often, Louis missed the few remaining red-letter days of his father's public existence, and experienced them only vicariously. In March 1866 he had to leave Paris just before Pasdeloup conducted the *Trojans* Septet in the Cirque Napoléon, with thrilling success. He felt his absence keenly. "So I shall never be with you at one of those moments which soothe your wounds a little, never be able to embrace you then, with tears, and show you how much I love and admire and venerate you. I was there in the opera house, but alas! what an opera house, what a butchery, what a mutilation of your lofty thoughts!"

The performance of the Septet, on 7 March 1866, gave Berlioz his last triumph in the Paris concert hall. Prices were tripled – it was a charity event – but the hall was packed. Pasdeloup had engaged Charton-Demeur to sing Dido. No one sent Berlioz a ticket, so he paid his 3 francs for a seat high up to one side of the vast arena. The Septet was encored with roars, and caused an even greater sensation the second time. It was, Massougnes recalled, "a tempest of bravos such as I never heard in my life". Then someone spotted the composer, the word spread, and the entire audience rose, pointing to him, waving hats and scarves, shouting "Vive Berlioz!" and, when he tried to hide, "Stand up, we want to see you!" Those near him grasped his hand and thanked him. Outside, well-wishers crowded round. Admirers called at the Rue de Calais to congratulate him; and a group of music-lovers sent a collective letter, adapting the one in *Evenings in the Orchestra* which Berlioz had written to Spontini after a performance of *Fernand Cortez*, beginning: "Dear Master, your work is noble and beautiful, but artists capable of appreciating its magnificence perhaps have a duty to tell you so. Whatever your present disappointments, you will easily forget them in the consciousness of your genius and the inestimable value of what it has achieved."

This year, 1866, was the last in which Berlioz was involved at all actively in the musical life of Paris. In January, with Saint-Saëns' help – "a first-rate musician who knows his Gluck almost as well as I do" – he coached Mme Charton in the great role of Armide for a production at the Théâtre-Lyrique. The project was abandoned, partly because the company was short of money, partly because the Opéra directors grudged Carvalho another success with Gluck and, having some vague idea of doing it themselves, put ministerial pressure on him to relinquish it; but while the daily rehearsals lasted Berlioz was a changed being. "Can you believe it," he wrote to Ferrand, "since I've been immersed in music again my pains have gradually disappeared. I get up every morning just like the rest of the world. [. . .] This morning, in the Hatred Scene, Saint-Saëns and I clasped hands. We could hardly breathe. No man has ever found such accents."

Presumably he was paid for the work on *Armide*. In any case he was better off than before. In January his librarian's salary was doubled.

(Three months later he succeeded to the post of Curator of the Conservatoire Museum left vacant by Clapisson's death, though not to the stipend, which reverted to Clapisson's widow.) That spring, too, a buyer was found for the farm at Murianette, above the Isère valley, which he had inherited from his father and which till then had been let at an uneconomically low rent.

Liszt was in the audience at the Pasdeloup concert. From his perch in the amphitheatre Berlioz caught sight of him in his black abbé's soutane – Liszt had taken minor orders the previous summer. Although Berlioz had hastened to assure the Princess that he would not dream of mocking him for it, this new incarnation was another stumbling-block to add to their musico-political disagreements. And though Liszt was happy to applaud the Septet – it was the first time he had heard any of his friend's magnum opus – Berlioz was unable to reciprocate when Liszt's Graner Mass was performed at St Eustache a week later. "An immense crowd was there," he told Ferrand. "But alas, what a negation of art." There are passages in this work of the Weimar years, recently revised, that he might have been expected to admire; but by now he was caught in the same kind of ideological bind that he had himself deplored in the more dogmatic futurists ten years before.

The Lisztian and Wagnerian literature still berates Berlioz for "refusing to review the performance" of Liszt's mass and "handing his column over to d'Ortigue to do it for him" – this when it was two full years since he had retired from criticism and the column had become d'Ortigue's. (As Berlioz might have said, that was how history was written.) What is true is that, at Liszt's request, their mutual friend Léon Kreutzer invited him and Berlioz, with d'Ortigue and Damcke, to an informal discussion at his house in the Rue de Douai, and Liszt talked and played for an hour, seeking to clear himself of the charge that his music subverted harmonic, rhythmic and melodic order and good sense. "I treated him with all the respectful consideration I owe him," wrote Liszt to the Princess. "I fancy that hour of friendly chat did not diminish the good opinion he perhaps has of my modest musical savoir faire. Naturally we spoke of you – and on that subject we will always be in agreement!" Berlioz does not seem to have been convinced by Liszt's exposition; but the two men were destined to conclude their long friendship on a less contentious note. The same evening, they were both at the apartment of the Princess's friend Mme de Blocqueville, Marshal Davout's daughter, on the Quai Voltaire. "Berlioz brightened up towards the end of dinner, apropos of Shakespeare. The conversation kept going most agreeably and at a lively and interesting level." It was the last time they saw each other.

Berlioz might feel benevolently disposed towards some of the younger composers like Reyer, Massenet, Bourgault-Ducoudray, Adolphe Samuel, the Dane Asger Hamerik and Saint-Saëns (whose gifts he greatly admired, though the young man was almost too precocious: "he lacks inexperience"). But he was happiest with the past: with *Don Giovanni*, a score massacred at the Italiens and the Opéra but which was being done quite respectably at the Lyrique, and with *Hamlet* and *Othello*, given far from inspiringly in Italian at the Théâtre-Italien by a company from Milan but with an actor of genius, Rossi, in the name parts. Berlioz went more than once to both plays, and attended eight consecutive performances of Mozart's opera.

That spring too, after urging the cause of Gounod as the worthiest successor to Clapisson's *fauteuil* at the Academy, he had the satisfaction of seeing him elected on the first ballot – a vote denounced in scabrous terms by Azevedo, who had backed his protégé Félicien David to win.*

If Berlioz still had a part to play, it was mostly on the fringes. In July (as mentioned in the previous chapter) he went to Louvain in Belgium for a few days, with Saint-Saëns, d'Ortigue and the St Eustache organist Batiste, to serve on the jury of the international choral-music competition. And in August, after Louis left, he travelled to Epernay in Champagne to preside over a gathering of local choral societies. What induced him to is obscure: he had to listen to them (he told Mme Massart) "yelling their heads off for seven hours by the clock". But he seems to have enjoyed himself; and perhaps he was well paid for his pains. The deputy mayor was a millionaire. He insisted on having Berlioz to stay in his brand new mansion, built on a wooded hill outside the town and surrounded by spacious gardens, and came in person to meet him at the station in a carriage drawn by two superb horses. The man had seven children. "When I heard it, I drew a singular portrait of their mother. I imagined a real fright – ungainly, gone to fat, blotchy complexion. Not a bit of it! She's charming, with a figure slim and straight as an English needle; pretty eyes, full of sparkle; natural; cool and composed but not cold; not too devout – on friendly but not

* "On the pediment of the Temple of Art is written in letters of gold the name F. D. On the steps below is dumped an excrement called Gounod."

compromising terms with the Good Lord; doesn't spoil her children; dresses well, with none of the usual provincial ideas. To think that a man can get all that – wife, children, house, millions – by selling champagne!''

In mid-September he spent three days in Geneva seeing Estelle, who was now living a mile from the lake, at Les Délices, Voltaire's villa (she had the room that had been his library). The visit, originally planned for August, had been put off because of some unnamed crisis in her life. What passed between them this time is not known. We have only a list of the expenses of the journey, in his hand, showing that he stayed as before at the Hôtel Metropole, had a haircut and shave, bought a pair of gloves and a book, and dined in Mâcon on the way back to Paris. The list includes the cost of a cab to the Forniers' house, but none back to his hotel: for the return journey and on other occasions he must have been conveyed by Charles Fornier. Presumably they discussed Estelle's unhappy son Auguste, who was living a precarious, debt-ridden existence in Paris and who had several times borrowed money from Berlioz. There is a gap in the surviving correspondence for the seven months following the visit. But it is clear that, as before, she continued to be central to his life. When Legouvé saw him home after the dinner given by Gounod to celebrate his election to the Academy in May of that year, Berlioz's talk as they walked the deserted streets had been all of Estelle. In December he spoke to Cornelius at length about her. Six months later, when disaster struck, it was she that he turned to first.

The trip to Geneva had to be squeezed into three days, and a projected detour to Vienne abandoned, because he was needed in Paris. Once more there was Gluck to lift him above his physical sufferings, this time at the Opéra of all places. The management had been coasting on the success of *L'Africaine*, which was still filling the house. But now it roused itself to put on *Alceste* again, and Berlioz was again asked to supervise. At intervals that summer and autumn he attended the chorus and orchestra rehearsals and coached the singers, infusing them with the spirit of the great score (and at one point bribing Alceste's two children not to smile as they embraced their stricken mother, by promising each of them a box of sweets). His labours revived him as nothing else could. "How beautiful it is, how beautiful," he exclaimed to Mme Massart. "The other day, at the first stage rehearsal, we all wept like stags at bay." After a day of rehearsing he would lie awake much of the night, his head full of the music's sublimities. It was hard going, and for a while he despaired of the feebleness of the conductor, his friend Hainl (who "knows nothing, feels nothing, and understands nothing"). Gradually it took fire. At times the soprano Marie Battu was transformed from a rather ordinary singer into something like a tragedienne (so that after one performance he was moved to write in her album: "Hail Mary, full of grace, but also full of nobility, force, tenderness and passion"). Though Berlioz was not officially in charge, it was recognized – by Joachim, by Ingres and other colleagues at the Institute, by Fétis himself – whose hand lay behind it. Perrin talked of following *Alceste* with *Armide*.

This was Second Empire Paris, however. Unlike *L'Africaine*, unlike Mermet's *Roland à Roncevaux*, *Alceste* failed to take. After eight performances it was cut down to two acts, sharing the bill with a ballet, and the *Armide* project was dropped. Like other things in Berlioz's career, his campaigning for Gluck would come to its greatest fruition after his death, with the publication of the edition of Gluck's main operas – the two *Iphigénies*, *Alceste*, *Armide* and *Orphée* – which his constant urging inspired and which was brought into being by Damcke, and later by Saint-Saëns, with the backing of the wealthy Fanny Pelletan.

For the moment, his work on *Alceste* gained him 1,206 francs and the joy of introducing the work to a new generation of musicians and music-lovers and, in addition, the curious blessing of a public fan letter from his one-time enemy Fétis. Berlioz, Fétis said, had "penetrated deeply into the great composer's mind"; such an interpretation bespoke "not only a great musician but a poet and philosopher as well". Berlioz's reply (also published in the press) was only lightly touched with irony: "If anything could restore the courage that I no longer need, it would be approval such as yours. But in the small band that fights – *nullam sperante salutem* – against the Myrmidons, you are still a spear while I am now only a buckler." This drew a response full of friendly chiding. What was all this talk of spears and bucklers, and courage no longer needed? "You are twenty years younger than I. Unhappily, I know, you do not enjoy the robust health that God has given me; but you have strength of spirit, and it has only to be reawakened. The author of *The Childhood of Christ* cannot condemn himself to silence." To work for the good of art helped one forget the decadence of these melancholy times. "Revive your courage, dear M. Berlioz, and take up your pen again. One cannot live in the void – and, for a choice spirit, discouragement and inaction are tantamount to it."

Others too did their best to persuade him that composition was what he needed; but he would not hear of it. After *Alceste*, discouragement took possession once more, together with the full force of his bodily ills which the experience of working on the marvellous score had relieved. When someone urged him to protest at the exclusion of Spontini from the composers represented on the façade of Garnier's projected new Opéra, he could only reply that it was symptomatic of the age they lived in and there was nothing to be done. Heller, writing to Charles Hallé that autumn, described him as "quite broken, worn out and fretting all the time, poor man. You would hardly know him for the old Hector – so spirited, such a fighter, cleaving his adversaries, and sometimes windmills too, in twain."

His sadness and sense of isolation were intensified by the sudden death, in November, from a stroke, of Joseph d'Ortigue, his friend of over thirty years. It made Paris seem more than ever a desert. D'Ortigue had been the first to champion his music, had been among his most intelligent and even-handed critics, had argued the case for him in two books published in the 1830s, and to the end continued to press his claims. One of his last articles in the *Débats* called on the government to commission from Berlioz a ceremonial work on the lines of the 1840 symphony for the opening of next year's exhibition: it would be a masterpiece, and it would recall the long-silent composer to his art, perhaps even to good health. But with d'Ortigue's death any faint hope of that had gone.

Conducting was an activity that he could still, just, contemplate. He turned down invitations from St Petersburg, Brussels and Breslau, pleading poor health, but accepted a request from his old friend Ferdinand Hiller that he come to Cologne to give a concert in February 1867, though he warned him what to expect: "I am constantly ill, in pain, bored and boring – more than I can possibly tell you." Meanwhile he had had another offer. When, during the *Alceste* performances, he received an invitation from Johann von Herbeck on behalf of the Gesellschaft der Musikfreunde, to come to Vienna in November and perform *The Damnation of Faust* with a large orchestra and chorus in the 3,000-seat Redoutensaal, he hesitated only briefly. Ill and weak as he was, it was not to be refused. "I have need of music." It was a chance to crown his career with one last grand appearance, and in a work whose diverse fortunes – defeat in Paris, victory in Dresden – embraced the two poles of his public existence.

The performance, planned for mid-November, was postponed by a month. Thanks to the delay, the very demanding chorus part was that much better prepared by the time the composer arrived on 7 December, after a day and night in the train. Exhausted, he rested while Herbeck, who knew the score inside out, went on with the rehearsals. Berlioz worked with the orchestra on the 11th (his sixty-third birthday, which prompted Cornelius, in Munich, to send him a verse telegram – "Gloire, salut, honneur! / Et croyez que mon coeur, / Quoique loin de vous, / Vous suit partout"), and again on the 12th, Herbeck interpreting for him with the players; but he was so worn out by it that he spent the 13th in bed and once more handed over to Herbeck, in whom he had complete confidence ("he knows my tempos exactly"). On the 14th he rallied and conducted the third and fourth parts of *Faust* himself.

By now Cornelius was there, occupying the room next to his at the Hôtel de Francfort. "As I entered Berlioz's room and received his joyful embrace, little Levi the music dealer, brother of the horn player and singing teacher, exclaimed: 'That looks like Cornelius. It can only be Cornelius. I knew you would come.'"

His moral support was just what Berlioz needed. The rehearsals were proving anything but smooth. On the morning of the 15th Cornelius reported that it was "still going badly". According to eyewitnesses in the hall (admittedly always a dubious source), the ailing Berlioz was having difficulty controlling the very large orchestra – forty violins, other strings in proportion, and double wind. He appeared to have a hazy memory of his music, buried his face in the score, and failed to give some vital leads, which made him exasperated with himself as well as with the players. When a cellist came in early he turned pale with anger and shouted, "Taisez-vous donc!" He threw his baton at the cor anglais player when the man made a mistake in Marguerite's Romance. Herbeck retrieved it for him; but he could only exclaim: "I am mortally ill." He could barely walk without the support of Herbeck's arm. Yet he told Cornelius that, though the least exertion tired him, "it's only music that can make me forget the pain for a few hours".

The negative reports of Berlioz's conducting should be read partly in the light of the typically Viennese feud then in progress between Herbeck's supporters and those of Dessoff, conductor of the Vienna Philharmonic, and the critics Hanslick and Zellner. Berlioz, as the protégé of Herbeck, was a natural target for their attacks.

He must eventually have found his way back into the work and established a rapport with his enormous forces, for the performance, on the afternoon of the 16th, Beethoven's birthday, was a triumph. Something of the old fire returned. He was recalled eleven times at the end. The concert rejuvenated him. Almost everything about it pleased him: the singing of Walter as Faust, "a delicious tenor, superior to any in Paris", and of Bettelheim the radiant Marguerite, whose "D'amour l'ardente flamme" (presumably with the cor anglais obbligato played correctly) was one of the highlights of the performance; his friend Hellmesberger's account of the viola solo in the King of Thulé; the precision of the chorus and its delicacy of nuance, and the freshness and perfect intonation of the women's voices; and all that Herbeck ("a conductor of the first rank") had done to make it possible. That evening his hotel room was full of flowers and well-wishers; and that night, according to Cornelius, he "slept well". All next day he was besieged by visitors – until it was time to dress for the gala supper hosted by Prince Czartorisky at the Hotel Munsch and attended by several hundred artists and music-lovers, including the 140 amateur sopranos and altos of the choir. Many toasts were drunk. Cornelius recited a long poem in Berlioz's honour. Berlioz spoke of his career as a critic. At the end Herbeck brought the house down by proposing "the health, in this hall where Mozart gave his concerts, of the distinguished man – no, the word is too pale – the man who has blazed new paths in music and who, a year after the death of the genius whose birthday we celebrate, gave us the Fantastic Symphony, destroyer of the dull-witted musical bourgeoisie. I raise my glass to Hector Berlioz, who for nearly half a century has fought against the miseries and misfortunes of life. Long live the genius of Berlioz!"

Writing to Reyer the same day, Berlioz felt he could say that "here is one of my scores saved. They will perform it now under the direction of Herbeck, who knows it by heart." Vienna, however, would take its time – as it usually did – before it admitted Berlioz. Some reviews were enthusiastic; but it was the conservative Hanslick – in his unregenerate youth a partisan of Berlioz, and of Wagner, but now the high priest of "absolute music" – who set the tone. He pronounced against the work. Berlioz had expected a "total slating" from Hanslick and he got it; it was, in Hugh Macdonald's phrase, "an influential castigation".

We consider that Berlioz's gifts are very much in decline in *Faust*. His fragile, feverish talent suffered a kind of minor stroke and has not recovered. Since then he has written only *The Childhood of Christ* and *The Trojans*, in both of which his powers of invention are bankrupt. [. . .] Berlioz's compositions, we believe, will soon cease to have a lively influence on the art of music; and, before long, public opinion, far from accepting a work such as *Faust* as real music, will reach the conclusion that it is not music at all.

Berlioz had to make do with the admiration of many of the younger musicians, not least Cornelius, for whom the *Damnation* was "one of our great musical masterpieces, to be ranked with *The Creation* of Haydn, Handel's oratorios and Beethoven's Ninth Symphony". Hearing it was among the supreme experiences of his life; to "share this triumph with him" sealed their relationship in a wonderful way. "Dear Berlioz! He has remained a pure musician and artist, unsullied by any mixture of the worldly politician claiming a special relationship with the Good Lord." The two men spent many hours together. Berlioz sang him passages from *The Trojans* and said he would like him to do the German translation of the libretto and of the *Memoirs*; and one evening he told him all about Estelle.

On the 18th he was taken to the Vienna Conservatoire to hear Hellmesberger and his student orchestra play *Harold*. Three days later he was back in the Rue de Calais, in a state of collapse. It was the coldest winter in Paris for years; the Seine was frozen over. Much of January he spent in bed; he was, he told Hiller, "one of the most horizontal men that exist – in so far as I exist at all". On the 11th he wrote to Ferrand:

Dear friend

It's midnight. I'm writing to you in bed, as always, and you'll receive my letter in bed, as usual. Your last note distressed me; I read your sufferings between the lines of its brevity. I wanted to reply at once; but intolerable pains, sleeping twenty hours at a stretch, doctor's mumbo-jumbo, rubbings with chloroform, draughts of laudanum – quite useless but precipitating wearisome dreams – prevented me. I see all too well how hard it will be for us to meet. You can't budge, and the least removal, for three quarters of the year at any rate, finishes me off. I have no way of picturing your place at Conzieux, your "home" as the English say, your existence there, your circle: I can't *see* you. This makes me sadder still when I think of you. But what's to be done?

The trip to Vienna killed me. Not all my success, my joy at such enthusiasm, the tremendous performance, etc., etc., could save me. I can't stand the cold of our terrible climate. The day before yesterday my dear Louis wrote describing his excursions on horseback in the forests of Martinique, and the tropical vegetation, and the sun, the real sun. That's what we could do with, you and I. But it's all one to Nature if we die far from her, ignorant of her sublimest glories. Dear friend! The senseless din of carriages disturbs the silence of the night. Paris – damp, chill, deep in mire, Parisian Paris! Now everything's quiet. It sleeps the sleep of the unjust. Roll on insomnia, and "no mincing", as one of those ruffians of the first Revolution remarked. [. . .]

Let me know if you have the full score of my Messe des morts. If I were threatened with the destruction of all my works save one, it would be for the Messe des morts that I'd beg grace. A new edition of it is being produced in Milan at the moment. If you haven't got it I can send it to you in six or seven weeks, I think.

Don't forget any of my questions, and reply when you have a little strength – alas, it's not leisure that you lack.

Farewell, dear friend, I shall lie awake thinking of you, since *non suadent cadentia sidera somnos*.*

In February, after twice cancelling it, he managed to keep his engagement with Hiller in Cologne. Stephen Heller had warned that Berlioz when ill was hard to bear, and Berlioz himself apologized in advance: "I will try to feel a little better when I come; if I'm not, I shall be insufferable." Afterwards Hiller was able to report that his visitor was on his best behaviour and that Hiller's wife and his two daughters were charmed by him. The orchestra had been well prepared and he was given three rehearsals. Though (Hiller remembered later) he spent much of the time in bed and could hardly drag himself to rehearsals, "the moment he stood on the rostrum he was a different man, vital, energetic, exuberant". The reviewer for the *Signale*, while trusting that Berlioz's music would not establish itself in the concert halls of Germany, conceded that *Harold* and the Nocturne from *Beatrice* made a deep impression on the audience. "Berlioz, with his white hair and pale aquiline countenance irradiated by his blue eyes, was received very cordially by our public, with loud applause after each piece and, at the end, cheers and fanfares by the orchestra." No doubt (the reviewer added) some

* "The sinking stars do *not* invite sleep": an adaptation of *Aeneid*, ii, 9.

of this could be attributed to the prestige of the man; but there was no denying that "the music itself achieved a real success".

Abroad was, as ever, where he thrived. In January the Grand Duke's chamberlain wrote from Weimar with news of a successful performance of the Fantastic Symphony. In April *The Childhood of Christ* was given in Lausanne – Estelle went to hear it – and in May in Copenhagen. *Harold* had been played five times the previous year in New York, and he was being urged to go there. If only his health were better! All this was coming too late.

That spring the American conductor Theodore Thomas called at 4 Rue de Calais, as he noted in his diary for 8 May:

> Spent a delightful hour with Berlioz, in which we talked over all his larger compositions. It seems he had heard already that I played his music, and, as I was leaving, he asked me if there was anything of his that I would like which I did not already have in my library. I told him yes, there was one thing that I wanted very much, and that was his great Requiem Mass. Hearing this Berlioz went to the music case, took down his own copy of the score, and inscribed it, "To Theodore Thomas in remembrance of the grateful author, Hector Berlioz", and presented it to me.

The revised Ricordi edition of the Requiem was published that month. Berlioz was very pleased with it – "It puts our French, Schlesinger edition in the shade" – and sent copies to Hiller and Herbeck as well as to Ferrand. In March Cosima von Bülow wrote him an account of *Romeo* in Basel, performed complete under the aegis of her husband. In Paris, by contrast, the Société des Concerts merely talked of giving extracts from the work, before proceeding not to. A complete *Romeo* was made even less likely – if that were possible – by the success of Gounod's *Romeo and Juliet*, which opened at the Théâtre-Lyrique on 27 April. It was the second time Gounod had used a subject Berlioz had treated in the concert hall. The new score showed clear traces of the influence of the old. Some critics even compared the opera unfavourably with the symphony. But what use was that?

Meanwhile, as an academician he was required to serve on several juries awarding prizes in connection with the Exposition Universelle des Beaux-Arts. The exhibition, in tandem with the Exposition Agricole et Industrielle, opened on 1 April. With Franco-Prussian relations heading for breakdown and French intervention in Mexico in ruins, it was not the best of times for celebrating the arts of peace; but the double event drew huge crowds. Paris went *en fête*, and the whole world converged on it. Much more than 1855 had been, it was Napoleon III's resplendent answer to Queen Victoria's Great Exhibition of 1851. For Berlioz, the extravagant cosmopolitanism might once have been entertaining. Now it largely passed him by. The exhibition merely added to the difficulty of getting about the city: the streets seethed with tourists and there were no cabs to be had. He had none the less to attend the meetings of his juries. On 11 June he was at the Conservatoire when the prize for the best cantata was awarded, unanimously, to Camille Saint-Saëns. The victory galvanized him and, finding a cab, he hurried to the Rue du Faubourg St Honoré to tell his young friend the news without delay. Saint-Saëns was out, so he left a note.

One other duty fell to him: to organize a grand concert in one of the halls in the exhibition building on the Champ de Mars, as he had done in 1855. He chose a familiar programme: excerpts from Gluck, Rossini, Auber, ceremonial pieces by Méhul and David, and his own *Hymne à la France*. The concert was to be given twice, on 8 and 15 July; in all probability it would mark his last public appearance in Paris. In the event he was not there to witness it.

When Louis said goodbye to his father in August 1866 both of them knew they might not see each other again: Berlioz could well be dead by the time Louis returned to France. He expected to be in the Antilles for at least a year; he was now a captain, in command of his own ship. The company was engaged in evacuating troops and French nationals from Mexico, in the aftermath of Napoleon III's bungled attempt to establish a Catholic Empire in America.

Louis kept track of his father's doings by means of letters and the newspapers that Berlioz sent to St Thomas, the port in the Virgin Islands where he regularly put in. Very little of their correspondence from these months has survived; but we can deduce from what Berlioz told his friends that they were in fairly regular contact. In late September 1866 Louis wrote to his father in high spirits, posting the letter in St Thomas. He reported himself as "thoroughly launched in the beau monde of Martinique. I was received in splendid fashion at Morne Rouge by the mayor of St Pierre. If only you had been there! I thought of you a lot, and talked a lot about you with those gentlemen. On the road from St Pierre to Morne you would find everything you ever dreamed of in

natural grandeur and richness and ideal beauty – it's overwhelming."
Louis was the talk of the island. The son of Berlioz, they kept exclaiming.
"I can't fart without the inhabitants complimenting me on it." The son
of Berlioz – the son of the man who wrote *L'Africaine*: "one of them
assured me I was wrong when I said he didn't!"

At the beginning of April Berlioz told Estelle that he had just had
news of his son, "who's still navigating the waters of the Gulf of
Mexico". In May he was "hearing quite often from Louis". By then
Juarez's forces were in control and the French were getting out when
and how they could. On 11 June Berlioz told Ferrand it was "a long
time" since he had had any news of Louis. He was "racked with anxiety"
and "fearful of what those Mexican brigands may do". In the end,
though, it was not the brigands.

Louis' latest surviving letter is dated "4 February 1867, at sea", and
addressed to Félix Marmion. Having commanded the *Caravelle* and
the *Caraïbe*, he was on board the *Nouveau Monde* en route for Mexico
to take command of his new ship the *Sonora*. He was sailing into
dangerous waters, he wrote, but didn't doubt that before long he would
be back, telling his great-uncle about *his* campaigns.

> After enduring the terrible epidemic at St Thomas and losing men from
> yellow fever, I'm off to find fresh troubles at Vera Cruz. In all probability
> I shall leave with the iron-clad squadron. All Mexico having risen in
> revolt, I can't simply wait and have my ship seized and be myself taken
> prisoner.
>
> I didn't write sooner, having only rather depressing news to give you,
> but now that I shall be running greater risks, such as fever, gales and
> bullets, I'm sending you these few lines to tell you that your great-nephew
> still loves you with all his heart, as in the past, and to say that I have
> accepted my dangerous mission in the hope of getting the little red ribbon
> that all the members of our family have won with honour, and finally
> because I owe the company I serve my entire devotion.
>
> Although misfortune has struck my predecessors, I hope to get away
> from this unpleasant region safe and sound. My health is solid, I am still
> as lean as I was as a child, I am wiry and shaggy; I have paid all my dues
> and am weaned.
>
> My father at present knows everything. God knows what anxiety he
> must be in!

Whether Berlioz heard from Louis again after he wrote to Ferrand on 11 June is not known. He could just have done. Letters to France could take many weeks. In any case the official news from Mexico did nothing to relieve his anxiety. The capture of the Archduke Maximilian had been known in Paris since the beginning of June, and there were continual rumours of his impending execution.

Berlioz's friends did what they could to distract him. Much of the time he was confined to his bed; but on 31 May he attended a soirée at Mme Erard's and heard Saint-Saëns and Planté play three of Liszt's symphonic poems, arranged for two pianos.

Late in June a surprise party was arranged at the nearby studio of the Marquis Arconati-Visconti in Boulevard Rochechouart. The Marquis, a rich collector, traveller and music-lover, had attended every performance of *The Trojans at Carthage*. He and Théodore Ritter, the Massarts, the Damckes and Reyer pooled their ideas. On arriving, Berlioz would find the studio hung with Egyptian fabrics, in the middle of one wall his portrait bust surrounded by palms and flowers, on the others scrolls bearing the names of his works, and many friends and admirers assembled to honour him. Music – his own – would greet the unsuspecting guest on his entrance. It was agreed that, at a given hour, Berthold Damcke, who lived practically next door to Berlioz, would call at the Rue de Calais to take him to the party, while the others waited for them at the studio.

They waited; but the two men did not come. Eventually, Ritter was deputed to go and look for them.

The exact sequence of events is hard to disentangle from the various conflicting accounts written soon after; but it seems most likely that news had reached 4 Rue de Calais that morning which Mme Martin communicated to their neighbour Damcke but which both Berlioz and the friends gathered at the studio were still ignorant of. Damcke arrived at the Rue de Calais as planned but left again abruptly. Mme Martin, in tears, explained that Damcke had suffered a serious misfortune. At this, Berlioz went straight round to see him. Damcke did his best to fend off his questions: he would tell him later. With Louise Damcke they set out for the studio. Before they got there a friend of Louis' came up to them in the street and offered condolences. Yes – yellow fever. He had been dead three weeks.

28

Last Rites

Berlioz fled home to the Rue de Calais, where Ritter found him weeping helplessly. "It was for me to die," he kept saying. The rest of that day he lay on his bed, not speaking. The following day, 29 June, he wrote to Estelle – "Forgive me for turning to you at the moment of the most terrible grief of my life. My poor son has died at Havana, aged thirty-three" – and, laconically, to his nieces Joséphine and Nanci: "Louis has died at Havana." The day after, he sent brief notes to Ferrand and Félix Marmion. Friends left messages of loving sympathy, but he would see no one. The Exhibition concerts took place without him; his *Hymne à la France* was cheered, though he seems to have known nothing of it till Ferrand mentioned having read a newspaper report.

By the middle of July, though still numbed, he was having to respond to communications from the Compagnie Transatlantique and wind up Louis' affairs. The clothes and books and papers in Louis' cabin at the time of his death had no doubt been destroyed – the last surviving letter from his father dates from two years earlier (it contains the prophetic phrase "Dearest Louis, what would I do if I didn't have you?"). But there were his effects in the apartment at St Nazaire to dispose of – for Louis, not long before, had finally stirred himself to give up the rooms above cafés that he so disliked and invest in a comfortable, well-furnished home. All this, and the will that Louis had had his uncle Marc Suat make for him, had to be dealt with. Luckily a friend of Louis' was helping.

On 29 July Berlioz drew up his own will, appointing his three nieces his heirs and bequeathing annuities to his mother-in-law, his Swiss maid Caroline Scheur, and Estelle Fornier, "whom I entreat to accept this small gift [1,600 francs a year] in remembrance of the feelings I have had for her all my life". Damcke and Edouard Alexandre were named executors. To the first he left all his published scores, "in the bookcase in my study", to the second the presentation batons given him in Germany; to Mme Massart his one-volume English Shakespeare, to the lawyer Nogent Saint-Laurent his Latin Virgil, and to Reyer his annotated *Paul et Virginie*.

A large part of the will was taken up with the future of his operas, especially the two parts of *The Trojans*, the full scores of which his executors were enjoined to have published, Choudens having "failed to keep" his undertaking to publish *The Trojans at Carthage*. "I was unwilling to sue him. My executors will act as they see fit, to make him do so. But I insist that, if M. Choudens does decide to, the score be published absolutely as it is, *without cuts, without changes, without the slightest suppression of text*." The German translation of the two parts were to be entrusted to Peter Cornelius and that of the *Memoirs* to his sister Mlle Cornelius, herself an experienced translator from the French, or, if not to her, on no account to those who translated his three collections, *Evenings in the Orchestra*, the *Grotesques* and *A travers chants*, "which are teeming with mistakes". The will, together with his share certificates, was deposited with Gatine the notary, 51 Rue Ste Anne.

He also busied himself seeing lawyers on Ferrand's behalf and obtaining parole for Ferrand's adopted son, Joanny Blanc-Gonet, who was serving a ten-year sentence for burglary. For his own future he no longer greatly cared. With Louis gone and Estelle a physically distant presence, what future did he have? He longed only for an end to his torments. The intestinal pains had returned and spread to his stomach. Whole days and nights were passed in agony. He ventured out less and less. When he did he was sometimes seized in the street with spasms so intense he could hardly move. Once he only just reached his barber's in the Passage de l'Opéra before vomiting convulsively. Though Death was "still playing" with him, it surely could not be much longer.

As if symbolically to sever the remaining threads, he went to the Conservatoire one morning in July and with the help of the library attendant emptied the contents of a trunk that he kept in his room, and made a bonfire of them all – concert programmes, cuttings, pamphlets, citations, everything, including the skull he used for his writing sand, picked up in an Italian cemetery thirty-six years before and which the attendant assured Tiersot had been "*the skull of his wife*".

At the beginning of August his doctor, alarmed at his physical and mental condition, ordered him to Néris les Bains in the Auvergne to try the effect of the waters. He went, but after a few days the physician in charge, hearing his croaking voice and feeling his pulse, diagnosed laryngitis and packed him off to his nieces and brother-in-law in Vienne, where he stayed for a month. Most of it was spent in bed. It was from bed that he wrote to Félix Marmion, in late August or early September.

> Dear Uncle
>
> I need to see you. My nieces tell me that I shall, quite soon. In the meantime I can't resist writing to you. I'm in bed, as I am nearly all the time, in frightful pain from my neuralgia, which the baths at Néris were powerless to combat without danger to my health, the doctor said. Suat and his daughters have kept me in Vienne so that I can be here for the wedding [of the elder daughter, Joséphine]. I realized that it would upset them if I went back to Paris so I've stayed on. But I'm no company for them. Those poor children spend three quarters of the time working beside my bed. I can't even go with them on their evening walk. If I'd not felt so dreadfully weak I would have come to see you. But there's no way I could have, never knowing if I am going to have five or six hours that are bearable. It was all I could do to make two brief visits to St Symphorien, a few miles from here [to visit Estelle, who had moved there from Geneva]. The weather is so beautiful it breaks my heart. Since this morning I've not been able to think of anything but Meylan. I see you there, clearly, fifty years ago. Dear Uncle, you are the only one of the family I have left, and you are perhaps too the one person who can understand the sad enchantment of such memories and will forgive me for speaking of them. I am so alone now. The chief tie that bound me to the present is broken, and my whole soul flies backward to the past. Poor Louis . . . Dear Uncle, I must stop, I feel my mind blurring, and in it only thoughts beyond utterance.
>
> > With much love
> > Remember me to my aunt
> > H. Berlioz
>
> PS. I think I'm a little better and will sleep – for which I have you to thank.

On 9 September he saw Estelle once more; she too was in mourning (her son Auguste had died in April). Next day he was a witness at Joséphine Suat's wedding to Auguste Chapot, a major in the French army, seventeen years older than the bride but "charming in every respect", Berlioz told Mme Damcke – "if he hadn't been I would not have witnessed". Camille Pal held aloof – the enmity between him and Suat had never abated – but Mathilde and her husband and her two young children were there, and thirty other members of the family. "It was the oldest that I was most pleased to see, my uncle the colonel, who is eighty-four. We both cried when we met. He seemed ashamed to be alive. I am much more so."

Three days later, dosed with laudanum, he took the night train to Paris. On Sunday 15 September he visited Mme Charton at Ville d'Avray on the south-western outskirts of Paris and walked in the woods in perfect early autumn weather, returning to the singer's villa for "an excellent dinner". Such is the sense of well-being expressed in his letter to his niece Nanci recounting the excursion that his words, "tout heureux, tout aise", echo – unconsciously, it may be – the first *Nuits d'été* song, which describes the happiness of the poet returning from an idyllic day in the woods.

Days like that came rarely, however. Much more typical was the nihilism he gave vent to, that October, to the Princess Wittgenstein, which brought their long and passionate correspondence to a jarring end. Perhaps her continually preaching to him the consolations of religion and the need to turn to God finally irritated him to the point where his exasperation boiled over. "You don't know what *unremitting* physical and mental pain is like – not to have an instant's respite. Otherwise you wouldn't be astonished at what you call my coldness. I'm not aware of what it was that offended you." He then spoke of Néris, Vienne and St Symphorien, and asked her if she supposed such impressions were capable of softening the effect of his loss. As for the festival at Meiningen (two movements from *Romeo and Juliet* had just been played with great success), all that kind of thing was a matter of indifference to him.

> The absurd seems to me man's natural element, and death the noble object of his mission. That was already more or less my state of mind when I called on the young princess, your daughter, in Vienna; it was that that made her find my manner cold, as you tell me she did. But I also found her greatly changed. That's life! Farewell, dear Princess, my letter will strike you as quite ridiculous amid all your Roman excitements, which are a hundred times more so. I kiss your hand.

Three years before, he had begged the Princess not to cast him out if he ever did anything to merit the loss of her affection ("with wretches like me one can never be sure"). She duly forgave him; and her name stands high in the record of his life as the one who persuaded him to compose *The Trojans*, an action commemorated in his autobiography and in the dedication of the score. But she seems not to have answered his letter and he never wrote to her again.

Yet if Berlioz in the autumn of 1867, like Hamlet, did not "set his life at a pin's fee", it was different where the things he had fought for were concerned. As he said to Fétis, he still defended his gods. Music, though in his lowest moments he might deny the fact, could still galvanize him. He might almost boast to the Princess, in a mood of black despondency, that reports of the success of his works left him unmoved: to his niece Joséphine it was another story. The fan letter he had from a music-lover who was at Meiningen "stirred me to the heart. I am happy that my *Romeo and Juliet* Love Scene made so many people weep." What happened to his works, above all what happened to *The Trojans*, remained of supreme importance to him. When the Russian composer Cesar Cui called at the beginning of August and asked to be allowed to make a copy of the full score of the opera to take back to St Petersburg – where all his colleagues and friends at the Free Music School knew it by heart from the vocal score and were longing to perform extracts at their concerts – his first excited reaction had been to jump at the offer and ignore Choudens and his deeply compromised copyright to the work. He might himself have no future, but the future of the music he believed in, including his own – he cared passionately about it and must go on fighting for it till his strength gave out. He could not abandon the struggle.

That is why, with all its harrowing details of disease and disintegration, the spectacle of his final months is not all darkness but, as befits someone of his nature and name, is touched with heroism.

When the Grand Duchess Elena Pavlovna, aunt of Tsar Alexander II and patron of the Russian Musical Society, came to Paris in September for the Exhibition and invited him to conduct the Conservatoire Orchestra in St Petersburg during the coming winter season, he let himself be persuaded – this although he had just turned down a more lucrative offer from the head of Steinway in New York (who had to be content with a bust of the composer instead). The Grand Duchess, he said, was an exceptionally charming and cultivated old woman who could get round anybody, she spoke perfect French, and she was a musician into the bargain. The money, without being spectacular, was good – 15,000 francs, 6,000 of it in advance, plus expenses, a sumptuous and well-heated apartment in her palace, and use of one of her carriages. His nieces and brother-in-law feared he would not be up to the fatigue of the rehearsals, but his friends knew it was what he needed.

Berlioz himself, who worried more about money as he got older, gave financial necessity as the reason for venturing to northern Russia in the depths of winter. He had to "make ends meet", he "earned nothing" in Paris; here was a chance to "gain myself a little momentary affluence". "If it kills me, at least I'll know it was worth it." Yet, having recently sold the farm at Murianette and decided to sell the one on the outskirts of La Côte (the Ferme du Nand at Le Chuzeau), he was hardly in want. It was surely the musical prospect that enticed him: to be among musicians who admired his work and performed it frequently (Cui confirmed what Wieniawski had told him the year before), to make music again in sympathetic surroundings, to return to the scenes of his triumphs twenty years before, when "holy Russia" saved him at the worst moment of his career, to proselytize among the new generation of Russian composers of whom Cui had told him and perhaps establish a tradition for the interpretation and performance of his music, to conduct Beethoven as he felt he knew how and introduce them to the great Gluck while there was still time. With such possibilities in view, even the rigours of the long journey lost their sting – especially as the Grand Duchess's officials assured him that the train he would board at Berlin had roomy, heated compartments, with bed and everything else one required.

Between them, Berlioz and the Grand Duchess worked out the programmes of the six concerts. The first five would feature the "classical" masters: five Beethoven symphonies (nos. 3–6 and no. 9) and *Leonore no. 2*, scenes from *Armide*, *Orphée* and *Iphigénie en Tauride*, three Weber overtures, Mozart's C minor piano concerto, *Ave verum*, "Deh vieni" from *Figaro* and extracts from *The Magic Flute*, Mendelssohn's *Hebrides* overture, Haydn's "Emperor" hymn and variations played by all the strings of the orchestra, and of his own music only the Nocturne from *Beatrice and Benedick*. The sixth would be an all-Berlioz programme: movements from *Romeo*, the Elbe scene from *Faust*, *Absence, La captive*, and *Harold in Italy*. At Wieniawski's request *Rêverie et caprice* was added to the fourth concert; but when the director of the Russian Musical Society, Kologrivov, on receiving the programmes, wrote back to say there should be more Berlioz, the composer thanked him for his "friendly reproaches" but declined to make any further changes: the programmes had been agreed with the Grand Duchess and it was not for him to alter them. Instead two further concerts were projected, after the Conservatoire season, at which the Tibi omnes from his Te Deum might be heard (the autograph score of the work, which he had given to Stasov five years before, was in the municipal library at St Petersburg), together with scenes from *Alceste*.

With less than two months to go before his departure he was plunged into a stimulating rush of preparations. Letters and telegrams flew back and forth. He had to establish what performing material was not available in Russia and therefore must be brought with him, see that the chorus and orchestra parts of *Orphée*, Act 2, were altered so as to conform to the new, correct edition published by Heinze in Leipzig, arrange for Alfred Dörffel, editor of the score, to coach the young contralto Lavrovskaya in her part (the Russians had no Gluck tradition and knew the operas, if at all, only in garbled versions), and make sure that the extra players needed for his own music were procured: two more bassoons, a third flute, a cor anglais, two cornets, a couple of harps (ideally, four) and an extra timpanist. During the rest of September and throughout October he was busy with these and other matters (including sittings for the Steinway bust, which was being sculpted by his Institute colleague Perraud). On 1 November Berlioz told Suat that everything was in train: parts were being copied and preliminary rehearsals held in St Petersburg, he'd managed to buy quite cheaply an excellent fur coat, hat and rug, and two artists of his acquaintance (Dörffel and the soprano Mlle Regan) would be picking him up in Berlin and travelling with him the rest of the way. All he was waiting for was the advance of 6,000 francs. Soon afterwards he had that too.

He had misgivings as well. There were times when he wondered whether, quite apart from his health, he hadn't been naïve to take on such a burden. Despite the Grand Duchess's assurance of unlimited rehearsals it transpired that the Conservatoire orchestra never rehearsed for a concert more than twice. Two rehearsals, he exploded to Dörffel – two sight-readings, rather. "If they won't rehearse my scores they won't perform them – that's all there is to it." True, two was all the Paris Conservatoire orchestra ever had; but they knew their repertoire by heart, whereas the young Russian orchestra was not yet at that stage. There was no way they could do Beethoven's Ninth on fewer than four.

"In London we had seven. When I put on *Romeo and Juliet* in Baden with the combined Baden and Karlsruhe orchestras we had eleven the first year and nine the second." Clearly he was going to have his work cut out. And then, how much socializing would be expected of him? What if the Grand Duchess kept inviting him to her salon?

On the eve of his departure he wrote to Félix Marmion:

> I am full of enthusiasm for my Russian journey, in the afternoon – the mornings, when I'm in pain, are another matter; but once I am launched on my rehearsals I shall be more in control of my troubles. The Grand Duchess has sent word that I shall be asked to give two more concerts after the Conservatoire ones. I don't know whether I shall have the strength to do so much. Otherwise Her Highness is kindness itself. She's already had me paid 6,000 francs, and I'm not leaving till tomorrow. I'll find hardly any of my acquaintances from 1848 [1847], they're almost all dead. Only General Lvov is still alive, and he's stone deaf. I'll have the Italian singers Mario, Tamberlick and Tagliafico, who are threatening to come and entertain me on the evenings when they're not performing ... There's an engineer in the Russian army that I know who will entertain me rather better and who is a genuine lover of music [Cui]. We spent a few hours together in Paris recently.

Berlioz was in Berlin on the evening of 13 November. On the 14th he rested in his hotel. Next day he set out with his two companions, arriving at St Petersburg's station on the 17th to be met by a carriage sent by the Grand Duchess and driven through the white streets to a "superb apartment" in the Mikhailovsky Palace, where his own French-speaking servants were waiting to attend his every need. Already, despite nearly four days in the train, he felt twice the man he had been when he left Paris.

He was hardly installed before the big salon of his apartment was full of visitors. Luckily there was no need to go out – everybody was coming to see him. Outside the windows the snow fell in bucketfuls. "God, what snow," he wrote to his niece Nanci. "And swarms of sparrows and pigeons, unafraid of getting their feet frozen, searching in it for grains of oats dropped by the horses; people passing in sledges, their heads covered in thick hoods; and the huge square, glacial and silent. But in a few days all these impressions will have vanished: I shall be plunged in music and thinking of nothing else."

To be conducting again – and, though there were the usual problems with the singers and the chorus, conducting such a fine orchestra – gave fresh meaning to his whole existence. The orchestra, about seventy-strong, made up of the leading players from the imperial theatres, proved to be first-rate. It knew a lot of the music already and mastered the rest quickly, so that the sessions were true rehearsals, not the sight-readings he had feared.

The first six weeks of Berlioz's visit to Russia were the climax of his career as a conductor. Notwithstanding days when he felt "sick as eighteen horses" and coughed "like six donkeys with the glanders", and was forced to rehearse sitting down, the experience rejuvenated him. Again and again his letters spoke of the restorative power of music-making. "I recover my strength when I conduct these master-pieces. Beethoven's Pastoral Symphony the other day set me up again completely." It was "necessary to leave Paris to rediscover my life". These Russians might inhabit a world of snow and ice but they had fire in their veins and a deep love of music in their blood. Their company, their admiration and the affinity they clearly felt with his music, renewed his spirits. Here was a community of musicians who understood him, who regarded what he had done as of the utmost importance to them.

There were formal receptions to be gone through; and from time to time the Grand Duchess invited him to private audiences and at her request he would read to her, in French, from Shakespeare or Virgil or Byron. But what he liked best was when his new friends came to visit him, to dine or just to talk, bringing others with them, writers as well as musicians. They were often there during these weeks. As often as not he received them unceremoniously from his bed and stayed there while they sat round. Nearly all of them spoke French fluently. Stasov, the writer and art critic whom he had met in 1847 and who had called on him in Paris in 1862, and who at forty-three was a good ten years older than the young composers he championed – "the Mighty Handful" he had christened them – was prominent among them, as were the thirty-year-old Balakirev, who was preparing the chorus for the concerts, and Cui, and the Russo-German writer and pianist Wilhelm von Lenz. Stasov brought his lawyer brother Dmitri. Borodin came; Mussorgsky too, perhaps – it is hard to imagine that a musician who venerated Berlioz as he did would fail to get himself introduced. Rimsky-Korsakov's complaint, made in his autobiography of many years later, that Berlioz took no interest in the young Russian composers and behaved in a high and mighty and generally unapproachable way, is not borne out by the evidence. On the contrary: there is abundant testimony to what Stasov called his frequent contact with the musicians of the new Russian school and to their many animated conversations. It was an integral part of the whole experience.* They attended the birthday supper given on 11 December by the members and associates of the Russian Musical Society (Kologrivov and Dargomizhky among them), when Berlioz, "one of the creators of the new school", was made an honorary member of the society in recognition of his "immense role in the history of art" and "in the hope that the ties which unite one of the great originators of contemporary art with our musical circle will exert a favourable influence on the development of music in this country".

Under their passionate urging he even thought, momentarily, of composing again. They could not accept that he had no further works to give the world; it was (they insisted) wrong of him, as the greatest living composer, to persist in such a resolution. Though nothing could really shake it, their insistence was gratifying in the extreme. He was pleased, too, when at a gathering in his apartment on 25 November they reproached him for having brought nothing from *The Trojans*. This time he complied, and wrote asking his neighbour Damcke to send "the copy of the complete full score made by Roquemont", which Damcke would find in the glass-fronted cabinet in his bedroom, together with the orchestral parts ("on the piano") and a libretto. At the same time he wrote to Choudens to obtain his authorization. The transaction was sealed in a document signed by the composer and Kologrivov, which for a down payment of 500 francs (to be handed by Berlioz to Choudens) gave the Musical Society the Russian rights to the opera.

By the time of his birthday supper Berlioz was in the thick of things and had given his first two concerts. His new friends had again protested that the programmes contained too little of his music; and with the Grand Duchess's consent they were modified. The Fantastic Symphony was added, on his stipulating three rehearsals. So were the Offertorium

---

* Stravinsky remembered Rimsky (his teacher) telling him of going to one of Berlioz's concerts "with the other young composers of the group. They saw Berlioz – in a tailcoat cut very short at the back, Rimsky said – conduct his own music and Beethoven's. Then they were shepherded backstage by Stasov, the patriarch of St Petersburg musical life. They found a small man – Rimsky's words were 'a little white bird with pince-nez' – shivering in a fur coat and huddled under a hot pipe which crossed the room just over his head. He addressed Rimsky very kindly: 'And you compose music too?', but kept his hands in his coat sleeves, as in a muffler."

from the Grande messe and three overtures, *Francs-juges*, *Benvenuto Cellini* and *Roman Carnival*; but *La captive* and the Nocturne were dropped (though the latter was sung at a private soirée of the Grand Duchess). Other changes were made. The Mozart concerto disappeared, as did the *Hebrides* overture (surely to the regret of Berlioz, who loved the piece); the Ninth Symphony was first shorn of its finale, for lack of suitable singers, and then dropped altogether and the Emperor Concerto (with Dörffel as soloist) substituted; the overture to *Euryanthe* was replaced by Agathe's scena from *Freischütz*, the Haydn quartet movement by an aria from *The Creation*, and the *Armide* excerpts by Act 1 of *Alceste*. But, though the details were different, the three bases of the series – Gluck–Beethoven–Berlioz – remained the same. At the opening concert they gave the Pastoral, at the second the Fantastic, at the third Act 2 of *Orphée* (sung in Russian) and the Beethoven C minor, at the fourth the Eroica, the Offertorium, *Alceste*, Act 1, and the *Francs-juges* overture. Berlioz was lifted out of himself. On the days following he might be forced to take to his bed; but, however ill he felt, whenever it was time "to mount the rostrum and I see all that sympathetic world around me, I come alive, and conduct as I have perhaps never conducted before". The Fantastic Symphony, in the big Hall of the Nobles, was brought off with thrilling verve and authority. Received with prolonged applause on entering – so that "after bowing to right and left, before, behind, to the orchestra, to the choir, I had to stand still and wait till the storm of applause stopped" – he was recalled half a dozen times at the end. It was more than ten years since he had heard the work. In bed that night, remembering it, he wept. The ovation for *Orphée* at the third concert was as great. It had taken him and Balakirev many hours to bring the large amateur chorus up to scratch but in the end all went beautifully, with lovely singing by the young contralto Lavrovskaya and applause after each movement. "What a joy it has been to reveal to them the masterpieces of that great man!"

Cui, in one of several long reviews in the *S.-Petersburgskie Vedomosti*, gave a glowing account of Berlioz's conducting: there was no one, he wrote, whose performances were truer to the composer's intentions, who had greater understanding of the spirit of a work or who observed all the nuances so faithfully.

What a grasp he has of Beethoven, how exact, how thoughtful his performances are, how effective yet without the slightest concession to the false and the tawdry. I prefer Berlioz as an interpreter of Beethoven to Wagner (who, with all his excellent qualities, is at times affected, introducing sentimental rallentandos). Gluck he has made new to us, alive, unrecognizable – outmoded by now, maybe, but undeniably a brilliant innovator, a genius. As for Berlioz's own works, the magnificent performances under his direction have revealed wonders we had not suspected even after careful study of his enormous, complex scores. And how simple and restrained he is on the rostrum, and yet how precise his gestures are. And how modest he is! When the audience called for him after the first piece, he came out and with a charming wave of the hand indicated that it was the orchestra, not he, that deserved the applause. Of all the conductors we have heard in Petersburg, Berlioz is unquestionably the greatest.

His impact on Moscow audiences was as remarkable when, at the behest of the local conservatoire, he gave two concerts in the first fortnight of January, one to an audience of more than ten thousand in the Riding School, the other in the Hall of the Nobles. The Offertorium, listened to with religious attention by the huge throng, unleashed at the final "Amen" such an explosion of cheering as he had rarely experienced. It was the same when the piece was given at the second concert, at which he also conducted *Harold*, *King Lear* and the Beethoven violin concerto. At a banquet afterwards the toast was proposed by the twenty-seven-year-old Tchaikovsky.

Berlioz had at first declined the Moscow invitation; and, despite the musical delights afforded by an orchestra and chorus far finer than he had found twenty years before, the experience exhausted his last reserves of strength. He returned to St Petersburg in mid-January with his health in ruins.

Waiting for him in the apartment, to his joy, was a letter from Estelle, and one from his dear friend Mme Massart with news of far-distant Paris.

You wouldn't believe, my dear Monsieur Berlioz, the pleasure your letter gave us. I know that "nor gold nor greatness cause us to be happy", but they can cause one to forget, and that would have been sad, for we are very fond of you. You can therefore imagine the delight it has given us to see you appreciated and fêted like that. The colder a country is, then, the more generous and warm-hearted? In that case you'll find us on fire: for the last week we've been enjoying Siberian weather; we're all prostrated by it, man and beast. The carriages are stuck fast, and it was all we could do, last Friday evening, to reach Vieuxtemps', where there was music. Carlotta Patti – what a goose! And Mme Escudier-Kastner, as pianist – I shan't say a word; but it was enough to make one hold one's nose and block one's ears. And there were so many ugly people. None of the senses had a good time, except when Vieuxtemps played a romance and a rondo. I talked of you to Mme Damcke, who was surprised that I hadn't been to see her to hear your news. I proudly replied that I had had my own *personal* letter and, before that, had seen your mother-in-law, who told me everything: sending off *The Trojans*, the Grand Duchess's treats, the artists' reception, etc.

So you're going to become very rich. I imagine you springing a surprise on us: on your return, collecting a grrrrand full-size orchestra and regaling us with *Romeo* and the Fantastic Symphony and the Pilgrims' March from *Harold*. That would be neat! You should do it for your friends and fellow-artists. You have the money – and the strength, for, you see, your health is much better than you suppose. What do you care about making your life easier? Are not the delights of the mind superior to all others? I can tell you that there is a great deal of interest in you and your travels, and the new generation is curious to hear your works in their entirety.

But I'm chattering – and I've forgotten to tease you. That must be the first time. I was intending to, and the fine Russian ladies would have been the ideal theme!

Of course I still know English. And the proof is that I am

"Yours for ever"

A. Massart

There could be no more dreams of that sort, however. He had used up what was left of his strength. In St Petersburg it was colder than ever. The birds were falling from the trees, the coachmen from their boxes. "What a country! And in my symphonies I sing of Italy, and the sylphs and the rose bowers on the banks of the Elbe." He would get through the two remaining concerts somehow, and the social obligations, and then set off home and thence to Nice and Monaco. They were pressing him to stay a few more weeks and conduct once more, a benefit concert at which all the musicians would give their services and he would earn an extra 8,000 francs; but it was all one to him now. The unremitting snow and ice had got to him at last. He needed the sun and the smell of violets and the sight of a southern sea.

He struggled through the final weeks but it was not the same. His strength was gone. There were days when the rehearsals left him half dead. Settling the programmes and dealing with singers and their anxieties and vanities was now not a challenge but a burden. Things no longer seemed possible. When he was asked to give the Royal Hunt and the *Trojans* ballet music at the penultimate concert, on 25 January, he refused, on the defeatist grounds that "breaking the opera up like that" would "make it look as though it were an instrumental work". If they could have included the Septet as well, it might have been different; but, though it had been talked of, they didn't have the singers. He heard this for himself when Stasov and Balakirev took him to the Russian Opera to see *A Life for the Tsar* from Kologrivov's box. As he reported to Demeur, the singers were wretched, though Glinka's work struck him as "most original".

The spell could still work. "What an orchestra I have," he wrote to Reyer on 23 January. "It understands so quickly and well. And it knows almost all my music. As for Beethoven's, it plays it practically by heart. This morning I was profoundly moved by the Symphony in B flat [no. 4], which we went through without stopping once." Music, he adds, "would have cured me on this trip if I could have recovered my health".

On 7 February he rehearsed the orchestra and chorus for the last time and made his adieus. After three hours on the rostrum he was a wreck, though "happy to see the players so proud of themselves". Everything had gone well – the Love Scene, Queen Mab, the Sylphs, *Harold* – so it is permissible to suppose that at the concert next evening he found the necessary energy and summoned his best. But when they again begged him to stay on for a further concert, he declined. He was finished. He gave his baton to Balakirev, and to the Russian Musical Society the pair of antique cymbals, with the magical ring to them, made in Paris for *Romeo* in 1839 and used by him ever since. It was a farewell to more than Petersburg. He knew he would never conduct again.

Perhaps it was in this last week, just before the final concert, that he posed for the full-length studio photograph which shows him standing in evening dress, baton raised, left hand on hip, decoration in lapel, eyes staring from dark sockets beneath a mane of snow-white hair: a ghost, yet awesome, still a force.

Some time between the concert of 8 February and his departure five days later there was one last grand supper. On the 13th his friends put him on the train to Berlin. Four days later he was back in Paris, more dead than alive.

Joséphine and her husband were in town; he dined with them the day after his return. He went to the Institute to see the sculptor Perraud about casting another copy of the Steinway bronze for the St Petersburg Conservatoire. But mostly he lay in bed, dulling the pain with laudanum and trying to gather strength for the journey south. Brief business letters were sent to his brothers-in-law: he wanted to get his affairs in order before setting off.

Paris was much as he had left it. "That blockhead" Pasdeloup was still performing extracts from his works, this time the Fête from *Romeo*. "God knows how it will go . . . I'm in bed and have the great good fortune not to be hearing it." To balance that, a young admirer, Georges de Massougnes, sent him two splendid articles he had written for the *Redressement*, a small review published in the Latin Quarter; on the strength of it the two men became friends.

On 1 March Berlioz wrote to Stasov to "say hello" and tell him he was leaving that evening. "Oh, when I think that I shall lie stretched out on the marble steps at Monaco, in the sun, by the sea! . . . Don't be too strict with me, write to me in spite of my brevity. Remember that I am ill, that your letter will do me good; but don't talk to me about composing – no nonsense like that . . . Be sure to tell me that you have remembered me to your charming sister-in-law, your gracious daughter and your brother. I can see all three of them as if they were here. Music – Ah! I was going to say something to you about music but I'll forgo it. Farewell, write to me soon, your letter will revive me – it and the SUN. Poor unfortunate! you live amid snow."

He stopped briefly with the Suats in Vienne and then continued south to Monaco, having decided against visiting Morel and Lecourt in Marseille. "I should be shattered by your company more than by any other. Few of my friends loved Louis as you did. And I cannot forget."

Berlioz had set his heart on the Riviera; the thought of it had kept him going through the last weeks of the Russian winter. Its healing balm, as in 1831 and 1844, would be his return to life. Instead, it was the beginning of the end.

At first the weather, disappointingly, was overcast. On about the 6th it cleared and, having booked a seat on the omnibus for Nice, he thought he would enjoy the sun by the water's edge. As he was starting to clamber down the rocks his foot slipped and he fell, cutting his face and nose and, for a few minutes, losing consciousness. Bleeding profusely, he managed to get himself back to the Hôtel de Paris, where they cleaned his wounds and put him to bed. Next morning he felt well enough to take the early coach to Nice. On arriving, and having checked in to the Hôtel des Etrangers, he crossed the road to the terrace and sat down on the nearest bench overlooking the sea. After a moment he got up again to move to a seat with a better view. He took a few steps, then without warning fell head first. Two young men who were passing picked him up, his face covered in blood. They helped him to the hotel, where he stayed in bed for a week, refusing to see a doctor, writing to no one, admitting no one except the hotel staff, and speaking only with difficulty. The second fall, he recognized, had been caused by a stroke. He had intended to visit Dauphiné on his way back; but all he could do was to return to Paris, where his mother-in-law and Caroline the maid greeted his scarred face and swollen nose with cries of horror. This time the doctor came and put him on a strict diet; he was to stay in bed and not go out without permission.

Gradually the superficial consequences of the two falls diminished. He had at least one relapse; but by the last days of March his nose was almost back to normal, and he could walk holding on to the furniture. With the return of warm weather he was allowed to go out, for a drive or to the Institute for the Saturday signing on, but always with his mother-in-law in attendance or Caroline's husband Schumann: for the first time in his life he had a manservant. In June he sent for his will and wrote a codicil, adding 1,800 francs to his mother-in-law's annuity.

Speech remained difficult. When friends came to the house Mme Martin did most of the talking (in her imperviously Spanish French); he was a silent witness of their conversations. Reading was mostly beyond him – his mind was still too confused to concentrate – and writing an enormous labour. The letter to Stasov describing his accidents begins brightly enough – "My dear Stasov, you called me 'Monsieur Berlioz' in your last letter, and so did Cui. I forgive you both. But you see, your two letters will have to be written again" – but breaks off in the middle: too exhausted to continue, he had to wait till next day. In June it took him two days to complete four sides to the Grand Duchess. Once he had told his regular correspondents about his falls, the letters dwindled almost to nothing. There are none to Ferrand later than October of the previous year, when Berlioz was occupied with the affairs of Ferrand's adopted son Blanc-Gonet. He may not even have heard of the murder of Ferrand's wife on the night of 25–26 May – when Gonet broke into the house, smothered Mme Ferrand and made off with her jewels – nor of Gonet's execution in September and Ferrand's death a few days later.

Those he managed to write are pitiful to see. His handwriting – in Boschot's words, that "admirable script, elegant, artistic, imperious" – had begun to collapse some time before the journey to Russia. Now it disintegrated. A brief note to Reyer in the last week of June gives the impression that each character has been formed, or half-formed, with painful effort.

Only Estelle, and Stasov, had power to galvanize him. In June he received an anxious inquiry which must have gladdened his heart. "Since the 25th March," she wrote, "the date of your last letter, in which you told me of the accidents you had when you were alone at Menton and Nice, and the sufferings that resulted from them, I have had no further news of your health." She had hastened to reply, begging him to write if he could do so without undue fatigue; and now nearly three months had passed.

> Perhaps a letter has gone astray, thus preventing me from knowing how you are, for I cannot explain this long silence otherwise – you who are so punctilious in replying. So I beg you to be so good as to give me your news, or to have someone send it to me if you are not yet able to do so yourself; for you cannot doubt how concerned I am to learn how you are. My children are as eager to know as I am.

This time he answered at once. And this time, too, he broke the rule of their relationship and kept her letter to read and reread: it was too precious a proof of interest to be destroyed.

The letter of 21 August to Stasov (written after the journey he made that month to Grenoble), though full of woes and penned with obvious difficulty, is the last to show a flash of the true Berlioz.

> My dear Stasov
> You see, I omit the Monsieur. [He then describes his visit to Grenoble.]
> I'm worn out. And I get letters from Russia and from Loewenberg asking me impossible things. They want me to speak highly of a German artist – of whom I do indeed think well – but on condition that I speak ill of a Russian artist whom they want the German to replace and who on the

contrary deserves the highest praise. For God's sake, what kind of a world is that?*

I feel I am going to die. I no longer believe in anything.

I should like to see you. You would cheer me up, perhaps. Cui and you might put some fresh life into me. But there's nothing to be done.

I'm extravagantly bored. There's not a soul in Paris. All my friends are away, in the country, or at their country houses, or shooting. Some of them have invited me to visit them, but I don't have the strength. What are you up to? And your brother, and your charming ladies? Oh, please, please write to me, no matter how briefly. But I still feel the effects of my fall on the rocks at Monaco; I've some souvenirs of Nice too. Perhaps you're away and my letter won't reach you. I'm prepared for anything. If you're in Petersburg send me six lines – I'll be eternally grateful.

A thousand greetings to Balakirev.

Farewell. Writing is very difficult for me. You are kind. Prove it to me once again.

I shake your hand.

Hector Berlioz

Why, given his enfeebled state, he decided to go to Grenoble, a town he never cared for, and in the turmoil and heat of a summer fête, is a puzzle. To inaugurate a statue of Napoleon I on the ninety-ninth anniversary of the great emperor's birthday might have appealed to him once; but not now. He told his niece Mathilde in April that nothing would induce him to. It would mean having to speak at the ceremony – but "I can't say six words properly." A month later he wrote to tell Camille Pal that he would not be leaving Paris that year. Then the Napoleonic invitation was replaced by one asking him to preside over a choral competition for Orpheonists from the surrounding region, and he agreed to do it. Perhaps he thought that by seeing Camille Pal in person he could finally settle his financial affairs, apparently an obsessive preoccupation during these months (the last two extant letters, both to Pal, are concerned with it). Perhaps he imagined it would be an

* The Russian was Balakirev, the German Seifriz, conductor of the Loewenberg Orchestra, which Berlioz had spoken of to the Grand Duchess. The Grand Duchess had earlier mentioned the idea of engaging Seifriz for some of the concerts, in alternation with the resident conductors. According to Stasov Berlioz did not reply to the Russian Musical Society's letter.

opportunity to say goodbye to other relations and friends, like Félix Marmion, Estelle, Albert Du Boys, though he seems to have seen none of them except possibly Estelle.

Yet by a curious concatenation of nature and human contrivance the visit became a kind of apotheosis. At the banquet in the town hall on the evening of 14 August Berlioz, all accounts agree, looked more like a spectre than a living person. The mayor toasted him in the name of a Dauphiné proud of its famous son, then, sensing that the occasion called for a special gesture, took a silver-gilt crown from a casket standing on a nearby table and placed it on the head of the guest of honour, who rose to his feet. In that instant one of those freak storms familiar in the region (and celebrated in his music) burst on Grenoble. A wind like a hurricane rushed through the open windows of the hall, scattering the flowers and extinguishing the candelabra, a flash of lightning lit up the surrounding Alps, the thunder cracked, and in the ensuing darkness (an eyewitness reported) the startled banqueteers saw – "illuminated in the light of some candles the wind had spared, standing erect in his marmoreal pallor like one transfigured, his gaze profound, his features inspired and imprinted with the peculiar nobility that the approach of death confers – the author of the Fantastic Symphony".

A moment later, amid total silence, supported by two companions, the crown clutched in his hand, he left the hall. He did not attend the unveiling of Napoleon's statue next day. But, if Tiersot is right, on the way to Lyon he visited Estelle.*

After Berlioz's return from Grenoble his life ebbed rapidly. He was now a barely walking shadow. It may have been that autumn, one evening as he was leaving the Institute, that the critic Blaze de Bury met him, and saw, on the quay, "an apparition like a ghost, ashen, emaciated, bent, shaking; even his eyes, those great commanding eyes, had extinguished their spark".

The letter of 21 August to Stasov, quoted above, is the last of any substance. Stasov replied but received no answer. He wrote again in

---

* Tiersot, then a boy of eleven, was in Grenoble that day and remembered the storm and the havoc it caused. He also remembered the true history of the silver-gilt crown which, as he remarks, in its mixing of the sublime and the grotesque enhanced the romanticism of the scene. The mayor had snatched it up on impulse, but should not have done: it was due to be presented next day to the winning Orphéon. The organizers, realizing they could not very well ask for it to be returned, had to go back to the original donor, the abbot of the Grande Chartreuse, and ask him to pay for a replacement.

October, enclosing a long missive from Balakirev which contained the scenario of a four-movement symphony on Byron's *Manfred*: for (Balakirev said) "your resolution not to compose any more is very upsetting to us, and we for our part will not cease to protest with all our might against such a *wicked idea*". Stasov was equally insistent. "Forgive me for saying once again what you are unwilling to hear." He also announced good news for the coming season: "It goes without saying that there will be lots of Berlioz at the concerts; and at the two concerts of the Free School of Music we shall at last have the joy of hearing, for the first time, your Te Deum, complete, as well as the descriptive symphony [Royal Hunt and Storm] from *The Trojans*. Imagine how we are looking forward to the performance of these monumental works by the orchestra, when we are mad about them just from reading the scores or trying them out at our pianos. If only you could be with us!"

Three months before, reports of the Requiem and the Fantastic Symphony performed with success at the Altenburg Festival in Germany had stirred an unexpected joy, and he had written at once to tell Estelle. Now the news from Russia roused no response. He was beyond it. Life had receded too far. There was nothing to hold him back. So many of his contemporaries were dying: Kreutzer, Stephen de La Madelaine, Edouard Monnais, the editor of the *Gazette*, and now the great Rossini himself, whose *Barber* and *Comte Ory* and *William Tell* he had admired and whose wit he had delighted in, though he had hated what he stood for. None of this mattered any more. It was only a question of time before he followed them. Dr Nélaton had told him how long it would be. He could let go at last. For some time his memory had been failing him. When Reyer asked him to sign his copy of the vocal score of *Benvenuto Cellini*, Berlioz wrote "A mon ami" and then stopped: he could not recall his name. The inscription is hardly more than a scratch.

He could still show some life. His cousin Odile's son, Ernest Caffarel, called at 4 Rue de Calais on 18 November and reported finding him "a lot better; he spoke to me as he had before his illness. He eats like you and me. I sat while he had dinner; and to reassure you even more I can tell you that he went to the Français recently with the Charton-Demeur family to see [Balzac's] *Mercadet*". Stephen Heller remembered him, after an evening spent at Damcke's house only a few months before his death, insisting on searching in thick fog for the large white paving-stone, not far from the front door, on which he always stood when wishing

Heller good night (an idea which Berlioz clearly derived from Rabelais, who in *Gargantua and Pantagruel* notes that the ancient Greeks used to mark joyful occasions with white stones). "We parted hurriedly, for it was cold and a dense yellow fog blanketed the streets. Hardly had I gone ten paces when I heard Berlioz's voice: 'Heller! Heller! Where are you? I didn't say good night to you on the white stone.'" Heller struck match after match but in the damp air none would light, and the two of them almost crawled over the pavement before the stone loomed into view, and Berlioz, "placing both feet on it with great gravity", was able to say: "God be praised! I'm standing on it. And now – good night."

On 25 November, prompted by his friend Lassabathie the administrator of the Conservatoire, and accompanied by his manservant Schumann, Berlioz went to the Institute to vote for the historian and art critic Charles Blanc, who was elected. He was repaying a debt of twenty years' standing. Blanc had saved his librarian's job in the far-off republican days of 1848.

It was, as Blanc said, a heroic effort, but it was almost the last. The Institute archives show him as having attended the quarterly meeting of the five academies on 6 January 1869. Otherwise, the record for the final months is practically void. His account books, in which he noted income and household expenditure, fade away to nothing. The last entry, in an almost illegible hand, is for 4 February. Some time before that he became partially paralysed, perhaps by another, more severe stroke, and lost the power of speech. Once – George Osborne remembered – he took Mme Charton-Demeur's album and traced the refrain, words and music, of *Absence*: "Reviens, reviens, ma bien-aimée". But when visitors called, though he half sat up to greet them, he could only smile. At the beginning of March he sank into a coma. Friends took turns at the bedside. On the morning of the 8th Reyer scribbled a note to Dr Denau to come at once: it could not be long now. Mme Martin, Marie's friend Mme Delaroche, and Mme Charton were with him when he died, at half past noon. According to Reyer the last words anyone heard him speak were "They are finally going to play my music."

Epilogue

The funeral, three days after his death, on a chill March morning, was celebrated with the moderate degree of pomp proper to a member of the Institute and an officer of the Legion of Honour. Auber, Gounod, Ambroise Thomas, Reyer and Baron Taylor were among the pallbearers. So was Perrin, representing the Opéra, to which Berlioz had been of use when works by Weber or Gluck were revived. Trumpets of the National Guard directed by Adolphe Sax saluted the coffin as it was carried from the house and lifted on to its bier, and music from the Symphonie funèbre resounded as the two-horse cortège, with the deceased's mainly German decorations prominently displayed and a uniformed delegation from the Institute in attendance, proceeded down the steep incline of the Rue Blanche to the recently completed Eglise de la Trinité. After the service the Symphonie funèbre again accompanied the procession on its route northward to the Cimetière Montmartre.

Berlioz would have been pleased with some aspects of the church ceremony and could have predicted the rest. The music, performed by musicians from the Conservatoire, the Opéra and elsewhere, included the allegretto of Beethoven's Seventh Symphony, the march from *Alceste*, the Hostias from the Grande messe, and movements by Cherubini and Mozart – but conducted, turn and turn about, by Pasdeloup and Hainl, two leading champions of the cult of the approximate which his life had been dedicated to opposing. At the graveside there were speeches: among others, a dignified tribute by the sculptor Guillaume, president of the Institute, and one on behalf of the Conservatoire by Elwart, who exasperated Bizet by referring to the dead man as "our colleague" ("If you are going to make a speech," Berlioz had said to Elwart, "I'd just as soon not die.") The story, recounted by Boschot, of the undertakers' black horses bolting and dragging the hearse into the cemetery at full gallop – like their counterparts in *The Damnation of Faust* ("A moi,

Vortex, Giaour!") – sounds almost too good to be true. But Berlioz would have recognized the authentic Parisian character of the blunder which marred the service at what should have been its most numinous moment: the organist's rendering of the Septet ("Tout n'est que paix autour de nous") barely begun before it was cut off by the brass striking up Litolff's funeral march for Meyerbeer.

"Enfin on va jouer ma musique." Berlioz's dying remark was generally interpreted as sarcastic, in conformity with the image of a man consumed with bitterness if not fundamentally *méchant* (though Saint-Saëns would protest against the charge, asserting that "on the contrary, he was good and kind, to the point of weakness, and full of gratitude for the least sign of interest and affection that one showed him"). The words might more appropriately be seen as a prophecy, coming as they did from someone whose familiar spirits were the heroes of the ancient world, among whom – to quote Berlioz's footnote to the final scene of *The Trojans* – there was "a belief that at the moment of death one was granted foreknowledge of the future". After all, the prophecy has been largely fulfilled. His music may have had to "create its own posterity" (as Proust said of Beethoven's late quartets). But it has done so.

In France, however, it has undeniably taken its time – and, clearly, France was what he meant, since his music had already established a foothold in Britain and America and was being performed regularly in Germany and Russia. On the morning of his death a telegram delivered to the house announced the performance of scenes from *The Trojans* in St Petersburg. It was in Moscow, not in Paris, that the Grande messe des morts, a month later, commemorated his passing. In Paris he would have to wait longer.

In Britain, where his music had excited interest and made partisans, there were just enough conductors of understanding and ability to keep it alive, even while it remained controversial. William Ganz, who had played under him, introduced several works to London in the 1870s and 1880s, as did August Manns, and in Manchester Berlioz's friend Hallé and the orchestra named after him gave what Shaw said were exemplary performances, on occasion coming south and showing London how it should be done. Then came Hans Richter, and after him Harty and Beecham.

In Germany a whole school of first-rate musicians – Wagnerians almost to a man – took him up. Critics and professors might carp, but that was normal (as late as the early twentieth century the Berlin Conservatoire refused to allow Wagner's music on the syllabus). What mattered was that Bülow, Mottl, Richter, Mahler, Weingartner, believed in Berlioz and performed him. When news reached Vienna that a statue of the composer, by Lenoir, was to be unveiled in October 1886 in the Place Vintimille, Richter had a special crown carved, in the name of the Vienna Opera and Philharmonic Society, which reached Paris on the morning of the ceremony. Following Bülow's revival of *Benvenuto Cellini* at Hanover in 1879 the opera was taken up in twenty German cities. Festivals frequently featured the Requiem. Mottl, who would not tolerate criticism of Berlioz ("there is no 'but'!"), gave the complete *Trojans* – still thought of as a work in two separate parts – on successive evenings in Karlsruhe in 1890, and later in Munich and Vienna. The young Mahler conducted the Fantastic Symphony so often that its linear style became part of him; one can almost describe the texture of his music, which takes the sustaining pedal out of the Romantic orchestra, as the result of passing the Austro-German symphonic tradition through the clarifying filter of the Berliozian sonority. Weingartner, having been prejudiced against Berlioz's music (as he acknowledged), became one of its foremost champions.

For Bülow, as for Cornelius, Berlioz was spiritually a German. In Cornelius' words, it was as if the blood in his veins were German blood and he had been "nourished on German milk". For Berlioz, on the other hand, such nationalistic ideas were alien and meaningless. Austro-Germany was music's *alma parens* not for reasons of "blood" but because music was accorded unique importance there, and it was where Beethoven and Weber and Gluck came from. Equally, he could never have described himself, like Debussy, as "musicien français". He was a musician. That was sufficient.

At least by dying in 1869 he was spared the disasters of the next two years: the foolhardy conflict with Prussia, the humiliation of his admired Emperor, quondam "saviour of France", the siege and surrender of Paris, the annexation of Alsace-Lorraine, the civil war and Thiers' brutal destruction of the Commune, which he might have shocked some of his supporters by approving – though, on balance, I think it would have horrified him.

Nor might he have greatly relished being elevated, in the immediate aftermath of the war, into a kind of temporary patriotic icon, an eminent French composer to set against the conquerors' Wagner. But nationalism was the great rallying-cry in the second half of the nineteenth century; nationalistic rivalries and debates were the norm, and the search for national identity preoccupied French musicians in the decades following their country's shameful defeat. Berlioz and his music could play only a minor part in all that. He was an ambiguous figure. Where did he fit in? Under what banner could he be enrolled? He was undeniably French – Romain Rolland called him "perhaps the first great composer who dared to think in French". Yet it was France's enemy that seemed to admire and champion him most.

The *Memoirs*, published in 1870, did not help. They might kindle the sympathy and devotion of individual readers: they hardly assisted the larger cause. The book was too much of an oddity. Like the man's music it was difficult to pin down. It confronted people with the same mixture of enthusiasm and mockery, outspokenness and reticence as had perplexed them in the author during his lifetime. They tended to assume that, if not a congenital liar, he was guilty of trying it on. An industry of refutation grew up. Hippeau, and after him Boschot, made much of the supposed inaccuracy of what Stanford called "Berlioz's masterly work (of fiction?)". Its essential truthfulness took many years of research and patient demonstration to establish.

Gradually his reputation in his native country grew. But it continued to be linked to and overshadowed by that of Wagner. The anti-futurists saw the two men, however improbably, as partners in crime. When it became no longer safe to attack Wagner, because of his enormous popularity in Paris, they concentrated on attacking their other *bête noire*.

Berlioz, however, was accustomed to the disapproval of the Scribes and Pharisees. What he had feared most, in his last years, was not the hostility of individual critics but that there might be no interpreters left who knew how to perform his music: "the great Hector's sword" would "lack a master". The advent of Edouard Colonne was therefore crucial. In 1877 Colonne conducted *The Damnation of Faust* at a concert in the Châtelet and scored a triumph. The work became an instant success. Six more performances followed that season. By 1903, the centenary of the composer's birth, it had been given 117 times at the Concerts Colonne alone. Pasdeloup's gallant but approximate efforts were eclipsed. The triumph, maybe, was two-edged. Though Colonne performed most of the other major works, they did not catch on to anything like the same extent. Berlioz was accepted – as the composer of a single work, at most of two: *Faust* and the Fantastic Symphony. But the oeuvre was now in good hands. One perceptive and capable conductor outweighs a dozen obtuse commentators. In 1890 the fifteen-year-old Pierre Monteux became a violist in Colonne's orchestra and learned the music from the inside. In due course he and his younger contemporary Munch succeeded to the tradition. Berlioz's reputation in his native country might continue to have its ups and downs. But the line held.

Given that nationalistic sentiment meant little or nothing to him, why did he set so much store by his reception in France? Because, as Tiersot says, "France was one of his loves" – a love which "held him at arm's length and made him pay dearly for it. He could have said of her what he said of his first wife: 'I found it impossible either to live with her or to leave her.'" In spite of everything, Berlioz wrote, "I love our absurd country." How could he not wish to be loved in return?

Slowly, little by little, he has been. His French admirers have ceased to be a small minority, a sect. Articulate, well-informed champions of the music have grown more numerous. Only to *The Trojans* has French opinion remained generally resistant. It was a whole century after the composer's death before Claude Rostand, reviewing the Colin Davis recording in *Le Figaro littéraire*, made formal recantation in the name of his "wilfully blind" countrymen who, "relying simply on received opinion", had "always refused to accept that *The Trojans* is a great masterpiece, the summit of its composer's genius".

> According to the official view that we were taught, it was an operatic "monster", fruit of the old age of an artist in decline, its occasional beauties set in an ocean of feebleness, and in any case humanly impossible to perform or listen to in one evening. This judgement, this summary condemnation, repeated ad nauseam till recently even by the most enthusiastic Berliozians, was based not simply on incomprehension but on a large measure of pure ignorance.

It was, Rostand said, "one of the most astonishing musical scandals of all time".

Since then the opera has been staged complete, twice, in Lyon (where Munch's pupil Serge Baudo carried out his master's dream of starting a Berlioz festival in France), but in Paris not quite complete and only half-heartedly, after a fashion. It still awaits consecration by the city which cold-shouldered it. If that happens in 2003, the bicentenary of the composer's birth, the dying Berlioz's prediction will finally have been fulfilled.

Perhaps by then the dust of controversy that he raised almost from the moment of his coming into the world will have settled, and it will be possible to see his life clearly, in perspective and in all its unity-in-diversity. The processes of musical history will have run their course, its ancient disputes and unreal generalizations will have receded for good and all, and he will take his place among the great composers, his work explored without preconceptions and loved and cherished on its own terms, his existence recognized as complete. Though disease and exhaustion cut it short – what would one not give for the opera on *Antony and Cleopatra* that he nearly wrote! – the sense of defeat it once conveyed will not after all be unrelieved. It will be seen that he did fulfil himself, that the life, with its miseries as well as its splendours, was necessary to the art. If his capacity for grief, for regret, had not been so cruelly sharpened, his music might not be what it is. Sadness, suffering, mark many of his most characteristic utterances, from the opening of the Fantastic Symphony to Dido's "inutile prière d'un coeur qui se déchire" – the suffering of a nature in love with unattainable beauty, capable of infinite tenderness but estranged from the universe, proud and exalted yet naked to the whips and scorns of time. A tragic life – but, for us at least, worth the cost.

Bibliography, References, Abbreviations

Académie des Beaux-Arts, Paris, Archives of   BA

Adam, Adolphe, *Lettres sur la musique française*, ed. Joël-Marie   ADAM
Fauquet, Geneva, 1996 (reprinted from *La Revue de Paris*,
1903, Aug.–Oct.)

Almanach des Spectacles, Paris, 1822–   SPECT

Archives Nationales, Paris   AN

Association Nationale Hector Berlioz, *Cahiers Berlioz*, no.2, ed.   CAHIERS
Peter Bloom and Hervé Robert, La Côte St André, 1995

Banks, Paul, "Byron, Berlioz and Harold", Royal Musical   BANKS
Association conference, Birmingham, 1982

Barraud, Henry, *Hector Berlioz*, Paris, 1979   BARRAUD

Barzun, Jacques, *Berlioz and the Romantic Century*, 2 vols.,   BARZUN
Boston, 1950; rev. edn, New York, 1969

Berlioz, Hector, "Lettre d'un enthousiaste sur l'état actuel de   LE
la musique en Italie", in *Revue Européenne*, March-May
1832, 47–64

     Autobiographical Sketch (BN, Berlioz Papiers Divers, no.   AS
38a)

     "Voyage musical" and "Académie de France à Rome" in   IP
L'Italie pittoresque, Paris, 1834

     Grand Traité d'instrumentation et d'orchestration modernes,   TRAITE
Paris, 1843; rev., plus *L'Art du chef d'orchestre*, Paris, 1855

     De l'instrumentation, ed. Joël-Marie Fauquet, Paris, 1994   INSTR

     Voyage musical en Allemagne et en Italie, 2 vols., Paris, 1844   VM

     Les Soirées de l'orchestre, ed. Léon Guichard, Paris, 1968   SO

     Les Grotesques de la musique, ed. Léon Guichard, Paris, 1969   GROT

     A travers chants, ed. Léon Guichard, Paris, 1971   ATC

     Mémoires de Hector Berlioz, ed. Pierre Citron, Paris, 1991   MEM
     (roman numerals refer to chapter numbers)

     The Memoirs of Hector Berlioz, tr. and ed. David Cairns,   MEMC
London, 1969; rev. 1990

Les Musiciens et la musique, ed. André Hallays, Paris, [1903] MM
(articles from the *Journal des débats*)

Hector Berlioz, cauchemars et passions, ed. Gérard Condé, CONDE
Paris, 1981 (articles from various journals)

La Critique musicale d'Hector Berlioz, 1823–1863, ed. H. BCRIT
Robert Cohen and Yves Gérard, Paris, vol. 1 (1823–34),
1996; vol. 2 (1835–36), 1998

Correspondence inédite de Hector Berlioz, 1819–1868, ed. CI
Daniel Bernard, Paris, 1879

Lettres intimes, Paris, 1882 (serialized earlier in *La Nouvelle* LI
Revue, 1880, which in one or two cases published a fuller
text. The recent discovery of the original letters from
Berlioz to Humbert Ferrand, for more than forty years
believed lost, has revealed many editorial changes, cuts,
incorrect datings, etc., in the published texts)

Briefe von Hector Berlioz an die Fürstin Carolyne Sayn- SW
Wittgenstein, ed. La Mara, Leipzig, 1903

Une Page d'amour romantique: Lettres à Mme Estelle F., EST
(Editions de la *Revue bleue* et de la *Revue scientifique*),
Paris, 1903

Hector Berlioz, les années romantiques, 1819–1842, ed. Julien AR
Tiersot, Paris, 1904

Hector Berlioz, le musicien errant, 1842–1852, ed. Julien ME
Tiersot, Paris, 1919

Hector Berlioz, au milieu du chemin, 1852–1855, ed. Julien MC
Tiersot, Paris, 1930

Nouvelles Lettres de Berlioz, 1830–1868, ed. Jacques Barzun, NL
New York, 1954

Correspondance générale d'Hector Berlioz, ed. Pierre Citron, CG
8 vols., Paris, 1972– (NB. CG references in arabic
numerals are to page numbers, not to letter numbers)

Selected Letters of Berlioz, ed. Hugh Macdonald, tr. Roger BLET
Nichols, London, 1995

Berlioz Papiers Divers, Bibliothèque Nationale de France BPD
(Musique)

Berlioz, Louis, *Livre de Raison de Louis Joseph Berlioz, Docteur* LR
médecin résidant à La Côte St André (Reboul-Berlioz
Collection)

Mémoires sur les maladies chroniques, les évacuations sangu- LBMAL
inaires et l'acupuncture, Paris, 1816

"Berlioz and the Romantic Imagination": catalogue of the Ber- BVA
lioz Centenary Exhibition at the Victoria and Albert

Museum, London (Arts Council), 1969

Berlioz Society (London), Bulletin, 1952– — BSOC

Bibliothèque Municipale, Grenoble — BGREN

Bibliothèque Nationale de France (Musique), Paris — BN

Bibliothèque de l'Opéra, Paris — BOP

Bloom, Peter, *The Life of Berlioz*, Cambridge, 1998 — BLOOM

François-Joseph Fétis and the Revue Musicale (PhD, University of Pennsylvania), University Microfilms, Ann Arbor, Michigan, 1973 — BLOOMFET

"La Mission de Berlioz en Allemagne: un document inédit", in *Revue de musicologie*, 66 (1980), [70]-85 — BLOOMMISS

"Berlioz and Officialdom: Unpublished Correspondence", in *19th Century Music*, IV, no. 2 (Fall 1980), 134–46 — BLOOMOFF

"Episodes in the Livelihood of an Artist: Berlioz's Contracts with Publishers" in *Journal of Musicological Research*, vol. 15, 219–73 — BLOOMCON

Music in Paris in the Eighteen-thirties, ed. Peter Bloom (vol. 4 of *Musical Life in 19th-century France*), Stuyvesant, NY, 1987 — BLOOMPAR

Berlioz Studies, ed. Peter Bloom, Cambridge, 1991 — BLOOMSTUD

ed., *Hector Berlioz: Benvenuto Cellini, dossier de presse Parisienne, 1838 (Critiques de l'opéra français du XIXème siècle)*, 1995 — BENBLOOM

Bongrain, Anne, and Gérard, Yves, eds., *Le Conservatoire de Paris, 1795–1995*, Paris, 1996 — CONS

Boschot, Adolphe, *La Jeunesse d'un Romantique: Hector Berlioz, 1803–1831*, Paris, 1906 — BOSCHOT I

Un Romantique sous Louis-Philippe, 1831–1842, Paris, 1908 — BOSCHOT II

La Crépuscule d'un Romantique, 1842–1869, Paris, 1912 — BOSCHOT III

Bourgault-Ducoudray, Louis, "Les Musiciens célèbres: Berlioz, souvenirs intimes", in *Le Conseiller des dames et des demoiselles*, 39e année, 1 février 1886 — DUCOUDRAY

Bouvet, Charles, *Cornélie Falcon*, Paris, 1927 — BOUVET

Brenet, Michel, *Deux pages de la vie de Berlioz*, Paris, 1889 — BRENET

Bülow, Hans von, *Briefe und Schriften*, ed. M. von Bülow, 8 vols., Leipzig, 1899–1911 — BULOW

Charlton, David, "Romantic Opera, 1830–1850", in *Romanticism, 1830–1890*, ed. Gerald Abraham (*New Oxford History of Music*, IX), Oxford, 1990 — CHARLTON

Chateaubriand, François-René de, *Génie du Christianisme*, 5 vols., Paris, 1802 — CHAT

Comboroure-Thompson, Cosette, *La Carrière dramatique en* — COSETTE

France de Harriet Smithson, thèse doctorale, 3e cycle (La Sorbonne), 1973

Cone, Edward, *Music, a View from Delft*, ed. Robert P. Morgan, Chicago, 1989 — CONE

Cornelius, Peter, *Literarische Werke*, 4 vols., Leipzig, 1904–5 — CORNELIUS

Crabbe, John, *Hector Berlioz, Rational Romantic*, London, 1980 — CRABBE

Crombie, Peter, *Hans von Bülow* (forthcoming) — CROMBIE

Curtiss, Mina, *Bizet and His World*, London, 1979 — CURTISS

"Gounod before *Faust*", in *Musical Quarterly*, xxxviii (1952), 48–67 — CURGOUNOD

Delacroix, Eugène, *Correspondance générale d'Eugène Delacroix*, ed. André Joubin, 5 vols., Paris, 1935–7 — DELCOR

Journal, ed. André Joubin, 3 vols., Paris, 1932 — DELJOUR

Deldevez, Ernest, *La Société des concerts*, Paris, 1867 — DELDEVEZ

Dupuy, Ernest, "Alfred de Vigny et Hector Berlioz", in *Revue des deux mondes*, 15 April 1911, [837]–65 — DUPUY

Ellis, Katharine, *Music Criticism in Nineteenth-century France: La Revue et gazette musicale de Paris, 1834–1880*, Cambridge, 1995 — ELLIS

Elwart, Antoine, *Histoire de la Société des Concerts du Conservatoire Impérial de Musique*, Paris, 1860 — ELWART

Engel, Louis, *From Mozart to Mario*, 2 vols., London, 1886 — ENGEL

"Berlioz", in *Temple Bar*, October 1883, 204–25 — ENGBER

Fauquet, Joël-Marie, "Hector Berlioz et l'Association des artistes musiciens", in *Revue de musicologie*, 67 (1981), 211–36 — FAUQUET

Fouque, Octave, *Les Révolutionnaires de la musique: Lesueur, Berlioz, Beethoven, Richard Wagner, la musique Russe*, Paris, 1882 — FOUQUE

François-Sappey, Brigitte, "La Vie musicale à Paris à travers les *Mémoires* d'Eugène Sauzay (1809–1901)", in *Revue de musicologie* 60 (1974), 159–210 — SAUZAY

Ganz, A. W., *Berlioz in London*, London, 1950 — GANZ

Ganz, William, *Memories of a Musician*, London, 1913 — WILGANZ

Glinka, Mikhail, *Memoirs*, tr. Richard B. Mudge, Norman, Oklahoma, 1963 — GLINKA

Goncourt, Edmond and Jules de, *Pages from the Goncourt Journal*, ed. and tr. Robert Baldick, Oxford, 1978 — GONCOURT

Griepenkerl, Wolfgang Robert, *Ritter Berlioz in Braunschweig: zur Charakteristik dieses Tondichters*, Brunswick, 1843 — GRIEP

Hallé, Charles, *Life and Letters of Sir Charles Hallé*, London, 1896 — HALLE

Hanslick, Eduard, *Aus meinem Leben*, 2 vols., Berlin, 1894   HANSLEBEN

Heidlberger, Frank, ed., *Hector Berlioz: Les Troyens à Carthage,*   TRAC
*dossier de presse Parisienne, 1863 (Critiques de l'opéra
français du XIXème siècle)*, 1995

Heller, Stephen, *Lettres d'un musicien romantique à Paris,*   HELLER
ed.J.-J. Eigeldinger, Paris, 1981

Hensel, Sebastian, *The Mendelssohn Family*, tr. C. Klingemann,   HENSEL
2 vols., London, 1881

Hiller, Ferdinand, *Künstlerleben*, Cologne, 1880   HILLER

Hills, Joan, "Ariel in Vienna", in *Bulletin of the Berlioz Society*,   HILLS
XLIX (January 1965), 2–9

Hippeau, Edmond, *Berlioz intime*, Paris, 1883   BI
Berlioz et son temps, Paris, 1890   BT

Holoman, D. Kern, *Berlioz*, London, 1989   HOLOMAN
The Creative Process in the Autograph Musical Documents of   HOLDOC
Hector Berlioz, c. 1818–1840, Ann Arbor, Michigan, 1980

Catalogue of the Works of Hector Berlioz (New Berlioz   HOLCAT
Edition, vol. 25), Kassel, 1987

"The Present State of Berlioz Research", in *Acta Musicologica*   HOLRES
(International Musicological Society), vol. XLVII (1975),
31–67

"Berlioz au Conservatoire: notes biographiques", in *Revue*   HOLCONS
de musicologie, 62 (1976), 289–92

"The Berlioz Sketchbook Recovered", in *19th Century Music*,   HOLSK
VII, no. 3 (Spring 1984, "Essays to Joseph Kerman")

Hopkinson, Cecil, *A Bibliography of the Musical and Literary*   HOPK
Works of Hector Berlioz, 1803–1869, 2nd ed., rev. and
ed.Richard Macnutt, Tunbridge Wells, 1980

[Hugo, Adèle], *Victor Hugo raconté par un témoin de sa vie*, 2   VHR
vols., Brussels, 1863

Janin, Jules, *735 lettres à sa femme*, ed. Mergier-Bourdeix, 3   JANIN
vols., Paris 1973–9

Jullien, Adolphe, *Hector Berlioz: sa vie et ses oeuvres*, Paris,   JULLIEN
1888

Kemp, Ian, ed., *Hector Berlioz: Les Troyens*, Cambridge, 1988   KEMP
"*Romeo and Juliet* and *Roméo et Juliette*", in *Berlioz Studies*,   KEMPROM
ed. Peter Bloom, Cambridge, 1992, 37–79

Langford, Jeffrey, and Graves, Jane, *Hector Berlioz: a Guide*   LANGFORD
to Research, London, 1989

Legouvé, Ernest, *Soixante ans de souvenirs*, 2 vols., Paris, 1886   LEG

Lesure, François, ed., *La Musique en France à l'époque*   LESURE
romantique, Paris, 1991

Levy, David B., '"Ritter Berlioz' in Germany", in *Berlioz*   LEVY
    Studies, ed. Peter Bloom, Cambridge, 1992, 136–47

Linden, A. Vander, "En marge du centième anniversaire de la   LINDEN
    mort d'Hector Berlioz (8 mars 1869)", in *Bulletin des*
    beaux-arts, Académie Royale de Belgique, li (1969), 37–
    75

Liszt, Franz, *Artiste et société*, ed. Rémy Stricker, Paris, 1995   LISZT
    Franz Liszts Briefe, ed. La Mara, 8 vols., Leipzig, 1893–1905   LBRIEFE
    Correspondence de Liszt et de la Comtesse d'Agoult, ed.   OLLIVIER
    Daniel Ollivier, 2 vols., Paris, 1933–4
    Briefwechsel zwischen Franz Liszt und Hans von Bülow, ed.   LBULOW
    La Mara, Leipzig, 1898
    Briefe hervorragender Zeitgenossen an Franz Liszt, ed. La   LZEIT
    Mara, 3 vols., Leipzig, 1895–1904

Locke, Ralph P., *Music, Musicians and the Saint-Simonians*,   LOCKE
    Chicago, 1986

Macdonald, Hugh, *Berlioz*, London, 1982   MACB
    Berlioz Orchestral Music, London, 1969   MACO
    "One Hundred Years Ago", *Berlioz Society Bulletin*, April   MACBSOC
    1961–April 1969 (most numbers)

Maclean, Charles, "Berlioz and England", in *Sammelbande der*   MACLEAN
    Internationalen Musik-Gesellschaft, v (1904), 314–28

Maréchal, Henri, *Paris: souvenirs d'un musicien*, Paris, 1907   MARECHAL

Maretzek, M., *Revelations of an Opera Manager in 19th-century*   MARETZEK
    America: Sharps and Flats, New York, 1890

Massenet, Jules, *Mes souvenirs*, ed. Gérard Condé, Paris, 1992   MASSENET

Massougnes, Georges de, *Hector Berlioz: son oeuvre*, Paris,   MASSOUGNES
    1919

Mathieu de Monter, Emile, "Etudes biographiques et critiques: MATHIEU
    Hector Berlioz", in *Revue et gazette musicale*, nos. 24
    (1869) – 27 (1870)

Mellers, Wilfrid, *Man and His Music*, London, 1962, (Berlioz   MELLERS
    chapter) 759–73

Meyerbeer, Giacomo, *Briefwechsel und Tagebücher*, ed. Heinz   MEYERBEER
    and Gudrun Becker, 4 vols., Berlin, 1960–85
    Giacomo Meyerbeer: a Life in Letters, ed. Heinz and Gudrun   MEYBECKER
    Becker, tr. Mark Violette, London, 1989

Mongrédien, Jean, *Jean-François Le Sueur*, 2 vols., Berne, 1980   MONGLES

Murphy, Kerry, *Hector Berlioz and the Development of French*   MURPHY
    Music Criticism, London, 1988

Newman, Ernest, *The Life of Wagner*, 4 vols., London, 1933–   NEWW
    47

Newspapers and periodicals cited most often:

Correspondent	CORR
Corsaire	CORS
Figaro	FIG
France musicale	FM
Gazette musicale	GM
Illustrated London News	ILN
Journal des débats	DEBATS
Ménestrel	MEN
Music and Letters	ML
Musical Quarterly	MQ
Musical Times	MT
Musical World	MW
Neue Zeitschrift für Musik	NZfM
Nouvelle Revue	NR
Rénovateur	REN
Revue des deux mondes	RDM
Revue et gazette musicale	RGM
Revue musicale	RM

d'Ortigue, Joseph, *Le Balcon de l'Opéra*, Paris, 1833 — D'ORT

De l'Ecole musicale italienne et de l'administration de l'Académie royale de musique à l'occasion de l'opéra de M. Berlioz, Paris, 1839 — ORTCEL

Osborne, George, "Berlioz", in *Proceedings of the Musical Association*, v (1878–9), 60ff — OSBORNE

Pavans, Jean, "Hector Berlioz: un art de la fiction", in *Cahiers de la différence*, 9/10 (January–June 1990), Paris, 17–24 — PAVANS

Payzant, Geoffrey, *Eduard Hanslick and Ritter Berlioz in Prague*, Calgary, 1991 — PAYZANT

Primmer, Brian, *The Berlioz Style*, Oxford, 1973 — PRIMMER

Prod'homme, J.-G., *Hector Berlioz: sa vie et ses oeuvres*, Paris, 1905 — PROD

"Beethoven en France", in *Mercure de France*, no.690 (15 March 1927), 590–626 — PRODBEET

Raby, Peter, *Fair Ophelia: a Life of Harriet Smithson Berlioz*, Cambridge, 1982 — RABY

Reboul-Berlioz Collection (formerly Paris, now divided between the three children of the late Yvonne Reboul-Berlioz) — REBOUL

Reeve (Kolb), Katherine, *The Poetics of the Orchestra in the Writings of Hector Berlioz* (PhD, University of Yale), University Microfilms International, Ann Arbor, Michigan, 1978 — REEVE

Rey, Etienne, *La Vie amoureuse de Berlioz*, Paris, 1929 — REY

Reyer, Ernest, "Hector Berlioz: biographical notes and personal reminiscences", in *Century*, XVII (December 1893), 305–10 — REYER

Notes de musique, Paris, 1875 — REYNOTES

Richard Macnutt Collection, Withyham, Sussex — MACN

Roger, Gustave, *Le Carnet d'un ténor*, Paris, 1880 — ROGER

Rolland, Romain, *Musiciens d'aujourd'hui*, Paris, 1908 — ROLLAND

Rushton, Julian, *The Musical Language of Berlioz*, Cambridge, 1983 — RUSHTON

Berlioz: Roméo et Juliette, Cambridge, 1994 — RUSHROM

"The Genesis of Berlioz's *La damnation de Faust*", in *Music and Letters*, lvi (1975), 129–46 — RUSHFAUST

Saint-Saëns, Camille, *Regards sur mes contemporains*, ed. Yves Gérard, Arles, 1990 — SAINT-SAENS

Sand, Georges, *Correspondance*, ed. Georges Lubin, 25 vols., Paris, 1964–91 — SAND

Schumann, Robert and Clara, *The Marriage Diaries of Robert and Clara Schumann*, tr. Peter Ostwald, London, 1994 — SCHUMANN

Stasov, Vladimir, *Selected Essays on Music*, tr. Florence Jonas, London, 1968 — STASOV

Stricker, Rémy, *Georges Bizet*, Paris, 1999 — STRICKER

Franz Liszt: les ténèbres de la gloire, Paris, 1993 — LSTRICKER

Tiersot, Julien, *Hector Berlioz et la société de son temps*, Paris, 1904 — TIERSOC

Berlioziana: series of weekly articles in the *Ménestrel*, 70–72 and 75–7 (1904–6 and 1909–11) — TIERMEN

Lettres de musiciens écrites en français, ed. J. Tiersot, 2 vols., Turin, 1924, 1936 — LM

Viardot, Pauline, "Pauline Viardot-Garcia to Julius Rietz: Letters of Friendship", in *Musical Quarterly*, i (1915), 350–80, 526–59; ii (1916), 32ff — VIARDOT

Vier, Jacques, *La Comtesse d'Agoult et son temps, avec des documents inédits*, 6 vols., Paris, 1955–63 — VIER

Vigny, Alfred de, *Journal d'un poète*, ed. Louis Ratisbonne, Paris, 1882 — AV

Waddington, Patrick, "Pauline Viardot-Garcia as Berlioz's Counsellor and Physician", in *Musical Quarterly*, LIX (July 1973), no. 3, 382–98 — WADDINGTON

Wagner, Richard, *My Life*, tr. Andrew Gray, ed. Mary Whittall, Cambridge, 1983 — MY LIFE

Wagner Writes from Paris, ed. and tr. Robert L. Jacobs and Geoffrey Skelton, London, 1973 — WCRIT

Briefwechsel zwischen Wagner und Liszt, 2 vols., ed. Erich Kloss, Leipzig, 1910 — LWAGNER

Walker, Alan, *Franz Liszt*, vol. 1, *The Virtuoso Years, 1811–1847*, London, 1983 — WALKER I

Franz Liszt, vol. 2, *The Weimar Years, 1848–1861*, London, 1989 — WALKER II

Franz Liszt, vol. 3, *The Final Years, 1861–1886*, London, 1996 — WALKER III

Warrack, John, *Carl Maria von Weber*, London, 1968; rev. 1976 — WARRACK

Wotton, T. S., *Hector Berlioz*, London, 1935 — WOTTON

Wright, Michael G. H., *A Berlioz Bibliography: Critical Writing on Hector Berlioz from 1825 to 1986*, Farnborough, 1988 — WRIGHT

Notes

I

1   ... Heinrich Heine: see RGM 4 Feb. 1838.

1   The words are Berlioz's: MEM XLIV 256.

2   As Peter Raby remarks ... : RABY 132.

2   ... "like Othello": CG II 62.

2   "Eh bien, Berlioz ...": quoted CG II 60.

2   he told ... Nancy: CG II 62.

2   "elated with wild hopes ...": MEM XLIV 259.

2   ironic, he told his father: CG II 84.

2   an earlier letter ... : CG II 62–4, where it is dated 7 Jan. 1833; but more likely 14 Jan.

2   She dismissed it: see CG II 74–5.

3   Berlioz watched him parade ... : see CG II 70.

3   [Félix Marmion] wrote to Nancy: REBOUL, 2 Feb. 1833, quoted CG II 70n–71n.

3   ... Edouard Rocher hints: see CG II 93–4.

3   [Marmion] sent a report to Nancy: REBOUL, 10 Feb. 1833, quoted CG II 75n.

3   "Our one resource": see CG II 86.

4–5   "Oh my father ...": CG II 83–4.

5   "In the last resort": CG II 79.

5   And to Adèle: CG II 97.

5   "Will they prevent my marrying ...": CG II 101.

6   ... her sister Anne: her name on B's and Harriet's marriage certificate is given as Anne-Cécile (see CAHIERS 21).

6   Berlioz was actually mad: see CG II 121.

6–8   Félix Marmion in a letter of 6 March: REBOUL (shorter quotation, CG II 82n–83n).

9   ("which wasn't true"): CG II 88.

9   "The one thing that frightens me ...": CG II 63.

9	he wrote to Edouard Rocher: CG II 90.
9	Nancy regretted . . . : REBOUL, quoted CG II 90n.
9	. . . Berlioz was telling Rocher: CG II 92.
9	"cold and impassive . . .": CG II 106.
9	Even Nancy was touched: REBOUL, quoted CG II 107n–108n.
9–10	"This evening I shall see Harriet . . .": CG II 104.
10	"once more hesitated . . .": CG II 111–12.
10	He had . . . waited nearly six years: cf. RABY 144.
10	. . . a young woman of eighteen: see CG II 112.
11	. . . British Embassy . . . Faubourg St Honoré: near the Place de la Concorde. The former Hôtel Borghèse, residence of Napoleon's sister Princess Pauline, was bought by the British government in 1814. The marriage contract was signed the previous day, 2 Oct. (BLOOM 60).
11	The account in the *Memoirs*: XLIV 260.
11–12	. . . in Barzun's phrase: BARZUN I 410.
12	. . . says Hippeau: BI 341.
12	. . . says Tiersot: TIERSOC 79.
12	"the thousand and one absurd slanders": CG II 121.
12	. . . forced him to take [the money] back: MEM XLIV 259.
12	"glad he had nothing . . .": CG II 63.
13	"changed in every respect": CG II 38.
13	Janin . . . in the *Journal des débats*: 8 Jan. 1833.
13	in Antoine Fontenay's box: see Fontenay, *Journal intime*, Paris, 1925, 166–7. F saw Harriet as Jane Shore a month before and recorded her, in his diary, as having been "très belle".
13	Dorval . . . to Vigny: quoted COSETTE 275.
13	Adèle Hugo: CG II 388–9.
13	The newspaper accounts: the press continued to cover the company even after it had moved to the Rue Chantereine.
14	. . . the *Débats* reported: 7 Dec. 1832, where the "modesty" of Nature is printed as "majesty" (COSETTE 155).
14	in January 1833, another critic . . . : in *L'Artiste*, quoted RABY 139.
14	"illuminating the whole heaven of art": MEM XVIII [112].
14	(he writes to Albert Du Boys): CG II 60.
15	she is "Ophelia in person": CG II 127.
15	no longer the slim and graceful beauty: CG II 63.
15	"Her character is really amazing": CG II 104.
15	"One day she saw me so moved . . .": CG II 102.
16	She is his "star": CG II 49.
16	the "excessive" Berlioz . . . the texts . . . : CG II 42, 103, 59, 79, 111–12. See also the letter to d'Ortigue, CG II 68.

16	sobbing in Liszt's arms: OLLIVIER I 19–20 [4 April 1833].
16	telling Hiller . . . : CG II 108.
16–19	Ernest Legouvé . . . : LEG I 291–5.
19	. . . a plea to Liszt: CG II 49.
19	Edouard Rocher . . . urged him: CG II 94.
20	Hiller described . . . : HILLER 85.
20	Harriet . . . "was already too old": LEG I 301.
20	Etienne Rey's phrase: REY 112.
20	Jonathan Keates . . . : in a review in the *Observer*.
21	"the two wings of the soul": MEM Travels in Dauphiné 602.
21	his "sole and unique chance": CG II 79.
22	"jolie petite maison . . .": CG II 117.
22	he told Ferrand . . . To Liszt . . . : CG II 122, 119.
23	Chopin . . . "Your charming letter": CG II 121.
23	Years later he recalled: DEBATS 6 Sept. 1846.
23	"When I feel I have misspent": CG II 117.
23	"followed . . . her recovery": CG II 107.
23	". . . thinks the whole world" . . . lacking in confidence: CG II 115–16.
23	he was at Hugo's house: see CG II 119.
23	. . . a go-between for Schutter: see CG II 120.
23–4	. . . the Comtesse de Vigny's album: see CG II 117n ; DUPUY 842–3; and the album (private collection).
24	a clause in . . . marriage contract: see CG IV 474; CAHIERS 20.
24	Harriet asked Mlle Mars: CG II 103. The letter was written by B and signed by H.
25	according to the *Revue musicale*: 1833, 348–9.
25	Berlioz on his own admission: MEM XLV 263.
26	one of the harpists . . . tripped: SAUZAY 170.
26	"As the clamour increased" . . . d'Ortigue: QUOT 4 Dec.1833.
26	A supporter yelled . . . : see CG II 135.
27	. . . Berlioz treats it in the *Memoirs*: XLV 262.
27	Harriet . . . "showed herself . . .": MEM XLV 264.
27	"sleep on straw": CORNELIUS I 157.
27	Schlesinger . . . to Meyerbeer: MEYERBEER II 355.
27	. . . wrote d'Ortigue in the *Quotidienne*: 17 Jan. 1834.
28	Berlioz described [Harriet] to Adèle: CG II 143–4.
28	"on the point of leaving for Germany": CG II 156–7.
28	*L'Europe littéraire*: at 50c. a line (see CG III 120). 12 June, 19 July 1833. Also "Journal d'un enthousiaste", an edited version of the *Revue Européenne* article on Italy, 8 May 1833.
28	*Rob Roy*. . . in April: 14 April 1833, with Beethoven Sym. 4 and

arrangements of string quartets, music by Meyerbeer, Cherubini, etc.

29   He had written to Spontini: CG II 136–7.

29   [Harriet and Alphonse Robert]: CG II 144.

29   biographers have scoffed: e.g. BARRAUD 73–4.

30   . . . he sketched the Pilgrims' March: MEM XLV 266.

30   "Oph.'s love . . .": CG I 232.

30   A letter to Ferrand . . . "horribly sad": CG II 184.

30–31 Another, to Liszt: CG II 177–9 [May 1834].

30   "my artistic affections" . . . Spontini: B was stirred to write a vigorous defence of *La Vestale* in REN on 18 May.

31   [Adèle, Harriet, Nancy]: CG II 125–6, 131–2, 167.

31–2 [B accosted by Paganini]: see MEM XLV 264.

32   Beethoven's choral symphony . . . review of themes: see BANKS.

32   His original scheme for *Harold*: see CG II 164.

2

35   They . . . "talked and argued art": CG II 181.

36   "pastorally seated in the garden": CG II 189–90.

36   . . . reply which, he told Ferrand: CG II 195.

37–8 "Yes, my dear Adèle": CG II 198–201.

39   "below the level of her talents": CG II 240.

39   [Th.Nautique, plans for opera, German chorus]: see REN 2 July, 14 Dec.1834 (BCRIT I 283–5, 476).

39   Janin, in the *Débats*: DEBATS 1 Dec.1834.

40   . . . review in the *Gazette*: 7 Dec.1834.

40   . . . *Galignani's Messenger*: 29 Nov.1834.

40   . . . still mentioning [Paganini]: CG II 196.

40   d'Ortigue's review: QUOT 27 Nov.1834.

41   . . . the Boulogne press . . . the Paris papers: *L'Annotateur* 26 June; DEBATS 2 July; GM 6 July; DEBATS 9 July; GM 13 July 1834.

41   [Janin and Paganini]: DEBATS 15 Sept.; GM 21 Sept.; DEBATS 22 Sept.1834.

41   D'Ortigue . . . clearly implies . . . : QUOT 27 Nov.1834.

41   Chopin . . . at the third concert: see BLOOMPAR 276–7. Liszt too had at first been going to appear.

41   . . . had to ask . . . Gounet: CG II 133.

41–2 [letter to Duc d'Orléans, . . . cheque]: BLOOMOFF 138–9.

42   Fétis' *Revue musicale*: 4 Jan.1835.

42   The *Revue du théâtre*: quoted BOSCHOT II 275.

42	... Janin ... : DEBATS 24 Nov. 1834.
42	Berlioz told Ferrand: CG II 209.
43	He informed d'Ortigue: CG II 213.
43	Schlesinger wrote to Meyerbeer: MEYERBEER II 430.
43	[Girard] failed to correct the harpist: see MEM XLV 266.
44	"Ha! ha! ha! haro! ...": quoted MEM XLV 266-7.
44	In *Lettres d'un voyageur*: Paris 1857, 335. HOLOMAN 171 places the incident, wrongly, in December 1835.
44	Antoni Deschamps ... : 15 Nov.1834, quoted CG II 204n-205n.
44	d'Ortigue ... the "magical moment": QUOT 12 March 1833.
45	encouraged by Harriet, he had risked: see CG II 316.
45-6	[letters about journalism]: CG II 225, 232, 243-4, 247-8, 263, 264.
46	Delacroix ... : quoted J.-M. Bailbé, *Le Roman et la musique en France sous la Monarchie de Juillet*, 1969, 140.
46	"wings too wide ...": CG II 198.
46	Clapisson ... : see ROGER 1.
46	Berlioz's studio ... Gastinel ... : see AR 269 n1.
47	"doomed to be different": MEM XXX 164.
47	"Ten francs for an idea!": CG II 109-10; MEM XLVII 279.
49	the "Opéra and Conservatoire crowd": CG II 109.
49	"working outside the theatre ... idiot directors": CG II 233, 230.
49-50	Liszt shut himself away: see OLLIVIER I 22-3, 25-6; VIER I 380.
50	George Sand ... "la fraternité ...": SAND III 612.
50	Bertin de Vaux: see BOSCHOT II passim.
51	Thiers ... in ... Goncourt's phrase: GONCOURT 196.
51	Guizot told Legouvé: LEG I 327.
52	his ... ideas on tone-painting: RGM 1 and 8 Jan.1837.
52	d'Ortigue ... tell the story: QUOT 17 Jan.1834.
52	as Berlioz said of Heine: MEM Germany I 361.
52	Most criticism of Balzac: see David Bellos, *Balzac Criticism in France, 1850-1900*, Oxford, 1976, 13-14.
53	The article ... in the *Débats* in 1837: 10 Nov.
53	Legouvé ... "few felt easy ...": LEG I 315.
53	who did not ... play the game [or] take bribes: TIERSOC 178 ("l'intérêt n'avait pas de prise sur ses jugements").
53	"Cab, sir?": by Cham (*Charivari* 18 Nov. 1855, reproduced JULLIEN 228).
54	"It's all in my orchestra": GM 18 Jan. 1835.
55	... "symphony on a new ... plan": CG II 230.

56	"as one having authority . . .": *Matthew* vii 29.
57	". . . *Gazette musicale*": 5 Oct. 1834.
57	"desperate for a few francs": MEM XLVII 279.
60	Italian musical culture . . . Liszt: cf. Liszt at La Scala, in Franz Liszt, *Lettres d'un bachelier ès musique*, ed. Rémy Stricker, Paris, 1991, [71]ff.
60–62	"The other day . . . the Théâtre-Italien: REN 5 Dec. 1834.
62–3	His review of Donizetti . . . : REN 29 March 1835.
63	Carafa: cf.CG III 401: "a musical odd-job man whose only recommendation is that he's not French". Carafa more than once got a lucrative post that B aspired to.
63	"*La grande duchesse* . . .": REN 3 Dec. 1835. B in MEM wrongly recalled his review as consisting simply of the Bossuet quotation.
63–6	*Débats. . . Zampa*: 27 Sept. 1835.
66	"walking on eggshells": GROT 117.
66	"I find Paër's opera . . .": CG II 190–91 (1835, but dated 1834 in CG).
66	"Despite M. Bertin's request . . .": CG II 229.
66	"my position has not allowed me": CG II 164.
66	(in a letter to . . . Rellstab): CG II 434.
67	"Recently Jules Janin . . .": CG II 333.
67–8	"My old chest complaint": CG II 552–4.
68	that "infernal chain": CG VI 200.
68	"How rarely am I able . . .": CG VI 22–3.
68	Janin confirmed it: reference mislaid.
68	"I am trying to support . . . Gounod": CG VI 277. Cf.CG III 745: "je n'ose aller la [Mme Viardot] voir, je ne saurais que dire . . . et que vais-je écrire dans mon feuilleton?"
68n	a review of . . . Lenz's *Beethoven*: DEBATS 11 Aug. 1852 (SO 398–411).
68–9	He enlarges . . . in his *Memoirs*: XLVII 281.
69	The methods devised by . . . Castil-Blaze: see MURPHY 66.
69	to quote Katherine Kolb: see Katherine Kolb Reeve, "Hector Berlioz", in *European Writers: The Romantic Century*, New York, 1985, vol.6, 785.
69–70	"M. Duponchel – the Opéra Chorus": REN 31 Aug. 1835.
70–71	"One day on its long legs . . .": DEBATS 24 Dec. 1846.
71	"Mlle Falcon, so energetic . . .": REN 6 March 1834.
71	reviewing the dreaded Mlle Nathan: DEBATS 28 May 1839.
71	"To write nothing about nothing": MEM LIII 420.

72   as Tiersot says: TIERSOC 173–4.

72   "they should take the channel ferry . . .": quoted RABY 128.

72   Louis Gouin . . . : letter of 23 July 1833 (MEYERBEER II 321).

72   Janin . . . ready to exploit his position: see MURPHY 62.

72–3   Heine . . . "just as the apostle": quoted BOSCHOT II 328.

73   Meyerbeer owed [Fiorentino] 3,000 francs: see ENGEL I 197ff, and Baron de Trémont in "Le monde musical à l'époque romantique: souvenirs inédits (1re série)", ed. J.-G. Prod'homme, MEN 30 LXXXIX, 30 Sept.1927.

73   Gifts of money . . . : see Adam to Fiorentino, LM II 108–9.

73   "In justice to myself . . .": MEM XLVII 281.

74   Berlioz responded with . . . enthusiasm: e.g. DEBATS 17 March 1839.

74–5   "The historical concert . . . M. Fétis": REN 29 April 1835.

75   to quote Gérard Condé: CONDE 14, 15.

75   "capture the attention . . .": CONDE 16.

75–6   "Why must this stately . . .": RGM 9 April 1837.

76–7   "If I were rich . . .": RGM 28 Jan.1841.

77–8   "Following our admirable custom . . .": DEBATS 25 April 1835.

78   the struggle had taken its toll: cf.BARZUN I 245: "in a man of artistic faith the continual dissent of mankind engenders at last a spiritual weariness".

78   "good to be alive . . .": MEM Travels in Dauphiné [583].

78   the critic's true role: see my vol.1, 217, 289.

79   Schumann . . . : NZfM 2 [1835] 42, quoted Kolb (Reeve), Colloque Berlioz, Grenoble, 1980.

79   on the slow movement of the Eroica: DEBATS 25 Jan.1835; RGM 9 April 1837.

79   . . . Pastoral Symphony: RGM 4 Feb.1838.

79–80   . . . Seventh Symphony: RGM 11 Feb.1838.

80   . . . the Fourth . . . in the *Débats*: 12 April 1835.

81   came "uniquely . . . out of Beethoven's genius": RGM 28 Jan.1837.

81   the Grande Armée veteran: DEBATS 18 April 1835.

81   "At the first five or six performances": REN 27 April 1834.

82   *Fidelio*. . . in the *Débats*: 19, 22 May 1860.

82   There exists, as Condé says: CONDE 16.

82   a distinction . . . between "criticism" . . . and "feuilletonizing": e.g. MEM LIII [418].

83   "May the fires of heaven . . .": CG III 627.

84   "Meanwhile I must go on writing": CG VI 200, 14 Feb. 1861, to Louis.

84   "Oh the brutal, brainless . . .": REN 5 Oct. 1835, BCRIT II 305.

4

85	. . . a detailed plan: BPD 10. This is usually assigned to 1835 (e.g. HOLOMAN 169), but the day and month – Thursday 22 Nov. – and the fact that Duprez (still in Italy in 1835) is mentioned among possible singers both point to 1838.
85	camping out at 34 Rue de Londres: cf.CG II 276, 23 Jan. 1836: "Je n'ai pas trouvé le moyen d'acheter la moitié des meubles qui nous sont nécessaires."
86	A letter of December 1834: 18 Dec. (Pierpont Morgan Library).
86	Ministry of the Interior refuse . . . permission: BLOOMOFF 146.
86–7	She and Berlioz went to see Victor Hugo: see CG II 233.
87	the Conservatoire was "the one hall . . .": CG II 229.
87	. . the best season . . . was unavailable: CG II 232.
87	Liszt's programme . . . included . . . : but not the Fantastic (as in HOLOMAN 614): see REN 25 April 1835.
87	The concert, he told his father: CG II 239–40.
87	". . . musical performance was detestable": d'Ortigue's review (GM 10 May, an impassioned defence of B's genius and courage) confirms this, at least so far as the choral singing in *Lélio* is concerned.
88	no fewer than eight . . . reports: see BCRIT 1 passim.
89	*Othello* at the Porte St Martin: see Robert Baldick, *The Life and Times of Frédéric Lemaître*, London, 1959, 149–50.
89–91	"My dear Papa . . .": CG II 238–41.
91	"Your former piano teacher Camille Moke": MEYERBEER II 459.
91	a summer-house built by Henri IV: CG II 255.
91	"the élite of . . . young writers": CG II 255–6; BLOOMSTUD 87.
91	stipend due on 1 July: by mid-June he was asking the ministry to "expedite it as quickly as possible" (CG II 242).
91–2	an early version of . . . the first movement: the Symphonie funèbre comes before *Romeo* in B's chronological list of mss (MUSEE).
92	review of . . . *Le cinq mai*: RGM 29 Nov.1835, by the pseudonymous Germanus Le Pic. *Le cinq mai* would fit plausibly into the scheme of such a work.
92	the Panthéon . . . as he told Ferrand: CG II 248.
93	Berlioz's . . . article . . . in the *Débats*: 9 Aug.1835.
93	"quarry . . . long lain in wait for": MEM XLVI 270.
93	"The whole thing . . . finished": CG II 248, 247.
94	the first night of . . . *Chatterton*: Théâtre-Français, 12 Feb. 1835. B's letter: CG II 227.
94	"Harriet hates to see me so enslaved": CG II 244.

94	letter, to Edouard Rocher: CG II 277.
95	the baby . . . seriously ill: see CG II 254–5.
95	[Harriet and B's family]: see CG II 285, 266, 279, 274.
95–6	the two on Meyerbeer's piano music: 18, 25 Oct. 1835.
96	the abuses of the operatic establishment: see Louis Gouin to Meyerbeer, MEYERBEER II 366.
96	Rellstab: RGM 9–30 Aug.1840.
96	Stoepel's eloquent account: 2 Feb.1834.
97	a "ruthless . . . businessman . . .": Katharine Ellis, *La Revue et Gazette Musicale de Paris: The State of Music Criticism in Mid Nineteenth Century France* (doctoral dissertation, 1991), 35–6.
97	a favourable notice . . . Herz's concertos: 6 March 1842, by Henri Blanchard.
97	Stoepel's review of . . . *Neuf mélodies*: 25 May 1834.
98	a counter-attack by Schumann: see CG II 263, where B says he has received "a bundle of articles from journals in Leipzig and Berlin, in which Fétis has been given a good thrashing on my account".
98	lists of . . . musicians: BPD 9. The many pages in B's hand are a particularly vivid illustration of how much work went into arranging such concerts, and how much they cost. The documents list the musicians' fees and ancillary costs: hire of hall, heating, candles and the remuneration of the orchestra attendant, Hottin.
99	again Girard made a bad mistake: see MEM XLV 266.
99	only one rehearsal: see CG II 260–61.
99	to Adèle . . . to Liszt: CG II 265, 282.
99	. . . work as organizer . . . : a new art: See HOLOMAN 23.
100	he wrote to Adolphe Samuel: CG V 394.
100	Spontini chided him: CG III 138.
100	according to Charles Hallé: HALLE 68.
100	von Bülow: Bülow, however, later modified his opinion.
100	as Louis Engel said: ENGEL I 68.
100	Pierre Boulez's dicta: in William Glock, *Notes in Advance*, Oxford, 1991, 133, and as reported in David Cairns, "How the Past Makes the Present Take Note", *Sunday Times*, 3 Dec. 1989.
100	the "uplifting fatigue": quoted in D. Kern Holoman, "The Emergence of the Orchestral Conductor in Paris in the 1830s", BLOOMPAR 428.
101	the management . . . new concert hall: see CG II 283–4, 281.
101	the current minister, Thiers: who was not a member of the Bertin circle (Thiers' newspaper was the *Constitutionnel*).
101	"profound dejection" (he told Liszt): CG II 281.
102	Music . . . emancipator of the masses: see Anik Devriès, "La 'Musique

à bon marché' en France dans les années 1830" in BLOOMPAR.

103   "that hellish ministerial world": CG II 277.

103   The history of *Benvenuto Cellini*: see NBE vol.1a, foreword by Hugh Macdonald, on which this account of the genesis of the libretto is partly based. Barbier's different account (see *Etudes dramatiques*, Paris, 1874, and *Souvenirs personnels et silhouettes contemporaines*, Paris, 1883) does not accord with the facts as known.

103   "simpletons that we were": CG II 197.

104   undated letter from Armand Bertin: listed in Librairie Henri Saffroy, Catalogue no. 7, Dec. 1968, no. 1223. It refers to a 3-act libretto, but this could have been *Cellini* at an earlier stage.

104   . . . so long as Véron was there: CG II 245.

104   Duponchel "imagines he likes my music": CG II 245–6.

104   The Bertin influence had . . . waned: see CG II 281.

5

106   the scene of the bathing beauties: see Louis Gouin to Meyerbeer, 10 Dec.1833, MEYERBEER II 353.

107   [the duet's] rehearsal with orchestra: see BOUVET 99ff.

107   scornful of the "platitudes": CG II 233.

107   "I am very curious . . .": CG II 231.

107   what Louis Engel called his "clever head": ENGEL II 54–5.

107   ". . . so many interests . . . are at stake": CG II 288.

107   Meyerbeer "enduring the complaints": RGM 6 March 1836.

108   "The influence of Meyerbeer": MEM LIX 551.

108   talking during *Robert le diable*: SO Fifth Evening,

108   the Blessing of the Daggers: MEM LIII 425–6. See also CG III 195–6, letter to Meyerbeer.

108   the Michelangelo of music: see Bizet in STRICKER 51 (BARZUN I 551n).

109   Mendelssohn . . . found it heartless: see J. M. Bailbé, "Mendelssohn à Paris en 1831–1832", in BLOOMPAR 32–3.

109   Liszt . . . to Marie d'Agoult: OLLIVIER I 170.

109   Verdi . . . "the power of Meyerbeer's genius": quoted Julian Budden, *The Operas of Verdi*, vol. 2, London, 1978, 153 n7.

110–11   to dictate the conditions: cf. ENGEL I 208. (See also ROGER 208 on M's active enjoyment of theatre politics.

111–12   The account . . . in the *Memoirs*: XLVIII 289–90.

112   "having the best heart . . .": CG II 451, undated, *c.* 25 April 1836, wrongly attributed to July 1838.

113   as Liszt said, ". . . the crowd speaks": NZfM, quoted BARZUN I 304.

114   induced, with Meyerbeer's aid: cf. Prosper Pascal, review of *The Trojan at Carthage* (TRAC 17): "l'intervention d'un allié puissant l'y fait entrer".

114   Hoffmann's *conte* "Signor Formica": see NBE vol. 1a, Foreword, and Raymond Hyatt, "Hoffmann's 'Story of Salvator Rosa' and the libretto of *Benvenuto Cellini*", in BSOC 119 (winter 1983–4), 11–15.

117   Robert Craft remarks: in *Prejudices in Disguise*, New York, 1974, 155.

117   the huge shining Perseus: actually an idea thought up by B for the Weimar production, not in the original scenario.

118   another transformation: see also Bernardino's "Tra-la-la" in Tableau 2, sung to a reminiscence of the opening scene's "De profundis".

119   As David Charlton remarks: CHARLTON 111.

120   the multiple bells and saxhorns: see CHARLTON 111.

121   a task . . . "delicate and difficult": CG II 284.

121   Berlioz conceded that the . . . *débats*: CG II 285.

121   Mlle Bertin's talent: MEM XLVIII 285.

121   "some really remarkable things": CG II 306.

121   "What an inferno . . .": CG II 308–9.

122   A gesture of Rossini's . . . : see HALLE 98–9.

122   Charles Hallé . . . described Louise Bertin: HALLE 98.

122   the violinist Sauzay: see SAUZAY 174–5.

122   ". . . satisfying to . . . the Bertin family": CG II 303.

122   as the *Figaro*. . . put it: quoted BOUVET 111.

122   "with . . . his mulatto lungs": CG II 319.

122   (wrote Nourrit . . . to his brother): LM II 259.

122   Janin['s] review: 17 Nov. 1836.

122   In a subsequent article: 17 Dec. 1836.

123   (an impression . . . confirmed): see VHR 379, where Adèle Hugo also records that disaster struck two of the leading members of the cast, Falcon and Nourrit.

123   planned to be rid of the piece: see Nourrit (LM II 259): "We are going to give it five or six times, and I trust that that will be the end of it."

123   a memorandum in his hand: see "The Berlioz Sketchbook, 1832–1836", ed. D. Kern Holoman, in *19th Century Music*, VII/3 (3 April 1984).

124–5   "I was assassinated with demands": CG II 317.

125   the *Courrier français* . . . the *Carrousel*: quoted CG II 317n, 318n.

125   In the *Monde*. . . Liszt: 11 Dec. 1836.

125   He told Adèle . . . : CG II 316.

126   "I announced my two . . . symphonies": HOLOMAN 180 wrongly states that they had been performed together two years earlier. This was in fact the first time.

126   Liszt . . . , wrote Berlioz in the *Gazette*: 12 June 1836.

126   Liszt and Berlioz . . . , wrote Heine: RGM 4 Feb. 1838.

126   "truncated and hacked about": B to Liszt, CG II 294.

126   ". . . I shall have made in two weeks . . .": CG II 316.

127   "never has the great tragedienne": QUOT 24 March 1836, quoted RABY 156–7, CG II 289n.

127   Janin took flamboyant exception: 19 Dec. 1836.

127   a letter from Harriet to Butler: Garrick Club, quoted COSETTE Appendix II.

128   The parents . . . Hector's advice: see CG II 300–301, 304, also Félix Marmion to Joséphine B, 6 Sept. [1836] (REBOUL).

128   [B to Nancy]: CG II 287.

129   "lazy, insolent and dishonest": CG II 274–5.

129   Louis can "run about", etc.: CG II 277, 286.

129   writing fewer articles for the *Débats*: 11, as against 19 in 1835 and 20 in 1836.

129   Luckily (Berlioz told Adèle): CG II 320–21.

130   written agreement with Duponchel: see CG II 252, 2 Oct. 1836 (wrongly dated 1835 in CG).

131   Berlioz, in . . . the *Gazette*: 4 Dec. 1836.

131   an intimate of Agenor de Gasparin: see MEM XLVI [268].

131   Boschot remarks: II 343.

131   "belonging to the small community": MEM XLVI [268].

131   subscribers to the Société des Concerts: see Elisabeth Bernard, "Les abonnés à la Société des Concerts du Conservatoire", BLOOMPAR 46.

131–2 Berlioz reported to his father: CG II 337, dated 8 March, postmarked the 9th.

6

133   [save] the Messe des morts . . . from the flames: CG VII (11 Jan. 1867); LI 302–3.

134   *Le dernier jour du monde*: see my vol. 1, passim.

134   the funeral of Marshal Lannes: see CG II 373.

134   the journalist who in December 1837: *Figaro* 5 Dec., quoted PROD 170.

135   he recalled the trouble he had: CG II 344–5.

135   in Saint-Saëns' phrase: *Guide musical* (Berlioz centenary numbers), 1903, 627.

135–6   Paul Rosenfeld: in *Musical Impressions*, ed. Herbert A. Leibowitz, London, 1970, 97.

136   Wordsworth's "visionary gleam": cf. MELLERS 771.

136   "It is thou that art our father": MEM LIX 543.

136   the very loss . . . permanent mark: see the recurring religious imagery in B's works – *Harold*, *Romeo*, *Faust*, Fantastic I (coda), etc. – and the fact that the impulse for his three large-scale sacred works came from himself.

137   "I felt as if my brain . . .": MEM XLVI 270.

137–8   Edward Cone's classic essay: CONE 139–57.

139   what he called his architectural works: MEM Postscript 561.

140   "promisisti" . . . the last word: pointed out by Katherine Jang during a graduate seminar which Kern Holoman and I took at the University of California, Davis, in 1994.

140   28,000 francs, protested . . . Adam: ADAM 20–21.

140   "not devoid of talent": MEM XLVI 269.

141   a timetable of what remained to do: autograph full score p. 21 (BN ms 1509). It raises the possibility that the Agnus was originally an independent movement (perhaps even based on the G minor Agnus of the *Messe solennelle*) and that the return of the Requiem aeternam music and the crucial framing it achieves came quite late in the composition of the work. But it should be noted that the list, in pencil, is difficult to decipher, owing to the waxes used in restoration of the score, and none of the published transcriptions are reliable.

141   preparation of . . . parts: see CG II 348.

141   his copyist Rocquemont: see HOLOMAN 232–3; HOLCAT 159; HOLDOC passim.

141   (at one point mounting guard . . .): see MEM LIII 424.

141–2   "a man of uncommon intelligence . . .": MEM LIII 424.

142   Montfort . . . enrolled . . . percussion: see BPD 11.

142   "The Requiem exists": CG II 354–5.

142   to Liszt: "Fortunately . . .": CG II 357.

143   the *National* remarked: quoted CG II 354n.

143   Berlioz . . . logical in pointing out: CG II 360.

143   Armand Bertin . . . a "stinging" letter: see CG II 361.

143   prompted by Félix Marmion: see CG II 358n.

144   "to do a lot of running about": CG II 363.

144   "with all possible insistence": CG II 369.

144–5   "The First Opera": RGM 1, 8 Oct. 1837.

145	He writes to Dumas: CG II 371, where it is assigned the date 30 Oct. However, 16 or 23 is more likely.
145	Halévy tries to get the Bertins . . . : MEM XLVI 271–2.
145	He corresponds with Vatout: CG II 373–4 (also 369–70).
146	the Conservatoire's . . . prizegiving: DEBATS 20 Nov. 1837, quoted PROD 169.
146	"not lost anything by waiting": CG II 394.
146	"a very sad ceremony": CG II 368.
146	the number of performers was reduced: see BPD 11 and 16.
147	Louise Vernet-Delaroche: see CG II 380.
147	a pinch of snuff: my placing it at the public dress rehearsal, not at the performance, is conjectural, but based partly on the assumption that a relatively unknown musician like Hallé would be more likely to have been at the public rehearsal than among the bigwigs at the grand ceremonial occasion itself. For the veracity of the incident, see my discussion in BMEMC 520–21.
147	Vigny . . . : AV 72.
147	Louis was "enraptured . . .": CG II 384.
147	famous operatic names like Levasseur . . . : see BPD 12.
148	as the *Siècle* reported: quoted PROD 172.
148	the curé of the Invalides . . . the Duc d'Orléans: see CG II 383, 391.
148	the *Constitutionnel* ascribed his triumph: quoted PROD 171–2. The same paper found the chanted De profundis "altogether more vivid and poignant than M. Berlioz's Dies irae".
149	Bottée de Toulmon . . . : RGM 10 Dec. 1837.
149	. . . moved d'Ortigue to thank him: LM II 207–8.
149	Legouvé . . . General Bernard . . . Liszt: CG II 382, 381, 387.
149	They "merely added a nought": MEM XLVI 276.
149	the *Morning Post*: 8 Dec. 1837, reproducing *Galignani's Messenger* of the 6th.
149	to Schumann in an open letter: reproduced CG II 327–32.
150	the retirement of . . . Nourrit: DEBATS 5 April 1837.
150	to review . . . Duprez: DEBATS 19 April, 17 May 1837.
151	Falcon was unable to answer . . . : BOUVET 115.
151	Marmion was at Duprez's debut: see CG II 346.
151	Relations with La Côte: see CG II passim.
152	"from Aunt Adèle": CG II 407.
152	"Harriet too complains . . ." CG II 368.
152–3	memorandum . . . [duke's] . . . secretary: see BLOOMOFF 143. The duchess expressed her regret at not having "been able to find an occasion of admiring [Harriet's] talent during the [wedding] festivities at Versailles" (CG II 362).

153 the "hours of smoke-filled talk": CG II 523.

153 Liszt's "duel with . . . Thalberg: see WALKER I 237ff.

153 [Trio concert]: RGM 19 Feb. 1837; OLLIVIER I 186–7; HALLE 39. CORNELIUS I 176 shows that Liszt was still recalling it, with amusement, in 1854.

153–5 [Berlioz–Marie d'Agoult–George Sand correspondence]: see VIER I 257, 405; CG II 348–9, 351, 352–3, 356, 365.

156 Berlioz applied for a licence: CG II 409–10.

7

157 [Joséphine B's death]: at 2 a.m., witnessed by Dr B's tenant, the blacksmith Claude Ferlet (Actes civils, Mairie, La Côte St André).

157 "too weak to write": undated, postmarked 1838 (REBOUL).

157 The last . . . letter: CG II 407.

158 Berlioz's letter to his father: CG II 429–30.

158 His . . . submissions to the minister: CG II 414–20, 731–5.

159 "The whole thing has caused me . . .": CG II 444.

159 Bienaimé: see BLOOM 93; MEM XLVII 278.

160 . . . published in the Gazette: 1 July 1838; CG II 443.

160 Danton . . . portrait-bust: B sent each of his sisters a copy.

160 "I am at the crisis point": CG II 437.

161 according to Adolphe Adam: ADAM 32.

161 [Preparations for Benvenuto]: see CG II 430–50 (passim).

161 appeal to Legouvé for another loan: to pay a debt incurred the previous summer which fell due at the end of July.

161 The Memoirs' account: XLVIII 286–8.

162 "the enemy of music . . . war of ridicule": CG III 617, 564; DEBATS 26 Sept. 1840; SO 145–7.

163 . . . wrote the Artiste: quoted BRENET 54; BENBLOOM 1–12.

164 Galignani's Messsenger: reprinted MW 20 Sept. 1838.

164 Janin['s] . . . feuilleton: DEBATS 15 Sept. 1838.

164 Méhul remarked: LM II 89.

164 Reicha noted: "From the Unpublished Autobiography of Antonin Reicha", ed. J. G. Prod'homme, MQ vol. 22 (1936) 350.

164 "The rabid enemies": CG II 457.

165 what Boschot calls "l'esprit français . . .": II 442.

165 "the audience . . . went to sleep": quoted WCRIT 157.

165 La France musicale: 16 Sept. 1838.

166 [Duprez's] autobiography: Souvenirs d'un chanteur, Paris 1880, 153–4.

166 [Duprez] roughly handled by the press: see BRENET 61–2.

166   Hugo, who wrote: CG II 453.

166–7   Liszt . . . in the *Gazette*: 13 June 1839.

167   "Impossible to tell you . . .": CG II 457.

167   Dupont . . . took longer . . . The director: see NBE vol.la xv–xvi.

168   Duponchel . . . not committed: see P. Pascal, J. Weber (TRAC 17, 144). Marie Escudier's review of Maillot's *La Musique au théâtre* in FM, 14 June 1863, quotes Maillot: *Benvenuto Cellini*, "qui fut représenté au milieu d'un fâcheux concours de circonstances ayant pris naissance dans l'intérieur même du théâtre".

168   "We're now told Berlioz's music . . .": MEM XLVIII 288.

168   "the *bons mots* of the tenor . . .": SO 122.

168–9   [arranging loans]: see CG II 437, 444–5, 448, 492, 498.

169–70 [Notes to Réty]: CG II 474, 480, 483–4.

170   500 francs from the Duc: see BLOOMOFF 143 and CG II 652. I take it that B's draft letter of thanks to the duke, assigned by the editor of CG II to 1840, belongs here. On the back is written the programme for the concert of 25 Nov. 1838.

170   Heller . . . in the *Gazette*: 2 Dec. 1838.

170   The English were "execrable musicians . . .": CG II 481–2.

171   "Harriet is greatly looking forward . . .": CG II 464.

171   Alexandre Rocher: son of Louis R and the so-called Madame Sabine, nephew of Joseph R, Mélanie Thomas and Nancy's friend Rosanne Goletty.

171–2   Berlioz wrote to tell his father: CG II 477.

172   "my sisters judged him too severely": see also letter to Nancy from Elise Julhiet, who had seen the two boys in Paris (16 Nov.1838, REBOUL).

172   "Prosper, I repeat . . .": CG II 482.

172   An oral tradition . . . La Côte: BOSCHOT II (rev.edition) 268.

172   his brother's concert – the culmination: "l'exécution a été au-dessus de tout", "je n'ai jamais été exécuté ni compris comme ce jour-là". (CG II 512, 522).

172   Paganini . . . : see MEM XLIX [291]–5; CG II 488–512 (passim). See also the violinist A. J. Oury to Cook of the Royal Philharmonic Society, proposing "to your *serious attention* the best means of procuring an engagement for the *Living Beethoven*!! Berlioz at the Society Philharmonic [etc.]". Oury goes on to narrate the events following B's second concert (18 Dec. 1838, RPS archives, information supplied by the late Charles Reid).

173   If it had been Rome, he told Liszt: CG II 522–3.

174   Janin to Berlioz: see also J's feuilleton "Paganini et Berlioz", DEBATS 24 Dec.1838.

174–5   to accept such an improbable ... event: cf. ENGEL II 242: "a lot of small creatures tried with stories and inventions, and by malicious interpretations, to throw their own darkness over the light and lustre of one of the greatest illustrations of contemporary art".

175   the story Hallé claimed to have heard: HALLE 69–70. See also HILLER 89.

175   *Journal de Paris*: 18 Jan.1839.

8

176   half [the 20,000 francs] went instantly: see CG II 684.

176   "a new dress and hat ...": see BPD 34.

176   not only sorrows, he told Adèle: CG II 494.

176   [the library job]: Cherubini had proposed B for it the year before (BLOOM 91–2). This appears to contradict B's statement in MEM XLVIII [284] that Ch opposed it.

177   (Tiersot remarks ...): TIERSOC 166.

177   "a banal honour": CG II 551. See also MEM XLVI 276.

177   the plan mentioned in the *Memoirs*: XLVII 282–3. See also CG III 165–7.

178   ... symphony on Schiller's *Joan of Arc*: see GRIEP 10.

178   "... you know best": MEM XLIX 295.

178   Emile Deschamps ... recalled: *Oeuvres complètes*, Paris, 1874, VI, i.

178   he had ... "often imagined ...": MEM XXV [144]–5.

178   ... June ... mentioning ... to Mendelssohn: I am assuming that the riding excursions took place after B's stay in Nice, not before.

179   ... written ... to a fellow-Gluck enthusiast: CG II 545.

180   the "fever of my choral symphony": CG II 555.

180–81   "moved him too much": see CG V 353.

181   a draft of [the Convoi funèbre]: reproduced NBE vol.18 380.

181   in a state of "exaltation": CG II 563.

181   "At the name 'Romeo' ...": ATC 358–9.

182   ... exasperation in his letters: CG II 537–8, 552, 557, 583–4.

182   [Harriet's illness]: CG II 525, 531.

183   [letters] to Edouard Rocher: CG II 515, 525.

183   [Nourrit's death]: see CG II 554n.

183   Chopin played the organ: WALKER I 166.

183   Berlioz described it to his father: CG II 554–5.

183   M. Petit ...: see letter of 3 March 1839 from Adèle to Nancy (REBOUL).

183   ... thought she could have done better: see CG II 551 and n.

184   Adèle . . . told Nancy: letter of 28 April [1839] (REBOUL).

184   "pride at sending . . .": CG II 547.

184   Adèle . . . begged Nancy: 12 May 1839 (REBOUL).

184   Hector wrote to his father: CG II 551, 555.

185   He wrote to Duponchel: CG II 540–41 (undated).

185   As he said to Legouvé: CG II 529, undated, assigned to late Jan., but
        probably later, after the work was withdrawn.

186   Duponchel insisted: see CG II 575.

186   Other directors . . . showing . . . interest: see CG II 529, 541.

186   a big retrospective concert: programme given in BPD 35.

186   Antoni Deschamps . . . : quoted CG II 554n.

186   To Liszt . . . To Schumann: CG II 523, 533.

186   The lioness of the season: Clara Wieck, however, felt that the journals
        associated with B had not done her justice.

187   "He . . . began talking of you": quoted MEN 5 April 1903, 108–9.

187–8   The open letter to Liszt: reproduced CG II 565ff.

188   it was Duprez . . . who was intended: see CG II 580: "une homilie à
        l'adresse de Duprez".

188   (giving high praise . . . to his singing . . .): DEBATS 17 March; RGM
        24 March 1839. See also DEBATS 5 Dec. 1848.

189   [Suats' visit, correspondence]: REBOUL; CG II 556–7, 564n, 636.

189   tickets for . . . *Mademoiselle de Belle-Isle*: they saw it on 4 June.

191   "You can imagine how delighted . . .": CG II 563.

192   "My dear collaborator": CG II 561.

192   "I have finished the symphony": CG II 576, undated, assigned to 9
        Sept., but must be later (see reference to "la folle").

192–3   [Preparations for *Romeo*]: see CG II 582–93.

193   list . . . of "Billets à donner": BPD 4.

194   Gounod . . . recalled . . . the excitement: preface to *Hector Berlioz,
        Lettres intimes*, LI, viii–ix.

194   Harriet . . . encouraged him: see CG II 616.

194   he wrote . . . to Jules David: CG II 594.

195   The introductory movement (etc.): see BOSCHOT II 505–6.

195   Marie d'Agoult . . . to Liszt: OLLIVIER I 298–9.

195   a "tour de force . . .": CG II 598–9.

195   the third performance: HOLOMAN 615 suggests it may have been
        cut, but see RUSHROM III n4.

196   letters of congratulation: CG II 595–7.

196   opponents "forced . . . to be all smiles": CG II 599.

196   a badly oiled syringe: quoted MEM XLIX 296.

196   the *Nouvelliste*: 20 Dec. 1839.

196n   Balzac . . . : quoted CG II 599.

196   Gautier . . . : *Presse* 11 Dec. 1839.

197   Janin's review: DEBATS 24 Nov. 1839.

197–9 Heller . . . the *Gazette*: 19, 22 Dec. 1839.

199   Berlioz in the *Memoirs* treats *Romeo* . . . : XLIX 295–7.

199–200 a note added . . . the Fantastic: see NBE vol. 16 167–8.

200   "genre" as something not set: see Katherine Reeve (Kolb), "The Damnation of Faust" in BLOOMSTUD 152.

200   [Wagner's] . . . novella: RGM 19, 22, 29 Nov., 3 Dec. 1840.

200–201 Marie d'Agoult . . . Sainte-Beuve: OLLIVIER I 317.

201   Ian Kemp's essay: KEMPROM 37–79.

201   more than he could bear: his friend and champion d'Ortigue confessed that the music of the Tomb Scene "left him cold" (QUOT 26, 27 Dec. 1839, quoted RUSHROM 77).

202   the formal plan of *Romeo*: its novelty is matched by the novelty of the form of the seven movements, each forged anew for its particular musical and poetic purpose. As Kemp shows, even the scherzo transforms the traditional model.

203   the "law of crescendo": RGM 4 March 1838.

203   The crescendo operates . . . emotionally: see Ellis, thesis (op. cit.), 150 n9: the Convoi is, in this respect the "pivotal movement".

204   bell-like tolling: an idea perhaps partly inspired by the bell which figures in a stage direction in Le Tourneur's translation of the play.

204   the rising cor anglais phrases: NBE vol. 18, movement 3, bars 155–68.

205   *Romeo and Juliet*, in Boschot's phrase: II 486.

205   Wagner, by his own confession . . . : MY LIFE 191.

206   "No one," he told Adèle: CG II 616.

9

207   Adolphe Adam complained: ADAM 77.

208   what the *Memoirs* call . . . : L [298].

208   where the band took its place: see VMII 103n.

209   a failure of communication: see letter from Cavé to B, CG II 647–8.

209   Adam swallowed his scorn: ADAM 80–81.

210   Habeneck . . . : MEM L 300.

210   Even Mainzer . . . : see CG II 649.

210   Dresden *Abendzeitung*: 5 May 1841 (WCRIT 132–3). See also BLOOM 97.

210   Berlioz was asked to add a triumphal march: see CG II 670.

210   . . . the *Ménestrel*: 20 Dec. 1840 (quoted CG II 671n), signed A. E. – probably Antoine Elwart.

211 a . . . concert in the Panthéon: see CG II 637–8 and n.

211 "Festival de M. Berlioz . . . *Charivari*: quoted BOSCHOT II 549, 552.

211–13 provoked from . . . Scudo a review . . . : RDM 15 Nov. 1840.

214 He wrote to the . . . *Revue des deux mondes*: Nov. 1840 (see CG II 668–9).

214–16 Scudo . . . returning to the attack: RDM 15 Dec. 1840.

216 one of the papers Dr B saw: the *Revue* had a wide circulation. Le Fanu's Silas Ruthyn (*Uncle Silas*, 1864) had it sent to his Derbyshire home.

217 a note from Balzac: CG II 669.

217 a deficit of twelve hundred francs: see CG II 684–5.

217 (as Adèle reported to Nancy): 8 Nov. [1840].

217 "paid a thousand francs for it": CG II 663.

218 . . . attacked [Montalivet] verbally: see CG II 667.

218 "Music on a large scale . . .": CG II 685.

218 "Is it not sad to have to recognize": CG II 626.

219 "could have massacred the Eternal Father": CG II 630.

219 "a hundred years old": CG II 627.

219–20 [family correspondence over Janin's article]: CG II 608–10, 615–16.

220 [Paganini] wrote from Nice: CG II 624.

220–21 Paganini to his Genoese lawyer: quoted BARZUN I 345 n.

221 Allyre Bureau . . . wrote . . . : 1 Jan. 1840, quoted BLOOMSTUD 99 and n.

221 The account in the *Memoirs*: LIII 297.

222 as Barzun remarks: BARZUN I 403.

222 Reviewing the final Conservatoire concert: RGM 17 May 1840.

223 "There was talk of . . . *Freischütz*": RGM 17 May 1840.

223 two days' detention: see CG II 660, 665 and n.

223 . . . wrote Liszt in the *Gazette*: 24 Oct. 1840.

223 reprinting of his *Débats* articles: one or two from the *Gazette* as well. The *Débats* articles were reproduced with the same regularity in 1841.

223–4 [Lobe's] open letter: NZfM 1837, VI, 147.

224 [letters about projected German trip]: CG II 496, 533, 537, 579, 585, 638.

224 In March he told Adèle: later in the month he writes to Nancy of a projected family reunion "before my departure for Germany".

225 he "daren't leave Paris": CG II 687.

225 "On one pretext or another . . .": LI [302]

225 "a resonant memory": RABY 164.

226 a note from Félix Marmion: CG II 636n.

226 Berlioz to Alfred de Vigny: CG II 636.

226   a later remark of Berlioz's: CG III 723.

226   the visit took place . . . June 1840: whether with or without Camille
       and Mathilde is uncertain.

226–7 letters . . . from Nancy Clappier: REBOUL.

227   a letter of January 1840 to Ferrand: CG II 627.

227   Dr Berlioz . . . deep depression: see Dr B's letter of 16 Feb. 1840
       (REBOUL) and MEM II 42. He attempted suicide.

227–8 Berlioz wrote [to his father]: CG II 659.

228   When . . . Marmion visited her: see letter of Friday 26 May [1843]
       (REBOUL), wrongly assigned to 1842 in CG II 726n.

229   . . . Harriet's solitariness in Montmartre: CG II 285–6.

230   he pitied her more: see MEM LIX 542–3.

230   Legouvé's statement that her ardour grew . . . : LEG I 300.

231   Legouvé's story: LEG I 302.

IO

232   his "first musical expedition . . .": LI [302].

232   Sotera de Villas . . . Major Martin (. . . never married): see BLOOM
       103.

232   Henry Barraud accuses Marie . . . : BARRAUD 103.

233   . . . The weight of contemporary witness: Pauline Viardot thought
       Marie "most unpleasant", "dreadful" – "how could such a man
       marry a woman like that?" (VIARDOT 373).

233   Wagner asked Liszt . . . : WAGNER II.

233   Louis Engel . . . : ENGEL I 85.

233   Hanslick recalled her . . . : HANSLEBEN I 57.

233   Morel complained to Lecourt: letter in Librairie Simon Kra catalogue
       no.19, June 1929, no.7649.

233   In Legouvé's reminiscences: LEG I 318–19.

235   "les années mystérieuses": BOSCHOT II 563–622 (chapter heading).

235   recently discovered documents: see Ralph P. Locke, "New Letters of
       Berlioz", *19th Century Music*, I (1977), 73–4.

236   he went on sending Ferrand letters: this is clear from the numbering
       in *La Nouvelle Revue*, where the Ferrand letters were serialized in
       1880.

236   "Two months from now": CG II 682–3, where the addressee is given
       as Adèle; but it was Nancy: see letter of late March 1841 from
       Adèle to Nancy, thanking her for sending their brother's letter
       (REBOUL).

236–7 "You would be right . . .": CG II 684–5.

238 "Liszt and Berlioz are friends . . .": published 17 June 1841, WCRIT 133–4.

238 Berlioz's account in the *Débats*: 16 May 1841.

239 his letter to Léon Pillet: CG II 680.

239 [exchanges with Pillet]: see MEM LII [413]ff.

239 Wagner . . . in the *Gazette*: 23, 30 May 1841.

239 . . . in the Dresden *Abendzeitung*: WCRIT 142.

240 Wagner found them anonymous: Adolphe Jullien remarks (JULLIEN 152) that it was a pity W did not follow their example when he revised *Iphigénie en Aulide*.

240 The fault lay in the heavy way . . . : CG II 681.

240 (Habeneck was unwell): according to JULLIEN 152, Habeneck stood down rather than "apprentice himself" to B.

240–41 Wagner himself, in a second article: WCRIT 156.

241 . . . protest in the *Memoirs*: LII 417.

241 He received . . . the first act [of *La Nonne*]: see CG II 692.

242 he reads the scenario to Harriet: see CG II 672.

242 "this time no one will complain": CG II 699. The plot had undergone some changes by the time Gounod set it, to judge by the version in CURGOUNOD 63–5.

242 "Duprez has only six . . .": CG II 717, also 699.

242 "travelling about the Normandy countryside": CG II 724.

243 an album leaf . . . "à Marie": see MACB 39.

243 Berlioz's letter of 3 October 1841: CG II 701. Much has been made (e.g. RABY 166) of the fact that the letter does not mention Harriet. But it does, in a PS, omitted from the published text, but itself, in its choice of words, seemingly loaded with hidden meaning: "Ma femme a conservé de vous une véritable admiration. C'est à la lumineuse rectitude de votre esprit et à l'élévation de votre coeur qu'elle s'adresse."

243 Boschot is surely right: BOSCHOT II 595.

243 the management would hardly . . . engaged her: BLOOM 103 suggests that Banderali may have had a hand in her engagement by the Opéra.

243 "the bad habit she has . . .": *Moniteur des théâtres*, quoted by Boschot.

244 the sketchbook which Berlioz kept . . . : MUSEE.

244 Berlioz reviewed both débuts: DEBATS 2/3 Nov. 1841, 30 Jan. 1842.

244 . . . Mme Stoltz: the singer is named in the next sentence: "Mlle Recio, without copying Mme Stoltz, . . .".

245 The conversation Legouvé reports: LEG I 320.

245 Napoleon's dictum: quoted REY 150.

245 "nothing short of a coup d'état: MEM LI [302].

245   "not one coup d'état but . . .": CG III 462.

246   "We conversed . . . painful subject": OSBORNE.

246   Marie Recio [not] the source of . . . *Nuits d'été*: or even the occasion of it, as Camille Moke was of the Fantastic by releasing B from the paralysing effect of his obsession with Harriet.

246   Stephen Heller in the *Gazette*: 4 July 1841.

247   the cycle's publication: by 1 Sept., when it was mentioned in NZfM 43, 718 (quoted BLOOMSTUD 81 n4, 85).

247   announced for a concert: RGM 5 Nov. 1840.

247   Gautier was pleased when composers . . . : see BLOOMSTUD 88–9.

248   three-note figure (D–E flat–D): C–D flat–C in the (transposed) orchestral version. The same figure runs through the Offertorium in the Grande messe of three years earlier.

249   [Harriet's] suspicions . . . groundless: Legouvé's assertion that B had a succession of affairs with singers and dancers is now generally discredited.

249–50   [References to Louis]: CG II 672, 692, 702, 722, 724.

250   "Harriet never goes out": CG II 715.

250   a buzzing in his head: CG II 717.

250   giving away more than 250 tickets: see BPD 14.

250   "If my father had been there": CG II 716.

250   The cabinetmaker's letter: REBOUL. B enclosed it in the envelope, and it was preserved in Nancy's papers.

250   the second concert: for the programme, see the review in RGM 20 Feb. 1842.

251   Heller's account: HELLER 102.

251   he reviewed [Kastner] in the *Débats*: 2 Oct. 1839.

252   sitting in on [Dieppo's] trombone class: see BLOOMPAR 373.

252   A performance of *Don Juan* . . . : see DEBATS 16 May 1841.

255   [the viola in Orestes' scena]: this passage not in RGM.

255   ("My dear Coche . . ."): CG II 706.

256   Maurice Bourges' review in the *Gazette*: 20 Feb. 1842.

256   "Everyone thinks I am rich": CG II 687.

256   the Opéra post: according to a letter of March 1841 (CG II 683) he had been as good as offered it, provided of course that Habeneck, who was reckoned to have grown too old for the job, could be persuaded to retire.

256   Wagner . . . reported: WCRIT 134.

256   "But the grand old man": CG II 683.

256   Auber got the job: cf. Hottin's remark, MEM IX 74.

257   Berlioz's obituary of Cherubini: 20 March 1842, CONDE 141–4.

257 his article on . . . *Les deux journées*: 13 April 1842, CONDE 179–85.

257 as Barzun remarks, he "knew better . . .": BARZUN I 414.

257 As he said of Spontini . . . : CG II 700.

257 Boschot may be right . . . : BOSCHOT II 613.

257 Berlioz, in a letter to Nancy: CG II 725.

257 When he told the Comte de Rambuteau: see CG II 721–2.

258 A letter from Adèle to Nancy: REBOUL.

259 Balzac, that "innocent galley-slave": CG II 724–5.

259 "a ruinous art": CG II 687.

259 Berlioz wrote Snel . . . : CG III 11–13. This letter should have appeared in CG II.

260 he sent word to Rocquemont: CG II 728.

I I

261 [1st Brussels concert]: see *Belgique musicale*, 29 Sept. 1842; LINDEN 64.

261 Fétis, denouncing the music: see CG III 17.

261 . . . they broke into applause: see Ernst to Liszt, LZEIT I 52.

261 Zani de Ferranti: MEM LI 303, and unpublished papers in the Ferranti family.

262 till "the man in the street . . . a poet": *Emancipation*, 14 Oct. 1842; LINDEN 65.

262 the Salle Cluysenaer: the former Hôtel d'Angleterre, converted to a concert hall by the architect Alfred Cluysenaer (LINDEN 41).

263 his head full of Goethe and Hoffmann: see CG III 24.

263 the theatre was busy: see CG III 25.

264 Lindpaintner . . . "Since you are here": MEM Germany I 323.

264 ". . . 'Wilkommen' to Germany": MEM Germany I 342.

265 . . . Molière: *Le dépit amoureux*, I, iv.

268 a plea to Guhr . . . he dispatched: CG III 20, 21.

268 Berlioz wrote . . . to Bottée: CG III 29, 17 Nov 1842.

269 "M. Berlioz being entrusted . . .": AN F21 1282, draft dated 28 Nov. 1842, quoted BLOOMMISS 70.

269 the Foreign Minister, Guizot . . . : REBOUL.

269 "Our brilliant Berlioz . . .": MEYERBEER III 421; MEYBECKER 92.

270 he told Dufeuillant: see letter from Adèle to Nancy [6 Dec. 1842] (REBOUL).

270 she had felt "quite desperate": CG III 23.

270 "Harriet is finding it very hard . . .": CG III 35–6.

270   [correspondence with and about Harriet]: REBOUL.

270   the loftiest ideas of German culture: cf. GONCOURT 179.

271   "far removed from the . . . intrigues . . . of Paris": MEM LI 309.

271   old Schott: MEM Germany I 315.

272   Frankfurt . . . by slow train: the line from Wiesbaden to Frankfurt, which passed through Castel (on the Rhine opposite Mainz) had opened two years before.

272   According to . . . Hiller, Guhr had . . . : HILLER 91.

272   [Relationship with Guhr]: CG III 42, 54, 339.

272   ". . . he seemed destined . . . embarrassment": MEM Germany I 321.

272   "that bloody town of Frankfurt": CG III 42.

272–3   "Guhr is a small man . . .": MEM Germany I 316–17.

274   friends had advised . . . large centres: MEM Germany I 351.

274   [Stuttgart concert, etc.]: MEM Germany I 321–8; CG III 43, 53.

275–6   [Hechingen]: MEM Germany I 328–31.

276   Johann Christian Lobe: CG III 37–40.

277   he wrote to Morel: see CG III 55.

277   a wry reference . . . in his album: MUSEE.

277   [B gives Marie the slip]: see HILLER 91ff.

277   his account of Weimar: MEM Germany I 338ff.

278   Berlioz, writing to Morel: CG III 71–2.

279   in a dark-red waistcoat: see CG III 65–6.

279   [letters to and from Mendelssohn, etc.]: CG III 58–64.

280   . . . Letter . . . described their meeting: MEM Germany I 345–6.

281   [Leipzig] the bastion of conservatism: see WALKER I 347–8.

281   Critical comment . . . in Leipzig: see LEVY 140–41.

282   Berlioz wrote . . . to . . . d'Ortigue: CG III 73.

282   [Schumann, meetings, etc.]: SCHUMANN 181–6, 189. See also LEVY.

283   Meyerbeer to Reissiger: quoted NL 48.

283   *Absence* [with orchestra, 17 Feb.]: not with piano, as stated in HOLO-MAN 616 and HOLCAT 226.

284   "mistaken regard for the old": MEM Germany I 358.

284   Wagner, who in *Mein Leben* . . . : MY LIFE 284.

284   Parish-Alvars, the "Liszt of the harp": MEM Germany I 357.

285   (As he told Lipinski . . .): CG III 117.

285   excessive . . . tremolo: B is speaking of the original version of *The Flying Dutchman*.

287   With a hall like that . . . d'Ortigue: CG III 73–4.

287   a letter . . . from Meyerbeer: CG III 74.

287   the travellers reached Brunswick: the first part of the journey, as far as Magdeburg, by train.

287   [Brunswick visit]: see MEM Germany I 362–8.

287   the Müller Quartet: see B's review of its Paris concerts in REN 28
       Feb. 1834 (BCRIT I 177).

288–9 "Dear Father . . .": CG III 79–80.

289n   Dr Berlioz wrote to Nancy: REBOUL.

290   *Ritter Berlioz. . . a trenchant rebuttal*: see GRIEP, and LEVY 137ff.

290–91 [Hamburg visit]: see MEM Germany I 369–70.

291   Joseph Reichel: see CG III 85.

291   [Berlin visit]: see MEM Germany I 371–401; CG III passim.

291   (a copyist manuscript . . .): see HOLCAT 199.

292   Queen Mab almost as good as . . . at Brunswick: the Berlin players
       had fewer rehearsals (2 as against 4), but half the programme was
       repeated from the first concert.

293   to the "Artists of the Royal Chapel": CG III 90–91.

293   [visits to Hanover, Darmstadt]: see MEM Germany I 402–12; CG III
       passim.

293   Marie . . . in the shade in Berlin: however, she gave a recital on 18
       April.

293   no mention of [Marie] having "sung really well": see CG III 76, 85.

294   Everyone . . . eager to rehearse: cf. HALLE 28–9.

294   Louis Schloesser . . . : see Adolph Schloesser, "Personal Recollections
       of [. . .] Hector Berlioz", in *The R[oyal] A[cademy of] M[usic]
       Magazine*, Feb. 1911, 4–7.

294   Hanslick . . . "whoever lived and cheered . . .": quoted BARZUN I
       399.

295   "If I had been born in Saxony . . .": CG III 98.

295   his report to the Minister: see BLOOMMISS [77]–85. The minister's
       letter of thanks: 73, and BLOOM 106.

296   most up-to-date [instruments]: like the bass tuba and the valve trum-
       pet, "which we have not yet decided to introduce into our bands".

297   benefit concert: see CG III 141–2; BLOOM 109.

298   "Principal Composers in 1843": "PANTHEON MUSICAL", by
       Traviès, reproduced JULLIEN between pp.166 and 167.

12

299   . . . monster concerts pictured in his *Memoirs*: LIII.

299   [compositions 1843–5]: also Thalberg's arrangement of the Apothe-
       osis (HOLCAT 314).

299   grocer's assistant who hissed *Freischütz*: RGM 3 Dec. 1843.

300   reform of French military bands: DEBATS 1 April 1845.

300   *Euphonia*. . . in the *Gazette*: 18, 25 Feb., 3, 17, 24 March, 28 April, 2 June, 28 July 1844.

300   Louis told his Aunt Nancy: REBOUL, reproduced CG III 138n.

300   Spontini . . . was moved to write: CG III 138–9.

301   His "great beast of an orchestra": CG III 181.

301   [concert] of 1 August 1844: see MEM LIII; CG III 194–8. In REBOUL there is a letter communicating the detailed and enthusiastic report on the concert by one of the bass-drum players.

302   *Voyage musical*. . . excellent reviews: but not in the *Siècle*, one of the papers B's family read.

303   "M. . . . Berlioz may now walk . . .": quoted BOSCHOT III 71.

303   projects for visits abroad: see CG III 100, 101, 103, 104, 156, 201, 364.

303   what George Eliot called . . . : in her essay "German wit: Heinrich Heine", in *Essays*, ed. Thomas Pinney, London, 1963.

303   "the electrifying city": CG III 366.

304   "the intelligent people . . . found there": CG III 325. See also MEM XXV 147.

304–5   [two letters to Nancy]: CG III 108–9, 112–14.

306   championed [Glinka] in the *Débats*: 16 April 1845.

306   . . . Emperor concerto played by Hallé: HALLE 68 says it was the G major, no.4.

307   A letter of late February 1845: CG III 229–30.

307   to Michel-Maurice Lévy: CG III 232–3.

307   Glinka describes . . . : GLINKA 192.

308   the "heartbreaking rotunda": MEM LIII 429.

308   Glinka remarked . . . the contrast: GLINKA 191.

308   Heller . . . protest in the *Gazette*: RGM 21 Jan. 1844.

309   Félicien David [at the Conservatoire]: *Le désert* 8 Dec. 1844, *Christophe Colomb* 7 March 1847. Elwart also gave a big concert of his works in the Conservatoire Hall on 12 Dec. 1847.

309   [Habeneck] in the green room: see MEM XLVIII 287–8.

310   he described Pillet . . . on his side: CG III 110.

310   "I'm on bad terms with the administration": CG III 278.

310   "on the principle of the Gospels": quoted BOSCHOT III 81.

310   Berlioz and . . . Dartois: CG III 192–3, 759–63.

311–12   petition . . . to . . . Duchâtel: CG III 165–7.

312   Berlioz wrote a month later: CG III 173.

312   Amussat . . . "Go south . . .": MEM LIII 429.

313   [Harriet] drinking heavily: CG III 266 implies that H's drinking was the cause of B's getting involved with Marie.

313   their brother "must be suffering cruelly . . .": Adèle to Nancy, 16 July [1844] (REBOUL).

313, etc. [Louis' letters]: REBOUL.

314   the presence of a mistress: *La belle Isabeau*, to a text by Dumas about a knight who elopes with a young woman imprisoned in a tower, was published in Dec. 1844 with the dedication "à Marie Recio".

314   *La France musicale*: 20 Aug. 1843.

314   Berlioz told . . . Lipinski: CG III 118.

314   The *Corsaire*: quoted BOSCHOT III 44.

314   to Louis Schloesser: CG III 161.

314   he asked Saint-Georges: CG III 144.

315   Dr Berlioz wrote to Nancy: 11 July 1843 (REBOUL).

315–17 [letters about Harriet]: CG III 148, 156, 181, 188–9, 199, 202–3, 206–7.

317   Adèle . . . "It would . . . relief to me": 22 Aug. [1844] (REBOUL).

317   A friend of Adèle's: M. Pennet. Adèle to Nancy, Thursday 22 Aug. [1844 – postmark].

319   the "amicable separation": MEM LI 303.

319   43 Rue Blanche . . . 41 Rue de Provence: see CG III 249.

319   any further ambition . . . his concerts: the Salle Herz concert of 3 Feb. 1844 was her last.

320   Napoleon III's annexation . . . : DEBATS 26 June 1860.

320   The brief paragraph in the *Memoirs*: LIII 429.

320   passages in the "Italian journey" . . . to be done: see my vol.1, 457–62, 510–11, (also 481–2).

321   [Harriet] sent . . . Marmion . . . a note: REBOUL, dated 22 mai only: but 1845 was the sole year between 1844 and 1848 when B was in Paris in May. (After 1848 H was semi-paralysed and bedridden until her death.)

321   (the inhabitants of Dauphiné . . .): MEM XLIII 250.

321   (Adèle Suat wrote rapturously . . .): REBOUL, 4 March 1845.

322   the account . . . published . . . in the *Gazette*: 10 Sept. 1848. See also MATHIEU RGM 5 Dec. 1869 on B's frequent quoting of the omnibus driver's "manque un Tur".

322   . . . the Apotheosis: B often uses it as a joint title for the second and third movements.

322   he wrote to both Liszt and Mendelssohn: CG III 254, 255.

323   "SUBLIME, trois fois SUBLIME": quoted BOSCHOT III 87.

323   [Dorant] had just arrived: RGM 15 Oct. 1848 (GROT 289–90).

324   "Before rehearsals have even started": MEM Germany I 349.

325   a letter from Adèle . . . : 10 July (REBOUL).

325   (he wrote to Hainl afterwards): CG III 272–3.

325   explain . . . the situation to Nancy: CG III 265–6.

326   Liszt . . . Grande messe . . . Berlioz–Liszt concerts: see CG III 246–7, 269.

326   "Where are they going to put us all?": CG III 272.

326   the committee . . . running the festival: see WALKER I 418n.

326   (. . . Kreutzer noted in the *Gazette*): 17 Aug. 1845.

326   "He was beset with . . . cabals": CG III 277.

326   Berlioz's . . . report in the *Débats*: 22 Aug., 3 Sept. 1845.

328   Liszt's conducting, which he described . . . : CG III 277.

328   the ceremonial lunch: see WALKER I 424.

328   Liszt . . . upbraided by Chelard: see Walker II 98n.

329   His goal . . . Vienna: at one point he hoped to take in Munich on the way (see CG III 285–6).

330   Boschot . . . evokes Berlioz . . . : BOSCHOT III 88–92.

330   One of the [*Eight Scenes*] . . . announced: RGM 28 Jan. 1844.

330   indications . . . choral and orchestral material: see NBE vol. 8b 456.

331   wrote the score . . . "with an ease . . .": MEM LIV 489.

331   sampling the summer festivals: see CG III 276.

331   a letter of 3 October [to Gandonnière]: CG III 283–4.

331   he had with him the text . . . : see NBE vol. 8b 484.

13

332   The . . . customs officer: MEM Germany II 435.

332, etc. [visits to Vienna]: see MEM Germany II 434ff; CG III 288–99, 310–15, RGM 21 Dec. 1845.

333   Berlioz cameos: see Daniel Bernard, "Notice sur Berlioz". CI 41.

334   Louis Engel recalled: ENGEL I 105.

334–5   Marie Recio . . . to Desmarest: CG III 298n.

335   (Joseph Fischoff . . . *Musical World* . . .): 5 Feb. 1848.

335   Others welcomed his advent: Bacher, Becher, Wesque von Puttlingen, etc.

336   wrestling with Queen Mab: see CG III 733: "j'ai eu beaucoup de peine à le faire marcher à Vienne".

336   The end of the scherzo . . . more telling: on the advice of Ernst's secretary, Frankoski – see MEM XLIX 296.

337, etc. [visits to Prague]: see MEM Germany II 461ff; CG III 305–15, 324–37; PAYZANT.

337   "the city . . . most passionate about my music": CG IV 164.

337   As one of them, . . . Hanslick, put it: HANSLEBEN I 56.

337   "a Frenchman" (in Hanslick's words): quoted PAYZANT 107.

338	. . . article by . . . Ambros: *Wiener Allgemeine Musikzeitung*, 3 instalments, beginning 7 Oct. 1845 (see PAYZANT 10ff).
338–9	[the] itinerant harpist: see RGM 23, 30 July 1848 (SO 2nd Evening).
339	". . . neared the contrapuntal residence": HANSLEBEN I 58–9.
339	Tomaschek: see also MEM Germany II 483–4.
340	Hanslick . . . "total absorption": quoted PAYZANT 64.
340	"we expected a . . . bewildered . . .": quoted PAYZANT 81.
342	precious glimpses of Marie: HANSLEBEN I 57.
342	"inexorably beating down the cost . . .": Hanslick, *Aus dem Concertsaal*, Vienna, 1870, 545–6.
343	"this time I shall go *alone*": CG III 519.
343	Gordigiani . . . in a letter to Marie: REBOUL.
343ff	[visit to Pesth]: see MEM Germany II 451–61; CG III 316–19.
344	when Liszt played his arrangement: see WALKER I 320.
347–8	[visit to Breslau]: see MEM LIV; CG III 320–27.
348	Hanslick received a note from Prague: see HANSLEBEN I 60.
349	. . . anonymous review in *Ost und West*: PAYZANT 99–100, where the review is attributed to Ambros.
350	grand supper . . . in the Three Lindens: it was to have followed the concert, originally scheduled for the 14th.
351	the positions . . . into his lap: his friends had urged him to cut short his journey so as not to miss the chance: see CG III 328.
351	enmity "all the greater since my German tour": CG III 366.
351	"Spontini," he wrote in the *Débats*: 29 Sept. 1846.
352	The lack of a hall [in Paris]: see DEBATS 6 Sept. 1846 (CONDE 81–2), where B discusses the "projet d'une salle de concert par M. Barthélemy".
352	Léon Kreutzer . . . to d'Ortigue: LM II 208–9.
352	". . . everything went perfectly": cf. CG III 361.
353	Prague (as *Ost und West* reported): 21 April 1846, quoted PAYZANT 101.
353	Louis . . . first communion: see letter of Nancy to Louis, 4 June 1846 (REBOUL).
353	the account [of Lille] in the *Gazette*: 19 Nov. 1848 (GROT 301ff.)
353	"the fresh-sounding voices . . .": CG III 346.
354	in cafés, in the Tuileries Gardens . . . : see MEM LIV 491.
354	one warm Sunday, . . . for Enghien: DEBATS 6 Sept. 1846.
354	"four large pieces" referred to: CG III 336, 16 April.
354	"still far from . . . finished": CG III 349.
355	"polish the different sections": MEM LIV 491.
355	Legouvé describes listening . . . : LEG I 310–11. See also CG IV 700.
356	"himself a Faust": see CG III 336n.

| 357 | . . . album leaf of . . . Romance: NBE vol. 8b 485. |

357 . . . album leaf of . . . Romance: NBE vol. 8b 485.

357 . . . Katherine Kolb . . . : BLOOMSTUD 152.

357 "an opera without decor . . .": B to the Duchesse d'Orléans, 30 Nov. 1846, quoted BLOOMOFF 144.

357 As John Warrack has said . . . : in a BBC programme note.

361 the being who cannot love or die: cf. B to Scribe, CG III 485.

361 Gautier might proclaim: in the *Presse*, 7 Dec. 1846.

361 the correspondence . . . October and November: CG III 370–82, 386–90.

362 "nothing in my career . . .": MEM LIV 492.

362 a recent review . . . Mme Stoltz's vocal line: DEBATS 6 Sept. 1846.

362 (Berlioz told Hainl): CG III 352–3.

362 Pillet had enough influence . . . : see CG III 401.

363 the postponement of the performance: 27 Nov. See RGM 29 Nov. 1846; CG III 382.

363 Maurice Bourges, in the *Gazette*: 13 Dec. 1846.

363 according to . . . Escudier: FM 13 Dec. 1846.

363 Azevedo: quoted BOSCHOT III 142–3.

363 the *Siècle*: quoted CG III 400n.

363 Even Adolphe Adam . . . : ADAM 182–3.

364 in d'Ortiguc's words: quoted BOSCHOT III 141.

364 "Happy, thrice happy . . .": DEBATS 7 Dec. 1846.

364 a dinner in his honour: see CG III 400, 408.

364 the Pandaemonium scene: it was given at the second performance (see CG III 435).

365 "I am checked for want of a hall": CG III 401.

365 Never again, he vowed . . . : see MEM LIV 492.

14

366 in correspondence with . . . Lvov: CG III 270–71. See also the profile of Lvov in RGM 25 Oct. 1840. (Also, shorter pieces by Schumann, Wagner and Henri Blanchard, respectively 6 Sept., 11 Oct. and 4 Nov.).

366 Letters . . . were dispatched: see CG III 399, 404.

366 Friends came to his aid: see MEM LIV 492–3; CG III 414. Though every cent had long been repaid by the time he wrote the *Memoirs*, his gratitude was still overflowing.

367 the Duc de Montpensier: see CG III 368.

367 he proved "less inflammable": CG III 370.

367 as Berlioz . . . in the *Débats*: 2/3 Jan. 1847.

368   Mme Rossini sprang to the defence . . . : see LM II 30.

369   a brief shooting holiday: see CG III 449.

369   "My dear Rocquemont: CG III 398.

369   . . . near to a complete break: perhaps it was this occasion that
       Osborne recalled.

369   . . . Adèle to Nancy: 27 Feb. [postmark 1847] (REBOUL).

370   Berlioz sent Balzac a note: CG III 405–7.

370   . . . the novelist late one night . . . : MEM LV 495.

370   in a bass drum: quoted BOSCHOT III 150.

370   *Charivari* suggested . . . : quoted STASOV 149.

370   letter of recommendation . . . to . . . the Tsarina: cf. Adèle, 27 Feb.:
       "la lettre du roi de Prusse lui sera précieuse", etc. (REBOUL).

370–71 Frederick William IV . . . : LM II 209–10, 18 Feb. (Russian calendar).

371ff [visit to Russia]: see MEM LV, LVI, Suite du Voyage en Russie; CG
       III 407–40; STASOV.

372   his cello-playing brother Matthew: see CG V 159n.

372   no adequate Marguerite . . . available: see FOUQUE 209–10; PROD
       281, quoting the *Abeille du Nord*.

372   . . . audience described by Odoyevsky: in an open letter to Glinka in
       S.-Peterburgskiye Vedomosti, 5 March, quoted STASOV 151.

373   Prince Galitsin . . . 29-stanza ode: REBOUL.

373   "friendly, sympathetic . . .": in "Liszt, Schumann and Berlioz in
       Russia", STASOV 154–5.

374   Carolyne Sayn-Wittgenstein: see LSTRICKER 238 ff; WALKER II
       504–5.

374   Odoyevsky was struck . . . : quoted STASOV 151–2.

374   "the reputation he enjoys . . .": STASOV 23–4.

375   Stasov thought . . . the seminal visit: STASOV 157–8.

375   Russian music . . . was not mentioned: STASOV 58–9.

376   (the games of billiards at Vielhorsky's): see CG III 597.

376   . . . he liked the tea: see CG III 626.

377   "with as much care as a new opera": MEM XLIX 297.

377   the . . . performance [of *Romeo*]: B "had to come to Russia to hear
       a really good reading of it" (CG III 423).

378   "one of my attacks of *isolation*": the spleen made B morose company,
       according to Tajan-Rogé: he and his friends found B "unbearable:
       adorable every time it was a question of music and musicians" but
       otherwise absorbed, preoccupied and boring (CG III 480).

379   Bortniansky: see, however, Liszt's much less enthusiastic opinion,
       LBRIEFE IV 223.

379–80 he wrote . . . to Tajan-Rogé: CG III 462–3.

380   [Marie] . . . aroused no longer: see CG III 498 and n, which suggests

that his feelings for M may possibly have been deeper at first than
is assumed.

381ff [visit to Riga and Berlin]: see MEM 517–21; CG III 431–40.

383 intending . . . concerts in Hamburg . . . Bremen: despite the meagre
financial returns in Germany compared to Russia (see CG III 436).

383 "the same old camel . . .": REBOUL, quoted CG III 426.

384 His duty . . . "not in smoothing their path": MEM LVII 525.

384 he cancelled a long-planned visit: see CG III 449.

384 had not stopped Halévy: nor Dietsch who, though chorus master, had
had his *Flying Dutchman* (based on Wagner's sketch) performed at
the Opéra.

385 in the *Gazette* and the *Monde musical*: 5 Sept., 2 Sept 1847.

385 [Louis] (A letter of the previous June): REBOUL, 16 June 1847.

386 Adèle complained: undated letter, "La Côte, dimanche". "Il faut que
notre pauvre père soit de fer pour résister à son régime d'opium
et de purgations tous les deux jours."

386 a happier glimpse of Dr Berlioz: MEM LV 496.

386 The old man . . . returning to the Requiem: MEM LVIII [531].

386 Berlioz . . . reasoned with her: see his letter to Nancy, CG III 480.

387 [Louis] met his cousins: he may have already met Mathilde (if she
was in Paris with her mother in June 1840), but not Joséphine or
Nancy.

387 presented him with a watch: see CG IV 480.

387–8 "Dear Aunt": 30 March 1847, REBOUL.

388 "Dear Father": REBOUL, reproduced CG III 454. A subsequent
letter, of 25 Jan. 1848, shows him doing better in class.

389 ". . . series of coups d'état": CG III 462.

389 Harriet . . . was still drinking: see B's unpublished letter of 16 March
1848 to Nancy: H "dépense plus que jamais (et toujours par la
même raison)" (MACN).

389 Castil-Blaze . . . a new version of *Fidelio*: see RGM 14 Nov. 1847
("Nouvelles").

389 Fétis . . . a three-part essay: RGM 9 May, 6 June, 4 July 1847.

389 "renouncing *la belle France*": CG III 450.

389–90 a letter written from London: CG III 503–4.

390 "rich enough to *give* concerts": cf. CG III 433: "Oh, si j'étais
immensément riche, quelles représentations je me donnerais à moi
et à mes amis".

391   "the old familiar story": MEM LVII 527.

391   Escudier ... a counter-deed: see CG III 509.

391   Jullien ... "made his own fortune": CG III 460–61.

391–2   ... observed Lumley: quoted MARETZEK 72.

392   ... part of the impresario's game: cf. Shaw: "all the impresarios, from Handel to Laporte and Lumley, lost money and lived, as far as one can make out, chiefly on the splendour of the scale on which they got into debt".

392   "the world laughed at him ...": Dutton Cook, "Berlioz and Jullien", *Belgravia* May 1880, 295.

392   Louis Engel ... in no doubt: ENGEL II 206, 209.

392   a jewelled baton ... : GANZ 16–17.

393   Gruneisen sprang on to the quay: see CG III 458.

393   "a footman in a blue-velvet ...": MARETZEK 71.

393   Coutts' Bank: see Alastair Bruce, BSOC 146 (autumn/winter 1992), 8–10.

393   ("a lot of hard work to be done"): CG III 459.

394   chorus of over a hundred: B gives it variously as 110 and 120 voices.

394   "The new drop scene": quoted GANZ 29. See also *Morning Post* 7 Dec. 1847.

394   Mme Jullien ... to Paris: see letter of 16 Oct. 1847 from J to Mme J (MACN).

394   the services of Dorus-Gras: see MW 19 Feb. 1848. She had been visiting London for the past half-dozen years.

394   [B] exchanged letters with ... Barthe-Hasselt: see CG III 472.

394   Staudigl: ILN 13 Nov. 1847 says he couldn't obtain release.

394   *Iphigénie en Tauride*: RGM 12 Dec. 1848 says *Aulide*.

395   [London letters, first weeks]: CG III 457ff.

395   ... exchanged letters with Scribe: CG III 466–7, 473–6, 484–5.

396   Grimblot: Paul Grimblot, a writer on history and philosophy as well as a diplomat, was first proposed for temporary membership of the Athenaeum in 1846. His proposer, Henry Hallam, also proposed Berlioz, on 23 Nov. 1847, "for the usual period of two months". This was renewed, on the proposal of Lord Mahon, on 15 Feb. 1848, which suggests that B did use the club.

396   *Elijah*. . . "a magnificent work: CG III 513–14.

397   Reeves ... "the greatest sensation": ILN 12 Dec. 1847.

397   Dorus-Gras' vocal agility: MW (19 Dec. 1847) speaks of her incomparable vocal agility but finds her less remarkable for purity of tone

or volume and far below Mme Viardot in passion and energy.

397–8	Berlioz to Belloni: CG III 489.
398	Berlioz . . . his [music] . . . to Grimblot's: see CG III 565.
398	English Grand Opera's committee: see MARETZEK 76.
399	the rump of the orchestra: MW 15 Jan. 1848: "M. Jullien's present tour has somewhat thinned [the] ranks".
399	"treatment by fatigue and theatre draughts": CG III 502.
399	. . . he told General Lvov: CG III 513.
399	Maretzek . . . describes Berlioz's mood: op.cit., 78.
400	so much hung on this . . . trial: see CG III 547, also 503, 505.
400	Julius Benedict . . . "the musical event": LM II 210.
401	Charles Godfrey . . . told him: see CG III 518.
401	Morris Barnett . . . Morning Post: 8 Feb.1848, quoted GANZ 43.
401–2	Edward Holmes: Atlas 12 Feb.1848.
402	letters to Morel . . . Vigny: CG III, 517, 516.
402	the losses . . . faded before the joy: letter of 14 Feb.1848 to Gruneisen (MACN. Short précis – misdated – CG III 520).
403	Fraser's Magazine. . . Holmes: quoted GANZ 74.
403	"Now that Jullien . . . no longer paying": CG III 517–18. If Maretzek (79–80) is correct, the chorus and orchestra only took part in B's concert after M persuaded them to have pity on "their conductor, a stranger, who worked for two months for nothing, and thus helped them to get, so far, their own salaries".
403–4	Berlioz wrote to Kittl: CG III 518–19.
404	treat [Jullien] in . . . Memoirs: LVII 528–9, Postface 567.
405	Frederick Beale . . . evening of his music: see CG III 523.
405	patriotic pieces arranged by Berlioz: see CG III 536, HOLCAT 100, 216, 295; and Cecil Hopkinson, "Berlioz and the Marseillaise", ML Oct.1970 (51. no. 4), 435–9.
407	Musical World. . . "polished manners": quoted GANZ 52.
407	letter of mid-March to d'Ortigue: CG III 527.
408	concert by the . . . Amateur Musical Society: MW 15, 22 April; ILN 15 April.
408	Wilhelm Ganz in his diary: see GANZ 55–6.
408	Jim Davison . . . contemporary music: see Charles Reid, The Music Monster, London 1984, passim.
408–9	He visits Maretzek: op.cit., 78–9. M dates the episode 11 Dec., B's birthday, when, however, the weather was not foggy.
409	He sits up late . . . with . . . Wallace: see SO 46off.
409	Charles Hallé visits [B]: see HALLE 102; CG III 532; MW 8 April 1848.
409	("everyone is terrified . . ."): CG III 534.

410   "sit on the street corner": CG III 543.

410   Germany . . . (in Hallé's word): HALLE 229.

410   profound discouragement: see CG III 652, 654.

410   "Poor father, he sees . . ."; CG III 534.

410–11   [longing to travel]: CG III 538–9, 652, 644, 546.

411   pored over his father's atlas: MEM II 42–3.

411   "London, 21 March 1848": MEM II [37]-8. My following paragraph is indebted to Pierre Citron's masterly introduction to his edition of the *Memoirs*.

411   Chateaubriand: Peter Bloom (BLOOM 119–20) suggests that Armand Bertin, who had been Chat.'s private secretary, may have encouraged B to write his memoirs, in emulation of the author of *Mémoires d'Outre-Tombe*.

411   Jullien's project . . . *Voyage musical*: see CG III 500.

412   bailiffs . . . possession of the house: see unpublished letter of 28 April 1848 to Nancy (MACN); also HILLER 93–4.

413   Claire Clairmont: my thanks to David Hayes for the information. He points out that the date of a letter from Mary Shelley to CC antedates B's departure by several days, but that does not mean that CC was back from her holiday in Ireland by then. It seems likeliest that B never met her. If he had he would surely have mentioned it.

413   "God grant it lasts . . .": CG III 536.

413–15   letter to Duc: CG III 545–8.

414   Brooke [Hamlet]: see GANZ 65 and n.

415   the reactionaries . . . Stasov complained: STASOV 53.

415   ambivalence [about revolution]: CG III 587–8, 597, 564, 534.

417   Hanover Square Rooms: on east side of the square, and seating up to 900 people.

417   According to Albert Ganz: op.cit., 66.

417   [playing without pay]: B's letter to Duc confirms this.

417   Two invitations . . . : GANZ 67 (CG III 554, résumé).

417   music . . . performed before: the *Invitation* had not figured at the concert of 7 Feb., but was in Jullien's repertoire.

418   "ashamed to be making music . . .": 11 July (MACN, précis CG III 557). The letter tells of Harriet's near escape.

419   he and Roger called on Barnett: see ROGER 64–5.

419   Paris "completing the burial . . .": MEM IV 55. See also Delacroix's impressions, quoted BARZUN I [542]n.

420   . . . wrote again to . . . Minister of the Interior: CG III 559, 560–61, 571.

16

421 "a state of calm acceptance": letter of 17 Aug. to Rosanne Goletty (REBOUL).

421 [details of Dr B's final days]: letters of Adèle and Nancy, MEM LVIII 532–3.

421 "Two lines . . .": CG III 566–7. The Pals' explanation is a little hard to credit. Camille had written to B in Paris in mid-July (see CG III 561).

423–6 [visit to Meylan]: MEM LVIII 533–40.

426 Next day he visited his uncle and aunt: see CG III 589.

426 The [family] document: written by Nancy (MACN).

426 A separate deed . . . Monique Nety: MACN.

426 he took his father's book . . . : see CG III 652.

17

429 Bourges, reviewing the [Te Deum]: RGM 6 May 1855.

429 Hasse['s] . . . Te Deum: MEM Germany I 359.

430 the catalogue . . . November 1846: the so-called Labitte Catalogue.

431 a note . . . Berlioz to Stasov: CG III 430; see also STASOV 161.

431 ". . . like Pope and Emperor": TRAITE 168.

431 by the autumn of 1848 . . . at work: CG III 628 (28 April 1849) refers to a Te Deum "begun more than six months ago".

431 On 1 September 1849 . . . to Nancy: CG III 653–4.

432 [abortive encounter . . . Prince-President]: see CG III 664.

432 sins castigated in his reviews: e.g. DEBATS 5, 15 Dec. 1848, 7 Jan., 28 Sept. 1849.

433 *Débats* report of . . . Charles Blanc: 5 Dec. 1848.

434 "Girard – who . . . did well . . .": CG III 625.

434 "great walls of China . . .": CG III 621.

434 The deaths of several friends . . . : see CG IV 15.

435 his London friends . . . Te Deum: see CG III 657, 658–9.

435 . . . hold on to what he had: "le peu que j'ai m'oblige à rester en France" (CG III 580).

435 "perhaps in the end the mountain . . .": CG III 615. See also B's draft note to Janin for his review, CG III 622.

435 "a dog of a trade": CG III 745.

435 Halévy's new opéra-comique: DEBATS 14 Nov. 1848.

435 "I said what I thought": CG III 594, to Michael Vielhorsky.

435 Clapisson's *Jeanne la folle*: DEBATS 9 Nov. 1848.

437	Meyerbeer's . . . letters: CG III 618, 619–20.
437	[B's] notice [of *Le Prophète*]: DEBATS 20 April 1849.
437	Reporting on the revival . . . : DEBATS 27 Oct.1849.
438	art ". . . the only thing in this world . . .": CG III 655.
438–9	"If you liked . . . Hoffmann": DEBATS 4 April 1849.
439	Louis . . . home from boarding-school: see CG III 660.
440	"Montmartre 19 October [1849]": MACN.
440	Harriet's sufferings . . . "only more dear": MEM LI 303.
441	"It appears, my dear sister . . .": CG III 643–4.
441	he admitted . . . the Montmartre establishment . . . : CG IV 102.
442	"Yes . . . poor Harriet's house": CG IV 92.
442	as [Louis] explained to . . . Nancy: CG III 592n.
442–3	[letters about Louis]: CG III 578, 580, 586, 654, 664, 636–7, 699, 696.
443	"George Sand herself . . .": CG III 667.
443	raising loans: see CG III 636–7, 654.
443–4	[Nancy's illness and death]: CG III 651, 631 ("je vois . . . quelle ressemblance il y a dans nos idées et nos sentiments"), 652, 698. Boschot (III 236) states, though without giving any evidence, that no one could bring themselves to help Adèle because of the terrible smell in the sickroom. But Adèle's letters speak of at least four other devoted carers.
444	"The traces of his pen . . .": CG III 652.
444	"No doctor dared . . .": MEM LIX 541–2.
445	"At least let me have news . . .": CG III 713.
445–6	"My dear, dear sister": CG III 713–15.
446	[a present for Monique Nety]: Adèle advised B to buy her a dress in Paris (see CG III 720).
446	The place . . . smelled of horses: see MATHIEU 5 Dec.1869.
446	Berlioz hailed its advent: RGM 28 Jan.1849.
447	only three . . . music by Beethoven: 19 Feb.1850 – overture *Leonore no.2*; 22 Oct.1850 – Symphony 5; 25 Feb.1851 – Sonata in F minor, op.57 (Appassionata).
447	The membership of the orchestra: see BPD 25.
447	Berlioz's [letter] on . . . headed paper: CG III 690–91.
448	"discussions without end," he told Liszt: CG III 679. It was the endless contentious committee meetings that made Seghers eventually give up the Société Ste Cécile.
448	. . . to take the company . . . to Rouen . . . Amiens: see CG III 703.
448	first two parts of the *Damnation*: minus, for some reason, the Rat and Flea songs.
449	Kreutzer . . . in the *Gazette*: 27 Oct. 1850.
450	In the *Gazette* Kreutzer noted . . . : 5 May 1850.

451   the ladies . . . presented Berlioz: see CG III 744.

451   white satin cushion . . . [gold] coronet: CG IV 35–6.

451   a society lady of [Duc's] acquaintance: see GROT 187–8 and CG IV 636n.

451–2   the musicians . . . "practically nothing": CG IV 103–4.

452   inauguration . . . Salle Barthélemy: see RGM 29 June 1851.

452   he told Morel . . . seven rehearsals: CG III 744; see also 749.

452   review of *The Monk*: 11 May 1851, quoted CG IV 62n.

452   Niedermeyer . . . rapturous letter: CG IV 34.

453   "Ste Cécile, Berlioz & compagnie": quoted BOSCHOT III 272.

453   Berlioz told Liszt . . . compositions: CG III 679.

453   describing [Schubert's Great C major]: DEBATS 27 Dec. 1851.

453   Berlioz's attempts . . . new music: see unpublished letter of 27 March 1850 to L. Lambert (MACN).

453   (84 francs . . . he told Adèle): CG III 731.

453   projected visit to Dauphiné: see CG III 723.

454   [letter to Pontmartin]: CG III 650–51. 9 Aug., assigned by CG to 1849; but I incline towards 1850.

455–6   [Louis]: Berlioz reported to Adèle: CG III 728–32.

455   "a light westerly wind": probably a slip of the pen for easterly: see later in the letter – "si le vent d'est continue à souffler".

456   Louis . . . was enjoying everything . . . : see CG III 748.

457   the sea air . . . : CG IV 46.

457   applying "reluctantly" . . . the . . . Academy: CG IV 40.

457   dinner with Spontini: CG III 611.

458   [Spontini's death] "affected me deeply": CG IV 26; also 42.

458   a long article . . . for the *Débats*: 12 Feb. 1851 (SO 198–228).

458   the Festival du Nord: see CG IV 41.

458   "a singular idea for a Frenchman": CG IV 62.

459   plans . . . series of concerts: see CG IV 62–3, 71.

459   Berlioz . . . lists of performers: see GANZ 89–90.

459   regular reports [in the *Débats*]: 31 May, 20 June, 1 July, 29 July, 12 August 1851.

459   Purcell's anthems . . . left him cold: the singing, however, may not have done much to recommend them, the mid 19th century not being a high point in the history of English cathedral choirs.

460   the celestial Sontag: three years later, at the time of her death, he recalled her exquisite singing of "Deh vieni" in *Figaro*, which till then he had "only heard coarsely performed": it was S the German with her innate understanding of great music and her mastery of mezza voce and command of nuance who sang it as it ought to be sung. She "sang piano as finely and surely and mysteriously as twenty good violins

under a capable conductor" (DEBATS 5 Oct.1854; GROT 254–7).

461–2 Charity Children's service: cf.Haydn: "I was more touched by this innocent and reverent music than by any I ever heard in my life".

465 . . . Erard [the prize] for piano: MW later claimed that Broadwood should have been awarded it.

465 . . . in the *Débats* that November: 27 Nov.1851.

466 schemes . . . for . . . the Te Deum in Paris: see CG IV 70–71, 76, 80–81.

466 attempts to resuscitate the . . . Philharmonique: see CG IV 88, 89n, 103–4.

466 "Nothing is possible . . . damned country": CG IV 93–4.

466 ignore . . . promptings . . . new composition: see MEM LIX 552–4.

466 refurbished Exeter Hall: see MW 6 Nov.1852, "Exeter Hall".

18

467 the Institute (. . . fifth attempt): i.e. including 1853, when he applied, but his application, sent from Germany, arrived too late. Reyer is emphatic that *The Childhood of Christ* tipped the scales.

467–8 explain it to . . . Baron von Donop: CG IV 396–7, 16 Nov.1853.

468 the . . . Richault Catalogue: HOLCAT 495–9.

468–9 Liszt wrote to Belloni: REBOUL, unpublished.

470 Liszt . . . "the renewal of music . . .": quoted WALKER II 339.

470 orchestral touches: inspired, respectively, by Fantastic V, *Cellini* carnival scene, Fantastic III (the two works of B that L was most closely associated with). Alan Walker (II 314, 316) mistakenly singles them out as Lisztian innovations.

470 to see his "Lazarus" rise again: B's own term (CG IV 128).

470–72 Berlioz wrote to Liszt . . . [the package]: CG IV 83–4.

472 *Beck et ongles*: CG IV 138.

472–3 "the truth and only the truth": CG IV 122–3.

473 "Honour to the master metalworkers": RGM 4 April 1852 (part of the text in CG IV 125).

473 Princess Carolyne confirmed . . . : CG IV 131.

473 Berlioz to the Grand Duchess: CG IV 130.

473 seriously short of money: see CG IV 87, 93.

474 "a genuine *desire* to like music": CG IV 104.

474 Ernst . . . two concerts: 14 Jan., 4 Feb. 1852.

474 Like Delacroix . . . : see BARZUN II 38–9.

474 Adam . . . knocked senseless: see RGM 4 Jan. 1852.

474 "we artists . . . state of death": CG IV 104.

475 *Débats*. . . writing every week: in Jan.-Feb. he wrote six articles.

476 gala performance ... *Prophète* ... 6 January 1852: see report in RGM, 11 Jan. (Nouvelles).

476 congratulatory letters and visit: see CG IV 118–19.

476 The [New Philh.] prospectus: quoted *Morning Post* 25 March.

477 "exclusiveness ... not be tolerated": but one notice describes the entire audience as in evening dress.

477 "stock favourites" of the old society: MW 8 May 1852.

477 the *Musical World*. . . sarcastically: 20 March 1852.

477 ... a hallowed tradition: see MW 31 Jan. 1852, Letters to Editor, no.1.

478 ("in Paris ... women's voices in England"): CG IV 174.

478 four full orchestral rehearsals: see GANZ 124, quoting Wilhelm Ganz's diary.

478 A letter from Berlioz to Jarrett: CG IV 142–3.

478 Another ... to Jarrett: CG IV 160–61.

479 *The Isle of Calypso*: see MW 1 May; Reeve's reply, 8 May.

479 *Oberon* overture "with a fire...": MW 27 March 1852.

479 Harriet Grote . . . : quoted BARZUN II 41.

480 "Dear Lady ...": CG IV 169.

480 [Berlioz at St Paul's]: see MW 3 June 1852; OSBORNE.

480 "a look of pleasure on his face": this was how Barnett used to describe him, according to GANZ 128. But Barnett's *Musical Reminiscences and Impressions* (London, 1906) gives a different account.

480 at Caldwell's Rooms: see GANZ 123.

481 The letter to Ella: reproduced MW 20 May 1852, also MEN 30 May, later as preface to the full score of *The Flight into Egypt*, and GROT 185–9.

481 a project ... a few years before: see CG III 667.

481 in Barzun's words: *Evenings with the Orchestra*, trans. Jacques Barzun, New York, 1956, Introduction, x.

481 On 10 May he asked Rocquemont: CG IV 153.

481–2 he gave d'Ortigue an account ... : CG IV 151–2.

482 "I had the weakness ... heartbroken": CG IV 146.

483 *Illustrated London News*: 1 May 1852, 342.

483 Berlioz's ... letter to Gounod: CG IV 154–5.

483 The *Musical World* reported: 1 May 1852.

483 the *Morning Post*: 1 May.

483 what he had to say ... *Débats*: 16 April 1845.

483 Wilhelmine Clauss: DEBATS 21 Feb. 1852.

484 Silas ... "When I got there...": quoted GANZ 147.

484 As Barzun remarks: BARZUN II 43.

484 preparations for ... Ninth Symphony: B mentions five rehearsals, MW seven, RGM six.

484–5   the *Times*: 13 May, reproduced MW 15 May. Davison was critic on both journals.

485   *Morning Post*: 13 May.

485   *Illustrated London News*: 15 May.

486   *Musical World*. . . Italian Symphony: 5 June.

486–7   *Illustrated London News*. . . "the ovations . . .": 12 June, by Gruneisen.

487   reported the *Literary Gazette*: quoted GANZ 148n.

487–8   Beale, wrote Berlioz to d'Ortigue: CG IV 162.

488   in Barzun's words, "conditions . . .": *Evenings* xi.

488   "tremulous stick . . ." (Gruneisen): ILN 12 June 1852.

488   "She is perhaps less unhappy . . .": CG IV 203.

489   Berlioz . . . in late October: see CG IV 216.

489   for [Louis] to come to England: see CG IV 124–5.

489–90   "You say you are going mad": CG IV 148–9.

490   "The dear child knows . . .": CG IV 202–3.

490   Goncourt . . . [Lévy] . . . "legal robber": GONCOURT 290, also 299.

490   extracts of [the *Evenings*]: RGM 26 Sept., 3, 10, 17 Oct., DEBATS 31 Oct. 1852.

491   [Trémont] low opinion of Berlioz's music: see MEN 2 Sept. 1927, 371.

491   "Grand, if lacking in finesse": CG IV 219.

491   attempt . . . spoil the performance: CG IV 214.

492   the assurances the composer received: see CG IV 273.

492   Berlioz's reply of 2 July: CG IV 178–81.

492   festival . . . at Ballenstedt: for the programme see WALKER II 287.

493–4   Bülow's letters: see BULOW I 412, 437.

494   "the uselessness . . . last act": the original two acts/four tableaux became four acts in the first Weimar performances.

494   adaptability . . . disconcerting to . . . admirers: cf. Shaw, commenting on Landon Ronald's dismay at Elgar's quick tempos in *Falstaff*: "He wants to make more of every passage than you [Elgar] do. A composer always strikes an adorer as being callous."

494   [Liszt's] observations "perfectly fair": CG IV 179–80.

495   he sent Liszt a long letter: CG IV 182–9.

495   further detailed changes: see NBE vol.la XVIII-XIX.

19

499   "an important week for art": LBRIEFE I 116, 146.

500   Adelheid von Schorn: *Zwei Menschenalter*, 1901, tr. L. de Sampigny

as *Franz Liszt et la Princesse Sayn Wittgenstein*, Paris, 1905, 28.

500–501 the notes in Berlioz's hand: CG IV 227n.

501   [Liszt] told Fischer: 4 Jan.[1854], LBRIEFE I 146.

501   The response of the audience: CG IV 227 (to Adolphe Duchêne and not, as stated, to Joseph-Esprit Duchesne).

501   The contrast . . . a few tears: CG IV 226, also 232, 239.

501   Ignaz Moscheles: Emil F. Smidak, *Isaak-Ignaz Moscheles*, Aldershot, 1989, 177.

502   [banquet at the Stadthaus]: see also PROD 315–16 and n.

502   trombonist . . . collect their names: see CG IV 234.

502   "Dear friend . . .": CG IV 228.

502   "*For ever*": in English.

502   Liszt . . . a note to the Princess: LBRIEFE IV 132.

502   "a category of ideas . . .": CG IV 239.

503   "As for Paris" . . . Gruneisen: CG IV 275.

504   not the one to help "Dr W. . . .": CG IV 275, also 240.

505   [Liszt's] piano organ: see WALKER II 77 and n.

505   "your zigzags console me . . .": CG IV 282–3.

506   he had Meyerbeer to dinner: this assumes M accepted the invitation (CG IV 235).

506   "Schubert trios": CG IV 244.

506   review of Pasdeloup: DEBATS 17 March 1853.

506   [Louis] "The poor dear child": CG IV 246.

507   "Two strenuous rehearsals . . .": CG IV 317–18, to George Hogarth.

507   *Harold*: Henry Hill, who was to have played solo viola, was ill; his place was taken by B's friend Prosper Sainton.

508   wrote Gruneisen . . . *Illustrated London News*: 4 June 1853.

508   Davison reminded readers . . . : MW 26 March 1853.

508   the voice he had "dreamed of . . .": CG IV 310–11.

508   Smythson, the best [chorus-master]: CG V 197.

509   dinner . . . for the entire cast: CG IV 326.

509   "After the French Season . . .": DEBATS 26 July 1853 (GROT 137–44).

510   Adolph Schloesser: see above, RAM Magazine.

510   as he told Barbier . . . : CG IV 326.

510   Queen Victoria . . . her diary: see George Rowell, *Queen Victoria Goes to the Theatre*, London, 1978, 37.

510   the Italian faction: joined, according to CG IV 341, by reinforcements from Paris.

511   . . . the words of Wilhelm Ganz: WILGANZ 59–60.

511–12 Holmes to Clara Novello: Averil Mackenzie-Grieve, *Clara Novello*, London [1955], 250.

512   [B's letters after *Cellini*]: CG IV 333, 342, 335.

512   an open letter to the *Musical World*: 9 July (CG IV 340).

513–14 "The engraving of *Faust* . . .": CG IV 349–52.

514   shared the revulsion of Turgenev: cf. CG IV 363: "ces niais de joueurs", etc.

515   Every morning . . . the seven o'clock train: see CG IV 362.

515–16 [visit to Frankfurt]: CG IV 356, 392, 361; see also GROT 49–50. The concerts were on 20 and 24 Aug.

516   two feuilletons "sprang" at him: CG IV 361.

517   [Wagner] "had a great weakness . . .": MY LIFE 501.

517   at the house of Liszt's children: MY LIFE 503. WALKER II 437 says B was there already, having arrived with Liszt. The children's musical preceptor was Seghers.

517–19 [visit to Brunswick, Hanover, Bremen]: CG IV 375, 386, 387, 393, 394, 398, 407.

518   silver-gilt baton . . . with garnets: now at MUSEE.

518   "All right – let him die . . .": MEM Postscript 560.

520–24 [visit to Leipzig]: CG 402ff. See also CORNELIUS I 149 and William Mason, *Memories of a Musical Life*, New York, 1901.

520   *Faust*, Parts 1 and 2: apparently without the Elbe scene (see programme in B's hand, CG IV 409n).

521   Brahms [and *Flight into Egypt*]: letter to Clara Schumann, quoted BARZUN II 75 n19.

521   Cornelius . . . his sister: CORNELIUS I 149.

521   The *Signale* . . . : 8 Dec. 1853, translated MEN 25 Dec. (quoted PROD 321–3).

522   evening . . . at Brendel's: 7 Dec.

522   Brahms to Joachim: see *Johannes Brahms: Life and Letters*, ed. Styra Avins, Oxford, 1997, 29.

522   Schumann's . . . "New Paths": NZfM 26 Oct. 1853.

523   His refusal (in Barzun's words): BARZUN II 73.

523–4   [B's] thoughts . . . current state of music: CG IV 403–5.

524   a related point . . . to . . . Duchêne: CG IV 400.

524   both the Requiem and the Te Deum . . . Brunswick: see CG IV 425, 428–9.

524   . . . *The Arrival at Sais*: see CG IV 460, 462.

525   The *Ménestrel* reported: 25 Dec. 1853.

525–6   [B's reaction to the case]: see CG IV 447–8, also 432n, 444n.

525   *Débats . . . Gazette . . . Siècle*: respectively 22 Dec., 25 Dec., 29 Dec. 1853; also a mention in MEN 1 Jan. 1854.

526   His correspondent . . . read the libels . . . : CG IV 446–7.

526   the ladies of [David's] choir: see CG IV 451.

526   a fresh effusion of gratitude: CG IV 453.

526   *La France musicale*: 18 Dec. 1853, also 1 Jan. 1854.

526   a sardonic letter to the *Gazette*: 22 Jan. 1854.

527   Never (he told d'Ortigue): CG IV 456.

527   review of *L'étoile du nord*: DEBATS 21 Feb. 1854.

528–9   "Dear sister": CG IV 467–9.

528   "A large number of men of letters . . .": contrast MEM LIX 544: "deux ou trois hommes de lettres [. . .], plusieurs artistes [. . .] et quelques autres bons coeurs".

529–30   "My poor dear Louis": CG IV 469–70.

530   "Dear, wonderful sister": CG IV 473–4.

530–31   "My dear Aunt": CG IV 474n–475n.

531   "Dear friend": CG IV 480–81.

533   "She inspired you . . .": quoted MEM LIX 546 (CG IV 484).

20

534   What Peter Raby calls . . . : RABY 174.

534   "romantic egotism . . .": quoted BARZUN II 79n.

534   . . . Goethe's "Wer nie sein Brot . . .": e.g. OLLIVIER I, 46, 57.

534   reciting passages from roles . . . : see MEM IX 554. B mentions only Cordelia, but other roles too are highly likely.

535   [disposing of the lease]: see CG IV 485–6, 504.

535–6   [visit to Hanover, Brunswick]: CG IV 486–96, 498–505.

535   Joachim . . . to Liszt: LZEIT I 329–30.

536   he spoke of Harriet's death: CG IV 500.

536–9   [visit to Dresden]: CG IV 506–32.

538–9   Bulow to Liszt: LBULOW 76–9, 82–3.

540   Cornelius . . . wrote to . . . his mother: CORNELIUS I 153–4.

540   in June he told Morel: CG IV 547.

541   [Liszt] "had to be stopped": WALKER II 393.

542   centre of gravity . . . to Paris: the old chimera, recognition in his native capital: Paris must be brought to concede his worth – this though he was well aware how much value that would have, given his opinion of Parisian musical culture.

542   "adders fanged": Adolphe Adam, who was backing Clapisson, duplicitously offered B his support (see CG IV 566). Commenting on the result of the election in the *Artiste* (1855, 40, reproduced MEN 1903 391), Offenbach, at the time still music director of the Théâtre-Français (the Bouffes Parisienne opened the following year), described a visit to an ancient academician who had never heard

of the *Damnation* or *Romeo and Juliet*, and had in any case promised his vote "to the celebrated author of *Le Postillion de Madame Ablou*, which is known in the five continents of the world". "And in the cafés-chantants," Off. replied.

542   ". . . till the next vacancy": CG IV 571.

544   St Valery . . . two years before: see CG IV 304.

544   "God keep you, my dear Morel . . .": CG IV 572.

544   "what the poor child . . . felt": CG IV 567.

544–5 [visit to La Côte]: REBOUL; CG IV 568, 608, V 165.

545   "My dear Casimir . . .": CG IV 584. They had corresponded sporadically but had not seen each other.

545   [B and Marie] were married: see CG IV 602.

546   John Ella: HALLE 249–50.

546   Berlioz wrote to Louis: CG IV 596–7.

546   a letter from [Aunt Marmion]: REBOUL.

547   "Russian columns on the . . . Alma": CG IV 588.

548–9 "My passion for music . . .": CG IV 568–70.

549   "I know my Paris too well": CG IV 554.

549–50 [planning the performance of *The Childhood*]: CG IV 597, 598, 606, 626, 638n, 666.

550   "The whole hall," wrote Cosima . . . : quoted Richard du Moulin-Eckart, *Cosima Wagner*, tr. Phillips, 2 vols., London, 1930, I, 40.

550–41 congratulatory letters: a selection is given in CG IV.

551   the *Moniteur officiel*: quoted BARZUN II 86.

551   Scudo . . . Jouvin: 15 Dec., 17 Dec. 1854. Liszt, writing to Brendel, described Scudo as a critic who for years had "set himself up in spiteful opposition to our view of Art and to those we honour and support" (LBRIEFE I 193–4).

551   "insulting to its older brothers": CG IV 645–6.

552   as Gautier . . . argued: *Presse* 28 Dec. 1854.

554   ". . . to live only in the past": CG IV 568.

555–6 Roger wrote: 7 Jan. REBOUL (reprod. CG IV 689–90).

557   Liszt . . . delighted to produce it: see LSTRICKER 77 n. 2.

557   "I am being encouraged, urged . . .": CG IV 725.

558   a chapter on new instruments: printed DEBATS 9, 12 Jan. 1856.

558   nor in Hanover: as he was preparing to set out, the King wrote asking
        him to postpone the complete performance of *Romeo and Juliet*
        for a year because of "problems in his orchestra and chorus".

558   Berlioz who suggested . . . monodrama: CG IV 681.

559   the Aeolian Harp . . . moved him . . . : see CG IV 724.

559   New Weimar Association: see WALKER II 752.

560   "homonym of the great Fantastical": CG V 43.

560   he thanked Hoffmann: see CG IV 717.

560–61 "Waltz sung by the wind . . .": See HOLCAT 346.

561   in the . . . *Gazette*. . . Cornelius: RGM 27 May, 3 June 1855.

561   Cornelius told his mother . . .: CORNELIUS I 149.

561–2   [Brussels concerts]: see CG V 32, 37, 38, 50, 55. Press criticism of B
        was somewhat more favourable than in 1842.

562   Edgar Quinet: *Lettres d'exil*, Paris, 1885, I, 217–18.

563   [Fétis] wrote to Liszt: LZEIT II 16–17.

563   [Marie] his "homme d'affaires": CG V 32.

563   [Marie's gambling] a note from Berlioz: 21 May 1858 (MACN).

564   Meyerbeer often ill . . . : and, according to William Ganz, terrified of
        being buried while still alive (WILGANZ 165).

564   Heine . . . ("at death's door"): CG IV 44.

564–5   [preparations for Te Deum]: CG IV 716, V 71, etc.

565–7   [letters about Louis]: CG IV 705, 706, V 23, 50, 92, 145–6.

567   [Te Deum]: see HOLOMAN 471–2; NBE vol.10; CG V 77–8, 81–
        2.

567   One critic . . . worldly pomp: Fiorentino in *Moniteur universel*, quoted
        CG V 83n-84n.

568   He . . . appealed to Wylde: CG IV 665. The autographs of this letter
        and the one to Davison (650–51) are lost. There is an evident
        editorial confusion of dates. The letter to Davison, written after
        the one of (?) 26 Dec. to Wylde, should perhaps be dated 28 Dec.,
        not 23.

568   English aversion . . . rehearsing: see CG V 420: "Je tremble en pensant
        aux habitudes anglaises pour les répétitions."

568–9   Klindworth: "Wagner in London", MT 1 Aug. 1898, 516.

569   Dr Wylde . . . assured him: see CG V 116.

569   a letter to the *Musical World*: 30 June 1855 (reprod. CG V 118–20).

569   he hopes . . . "we can do better": CG V 349.

570   Both [W and B] conscious of the opportunity: e.g., CG V 100.

570–71 "Dearest friend . . .": CG V 115–18.

571 [the Beneke family]: one of them, Carl Victor, married Mendelssohn's daughter Marie in 1860.

571–2 Wagner wrote to Liszt from Zurich: LWAGNER I 433–4..

572 "so much progress in French": perhaps from his daily contact with Sainton, concert-master of the Philharmonic.

572 ". . . charming letter" (Berlioz told Liszt): CG V 149.

572–3 Berlioz's reply [to Wagner]: CG V 150–52.

573 Berlioz had written to Morel: CG V 94.

574–5 letter to Théodore Ritter: CG V 123–6.

574 "concerto by Henselt . . . M. Klindworth: Klindworth, in MT, op. cit., remembered B falling asleep during the rehearsal of the concerto's slow movement.

576 second . . . New Philharmonic [concert]: see GANZ 204.

576 Marie told . . . Mme Duchêne: CG V 123n.

576 in A. W. Ganz's words: GANZ 208.

577 by no means committed himself: "I have impulses towards composition which I hold on a tight rein and which, I trust, will not force my hand" (CG V 167).

577 possible visits [to Germany]: including a Requiem or Te Deum at the Thuringia Festival – see CG V 148.

577 jury on musical instruments: see CG V 144, 146, 147, 157, and HOLOMAN 475–6.

577 Holoman . . . argues . . . a baton: HOLOMAN 354.

578 L'Art du chef: B's call, in the pamphlet, for a class in percussion at the Conservatoire went unheeded until after the First World War.

578 Princess . . . in Paris: B, monopolized by the jury, saw less of her than expected.

578 Memoirs which Berlioz . . . sent [Liszt]: see CG V 87, 99. L, in his reply, was merely to acknowledge "the parcel", so that Marie could continue ignorant of the book's existence.

578 "My Benvenuto Cellini": CG V 150, 10 Sept. 1855. It had been, as B wrote to Liszt, "the late Grand Duke, or perhaps she herself, who gave you the means to galvanize my poor opera". L's opinions are in LBRIEFE IV 188–9.

578–81 [Exhibition concerts]: see CG V 175, 179, 180, 183, 187, 239.

581 "That great imbecile of a theatre": CG V 37.

581 The Sicilian Vespers. . . [B's] notice: DEBATS 2 Oct. 1855.

581 Berlioz, quoting Racine: CG V 166 (repeated 171).

581 "But he'll end . . . Emperor's head of music": CG V 240–41.

582 with . . . Ritter to Legouvé's house: see LEG I 310–11; CG IV 700.

582 "My dear, very dear Théodore": CG V 244–5.

582–3   [B] expounding the Ninth Symphony: LEG I 306–7.

583   "So the learned men of Berlin": CG V 212–13.

584   "your magnificent composition": CG V 31, 229.

584   "When will your Berlin plans . . . ?": CG V 199.

585   the request of his cousin Raymond . . . : see CG V 189–90.

585   . . . to chase up Adolphe Sax: see CG V 185, 186.

585   he twice wrote to Sainton: CG V 245–7, 247–8.

586   . . . a notebook in his hand: MUSEE.

586   the [Gotha] performance . . . "quite good": CG V 268.

586   feuilleton [on *Santa Chiara*]: DEBATS 2 Oct. 1855; CG V 164.

587   . . . possibly one other [*Nuits d'été* song]: see BLOOMSTUD 93.

587   the score . . . "shining like a . . . sword": CG V 266, also 272.

587   "a second *Fidelio*": quoted WALKER II 399.

588   (Liszt wrote to . . . Agnes Street): LBRIEFE III 64.

588   Liszt told Bülow: LBULOW 173–4.

588   writing to . . . Hippeau, Liszt: LM II 387.

588–9   [B] misrepresenting [W] . . . "music without melody": MEM Post-
        script 560.

589   Marie . . . [disparaging Johanna Wagner]: quoted CG V 304n.

589   a letter from Bülow . . . [B's response]: CG V 263–4, 267.

589   Liszt . . . "less than friendly attitude": LBRIEFE IV 368.

22

591   "For the last three years . . .": MEM LIX 550.

591   *Orphée*. . . "but for . . . anachronism . . .": DEBATS 17 March 1839.

591   *Sapho* . . . : DEBATS 22 April 1851 (CONDE 283–94); KEMP 5 (B
        "providing Gounod with an extended composition lesson").

592   *Sapho* revived: DEBATS 7 Jan. 1852 (CONDE ibid.).

592   in *Evenings*. . . the narrator: SO 140.

592   Cassandra, "prophetic virgin . . .": SO 383.

592   the libretto, he told . . . Marmion: CG V 328.

593   he quotes the Latin words: DEBATS 6 Sept. 1854 (GROT 124).

593   a letter to Bülow . . . : CG IV 574.

593   [Sontag] "would have been worthy": DEBATS 5 Oct. 1854 (GROT
        257).

593   . . . April he quotes it again: DEBATS 17 April 1855.

593   when he is . . . in Weimar: the *Aeneid* is twice quoted in letters written
        there (CG V 713, 717).

594   . . . to buy an apartment: see CG V 283, 288, 296.

594   5 May . . . "an epic date": CG V 328.

594 "only doing the words . . .": CG V 299.

594 (The English pianist Alice Mangold . . .): see A.M. Diehl, *Musical Memories*, London, 1897, 64ff. The writer speaks of her first visit "to the great critic".

595 Beale had . . . intended: see Beale's letter of 25 June 1856 (REBOUL).

595–6 Duchesne wrote: 23 June 1856 (REBOUL).

596 a letter from the imperial household: REBOUL, from the Ministre d'état et la maison de guerre. See also CG V 357.

596 "I was sitting on a bayonet . . .": CG V 328.

596 January . . . photographed by Nadar: 13 Jan. 1857, when B signed N's visitors' book.

597 relatively free of anxiety . . . Louis: see, however, CG V 354–5.

597 He tried various doctors: a note from a Dr J. Sichelataire, dated 4 Jan. 1856 and enclosing "my little prescription – but I don't guarantee to cure you *instantly*" was preserved among B's papers (REBOUL).

597 located . . . in the intestines: "gastritis" was a familiar ailment in the Berlioz family. Dr B, in a pencilled note in his copy of his *Mémoires sur les maladies chroniques* (MUSEE), identifies it as a common affliction of those "given to nostalgia".

597 Tovey's verdict: *Essays in Musical Analysis*, London, 1936, IV, 89n.

598 [Boschot's misdating]: the entire work, text and music, was written in a little under two years, and in a form as long as we now have it (though two of the Act 4 ballets and the Dido–Aeneas scene in Act 5 were added later, the finale was much longer, and the Sinon scene had not been removed).

598 "Gluck . . . was a Romantic": see my vol. 1, 235–6.

598 As Kemp says, "everything . . .": KEMP 93.

599 A Virgilian opera "on the Shakespearean plan": MEM Postface 568.

599 Donald Grout: *A Short History of Opera*, New York, 1947, I, 320.

600 he had "spent his life . . . demigods": CG V 694.

600 Hector, "recalled to life . . .": CG V 619.

600 "the melancholy voice of Virgil": MEM XLI 238.

602 large-scale tonal design: see KEMP 113–18 (disputed, however, by Rushton, KEMP 120, 122–4).

603 [Caasandra's] heartache . . . projection: this idea in KEMP 107.

603 the "ardent existence": CG V 648.

603–27 [letters on *The Trojans*]: CG V 286, 300–301, 307–8, 310–11, 317, 322–3, 330, 332, 337–8, 350–53, 361, 366, 378–9, 382–3, 388–9, 391–2, 401–2, 413–14, 417–19, 424, 427–9, 432–4, 436–8, 445–6, 451–2, 470–71, 475–7, 485–6, 501–2, 508, 509–10, 518, 528–9, 533–4, 539–40, 541–4, 545–6, 547, 548–9, 551.

615   [B's march and Spontini's in *Olympie*]: see KEMP 160.

627   *Quidquid erit* . . . : *Aeneid*, v, 710.

23

629   "Come a Cassandra . . .": CG V 561.

629   turning down invitations: see CG V 558, 560, VI passim.

629   his alarm when . . . Schwab: see CG V 595.

629   an appeal to the Emperor: the letter is given in MEM Postface 568–9.

629   Morny (whom Alphonse Daudet . . .): GONCOURT 220.

629–30   [démarches at the Tuileries]: see CG V 564, 567, 568–9, 575, 597, 679.

630   "The Emperor complained . . .": GONCOURT 77.

630   distribute . . . the poem . . . hold readings: see CG V 604, 608–9, 612, 671, 673, 703; also 529, 535.

631   "Indeed . . . your great reputation . . .": CG V 621–2; also 627.

631   Coriolanus . . . "that great-hearted patrician": CG V 706.

632   "the joy I feel . . . my *Trojans* scenes": CG V 713–14.

632   "magnificent and moving": CG VI 19.

632   Adèle['s] . . . sickly daughter: seemingly some kind of nervous complaint. It lasted several years.

632   Ernest Reyer . . . a masterpiece: quoted BARZUN II 164. See also Paul Smith in the *Gazette*, 4 Sept. 1859.

633   [Pauline Viardot's varied talents]: see WADDINGTON 383.

633   one of her "four true friends": letter to Louis V, 14 Jan. 1858, quoted WADDINGTON 383.

633   she told Julius Rietz: VIARDOT 41.

634   B . . . to Louis . . . Mme Viardot . . . exclaimed: CG VI 30.

634   "The sight of this man in . . . pain": VIARDOT 43.

635   "I could talk to you . . .": CG VI 32.

636   "What do you think of Gluck's critic?": CG VI 70.

636n   exchange of letters . . . with Delsarte: CG V 457–62.

636   "colossal sphinxes . . .": GROT 211–12. B quotes *Henry VI Part I*: "Glory is like a circle in the water", etc.

637   complimenting . . . Massenet: see MASSENET 46n.

637   "you say support Carvalho . . .": CG V 447, 24 March 1857.

638   whether the director's "good intentions": CG VI 24.

638   "I'm writing ballet music . . .": CG VI 75.

638   Delacroix said, "Dido . . . a titmouse": CG VI 35.

639   "The Prince has a work . . .": CG VI 73.

639   (Marie Sax . . . "ignorant as a carp"): CG VI 83.

639   [Pauline Viardot's verdict]: VIARDOT 47.

639n   "That's M. Gluck . . .": see CG VI 87 and n.

639–40   [B on Viardot's Orphée]: see CG VI 76; DEBATS 22 Nov., 22
           Dec. 1859.

641   [Litolff concert]: 2 May 1858. The programme also included *La
           captive*, sung by Falconi.

641   . . . perform "the whole of his repertoire": CG V 568.

641   B . . . assembled tuning-forks: see HOLOMAN 490–91.

642   The collection (he told Pohl): CG V 660.

642   the press, generally, . . . : see "L'accueil de la presse", GROT 401–4.

642   "Mme Viardot, pen in hand . . .": quoted CG VI 41n.

642–3   he went to see General Mellinet: see CG VI 43.

643   "I heard Dido's farewell . . . : CG VI 56. The soirée was on 24 Oct.

644   Berlioz . . . mobilizing support: see CG VI 58–60.

644   "Flattering for Verdi . . .": CG VI 83–4. B's memory seems to have
           conflated *Gulliver's Travels* (where the hero merely puts out the
           fire) with two passages in Rabelais where both Gargantua and
           Pantagruel drown hundreds.

644n   "Give my warmest greetings . . .": 20 Feb. 1860, "Lettres inédites de
           G. Verdi à Léon Escudier", *Rivista musicale italiana*, xxv.

645   article on the operatic *Romeos*: DEBATS 13 Sept. 1859, ATC 349–60.

645   Liszt . . . "not long for this sad world": LBRIEFE V 495 (CG VI 47n).

645–7   [letters on *Antony and Cleopatra*]: CG VI 51, 60–61, 75, 84–5, 350.

647   his "Penelope's robe": CG V 558.

647   he told Adèle . . . his "névralgie": CG V 713.

648   ("the Good Lord . . . keep his hand in"): CG V 594.

648   Saint-Saëns . . . dined on oysters: see MEN 21 Oct. 1921.

648   hymn for [Vries'] tabernacle: see HOLCAT 396–8.

649   the doctor . . . ". . . between the pads": CG VI 39, "Friday". CG
           suggests 7 Oct. 1859; 21 seems to me more likely.

649   "just as . . . in Molière's day": CG VI 49.

649   wrote Wagner to Mathilde . . . : *Richard Wagner an Mathilde Wesen-
           donk*, Berlin, 1904, 186.

649–50   [meetings, correspondence with Wagner]: CG VI 53n-54n, 62n, 64,
           89, 107, 111 and n.

650   [copyist full score of *Tristan*]: BN Rés. VM^3 5.

24

651   "His first name, Hector . . .": LBRIEFE VI 384.

652   Cornelius could describe himself: quoted BARZUN II 76.

654   "Only one thing can save him . . .": W suggested that B set his libretto *Wayland the Smith*.

654   Cosima, in her diary: *Cosima Wagner's Diaries*, tr. Geoffrey Skelton, New York, 1978, II, 179.

654   as [Marie] told Berlioz's nieces: 20 March 1861, MUSEE, quoted BLOOM 154–5.

654   Reyer describes Marie . . . : REYER 309. She was, presumably, referring to the "reminiscences" of B's music in W's.

655   he warned her . . . diminished sevenths: CG VI 125.

655   "Wagner . . .," he told . . . Samuel: CG VI 117.

655ff   [B's review of W's concerts]: DEBATS 9 Feb. 1860; ATC [321]-32.

657   . . . doctrines . . . obstructed [the future]: cf. PAVAN 23: B's "réticence envers Wagner provenait d'un dégoût pour toute *obstruction* de l'avenir".

658   the painful impression . . . Bronsart: CG V 447–8. It may be significant that a gap of eight months ensues in the surviving correspondence between B and the Princess.

659–60   [Wagner's] reply: reprod. CG VI 127–31.

660   Berlioz told Hallé . . . : CG VI 142.

660–61   [letters about the Théâtre-Lyrique]: CG VI 157, 159, 170, 178–9.

661   According to Wagner's *Mein Leben*: MY LIFE 618.

661   a cabal . . . led by Héquet . . . and . . . Scudo: see ELLIS 213n.

661   according to Wilhelm Ganz: WILGANZ 180.

662   his protest . . . made silently: CG VI 207.

662   "God in heaven . . .": CG VI 207. BLOOM 154 quotes a description by Victorin Joncières of B in his box listening to *Tannhäuser*.

662   "The second performance . . . *Tannhäuser*: CG VI 213.

663   Nancy Suat . . . to . . . Mathilde: 7 Oct. 1861 (REBOUL).

663   "I desire nothing but sleep . . .": CG VI 144.

663   Hanslick . . . the summer of 1860: HANSLEBEN I 60–61.

663   to judge by the letter to . . . Samuel: CG VI 117.

663   Reyer speaks of evenings . . . : REYER 306.

664   The friendship . . . Pauline Viardot: after July 1860 there is a gap of nearly 11 months in his surviving letters to her.

664   [letters about Adèle's death]: CG VI 136, 143.

664   [*Fidelio* articles]: 19, 22 May 1860.

664–5   "If only . . . better . . . how happy: CG VI 170–71, to Nancy Suat.

665   General Mellinet . . . commission: see CG VI 206n, 213 and n.

665   *Le temple universel*: see CG VI 194, 197, 201, 208; HOLCAT 399–401.

665–6   [Cornelius' letters, B's replies]: CG VI 176, 275–6, 282–3, 288–91.

666   "a caprice . . . point of a needle": CG VI 320.

667   1850s . . . sketched an outline: see NBE vol. 3 VIII.

667–8   [composition of *Beatrice*]: see CG VI 174, 178, 182.

668   words of the Nocturne . . . Baden: see DEBATS 11 Sept. 1861 (ATC 299).

668   the music . . . sketched . . . Institute: see MEM Postface 579.

668   "one of the liveliest . . . things": MEM ibid.

669   "I have taken as my text": CG VI 318–19.

669   Tiersot called it . . . Virgil's *Per amica* . . .": TIERSOC 200–201.

671   Louis' "matrimoniomania": CG VI 199.

671   except . . . his father's money: see CG VI 353, to Legouvé.

672   Berlioz . . . a defensive reply: CG VI 252–3.

673–4   "Dear Father" . . . 24 November 1861: MUSEE.

675   [Louis' post] "not through influence: CG VI 261–2.

675   ends "I adore you": REBOUL, Marseille 7 Jan. 1862.

675   "They must think I'm dead": CG VI 215.

675   [*Alceste*] the equivalent (he told Royer): CG VI 221–2.

676   to Pauline Viardot . . . "Nothing happened": CG VI 223–4.

676   Royer, reporting to the minister: BOSCHOT III 540.

677   told Ferrand . . . ". . . fold my arms": CG VI 237.

677   Sinon scene: orchestrated by Hugh Macdonald, the scene has been included in a few modern productions. However, B seems to have wanted it cut: when the work was divided into two, *La prise de Troie*, which lasts under 90 minutes, could easily have accommodated it if he had wished.

677   [performance of *Alceste*]: see CG VI 246–7, 355.

678   *Harold*. . . "performed . . . as I want it": CG VI 271.

678   "It's in the image of God": CG VI 245.

678, etc.   [Preparations for *Beatrice*]: see CG VI 250, 270, 272, 281, 290, 308, 315–16, 318–20, 321–2.

679   a sigh of relief when Beulé . . . elected: see CG VI 294.

680   "My nieces . . . offered": CG VI 299.

681   [letter to Louis, 12 July]: CG VI 312–13.

681   Liszt . . . "Like a nightmare": LBRIEFE V 171.

681   the notice of [Marie's] death: FM 22 June 1862.

682   [*Beatrice* at Baden]: see CG VI 323ff.

682   Reyer to Bizet: CURTISS 116.

682   Reyer . . . "a *succès d'estime* . . .": CURTISS 118–19.

683   wrote Gounod: see J. G. Prod'homme and A. Dandelot, *Gounod*, 1911, II 45.

683–4   Berlioz talked to Legouvé: LEG I 321–3.

684   "a love which came to me . . .": CG VI 409.

685   offering Stasov . . . Te Deum: see CG VI 335–6.

685   The account . . . he sends to Pauline Viardot: CG VI 341.

686   he wrote to Perrin: CG VI 391–2.

25

688   Berlioz . . . *The Flight into Egypt*: 8, 22 Feb.1863. Also (cond. Tilmant) Félicien David's Symphony in E flat, Bizet's *Vasco da Gama*.

688   offering the society his . . . scores: CG VI 424–5.

688   the committee . . . voted in favour: HOLOMAN 560.

689   Louis . . . draft contract: REBOUL (CG VI 549–60), undated, *c.*March-April 1863.

690   "some really beautiful things . . ." [*Tannhäuser*]: CG VI 422.

690   Mme Milde . . . Beatrice: CG VI 425–6.

691   "Poor Grand Duke": CG VI 446.

691   "a man of refinement . . .": *Hektor Berlioz Leben und Werk*, Leipzig, 1900, 252.

691   [visit to Weimar]: see CG VI 418–19, 433, 436, 449, 450.

692–3   Berlioz's letter to the Massarts: CG VI 430–33. See also MEM Postface 576–8

694   he told the prince . . . the two sentries: CG VI 440.

694   Berlioz arrived from Paris: having left by the 10 p.m. train from the Gare de l'Est.

694–6   [visit to Strasbourg]: see CG VI 413, 437, 441–2, 444, 454, 463–6.

695   [Berlioz's speech]: see CG VI 464n.

696   [Preparations for *The Trojans at Carthage*]: CG VI 473–4, 477, 498, 499.

698   how cooperative they had been: one reviewer remarked that "everyone understood that the fate of a great work was in their hands", TRAC 92; MEN 8 Nov.1863.

698   "nothing but devotion": CG VI 537.

699   arguing . . . for . . . Massenet: MASSENET 45, where Ambroise Thomas is quoted as saying: "Embrassez Berlioz. Vous lui devez beaucoup de votre prix!"

699   Baden . . . revival of *Beatrice*: I assume that Louis, who intended to go, was there, but there is no evidence either way.

699   the performance as a whole was worse: see CG VI 487.

700   ". . . it's so beautiful": quoted Daniel Bernard, CI 55.

701   Carvalho's . . . plan to [divert] the Seine: KEMP 181.

701   "the leaping satyrs . . .": MEM Postscript 574.

701   the sentries' scene: it was sung at the public dress rehearsal – see Marie d'Agoult's letter, CG VI 502.

701   "out of place in an epic work": MEM Postscript 575.

701   Saint-Saëns called it a "mania": see CURTISS 136.

702   as the *Memoirs*. . . recalled: Postscript 571–2.

702   Mercury . . . survived: see TRAC 126.

702   "Why," asked the *Constitutionnel*: TRAC 15.

702   a cartoon by Cham . . . "M. Mangin . . .": *Charivari* 22 Nov. 1863.

702   "still in need . . . strenuous . . . rehearsals": MEM Postscript 572.

703   Meyerbeer . . . "for my pleasure . . .": see BOSCHOT III 592–3.

703   Corot: see BARZUN II 242n.

703   "such music . . . not *allowed*": see CG VI 525.

703   Marie d'Agoult['s letters]: CG VI 502, 516.

703   [other congratulatory letters]: REBOUL; CG VI 503, 506–10, 512–13, 518, 542.

703   the audience naturally expected: see TRAC 51.

704   Soldiers' chorus from . . . *Faust*: See Louis Gallet, *Notes d'un librettiste*, Paris, 1891, 299–300. I have found no other similar report. Perhaps Gallet's memory confused it with one of Gounod's less successful first nights

704   "Non-symphonic interlude": *Journal amusant*, 28 Nov. 1863.

705   Bernard Jouvin . . . *Figaro*: TRAC 40–48.

705   Scudo: TRAC 128–31.

705   Kreutzer . . . Durand: respectively *Union*, *Ménestrel* and *Peuple*, *La France*, *Débats*, *Temps*, *Courrier de dimanche*, *La France musicale*, *Esprit public*.

705   the orchestra "goes confidently" . . . "but . . .": CG VI 526.

706   Deloffre . . . unclear: quoted by Hugh Macdonald, doctoral thesis on *The Trojans*, 59–60.

706   "experienced but rather feeble": JULLIEN 276.

706   "if Mlle Dubois . . .": TRAC 127. She ruined the Dido–Anna duet, according to MASSOUGNES 50.

706   "impossible" . . . "more impossible still": 18 Aug. 1864. The present published volumes of CG go up to the end of 1863; 1864–9 will be covered by CG VII. Letters quoted in the following notes which carry no reference are at present unpublished.

707   Audiences . . . had fallen off: see BLOOM 165 and 197 n20.

707   "Never mind," he wrote to the Princess: CG VI 544.

707   "22 performances": in fact 21 plus the public dress rehearsal.

707   "The agony of seeing a work . . .": MEM Postface 575, 574.

708   Gounod . . . "beneath the walls of Troy: LI vii.

26

709	Verdi . . . "a poor sick man": 5 June 1882, to Arrivabene, *I copialettere di Giuseppe Verdi*, Milan, 1913, 628.
709	Liszt, as early as 1861: quoted LBRIEFE V 717.
709–13	Bourgault-Ducoudray: DUCOUDRAY.
713	Reyer . . . "if he gave us . . .": *Guide musical*, Aug. 1903, 23–30.
713	Tiersot . . . "he realized . . . had come": TIERSOC 238.
714	Most Saturdays . . . at the Institute: see HOLOMAN 502.
714	[Meyerbeer's] obsequies: see HOLOMAN 573.
714	Marshal Vaillant . . . his note: 12 Aug. 1864.
714	As . . . Mérimée told him: see CI 307.
715	Dr Blanche['s] . . . party: LI 278–9, 10 Nov. 1864.
715	("they've lost their deposit"): CI 306 (text heavily edited), 15 March 1864.
715	retirement . . . announced . . . 20 March: and in RGM on 3 April.
715	he wrote . . . anonymously, in the *Gazette*: 20 Aug. 1865.
715	"No more platitudes . . .": MEM Postface 576.
715–16	walking past the Opéra . . . : CI 308, 21 Aug. 1864.
716	*Mireille*: 20 March 1864, to Louis.
716	Ritter . . . Beethoven . . . concertos: see LI 269–70. I have found a press reference to only one of the concerts.
716	"music of the starry spheres": LI 288, 26 April 1865.
716n	Stephen Heller: RGM 2 March 1879.
716	[neighbours]: also the d'Ortigues in the Rue St Lazare, and Reyer in the Rue de la Tour d'Auvergne.
717	It became, Heller said: op.cit.
717	[cigars and Shakespeare with Balfe]: see CI 319, 11 July 1865.
717	Benoit Hollander['s description]: quoted GANZ 213.
718	competition at Louvain: see letters to Estelle Fornier (EST 38–9) and Marmion (31 July 1866).
718	"I own a fine garden": CG VI 342.
718	To Ferrand . . . in May 1864: LI 268–9, 4 May.
719	In August he tells the Princess: SW 137–8, 3 Aug. 1864.
719n	parrot . . . "Cochon": CG V 552. See also CG V 98–9 (the same parrot?).
719n	letter to the Princess . . . [1862]: CG VI 318.
719–20	"I confess it saddens me . . .": SW 141–5, 30 Aug. 1864.
721	the Goncourts . . . "nothing of Balzac's world": GONCOURT 53. "Philadelphia, St Petersburg, what you will" (Gautier, ibid.)
721	[Montmartre exhumation]: MEM Postface 580–81. BOSCHOT III

593 says 3 Feb. but gives no supporting evidence. HOLOMAN 569 and 669 n3 opts for 3 March.

722   he slept for two hours . . . : see CI 308.

722   "My favourite walk . . .": SW 143, 30 Aug. 1864.

722   Offenbach . . . in . . . his copy: formerly André Meyer Collection.

723   [memories of Adèle]: see SW 149–50, 19 Oct. 1864.

723ff   [visit to Meylan, meetings with Estelle]: MEM Travels in Dauphiné 585–90.

723   "I saw her," he told the Princess: SW 147–8, 9 Oct. 1864.

724   [B and Patti] had become friends: he dined with her on 4 Feb.

725ff   [published exchange of letters with Estelle]: MEM Travels in Dauphiné 591–602.

725   "I was born to trouble": SW 149, 9 Oct. 1864.

726   "the other" . . . beginning to influence her: SW 151.

727–8   "First of all, don't imagine: EST 31–3, 17 Nov. 1865.

728   "I tire you with my admiration": EST 13, 27 April 1865.

728   "Oh what a happy evening": EST 10, 16 Feb. 1865.

729   "But it wouldn't be worthy": EST 14–15, 27 April 1865.

729   "famous . . . to make you dear . . .": EST 2, 22 March 1865.

729   His letters kept her up to date: EST passim.

729   *Francs-juges* overture . . . Pasdeloup: 22 Jan. 1865.

730   "My visit to Mme F.": letter to Louis, 19 Aug. 1865.

730   the *Memoirs*: B borrowed Estelle's copy back to correct the misprints – see EST 24, 21 Aug. 1865.

730   "senseless struggle . . . impossible": CI 376, 4 or 5 Sept. 1865, to Heller.

730–31   "My dear doctor": EST 24–5, 30 Aug. 1865.

731   the ". . . testing of his love-illusion": BARZUN II 248.

731   at its most heartbreaking: SW 177, 13 July 1866.

27

732   a testy . . . letter: CI 317–18, 28 June 1865.

732   Louis . . . firmly argued reply: 4 July (REBOUL).

733   [Louis' letters]: REBOUL, MUSEE.

733   he revelled in [article] by Reyer: 2 Jan. 1865.

733   roused to rage: "Dimanche" [Oct. 1864].

733   the "gangrenous" society: 12 March [1864].

733   "Oh! I would sacrifice . . .": [*c.* Nov. 1865.]

733   "Alexis writes": [March 1866].

734   in his cabin on the *Louisiana*: "En mer, 29 avril 1865".

734	reread . . . *Aeneid*: "Dimanche 4 septembre" [1864].
734	"a noisome night-soil man": 11 Dec. [1862].
734	"To say my prayers": "jeudi" [? Sept. 1865].
734	"defied any intelligent man": "Dimanche" [*c*. Sept. 1865/6].
735	he felt bereft: "mercredi" [12 July 1865].
735	"It's midnight": [undated].
735	If only (he cried) . . . *Don Giovanni*: 30 June [1866].
736	"playing with this immense machine": 13 Oct. [1865].
736	"I adore the sea": "le 25".
736	"Louis and I . . . like brothers": 10 Nov. 1864. The same day he wrote to Lecourt: "Louis is in Mexico. I count the days till his return. We grow fonder of each other all the time."
736	he was not to be alarmed: 14 Jan. [1865].
736	"I would be easier in my mind": 2 Jan. [1865].
736	"who knows which of us . . .": [*c*. early 1865].
736	invited him to come: [22 Dec. 1864].
737	a room with a comfortable bed: "le 27 soir".
737	"Everyone is talking of you": "mardi" [11 April 1865].
737	"between sky and sea": [6 Jan. 1865].
737	"I love you so much": "dimanche".
738	"If you could read what I say": "mardi 28 mars" [1865].
738	There was "no circumstance . . .": "dimanche".
738	"many mistresses . . .": "le 1er janvier" [?1866].
738	"Poor father! I now feel . . .": "lundi".
738	"So I shall never be with you . . .": 9 March [1866].
739	Septet . . . encored with roars: see MASSOUGNES 100–101.
739	a group of music-lovers . . . collective letter: see LI 295, 9 March 1866.
739	Saint-Saëns . . . "a first-rate musician": LI 291, 17 Jan. 1866.
739	*Armide*. . . abandoned: see LI 295, 8 March 1866; SW 175, 30 Jan. 1866.
740	a buyer was found . . . Murianette: see letter of 20 March 1866 from Camille Pal, and B to Pal, 6 April 1866.
740	Berlioz . . . hastened to assure the Princess: SW 161, 11 May 1865.
740	"An immense crowd was there": 15 March. LI 296, 16 March 1866.
740	Berlioz . . . "refusing to review . . .": e.g. WALKER III 101.
740	wrote Liszt to the Princess: LBRIEFE VI 113–14.
741	*Don Giovanni*. . . *Hamlet*. . . *Othello*: see EST 37–8, 29 May 1866, and to Félix Marmion, 31 July 1866.
741–2	gathering of . . . choral societies: see CI 331, 3 Sept. 1866.
742	unnamed crisis in her life: BOSCHOT III 634–5 thinks it was financial – Estelle hoped to "touch" B. It could equally well have been concerned with one of her children (see below).

742   list of the expenses: MACN.

742   Estelle's unhappy son Auguste: there are several desperate letters from the young man, who was in Paris, to B, who helped him.

742   Legouvé . . . after [Gounod's] dinner: LEG I 324–6.

742   *L'Africaine*: B remarks to the Princess that the publicity for Meyerbeer's opera is ubiquitous and inescapable: "Je crois que dans la hutte d'un Esquimau on en trouverait encore" (SW 175–6).

742   bribing Alceste's two children: see letter of 28 Sept. 1866 to Joséphine Suat.

742   "we . . . wept like stags at bay": CI 332, 3 Sept. 1866.

743   Hainl . . . ("knows nothing . . ."): 5 Oct. 1866, to Jos. Suat.

743   "Hail Mary full of grace": 18 Oct. 1866.

743   Joachim: quoted NL 256 n67.

743   Fétis: see below.

743   [Gluck] edition: see HOLOMAN 571.

743   [correspondence with Fétis]: REBOUL. ("Myrmidons" = futurists.)

744   Others too did their best: see letter of 29 March 1866 from Tournière-Blondeau, with a project for a Ulysses opera.

744   exclusion of Spontini from . . . [Palais] Garnier: see letter of 22 June 1866 to an unnamed correspondent. In the event Sp was included.

744   Heller . . . to Hallé: HALLE 292, 18 Oct. 1866.

744   d'Ortigue . . . in the *Débats*: quoted BOSCHOT III 637–8.

744   "I am constantly ill": 6 June 1866 (to Marc Suat) and others.

744   invitation from . . . Herbeck: Daniel Bernard (CI 57–8) says Mme Falconi acted as intermediary.

745   ("he knows my tempos"): letter to Damcke, "jeudi soir dans mon lit/vendredi matin", 13 Dec. 1866.

745   By now Cornelius was there: see CORNELIUS II 460.

745   Hôtel de Francfort: see letter of 24 Dec. 1866 from Charles Fornier to B (REBOUL).

745   "Taisez-vous donc!": quoted PROD 402n.

746   a delicious tenor . . .": CI 334, 17 Dec. [1866], to Reyer.

746   his friend Hellmesberger: H was a fellow-member of the jury at the 1855 Exhibition.

746   Writing to Reyer . . . : CI 335, 17 Dec. 1866.

746   "an influential castigation": MACBSOC 57 (July 1967), 16.

747   Cornelius . . . the *Damnation*: CORNELIUS II 464.

747   "one of the most horizontal men . . .": CI 336, 12 Jan. 1867.

747–8 to Ferrand: LI 301–33.

748   Berlioz apologized [to Hiller] in advance: CI 336, 12 Jan. 1867.

748   (Hiller remembered later . . .): HILLER 95.

749   Theodore Thomas: see Rose Fay Thomas, *Memoirs of Theodore*

Thomas, New York, 1911, 37. The score is in the Newberry Library, Chicago (HOLOMAN 582–3).

749   "It puts . . . in the shade": 12 May 1867, to Morel.

749   sent [a copy] to Herbeck: see NL 258, 15 March 1867.

750   On 11 June . . . the Conservatoire: see LI 305.

750   *Hymne à la France:* on 27 June B wrote to Barbier to invite him to the final rehearsal on the 29th. (Barbier was author of the text of the *Hymne*.)

751   Berlioz told Estelle: EST 44, 6 April 1867.

751   In May . . . still "hearing quite often": 20 May, to Nancy Suat.

751   Berlioz told Ferrand: LI 304.

752   various conflicting accounts: JULLIEN 303–4; REYNOTES 266.

28

753   "It was for me to die": the full quotation in JULLIEN 304 – "ne pouvais-tu donc pas m'attendre?" – sounds almost like an unconscious echo of *Sur les lagunes*: "sans m'attendre elle s'en retourna".

753   "Forgive me for turning . . .": EST 45.

753   Friends left messages: including Heller, Stephen de La Madelaine, Emile Ollivier, Mme Ernst, Barbier, Szarwady (REBOUL).

753   Ferrand mentioned . . . report: 15 July 1867, omitted from LI.

753   "Dearest Louis, what would I do . . .": CI 327, 13 Nov. 1865.

753   Louis . . . a home . . . will: see B's letters to Marc Suat, 6 June and 22 July 1866.

753   Berlioz['s] . . . will: REBOUL.

754   seeing lawyers on Ferrand's behalf: see LI 307–11.

754   the attendant assured Tierzot . . . : see TIERSOC 348.

755   "Dear Uncle . . .": 5 September or 29 Aug. (MACN).

756   Berlioz told Mme Damcke: CI 338–9.

756   visited Mme Charton: see letter of 19 Sept. to Nancy Suat.

756   the nihilism . . . the Princess: SW 182–4, 27 Oct.1867.

756   Three years before . . . begged [her]: SW 145–6, 24 Sept.1864.

757   to his niece Joséphine: 23 Oct.1867.

757   Cui . . . asked . . . [*The Trojans*]: see FOUQUE 246.

758   His nieces and brother-in-law . . . but his friends: Heller, Hiller (in Paris for the Exhibition), the actor Bressant, etc.

758   to "make ends meet": LI 310, 8 Oct. 1867.

758   "If it kills me": CI 339, [24 Sept.], to Mme Damcke.

758   Wieniawski had told him: see B's letter of 31 July 1866 to Félix

Marmion: W "m'apprend que plusieurs de mes partitions sont fréquemment exécutées à Petersburg et à Moscou, avec des enthousiasmes Russes".

759   thanked him . . . "friendly reproaches": 22 Oct.1867.

759   Two rehearsals, he exploded: 9 [Oct.1867], to Alfred Dörffel.

759–60   Beethoven's Ninth . . . "In London . . . seven": see, however, above, where B says *five* (but RGM seven).

760   he wrote to Félix Marmion: 11 Nov.1867.

760   "God, what snow!": 18 Nov.[1867].

761   "sick as eighteen horses": CI 344, 22 Dec.1867, to Mme Massart.

761   "I recover my strength . . . Pastoral Symphony": 28 Dec., to Nancy Suat.

761   private audiences . . . Shakespeare . . . : see STASOV 166.

761   received them . . . from his bed: see Lenz's letter of 21 Feb. 1868: "J'aime à croire que ces lignes ne vous trouvent pas au lit comme je vous trouvais toujours, vous, au Palais Michel" (REBOUL).

761   [B's visitors]: see FOUQUE 255–6; B's letter of 1 March 1868 to Stasov.

761   Musorgsky: the influence on him of both *The Trojans* and *Benvenuto Cellini* (especially the latter's choral writing) is palpable.

762n   Stravinsky: Igor Stravinsky and Robert Craft, *Conversations with Igor Stravinsky*, London, 1958, 29n.

762   honorary member of the society: see FOUQUE 254; STASOV 167.

762   he even thought . . . of composing: see FOUQUE 253.

762   wrote asking . . . Damcke: NL 264–8, 26 Nov. [1867]. D was also asked (11 Dec.) to send a copy of the *Memoirs* to the Grand Duchess.

762   a document . . . Kologrivov: FOUQUE 247–50.

763   Pastoral . . . : "How we sang that amazing poem! What a fine orchestra – they do what I want, these brave artists" (8 Dec. 1868[1867] to Félix Marmion). Other letters describing the concerts include: to Estelle (EST 49–51, 14 Dec.), Edouard Alexandre (CI 343, 15 Dec.), Estelle (EST 51–3, 23 Jan.), Reyer (23 Jan.), Demeur (MACN, 7 Feb.).

763–4   Cui['s] review: quoted STASOV 166.

764   [visit to Moscow], rehearsals: 4, 5, 7, 10 Jan., concerts 8 and 11. B stayed at the Hôtel de France. The first programme included Beethoven 5, *Roman Carnival* and Fête from *Romeo*. The violin and viola soloist at the second was Laub.

764   Berlioz . . . at first declined . . . Moscow: see EST 51.

764–5   letter . . . from . . . Aglaë Massart: 5 Jan. 1868.

765   "What a country! . . .": to Alfred Holmès, CI 377–9, 1 Feb.1868.

766   "breaking the opera up": to Reyer, 23 Jan.1868.

766   took him . . . to see *A Life for the Tsar*: 5 Feb.

766   antique cymbals . . . last grand supper: see FOUQUE 255.

767   [letters after B's return]: to Camille Pal, Marc Suat, Stasov (CI 349–51, but omitting the remark about "that blockhead Pasdeloup"), Massougnes (NL 270), Stasov (CI 351–2)

767   stopped . . . with the Suats: see B's accounts (MACN): "J'emporte à Monaco en passant par Vienne 1256 fr."

767   "I should be shattered by your company": CI 353, 26 May 1868, to Morel.

767   about the 6th it cleared: see letter of 24 April to Stasov "trois jours après mon arrivée . . ." (April).

768   caused by a stroke: see letter of 22 [?28] March to Nancy Suat: "Je suis tombé raide d'une congestion."

768   almost back to normal: see letter of 24 March to Stasov.

768   codicil: 12 June.

769   "that admirable script": BOSCHOT III 651.

769   brief note to Reyer: 24 June.

769   "Since the 25th March . . .": unpublished letter (MUSEE).

769   he answered at once: *c*.13–14 June. The date 12 June pencilled on Estelle's letter must be wrong. B's is clearly a reply to hers, "reçue ce matin".

770n   According to Stasov . . . : STASOV 169n.

771   [Grenoble banquet] (an eyewitness reported): MATHIEU RGM 13 June 1869. See also RGM 23 Aug. 1868.

771   Tiersot: see TIERSOC 41–2, 328, and TIERMEN.

771   Blaze de Bury: see *Musiciens du passé et du présent et de l'avenir*, Paris, 1880, 351.

772   reports of the Requiem and the Fantastic: see EST 57–8 [*c*. July] 1868.

772   The inscription . . . a scratch: reprod. JULLIEN 309 (see also 312).

772   Ernest Caffarel: "Paris 20 novembre 1868" (REBOUL).

772–3 Heller . . . the white . . . stone: RGM, op.cit.; cf. CG V 585: "je crois que vendredi [Baden concert, 1858] sera une journée musicale à marquer avec une pierre blanche".

773   The Institute archives . . .: see Peter Bloom, "Berlioz à l'Institut Revisited", *Acta Musicologica*, vol. LIII, FASC. II.

773   Charles Blanc . . . a heroic effort: see Blanc's letter of 27 Nov. to Lassabathie: "I am indebted to you for the heroic effort Berlioz made to go and vote for me. I shall never forget" (*Catalogue de la Collection Bovet*, Paris, 1887, 336, no. 9919).

772   His account books . . . : MUSEE.

773   Osborne remembered: op.cit., 70–71.

773   According to Reyer the last words . . . : REYER 305. Reyer also
       says (310) that B's servant Schumann, acting on B's instructions,
       delivered his master's Academician's coat and sword to him, on
       his (Reyer's) being elected to the Academy. Schumann had kept
       them safely and had hidden them from the Prussians.

Epilogue

774   Elwart, who exasperated Bizet: see BARZUN II 297.

774   "If you are going to make a speech": quoted BOSCHOT III 661.

774   the . . . horses bolting: Reyer, on the other hand, remembered that, on arriving at the church, they "reared and refused to advance" (REYER 309).

775   Saint-Saëns would protest: MEN 21 Oct 1921.

776   [Lenoir's] statue . . . Square Vintimille: see JULLIEN 364.

776   twenty German cities: the list is given ROLLAND 18.

776   Mottl . . . ("there is no 'but'!"): quoted MASSOUGNES 138.

776   Weingartner, having been prejudiced . . . : see *Akkorde*, Leipzig, 1912, 171–3.

777   Romain Rolland called him . . . : ROLLAND 50.

777   what Stanford called . . . : *Pages from an Unwritten Diary*, London, 1914, 68.

778   Tiersot . . ." France . . . one of his loves": TIERSOC 147.

778   "I love our absurd country": MEM XXV 147.

778   Claude Rostand . . . : *Le Figaro littéraire* 21–27 Sept. 1970.

Acknowledgements

The generosity of several institutions and individuals helped to make possible the writing of this second volume: the Getty Center in Santa Monica, California; the Authors' Foundation; Mrs Drue Heinz and the Trustees and staff of Hawthornden Castle; the Warden – John Roberts – and Fellows of Merton College, Oxford, where I spent a term as a visiting fellow; Deirdre and Nick Wollaston; Janet and Richard Macnutt; Beth and Hugh Macdonald; Edith Stokes, George Crawshay and the staff of Mount Pleasant, where over half the book was written; Francis Reckitt, who first established that hospitable haven; and, not least, John M. Anderson, benefactor and fellow-Berliozian.

Many of the French friends and colleagues listed in the first volume again gave me aid and encouragement, for which I thank them; but I am especially grateful to Lucien Chamard-Bois, Thérèse Husson, and Catherine Massip for their response to frequent requests for help and information.

Catherine Butler-Smith kindly shared with me some of the fruits of her researches into the psychology and stresses of creative and performing musicians, Hugh Cobbe his knowledge of the railway networks of nineteenth-century Europe, and Ian Kemp his deep insight into Berlioz's music. Peter Bloom was a mine of information, ungrudgingly provided, as were Hugh Macdonald, Gunther Braam, and David Charlton. Mark Le Fanu gave me invaluable advice over a period of many months. Jacques Barzun, to whom Berlioz's renascence in the second half of the twentieth century owes so much, was a constant presence and guide.

Thanks also to Edward Anderson, Simon Blundell, Thierry Bodin, Anne Bongrain, Hildburg Braun, Thomas Braun, Adrian Brown, my cousin Julian Bullard, Bridget Cairns, Brian Chenley, Loïc Chotard, Eric Clark, Pamela Clark, Emmanuel Cooper, Catherine Cunaud, Oliver Davies, Donna Di Grazia, Sarah Dodgson, Kenneth Dunn, Jonathan Elkus, John R. Elliot junior, Katharine Ellis, Angela Escott, Annagret Fauser, Ernest Fleischmann, Ken George, David Hayes, Auriel Hill, Katherine Kolb, Jean-Pierre Maassakker, Bidgy Mahilian, Ian Martin, Eve Morath, Roger Nichols, Bridget Palmer, Geoffrey Payzant, Martine Perrin, Jack Pole, Charles Reid, Michael Rose, Alain

Rousselon, Julian Rushton, Mme Sicard of Météo-France, and her assistant M. Cholet, Elizabeth Csicsery-Rónay-Smith and her late husband Clifford Smith, Rémy Stricker, Kit Wynn-Parry, and Heather Yasamee.

For help with the illustrations: Gunther Braam, Philip Burnam-Richards, Lucien Chamard-Bois, Ute Krebs, Alison Latham, Jenny Page, Cécile Reynaud, Rigbie Turner, Jo Wallace, and above all Richard Macnutt.

The following read the manuscript and made criticisms and suggestions from which it greatly benefited: my wife Rosemary; Elizabeth Davison (the early chapters only – her illness and death deprived the book of a faithful ally and the author of a dear friend); Kern Holoman; Hugh Macdonald; Richard Macnutt; Esther Sidwell; and Tom Rosenthal, who commissioned the biography and, as chairman of André Deutsch, published the first volume. To all of them, heartfelt thanks. Tom continued to advise and support me with the same enthusiasm and shrewdness after he had retired from Deutsch, and after his successor had decided not to go on with the book. From this limbo I was rescued by Stuart Proffitt, whose arrival at Penguin just when I found myself in need of a publisher and a sympathetic, Argus-eyed editor was like an answer to prayer.

Lastly, gratitude – more than I can express – to my wife, who has lived with the project through all its many stages, and to whom, and to our grandchildren, this second volume is dedicated.

Index

Berlioz, Hector (*Works*) – *contd.*
lagunes, 247, 248, 655;
Symphonie funèbre et
triomphale (previously
Symphonie militaire), 22, 55,
91–2, 209–10, 218, 235, 246,
250, 253, 259, 268, 271, 283,
289, 299, 300, 321, 322, 323,
324, 351, 354, 372, 376, 400,
404, 405, 406, 413, 415, 579,
580, 581, 774; *Tantum ergo*,
713–4; Te Deum, 55, 251, 284,
427–32, 435, 448, 449–50, 459,
462, 466, 467, 474, 475, 492,
503, 506, 513, 524, 549, 552,
558, 564–5, 567, 572, 576, 577,
578, 579, 598, 618, 621, 685,
759, 772; *Le temple universel*,
665; *32 Mélodies*, 699; *Tristia*
(3 entr'actes for *Hamlet*), 711;
The Trojans, 55, 108, 133, 251,
255, 365, 395, 432, 467, 556,
568, 591, 592–3, 595, 597–627,
628–9, 631, 632, 635, 638, 641,
642, 646, 647, 651, 653, 654,
655, 658, 660, 663, 665, 666,
667, 674, 675, 676, 677, 678,
680, 685, 686, 687, 689, 690,
693–4, 696, 697, 699–708, 712,
713, 714, 715, 726, 733, 734,
738, 739, 740, 747, 752, 754,
757, 762, 765, 766, 772, 775,
776, 778; *Veni creator*, 713–14;
Villanelle, 247; *Vox populi*
(combining *Le menace des
Francs* and *Hymne à la France*),
443; *Waverley*, 44, 88; *Zaïde*,
299, 334n, 341, 351, 417
Berlioz, Joséphine (Finette), née
Marmion, mother of HB, 6, 38,
90, 95, 129, 152; and bequests,
158; breach with HB healed, 36,
128, 151–2; death, 157

Berlioz, Laure, aunt of HB, 426
Berlioz, Dr Louis, father of HB, 2, 9,
17, 31, 38, 152, 157, 158, 183,
184, 190, 216, 219, 249, 251,
289n, 315, 322, 324, 326; breach
with HB healed, 36, 128, 151–2;
death, 420, 421–2, 427;
depression, 227, 410; his estate,
422, 426, 544–5; and Louis,
317–18, 385–6; quoted, 3;
refuses his consent to HB's
marriage, 3–4; *Mémoires sur
les maladies chroniques*, 426,
444
Berlioz, Louis, son of HB, 155, 171,
176, 230, 270, 384, 467, 489–90,
544, 559, 605, 606, 622, 664,
671, 680, 688–9, 700, 703, 705,
706, 717, 718, 720, 721–2, 728,
741, 748; Adèle and, 189–90,
191; appearance, 37, 457, 529;
birth, 36, 37; childhood, 90, 95,
128, 129–30, 147, 152, 182,
184–5, 189, 197, 227–8, 231,
249, 300, 315–16, 385–7;
commands his own ship, 750;
his daughter, 566, 672; death,
752, 753; the death of his
mother, 528, 530–31;
education, 152, 194, 315, 317,
318, 353, 388–9, 442, 443; and
HB's marriage to Marie, 546–7;
health, 565, 566; and his
grandfather, 317–18, 383–4; on
his mother's situation, 313; last
surviving letter, 751; naval
career, 442, 443, 454–7, 458,
473–4, 489, 506–7, 514, 543,
544, 597, 618, 642, 671, 675;
relations with HB, 565, 671–5,
681, 732–9; temperament, 442,
489, 565, 672
Berlioz, Nancy, see Pal, Nancy